GLAISTER'S GLOSSARY OF THE BOOK

'*A good book, particularly when read in conjunction with others, produces a lasting impact at a level of complexity which no other medium can match. A book demands prolonged contact; its pages are "recoverable" in the sense that they can be turned back and reappraised. . . . While not providing hyper-stimulation at any one moment of time, the book draws the willing reader into a personalized, critical and therefore active state of mind.*'

David Caute, The Times, *14 October 1972*

Glaister's Glossary of the Book

GEOFFREY ASHALL GLAISTER

Terms used in Papermaking,
Printing, Bookbinding and Publishing
with notes on Illuminated Manuscripts
and Private Presses

Second edition, completely revised

UNIVERSITY OF CALIFORNIA PRESS
BERKELEY AND LOS ANGELES

First published in 1960 as *Glossary of the Book*
  (*Encyclopaedia of the Book* in USA)
This second edition, completely revised and reset, published
  in the United States in 1979 by University of California Press

Library of Congress Catalog Card Number: 76–47975
ISBN: 0–520–03364–7

Printed in Great Britain

This edition is offered to
Bernardus de Hortis Vernalibus
with the affection and
admiration of
its author

CONTENTS

COLOUR PLATES

PREFACE TO THE SECOND EDITION

A fundamental difference between this and the first edition is in the alphabetical order of entry words. The former arrangement was word by word giving, for example, mill finished, mill ream, millboards, mille and Miller. Entries are now arranged letter by letter (as are those in the OED) so that the above appear as millboards, mille, Miller, mill finished and mill ream. This has been done for consistency when placing words found in both combined and separated form, e.g. paper back or paperback.

Users of the first edition may welcome a note of other changes made for the second which, following eighteen years of revision, has become virtually a new book. Of the 3,269 original entries 481 of diminished interest have been omitted. Of the remaining 2,788 most two or three-line entries remain unchanged beyond minor additions, deletions or updating to maintain their usefulness, but 1,050 have been rewritten and extended as sample word-counts will show: arabic type (from 38 words to 1,364), Bible printing in England (240 to 2,985), Caxton (330 to 2,053), Benjamin Franklin (123 to 363), morocco (41 to 284), pharmacopoeia (180 to 469).

Revised entries on Intertype, Kodak, Linotype, Ludlow, 'Monotype' and Photon machines have been supplied by their makers. Elsewhere revision has included the excision of mechanical data from some entries and the clarification of others.

Of the 3,932 entries in this edition 1,144 are new. Random examples are Bengali printing and typography (3,076 words), ethiopic type (1,412), Hebrew printing before 1600 (2,077), Islamic bookbinding (986), manuscript book writing (2,100), Persian illumination (1,030) and toy books (408).

Of the 390 entries wholly or partly the work of others 220 are translated extracts from the Swedish 'Grafisk Uppslagsbok' (signed GU), 90 were written by the late Dr Muriel Lock (ML), 4 on colour printing by John Jarrold (JJ), 64 on trade bookbinding by Lewis Kitcat (LK) and 10 on Americana by David Welsh (DW). Where necessary they have been amended for this edition.

It may be unusual for a book of this scope to remain so largely a personal compilation, but since 1947 the formidable tasks of collecting material and writing it have been a way of life, rarely set aside. Continuous and extensive reading for the second edition has ranged from pre-printing history to the microwave drying of paper. And if the drudgery implicit in Samuel Johnson's definition of a writer of dictionaries has been at times hard to bear, it was made worthwhile in an Addis Ababa library when a printer, chancing to see the first edition on a shelf, was overheard to say: 'We have a copy of that in our works library. It's our Bible.'

Roundhay, Leeds　　　　　　　　　　　　　　　　　　　　　　　　　　　　　　　　　GG
1978

　　　　　　　　The jacket, title-page and dedication panel for this edition were
　　　　　　　　designed and executed by Michael Harvey.

　　　　　　　　The griffin on the front board was adapted for the first edition of
　　　　　　　　this work from a design made for the author by Kurt Kierger of
　　　　　　　　Vienna.

SHORTENED PREFACE TO THE FIRST EDITION

In the 15th century, when the bookcrafts as now practised may be said to have begun, the printer often combined the roles of typefounder, editor, printer, binder, publisher and seller of his productions; a time-consuming but surely very satisfying occupation. As the years passed, and the processes of making books grew into separate trades, each with its own master craftsmen, special terms were evolved to describe the technicalities particular to every stage of creating a book. This evolution has never ceased, yet an exhaustive search must be made in the many handbooks available before the interested bibliophile, the apprentice printer and binder, the publisher or the bookseller, the papermaker or the librarian can find clear explanations of these terms and something of their history. May this be offered as a reason why a librarian, although outside the book trade proper, has ventured to write a book for its use, claiming that the detachment of a broad general viewpoint is a not unsuitable qualification for doing so, even in an age when specialization discourages the polymath.

In the preface to his 'Dictionary of the English language', 1755, Samuel Johnson states that 'to explain, requires the use of terms less abstruse than that which is to be explained, and such terms cannot always be found. For as nothing can be proved but by supposing something intuitively known, and evident without proof, so nothing can be defined but by the use of words too plain to admit of a definition.' I have taken this as a guiding principle in compiling this glossary which aims at providing a reference-companion to be constantly available when studying or practising the processes of making a book.

It is doubtful if any one person could pronounce with certainty on the accuracy of all the terms in this book, and the publishers sent the typescript to several specialist and practising craftsmen for scrutiny and comment (listed in the first edition). The words of Thomas Watts in his 'Treatise of mechanicks', 1716, seem particularly appropriate here, 'should there notwithstanding all the Care that has been taken be some Errata found in this Book, which we are persuaded are not many, it is hop'd the Publick will have the Goodness to pardon 'em, when they reflect what little Time I can have to spare from my daily Employment, and even what Interruptions must accompany those Moments'.

The Glossary includes illustrations and translated extracts from the Swedish 'Grafisk Uppslagsbok'. This manual for the graphic trades was prepared under the auspices of the Sveriges Litografiska Tryckerier and published by Esselte, Stockholm, in 1951. Extracts were translated by E. Wesander and E. Birse. Those merely edited by me are marked (GU). Those combined with my previous notes are marked (With GU).

'I have to acknowledge the benefits of a management at once businesslike and gentlemanlike, energetic and considerate' wrote Charlotte Brontë to her publisher in 1847. I wish to echo her words here; Sir Stanley Unwin believed in the possibilities of my first typescript when others were unable to see them, while his Production Manager, Ronald Eames, guided my labours for eight years, encouraging me to continue when I would have gladly renounced the project for a less exacting task.

Dacca   GAG
Pakistan
1960

ACKNOWLEDGEMENTS

Through the years 1960–78 there have been several persons whose help and interest have furthered the compilation of this book. Certain single entries have benefited from essential information supplied by Anthony Hobson of Sotheby & Co., Fred Hutchings, retired City Librarian of Leeds, Professor F. B. J. Kuiper of Leyden University, Osmund Lewry of Oxford University and Professor David Pye of the Royal College of Art.

New notes and photographs were supplied by Harris-Intertype Ltd, International Photon Ltd, Kodak Ltd, Linotype-Paul Ltd, Ludlow Industries (UK) Ltd and the Monotype Corporation Ltd. Raoul Curiel of the Bibliothèque Nationale and Bernard Adams of the British Council (to whom this edition is dedicated) have helped me for years with books, photocopies and detailed answers to queries. Perhaps more important they, with my colleagues Joanna Collihole and Hazel Talbot of the Council, have believed in what I was doing.

When the typescript was ready for expert scrutiny Howard Nixon, Librarian of Westminster Abbey, not only read and annotated entries on the history of bookbinding but permitted me to use his own authoritative writings and unpublished notes. Equally generous with their time and expertise were C. M. Thompson and C. G. Ingamells of John Dickinson & Co. who read the papermaking entries, and D. P. Brooks of Staples Printers Ltd who dealt with letterpress printing. Sections on publishing and bookselling were read by the late Ronald Barker and Philip Unwin: again resulting in detailed suggestions, generously given.

At a later stage assistance with final checking was given by G. R. Davies, Director of the Booksellers Association; John Dreyfus, Typographical Consultant to Cambridge University Press; the Society of Authors; Edward Miller, Libraries Adviser to the National Trust; James Mosley, Librarian, St Bride Printing Library; and Stanley Rackham, formerly Managing Director, William Clowes Ltd.

The Publisher joins me in thanking Professor David Welsh of the University of Michigan, Ann Arbor, who in 1976–7 scrutinized the complete typescript, corrected details and supplied useful notes to extend the coverage of the history of the book in America. We appreciate, too, the assistance given to him by staff of the Hatcher Graduate Library and the School of Library Science, University of Michigan in locating material.

Finally the Publisher's own sponsors of this edition merit a special mention. They include Ronald Eames, formerly Design Director, who might well have thought eighteen years ago that one *Glossary* in his career was enough, but continued for a decade to supervise the second edition and to extend the Appendix of type specimens. The 1300-page manuscript was then taken over by John Newth who, undaunted, guided it to publication. His colleague, Michael Radford, checked the cross-referencing. No author of a complicated typescript will need reminding how valuable the assistance recorded above can be. It is gratefully acknowledged.

A

ABA: see *American Booksellers Association.*

Abbey, John Roland, 1896–1969: an English bibliophile who from 1933 assembled an important collection of fine bindings of all periods. He also commissioned work from craftsmen, seeking by his patronage to encourage a greater interest in their skill. Although many of his bindings were sold at Sotheby's between 1965 and 1967, realizing £355,410 (see the sale catalogues), he bequeathed an impressive group to the British Museum.

Scarcely less outstanding for its quality was his collection of colour plate books, mostly reproduced by aquatint or lithography, issued between 1770 and 1860. All that survives in England is the set of catalogues he published, the books now being owned by the American collector Paul Mellon who has added substantially to them. See G. D. Hobson, 'English bindings in the library of J. R. Abbey', 1940, and A. R. A. Hobson, 'French and Italian collectors and their bindings illustrated from examples in the library of J. R. Abbey', 1953.

abbreviations: words which are shortened by removing the end letters and adding a full point, thus *volume* becomes *vol.* Words which are shortened by removing internal letters are in linguistic usage known as *suspensions,* and by printers as *contractions,* thus *Doctor* becomes *Dr* and *volumes* becomes *vols* which are not, in British typography, followed by a full point.

The long tradition of shortening words was begun by monastic scribes seeking to fit as much as possible on to a costly parchment page, and was continued by the first printers. Latin was the language in which both worked and the abbreviations were understood throughout Europe. See *Latin abbreviations.* See also *publishers' abbreviated answers.*

abecedarium: a book containing the alphabet, spelling rules, tables, or an elementary grammar. These primers were in use in Europe before the invention of printing. Those for learning Latin usually contained abstracts from the writings of *Aelius Donatus,* q.v.

The English abecedary was known in the 14th century; in the 16th century the privilege for ABC books, as they became known, brought much profit

to *John Day,* q.v. See also *Costeriana, horn book, Primer.*

Abraham ibn Usque: a Portuguese printer who settled in Ferrara where, in 1553, he printed the *Ferrara Bible,* q.v., for Jewish refugees from the Spanish Inquisition. In the same year he may have published his brother Samuel's 'Consolacam as Tribulacoens de Israel' written in Portuguese; however, the BM claims this is a fictitious imprint and that the work was printed at Amsterdam in 1660.

abridged edition: a shortened version of a book, made to extend sales to readers who because of its length, complexity or cost need an alternative to the original. Although the remaining words are still those written by the author, the less essential passages, illustrations, lengthy notes and appendices are reduced or omitted.

Government reports may be popularized in this way, while the 'Shorter Oxford English dictionary' is a well-known abridgement in two volumes of a thirteen-volume original. Literary classics may be issued in abridged editions so that overseas learners of English as a second language can appreciate something of an author's language and style without being discouraged by a book of formidable length. The editor who reduces the text may add notes and a glossary. Cf. *simplified edition.*

absorbency testing: see *paper testing.*

absorption: in printing, the penetration of paper by ink deposited on it. Its extent is affected by the fibre structure, the constituency of the ink, and the pressure of type or plates. Too rapid penetration of an open-structured paper may cause *strike through,* q.v., or with coated stock to a powdery deposit of pigment remaining on the sheet. Should the paper be insufficiently absorbent set-off and even total drying failure may result.

The absorptive quality of paper is of great importance and is checked by various laboratory tests as, for example, the PIRA surface oil absorption tester. See also *paper testing, powdering.*

acanthus: the leaf of the plant *Acanthus spinosus* was much favoured as a decorative feature by illuminators of manuscripts, particularly by Carolingian artists in the 9th century, as still earlier by Greek and Roman sculptors. It became one of the principal leaf ornaments for borders, and a symbol for trees, used by artists of the *Winchester School*, q.v. See also *arabesque*.

accents: diacritical signs placed over or under various letters in the alphabets of several languages to show the nature or stress of the sounds they represent. While lower-case accent-bearing letters are cast as units, in display work it may be necessary to use separately cast, or *floating accents*; these are adjusted with leads.

Standard accents are:

acute	´	diaeresis or Umlaut	¨
cedilla	¸	grave	`
circumflex	ˆ	tilde	~

e.g. áàâä éèêë ç ñ

See also *peculiars*.

Ackermann, Rudolph, 1764–1834: a native of Saxony where he was a designer in the family coachbuilding business. About 1790, after working in Paris, he came to London, designing, *inter alia*, Lord Nelson's hearse. In 1795 he opened his famous Repository of Arts in the Strand. In addition to selling aquatints, artists' materials and books there was a reading room and a print lending library with an annual subscription of four guineas. The premises, of no little elegance, quickly became a fashionable meeting place.

From the Strand Ackermann issued numerous topographical works, many with aquatints by Rowlandson and Alken. An outstanding publication was 'Microcosm of London', 1808–11, for which Pugin drew the buildings and Rowlandson added the people in the streets. The edition of 1,000 copies, each with 104 plates, called for hand labour on mass production lines. From a single plate the engraver gave an inking to neutral tone areas. Rowlandson would colour a proof. Then, in what was euphemistically called a 'drawing school', a team of women and children, many of whom were European refugee aristocracy, would hand-colour the prints, some doing the faces, some the dresses, some the buildings, and so on until the 104,000 prints were finished.

Ackermann's other publications included his magazine of fashion 'Repository of Arts', 1809–28; 'Poetical magazine', 1809–12, and the annuals he pioneered in 1822 by introducing this popular format from Germany. The first was 'Forget-me-not: a Christmas and New Year present for 1823', edited by F. Shoberl. The last of the twenty-five volume run was issued in 1847. He made lithography better known in England, starting a lithographic press in 1817, and publishing in 1819 a translation of Senefelder's manual.

acquisitions editor: see *sponsoring editor*.

acronym: a word formed with the initial letters or syllables of its components. NATO, radar, and UNESCO are examples, but ARCP and FRGS are not since they are not words.

acting edition: an edition of a play specially prepared for use within a theatre and usually distinguishable from other editions by its low price, thin cut-flush covers, and sometimes fuller stage directions.

Adams, Katharine, 1862–1952: an English bookbinder who in 1897 was a pupil of *S. T. Prideaux*, q.v. She opened her workshop in 1901. Characteristic styles were dotted outlines and lettering on the covers. Her designs were sometimes pictorial. In 1907 she began teaching bookbinding to the nuns of *Stanbrook Abbey Press*, q.v.

She worked for wealthy collectors and by the time of her last commission, about 1924, she had 'bound or mended' 99 books for Fairfax Murray, 70 for St John Hornby of the *Ashendene Press* and 27 for *Emery Walker*, qq.v., though as late as 1943 she made an occasional half-binding for her own pleasure.

Adams press: a bed and platen printing machine invented about 1830 by the brothers *Isaac* (1803–83) and *Seth Adams* of Boston, Mass. It had a wooden frame and a stationary platen to which a frisket-held sheet and the bed were mechanically raised for impression. Three operatives were needed. Later models were steam-powered. In 1834 Isaac invented a form of mechanical *delivery*, q.v., by means of a frame and tapes, known as a 'fly'.

In 1859 Robert Hoe bought the business, making improved models. The extensive use for book printing of the Adams press continued until the early 1880s when it was superseded by cylinder machines.

adaptation: a work which has been rewritten or modified for a special purpose, usually by someone other than the author.

addendum (pl **addenda**): 1. matter to be included in a book after the body of it has been set. This is printed separately at the beginning or end of the text and is less extensive than a *supplement*, q.v.

2. a slip added to copies of the finished book as an *insert* (2), q.v. See also *appendix*, *erratum*.

Adelkind, Cornelius, fl.1515–46: one of an exiled family of German Jews who migrated to Padua and Venice at the end of the 15th century. It is possible that his father, *Baruch*, was employed by Aldus. Cornelius, who converted to Christianity, was chief pressman and later corrector of the *Bomberg* establishment, q.v. When Bomberg died about 1550 Adelkind worked for Giustiniani who also issued Hebrew books. See also *Hebrew printing before 1600*.

adhesive binding: a method of machine binding books without sewing or stitching their sections. There are many makes of machine, all operating on the same principle. After gathering the books are fed singly to the machine where they are clamped and carried against a device which removes the back folds, leaving the book as a clamped block of single leaves with roughened edges. The type of roughener chosen to do this will depend on the paper surface and the degree of roughness required. Rotary knives and sanders which quickly expose the fibres of soft, porous stocks can be used with slow-penetrating animal glues. If such knives were used with highly finished stock the coating of filler on the fibres would not be removed sufficiently for the adhesive to reach them effectively, so pattern roughening by a face-milling cutter is more satisfactory. This leaves a series of notches along the back which increase the area gripped by the adhesive. It is possible to leave the signature folds intact at head and tail, giving the illusion of sewn sections to the finished book.

The sheared back is next carried across gluing mechanism and a strip of lining cloth is applied, its overlapping edges being turned over the sides of the book to receive the end-papers and cover. The choice of adhesive and the manner of its application will depend on the paper, the publisher's budget and the quality of product required. Flexible adhesive is essential. The following are used: animal glue, a cold polyvinyl or emulsion adhesive which is allowed to dry out before trimming, a single-shot hot-melt adhesive which dries quickly and does not shrink, or an application of cold polyvinyl which is dried under intense heat while the book is on the binding machine followed by a second application using a hot-melt adhesive. If a polyvinyl is used it is possible to round and back the book and case up in the usual way. Such books will open quite flat without splitting. It is important that the grain direction of end-papers runs down the page.

In some machines no lining cloth is used and the paper cover is stuck direct to the roughened back and subsequently cut flush. A disadvantage of all adhesive-bound books is that they cannot be re-bound by normal sewing but only by the further shearing of the back margins, and a disadvantage of some is that in tropical climates they disintegrate into a pile of leaves.

Alternative names are *cut back binding, perfect binding* and *unsewn binding*. See also *caoutchouc binding, hot-melt adhesives, Maybury binding process, Steamset, thermoplastic binder*.

adhesive stitch binding: see *stitching*.

ad. loc.: an abbreviation for the Latin 'ad locum', i.e. at (or concerning) the place (passage in a text) cited.

ad usum Delphini: the name given to the series of carefully edited Latin classics, each with a vocabulary, ordered to be printed by Louis XIV for the eduction of the Dauphin. Publication began in Paris in 1671, and the cost to Louis was 200,000 francs.

In 1783 Louis XVI ordered from *F. A. Didot*, q.v., a series of French classics issued with the imprint 'Imprimé par ordre du Roi pour l éducation de Monseigneur le Dauphin'.

advance copies: copies of a book bound up to enable the publisher to check that all is well before binding proceeds and to have a specimen which the bulk must match. They are also given to reviewers and book-club selection committees. These copies may be final proofs or the earliest of the main printing and enclosed in plain or printed wrappers. Alternatively, they may be bound in a colour, fabric or style differing in some way from the book as finally published. They were at one time given to publishers' representatives 'subscribing' a book to booksellers, but proofs and jackets are now mostly supplied instead. See also *blad, review copies*.

advance jackets: dust jackets of forthcoming books sent to booksellers and others as part of publishers' sales promotion. See also *crystal*.

advance sheets: see *folded and collated copies*.

adversaria: a collection of notes or commentaries, originally referring to Roman works with the text written on one side of a diptych, the notes on the opposite side. The term was extended in scope, both by the Romans and later by the Humanists, to include collections of textual criticism, also rough note books.

See also *association copy, scholium*.

advertisements: publishers' announcements of selected books; they may be printed at the end of the book (generally to use up blank pages at the end of a working) and on the back of the jacket, or they may be printed separately and included as an *insert*, q.v.

The earliest known printed advertisement of books was issued by Heinrich Eggestein at Strasbourg in 1466. His contemporary Peter Schöffer of Mainz advertised his books by printing broadsides with a space for the addition of an agent's name and address, often an inn, a common practice 500 years later.

advertising card: an American term for the list of an author's works, or of works issued in the same series, printed opposite the title-page.

3

against the grain: across the direction in which the fibres of paper lie. See also *grain direction*.

agate: a former size of type, between pearl and non-pareil, approximating 5½-point.

agent: see *literary agent*.

airbrush: a pressure spray used for retouching, spray painting, and in lithography. It was invented in America about 1900.

air dried: said of hand-made, mould-made, or the better machine-made papers which, after sizing, have been dried by exposure to air at a controlled temperature while moving on a series of drums. If the paper is coated it is passed through a heated chamber before reeling. See also *loft dried, relative humidity*.

air-knife coater: a device on a *coater*, q.v., whereby a jet of compressed air removes surplus coating from the moving web of paper.

Aitken, Robert, 1735–1802: a bookseller and binder of Paisley whence he emigrated to America, settled in Philadelphia in 1769, and opened a bookshop. Two years later he added printing and binding equipment to his business, and he became the most important American binder of the period.

Fortunately his Waste-book (rough account book) survives with the Library Company of Philadelphia, for whom he bound, providing an unusually detailed account of his career. We learn, for example, that in 1774 his bindery produced some 5,000 plain bindings and 400 gilt calf or morocco bindings, that in 1793 he bound up books from his press in styles ranging from plain wrappers to extra gilt, and in the same year he bound 419 copies of a single title for the printer John Dunlap (of Declaration of Independence fame). It was Aitken who in 1782 issued in 12mo format the first complete Bible in English to be printed in North America.

His daughter *Jane Aitken*, until about 1817 a printer, binder and bookseller in her own right, took over her father's remarkably large collection of roll tools (42) and stamps (*c.* 230) and continued his work as binder to the American Philosophical Society and the Library Company. See W. & C. Spawn, 'The Aitken Shop', *Papers Bib. Soc. of America*, 57, 1963.

ajouré: a style of decorating book covers practised in Venice in the late 15th century by craftsmen from the Near East. Features were patterns of cut-out leather, gilded arabesques, and a coloured background.

à la cathédrale: 1. a name given to the *eau-forte* frontispiece illustrations in which a single plate showed a confused interpretation of the main incidents or characters of a story. Most notable were those of Célestin Nanteuil for the works of Victor Hugo.

2. the name given to the richly gilded bindings with elaborate onlays of coloured leather, inspired by stained glass windows, which were introduced in Paris in the early 19th century when there was considerable interest in Gothic art. Trade binders introduced a cheaper style using embossed blocks with motifs ranging from a few Gothic windows, pillars and pinnacles to a complete West Front. See also *embossed bindings*.

à la Duseuil: a French binding style characteristic of the early 17th century. Red morocco covers had as their principal decoration an outer three-line frame near the edges, and an inner three-line frame embellished at the corners with fleurons, leaving a space in the centre of each cover for the arms of the owner. Numerous examples survive from the libraries of Richelieu and Louis XIV.

The style is often erroneously attributed to the 18th century binder *Augustin Du Seuil*, q.v., but it was fashionable forty years before his birth, and Cardinal Mazarin (1602–61) had many of his books covered in this way.

Alaska seal: an imitation sealskin made from sheepskin or cowhide.

Albatross Library: the imprint of a series of reprints founded in 1932 in Hamburg by J. Holroyd Reece, Kurt Enoch, and Max Christian Wegener. Covers for the series, which eventually reached some 400 titles, were designed by Mardersteig. In 1936 Albatross took over management of the *Tauchnitz* firm, q.v., though each kept its identity. From the outbreak of war in 1939 Tauchnitz publishing was limited to German books and the once more independent Albatross books were published for a while by Collins of Glasgow and later by Bonnier in Sweden.

Albert, Joseph, 1825–86: a Munich photographer who sought to reproduce paintings in local museums. In attempts to make multiple copies of these he experimented with photolithographic methods, basing his work on that of Poitevin who had discovered the sensitivity of chromo-gelatine in 1855; the efforts of Poitevin had been improved by M. Tessié du Motay and C. R. Maréchal of Metz in 1865, but it was Albert who made these discoveries into the practical printing process now known as *collotype*, q.v., but at first named *albertype* after him.

His first collotype impression from a glass plate was made in 1868. Albert also made important contributions to the development of colour photography. See also *Talbot, W. H. F.*　　　(With GU)

4

Albion press: a hand printing press devised and first made about 1822 by *R. W. Cope*, q.v., in London. Type lay on a horizontal sliding bed, pressure being exerted by an elbow-shaped lever joint called a toggle which forced the platen on to the forme.

Advantages claimed for it by the maker were simplicity, compactness and lightness. Experience in use was to prove it long lasting. Successors to his business made improvements. Other firms made presses of the Albion type, Dawson, Payne & Elliott of Otley doing so until 1940. They are still found in use by private presses and art schools. See Reynolds Stone, 'The Albion press', *Jnl. Printing Historical Society*, 2, 1966.

albumen: the chief protein content of egg white; soluble in water and coagulated by heating. It is an ingredient of *glair*, q.v.

albumen process: an obsolescent method of lithographic printing from plates made by coating a base with a solution of albumen and ammonium dichromate. The image to be reproduced is printed down from a negative under a strong light source. In passing through clear areas of the negative light hardens and renders insoluble the corresponding areas of the plate. When a greasy base is applied it adheres to the hardened coating. Washing in water removes the non-hardened areas (water-retaining) about the greasy image. In Britain lithography from *pre-sensitized plates*, q.v., has superseded the albumen process, proving more stable for fine work and long runs.

alcuinian script: see *Carolingian script*.

Aldine bindings: the variously-tooled bindings made in Venice at the end of the 15th century and the first quarter of the 16th century for Aldus and his followers. Boards of thin wood or pasteboard were covered with red, blue, green or brown morocco, early examples being decorated in blind with an outer frame and a central device. See also *Aldine leaves, Venetian bindings*.

Aldine device: a dolphin entwining an anchor. This symbol, known to ancient philosophers, was later used on coins of Titus Vespasianus. According to Erasmus, a friend of Aldus, the anchor represents the period of deliberation before a work is begun, the dolphin the speed of its completion. As a printer's device it was used in five variant forms by Aldus, inspired to do so either by seeing the coin or when printing Colonna's manuscript of 'Hypnerotomachia Poliphili' in 1499 in which the dolphin and anchor with the motto 'festina tarde' appear in one of the woodcuts. When Aldus first used the device in his edition of 'Poëtae christian veteres', 1502, he added the motto 'festina lente' and the name Aldus (from Theobaldus).

Aldus complained of the use of his device by other printers, saying that it could be seen to be an impudent fraud 'for the head of the dolphin is turned to the left, whereas that of ours is well known to be turned to the right'. Printers who used his device were Jehan de Channeu of Lyons and Avignon from 1510–36, Nicolas Le Riche of Paris in 1548, the Parisian publisher Bernard Turrisan from 1554–71, and his successor Robert Colombel from 1571–1602, Ambroise Brillard of Bourges about 1580 and his contemporary Antoine Tardiff of Lyons (with the motto 'festina tarde'). See also *Munsell, Pickering*, and the illustration under *device*.

Aldine leaves: small binders' stamps cut with a vine leaf and stem design, adapted from the *arabesque*, q.v., but originating in classical art. They were used from 1499 as part of the restrained cover decoration on books bound for Aldus. It is likely that printers were thus inspired to use them as *flowers*, q.v., on title-pages, e.g. Estienne from 1509. In Italy the binding tools were known as *piccoli ferri*, and in France, where they were much used, as *petits fers*.

Aldines: a group name for books printed in Venice and Rome by the Manutius family.

Aldus Manutius: the latinized name of the famous Venetian printer *Teobaldo Manucci* (1450–1515), also known as *Aldo Manuzio*, who was born at Sermoneta in Italy.

Early studies in Rome and Ferrara convinced him that Greek and Latin classics offered a moral philosophy relevant to daily conduct and decision, and being aware of the absence of printed texts he decided to set up a press in Venice to print them. In this he was financed by Alberto Pico della Mirandola.

The wealthy commercial port of Venice was a logical place for his enterprise since from the mid-15th century a large community of exiled Greeks (mostly Cretans) had settled there (known corporately as 'La Scuola e Nazione greca'). It was a centre of Greek studies and had in the Temple of St Mark the important collection of 500 Greek MSS donated in 1468 by Cardinal Bessarion. Texts were thus at hand.

Aldus had as principal editor the Cretan Marcus Musurus (d. 1517) who was responsible for a dozen of the Aldine editiones principes. Another Cretan was Yannis Gregoropoulos, chief compositor, well able to read difficult manuscript originals. The two lived on the premises. From 1494 to 1515 a steady flow of Greek texts came from the press. The first dated book was Lascaris's 'Erotemata, cum interpretatione latina', 1494/5; the most important was a folio edition in five volumes of Aristotle's works, 1495–8.

In 1498, 1503 and 1513 Aldus issued lists of his publications stipulating minimum sale prices, e.g. *veduntur non minoris* or *veduntur minimo*.

In 1500 he formed an Academy at his home (*Neakademia*) at the meetings of which only Greek was spoken. Among scholars working with him was Erasmus who in 1507 gave Aldus two Greek tragedies, 'Hecuba' and 'Iphigenia', suggesting publication in small octavo with italic type. He asked for a few copies in return. In 1508, when he lived with Aldus to see his 'Adagiorum collectanea' through the press, type composition proceeded as Erasmus wrote. The latter recorded that Aldus's large library was notable for its Greek texts, also that Poles and Hungarians were among the many scholars who brought or sent him old manuscripts to print, often with money to do so. Another scholar working with Aldus was the Latinist Hieronymous Avantius whose edition of Lucretius, 1500, was well known.

Italian classics printed by Aldus included Petrarch's 'Canzoniere', 1501, important for its moral message and excellent poetic writing. It was edited by Pietro Bembo, as was Dante's 'La Divina commedia', which Manutius printed in 1502. Bembo's 'Gli Asolani', a prose dialogue, appeared in 1505.

The greek type used by Manutius was modelled on the writing of Marcus Musurus and cut by Francesco Griffo. Manutius was shrewd enough to realise that publication in small format would ensure the wide circulation of his books and that this would need small type. He therefore commissioned Griffo to cut for him a distinctive sloping type which had more than sixty tied letters to emphasise its cursive quality. We know this type, and its many successors, as *italic*, q.v. It required some 150 punches and first appeared in an edition of Virgil in 1501. He called his small books 'libelli portatiles in formam enchiridii' (handbooks). Both format and type were speedily copied elsewhere, notably in Lyons.

When *Jenson*, q.v., pioneer of the roman letter, died in 1481 his punches, matrices and types were bought by Torresano, the father-in-law of Aldus. It was, however, the roman face which Aldus commissioned from Griffo in 1495, and not the earlier Jenson, which was later to influence Garamont's roman and its successors.

From 1515 to 1533 the press was managed by Aldus's brothers-in-law, but they dispersed the body of scholars and so editorial standards fell. However, in 1533 *Paulus Manutius* (1512–72), youngest son of Aldus, took over the press. He concentrated on editions of Latin classics, particularly Cicero. Between 1561 and 1570 he was in Rome as director of the *Tipografia del Popolo Romano*, q.v. The Venetian press eventually passed to *Aldus II*, grandson of the founder. He, too, was invited to Rome to assist with the newly established *Typographia Apostolica Vaticana*, q.v.

It was Aldus I who established Venice as a centre for Greek printing, and until the end of the 19th century almost all Orthodox ecclesiastical books used in the Greek-speaking world continued to be printed there. See also *Aldine device, cursive, Francesco da Bologna, Torresano, Venetian bindings*.

alfa grass: a variety of esparto used in papermaking.

all along: the method of hand sewing the sections of a book on cords or tapes when the thread goes from kettle-stitch to kettle-stitch inside the fold of each section. Also used to describe a machine-sewn book in which each section has the full number of stitches. See also *hand-sewing*.

Allan, George, 1736–1800: see *Grange Press*.

Allde, Edward, fl.1584–1628: a London printer, the son of *John Allde* whose business he appears to have continued. About 370 works have been traced to his press, two-thirds being printed for sale by others. They include devotional books, news pamphlets, a popular cookery book, and one on gardening. The remainder were sometimes printed for their authors, e.g. John Speidell's mathematical textbooks.

allonym: a person's name used by a writer instead of his or her own. Hence 'allonymous' books.

All rights reserved: a claim of copyright sometimes printed on the back of a title-page; now generally superseded by the *copyright notice*, q.v. Originally, the words were added to the copyright notice in books published in the United States in compliance with the Buenos Aires Convention of 1910. This was later replaced by the *Universal Copyright Convention*, q.v.

alluminor: one who illuminated manuscripts. Later terms were *enlumineur* and *limner*.

all up setting: see *keep up*.

almanac: a book containing the days, weeks and months of the year together with information about festivals, astronomical data and other items of interest.

The word derives from the Arabic 'al manākh', meaning a calendar. An early counterpart was the list of days when legal business was allowed and also the festivals and games for each day of the year. The Moors introduced the word *almanac* to Spain. It was used by Chaucer to refer to tables of celestial eclipses, conjunctions of the sun and moon, and the dates of movable feasts. The tables were illustrated by diagrams. Roger Bacon used the term in 1267 in his encyclopaedia 'Opus maius' for a table giving the movements of celestial bodies. In 16th century

England most almanacs were written by 'doctors in physick and astronomie' and they were used by students of astronomy, law, and medicine. One of the earliest almanacs printed in England was de Worde's for the years 1507–19, issued in 1508.

Between 1557 and 1775 the privilege for almanacs was held by the Stationers' Company and the two universities. Dr Francis Moore's almanac first appeared in 1700 as 'Vox stellarum', and it is still issued as 'Old Moore's Almanack'. The important navigational aid the 'Nautical Almanac' was initiated in 1766 (for 1767) by the Astronomer Royal, while 'Whitaker's Almanack', which is widely accepted as an authoritative reference book, dates from 1868. See also *ephemeris, prognostications*.

alphabet: see *letters – forms and styles*.

aluminium plates: lithographic printing plates used as an alternative to zinc. They have the disadvantage of oxidizing quickly, but *anodized aluminium plates*, introduced to the trade in the 1950s, do not oxidize, and their finer grain improves print quality. They are particularly suitable for the *deep-etch process*, q.v.

Amazeur, Jean, fl.1534–55: a Parisian printer of illustrated Missals and Breviaries, mostly for the publishers Godard and Merlin.

Ambrosian Iliad: fragments of an illustrated Iliad on vellum, believed to have been written prior to 500 at Constantinople. Only fifty-eight miniatures survive, with portions of the Greek text written in uncials on the backs: they are thought to represent a quarter of the whole work which may have been a copy of an earlier original. The pictures, all within blue or red frames, are painted in tempera on a buff wash ground. In style they are considered to represent a group of Homeric illustrations based on the traditions of many periods, here collected and painted by one artist. Since 1609 the work has been in Milan.

Amerbach, Johannes, *c.* 1430–1513: a printer, born at Reutlingen in Germany. He studied at the Sorbonne under *Johann Heynlin* before working in Nuremberg as a press corrector for *Anton Koberger*, qq.v. In Basle, where Amerbach established a press about 1475, he was joined about 1482 by Jakob Wolff (d. 1519). His partners from 1490 were Johann Petri von Langendorf (d. 1511) and *Johannes Froben*, q.v. Initially Amerbach was probably the business manager and editor-publisher rather than a practising craftsman.

He became the leading printer in Basle, issuing at least seventy works, among them a Latin dictionary, eleven Latin Bibles, classics and theological books. He was the first Basle printer to use roman type.

He had a considerable reputation in Germany where Koberger acted as his publisher. Heynlin von Stein left the Sorbonne for Basle to advise him on what texts to print and to supervise the editing. Amerbach planned accurate and well produced editions of the four doctors of the Church, issuing St Ambrose in 1492 and St Augustine in 1506. Reuchlin and Reisch helped with the Hebrew and Greek texts of St Jerome but Amerbach died before the work was finished. The business was then directed for a time by his former partner Froben, and later by his younger son *Boniface Amerbach* (1495–1562). See 'Die Amerbach-Korrespondenz', 5 vols, Basle, 1942–58.

American Bookplate Society: a society formed in New York in 1913 with the aim of increasing knowledge and appreciation of bookplates by means of exhibitions and the publication of a monthly journal.

American Book-Prices Current: established by Luther S. Livingston in 1895 (from September 1894) as an annual guide to sale prices, compiled from catalogues of the more important sales of literary properties sold at auction in the United States and London.

The work has four main sections: books, autographs and manuscripts, broadsides, maps and charts. Occasional cumulative indexes have been issued.

Since 1969 publication has been under the auspices of Columbia University Press.

American Book Publishers Council Inc.: founded in 1920 as the *National Association of Book Publishers*, reorganised as the *Book Publishers Bureau* in 1937, and given its present title in 1946. It is a non-profit making corporation which exists to further the interests of book publishers. Its objects include the encouragement of reading, the maintenance of credit information on bookstores and other outlets; the administration of a group insurance plan for the book trade; developing of sales outlets and publicity methods; the advising on copyright problems; the opposing of censorship; and liaison with government departments, libraries, and educational organizations. Headquarters are in New York. In 1970 it was absorbed by the *Association of American Publishers*, q.v.

American Booksellers Association: or *ABA*, founded in 1900. The oldest American organization for booksellers. Annual conventions are held at which there are trade exhibits by associate member publishers for bookstore buyers, and at which trade methods and problems are discussed. The Association issues a monthly bulletin and also the annual 'Book Buyers' Handbook' which is one of the basic American book trade reference books. It also publishes a monthly journal *The American Bookseller*. Address: 122 East 42nd Street, New York 10017.

American book sizes: common book sizes in the U.S.A. are given here though they are not absolute. It will be seen that the word 'octavo' or 'quarto' alone does not indicate size since octavo books vary in vertical height from Cap Octavo, 7 inches, to Imperial Octavo, $11\frac{1}{2}$ inches.

Name	*inches*
Thirtysixmo	$4 \times 3\frac{1}{3}$
Medium Thirtytwomo	$4\frac{3}{4} \times 3$
Medium Twentyfourmo	$5\frac{1}{2} \times 3\frac{5}{8}$
Medium Eighteenmo	$6\frac{2}{3} \times 4$
Medium Sixteenmo	$6\frac{3}{4} \times 4\frac{1}{2}$
Cap Octavo	$7 \times 7\frac{1}{4}$
Duodecimo	$7\frac{1}{2} \times 4\frac{1}{2}$
Crown Octavo	$7\frac{1}{2} \times 5$
Post Octavo	$7\frac{1}{2} \times 5\frac{1}{2}$
Medium Duodecimo	$7\frac{2}{3} \times 5\frac{1}{8}$
Demy Octavo	$8 \times 5\frac{1}{2}$
Small Quarto (usually less)	$8\frac{1}{2} \times 7$
Broad Quarto (varies up to 13 × 10)	$8\frac{1}{2} \times 7$
Medium Octavo	$9\frac{1}{2} \times 6$
Royal Octavo	$10 \times 6\frac{1}{2}$
Super Royal Octavo	$10\frac{1}{2} \times 7$
Imperial Quarto	11×15
Imperial Octavo	$11\frac{1}{2} \times 8\frac{1}{4}$

American Book Trade Association: the name chosen at a booksellers' convention at Ohio in mid-1874 for the *Booksellers' Protective Union*, formed in 1873. Such was the disagreement among members about price maintenance, underselling and piracy that the Association ceased in 1877.

American Company of Booksellers: formed in 1801 in New York to prevent price cutting and to regulate book sales by means of annual trade fairs. It also offered prizes for improved manufacturing methods. Following disagreements the Company ceased in 1805.

American Institute of Graphic Arts: founded in 1914 by a group of members of the National Arts Club in New York. They aimed 'to do all things which would raise the standard and the extension and development towards perfection of the graphic arts in the United States'. These aims have been reached in many ways. In addition to occasional exhibitions featuring a single personality or aspect of graphic art there are two regular exhibitions: 'Printing for Commerce' (annually 1924–41, and since 1950), and 'The Fifty Books of the Year' (annually since 1923). A Trade Book Clinic was established in 1930, of which most of the participants are members of the production staffs of New York publishers who meet for lectures and discussions at which the quality of their current publications is appraised.

In 1948 the Institute started a workshop where the office workers of printing and publishing firms can handle type and machines. In addition to occasional publishing, the Institute has issued the *News-letter* (1922–45), which in 1947 was superseded by the *Journal*.

At its annual meeting the Institute's medal is presented to some personality in the graphic art world. Among recipients have been W. A. Dwiggins, Frederic Goudy, Dard Hunter, Stanley Morison, Bruce Rogers, Carl Rollins, and D. B. Updike.

American joints: see *french joints.*

American point system: see *point.*

American Publishers Association: founded in 1900. Its aims were to establish and maintain fixed selling prices for books. To a degree never known in England the 1890s had seen a tremendous spread of the practice of selling books as loss-leaders in general stores, thereby damaging the legitimate book trade. Matters reached the stage when it was cheaper for a bookseller to buy his stock from a store than from the publisher. The new Association sought to deny their books to the big department stores. One such, Macy & Co. of New York, sued the Association and were in 1914 awarded $140,000 by the Supreme Court. That was the end of the Association. For subsequent organizations see *Association of American Publishers, Inc.*

American russia: strong, split cowhide used for book covers. Also known as *imitation russia.*

American Society of Indexers: formed in 1969 with aims similar to those of the British *Society of Indexers*, q.v., to which it was affiliated in 1971.

American Type Founders Company: a company begun in 1891 and organized a year later as 'a consolidation of twenty typefoundries'. It developed into the leading type and printing equipment business in the United States. The first complete general specimen book of 1900 included 525 series of job founts and thirty-seven of body type.

Prominent typographers associated with its early fame were *Lynn Boyd Benton*, q.v.; Will Bradley, who was art director and editor of 'The American Chap-book' and other occasional pieces issued by ATF; and *Henry Lewis Bullen*, q.v., who founded the typographical library and museum which since 1936 has been at Columbia University.

In 1902 the ATF issued the popular Cheltenham type face devised in 1900–1 by Ingalls Kimball (1874–1933). The working drawings for this were made under his direction by *Bertram Goodhue*, q.v. See also *ATF typesetter*.

Ames, Joseph, 1689–1759: notable as the author of 'Typographical antiquities, being an historical account of printing in England . . . from the year 1471–1600 . . .', London, 1749. There were later revisions.

Amharic: see *ethiopic type*.

Amman, Jost, 1539–91: a famous draftsman, copper-plate engraver and woodcutter, born in Zurich. In 1560 he settled in Nuremberg, and in 1562 took over and completed the commissions of Virgil Solis for

with extra illustrations and a text by Hartmann Schopper, had the title 'Panoplia omnium . . . artium', and was also issued in 1568.

Amos, Charles Edward: an English millwright and engineer who in 1840 invented a consistency regulator, which he called a 'pulp regulator', for delivering a proper proportion of pulp and backwater according to the speed of the paper machine. He also invented a paper cutter. (ML)

ampersand: &, a monogram which derives from the scribes' ligature for the Latin word *et*, meaning 'and'. The origins of this may be traced to graffiti of

Type-founder

Printer

Bookbinder

Three of Amman's woodcuts to Hans Sach's stanzas in 'Eygentliche Beschreibung aller Stände auf Erden', printed in 1568 by Sigmund Feierabend of Frankfurt. (Here reduced)

Sigmund Feierabend, q.v., for whom he worked for the rest of his life. In 1577 he was given the citizenship of Nuremberg.

He was noted for his title-pages, book illustrations and woodcuts which appeared in the Bible, herbals, cookery books, books of costumes, heraldry and playing cards. One of his best-known works was 'Ein neuw Thierbuch', Frankfurt, 1569, of which there were many reprints. Some of his cuts in this and in his 'Kunst und Lehrbüchlein', Frankfurt, 1578, served as patterns for jewellers who made gold and enamel pendants. Amman was related to practising goldsmiths. A reprint of the 4th edition (1599) of the 'Kunstbüchlin' (as it was orginally misnamed) was issued by Dover Publications Ltd in 1968.

Reproduced here are three of his woodcuts from the book 'Eygentliche Beschreibung aller Stände auff Erden', 1568. This included over 100 cuts with a poem by Hans Sachs under each. The Latin edition,

the 1st century AD, and in one form or another & has been used by writers and printers ever since.

The word *ampersand* is a corruption of 'and per se = and', i.e. & by itself. In his 'Diggings from many ampersand-hogs' L. C. Wroth wrote 'To exist as a corruption descriptive of a contraction seems an ignoble destiny. To be called "ampersand" not because of descent from one of the great languages of antiquity, but for the shameful reason that for centuries snuffling little Britishers refused to enunciate properly the tag at the end of their alphabets is not the best basis for a life of dignity . . . Droning their *hornbooks* in unison or alone those speech-lazy boys and girls of the past gradually allowed their "X, Y, Z, &" their "ex, wye, zed, and per se and", to become "ex, wye, zed, ampersand", creating from four monosyllables, without thought or design, a lovely liquid word that not only sounds as if it meant something, but that belongs to the hierarchy of poetic sounds.' See J. Tschichold, 'The Ampersand: its origin and development', translated by F. Plaat, *British Printer*, January 1958, where nearly 300 examples are shown. See also *horn book*.

Amsterdam Typefoundry: see *Typefoundry Amsterdam*.

ana: 1. 'books so called from the last syllables of their titles . . . they are loose thoughts, or casual hints, dropped by eminent men and collected by their friends', Samuel Johnson's 'Dictionary', 1755. Paradoxically, the best exemplar of his definition was entitled 'Life of Johnson' by Boswell, and not 'Johnsoniana'.

The collections of 'ana' made in classical Greece and Rome were not so named, and the term seems first to have been used by a friend of Poggio for the *bons mots*, anecdotes, historical incidents, and sundry items collected by the Italian Humanist (though not until 1720, in Amsterdam, did a printed edition of them appear as 'Poggiana').

In Germany an edition of Luther's table-talk, recorded by his friends, was published in 1566 as 'Tischreden': it could appropriately have been entitled 'Lutherana' (as was an 1892 edition of it) and was the first 'ana' to be published. The 'Scaligeriana', Utrecht, 1666, was the first book printed with the name (later editions gave 'Scaligerana'). This began a fashion for comparable works, particularly in France where the vogue continued until the mid-18th century. Here the content was scholarly and literary as in the well-known 'Menagiana' of 1693. In England John Selden's 'Table talk . . .', 1689, was issued as 'Seldeniana' in 1789.

2. a writer's miscellaneous papers which may have been assembled after his death and include some previously published, as 'Baconiana', 1679. (This may be the first occurrence of the suffix in an English title.)

3. an anthology of a single subject, thus Heinrich Bebel's collection of German proverbs published as 'Bebeliana', Augsburg.

4. a group heading used in antiquarian booksellers' catalogues for books having a common theme, thus 'Americana', 'Shakespeariana'.

Anabat, Guillaume, fl.1505–10: a Parisian printer who produced some twenty-six Books of Hours, most of them for the Hardouyns. They were richly illustrated, mostly in the style of Pigouchet and Vostre. As the second part of a work begun in 1510 for Jean Granjon was completed by Nicolas de Prez in the same year it is possible that Anabat may have died.

anagnostes: see *dictation of copy*.

anastatic printing: an obsolete process for multiplying facsimiles of writing, drawings or letterpress. It involved soaking the original in diluted nitric acid and transferring the image to a zinc plate for printing in a lithographic press.

The process as developed in England originated in Berlin about 1840. In 1844 Joseph Woods (d. 1849) registered a patent in London and gave the process its name. From 1848 the Ipswich firm of Cowell used it until the 1890s by which time photographic transfer methods had made it obsolete.

Notes on the history of this and similar minor processes are given in G. Wakeman's 'Aspects of Victorian lithography: anastatic printing and photozincography', Wymondham, Brewhouse Press, 1970.

anathema: a formula for consigning to damnation those who might be tempted to damage or steal a book. During the 13th and 14th centuries a phrase to this effect, written in Latin, would often accompany a formal inscription of ownership at the beginning of books belonging to certain English monastic libraries.

Hans Christian Andersen Medals: see *International Board on Books for Young People*.

André, Jean, fl.1535–52: the principal printer in Paris during this time of the acts and ordinances issued by the parliaments of François I and Henri II, and an official printer to the University.

He published some anti-Lutheran tracts, and by denouncing them to the authorities was responsible for the death or imprisonment of several Calvinists, including François and Robert *Estienne*, q.v.

Andrewe, Laurence, fl.1510–37: a native of Calais who worked in London and Antwerp as a translator and printer of scientific works. His first published translation was printed by *Jan van Doesborgh*, q.v., and the latter may have taught him the craft of printing.

Andrewe issued an undated edition of 'The myrrour & dyscrypcion of the world', taking Caxton's 1481 text and also some of the original blocks (STC 24764).

Angerer, Carl, 1838–1916: the founder in 1870 of the Viennese firm of Angerer & Göschl, plate-makers and reproducers. Having acquainted himself while working for Firmin Gillot with the latter's process for making blocks, Angerer worked independently in 1865. In 1870 he developed the so-called Vienna process to which he gave the name 'chemigraphy'. He also contributed to the practical development of the half-tone block method. (GU)

Anglo-Norman: the name given in England to *lombard* capitals, q.v. They were sometimes given emphasis by adding a shading stroke in red ink.

Anglo-Saxon Chronicle: a chronological history of

England which survives in six complete manuscripts, each devoted to a particular area and period: 1. from 891–1070, written in Winchester and Canterbury, now in Cambridge University Library; 2. up to 977, including a Mercian chronicle for 902–42 in the British Library (Cotton, *Tiberius* A.vi); 3. an Abingdon chronicle up to 1066 (BM, Cotton, *Tiberius* B.i); 4. from Worcester and Northumbria, begun 1016 and extending to 1079 (BM, Cotton, *Tiberius* B.iv); 5. a Peterborough chronicle, written 1122–54, now in the Bodleian; 6. a Saxon and Latin MS. from Canterbury, belonging to the 12th century (BM, Cotton, *Domitian* A.viii). Other parts were lost in the fire which damaged the Cotton collection in 1731.

Anglo-Saxon illumination: see *Hiberno-Saxon illumination*.

aniline printing: see *flexography*.

animal-sized: paper hardened or sized with animal glue or gelatine by passing the finished sheet or roll through a bath of glue. See also *engine-sized, tub-sized*.

annals: a historical record of the events of a year, published after the end of it; usage of the term dates to ancient Rome (the 'Annales Maximi').

Annual Bibliography of the History of the Printed Book and Libraries: since 1973, when vol. 1, listing the publications of 1970 was issued in The Hague.

The editorial board then included representatives of twenty-four member countries of IFLA, with H. D. L. Vervliet as editor. It was stated in vol. 1 that the bibliography 'aims at recording all books and articles of scholarly value which relate to the history of the printed book (from the first half of the 15th century), to the history of the arts, craft, techniques and equipment, and of the economic, social and cultural environment involved in its production, distribution, conservation and description'. Books and articles on modern technical processes are excluded.

Acknowledgement was made to J. Simmons, editor of *Bibliography in Britain*, q.v., the classification plan of which was borrowed.   (HDT)

annuals: 1. serial publications issued once a year. 2. literary anthologies, popular in the 19th century, usually illustrated by steel engravings. The latter, known as 'embellishments', were a more important sales factor than the text. This class of book originated in Germany, being introduced to the English trade in 1822 by *Ackermann*, q.v. Ladies were the intended recipients if not the purchasers, and the success of early annuals led to many imitations. 'The Keepsake'

and 'Friendship's offering' (1824–44) were two of the better known, 35,000 of the first edition of the latter being sold within weeks.

Among famous illustrators was John Martin whose romantic engravings may have influenced Charlotte Brontë who had framed prints in her home and read the annuals. See F. W. Faxon, 'Literary annuals and gift books: a bibliography, 1823–93'. London, 1973. See also *keepsake, table book*. 3. in modern publishing, a term used for the illustrated anthologies for children based on sports, comic papers and so on. Publication is often timed for the Christmas trade.

anodized aluminium plates: standard litho plates, suitable for large or small machines and superior to normally grained zinc or aluminium plates which quickly oxidize.

Plates are first given a fine grain by mechanical or chemical *graining*, q.v., and are then electrolytically given a stable, hard water-receptive surface suitable for the deep-etch image. Such plates are suitable for runs of up to half a million.

In the United States grained aluminium plates are still widely used, the image areas being strengthened by copperizing.

anonymous: a publication of undeclared authorship.

anopisthographic printing: the manner of printing early block books on one side of the leaf only since the brown or grey water-based ink used was absorbed through the paper. Later, when oil based inks were used, block books were printed on both sides of the dampened leaf, being described as *opisthographically* printed.

answering code: see *publishers abbreviated answers*.

anthology: a collection of extracts from the writings of one or several authors. Early Greek examples date from the 2nd century BC, and anthologies, particularly of poetry, have been continuously popular in most European literatures. See also *chrestomathy, florilegium, garland*.

Antiphonary: one of the present liturgical books intended for use in choir. Generically includes antiphons and antiphonal chants sung at Mass and at the canonical Hours, but now refers only to the sung portions of the *Breviary*, q.v.

antiqua: 1. roman types based on scripts developed by the Italians *Niccoli* and *Poggio*, qq.v., who had modelled them on early manuscript hands used in North Italy during the 11th and 12th centuries.

2. the German name for roman type as distinct from *Fraktur*, q.v.

antiquarian: the largest known size of hand-made paper, 53 in. by 31 in., introduced to the trade by James Whatman in the 18th century.

Antiquarian Booksellers' Association (International): the secondhand book trade association, founded in London in 1906. Membership is open to any British or foreign bookseller dealing mainly in books no longer in print.

The aims of the Association are to promote and extend the sale of antiquarian and rare books, to improve the status of the trade, to promote honourable conduct in business, to provide funds to assist members or their dependants in distress, to promote exhibitions or co-operate with other organizations to further the distribution of books, and to act as an Association in matters where individual action would be less likely to succeed. See also *The Clique*.

antique binding: see *monastic bindings*.

antique gold edges: said of the finish given to gilt edges which are either left unburnished, or burnished and washed over with water. When bound in stout or bevelled boards designs are sometimes tooled on book edges, a diapered pattern with centre tool being generally used. Cf. *rough gilt*.

antique laid: 1. originally, descriptive of paper made on moulds which had the chain wires laced or sewed direct to the wooden ribs, or supports, of the mould. This caused the pulp to lie heavier along each side of every chain line in the sheet of paper.

2. now, any rough-surfaced laid paper. Better qualities have an esparto furnish; cheaper varieties may include sulphate pulp or even mechanical wood.

antique wove: a light bulky rough-surfaced paper of good quality. The finish is matt, the paper being neither calendered nor coated. It is suitable for printing type and line engravings, but not half-tones unless by offset litho, and is used for most books without blocks.

anti-set-off sprayer: an apparatus attached to a printing machine to prevent *set-off*, q.v. It is a spray gun which blows a mixture of resinous solution or powder on to each printed sheet as it falls on the delivery tray of the press. The tiny globules or grains keep the sheets momentarily separate.

In modern practice either a dry powder such as limestone, starch or hartshorn, or a solution of dextrin or gum arabic is used. Advantages claimed by the makers of powder sprays are that higher running speeds are possible; less escapes into the atmosphere, thus more reaches the sheet, and the equipment is easier to clean.

APA: see *American Publishers Association*.

Apocalypse: the Revelation of St John the Divine which, with its message of the triumph of Christianity over the forces of evil, was a favourite text in Europe for copying and illuminating.

It began to interest English artists in the 13th century, preceded elsewhere by Carolingian and particularly Spanish artists who interpreted the Beatus commentaries in the vivid *Mozarabic* style, q.v. One of the earliest and certainly the most sumptuous is the Trinity College Apocalypse (MS.R.16.2) which was probably made in the second quarter of the 13th century in an undetermined scriptorium. The text is in French. (A superb facsimile was issued by the Eugrammia Press, London, 1965). Scarcely less important were copies made by artists of the *St Alban's School*, q.v. The text was often subordinate to the delicate lightly-tinted drawings, with tall slim figures for the virtuous and ugly shapes for the powers of evil. A famous example is the Douce Apocalypse (named after *Francis Douce*, q.v.) made prior to 1272 for Edward I and now in the Bodleian Library (MS. *Douce* 180).

The earliest printed Apocalypse, probably of Flemish origin, was a block book with cuts closely resembling scenes in late 14th century illuminated manuscripts of French or English origin, but because of problems of interpreting in wood, showing simple outlines for the figures. Apocalypse block books, of which some six editions with different suites of blocks are known, were printed in the Netherlands and Germany in the era 1460–7. Some were hand coloured.

Of Apocalypses printed from movable type the most famous are the German and Latin editions of Anton Koberger in 1498 which included Albrecht Dürer's dramatic suite of woodcuts (for an illustration see *woodcut*). See M. R. James, 'The Apocalypse in art', 1931.

apocryphal: of doubtful authenticity.

apograph: an exact transcript of an original manuscript.

Apollo and Pegasus bindings: see *Grimaldi, Giovanni Battista*.

appendix (pl appendices): matter subordinate to the text of a work and printed immediately after it. An appendix differs from an addendum in that the need for the latter is only discovered when the book is set; the former is planned from the beginning as an integral part of the work.

Appledore Private Press: an American private press founded *c.* 1870 at Hamden, near New Haven, by

William James Linton who had previously lived in England.

In addition to being a poet and champion for the freedom of the press Linton was a wood engraver of merit. Publications were mostly of verse.

Applegath, Augustus, 1788–1871: born in London; a printer and machinery maker. About 1817 he took into partnership his brother-in-law *Edward Cowper* (1790–1852). They were interested in the printing of bank notes (with official approval and financial support) for which in 1819 they devised an early form of offset printing with curved stereos. The first revolution of the impression cylinder, made without paper, imprinted the design on leather pads; a second revolution, made with paper in position, impressed the same design on the front of the sheet by direct contact and on the back of it by contact with the pads, the two impressions being in perfect register. As it was found that their notes could be copied the project was abandoned.

They also worked on the simplification and improvement of the König and Bauer perfector presses installed by Thomas Bensley and *The Times*.

In 1821 Applegath alone took premises to build his own improved cylinder machines. These were used in London, Paris, and Petersburg by state printers as well as by newspaper printers. Financial difficulties led Applegath to sell his workshop to William Clowes, and he turned his attention to silk printing from engraved curved copper plates, opening a factory at Crayford in 1826.

In 1844 he sold his second business and opened anew in Dartford with a silk-printing works as well as separate premises for building printing machinery. His most famous product was the eight-feeder vertical press he made for *The Times* in 1848. This could print 8,000 four-page sheets an hour on one side. By 1858, however, *The Times* turned to the ten-feeder presses of Richard Hoe, and Applegath's business had passed its peak. In 1868 he retired, his remaining label and bank note printing shop passing to his son *Louis*. In 1889 he sold it. See also *König, letterpress machines*.

apud. the Latin for 'at (or obtainable at) the house of' (in the context described here). The word, followed by the name of the printer, publisher, or bookseller, appears frequently on early title-pages. E.g. APVD SIMONEM COLINAEVM (Obtainable at the house of Simon Colines).

Apud Sanctum Jacobum de Ripoli: the imprint used on books issued from the press of the convent of Dominican nuns in the Via della Scala, Florence. It was active from 1476–84, being principally inspired by two convent officials, Fra Domenico da Pistoia and Fra Piero da Pisa.

Johannes Petri, who supplied a roman type in 1477, and Nicolaus Laurentii were among professional craftsmen who assisted, but it was the nuns, already skilled in calligraphy and illumination, who worked as compositors and, suggests BMC, probably also on presswork. They were not, however, particularly skilled or careful. They issued between seventy and eighty works; copies of the first to appear, a Donatus of 1476, have disappeared. Others included a life of St Catharine, 'Fior di virtù', Perottus and Latin classics.

aquatint: 1. an intaglio process for reproducing illustrations which are normally tones (rather like black ink wash drawings), but often a combination of tones and etched lines. The design is first etched or engraved on a copper plate before the aquatint ground is applied. The design is one of varying degrees of tone, and these will be stopped out with varnish as etching proceeds and the plate is etched to different depths. The purpose of the aquatint ground is to divide the surface of the plate into microscopically small ink cells. The special granular effect of the ground is applied by either dry or wet methods. In the former case the plate is placed in a bitumen powder cupboard in which a fine dust of the powder is whirled about and allowed to settle uniformly on the upturned surface of the plate. This dust is melted by a heater under the plate. The size of the granules depends on the time which passes between setting the dust in motion and laying up the plate in the cupboard, and its density on how long it is allowed to remain there. By the wet method liquid aquatint ground consisting of resin dissolved in alcohol is flowed over the plate, when after the evaporation of the alcohol the resin remains as a grain layer on it.

After laying on a ground by one of these methods and painting the back of the plate with varnish as a protection against the acid, etching is done with dutch mordant or perchloride of iron. The lightest grey tones will be etched first, and after the plate has been dried these areas are stopped out with varnish. The varying depths of tone are achieved by further controlled etching. If tones are etched too deeply they can be lightened with a burnishing tool. Aquatint and dry-point plates can be combined, the latter bearing the design in outline, the former the surface tinting.

A variant of the aquatint is the *aquatint wash*, when nitric acid of different strengths is painted with a brush on the copper plate in a manner similar to tinting in water colour painting.

Sugar or *reverse aquatint* is another etching method by which the plate is cleaned and the drawing is made on it with a pen or brush using a solution of sugar and indian ink (or a solution of gum arabic, sugar, and ox gall). After drying the plate is then given a thin coat of hard etching ground. This having dried (quickly) the plate is immersed in water which causes the sugar layer to swell and 'lift' the varnish off the design areas, exposing the metal. The remaining varnish acts as a resist to the etching acid in which the plate is now immersed. The etching is repeated if tones are required.

To control the etching more closely the artist often works with a plate sufficiently large to allow for a marginal key strip; on this he makes a number of tones corresponding to those of the main picture. When the plate is finished this strip is cut off. On completing the etching any remaining varnish and ground are washed off with benzol, after which printing takes place as in other copperplate printing.

Claims for the invention of aquatint are made for Abbé St Non, 1750, and for J. B. Le Prince (1734–81): coloured aquatints were introduced by F. Janinet (1752–1814). The process achieved its finest results at the hands of Francisco de Goya (1746–1828) who combined etching and aquatint. Paul Sandby (1725–1809) introduced it into England in 1775, and Thomas Malton (1708–1804) was an important worker in this medium, while the topographical works of *Rudolph Ackermann*, q.v., provide noteworthy examples.

2. a print taken from the plates described above.
(With GU)

Aqua-trol: the trade name of an American device for the continuous removal by heated air of moisture from the inking system of a lithographic press. It was developed by the American Type Founders Company.

arabesque: the style of Islamic ornamentation deriving from the classical acanthus leaf and vine. As perfected by the Fatimids for decorating the mosque of al-Azhar in Cairo, 970–1003, the forms were less naturalistic than the original. Division into the basic elements of stem, leaf and blossom made the arabesque adaptable for infinite variation ranging from the partly figurative to the abstract, and suitable alike for the decoration of a small box, a tooled bookbinding, or the dome of a mosque. The Muslim artist or craftsman filled an entire surface with ornament, and the arabesque was combined with geometrical units and also with calligraphy.

Arabesque-patterned embroidery made by Muslim craftsmen at Palermo in the 11th century probably marks the beginning in Europe of an art theme which culminated in its final formal brilliance during the later Italian Renaissance. Familiarity came from Islamic leatherwork, pottery, embroidery and metalwork imported into Venice and Spain from the Levant and North Africa as well as from migrating settlers. Early Venetian bindings with arabesque motifs, the work of Muslims, may date from the 1480s. As interpreted by non-Muslims the arabesque lost its original calligraphic quality, becoming simpler and less closely packed. Basing their work on such

14

compilations as Tagliente's pattern book 'Essempio di recammi', Rome, 1527, Italian and French bookbinders and printers created designs built up from curving stems, leaves, fruit or flowers into graceful convolutions for cover, title-page and border decoration. See also *acanthus, ajouré, Arabic calligraphy, entrelacs, flowers, leaf, mudéjar bindings, white vine.*

Arabic calligraphy: formal writing based on the two main groups of script used for Arabic: *Kufic* and *Naskhī.* The original Kufic, thick, angular, and with long horizontal strokes, is named after Kufah in Iraq where, according to tradition, it was devised during the reign of 'Ali (36–41 AH/AD 656–61) and used in a theological school. As the earliest form had no pointing or diacritical signs variant meanings could be given to one symbol. By the 2nd century AH/AD 8th a fully pointed Kufic was established as the only script for copying the Koran, though pointing is often omitted for other texts. As all Arabs knew the Koran by heart legibility was less important than a dignified presentation of its message. The use of gold and colour to mark divisions began in the 3rd/9th century. For contemporary lapidary inscriptions, particularly Egyptian, foliated and floriated Kufic were used in which vertical strokes ended in lobed-leaf and half-palmette forms.

By the 6th/12th century the Muslims of Andalusia and North Africa were using two cursive derivatives of Kufic known collectively as *Maghribi* which, when merged into one by the 10th/16th, was marked by a general lightness of stroke, deep curves below the line and fewer angles.

The cursive *Naskhī* and its more elegant form *Thuluth* (used for headings, titles and inscriptions) are attributed to Ibn Muqla of Baghdad in the early 10th century AD and were perfected by Ibn al-Bawwab by the end of the same century. They remained the principal scripts for copying the Koran in eastern Islamic countries. Naskhī, found in several styles, was locally modified for sounds either additional to or not required in the original.

Of considerable importance was *Nastalīq*, developed in Persia in the later 14th century by Mir Ali Tabrizi, with flowing horizontal strokes and downward oblique strokes, and used mostly for secular writing. This script of great elegance predominated in Iran, Turkey (until 1928), Afghanistan and Mughal India.

Calligraphy in its various forms was an important element in Islamic art, being found subtly integrated with the *arabesque,* q.v., but the sole reason for its creation and development was the need to preserve the integrity of the Koran and proclaim its message. Copying the Koran was an act of the highest piety. The message was also cut in stone for permanence, thus the earliest important surviving Muslim shrine, Abd al-Malik's Dome of the Rock at Jerusalem, completed 72 AH/AD 691, included in its decoration an elaborate epigraphic frieze 240 m. long in a hieratic form of Kufic. It was, and is, difficult to read from the ground and was intended more as an affirmation of faith, addressed to God.

Arabic is still the second most widely used script in the world. It is written from right to left: numerals from left to right.

See also *arabic type, Islamic illumination, Koran.*

arabic numerals: 1 2 3 4 5 6 7 8 9 0. A misnomer given to the system of numerical notation used in the western world. In spite of the name the numbers are widely accepted as tracing their origins to Hindu symbols used in India where written numerals, without the zero, are found in the inscriptions of Ashoka who reigned from 264–230 BC. The dot as a zero symbol was known by 200 BC. The earliest known inscription recording the date by a system based on nine integers and a zero comes from Gujerat and is dated AD 595. By the 8th century AD the Hindu *devanagari* numerals, which by then included a small circle as a symbol for zero, were used by traders in Baghdad through contact with visiting Arab merchants and those who had conquered Sind in 712. The Arabs called mathematics *hindi sah* (the Indian art; or, the art of the engineer), and the numerals are to this day known in Arab countries as *al-Arq'ām el-Hindīye*, thereby perpetuating a belief in their Indian origin.

The original symbols were modified by the Eastern Arabs of Baghdad and, as usage spread, by the Moors of North Africa and Spain. The latter called them *gobar* numerals, after the Arabic *hurūf al-gubār*, i.e. dust numbers, from the Hindu dust abacus. It is the early Baghdad form which survives today in Arabic-speaking countries, Pakistan and India, i.e. ١ ٢ ٣ ٤ ٥ ٦ ٧ ٨ ٩٠. The *gobar* numerals developed into our 1 2 3 4 5 etc.

In the Near East the great Arab geographer, astronomer and mathematician Mohammed ibn Musa al-Khwarizmi (died c. 831) explained the use of Hindu numerals in his little treatise on algebra, the first of its kind, 'Hisāb al-Jabr wa al-Muqābalah' (algebra and theory of equations), written about 825. Al-Khwarizmi's works are known only from several Latin translations made in the 12th century by English scholars working in Spanish universities, notably of his trigonometrical and astronomical tables by Adelard of Bath in 1126 who also translated an arithmetic, ascribed to al-Khwarizmi, as 'Liber ysagogarum Alchorismi'. The algebra was translated in 1145 by Robert of Chester as 'Incipit liber restauracionis numeri quem edidit machumed filius moysi algauriszmi quare dixit machumued' (*sic*), now in Dresden, and by Gerard of Cremona (1114–75) who latinized the Arabic title as 'De jebra et almucabala'. These medieval latinized distortions of al-Khwarizmi's name and his titles led to the words *algebra*, *algorism*, and *algorithm* gaining currency for algebra and the new written decimal system of arithmetic.

The earliest known European manuscript to include arabic numerals was the 'Codex Vigilanus' written at Albelda in Spain in 976, and now in the Escorial Library. Only 1 2 7 8 and 9 of the *gobar* numerals used in it approximate the form now familiar. Gebert of Rheims, who studied in Spain after 967, prior to becoming Pope Sylvester II, is credited with the introduction into Europe of an improved abacus which had counters marked with numbers, known as *apices*, which were clearly of Hindu origin. Indeed, until the 16th century the name *apices* was often given to the Hindu-Arabic numbers.

A factor necessary before calculations could be done on paper instead of on an abacus was the zero symbol. The Hindus used a dot called a 'çūnya bindu' (the dot marking a blank). The Arabs still use a dot for zero. They rendered the Hindu word as 'sifr', whence the Latin 'zephirum' of the 13th century which became the Italian 'zero' by the mid-14th century. The English 'cipher' is clearly from the Arabic.

Inevitably the merchants of Venice, Florence, Genoa, Pisa and Milan, who traded with Arab countries, became aware of the new numbers. Influential in their adoption was Leonardo Fibonacci, or Leonardo of Pisa as he was known at the time, who wrote a book 'Liber abaci' in 1202, advocating the Hindu-Arabic numerals for all commercial calculations. This was the first systematic introduction into Europe of the decimal notation and the Arabic method of numbering. Another well-known mathematician was the Englishman John of Halifax, fl.1230–56, better known as Johannes de Sacro Bosco, whose 'Algorismus vulgaris', c. 1250, was circulated in manuscript copies until the editio princeps of Pruss, Strasbourg, 1488. There was also Alexander Gallus' elementary arithmetic in Latin 'Carmen de algorismo', c. 1220, which may have inspired the anonymous compiler of the English book 'The crafte of nombrynge', written about 1300 and now in the British Library.

Thus by the beginning of the 14th century, and in spite of much opposition from German law courts and Italian bankers, Europeans generally were familiar with arabic numerals although the abacus for counting and roman numeration for writing were not superseded until the mid-16th century. The first printer to date a book in arabic numerals was Ratdolt in his 'Calendario' of 1476. See D. E. Smith & L. Karpinski, 'The Hindu-Arabic numerals', Ginn, 1911.

arabic type: type based on the two main groups of script used for written Arabic (see *Arabic calligraphy*). The basic cursive alphabet has twenty-nine letters used in simple form at the beginning of a word. In the middle of a word a linking stroke is added. At the end of a word and solus a terminal flourish is added. Letters of similar shape are distinguished by dots placed above or below. The printer's basic fount calls for 102 individual characters exclusive of punctuation sorts, accented letters, and so on. As overlapping is required for all-metal setting in arabic, and up to five elements may be combined to form a single character, a type case of, for example, Monotype Naskh Accented, has some 270 elements.

The Arabic alphabet, impressed from a wooden block, was first seen in print as one of several exotics included in Breydenbach's 'Peregrinatio . . .', Mainz, 1486.

For a printer using movable type the alphabet presented particular difficulties as in scribal practice only a portion of a letter was used according to its position, solus, at the beginning, interior, or end of a word. This involved the cutting of many ligatures to reproduce the cursive script. In 1505 Juan Varela at Granada printed Pedro de Alcalá's 'Arte para ligeramĕte saber la lĕgua araviga' using a rotunda type with points over letters and a woodcut table of arabic characters.

Some years later the first metal type for arabic was cut and cast by *Gershom Soncino*, q.v., and used by Gregorius Gregoriis at Fano in 1514 to print the 'Kitāb ṣalat al-sawā'i'. Pope Julius II had instigated this translation of the 'Septem horae canonicae' from a Latin Book of Hours. It was printed in red and black, twelve lines to a page, surrounded with foliated woodcut borders in the style later called *arabesque*, q.v. Two years later Petrus Paulus Porrus printed a polyglot Psalter in Hebrew, Greek, Arabic and Syriac, Genoa, 1516.

An unsuccessful attempt to cut an arabic fount without ligatures was made in Paris when Pierre Gromor printed Postel's Arabic grammar in 1538/9. In a German-speaking country Michael Zimmermann had an arabic fount cut for him by Kaspar Kraft at Vienna in 1553. In Germany the first fount cast there was used for Rutger Spey's Arabic and Latin version of the 'Epistola Pauli ad Galatos' issued at Schönau in 1583. The Nuremberg typecutter Johann Lobinger cut an arabic type for Franz Mesgnien-Meninski of Vienna who paid for the setting up of a press to print oriental works. His 'Thesarus linguarum orientalium' of 1675 was reprinted in three volumes, 1680–7.

When, from the later 16th century onwards, the expansion of trade and diplomacy with Middle East countries led to the study in universities of the Arabic language as a key to Muslim science and philosophy *Leyden* became the leading European centre for printing oriental studies. Of particular importance were the works of Jacob Golius and the wealthy scholar Thomas Erpenius (1584–1624) who commissioned from the Raphelengius establishment a fount of arabic for his private use. Franciscus Raphelengius had shown his first arabic type in the

'Specimen characterum arabicorum Officinae Plantinianae', 1595, and his 'Lexicon arabicum' with notes by Erpenius was posthumously issued in 1613. Erpenius issued his own 'Proverbiorum arabicorum' in 1614, his Arabic edition of the New Testament in 1616, his famous 'Grammatica arabica', 1617, and other works in Arabic including 'Historia Josephi Patriarchae ex Alcorano', 1617, which was an extract in Arabic of the Koran with a Latin translation and his own commentary. The types were acquired by the Elzevirs in 1625 and were later recut by *Fleischman*, q.v.

Elsewhere by far the most successful and important supplier of arabic type in the 16th century was *Robert Granjon*, q.v., whose founts were commissioned by the *Stamperia Orientale Medicea*, q.v. Granjon took the refined Naskhī script as his inspiration. Another Frenchman, Savary de Brèves, while ambassador to Turkey had a fount of arabic cut in Constantinople and finished by Le Bé in Paris. It was used to print an Arabic version of the Psalter at Rome in 1614. De Brèves died in 1627 and on the instructions of Richelieu his arabic types were purchased in 1632 by Antoine Vitré, printer to Louis XIII. In 1640 they passed to the Imprimerie Nationale, but were used in the Paris Polyglot, 1645, printed by Vitré and others.

The Breslau physician and scholar Peter Kirsten (1575–1640) established a press at his house and commissioned a fount of arabic from Peter von Selau, using it for a number of Arabic texts which he edited and published between 1608 and 1611 from the press of Baumann. His specimen 'Tria specimina characterum arabicorum' of 1608 included an extract from the Koran. Noteworthy was his three-volume 'Grammatices arabicae', 1608–10. In 1636 he moved to Uppsala, printing Arabic works there. On his death the arabic types passed to Uppsala University.

In England Wynkyn de Worde used woodcut arabic letters in Wakefield's 'Oratio de laudibus trium linguarum' in 1528, and even eighty years later, when William Bedwell issued his Latin and Arabic edition of the St John Epistles, printing had to be done in Leyden. Bedwell bought type from the Raphelengius firm and in 1632 bequeathed it to Cambridge University. In 1637 Oxford University Press bought punches and matrices for an arabic fount from Cornelisz van Hoogenacker of Leyden. It was a copy of one made for Erpenius in 1614. A source book for later writers on Islam was the compilation 'Specimen historiae Arabum' of Edward Pococke (1604–91), printed by Henry Hall at Oxford, 1648–50. This was the first book printed in England to include substantial portions in arabic type. The first part, issued in 1648, was a set of notes by Pococke on a short description of the Arabs written by Bishop Gregorius (d. 1286). The latter's full Arabic text with Pococke's Latin translation and the 1648 notes was issued in 1650.

A better fount of arabic was cut in English (14-point) size by Caslon in 1725. It was commissioned by the SPCK for the printing of works for the Christian communities in the Middle East and was used in 1725 for a Psalter and in 1727 for a New Testament.

In 1781 Oxford University Press bought a fount of arabic cut by Joseph Jackson, used earlier for John Richardson's 'Persian, Arabic, and English dictionary' in 1777. For Bulmer's edition of this work, 2 vols, 1806–10, a new fount of arabic was used for which the editor *Charles Wilkins*, q.v., designed the type and William Martin cut the punches.

Printing in an Arabic speaking country began in Egypt in 1798 when J-J. Marcel set up a press at Alexandria to print the proclamations of Napoleon. The latter had confiscated the press from the Congregatio in Rome and taken it together with Maronite translators and founts of type to Egypt. The first books to be printed there were Marcel's 'Exercices de lecture d'Arabe littéral . . .', 1798, containing extracts in Arabic and French from the Koran, and 'Alphabet arabe, turk, et persan', 1798. The press was moved to Cairo in 1799. After issuing a 'Grammaire arabe vulgaire' in 1801 Marcel took the press to Paris to print oriental works.

The first Egyptian government-owned press was established by Mohammed Ali at Bulaq in 1821 under the management of a printer who had been trained in Italy for this purpose. When the educational reforms of Ali Mubarak Zaki in 1867/8 extended to printing the number of characters required to compose arabic type was halved and an improved fount was made for the Bulaq press.

The first non-government press in Cairo for printing in arabic type was set up about 1855 at the instigation of the Coptic Patriarch Cyril IV.

Arabic type continued to be hand set until well into the 20th century when the various composing machine makers in America and Europe overcame the problems of fitting cursive characters to the unit system and of delivering matrices in reverse. In 1928 the American Linotype firm showed their Arabic Old Style in 24-point size. The Intertype arabic was designed by the Egyptian Haddad who named it Ahram. In 1934 Monotype cut a new Naskhī type for the Government Printing Office in Hyderabad, India. With additional diacritical signs it was suitable for transcribing Berber, Malay, Persian, Pushto and Urdu. Duplicate keyboards were made for the different regions, but in spite of this progress most Urdu newspapers in Pakistan were still being written out by hand in the mid-1970s for subsequent litho plate making. To improve legibility and encourage reading skills attempts have been made in the 1970s to simplify and rationalize traditional calligraphic-based type designs. One experiment, made in Algiers

by Roberto Hamm, resulted in two founts of basic shapes, one with vowel accents and one without.

Lund Humphries and Cambridge University Press are among British specialists for printing scientific and literary works in the Arabic language; and wherever printed, the range and clarity of *Monotype* founts for hot-metal and Filmsetter machines have been recognised as a major contribution to Arabic typography. In the *Linotype-Paul* computerized typesetting system Arabic copy can be tapped off on the standard roman keyboard. All decisions for selecting form of character (i.e. initial, medial or terminal) with calligraphic linking strokes and the positioning of diacritical marks are controlled by the system. The type design used is that of Osman Huseini of Damascus.

A development announced in London in 1976 was a computer line printer for printing in Arabic and/or English at a speed of 500 lines a minute. It was based on an electrostatic printer plotter and a micro-processor with a high-resolution character matrix giving print quality comparable with typeset even for the fine curves of arabic script. See also *Koran* and Appendix A.

Arber, Edward, 1836–1912: a London man of letters who between 1868 and 1896 issued as cheap reprints the texts of famous and also little known works written from the time of Caxton to Addison. He added critical introductions and notes.

More important today were the privately printed and published 'Transcription of the registers of the Company of Stationers of London, 1554–1646', 5 vols, 1875–94, and the 'Term catalogues, 1668–1709', 3 vols, 1903–6. The last work was edited from London booksellers' quarterly lists.

arbitraries: synonymous with *peculiars*, q.v.

Arches paper: currently the name and watermark of a high-grade paper made by hand at Arches, Vosges, France where the pure water led to the setting up of a mill as early as 1469. Since 1747 the mills of Arches and nearby Archettes have been associated.

archetypal novels: the earliest romances in verse and prose, popular in the Middle Ages, which in England, via translations of such Italian writers as Boccaccio, led to Defoe and the novel as now understood. Thus William Painter's 'Palace of pleasure', 1566, in which he writes 'In these histories (which by another term I call Novelles). . . .'

archetype: said of a manuscript accepted as textually correct and used for amending copies.

architectural bindings: bindings with architectural designs delineated by tooled outlines of base, columns, pediments, etc., done with straight and curved fillets. Some were made for Grolier about 1545. In Parisian examples, made between 1565 and 1572, onlays of coloured calf and morocco gave emphasis to the architectural features. That the contents of the books rarely related to architecture was apparent from the title lettering sometimes placed between the columns. See also *à la cathédrale, embossed bindings*.

architectural title-page: a decorated title-page having as its main feature an engraving of columns resting on plinths linked by an arch or pediment. The author's name, the title and the name of the publisher or printer appeared between the columns. Their use in printed books began in Venice about 1490, but this was merely the continuation of a style found on humanist manuscript title-pages. Roman monumental inscriptions of the kind collected by the epigraphist *Ciriaco d'Ancona* were the inspiration for title-page displays which might even include a sarcophagus bearing on one side the book title. Elaborate architectural motifs set against scenic backgrounds appear in many Italian manuscripts of the later 15th century.

The engraved architectural title pages of printed books had the advantage that the same design could be used for several titles merely by changing the lettering. See also *Pablos, title-page*.

archive: 1. the building in which public records or historical documents are kept. 2. as archives, the documents. 3. a title-word for scientific or academic periodicals, this being a usage dating from the early 18th century, particularly in Europe.

Arden Press: a printing business founded in 1904 by *Bernard Newdigate*, q.v. It had its origins in his father's firm The Art and Book Company. In 1908 it was absorbed by W. H. Smith for whom Newdigate worked until 1914. Fine printing was done for various publishers as well as high quality jobbing work.

Argonaut Press: a publishing imprint founded in London in 1926 for the purpose of issuing reprints of famous works of travel and discovery. When the series concluded in 1938 eighteen titles had been issued, each with facsimiles of original maps, portraits, etcetera. Printing was done by C.U.P.

Ark Press: a small private press established by Kim Taylor at Foxhole, Dartington, in 1954. In addition to printing pamphlets and jobbing work Taylor issued small editions of well-designed illustrated books. The first to appear was an edition of St Matthew Passion limited to twenty-five copies printed on vellum. By close collaboration between author, artist,

designer and printer, and choosing materials with care Taylor produced books of high standard to sell at low prices. Machining was done by Kenneth Worden, a commercial printer of Marazion, Cornwall. The press continues to print carefully made books but to make it more commercial editions published in the late 1960s were of 1,000 copies.

armarian: the monk responsible for the care and maintenance of the books in a monastery library, of which he also made a catalogue. The scriptorium, and the supervision of the writing and copying done in it by other monks, were usually within his charge.

In ancient Rome an *armarium* was a bookcase: in the Middle Ages the usage of the word was extended to refer to a library, particularly in a monastery.

Armenian bole: a powdered red clay which is dusted on the edges of books before gilding as a base for the gold, to which it gives a greater depth and lustre. Bole is mostly obtained from Bohemia, Italy, and Silesia.

arming press: originally, a hand-press in which heated blocks were used to stamp arms on the sides of leather-bound books, an *armorial binding* being a book decorated in this way.

In 1832 the screw action of former presses was replaced by the lever action of the Imperial press and this machine was found suitable for gold blocking on cloth.

Such presses are adaptable to any sort of blocking and are much used today for single-copy work and short runs. Cf. *embossed bindings*.

Arnoullet, Balthazar, 1517–56: a French publisher who pioneered the use of copper engraving. In 1546 he issued from his Lyons press 'Epitome des rois de France . . .' with Claude Corneille's engraved portraits of the kings of France. His most important work was an edition of the Bible in 1550.

Arrighi, Ludovico degli, da Vicenza, fl.1510–27: a bookseller, publisher, scribe, printer and type designer who worked in Rome where he was principally employed as a 'scriptor brevium' in the Papal Chancery. His writing manual entitled 'La operina . . .', Rome, 1522, contained thirty-two pages, all printed from wood blocks engraved by Ugo da Carpi, and showed the *lettera corsiva* or *cancellaresca* of which he was an undoubted master. It was the first manual of instruction in chancery script to be written and printed for general instruction. (Leaf A XIIv of this book is reproduced under *letters – forms and styles*, q.v.)

Arrighi's second work, 'Il modo de temperare le penne', 1523, was issued in Venice in association with

18

the engraver Eustachio Celebrino who cut the blocks. It included the first use of his italic type.

Of books written in his hand there is a fine Book of Hours in the Fitzwilliam Museum, Cambridge.

Arrighi's italic printing types, less sloped and more formal than the earlier Aldine, were particularly elegant and had much influence on the italics of other 16th century designers. The first use by him of his earliest version was in Trissino's 'Canzone', Rome, printed at the end of 1523 or early in 1524. See O. Ogg, 'Three classics of Italian calligraphy', Dover Publications Inc., 1953, which gives an unabridged facsimile reprint of the above two works in addition to manuals by *Tagliente* and *Palatino*, qq.v.

Arrivabenus, Georgius, fl.1483–c. 1500: an early Venetian printer of the classics and legal works. He sometimes printed in partnership with Paganinus de Paganinis, notably a Missale Romanum, 1484. Alone he issued a Latin Bible in 1487/8, Horace, 1490, and works by Justinian.

ars artificialiter scribendi: a Latin phrase, often found in the colophons of 15th-century printed books, indicating that the printer's craft was that of artificial writing.

Ars memorandi: a guide to the clergy for remembering the chapters of the four Gospels. It survives in three block book editions, c. 1470, notable for their well-cut lettering. Extant copies are few.

Ars moriendi: literally, 'the art of dying'. This was the name of an anonymous work, probably intended for those advising the dying how to overcome temptation. It appears to have been first printed as a block book in the southern Netherlands in both French and Latin editions. The date formerly assigned to it was between 1420 and 1450, but in 1966 Dr Allan Stevenson proved that the paper was not made until c. 1466. The illustrations were notable for the introduction of panelled shading. It has been suggested that they were enlargements by the Master E. S. based on eleven of his own small line engravings.

Block book editions of this popular work were followed by numerous editions printed from movable type. Among these were 'L'Art et disposition de bien mourir', Lyons, J. Syber (?), c. 1485; 'Ein Büchlein von dem Sterben', Leipzig, Kachelofen, 1494; 'Ars moriendi, that is to saye the craft for to deye for the helthe of mannes sowle', attributed to Caxton, 1491; and 'Arte or crafte to lyve well and to dye well', London, Wynkyn de Worde, 1505.

See Sir Lionel Cust, 'The Master E. S. and the Ars Moriendi', Oxford, which includes both the block book and the E. S. illustrations.

Ars Typographica: an American miscellany of the graphic arts edited by *Frederic Goudy*, q.v., and published in New York by the Marchbank Press. The first issue appeared in 1918: the last in 1926. Goudy used the periodical for the first display of many of the types which made him famous. Dard Hunter and Douglas McMurtrie were among the contributors who sought to stimulate an interest in fine printing, not only of books but also of periodicals and advertisements.

art canvas: a rough-surfaced cloth used for cased book covers.

art comp.: see *jobbing printing*.

art gilt edges: book edges coloured under the gold to tone with the colour of the binding material.

art paper: high quality coated printing paper. In the past such papers had a coating of china clay, casein and latex applied by brushes to an esparto base paper. This brush coating method is largely obsolete and 'art papers' are coated by other processes such as *air knife* or *blade coaters*. It is more usual to use a woodfree base paper instead of a pure esparto sheet.

Art papers are designed for quality letterpress half-tone work, but are suitable for other printing processes, laminating and varnishing. For work involving bending, folding or scoring tougher stocks are used. Such papers, known as *strongfold*, permit folding to be done during the print run. See also *coated paper, imitation art paper*.

art vellum: a strong thick paper which, as a result of calendering or plate-glazing, has a surface which simulates animal parchment. Also known as *vellum parchment*.

Apart from its suitability for certificates, diplomas and special printings of limited editions it had a certain vogue in the 1890s for publishers' bindings. It has a pleasing appearance whether blocked in gold or ink, and less tendency to warp and curl than the natural skin.

artwork: a general term used in publishing for illustration originals however produced. See also *mechanical*.

Arundel MSS: the collection of 550 manuscripts forming part of the library assembled by *Thomas Howard*, q.v., which in 1831 passed to the British Museum from the Royal Society (the recipient of most of his library). In addition to Biblical and ecclesiastical writings are works on French literature and French history.

Arundel Psalter: two Psalters bound together neither being complete and the first pre-dating the second by some twenty-five years. The book is known as the Psalter of Robert de Lisle. The first, probably done by an early 14th century Court artist, contains simple borders and miniature-filled initials. The second has full-page scenes from the Passion and a number of allegorical scenes, all typified by rich and elaborate detail in the East Anglian manner. The work is now in the British Library, (*Arundel* MS.83).

ascenders: the upper portion of lower-case letters above the x-height, ie. b d f h k l t. They are known as *ascending letters*. Cf. *descenders*.

Ascensius: see *Badius Ascensius, Jodocus*.

Ashburnham, Bertram, fourth Earl of, 1797–1878: a wealthy bibliophile whose library included some 3,800 manuscripts and many incunabula, among which were a 42-line Bible, Caxtons, Shakespeare Folios, a block book Biblia pauperum and the famous Pentateuch (see next entry). He bought an important group of nearly 2,000 early Italian and French manuscripts from Guglielmo Libri, a second group of 700 French manuscripts from Joseph Barrois, and 996 manuscripts from the Stowe collection.

The Ashburnham Library was dispersed by sale in 1897–8, the *Stowe MSS*, q.v., being acquired by the Government for £50,000 almost entirely for the British Museum. It was later found that Libri and Barrois had stolen many of the books from French libraries.

Ashburnham Pentateuch: a 7th century codex of uncertain but possibly Spanish origin. The text, written in uncials, survives on 142 folios and is illustrated with Old Testament scenes from the Creation to Moses. Nineteen of the pages bear miniatures painted in watercolours upon monochrome grounds. They show costumes, furniture and buildings of much interest and may be a Christian interpretation of earlier Jewish originals. The work is now in the Bibliothèque Nationale, Paris, (Lat. 2334) where it is catalogued as 'Pentateuque dit de Tours' from its location there in the church of S. Gatien from the 9th century.

Ashendene Press: a private press founded by C. H. StJ. Hornby in 1894 at the family residence at Ashendene, Herts., and in 1899 moved to his home in Chelsea. He began in 1895 by printing a few miscellaneous pieces in Caslon type, followed by ten small works in Fell (loaned through Dr Daniel). He then had a fount cut as his proprietary type, copied for him by *Emery Walker*, q.v., from that used by Sweynheym and Pannartz at Subiaco in 1465. As was to be expected the type was cut by *E. P. Prince*, q.v., and given the name Subiaco by Hornby. It was first used in 1902 and frequently thereafter.

As a rich man, printing for his pleasure, Hornby could afford the finest materials including special makings of Batchelor's paper with his private watermark, fine black ink made by Jänecke of Hanover and Winsor & Newton's pure vermilion for the hand-inscribed initial capitals designed for him by Graily Hewitt and Eric Gill (for More's 'Utopia', 1906). These were later cut in wood.

In using the finest materials for his carefully planned pages of closely spaced type Hornby continued the Kelmscott Press traditions but without the elaborate decoration which marked them. He acknowledged the inspiration and help of Walker and Sydney Cockerell, both previously associated with Morris.

His editions, at first printed personally on an Albion press, were small, in the case of 'The song of Solomon', 1902, of only forty copies, all on vellum; while the finest production of this press, which closed in 1935, is generally held to be a folio edition of Dante ('Tutte le opere') in 109 copies. They were thus too few to affect directly the commercial printing standards of the day, but the gifted craftsmen he recruited to the family printing concern (W. H. Smith & Son) did much to raise them and had considerable influence. See C. H. StJ. Hornby, 'A descriptive bibliography of the books printed at the Ashendene Press, MDCCCXCV–MCMXXXV', 1935, repr. 1975.

Ashkenazi: a family of German refugee Jews who in 1486 founded the first Hebrew press at Naples. ('Ashkenazim' was the name given to the Jews of Germany and East Europe: those in Spain and Portugal were known as 'Sephardim'.) *Joseph ben Jacob* and his son *Azriel* added the word to their names. They printed works on religion, philosophy, a Hebrew-Arabic-Italian dictionary, 1488, Jacob Landau's code of ritual law ('Sefer Agur'), c. 1490, and in 1491 the first medical book printed in Hebrew. This was a translation of Avicenna's famous 'Al-Qanūn fi'l-Tibb' ('Canon'). They appear to have ceased printing in Naples in 1492, probably when plague decimated the city's Jewish community. See also *Hebrew printing before 1600*.

Ashmole, Elias, 1617–92: an antiquarian whose collection of curiosities was given to Oxford University in 1682. In 1860 the Bodleian received the libraries of four antiquaries: – Ashmole, John Aubrey, Sir William Dugdale, and Anthony à Wood. The 706 manuscripts included scientific, medical and heraldic works. The 3,000 books included works on astrology and astronomy as well as pamphlets and official papers of the Civil War period.

Asphodel Press: a hand-press established by Phyllis Gardner at Hampstead, London, in 1923. Several of the small editions of minor poetry she printed included wood engravings by the founder. It appears to have closed by 1929.

assembler box: the Linotype machine equivalent of a composing stick to which matrices and spacebands are automatically conveyed as the operator taps off copy.

assembling: see *gathering*.

assico: a corruption of the Latin *asse(ribus) corio*, meaning 'in boards (covered) with leather'. The word is used in the Day Book of the Oxford stationer John Dorne (fl.1524–8).

assisted morocco: inferior goatskin, embossed with the characteristic grain of better qualities and boarded.

Associated Booksellers of Great Britain & Ireland: from 1895 to 1948 the name of the *Booksellers Association of Great Britain and Ireland*, q.v.

association copy: a copy of a book which belonged to the author or to a person identified in some way with it or its subject.

Association of American Publishers, Inc.: or *AAP*, founded in 1970 by the merger of the American Book Publishers Council (ABPC) and the American Educational Publishers Institute (AEPI). The Association furthers members' trade and professional interests by group action through its committees, e.g. copyright, promotion of books and reading, statistics, international trade, and relations with national and international agencies. Address: 1 Park Avenue, New York.

The *American Book Publishers Council* was founded in 1946 for publishers of all books except encyclopaedias and textbooks. The *American Educational Publishers Institute* originated in 1942 when a group of elementary and secondary textbook publishers formed the *American Textbook Publishers Institute*. The change of name came when they were joined by publishers of encyclopaedias and college textbooks.

The earliest representative trade group was the *American Publishers Association*, founded in 1901 as a general association of all book publishers: it ceased activity in 1914. In 1921 the industry formed the *American Association of Book Publishers* which existed until 1937, although its subsidiary, the *Book Publishers Bureau*, continued until 1946 to administer a credit information service. During World War II the Council on *Books in Wartime* coordinated the trade production of paperbacks for the armed forces. A small independent group, the *Association of American University Presses*, founded about 1937, arranges an annual Book Show at which what are judged to be the twenty-five best-produced books issued by university presses are displayed.

Address: 1 Park Avenue, New York.

Association of Little Presses: formed in London in 1966 as a loosely knit group of individuals wishing to further the interest in and sale of poetry printed or published by its members. They believed much modern poetry merits publication in broadside, pamphlet or book form, and hoped that with official support and an organised joint mailing list a bigger public for their work would develop. The Association's first catalogue, issued in 1970, listed the output of sixty-five members: the 1974 edition had a hundred and twenty.

Association of Publishers' Educational Representatives: or *APER*, established in London in 1898 to systematize the direct canvassing and sale to schools of new textbooks. Between 1906 and 1945 representatives in the north had an independent association, *NAPER*, but were then reunited with APER which by 1976 had 240 members. They are issued with permits to visit schools. Exhibitions are also held.

Association Typographique Internationale: or *A.TYP.I.*, founded in 1957, largely on the initiative of Charles Peignot. Through his family typefounding business and his experience in making type faces for the *Photon* (*Lumitype*) *machine*, q.v., Peignot realized that new methods of photosetting might cause both a decline in typographical standards and the unauthorised copying of type faces (because of the cheap and speedy methods available for their manufacture). Representations by A.TYP.I. led in 1973 to the signature at Vienna of an international treaty for the protection of typefaces and their international deposit. A series of congresses organised by A.TYP.I. has helped to extend a better appreciation of typography, while working seminars have been arranged to increase the technical knowledge needed by designers of new type faces. Headquarters are in Geneva. See also *Vox classification*.

asterisk: a star-shaped sort, *, used as a reference mark in the text to draw attention to a footnote, to mark a word which is conjectural or obscure, to cover identity (Mrs S***h), to make legally printable and inoffensive such words as s**t, as a hiatus mark, or as a printer's flower.

astronomical symbols:

♒	Aquarius	☌	Conjunction
♈	Aries	⊕ ♁	Earth
♋	Cancer	♊	Gemini
♑	Capricorn	⚴	Juno
⚳	Ceres	♃	Jupiter
☄	Comet	♌	Leo

♎	Libra	♇	Pluto
♂	Mars	⚻	Quincunx
☿	Mercury	♐	Sagittarius
◍	Moon	♄	Saturn
⊖	Moon, eclipse of	♏	Scorpio
☽	Moon, first quarter	⚺	semi-sextile
○	Moon, full	△	semi-square
☾	Moon, last quarter	⚼	sesqui-quadrate
☽	Moon, lower limb	⚹	sextile
●	Moon, new	⚹	star, fixed
☾	Moon, upper limb	☉	Sun
♆	Neptune	☉	Sun, lower limb
☊	Node, ascending	☉	Sun, upper limb
☋	Node, descending	♉	Taurus
☍	opposition	♅	Uranus
⚴	Pallas	♀	Venus
♓	Pisces	♍	Virgo

In 1491 Gershom Soncino used small woodcuts of the traditional pictorial emblems of the zodiac, and astronomical signs, cast in type metal, were used in the early 16th century, notably by the Giunta of Venice.

atelier Louis XII–François Ier: the workshop whence came a group of French bindings made between 1503 and 1519 for the monarchs and their circle. At first the calf covers were decorated with alternating vertical bands of blind and gold stamped tools. This was the first regular use of gold tooling in France. Later, in an attempt to unify what was a combination of old and new techniques, blind tooling was abandoned and superseded by gilding with roll tools including a fleur-de-lis roll.

They were long known as *Blois bindings*, but are now attributed to the Parisian bindery of *Simon Vostre*, q.v. Some thirty-three have been identified.

ATF: see *American Type Founders Company.*

ATF typesetter: a system of keyboard photosetting announced in 1958 by the American Type Founders Co. Inc. and subsequently improved. It is intended for the small user. Two portable machines comprise the equipment: a keyboard unit and a photographic unit.

The keyboard unit has a standard electric typewriter keyboard with the addition of code keys and a control panel. It produces a 'common language' perforated tape and a typewritten proof. There are controls for the coding of justification, letterspacing, interlinear spacing, quadding, and tabular setting.

The photographic unit automatically produces typeset matter according to the coded tape on either film or activate/stabilize photosetting paper.

Type is reproduced from 6in. plastic discs, each carrying two founts. There is no optical enlargement, a separate disc being used for each point size. Type can be from 5- to 14-point, and a special headline setter is available for 18- to 84-point.

Athelstan Psalter: an early tenth-century Psalter of German origin, presented to King Athelstan about 925. Some illustrations were by Frankish painters, but the four full-page illuminations were added later by Saxon artists, the animal head initials being typical of the latter. A Syrian Christian influence is noticeable in some of their figure drawing.

The work is now in the British Library (*Galba*, A. xviii).

atlas: a collection of maps published in book form. The name was first used in this connection by Gerard Mercator for his 'Atlas sive cosmographicae meditàtiones de fabrica mundi et fabricati figura', Parts I–III, Duisberg, 1585–95, although maps had been bound together from early times.

The figure of Atlas holding the globe, from which Mercator took the name, had appeared on the title-page of an earlier work, viz. 'Geographia, tavole moderne di geografia' by Antonio Lafreri, Rome, 1570. See also *mappae mundi*, *periplus*, *pilot*, *portolano*, *ruttier book*, *wagoner*, *wind rose*.

atlas folio: the largest folio size, 17 in. by 26 in.

attaching: the binding process of joining the boards to the body of a book, not to be confused with *casing-in*, q.v. A difference is made between attaching to a french joint or to a tight joint, single attaching or double attaching, made boards and whole boards. For the attaching joint a narrow strip of tough paper is introduced outside the end leaf to serve as a first link

Attaching

with the boards when attaching these. When using the *french joint*, q.v., the tapes are placed directly on the attaching joint. (GU)

Attaingnant, Pierre, fl.1528–51: a punchcutter, typefounder, printer, publisher and bookseller who may have been born and educated near Douai. By 1514 he was established in Paris where he married into the Pigouchet family.

He was France's first music printer, and the first to use the single-impression music type once attributed to *Pierre Haultin*, q.v. His earliest work was a book of part songs issued in 1528. Motets and lute music followed in 1529, keyboard music in 1531, and folio Masses in 1532. From 1537 until 1551, when his last volume appeared, he styled himself 'imprimeur du musique du Roi' for 'lutz, flustes, et orgues'. Over 170 of his musical editions are known.

From 1553 his second wife continued the business until 1567 if not 1571. See D. Heartz, 'Pierre Attaingnant: royal printer of music', U. of Calif. Press, 1969.

A.TYP.I: *Association Typographique Internationale,* q.v.

Aubert, David: born in Hesdin in Artois. A scribe who worked in Brussels from 1459 to about 1462 when he established an atelier in Bruges to produce books for Philip the Good, Duke of Burgundy and his circle. In 1475 he was working in Ghent for Margaret of York, wife of Charles the Bold.

Aubert was typical of the entrepreneur who employed miniaturists, gilders, and other craftsmen to make books for secular needs, always in the service of rich patrons. Among artists he employed were Simon Marmion of Valenciennes, Jean Le Tavernier and Loyset Liédet.

Aubert wrote a somewhat thick bastard script. Notable works from his atelier were 'Conquêtes de Charlemagne', 3 vols, 1458–60, now in Brussels, which had superb miniatures painted in grisaille by Le Tavernier; Ludolf of Saxony's 'La Vie du Christ', 1461, illuminated by Liédet, a volume unusual for its absence of marginal ornament; and Guy de Thurno's 'La Vision de l'Âme', 1474, now in the Hofer collection, Cambridge, Mass.

Augereau, Antoine, 1485–1534: born at Poitou, France. He was a Protestant scholar, printer and publisher who worked in Paris. He was also an engraver of punches, and it is believed that Claude Garamont was his apprentice.

In 1531 he reprinted in his own type the 1530 edition of Andrea Navagero's 'Orationes duae', published by Jean Petit. It was one of his earliest books and within two and a half years he had produced about forty works. He was strangled and burned for heresy.

All Augereau's printing was in roman type of which he engraved three series. His type of 1532, based on a copy he made of that cut by Griffo in 1495 for Manutius, was later re-cut by Garamont. His types were used by others, and Augereau influenced the decline of gothic founts in Paris. In a work on French orthography, issued in 1533, he printed for the first time the accents now common to written and printed French. See J. Veyrin-Forrer, 'Antoine Augereau', Paris, 1957.

Augustine Gospels: the two Latin versions of the Gospels, written in roman half-uncial script, thought to have been brought by St Augustine from Rome to Canterbury in 597. They are now in the libraries of Oxford and Cambridge Universities.

aumbry: in medieval times, a cupboard or press for books (and for other things). See also *magister almarii.*

Aurich, Erich, b. 1906: a leading carftsman-bookbinder of Germany with an international reputation. He was born in Leipzig where he studied book design and bookbinding under such authorities as Ignaz Wiemeler, Walter Tiemann, and Anna Simons. He later lectured at the Staatliche Akademie der Bildenden Künste in Stuttgart.

Aurispa, Giovanni, *c.* 1369–1459: a famous Italian scholar and collector of manuscripts which he gathered on journeys to the Middle East. His 300 Greek works included Aeschylus, the Iliad, Plato, Plutarch and Sophocles, and he did much to encourage the study of Greek in Italy.

Austin, Richard, fl.1788–1830: a London punchcutter and wood engraver who worked for John Bell's *British Letter Foundry,* q.v. He also cut punches for the Wilsons of Glasgow and for William Miller of Edinburgh.

He opened his own business under the name Imperial Letter Foundry, being assisted by his son George who succeeded him in 1824. They claimed that the use of a secret formula for casting made their punches the best in London.

Australian Children's Book Award: two annual awards to the author and/or illustrator, born or resident in Australia, responsible for what are judged to be the 'Book of the year' and 'Picture book of the year'. The books can have been published anywhere but must be on sale in Australia when the award is announced.

The award is administered by the Children's Book Council of New South Wales, Sydney.

Australian National Book Council: established in late 1973 by nominees of associations representing booksellers, publishers, librarians, authors and the book trade. Planned activities included the sponsorship of the Australian Book Week, the establishment of a

$10,000 National Book Council award for Australian writers, liaison with adult education and education authorities in all States, work with large community (educational and library) groups, literary luncheons, and a publishing programme.

authorized edition: an edition of a work published with the consent of the author or copyright owner. It is thus distinguished from pirated or other editions which appear without this blessing.

author's binding: copies of a book bound to the specification of the author for presentation.

author's corrections: textual deviations from the original copy made by the author on his proof. As these are not printer's errors the publisher and author are charged for their insertion or deletion. Far from being discouraged by thoughts of personal expense the arrival of an author's galley proofs is often followed by extensive rewriting, so heady is the exaltation thereby occasioned (or so deep the dismay).

The Authors' League of America: founded in 1912. Services to author members include manuscript reading, help in placing, financial aid, and advice on contracts and copyright. Its British equivalent is *The Society of Authors*, q.v.

author's proof: 'marked' proofs supplied to an author for correction. Printing errors are first marked by the printer's reader, and the author's proof embodies these. The author returns the proof for any further corrections to be made by the printer. Revised page proofs, free from these errors, are then supplied for the printer to check.

autolithographer: an artist who creates his original directly on the lithographic surface from which it will be printed. Cf. *lithographic artist*. See also *Plastocowell*.

autolithography: the oldest and fundamental method of *lithography*, q.v., is brush and pen drawing in which a lithographic artist draws directly on a ground stone or plate, using a brush or steel pen and liquid litho ink. Auxiliary key lines are transferred by tracing. Full covered surfaces are painted with a brush which can also replace the pen for drawing lines. Shaded surfaces can be obtained by drawing a network of lines of varying thickness. More delicate tones are obtained by dotting which gives a more durable surface than crayon-drawing with soft or hard crayons. Crayon and pen drawing are often combined for actual autolithography by an original artist.

For shaded tones various means are used. A grained tone can be obtained on smooth surfaces by the *splash manner*, q.v., for which a hard brush is dipped into a solution of litho ink and drawn across the edge of a ruler or wire mesh causing ink to drop on the stone or plate below. Varying the mesh and the distance between the ruler or net and the stone gives differences in tone. More delicate tones and shades result from *airbrush* spraying, q.v. Other means include *mechanical tints*, q.v., and the transfer of 'hatched tints' from original stones.

There are also ruling machines and pantographs, used chiefly in *stone engraving*, q.v., a method based more on the gravure principle than on ordinary litho printing. On a grey or blue stone, which has been given a smooth closed surface with oxalic acid solution, an image is engraved to a slight depth, after which the stone is inked. In order to check his work the lithographer gives the stone surface a thin coloured ground. Deep engraving is then done with nitric or acetic acid. After inking with a tampon or nap roller printing can be done directly from the stone on soft, damped paper. It is usual, however, to transfer the engraving to a yellow stone or plate.

Lithographic drawing on a metal plate is more common than on stone, but as it is difficult to work on, plastic surfaces, plain or grained, are also used. The final printing surface is then made by printing down to metal using light-sensitive coatings in the usual photo-litho manner. See also *Plastocowell*, *transfer*.

automated publishing systems: see *computer-assisted typesetting*.

autoplate machine: the moulding cylinder around which flong is placed to make a curved stereo for rotary printing. See also *plate-boring machine*.

aux petits fers: the decoration on a book cover resulting when small individual tools are impressed upon it to build up complete patterns. See also *Aldine leaves*, *flowers*.

aviary: a book of birds, and particularly a manuscript volume illustrated in the manner of a *bestiary*, q.v., with depictions of real or imaginary birds.

azure: in the papermaking industry azure refers to lighter tints of blue and applies to both laids and woves.

azured tool: a binder's finishing tool which has hatching within the outline of the design it carries, e.g. a leaf or petal.

azured tooling: the use of tools which have a hatched surface, seen on the leather as contained areas of close parallel lines which may be horizontal or diagonal. The name derives from the use in heraldry of fine horizontal parallel lines to indicate blue. When flowers and leaves are azured-tooled this alternative to unfilled outlines emphasises their shape and enhances the general richness of a cover.

The use of azured tooling dates from the second quarter of the 16th century.

B

BA: see *Booksellers Association of Great Britain and Ireland.*

babewynes: the name given to the grotesque animals and other figures which were a feature of sculpture, wood carvings, and manuscripts in the 13th and 14th centuries. The term is probably of Italian origin (from *babuino* = monkey) and derives from the popularity of monkeys in contemporary decorative art; by extension it includes all grotesque animals. Many of the lively and vigorously drawn creatures which fill the margins of religious manuscripts were common to bestiaries and fables, being in no way related to the accompanying text. They may, indeed, have their origins in the pagan imagery of pre-Christian art.

The use of babewynes for both manuscript decoration and church architecture continued in England long after Continental artists were interpreting only orthodox Christian iconography in their work. See also *bestiary.*

Bac, Govaert, fl.1493–1511: or *Godefroy Back.* An early printer and bookbinder of Antwerp, where, in 1492, he married the widow of Antwerp's first printer, Mathias van der Goes, and acquired his business. He was notable for the books he printed in Dutch (including Sir John Mandeville's 'Itinerarium', 1494) as well as a few Latin works.

back: the part of a book formed where and when the sections of it are united by sewing or stapling. The back may be left flat, but is usually given a convex shape by *rounding*, q.v. While back is also used to describe the portion of outer cover which encloses this, the term *spine* is to be preferred. See also *flat backs.*

A firm flexible back gives a good opening

A firm stiff back is less satisfactory

A hollow back also gives a good opening

back cornering: the cutting away of a small chip off the boards of a book from their four inner corners. This is done by the forwarder before he attaches the leather cover. The easier opening of the boards is facilitated.

backed: 1. said of a sheet in printing when it has been backed up, i.e. had the second side printed. See *backing-up* (1).

2. said of a book in binding after *backing*, q.v.

back-edge curl: a post-impression difficulty which may arise when light-coated papers are used on a high-speed sheet-fed lithographic press. After the sheet has passed the point of nip between the impression cylinder and the blanket it clings to the blanket surface until the grippers pull it off.

It is the angle at which peeling takes place which causes curl. Curl may result in mis-register in subsequent printings in process work. Also known as *tail-end hook.*

backing: in hand binding, after the sections have been sewn and glued their backs are splayed outwards from the centre of the book as shown on the following page. This adds to the permanence of the *rounding*, q.v., and provides an abutment for the boards. For mechanical binding a backing machine was invented in America by Charles Starr who took out a patent in London in 1850. See also *Steamset.*

backing boards: wedge-shaped boards between which an unbound book is held in the lying press for backing.

backing strip: synonymous with *lining*, q.v.

backing-up: 1. printing on the reverse of a printed sheet which is then said to be *backed* or *backed up.* See also *perfecting.*

Backing by hand

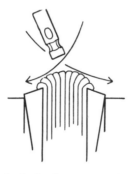

The correct angle for backing. Note the backing boards

2. in electrotyping, the process of filling in the thin copper shell with metal in order to give a solid back.

back-lining: in *edition binding*, q.v., the gluing of a brown paper strip to the back of sewn sections held in a clamp. In 1977 *synthetic hot melts* were introduced as an alternative for animal glue. Advantages claimed were a clean stable adhesive, ease in handling, quick setting, greater adhesion and a stronger and better finished book.

back margin: the inner page margin, parallel with the fore-edge or outer margin. See also *gutter*.

back mark: 1. the impression made in sheets of hand-made paper by the wire or cord on which they are hung to dry. It is smoothed out when glazing.
   2. See *collating mark*.

back matter: another name for end-matter or *subsidiaries*, q.v.

back pages: see *verso*.

backs: the back margins of pages, i.e. those next to the spine or hinge of a book. See also *gutter, gutter margin*.

backslanted type: display type which slopes to the left of a vertical axis. An example is Clearface Extra Bold backslanted. See also *contra italic*.

back-tenter: the operator of the dry end of a paper-making machine. Also known as *back-tender*.

backwater: surplus water which drains off the wet end of a papermaking machine. The fibre, loading, and other substances suspended in it are extracted for re-use, e.g. to dilute the stuff, or in the Hollanders. Also known as *pulp water, size water, white water*. Cf. *retention*.

bad colour: an impression of uneven colour, due to faulty ink distribution, poor cylinder packing, etcetera. See also *ink coverage*.

bad copy: a manuscript which has been heavily corrected by its author. It is thus difficult to read and slows composition.

Badier, Florimond, fl.1645–60: a Parisian bookbinder who may have been one of several master binders and gilders working in a joint atelier established about 1630 and continuing until 1668 when it appears to have ceased. Clients included Louis XIV and Marie Thérèse. Their considerable production of de luxe bindings in pointillé tooled fanfare style with rich doublures and onlays was noteworthy, as between 1633 and 1640, was the use of a small pointillé-tooled man's head. This was once thought to have been Badier's personal device, but some fifty bindings with at least five similar heads have been traced by French scholars: they cover the period 1620 to 1660 and appear to be the work of several craftsmen.

Badier began his apprenticeship to a gilder in 1630 and received his brevet as master-binder in 1645. Only three bindings signed by him are known, the most celebrated being on a folio copy of 'De imitatione Christi', Paris, 1640, now in the Bibliothèque Nationale (Impr. Rés. D. 714); the crimson morocco boards have mosaic compartments of yellow, green and fawn leather, and show the 'head' motif. See E. Dacier, 'Les Trésors des bibliothèques de France', 4 vols, Paris, 1930–1.

Badius Ascensius, Jodocus, 1462–1535: the latinized name of *Josse Bade*, a Parisian printer born at Asch near Ghent. After a classical education begun at Louvain and completed in Italy he went to Lyons in 1492. He taught and wrote commentaries on the classics. Recognising the importance of printing to further his ideas he formed a close association with the printer Jean Trechsel, one of whose daughters he married, and for whom he acted as literary editor and proof corrector. A product of this association was an illustrated edition of Terence with a commentary by Badius, printed in 1493 and reprinted thirty-one times by 1517.

When Trechsel died in 1498 Badius worked for other Lyons printers before settling in Paris in 1499, at first as an associate of Jean Petit, the leader of the Parisian book-trade, who in 1503 helped him to set up his own press. Badius was only one of many printers commissioned by Petit, nor did he work solely for him. As in Lyons the Badius household was a meeting place for humanist scholars and writers: he called them the 'Ascensiani' (from the latinized name of his birthplace) and published many of their works.

Badius issued about 800 works and was noted for the accuracy of his classical texts on nearly all of which he wrote commentaries. Some of his editions were quite large, thus his translation of Thucydides, 1528, was printed in 1,225 copies, using types bought from Froben.

Badius was succeeded by *Robert Estienne*, q.v., who married his daughter. See P. Renouard, 'Bibliographie des impressions et des oeuvres de Josse Bade Ascensius', Paris, 1909.

bad sheets: see *imperfections*.

Bagford, John, 1650–1716: a notorious book collector who acted as agent for such bibliophiles as *Robert Harley*, q.v. His notoriety derives from his alleged destruction or mutilation of countless books in order to amass a collection in 216 volumes of title-pages, bookplates, paper specimens, etc., for a history of printing and the book crafts. The British Library, owner of the collection, published a catalogue of it in 1974.

Bagguley, G. T.: see *Sutherland bindings*.

Baildon, J.: see *Beauchesne*.

Baine, John, 1713–90: an Edinburgh typefounder who between 1742 and 1749 partnered *Alexander Wilson*, q.v. Their first foundry was at St Andrews but was moved to Camlachie near Glasgow in 1744. After 1749 Baine may have worked in London until about 1768 when he settled in Edinburgh. In 1787 he and his grandson emigrated to Philadelphia, taking foundry equipment with them. Their venture was the first

regular typefounding business in America to be successful.

Bak, Jacob: see *Kohen*.

Bakalar, Nicolaus, fl.1498–1513: properly Mikuláš Stétina, a graduate of Cracow University who worked in Pilsen as a printer. Within two years he produced nine of his translations into Czech. His output included an abridgement of Breydenbach's famous 'Pilgrimage' and an edition of Thomas à Kempis.

baked: said of type ready for distribution which, after rinsing, adheres closely together and cannot easily be separated. This probable trouble with new type may be prevented by soaking in a solution of soft soap and water before type is laid in case.

Bale, John, 1495–1563: the compiler of the first bibliography in England, 'Illustrium Majoris Britanniae scriptorum . . . summarium', Gippeswici, 1548.

ball: see *ink ball*.

Ballantyne, James, 1772–1833: the Scottish printer-publisher who founded his press in 1796 at Kelso, and is remembered for the high standard of his work. He was the publisher of Sir Walter Scott, the latter having a financial interest in the business. See 'The Ballantyne Press and its founders, 1796–1908'. 1909.

Balligault, Felix, fl.1492–early sixteenth century: a Parisian printer who worked for many booksellers and publishers including Gilles Gourmont, Claude Jaumar, and Antoine Vérard.

Balston, William, 1759–1849: one of England's leading papermakers. In 1774 he was apprenticed to *James Whatman II*, q.v., at Turkey Mill near Maidstone. When the firm was sold to the Hollingworth brothers in 1794 Whatman lent Balston £5,000 to buy a partnership, the firm being known as Hollingworths & Balston. This lasted until 1806 when Balston established his own business at Springfield Mill, Maidstone, installing there one of the earliest steam power plants. He did not, however, acquire a Fourdrinier, and as in time printers came to find machine-made papers cheaper, it was the manufacture of writing and drawing papers, with the Whatman mark, that brought Balston fame and (much later) wealth. Financial difficulties led to a partnership in 1814, and the firm operated as Balston, Gaussen & Bosanquet until 1849, when it was re-named after William's sons who later assumed control and became W. & R. Balston. It now trades under the name Barcham Green & Co. Ltd. See T. Balston, 'William Balston, papermaker, 1759–1849', Methuen, 1954.

Bämler, Johannes, fl.1472–95: a noted printer of Augsburg who lavishly illustrated his books with woodcuts. He is also remembered as a painter of miniatures and as a rubricator.

Bampton Press: a private press established at Bampton Vicarage, Oxfordshire, about 1848, by the Rev. J. A. Giles. The works issued from it were mostly of a religious or local character, many being written or edited by Dr Giles. The best work, and perhaps the last to appear, was Joseph Bosworth's translation of King Alfred's 'Description of Europe', 1855. This was printed in an Anglo-Saxon letter, and was apparently set by a professional compositor. No work bears the name of the printer, the usual imprint being 'Printed at the author's Private Press'.

Bancroft, John Sellers: a mechanical engineer and manager of Sellers & Co. of Philadelphia. In 1894 the firm was given a contract to build fifty casting machines from Tolbert Lanston's drawings (see *Monotype*). Bancroft was invited to redesign the casting machine and he introduced several basic improvements.

banderole: a ribbon-like scroll bearing writing, as *phylactery*, q.v.

bands: in hand binding, the cords of flax or hemp to which the folded sheets of a book are attached by sewing across them. Sometimes the bands show on the spine of a book, but they are often sunk into the back by sawing grooves across the folds of the collated signatures.

Sewing on bands probably originated in Europe at the time of Charlemagne. From the 9th to 12th century the bands to which the gatherings were sewn were threaded through tunnel-like holes made in the thickness of the boards. They were then twisted together and securely pegged.

The sewing frame was in use in 12th century Europe. See also *false bands*, *flexible sewing*, *hand-sewing*, *raised bands*, *sawn-in back*.

Sewing on unstranded bands

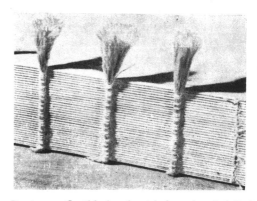

Sewing on flexible bands with frayed ends (*slips*)

bank: a printer's bench on which sheets are placed as printed, or on which standing type rests. Also known as *random*.

Bankes, Richard, fl.1523–45: a London printer, few of whose thirty-odd books are extant, who in 1540 received from Henry VIII a privilege for Epistles and Gospels. In 1525 he issued the first edition of an anonymously compiled herbal, and in 1545 an early book on cookery.

bar: the long handle on a hand-press which is pulled over to give the impression.

Barbédor, Louis, c. 1589–1670: a Parisian calligrapher and writing master who was commissioned to revise the scripts used by the Court. His decoratively paged manual 'Les Écritures financières et Italienne bâtarde...', Paris, c. 1647, had considerable influence in France where the adoption of his rounded scripts for state papers officially replaced gothic cursives, and also on his English contemporaries.

Barbou: a French family of printers and publishers, operative from 1524 to 1820. They had branches in Paris, Limoges, and Lyons, where Jean Barbou began printing in 1536. His son Hugh set up business in Limoges. The Paris house was begun in 1704 by Jean-Joseph (1688–1736) who had previously worked in Limoges. In 1752 it was directed by *Joseph-Gérard* (1723–c. 90) who was one of the leading printers in the great age of the French printed book. From 1753 he re-issued and continued the series of illustrated classics in small format begun in the 1740s by Antoine Coustelier. In a series of 12mo and 16mo editions he made elegant use of Fournier's types and ornaments and commissioned such engraver-illustrators as Jean Papillon and Nicolas Cochin to make decorations for title-pages, borders and headpieces. Notable was his edition of La Fontaine's 'Fables', 1762, which had fine engravings.

In 1764 he printed P.-S. Fournier's 'Manuel typographique' Vol. I, with Vol. II in 1766, followed by Louis Luce's 'Essai d'une nouvelle typographie' in 1771. Both were famous collections of printers' types and ornaments. See also *Fournier*.

Barclay, Andrew, 1738–1823: a Scotsman who emigrated to Boston where from 1765-75 he published, bound and sold books. He moved to New York in 1776 and to Nova Scotia in 1783 where he was a farmer.

There were at this time several Scotsmen working as binders in Colonial America. Barclay's bindings were tooled in a simple style, their association with Scotland appearing only by the use of thistle tools and the cross of St Andrew. In his advertisements he asked for 'Sheepskins suitable for Binding'.

barge: a small wooden case having divisions. Used for holding spaces during the correction of type matter.

Barker, Christopher, *c.* 1529–99: a London publisher who, with his assigns and deputies, held the valuable appointment of printer of Bibles, service books and parliamentary publications to Queen Elizabeth I. He issued the first edition of the Geneva Bible printed in England, 1575, printed for him by *Thomas Vautroullier*, q.v.

As Queen's Printer he published officially sponsored translations into several European languages of pamphlets explaining British foreign policy and actions to further it. The royal warrant was continued by his son *Robert* (d. 1645) who printed the Authorised Version of the Bible, 1611, for James I.

barrels: wooden barrels used for despatching bulk copies of books in sheet form as the European book trade developed in the later 15th century. The recipient gathered the copies, inserted any hand-painted initials or rubrics, and had them bound. Books reached England in this way from the great trade fairs at Antwerp, Cologne, Frankfurt, Lyons and Paris.

Until the mid-16th century almost all education in Europe was in Latin, and printer-publishers could be sure of an immediate demand for their products far beyond the town or even country of printing. Thus even by 1490 Baptista de Tortis of Venice was printing Justinian's 'Digests' in editions of over three thousand copies. See also *rums*.

Bartlett, Roger, *c.* 1633–1712: a London bookbinder who was apprenticed in 1647 to a stationer and freed in 1654, then working as a bookbinder. After losing his shop in the Great Fire of 1666 he moved to Oxford where he worked without having regularised his position by matriculating with the University. This meant he could not have an apprentice and was not recognised by other binders.

He bound a number of presentation bindings which it was the custom of the University to give to distinguished visitors, those associated with his name being in crimson, orange or blue morocco and usually having cottage roof tooling. His tools are distinctive and a considerable number of bindings from his workshop are known. A fine lectern Bible printed in 1685, now in York Minster, shows what may be his only mosaic covers. See I. G. Philip, 'Roger Bartlett, bookbinder', *The Library*, 5th ser., x 4 1955; and H. M. Nixon, 'Roger Bartlett's bookbindings', *The Library*, 5th ser., xvii 1962, which shows rubbings of his tools.

Bartolozzi, Francesco, 1727–1815: an Italian painter and engraver who from 1764 to 1802 worked in London as a pioneer of *stipple engraving*, q.v. Examples of his work illustrate Thomson's 'The seasons', Bensley, 1797.

Barton, Thomas P., 1803–69: of Philadelphia, and 'the first American to form an extensive, purposeful collection of Shakespeariana' (PBSA 1964). From the early 1830s European antiquarian booksellers supplied him with the largest and finest copies of Americana, belles-lettres, history and Shakespeare. He bought a copy of the First Folio in 1845, subsequently adding the other three plus many Quartos. He had many books rebound by leading English, French and Italian craftsmen: these await study and publication. Since 1873 the collection has been in Boston Public Library.

baryta paper: paper coated with barium-sulphate gelatine. It is suitable for repro proofs both in galley for paste-up and in made-up pages ready for lithographic platemaking.

Basa, Domenico: a printer from the Manutius office in Venice who settled in Rome. In 1585 he printed 'Salamese ben Cand Ghadi' using an arabic type cut for him by Robert Granjon. He later sold it to the *Stamperia Orientale Medicea*, q.v. In 1587 he was appointed first director of the *Typographia Apostolica Vaticana*, q.v.

base line: the imaginary line on which the bases of capitals and minuscules without descenders align.

base planer: see *planing machine*.

basil: unsplit sheepskin, vegetable tanned. It is poor quality but is sometimes artificially grained to simulate more costly leathers. Its use in England dates from the early 19th century while in America *Andrew Barclay*, q.v., on a broadside sales-list of books imported in sheets from Britain offered cash for 'Sheepskins fit for Bookbinding'.

29

Baskerville, John, 1706–75: the typefounder and printer of Birmingham who designed the famous transitional type which bears his name. After an early career as a writing-master and engraver he made a fortune in japanning and began printing, building his own press in 1751/2. His first book was an edition of Virgil, 1757. His presswork was of the finest, and though not commercially successful he did much to improve the standards of his day. He had wove paper made to his requirements, probably at Whatman's mill. Printed sheets were finished by pressing between hot copper plates. He made his own ink, 'shorter' than usual.

Baskerville's types were bought by Beaumarchais in 1779 for a ninety-two volume edition of Voltaire (1780–89). The original punches were lost for many years, being found in Paris in 1929; in 1953 the surviving originals plus some modified and replaced characters (a total of 2,750 punches) were presented by the French firm Deberny & Peignot to the Cambridge University Press, to which Baskerville had been Printer of Bibles and Prayer Books, (1758–63). His folio Bible, 1763, was among his masterpieces, though, as were others of his books, marred for some by excessive letterspacing. See P. Gaskell, 'John Baskerville: a bibliography', C.U.P., 1959, corrected and reprinted, 1973, and F. Pardoe, 'John Baskerville', Muller, 1975.

Bassandyne, Thomas, d. 1577: a printer, binder and bookseller of Edinburgh. He is remembered for his use of Granjon's civilité type in an edition of Robert Henryson's 'Morall fabillis' (Aesop), 1571, and for his work on the first printing in Britain of the English Bible (Geneva version). He used roman type for it, itself an innovation, but had only finished the N.T. by 1576. The work was completed in 1579 by his former associate Alexander Arbuthnot to whom, because of a dispute, Bassandyne had been obliged to cede his rights in the enterprise.

bastard: 1. a letter foreign to the fount in which it is found.

2. an obsolete paper size, 33 in. by 20 in.

3. any non-standard size of paper.

4. a type cast on a body larger or smaller than that for which it was cut.

bastard title: see *half-title*.

bastarda: a cursive gothic letter which developed as a quickly written script in France in the late 13th century. It had pointed descenders and a looped form of b d h and l. As a printing type it was used until the mid-16th century in France and the Low Countries and was introduced into England from Bruges by William Caxton. German Schwabachers and Frakturs are later bastardas. See also *letters–forms and styles*.

Batchelor, Joseph: a papermaker of Little Chart near Ashford in Kent whose fine hand-made sheets were used by the Ashendene, Doves, Essex House, Gregynog, and Kelmscott presses. Watermarks were designed by his clients.

Bateman, Abraham & John: two London binders who in 1604 were appointed Court binders to James I. The use of small flowers, decorated corners, and the Royal arms as a centre-piece were features of their work.

batter: type or blocks which are damaged or worn so that defective impressions result. See also *hell-box*.

battledore: a variety of school primer made of folded paper varnished on the inside and used in the late 18th century. When opened it resembled a *horn book*, q.v., which it superseded, but was sometimes without a handle. The outside was usually covered with *Dutch paper*, q.v.

Bauer, Friedrich Andreas, 1783–1818: a German who came to London in 1805 where he was associated with *König*, q.v., as a maker of printing machinery.

Bauersche Giesserei: until 1971, when it was closed, one of the largest typefounding firms in Germany. It traces its origins to a workshop established in Frankfurt on 25 July 1837 by *Johann Christian Bauer* (1802–67). He was born at Hanau and learned his craft from Andreas Schneider, a famous punchcutter of Frankfurt, continuing to work with him until 1835. Between 1839 and 1847 Bauer worked to improve his skill at the Wilson foundry in Edinburgh.

In 1861 he introduced his Neue Kirchenschriften, modelled on 16th century designs, in an attempt to popularize roman types in Germany. The firm's types were widely used, and at his death Bauer left 10,000 punches which he had cut, among which those for his $3\frac{1}{2}$-point Brilliant roman were considered an achievement.

His son *Friedrich Wilhelm* continued the business which, after 1868, was known as *Bauersche Giesserei*. There were eventually agencies in Russia, Spain, and America (where a branch was opened in 1927).

In 1898 the firm was acquired by *Georg Hartmann* (d. 1954), who was quick to realise that typecasting machines installed by printers would diminish the demand for his bread-and-butter types, so he engaged such notable young artists as *Friedrich Kleukens* and *Emil Weiss*, qq.v., to design a range of proprietary faces. In 1916 Hartmann added the foundry of *Heinrich Flinsch*, q.v. With it came types by F. H. Ehmcke and Lucian Bernhard. Other famous designers associated with the firm have been Paul Renner, Imre Reiner, Heinrich Jost, and Max Caflisch.

Much of the Bauersche Giesserei was destroyed

during the 1939–45 war, and the foundry was largely rebuilt by Hartmann in 1948.

Of note is a series of publications by the firm's private press 'Der goldene Brunnen', and Konrad Bauer's sumptuous 'Aventur und Kunst: eine Chronik des Buchdruckgewerbes von der Erfindung der beweglichen Letter bis zur Gegenwart', issued in 1940 to commemorate the 500th anniversary of the invention of printing. Konrad Bauer died in 1970.

Baumgarten, Johann Ernst, fl.1759–82: a German binder working in London where he had considerable influence on English binding. Much of his work was done on new books sold by the London bookseller Benjamin White of Fleet Street in whose catalogue of 1779 nearly seventy bindings by John Baumgarten are listed, many in tree-marbled calf, a style he may have initiated. For his most sumptuous bindings he used elaborate chinoiserie or 'Chippendale' patterns including tools of pagodas, junks, birds on twigs, and rococo leaf ornaments.

Among the many workmen he employed were *Walther*, *Kalthoeber*, and the Spaniard *Carsi y Vidal*, qq.v.

When Baumgarten died in 1782 he was succeeded in business by Kalthoeber.

Bauzonnet, Antoine, fl.1830–48: a Parisian binder and gilder who worked with *Purgold*, q.v., later marrying his widow and continuing the business. He was an excellent gilder who specialized in the creation of patterns composed solely of multiple straight lines to make bindings of sober elegance and distinction.

Bauzonnet, and his son-in-law *Trautz*, q.v., had the leading bindery in mid-19th century France.

Baxter, George, 1804–67: artist, engraver and colour printer. In 1836 he patented his letterpress process for the mass reproduction of colour prints in oil-based inks. His early experiments followed the method outlined by the German printer *Jacob Christoph Le Blon*, q.v. Baxter copied the subject for a print in reverse on a copper or steel plate, etched it with acid, and deepened the lines with a stippling needle. A neutral-tint pull was taken from this key plate, and then wooden blocks were used to add colours. As many as ten or more were needed, a block for each colour, printed in turn.

Baxter used the best materials, with inks of his own grinding. While remembered chiefly for his 'Baxter prints' he also worked for book publishers of whom the earliest was Robert Mudie whose 'Feathered tribes . . .', 2 vols, 1834, had two coloured title-page vignettes. About a hundred titles are associated with his name as printer of illustrations. His colour process was used under licence by others during the 1850s. See C. T. C. Lewis, 'George Baxter, the picture printer', Low, 1924.

Bay Psalm Book: the first book printed in Colonial America. The title-page reads: 'The whole Booke of Psalmes, faithfully translated into English Metre'. It was printed in 1640 by *Stephen Daye*, q.v., of Cambridge, Massachusetts Bay, whence the common name for it. Of the edition of 1,700 copies believed to have been printed only eleven are known of which three are perfect.

BBIP: see *British Books in Print*.

bead-roll: a roll of parchment on which prayers and commemorative verses were inscribed to honour the dead. From about the 9th century such rolls were taken from monastery to monastery when an abbot died, further verses being added at each. Examples of the 16th century sometimes contain drawings depicting the abbot's life and death, with backgrounds of his Abbey.

Alternative names are *bede-roll* and *obituary roll*.

beard: 1. in Great Britain, the space on a type between the bottom of the x-height and the upper edge of the shank or body. This space comprises the shoulder on which the face rests and the bevel by which it is raised from it, and is the area in which the descenders of lower-case letters extrude.

2. in U.S.A., the bevel between the face of a type character and the shoulder.

bearers: 1. part of the printing press on which cylinders rest.

2. thin strips of type metal 0.918 in. high by ⅛ in. wide, which are put in a forme to facilitate the smooth running of ink rollers.

beater: the machine in which half stuff produced in the breaker/potcher is defibred. The *Hollander*, q.v., was the most-used beater until modern technology evolved machines known as *disintegrators* which are quicker and more efficient. See also *deflaker*, *Jordan*, *potcher*.

beating: 1. converting half-stuff into paper pulp.

2. the original method of inking type with ink balls.

3. a stage in the hand binding of books for which a large-faced hammer was used to beat folded sheets, several at a time, to make them more compact before sewing commenced.

beating hammer: a heavy bell-shaped hammer of cast iron, held by a short wooden handle, used to press and flatten the folded gatherings of a book before sewing. These hammers were used in bookbinding until they were gradually superseded by the rolling machine introduced by William Burn in 1827.

Beatty, Sir Alfred Chester, 1875–1968: a renowned

book collector who acquired a series of manuscripts on papyrus of the Greek Bible written about the 2nd or 3rd century, and a series of ancient Egyptian papyri. The most important of these, written in hieratic characters on both sides of a roll, contains the mythological story of the Contendings of Horus and Seth, and, in addition, groups of love songs.

He assembled one of the greatest private collections of Oriental and Western MSS. and printed books. After 1953 he built in Dublin a special library and exhibition gallery for the housing and display of his treasures (open to the public). There are Turkish, Russian, Armenian, Persian, Ethiopic, Indian and Arabic MSS. all in the finest state. Several scholarly monographs on parts of the collection have appeared.

Beatus: the first word of the first Psalm. When a handwritten Psalter was being decorated the medieval illuminator's initial B sometimes filled a whole page and was a traditional display of his skill.

Beauchesne, John de, b. 1538: a Huguenot immigrant to London in 1565. With John Baildon as translator and editor he compiled the first writing book to be printed in England 'A booke containing divers sortes of hands', Vautroullier, 1570, of which the 'Italique hande' was one.

Beauchesne was also the writing master of Elizabeth of Bohemia, daughter of James I, for whom he wrote a copy book which is now preserved in the Newberry Library.

Beauclair, Gotthard de, 1907: born in Switzerland, and one of the leading book designers in Europe. He trained as a compositor in Offenbach and then worked with *Rudolf Koch*, q.v. Later he moved to the Offizin Haag-Druglin in Leipzig and in 1928 to the *Insel-Verlag*, q.v.

Of considerable influence on post-1945 typography in Germany was the programme of new type designs he instigated and supervised while employed as typographic consultant to the Stempel A.G. of Frankfurt. See also *Trajanus-Presse*.

Beaumont Press: a private press founded in London in 1917, its purpose being to issue hand-printed editions of original work by contemporary writers who included Edmund Blunden and D. H. Lawrence. The books were quarter-bound in canvas with paper sides especially designed for each by Cyril Beaumont. The press closed in 1931. See C. W. Beaumont, 'The first score', 1927, and B. T. Jackson, 'The Beaumont Press', *Private Library* 1975.

beauty: a collection of extracts from an author, often selected to present the more wholesome passages. This form of censorship was practised in England during the 18th and 19th centuries, Shakespeare being among the writers so treated.

Beckford, William, 1759–1844: a wealthy book collector who amassed a great library at Fonthill, Wilts. He spent large sums of money on binding. Most of his early collection he sold in 1822 when he moved to Bath, but between 1829 and 1844 he formed a second library. On his death, his son-in-law, the 10th Duke of Hamilton, transferred the books to Hamilton Palace. The library was sold by Sotheby between 1882–4 for £86,000.

The collection included Jenson's Latin Bible, 1476; the Lactantius of Sweynheym and Pannartz; Greek and Latin classics from the press of Manutius; French and Italian literature, as well as Grolier, Maioli, Ève, and Padeloup bindings.

bed: the steel table of a printing press on which the forme of type is placed for printing. When the forme is secured it is sometimes described as having been 'put to bed'.

bede-roll: the earliest name for a *bead-roll*, q.v.

Bedford, Francis, 1799–1883: a London binder who worked for Charles Lewis until the latter's death in 1836, ran the firm for his widow until 1844, and then was in partnership with John Clarke until 1851 when he opened his own bindery. For the bindings he made for wealthy collectors Bedford revived earlier Lyonnese and Italian styles, often copying the tools used. His *forwarding*, q.v., was reputed to be the best in England.

Bedford, John of Lancaster, Duke of, 1389–1435: the third son of Henry IV. He was Regent of France from 1422–35, and finding it politically in his interest to patronise learning he employed scholars in his household to write medical and scientific works. He also commissioned several splendid illuminated manuscripts of which four are now in public collections.

1. *The Bedford Missal*, a Book of Hours of Paris use, begun in 1423 as a wedding gift for his wife. Three schools of painting are represented, English, Flemish, and French, and it took seven years to complete. Each page of text is bordered with leaves and flowers, interspersed with medallions showing scenes from the lives of the saints. There are also four full-page Biblical scenes.

Bedford's wife gave the book to Henry VI in 1430. Subsequent owners included Catherine de Medici; Edward Harley, Earl of Oxford; James Edwards of the Halifax binding family, and the British Museum which paid £3,000 for it in 1852 (Add. MS. 18850).

2. *Psalter and Book of Hours*, of Sarum use, illuminated in England by Herman Scheerre, *c.* 1420–2. Bought in 1929 by the British Museum for £33,000 (Add. MS. 42131).

3. *Sarum Breviary*, begun in 1424 and belonging to the same schools as the Missál. Now in the Bibliothèque Nationale, Paris (MS. Lat. 17294).

4. *Le Pèlerinage de l'âme*, of French workmanship, prior to 1427, now in Lambeth Palace Library (MS. 326). This has a miniature showing the Duke receiving the book. See E. C. Williams, 'My lord of Bedford', Longmans, 1963.

begin even: an instruction to the compositor to begin setting copy without indenting the first line of it.

Bekk apparatus: see *paper-testing*.

Beldornie Press: the private press which Edward Vernon Utterson (1776–1856) installed at his house in Ryde, Isle of Wight, in 1840. He was an antiquary, artist, book collector and founder member of the *Roxburghe Club*, q.v., and for some years prior to setting up his press he had commissioned reprints of 16th and 17th century literary pieces for distribution to friends.

Between 1840 and 1843 he edited and issued some thirty small items, some in as few as twelve copies. The original woodcuts, headbands and ornaments were faithfully copied. Utterson did not work the press, but brought local compositors and printers to his house. See R. V. Turley, 'Edward Vernon Utterson . . .', *Book Collector*, Spring 1976, 21–44.

Bélin machine: an electronic scanning machine, made in France, which produces a continuous tone negative or positive. It is known in America as the *Consolidated Color Selector*.

The original to be reproduced is fitted around a revolving drum. A beam of light is directed on to the picture which, in revolving, reflects light of an intensity varying in proportion to the dark and light parts of the picture. The reflected light is received by a photoelectric cell which transmits impulses of related intensity to a drum containing a roll of sensitized film. This drum revolves at the same speed as that bearing the original so that the film is exposed, in dots, to a beam of light having an intensity proportionate to that reflected by the original. The exposed film is printed on to a sensitized plate and prepared by customary stages for use as a half-tone block. See also *photoengraving*.

Bell, John, 1745–1831: an enterprising London bookseller and publisher in whose edition of Shakespeare, 1785-8, the traditional use of the long 's' was discontinued. He issued a library of poets in 109 illustrated 18mo volumes, 'The poets of Great Britain complete from Chaucer to Churchill', Edinburgh, 1776–83. The series was reprinted in 1807 by Samuel Bagster.

In 1787 he started his British Letter Foundry, commissioning the engraver *Richard Austin*, q.v., to cut for him the transitional-modern type face for which Bell is now remembered. It had considerable influence on English newspaper typography. The accompanying ranging numerals were probably the first made in Britain. Early use of them was in Hunter's Logarithm tables. Bell also had a white-lined blackletter type. Its use for newspaper title lines dates from 1787 when he published *The World*, a London daily.

A casting of Bell's type of 1788 was made from the original matrices in 1864 for the American Henry Houghton of the *Riverside Press*, q.v. When using them there *Bruce Rogers*, q.v., gave them the name Brimmer, after the Boston writer Martin Brimmer. When used by *Updike*, q.v., at his Merrymount Press the type was known as Mountjoye. In 1931 Monotype began their revival from the original punches, now at the Stephenson Blake foundry. See Appendix A.

Bellaert, Jacob, fl.1483–86: a printer who may have worked as a compositor for Gerard Leeu in Gouda before setting up his own business in Haarlem and later in Antwerp. After he ceased printing his illustration material passed to others including Leeu. Bellaert was noted for his fine woodcuts.

belles-lettres: the publishing term for literary studies, essays, orations, letters and criticism.

bellows press: originally, a portable hand-press suitable for printing visiting cards, trade cards and labels. An early model was devised by the Bristol printers Isaac Moore and William Pine in 1770. It consisted basically of two hinged boards of which one had a recess to hold a few lines of type. The terminal handles of the two boards were squeezed together to effect impression.

Edward Cowper's *Parlour* press, c. 1840, was based on this principle but he substituted a toggle-joint for the handles. This gave sufficient pressure for sheets up to 20 in. × 13 in. to be printed on his largest models. The press was easy to set up and use, and in India it was a Parlour that William Sleeman bought to print eighteen copies of his 607-page confidential 'Diary . . .', at Lucknow in 1852.

The later *Adana* miniature flatbed press devised in 1922 by D. A. Aspinall perpetuated the principle: marketing began in 1923.

belly: the front or nick side of type.

bench press: see *standing press*.

Ben Day tints: a proprietary series of *mechanical tints*, q.v., conceived in America by Benjamin Day (1838–1916) as an aid to draughtsmen in the preparation of illustrations for reproduction in line and/or tone. They are now obsolescent.

Benedicht, Lorenz, fl.1561–1601: a printer and woodcutter of Copenhagen. He and his rival *Mads Vingaard* (fl.1562–1600) practically controlled Danish printing for forty years.

Benedictional of St Aethelwold: the finest example of the Winchester School of English manuscript printing. It dates from about 963–84. The Carolingian minuscule text, in Latin, written by Abbot Godeman, includes twenty-eight large illuminated pages, each a complete design, in which foliated borders, often terminating in corner rosettes of acanthus leaves, frame vividly coloured scenes from the Bible and lives of the saints which owe something in their presentation and lavish use of gold to continental iconography. (An influence probably transmitted by visiting monks from Rheims.)

The Benedictional was acquired by the British Museum in 1957 (Add. MS. 49598).

Beneventan: a cursive minuscule script used from the 8th to 13th century by monastic scribes in the Italian duchy of Benevento. The chief centre was the Benedictine monastery of Monte Cassino.

The script was highly developed yet quite independent of the Carolingian minuscule then in use in northern Europe. Certain unusual letter forms and the fusion of adjacent round letters make it difficult to read without study.

As used in parts of northern Italy it is sometimes referred to as *Lombardic*. See E. A. Lowe, 'Scriptura Beneventana', 2 vols., O.U.P., 1929.

Bengali printing and typography: Bengali is the spoken and written language of Bangladesh, West Bengal in India, and bordering areas of neighbouring states. The modern Aryan language derives from Sanskrit via Magadhi Prakrit (Grierson), and the literary language still includes many *tatsamas* from Sanskrit. Bengali, based on the usage of Calcutta and district, was the first language in which modern Indian literature developed and flourished. In this the introduction of printing by the British was significant.

Bengali script closely resembles *devanagari*, q.v. It has fourteen separate vowel characters or diphthongs, modified when preceded by a consonant, by inferior or superior symbols. The thirty-four consonant forms can be combined side by side or one above the other. A particular feature is a bar, or *matra*, over letters from which they appear to hang. Writing is from left to right, and there are no majuscules. The semi-syllabic nature of the alphabet together with the intricacy and delicacy of the script present problems to the typefounder who is called upon to fit characters of uneven length and size in hundreds of permutations.

Up to seven double cases are needed for a bookwork fount of bengali type which averages 600 sorts. Founts for mechanical typesetting and photosetting are available, but the thousands of small printing shops in the Subcontinent lack capital, and scarcely need

quicker production since fewer men would be employed.

Historical note
1. *Europe*
An unsigned engraved copper plate included in 'Observations physiques et mathematiques . . .', Paris, 1692 (reports of Jesuit missionaries to the Far East) may be the first depiction of the handwritten Bengali alphabet to be printed in Europe. The plate has three columns headed 'Caracteres des lettres des peuples de Bengale (41 shown): Chiffres de Bengale: Caracteres des peuples de Baramas (i.e. Burma)'.

In Georg Jacob Kehr's 'Monarchae mogolo-indici . . .', Leipzig, 1725, an engraved plate included the 'Alphabetum Bengalicum'. J. J. Ketelaar, Leyden, 1743, and J. F. Fritz, Leipzig, 1748, offered similar specimens of no commercial significance.

Then at Nagori, in what is now Bangladesh, a Portuguese missionary, Manoel da Assumpção, compiled a 'Vocabulário em idioma Bengalla e Portuguez em duas partes', printed at Lisbon in 1743. This was the first printed book to include words in the Bengali language, represented, however, in roman characters.

The renegade Dutchman William Bolts, who had been deported from India to London in 1768, commissioned a fount of bengali type from *Joseph Jackson*, q.v., before leaving for India to found the Austrian East India Company. It was intended for his Bengali grammar but the book was never printed. Writing of this in 1778, Halhed (see below) said that Bolts '. . . egregiously failed in executing even the easiest part, or primary alphabet, of which he has published a specimen . . .' In 1773 Jackson listed the type as 'Bengal, or modern Shanscrit'. It eventually passed to the Caslon foundry where it was improved and completed (Reed-Johnson). Copies of Halhed's 'Gentoo laws', London, 1777, showed the Bengali alphabet in an engraved plate: bengali type was still to be created.

2. *British India*
In the second half of the 18th century Portuguese was the lingua franca of foreign settlers and the indigenous peoples of the Bay of Bengal (Clive reputedly spoke it well). When the East India Company acquired rights from the Nawab in 1760 the official language of the new English law courts continued to be Persian which Company servants were required to learn. Educated Hindus and Muslims generally sought competence in Persian. The two dialects then common in Calcutta were *Hindi*, used by North Indian traders and written in *devanagari*, and *Urdu* (known by the British as *Moors*), used by sepoys and lower-class Muslims, written in the *Persian-Arabic* script. Sanskrit was confined to Brahmin *pandits* and had no place in public life. The status of Bengali was low, although the mother tongue of most of the population.

It was an Englishman, Nathaniel Brassey Halhed, who urged on British officials in Calcutta the need to learn Bengali for the furtherance of their duties. He wrote a 'Grammar of the Bengal language', printed on the press of Mr Andrews at Hoogly in 1778. This was the first occasion on which any Indian script had been mechanically reproduced in regular printed form. The bengali type used was the creation of *Dr Charles Wilkins* (c. 1751–1836), employed in Calcutta from 1770 to 1786 as a Writer in the Company's civil service. He cut the punches, made matrices and cast the type. In the Preface to his 'Grammar' Halhed praises the work of Wilkins, but John Gilchrist stated in *East Indian Chronologist*, 1802, that in 1778 Wilkins was aided by a Birmingham die-sinker, Joseph Shepherd, in the completion 'under the patronage of Governor Hastings of two elegant founts of Persian and Bengalese types . . .'. Shepherd claimed most of the credit for the type used in Halhed's 'Grammar'. Gilchrist wrote that 'Shepherd assisted Mr Wilkins from the first, and through the whole process of forming his Persian and Bengali founts' although 'the exclusive merit, with its subsequent profit and praise passed to Wilkins'.

In 1780 the Company asked Wilkins to set up a foundry and press in Calcutta for the printing of oriental languages, and thereafter Company promulgations were translated from English into Bengali for public circulation. Wilkins trained a local blacksmith, *Panchanan Karmakar*, as punchcutter and founder, later appointing him foreman. After Wilkins returned to England in 1786 Panchanan was employed by H. T. Colebrooke and later by the Serampore Press.

A notice in the Calcutta Gazette, 23 April 1789, announced 'The humble request of several Natives of Bengal: We humbly beseech any gentleman will be so good to us as to take the trouble of making a Bengal Grammar and Dictionary in which we hope to find all the common Bengal country words made into English. By this means we shall be enabled to recommend ourselves to the English Government and understand their orders: this favor will be gratefully remembered by us and our posterity for ever.'

Eventually Halhed's 'Grammar' was followed by such officially sponsored works as A. Upjohn's Bengal and English vocabulary of 1793, dictionaries, grammars, and Miller's (?) 'Tutor . . . well adapted to teach the Natives English', 1797. A second and improved fount of Wilkins' type was used to print a Bengal translation by Henry Pitts Forster of the Cornwallis Code, 1793. Forster's ambitious vocabulary 'English and Bangalee and vice versa' was printed at the Chronicle Press, 2 vols, Calcutta, 1799–1802.

James Augustus Hicky's weekly *Bengal Gazette* (1780–82) was the first newspaper printed in India. Other English newspapers published in Calcutta before 1800 included the government-sponsored *Calcutta Gazette* (from 1784). All were small and short-lived with average print runs of 200 copies. The first Indian-owned newspaper to be printed could be Gangakishore

Bhattacharya's '*Vangal Gejet*' (Bengal Gazette), c. 1818, if only a copy survived to prove it ever existed. Raja Ram Mohan Roy, publisher, writer and educationist of note, issued the weekly *Sambad Kaumudi*, c. 1821. Until mid-century handwritten Indian-language newspapers had a wider readership than those printed, and it was lithography, not type, which superseded the multiple hand-copying of news-sheets.

3. *Missionaries in India*
The Serampore Press
Printing in Bengal prior to 1800 was for British officials and their families: it was the 19th century missionaries who began printing for Bengalis. In 1794 the Baptist *Dr William Carey* (1761–1834), who had earlier started a village school at Madnabati in North Bengal, translated the New Testament into Bengali. His employer bought and gave him an English wooden press (cost £46). In 1799 Carey was joined by other missionaries including *Joshua Marshman* (1768–1837) a Bristol charity-school teacher, and *William Ward* (1769–1823) a Derby-born printer and one-time editor of the *Hull Advertiser*. Prior to 1813 the Company banned missionary work in Calcutta so in January 1800 the three set up their mission at Serampore (Sri Ram Pur) sixteen miles from the city. (Between 1676 and 1845 Serampore, also known as Frederiksnagore, was in an independent Danish enclave.)

The Trio's programme included founding elementary schools for vernacular education and the large-scale production in local languages of educational and Christian literature (for which Ward set up Carey's press). They also campaigned against such quaint Hindu customs as burning widows (*sati*, or *suttee*, abolished in 1829) and the sacrificial drowning of babies at the annual *mela* on Saugor Island when, in fulfilment of parental vows, as many as 100 would be thrown in the Ganges to be eaten by crocodiles (outlawed in 1802).

By 1805 the Press had thirty employees, and eventually became the largest multi-language printing business in the entire East. Between 1801 and 1832 the Serampore Press issued 212,000 books in forty languages (Grierson): they included grammars, Indian classics and original works, and the scriptures. The thirty or so *pandits* employed to translate or write texts included Ram Ram Vasu of Fort William College whose 'Raja Pritapaditya Charitra', 1801, and 'Lipi Mala', 1802, were the first full-length Bengali literary works ever printed. Another was Mrityunjaya Vidyalankar, author of 'Butrisha-Singhasan', 1802, and 'Raja Vali', 1808. He also assisted with Biblical translation into Sanskrit.

The printing of Carey's New Testament began in May 1800 and ended in February 1801, the whole Bible in five volumes being completed by 1809. It had the Bengali title 'Dharma-pustak', and in revised form was still being sold by the Baptist Missionary Society in Dacca in 1976. By 1826 six complete and twenty-four partial Bible translations were finished. Carey, who claimed he made the Bengali, Hindi and Sanskrit versions, checked all translations with the Greek and Hebrew originals and read all proofs twice. Critics have attacked the grammar, syntax and idiom of the Press translations, claiming that the writers were unfamiliar with the spoken forms of the languages used, but as the missionaries rightly realised it would be fallacious to hope that people could be taught or converted in a language not their own the translations had to be attempted.

Carey's contribution to the textbook programme included 'Kathopakathan, or dialogues intended to facilitate the acquiring of the Bengali language', 1801, which was an interesting account of local social life. His son Felix made Bengali translations of 'Pilgrim's progress' and 'Vicar of Wakefield'. Other books were written on history, ethics, geography, astronomy and science, notable being John Mack's 'Principles of chemistry', 1824, the first Indian textbook on the subject to be based on European teaching. Additionally the Press accepted other printing jobs to increase Mission funds, including Danish and English government publications.

From 1818–20, under the editorship of *John C. Marshman* (1794–1873), Joshua's son, the Mission published the monthly *Dig Darshan* (*The Signpost*) or *Magazine for Indian Youth*, the first vernacular paper in India. It had articles in Bengali and English on history, geography and current affairs, and was used in schools. The Calcutta School Book Society took 1,000 copies of each issue. Marshman also edited the weekly *Samachar Darpan or News Mirror*, 1818–41, which he claimed was the first western-style newspaper printed in any original language. It was for adults, and was issued in Bengali only until 1829, thereafter appearing bi-lingually and bi-weekly.

The Mission's influential journal *Friend of India*, monthly series 1818–28, with a quarterly series for longer articles 1820–27, was edited by Carey and Joshua Marshman. There was a break from 1828 until January 1835 when John Marshman restarted it as a weekly. He and others, notably Meredith Townsend, edited it until 1859, being succeeded by George Smith. In 1875 it was sold for Rs.30,000 to Robert Knight and published from Calcutta. It was renamed *Statesman and Friend of India*, later becoming *The Statesman* which is still Calcutta's leading English daily.

Serampore type

The Mission needed large quantities of type. Before joining Carey in 1801 Panchanan Karmakar, then in Colebrooke's employ, had offered to supply him with type at a twelfth of the prices asked by the London founders Fry and Figgins who quoted £500 for a fount of persian and £700 for 300 punches of 'nagree'. Carey induced Panchanan to set up a foundry at

Serampore where production could be supervised, readily available, and profitably sold to other printers. The industrious Panchanan cut founts of standard size (14-point) bengali and devanagari. He also made, either as *sand letters* or *woodletter type*, qq.v., an extra large alphabet for printing the wall placards used in Mission schools. More significant, ultimately, was his training of apprentices including his son-in-law *Manohar Karmakar* who succeeded him as master founder on his death in 1803.

For their earliest publications in Chinese the Press engaged twelve Bengali sari-blockcutters to cut ideograms in wood. These were used for the first volume of Joshua Marshman's edition of Confucius with a Chinese text and an English translation, 1809. In 1811, under Marshman's direction, Manohar began the cutting and casting of characters in metal. However, the March 1812 fire (see below) destroyed four cases of the new metal type as well as the wooden ideograms. A fresh start began in August 1812 when an English typecutter, John Lawson, arrived and, with Manohar, made what may have been the first complete fount of metal type for printing Chinese. It has 6,000 characters and was used for Marshman's 'Clavis sinica' (Chinese grammar), 1814. The latter's translation of the Bible into Chinese, done with the assistance of an Armenian, Johannes Lasser, was issued in 1822.

Lawson also guided Manohar in the cutting of a reduced size of bengali type intended 'to diminish the expense of paper, and the size of a book by at least one fourth without diminishing the legibility of character'.

Manohar served the foundry for forty years cutting founts for at least fifteen oriental languages. He was succeeded by his son *Krishna* who continued the foundry until his death in 1850. Many of their punches survive at the Baptist Mission Press in Calcutta.

Serampore paper

Paper locally available to Carey was made of cotton, known as *tulat*, mixed in the vat with copper sulphate. It proved unsuitable so he bought Patna paper which was sized with rice starch. But as insects found this irresistible, and ate the sheets even before a work was printed off, he had it treated with arsenic which discoloured the sheets. For Bibles the Press used large quantities of good English paper. By 1809 Joshua Rowe, the Mission secretary, set up a papermill where relays of coolies worked a treadmill. This was replaced in 1820, after a man died in action, by a 12 h.p. steam engine with heated drying cylinders. The mill ceased production in 1857.

Serampore pressroom

Carey's partner Ward, writing about 1812, described the pressroom which was more than 170 feet long. It included Carey's original wooden press and four English iron presses. 'There you find Indians translating the scriptures into the different tongues, or correcting proof sheets. You observe, laid out in cases, type in Arabic, Persian, Nagari, Telinga, Panjabi, Bengali, Marathi, Chinese, Oriya, Burmese, Kanarese, Greek, Hebrew and English (i.e. roman). Hindus, Mussulmans and Christian Indians are busy composing, correcting, distributing. Next are four men throwing off the scripture sheets in the different languages, others folding the sheets and delivering them to the storeroom, and six Mussulmans to do the binding. Beyond the offices are the varied type casters besides a group of men making ink, and in a spacious open-walled round place, our paper mill for we manufacture our own paper.'

In 1812 fire largely destroyed the Mission Press including manuscripts for printing, books, over 1,000 reams of English paper, 40 imposing stones, 143 founts of oriental type of which 104 had been cast on the premises, and 100 cases of roman. The damage was estimated at £10,000. However, 4,000 steel punches, many undamaged matrices, and hundredweights of re-usable lead were salvaged, and aided by public donations from England and America in just over a year books were being printed in more languages than before the fire. In 1837 the Serampore Mission was reunited with the Baptist Mission Society in Calcutta which later took over the printing and typefounding programme. Printing at Serampore ended in 1873.

Other presses

An important press for printing in Bengali was owned by the *Calcutta School Book Society*, founded in 1817 under Hindu and British management, and with government support from 1821. They concentrated on publishing elementary textbooks and by 1821 had produced 48,750 copies of sixteen titles, all in Bengali, plus others in Sanskrit and English. The Serampore Press supplied extra copies of its own books. By 1823 the Society was the principal source of textbooks in lower Bengal, complementing and continuing Carey's pioneer work in promoting education in Bengal.

In 1819 the *Calcutta Baptist Missionary Society* set up a press under W. H. Pearce, formerly of Oxford's Clarendon Press. His work was of the highest standard and the business was commercially successful. In one year alone, 1837, Pearce printed *inter alia* 250,000 copies of Indian language Biblical translations and tracts.

From 1835 English replaced Persian in the higher courts. Bengali was used in the lower courts. By 1840 the latter was the main language of the press, lower civil administration and primary education. For the upper and middle classes (particularly the Hindus) English became the language of commerce and the socially superior. By 1850 there were many adequate papermills and vernacular printing presses in Calcutta, but Bengali typography ceased to be of historical interest.

In spite of Indian charges, still made, that the British were no more than merchant adventurers and proselytizing zealots they made an enduring contribution to Bengal. Before 1790 Bengali had little status, being the language neither of government, commerce, law nor religion. Its literary tradition was based on orally transmitted verse and drama, and the educated preferred to read in Sanskrit, Persian or English.

It was the British, beginning with Wilkins and Halhed, who praised the elegance and beauty of Bengali, followed by Carey and his colleagues at Fort William College and Serampore, who encouraged Bengalis to experiment with prose narrative, the novel, short story and journalism in their own language. It was thereby raised from its debased condition as an unsettled dialect to a regular and permanent form of speech and made a vehicle for both Bengali culture and Western learning. And it was British presses in Calcutta and Serampore which printed their work, gave existing scripts their final shape, and made possible the production of vernacular textbooks (of which there were none previously) well ahead of comparable progress in other parts of India.

I am indebted to Siddiq Khan, friend and former Librarian of Dacca University, for making his researches available for this entry. See G. A. Grierson, 'The early publications of the Serampore missionaries', Bombay, *Indian Antiquary*, xxxii 1903; S. K. De, 'History of Bengali literature, 1800–1825', Calcutta, 1919; P. Carey, 'William Carey, D. D. . . .', London, 1934; and M. A. Laird, 'Missionaries and education in Bengal', O.U.P., 1972.

Bensley, Thomas, 1760–1833; a distinguished London printer, noted for his careful presswork. He interested himself in König's development of the powered printing press. Of his many fine books he is remembered for his 'History of England' by David Hume, 10 vols, 1806; and for the Macklin Folio Bible, 7 vols, 1800 (with the Apocrypha as an 8th vol. in 1816). He had types cut by Joseph Jackson and Vincent Figgins.

His working life ended in 1819 when fire largely destroyed his plant and premises. See also *König*.

Benson Medal: an award of a medal made by the Royal Society of Literature to an author of belles-lettres, biography, fiction, history or poetry. It is named after A. C. Benson, a one-time Master of Magdalene College, Cambridge.

Bentley, Richard, 1794–1871: a London printer-publisher who, with his brother Samuel, was noted for his careful work. He is remembered for 'Bentley's Miscellany' which began in 1837 and was for a time edited by Dickens, also for a fiction library of 127 volumes, 1831–55. Samuel was noted for his work of antiquarian interest. See R. A. Gettmann, 'A Victorian publisher', C.U.P., 1960.

Benton, Lynn Boyd: the American inventor in 1884 of the *punchcutting machine*, q.v., which used the pantograph principle to follow the outline of an enlarged letter or other character cut in a sheet of thin brass while a diminutive router, linked to it, cut the punch. While theoretically possible to cut any size from 6- to 36-point, for example, as reductions from a single enlarged original, certain changes of proportion must be made if all sizes of type in one design are to be aesthetically satisfying, so several brass templates must be made.

Morris Fuller Benton, his son, designed revivals of many classic faces for the American Type Founders Company, Bodoni, Cloister and Garamond being examples (See Appendix A).

Bergmann von Olpe, Johann, 1460–1526: a notary public, chaplain and scholar of Basle, who opened a printing shop about 1494 with Michael Furter as manager. He issued works by humanist writers. His finest typographical production was the 1494 edition of his friend Sebastian Brant's '*Das Narrenschiff*', q.v. In 1497 he issued Jakob Locher's Latin translation of it entitled 'Stultifera navis'.

His last dated book was issued in 1499.

Berne Convention, 1886: an international copyright agreement ratified in 1887 by several European countries and their former colonies. Non-signers then included the U.S.A., Russia, China, Turkey, and certain South American republics. In 1974 there were sixty-four member countries. Convention has been periodically revised: in Berlin, 1908; Rome, 1928; Brussels, 1948; Stockholm, 1967 and Paris, 1971.

See also *Copyright Act, Model Copyright Law, Universal Copyright Convention, World Intellectual Property Organization.*

Berner, Konrad: see *Sabon.*

David Berry Prize: a prize of a gold medal and the sum of £50 awarded triennally for a work dealing with Scottish history within the reigns of James I to James VI, the subject to have been previously approved by the Royal Historical Society, London.

Berry, Jean, duc de, 1340–1416: a wealthy patron of French manuscript painting for whom was made a series of Books of Hours including the 'Petites heures', the 'Grandes heures', and the 'Très riches heures'. The latter, now in the Musée Condé, Chantilly, was begun about 1411 by the three Limbourg brothers who came from Holland. The splendour and detail of the full-page scenes of town and countryside and the famous calendar of the months have led to its general acceptance as the finest example of the illuminator's art in France. The work was completed by Jean Colombe after the duke's death. Other artists he commissioned were André Beauneveu and Jacquemart de Hesdin, who painted the 'Très belles heures' now in Brussels.

Berry and his brothers Charles V of France and Philip the Bold of Burgundy were patrons in the grand manner, giving impetus and opportunity to artists who could only develop and flourish with support from the rich and cultured. See M. Meiss, 'French painting in the time of Jean de Berry', Vol I, Phaidon, 1967; Vol II, Thames and Hudson, 1975.

Jean Berté process: a printing process in which blocks of rubber, linoleum, or composition are used for printing flat water-colours on matt paper. It has been used in France for illustrated books for children.

Berthelet, Thomas, fl.1528–55: a London printer who, for a time, was King's Printer to Henry VIII. There is no evidence that he was binder to the King, as used to be thought; presentation copies to the King of books which he printed were bound in at least three different workshops. A bill survives for books supplied by him to the Royal Library in 1542–3 in his capacity as a bookseller, in which some of the bindings are described.

As a printer he is remembered for the first Bible (Vulgate) to be printed in London, for law books, and for Lily's Latin grammar of 1540. He issued an edition of the great encyclopaedia on natural science 'De proprietatibus rerum' of Bartholomeus Anglicus, translated by John de Trevisa, 2nd ed., 1535; the Latin dictionary of Sir Thomas Elyot, 1538; and translations of Erasmus.

Berthold, Hermann: the founder, in 1858, of a Berlin business known as 'Institut für Galvano-Typie'. In 1865 he opened a brass rule works which, as Hermann Berthold AG, has developed into one of the world's largest typefoundries. In 1878 Berthold established a unit of measure for type which was adopted by all German founders; one point equals 0·376mm. and there are 2,660 per metre (one Anglo-American point equals 0·351mm.).

The firm is noted for its extensive range of display types. Included are designs by Gunter Lange, Herbert Post, Imre Reiner, Georg Trump, and Martin Wilke. Founts are supplied in both Didot and Anglo-American point systems. The business is now a leading supplier of phototypesetting equipment. See also *Diatyp.*

Besançon, Jacques de: a Parisian illuminator of the late 15th century. He worked for a time with Antoine Vérard for whom he painted initials in books the latter printed on vellum.

Bessemer, Anthony: a Dutch punchcutter who worked in Holland and France before coming to England about 1794. He worked for the Caslon foundry. His son, *Sir Henry Bessemer*, was associated with the *Young-Delcambre* machine, q.v.

Besterman Medal: an annual award established by the Library Association in 1971 for an outstanding bibliography or guide to the literature of a particular subject. It is named after Theodore Besterman, the bibliographer.

bestiary: a book containing myths and folklore about real or imaginary animals and places. These mythical legends were used to illustrate Christian teaching. The text was allegorical and the morals were made clearer by the inclusion of drawings, sometimes coloured, of the strange beasts.

A 2nd century Greek collection of animal lore of Alexandrian origin, known as the 'Physiologus', which was widely copied and translated, served as an inspiration for the medieval bestiarist. Fine English examples date from the 12th-14th century. Woodcarvers, stone masons and limners may have used them as source books. See T. H. White's 'The book of beasts', Cape, 1954, which is a translation from a 12th century English bestiary now in Cambridge University Library (CUL.II.4.26). The original was in Latin. See also *grotesques, Physiologus*.

bestseller: a book of general interest of which skilful advance publicity, quotable reviews, the announcement that paperback and film rights have been arranged, frequently result in large numbers being sold within a few months of issue. Though interest may be sustained for a time by such announcements as 'Tenth big printing' many of these books are forgotten a few years later. Long-term steady sellers are such backlist books as Chaucer, Shakespeare, the Bible, classics and school textbooks which continue to sell for generations with little or no publicity.

Beta Ray substance gauge: an instrument for indicating continuously the substance of the web of paper as it moves off the papermaking machine. A radioactive source in the head of the instrument emits a continuous stream of electrons which penetrate the web of paper. The thicker the paper the weaker the stream as it is collected by an electronic apparatus below the web. This can indicate the paper substance with an approximate accuracy of $1 g/m^2$.

bevel: 1. the sloping surface of a type rising from the shoulder to the face. See also *beard*.

2. the outer edge of a printing plate. Its purpose is to hold the pins which secure the plate to its mount.

bevelled boards: strong boards with bevelled edges used for large books.

beveller: a machine for removing surplus metal from the edges (or elsewhere) of a block thus making a flange by which the block can be secured to its mount.

Bewick, Thomas, 1753–1828: a famous British wood engraver. He was an apprentice and later partner of Ralph Beilby, a Newcastle metal engraver. Subsequently he trained and partnered his younger brother John. He is remembered for his finely observed and detailed vignettes depicting country scenes, used as chapter endings in 'A general history of quadrupeds', 1790, and 'History of British birds', 2 vols, 1797 and 1804 of which six editions were printed before he died. His friend *William Bulmer*, q.v., published books with Bewick engravings, notably 'Poems by Goldsmith and Parnell' in 1795. See also *wood engraving*.

BFMP: the customary abbreviation for the *British Federation of Master Printers*, q.v.

Bible moralisée: a book of religious instruction popular in 13th and 14th-century Europe. It was essentially a picture book, arranged with eight Biblical scenes to a page, each set in a square or roundel and interpreted by a Latin text. Some examples had rough outline drawings, but others were fully illuminated and when complete had nearly 2,000 miniatures, the work of teams of artists.

Bible paper: thin, tough, opaque paper used mostly for printing Bibles and prayer books. It is made from new cotton or linen rags with titanium dioxide or calcium carbonate as loading. Bible paper, also called *Bible printing*, is erroneously referred to as *india paper*, q.v.

Bible printing: of all books the Bible has been issued in the largest number of editions. Already prior to 1500 there had appeared no fewer than ninety-four, most of which were in Latin. The 42-line, or Mazarin Bible printed by Gutenberg was apparently begun about 1450–2 and completed about 1456. Its two volumes consist of 643 folio 2-column leaves. It is thought that thirty-five copies were printed on parchment and 165 on paper; of this total only forty-eight are known. Of similar importance is the 36-line Bible printed about 1459 by an unknown printer who may, however, have been Heinrich Keffer if not Gutenberg himself. Its 884 printed leaves, two columns to a page, are usually bound in three volumes. The 48-line Bible printed by Peter Schöffer of Mainz in 1462 is also important. See also *Cracow fragments*.

Among Bibles printed in national languages may be mentioned the Low German versions printed by Quentell of Cologne in 1478 and by Arndes of Lübeck in 1498 (both famous for their illustrations); the first Bible in Italian appeared in 1471, in Catalan in 1478, in Bohemian in 1488, and in French in 1498. The original Hebrew text of the Old Testament was first printed at Soncino in 1488, and the Greek text of the New Testament by Froben in 1516. The complete Bible of Martin Luther was printed at Wittenberg by Hans Lufft in 1534, although the New Testament printed by Melchior Lotter and with illustrations to the Apocalypse by Lucas Cranach had appeared in 1522. It is said that Lufft sold 100,000 copies of Luther's Bible in forty years.

The Bible now exists in about 850 languages. See also *polyglot edition*.

Bible printing in America: the first Bible printed in America was John Eliot's Algonquin Indian version published by Samuel Green at Cambridge, Mass. The N.T. appeared in 1661, the O.T. in 1663.

The first Bible to be issued in a European language from an American press was Christopher Sauer's German quarto printed in Fraktur type at his German-town press in 1743 for which the type had been given by the Luther Foundry of Frankfurt. Sauer used the German edition of Baron Canstein which was without the prefaces and glosses of Luther.

Until 1781 the Bible in English for use in America was supplied in sheets from London, although a pirated edition of the Thomas Baskett Bible, Oxford, 1749, printed at Boston by Kneeland and Green in 1750–2 could be the first English Bible printed in America. In 1781–2 the first complete American Bible in English was issued by *Robert Aitken*, q.v., of Philadelphia. The Congress of 1782 recommended the Aitken Bible to 'the inhabitants of the United States'. It was followed in 1791 by America's first Folio Bible, issued by *Isaiah Thomas*, q.v.

For the origins of the *American Standard Version* of 1901 see *Bible printing in England*. Currently the largest producer of Bibles in English, not only in America but the world, is the World Publishing Company of Cleveland. Their Bruce Rogers folio World Bible of 1949 is probably the finest to have appeared in America. It was printed in a special cutting of Goudy's Newstyle type with decorated initials, head- and tail-pieces. The *New American Bible*, 1970, is a Roman Catholic Bible in modern English, being a new translation for which a team of fifty-one scholars based their work on Hebrew, Greek and Aramaic scriptures as well as the Dead Sea Scrolls. An *ecumenical* Bible was published in 1973.

Bible printing in England: Not until the 14th century was there a complete translation of the Bible in English. From certain early works such as 'Ormulum', 'Piers Plowman', Richard Rolle's prose version of the Psalms, and the miracle plays the general story of the Bible was by then fairly well known but there was no *text* for those ignorant of Latin. Then came the *Lollard Bible* inspired by John Wycliffe (*c.* 1330–84)

which was the first complete translation into English. There were two versions: the first, a literal rendering of the Vulgate, is thought to be the work of Nicholas of Hereford and was completed about 1380–4; the second, the work of John Purvey, was completed about 1396. It was the prologues and glosses of Wycliffe attacking such beliefs as transubstantiation which alarmed ecclesiastical authorities who held that 'the jewel of the church is turned into the common sport of the people'. Nonetheless, the Lollard Bible was widely known and nearly two hundred manuscript copies survive, many richly illuminated and mostly dating from the first decade of the 15th century.

Thus when printing was invented, which would have made possible the rapid multiplication and distribution of an English Bible, there was no approved text to hand. The absence of a text was not the only difficulty. Not until 1537 was there an English printer who could surmount the difficulties and problems of printing the Bible. There was in London no counterpart of such scholarly merchant-printers as Estienne, Froben, Fröschauer, or Koberger. The project needed time, capital to acquire large stocks of paper, an ability to organize the flow of work for producing stocks of copies in three sizes, absolute accuracy (of itself a major problem when setting 700,000 or more words in a 16th century pressroom), official approval, and a ready market to bring in an adequate financial return.

However, the stirrings of the Reformation, Henry VIII's restiveness under Papal supremacy, and the need of the church to provide an official English version to counteract unofficial ones stimulated scholars to produce a new text. The church was quick to recognise the danger of uncontrolled printing. A Bull issued by Pope Leo X in 1515 required bishops to read texts before they were printed; in many places it was an offence to issue a book without an imprint (hence the use of fictitious ones). There were public book burnings, beheadings, burnings at the stake, and imprisonments as works inimical to Catholic authority spread throughout Europe during the Reformation of the early 16th century. Censorship of the press led Wolfgang Stöckel of Leipzig to protest that printers would be ruined if they might not print what would sell, or had to print what would not. But although in 1545 Henry VIII said in Parliament that 'the most precious jewel, the Word of God, is disputed, rhymed, sung and jangled in every alehouse and tavern', the public demand for an English Bible continued.

The main versions to appear have been the following: *Tyndale's New Testament*, 1525/6. The first printed English translation of the New Testament, made by William Tyndale (*c.* 1494–1536) was based on the third printed Greek edition of Erasmus and itself influenced the compilers of the *Authorised Version*, q.v. With the financial help of a London cloth merchant, Humphrey Monmouth, a fragment of eighty quarto pages (ten sheets), with Lutheran glosses, was printed at Cologne by Peter Quentell in 1525. The city senate then forbade further work. Tyndale moved to Worms where the text, minus glosses, was re-set for the octavo edition printed by Peter Schöffer in 1526.

Copies were brought to England by the colporteur friar Robert Barnes who sold them for 3/2d (a craftsman's weekly wage). The prefatory matter helped to spread Lutheranism among Lollard groups in England, and understandably many copies were burned in London, by order of Henry VIII, at Paul's Cross in 1527.

Tyndale's translation from the Hebrew of part of the Old Testament was printed in 1530/1 by Hoochstraten of Antwerp who used the fictitious imprint 'Hans Lufft of Malborow' (Marburg). Two reprints of the N.T., revised by Tyndale, were published: the first by Martin de Keyser of Antwerp in 1534, and another for Godfrid van der Haghen in 1535. It was the 1535 edition, Tyndale's final revision, which had a lasting influence on future translators. There were also pirated editions, probably printed by Christopher Endhoven of Antwerp, in 1526, 1530, and 1534. The first Tyndale N.T. to be printed in England was the 1536 edition by Thomas Godfray.

The prose of Tyndale, his vocabulary and sentence structure, survived in the Authorised Version as part of the fabric of English national life. It was he who gave it its unity of style, a 'spoken' style which had been used since the prose chronicles of Alfred the Great. That the language was already archaic by 1611 mattered little, it being thought appropriate for a sacred subject to be heard in a sacred place.

Coverdale's Bible, 1535. The illustrated folio Bible translated by Miles Coverdale (1488–1569) 'oute of Douche (i.e. German) and Latyn into Englishe' was the first complete English Bible. The text was based on the Vulgate; the Pagninus translation from Hebrew and Greek printed at Lyons by Du Ry in 1528; Luther's German version of the N.T., 1522; the Swiss-German version of Zwingli, published at Zurich in 1531 and 1534; and Tyndale's translation. It was probably printed at Marburg by Cervicornus and Soter, and was unofficially dedicated to Henry VIII. Some twenty-three copies are known, all imperfect.

Coverdale's version of the Psalms, which he revised for the *Great Bible* of 1539, survives in the Book of Common Prayer, and his Bible was the first to introduce chapter summaries. It was issued in London in 1535 by James Nicholson of Southwark who bought the sheets from Jacob van Meteren, an Antwerp merchant, and then reprinted folio and quarto editions in 1537. The 1537 folio was the first edition of the whole English Bible to be printed in England. The quarto edition bore the title-page inscription 'Set forth with the kinge's most gracyous licence'. The Coverdale Bible was further reprinted in 1550 by *Froschauer* and in 1553 by *Jugge*, qq.v.

Matthew's Bible, 1537. This was a composite version of Tyndale's Pentateuch of 1530 and his revised N.T. of 1535, Coverdale's Ezra-Malachi and Apocrypha, and a translation of minor portions from the Calvinist Pierre Olivétan's French Bible printed by Pierre de Wingle at Neuchâtel in 1535. The prefaces and glosses owed much to Luther. The English text was edited by John Rogers, a former associate of Tyndale, but the title-page bore the pseudonym Thomas Matthew.

It was published by Richard Grafton and Edward Whitchurch but printed at Antwerp by Matthew Crom. What made it remarkable was the inscription 'Set forth with the kynges most gracyous lycence' which meant that it could be circulated freely in England in addition to the Coverdale Bible. To further the sale of this costly folio volume Grafton persuaded Cromwell in 1538 to issue an injunction ordering all parish churches to acquire a copy. An edition revised by Richard Taverner appeared in 1539.

Great Bible, 1539. This was a revision by Coverdale made at the behest of Thomas Cromwell of the Matthew Bible, and thus, by extension, of Tyndale. The work was influenced by Sebastian Münster's Latin translation of the O.T., 1535, which had a parallel Hebrew text.

Printing of it began in 1538 in Paris where Regnault was advised by Grafton and Whitchurch who had been appointed publishers and subsequently as printers. Parisian authorities stopped work during impression, and the work was completed in England. The imprint of Grafton and Whitchurch included the words 'Cum privilegio ad imprimendum solum'. Unbound copies sold for ten shillings.

The second and revised edition of 1540 bore the words 'This is the Bybble apoynted to the use of churches', in other words, the one to which Cromwell's injunction of 1538 was henceforth to apply. This edition had a preface by Cranmer and it is sometimes misknown as *Cranmer's Bible*. There were further editions by the end of 1541. In spite of the monopoly, in 1540 Berthelet was allowed to print a cheap edition to be used by private persons.

Geneva Bible, 1560. This Bible, the most widely used (in an octavo edition) by the laity in Elizabethan and Jacobean England, was a new translation, based on original texts, made by English Protestant exiles living in Geneva. Their leader was John Knox. The translators were Whittingham, Gilby, and Sampson, with some assistance from Coverdale. Their work for the O.T. was based on the 1540 edition of the Great Bible, carefully revised with the Hebrew text, the Latin version of Pagninus, 1528, and other Latin versions. For the N.T. they revised Tyndale's version in the light of Theodore Beza's Latin edition of 1556 and the fourth edition of Robert Estienne's Greek Testament, Geneva, 1551, which had numbered verses. The influential preface and notes owed much to Calvin's revision of the French Bible, Geneva, 1558.

This quarto Bible, also known as the *Breeches Bible*, was printed at Geneva by the Englishman Roland Hall and it was the first English Bible to be printed in roman type. Features of it were the division of chapters into numbered verses and the provision of a concordance and maps. It was illustrated.

In England Elizabeth I granted John Bodley (father of Sir Thomas) the exclusive right to print it, and he printed a folio edition at Geneva in 1561, but the first edition printed in England was that published by Christopher Barker in 1576. His warrant as Queen's Printer was the first to specify the right to print Bibles, Testaments, and the Book of Common Prayer, yet he complained of the expense of Bible printing, claiming in 1582 that his editions of the Geneva Bible had cost him £3,000 (now about £30,000) in eighteen months.

There were about 150 editions of all or part of this Bible, the last being printed in 1644. It was the first Bible printed in Scotland, where it was appointed to be read in churches. This was the work of Alexander Arbuthnot and the printer *Thomas Bassandyne*, q.v., dated 1579.

Bishops' Bible, 1568. Work on this revision of the Great Bible was begun in 1566 by a committee of bishops. The instigator of the plan, and also the editor, was Archbishop Matthew Parker. The revisers collated the O.T. with the Latin versions of Pagninus, 1528, and Münster, 1539. The Bible was printed by Richard Jugge and John Cawood, the N.T. on thicker paper to withstand greater use. After Jugge's death in 1577 Christopher Barker acquired the royal patent. He issued the Bishops' Bible in 1584. In all there were three editions in nineteen printings up to 1606: they were not annotated.

Although it was ordered from Canterbury that a copy should be kept in every bishop's house and every cathedral it was never formally recognised by the Queen. The principal importance of the Bishops' Bible was its use as the foundation of the Authorized Version.

Authorized Version, 1611. This is also known as the *King James Bible*. The A.V. was prepared by a committee of scholars, formed in 1604, who worked at Westminster, Oxford and Cambridge. Their brief enjoined them to follow the Bishops' Bible as far as it was consistent with 'the truth of the original', modified by the various versions of Tyndale and Coverdale where they agreed better with the text. There were to be no notes. The committee of translators referred to the Antwerp Polyglot, 1572, and the Tremellius Bible of 1579 in addition to earlier sources.

The completed manuscript (now lost) was sold to the King's Printer, Robert Barker, for £3,000. He had to pay the committee of revisers. The work was seen through the press by Thomas Bilson and Miles Smith. The first edition, a folio, sold for 30/- a copy. There was a handsome engraved title-page by Cornelis Boel. It bore the inscription 'Appointed to be read in Churches'. In addition to the black letter folio edition other sizes were printed in roman type.

In spite of James I's enthusiasm for its preparation the A.V. was not officially prescribed by Act of Parliament for use in churches (as was the Prayer Book), though its subsequent adoption was ensured since no other folio Bible was printed after 1611, and there were three further editions in the same year. With time the majesty and rhythm of its prose were regarded as wholly appropriate for the Word of God, the archaic solemnity of its language emphasising its authority, and it is still widely preferred to other versions.

The copyright for the A.V. is vested in the Crown, authority to print it in England being granted by charter to Oxford and Cambridge University Presses, and by licence to the Queen's Printer (Messrs. Eyre & Spottiswoode). This latter appointment is by Letters Patent and is held during the Queen's pleasure. The current Patent was issued in 1901 to the then three partners of Eyre & Spottiswoode by name 'and each of them and each of their executors, administrators and assigns severally and respectively'. The appointment is not affected by the demise of the monarch, and consequently does not come up for renewal at the beginning of each reign. The appointment, being held during pleasure, can at once be revoked in the case of misconduct.

Interesting sequels to the foregoing are that Eyre & Spottiswoode came under Catholic control, and that in 1957 the firm was sold to Methuen. Thus for a time the right to print the Bible for the Church of England came into Catholic hands, and the right was subsequently sold, though technically Eyre & Spottiswoode still exist in the Associated Book Publishers group.

Revised Version, 1885. This was the work of two committees set up in 1870. It was preceded by other revisions of parts of the Bible during the 18th and early 19th centuries, notable among them being John Wesley's translation of the N.T., 1755, and the American Noah Webster's revision of the Authorised Version which was published in New Haven in 1833. The R.V. stemmed from an awareness that two centuries of Biblical scholarship had resulted in a more accurate interpretation of the ancient text and its meaning. It was a literal word-for-word translation of the Hebrew and Greek, expressed as far as possible in the language of the A.V. or earlier English versions, which meant the result was somewhat laboured. The N.T. was published in 1881: the complete Bible in 1885. The R.V. is owned jointly by Oxford and Cambridge University Presses. They financed the revision and production.

American Standard Version, 1901. An American committee cooperated in the preparation of the R.V. As all their textual preferences were not accepted by the English committee a separate edition for America appeared in 1901 under the imprint of Thomas Nelson & Sons, New York. The A.S.V. was subsequently revised under the auspices of the International Council of Religious Education which acquired the copyright in 1928. (In 1950 this body and others merged to become the National Council of Churches of Christ in the U.S.A.). The N.T. appeared in 1946. The complete *Revised Standard Version*, printed in Toronto, New York, and Edinburgh for Thomas Nelson was published in 1952, and within twelve years had sold more than twelve million copies.

New English Bible, 1961–70. This was the work of a committee set up in 1947 representing the Churches of Scotland and England, the principal Free Churches, and the two universities. Their intentions were to render the English text as far as possible into idiomatic English free from the archaisms of King James and transient modernisms of later versions. The result, as seen in the N.T., published jointly by Oxford and Cambridge University Presses in 1961, is doubtless clear and readable but marred for some by the impersonal style associated with committee composition. It has been widely accepted, particularly overseas, where the language of 1611 presents unnecessary difficulties of comprehension, but there will always be those who prefer the A.V.

The Bible was completed when the Apocrypha and Old Testament portions were issued in 1970. The team of scholars who compiled it took note of the Dead Sea Scrolls and much modern research into Semitic languages. The one-volume version of the N.E.B. included slight revisions to the N.T. of 1961.

The Catholic Bible

Douai Bible. This is the version of the Bible in English which is approved for Roman Catholics in Britain. As now used it is a revision made in 1749 by Bishop Challoner (1691–1781) of the translation into English of the Vulgate made by Gregory Martin of the English College at Douai and Rheims. The N.T. was printed by John Fogny at Rheims in 1582; the O.T. by Laurance Kellam at Douai in 1609/10. The Challoner revisions were published in 1749 (N.T.) and 1750 (O.T.).

Knox Bible. This is a translation by Mgr Ronald Knox from the Latin Clementine Vulgate, i.e. the Latin Bible authorised by Pope Clement VIII in 1592 which is still the standard text for the Roman Catholic Church. Knox did not use the Jerome text. The N.T. appeared in 1945; the O.T. in 1949.

Revised Standard Version (*Catholic Edition*), 1965. This is a special edition of the American R.S.V. prepared by the Catholic Association of Great Britain.

Jerusalem Bible, 1966. A translation from the primary Hebrew and Greek texts, not the Vulgate, tracing its origins to an annotated French version prepared by the Dominican Biblical School at Jerusalem. This was first issued in fascicles from 1948. A one-volume abridgement appeared in 1965 and it is this which has been translated into present-day English by a team of scholars. It bears the imprimatur of the Archbishop of Westminster.

Common Bible, 1973. An ecumenical edition of the R.S.V. simultaneously published in America and Britain where Collins issued both hardcover and paperback editions.

See 'The Cambridge history of the Bible', C.U.P., 1963–1970; T. H. Darlow and H. F. Moule, 'Historical catalogue of printed editions of the English Bible, 1525–1961', 2nd ed. revised by A. S. Herbert, 1968; and J. Strachan, 'Early Bible illustrations', C.U.P., 1957.

For notes on other printed Bibles and Bible printing in other countries see under *Bible printing in America, Ferrara Bible, Froben, Hebrew printing before 1600, Irish type and printing, Malermi Bible, Mazarine Bible, Norton, Plantin, polyglot edition, Salomon, Scottish early printing and publishing, Vinegar Bible, Vulgate, Welsh printing and publishing, Whitchurch*.

Bible text: see *great primer*.

Biblia pauperum: a Latin name, meaning 'poor man's Bible', which came to be generally applied in and after the 18th century to the manuscript and block book

Page from a German 'Biblia pauperum', printed at Nuremberg by Hans Spörer in 1471

compendiums on the comparison of Old and New Testament subjects used in the 14th and 15th centuries by the lesser clergy and later by laymen. From early times the Christian Church taught the significance of O.T. incidents which prefigured those in the N.T., e.g. Jonah being swallowed by the whale suggested the entombment of Christ, and his emergence after remaining there for three days suggesting the Resurrection. In the Biblia pauperum each page showed a scene from the N.T., accompanied on either side by a prefiguration from the Old. A short verse or simple explanatory text completed the page.

The Biblia pauperum was developed in South Germany at the end of the 13th century and its use spread over Western Europe. An early example, dating from c. 1325, was made at Klosterneuburg near Vienna: the nine folios now surviving in the Österreichische Nationalbibliothek, Vienna, comprise seventeen pen drawings, some coloured. The first chiroxylographic version, made in Germany c. 1455, had simple woodcuts resembling in style the pen and ink outline illustrations of its predecessors. It had a German manuscript text, and survives in a single copy now in Heidelberg University Library.

The earliest typeset version has been assigned to the year 1465, largely on the evidence of watermarks in the paper, and was probably from a Brussels workshop. The drawings on which the woodcuts for this edition were based may have come from the hand of Rogier van der Weyden or one of his associates. There were other printed editions in the Netherlands and Germany, notable being that of Albrecht Pfister of Bamberg.

Biblical uncial: see *uncials*.

Bibliographical Society: founded in London in 1892 at the instigation of W. A. Copinger and Sir John MacAlister. The objects of the society are to promote and encourage bibliographical studies and research; to hold meetings at which papers are read and discussed; to form a bibliographical library; and to print books and papers dealing with different aspects of bibliography. The society's numerous publications are of considerable importance to librarians, scholars, and bibliophiles; perhaps the best known are Pollard and Redgrave's *Short-Title Catalogue*, q.v., and the journal *The Library*.

Bibliographical Society of America: founded in 1904. It aims 'by uniting individuals and institutions with predominantly bibliographical interests, to advance and support bibliographical research, particularly as it relates to America'. The Society's *Papers* (PBSA) have an international reputation.

Bibliographical Society of the University of Virginia: founded in 1947 with similar aims to the BSA above.

Records of papers read at meetings were published first as *Papers . . .*, Vol I, 1948–49, but with volume II the title was changed to *Studies in Bibliography* (SB), and as such it continues.

Bibliographie de la France: the official French bibliography. It began in 1811 as 'Bibliographie de l'Empire français', and lists books entered in the copyright office at the Bibliothèque Nationale. Weekly parts are supplemented by monthly, quarterly, half-yearly and annual cumulations.

bibliography: 1. 'the study of the material transmission of literary and other documents: its ultimate aim is to solve the problems of origin, history and text, in so far as this can be achieved through minute investigation of the material means of transmission' (W. W. Greg). This is *analytical* or *critical bibliography* and calls for a knowledge of the history of printing methods. It leads to *descriptive bibliography* which is an arrangement and full description of primary documents (books and manuscripts), and should be based on a personal examination of them. It also leads to *textual bibliography* and is concerned, in the case of a manuscript, with a study of the paper, ink, and form of script. With a printed book there is a need to study how a text (words and punctuation) given to a printer was affected by him when transferring it to the printed page. The best known single body of work troubled by problems of the printer's interpretation of copy has been the Folio and Quarto editions of Shakespeare about which scholars still dispute. In this connection the Hinman *collating machine*, q.v., enabled its inventor to identify the work of five compositors in the First Folio solely by tracing the imperfections in pieces of type.

2. *enumerative* or *systematic bibliography* is the 'listing according to some system or reference scheme of books (and articles in periodicals) that have a formal relationship' (Bowers). This may be (a) a list of material arranged by language, historical period, or place of origin; (b) one arranged by subject or a group of subjects, and divisions; (c) a list of writings by or about an author. The *GKW*, q.v., is an example of (a), Garrison and Morton's 'Medical bibliography' is an example of (b), and the Soho Bibliographies of (c). Items may be identified only by author, title and date, just sufficient to record the existence of a work.

Bibliographies which would be better termed *reading lists* or *sources* are often included in nonfiction books, either as an appendix to the text, at the ends of chapters, or as footnotes to pages.

3. in the booktrade the word is used for the list of previous titles by an author, or of books in a series, printed on the back of the half-title; also for the date of first publication, reprints and revised editions, printed on the verso of the title-leaf. This last is often

referred to by the trade (though not by librarians) as the *biblio*.

Bibliography in Britain: an annual classified list of books, articles and reviews published in the United Kingdom on the 'history of the printed book and of the arts, crafts and techniques involved in its production, distribution, conservation, description and analysis'. It is compiled by members of the Oxford Bibliographical Society. Vol 1, for 1962, appeared in 1963. It has now ceased.

bibliology: the scientific description of books from the earliest times to the present, and including all the materials and processes involved in their making. See also *codicology*.

Bibliomites: see *Society of Antiquarian Booksellers' Employees*.

bibliopegy: bookbinding viewed as a fine art. (OED)

bibliophile: literally, a friend of books, by which is now implied a collector of them. In the days of Plato and Aristotle (both of whom had libraries) books were collected to be read, and while later the Livres d'Heures so exquisitely illuminated for such patrons as the Duc de Berry were made to delight the eye rather than improve the mind, the great libraries of Sir Henry Savile and others of his day were collections of books to be studied by scholars and friends.

It was during the later 16th century and after, when increasing numbers of noblemen, statesmen, and the higher clergy developed their libraries, that a collection of books came to denote wealth and sometimes taste. Books were bought because they were rare, finely printed or sumptuously bound (and if they were not this would be rectified by rebinding, to the peril of an often important original cover).

By the 19th century a library of calf or morocco was the mark of success in business, and it was during this era, too, that another reason for collecting books developed: this was the limited edition from a private press (press books, as they are called).

The history of Quaritch (from 1847) or Sotheby (from 1744) shows how books were bought and sold for their incidental qualities rather than for their texts. The 19th century was not without tragedy for the British bibliophile since many great collections went to the salerooms, and while the Bodleian or British Museum occasionally benefited from a legacy or purchase, whole libraries were shipped across the Atlantic to a richer country anxious to acquire the cultural heritage of Europe. Thus it is that the greatest collections of the 20th century have developed in America. See A. N. L. Munby, 'Sale catalogues of libraries of eminent persons', 12 vols, Mansell-Sotheby, 1971–6.

Bickham, George John, 1684–*c*. 1758: one of a London family of engravers. He is remembered for his influential writing manual 'The universal penman' which was a compendium of all scripts in current use to which twenty-five writing masters contributed. It was issued and reprinted in parts between 1733–41. See Sir Ambrose Heal, 'The English writing-masters and their copy-books', C.U.P., 1931.

Billingsley, Martin, 1591–1622: a skilled writing master and tutor in calligraphy to Charles I. He is remembered for his manuals 'The pen's excellencie', Humble, 1618, and 'A coppie book . . .', 2nd ed., 1637, in which he illustrated three kinds of secretary, then the usual hand in England for most business. It was thought to be quicker than Italian cursive which was slow to gain influence.

bill of fount: see *fount scheme*.

bill of type: see *fount scheme*.

bimetallic lithographic plates: printing plates made of two dissimilar metals, chosen for their wetting properties. Copper, brass, zinc, and silver are readily wetted by oils; aluminium, magnesium, lead, nickel, chromium, and stainless steel by water. Chemical treatment can, however, affect the receptivity of any metal to either fluid.

Although such plates require special electro-plating equipment, and are costly, there are certain advantages. The hardness of such metals as chromium permits long runs on high-speed offset presses; image areas on copper are more permanent than the albumen images on zinc; the plate may be used without graining to make it water retentive (or with only a minimum grain) and will thus need less damping water than normal grained plates, thereby minimizing water-ink emulsification.

In most cases the image on these plates is formed by a combination of photomechanical stencil and electroplating, though chemical deposition is also possible, e.g. a deep-etched zinc plate can be copper-coated on its image areas by immersion in a copper sulphate copper oxalate solution, or in the *Ahlen and Akerlund* process where a chromium or stainless steel plate is coated with a light-sensitive dichromated film, exposed under a positive, developed, and immersed in a copper solution.

There are two groups of electrolytic methods. In the first, negatives are used when exposing the plate. The finely-grained aluminium *Alkuprint* plate of M. Horn is given a copper deposit in an electrolytic bath. It is then given a light-sensitive coating and exposed under a negative. After development, the bared copper areas are etched off, and the non-image aluminium base thus exposed is treated with dilute nitric acid to make it ink-repellent. The difficulty of plating copper on aluminium limits the use of this process.

An iron base-plate coated first with lead (non-image) and then with copper (image) is the method of *W. A. Boekelmann and A. Elfers.* The printing rollers must be set with care when using these plates due to the softness of the lead.

In the *Electron intaglio plate* method of E. Blau a zinc or brass plate is coated with dichromated shellac. After exposure under a negative, it is developed in alcohol, washed, dried, and heated to harden the shellac. Nickel or zinc is then electroplated on to the non-image areas. In the *Hausleiter* process a polished brass plate is sensitized, exposed, and developed; then the non-image areas are plated with nickel steel.

Positives are used in the second group of electrolytic methods.

In *Carl Aller's* process a stainless steel base-plate (with a 12 per cent chromium content) is coated with copper. It is then given a layer of dichromated gum arabic and exposed in contact with a half-tone positive. After development, the exposed copper image areas are protected with an electrically deposited resist, while the copper on the non-image areas is etched away with ferric chloride solution. These plates are known as *Levy plates.*

In the *Nu-chrome* process, announced in Britain by Coates Bros in 1957, a thin steel base is plated with copper and then chromium. The steel is solely for strength. A patent polyvinyl light-sensitive coating replaces the usual dichromated gum. After exposure, the image is dyed, dried, and retouched. Etching follows, leaving the exposed copper image slightly below the matt-finished water-absorbing chromium layer. Treatment with phosphoric solution enhances the ink receptivity of the copper and the water receptivity of the chromium. Cheapness, stability, durability, and good definition are among advantages claimed for these plates.   (With GU)

binder's boards: see *boards.*

binder's brass: a brass block bearing relief letters, or a design in relief, used for blocking the cover of a book. The binder or publisher sends the brass engraver a layout of his requirements. This layout may be a good pull, a sketch, or a careful reproduction in black and white. The lettering is set up in type, or drawn by hand, and photographed to the required size. The resulting negative is printed down on a 5-gauge brass plate of suitable size, the negatives from several jobs being printed at the same time. The plate is then shallow-etched.

It is next sawn into separate blocks which are given to a machinist who removes all the metal surrounding the design or lettering: this is where the brass gets its depth. Each block now receives the attention of a hand-engraver to take the burrs off, give shape and

precision to the block, and give it the final finish. It is this hand craftsmanship which gives the brass block its superiority over the cheaper soft-metal zinco, cast from type, which is sometimes used as an alternative.

binder's cloth: see *book cloth.*

binder's title: the title as lettered on the binding. It may be contracted from that on the title-page, or original cover of a book being rebound.   (LK)

binder's waste: surplus printed sheets used by hand-binders for lining end-papers and the like.   (LK)

binding: 1. a difficulty arising when locking up type, caused by using furniture which is longer or wider than the type and 'binds' at the ends.
   2. see *bookbinding.*

binding proof: see *witness* (2).

binding variants: differences of colour, fabric, lettering or decoration occurring between copies of the same edition as issued by the publisher. These may occur when not all copies are bound at one time or in one bindery. See also *primary binding, remainders, secondary binding.*

Binny, Archibald: a Scot who with *James Ronaldson* established a typefoundry in Philadelphia in 1796 from which the first American type-specimen book was issued in 1812. Their transitional roman face No 1, the first noteworthy type to be designed in America, was later revived by Updike, who called it Oxford, and by American Type Founders Company who called it Monticello.

Binny and Ronaldson acquired Fournier material, formerly owned by Benjamin Franklin. When their business was sold in 1833 it passed to the firm later (1860) known as MacKellar, Smiths and Jordan which, in 1892, became part of the American Type Founders Company.

Birckmann, Franz: the founder at Cologne, early in the 16th century, of a well-known bookselling and printing business which continued until the end of the century. He made journeys to Paris, Basle and London where he established branches for the exchange and import of books.

In 1526 he began printing on his own account, issuing law books and an octavo Latin Bible. After his death in 1530 his son *Franz II* and brother *Arnold* were among the more notable of his numerous heirs and successors who extended the business in Antwerp and specialized in medical, scientific and theological printing. Several members of the family settled in London and it is probable that the first printer of Cambridge, *John Siberch*, q.v., who was a relative by marriage to the Birckmanns, was their sometime book-selling agent for the Cologne-London trade.

birthday book: a variety of book, popular in the Victorian era, which gave a quotation for each day of the year, and had blank leaves for autographs. The first was published in 1866 by Mack of Bristol and was 'The birthday scripture textbook'. Other 'birthday books' offered a daily quotation from the works of a celebrated poet, and the term has since been extended to include those amorphous conflations of essays published to mark a prominent person's birthday (see *Festschrift*).

bis: twice, used after a page number in indexes to indicate that the item is referred to twice on that page. Thus *ter* or *quat* to denote thrice or four times.

Bisticci, Vespasiano da, 1421–98: a Florentine scholar-bookseller who collected classical manuscripts for such wealthy patrons as Niccolò de' Niccoli and Cosimo de' Medici. He is said to have employed forty-five scribes to copy two hundred works for the library of Fiesole which Medici founded *c.* 1440.

BL: an abbreviation, used in catalogues and lists, to indicate that a book in English is printed in *black letter*, q.v. Cf. *GL*.

black: a blemish on a printed sheet made by a lead space which has risen to type height and left an impression. Cf. *monk*.

black face: see *black letter*.

James Tait Black Memorial Prizes: the prizes founded in 1918 by Mrs J. C. Black, widow of a partner in A. & C. Black Ltd of London. They are awarded each spring for the best biography and best work of fiction published during the previous year.

black letter: or *gothic*. A general term, 'as confusing as it is convenient' (Morison), for the group of scripts which developed in Europe in the 12th century. Its final form, then known as *text* or *textura*, evolved in Paris in the early 13th century. The several regional forms of black letter scripts and later type may be broadly grouped as:
1. *for Bibles and service books* lettre de forme, text hand, textura, textus, textus quadrata;
2. *for scholastic works in Latin* fere-humanistica, gotico-antiqua;
3. *for copyists' formal vernacular use* Italian rotunda, lettera Bolognese, lettre de somme, litterae Venetae, textus prescicus;
4. *cursive scripts* Fraktur, lettre bâtarde, Schwabacher.
Inevitably black letter scripts inspired the design of early printing types varying, as did the scripts, according to the locality in which cutting was done. In Germany, due to the influence of Maximilian, *c.* 1517, Fraktur became the national script and type, retaining a dominant position until abolished by Hitler in 1941 as being Jewish. In England black letter for books in English was used from the 1560s until abandoned for general publishing in the 17th century, but, as the specimens of Thorowgood, 1824, and Figgins, 1825, show, founts were still available and continued in occasional use for ecclesiastical and legal publications during the Gothic revival of art and architecture in the 19th century. See also *letters – forms and style*.

blad: 1. formerly, a sample of a forthcoming book, made up for the publisher's traveller to show to the trade. It usually consists of the first thirty-two pages, including prelims, bound up in the same cloth as the edition run. 'Dummies' for Frankfurt are more common today.
2. publishers' publicity material in fold-out format, opening up like a concertina to show a sequence of specimen pages of text and pictures.

blade coater: an 'off-machine' coating unit. Briefly, a moving web of paper is carried on a large rubber-covered roll against which a flexible steel blade is held at the point where the web has received its layer of clay-casein-latex coating slip. After drying it can then be given a second coating by either a blade or air-knife coater. Varieties of blade coater include the Flexiblade and the *trailing blade coater*, q.v.

Blades, William, 1824–90: a London printer who wrote on printing and bibliographical subjects. His major interest was Caxton, and he was the first to make a professional examination of Caxton's output by considering the type used in over 400 copies of his books. The result was 'The life and typography of William Caxton, England's first printer . . .', 1861–3. On this work he based his 'The biography and typography of William Caxton', 1877, reprinted with an introduction by James Moran, 1971.

His firm Blades, East & Blades issued facsimile reprints of Caxton's 'Gouernayle of helthe' in 1858 and 'Moral prouerbes' in 1859 from reproduction type specially cast in pewter.

Blades' impressive collection of 2,000 or so books, pamphlets and miscellanea on printing was acquired by the St Bride Foundation for its library.

Blado, Antonio, 1490–1567: privileged printer to the *Tipografia Camerale*, q.v., in Rome. He acquired a cursive type face, probably designed by Ludovico degli Arrighi in 1526. With it he printed in 1535 the important philosophical work by Leone Hebreo 'Dialoghi d'Amore', while his use of it in 1539 for the 'Vita

Sfortiae . . .' of Paolo Giovio inspired its recutting in 1923 as the Blado chancery italic of the Monotype Corporation. See also *greek type*.

Blaeu, Willem Janszoon, 1571–1638: a map engraver, bookseller, and printer of Amsterdam. Between 1594 and 1596 he was an assistant to Tycho Brahe in Denmark, then returning to Amsterdam where he began making globes and astronomical instruments. He began publishing single-sheet maps about 1604, and also printed books for which some of the types he used were cut by Nicholas Briot, but it was the great series of atlases issued between 1629 and 1662 which brought fame to Blaeu and his sons *Cornelius* (d. 1648) and *Johann* (1596–1673). Of these the 'Atlas magnus', 1650–62, in eleven folio volumes was particularly notable. Their foundry was sold to Voskens in 1679, the printing presses in 1695, but publishing and bookselling continued until 1712. After 1673 the atlas plates were bought by Albertus Magnus.

The elder Blaeu is also remembered for his improvements, about 1620, to the screw and lever printing press. These were the substitution of the wooden hose by an iron one and the fitting of two long screws with butterfly nuts for the closer control of the platen after positioning. This facilitated the use of a larger platen and thereby the printing of bigger sheets, and diminished the risk of slurring the impression. See also *hand-press*.

Blake, William, 1757–1827: one of the greatest English artist-illustrators, remembered particularly for his engraved 'Prophetic Books', 'Milton', 'Dante', and 'Jerusalem'. He described his books of illustrated verse as 'illuminated printing'. Beginning in 1788 he experimented with printing from relief-etched copper plates on which illustration and text were outlined; some of the etched plates were finished off with a graver. He used a hand-press.

To increase the effect of an illuminated manuscript Blake varied during the printing the tints in which a plate was coloured, changed the order of plates, and transposed parts of the text; while to many impressions he and his wife added colour-washes by hand. Gold and silver further embellished some of his later work. See G. Keynes and E. Wolf, 'William Blake's illuminated books: a census', New York, Grolier Club, 1953; G. E. Bentley, 'Blake books: annotated catalogues of William Blake's writings', O.U.P., 1977; and D. Bindman, 'Complete graphic works of William Blake', Thames & Hudson, 1978.

Blakeney Press: a one-man private hand-press set up by Edward Henry Blakeney at Ely in 1908. Small editions of his own poetry were issued, not for public sale, in addition to occasional prose pamphlets. Before he died in 1955 Mr Blakeney printed about eighty works.

blanc fixe: an artificially produced form of barium sulphate which can be added as a filler to paper pulp, giving colour and softness to the sheet.

blanket: 1. on an offset press, the layer of rubber or synthetic material which covers the transfer cylinder. See *offset blanket*.
2. in letterpress, a composition, cork, plastic, rubber or textile covering for the impression cylinder.

blanket-to-blanket press: a unit perfecting press used for web offset printing and sheet-fed offset perfectors. The web of paper passes between two blanket impression cylinders so that both sides of it are printed simultaneously. In colour work up to four of these double units are installed in linked sequence, the web passing horizontally through them. There are limitations to successful operation: extra make-ready is needed, simultaneous drying of both sides of the web may cause blistering, the wide intervals between printing impacts make hairline register difficult to maintain, and the wastage from web breakages tends to be high. See also *drum press, unit principle*.

blank line: see *white line*.

blanks: see *white out*.

bleaching: the use of chemicals to remove impurities in the fibrous materials of paper pulp and to improve the colour. The potential use of chlorine as a bleaching agent, made known in 1786 by the French chemist C. L. Bertholet, was important to papermakers since by it coloured rags could be made white. They could thus produce more superior quality paper. The use of chlorine by English papermakers began about 1790. Earlier attempts to bleach rags had included their immersion in a solution of quicklime and pearl ash followed by exposure to sunlight. Joshua Gilpin was the first in America to use chlorine.

bleaching paper: fox marks on printed paper can be removed by bleaching. This is done in three stages: 1. immersion of the sheet in a weak solution of permanganate of potash and rinsing; 2. immersion in a hot weak solution of sulphurous acid and rinsing in water; 3. immersion in a solution of hyposulphate of soda and a final rinsing. The paper then requires re-sizing.

bleach-out: a weak photographic print which has not been fixed. It is used as a basis for an outline drawing of the subject. The unwanted part of the photograph is then bleached out without affecting the inked outline.

bled-off: said of illustrations which spread to the edge of the page, leaving no margins. Blocks from which such illustrations are to be printed must exceed the trimmed size of the page at the edge or edges where it bleeds.

bleed: a margin which has been overcut is said to bleed.

blind blocking: *blocking*, q.v., without the use of gold.

blind folio: a leaf in the prelims of a book which has no page numbers printed (or written) on it. Thus when numbering begins the introduction may bear a 9: counting the unnumbered pages shows the half-title to be page 1, the title-page to be page 3, the dedication to be 5 and the contents page to be 7. Numbered folios are said to be *expressed*.

blinding in: see *tooling*.

blind, printing for the: see *Braille, Moon*.

blind-stamped panels: designs impressed on the leather cover of a book by means of a single engraved wood or metal *panel stamp* bearing a complete design. This was done in a *blocking press*, q.v.

An early panel-stamped book cover was made in Antwerp about 1240. The panel shows a priest kneeling before the Virgin and Child. The priest, Wouter van Duffel, canon of the church of Notre Dame, 1249–85, is named on the binding in French, and also on an extant document in Latin, dated 1283: his armorial motif is common to both. The brown calf binding, transferred to a 15th century treatise on heraldry written in English, is in the Plantin-Moretus Museum (O.B.5.6).

Panel stamps came into wider use in the later 13th century, chiefly in the Netherlands. As printing spread in the late 15th century the production of large numbers of books, sold to the purchaser in sheets or quires, called for quicker binding. This led to the use of panel stamps and roll tools as a means of adding decoration to the covers.

In France large historiated panels which could effectively embellish a whole octavo or quarto board were used during the period 1488–1528. Similar stamps were much used in Germany, particularly on pigskin covers.

In England the era of these panels was from 1485 to 1550, the royal arms and heraldic devices being favoured designs. Calf was the usual leather and gilding was rarely applied.

There was a revival of panel-stamping in England, *c.* 1820–50, for the *architectural bindings*, q.v., used on Bibles and prayer books. The leather was blocked in an enormous *fly embossing press* or in an *arming press*, qq.v., before attaching. See illustration under *bookbinding*. See also *embossed bindings, Richenbach*. See J. B. Oldham, 'Blind panels of English binders', C.U.P., 1958.

blind tooling: the use of heated tools to impress a design on the cover of a book without the use of gold, ink or foil. The tools are pressed into the leather by hand. The amount of pressure directly affects the result since on some leathers the skin is darkened in proportion. The tools are used at lower temperatures than when working with gold leaf.

The use of a die or stamp in a press is known as *blocking*, q.v.

blistering: a defect which may occur under the surface of coated stock as the printed web passes through the oven on a heat-set web offset press. It may be due to a high moisture content or air resistance. See also *delamination, heat-set inks*.

block: 1. an etched or engraved plate of aluminium, copper, magnesium or zinc after it has been mounted to type height for letterpress printing. *Line blocks*, q.v., are used to reproduce an original consisting only of lines, dots, and fully covered solids. *Half-tone blocks*, q.v., reproduce originals consisting of continuous tones. A *combined block* can be made from a line block and a half-tone.

Two-, three-, or *four-colour blocks* are sets made for printing the component colours of a coloured original. A *duplex block* is a special two-colour block, not intended to give a two-colour impression, but a mellower picture than a one-colour half-tone.

A block can be duplicated as an *electro* or *stereo*, qq.v. Blockmakers charge for blocks according to their surface area, a certain minimum price being charged (a *minimum block*). For printing on paper with a dull or rough surface special *deeply etched blocks* are used, or else *relief blocks* which cost more. See also *photoengraving*.

2. a metal stamp, usually of brass, used to impress a complete design or lettering on a book cover. See also *arming press, binder's brass, blocking press*. Cf. *tooling*.

3. to stamp a book cover or case with the block described in (2).

block book: a book either of text or text and pictures printed entirely from woodcuts. Such books were usually of a religious nature. The Apocalypse, Biblia pauperum, Ars moriendi and Canticum canticorum were popular subjects, appearing in numerous editions, often with crude cuts by unknown artists. The block cutters were members of the Guilds of Carpenters, not of Scriveners or Stationers.

A block book was usually a series of folio leaves, printed on one side. The text was normally limited to a description of the pictorial design, although whole pages of text were also cut in wood. In some cases a block filled one page but in others it filled a two-page opening with a blank page preceding and following the double spread. This gave a regular sequence of two printed pages followed by two blank pages all through the book. The blanks were sometimes pasted together to assist continuity.

At first prints were obtained by rubbing (see *frotton printing*) and the ink was either grey or brown but towards the end of the 15th century blocks were printed in black ink in a press and both sides of a leaf were used. Sometimes the pictures were crudely hand-coloured.

When block books originated is uncertain but extant examples in Europe belong to the era 1455–1510, and the Netherlands and Germany were the main centres of production. No English or French examples are known. It may be wondered why they should have been made when printing from type had begun and was spreading. Firstly, they were simpler to produce, requiring neither types nor press, and secondly, they were intended for a relatively poor and unsophisticated public for whom printed books of the kind then produced were unintelligible and too costly. Two centuries later books printed from wooden blocks were made in Russia (from about 1725) marked by the prevalence of figurative elements. They were the work of anonymous printers, issued without an imprint, and sold by chapmen. Subjects included biblical scenes and saints' calendars, folk literature, simple education and official publications of the civil presses in Moscow and St Petersburg.

In China the stamping of designs from wooden blocks on to paper may have begun about AD 600 if not earlier, and in Europe block books were preceded by single leaves printed from a block bearing text and pictures. For an illustration see *Biblia pauperum*. See also *anopisthographic printing*, *Apocalypse*, *Ars memorandi*, *Ars moriendi*, *Canticum canticorum*, *chiroxylographic book*, *Exercitium super Pater Noster*, *(Die) Kunst Chiromantia*, *opisthographic printing*, *Speculum humanae salvationis*.

block diagram: in technical-book illustration, the representation of the units of a machine or sequence of processes by outline squares or rectangles having printed within them the names of each.

blocked up: composed type which cannot be printed off, probably because author's corrections or special sorts or paper are awaited. See also *good*, *live matter*.

blocking: the impressing of a design or lettering on a book cover by machine. The blocking may be blind, ink, foil or gold leaf. See also *binder's brass*, *gold blocking*. Cf. *tooling*.

blocking foils: a foil in its strict sense is metal rolled or beaten to a thin leaf. Imitations of gold leaf, but using bronze powder as the colouring medium and made up in leaf form, are known as foils and used by bookbinders for blocking, as are similar leaves using aluminium or other white metals to imitate silver. White and coloured pigments and also coloured metal powders are made up in the same way. All are used as is gold leaf, the impression being obtained from a heated die and the surplus leaf brushed away. Modern practice, and especially with power-operated blocking presses, is to use foil made in the form of a transfer, the metal or pigment being held on a continuous web of thin paper or material of the cellophane type which is drawn over the heated blocks so as to present an unused portion for each impression. The use of any of the foregoing materials is known as *foil blocking* as distinct from blocking in gold or other precious metals. See also *blocking press*. (LK)

blocking press: a press in which heated blocks are used to stamp designs and lettering on book covers and cases. In machine bookbinding this is done mechanically, gold or pigment foil being fed through the machine on a plastic or paper ribbon which embodies its own size or adhesive. The press is also used for blind or ink blocking (for the latter heat being unnecessary). When gold leaf is used it is first laid on the book cover. See also *butter stamp*, *embossed bindings*, *glair*, *gold blocking*, *tip*.

blockmaking: see *photoengraving*.

block mounting: the final treatment of a prepared photoengraved plate (half-tone, line block) before it is supplied to the customer. Finishing includes spot etching, the hand retouching of surfaces, and routing away large background areas. Unless required unmounted the plate is usually squared up, trimmed, given a bevel, and mounted to type height on wood. Not all blocks are squared up: they may be given an irregular shape by routing, e.g. cut-out or vignetted (see illustrations). The bevel is not made if the plate is to be stuck to a metal base with a two-sided adhesive.

A block mounted on wood is normally only used for making an electro or stereo: for printing purposes mounts of iron, lead, synthetic materials, magnesium or duralumin are used. See also *photoengraving*, *plate dog*, *router*.

block quotation: a quoted passage set off from the text it accompanies. See *quotations* (1).

block stitching: an alternative name for *wire stitching*, q.v.

Blois bindings: the former name for a group of thirty-four French bindings once thought to have been made by craftsmen working at Blois. This being doubted by scholars the bindery whence they came is referred to as the *atelier Louis XII – François Ier*, q.v.

blooming letters: large (144-point) display capitals deeply engraved in boxwood. The strokes of the letters were formed by splayed stalk, leaf and flower motifs. With those used as initial capitals at Oxford in 1674 one letter ranged with as many as twelve lines of accompanying text. There were smaller sizes.

In Watson's 'History of the art of printing', 1713, are twenty-six pages misleadingly headed 'blooming letters', but these are properly *floriated initials*, being examples of the woodcut initial capitals set against a pattern of leaves, flowers, and sometimes birds, used extensively since the days of Ratdolt of Venice. They were used at the beginning of each chapter much as had been painted initials in manuscripts.

Something akin to blooming letters were revived in Victorian England but in these the flower and leaf motifs were contained *within* the outline strokes of roman or sloped roman letters as distinct from forming them. See also *criblé initials, factotum*.

Blooteling, Abraham, 1640–90: a Dutchman, and the reputed inventor, about 1671, of the *mezzotint* rocker, q.v.

Blower Linotype: the first Linotype in commercial use (in the office of the *New York Tribune* in 1886). It was so named because matrices were carried to the assembler by a blast of compressed air.

Blue Book: an official report of the Parliament of the United Kingdom and the Privy Council: issued in a blue paper cover.

blurb: a colloquialism coined in America in 1907 for the short note by the publisher or author describing and recommending a book and introducing the author. It is usually printed on the jacket flaps and may be repeated in the prelims. See also *browse, gutting, jacket, puff*.

BNB: see *British National Bibliography*.

board: an imprecise term assigned for British statistical and customs duty purposes to paper with a substance exceeding 220 gsm. See also *boards*.

board covers: 1. an inexpensive binding style used by English publishers before book cloth was introduced in the late 1820s. By a method known as *boarding* thin boards were secured to the book by its sewing cords. Then, prior to cutting, a paper cover was pasted on. Three pieces of paper were used, usually one colour for the spine and a different colour for the two sides. The edges were then trimmed. If a single piece of paper was used instead of three the

style was named *extra boards*. Most books were given a more durable binding after purchase, and surviving examples not so treated are said to be in *original boards*. See L. Darley, 'Bookbinding then and now', Faber, 1959.

2. the 20th century counterpart in which machine-fitted paper-covered boards are used for cheaper books.

boarded leather: dampened leather which is pressed between boards or rollers to emphasise or modify the natural grain. See also *graining boards, straight-grain morocco*.

board glazed: a paper finishing process in which boards are used instead of metal plates. The resulting surface is smooth but not highly glazed.

board paper: see *end-papers*.

boards: 1. a general term for *chipboards, millboards* and *strawboards*, qq.v., as used for cased or hand-bound books. The substitution of fibrous boards for the wooden boards previously used is attributed to Aldus Manutius. See also *grooved boards, liners, split boards*.

2. certain types of card used in printing. *Bristol* boards are the best quality, and are sometimes made from rag. *Ivory* are good quality, made from wood. *Pasted* boards are built up by laminating several thin layers with an adhesive. See also *fashion boards*.

Boar's Head Press: a private press founded by *Christopher Sandford* in 1930 at his home in Devon. Some eighteen books were issued in small editions before the press closed in 1936. Some had engravings by his wife, Lettice. The books were printed for him at the *Chiswick Press*, q.v. Sandford was for a time co-owner of the *Golden Cockerel Press*, q.v.

bocasin: a fine quality buckram.

BOD: see *Booksellers Order Distribution*.

bodkin: a pointed steel tool used to lever up type when making corrections. Also known as a *spike*.

Bodley, Sir Thomas, 1545–1613: the diplomatist and scholar who financed the rebuilding between 1598 and 1602 of Oxford University Library which bears his name. From 1600 he sought donations of books from the wealthy and learned, and employed agents abroad to buy books and manuscripts. The library was opened in 1602 with a stock of about 2,000 volumes, and it may be considered the first semi-public library in Europe.

In 1611 the Stationers' Company agreed with the University that a copy of every new book published by its members should be delivered to Sir Thomas;

this was a fore-runner of the *statutory copies*, q.v., still received. At the time it was not always observed.

The reputation of the library spread. In 1710 Zacharias Conrad von Uffenbach wrote of the world-famous public library where one was required 'to take an oath pro admissione ad Bibliothecam Universitatis', and where 'it costs about eight shillings and some trouble to gain an entrance . . .' He also wrote of the disturbing presence of spectators who had no access to the books 'amongst them peasants and womenfolk who gaze at the library as a cow might gaze at a new gate . . .' See W. D. Macray, 'Annals of the Bodleian Library, Oxford, AD 1598–AD 1867', Rivingtons, 1868; and Sir Edmund Craster, 'History of the Bodleian Library, 1845–1945', O.U.P., 1952.

Bodmer, Martin, 1899–1971: a Swiss banker, born in Zurich, who had one of the world's finest private collections of Shakespeariana, forming part of his 'Bibliothek der Weltliteratur' at Grand Cologny, Geneva. Dr Bodmer began collecting books after a trip to the U.S.A. in 1919, where he acquired his first English sets; but the kernel of his collection was formed around first editions of Goethe and the German classics and romantics of the same period. From Goethe came the idea of 'Weltliteratur', i.e., the great texts from Homer and the Bible to the present; in general poetry and literature in its proper sense, but including all important religious, philosophical, and scientific texts. All major languages are represented.

Dr Bodmer wrote 'I have always tried to have texts as near as possible to their origin. If this is not possible by manuscripts, I have the first prints, beginning with the Gutenberg Bible, about 500 incunabula, and all the important firsts from the 16th to the 20th century. From all eminent authors, from the Renaissance to our time, I try to have also an important or significant specimen in holograph MS. The collection contains over 1000.

'The "big five" – Homer, the Bible, Dante, Shakespeare, and Goethe – are specially developed. From Homer I have a very important papyrus scroll from the second century AD, containing the 5th Canto of the Iliad, and also a 2nd-century papyrus with the almost complete Gospel of St John in Greek.'

The Shakespeariana was said to include the most perfect set in existence of the four Folios; an extensive group of quarto editions of the plays, and an uncut copy of 'Troilus and Cressida' (STC 22331) made unique as the only copy of any of Shakespeare's plays, printed during his lifetime, to survive in this state. This magnificent collection of folios and quartos was assembled over a period of years by the late Dr A. S. W. Rosenbach, and sold to Dr Bodmer in 1952.

Bodoni, Giambattista, 1740–1813: an Italian printer and punchcutter, born at Saluzzo, Piedmont, where his father was a printer. Bodoni was a pupil of the Abbate Constantino Ruggieri, superintendent of the printing office attached to the Congregatio de Propaganda Fide in Rome. It was here that he printed his first book, a Missal in Coptic arabic, 1762, and the 'Alphabetum Tibetanum', 1759.

In 1768 he undertook the management of the Duke of Parma's private press, the Stamperia Reale, at Parma. For his early work he used Fournier types, but soon began designing his own. His first specimen book of 1771 was overshadowed in importance by his 'Manuale tipografico' which appeared in 1788. Bodoni was in no sense a scholar-printer in the tradition of De Tournes or Froben, he had no urge to print for the masses, yet he became the most celebrated printer in Europe. About 1790 the Duke of Parma set up for him a model printing office in his own palace. Books issuing from the two presses which he now managed had an impressive, if chilly, elegance: they were books in the grand manner. Notable were his editions of Horace, 1791; Virgil, 1793; Catullus, 1794; and Homer's 'Iliad', 1808 (a vellum copy of which he presented to the dedicatee Napoleon in 1810).

The London bookseller James Edwards commissioned from him editions of Greek and Latin poets, while other commissions were for limited editions of Walpole's 'Castle of Otranto', 1791; Gray's 'Poems', 1793; and Thomson's 'Seasons', 1794.

He set up a foundry as part of the ducal printing office, engraving his own punches, and he claimed to have designed all the faces subsequently shown in the second edition of 'Manuale tipografico' which was issued by his widow in 1818. The most famous of his roman types was the modern face he designed in 1790. Under the name 'Bodoni' recuttings of this, with slight variations, are still supplied by most large foundries and matrix makers. (See Appendix A.)

In 1923 the *Officina Bodoni*, q.v., was granted by the Italian government the sole right to use the original Bodoni matrices. See also *Museo Bodoniano*.

body: 1. the shank of a type.

2. the measurement of thickness of a type, slug, lead, or rule, etc. The standard measurements according to the British-American Point System are:

5-point 0·0692 in.	14-point 0·1937 in.
6-point 0·0830 in.	16-point 0·2213 in.
7-point 0·0968 in.	18-point 0·2490 in.
8-point 0·1107 in.	24-point 0·3320 in.
9-point 0·1245 in.	30-point 0·4150 in.
10-point 0·1383 in.	36-point 0·4980 in.
11-point 0·1522 in.	48-point 0·6640 in.
12-point 0·1660 in.	

3. the main portion of a book, excluding the prelims, appendices, etc.

body-em: the em of any fount. The width is the same

as the body, i.e. the em is square in section except in types cast on Monotype machines where the width of the em is related to the comparative width of the type design, e.g., in a 10-point fount of 9½ set the em will measure 10 points in body and 9½ points laterally.

body paper: the paper forming the base of coated stock.

body type: the type used for the main body of a work, excluding displayed matter.

bogus: a word used in the United States when advertisements which are received by a newspaper in matrix or plate form are re-set in type. The re-set type is not used but is consigned at once to the hell-box. This wasteful and costly procedure appears to have been insisted upon by the International Typographical Union in 1871, but it continues today. In 1960, for example, the *New York Times* estimated that it paid for some six million lines of display matter to be set in this way. Bogus is also known as *dead horse.* (The purist may claim that this definition is outside the deliberately assumed limits of this book: it is too interesting to omit.)

Bohn, Henry George, 1796–1884: a London publisher and antiquarian bookseller. He achieved fame and success as the publisher of several series (*Bohn Libraries*) totalling over 600 post octavo volumes.

Also important was his acquisition about 1835 of the copyright and stock of 'The bibliographer's manual' by *Lowndes,* q.v. Bohn's corrected and updated edition of this was issued in parts between 1857–64. The work formed ten volumes, with an appendix volume compiled by Bohn. When he retired in 1865 copyright and stock were bought by Bell & Daldy (from 1873 George Bell & Sons). They issued the 'Manual', unchanged, in a six volume edition in 1869, and in this form it remained in print until 1914. The Gale Research Company of New York issued a reprint in 1968.

Bohn, John, 1757–1843: a German binder who opened premises in London in 1795. He was noted for such finishing details as gilded doublures, paper marbling, etc., and supplied these items to other binders.

boiler: the container in which such raw materials of paper as esparto, rags, straw, etc., are boiled. Cf. *digester.*

boiling agent: chemicals with which wood chips are boiled, or cooked, in a *digester,* q.v., as a preliminary stage of making *chemical wood pulp,* q.v.

bold face: type having a conspicuously heavy appearance, but based on the same designs as its *medium*

weight in the same *fount,* qq.v. Bold can normally be set or tapped in the same line, as in the entry words of this book.

bole: 1. to reduce height of type by shaving the feet. The width of a type character can be reduced by boling to make it fit.
2. see *Armenian bole.*

Bollingen Prize: established in 1945 by Paul Mellon as an annual award of $2,500 to a distinguished American poet. It was then administered by the Library of Congress, subsequently by Yale University Library. Since 1962 the award has been one of $5,000 made every other year. Recipients have included Ezra Pound, W. H. Auden, and Robert Frost.

bolts: three of the edges of a folded sheet in bookbinding. Hence, head bolts, fore-edge bolts, tail bolts. The folded edge at the back of a sheet is not referred to as a bolt; it is termed the *last fold* or *back fold.* Until the folds have been cut away by machine, or cut through by hand, the leaves cannot be opened. See also *opened, uncut.* (LK)

Bomberg, Daniel, d. 1549/50: an Antwerp Christian, son of Cornelius Bomberg who taught him typefounding and printing. He learned Hebrew, and settled in Venice about 1515, obtaining a privilege to print Hebrew books for Jews in 1516. In 1517–18 he issued in twelve folio volumes the first printed rabbinical Bible (Mikraot Gedolot) edited by the apostated Jew Felice da Prato (Felix Pratensis). It included the massoretic notes which comprised traditional information fixing the Biblical text beyond the possibility of change. On either side of the text Bomberg placed the commentaries of *Rashi,* q.v., and his disciples, and this form has remained the definitive setting until the present day. The work was embellished with fine floriated Hebrew capitals. A second edition in four volumes, which included the Massora, appeared in 1524/25: it was edited by Jacob ben Hayyim of Tunis, a famous scholar closely associated with Bomberg. Hayyim also edited the first complete Babylonian Talmud which Bomberg issued in fifteen volumes, 1520–3, and the Jerusalem Talmud, issued in 1522/23. The Talmud and many of the 250 other Hebrew works printed by Bomberg appeared under the direct patronage of Pope Leo X.

Although Jews in Venice could not own presses Bomberg employed them as craftsmen after first obtaining permission for them to discard their distinctive yellow caps. Bomberg, who gradually replaced *Gershom Soncino,* q.v., as Italy's leading printer of Hebrew, spared no effort or money to ensure accurate texts, and in addition to ben Hayyim he employed other scholars for proof reading and editing, among them being the famous Hebrew grammarian Elijah Levita (1468–1559). His chief printer was *Cornelio Adelkind*, q.v.

After 1527 his son David began to work at the press and when Daniel went back to Antwerp in 1539 he managed it until 1548. When Daniel Bomberg died most of his material passed to the Venetian printer Giovanni di Gara, but a Plantin specimen sheet of 1579 shows hebrew type seen in earlier Blomberg books. See also *Hebrew printing before 1600, Talmud.*

Bonet, Paul, 1889–1971: a Belgian by birth who became the leading French designer of craft bookbindings. He began to design bookbindings about 1925, experimenting with many unusual materials and artistic styles, and employing the most gifted craftsmen to execute them. Many of his *Surréaliste* designs with extravagant and exotic coloured inlays appear on sumptuous *livres de peintres*, q.v., for which they are entirely appropriate. Designs were not repeated, even on two copies of a single title. The importance he gave to lettering is of note.

Bonet also designed edition bindings for the Parisian publisher Gallimard, and was the principal instigator of the *Société de la Reliure Originale*, q.v. See 'Bibliothèque Paul Bonet', Paris, Blaizot, 1970, which is a catalogue of his personal collection.

Bonhomme, Pasquier, fl.1468–83: a Parisian seller of manuscripts who also had a printing press. From this he issued the first book in the French language to be printed in France. This was 'Les Grandes chroniques de France' or 'Chroniques de Saint-Denis', Paris, 1476/7. The type used was a lettre batârde. Blank spaces were left for the later insertion of illuminated miniatures to the purchaser's taste. Five unsigned works have been attributed to him before 1483. He died in 1501.

In 1484 the business was continued by his son *Jean* who issued legal and theological works, also an illustrated herbal as well as Pierre de Crescens' 'Le Livre des ruraulx prouffitz du labeur des champs', 1486, which had excellent woodcuts showing lively scenes of rural life, the hunt, etcetera. They may have been adapted from a manuscript original.

Jean appears to have ceased printing about 1490, but he lived until about 1529.

book: for statistical purposes the British book trade once assumed that a book was a publication costing sixpence (2½p) or more. Other countries define a book as containing a minimum number of pages, but have not agreed on a standard number. At a UNESCO conference in 1950 a book was defined as 'a non-periodical literary publication containing forty-nine or more pages, not counting the covers'.

The term is also used for divisions of a larger work, as in the Books of the Bible.

In 18th-century England the word was often synonymous with *copy*. Thus in the minutes of the Oxford Delegates for April 1703 we read: 'Rec'd of Mr John Hull 30 books of the 1st and 2nd vol. of Dr Morrison's herbal at £2.10.0'.

book annotators: people who write personal comments or notes in the margins of books, either their own or those they have borrowed from public libraries. In the early 14th century *Richard de Bury*, q.v., wrote of this habit as follows: 'We must specially keep from all touch of our books those shameless youths who, when they have learned to shape the letters of the alphabet, straightway become incongruous annotators of all the fairest volumes that come their way, and either deck with their monstrous alphabets all border margins that they can find around the text, or rashly presume to write with unchastened pen whatsoever frivolous stuff may happen to run at that moment in their heads . . .'.

book auction: the selling of books to the highest bidder. For the last three centuries this has implied the sale by numbered lots of which a catalogue was made in advance.

Auctions of slaves, though not books, date from Babylonian times, but books are known to have been sold by auction in Islamic countries of the Mediterranean and in the book bazaar of Cordova in the 10th century. When the library of a rich Palestinian Jew was auctioned in the 13th century a public notary recorded the title, purchaser and price of each. Some centuries later a library was auctioned in Istanbul in 1578, and further north the library of Philip van Marnix (1538–98) was auctioned at Antwerp in 1599. At this time, too, book auctions were frequently held in Spain and a notable sale in Italy was of the Pinelli library in 1608 (see *sale by candle*).

Book auctions in the modern sense, with numbered lots and a catalogue, seem to have begun at the end of the 16th century in Holland. The earliest English example of which a catalogue survives was held in 1676 by William Cooper of Little Britain: he sold the collection of Dr Lazarus Seaman for about £3,000. By 1700 London auctioneers were commissioned to sell collections in the provinces. Taverns and coffee houses were often used for sales until well into the 18th century.

It was not until 1744 that Samuel Baker of Covent Garden founded the first auction room in England solely for the disposal of books, manuscripts and prints. (For the subsequent history of this firm see *Sotheby & Co.*)

It was customary at the early German book fairs for a printer-publisher to auction off unsold copies of his books as an alternative to paying for storage with a local man until next year's fair or taking them home.

In France the first important auction of rare and

valuable books was the sale in Paris during 1738 of the library of Count d'Hoym. The earliest book auctions in America were held in Boston coffee houses from about 1716. See also *book ring*, *trade sales*.

Book-Auction Records: first edited by Frank Karslake, and published since 1904 by Henry Stevens, Son & Styles, as a quarterly record of London, New York, etc., book auctions, with annual cumulations. Vol. 1 appeared in 1903 (from June 1902), and the work continues. General indexes have been issued from time to time. In 1969 BAR was acquired by Dawsons of Pall Mall. It now appears as *BAR Quarterly*, published by Wm. Dawson & Sons Ltd.

bookbinding: the hand or machine processes of fastening together the printed sheets of a work and enclosing them within a protecting cover. For comprehensive references see *bookbinding materials*, *bookbinding methods*, *bookbinding styles and binding features*, *bookbinding tools and machines*.

Historical. As a protection for medieval manuscript books thin wooden boards were used for covers and during the early Middle Ages these were given a full leather covering to join across the spine the back and front board, thereby giving rise to full binding in the modern sense. Deerskin, sheepskin and pigskin were used; calf was introduced in the 15th century when sheepskin and parchment bindings also became popular. About 1500 pasteboard was substituted for wooden boards in Italy where, at the same time, coverings of imported goatskin were used. In Germany wooden boards continued in occasional use until the 18th century. *Full leather* bindings, though modified to the requirements of modern techniques, maintain their superiority, but in general use (particularly on the Continent) are *half-bound* books, and in England and America *cased* books.

If cloth is substituted for leather we have a *cloth* or *half-cloth* binding, and if only boards and paper are used the term *paper boards* applies. If the covering is of paper without boards we speak of *paper covers*.

Before the invention of printing books were relatively scarce and valuable, rarely found in large enough numbers to warrant their being shelved in vertical rows. Books were kept laid flat on shelves in a cupboard (*armarium*) or on reading stands, and ornamentation, if any, was concentrated on the front cover which, in the case of Bibles and Gospels for altar use, might receive the skilled attention of a jeweller. When decorated, leather bindings would be stamped in relief with dies or panel stamps. About 1500, roll tools for impressing continuous patterns were introduced. In southern Europe, where Venice was the chief centre of the trade, the decorative skill of the oriental craftsmen employed was seen in the interlaced strapwork and gilded arabesques used for corner pieces and centre panels. When the custom of shelving books vertically spread they were often placed with the spine innermost, the title being inscribed on a small piece of vellum stuck on the cover or written on the fore-edge. By 1560, however, books were generally shelved as now, and it was a natural consequence to decorate the spine.

Lettering on the spine is thought to have been introduced about 1535. As the leather cover was attached direct to the back of the stitched sheets the raised bands divided it into panels where lettering and tooled patterns were placed.

Practical. The main stages of *hand-binding* are: folding the printed sheets into sections, gathering these in sequence, beating or rolling, collating sections and plates or maps, pressing, knocking up and marking up for sewing. There are two methods of sewing: *ordinary*, for which grooves are sawn in the back to take the cords and kettle stitches. Sewing thread goes in and out of holes pricked along a section passing over but not round the cords. In *flexible* work there is no hollow and no saw cuts are made in the back (to which the covering leather will be stuck direct). As sewing proceeds thread encircles each of the four or five cords and terminates in a kettle stitch which links one section to the next. End-papers are attached, the back is glued, rounded and put in a press to form the grooves in which the edges of the two book boards will fit. Boards are lined with paper on one or both sides, cut to the final size and attached to the body of the book by lacing on. Cord ends are pasted, tightened and hammered flat. The book is pressed. Then top-, tail- and fore-edges are cut in a cutting press: this is known as *cut in-boards* (cf. *cut out-of-boards*).

Book edges are next coloured, marbled or gilded. Headbands are fixed and the book is covered. Collectively, the foregoing are known as *forwarding*. *Finishing*, which follows, is the lettering and creation by a skilled craftsman of a design on the cover, worked with heated hand-tools and often onlays of coloured leather. End-papers are stuck to the inner sides of the boards, the spine and covers are polished and lightly varnished, and the book is pressed.

The main stages of *edition binding* are: folding, gathering, cutting edges, rounding and backing, lining backs, casemaking is done separately and, after blocking, cases are secured to the prepared books to produce the finished article. Printed matter is delivered to the bindery in large flat sheets which are folded to book size. One sheet usually comprises 16 or 32 consecutive pages, but sheets with a lesser number are used as convenient. A complete set of sheets comprises one book, and before sewing it is necessary to arrange folded sheets consecutively by gathering. End-papers and single-leaf illustrations are tipped to the sections where desired while four-page illustrations are inserted in a section and sewn with it. After sewing

Polaire. 15th century

Chained book. 16th century

Oriental binding with typical flap

*16th-century binding
with title on
fore-edge*

Incised and painted edge of Jacob Krause (1526–85)

56

16th-century blind stamped binding

Grolier binding, c. 1550

German renaissance binding by Jacob Krause
(Nationalbibliothek, Wien)

16th-century fanfare binding attributed to Nicolas Eve
(Bibl. Sainte-Geneviève, Paris)

Swedish embroidered binding. 17th century

17th-century fan binding

Derome dentelle binding. 18th century
(Bibl. Mazarine, Paris)

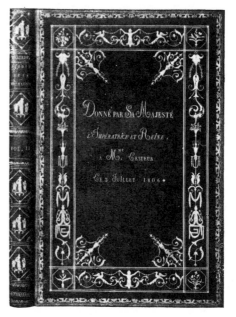

19th-century French Empire binding
(Béraldi collection, Paris)

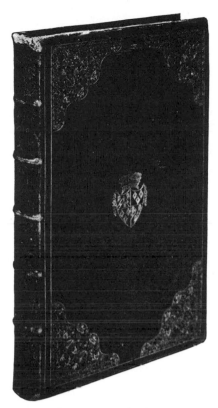

*Roger Payne binding
18th century*

*Swedish binding
dated 1796*

Jewelled binding on a medieval Spanish manuscript

Swedish binding of silver. 19th century

the sections the book is pressed and the traditional method of binding calls for cutting the edges followed by coating the back with glue. When the glue is dry the book is rounded and backed, lined with mull and with paper and finally pasted into its case.

Cases consist of a covering material, such as bookcloth or linson, which is glued to the boards with the edges turned in and subsequently blocked. Alternative methods of binding are by the use of *expandable cloth*, q.v., and for cheaper work *adhesive binding*, q.v., is common. Books may be given coloured edges, the colour being applied by a spray gun, or exceptionally one or more edges may be gilt. Back linings may be topped with headbands to improve the finish.

While machines perform most of the foregoing processes they originated as hand work and, when dealing with small quantities, hand-binding remains the only practical procedure.

Production statistics show that most books in Britain and America are now sold in paperback form, and while the custom of casing is widespread on the Continent many books are sold there in paper covers to be bound according to purchasers' wishes.

bookbinding materials: see *American russia, Armenian bole, art vellum, Balacuir, bands, bevelled boards, block, blocking foils, boarded leather, boards (1), buckram, calf, case (1), chipboard, Cobb's paper, cords, decorated papers, deerskin, dutch gilt paper, dutch leaf, écrasé leather, Elephant hide, expandable cloth, french shell, glair, gold, gold leaf, imitation leather, imitation morocco, jute board, leatherette, liners, linson, millboards, mordant (1), morocco, nonwoven binding materials, ooze leather, oriental leaf, palladium, parchment, pigskin, reel gold, russia, scabbards, scratted paper, seal, sewing thread, sheepskin, size, slips, smooth washed, split boards, strawboards, thongs, Turkey leather, vellum, vinyl binding materials, watered silk.*

bookbinding methods: see *adhesive binding, all along, attaching, azured tooling, back cornering, backed, backing, beating, blind tooling, blocking, bundling, capping up, casing-in, chain stitch, cloth joints, covering, craft bookbinding, creasing, cut back binding, cut flush, cut in-boards, cut out-of-boards, doreur sur cuir, edition binding, embossing, extra bound, extra cloth, false bands, finishing, flexible sewing, forwarding, french sewing, gathering, giggering, gluing-up, gold blocking, gold tooling, guarding, hand-binding, hand-sewing, holing out, hollow back, hollows, ink blocking, inlaying, joints, kerfs, kettle-stitch, laced on, lamination, laying on, lining, machine binding processes, marbling, marking up, Maybury binding process, meeting guards, miscellaneous binder, onlaying, overlaying, paring, pasting, prebinding, pulling, recessed cords, reinforced binding, reinforced signatures, rounding, saddle stitch, sawn-in back, sewing, side-stitch, siding, smashing, spine, stabbing, Steamset, stitching,*

sunken cords, sunken flexible, thread sealing, tipped in, tooling, trimming, triple lining, turning-in corners, two sheets on, ultrasonic binding, underbanding, unsewn binding, vellum binding trade, warehouse work, warping, whipstitching, wire stabbing, wire stitching, wrappering.

bookbinding styles and binding features: see *ajouré, à la Duseuil, antique gold edges, arabesque, architectural bindings, art gilt edges, atelier Louis XII-François Ier, author's binding, aux petits fers, azured tooling, back, bands, binder's title, binding variants, blind-stamped panels, Blois bindings, board covers, bosses, bound, burnished edges, Cambridge-, cameo-, Canterbury bindings, caoutchouc binding, chamfered edges, champlevé, chased edges, chemise, Chudov bindings, circuit edges, clasps, cloisonné, cloth boards, cloth joints, colonial cloth, coloured tops, Coptic bindings, corners (2), Corvinus, Cosway bindings, cottage binding, cuir bouilli, cuir ciselé, curtain-, dentelle bindings, diapered, diced, divinity calf, dos à dos, doublures, drawn on, Ducali bindings, edge rolled, embossed bindings, embroidered bindings, end-papers, English bookbinders, Etruscan bindings, extension cover, extra, false bands, fan bindings, fanfare, fillet (1), flat back, flexible binding, flexicover, floriated, flush boards, fore-edge painting, French bookbinders, french fillet, french joints, full bound, full gilt, gilt edges, gilt solid, goffered edges, gótico mudéjar, Greek binding style, Grimaldi, Grolier, grooved boards, guards, guinea edge, Günther, half-bound, half-cloth, half-leather, headband, headcap, hinges, Hollis, hollow back, imbrication, in boards, in boards extra, inlaying, interleaved, Irish bindings, Islamic bookbinding, Jansenist bindings, jewelled bindings, labels, lace bindings, lacquered bindings, leather joints, Lederschnittbände, lettering on the spine, letterpress binding, library edition, limp binding, Little Gidding bindings, Lyons bindings, Magnus, Maioli bindings, marbling, mitred (1), monastic bindings, mudéjar bindings, olivined edges, one on and two off, onlaying, open back, Oxford hollow, padded sides, palleted, panel (1), panel back, paper boards, paper covers, peasant bindings, Pillone, plaquette, pointillé, pot cassé, powdered, publisher's binding, publisher's cloth, quarter bound, raised bands, re-backed, remboîté, Restoration bindings, Rospigliosi bindery, rough gilt, Roxburghe, run-up spine, Safavid bindings, Scottish bindings, secondary binding, self ends, semi-yapp, shelf back, signet, slip case, solander, sombre bindings, spine, spirex, sprinkled edges, squares, start, stilted covers, tailband, tail cap, textile bindings, three-quarter binding, ties, tight back, top edge gilt, trade binding, transparent bindings, trimmed edges, velvet bindings, Venetian bindings, vernis sans odeur, votive binding, wallet-edged, Wiemeler, woodcut bindings, wrappering, Yapp, yellow backs.*

bookbinding tools and machines: see *arming press,*

beating hammer, block (2), *blocking press, burnisher, butter stamp, fillet* (2), *floret, fly embossing press, gilding rolls, gold-blocking press, gold knife, gouge, graining boards, guillotine, hand letters, jacketing machine, key* (1), *lying press, machine sewing, pallet* (2 & 3), *panel stamp, plough, pressing unit, roll* (2), *rubbing-off chest, standing press, tip, trindle.*

Book Centre: a limited company founded in 1938 by a publishing house which, in addition to distributing its own books offered to other publishers the advantages of large-scale warehouse, trade distribution, recording and accounting facilities. Details of every title are stored in a computer which provides speedy identification when processing orders and also facilitates stock control. A computer bureau produces invoices at the rate of 70,000 a week.

Ancillary services include the *Publishers and Booksellers Delivery Service* (PBDS) for the UK book trade, an *Overseas Booksellers Clearing House* to which an overseas client can send a single remittance in payment of several publishers' accounts, and a *Publishers Computer Service* for invoicing, collecting accounts, sales analysis and stock control. Regional depots are maintained. The principal office is POB 30, North Circular Road, Neasden, London NW10 0JE. See also *Orders Clearing, International Book Information Service.*

book cloth: dyed and coated calico used for book covers. The first cloth specially woven for this purpose was made for *Archibald Leighton*, q.v., in 1825. He developed a 'filler' for the calico so that it would accept glue, and popularized it by embossing the surface to simulate grained leather or silk. A few years earlier *Pickering*, q.v., had used a furnishing fabric to cover books. By the 1840s the manufacture of book cloth was commercially viable, the first firm in Britain to make it being Thomas Hughes of Bunhill Row, London, EC1. With its adoption for *edition binding*, q.v., the publisher met the cost. In former times, when books were sold in folded sections, sewn or unsewn, and protected only by a wrapper, a buyer commissioned whatever style of binding he was prepared to pay for, a custom which has not ceased in France.

The first cloth bound book to be published in America was Eaton's 'Rome in the 19th century', issued by Harper in two half-cloth volumes in 1827.

In modern usage there are two main groups of woven cloth: thin, hard-surface cloths which contain a starch-based filling, and matt, unglazed cloths resembling heavy linen and having less starch than the former. Increasing use is now made of polymer-coated cloths which are hard-wearing and resistant to moisture, dirt and insects. If wished the surface can be given a textured finish by passing the cloth between engraved rollers. See also *cloth used in bookbinding, graining boards, linson.*

book club: 1. in the 18th and early 19th centuries several book clubs or literary societies were active in England. Members were usually well-to-do and met regularly for literary discussions and to borrow books from the club collection. Annual sales of surplus stocks were held. See. P. Kaufman, 'Libraries and their users', L.A., 1969.

2. a business organization which selects from newly published books a monthly choice for postal supply to its members, usually at the full published price. Subscribers undertake to purchase a book a month but are offered alternatives, e.g. a work of fiction if the 'book of the month' is nonfiction and vice versa. (These are known in the U.S.A. as *alternates.*) A house journal giving news about forthcoming books and literary events is often included in the despatch.

The mail-order distribution of books began in Germany in 1919 when cheap special editions of the classics were supplied by post to *customers*: they were not available in bookshops. The first book club anywhere for the supply of books to *members* began when the Deutsche Buch-Gemeinschaft was founded at Darmstadt in 1924. There was at that time no interest in the idea in British book trade circles.

In America a mail-order firm for distributing pocket editions of the classics (The Little Leather Library) was begun in 1916 by Harry Scherman: in ten years he sold 50 million. He then helped to found the *Book-of-the-Month Club* (BOMC), organizing a board of distinguished editorial advisers who chose newly published books for members. The first selection was posted to some 5,000 subscribers in April 1926. Another American organization, the *Literary Guild* (LG), first incorporated in 1922 and reincorporated in 1926, began operating in January 1927. Thirty years later BOMC had about 500,000 members: LG had nearly a million.

American book clubs were enormously successful. By 1956 BOMC was mailing 4,000,000 circulars a month, and although in 1926 its loss on operations was $24,054 by 1947 it could afford to give away some $16,000,000 in free books. Part of this success was doubtless the value members placed on the advice, untainted by publishing trade hyperbole, given by the boards of respected selectors. There was also the psychological appeal of being a member of a club and a name on someone's list. Lastly, mail-order selling of goods was already part of the American way of life, firmly established as a means of bringing goods to remote communities. For the British counterpart of BOMC see *The Book Society.*

3. a similar organization which publishes books for members who undertake in advance to purchase a minimum number of specially produced books a year. They range from the semi-de luxe editions of reprints, e.g. *The Folio Society*, to cheaper editions put out for a larger general public, e.g. *The Reprint Society* (sold in 1966) which in 1939 issued T. E. Lawrence's 'Seven

pillars of wisdom' Vol. I as its first choice. Initially RS books could be collected from an agreed bookshop of the member's choice.

After September 1968 British book clubs were allowed to offer members *original* titles on the date of regular trade publication, i.e. *simultaneous publication* of the two editions, instead of waiting twelve months to issue their club reprints. The only condition was that editions must be clearly marked and specially bound. Books given away as *lead-in titles*, q.v., were excluded from this permission unless they had previously been offered as alternative choices in which case they need only be six months old.

Although initially viewed by the retail trade as likely to deprive bookshops of business, by the 1970s lavishly-promoted book clubs were well established, enabling a new public to acquire by post books they would never have troubled to buy in a bookshop. They ranged in subject specialization from cookery and crime to religion and romance.

Book Club of California: established in 1912. Standards of scholarship and book production are among the highest in the Americas. An example is Charles Muscatine, 'The book of Geoffrey Chaucer', S. Francisco, 1963, which is a chronological account of editions from Caxton to Kelmscott. The club publishes a quarterly newsletter. (DW)

book clubs and literary societies: bodies formed for the printing of works which would not, because of their specialized nature, be published as commercial ventures. While often characterized by scholarly editing, they are not always typographically remarkable. In America there are several book clubs which antedate by many years the modern 'book club' noted above and are akin to the 19th century literary societies of Europe. They publish new material and reprints in the service of bibliography. Notes on the following clubs and societies are given under their names: *Bibliographical* (U.K.), *Bibliographical* (U.S.A.) *Book Club of California, Bradford, Cambridge Bibliographical, Camden, Chaucer, Chetham, Early English Text, Edinburgh Bibliographical, First Edition, Fleuron, Galley, Gesellschaft der Bibliophilen, Grolier, Hakluyt, Harleian, Malone, Pipe Roll, Prince, Rowfant, Roxburghe, Scottish Text, Ye Sette of Odd Volumes.* See also *private press.*

Book Clubs Group: formed in 1951, within the Publishers Association, to bring about cooperation between book clubs in their dealings with publishers, to ensure adherence to regulations drawn up for the conduct of book clubs, and to establish community of outlook towards other parties concerned with various subsidiary rights.

The Book Collector: since 1952, a quarterly journal published in London for those interested in the collection and study of printed books and manuscripts. It incorporates the earlier *Bibliographical Notes and Queries* and *Book Handbook*. Articles are specialized and of high standard.

This elegant journal was for many years printed at Hertford by the Shenval Press on Grosvenor Chater's Basingwerk Parchment paper, resulting in a most felicitous combination of scholarship and good taste. It is now published by The Collector Ltd and printed by the Scolar Press to the same high standard.

The Book-Collector's Quarterly: a periodical devoted 'wholeheartedly to the interests of those who collect books of any kind'. It was edited by Desmond Flower and A.J.A. Symons, and was first published in London in December 1930 by Cassell & Co. Ltd and The First Edition Club (whose official organ it was). The origin of this periodical lay in Flower's desire to revive the 'Bibliophile's Almanack', founded in 1920 by Harold Child and Oliver Simon, and printed at the Curwen Press. This had lapsed in the 1920s.

The Quarterly, also printed at the Curwen Press, maintained a high standard of production and editorial excellence. The final number, XVII, appeared in 1935.

book design: see *copy fitting, margins, parts of a book, technical book illustration, typographer.*

Book Design and Production: from 1958, an illustrated quarterly of high standard with articles describing practical ways in which improved production methods could serve the book trade. An important feature was, for a time, the reporting of private press activities. When, in 1965, the title was changed to *Print Design and Production,* and the frequency of issue to six numbers a year, the scope of the articles became less specialized. It ceased publication in 1967.

Book Development Council: or *BDC*, a non-profit making body established in London in 1965 by the Publishers Association. In 1970 the BDC became the export division of the Association which assumed full financial responsibility for it.

The Council seeks by co-operative action, in Britain and overseas, to make available the skills of British publishing wherever they can be used, and particularly in developing countries; to ensure that adequate supplies of British books are available on reasonable terms wherever they are needed; and to support or complement local educational or publishing and bookselling enterprise. To these ends it has become the export arm of British publishing. See also *International Book Information Service.*

Booker Prize: an annual award of £10,000 for the best novel, in the opinion of the judges, to have been published by a writer from Britain, the Commonwealth, Eire or South Africa. It was established under the sponsorship of Booker McConnell Ltd in 1968 for a period of seven years (later extended for a further seven), the first award being made in 1969 to P. H. Newby for his 'Something to answer for'. The award is administered with the assistance of the National Book League.

book fair: see *Frankfurt Fair*.

book-fell: an obsolete term for a sheet or manuscript of parchment or vellum.

book form: said of a work which is issued within covers after having previously appeared in a journal, pamphlet, or newspaper. An example was Ernest Hemingway's novel 'The old man and the sea', issued in book form in the U.K. by Jonathan Cape after first publication in *Life Magazine*.

book hand: any of several scripts used for manuscript books before the introduction of printing. Among examples are *black letter, cancellaresca formata, Carolingian script, cursive, half-uncial,* and *uncials,* qq.v. See also *letters—forms and styles*.

Book Handbook: a periodical for book collectors, edited by Ronald Horrox, and first published in London in 1947. One volume was issued between then and 1950. The second and final volume, issued in 1951, was printed and published by the *Dropmore Press,* q.v. The 'Book Handbook' was then incorporated in *The Book Collector,* q.v., which until mid-1955 was also printed by the Dropmore Press.

bookhandler: an alternative designation for the member of a publisher's office who deals with authors and organizes the design and production of books from typescript to bound copies; in short, an *editor* or *production manager*. This unusual term, with overtones of a police officer controlling and training Alsatian dogs, was seen in a trade advertisement in the 1970s.

Book Impositions, 1975: a book giving diagrams of the impositions required for the various types of book-folding machine. It is published by the BPIF and is the standard work on the subject, containing full information for printing sheets for machine folding.

The 1975 edition is a revision of earlier editions, the first having been compiled in 1927 by the Master Bookbinders Association (later the Master Binders Alliance of London) with the object of 'removing misunderstandings between Publishers, Printers and Binders on matters relating to machine folding'.

(LK)

book jacket: see *jacket*.

Book of Common Prayer, 1549: the first complete service book in English which, with modifications, has been the official order of the Church of England service since the Elizabethan Act of Uniformity of 1559. It was first printed by both *Grafton* and *Whitchurch,* qq.v., the latter also issuing the first of several editions of the Second Book of Common Prayer, the First not having won official acceptance by the Church.

During the brief reign of Queen Mary (1553–8) the Sarum primer, in Latin or English, known as the *Marian Primer,* was prescribed for use instead, after which it was suppressed. (See also *Primer*.) The Book of Common Prayer was inspired by Archbishop Cranmer, who wrote most of, and was mainly an English translation of the medieval Latin Sarum use with additions from several English and Latin devotional books, and with the Psalms and other biblical passages from the Great Bible of 1540. Cranmer achieved an English prose for oral delivery which was both rhythmic and resonant. It is to his prayer book as much as to the Great Bible and Shakespeare that the language of 16th century England remains familiar, with many of its phrases and expressions still current. See F. Proctor & W. H. Frere, 'A new history of the Book of Common Prayer', 1902.

Book of Hours: a book of personal prayers for use by the laity. In England and France the use of such books began in the 11th century and continued until the 16th. In France they were known as *Livres d'Heures* or *Horae Beatae Virginis Mariae* (more simply as *Horae*), and in Germany as *Stundenbücher*. The usual contents were: 1. Calendar; 2. Four lessons from the Gospels; 3. Service for the Canonical Hours, the preparation and first few words of the Psalms, prayers, and hymns; 4. Seven penitential Psalms; 5. Choral portion of the Office for the Dead; 6. Miscellaneous meditations. From the common practice of writing in them the saints' days and feasts in red ink comes our expression 'red-letter day'.

Quite apart from the splendidly illuminated examples made specially for such wealthy patrons as the Dukes of Burgundy or the Duke of Bedford there were, in 15th century Belgium and France in particular, ateliers concerned solely with their production. Teams of illuminators worked on the scenes traditionally included (e.g. the Zodiac Man, the history of the Virgin and of Christ, the Prodigal Son, and the Seven Capital Sins), while a corpus of scribes copied the text with calendars for the usage of different dioceses. They were sent for sale to various European cities and represent a form of mass production. (See *manuscript-book writing*.)

French illuminated examples of the 15th century were the inspiration for the printed Books of Hours issued by Parisian presses from about 1485. They were typified by small format, borders printed from blocks surrounding the text on every page, bâtarde type, and from about 1496 a dotted (*criblé*) black ground as part of the decoration. The double-page spread was the designer's basic unit. The delicate black grounds and the decorative initials appear to be printed from copper blocks (vide Dupré's Horae, Paris, 1488 which states that the initials were 'imprimées en cuyure'). The printing of copies on vellum and a general air of elegant craftsmanship emphasised the fact that these books, like their manuscript forebears, were intended for the wealthy and cultured.

Most of the Horae were small (about 4½in. high up to 6½in.) but there were also editions referred to as 'Grandes Heures' issued by Vérard for special patrons which had a woodcut surface of about 8in. × 5in. The blocks extended to the edges of the pages.

In the last years of the 15th century the style of illustration in French Books of Hours underwent a change. The new manner, a fusion of sacred and profane art, owed something to German illustrators who came to France, and later, much more to the Italian Renaissance: architectural groupings of classical columns, caskets, sculptures and arches formed settings for Biblical scenes, but the delicacy of interpretation was essentially French.

It was not until 1525, when Simon de Colines printed Geofroy Tory's 'Heures de la Vièrge' that the true elegance and simplicity of Venetian Renaissance decoration was seen in a French Book of Hours. Tory's emphasis on the unshaded black line and the substitution of roman for gothic type were further steps from the old manuscript tradition.

Few Horae of artistic importance were published outside Paris, although in London Caxton, Machlinia, Pynson, and Worde issued Sarum Horae (Caxton's were printed in Paris).

The principal names associated with the Parisian Books of Hours include *Simon de Colines*, *Jean Dupré*, *Thielman Kerver*, *Philippe Pigouchet*, *Geofroy Tory*, *Antoine Vérard*, and *Simon Vostre*, qq.v. See H. Bohatta, 'Bibliographie des Livres d'Heures', 2nd ed., Vienna, 1924.

book papers: a generic term for all papers used in book production; *furnish*, q.v., may be anything from rag to mechanical pulp.

book pedlar: see *colporteur*.

bookplates: printed labels of ownership pasted on the inside front cover of a book. The best known early examples are those of Bilibald Pirckheimer (1470–1530) which were designed by Albrecht Dürer *c.* 1504. In addition to the owner's name the words 'ex libris' may form part of the design, and it is by the latter that bookplates are known on the Continent. See also *American Bookplate Society, ex libris, supralibros*.

A 16th-century bookplate, now in the University Library, Graz, Austria

Book-Prices Current: published in London by Elliot Stock (1837–1911). It began as a monthly in December 1886 and until 1921 was edited by J. H. Slater 'being a record of the prices at which books have been sold at auction, the titles and descriptions in full, the names of purchasers, etc.'. The first annual volume was dated 1888 (for 1887) and it continued until 1956. Occasional cumulative indexes were issued.

book prizes: see *literary awards and prizes*.

Book Production Managers Group: a group within the Publishers Association, founded about 1959 with the aim of improving the status and quality of production methods by starting training courses, forming study groups and holding seminars on trade problems (e.g. on the warping of boards).

Book Publishers Representatives Association: established in London in 1924 for social and charitable purposes, its objects being to promote co-operation and good fellowship among members. With funds collected through the years assistance is given confidentially to needy members. Regional branches were opened in Manchester in 1963 and in Scotland in 1972.

Bookrest: the name given to an appeal set up by the *Book Trade Benevolent Society*, q.v., to establish a fund to enable further homes to be built at the Booksellers Retreat, King's Langley, for retired members of the book trade. Address: 4 Little Essex Street, London WC2.

book-ring: a group of persons, usually dealers, who at an auction sale of books have agreed in advance not to bid against each other. Sale prices are thus kept low, which cheats the original owner. When the sale closes the dealers meet for a private auction and divide among themselves the difference between the public and private sale price.

The Bookseller: the principal trade journal for the British book trade. It was founded in 1858 by Joseph Whitaker, and now appears as an interesting and lively weekly journal giving trade news and an alphabetical list in which new books of the week are entered under author and title. These weekly lists were cumulated in the last issue of each month until 1969 when a new monthly, *Books of the Month & Books to Come*, took over this function. Since 1924 cumulative editions of the bibliographical entries have been published annually (see *Whitaker's Cumulative Book List*).

Of particular value to booksellers overseas are *The Bookseller's* massive Spring and Autumn surveys of forthcoming books. See also *British Books in Print*. Address: 12 Dyott Street, London WC1A 1DF.

booksellers' and publishers' abbreviations: see *publishers' abbreviated answers*.

Booksellers Association Charter Scheme: introduced in 1964 to encourage the definition and raising of standards in bookselling practice. It required members to carry in their shops a prescribed minimum value of book stock, to have a minimum floor and window space and to keep certain trade bibliographies. Members also undertake to enter staff for training courses and to provide the basic statistical data which enables the BA to publish annual reports on bookselling economics.

Booksellers Association of Great Britain and Ireland: since 1895, an association open to bona-fide bookselling establishments. It exists to further the sale of books, to protect the interests of booksellers, to provide training courses and correspondence courses for members' staffs, to uphold the status of the trade and support the practice of price maintenance. The BA owns two subsidiary companies, Book Tokens Ltd and BA Service House Ltd. Address: 154 Buckingham Palace Road, London SW1 9TZ.

Booksellers Association Service House Ltd: or *BASH*, formed in 1977 to take over and develop the trading activities and some of the membership services built up by the Association, and to provide additionally an organization for administering new collective promotion schemes to encourage greater sales through bookshops.

Booksellers Clearing House: founded in 1948 by the BA to enable bookseller members to pay their accounts to all publishers by one monthly cheque. Similarly, publishers receive from the Clearing House a single cheque for the gross amount due from all bookseller members. The saving on time, postal and bank charges is considerable. The Clearing House is operated by the BA's company Book Tokens Ltd.

Booksellers Order and Reorder Documentation: or *BORD*, a scheme researched by the joint Distribution and Methods Committee of the BA and PA to assist booksellers in stock control. Briefly, prior to supplying books to booksellers publishers would insert a card in each. The card would state ISBN, author, title and price. At the time of sale the bookseller, who would keep a master card for every title in stock, would remove the card and thus have at the end of the day his data for reordering and stock control. For books published below a minimum price the cost of the cards and their handling could be uneconomic; the scheme was not, therefore, developed in this form, and further research in stock control provision was made by the BA Trade Practice and Distribution Committee, culminating in the provision of Standard Stock Control Cards by the BA.

Booksellers Order Distribution: or *BOD*, begun in 1970 by a group of London booksellers dissatisfied with the operation of the Orders Clearing scheme then administered by IBIS. A bookseller anywhere in the world can despatch in one envelope his orders to several publishers. After checking, BOD forwards them on the day of receipt to individual British publishers and certain overseas suppliers. Costs are covered by small clearance fees. See also *Orders Clearing*.

bookselling organizations: see *publishing and bookselling organizations*.

book shrine: see *cumdach*.

Books in English: announced in 1970 as a combined bibliography of English language books published anywhere in the world which are contained on Library of Congress and British National Bibliography

MARC tapes. (MARC stands for *Machine Readable Catalogue*.)

The first issue, on only three microfiche, contained 150,000 entries for 40,000 books published during the period January–June 1970 for which catalogue data had been prepared by LC and BNB.

Catalogue information of every book received by BNB is stored on magnetic tapes which are fed to a computer output microfilming machine (COM). The product of this is a 35 mm microfilm which is reduced to ultra-microform level on a camera-recorder machine developed by the National Cash Register Co. One microform, known as a PCMI (photo-chromic micro image) can accommodate 3,000 A4 pages on a single 105 mm by 148 mm transparency with the pages positioned in rows and columns. Duplicates can be made as needed. To be consulted the microform must be fed into a 'reader' with a viewing screen. A separate unit will give print-outs. See also *microform publishing*.

Books in Print: an American booktrade reference work, indexing separately by author and title the books listed in the 'Publishers Trade List Annual'. It is published yearly by the R. R. Bowker Company of New York.

book sizes: see *American book sizes, British book sizes*.

The Book Society: an organization founded in London in 1928 by Alan Bott for distributing to its members recommended new books at the full published price. (It was thus not a book club in the usual sense of the term since editions were neither printed specially for it nor offered as bargains.)

A company was formed under the management of Bott (who later founded 'The Reprint Society' and Pan Books Ltd) with an independent literary committee assembled by Sir Hugh Walpole to select books. Advance copies of likely titles were submitted by publishers and the first 'choice' was Helen Beauclerk's 'The love of the foolish angel', posted to the first 2,000 members in April 1929. Members also received *The Book Society News* which gave notes on new books.

The constitution of the selection committee frequently changed and included many distinguished authors, but its terms of reference did not alter. The Society neither claimed to find masterpieces nor dictate to its members what they should read. Membership was world wide, and there were many among them overseas who welcomed the monthly recommendations of worthwhile reading, and respected the standard implied by the book wrapper legend 'Recommended by the Book Society' or 'Chosen by the Book Society'. The Society was sold in 1966 and has ceased to operate as here described.

Book Tokens Ltd: a company owned by the Booksellers Association to operate the scheme devised in 1928 by Harold Raymond, a director of Chatto & Windus and the Hogarth Press. Until 1943 the book tokens scheme was managed for the trade by the National Book Council (now the *National Book League*, q.v.). The scheme exists to encourage the sale of books by simplifying the giving of them as presents by means of a greetings card bearing stamps worth a stated amount. The recipient can use the token for a book of his or her choice at any bookshop in membership of the BA.

Book Trade Benevolent Society: formed in 1967 when several old-established book trade Friendly Societies were brought together under one name, with a change of their scope and status so that an increasing number of people could benefit.

In 1955 the Book Trade Benevolent Committee was set up to be responsible for the collection of donations for the benefit of the *Booksellers Provident Institution*, formed in 1837, the *National Book Trade Provident Society*, formed in 1902, the *Booksellers Provident Retreat* and the *Book Trade Hardship Fund*. All these were book trade charities, the Booksellers Provident Institution being the largest and oldest. They were mainly concerned with the relief of distress among members and former members (and their dependants) of the trade. The Retreat offered accommodation for retired members of the trade in homes at Abbots Langley, Herts. The Hardship Fund was set up as a means of giving assistance to those deserving it who were not eligible for help within the rules of the other bodies. This is no longer an obstacle for the present Society.

In 1961 the National Book Trade Provident Society, the Booksellers Provident Institution, and the Booksellers Provident Retreat were amalgamated as the National Book Trade Provident Institution. In 1967 followed the change recorded above.

bookwork folding chases: see *folding chases*.

BORD: see *Booksellers Order & Reorder Documentation*.

border: in bookwork, a border is a continuous decorative design arranged around matter on a page. Borders can be continuous cast strips of rule, plain or patterned, or they can be made up from repeated border units or *flowers*, q.v. An extensive range of proprietary borders is available.

border decoration: the ornamentation of a page by surrounding the printed matter on it with a decorative border. This treatment of a page had long been a feature of the illuminator's art, and it was in imitation of this that Günther Zainer of Augsburg first used a woodcut initial with foliage trailing from it for a calendar he printed in 1472 (GKW 1292). He later developed the idea into a left marginal border and head border in which he included figures and birds. Other early printers did likewise, often adding gold and colours. Particularly fine examples embellished the Livres d'heures printed in Paris by Pigouchet at the end of the 15th century.

By the mid-16th century borders made up of type ornaments had appeared (see *flowers*), and the slavish imitation of the manuscript ceased. See also *arabesque*.

Börsenverein der Deutschen Buchhändler zu Leipzig: the name since 1945 for the organization founded in Leipzig in 1825 by the Nuremberg publisher Friedrich Campe to represent the professional interests of the German book trade. Its former name was without 'zu Leipzig'. The association also had considerable influence in Austria and Switzerland. Publication of the book trade's first news periodical *Börsenblatt für den deutschen Buchhandel* began as a weekly in 1834; after 1863 it was issued daily. It developed into an important authority for recording the bibliography and history of the trade.

Beginning in 1841 with material amassed for the 400th Gutenberg anniversary the association set up a library, now housed in the Deutsche Bücherei, Leipzig.

After 1945 the Börsenverein in Leipzig, while still organizing book exhibitions and trade fairs, has been active in promoting Soviet literature and publishing Marxist-Leninist writers. See *Beiträge zur Geschichte des Buchwesens*, Leipzig, VII 1975.

Börsenverein deutsche Verleger-und-Buchhändlerverbände: since 1945 the national organization of the West German book trade with headquarters in Frankfurt-am-Main. Its *Börsenblatt* appears twice a week and is a well-edited publication of use to bibliophiles and librarians as well as to the book trade.

The Börsenverein is currently sponsoring research into book publishing within the wider context of social history. See also *Historische Kommission des Börsenvereins des deutschen Buchhandels*.

bosses: small raised ornaments of brass or silver usually fixed at the corners of both upper and lower cover of a book for protection against rubbing. They are associated with medieval bookbinding and were rarely used after the 16th century.

botanical symbols:

⊙ ①	annual	♂♀	dioecious
♂	antheridia	△	evergreen
◐	autumn flowering	♀	female
②	biennial	×	hybrid
∧	climbing plant	♂	male
⊙	monocarpus	♂♀☿	polygamous
♂–♀	monoecious	◑	spring flowering
∞	number indefinite	◓	summer flowering
♀	oogamia	♄	tree
♃	perennial	◑	winter flowering
!	personally checked		

Bottcher rollers: printing ink rollers made of synthetic nitrile rubber and known after their inventor, Felix Bottcher.

bottomband: an inelegant if logical term, found in a London publisher's handout, to distinguish a *headband*, q.v., placed at the foot of the spine from one at the top.

bottoming: a printing fault which may occur when using shallow relief plates whereby roller sag causes low areas to pick up ink direct. Very careful setting of the forme roller so that only the top of the image is inked may help to prevent it. The squeeze between plate and blanket should be from 0·002 in to 0·003 in.

bound book: one with boards attached to hand-sewn sections before they are covered with leather or cloth. The term is now widely, if loosely, extended to include *cased books*, q.v. See also *bookbinding*.

bourgeois: the name for a former size of type, now standardized as 9-point. The name may derive from Bourges, the birthplace of Geofroy Tory, who mentions it in 'Champ Fleury', or from the writing used in commerce by the bourgeois of France. The type size was first used in 1498 by Andrea Torresano of Venice.

boustrophedon: literally, 'in the manner in which an ox turns' when ploughing. The word is descriptive of the early Greek manner of writing in which the letters on alternate lines were written from right to left. Examples are known of writing in which alternate lines are also written upside down so that the feet of letters on a lower line touch the feet of letters on the line above. During the 5th century BC Greek writing from left to right on all lines became the rule.

bowl to bend an imperfect type so that it cannot be used by mistake. It will then be put in the *hell-box*, q.v.

Bowater Awards: since 1973, annual awards of cash and book tokens made by the Bowater (Paper) Corporation for essays on book design and production. Their purpose is to raise standards.

bowdlerized: said of an edition of a work from which, prior to printing, words or passages likely to offend readers have been removed by someone other than the author. The term derives from Dr Thomas Bowdler (or possibly his sister Henrietta Maria) who published an expurgated 'Family Shakespeare' in 1807, with a second edition (in which he was first named) in 1818: Gibbon's 'Decline and fall . . .' was similarly pruned.

The ridiculous lengths to which bowdlerization has been carried, particularly in Victorian England, are described in Noel Perrin's 'Dr Bowdler's legacy: a history of expurgated books in England and America', 1969.

Bowen, Emanuel, fl.1740–80: map engraver to George II and to Louis XV, best known for his atlases and county maps, the latter often embellished with vignettes of towns, coats of arms and historical scenes: some were annotated. His son *Thomas* was also a map engraver of merit.

Bowker, Richard Rogers, 1848–1933: a distinguished American bibliographer, editor and publisher. Between 1868 and 1878 he worked in New York as a part-time journalist and newspaper editor. He then joined *Frederick Leypoldt*, q.v., for whom he edited *Publishers' Weekly* before acquiring it in 1879 (it continues today without the apostrophe). In 1876 he was associated with Melvil Dewey and Charles Cutter in producing *The American Library Journal*.

Bowker was an active and influential campaigner for an international copyright law and for greater cooperation within the book trade. While not a librarian he served the profession in various ways.

His business was incorporated in 1911 and continues to be one of the two leading publishers for the American book trade and library profession. See also *Halsey William Wilson*.

bowl: the curved main strokes of a letter enclosing a *counter*, q.v. An alternative name is *cup*.

bowls: the non-metallic rolls of a *super-calender*, q.v. They may be made of compressed paper, cotton, linen or asbestos. See also *crown* (2).

Bowyer, William, 1663–1737: the London printer for whom *William Caslon*, q.v., designed the fount of roman and italic type which brought the latter fame. Bowyer was a leading printer and a liveryman of the Stationers' Company. His son *William* (1699–1777), 'the learned printer', entered the business in 1722 and worked for some years as corrector of the press. In addition to scholarly editing he published several of his own writings. In 1761 he was appointed printer to the Royal Society.

On moving to larger premises in 1767 he placed the sign 'Cicero's Head' above the entrance and it is guessable that he may have influenced Caslon in his choice of the famous *Quousque tandem* quotation for his specimen sheet of 1734. See 'Anecdotes of William Bowyer', written, printed and published by John Nichols, 1782.

box: see *hell-box, reader's box*.

box-in: to surround type matter with rule so that the printed result appears in a rectangular frame or box.

Boydell, John, 1719–1804: a London publisher who, with his nephew Josiah as partner, decided in 1786 to publish an illustrated folio edition of Shakespeare's works (at that time often spelled Shakspeare). He was assisted by George Nicol, later a partner, the King's bookseller who founded the *Shakspeare Printing Office* with William Bulmer as printer, William Martin as type-cutter and founder, and George Steevens as textual editor. The illustrations were stipple engravings from originals specially painted by such eminent artists as Reynolds, Romney, and Stothard. The plays were issued in parts from 1791–1802.

Boyet bindings: the manner of book decoration practised by Luc-Antoine Boyet, binder to Louis XIV from 1698–1733. His style was simple, consisting of a rectangular fillet of gold lines, ornamental corners, and a coat of arms in the centre of the upper cover. Other binding features he used were pointillé, leather doublures, and dentelles.

Boys, Thomas S., 1803–74: a London lithographer of distinction whose skill as a book illustrator may be assessed in his 'Original views of London as it is', 1842. His 'Picturesque architecture in Paris . . .', 1839, was the first English book with chromolitho illustrations.

Bozérian brothers: two Parisian binders, the elder fl.1793–1814, the younger fl. 1802–17. They bound whole libraries for a new generation of wealthy patrons who, after forming collections with purchases of fine bindings sold by ruined aristocrats, sought to develop them. This binding in bulk, while technically sound and carefully done, rarely approached the highest standards of skill and taste, thus later in the century many Bozérian bindings were rebound by others.

For their best work they used the then fashionable English straight-grained morocco, principally in shades of light red, dark blue, lemon, and pale green. Decoration on the boards was mostly limited to a bordering frame enclosing the popular Empire style of Egyptian and classical motifs.

The elder Bozérian regarded the spine as the main decorative feature; the younger usually divided the spine into panels with tooled fillets, since they were without raised bands; one or two panels bore the title and volume number in large letters, the remainder being covered with small tooling. On some of their best work they added mosaics of coloured leather to the spine, but not the sides.

Exceptionally, apparently, they bound a copy of Baskerville's 1772 edition of Terence after the Edwards of Halifax manner, using vellum boards decorated with a landscape in grisaille, and with a disappearing fore-edge painting. A note in the book, which is now in the Bibliothèque Nationale, claims that it was the first book so decorated to be made in Paris. The note is dated 1793.

BP chromo: see *proofing chromo.*

Bracciolini, Poggio: see *Poggio.*

brace ends: type sorts, viz: ⌒⌒ See also *cock.*

bracket: a punctuation mark, used in pairs, [ ], to enclose words, phrases, figures, etc., to be separated from the text, and elsewhere for various purposes.
(ML)

Bradel binding: a style of temporary binding with uncut edges, the top sometimes gilded, and a spine of linen or leather. It was of German origin but used in France by, it is thought, Alexis-Pierre Bradel, a nephew of Nicolas-Denis Derome, after whom it became known. There were, however, many binders named Bradel in Paris.

Bradford Club: a New York book club named after the city's first printer (see next entry). Between 1859 and 1867 the club issued eight volumes in limited editions, all concerned with American history and literature.
(DW)

Bradford, William, 1663–1752: a printer from Leicestershire who in 1685 established the first press at Philadelphia from which his first signed and dated work was Daniel Leeds's 'Almanac', 1687. He also printed many Quaker tracts and it was due to a difference with local Quakers that he moved his press to New York in 1693, his being the first press there. He held the appointment of 'Printer to King William and Queen Mary'. *The New-York Gazette*, which he started in 1725, was the city's first newspaper.

Partnered by Samuel Carpenter Bradford built the first American papermill, this was erected in 1690 at Germantown, Pennsylvania, and was managed for them by *William Rittenhouse*, q.v.

The Bradford family were important Colonial printers for several generations.

Bradshaw, Henry, 1831–86: a scholar and bibliographer who for many years worked in Cambridge University Library. He is important for his researches into typographical history and the activities of early English and Continental presses.

His writings, edited by F. Jenkinson, were published in 1889 as 'Collected papers of Henry Bradshaw'.

Brailes, William de, fl.1238–52: a cleric and illuminator, more remarkable for having signed his work than for its quality. He may have worked in Oxford or London. His filling of medallions with miniatures shows a French influence, as does the careful drawing. Most accessible of the few known examples of his work is a Book of Hours of Sarum use which the British Museum acquired from the Dyson Perrins collection in 1958. See Sir Sydney Cockerell, 'The work of William de Brailes', Roxburghe Club, 1930.

Braille: a system of embossed printing used to make books for the blind. It was invented in 1829 by *Louis Braille* (1809–52) of Paris who was blind. Cells of six dots are used for the alphabet and certain defined contractions. Printing is done with type, cast and composed as in normal typesetting, and also with thin brass plates having characters raised on the surface.

In 1952 an alternative method was announced and named 'solid dot Braille'. A transcribing machine interprets letters into dots and cuts a stencil. Plastic ink is forced through the stencil holes on to paper. Infra-red drying welds dots to paper. Advantages are sharper dot images, improved legibility, and reduced weight and thickness per volume since thinner paper is used. Cf. *Moon.*

Bramah, Joseph, 1749–1814: a versatile engineer who invented the first cylinder machine for papermaking. His patent (No. 2840 of 1805) was for making paper in 'endless sheets of any length' and had a gauze drum mould. A felt-covered roller in gentle peripheral contact with the mould wheel took the paper as it formed. There were also pressing rollers to assist drying. Bramah's method was eclipsed by the *Fourdrinier*, q.v.

As an alternative to screw presses for drying paper made in sheets he used a number of platens, in pairs, between which sheets were clamped and pressed hydraulically. Final drying was on frames which slid up and down grooved uprights in the manner of sash windows. See I. McNeil, 'Joseph Bramah: a century of invention, 1749–1851', David & Charles, 1968.

Branston, Robert, 1778–1827: a wood engraver working as a book illustrator and blockmaker in London where he was regarded as a rival of *Bewick*, q.v. His work is to be seen in 'History of England', Wallis & Scholey, 1804–10.

brass rule: strips of brass, type high, used to print lines and simple borders. They are also used as column rules in dictionaries, Bibles, etc. See also *mitred* (2), *Oxford corners*, *rule.*

brayer: formerly, a wooden pestle, three inches diameter, flat at one end and with a handle on the other, used to spread out ink to be taken from the ink block by the balls. See also *ink slice*. (ML)

breaker: a machine built on the *Hollander* principle, q.v., in which the raw materials of paper are broken into separate fibres known as *slush*. Other machines such as the Hydrapulper have twin rotors on the centrifugal principle and are suitable for some types of furnish: they are quicker and more efficient. See also *beater, deflaker, Jordan, potcher*.

breaking length: an indication of the *tensile strength*, q.v. of paper, being the length at which a suspended strip of paper will break due to its own weight.

breaking-off boy: a foundry boy employed to break off the jet from newly cast type.

break-line: the last line of a paragraph. Quads are used to fill the space. See also *end a break, end even, run on*. (ML)

break up: to unlock a forme and distribute the type.

breast box: the container from which a uniform and controlled flow of stock passes to the Fourdrinier wire. Also known as *flow box* or *headbox*.

Brehmer, August, b. 1846: a designer of Lübeck who with his brother Hugo, b. 1844, constructed stitching and folding machines. In 1871 he went to America where in Philadelphia in 1872 he patented his invention of the first machine for stitching cardboard by wire, to be followed by one for stitching books. The wire tended to rust. In 1879 he returned to Leipzig to found the firm of Gebr. Brehmer, subsequently world famous. In the 1880s they designed machines for thread sewing books. The firm continues as a leading manufacturer of mechanical binding machines.

Breitkopf, Bernhard C., 1695–1777: a journeyman printer who in 1719 began a typefounding business in Leipzig. His first specimen book, in 1739, showed some fifty founts, all from punches engraved in his own premises. In 1745 he was joined by his son Johann (1719–94) and they developed the founding, printing, publishing and bookselling firm into one of world renown.

Of major commercial importance was a method of music printing with a fount of 257 sorts which Bernhard completed in 1754 (see *music printing*). It was, however, costly, and users often made stereos to save wear. Among experiments not exploited commercially was a method of printing maps with movable type, 1777, and the casting in type metal of some twenty characters for printing Chinese.

From 1795 the firm traded as Breitkopf & Härtel, continuing to do so until 1951 when the main Leipzig

office was expropriated, a much diminished branch remaining, after 1945, in Wiesbaden.

Bremer-Presse: a private press founded in 1911 at Bremen by Ludwig Wolde (1884–1949) and Willi Wiegand (1884–1961). The first work to appear, Hugo von Hofmannsthal's 'Die Wege und die Begegnungen', with woodcut initials and tail-piece designed by Rudolf Schröder, was dated Christmas 1913. In 1918 the press was at Tölz, in 1921 was moved to nearby Munich. Wiegand designed a roman and a 'greek face, cut by Louis Hoell (d. 1935), for use in the series of translations of classical and modern poetry issued by the press. Decoration was mostly limited to hand-drawn title-pages and initials by *Anna Simons*, q.v. Many books were hand bound by Frieda Thiersch. Nothing was printed after 1935 and the press was destroyed by bombing in 1944. See 'Die Bremer-Presse: Königin der deutschen Privatpressen', Munich, 1964.

Brethren of the Common Life: see *Fratres Vitae Communis*.

Breviary: the book of daily Divine Office used in the Roman Catholic Church. It properly contains: 1. Calendar, 2. Psalter, 3. Proprium de Tempore (collects and lessons), 4. Proprium de Sanctis (collects, etc., for Saint's Days), 5. Commune Sanctorum (collects, etc., for Saints without special services), 6. Hours of the Virgin (burial services and Small Offices). It does not contain the Communion Service or Mass.

The Breviarum Romanum issued by Jenson in Venice, 1478, was the first to be printed. Before 1500 printers in Italy, South Germany and Switzerland had issued about a hundred editions for the 'usage' of particular dioceses and religious orders.

breviate: an abridgement or summary of a work, as, for example, 'Breviate of Parliamentary Papers'.

brevier: the name for a former size of type, now standardized as 8-point. The name cannot derive from its use for printing Breviaries, in spite of the attractions of this theory, since larger sizes were mostly used.

brilliant: the name for a former size of type, $3\frac{1}{2}$-point, now standardized as 4-point.

bring up: to underlay or interlay a printing surface (plate or block) to raise it to impression height.

bristol boards: fine cardboard, made in various qualities and thicknesses, usually with a smooth finish, used for printing and drawing. It is so named because it is said to have been first made at Bristol. (ML)

British Book News: since September 1940, a monthly annotated list of the more important books published in Britain and, since January 1949, the Commonwealth. It is published by the British Council in London.

Books are grouped according to the Dewey classification scheme, the reviews being short appraisals by specialists of each title. Fiction, reprints and children's books are included, while regular features are authoritative surveys of recent literature on a particular subject, details of some 700 forthcoming publications, and publishing trade news. The work gives valuable assistance to overseas librarians and booksellers when selecting books.

British Books: after 1959 the title of the former *Publishers' Circular*, q.v.

British Books in Print: the name chosen in 1965 for the *Reference Catalogue of Current Literature*, q.v., with the former name as a subtitle and with annual publication after 1967. From 1970 the work appeared in two volumes, computer controlled photosetting being first used for the 1971 edition.

Starting in January 1978 publication of the complete updated information in BBP, including price changes, began on microfiche (reduced 48×). The annual volume continued in its regular format.

British book sizes: prior to 1969 the standard sizes, with abbreviations used in trade catalogues were:

abbrev.	name	in.	cm.
Pott 8	Pott Octavo	$6\frac{1}{4} \times 4$	15·8
F'cap 8	Foolscap Octavo	$6\frac{3}{4} \times 4\frac{1}{4}$	17·1
Cr. 8	Crown Octavo	$7\frac{1}{2} \times 5$	19·0
L. Post 8	Large Post Octavo	$8\frac{1}{4} \times 5\frac{1}{4}$	20·9
Dy 8	Demy Octavo	$8\frac{3}{4} \times 5$	22·2
Med. 8	Medium Octavo	$9 \times 5\frac{3}{4}$	22·8
Roy. 8	Royal Octavo	$10 \times 6\frac{1}{4}$	25·4
SuR 8	Super Royal Octavo	$10 \times 6\frac{3}{4}$	25·4
Imp 8	Imperial Octavo	$11 \times 7\frac{1}{2}$	27·9
F'cap 4	Foolscap Quarto	$8\frac{1}{2} \times 6\frac{3}{4}$	21·5
Cr. 4	Crown Quarto	$10 \times 7\frac{1}{2}$	25·4
L. Post 4	Large Post Quarto	$10\frac{1}{2} \times 8\frac{1}{4}$	26·6
Dy 4	Demy Quarto	$11\frac{1}{4} \times 8\frac{3}{4}$	28·5
Med. 4	Medium Quarto	$11\frac{1}{2} \times 9$	29·2
Roy. 4	Royal Quarto	$12\frac{1}{2} \times 10$	31·7
F'cap fol	Foolscap Folio	$13\frac{1}{2} \times 8\frac{1}{2}$	34·2

(The centimetre figure is for vertical height)

In 1969 metric equivalents of former sizes and new ISO sizes were agreed for use in British book production. The principal sizes are:

Metric equivalents (in mm)

	trimmed	untrimmed	'Quad' paper
Cr. 8	186 × 123	192 × 126	768 × 1008
L. Cr. 8	198 × 129	204 × 132	816 × 1056
Dy 8	216 × 138	222 × 141	888 × 1128
Roy. 8	234 × 156	240 × 159	960 × 1272

ISO sizes

	in.	mm
B6	6·90 × 4·90	176 × 125
A5	8·25 × 5·80	210 × 148
B5	9·80 × 6·90	250 × 176
A4	11·60 × 8·25	297 × 210

See 'Metric sizes for book production', Publishers Association, 1969. See also *American book sizes*.

British Copyright Council: since 1965, when it was reconstituted from the former British Joint Copyright Council, a body formed to represent authors, composers, artists and others in order to defend and foster the principles of copyright, to work for their world-wide acceptance, to make representations to official bodies on matters relating to copyright and possible infringements.

Address: 29–33 Berners St, London W1P 3DB.

British Federation of Master Printers: the voluntary national organization of employers in the general printing industry including branches such as bookbinding, stationery manufacture, etc. It was founded in 1900. Membership is open to any individual, partnership, company or other organization engaged in the printing industry which is the owner of an operating plant. Members belong to one of the local Associations or regional Alliances comprising the Federation. In 1974 the name was changed to *British Printing Industries Federation*.

British Letter Foundry: the typefounding business started in London in 1787 by *John Bell*, q.v. It closed in 1797.

The British Library: established 1 July 1973. It includes within its *Reference Division* the former library departments of the *British Museum*. Both names occur in this Glossary, thus 'The British Museum acquired the collection in 1836', and 'His books are now in the British Library'.

British Museum Catalogue of XVth Century Printed Books: see *Proctor*.

British National Bibliography: first issued in January 1950, with the purpose of listing all new works published in Britain, giving a format description of each, and classifying the subject. Brief annotations are sometimes included. It is compiled from items deposited at the Copyright Office of the British Library, and entries are grouped according to the Dewey Decimal Classification, with author, title and subject indexes. Cheap novelettes, musical scores, maps, minor Government publications and periodicals (except for the first issue of new or revised titles) are excluded.

BNB is published by the Bibliographical Services Division of the British Library and appears weekly, with monthly cumulated indexes, plus three larger cumulations, the last being a cloth-bound annual volume. Quinquennia have also been issued.

The British Printer: founded in 1888 by Raithby, Lawrence & Co. of Leicester, at first as the official journal of an association of printers known as *The British Typographia*, q.v. It continues as one of the leading independent journals of the printing trade. In addition to authoritative articles for trainee printers its illustrated review of new machinery and technical developments make it essential reading for anyone interested in or concerned with printing. The publisher, Maclean-Hunter Ltd, also issues the annual *British Printer Specification Manual*, first published in 1954.

British Printing Industries Federation: since April 1974 the name of the former *British Federation of Master Printers*, q.v.

British Publishers Guild: a company formed to pursue activities of benefit to its publisher members. During the 1939–45 war a group of twenty-six leading publishers cooperated to produce a series of paperback 'Guild Books' for free distribution through the Services Central Book Depot to HM Forces. Titles were chosen from backlists of fiction, biography, poetry and philosophy. For a short time thereafter they were published commercially.

Another venture was the simultaneous publication of hard-cover and paperback editions: the former under the publisher's own imprint, the paperbacks as 'Guild Originals'. After the war the need for the Guild was diminished but from 1958–65 its resources were used for the *Publishers Accounts Clearing House* scheme, q.v., which was continued by Book Centre until the scheme closed in 1968.

British Publishers' Market Agreement: introduced at the end of World War II to preserve to members of the Publishers Association (the only signatories) the territories they considered their traditional export areas. Its intent was to control the extent of American market penetration by obliging United States copyright owners who offered books to British publishers to convey all territorial rights as set out in the Agreement.

In 1975, following a United States anti-trust suit against twenty-one American publishers, the latter agreed to sign a Consent Decree requiring them to trade in rights only on an individual basis. The Publishers Association Council then withdrew the recommendation contained in the Market Agreement, covering contracts with some seventy countries, and abandoned the protection formerly given by it.

British Standard letterpress inks: specifications for the hue, saturation and light fastness of inks for four- and three-colour letterpress printing. Colours are yellow, magenta, cyan and black. See BS 4160:1967.

British Standard offset-lithographic inks: a specification in respect of the hue, saturation and light fastness of five inks for offset lithography, published as BS 2650:1955 (see also the related BS 4666:1971).

Colours are yellow (opaque), yellow (transparent), magenta, cyan and black. The inclusion of transparent as well as opaque yellow permits the sequence in which the colours are printed down to be at the discretion of the printer.

British Typographers' Guild: see *Society of Typographic Designers*.

The British Typographia: an association of printers founded in 1887 by *George W. Jones*, q.v. They sought to raise printing standards and propagate new methods, particularly for photomechanical reproduction. See also *Penrose Annual*.

Brito, Jean: a professional scribe of Tournai and, from the late 1470s, a printer of Bruges where he died *c.* 1494. Claims were once made on his behalf that he invented printing prior to Gutenberg. There is a pamphlet printed by him in the Bibliothèque Nationale, Paris, which includes a verse colophon (here translated) 'This was printed by the Bruges citizen John Brito who invented ("inueniens") the wonderful art of printing, and all the remarkable apparatus pertaining to it, without being shown by anyone'. However, he was not a citizen of Bruges until 1455, and the paper of the pamphlet has subsequently been dated as post-1467, so Brito was probably only claiming that he was a self-taught printer. His use of printed signatures and catchwords also precludes the earlier date.

Of his printing activity little survives of the six or so undated editions attributed to him. They included French versions of Cato's 'Disticha' and 'Haro Martin'. The National Library of Scotland has a unique copy of the 'Ecloga' of Theodulus with a French translation, printed by Brito. See also *Waldvoghel*.

Britwell Court Library: see *Miller, William Henry*.

broad: an obsolete term for wooden furniture four ems wide.

broadside: originally, a sheet of paper printed on one side only. Broadsides were used soon after the beginning of printing for royal proclamations and official notices. They were later a vehicle for political agitation and the expression of opposition to authoritarian rule. They were even used for the dissemination of scaffold speeches by criminals on the point of execution.

Early in the 16th century poems and ballads were printed in this form in England, and black letter fount continued to be used long after the introduction of roman for books.

Broadsides are also known as *broadsheets*, *single sheets*, *street-* or *stall-ballads*, and *black-letter ballads*.

The term broadside is now applied to a variety of large regular and special-fold sheets, printed on one or both sides. A broadside may also contain one job or a number of jobs. (ML)

Brocar, Arñao Guillén de: an important itinerant printer of Spain. He worked at Pamplona, 1490–1501; Logroño, 1502–11; Toledo, 1518–21; and Alcalá de Henares, 1511–24. Among the 170 or so works he issued he is remembered for several editions of Antonio de Nebrija's Latin grammar, which brought him much profit, and for the Complutensian polyglot Bible. He died about 1524. See also *polyglot edition*.

brochure: a pamphlet or other short work which has its pages stitched and is not bound. The term derives from the French 'brocher', to stitch.

broke: paper rejected during manufacture and usually repulped or sold as *retree*. *Wet broke* may accumulate at the wet end of the *Fourdrinier*, q.v. *Dry broke* includes shavings from cutting and slitting as well as paper rejected in the *salle*, q.v. See also *fine whites*, *recycled paper*.

broken matter: 1. type-matter out of order. 2. composition which has short paragraphs, headings, etc. (ML)

broken off: see *quotations* (1).

broken over: see *hinged*.

Brotherton, Edward Allen, 1856–1930: a wealthy industrialist and book collector (created a baron in 1929) whose gifts totalling £200,000 provided for Leeds University the building known as The Brotherton Library. In 1935 his private library was presented to the University, on trust for the nation, and every facility for studying its contents is offered to accredited students.

Lord Brotherton began to form his collection in 1922, and at the time of its transfer to the University it included some 35,000 printed books and pamphlets, 400 manuscripts, and several thousand deeds and

letters. Additions by gift and purchase are still made.

Among important manuscripts are an 11th- or early 12th-century copy of Bede's 'Expositio super septem epistolas canonicas' and a 14th-century German copy of Jacobus de Voragine's 'Legenda aurea sanctorum', as well as several French Livres d'heures.

The 251 incunabula include works from the presses of Jenson, Ulrich Han, the da Spira brothers, Ratdolt, de Worde, and Pynson, while notable is a copy of Schedel's 'Liber chronicarum', 1493.

The greater part of the collection is devoted to English literature and history from the 16th to 19th century. There is also a virtually complete set of the Kelmscott Press books.

Brown, John Carter, d. 1874: the most important of an American family of book collectors who greatly added to the library of Americana begun in the 18th century by Nicholas Brown. In 1904 the collection was given to Brown University, Providence, R.I., and is still being increased by members of the family.

browse: to dip at random into books in a bookshop or library. The American Gelett Burgess wrote somewhat cynically on the blurb (a term he is considered to have coined) of his 'Are you a bromide?', N.Y., 1906, '. . . Never buy a book when you can look it over and suck its blood from the bookstalls, or get it from the library. It is liable to make the Author and the Book-seller too conceited and Affluent'.

Bruce, David, 1770–1857: a Scottish printer who emigrated to America in 1793, establishing his own premises in New York in 1806 with his brother *George* (d. 1866) as partner. They subsequently sold the printing business and took up typefounding. David Bruce made a trip to England about 1812 to learn the craft of stereotyping which he then introduced into America (although Francis Shield from London, who was established in New York as a printing press maker, announced in 1811 that he could supply stereotype plates). The Bruces were the first commercial typefounders in New York.

A son *David* II invented a typecasting machine in 1838 which was widely used in Europe and America. The machine was built by a locksmith named Brandt, under whose name it was sold in Europe, posing a considerable threat to traditional casters of type.

Brüder vom gemeinsamen Leben: see *Fratres Vitae Communis*.

Brugalla, Emilio, 1901– : of Barcelona, the leading bookbinder of Spain who has won an international reputation for the technical perfection of his work. When only twelve he was apprenticed to the now defunct commercial binding firm of Gibert y Trillas, and at the same time studied craft binding under Hermengildo Alsina, recently arrived from Paris. In 1921 Brugalla moved to Paris to perfect his technique of gilding and other aspects of finishing by studying at the Chambre Syndicale de la Reliure.

After two years he returned to Spain where in 1929 fifty of his bindings were shown at the International Exhibition, Barcelona.

In 1931 he set up his own bindery near the University of Barcelona, being joined by his brother José who specialized in the restoration of old books. His son Santiago later joined the firm and is now an excellent craftsman in his own right.

Brugalla has lectured on his craft, most notably at the Stockholm Congress of Master Binders, 1966, while his writings on the subject have appeared in several foreign journals, e.g. 'La Reliure' (Paris), 'Craft Horizons' (New York), and 'Allgemeines Anzeiger für Buchbindereien' (Germany). More than a hundred of his bindings in classical and modern styles were shown in 1963 at the International Congress of Bibliophiles, Barcelona, while in 1970 his work was recognized by the award of the silver medal of the German 'Meister der Einbandkunst Internationale Vereinigung'.

I am indebted to Señor Brugalla for the information on which this note is based and to Alan Evans for translating it.

bruising: a grey or mottled effect, most noticeable in coated papers, caused by undue heat or pressure in the calenders.

Brunet, Jacques Charles, 1780–1876: a French book-seller and bibliophile remembered for his 'Manuel du libraire et de l'amateur de livres', 3 vols, Paris, 1810. The fifth edition in six volumes and supplement, 1860–80, is best known. This gives particulars of some 40,000 rare and valuable books, especially in French and Latin.

brush-coated paper: an expensive coated paper with high opacity and good dimensional stability. There is often a proportion of esparto in the stock. The final finish is given by a series of reverse smoothing rolls. See also *coater*.

brush graining: see *graining*.

Brut: a history of England from the arrival of Brutus the Trojan to Cadwalader (AD 689) written in Middle English verse by Layamon, a priest of Ernley, Worcester, about 1207. It survives in two manuscripts, both in the British Library, to be dated *c.* 1225 and *c.* 1250. The first of his two sources was Geoffrey of Monmouth's 'Historia regum Britanniae', a somewhat fanciful account in Latin of the early rulers of Britain, completed *c.* 1140. It was very popular and widely circulated, and by it the legends of Arthur, Merlin, Lear, Cymbeline and Brutus began to gain still greater currency beyond England. Even before the 'Historia' the Arthurian legend had been 'pleasantly rehearsed from memory by word of mouth' by many 'histriones' in the baronial halls and courts of England and France, and also by Breton 'conteurs' as far as Sicily, Asia Minor and Syria. (The editio princeps of the 'Historia' was issued in Paris in 1508.)

Layamon's second source, which had been written in 1155, was an adaptation into French verse by the Norman poet Wace who lived at Caen. He gave it the title 'Roman de Brut', and while omitting certain cruder incidents in the 'Historia' added other material, probably from Breton sources, including the first extant reference in literature to the Round Table. As a poet writing for the rich his style was livelier, he being more concerned than Geoffrey to entertain his hearers or readers.

The priest Layamon (or Laghamon, meaning Lawman) wrote his adaptation of the Brut legend largely as a free paraphrase and expansion of Wace, thereby giving us the first account in English of these early legends which were later to inspire Dante, Chaucer, Shakespeare, Wagner, and Tennyson. Laghamon introduced more brutality and cruelty into his account than either of his predecessors.

There were additions by other hands up to 1479. These were written in simple English prose, rhythmic and dignified, in what became the established chronicle style of the 15th century.

Caxton, q.v., used material from Brut for his 'Chronicles of England', 1480 (STC 9991) and to add to Ranulph Higden's 'Polychronicon', written about 1327, which he edited and printed in 1482 (STC 13438). See R. S. Loomis, ed., 'Arthurian literature in the Middle Ages', O.U.P., 1959.

Bry, Theodore de, 1528–98: a refugee from Flanders who worked in Frankfurt as a copper engraver for *Sigmund Feierabend*, q.v.

After visits to England in 1586 and 1588 (where he worked with *Hondius*, q.v., on the plates for Wagenhaer's 'Mariners mirrour'), he married a rich Frankfurt woman, becoming a citizen in 1590. He then established his own business as a publisher of travel books illustrated with copper engravings.

His magnum opus, a record of discovery and travel with illustrations based on English sources, was published as 'Collectiones peregrinationum . . .'. It was begun in 1590 by de Bry and his two sons. After his second son died in 1623 part of the business was acquired by a son-in-law Matthäus Merian (1593–1650), an artist and etcher of Basle. It was he who in 1634 completed the 'Collectiones' of which much illustrative material consisted of etchings. Merian's work in Frankfurt included a remarkable topographical survey in thirty-one parts (with 85 maps and 1,467 plates) of France, Germany, Italy, the Netherlands and Switzerland. Publication began in 1647.

buckle folder: or *plate folder*. See *folding machine*.

buckram: a strong fabric made of jute, cotton, or linen, glazed and stiffened by size or glue, and used since 1860 for book covers. It gives a pleasant feel to the book when handling. The term was originally applied to woven cotton impregnated with starch. There are two kinds, 'single warp' and 'double warp'. See also *bocasin, book cloth*.

buckskin: see *deerskin*.

Buell, Abel, 1742–1822: of Connecticut, a jeweller and lapidary who, after experimenting at Killingworth, set up at New Haven what may have been America's first typefoundry. This was in 1769 when he cut and cast two small founts of roman type. He did not develop his business, however, and commercial punchcutting and casting of roman type was inaugurated in 1775 either by Justus Fox or Jacob Bay of Germantown, Penn. See L. C. Wroth, 'Abel Buell of Connecticut . . .', rev. ed., Conn., Wesleyan U.P., 1958. See also *Sauer*.

buffing: the final polishing of a reproduction plate before etching.

building-in machine: a machine used for the rapid drying of cased books. By means of several applications of heat and pressure books are dried in a few seconds. This is an alternative to lengthy pressure in a *standing press*, q.v.

bulk: 1. the thickness of a book exclusive of its covers.
 2. the volume, in cubic centimetres, occupied by one gramme of paper in the form of a pack of superposed sheets when a static load is applied. *Bulking thickness* is the thickness of a single sheet of paper calculated from the measurement of the thickness of several superposed sheets called a *pack*, when a static load is applied (BS 3983:1966).

bulking dummy: see *dummy*.

Bullen, Henry Lewis, 1857–1938: creator and one-time custodian of the American Type Founders Company library and museum in Jersey City. The collection, now in Columbia University, includes technical works for the printer as well as type specimens and examples of printing from the 15th century to the modern private press.

Beatrice Warde claimed for him the introduction of the term *type family*, q.v., and said that he was the first to 'realize and exploit the implications of the

Benton mechanical punchcutter'. Bullen was a frequent contributor to American printing trade journals.

Bullock, William, 1813–67: of Philadelphia, the inventor of a rotary web-fed letterpress machine which had two printing and two impression cylinders. It was patented in 1863 and the first model, made in 1865, was used for newspaper work. Although fed from a web the paper was slit into sheets before reaching the first impression cylinder. Bullock's machine, which printed from curved stereos and on both sides of the paper, has been described as 'the first really automatic printing machine', printing 10,000 full-size eight-page newspapers an hour. By 1869 a folder had been added. For an illustration see *rotary press*.

Bulmer, William, 1757–1830: of Newcastle, where he was a friend of *Bewick*, q.v., and where he learned to print. He later went to London, probably working for John Bell prior to 1790 when he was appointed printer to the newly established Shakspeare Printing-Office of *Boydell* and *Nicol*, qq.v. He proved one of the best printers of the time, striving to raise the standard of English typography. To this end he perfected his own ink, used good paper and specially cut types. He printed fine editions of Milton, 1794–7, and Goldsmith, 1795. The latter was printed on Whatman paper and had cuts by the brothers Thomas and John Bewick.

Bulmer was commissioned to print for Dibdin, the Royal Society, and the Roxburghe Club among others. He continued to work until about 1821, but may have ceased active control of the Shakspeare Printing-Office in 1819. See also *arabic type, devanagari, Stanhope Press, Wilkins*.

bumped out: said of a line of letters to which extra spacing has been inserted in order to square it up with the measure of a longer line.
 2. said of matter which is widely leaded.

bumping: see *smashing*.

bumping up: the making ready of half tone plates for printing on a rotary press. This is a form of interlaying the original plates, before stereos are cast, in which a sheet of paper, card or thin zinc is used to press the back of the original. This causes the deep tones to be raised higher than the mid tones or high lights.

bundling: the tying together in bundles of the folded sheets of a book to promote orderliness. Machines, called bundlers, are largely used for this work and exert considerable pressure upon the sheets thus expelling air from between the pages and producing compact bundles.　(LK)

75

Burgkmair, Hans, 1473–1531: a German artist who, after Dürer, was the leading book illustrator of 16th-century Germany. He worked for, among other patrons, the Emperor Maximilian for whom he made as book illustrations a number of woodcuts. Burgkmair, or rather his cutter Jost de Negker, was an early worker in *chiaroscuro,* q.v.   (GU)

burin: an engraving tool used by wood and metal engravers.

Burney, Charles, 1757–1817: a classical scholar whose important collection of some 13,000 works by Latin and Greek authors was bought by the nation in 1818 for placing in the British Museum. Equally valuable was a series of bound 17th-century newspapers, and some 525 manuscript volumes, mostly Greek and Latin (including the Townley Homer).

His father's music library had been acquired by the Museum in 1815.

burnished edges: the coloured edges of a book which have been smeared with wax and rubbed with a burnishing tool to impart a polished surface.

burnisher: 1. a costly hand-tool of agate or bloodstone used for polishing book edges.

2. a smooth, curved metal tool, used in photo-mechanical processes for removing rough spots from plates and half-tones.   (ML)

burr: a rough edge left on a block by the routing machine. It must be removed before printing.

A burr is also characteristic of the surface of a *dry-point* plate, q.v.

Bury, Richard de, 1287–1345: a civil servant and patron of learning who, as Bishop of Durham (1333–45), rescued many classical manuscripts from oblivion or destruction. He employed agents in Europe to collect for him, and also received books as gifts from those who sought his influence with the court. He employed friars to collate his manuscripts, and his household included scribes, limners, and binders.

He is remembered for 'Philobiblon', written in praise of books, learning and libraries. This may have been written by Robert Holcot, a member of his household, but the views expressed are Richard's. The first printed edition was published at Cologne in 1473. A notable English edition was issued by the Shakespeare Head Press in 1960.

No catalogue of Bury's books has been found, and only four of them are known: two are in the British Library, and two in Oxford libraries. See N. Denholm-Young, 'Collected papers on medieval subjects', Oxford, 1946. See also *book annotators.*

butted: said of slugs placed end to end to form a continuous line.

butter stamp: the name for a binder's tool used to impress a complete panel on the spine at one strike. They were used in 19th century England when binding library sets of such authors as Dickens as a quick alternative to the careful building up of a pattern of small tools, separately impressed. See also *blocking press.*

Buyer, Barthélemy, d. 1483: an educated merchant of Lyons who about 1473 set up in his house the town's first printing press. He employed *Guillaume Le Roy,* q.v., to work it, Buyer's name appearing on the title-pages as publisher. It is assumed that Buyer selected the works to be printed. He established sales agencies for his own books (mostly religious works in French) and those of other Lyons publishers (mostly legal works) in Paris, Toulouse, and Avignon, and probably in Spain and Italy. He was assisted in his enterprises by his brother *Jacques.*

Byddell, John, fl.1533–44: a London printer and bookseller, who held a patent for printing the English primer. His name sometimes appears as Bedel, and also with the appellation of Salisbury, thus the colophon of the 'Lyf of Hyldebrande', 1533, states that it was 'Imprinted by Wynkyn de Worde, for John Byddell, otherwise Salisbury'.

Bynneman, Henry, fl.1566–83: one of the few English printers of distinction at work in 16th-century London. His presswork was careful, and his use of ornaments and borders on title-pages and elsewhere was often artistic. In 1559 he was apprenticed to Richard Harrison and their names occur on the title-page of Harrison's Bible of 1562. In addition to a printing shop in Knightrider Street, Bynneman had a bookseller's shop at St Paul's, but his main work was printing commissioned by others. In 1574 he appears to have acquired the types and ornaments of Reginald Wolfe (d. 1573). Both Archbishop Parker and Sir Christopher Hatton were among his patrons.

Bynneman printed editions of Latin and Greek classics, using good italic and greek founts. His most important work, issued without his name, was the printing of Raphaell Holinshead's 'Chronicles', 1577. The borders, ornaments, and types are considered sufficient proof that Bynneman was the printer.

Byzantine illumination: the manuscript illumination of the Byzantine Empire, which was centred at Constantinople from 330 to 1453. Professor Runciman has described Byzantine art as 'the truest mirror of the synthesis that made up Byzantine civilization, lasting in its fundamental characteristics as long as Emperors reigned on the Bosphorus'. Briefly stated, the synthesis was drawn from (1) *Hellenistic art*, typified by continuous scenes not separated into single pictures, a naturalistic style, scenic backgrounds, the absence of extraneous decoration, and the use of delicate colours; (2) *Near-Eastern art* which was dramatic and lively, with simple composition, borders, decorative flora and fauna, marginal scenes and brilliant colours. The specifically Islamic contribution was geometrical ornament, the foliate motif known as the arabesque, and the use as ornament of Kufic script; (3) *Mosaic art* which had a static quality, anti-realistic, with solemnly-posed figures in carefully arranged robes, and colouring which formed patterns of light and shade; (4) *Oriental art* (particularly from the 10th century) seen in the harmony of colours and ornamental composition, the aim being formal design, lacking perspective, rather than representation even though landscaped and naturalistic details were present; (5) *Christianity*, with its direct appeal to the emotions. The Eastern Church prescribed rules for the depiction of sacred scenes. Their effect was to establish an iconographic tradition enduring until the 15th century, a tradition which influenced painting in Western Europe, and which flourished in Russia before and after 1453.

The main centres of illumination were Constantinople and Antioch, where work tended towards the Greek and classical, and Alexandria and Ephesus, where it tended to be oriental and decorative.

Byzantine manuscript production is often grouped into four periods. Surviving works from the early and formative period are few. They include the Cotton Genesis (*c.* 5th century) in the British Library; the *Vienna Genesis*, q.v., with gold and silver writing on murex-stained pages, and one picture showing several incidents; the *Codex Rossanensis*, q.v., with its decorated Canon Tables; and the incomplete Codex Sinopensis in Russia. Typical of this period was the full-page depiction of an Evangelist shown writing his Gospel. The four pages of the Evangelists, with a fifth showing Christ in Majesty became a tradition in Gospel books. This period culminated in the first Golden Age during the reign of Justinian.

There was a period of decline in art between the late 7th and the late 9th century, particularly during the iconoclastic schism (726–843) when lavish ornament was forbidden. Inevitably, many artists migrated, particularly to South Italy where, in the work they did, Byzantine solemnity was softened and enriched by Italian influences.

The 10th century revival of learning led to a second Golden Age which lasted until the 12th century. Work was now based on classical originals but with little innovation. The Bible, Psalter, Gospels, lectionary, and menologium were produced in great numbers, always richly decorated and with an extensive use of gold backgrounds. The use of Islamic art motifs, greater dramatic tension in figure drawing, and elaborate Eusebian Tables in the Gospel books were features of the period. In general the function of the images in the book was no longer to illustrate the text but to serve as evocative icons in their own right.

The influence of Byzantine illumination on the scriptoria of Western Europe was considerable, being seen in the rigidity of figure drawing, bearded Evangelists, grouped illustrations preceding the text, and gold backgrounds. See K. Weitzmann, 'Studies in classical and Byzantine manuscript illumination', Chicago, 1971. See also *chrysography*, *illumination*, *menologium*, *tetraevangelium*.

C

©: the symbol for copyright. See *copyright notice*.

cabinet: an enclosed rack for holding type in case; formerly of wood, now also of pressed sheet steel.

Cabinet des Poinçons: the official collection of punches, matrices and types acquired or created for what is now the Imprimerie Nationale, Paris, where it is housed.

The reign of François I (1515–47) marked the beginning in France of royal interest in type design, but only with the appointment in 1561 of Robert Estienne II as the first 'garde des caractères et poinçons du Roi' was an attempt made to organize a royal collection. Significant additions came later. The oriental founts cut in Constantinople for Savary de Brèves, and reworked in Rome by Le Bé, were bought in 1627 by Antoine Vitré on behalf of Louis XIV. Vitré was ordered to commission founts of ethiopic and armenian from Jacques de Sanlecque, but only the second of these was made. When Vitré died in 1674 his typographic material was deposited in the Bibliothèque Nationale, later passing to the Cabinet. The Garamont greek matrices were restored to royal ownership in 1674, followed by the punches in 1683.

The Imprimerie Royale, established in 1640, was dedicated to 'la gloire de la France' and to the production of works 'des bons auteurs en caractères dignes de leur travaux', and from that time there were no more independent 'imprimeurs royaux'. It was Jean Anisson, director of the Imprimerie from 1691 to 1707, who gathered together many of the dispersed early types and commissioned Philippe Grandjean to refurbish and complete them for further use, as well as to create new types.

In 1725 the royal typefoundry became part of the Imprimerie, but even after amalgamation many accredited royal typefounders worked in their own premises to maintain their independence from the civil service. For the remainder of the 18th century the Cabinet was in a state of 'demi-sommeil'.

Between 1799 and 1812 oriental types from the *Congregatio de Propaganda Fide*, q.v., were 'appropriated' and lodged with the Imprimerie. Later, Napoleon's ambitiously conceived programme for publishing French and oriental works led to the creation during the 19th century of many exotic types.

The Cabinet, since 1946 classed as a historical monument, has more than 3,000 non-roman founts representing seventy-three scripts. The Imprimerie continues to produce types, an example being Louis Gauthier's roman of 1972. See 'Cabinet des Poinçons', 2nd ed. Paris, 1950. See also *devanagari, Didot, Fournier, Garamont, Grandjean, Granjon, grecs du roi, Le Bé, Luce, romain du roi, Sanlecque*.

caddying: the adding of fibrous materials, sizing, and loading to paper pulp. The word is particular to papermakers in southern England and is elsewhere replaced by *furnishing*.

Caflisch, Max, 1916– : a graphic artist, book designer and teacher who trained with *Tschichold*, q.v. For many years he worked in Berne as art director to the firm of Benteli for whom his attractive display face of open capitals with accompanying ranging numerals, Columna, was made in the 1950s. He was later appointed head of the graphic arts department of the Zürich Kunstgewerbeschule.

cake diagram: in technical book illustration, a line drawing of a circle with segmented divisions to show portions of a whole.

calamus: a sharpened reed used for writing on papyrus or parchment.

calcium sulphate: a filler occasionally used in papermaking to give brightness and good colour to the sheet. It also improves the feel. Other names for calcium sulphate are *alabaster* or *pearl filler*.

Caldecott Medal: since 1938, an annual award made by the American Library Association to the illustrator of an outstanding picture book for children. It is named after the English illustrator Randolph C. Caldecott (1846–85) who in 1871 abandoned his career of bank clerk to concentrate on illustration. His fame rests on a series of *toy books*, q.v., of which he produced two every Christmas from 1878 until his death. Over a million copies have been printed through the years.

calender: part of the dry end of a papermaking

78

machine, being a column of iron or steel rolls (usually five). When paper is passed under pressure through these the action closes the pores and smooths the surface. See also *finish*, *super-calender*.

calender crush: a fault in papermaking seen as hard discolorations in the sheet: caused when the calender rolls crush a thickening of the web.

calendered paper: paper which has been finished in a calender. The varying degrees of gloss may be characterized as *low machine finish* or *high machine finish*. See also *machine finish*.

calendered varnish: the finishing by a heated cylinder of printed sheets which have been coated with a specially formulated varnish. This gives a hard, glossy, dry finish. Pressure between heated platens gives a similar result. See also *varnishing*.

calf: calfskin with a smooth finish used for book covers. In England it became the usual material for trade bindings, but not in the rest of Europe where books were usually sold in paper covers. Thus when visiting London in 1710 the German writer Zacharias Conrad von Uffenbach wrote '. . . in the booksellers' shops here one buys neatly bound volumes, and never even sees unbound books; and all are in neat calf leather such as English books are renowned for.' However somewhat contradictorily he went on to advise that 'Books are so dear in England that it would be the greatest folly to purchase Latin books, which in Holland can be had for a third of what one must pay here'. See also *Cambridge-*, *extra-*, *fair-*, *law-*, *marbled-*, *mottled-*, *reversed-*, *smooth-*, *Spanish-*, *sprinkled-*, *stained-*, *tree-calf*, *vellum*.

calf-finish lambskin: a split sheepskin with a smooth finish resembling calf.

caliper calender: basically two iron rolls with a gap between them which can be adjusted to give a moving web of partly dry paper the thickness required.

calipers: compasses-type calipers are used by finishers for marking out the position of lettering and ornamentation before commencing tooling.   (LK)

Callierges, Zacharias, fl.1499–1523: a Cretan who had a press in Venice where, in 1499, he printed Greek works for his countryman the bookseller Nicolaus Blastus. The fine type they used was the result of five years effort. Accented letters were cast in one piece which was held to be an advantage over the separately accented types of Aldus and his imitators.

An 'Etymologicum' and three other Greek works, all in folio, with woodcut capitals and borders printed in red, were issued up to October 1500 when Blastus

may have died. Callierges' next book appeared in 1509. Between 1515 and 1523 he was active in Rome.

calligrapher: one who writes elegantly, especially a skilled transcriber of manuscripts.

calligraphy: literally (from the Greek) beautiful handwriting, penmanship. From Roman times to the 16th century such scripts as half-uncial, Carolingian, humanistic, and their derivatives attained their finest forms in the service of religion, law, and commerce.

Printing did not immediately eclipse interest in calligraphy, especially in 16th-century Italy where such writing masters as Arrighi, Tagliente, Cresci, and Palatino were famed, as were their English contemporaries Baildon and Ascham, and later, Billingsley and Bickham. See H. Child, 'Calligraphy today', 2nd ed., Studio Vista, 1976.

See also *Arabic calligraphy*, *cursive*, *humanistic scripts*, *letters – forms and styles*, *striking*, *writing manual*.

camaïeu: a French term for *chiaroscuro* prints from two wood blocks, q.v., and also, in the 19th century, a term sometimes used for *tinted lithographs*, q.v. Two-block printing was said to be *en camaïeu*.

Camaïeu-gris was a name for the grey-black ink drawings enlivened with a few touches of colour produced by the Parisian miniaturist Pucelle and others in the 14th century. See also *grisaille*.

Cambridge Bibliographical Society: a society founded in 1949 to encourage an interest in all forms of the printed book, with a particular emphasis on Cambridge books and men. The annual dues include the yearly volume of the 'Transactions', as well as extra monographs which are issued free to members from time to time. A regular programme of lectures, meetings, and visits is also arranged.

Cambridge bindings: bookbinders are mentioned in Cambridge records from 1355, presumably working under the control of university stationers, though no decorated Cambridge bindings before the 1480s are known to survive. Blind stamped bindings on red-stained calf made by more than a dozen un-named binders during the next sixty years are known. More important were *Garrett Godfrey*, *Nicholas Spierinck*, and *John Siberch*, qq.v.

There was a group of craftsmen working in Cambridge from 1610–30, notable being Daniel Boyse. Typical covers, on brown calf or morocco, were tooled with a centre circle and four corner ornaments often coloured red.

Cambridge-calf: a style introduced in Cambridge in the late 17th century, but also used in London, in

79

which a central panel or frame is acid-stained or mottled.

Cambridge india paper: the trade name of a *Bible paper*, q.v., of high quality, which used to be made at Bury, Lancs, by J. R. Crompton & Bros.

Cambridge University Press: the second oldest learned press in Britain, which originated in 1521 with John Siberch as the first printer. The 'Oration' of Henry Bullock was the first book published. Siberch was not appointed by the University, which did not receive a Royal Charter permitting the appointment of a printer until 1534. The first genuine University Printer was Thomas Thomas, who took office in 1583. Mr Brooke Crutchley, when University Printer, kindly supplied the following annotated list of printers; an asterisk precedes the names of those to whom patents were issued but who are not known to have printed anything.

Cambridge Printers

1521	John Siberch	He disappears after 1523
1534	*Nicholas Speryng	
	*Garrett Godfrey	
	*Segar Nicholson	
1539	*Nicholas Pilgrim	
1540	*Richard Noke	
1546	*Peter Sheres	
1577	*John Kingston	
1583	Thomas Thomas, M.A.	d. 1588
1588	John Legate	d. 1620
?	*John Porter (before 1593)	
1606	Cantrell Legge	d. 1625
?	Thomas Brooke, M.A. (before 1608)	Resigned (?) 1625
1622	Leonard Greene	d. 1630
1625	Thomas Buck, M.A.	At least till 1668
	John Buck, M.A.	At least till 1668
1630	Francis Buck	Resigned 1632
1632	Roger Daniel	Patent cancelled 1650
1650	John Legate, jun.	Patent cancelled 1655
1655	John Field	d. 1688
1669	*Matthew Whinn	
1669	John Hayes	d. 1705
1680	*John Peck, M.A.	
1682	*Hugh Martin, M.A.	
1683	*James Jackson, M.D.	
1683	*Jonathan Pindar	
1693	*H. Jenkes	
1697	*Jonathan Pindar	At least till 1730
1705	Cornelius Crownfield	Pensioned 1740
1730	William Fenner Mary Fenner Thomas James John James	Lease relinquished by Mrs Fenner in 1738

1740	Joseph Bentham	Resigned 1766
1758	John Baskerville	Nothing after 1763
1766	John Archdeacon	d. 1795
1793	John Burges	d. 1802
1802	John Deighton	Resigned 1802
1802	Richard Watts	Resigned 1809
1804	Andrew Wilson	1811 (?)
1809	John Smith	Pensioned 1836
1836	John William Parker	Resigned 1854
1854	George Seeley	Retired 1856
1854	Charles John Clay, M.A.	Retired 1895
1882	John Clay, M.A.	d. 1916
1886	Charles Felix Clay, M.A.	Retired 1904
1916	James Bennet Peace, M.A.	(?)
1923	Walter Lewis, C.B.E., M.A.	Retired 1945
1946	Brooke Crutchley, C.B.E., M.A.	Retired 1973
1974	Euan Phillips	1976
1976	Harry Myers, M.A.	

See S. C. Roberts, 'History of the Cambridge University Press, 1521–1921', C.U.P., 1921; and D. F. McKenzie, 'The Cambridge University Press, 1696–1712: a bibliographical study', C.U.P., 1966. See also *Curatores Praeli Typographici*, *Pitt Press*, *Siberch*, *Syndics*.

Camden Society: founded in 1838 for the printing of inedited manuscripts and the reprinting of rare works on the 'civil, ecclesiastical or literary history of the United Kingdom'. It was named after the historian and antiquary William Camden (1551–1623), editor of 'Britannia', which was a county by county guide book, written in Latin, first published in 1586 (edition in English, 1610).

cameo bindings: book covers decorated with an inset or stamped cameo, especially important being those made in Italy from 1500–60. The cameos were often made from casts of ancient coins or medals or from specially cut dies. Cf. *plaquette*.

cameo coated paper: an American coated paper which has a dull finish. Its English counterpart is *matt art*.

camera: in principle, a lightproof enclosed space in one wall of which a lens is fixed, while the sensitized material on which a photograph is taken is on the opposite wall.

The *process camera* is a large stand camera with solid front and back joined by strong bellows. Easily changeable lenses can be fixed in the front, and a focusing screen or dark slide in the back. Both parts are movable and can be turned as needed. The base rests on a horizontal stand, along which it can be moved on rails (hence the former name *travelling camera*). The stand is suspended or rests on strong springs. A copyboard is also fitted on the stand which, in its normal position, is at a right-angle to the optical main axis, and is intended for mounting the originals to be reproduced. Control is from the rear.

Many *dark-room cameras* are constructed with the back built into the wall of the dark room. This ensures rigidity. (The prism problem can be solved by a 'double prism'.)

The prism position is so common when photographing in a reproduction studio that special cameras have been built with a fixed prism position, i.e. the camera always has the dark slide positioned at right angles to the copyboard. To save floor space some cameras of this kind are made in the form of *vertical cameras* in which the lens is placed vertically above the horizontal copyboard. The latter can be raised or lowered, the lens is fixed, and the back is movable in relation to it. The action has been made more or less automatic so that the movements of the copyboard and the position of the dark slide are synchronized while the image at the focal plane is always in focus. As a rule process cameras have special lighting devices, formerly arc lamps, but now with mercury vapour tubes, pulsed xenon lamps, or incandescent bulbs. (With GU)

camera copy: pasted-up copy, either typewritten or typeset, which is used as an original in photomechanical process work.

camera-ready copy: copy tapped off on an electric typewriter, often unjustified, which is ready without further attention for photographing and platemaking.

Cameron System: an in-line letterpress system for producing books in an uninterrupted sequence from unprinted paper to finished volumes ready for despatch. It was developed by the Cameron Machine Company of America where the first system was installed in 1968. Runs from 2,000 to 400,000 are considered economic, and the end product can be paperbacks or adhesive-cased hardbacks.

Photopolymer image-bearing plates are mounted on continuous belts, adjusted to whatever length is needed for one book (belts can be stored for reprints). The paper web is printed on one side from the first belt, mechanically turned, and backed up in register from the second. The web is then perforated and slit into ribbons one or two pages in width. After machine folding and assembling into signatures of four to sixteen pages the signatures are sheared by a rotary cutter.

The next unit collates signatures in sequence and ejects them on to a conveyor belt as complete books ready for the *Sheridan adhesive-binding unit*. Covering,

stacking and trimming complete the sequence. The time from starting printing to taking off the finished books is about two minutes, thus, for example, 5,000 copies of a 320-page book could be produced in two hours.

The first Cameron System in Britain was acquired by William Collins & Sons of Glasgow in 1975. At that time systems printed only in monochrome and on uncoated stock.

camlet: to marble. See *marbling*.

Campbell press: a low-priced cylinder machine devised by the American Andrew Campbell in 1862. Its general accuracy and efficiency led to considerable sales. It was marketed as Campbell's Country Press.

Campe Prize: an award of 15,000 marks, made by the Hamburg publishing firm Hoffmann & Campe. It is named after Julius Campe (d. 1867) who published the works of Heine and belonged to the vanguard of the 'Jungen Deutschland' literary movement. The award is made to writers of promise whose work expresses the spirit of freedom in accordance with the European tradition.

cancel: a leaf containing an error or errors which is removed from its section and replaced by another, suitably amended. If the need is discovered before printing is completed the cancel leaf may be set up with the prelims, being later cut and inserted in its correct place. If the new leaf bears a signature an asterisk should precede the signature letter. While 'cancel' applies to both leaves, in bibliographical cataloguing the old is referred to as 'cancellandum', the new as 'cancellans'.

There are also MS. cancels for individual words or letters, and also *paste-over cancels*, e.g. on transfer of printed stock to another publisher. See also *stub* (2).

cancellaresca corsiva: see *cursive*.

cancellaresca formata: see *cursive*.

cancellaresca testeggiata: see *Cresci*.

cancel-title: a new title-page, often showing a changed imprint. Such a page may be inserted when a book of British origin is prepared for the American market.

Canevari bindings: see *Grimaldi*.

canon: a former size of type, about 48-point. The name may derive from the use by early printers of type of this size for printing the Canon of the Mass.

Canon Tables: concordances to the Gospels, compiled by Bishop Eusebius of Caesarea (*c.* 265–*c.* 340), setting out in columns references to corresponding passages in each. In medieval Greek and Latin Gospel books the tables were usually enclosed within architectural shapes and formed one of the principal display pages.

Canterbury bindings: a group of 15th-century bindings (of which some ten survive) probably made in the monastery of Canterbury. The main decorative feature of the front panel was a circle, or two interlaced squares, filled with repetitions of a small tool; a feature probably deriving from Italy.

Canterbury School: an important centre of manuscript illumination in England from the 8th to 13th century was at Canterbury. Such foreign developments as the 11th-century Rheims ink-drawing technique influenced the limners, many of whom came from Winchester. Distinctive features at this time are capitals in red, green, and blue, interlaced foliage borders, occasional figures in line, and a predominantly deep colour scheme. The main works written were Apocalypses, Bibles, and bestiaries; many examples are to be seen in various College libraries at Cambridge. See 'Canterbury school of illumination' by C. R. Dodwell, C.U.P., 1954.

Canticum canticorum: an allegorization of Solomon's 'Song of Songs'. The first of two known editions has been dated from a study of its paper to late 1465 or 1466. There are two horizontal blocks on each of sixteen pages. Scholars have tentatively attributed the drawings for them to Hans Memlinc working in the Brussels studio of Rogier van der Weyden (d. 1464).

canting mark: a printer's *device*, q.v., in which the design is based on a pun on the printer's name. Two famous examples are those used by Androw Myllar of Edinburgh (a windmill) and John Day (a sunrise and the legend 'Arise for it is Day').

canvas: as used in bookbinding, a strong cloth which while thicker and more durable than ordinary book cloth is inferior to *buckram*, q.v. Prior to the 17th century it formed a base for embroidered covers until superseded by velvet or satin. In the later 18th century plain canvas was used to cover school books and books sold by chapmen.

caoutchouc binding: a method of binding books by cutting away the back folds of the sections so that the book became a pile of single leaves. These were then roughened and united by applying a rubber solution called caoutchouc. No thread was used. The process was patented in England in 1836 by William Hancock and can be regarded as a precursor of *adhesive binding*, q.v.

82

Another form of this may have been used by the Parisian binder Pierre-Joseph Bisiaux (fl.1777–1801) who offered his clients books 'relié sans ettre (*sic*) cousu'.

As rubber perishes with time many of the books bound in this way have had to be reprocessed with polyvinyl acetate adhesives (not all of which are stable).

cap: the protecting cover of brown paper with which the binder encloses the whole book except the boards during finishing. See also *capping up*.

Cape Levant: see *French Cape Levant*.

capitals: large letters, e.g. Z, I, A, etc. The name derives from the inscriptional letters at the head, or capital, of Roman columns. Their use in proof corrections and manuscripts is indicated by three lines under the letter or letters concerned. Abbreviated as *c.* or *caps*. Also called *majuscules*. See also *small capitals*, *uncials*, *upper case*.

cap line: 1. a line of type set in capital letters.
2. an imaginary line which runs across the top of capital letters. Cf. *base line, mean line*.

capping up: the fitting of a thin paper cover around the body of a book but leaving the back exposed. This is done after sewing, edge trimming and gilding are finished, and serves to protect the edges while covering, headbanding, and finishing processes are carried out.

capsa: the cylindrical container in which papyrus rolls were kept.

caps and smalls: words having the first letter set as a large capital and the following letters of the same word set in small capitals. The first word of a chapter is often set in this way. The use of caps and smalls is indicated in manuscripts by three lines under the first letter and two under the remaining letters of each word concerned. E.g. WATERLOO BRIDGE.

caption: strictly, descriptive matter printed as a headline above an illustration. The custom of the composing room, however, is to refer also to descriptive matter printed underneath an illustration as a caption. See also *legend*.

Caradoc Press: a private press founded in 1899 by H. George Webb. He was a wood engraver and used this medium for initials, borders, etc. Printing and binding were hand done by Webb and his wife. The press appears to have closed in 1909 after issuing twenty small works. A typical production was Sir Philip Sidney's 'Defence of Poesie and certain sonnets', 1906, printed in Jenson type on Batchelor's Kelmscott hand-made paper.

carbon black: see *gas black*.

carbon print: one of the chromate methods of copying in photography. Carbon tissue (sold in various shades) is used which is sensitized by bathing it in a solution of potassium dichromate or ammonium dichromate, and then dried in darkness without heat. Carbon print was formerly known as *charcoal print* because finely powdered charcoal was often used as a black pigment.

The carbon process has been applied extensively in reproduction work, especially for *intaglio*, q.v. See also *photogravure*.

carbon tissue: paper coated with gelatine which is made semi-opaque by the addition of pigment. The gelatine usually contains some sugar and glycerine, to preserve its flexibility. Carbon tissue is used for various methods of photographic reproduction based on the sensitivity to light of gelatine treated with alkali dichromate. (See *photogravure*.)

Carbon tissue and carbon print were invented by Poitevin in 1855, but were perfected by Joseph Swan in 1862–4. The latter set up the first factory for making them.   (GU)

cardboard: see *boards*.

card fount: the smallest complete fount of type stocked and sold by a typefounder.

caret: Latin for 'it needs' and represented by the symbol ⋏. This was used by scribes in the early 13th century to mark the place in a line of text where something was to be inserted, a purpose it retains in modern *proof correction*, q.v.

Carey, Matthew: an Irish immigrant who settled in Philadelphia as a bookseller and publisher. It was, however, his son *Henry* (d. 1879) who between 1817 and 1838 developed the business as the first real general publishing house in America. He was partnered, albeit nominally, by *Isaac Lea*. At a time when the works of English authors were being pirated Carey, whose list included Austen, Byron, Dickens, Disraeli and Scott, made *ex-gratia* payments to foreign authors. He was the first publisher to do so.

He was also influential in promoting such American writers as Irving, Fenimore Cooper and Poe, as well as issuing American works on law, medicine, science and travel. He began the practice of sending quantities of *remainders*, q.v., to retailers who fixed their own prices. In 1827 his firm founded the *American Quarterly Review* as a literary periodical. See D. Kaser, 'Messrs Carey and Lea . . .', Philadelphia, Pennsylvania U.P.,

1954, and his 'The cost-book of Carey & Lea, 1825–1838', 1963. See also *publishers' agent*.

Carey, William: see *Bengali printing and typography*.

Carmelite Missal: an illuminated Missal, of Carmelite use, made for the London Whitefriars. It was probably written in London before 1390 and illuminated there during the next seven years. In the 19th century the Missal was cut up and pasted into scrap-books which were acquired by the British Museum in 1874. From 1933–8 Margaret Rickert of Chicago skilfully reconstructed the surviving portions: these are large initials decorated in various styles, some with grotesques in the East Anglian manner, others being finely drawn Biblical scenes.

Carnegie Medal: an annual award made by the Library Association of London for an outstanding book for children written in English and first or concurrently published in the United Kingdom during the preceding year. It dates from 1937. Selection is made by representatives of the LA Youth Libraries Group from suggestions made by LA members.

Caroline minuscule: see *Carolingian script*.

Carolingian illumination: the Carolingian renaissance in the 8th century led to the development of Frankish illumination. Many cultures met and fused in the court of Charlemagne, the influence of Byzantium being seen in the arcaded Canon-tables and the use of gold and silver lettering on purple grounds; the large initial page designs appear to be of Celtic origin, while the inclusion of exotic birds is Syrian. A frequently used scheme was the narrative scene arranged as a strip placed at the top of a page or between lines of text. Sometimes several strips placed one above another filled a rectangular frame, but a unified composition consisting of a few large scale figures within a vertical frame was not usual. Alternatively an arch framed a figure or a scene. Important centres, with stylistic differences particular to each, were Tours, Rheims, Aachen, Trier, Metz and Hautvillers.

It was at Trier that the Gospel-book of Ada (Charlemagne's sister?) was made in the early 9th century (now Cod. 22, Trier Library). This and other works of the *Ada-group*, shows rich colouring and greater fantasy in the lively figure representations of the Evangelists and their symbols, deriving, it is suggested, from the pictorial tradition of Italy and England. The Golden Psalter (*c*. 783–95) written in gold minuscules with gold or silver capitals by the scribe Dagulf is the finest example of this group. It is now in the Österreichische Nationalbibliothek, Vienna.

In Bibles written and decorated at the *Tours School* the Anglo-Saxon influence is especially marked. The

Metz School perfected the historiated initial. From *Rheims* came the *Utrecht Psalter*, q.v., held to be the most splendid example of Carolingian illustrative drawing. The *Palatine School* of Aachen saw the revival of pure classical Roman tradition.

Carolingian script: the clear round script with clubbed ascenders and a minimum of ligatures and cursive features which was developed at the Abbey of St Martin at Tours where, after 796, Alcuin of York (*c.* 730–804) was abbot. The Emperor Charlemagne, himself a scholar, drew others from various parts of Europe to assist at the Court School he founded for *inter alia* the revision of the Vulgate, service books and classical Latin texts. The adoption of clearer writing was already in progress when in 782 Alcuin was invited to direct the programme. Just what was his contribution to the perfected script, as distinct from the revised texts which were written in it, is unclear. The book hand was probably developed from Anglo-Saxon half uncial or early Merovingian, though modern scholars disagree as to the precise origin.

Alcuin introduced punctuation and the grouping of words into sentences which, for the first time, began with an initial capital. His revised Bibles were circulated in folios, the pages being set out with square capitals for the main titles, opening lines and rubricated captions in uncials, prefaces in half-uncials, and the body of the chapters in the newly perfected minuscule. This systematic combination of styles, together with ample margins, resulted in an impressive page.

Carolingian minuscule script was used in German, French and English scriptoria (in the 10th century). After a period of neglect it was revived in the 15th century by Italian humanists who called it *littera antiqua*. It is also referred to as *caroline minuscule* and *alcuinian script*. See T. A. M. Bishop, 'English Caroline minuscule', O.U.P., 1971. See also *letters – forms and styles*.

Carpi, Ugo da: see *Da Carpi, Ugo.*

carrells: the stalls or pews in a medieval cloister which were set apart for individual study. A desk for reading and writing was provided in each. The term survives for comparable study facilities in university and college libraries.

carriage: 1. on a hand-press, the assembly of plank, coffin, and the horizontal wooden frame with iron ribs which supported them. The *plank* and *coffin* were drawn along the ribs by turning the *rounce* until the forme was under the *platen* for printing the paper, qq.v. 2. the bed of a cylinder machine along which the forme is run in under the impression cylinder.

Carsi y Vidal, Pascual: a Spanish bookbinder who

was sent by his government to London to learn bookbinding with John Baumgarten and his partner Christian Kalthoeber. On his return to Madrid he bound books for Ferdinand VII and other patrons.

car stocks: stocks of newly published books carried by publishers' travelling representatives for sale to booksellers wanting only a few. This is important just before Christmas to help with immediate repeat orders.

Carter, Harry, b. 1901: a leading British authority on the history of typefounding whose work is internationally recognized. After legal training, followed by instruction from George Friend of the Central School of Arts and Crafts in the skills of punchcutting, he worked with the Monotype Corporation, the Kynoch Press and the Nonesuch Press. He was later chief typographic designer to HMSO, and in 1954 was appointed Archivist to Oxford University Press.

Notable books he has edited are Moxon's 'Mechanick exercises', 1958 (with Herbert Davis); More's 'Dissertation upon English typographical founders...', 1961; and Hart's 'Notes on a century of typography at the University Press Oxford . . .', 1970. Of major importance are his 'A view of early typography', O.U.P., 1969, and 'A history of the Oxford University Press', Vol 1, to 1780, O.U.P., 1974.

Carter, Matthew: a contemporary British freelance type designer, engraver and punchcutter who studied with Paul Koch. He has made original contributions to the series of faces available for photosetting. He began his working career with Enschedé, followed by Crosfield Electronics, Mergenthaler Linotype, and also for a time at O.U.P. with his father *Harry Carter*, q.v.

In 1965 he designed a text face, Series 654 (later named Auriga), for the Lumitype 540. A year later his elegant script type based on Snell's writing manual of 1694 and the display face Cascade Script were both made for Linofilm. In America his Auriga was released in 1970 for the Mergenthaler *Linofilm*, q.v.

Carter, Will: see *Rampant Lions Press.*

Cartoprint: a Danish device for setting and assembling lists as, for example, of names and addresses in a directory. An electric typewriter is used to type copy on a continuous roll of thin card, with a fixed distance between each entry. Each entry is located by a marginal hole. The completed roll is fed into a punching machine which stamps out individual cards. The cards are then made up into columns held in metal tracks and photographed for platemaking. Lists can later be altered or extended by the insertion of new cards.

cartouche: the enclosed space on a map within which an elaborate drawing of human figures, plant life, animals or heraldic devices and the name or title are printed. Alternatively the cartouche may be in the form of a scroll with rolled ends and the title in the centre. Splendid examples of the former are contained in the atlas of Abraham Ortel (Ortelius), 'Theatrum Orbis Terrarum', printed in 1570 by Christopher Plantin of Antwerp.

cartridge paper: a strong paper of good white colour, made with little or no loading, It is hand-sized and may be surface-sized. It is used for drawing, envelopes, jackets, wrapping, etc. See also *offset cartridge*.

cartulary: see *chartulary*.

Cary, John, *c.* 1754–1835: a leading London map-maker and publisher. His maps were accurate and carefully revised for the many editions called for. His London maps of 1782 and 1787 are interesting for the division of sheets into numbered squares and the inclusion of such items as a list of hackney coach fares and marginal references to churches and public buildings. See H. G. Fordham, 'J. Cary . . . 1754–1835', C.U.P., 1925, repr. Dawson, 1976.

case: 1. a book cover, usually made by machine, consisting of two boards, a paper hollow, and a binding material (cloth, linson, etc.). It is usual for

Cases ready for use

the edition binder to submit a *specimen case* for the publisher's approval. This will show the outer material, blocking (lettering), boards, size and squares.

2. the compositor's case, being a tray divided into small compartments in which letters, numerals and spaces are kept. Cases may be used in pairs, an upper and a lower, or a whole fount of type may be in a double case, i.e. one unit. A case is illustrated under *hand composition*, q.v. See also *frame, lay of the case*.

cased books: books which have had a *case* (1), q.v., attached by hand or machine to their sewn sections. Cf. *bound book*. The use of cases is thought to date from the early 1830s. See also *edition binding*. *Cased editions* are also known (imprecisely) as *hardback editions* and *hard-cover editions*.

casein: a substance obtained from curdled milk and used as an adhesive in the manufacture of coated papers.

Casing-in by hand

Casing-in machine

casing-in: the final stage in the production of cased books. After the cases are attached the books are pressed for several hours while they dry out. See also *building-in machine, pressing unit*.

Caslon, William, 1693–1766: an eminent English typefounder the excellence of whose work freed English printers from their overlong reliance on the Dutch to supply matrices and type. In 1716 he set up in London as a metal engraver and bookbinders' tool maker, this including lettering. Under the patronage of William Bowyer, printer, Caslon set up a typefoundry in 1720. He cut a fount of *arabic*, q.v., to be followed by a pica roman and italic. In 1722 he began the English (14-point) founts of roman and italic used in Bowyer's folio edition of Selden's works, 1726. These old-face letters, inspired by van Dijck and other Dutch types then popular in England, made his name, and by the time he issued his first specimen sheet in 1734 his work was known abroad. (See Appendix A.)

His son *William II* joined the business in 1742 being an excellent craftsman. Two apprentices at that time, later to become successful typefounders, were *Joseph Jackson* and *Thomas Cottrell*, qq.v. About the turn of the century the firm traded as Caslon & Catherwood. When the last member of the Caslon family died in 1874 the business was taken over by the manager Thomas Smith whose sons, adopting the name Caslon, continued it. See J. Ball, 'William Caslon', Roundwood P., 1973.

cassie: a derivation of the French word 'casser' = to break; said of damaged sheets at the top and bottom of a ream. An obsolete term.

See also *cording quires, outsides*.

cast: see *electrotype* and *stereotype*.

cast coated paper: the most expensive kind of coated printing paper with an exceptionally high finish, developed in America about 1950. Body paper unwinds from the reel and receives an application of coating. While still in a plastic state the surface is brought into close contact with a highly polished metal drum and there dried. It thus differs fundamentally from orthodox coated art papers where, after application to the body paper, the coating dries uninfluenced by any other surface and has a natural polish with characteristics dependent on the coating. The surface will fracture unless the paper is handled with care at all stages.

The soft, absorbent and uniformly flat surface of cast coated paper is suitable for letterpress, offset litho and gravure. For half-tone, screens of 120 to 150 lines give the best results. The choice of ink needs special care: for a high gloss in the printed result, quick drying inks with a high gloss varnish content are used. For letterpress printing, types with fine hair

lines and great contrast between their thick and thin strokes, e.g. Bodoni, are unsuitable. See also *art paper*.

casting: to found type by pouring molten type-metal (an alloy of lead, tin, and antimony) into an adjustable mould to the upper orifice of which is brought a matrix of a letter or character. See also *stereotype, typecasting*.

casting box: a device for casting stereos, the mould being connected to the melting pot. There are two main types of casting box for curved stereos, different

Winkler casting box for horizontal plates

The Junior Autoplate machine casts vertically with a large jet which is automatically cut off. Boring is done in a separate machine. Capacity—two plates a minute. (L & M)

in principle. In one the plate is cast in a horizontal position, usually without any jet; in the other the plate is cast vertically and has a jet.

casting-off: see *cast-off*.

casting-up: see *cast-up*.

cast-off: an estimate by the printer of the number of pages in a given type size and page area that copy, exclusive of headlines and white lines, will occupy when set up in type. The cast-off is the basis of the printer's estimate of production costs (see *cast-up*) which he submits to the publisher. There are several methods, choice being influenced by the nature and quality of copy: 1. a representative portion of copy is selected and a specimen page is set in type, including headline and folio; 2. the theoretical or 'en' method, suitable for *good* copy, for which the number of pages of type is found by averaging; 3. scientific calculations developed by Monotype and Linotype. See 'Estimating for printers', latest ed., BPIF. See also *copy fitting*.

cast-up: a calculation by the printer of the amount of mechanical setting a job will need, inclusive of headlines and two *white lines*, q.v. He determines the number of characters, ens, or words which can be accommodated on an average page. From the cost per thousand ens, plus charges for display setting and any extras, a total for composing the whole work, including an allowance for author's corrections, is reached.

CAT: the acronym for *computer-assisted typesetting*, q.v.

Catalan bindings: see *gotico-mudéjar*.

catalogue raisonné: a classified booklist in which a brief appraisal of the subject matter follows each entry.

catch-letters: see *catchword* (2).

catchword: 1. the word written underneath the last line of each page or section in a manuscript which was also the word with which the next page or section commenced; its purpose was to assist the binder in assembling the book. The use of catchwords in European printed books was not consistent: in Italian books of the era 1470–1500 they first appeared at the end of a section, later at the foot of every page. Their use in England was from *c.* 1530 to 1800, usually on every page. They served as an aid to the compositor in imposing pages of type in correct order, and to the binder in gathering.
2. the word printed in bold type or upper case type at the top of each page in a dictionary or encyclo-paedia. The first three letters are sometimes used as an alternative: these are *catch-letters*.

category fiction: as classified by librarians and the book trade, crime, mysteries, romances and westerns.

catenati: *chained books*, q.v.

Cathach Psalter: the earliest surviving Irish manuscript, probably written in the late 6th century, and traditionally attributed to St Columba (521–97). The script is a round Insular form of half-uncial, and pen-drawn outline initials surrounded by dots are the decorative feature.

The name derives from the curious use to which it was put. A cathach, protected in a *cumdach*, q.v., was carried into battle to ensure victory. The Cathach Psalter was credited with this magic power long after the death of Columba, and Irish refugees took it to France in the 17th century. In 1842 it passed to the Royal Irish Academy; the cumdach was taken to the National Museum, Dublin.

cathedral bindings: see *architectural bindings*.

Catholicon: a Latin dictionary and grammar written by Johann Balbus, a Genoese Dominican, in the late 13th century. It was first printed at Mainz in 1460 on 373 folio leaves. Although dated the printer is not named, and it has been ascribed, without proof, to Gutenberg, to whom is attributed the colophonic inscription of its completion 'non calami, stili aut pennae, sed mira patronarum formarumque concordia, proportione et modulo . . .' that is 'not with a reed, stylus or pen, but by the wonderful accord, proportion, and harmony of punches and types' has it been finished.

Wherever printed, the stock passed to Peter Schöffer by 1469 as, of course, did Gutenberg's equipment.

Catnach, John, 1769–1813: a printer of Alnwick, Northumberland, who *c.* 1790 published 'Beauties of natural history' in which were sixty-seven small cuts by *Thomas Bewick*, q.v., to be followed by other books with wood engravings by Bewick and Luke Clennel. From 1807–9 Catnach took William Davison as a partner. The latter published independently several works illustrated by Bewick and remained in business until 1858.

Catnach moved to Newcastle in 1808 and to London in 1813. He was here succeeded by his son *James* (1792–1841). From the Catnach Press at Seven Dials James issued between 1813 and 1838 ballads, chapbooks, cheap books for children, topical newssheets and sensational broadsides, mostly of murders, real or fictitious. There was no typographical merit in these productions but trade was enormous and he advertised 4,000 ballads as continually on sale. See C. Hindley, 'The life and times of James Catnach . . .', London, 1878, repr. Detroit, 1968.

Caumont, Auguste-Marie, comte de, 1743–1839: a wealthy French bibliophile who settled in London after the Revolution and opened a binding atelier. There was then a vogue for English bindings among the French émigré colony in London. Caumont is not known to have bound books himself but he employed four or five journeymen binders. Their work was elegant and competently finished but not artistically original. Caumont imitated styles of the day producing, *inter alia*, vellum bindings after Edwards of Halifax. The binder *Kalthoeber*, q.v., worked with him from 1808 to 1814 when Caumont returned to France.

Cawood, John, 1514–72: a London printer, apprenticed to *John Reynes*, q.v. In 1553 he was appointed with Richard Jugge as Queen's Printer, issuing numerous editions of the Prayer Book.

Among popular works he reprinted was 'Birth of mankynde', 1560, a book of midwifery translated by Richard Jonas from Eucharius Rosslin's 'Der swangen frauen', Hagenau, 1513, and first printed in 1540 by the London physician Thomas Raynold (or Reynoldes) with copperplate illustrations by an anonymous engraver.

Caxton, William: England's first printer. In the absence of records it is conjectured that he was born between 1420 and 1424 in a Kentish middle-class family. He went to school, and in 1438 was an apprentice to Robert Large (d. 1441), an important and wealthy Mercer who in 1439 was Lord Mayor of London. About 1445 Caxton went to the Low Countries, trading in cloth at Bruges. He was admitted to the livery of the Mercers' Company in 1462.

By 1462, rich and well-known, he was head in Bruges of the Merchant Adventurers or 'English Nation', formed by the Mercers to protect the English settlement's trading interests. As Governor, Caxton had powers of magistrate and judge, acting for Edward IV in trade treaties with the Burgundian court and the Hanseatic League. From these contacts with the noble and wealthy he would be aware of current taste in literature, and may have dealt in illuminated manuscripts as an extension of his business. For unrecorded reasons Caxton's governorship ceased in 1470/71, giving him time to develop the projects which were to ensure his fame: translating, printing and selling books.

In March 1469 he began translating into English the romance 'Le Recueil des histoires de Troyes' from Raoul Le Fèvre's French version, completing forty pages before setting the work aside. It was at the suggestion of Margaret of York, Duchess of Burgundy and Edward IV's sister, that Caxton resumed the translation, finishing it in Cologne during 1471. Margaret appears to have been his patron, as she was of other authors, translators and scribes, giving him an entry into English and continental circles of potential moneyed purchasers of the books he planned to print.

In late 1471 he began learning the printing business, probably with *Johann Veldener*, q.v., in Cologne where records show Caxton lived between July 1471 and late 1472. In Wynkyn de Worde's edition of the English translation of 'De proprietatibus rerum', 1495, is a statement that his late master, Caxton, was 'first prynter of this boke in Laten tonge at Coleyn . . .' (c. 1472). The edition referred to is attributed by scholars to Veldener, and the statement may mean that Caxton paid Veldener to teach him the craft, or lent him money to print the book in exchange for instruction, not that he personally printed it.

The type used in the work was made by Veldener who also supplied Caxton with seven of the eight bâtarde and gothic types he subsequently used (gothic for Latin texts and headings).

In 1473 Veldener settled in Louvain. At this time Caxton was assembling materials and workmen with Veldener's help before setting up in nearby Bruges where he began printing in 1474. Here he issued the first book printed anywhere in English, the 'Recuyell of the historyes of Troye', completing it late that year or early 1475, and five other undated works. They included the French version of Troye (which was one of the first books printed in that language) and 'The game of the chesse', 1475, based on two French translations of the Latin original by Jacobus de Cessolis. It was also in Bruges that Caxton formed a business association with *Colard Mansion*, q.v. Another printer with whom he is thought to have had trade connections was *Gerard Leeu*, q.v., who printed books in English. Caxton could have offered a sales outlet.

Caxton's bâtarde types were based on the semi-cursive bookhand of that name used in Flanders for writing the important manuscripts which his books simulated. The earliest fount was large and wide, calling for 160 sorts with many tied letters. It was used for the 'Recuyell' referred to above. Later versions were narrower, with fewer sorts, and required less paper.

In 1476, on establishing the first press in England at a shop by the Chapter House, Westminster Abbey, Caxton printed an Indulgence and other small undated items before issuing the first dated book printed in England. This was '*Dictes or sayengis of the philosophres*', 1477, q.v., to be followed before he died in early 1492 by seventy-three books in English out of the hundred surviving works from his press.

It is assumed that Caxton left composing, printing and even proofing to his foreman and workmen,

occupying himself with his vast translating programme and with business affairs. His foreman and
successor was *Wynkyn de Worde*, q.v., who had
joined him by 1479, while others who trained and
worked at the press may have included *Robert Copland*
and *Richard Pynson*, qq.v.

The 'Chronicles of England', 1480, was the first
work in which Caxton used justified line endings and
printed quire signatures, both by then accepted
practice. His 'Myrrour of the worlde', 1481, was the
first illustrated book printed in England. In this
translation of a French paraphrase deriving ultimately from the 13th century Latin prose 'Speculum
historiale', attributed to Vincent of Beauvais, Caxton
included very simple woodcuts and diagrams which
may have been copied in his workshop from illuminations in a Bruges manuscript. Two years later he used
more interesting blocks in the second edition of 'The
game of the chesse', and several later works were
illustrated.

It is of note that prior to 1483 Caxton's English
translations of seven French manuscripts preceded
original versions printed in France. He clearly saw a
market for them before the French. Caxton may
have printed his translation into English of a French
version of Ovid's 'Metamorphoses' since he refers to
it, but no copy is known. The complete text of his
translation, written by a Flemish professional scribe
in a bold lettre bâtarde and dated 1480 was printed
in facsimile in 1968.

His first major contribution to English literary
history was to print, about 1478, an edition of
Chaucer's 'Canterbury Tales' which had circulated
in manuscript copies since it was written about 1390
(about eighty survive). The second edition, 1483, was
a somewhat hastily corrected re-write of the first and
included changes in word order and in words. It was
illustrated by twenty-six crude woodcuts, later used
by de Worde (1498), and Godfray, and copied by
Pynson in their editions.

Ranulph Higden (d. 1364) completed his universal
history 'Polychronicon' in the 1320s (a hundred MS.
copies of it survive). The translation into English by
John Trevisa (1306–1402) with later continuations
was printed by Caxton in 1482. By 1479 he had rented
additional premises (at the Sign of the Red Pale) in
the Almonry at Westminster. They do not survive.
The site was by the main way into the Abbey for the
court and officials, potential purchasers of the books
in which he specialized. Anything more traditional,
such as law and school books, would have sold better
by distant St Paul's where London's booktrade
developed. In Westminster there was neither competition nor control.

His famous enigmatic *device*, q.v. (reproduced in
this book), occurs for the first time on the last page of
the Sarum Missal printed for him in Paris, 1487, by
Guillaume Maynyal who specialized in the printing

of rubrished books. The device is cruder than French
work of the time and was probably cut in London for
impression after sheets of the book reached England,
although the style of the decorative border suggests a
Gouda woodcutter (supplied by Leeu?). Why Caxton
worked for eleven years before using a device is not
known, nor has its true significance been established
beyond conjecture. It would be natural for him to
base it on his trading mark as a merchant. The device
combines exactly the form of arabic 4 and 7 used in
Europe in the 12th century (though modified by the
late 15th), and in 1976 several writers considered the
device stood for 47 and 74 (for 1447 and 1474), two
important years in his life. In the 16th century the
identical mark was carved on a roof boss in Llanengryn
Church, Merioneth (see F. A. Girling, 'English
merchants' marks', Lion & Unicorn Press, 1962,
where both are shown). Not on record is the suggestion that the device is a rebus or visual pun of a
horseshoe quoit *cast on* a stake (or *pale*) adapted from
his name and shop sign. Contemporary variants of
the family surname were *Cawston* and *Caston*.

In 1485 he published his second great contribution
to English literary history, 'Le Morte Darthur', the
title he gave to the series of Arthurian romances
translated from French by Sir Thomas Malory
(d. 1471), apparently to lead his readers into believing
they represented one continuous work. In creating
this artificial unity he rephrased archaic language
and occasionally abridged the original, dividing it
into twenty-one books. Caxton's edition, reprinted
and adapted through four centuries, remained the
only known text until 1934 when what was claimed
to be the authentic 15th century manuscript text was
found in Winchester College (since 1976 in the British
Library). Caxton may have read it.

Caxton remained an active businessman as customs
records show. He imported and exported manuscripts
and printed books. He had an eye for and printed
readily saleable works. They were fashionable and
exclusive because continental printers had not issued
English editions of them, and they appealed to the
growing public literate in English. Had he printed
classical and religious works in Latin, for which the
English market was limited, he would have needed
scholarly editor-correctors and to arrange for European distribution to make a profit. Nor, without
closer attention than he had time to give it, would the
overall quality of his presswork have competed with
that then being done in Italy, France and Germany.

He apparently sold bound copies of books since
thirteen Caxton works and four of de Worde's
survive in bindings made in a Westminster shop active
until *c.* 1510. They are usually in brown calf over
wooden boards, with panel designs tooled in blind of
lozenge compartments containing impressions of
small floral or animal tools. Not all copies of their
books surviving in contemporary covers were bound

at Westminster. (See H. M. Nixon, 'William Caxton and bookbinding', *Jnl Printing Historical Society*, 11 1975/6, one of eight papers presented to the Caxton International Congress, London, 1976.)

Caxton dedicated books to patrons, an essential step for popularizing unfamiliar texts. He did this in prologues or epilogues giving, as appropriate, a laudatory reference to his patron, an introduction to the translation, or a note on the difficulty of rendering foreign texts into the unstable English of his day, much in the manner of a modern preface. If a text to be printed already had a prologue he made changes or additions.

His great achievement was to make available to English readers a considerable number of popular and useful books. He saw the need for prose to be a stable and worthy medium of literary creation and his use in print of London English was a step to this end. Inevitably there were borrowings from Dutch and French in his prologues (e.g. *convenable*, *publique*, *royame* and *semblable* in 'The game of the chesse') though many borrowings were associated with particular works and did not permanently enrich his vocabulary. Since he was not by training a scholar and did not cultivate elegant prose his writing often lacked logical or syntactical cohesion (he referred to it as 'rude and simple'). Thus his influence on the style of future writers was less than is often claimed for him and did not extend to consistent spelling: we find, for example, variant forms of nine words on a single page of 'Book of Eneydos', printed late in life (1490). In the next century such writers as Roger Ascham, John Skelton and Edward Coote were among those still lamenting the rude simplicity and lack of rhetorical discipline of their native tongue (see *ink-horn terms*).

Caxton's haste to publish a text was common to continental printers, all aware of the need to keep pressmen busy and secure a quick return on capital invested in type and costly paper. Haste meant occasional careless translation, lines repeated or omitted, and poor proofing. It was left to Wynkyn de Worde to improve and standardize to some extent the spelling for new editions of his late master's works.

Nonetheless, Caxton's work began a concern among later English printers that the books they produced should embody one linguistic form of wide acceptance. In following Caxton's spelling conventions his immediate successors were doubtless aware that in Europe standardized Latin had contributed to the commercial advantages its universal acceptance brought. Even so, until printers adopted the norms of the Authorized Version of the Bible of 1616, and later, they would vary the spelling of words in order to justify a line of type, leading to inconsistencies: those in the Bible were largely particular to each of several compositors.

For punctuation Caxton followed manuscript-book writing practice and used a diamond-shaped full stop,

a colon and a solidus: the approach to modern punctuation, including the comma, began with Aldus in Venice. See G. D. Painter, 'William Caxton: a quincentenary biography', Chatto, 1976, and the works referred to in it. See also *Blades*, *Brut*, *English spelling by printers*, *manière*.

Cayme Press: a printing press founded in London by Humphrey Toulmin and P. Sainsbury in 1923 with the aim of printing 'in pleasant form . . . any work that was not merely commercial, or which involved no departure from good typographical standards . . . Particular attention was given to the designing, engraving, and printing of Heraldic and Genealogical books and Tabular Pedigrees.' It became a limited company in 1933.

The Cayme Press also installed an etching press for artists to pull their own prints. See also *Favil Press*.

cellulose: the fibrous substance obtained from wood, cotton, hemp, flax and other plants. It is used in papermaking, the quality of the paper depending on the quality of its cellulose base.

Celtic illumination: see *Hiberno-Saxon illumination*.

Cenninus, Bernardus, fl.1470: a goldsmith, and the presumed first printer of Florence. The only work he is known to have printed was the Commentary of Servius on Virgil, edited by his elder son *Petrus* who may also have acted as pressman. With his younger son *Dominicus* Bernardus may have cut the punches and cast the type. The work, in three volumes, appeared in 1471/2. As was then usual blank spaces were left for the Greek quotations to be written in by the purchaser of the book.

centred: type lines which are placed in the centre of a sheet or in the centre of a type measure.   (ML)

centre head: synonymous with *cross-head*, q.v.

centre notes: notes set between columns.

centre-stitching: in pamphlet binding, stitching with thread by working it through the fold or centre in a manner similar to wire saddle-stitching.   (ML)

centum: a unit of a hundred, used as an alternative to a *ream*, q.v., when counting paper or card.

Cerne, Book of: an illuminated manuscript of the Passion and Resurrection portions of the Gospels written at Lichfield in the early 9th century. Decoration is in a severely calligraphic style and the colours used are light shades with only occasional gold; small beasts enliven some pages.

The name comes from its former location at Cerne

Abbey, Dorset, but it is now in Cambridge University Library.

cerography: engraving on wax spread on a sheet of copper; this plate is used as a mould from which an electrotype is made. The process is used in making maps. Hence, *cerograph* or *cerotype*, a print made by this process. (ML)

cf.: the abbreviation for 'confer', i.e. compare, or refer to.

chained books: books secured by chains to a horizontal bar which extended above the reading desk on which they rested, or to a shelf over it. This method of securing books was used in monastic and other libraries from the early 15th century until, in English church libraries, the early 18th century. Also known as *catenati*. For an illustration see *bookbinding*.

chain lines: the heavier lines on laid paper, spaced from 1 in. to 2 in. apart, and running at 90° to the *laid lines*, q.v. See also *turned chain lines*.

chain stitch: the stitch made by the binder at the head and tail of a section before beginning to sew the next.

chalcography: properly, the art of engraving on copper, but in the 16th century a printer might refer to himself as *chalcographus* in a Latin imprint (e.g. Bynneman, 1569 and Purfoot, 1605 also Froben).

chalking: synonymous with *powdering*, q.v.

chalk overlay: see *mechanical overlay*.

chamber lye: urine. Until the early 19th century this was one of the traditional fluids with which *ink balls*, q.v., were kept supple by soaking them overnight in a pelt pot. Thus Stower, writing in 1808, 'The pressman's next care should be to look after his balls. They should be well rubbed with a blanket soaked with chamber lie, if they are inclined to be hard, that they may be in proper order for the next day's work'.

Urine was also used by early printers as a washing agent when scrubbing type after a job was finished, and by at least one London bookbinder in the 18th century, Charles Hering, for softening his morocco leather. The manner of its collection has not been recorded.

In AD 1000 Heraclius described in his 'De coloribus et artibus Romanorum' how red Cordovan leather was made by dipping white undyed skins in a copper vessel containing madder and urine which was heated until hand-hot. This versatile fluid was also used from classical times by the makers of colours for manuscript painting: thus in 'Traités sur la composition des couleurs', compiled by Jean Lebègue in 1431

from earlier writers, we learn that when preparing deep rose colour some brazil wood and alum are to be boiled over a carbon fire for one hour in the urine of a drunkard, with the addition of an ounce of honey (to give a satisfactory viscosity) before removing it from the heat.

Chambers' Awards: three annual awards, each of £1,000, made to encourage Scottish writing. They are open to any writer born in Scotland, of Scottish parentage, or resident in Scotland, or writing on a distinctively Scottish theme. Address: 11 Thistle Street, Edinburgh. (DW)

chamfered edges: bevelled edges. When heavy boards are used for large books the top, fore- and bottom edges may be bevelled. This makes for a neater turnover when fitting the leather cover.

Champflex coater: a *roll coater* with two reverse-running rolls which apply coating as the web of paper passes over them. Surplus is removed by a polished doctor roll (or *metering bar*) which rotates in the direction of web travel. It is usual to give a base coat, dry it, and then apply a second coat which can have a different formula.

Champion coater: an American machine for the mass production of coated paper, introduced into Britain in 1938. Briefly, an excess of coating is applied to one side of the still moist web of paper. After drying, the paper is passed over a second unit to coat the second side.

In 1969 a means of giving a still better surface was announced. After first coating it as above the paper receives an over-coating applied by a high-speed air knife. See also *coater*.

champlevé: enamelled book covers made by craftsmen during the 13th century. Designs were cut into thin sheets of gold or copper pinned on to supporting wooden boards and the cavities were filled with enamel. On other bindings enamelling was limited to the subsidiary decoration of borders and corners, an ivory plaque bearing the Crucifixion carved in relief forming the central ornament of the upper cover. Limoges was a centre of this art. Cf. *cloisonné*. See M. M. Gauthier, 'Les Reliures en émail de Limoges', Paris, 1968.

chancery: a name given to narrow italic types deriving in design from cursive chancery scripts. These formal scripts, known as *antica corsiva*, *cancellaresca* or *lettera da brevi*, were used in the 15th and 16th centuries by scribes in the papal chancery for official documents and letters. See also *Arrighi*, *cursive*, *Poggio*, *writing manual*.

Channel School: the name sometimes given to the interdependent north French and south English schools of manuscript painting in the 13th century. See *Gothic illumination.*

chapbook: a paper-covered booklet, costing a penny or so, as sold by travelling hawkers (*chapmen*) who included bundles of them with the buttons, threads, laces and so on which they carried from village to village. Chapbooks were usually about 6 in. by 4 in., had up to twenty-four pages illustrated with crude but lively woodcuts, and had a decorated cover-title.

At the end of the 17th century, when the popularity of broadside ballads diminished, London's ballad printers turned to chapbooks. In the 18th century they were the main recreational reading matter of the adult poor, and also became nursery classics for children of all classes. They offered a welcome alternative to the mass of 'improving' moral tales and pamphlets then being put out.

Although often altered or abridged, chapbooks were the sole means of keeping alive and transmitting fairy tales, traditional lore and the anonymous English and continental tales of adventure and romance told by the troubadours of medieval times. The somewhat dull metrical romance 'Guy of Warwick' was as familiar in book or ballad form in the later 16th century as it had been in the 14th. After a period of neglect during the 17th century it was revived in a prose version in the 18th, becoming one of the best-known chapbooks.

Among many printer-publishers of chapbooks during the 18th century William Dicey (d. 1757) of Northampton and his family were the most prolific. A Dicey trade list of 1764 gave the wholesale price of penny histories (i.e. chapbooks) as 104 copies for half a crown. As printing spread to the provinces during this century Newcastle led the provincial chapbook trade. James Catnach was the chief printer of them in the 19th century.

In America the chapbook era was from about 1725 to 1825, supplies being imported from England until the 1750s when printers in Boston and Philadelphia began issuing them. Many narrated the adventures of white captives among Red Indians, but in general they were not as educationally important as in England due to the wider availability of other reading matter.

See V. E. Neuburg, 'The penny histories: a study of chapbooks for young readers over two centuries', O.U.P., 1968. See also *colporteur, songster.*

chapel: an association of the journeymen in a printing office. The leader is known as the 'Father'. Thus to 'call a chapel' is to summon a meeting of the journeymen and 'to chapel' a man is to require his attendance at such a meeting for a disciplinary purpose.

This usage of the word 'chapel' is of obscure origin,

the earliest known printed English reference being that of Moxon who in 1683 wrote 'Every *Printing-house* is by the Custom of Time out of mind, called a *Chappel* . . .' supposing this to have been because Bibles and service books were printed there. Later writers have sought to link the word with the wholly suppositious location of Caxton's press in a chapel at Westminster. Much more plausible would be its introduction and use by French immigrant printers who were permitted by the Act of 1484 to work in London. Between that date and 1536, when permission ceased, two thirds of London's printers and binders were aliens, mostly French speaking. That they should bring with them the language and working conditions already firmly established in France must have been inevitable. They knew no other and found none. The 'chapelle' would be essential in maintaining their identity and unity in an alien land whether or not corporate worship in a London church took place (see *Saint-Jean*).

In any event from early times it would be necessary to establish rules of conduct relevant to method and behaviour in a printing office where, at each press, a group of men worked as an interdependent team for twelve or more hours a day. Lapses were fined, the money being put in chapel funds to pay for beer, communal feasting and outings. Unfair practices by the press owner, such as the engagement of extra apprentices for cheap labour, would find the chapel united against him. Even by 1540 the combined groups of printing operatives were sufficiently powerful in Paris and Lyons to stage a total strike for better conditions.

In English establishments various quasi-religious ceremonies formed part of chapel meetings, thus in *The Craftsman*, May 1740, we read that it was the custom when setting up a printing house to consecrate the premises by sprinkling the walls with beer and to sing an anthem. Dissident printers were 'excommunicated', and a boy being bound as an apprentice was made to kneel before the Father of the chapel who 'baptized' him by squeezing a beer-soaked sponge over his head. When a journeyman joined a printing office he had to pay a 'benvenue' to the chapel, a clear corruption of the 'bienvenue' charged in France. In general there were many customs common to printing offices in England, France, Germany and Holland. See F. C. Avis, 'The early printer's chapel in England', Avis, 1971. See also *companionship, copy money, smooting, waygoose.*

chapman: a hawker of *chapbooks*, q.v.

Chapman, Christopher, fl.1704–56: the London bookbinder who was one of the two who worked for *Robert Harley*, q.v., and his son Edward.

Chapter books: books published by members of the

Chapter Coffee House, an association of London booksellers formed in the 18th century, whereby they paid for shares in a book and its printing costs, receiving in return a proportion of the books at cost price. They were later known as *Trade books*.

chapter heading: the displayed heading at the beginning of every chapter. It is set to uniform height for each chapter of the book and may be embellished with a head-piece or illustration.

character: any single letter, number, punctuation mark or symbol cast as a type. Synonymous with *sort*.

character book: a work offering the reader moral edification by describing aspects of human nature to avoid. Such books were popular in England and France during the first half of the 17th century and were inspired by the 'Moral characters' of Aristotle's pupil Theophrastus (*c.* 370–287 BC). An early translation from the original Greek into Latin was made by Pirckheimer, Nuremberg, 1527. More important was Isaac Casaubon's French version, Lyons, 1592, reprinted many times during the following 200 years. An English translation by J. Healy appeared in 1616.

Among English works in the style of Theophrastus were Joseph Hall's 'Characters of vertues and vices', 1608; Thomas Overbury's 'A wife, and characters', 1614; and John Earle's well-known 'Micro-cosmographie: or a peece of the world discovered in essayes and characters', Oxford, 1628. Earle's name did not appear as author until E. Say's edition of 1732. Its title suggests the association as a literary form of character book and essay. This link was to lead to the short story when such essayists as Addison, Steele and Defoe invented people with modern names to replace the Virtues and Vices of earlier essays and character books.

In France Jean de la Bruyère's popular 'Les Caracteres ou les moeurs de ce siecle' (*sic*), Paris, 1688, was also a pointer to later fictional writing. His work, often bound up with a translation of Theophrastus, was published in an English translation in London, 1698. See G. Murphy, 'A bibliography of English character-books, 1608–1700', London, 1925. See also *physiologie*.

chart: 1. a navigational map.

2. a written or printed sheet which on one side gives tabulated or graphical information of any kind. The reverse is normally blank. See also *tabular work*.

charta bombycina: a name misleadingly given to the earliest paper imported into Europe from Baghdad. It was not made from bombyx (silk) but linen.

charta damascena: the name by which paper was widely known in Europe during the 11th and 12th centuries. At that time most of the paper in use was brought from Damascus where its considerable manufacture began about 985. The import of Damascus paper diminished in the late 13th century because the papermills of Italy, Spain and elsewhere could supply the trade.

charter: literally, a leaf of paper. It commonly describes a deed or document by which a sovereign or other authority grants a right or privilege to a person or corporate body, e.g. when founding a university, a borough, or a corporation.

chart paper: a good-quality paper with a strong furnish, often tub-sized or wet-strengthened, which is suitable for the lithographic printing of maps.

chartulary: 1. a collection or set of charters, especially the volume in which were copied out by hand the charters, title-deeds, etc., of the land and property of a monastery. Also known as *cartulary*.

2. a modern printed version of such a volume.

chase: a steel or cast-iron frame into which type and blocks are locked by means of wooden wedges or small metal expanding boxes called quoins. Chases vary in size. The term 'in chase' describes a book which is imposed ready for printing.

chased edges: the gilded edges of a book which have been decorated by the finisher with heated tools known as goffering irons. A wavy or crimped effect results. Also known as *goffered edges*.

Chaucer Society: a society formed in 1868 by F. J. Furnivall for the publication of parallel texts of Chaucerian manuscripts. The series continued until 1912 by which time ninety-nine volumes had appeared.

cheeks: the two main vertical timbers forming the frame of a hand-printing press. They normally extended from floor to ceiling.

chemical graining: see *graining*.

chemical printing: the name given by Senefelder to his invention of *lithography*, q.v.

chemical wood pulp: pulp obtained by the chemical treatment of wood, and often known as *chemical wood*. The Englishmen Charles Watt and H. Burgess pioneered the process in 1851, taking out an American patent in 1854. It differs from *mechanical wood*, q.v., since the resin, ligneous matter and oils contained in the wood are removed by boiling with acid or alkaline solution. This leaves the wood cellulose fibre isolated so that these dissolved impurities can be washed out preparatory to bleaching and further stages of paper-making. See also *soda pulp*, *sulphite pulp*, *wood free*.

chemise: a form of loose cover of chevrotain or other leather which was fitted over the wooden boards after these had been attached to the book. These covers were sometimes secured to the book with bosses.

They date from the 12th to 15th century. Towards the end of the period it was not unknown for a chemise to be made of silk. See also *girdle book*.

chemitype: 1. a process for producing maps, etc., by etching lines on a zinc plate covered with wax, filling them with fusible metal, and then eating away the zinc with acid, leaving the lines in relief.

2. a plate made by this method.　　　　(ML)

Chepman, Walter, *c.* 1473–*c.* 1538: the associate of Androw Myllar in establishing, in 1508, the first printing press in Scotland. They had a joint licence and monopoly from James IV for printing and selling all books in Scotland. The first work they issued was 'The Complaint of the Black Knight' by Lydgate, also known as 'The Maying or Disport of Chaucer'.

chessmen: the pieces used in games of chess have since the 15th century been represented in printing by standard symbols cast as separate types.

Chessmen

Chetham Society: a society founded in Manchester in 1843 for the printing of local records, memorials, chartularies, etc. It was named after the Manchester cloth merchant *Humphrey Chetham* (1580–1653) who left a fund to establish a library. Publication began in 1844.

In 1966 the Johnson Reprint Corporation of New York began an extensive series of reprints.

cheveril (or **chevrotain**): leather made from the skins of small guinea deer and used in the Middle Ages for *chemises*, q.v.

chiaroscuro: properly *chiaro-oscuro*, meaning light and dark, and the name for single-colour wood engravings printed from successive blocks of wood for solid masses of lighter or darker shades. A key block for the darkest tone is printed first followed by from one to three tint blocks to add either light shades of the same colour or tones of a different colour.

Inspired by the two-tone effect of the manuscript painter's *grisaille*, q.v., the German wood engraver *Georg Lucas Cranach*, q.v., experimented with this method about 1507, but it was successfully developed by *Ugo da Carpi*, q.v., who from about 1516 used three or four blocks for printing the popular Renaissance style of water colour drawings. He and Jost de Negker were prominent among the many Italian and German printers who used the process in the 16th and 17th centuries. In the late 18th century it was revived in England, notably by *George Baxter*, q.v. See W. L. Strauss, 'Chiaroscuro: the clair obscur woodcuts by the German and Netherlandish masters of the XVIth and XVIIth centuries', London, 1973.

china clay (or **kaolin**): at one time the commonest filler used in papermaking to increase gloss, smoothness, opacity and printability. It has now largely been replaced by *satin white* (artificial sulphate of lime) which gives a smoother and more receptive surface.

china paper: a thin hand-made paper of silky texture made from bamboo and used for proofing wood engravings. Its modern machine-made substitute is more accurately termed *Japanese paper*, q.v.

chipboard: thin cheap board made from recycled paper with other cellulose material in a cylinder machine with up to eight vats of pulp, a cylinder for each. As the layers of fibre are formed they are picked up and combined by pressing to make a board. Chipboard is suitable for edition-binding cases. Weights used vary according to purpose, thus 1,500 g/m^2 for a medium quality metric crown octavo book of 320 pages, average stock.

chirograph: to the archivist, a formal handwritten document.

chiroxylographic book: a *block book*, q.v., with printed illustrations and handwritten text.

Chiswick Press: the imprint first used in 1811 by the elder *Charles Whittingham*, q.v., when he moved his printing business to Chiswick near London. The name was later used by his nephew, Charles Whittingham II, for his premises in Took's Court, London.

From 1885 until 1919 the press was directed by Charles Thomas Jacobi (1853–1933), noted for his attention to design, and the firm continued to print high-class work until it ceased trading in 1962. When it was acquired by Eyre & Spottiswoode about 1962 much of the historic printing material was transferred on loan to the St Bride Printing Library in London.

Chodowiecki, Daniel Nikolaus, 1726–1801: a German artist-engraver who worked in Berlin. He is remembered, *inter alia*, for his illustrations to the works of Goethe, Shakespeare, Cervantes, Voltaire and others. His influence on contemporary illustrations was considerable.

Cholmondeley Awards for Poets: established in 1965 by the Marchioness of Cholmondeley for the benefit and encouragement of poets of any age, sex, or nationality. The first awards, made in 1966, were to Stevie Smith and Ted Walker. The award, which is non-competitive, is administered by the Society of Authors.

chrestomathy: a collection of extracts from the writings of one of more authors, especially from a foreign language, used as specimens of a literature or language. Cf. *anthology, florilegy.*

Chromagraph: an electronic colour scanner developed in Germany by Rudolf Hell and announced in Britain in 1965. It is a transistorised unit which produces colour-corrected continuous-tone colour separations for letterpress, offset-litho or gravure. See also *Klischograph.*

chromate process: any of several very important photographic or reproduction methods based on the fact that a combination of chromate and a suitable colloid (gelatine, glue, albumen, gum arabic, etc.) is sensitive to light in such a way that the colloid loses its solubility or its ability to swell under the influence of light; it is said to be *tanned* or *case-hardened.* This phenomenon was discovered by Fox Talbot in 1852. See also *albumen process, carbon tissue, collotype, enamel process, photogravure.* (GU)

chromium plating: a means of protecting blocks and other printing formes of copper, brass, or other metals, in the latter cases usually after previous copper depositing or nickel plating.

chromolithography: lithographic printing in several colours. The term has been in use since 1827 when Gottfried Engelmann obtained a French patent for stone engraving in colours, the component colours being produced in crayon drawing. He called his process 'chromolithographie'. Illustrations made in this way first appeared in English books about 1839, such names as Day, Humphreys, Hullmandel, and Boys being important. See also *autolithography, colour printing, lithography, Plastocowell.*

chromo-paper: paper which is more heavily coated than art paper. The surface can be dull or glazed. It is used for colour lithography.

chromorecta process: see *offset reproduction.*

chronicles: originally, a detailed contemporary record of events arranged in order of time but without any attempt at literary style. The monastic chronicles of medieval days recorded national as well as local events and are in many cases the only accounts of them to survive.

There was a later period of chronicle writing in Tudor England. These were printed and were in the nature of reconstructions of early British history. One of the earliest chroniclers was Edward Hall whose account of the families of Lancaster and York appeared in 1542. The well-known Holinshed's 'Chronicles of England, Scotlande and Irelande' first appeared in 1577. This was the work of several writers. Other chroniclers were John Stow (1525–1605), John Speed (1552–1629) and the famous William Camden (1551–1623). See also *Brut.*

Chronicles of England: see *Brut, Caxton.*

chronogram: a sentence or a verse in which certain typographically distinguished letters express a date; the sentence must also have some relevance to the date. In a chronogram every stressed letter stands for its own numerical value, and every letter in a sentence which has a numerical value must be counted, e.g.:

$$
\begin{array}{l}
\text{GVstaVVs ADoLphVs GLorIose} \\
\qquad\qquad \text{PVgnans MorItVr} \\
5 + 5 + 5 + 500 + 50 + 5 \quad + 50 + 1 \quad + 5 \\
\qquad\qquad\qquad + 1000 + 1 + 5
\end{array} = 1632
$$

(1632 was the year in which Gustav fell at the Battle of Lützen.)

Chronograms were most frequent in books printed in Austria, Bavaria, Bohemia and the Netherlands from the 16th to 18th century, and particularly in Jesuit books and tracts.

chrysographer: an artist who specialised in the embellishment of manuscripts in gold. Extant examples date from the 4th century, though writing in gold is mentioned by Jewish historians of *c.* AD. 50. See also *gold, illumination.*

chrysography: writing with liquid gold. This became a feature of Byzantine manuscripts, not only for books but also for letters to foreign rulers, diplomas and official documents. The vellum was often stained with *turnsole* or *murex,* qq.v., to give a richer effect. Elsewhere gold writing occurs in surviving manuscripts written from the late 4th century onwards, and later in those of the Carolingian era. The craft was also highly esteemed in the Muslim empire where numerous copies of the Koran were written in this way.

Chudov bindings: bindings made for if not at the Chudov (Miracle) Monastery in the Kremlin. They date from the late 15th century until the first quarter of the 16th.

Common characteristics are sewing on thongs laced to cut-flush boards covered in calf, rounded spines without raised bands, head and tailbands affixed as in *Greek bindings*, q.v., and grooved edges to all boards which have two clasps riveted to them. Decoration is by blind stamping, usually of ornamental tools within frames and borders. Roll tools were not used. See S. A. Klepikov, 'Russian bookbinding from the 11th to the middle of the 17th century', translated by J. S. G. Simmons. *Book Collector*, 1961 408–22.

Church, William, *c.* 1778–1863: a native of Vermont, U.S.A., where he was a practising doctor of medicine before emigrating to England about 1820 and settling in Birmingham. Here he took up mechanical engineering with some success, notable being his inventions of a typecaster, a printing press and a composing machine (patented 1822). The caster discharged types into a magazine from which they were selected and set up by keyboard operation. When printing was completed the types were thrown back into the casting pot. No commercial use of his composing machine has been recorded.

The Church press of 1821 was a flat-bed hand-press of iron with vertically applied pressure, a new feature being roller ink distribution. Writing in his 'Typographia' Hansard stated that the pressman 'has only to lay the sheet on the tympan, and immediately apply his hand to the rounce, by the turning of which the forme is inked, the frisket and tympan turned down, the press run in, and the impression given'.

cicero: a Continental unit for measuring the width or 'measure' of a line of type and the depth of a page. One cicero equals 4·511 mm. or 12 Didot points. The name is said to derive from the size of type cut and cast for Schöffer's edition of Cicero's 'De Oratore' in the late 15th century. See also *Didot point, point.*

circuit edges: limp-backed Bibles and prayer-books are sometimes bound with projecting covers turned over to protect the edges. The cover is split at the corners, allowing it to fold closely to the edges like a box. Also known as *divinity circuit*. See also *Yapp.*

circular: printed or duplicated advertising matter used to announce new publications.

circulating library: since the later 17th century, when London booksellers seem to have originated the idea, a subscription library of fiction and other popular books. The first recorded use of the term was in 1742. One of the largest circulating libraries in

Victorian England was established in 1842 by Charles Edward Mudie: this, like its less successful imitators, gave a great impetus to the publishing of fiction, particularly in the form of the *three-decker novel*, q.v. See G. L. Griest, 'Mudie's circulating library and the Victorian novel', David & Charles, 1971. See also *novel distributor.*

cista librorum: a chest for the safe keeping of books. Such chests were used in 14th century monasteries and colleges.

civilité: a cursive type face designed about 1556 by *Robert Granjon*, q.v., of Paris and Lyons. It was based on the current hand used in the royal chancery because he considered italic to be essentially Italian. It was given the name 'civilité' after its use in a work of Erasmus translated by Jean Louveau, 'La Civilité puérile', printed at Antwerp by Bellère in 1559.

The new type was never a serious rival to italic. Its main use was for dedications, prefaces, imprints and verse. It was also used until the mid-19th century for French and Netherlandish courtesy books for children: these included Protestant tracts and pious texts of an improving nature.

Although Granjon obtained from Henri II the right for ten years to its exclusive use very similar type was used in Paris by Philippe Danfrie (who cut his own) and Richard Breton in 1558. This was a year after Granjon had first used it at Lyons to print Innocent Ringhière's 'Dialogue de la Vie et de la Mort'. Versions of it were cut by Ameet Tavernier *c.* 1562, and Hendrik van der Keere about 1570. Plantin used both the original and copies. In England similar types were known as *secretary*, and elsewhere as *lettres françaises d'art de main'*. See H. Carter & H. D. L. Vervliet, 'Civilité types', Oxford Bibliographical Society, 1966.

Denyse Clairouin Translation Prize: a prize founded by 'Les amis de Denyse Clairouin' in memory of the Parisian literary agent of this name who died in a concentration camp in 1945. It is awarded annually to a translator whose work is of high quality and most usefully furthers literary exchanges between France, the U.S.A., and the U.K. The amount varies.

clarendon: a thick-faced narrow type with bracketed serifs designed and cut by Benjamin Fox of the London firm Thorowgood and Besley. It was registered in 1845 but when the proprietary rights lapsed after three years the type was widely copied and sold by others.

Clarendon, Edward Hyde, first Earl of, 1607–59: author of 'History of the Rebellion', first printed by Oxford University in 1702, 1703 and 1704. Clarendon had been Chancellor of the University and it is probable that the manuscript copy from which type was set up had been presented by the author's son.

Part of the profits of the copyright were used by the University to establish the Clarendon Press in 1713. See also *Oxford imprints*.

Clarke, John: a 19th-century binder associated with Charles Lewis in the use of *tree-calf covers*, q.v.

clasps: ornamental clasps of brass, or of a precious metal, were a feature of bookbindings from the late 14th to the early 17th century. They were fitted to the boards of books at the fore-edge, over which they fastened, their purpose being to prevent warping of the boards. This was a practical feature of bookbinding when books were stored flat on shelves or chained to a stand. The metal was often elaborately chased. See also *ties*.

classics: a term generally accepted as including all writings in Greek and Latin penned before AD 600 which were not specifically Christian in content. No comprehensive catalogue of those which survive has yet been made, although the use of an optical scanner and computer may make one practicable.

The term now has wider connotations and any outstanding book on any subject is often described as a 'classic'.

Claudin, Anatole, 1833–1906: a Parisian bookseller whose researches into the history of French printing were issued as 'Histoire de l'imprimerie en France au XVe et au XVIe siècle', 4 vols, Paris, 1900–14 (the last volume by Paul Lacombe); and the posthumously published 'Documents sur la typographie et la gravure en France au XVe et XVIe siècles', Paris, 1926.

Clavell, Robert, d. 1711: a London bookseller remembered for his *Term Catalogues*, q.v., for the years 1668–1709.

clay-coated paper: see *art paper*.

clean proof: a proof which is free of errors.

clearing: see *distribute*.

clearing the stuff: the papermaking process in which any knots or clumps remaining in the stuff after beating are brushed out as it is passed through a refiner.

clichage: an obsolete method of duplicating a forme of type without using a plaster mould. A page of type was suspended image side down over a tray of molten metal. When the latter had cooled to 'the point between fusion and fixity' (Applegath) the type was impressed on the surface to form a mould. Plates for printing were then cast from it. The method was invented in France in 1787 by Joseph Carez, and

patented in England by Applegath in 1818 (No. 4249). It was in occasional use between the 1830s and 1890s. See also *stereotype*.

cliché: the French word for a block, stereo or electro.

Clichograph: an alternative spelling of *Klischograph* q.v.

clicker: the foreman of a companionship of compositors.

The Clique: since 1890, a weekly journal for antiquarian booksellers. Used to advertise desiderata and available to the booktrade only. It is published by Clique Ltd., 75 World's End Road, Birmingham.

clogged: see *filling in*.

cloisonné: enamelled book covers made mostly by Greek and Italian craftsmen during the 11th century. The design was first outlined by soldering thin strips of metal on to a metal plate; coloured enamels were filled in the compartments formed. Cf. *champlevé*.

Cloister Press: a printing press set up in 1921 at Heaton Mersey as an adjunct to the Manchester advertising agency of Charles W. Hobson. His object was to produce high-quality work for his own agency and for others able to appreciate it. The remarkable team of specialists he recruited to assist him included *Walter Lewis, Stanley Morison*, qq.v., and Holbrook Jackson. In 1921/22 some books were printed for commercial publishers, notably Sterne's 'Eliza' for Heinemann, with a somewhat over-ornamented title-page. The press closed in 1923 and the group dispersed, but the London office, taken earlier to St Stephen's House, Westminster, was retained by Morison as premises for *The Fleuron*. See also *Fleuron Society*.

close: the second of a pair of punctuation marks, e.g. ")].

closed up: when work is divided among several compositors and each has completed his part, the matter is closed up. (ML)

close out: a title which the publisher is allowing to go out of print. The retail price may be reduced and stockists receive a rebate for copies held.

cloth: see *book cloth*.

cloth boards: stiff cloth binding, as distinct from limp or flexible covers.

cloth joints: reinforcement with cloth of the fold of

an end-paper. The cloth is visible as an embellishment in the joint of the book. (LK)

cloth used in bookbinding: for varieties and finishes see under: *art canvas, bocasin, canvas, crash, duck, expandable cloth, extra cloth, holland, jaconet, linen finish, manila, mull, super.*

Clover Hill Press: a private press established in the 1930s by Douglas Cleverdon at Bristol where he had a publishing and bookselling business. He used an Albion press for the production of a few limited editions as well as for catalogues of the rare books he offered for sale.

Club Bindery: a bindery established in 1895 in New York by a group of bibliophiles who wished to sponsor the production of bookbindings comparable with the best European work. French and English craftsmen were among those employed. The bindery closed in 1909.

club line: the first line of a paragraph if set at the foot of a page. Cf. *widow line.*

clumps: interlinear spacing material used in whiting out and for footlines at the foot of pages. They are made of lead and are usually from 6- to 12-point thick. If made of wood they are called *reglets.*

Clymer, George, 1754–1834: of Philadelphia. An American who invented or improved machines of various kinds. He is particularly remembered for his Columbian press (illustrated under *hand-press*). He began work on this about 1807 and it was built in its final form by 1813. In 1817 Clymer went to London, patenting his invention the same year. Advantages he claimed for it were the exerting of pressure by the fulcrum and lever principle instead of the screw, greater precision and the possibility of using larger formes. His press was more widely used in Europe than in America, was imitated by others, and had a long working life even after the invention of powered cylinder machines. He died in London.

coated papers: a general term for art, chromo, enamel and similar groups of paper on the surface of which a mineral (e.g. blanc fixe, china clay, satin white) is applied after the body paper has been made. Although the term was formerly associated only with clay-coated papers it now includes body papers coated with synthetic resins, plastics, waxes and emulsions. The work is done on a *coater*, q.v.

While the treatment of paper surface will improve the shade and bonding properties the harder sheet which results gives a less satisfactory result with letterpress or gravure printing. The impression may require more ink, thereby increasing the risk of set-

98

off of text matter. However, coated papers are essential for letterpress half-tone work. Also known as *surface papers.* See also *art paper, cast coated paper, holdout, imitation art paper, roll-coated paper.*

coater: a machine which deposits a coating slip on the surface of paper. The coating is evenly distributed, the surplus removed, and the paper dried and finished. Coating can be done *on-machine* by a unit built near the dry end of the papermaking machine: the result is *machine-coated paper.*

An alternative is to use an *off-machine* unit which is an entirely separate machine into which fully matured body paper is fed from reels. There are several types of off-machine coater, but the main two are the *blade coater* and *air knife* coater. Coating can also be applied by a *brush coater* but this method is obsolescent.

Blade and air-knife coaters are now used in 'on machine' installations as the speeds of modern paper-making machines approach those of the coaters. The more traditional on-machine coaters are the *Champion metering-bar* unit and the *Massey roll coater.* Coating can also be applied in the size press of the Fourdrinier. Paper can be coated on-machine with a prime coat and subsequently be coated off-machine to produce high quality double-coated printing papers. The weight of coating can be varied between 5 and 14 g/m^2 per side, depending on the end use of the paper. See also *drying tunnel.*

coating paper: synonymous with *body paper*, q.v.

coating slip: the liquid mixture of clay or other pigments, binders and additives used to coat paper.

Cobb's paper: a thin, matt, self-coloured paper at one time used for end-papers and the sides of half-bound books. It was invented by the London papermaker Thomas Cobb in 1796.

Cobden-Sanderson, Thomas James, 1840–1922: a pioneer in the Arts and Crafts movement in England, a bookbinder of distinction, and a printer. In 1883, when already in his forties, he spent six months learning to bind in the premises of Roger de Coverley, and completed his first binding in 1884. He then set up his own bindery in Maiden Lane, London, where he did all stages of work except sewing and head-banding which were done by his wife. Edge gilding was put out to Gwynn. Within four years he had become famous as a binder and lecturer on the craft.

In 1893 he set up his Doves Bindery near the Kelmscott Press in Hammersmith. Here he no longer bound himself but employed a group of skilled craftsmen from the Zaehnsdorf and Rivière binderies to interpret his designs. *Douglas Cockerell* was his apprentice and *Charles McLeish*, qq.v., his finisher. The American binder Edith Diehl studied her craft in the Doves Bindery during 1905.

Floral and leaf patterns of considerable beauty typify his earliest work, but later he made simple linear and geometric patterns and it was these which most influenced subsequent binding design in England. A list of 120 of his bindings was published in his 'Journals', 1926.

For his printing activity see *Doves Press*.

Cochin: 1. a celebrated French family of printers and engravers of whom the best known was Charles Nicolas Cochin (1715–90). He established a reputation for his engraved title-pages.

2. the name of a series of types made by the Parisian founders Gustave Peignot ct Fils. In the Cochin type, 1912 (Monotype 1923), it was sought to embody the spirit of 18th century engraved lettering; the Nicolas Cochin type, 1913, was designed by Gustave Peignot.

Coci, Georg, fl.1499–1537: a German printer working at Saragossa where, in 1499, he acquired the press founded by the Hurus brothers. His printing was of a high standard, and he issued breviaries, missals and choir books as well as classical poetry. His Livy of 1520 had a title-page printed in three colours.

cock: the middle portion of a *brace end,* q.v., when cast in three pieces, viz: ⌒ ⌄ ⌐.

Cocker, Edward, 1631–76: a London writing master who made some twenty-four specimen books. He engraved the plates. Characteristic of his work were elaborate decorations in which a continuous line linked marginal drawings of animals and figures (see *striking*).

Cockerell, Douglas, 1870–1945: one of the most influential British teachers of hand bookbinding methods. In 1893 he was apprenticed to the Doves Bindery, and from 1896 taught at the Central School of Arts and Crafts. He later advised on and designed bindings for W. H. Smith & Son. While controller of the bindery he merged his own with theirs, moving to Letchworth with them in 1906. Cockerell is remembered for his classic handbook 'Bookbinding and the care of books', Pitman, 1901, revised edition, 1978.

The firm Douglas Cockerell & Son was established at Letchworth in 1924. His son, and former apprentice, *Sydney Morris Cockerell* (b. 1906) while continuing his father's craft binding traditions has specialized in the restoration and rebinding of manuscripts (a notable example was the *Codex Bezae*, q.v., done in 1965 for Cambridge University Library). He is also known for his fine marbled papers (see *marbling*).

Between 1935 and 1947 *Roger Powell*, q.v., worked in the bindery. In recent years Cockerell has, 'in cooperation with the scribe Joan Tebbutt, made a number of vellum bindings using black ink decoration combined with gold tooling'. His most useful contribution to binding construction is the use of a free paper guard round the first and last gathering of a book as this simple device allows the end-papers to open freely without pulling.

In 1963 the bindery was moved to Riversdale, Grantchester, Camb.

cockled: said of paper which has its surface marred by wavy or puckered areas, due to incorrect drying or poor storage. It may be improved by *conditioning*, q.v.

cockroach: a colloquial expression for display matter set entirely in lower-case type.

cock-up initial: an initial that extends above the first line of the text and aligns with the foot of it.

codex: 1. a volume of manuscripts; generally applied to scriptures. Abbreviated as *cod*. See also *illumination*.

2. see *codices*.

Codex Alexandrinus: a Greek text of the Bible, written in uncial letters on vellum, probably dating from the 5th century. It was given to Charles I in 1627 by the Patriarch of Constantinople who was formerly Patriarch of Alexandria. Since 1757 it has been in the British Museum. See 'The Codex Sinaiticus and the Codex Alexandrinus', 2nd ed., British Museum, 1955. See also *Young, P.*

Codex Amiatinus: a manuscript of the Vulgate written in Northumbrian uncial *c.* 715 at Monkwearmouth or Jarrow under Abbot Ceolfrid (642–716). The illuminations were by a native artist working in the classical tradition and bear no trace of contemporary Northumbrian styles. He was probably influenced by works brought from Rome by ecclesiastical pilgrims. The frontispiece of the prophet Ezra the scribe is interesting for its depiction of an armarium on which rest the Novem Codices, the nine volume revision by Cassiodorus of the St Jerome Vulgate.

Ceolfrid intended the codex as a gift for Pope Gregory II but he died when taking it to Rome. From about 900 it was at the Abbey of San Salvatore on Mount Amiata in the Abruzzi mountains, and it was here that Ceolfrid's name was partly erased from the colophon.

The codex, which was one of the principal sources for the revision of the Vulgate, is now in the Laurentian Library, Florence.

Codex Argenteus: a 6th-century Italian manuscript of

99

the Bible. The work is a translation into Gothic, originally made by Bishop Ulfilas about 350, written mostly in greek characters with some roman and runic. The writing is done in gold and silver on purple-stained parchment.

The main portion of the New Testament, on 187 leaves, has been in the Library of Uppsala University, Sweden, since 1669; the silver binding is 17th-century work. Other fragments survive in Milan and Wolfenbüttel.

codex aureus: a manuscript volume in which the letters are written in gold on leaves of parchment stained with turnsole or murex. See also *chrysography*.

Codex Bezae: a 5th or 6th century manuscript of the Gospels and Acts of the Apostles, written in uncial letters on vellum. It was probably made in Sicily and is the oldest known version of the New Testament with Greek and Latin texts on facing pages. In 1581 it was presented to Cambridge University Library by Theodorus Beza (1509–1605) who had acquired it from the monastery of St Irenaeus at Lyons.

Codex Cenannensis: the *Book of Kells*, q.v.

Codex Friderico-Augustanus: the portion now in the Leipzig Library of the *Codex Sinaiticus*, q.v.

Codex Laudianus: a manuscript of the Acts of the Apostles, written in Greek and Latin, and brought from Italy to England in the 7th century, probably by Benedict Biscop. It is now in the Bodleian.

codex rescriptus: another name for a *palimpsest*, q.v.

Codex Rescriptus Aphraëmi: a 5th century palimpsest manuscript of the Bible on which in the 12th century some works of Ephrem Syrus were written. The surviving fragments are in the Bibliothèque Nationale, Paris.

Codex Rossanensis: a Greek manuscript of the Gospels of Matthew and Mark probably originating in Antioch in the 6th century. The silver uncial letters of the text are written on pages stained with murex. The illustrations are collected at the front of the book, separate from the text, and another innovation which was likewise to influence later work was a decorative Canon table.

The name dervies from its discovery in 1879 at Rossano Cathedral, Calabria. See A. Haseloff, 'Codex purpureus Rossanensis', Berlin, 1898.

Codex Sinaiticus: a manuscript of the Bible in Greek, written in uncials, four 48-line columns to a vellum page, probably dating from the 4th century. The place of its origin has not been determined. It is the oldest

extant vellum codex. In 1844 it was discovered at a monastery near Mount Sinai by Constantine Tischendorf. He secured at that time forty-three leaves of the Old Testament, taking them to the Leipzig Library (where they now are) and giving them the name *Codex Friderico-Augustanus*.

In 1859 he secured a larger portion of the Old Testament and all the New, presenting them to the Russian Czar at St Petersburg (who was patron of the monastery). Part of the O.T. and all the N.T. (347 leaves from an estimated original of 730) were acquired by the British Museum in 1933 for £100,000. See 'The Codex Sinaiticus and the Codex Alexandrinus', 2nd ed., British Museum, 1955.

codices (sing. **codex**): originally, wax-covered wooden or ivory writing tablets which were hinged together like the pages of a book, the writing on them being done with a stylus. Later, codices were made of vellum and used for manuscript purposes. Abbreviate as *codd*.

codicology: the study or science of manuscript books as physical objects in order to identify the workshops that produced them. See also *bibliology*.

cods: glass, porcelain or steel marbles used for *graining*, q.v.

co-edition work: the printer's job name for whatever stage of an internationally produced book is done in his pressroom. See also *co-publishing*.

coffee-table book: a term with pejorative overtones for large, lavishly illustrated and strikingly jacketed books. Being costly, and of a size which precludes shelving in the average domestic bookcase they may supposedly be found piled on low (coffee) tables in lounges where they impress visitors. They enjoyed a tremendous vogue in Britain in the 1950s and 1960s, their attraction lying in the number, size, and general excellence of the pictures. While the text may not satisfy really serious readers it is usually adequate for those seeking the general background of a subject.

Critics tend to sneer at coffee-table books. One such described them (in *TLS*) as ' a cunning invention for timorous middle-brows, smart ladies, and those with lazy minds who can turn the pages, look at the plates, and dip into the texts without losing the thread or feeling any strain on the mind'. But if the books did not give pleasure they would not sell, and by introducing readers to new subjects they serve a purpose. Cf. *table-book* (2) See also *co-publishing*.

coffin: 1. an ornamental box for the safe keeping of books. Cf. *cumdach*.

2. part of the *carriage* assembly of a *joiner's press*, qq.v., being a wooden frame with four corner irons

within which was a stone or marble slab laid on a bed of bran, sand or paper. The forme of type rested on this stone before and during impression.

cold composition: 1. the use of a special electric typewriter, e.g. the *IBM Executive, IBM 72,* or *Justowriter,* qq.v., to produce camera-ready copy for reproduction by offset lithography.

2. the composition of film images as on the *Fotosetter, Linofilm, Monophoto,* and *Photon,* qq.v., or similar photosetting machines. In neither (1) nor (2) is metal type involved, either hot or cold. See also *cold type, hard copy, near print, photosetting.*

cold enamel: a dichromated shellac used as a photoengraving resist for line or half-tone blockmaking. Known in America, where it is most used, as *cold top.* Cf. *fish-glue enamel.*

cold pressing: an operation employed in the better grade of books. After sheets are printed and dried they are placed under pressure in a screw press or hydraulic press to take out the indentations made by the type.   (ML)

cold top: see *cold enamel.*

cold type: properly, type supplied by a typefounder for the composition of text or display, as distinct from type cast on the Monotype, Linotype or similar casting machines. However, the term has been extended by trade usage to denote the composition of type *images* involving the use of film which can be produced directly as on the *Intertype Fotosetter, Linofilm, Monophoto,* or *Photon,* or by keyboarding justified copy as on the *Justowriter,* q.v. This seems to be a misnomer since no type is used at all. Cf. *hot type,* and see also *hard copy.*

Colines, Simon de, 1475–1547: a distinguished French printer who pioneered in 1528 the use in France of italic types, and furthered the use of the roman letter. He may have cut his own punches. In 1520 he took over the press of Henri Estienne, whose widow he married, printing more than 700 works.

He developed a trade in 16mo editions and printed numerous Books of Hours with woodcut borders by Geofroy Tory.

A legal work, 'Praxis criminis persequendi', by J. Millaeus, which he issued in 1541, contained in its thirteen large illustrations perhaps the finest French woodcuts of his era.

collate: 1. to put the sections of a book in order. In modern practice collating is the checking by the binder of the sections after gathering. The work will be easier if the printer has used *collating marks,* q.v.

2. to compare one copy of a printed and bound book with another copy of the same impression. See also *collating machine.*

3. to describe in terms of a standardized formula the physical make-up of a book. This gives a bibliographer a precise description of how the book was gathered when given to the binder by the printer, i.e. the number of leaves to each quire, the presence of unsigned leaves, cancels, extra leaves and so forth.

collating machine: a bibliographer's aid, invented by the American Charlton Hinman (1911–77), for comparing different copies or impressions of a book, map, etc. Differences in material to be compared must be limited to minor corrections and changes made to an author's text while a sheet was being printed off; different editions cannot be compared by the machine.

Two copies of a book are placed open on the machine. By means of strong lamps and a series of mirrors the text is superimposed page by page on a final mirror and there magnified. The two images are displayed alternately. If the two pages are identical, a single motionless image will be reflected. If they are not, the place where type has been altered will appear as a disturbed reflection.

collating mark: a quad mark, having a printing surface usually about 12-point deep by 5-point wide, which is printed in the back, between the first and

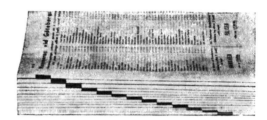

Collating marks

last pages of each section when in the forme. After folding and gathering the marks appear in descending order on the back of each section, a mistake in gathering being easily seen.

Collectarium: one of the service books used in the 11th century by the officiant at daily service. It contained the collects and short lessons, called chapters, which were to be read. In those days there were separate books for the Psalter, lessons, anthems and so forth. These later formed part of the *Breviary,* q.v.

collected edition: the publication in uniform format and under one imprint of the works of an author. Cf. *definitive edition.*

collecting drum: a revolving drum fitted to high-speed printing presses to catch copies or sheets coming out of the machine and collect them in stacks of five or ten before delivery so that final delivery can proceed at a slower rate. They are then delivered together as a flat layer which can be passed on with only one-fifth of the speed otherwise required.   (GU)

Collins Religious Book Award: established in 1969 to mark the 150th anniversary of the publishing house of Collins. It is a biennial prize of £1,000 for the book which in the opinion of a panel of judges has made the most distinguished contribution to the relevance of Christianity in the modern world to one of the following subjects: science, ethics, sociology, philosophy, psychology and comparative religion.

Collobloc: the trade name of a letterpress half-tone process which eliminates etching and metal printing surfaces. It derives in principle from the largely experimental washout gelatine relief processes of the 1870s which failed to give an image of sufficient depth.

The basic material of the printing surface is a three-layer laminated foil comprising a paper backing sheet; a black pigmented separation layer; a brown relief layer; and a clear layer of compounded colloids, blended to be hard yet not brittle, and of adequate printing depth. The foil is sensitized in a potassium or ammonium dichromate bath, dried by warm air, and is then ready for printing down. Other equipment needed is a patent vignette contact screen (65 or 133 ruling) instead of the usual cross-line glass screen, a vertical reproduction camera with vacuum back, a printing-down frame with arc illumination, a simple transfer mangle and a hot-water development system.

collodion: the vehicle on which a photographic image is deposited in the *iodized collodion process*, q.v. Collodion is a solution of pyroxylin in alcohol and ethyl ether. See also *wet plate*.

Colloplas: the trade name of a process for making non-etched gravure cylinders. It substitutes a rubber surface on which the printing image is impressed hydraulically for the copper-coated etched cylinders used in photogravure and was announced in 1954.

Instead of the continuous tone positive of normal photogravure, a continuous tone negative of the orginal, in the size finally required, is joined with a contact positive screen and printed down on a special Colloplas foil. The foil is sensitized in the same way as carbon tissue and printed down after drying. The exposed foil is next transferred to a polished sheet of brass and developed in hot water. This results in a matrix relief on which the screen lines appear as blank metal and the actual image as square-shaped mounds. The latter represent the ultimate cells, in depths varying according to the tone values of the original.

The printing cylinder is covered with a special unvulcanized rubber compound, and the brass matrix, when dried, is wrapped round it. The cylinder, as then prepared, is put in a Colloplas vulcanizing press which heats it to the 300°F necessary for vulcanization, and at the same time hydraulically presses the matrix into the rubber.

The narrow ridge, caused by the join of the matrix sheet, is ground away and polished, resulting in a seamless cylinder with a smooth glazed surface, but with the printing image impressed as an exact replica of the matrix. Duplicate cylinders can be made from the same matrix.

collotype: a planographic, photo-mechanical, non-screen printing process suitable for fine detail reproductions in monochrome or colour. Printing is done from a glass plate prepared by printing a negative on a gelatine film containing dichromate. Fox Talbot discovered in 1852 that a chromate gelatine layer was case-hardened by exposure to light. The first to employ this principle for the direct production of printing plates (lithographic stone) was A. L. Poitevin and sheets printed by him were exhibited in Paris in 1855. The method was given its practical adaptation mainly by Joseph Albert of Munich during 1867–71, who introduced the glass plate. In 1869 Jakub Husník of Prague issued an edition printed by Albert's process. Collotype came into general use under various names: glass printing, gelatine printing, albertype, etc. In 1871 Albert had the first collotype cylinder printing press built by Faber & Co. of Offenbach; the first satisfactory coloured collotype impression was made in 1875 and the first three-colour collotype was made in 1898.

As now practised collotype is done in the following stages: a negative is made of the subject with shadow masks and retouching as needed; a plate of aluminium alloy is gelatine coated by centrifugal force to a thickness of 0·0005 in. and dried; it is sensitized in a bath of dichromate and dried again; negatives are laid on the plate and exposed by mercury vapour light; the dichromate is washed off; finally the plate is dipped in glycerine and water, dried and mounted.

Although capable of the finest results collotype is slow and costly, depending on the printer's skill more than any other process. By 1975 only one firm in Britain was using it.

Instead of the former glass plate from which only 1,500 good impressions could be taken a film base fitted to flexible aluminium plates is used on a rotary offset machine, enabling long runs to be made. This variant of collotype is known on the Continent as *collography*. With rotary machines runs of 10,000 without appreciable loss of quality are possible. In America a run of 5,000 is regarded as the economic minimum.

collotype inks: soft, highly concentrated pigments in a medium of wax and lithographic varnish.

colonial cloth: descriptive of the cheap cloth-covered boards used for casing *colonial editions*, q.v.

colonial editions: originally, editions of novels bought in sheets from British publishers by exporting firms who issued them in cheap bindings for sale in the Colonies. Subsequently publishers produced their own colonial editions, bound in cheap boards, and with a title-page indicating that they were solely for export sale. They were retailed at a sum below the English net price.

It is not now usual to prepare special editions for oversea sale, but merely to supply copies of the home edition on special terms, and with the disappearance of colonies the term is obsolete. See, however, *English Language Book Society*.

Colonna, Francesco: a Dominican monk remembered for his 'Hypnerotomachia Poliphili'. This was written in 1467 in a mixture of Latin and Italian of his own devising and related the love affair of Poliphilo and Polia, set in a background of classical archaeology. It was first printed in 1499 by Aldus Manutius in a revised cutting of the type used for Bembo's 'De aetna', 1495/6.

Its importance and influence throughout Europe derived from the initial letters and some 168 wood-cuts, by an unknown designer, which were included. These inspired craftsmen, artists and decorators seeking models. A facsimile reproduction was published in London by the Eugrammia Press in 1963.

The Colophon: an American quarterly for book collectors first published by the Pynson Press of New York in 1930. It was issued until 1940, being continued as *The New Colophon* from 1948–50. It was then discontinued.

Subject emphasis was on fine books and manuscripts, American collectors, bibliography and book illustration; good materials and a cased cover gave it a certain permanence.

colophon: 1. in manuscript books, a concluding statement, not without overtones of pride in achievement, indicating some or all of the following: the title of the work, the name of the copyist, date and place of copying, a blessing for the patron or client who commissioned it, and threats of excommunication to unauthorized copiers. Shorter colophons named only the copyist and date.

The oldest known manuscript colophon concludes a copy of the Books of the Prophets written by Moses ben Asher in Tiberias in 827. During the later Middle Ages colophons were sometimes in verse. The Jewish copyist of the illuminated Worms Mazhor, Simhah ben Judah, noted in the colophon that copying had taken four weeks: that was in 1272.

Early printed colophons followed the manuscript tradition, occasionally including the date when printing began and/or ended, apologies for errors, the number of copies printed, and the name of the ruler under whose protection the book was issued. There were also colophons of full-page length such as in Gershom Soncino's edition of Rashi's Pentateuch, Rimini, *c.* 1525. In Hebrew books the length of the colophon was often adjusted to fill the whole space at the end of a text in the belief that there must be no blank. Probably for the same reason the colophon was sometimes printed in larger type than that of the text it concluded. In Italy early printed editions of the classics sometimes ended with a colophon in verse. By the early 16th century the practice of identifying a book and its printer on the *title-page*, q.v., was accepted and the colophon was abandoned.

The word colophon derives from the Ionian city of that name. It was held that the Colophonians, being good fighters, tipped the scale in favour of whichever side of a battle they fought, enabling it to finish. Hence the phrase of Erasmus 'Colophonem adidi' – 'I have put a finishing touch to it' and its use to describe the words at the end of a book.

A modern form of colophon is the production note at the end of private press books. In France this may begin with the words 'Justification du tirâge' or 'Achevé d'imprimer'. See also *cuneiform*, *explicit*.

2. a publisher's *device*, q.v., printed on the title-page. This is a misuse of the term. A device may appear on *every* book the publisher issues: a colphon is particular to *one title*.

coloured printings: cheap paper with a high mechanical wood content. It is used, *inter alia*, for covering pamphlets.

coloured tops (or **edges**): book tops (or all three edges) tinted with a dye or pigment, usually applied with a spray gun. Much used for publishers' binding. After colouring, the edges may be brushed with wax to give a gloss, and a still higher gloss is obtained by rubbing with an agate burnisher. For directories and similar books of reference bands of contrasting colour may be used on the edges of different sections to assist the user, further aid being given by rubber stamping section titles in ink. See also *thumb index*.
(LK)

colour engraving: a sheet printed in several colours by an intaglio method (*copperplate engraving*, *etching*). The term is also incorrectly used for wood engravings and lithographs in colour. Copperplate printing combined with some means of colouring (or hand-colouring) has been known since the 17th century. Both then and in the 18th century engravings were made by colouring different parts of the same plate in different colours.

colour gravure: the process of reproducing coloured originals in colour by *photogravure*, q.v. In contrast to colour work in letterpress and lithographic printing the colour picture in colour gravure is usually of almost continuous tone character, the dark and light colours being obtained by varying depth of the etched cells. In conventional gravure cylinder wear will reduce the depth of the shallow highlight cells proportionately much more than the deeper shadow cells, causing colour changes. The use of varying area dots something on the lines of half-tone letterpress or lithography has the advantage of better colour control. Several attempts have been made to combine the rich colour range of variable depth with the control possible with variable dot area (the *Dultgen, Henderson* and *McCorquodale-Gresham* processes). The technical problems are still much greater than in colour letterpress and colour lithography. The principal uses of colour gravure are in mass circulation colour magazines and packaging materials. (HJJ)

colour guides: 1. marginal marks on each of the three negatives used in making plates for colour printing. They enable the printer to superimpose them in register.

2. the set of progressive proofs supplied by the photoengraver to the printer.

colour key: a process for producing coloured line drawings. A line block is made of the original drawing and pulls are taken from it, printed in light blue ink. On these the colours are drawn and etched, a separate sheet for each printing.

colour lithography: see chromolithography.

colour photography: the photographic depiction of a subject in its natural colours. The different shades of nature are formed by the light of the spectral colours being mixed in different proportions. The *three-colour principle,* proclaimed in 1860 by J. C. Maxwell, as applied to photography calls for three negatives of a subject to be made with an identical adjustment of the camera. The first exposure is through a blue-violet filter which only admits light of wavelengths corresponding to the blue-violet third of the visible spectral area. The blue-violet content of the different parts of the subject is thus registered on the first negative. The second negative is exposed through a green filter and the third through a red filter. Thus a *three-colour analysis* of the subject is made and its proportions of blue, green and red are recorded separately. (See *colour separation.*)

Beginning with Kodachrome, introduced by Kodak in 1935 there have been many proprietary processes for making colour prints or transparencies. Kodachrome carried three emulsions on a single film sensitized to the three colours for direct processing to a three-colour transparency. Newer colour-negative processes have colour-correcting (masking) layers in the colour negative.

colour printing: printing in inks other than black. The earliest example of this occurs in the Mainz Psalter of 1457 in which Peter Schöffer printed in red and black with initial capitals in blue ink. Illustrations in the earliest books were woodcuts *coloured by hand,* and not until 1481 was colour printing from several blocks attempted. In that year Peter Brun and Pedro Posa of Barcelona printed the 'Ars brevis' of Lullus which included a table printed in red, violet and green. About 1485 Ratdolt printed Sacro Bosco's 'Opus sphaericum' with two-colour woodcut diagrams, using a separate block for each colour. By the same method he printed the first more artistic woodcut: this was the coat-of-arms of the Bishop of Augsburg, in four colours, in the 'Obsequiale Augustense', 1487.

In the early 16th century chiaroscuro engraving from successive blocks was introduced, a method used by Baldung, Burgkmair, Cranach, Dürer and others. The oldest dated print made in this way was printed by Ugo da Carpi in 1518. It was not, however, until the 18th century that attempts at actual colour printing were renewed. Cornelius Bloemaert (1603–83) had printed some sheets with outlines in copperplate engraving, colouring them with wooden blocks, but otherwise hand-colouring was usual. There were two methods: either the copperplate engraving was coloured after printing, or the uninked plate was impressed on the sheet leaving faintly visible outlines as a guide for the colours, a final impression from the inked plate completing the picture.

It was only when mezzotint, aquatint, and crayon engraving had been developed that there was any actual colour printing and attempted colour reproduction. Sometimes different parts of a plate were inked up in different colours, a method which may have been first used by the Dutchman Herkules Seghers (1585–c. 1650) and adopted in England and Germany. It was perfected by William Ryland who worked with Bartolozzi on stipple engraving, and who developed a combined etching and engraving technique. He inked a plate with a ground colour which was then dried. After which, various parts of the plate were coloured selectively by means of small dabbers called 'dolls' (Fr. poupées). From this the method took the name 'gravure à la poupée' (also 'manière anglaise', a term also applied to mezzotint). The plate was heated before printing so that the colours fused into one another to some extent.

Colour reproduction in its present sense may be said to have begun in the workshops of J. C. Le Blon (1667–1741) who worked in Holland, England and France. Inspired by Newton's theory of light and colour he tried to reproduce natural colours by printing with several plates, at first with seven for the seven colours of the spectrum, later with only three, for yellow, red and blue. His experiments appear to have begun in 1711 but it was not until 1720 that he found sleeping partners in London who formed a company ('Picture Office') for reproducing in colour the works of the Italian masters. The company was liquidated in 1723 in which year he published his manual 'Coloritto' which contained the first ever progressive prints. After being declared bankrupt in London he moved to Paris about 1735 where he perfected and patented his four-colour plate process, the foundation of true colour printing, thereby preventing his successor and rival d'Agoty from experimenting until after his death. The work done in Amsterdam by Le Blon's pupil Jean Ladmiral was technically of a higher standard.

In the 19th century lithography predominated in colour reproduction. Among early coloured lithographs were those printed by Barth of Breslau in 1816 and Zahn of Berlin in 1829. The term *chromolithography* occurs for the first time in Gottfried Engelmann's French patent in 1837. Other prominent workers were Lemercier in Paris, William Day in London, Arnz in Düsseldorf and the State Printing House in Vienna.

Present-day colour printing is governed entirely by the photoengraving (process) work which developed at the end of the 19th century and is used for letterpress, lithography and photogravure. (With GU) See also *Baxter, three-colour reproduction*.

colour printing   technical note: the age, quality and condition of paper are of considerable importance in colour printing. Large sheets, fresh from the mill, may shrink in the pressroom, affecting register. It is of assistance if a relative humidity of 60 to 65% is maintained: this will also reduce a tendency to wave or produce static.

If a paper-conditioning plant is installed sheets are held for some time before printing on a hanging conveyor while room air is circulated. The maintenance of condition during the run is also important since each printing adds moisture and paper should be checked after running off ream batches. These should be numbered and covered with a few sheets of interleaving to prevent dimensional changes in the top sheets. Batches will then be re-loaded in the press in the order of emergence. Paper should have the grain direction the narrow way of the sheet.

colour scanner: a machine which provides a set of continuous tone or screened separation negatives or positives ready for use in the preparation of printing surfaces for colour half-tone reproduction.

The many proprietary models available include Crosfield Electronics *Magnascan 450*, introduced in 1969, which was the first machine to give in a single step fully corrected separations of the required size.

Linotype-Paul's *Linoscan* will simultaneously scan two colours, making for speedier production.

Dr Rudolph Hell's *Vario Chromagraph* will make either continuous tone or directly-screened separations. The Hell *Chromograph DC 300*, introduced in the mid-1970s, uses an argon-ion laser as the light source for exposure, and a computer containing the half-tone dots preprogrammed on punched tape for different density values and screen angles. Faster exposure times than for contact screening and finer dot size are among advantages claimed. The Hell *Chromaskop*, shown in 1977, is a colour-monitoring system in which an original (transparency or reflection copy) can be corrected before separations are made. When the original is shown on a colour monitor screen the hue of even small areas of the transparency can be changed by means of a narrow band correction system. See also *scan plates*.

colour separation: photographic three-colour analysis, especially in the production of printing plates. This is mostly a question of smooth originals: paintings, coloured prints or transparencies. As in all three-colour analysis separating is done by exposure through filters and making three negatives in succession.

As colour reproduction is often done in four colours it is usual to make a fourth negative for black. If more than four colours are required for printing, additional colours are made from standard negatives. Colour separation by infra-red radiation is sometimes used as normal procedure for making the black negative.

Colour separation has certain defects so the negatives obtained and the positives made from them must be adjusted and retouched before reproduction can proceed. According to the method of printing employed this retouching is done in various ways. (See *masking, offset reproduction*.) In some cases the retouching can be done on the original picture; for example, it may be desirable when reproducing water-colours to avoid the black outlines in the coloured prints, in which they would otherwise appear automatically in all colours with subsequent register difficulties. There are methods of painting the outlines over with covering colours of shades matching the surrounding colour surface, this painting being done on a thin transparent film which is removed when exposing the 'black' negative.

The negatives obtained by means of colour separation are known as *colour-separation sets*.   (GU)

colour sequence: the accepted order of letterpress printing in four colours is yellow, red, blue, black. It was suggested in Germany in 1957 that to print yellow as the third colour would help to make *moiré*, q.v., less noticeable, since blue, usually printed third, is very intense. If yellow is not printed first a transparent yellow ink should be substituted for the normal near-opaque trichromatic yellow ink.

The engraver will, however, require notice of any departure from the normal sequence.

colour systems: colour can be described by three terms which can be three colours. This, the international system, is closely related to methods of colour printing. It has the disadvantage that it is difficult to visualize a colour in terms of its three colour co-ordinates, e.g. the relation between a pale green, a bright green and a duller version of the same hue would not be visually obvious. So for everyday use three different terms are preferable, i.e. *hue* (the content of yellow, red, etc., which gives it its name), *saturation* (the strength with which the hue emerges after dilution by white light) and *luminosity* (in comparison with the grey scale, the ends of which are black and white). The two principal systems are the Munsell and the Ostwald: both are American.

The *Munsell* system, 1915, defines colour in terms of hue, chroma (= saturation) and value (approximately = luminosity). The usefulness of the Munsell chart of numbered colours has been limited in Europe by its cost.

The somewhat similar *Ostwald* system, 1931, is available in an excellent colour atlas issued by the Container Corporation of America, while an essentially practical colour chart is that issued by the Lithographic Technical Foundation of New York. On a single sheet 22 in. by 29 in. it shows 1760 different colour combinations made with two, three and four colours.

The British Colour Council produces a cheaper and useful if less systematic chart. Tintometer Limited have several methods of colour measurement. (HJJ)

colporteur: a hawker or pedlar of books. From the late 15th century, particularly in France, Germany and Italy pedlars roamed the countryside carrying in a box or basket a selection of almanacs, prognostications, abcs, chapbooks, broadsides and religious prints as well as official proclamations. For the provincial reader there was often no other means of supply. In the 16th century, however, when the unregulated nature of their trade was recognised by publishers as an effective means of distributing banned pamphlets in towns their number increased. In the 1540s French colporteurs sold heretical writings issued from Geneva, and in both France and Germany an enormous number of them played a significant role in spreading the ideas of the Reformation.

Later in the century ineffective attempts were made, notably in Paris, to restrict bookselling to bookshops where it could be controlled and stocks seized. Colporteurs were hounded by the Parisian police who regarded them as little better than vagabonds. An edict of 1618, typical of several through

106

the years, forbade them to take apprentices, to own business premises, to print under their own name, or to sell pamphlets of more than eight leaves. But illicit hawking in French towns continued to the end of the 18th century, many colporteurs being imprisoned for daring to sell clandestine pamphlets 'qui dénonçaient les tares du régime et les turpitudes royales'. There was a similar situation in England in the 17th century when the Stationers' Company attempted unsuccessfully to suppress book hawkers who were considered a danger to the Company and the government. See also *chapbook*.

Columbian press: see *Clymer*.

column-face rule: a rule used to separate columns of text.

Combe, Thomas, 1797–1872: Superintendent from 1832 until his death of the Clarendon Press, Oxford. In 1855 he bought from the Duke of Marlborough the Wolvercote Mill and its adjacent properties on behalf of the Managing Partners and the Bible Committee of the Oxford University Press Delegates. The mill had been used for making fine paper suitable for books from about 1683 and is first recorded as a supplier to the Press in the accounts for 1694. See also *Oxford india paper*. See H. Carter, 'Wolvercote Mill: a study in paper-making at Oxford', 2nd ed., O.U.P. 1974.

combined line and half-tone: a printing plate suitable for reproducing originals with well defined areas of line and tone. Line areas were photographed on an unscreened negative and half-tone areas through a screen. The two results were fitted together by the finisher who stopped out the unwanted areas on each negative prior to printing down, in register, to metal.

This has been superseded by the use of *powderless etching*, q.v. The original is photographed twice, using an overlay and masking. The two negatives are then fitted together for printing to metal. Also known as *line and half-tone fit-up*.

combing wheel: part of the mechanical device on a printing machine which, with the forwarding sucker, passes sheets of paper singly from the stock pile to the feed board and thence to the impression cylinder.

come-and-go: the name for an imposition scheme whereby one set of type is imposed with the head of the first page laid to the head of the last page, and so on throughout the forme. The signatures are delivered *two-up*, q.v., so that the last signature is head-to-head with the first. If a book consists of an even number of sections the gathering of one of each will make a set, with another set turned upside down. This method gives two copies, one running from beginning to end and the other from end to beginning and upside down. The two copies are not separated until final trimming.

comma: a punctuation mark, which was already in use in 9th-century Greek manuscripts.

command of hand: synonymous with *striking*, q.v.

Command Papers: sessional papers printed by Command of Her Majesty and presented to either or both Houses of Parliament. A Treasury directive recommends that they should be 'limited to the case of documents likely to be the subject of early legislation or which may be regarded as otherwise essential to Members of Parliament as a whole to enable them to discharge their responsibilities.'

The serial numbers they bear run (theoretically) from 1 to 9999. As published they have been:

1st series	1833–1869	Nos 1 – 4222
2nd	1870–1899	C. 1 – C.9550
3rd	1900–1918	Cd. 1 – Cd.9239
4th	1919–1956	Cmd. 1 – Cmd. 9889
5th	1956–	Cmnd. 1 – proceeding

See J. G. Ollé, 'Introduction to British government publications', 1965.

Commelin, Jerome, fl.1560–97: a French scholar-printer who worked in Geneva and Heidelberg. He is remembered for his editions of Apollodorus, Chrysostom, Athanasius, and 'Rerum Britannicarum', 1587. His device, an emblem of 'Truth in Glory', appears to be the origin of the one used in 1606 by John Legate, then printer to Cambridge University Press. Legate added the words 'Hinc lucem et pocula sacra'. In a refined form the device is still used by C.U.P.

commission agreement: a contract between an author and a publisher by which the former assumes full financial responsibility for the production and advertising costs of his book and owns the stock: the publisher, in return for an initial cash payment plus commission on sales, publishes and sells the book. See also *publishers' agreements, vanity publisher*.

commonplace book: a personal notebook in which the owner copied passages of interest from the writings and speeches of others, or in which he wrote his own compositions. Such books were often circulated in manuscript and were popular in the 16th and 17th centuries. The first edition of Francis Bacon's 'Essays', 1597, included maxims and aphorisms from his commonplace books.

common press: another name for the *joiner's press*, q.v.

Commonwealth Poetry Prize: an annual award of £250 for a first book of poetry published by an author from a Commonwealth country other than Britain. It is administered by the Commonwealth Institute and the National Book League.

companionship: a group of compositors working together under a foreman. He is known as a *clicker*. See also *chapel, cut the line, smooting*.

Company of White Papermakers: an association of English makers of white paper, incorporated in 1686, to secure for themselves a fourteen-year monopoly for making better qualities of paper. (This meant any paper costing more than four shillings a ream.) The Company rented mills and employed Huguenot refugees, probably to nullify competition from refugee papermakers from France who had settled in southern England. For some years most English books had been printed on paper imported from France and Italy, only coarser grades being made in England. (See also *rag paper*.)

The Company was disbanded about 1696.

compass chart: a *portolano*, q.v. See also *wind-rose*.

compendium: an *epitome*, q.v.

compensation guards: narrow guards in the form of page-length stubs of paper which are bound up, to balance at the back, a book having bulky folding plates or maps. Also known as *filling-in guards*.

compiler: one who assembles or arranges for publication a selection from the writings of others, e.g. an anthology of plays, poetry or prose. Whereas an *editor*, q.v., may also assemble a collection of the writings of others, he may alter, amend, delete or annotate portions of the texts. A compiler usually presents exactly as written the works he brings together.

Complutensian Polyglot: see *polyglot edition*.

component-location diagram: in technical book illustration, an outline drawing with little detail but with important component parts labelled to assist identification.

compose: to set up type according to *copy*, q.v. See also *stamp*.

composing: the placing together of typographic material into a forme for letterpress printing in a printing press. Typographical material consists of *type*, the printed image of which is visible in the impression, and of non-printing *blanks* or whiting out material. The latter, also called *spacing*, is lower than type height so that it does not come into contact with the inking rollers or paper. Its object is to separate the characters so that they are legible and at the same time to hold them together in the units of which lines and pages consist. To facilitate this all typographical material must be dimensioned according to a definite system (see *point*). Letters which are to form words and lines of a given measure must have the same body size, as also the spacing material used between the words to justify the lines. For filling larger spaces *quads*, q.v., are used. For interlinear spacing *leads* of standard thickness and various lengths are used. Larger blank areas and margins are filled with *furniture*, q.v. For securing the forme firmly in the chase *quoins* are used. Composing is done from a manuscript, known as *copy*, either by hand or machine. Machine composition must also be prepared for printing by hand compositors. See also *hand composition, Intertype, Linotype, Monotype.*

In most cases composing is first done in galleys or slips, which means that type set up to a given measure continues in unbroken sequence in long columns for pulling *proofs*, q.v. After various proofs have been pulled and corrected the matter can be made up into pages, imposed in correct order for printing and subsequent folding, and locked up in a *chase*, q.v., being then known as a *forme*. When printing is completed, type (if not required for stereos or to be left standing) should be distributed, which means that typographical material is returned to the case or sent to the metal box (mechanically cast types are melted down for re-use in the composing machine).

Composing in many printing establishments is done to rules known as the *style of the house*, q.v. This term includes the physical setting up of matter, the use of spaces, headings, rules, marginal proportions, etc., and also orthographical style so that punctuation, word division, abbreviations, capitalization, etc., will be uniform even if a long manuscript is set by several compositors. As a general guide to authors preparing their copy, and printers working without house rules 'Rules for compositors and readers at the University Press, Oxford', by Horace Hart, 38th ed., O.U.P., 1978, and 'Authors' and printers' dictionary' by F. H. Collins, 11th ed., O.U.P., 1973, should be used.

composing room terms: see *bad copy, baked, bank, barge, batter, begin even, binding, blank line, blocked up, bodkin, border, bow, box-in, break line, break up, bring up, broken matter, bumped out, bumping up, butted, cabinet, cap line, caps and smalls, caption, case (2), cast-off, cast-up, catchwords, centred, chapel, chase, clicker, closed up, clumps, cock-up initial, collating mark, companionship, composition fount, compositor, copy fitting, copy holder, copy money, correcting, cross bars, cross heads, cut the line, dash, dead matter, direction line, dirty proofs, display, distri-*

108

bute, division of words, double, double column, double setting, dressing, drive out, em, emptying the stick, em quad, en, end a break, end even, end matter, even folio, even s. caps, fat matter, figure, flowers, flush paragraphs, follow copy, footline, footnotes, footstick, forme, foul case, founder's type, fount scheme, frame, furniture, galley, get in, good, gutter, hand composition, hand set, hanging paragraph, head, headline, hook in, imposing surface, imposition, indented, indention, initial letters, in pendentive, interlinear matter, justification, keep down, keep in, keep out, keep up, kill, laying the fount, lay of the case, layout, leaded, leaders, leads, legend, letterspacing, lifted matter, line gauge, literal, locking up, lock-up table, lower case, make even, make ready, make-up, margins, marked proof, mathematical setting, matter, measure, misprint, mixed composition, montage, mortise, nib, notes, open matter, ornaments, out, over matter, page-cord, page gauge, page proofs, penalty copy, photosetting, pie, pierced, planer, point, preliminary matter, pre-press work, proof, query, quoins, quotations, random, reglets, reimposition, removes, revise, rivers, rule, runners, run on, setting rule, shooting stick, side sorts, sidestick, signature, sorts, spacing, spacing material, special sorts, stamp, stet, stone, straight matter, style of the house, tack marks, teletypesetting, transpose, turned sort, two-line letters, tying up, type, upper case, white out.

composing rule: the former name for a *setting rule*, q.v.

composing stick: a metal holder in which the compositor sets up type in words and lines. The stick is adjusted to the required measure before setting. The compositor sets type upside down and from left to right. See also *setting rule*.

Two types of composing stick. In the upper illustration the setting rule is clearly visible

composite block: a combined half-tone and line block; also a plate made up of two or more originals.

composite book: a book made up of distinct parts, either different subjects or the works of several authors collected by an editor and bound in one volume. See also *fly title*.

composite work: a book written by several authors in collaboration.

composition: see *composing*.

composition fount: a loose description for any type-face used for book printing, as distinct from display, which is 'tapped' on a type-composing machine in sizes not larger than 14-point.

Composition Information Services: of Los Angeles, U.S.A. An organisation devoted to typesetting technology, established to assist in bridging the gap between the composition craft and the data processing sciences. A newsletter is issued.

composition roller: the usual *inking roller*, q.v., on a letterpress machine.

compositor: a craftsman whose work consists of setting up type by hand or machine, correcting machine-set composition, making up pages, imposing them, and performing all the necessary assembling of the type forme. See H. W. Larken, 'Compositor's work in printing', Staples, 1961.

compound printing: single impression printing, in two or more colours, from a forme made up of parts which are separately inked. See *Congreve print*.

comprint: to print a book for which the privilege had been granted to another printer. Thus in 1636 Oxford University obtained a charter permitting the establishment of three printers who were allowed to comprint all books. When the Stationers' Company challenged their right to print Bibles, almanacs, primers, and similar works for which its members held patents a 'covenant of forbearance' was drawn up by which the Company paid the University £200 a year not to print certain privileged works. This lapsed in 1672.

computer-assisted typesetting: the use of a computer programmed to produce coded tape for activating a photosetting, TTS, or line-casting machine. It is also known as *computer-controlled typesetting*. Investigation in America and Britain began in the early 1960s. In experiments at Kings College, Newcastle upon Tyne, copy tapped off on a tape-punching typewriter was edited on special equipment and fed into a computer programmed to divide copy into lines and justify them. The edited tape which emerged was fed into a five-hole tape reader driving a 31-channel Monotype tape-punch. The finished tape was ready for the caster.

By 1965 computer-assisted typesetting in Britain was a practical proposition, a computer typesetting system being defined as one 'performing after input at least the following primary function: all the typographical requirements of justification, hyphenation and formatting without human intervention'. Any system employing a form of computer which cannot carry out this primary function must be termed *computer-assisted typesetting* (e.g. the keyboarding space-computer on the early Photon and the Fairchild justifying tape perforator). A second requirement, to achieve more sophisticated advances without re-keyboarding the data, involves the ability to store text or data in computer-retrievable form (such as on magnetic tape). This leads to *computer typesetting systems* which can accept insertions or deletions under programme control, arrange the number of lines on a page, position page numbers and running heads, re-format text in any face or set (for different typesetting machines if needed), carry out multi-column justification and such data processing work as indexing and collating.

The first computer-set book commercially produced in Britain was Margaret Drabble's novel 'Millstone', 1965. It was set by Rocappi Ltd. In the same year the British & Foreign Bible Society commissioned from Stephen Austin & Sons Ltd. a computer-set edition of the Bible (RSV). Composition of the five million characters took nearly three years. It was tapped off on a 7-channel keyboard. Output was converted on a computer into tape for running through a Monotype spool caster. Chapter heads and initial capitals were later dropped by hand into spaces programmed into the computer. Plastic duplicates of plates were made for machining by Collins of Glasgow. By storing the 1,200 pages on two reels of tape the economic production of future editions in different formats and sizes of type became possible, justifying the high initial cost of computerization. It may also be noted that while computer setting an 800 page directory of tax tables may use 8 km. of paper tape its equivalent would be 3 tons of metal type.

The use of a computer as an aid to composition can take many forms ranging from the mini-computer contained in the keyboard or visual display unit to the large general purpose unit capable of carrying out simultaneously a wide variety of tasks. In the case of simple installations the 'idiot tape' is passed into the photosetter and the justified product is read, corrected and made up by paste-up techniques. As a further refinement more advanced systems can merge corrections with the first setting, and some can also divide the lines into pages (vertical justification).

A further variation uses a computer printout for

the first and second stages so that one pass through the photosetter produces made up and corrected pages complete with running headlines, display lines and folios.

Much printed material is created from data bases, such as parts lists which were initially keypunched for stock control purposes. The new material is prepared and formatted for a photosetter by a special computer programme. See A. Phillips, 'Computer peripherals and typesetting', HMSO, 1968, and 'Glossary of computer typesetting terms', Seybold Publishers Inc. See also *CRT photosetting, Fototronic, justification, Linasec, optical character recognition, Photon, precon.*

computer control of papermaking: the use of a computer to control the wet end of a papermaking machine, i.e. thick stock flow, clay flow, flow box pressure, slice gap and wire speed. The computer is programmed to set up in the correct sequence the machine running conditions proper to each grade of paper, thereby maintaining quality control, reducing waste and increasing output. It permits quicker grade changes to be made than would otherwise be possible.

This method was introduced in the 1960s at the Wolvercote Paper Mill at Oxford. In America the Harding Jones Paper Co. was one of the first to instal an IBM computer to improve control of the papermaking machine, and most large paper manufacturers now have some form of computer control.

computer terminology for the printer: the following are some of the commonly used terms: *alphanumeric data*, data consisting of alphabetic, numeric and commercial symbols (e.g. £ & $); *assembly language*, a symbolic program language which represents a particular computer's *machine code* and into which it is translated for operating the machine; *backing store*, programs and data stored on discs, drums or tapes; *central processing unit*, or *CPU*, a collective name for the memory, arithmetic and control units of a digital computer. The size of the CPU determines the range of functions a computer will perform; *character set*, the group of alphanumeric symbols which a computer will recognize and accept, i.e. letters, numerals, punctuation marks and typographic signs; *data bank*, information stored for a specific purpose on punched cards or magnetic tape for processing by a computer; *direct access*, a magnetic drum or disc holding stored data for retrieval; *edit*, to prepare data for printing by writing in the spacing and special symbols required; *hardware*, the machinery and storage components of a computer system; *indexed sequential*, a data-record location-indicator, consulted when retrieving matter held in the data bank; *inputting*, the transfer of data into a computer system; *machine-code program*, the basic instructions which a computer will interpret; *main frame*, the central processing unit and store of a computer system; *modem*, a device used at each end of a telecommunications link between a terminal and a computer to *mo*dulate and *dem*odulate a signal, i.e. the device converts data into signals which are sent on a telephone line to a receiver where the signals are reconverted and processed by a computer into reading copy (see *teleordering system*); *off-line*, said of a peripheral which is operating the main computer system but is not connected to it; *on-line*, said of a peripheral which is in direct continuing contact with a computer; *output*, data which has been processed by a computer and, after proofing, is ready for the photosetter; *peripherals*, ancillary equipment linked to the central processor unit of a computer for input, output or storage: this includes card punch, magnetic tape or disc and tape reader; *print-out*, a readable record on paper, produced on a tape-typewriter or a line-printer, and used for proof correction; *program* (not *programme*), a complete set of instructions prepared in a symbolic programming language (when it becomes a *source program*). A compiler then converts it into a *machine-code program* for loading into a computer; *software*, any program; *terminal*, a device which communicates input/output information to/from a computer system. Terminals include a telecommunications system, teleprinter, teletypesetter or video display unit; *write in*, to record data on to a magnetic tape or disc. See references under *computer-assisted typesetting.*

concordance: an alphabetically arranged index which shows where any selected word appears in the collected writings of an author, e.g. Bartlett's 'Concordance to Shakespeare'.

condensed book: a single volume containing condensations or long extracts from several books. Any books which an editor considers unduly wordy may be treated in this way, but fiction, whether classical or modern, is often chosen. In America condensed books are big business, e.g. the Reader's Digest Condensed Book Club which mails them to two million or so members. Cf. *abridged edition*, which differs from the above.

conditioning: the maturing of paper by the drying out or addition of moisture to it. This is done in a conditioning plant which consists of a series of vertical compartments into which conditioned air is blown while rolls of paper are fed through. See also *relative humidity.*

conducting roller: a roller for ferrying paper through a rotary press. Such rollers must rotate freely and be in static and dynamic balance; they usually have ball-bearings and are driven solely by contact with the paper. (GU)

conger: a group of from ten to twenty publishers and wholesale booksellers who combined to share the

Conditioning hand-made paper

publishing and selling of a work, and to use their power as wholesalers to protect the sale, of their books from undercutting and piracy. Congers were a feature of the London book trade in the late 17th and early 18th centuries when such famous men as Lintot, Longman, Rivington and Tonson were among those co-operating in this way.

The number of shares held by individual members of a conger was not always equal and the whole conger might own only part of a work, e.g. an encyclopaedia. A member could sell his rights, while on his decease they might be disposed of by legacy or auction. Thus title-pages of a work which appeared in several editions through the years would list different proprietors.

Congregatio de Propaganda Fide: a society established in Rome in 1622 by Pope Gregory XV. Pope Urban VIII added a printing office and foundry in 1626 to publish Bibles and religious texts for the use of missionaries in Africa and Asia. It was here that *Bodoni*, q.v., received his training. The first complete printed Arabic Bible was issued in 1671.

Because of its purpose the press acquired more than fifty founts of type for the setting of oriental languages, but between 1799 and 1812 these were appropriated by the French and lodged with the Imprimerie Nationale in Paris. See also *Cabinet des Poinçons, devanagari, Stamperia Orientale Medicea.*

Congreve print: a coloured print made by a process perfected if not invented in 1820 by Sir William Congreve (1772–1828) which in its essentials had already been used in 1457 for printing initials in the Mainz Psalter. It was devised to render more difficult the forgery of Bank of England notes and employed a compound printing plate divided into separate pieces which were removed for colouring, after which they were re-assembled and printed as one forme. Ornaments from such plates were occasionally used in scrapbooks popular in the early 1830s.

Congreve also designed a press in which the colouring as well as the printing could be done mechanically.

conjugate leaves: any two leaves of a book which together form one piece of paper.

Conradin Bible: an incomplete 13th century illuminated Bible, owing its name to its alleged ownership by King Conradin of Sicily who died in 1268. The surviving portion of the end of the O.T. and all the N.T. is on 164 vellum leaves, the text being written in a round Italian hand on pages which have unusually wide margins.

Large scale figures dominate scenes set in the side and bottom margins to illustrate the narrative of the books of the Bible. Backgrounds, often of dark blue spattered with large gold dots, have scalloped edges emphasising the outlines of the principal figure or figures. The latter are painted in vivid contrasting and even discordant colours.

Neither the artist not his location has been identified, nor has any other work been attributed to his atelier. Scholars have suggested Sicily and Bologna as the home of the artist, possibly a man familiar with mosaic and fresco painting working in the western Romanesque tradition with a Gothic influence.

The Conradin Bible is in the Walters Art Gallery, Baltimore.

Consolidated color selector: the name used in America for the *Bélin machine*, q.v.

Constance Missal: the English name for the *Missale speciale Constantiense*, q.v.

contact screen: a half-tone screen made on a film base and having a graded dot pattern. It is used in direct contact with a film or plate to obtain a half-tone negative from a continuous tone original. Contact screens give better definition than the conventional glass screen and excellent gradation. They can also be used for silk screen work. See also *screen.*

contents: part of the prelims where the separate divisions of a book are listed in the order in which they appear. Often set in type two points smaller than that used for the text, to a narrower measure, and printed on the next recto page after the dedication or title page.

continuous feed: a term used to describe the action of an automatic sheet feeder attached to a printing press, folder or other machine, so constructed that the supply of sheets can be renewed without interrupting the action of the machine. See also *feeder.*

111

continuous guard: a method used when sewing sections of vellum or other material which would be damaged by the glue or paste used for binding. A long strip of hand-made paper, as wide as the book is high, is either folded like a concertina before sewing or creased to about ½ in. round the back of each section as sewing proceeds. A flat wooden blade is used for creasing. The needle must pass centrally through the fold, and even tension is important. When gluing-up, the book itself remains untouched by the mucilage.

continuous tone: said of photographs, negatives of photographs, or coloured originals in which the subject contains shades between the lightest and darkest tones. Such originals as maps may be a combination of line (including type) and continuous tone: their reproduction may involve the preparation of separate negatives (masking), later combining the negatives in printing. See also *half-tone process.*

continuous tone negative: a photographic negative. The tone variation is inversely proportional to the subject. Dark areas (shadows) in the original are represented with minimum density in the negative; light areas (highlights) have a high density, and in-between tones vary according to the light reflected from the subject.

contract, forms of: see *publishers' agreements.*

contra italic: an italic *backslanted type*, q.v. An example is Minion Contra Italic Shaded.

contraries: such harmful impurities as pins, buttons, string or rubber which are found when sorting rags or waste paper in the paper mill.

Cope, Richard Whittaker, d.1828: a London maker and seller of printing machinery, particularly known for his *Albion press*, q.v. After his death the business was continued by his executor J. J. Barrett, subsequently joined in partnership by a former foreman John Hopkinson (d. 1864). During the minority of Cope's son *James* the firm traded as Hopkinson & Cope. In 1879 they acquired an interest in David Payne's works at Otley.

Copland, Robert, fl.1508–48: a London printer and translator from French. He was an assistant to *Wynkyn de Worde*, q.v., and even when working independently he may have printed under the latter's imprint until 1535. Of his own publications Copland had only issued a dozen in twenty years. See Sir Frank Francis, 'Robert Copland, sixteenth century printer and translator', Glasgow, Jackson, 1961.

Copland, William, fl.1548–*c.* 69: the presumed son of *Robert Copland* whose business he continued. In later life he printed only minor pieces, ballads and pamphlets, and apparently died in poverty since the Stationers' Company, of which he was an original member, paid his funeral expenses.

copper engraving: an impression taken from an engraved copper plate. The work is done on a brightly burnished copper plate (16 or 18 gauge) which is first coated with a ground on which the design is traced with a needle, then the ground is washed off. Guided by the lines, the artist engraves by cutting away metal shavings with a *burin* (graver), a narrow steel tool of varying section (oval, triangular, square, etc.) cut obliquely at the point, while the other end is

The workshop of the copperplate engraver Wolfgang Kilian of Augsburg (1581–1662), after an engraving of 1623

fixed in a wooden handle. The 'burr' lifted out of the metal may remain on the edge of the line, and this may be removed with a *scraper*, a three-edged cutting tool. The strength of the inked impression is in proportion to the depth of the line. In order to control the plate more easily during engraving the artist rests it on a rounded cushion of sand. The finished plate is warmed, inked, and together with the sheet to be printed, passed through a rolling press. For direct printing such plates should be steel-faced. See also *copperplate printing, dry-point, etching.*

Early examples of copper engravings in Germany and Italy date from *c.* 1440, but this graphic method was certainly used in the 14th century and may be even older. It has been suggested that it originated from the metal-engraved patterns used by armourers, but it is not known when it became an independent art-form in which the impression was the main object. Copper engraving was first used for making playing cards and religious pictures.

Its use for book illustrations began with Boccaccio's 'Du dechiet des nobles hommes et femmes' printed by Colard Mansion, Bruges, 1476 (GKW 4432), which probably had ten engravings pasted in, though no copy with more than nine survives. In Italy Antonio Bettini's 'Monte Santo di Dio' printed by Nicolaus Laurentii, Florence, 1477 (GKW 2204), was the first book to include engravings from copper plates. Among copperplate engravers of the 15th century may be mentioned Andrea Mantegna (1431–1506) with a few but skilfully done sheets, Martin Schöngauer, and several unknown artists now referred to as 'Meister des Hausbuches', 'Meister mit den Bandrollen', etc. About 1500 Albrecht Dürer and others contributed considerably to the development of this medium, both technically and artistically. In the 16th century the art was particularly flourishing in Italy.

The first English book to be illustrated in this way was 'Byrth of Mankynde', a translation by Richard Jonas of a German treatise on childbirth, 1540. The first English copperplate title-page was engraved for Thomas Gemini's 'Compendiosa totius anatomiae delineatio', London, 1545.

In France the art began about 1540 when Italian craftsmen at Fontainebleau trained Frenchmen, but the popularity for book illustration of separately printed copperplates came about 1573 when, among others, Gabriel Tavernier of Antwerp set up a press in Paris. Some French publishers continued to obtain prints from Antwerp until the turn of the century, believing the workmanship superior to that done locally. French supremacy in copper engraving specifically for book illustration as distinct from separate prints began with the work of Chauveau in the mid-17th century and that of Claude Mellan and Nicolas Poussin who both worked for the Imprimerie Royale. See also *livres à vignettes*.

Colour work was introduced in the mid 17th century in the Netherlands. Only one plate was used (often a combination of etching and engraving) bearing various colours, and needing fresh inking after each impression. Bartolozzi later developed this idea for his *stipple engraving*, q.v. Colour printing from three plates was devised in London about 1711 by Le Blon. See also *hand-coloured illustrations*.

Copperplate engraving was used extensively for illustrated books during the 17th and 18th centuries, particularly in France and England, but after wood engraving developed in the 1770s work in copper lost its popularity though it is still in occasional use for map work, security printing, book plates, etc., the plates often being made by mechanical means or process work. See A. M. Hind, 'A history of engraving and etching from the 15th century to the year 1914', Houghton Mifflin, 1923, repr. Dover, 1963.

copperplate printing: printing in a hand-press from plates made on an intaglio principle. In such plates the image lies below the surface. Ink is distributed over the whole plate by manual inking up, the surplus being wiped off, so that only the sunken image remains filled. A soft, absorbent sheet of paper is then pressed against the plate, the ink being transferred to it. In this way the printing of etchings is done, whether of zinc or copper, also of copperplate engravings.

copperplate printing ink: a pliable short ink made of pure weak linseed oil with a high pigment content. It is warmed before being rolled or dabbed on the plate.

copperplate printing press: a press which through the years has been little changed except that the first presses were made of wood whereas now they are made of iron and steel and are often powered. A strong iron plate forms the bed for the printing plate which, however, usually rests on an intermediate plate of softer zinc. Above the paper laid on the printing plate there are felts, then the bed, plate, paper and felts are driven forward between two revolving cylinders. Here strong pressure transfers ink from the cavities in the plate to the paper. It also impresses the bevelled edge of the plate on the paper, seen as a 'bevelled border', a characteristic of printing in a hand-press which is often reproduced artificially. The impressions, taken on damped paper, are first dried between sheets of cardboard, after which they are again slightly damped and dried on cords or in a press. See also *intaglio, photogravure*.
(GU)

copper plates: photoengraving plates of copper, suitable for fine-screen half-tone work and four-colour half-tone. Laminated copper-plastic plates are also used. Cf. *zinc plates*.

Coptic bindings: leather bindings made in the Coptic monasteries of Egypt of which survivals, sometimes fragmentary, date from the 4th to 11th century. About 120 bindings survive in museums and libraries, and they are of great importance in the history of the craft.

The method of binding was not unlike modern case-binding. Gatherings were sewn with chain stitches of thin cord or thread secured by kettle stitches. There were no thongs or cords across the backs. The body of the book was then glued to a strip of linen which extended across the back: this in turn was glued to the inner side of the spine. Parchment end-papers (often bearing writing) covered the marginal turnover of the linen. Early end-papers were left blank but later they were sometimes decorated.

Boards were made of layers of discarded papyrus pressed together and covered with leather (goatskin) to which might be stitched a design of cutout open-work over a gilded parchment foundation. Decorative variants included incised line work or a combination of impressed lines and curves in repoussé. A frame of tooled lines emphasised the importance of the central field on the covers. A much-used motif was the eight-pointed star or a square interlaced with a saltire cross, while strapwork, punched dots and rosettes, all within frames of parallel lines intersecting at the corners, were other features. Repetitions of small animal and bird stamps are found on 9th and 10th century covers. While both upper and lower covers were decorated it was usually not with the same pattern. Some covers made in the 7th and 8th centuries bore designs in black ink: either the design was painted on with a brush, or areas about an outline drawn on the leather were painted black (Arnold). Leather thongs on the front board secured the book when closed: they were fastened to ivory or bone pegs on the edge of the lower board. This reduced the tendency to warp of parchment leaves.

Modern historians of bookbinding have pointed out that the binding on the 7th century *Stonyhurst Gospel*, q.v., shows decorative and technical affinities with Coptic and Tunisian techniques, as does the 8th century Ragyndrudis Codex at Fulda, without, however, postulating a Mediterranean origin for either.

Coptic binding methods were later to influence early Islamic binding in Egypt.

co-publishing: the syndicated publication of books. This is practised internationally to effect economies in production, particularly when the potential home market sales for a book would not justify publication. Bigger print runs also make a lower selling price possible.

Publishers in English-speaking countries may contract in advance to take a significant number of sheets in a book. The work will be printed in country A and then supplied to a publisher in country B, usually with a revised sheet of prelims giving the latter's imprint. But it is the heavily illustrated art and children's books which form the largest part of the co-publishing trade. Projects are often hatched at the *Frankfurt Fair*, q.v., where publishers from several European countries, the U.S.A., Japan and Latin America may agree to join in publishing a book offered by one of them.

The initial sponsor will assemble text and illustra-

114

tions: the same or another will have, say, 100,000 sets of illustrations printed. They will either be distributed to the other countries for the overprinting of locally-made translations of the text, or the foreign language texts may be sent to the initial sponsor to have them printed. Binding for all the group may be done in a third country, not necessarily sharing in the project, but where capacity and low costs make it expedient to do so.

See also *co-edition work*.

copy – author's preparation: the author should prepare typescript on one side of the paper, double spaced, and with the same number of lines on each page. The typing should all be done on one machine, and a good left-hand margin is necessary.

Apart from the index, which cannot be compiled until page proofs are run off, the copy should be complete with title-page, dedication, preface, appendices, etc., and an indication must be given of any matter which is to follow.

Illustrations should be numbered, and the legends (with corresponding numbers) should be typed in order on separate sheets. Marginal numbers (encircled) in the typescript will show where the illustrations are to appear. Their insertion is known as *keying*.

Words which are to be printed in italic type should be underlined, words in bold type are indicated by a wavy underline, those in bold italic with a wavy line under a straight. Other typographical styling will normally be done by the printer who will submit a specimen page for the publisher and author's approval.

It is important that the copy shall be clean. Academic experimenters have estimated that a saving of 14% setting time can result from giving the printer a clean typescript instead of one which is heavily altered.

Various points require attention when submitting illustration copy for the process worker. Photographs should be glossy, at least half-plate size, and in any case larger than the reproduction, with a full range of tones. Line drawings should be on blemish-free white board, and be drawn twice the size of the ultimate result. Preliminary or layout lines should be in light blue pencil. Copper or steel engravings used as copy must be in rich black ink on good white paper, pencil sketch originals reproduce best when photographed to the same size or only slightly reduced. Colour prints and transparencies should not be too contrasty, while hand-coloured prints require bleaching otherwise the silver deposit will affect the three-colour negatives. Water-colours and oil paintings make good copy, as do pastel crayons if the colours have not been overlaid too much by the artist.

It may be added that the earliest extant example

of a manuscript used as printer's copy is that of St Augustine's 'De Civitate Dei', Subiaco, 1467, which survives at the St Scolastica monastery.

copy editor: the member of a publisher's staff who carefully marks up an author's typescript for the printer. This is done according to the publisher's house style.

copy fitting: calculating the printer's requirements for setting a given amount of copy. (See *cast-off*.)

After noting the publisher's planned format for a book the designer makes a character count of the copy (so many *ens*) as a basis for deciding the number of pages needed, line length and depth of text area. Copy to follow for prelims and index, as well as illustrations, are also considered.

The designer next chooses a type face in a size to give, say, eight to ten words per line (approx. 55–65 characters). By using copy-fitting tables, which relate character count to type face and point size, he finds which size will meet the publisher's quota of pages. He will also bear in mind the availability in the chosen face of any special sorts called for in the copy. Minor adjustments to margins may be needed, and for books of continuous text small margins are sometimes feasible by opening up lines of type with interlinear spacing.

The end product of the foregoing is a series of working layouts giving printer and binder clear specifications for all the constituent *parts of a book*, q.v.

The foregoing tasks call for skill and judgement, attention to detail, a knowledge of types, paper finishes, printing and binding processes, plus an instinctive feel for what will most effectively present an author's work to the reader. See also *margins*.

copyholder: one who reads copy aloud as the printer's corrector follows the reading in the proof. See also *reader's box*.

copying machine: see *step-and-repeat machine*.

copy money: money paid to printing house employees in lieu of the free copies of books to which, prior to 1635, they had been entitled by custom. In that year the Stationers' Company ruled that journeymen were to receive threepence a week instead of a copy of any book they had helped to print that week. This substitution of money for actual books was to discourage the illicit sale by workmen of copies at reduced prices, copies which were sometimes incomplete, made up from faulty sheets, or which had been run off in excess of the number laid down by the author or the master printer.

In 17th century France free copies claimed by workmen as their due were known as 'exemplaires de chapelle' and were sold for the benefit of the printers' chapel.

Copyright Act: an Act first introduced in 1709 to protect authors from the illicit printing of their works, either in whole or in part. In 1911 the scope of the Act was extended to include music, paintings, drawings etc. In general an author's works are protected for his lifetime and for fifty years after his death, which protection extends via the *Berne Convention*, q.v., throughout most countries of the world.

A new British Copyright Act was enacted in 1956. According to the new law 'copyright subsisting in a work shall continue to subsist for a full fifty years from the end of the calendar year in which the author dies, and shall then expire'. The provision made in the 1911 Act whereby during the last twenty-five years of the copyright life of a work that work could be published as of right on payment of a statutory royalty was repealed. In the case of a work of joint authorship the reference to author means the author who dies last.

In the case of works which have been commissioned and works made under contract of service, the 'commissioner' or 'employer' shall be entitled to copyright unless an agreement has been made to the contrary.

Provision is made for the copying of certain copyright material by libraries which are not established or conducted for profit. Such copies are only to be supplied to persons proving that they are required solely for research or private study, but control is scarcely possible.

One section relates to the use of extracts from a copyright work for 'fair dealing'. This covers extracts made for the purpose of conveying news of current events to the public, literary criticism and reviews, extracts published for schools, and the reading of extracts in public. Such usage is to be accompanied by a 'sufficient acknowledgement' which is elsewhere defined as one 'identifying the work in question by its title or other description and, unless the work is anonymous or the author has previously agreed or required that no acknowledgement of his name should be made, also identifying the author'.

Welcomed by the Publishers Association was the section which granted the publisher for twenty-five years the copyright of the typographical arrangement of a published edition of a work. This includes reproduction by photographic or similar processes. See J. M. Cavendish, 'Handbook of copyright in British publishing', Cassell, 1974, and 'Copyright and designs law' (Whitford report), HMSO, 1977 (Cmnd 6732).

copyright in America: the U.S. copyright statute of 1909 was replaced in 1976 when Congress passed a copyright revision bill, effective from 1 January 1978. While providing for various forms of publishing in respect of *books* its rulings included *inter alia* the extension of copyright to fifty years after an author's death; guidelines on photocopying by teachers for classroom use, by other individuals and by libraries; an interpretation of 'fair use'; protection for unpublished works without regard to the nationality or domicile of the author and (from 1982) the repeal of the former requirement that an English language publication must be manufactured in the U.S. to be granted full U.S. copyright: this last is intended to benefit American authors who first publish abroad.

The *form of notice* is ©, or the word 'Copyright' or the abbreviation 'Copr.', the year of first publication of the work and the name of the owner of copyright in the book.

Copyright (International Conventions) Order: an Order in Council of 1964 by which the United Kingdom accepts obligations to protect foreign copyright works under the Berne and Universal Copyright Conventions.

copyright notice: intimation of a book's copyright, which usually appears on the back of a title-page. To meet the requirements of the *Universal Copyright Convention*, q.v., publishers in subscribing countries must ensure that the first and all subsequent editions of a work bear the symbol ©, the name of the copyright owner, and the year of publication.

Unauthorized reprinting and plagiarism have bedevilled publishing since its earliest days. One writer to assert his rights on the title-page was Paul Rici, a German-Jewish physician who in 1519 issued his Latin translation of a medical treatise by the Spanish Muslim Albucasis. The title-page had a notice threatening papal excommunication as well as punishment by the Emperor Maximilian to anyone reprinting the work or selling such reprinted copies within six years. See also *privilege, Stationers' Company*.

cord: see *page cord*.

cording quires: a 16th century term for the outside quires of a ream of paper.

Cordovan leather: an imprecise term for leather originally made famous in Spain where it was used by Arab craftsmen for, among other things, bookbinding. See *mudéjar bindings*.

After the Arab conquest of Spain in AD 711 two kinds of leather were made. The first, known in Spain only as *guadameci*, described in its simplest form the soft alum-tawed male sheepskin (or goatskin) white or vivid red in colur, which had originated in the Libyan village of Ghadames. It was developed in Cordova (although alum-tawed goatskins were used in Europe and the Near East from pre-Christian

times). The red dye, which was probably the specifically Arab contribution, came from the kermes insect, but a Cordovan ordinance of 1543 specified only madder should be used.

The second kind, known in Spain as *cordobe*, was vegetable-tanned goatskin, not necessarily red or made in Cordova. Elsewhere in Europe, from the 13th century, various leathers, differing in finish, were made and known as *Cordovan* or *Spanish leather*.

In England the name Cordovan leather or *cordwain* was used for similar skins. They were sometimes used for bookbindings until morocco was introduced in the 18th century. A curious patent (No. 2285) was granted to William Akison in 1700 for making 'Spanish or Morocco Leather from horse hides'. Modern Cordovan leather is still made from horseskin but is not used for bookbinding. See J. W. Waterer, 'Spanish leather', Faber, 1971.

cords: lengths of flax or hemp placed across the back of a book; to these the sections are sewn.

cordwain: see *Cordovan leather*.

corcd type: large-size types and spacing of which the feet have been hollowed to reduce weight.

corium: the Latin for leather. The term 'in corio' or 'cor. turcico' is found in some 16th–18th century documents and booksellers' catalogues to describe books bound 'in leather' or 'Turkey leather' respectively.

corners: 1. in printing, material for setting corners in ruled frames, or connecting ornamental borders. See also *Oxford corners*. (GU)

Corner pieces

2. in binding, the triangular pieces of leather or cloth which cover the corners of half- or three-quarter bound books. See also *mitred* (1), *turning-in corners*.

corpora: initial capitals inserted by a rubricator in blank spaces left in a manuscript for that purpose by a scribe or early printer.

correcting: the alteration of errors or defects in printing galleys and formes, whether text, plates or blocks; also reproduction negatives, etc. See also *proof corrections*.

correctores peciarum: officials of a medieval university appointed to check the accuracy of the exemplar

Correcting composed type. The wrong letter is removed with a bodkin. A pair of tweezers lie on one side of the galley; a composing stick on the other. If an error is found in a Linotype setting the slug must be taken out, re-set and re-cast

made from an author's text prior to its multiple copying by a stationer. See also *hic nullus est defectus, manuscript-book writing.*

corrigenda: corrections of mistakes in a book which were not noticed during proofing. They are brought to the reader's attention by listing them on a separately printed correction leaf which is either loosely inserted in the book or tipped in. Alternatively they can be printed on an otherwise blank leaf at the beginning or end of the book. Also known as *errata.*

Corrosheet: the proprietary name of a British self-adhesive corrugated wrapping board for manually or mechanically sealing books for despatch. It was introduced to the trade in 1973 by Central Packaging of London and was claimed to be lighter and quicker than traditional packing methods, using neither string, glue nor staples. This water-resistant material is suitable for a book or books of 1·5 kg total weight.

Corvinus, Matthias: from 1458–90 King of Hungary. His interest in book collecting began in the early 1460s when he brought books from Rome for the library he planned at Buda under the guidance of Johannes Vitéz (d. 1472). His marriage in 1476 to Beatrice of Aragon was followed by the import of books and possibly master binders from Naples. During the next decade the king's librarian Taddeo Ugoleto travelled widely securing many unique Greek manuscripts. After they had been translated into Latin, with the addition of scholars' commentaries, teams of copyists were employed under the supervision of Felix Petancius to write them out.

Many of the humanist texts were written in Florence where such artists as Attavante, Boccardi and Antonio del Cherico were commissioned to illuminate them. The MSS. still unfinished in Florentine ateliers when Matthias died in 1490 were acquired by others.

Royal patronage extended to bookbinding. There were gilded leather bindings with floral designs framed by blind-stamped scroll-work and the royal arms on the boards. Edges were gilded and chased. Other volumes were covered in brocade, silk or crimson velvet with finely wrought bosses and clasps of silver. The textile bindings mostly perished with time.

After Suleiman entered Buda in 1526 much of the collection was transferred to Constantinople. The books returned by Sultans in the 19th century had been rebound in Turkish style. Other books were burned after the recapture of Buda in 1686 when 300 volumes were taken from the palace to Vienna where they remain. These were never part of the royal collection of which the surviving few hundred of the original volumes are now scattered among libraries in thirteen countries.

For an annotated illustrated catalogue of 180 known Corvinian manuscripts see C. Csapardi's 'Bibliotheca Corviniana', Budapest, 1969.

Corvinus Press: a private press founded in 1936 by the late Viscount Carlow. Editions were small and the work largely experimental.

In 1945 the equipment was acquired by the *Dropmore Press*, q.v.

Cosmocolor: the trade name of a British system for making high quality colour reproduction sets with good detail and resolution. Colour transparencies are the input, and the output is in the form of colour corrected screened three or four colour separations, negatives or positives, which are ready for immediate letterpress blockmaking or lithographic platemaking.

Costeriana: the name given to fragments of Latin grammars and a few other early works supposed to have been printed in Holland prior to Gutenberg's invention. In the absence of acceptable proof the claim for Dutch priority is largely based on two statements: the first, by *Ulrich Zel*, q.v., quoted in the 'Cologne Chronicle' of 1499, is that the art of printing in Mainz had been 'pre-figured' in a simpler form in editions of Aelius Donatus made at Haarlem about 1440. The second, printed in the 'Batavia' of Hadrianus Junius, Leyden, 1588, elaborates the foregoing by adding the name of Laurens Janszoon Coster (*c.* 1370–1440) who in the 1430s was living in Haarlem, as the one who made letters of lead, later of tin, and used thick ink to print on one side of a leaf only before pasting the blank sides of two leaves together. The statement adds that one of Coster's assistants, *Johann Fust*, q.v., stole his master's tools and equipment and took them to Mainz, there to print on his own account.

None of the surviving undated fragments, mostly recovered from the lining of bindings made in the 1470s, is identified by the name of printer or place.

Another undated work linked with the Costeriana fragments as being pre-Gutenbergian, is the 'Doctrinale' of Alexander Gallus. Evidence of its early existence in printed form comes from the diary of Jean de Robert, Abbot of St Aubert in Cambrai, which records his purchase at Bruges in 1446 and 1451 of copies of the 'Doctrinale' *jete en molle*, (i.e. *jetté en moule*, or cast in a mould). See also *Cracow fragments, donat, eponymous press, Gutenberg, metallography* (2), *Schöffer*.

Cosway bindings: richly-tooled morocco bindings having one or more miniatures, painted sometimes on ivory, set in one or both boards. A sheet of glass may protect the painting.

These bindings first appeared in the early years of the 20th century, and J. H. Stonehouse (1864–1937), manager for the London bookseller Henry Sotheran commissioned *Rivière*, q.v., to produce them.

From 1912 the paintings, which were mostly portrait miniatures, were the work of Miss C. B. Currie, and followed the style of water-colours done by Richard Cosway (1740–1821), many of which had been used for snuff-box and trinket-box lids. Miss Currie, who died in 1940, also painted fore-edges under the gilding.

cottage binding: a 17th-century style of book decoration popular in England (especially in the workshops of *Mearne* q.v.), in which the framework of the design tooled on the cover may be said to resemble a gable.

Cotton, Sir Robert Bruce, 1571-1631: a statesman, bibliophile and antiquarian. As early as 1588 he began buying books for the library he formed in his house at Westminster, and he continued to enlarge the collection until his death. Cotton was a founder-member of the Antiquarian Society (fl.1572–1604). He and his friends were anxious to ensure the preservation and collection in one place of the country's ancient historical records. Had such a collection as his not been assembled when it was much material would have been irretrievably dispersed in the troubled 17th century.

His possession of the *c.* 5th century Genesis and the *Lindisfarne Gospels*, q.v., is well known, but he also had the most important surviving manuscripts of pre-Conquest England, particularly the *Anglo-Saxon Chronicle*, q.v., Bede's 'Historia Ecclesiastica', King Alfred's translation of Orosius' 'Historia universalis', the unique manuscripts of 'Beowulf' and 'Sir Gawain and the Green Knight' and so on.

He acquired quantities of State Papers from the time of Henry VIII to James I, his manner of doing so being thought questionable even by his contemporaries. Nonetheless, recognizing the importance of his efforts at preservation many of his antiquarian friends bequeathed manuscripts to him.

A catalogue partly written by him records that in 1621 the library already included the major works. He is known to have been generous in lending his books.

In 1731, when his library was stored at Ashburnham House, Westminster, a fire destroyed or damaged over two hundred of the State Papers, deeds, abbey chartularies, as well as the Genesis. In 1753 the balance of the collection was acquired by the British Museum where, during the last two centuries many of the damaged volumes have been restored.

Cottrell, Thomas, fl.1757–85: a London typefounder who served his apprenticeship with the first Caslon before opening his own foundry. In his day he was notable for a fount of two-line Engrossing in imitation of the law hand used for legal documents; for a fount of Domesday characters; and for his refurbishing on behalf of William Bowyer the elder of the Anglo-Saxon types (cut from drawings by Humphrey Wanley) which had been used in 1715 for Mrs Elstob's 'Anglo-Saxon Grammar'.

Nine years after Cottrell's death his foundry was bought by *Robert Thorne*, q.v.

couch: 1. the board on which sheets of leaf are pressed in hand-made papermaking. See *leaf* (2). To couch is thus the action of lifting the sheets on to the board.

2. the felt blanket on to which sheets of partly dried leaf are transferred for drying into sheets of paper.

3. the roll from which the wet web on the paper machine is transferred unaided from the wire to the next section.

coucher: 1. the craftsman who lifts the newly formed (and still wet) sheet of paper from the mould in which it has been made, and skilfully transfers it to the couch board on which he builds up a *post*, q.v. See also *upper end boy*.

2. an obsolete term for a large book meant to rest on a table or stand, especially a chartulary, register, or antiphonary.

counter: 1. the inside area of a type-face, e.g. the centre of an 'o' the space between the vertical strokes of an 'n', etc. This is so called because the steel punch used to stamp the matrix is often counter-punched to form these areas.

2. an automatic device incorporated with printing and folding machines and the like for the purpose of recording the quantity of sheets produced.   (LK)

counter-etching: a stage in the preparation of lithographic printing plates, immediately after graining and before transferring the image, whereby the plates are sensitized or counter-etched. A zinc plate is washed in running water and then put in a solution of alum, nitric acid and water. The nitric acid will attack the metal and break up the film of zinc oxide, while the alum deposits a layer of water-insoluble aluminium sulphate. This aluminium salt is more sensitive to the image-forming materials than the original zinc surface.

counter-mark: a watermark often embodying the papermaker's initials which is placed in the second half of the sheet opposite the normal *watermark*, q.v.

courtesy book: a work of guidance on the varied accomplishments which ladies and gentlemen of fashion and breeding might be expected to have. Education, marriage, dress, recreations, behaviour and conversation were among the topics dealt with. There was a manuscript 'Boke of curtasye' in circulation in England about 1450, and an early printed one was 'Decor puellarum', Venice, Jenson, 1471.

Caxton printed a courtesy book, *c.* 1477 and such books remained popular in England, France, Italy and America until the end of the 18th century. Their tradition has been continued in the various books of etiquette published in the 20th century. Notable was Thomas Hoby's 'The courtyer', 1561, a translation from the Italian of Baldessare Castiglione, which inspired other writers.

'Advice to lovers . . . shewing them how to demean themselves so as not to miscarry in the grand affair of love', London, 1680; 'A vindication of man's natural right of sovereign authority over woman . . .', London, 1739; and 'Advice from a lady of quality to her children in the last stages of a lingering illness', Boston, 1796, are among the 1,500 titles listed in V. B. Heltzel's 'Check list of courtesy books in the Newberry Library', Chicago, 1942.

courtesy terms: special discounts off the published prices of books allowed by publishers, wholesalers and booksellers to their own employees, to the press and to members of allied trades. Such discounts do not customarily exceed those available to the retail trade except in the case of publishers' employees purchasing the publications of their own firms.

Court hand: a general term for all handwriting, other than *book* and *text hands*, qq.v., used in England from the 12th–17th century for business, accounts, proceedings, memoranda etc. In the 18th century the term applied only to legal hands. (A Court was an English administrative department.) See also *calligraphy*.

covenant of forbearance: an arrangement made between Oxford University and the Stationers' Company in 1637 whereby in return for an annual payment of £200 the University would cease to print certain privileged books. See also *comprint*.

cover: the paper, board, cloth or leather (used singly or combined) to which the body of a book is secured by glue and thread. The cover of a machine-bound book is called a *case*.

coverage: the degree to which the fibres of paper are covered and concealed by a coating. See also *coated papers*, *smoothness*.

cover board: book covering material made by pasting together two sheets of *cover paper*, q.v.

covering : 1. in hand binding, the fitting of covering material (usually leather) to the body of a book after lacing on the boards.
2. the mechanical securing of prepared covers to machine-sewn books, known as *casing-in*.
3. gluing a cloth cover solidly to the first and last pages of a book and over the spine. It is then trimmed. The cover is sometimes stiffened by a very thin cardboard lining, and there may or may not be endpapers. The style is suitable for school textbooks and is known as *limp flush*. Cf. *wrappering*.

cover paper: strong thick paper used as covers for booklets, brochures, etc. It is available in many colours and with plain or embossed surface finishes. The best are made from esparto.

cover title: the title of a book as stamped or lettered on the spine of a book. This may be an abbreviation of the full title.

Cowper, Edward, 1790–1852: a London mechanical engineer, printer, and sometime partner of *Augustus Applegath*, q.v., with whom he was associated in improvements to König's perfecting press. In 1816 he patented curved stereo plates for use on his rotary perfector on which four (on later models two) drums ferried the sheet from the first to the second impression cylinder; he also invented an ink-distributing table in 1818, and about 1839 developed the small *bellows press*, q.v., known as the *Parlour*.

crabs: a colloquialism for copies of a book returned by the bookseller to the publisher.

Crabtree: see *Mann*.

Cracherode, Clayton Mordaunt, 1730–99: a bibliophile of wealth and taste who formed a library of 4,500 volumes. Included were many first printed editions of classics, the Mainz Catholicon, Dante's 'Divine Comedy' (Florence, 1481) etc. Roger Payne was commissioned to rebind many of his books.

Cracherode bequeathed his library to the British Museum where it was the first library to be kept distinct and not dispersed among the collections.

Cracow fragments: portions of five printed leaves, belonging to the Jagiellonian University Library of Cracow, Poland. In the catalogue of the library's incunabula (1900) they appeared simply as 'Donati fragmenta'. They attracted considerable attention in 1937, however, when loaned to Dr Carl Wehmer, principal editor of the 'Gesamtkatalog der Wiegendrucke', for documentation.

Wehmer found the fragments were printer's proofs, all pulled on leaves taken from an account book which had been used by a cloth merchant of Mainz for business transacted between 1383 and 1393. This book had apparently turned up as waste in a Mainz printing shop. The five leaves were printed in an early state of the 36-line Bible type: three were from a Donatus grammar; the fourth was from a Bible, apparently 40-line; while the fifth was part of an astrologer's planetary table for January and February of an unspecified year. This last proved to be identical with fragments of an astronomical calendar discovered at Wiesbaden in 1901. The Berlin Astronomische Rechen-Institut had declared the Wiesbaden fragments to be planetary tables for 1448, leading one to infer that they were printed in 1447. If this were so, then the Cracow leaves belonged to the same year. This had upset all theories that Gutenberg's invention was dated 1454.

Gutenberg's 42-line Bible was completed by 1456, and the 36-line Bible by 1461 (or a little earlier). The Cracow Bible fragment was apparently set from an independent manuscript, and judged from its type vis-à-vis the 36-line version must have been printed about 1458. Experts also assigned the Donatus fragments to 1458. There remained the calendar.

Dr Wehmer, aided by authorities on medieval astrology, concluded that such tables were not intended for scientists but for popular travelling astrologers to whom it would matter little that their tables were ten years out of date. Thus 1454 may still be considered as the earliest date when printing from movable type began.

See Carl Wehmer, 'Mainzer Probedrucke in der Type des sogenannten Astronomischen Kalenders für 1448', Munich, Leibniz Verlag, 1948.

cradle: a bow-shaped steel rocker with a toothed edge used to roughen the surface of a copper mezzotint plate so that an even and deep grain is given to the entire surface. The cradle is drawn over the plate in one direction until the whole has been treated. The rocking is then repeated in another direction, and continued in several directions, determined by means of a special composing stick.

The invention of the cradle is attributed to Abraham Blooteling, 1672, who in any case perfected the technique of its use. Before this time graining was done in a more primitive way and even today an artist will do the preliminary roughening of the plate with sandpaper, a roulette, or a sand jet blower. See also *mezzotint.* (GU)

cradle book: see *incunabulum.*

craft bookbinding: or *hand binding,* being the processes listed under *forwarding* and *finishing,* qq.v., as well as the repair and restoration of books. There are currently two categories of craft binder: those whose main interest is in decorating the covers, and those who consider books as three-dimensional and articulated objects intended for preservation and use. Among British craftsmen *S. M. Cockerell, Bernard Middleton, Roger Powell* and *Peter Waters* typify the second.

Cramoisy, Sébastien, 1585–1669: a Parisian printer and publisher who was appointed first director of the Imprimerie Royale upon its establishment in the Louvre in 1640.

Cranach, Lucas, 1472–1553: a German painter, also a wood-cutter. His real name was Müller or Sunder, but he was called Cranach after his Bavarian birthplace Kronach. He worked in Bavaria and Austria before settling in Wittenberg where he employed a number of assistants, among others being his sons *Hans* (1500–37) and *Lucas,* jun. (1515–86). His work was mostly for religious books some of which bear his mark of a winged serpent with a ring in its mouth. Cranach was one of the most important and influential book illustrators of his day. He experimented with colour printing and also in copperplate engraving, a medium he chose for two portraits of Luther (1520–21) which were extensively circulated in pamphlets. (With GU)

Cranach-Presse: the private press planned at Weimar in 1912 by Harry Graf von Kessler, a diplomatist, politician and patron of the arts who was born in Paris in 1868. His advisers and helpers included Anton Kippenberg of the Insel-Verlag and a group of Englishmen associated with the graphic arts movement, notably Emery Walker, Eric Gill, Edward Gordon Craig, J. H. Mason and Gage Cole (a pressman from the Doves Press). Paper known as Maillol-Kessler Bütten as well as silk-paper for special copies came from a mill set up for the purpose.

The first book, prepared just before World War I, was an edition of Virgil's 'Eclogues'. This was eventually published in three editions in 1926 and

1927. During World War I Henry van de Velde managed the press. The most celebrated of the small output issued between 1926 and 1931 was an edition of 'Hamlet' with woodcuts by Craig, issued in German, 1929, and in English, 1930. Edward Johnston began designing the special Cranach Textura type in 1913 and the punches, begun by E. P. Prince, were finished by G. T. Friend. The press binder was Otto Dorfner. Nothing was published after 1931 and the printing equipment was sold. Kessler died in Paris in 1937. See R. Müller-Krumbach, 'Harry Graf Kessler und die Cranach-Presse in Weimar', Hamburg, 1970.

Crantz, Martin: see *Gering, Ulrich.*

crash: a loose-weave binding cloth.

crash finish: a variety of paper having a surface like coarse linen; it can be used in offset printing.

Crawford, Alexander William, twenty-fifth Earl of, 1812–80: a Lancashire bibliophile who by 1860 had established a library of 100,000 volumes at Haigh Hall. It was known as the *Bibliotheca Lindesiana.*

Much of it was dispersed in a series of sales in 1887, 1889 and 1924. In 1900 his collection of manuscripts was acquired for the John Rylands Library in Manchester and the important collection of books on astronomy was given in 1890 to the Royal Observatory in Edinburgh. See 'Bibliotheca Lindesiana', Aberdeen, 1910–13, in eight volumes, and N. Barker, 'Bibliotheca Lindesiana', Quaritch for the Roxburghe Club, 1978.

Rose Mary Crawshay Prize: a prize founded in 1888 by R. M. Crawshay as an annual award for writings on Byron, Keats, or Shelley. Since 1915 the scheme has been administered by the British Academy and the scope altered: it is awarded to a woman writer of any nationality for a work on English literature written or published within three years preceding the date of the award. (Preference is still given to a work on Byron, Keats or Shelley.) The amount is £100.

creasing: 1. a linear indentation made by machine in thick paper to provide a hinge. This makes for neater hand folding.

2. a printing fault seen as deep creases which may occur when paper is not stored at the correct humidity, or through other causes.

Cresci, Gianfrancesco, fl.1552–72: of Milan. Appointed a scriptor to the Vatican Library in 1556 and to the Sistine in 1558. He was the last of the great Italian writing masters, publishing specimens in 'Essemplare', printed by Blado, Rome, 1560, and 'Il perfetto scrittore', 1570. One of his styles of writing featured ascenders curving to the right with a thickened terminal stroke. This was later known as *cancellaresca testeggiata.*

Cretté, Georges, b. 1893: a Parisian artist-binder who first studied and worked in the Marius Michel atelier. For the skilful interplay of gold fillets on some of his work he has been called 'maître des filets'.

Creuzevault, Henri: a 20th century Parisian de luxe bookbinder noted for the abstract designs of coloured leathers which typify much of his work no less than for the doublures and end-leaves of black deerskin, cloth or suede which he favoured. He has now ceased binding.

criblé: minute punctures or depressions made in surfaces of wood or metal. De Vinne describes the process as being intended partly to offset the impossibility of obtaining a solid black background due to the imperfections of early presswork. Criblé backgrounds can be used to lighten borders which would appear too dark in relation to the text area of a page were they printed solid black.

criblé initials: decorated initials used at the beginnings of chapters, notably by the 16th-century French printer Geofroy Tory, in which the capital appears on an all-over ground of small dots or sieve-like pattern.

criss cross row: an alternative name for a *horn book,* q.v., which generally included the Paternoster and began and ended with Christ's cross. They were sold in considerable numbers by chapmen. See A. Tuer, 'History of the horn-book', Leadenhall Press, 1897.

Crivelli, Taddeo, fl.1452–76: one of the leading manuscript painters of the Italian Renaissance. In Ferrara he worked with other artists on the glorious Bible of Borso d'Este (now in the Estense Library, Modena), and after 1471 he moved to Bologna. See also *map printing.*

Crom, Matthew: the printer of Antwerp from whose press the Matthew Bible was issued in 1537 and a New Testament in 1538 as well as other books for the English book trade. In his later years he was an associate of *Steven Mierdman,* q.v., to whom his printing material passed.

Cromberger, Jakob, fl.1503–37: a German printer of Seville who worked for a time in Evora and Lisbon. He was noted for the fine books he issued, mostly essays, romances, poetry etc. In 1527 his son Johann (or Juan) succeeded him. In 1539 the latter sent a press and a printer, Juan Pablos, to Mexico where he printed eight works: one of these, 'Ordinarium sacri ordinis heremitarum Sancti Augustini', 1556, contained the first music printed in America.

Cromer Greek Prize: a prize founded by the first Earl of Cromer, being a biennial award of £150 for the best essay on the culture of ancient Greece. It is administered by the British Academy, subjects of Britain or Eire under thirty-five years the December preceding the award being eligible.

Crompton Bequest: a fund established by the late R. H. Crompton to assist the publication of works of merit and permanent worth which would not otherwise be published due to the unlikelihood of their being financially profitable. Awards are made by the trustees, the Society of Authors.

cropped: said of a book which has had its margins unduly trimmed. They are said to *bleed*.

Cropper: the popular name of the jobbing platen press manufactured by H. S. Cropper & Co. of Nottingham where production began in 1867. It was sold as the *Minerva*, and was very much an improved version of Gordon's *Franklin* press of 1856. Cropper presses were widely used in Victorian England and it was claimed that more than 9000 had been sold within twelve years.

cross: the following forms of cross are available as type:

⊕	*Manx (wheel) cross*
✝	*Greek*
✝	*Latin*
⊤	*St Anthony, or Tau*
✕	*St Andrew, or saltire*
卐	*Swastika, or Fylfot*
☦	*Patriarchal*
☥	*Papal*
✠	*St George, or Cross patée*
✴	*Maltese*
☨	*Cross of Lorraine*
✣	*Cross crosslet*

cross-bars: bars used to divide a chase into sections so as to lock up the pages more securely.

cross-grained morocco: goatskin having diagonally crossed lines produced artificially.

cross-heads: subsection or paragraph headings or numerals printed across the page and centred in the body of the text from which they are separated by one or more lines of space. They normally mark the first subdivision of a chapter. See also *sub-heads*.

cross reference: a reference from one part of a book to another where the same subject is dealt with, probably under an alternative name or a related aspect.

crown: 1. a standard size of printing paper, 15 in. by 20 in.
  2. the camber from the centre to the ends of a calender roll. See also *bowls*.

crowner: an item of publishers' publicity supplied to booksellers for use in counter or shop window displays. It is made of board, of varying size and shape, and is positioned over a book (or pile of one title) to draw attention by arrestingly designed printed or drawn wording. Cf. *streamer*.

crown octavo: a book size, 7½ in. by 5 in. In the U.K. the metric equivalent is 186 by 123 mm. See *British book sizes*.

CRT photosetting: a term referring to machines which utilize a *cathode ray tube* to project their final product on to film or paper. There are two main groups: those which store the whole of the character set in digital bits such as Digiset, Videocomp, Photon 7000 CRT/APS4, and those which contain visible characters which are scanned and reproduced on the CRT such as the *Linotron* range, q.v., and the Crosfield Magnaset. See also *Intertype Fototronic CRT*.

crushed Levant: large-grained goatskin, used for book covers. The surface is crushed before use, and after covering, the book is polished until smooth.

crystal: an album of book jackets. Several clear foil envelopes, each displaying jackets side by side, are secured by rings to the inner fold of a protecting cover. Sales representatives take them on overseas promotion tours.

crystallization: a printing fault, seen as a mottled or uneven effect, which may occur when using two or more colours on a letterpress working. This indicates that the first ink has been allowed to dry so hard by oxidation that it will not properly receive a subsequent impression. The trouble may be overcome by adding an ink solvent to the overprinting ink which will soften the crystallized first impression. Also known as *trapping*.

Cuala Press: an Irish private press founded in 1903 by Elizabeth Corbet Yeats as part of a group of craft industries for women. Until 1908 it was known as the *Dun Emer Press*, q.v., and in 1924 the press was moved from Dundrum to Dublin.

The press was largely concerned with the Irish literary movement. Among the authors of books and broadsides, issued in editions of between 50 and 300 copies, were MacNeice, Masefield, Pound, Synge, and Yeats. Writing in 1933 the poet W. B. Yeats said 'My sister's books are like an old family magazine. A few hundred people buy them all and expect a common theme.'

When Elizabeth Yeats died in 1940 the press was managed by the poet's wife until 1948 when the publication of books ceased. She died in 1968. In 1969 the press was revived, and in 1971 the Irish University Press began printing the entire output of the Dun Emer and Cuala presses. See L. Miller, 'The Dun Emer Press, later the Cuala Press', Dolmen, 1973.

cuir bouilli: animal skins without any oil dressing which were scalded in very hot water and resins. (In spite of the name they were not boiled.) As early as the 9th century they were found suitable, without boards, for covering books. It was possible to shape the damp leather over a wooden die, or alternatively to mark the outline of a design into the skin and then hammer it into relief. In drying, the skin hardened and retained its shape. Final dressing with wax or resin would assist this and act as a preservative. As used in the 14th century the background was punched, making it slightly sunk and leaving the design in relief. Motifs were mythical animals and interlaced foliage.

Leather so treated was extensively used in Europe for all manner of objects, not only book covers, thus, for example, Chaucer writes: 'His jambeaux (shin-guards) were of quyrboilly' in 'Canterbury Tales', (Sir Thopas, line 875).

cuir ciselé: a manner of decorating leather-bound books widely practised in the 15th century in south east Germany, Austria and Spain. The design was outlined on dampened leather by scoring it with a sharp tool or knife. A relief effect was then obtained by punching and deepening the leather round the outline. Sometimes the design was hammered from the back, giving an embossed effect. More recent, and superb, were examples made in France by Henri Marius Michel, c. 1866. See also *Jewish leather cutting*.

cul-de-lampe: the French term for a *head-* or *tail-piece*, qq.v.

cumdach: a jewelled and elaborately decorated box used in late 9th-century Ireland for keeping manuscript books. Also known as a *book shrine*. See also *Cathach Psalter*.

cum licentia: a Latin phrase appearing on the title-page of a book (or on a *licence leaf*, q.v.) to indicate that it is published by permission of some secular or ecclesiastical authority. See also *imprimatur, nihil obstat*.

cum privilegio regali: a Latin phrase found in the imprints of books printed in England during the 16th century. Henry VIII's proclamation of 1538 stated that no book in English was to be printed unless the text had been approved by officials acting in the King's name. The words *cum privilegio regali* signified this approval. The proclamation also required the addition to the formula of the words *ad imprimendum solum* to indicate that the printer had been granted the exclusive right to print the text. See also *privilege*.

Cumulative Book Index: one of the most important bibliographical works for the American book trade. This was established in 1898 by the H. W. Wilson Co. of New York as a monthly list of U.S. publications; since 1929 it has claimed to list all books printed in English wherever issued. The annual volumes are cumulated over periods of years, entries being arranged in one alphabetical sequence of author, title and subject.

cumulative list: a list of books which combines material previously published in separate lists.

cuneiform writing: wedge-shaped symbols (Lat. *cuneus* (wedge), *forma* (form or shape). This name is given to the system of writing used in varying forms and at different times from c. 4,000 to 100 BC by a number of Near Eastern peoples (Akkadians, Assyrians, Babylonians, Hittites, Persians and Sumerians).

Inscriptions were impressed with a *stylus* into clay tablets. Early writing was *pictographic*, i.e. each character represented an idea, not a letter, but by about 600 BC Assyrian syllabaries had been made. Cuneiform continued in occasional use for legal contracts and astronomy until c. AD 75.

Several scribal conventions used in later manuscripts and incunabula were already developed: thus an early extant use of *catchwords*, q.v., is on clay tablets made for the Neo-Assyrian king Ashurbanipal (668–626 BC) for whose library at Nineveh earlier tablets were copied. If a text continued on several tablets they were numbered and had a linking catchword to the next incised at the foot of each. The last tablet of a text traditionally ended with a *colophon*, q.v., in which references to gaps in the archetype or difficulties in interpreting it were noted.

Glossed and *interlinear* texts were made, as were word lists giving in parallel columns Sumerian ideograms and their Neo-Assyrian equivalents. Many tablets from the king's collection are in the British Library.

cup: an alternative name for *bowl*, q.v.

Cura Pastoralis: a copy of the 'Regulae' of Pope Gregory I in a version translated from Latin into Old English. This was thought to be the work of King Alfred but is more probably that of scholars at his court. It is now in the Bodleian Library, Oxford.

Curatores Praeli Typographici: the body formed at the instigation of Richard Bentley (1662–1742), in 1698, to direct the affairs of the Cambridge University Press. This control is now exercised by a University committee; its members being known as the *Syndics*, q.v.

curiosa: a bibliophile's term for works in some degree indecent. See also *erotica, pornography*.

Curll, Edmund, 1675–1747: a London bookseller, publisher and pirate. His occasionally unethical publishing activities brought him into conflict with many in the literary world, particularly Pope in whose 'Dunciad' he is satirized. In 1716, 1721 and 1735 he was ordered to appear at the bar of the House of Lords. It was as a result of his publishing the works of the Duke of Buckingham that a resolution was passed making it a breach of privilege to print, without permission, 'the works, life, or last will of any lord of this house' (i.e. House of Lords). This remained in force until 1845.

Curll was also prosecuted for libel, pilloried and publicly reviled for some of his actions. See R. Straus, 'The Unspeakable Curll', Chapman & Hall, 1927.

cursive: a running script. After the mid-15th century the slowly written *lettera antiqua* used by early Italian manuscript copyists was gradually replaced by cursive variants of it. For the writing of books and texts by scholars and for other non-official purposes a small informal *lettera corsiva* had been used throughout the 15th century. This was quickly written, had many tied letters and ligatures, and was usually but not necessarily sloped. It was this speedy form of cursive which Griffo cut as a type face for Aldus Manutius in 1500. It was used to set whole books so that they could be small, and plain roman capitals were used with it. The source which inspired Griffo or Aldus remains unidentified, but it was not Plutarch's handwriting (a once-held misconception due to the misreading of a statement in the Aldine Plutarch of 1502 that the text was based on a manuscript in Plutarch's hand). In his book 'The script of humanism', 1963, Wardrop speculates on the influence *Sanvito*, q.v., may have had on Aldine's types. Other printers in Venice, Lyons, Erfurt and Paris were quick to copy the Aldine italic.

A non-literary style of humanistic cursive writing was contemporaneously used in Italy for diplomatic and official letters. Inevitably, in view of its purpose, it was more regular and formal and was written by specially appointed scriptors. This script was to become known as *lettera cancellaresca corsiva* or *lettera da brevi*: i.e. chancery cursive or Brief script. A chancery was and is an administrative office from which letters were sent and in which they were received and filed; a Brief was a papal letter of a special kind, tracing its origins to the pontificate of Boniface IX (1389–1404) at which time gothic cursive was used for writing them. The earliest known humanist cursive Brief is dated 1446, but although *cancellaresca corsiva* had been developed and perfected in the papal chancery since the pontificate of Pius II (1458–64) it was not until 1522 that one of its finest exponents, *Ludovico degli Arrighi*, q.v., published a book of engraved specimens of the script and gave it its name. He used upright roman or swash capitals with the minuscules.

It was this diplomatic script which inspired the first italic printing types of Rome. The master of *cancellaresca corsiva formata*, Arrighi, had an italic face cut by Lautizio de Bartholomeo dei Rotelli, goldsmith and seal-cutter of Perugia, in 1524. The several versions made for Arrighi have had considerable influence on present-day italic faces cut for use with old-face romans. Unlike the Aldine types they were intended for emphasis or display, not for setting complete texts. Indebted to Arrighi were Antonio Blado, Robert Estienne, Simon de Colines, Granjon and Garamont.

Monotype revivals based on chancery cursive are Bembo italic, 1923; Blado italic, 1924; and Arrighi (hand) 1925, (machine) 1929. See also *humanistic scripts, italic, letters – forms and styles*.

curtain bindings: a distinctive style of book cover decoration, particular to Spain, and apparently limited to the years 1814–33, although it was used in 1849 by Tomás Cobo. Fillets and gouges were used to tool patterns which simulated a draped curtain or pair of curtains. The design on upper and lower cover was not always the same. Curtains onlaid or inlaid in leathers of contrasting colours and also acid staining were used. They were in questionable taste, set no fashion, and scarcely rank as major bindings.

Curwen Press: a commercial printing establishment, included here because of the good taste, faultless workmanship and fitness for purpose of its output. It was founded in 1863 as the Tonic Sol-fa Press by the Rev. *John Curwen* (1816–80) of Plaistow to promote his movement of popular education through singing from music printed in Tonic Sol-fa notation. He was subsequently assisted by his sons *John Spencer Curwen* (1847–1916) as the publisher and *Joseph Spedding Curwen* (1949–1919) as the printer. The two businesses were separate.

Printing done prior to 1909 has been described as 'technically good but undistinguished and merely functional'. In that year *Harold Curwen* (1885–1949), youngest son of Joseph, joined the printing firm and assumed control in 1914. By this time the business was trading as 'Curwen Press'. Harold had learned printing in Leipzig (then a lively centre for experimental typography) and calligraphy under Johnston in London. He soon replaced unattractive types by Caslon, Imprint and Kennerley, and in 1918 commissioned Lovat Fraser to work for him.

In 1921 *Oliver Simon* (1895–1956) formally joined the press, setting out to develop bookwork. The brilliantly successful association of Curwen and Simon led to a steady flow of fine books as well as jobbing printing of outstanding quality. New types, flowers, borders and illustrations were commissioned from, among others, Van Krimpen, Rudolf Koch, Edward Bawden, Paul Nash and Graham Sutherland.

In 1933 the printing side at Plaistow of the music publishing firm J. Curwen & Sons Ltd became The Curwen Press Ltd with independent directors.

Among important publications on typography printed by the Curwen Press were the first four volumes of *The Fleuron*, and *Signature*, edited by Oliver Simon. After his death his brother *Herbert Simon* (1898–1974) led the firm until 1969. In 1958 a subsidiary company *Curwen Prints Ltd* began under Oliver's son Timothy, d. 1970, principally to stimulate the production of autolithography by such artists as Moore, Hepworth, Piper and Ceri Richards. In 1966 a London sales gallery was opened. See H. Simon, 'Song and words: a history of the Curwen Press', George Allen & Unwin, Ltd, 1973.

cushion: the quality of resiliency or compressibility of paper. If the fibres are *dead*, q.v., the finished paper will lack cushion.

cut: 1. a wood, copper or steel surface bearing a design cut or engraved in it. While formerly restricted to woodcuts, the term is loosely used for half-tones, zinc etchings or other illustrative letterpress material.
2. an illustration printed from the above.
3. an instruction to the process engraver that part of an original must not be reproduced.

cut ahead: said of reeled paper which has been slit into sheets so that while each has a watermark it does not fall in the same position on each. Usually watermarks are arranged in diagonal lines across the sheet, an arrangement known as *staggered watermark*. Cf. *cut to register*.

cut-away: an illustration of a machine in which part of the outer cover or casing is shown cut away to show internal details.

cut back binding: another term for *adhesive* or *unsewn binding*, q.v. The name is appropriate because the folded and gathered sections are trimmed at the back leaving so many cut leaves to be stuck together.

cut edges: the three edges of a book which have been cut solid by machine so that all pages on each are flush. Cf. *trimmed edges*.

cut flush: said of a book which has its cover and page edges quite even, cutting being done after the cover is attached. Also known as *flush boards* or *trimmed flush*.

Cuthbert Gospels: the *Lindisfarne Gospels*, q.v., which were written in honour of St Cuthbert.

cut in-boards: said of a book which has its head, tail and fore-edge trimmed after the boards have been laced on by the sewing cords. Cf. *cut out-of-boards*.

cut-in heads: paragraph or section headings set in a bold or otherwise distinguishing type in the text, i.e. not in the margin.

cut-in side notes: notes to a work which are set in the text, the type being built around them on three sides. See also *marginal notes*.

cut-off: on web-offset and gravure machines, the length of the printed area along the web of paper. This is fixed by the relative positions of plate cylinder, folder, cutter etc. The size of cut-off determines the class of printing job for which a machine is suitable.

cut out half-tone: synonymous with *outline half-tone*, q.v.

cut out-of-boards: said of a book which has its edges cut or trimmed before affixing the boards. The latter are used for positioning during the cutting of head and tail edges. This method is used when boards are not laced on but fit closely in the grooves. (A hollow back is needed.) Cf. *cut in-boards*.

cut the line: a former printing trade expression which meant that if a member of a *companionship*, q.v., ran out of copy or type the whole companionship stopped work until fresh supplies enabled him to continue.

cutting: the separation by slitting in the printing machine or in a guillotine of a printed sheet which contains more than one job, e.g. in *work and turn* machining where each sheet has two perfected impressions which must be cut before folding can proceed. Cf. *trimming.*

cutting cylinder: a cylinder bearing a knife and forming part of a rotary press. It is used for cutting each copy from the web. See also *cutting stick* (2).

cutting machine: see *guillotine.*

cutting-off: a stage in *machine-sewing,* q.v., when a row of books sewn as a unit must be separated prior to subsequent processes.

cutting stick: 1. the strip of wood on which a guillotine knife descends when cutting.

2. the strip of wood, rubber or composition fitted to the folding roller of a rotary web machine. During cutting the knife presses against it.

cut to register: said of watermarked paper which has been cut so that the watermark appears in the same position in each sheet. Cf. *cut ahead.*

cut to waste: the trimming of standard-size sheets of paper to fit a particular printing job. The offcuts are waste.

Cuzin: a Parisian binder who began working about 1864. He revived the 15th and 16th century manner of sewing on raised cords, and his forwarding was excellent. His gilding, more restrained than that of *Trautz,* q.v., was generally also less derivative. His dentelles were notable.

cylinder dressing: the packing used for *dressing the cylinder,* q.v.

cylinder machine: a standard papermaking machine invented in 1805 by Joseph Bramah and considerably improved by John Dickinson in 1809. The sheet is formed on the surface of a cylindrical wire mould which revolves in a vat of stuff, the water draining through the mesh. The partly-formed sheet is then transferred to a felt with the aid of a roll which rides on the surface of the felt and presses it against the sheet, the subsequent stages of its manufacture being similar to those employed in making paper on the *Fourdrinier,* q.v.

cylinder press: a printing press in which the forme is carried on a flat bed under a paper-bearing cylinder for an impression to be made at the point of contact. The cylinder revolves against the forme with the same peripheral speed as the lateral speed of the

forme. The first cylinder machine in Britain was built in 1812 by Friedrich König.

Designs vary and include principally the *stop-cylinder machine* in which the cylinder is stationary during the return of the bed; the *two-revolution machine* in which the cylinder revolves continuously at a constant speed making one revolution during the forward movement of the bed and one during its return (for the latter the cylinder is raised to clear the forme and the sheet is delivered); the *single-revolution machine* in which the cylinder revolves at a constant speed, making half a turn for each of the movements of the bed.   (GU)

See also *front delivery, letterpress machines.*

cyrillic: the name given to one of the scripts used for writing the Slavonic dialect, now known as Old Bulgarian, taken by the brothers Cyril (827–869) and Methodius from Salonika to Moravia. It was there used to set down evangelical works for the early Slavonic Church including a translation of the Bible. There were two alphabets: *Glagolitic,* probably deriving from a modified non-cursive Greek minuscule hand, and *Cyrillic,* which to a basis of twenty-four Greek uncial letters has nineteen new signs for sounds peculiar to Slavonic. Although named after Cyril opinions differ as to which, if not indeed both, he created. Glagolitic was soon abandoned, surviving today only for the Slavonic liturgies of certain Balkan communities. The original Cyrillic, in the modified version known as *Poluustav,* remains as the liturgical script of the Eastern Church and served as the basis of the first *cyrillic types* used in the 15th and 16th centuries by the Russians, Serbs, Ukrainians and Bulgarians. They are known as Old Church Slavonic (available today as Monotype Series 597).

The use of cyrillic type dates from 1491 at Cracow where *Sweipold Veyl (Szwajpolt Fiol* in Polish) of Neustadt an der Esch used type cut by Ludolf Borchtorp of Brunswick to print four church books in 1491, the Oktoich (a collection of hymns designed for eight-part choral singing) and also a Book of Hours in 1493. Similar types were also used at the Obograd monastery near Cetinje (Yugoslavia) to print the Osnoglasnik but their use in Russia did not begin until 1564 (see *Fëdorov*), and not until the 18th century is there evidence of typefounding in Moscow. Type was imported from Holland and even there only two Dutch founders are known from surviving specimens of the 1690s to have had cyrillic type. They were the widow of Dirk Voskens and J. A. Schmidt, both of Amsterdam.

In 1698 Peter the Great granted a privilege to the Amsterdam printer Jan Hendrik Thesing to print for him in cyrillic. Thesing was assisted by a Belorussian from Latvia called Ilya Fedorovich Kopievich who remodelled and simplified certain letters to make an early form of Russian. In 1700 Kopievich assisted

Jan de Jongom who also printed a few Russian books for Peter. Very few of these Amsterdam books survive, but twenty-three are listed in Kopievich's bibliography, the first to be compiled. In 1698 the Dutch engraver Adrian Schönebe went to Moscow to train Russians in his art, being succeeded there in 1702 by his stepson Pitr Pikart. Peter the Great commissioned books on shipbuilding, military science and fortification, all with illustrations. Also of note was the work 'Symbols and emblems' printed by Heinrich Wetstein for Peter, with 840 copper engravings imported from Amsterdam, though most copies were lost in transit.

In 1708, when Dutchmen took punches and matrices from Amsterdam to Moscow, typecasting and printing there began with modern latinized russian type which is still known as *cyrillic*, although the older form continued in use for the printing of ecclesiastical works. Modernization was the result of Peter's decree that earlier types should be simplified and his decision to establish a state printing press in the new capital at St Petersburg where his 'civil alphabet' was used. The first book to show it was issued in 1713.

Cyrillic type was further simplified after the 1917 Revolution. Attempts made in 1921 and 1929 to replace cyrillic by roman were unsuccessful.

Cyrillic types were first used in England at Oxford in 1695, for a type specimen, and in 1696 for H. W. Ludolf's 'Grammatica russica'. They were from J. A. Schmidt, in the 1690s a typecutter of Amsterdam and formerly of Egenolff-Luther of Frankfurt.

See Appendix A for the modern Times Cyrillic. It is basically the Petrine version.

D

dabber: see *ink ball*.

da Carpi, Ugo, *c.* 1479–1533: a leading engraver of Venice and Rome associated with the method of making coloured woodcuts known as *chiaroscuro,* q.v., for which the Signoria at Venice granted him a privilege in 1516. In 1525 he issued 'Thesauro de scrittori', a compilation of scripts by Arrighi, Tagliente and Fanti. It was printed by Blado. Later editions included that of 1535 which was issued in facsimile by Nattali & Maurice in 1968.

dagger (or **obelisk**): a printer's sign † used in the text of a work as part of a recognized sequence of alternatives to superior letters or numbers to draw the reader's attention to a footnote. If placed before a person's name it denotes 'deceased'. See also *reference marks.*

Daguerre, Louis Jacques Mandé, 1787–1851: a French artist and inventor who interested himself in photography. In the 1820s he became well known as a result of a diorama he built in Paris. His efforts at photography were not really successful until 1829 when he entered into partnership with J. N. Niepce. After the latter's death in 1833 Daguerre invented the process which bears his name, *daguerreotype.* This was a means of making photographs on silver plates and is considered the first really practicable photographic method. (GU)
See H. & A. Gernsheim, 'Daguerre', Secker, 1956.

daguerreotype: a method of making and fixing a photographic image, invented in 1833 by L. J. M. Daguerre.

A silver plate or silvered copperplate exposed to iodine or bromine vapour is transformed on the surface into silver iodine or silver bromide respectively, thereby becoming light-sensitive. On exposure in a dark room the picture is developed in vaporized mercury which is deposited on the different parts of the plate in proportion to the amount of light influencing them. The plate is fixed in a solution of carbonate of soda and is often toned by gold chloride. Such daguerreotypes are unique in that they cannot be copied. The process was made public in 1839. In the 1850s it was superseded by a negative-positive

process by which any number of copies can be made. The few genuine daguerreotypes extant are considered fairly valuable. They are recognizable by the metal plate being reflecting, thus the picture with its soft and fine details appears positive only under certain light conditions; also the image is usually turned sideways. The image is very sensitive to any rubbing for which reason it is always kept mounted under glass with sealed airtight edges. (GU)

Dalziel, George, 1815–1902: a partner with his brother Edward (1817–1905) in the Camden Press, a wood-engraving business which they established in London in 1857, having worked there as engravers since the 1840s. They are remembered now for their series of illustrated 'gift books' which Routledge published for them in the mid-1860s.

dampeners: the cloth covered rollers on the *damping unit,* q.v., of a lithographic press.

damping: 1. the moistening of paper before using it in a hand-press to make the surface softer and more receptive to ink. The paper is laid between moist blotting or waste-paper, or sprinkled with water, the damping being followed by brushing. In earlier rotary presses damping was done by guiding the paper course over perforated steam rollers and then between smoothing rollers before printing.

2. the keeping moist of a lithographic plate. In a hand-press this is done with a sponge: in a machine press by means of damping rollers similar in construction to the inkers. The fluid used, known as *damping solution,* q.v., varies in composition according to the material used for the forme (stone, zinc, aluminium, magnesium, etc.)

The traditional method of applying a film of water to the litho-offset plate and rolling on the damping solution has the disadvantage that it is difficult to maintain the ink/water balance during long runs. An American alternative, successfully investigated in the mid-1970s, is to remove the damping rollers and fountain equipment and substitute a bank of nozzles to spray a fine air/water mist, not on to the plate, but on to two rollers running in with the *distributor rollers,* q.v. Each of up to eighteen nozzles in a spray unit has an

128

adjustable pump so that the discharge on particular areas of a plate can be controlled.

3. the damping with a sponge dipped in water of hand-set formes prior to breaking up the type for distribution.

damping paper: sheets of hand-made paper are moistened before printing. By reducing the hardness of the size this makes paper more receptive to ink and less likely to set-off. Also, the roughness and variations in thickness of dry paper call for greater pressure to obtain good sharp impressions than with damp sheets.

When preparing for the press piles of paper are interleaved with moistened *waterleaf*, q.v., one piece between every twenty sheets, and they stand for a few hours. They are then pressed. Printing should follow immediately, the floor being sprinkled with water so that sheets will not dry before they are back up. Printed sheets must then be dried to avoid mould.

damping solution: liquid used in the damping unit of a litho press. Formulas vary. An alternative to the normal solution of iso propyl alcohol calls for decreasing the wetting contact angle on the non-image areas of the plate and increasing the contact angle for ink. Ink-in-water emulsification is prevented and water-in-ink emulsification is reduced. Less water is used so the advantage of alcohol's high evaporation rate is not critical. Also known as *fountain solution*.

damping unit: a system of rollers for applying *damping solution*, q.v., to the non-image areas of a lithographic plate. The rollers in contact with the plate are covered with cloth or similar water-retaining material so that desensitization is maintained during printing. An alternative method of supply is to use banks of oscillating nozzles controlled from a panel. There are other methods. See also *fountain*.

dandy roll: a light hollow cylinder of stainless steel or phosphor bronze wire gauze which, in rotating above the partly formed web of paper, closes up the surface fibres. The dandy roll may be free running or powered and is usually placed between the first and second suction boxes of the Fourdrinier. Designs vary.

According to the weave of the wire gauze the impression left on the moving paper is either of ribs with parallel cross lines for *laid papers*, or the uniform effect of *wove paper*. If required, devices or monograms are worked into the gauze: they are made of wire which is soldered or sewn to it and serve to impress the *watermark* and *countermark*, qq.v

A *spiral-laid dandy roll* is one where the chain lines are along the length of the dandy and the laid lines run in the manner of a helix round the circumference.

Early models of the dandy roll, initially called a 'riding roll', were made in England by John and Christopher Phipps in 1825, by John Marshall in 1826, and by John Wilks in 1830.

Daniel Press: a precursor of the later private press movement. It was established by the Rev. C. H. O. Daniel in 1845 at Frome, then in 1876 at Oxford. Daniel revived the Fell types of the Oxford University Press. The Daniel Press ceased its activities in 1919 and is now used for student instruction in the Bibliography Room in the Bodleian Library. See 'Memorials of C. H. O. Daniel, with a bibliography of the Press, 1845–1919', Oxford, specially printed on the Daniel Press, 1921, repr. Dawson, 1974.

dark-room camera: a reproduction camera with the back portion let into the wall of a dark room so that dark slides are unnecessary. Modern dark-room cameras are automatic and mechanized and can be manoeuvred entirely from within the dark room.

Darlington Press: a private press established about 1768 at 'The Grange' (i.e. Blackwell Grange, near Darlington), the seat of George Allan (1736–1800). He was an enthusiastic printer and issued many pamphlets of antiquarian and topographical interest in addition to publishing the poetry and miscellaneous writings of his friends.   (With ML)

dash: 1. for decoration, a short strip of rule which may be plain or ornamented in several ways.

See also *border, french rule, rule, swelled rules*.

2. for punctuation, a short strip of rule cast in the following lengths: the two-em dash   ; the one em dash —— ; the en rule –; and the hyphen -. (Collins gives guidance on their usage.)

dates: when preparing copy for the printer the following principles for setting out dates are offered for guidance:

(a) 432 BC   AD 432   720 AH (i.e. the Muslim calendar in which the era begins from *al-hijra*, the date of Mohammed's flight from Mecca to Medina in AD 622.)

(b) Winter 1972/73

(c) 362/361 BC

(d) from 1968 to 1973: not from 1968–73

(e) from the 4th to 6th century: not 'centuries'

(f) between 1968 and 1973: not between 1968–73

(g) 9 October 1973.

Dawson, William: a printing machinery maker of Otley in Yorkshire. Assisted by an employee, *David Payne*, he made the first model of the *Wharfedale* stop-cylinder press about 1858. In 1864 he took Payne into partnership though their businesses were separate from 1866–1914 when their successors amalgamated. The Elliott firm was taken over in 1921, and now trades as Dawson, Payne and Elliott (although it is owned by Crabtree-Mann Ltd of Leeds).

The various types of printing press made by the Otley factory are used throughout the world. The sheet-fed rotary letterpress machine for wraparound plates which they successfully tested in 1959 was one of the pioneer models.

Day, Benjamin, 1838–1916: of New Jersey; the inventor in 1879 of *Ben Day tints*, q.v.

Day, John, 1522–84: born at Dunwich in Suffolk. He was a London printer, bookseller and typefounder who appears to have begun printing theological works about 1546 in association with William Seres. After 1549 he worked alone but spent some years in the Tower for having printed 'noythy bokes'. He resumed printing in 1557 and was an original freeman of the Stationer's Company and Master in 1580. He became one of the most important printers of the day. The high standard of his output was probably due to his employment of foreign refugee workmen of whom one, about 1576, was Gabriel Guyot, a Dutch typefounder whose family was connected with Plantin.

Day secured many valuable privileges and is remembered for his almanacs, ABC primers, psalms and the first English edition of Foxe's 'Book of martyrs', 1563, (entitled 'Actes and monuments of these latter and perillous dayes'). As this had over 2,000 folio pages and a copy was prescribed for every parish church the work was very profitable.

He was known for his efforts at music printing and his use of woodcut initials. He worked with roman and gothic types and about 1558 cut a fine double-pica roman with matching italic.

Day also printed 'De antiquitate Britannicae ecclesiae Cantuariensis' for Archbishop Parker on the latter's private press at Lambeth in 1572.

Of his twenty-two children, by two wives, only one, *Richard*, was a printer. After John Day's death his valuable rights, long enviously regarded by his rivals, were acquired for the *English Stock*, q.v. See C. L. Oastler, 'John Day: the Elizabethan printer', Oxford Bibliographical Society, 1975.

Daye, Stephen, fl.1638–48: an Englishman who worked the first press to be set up in North America. This had been taken from England by the Rev. Joseph Glover (of Sutton, Surrey) who died on the voyage and Daye and his son Michael had been engaged as pressmen. In late 1638 the press was erected in the house of Glover's widow who married Henry Dunster, first president of Harvard, at Cambridge, Mass. The first

publication of the press was 'The Oath of a Freeman', 1639, but no copy of this is known. The first book to be issued of which copies survive was 'The whole Booke of Psalmes, faithfully translated into English Metre', 1640. The book is also known as the *Bay Psalm Book* and there is a copy in the Bodleian Library, Oxford. (A facsimile reprint was issued in Chicago in 1956.)

From 1649 until it closed in 1692 the press was managed by Samuel Green. The original press was sold several times and is now preserved in the museum of the Vermont Historical Society. See G. P. Winship, 'The Cambridge Press, 1638–1692', Philadelphia, 1945.

dead: said of fibres which due to excessive action in the beater have had their strength and resilience destroyed.

dead line: a short line incised on the bed of a flat-bed cylinder press to guide the positioning of the forme. Should the latter be pushed over the line the grippers may damage the matter.

dead matter: type which has been printed and awaits distribution. See also *blocked up*, *live matter*, *standing type*.

Deberny and Peignot: the largest typefounding firm in France. Its origins can be traced to an association formed in 1827 by the novelist Honoré de Balzac, André Barbier, printer, and Jean-François Laurent, typefounder. They acquired material from the foundry established in 1748 by Joseph Gillé, but the business, which was primarily a publishing venture, failed in 1828. Laurent was then joined in setting up a foundry by *Alexandre de Berny* (1809–81) whose mother was a friend of Balzac. The partnership continued until 1848 when de Berny (by now Deberny) worked alone. The roman face he made at this time was considered less chilly in its effect on the printed page than the still popular Didot and Bodoni romans.

In 1877, on taking Charles Tuleu (d. 1881) into partnership, the firm was known as Deberny & Cie. Among the well-known designers who worked for them was Carlègle.

Amalgamation with the Parisian foundry Peignot & Fils, established in 1898 by *Gustave Peignot* (1839–99), took place in 1923. He had acquired the Pierre Leclerc foundry in 1868, incorporating with it a number of others. His sons Lucien (d. 1916) and Georges (d. 1915) gave new impetus to French type design. This began with a face by Eugène Grasset, 1899, and one by Georges Auriol, 1902. In 1912 the firm purchased the original matrices of Firmin Didot. Among faces well known outside France is the series Les Cochins which was begun in 1912.

The firm later operated a trade-setting house, made

composing-room equipment, and claimed to have the most complete collection of non-roman faces in the world. In 1950 they sponsored the invention of the *Photon*, q.v. Notable in the 1960s was the Univers range, designed by *Adrian Frutiger*, q.v., for which 40,000 punches were cut. In 1972 Deberny Peignot was acquired by *Haas*, q.v. See also *Baskerville*, *Cochin*.

decimal point: British 3·8, U.S.A. 3.8, Continent 3,8.

deckle, deckle strap: on the papermaking mould, the frame or border, usually of wood, which confines the paper pulp to the mould. On the papermaking machine, the strap on either side of the moving web which limits the lateral flow of the pulp and also controls the contour of the edge of the paper web. See also *deckle edge*.   (ML)

deckle edge: 1. the rough uneven edge of hand-made paper, caused by the pulp flowing between the frame and deckle of the mould. In machine-made papers this effect can be produced mechanically on the edges of the paper.

2. in bookbinding it is usual to leave the deckle edges of hand-made paper uncut as in the bound book they are thought to have a beauty of their own. As dust collects on them they are not very practical.

Declaration of Independence: see *Goddard, Mary Katharine*.

decorated papers: sheets of coloured paper, usually patterned, suitable for end-papers or for wrapping slim books.

By the end of the 17th century Germany was the centre of the decorated paper trade, particularly at Augsburg and Nuremberg, though dyed papers were known there in the 15th century. Some had patterns of flock put on glued paper. Dyed papers were made in Constantinople in the 16th century, often being dusted with gold or silver. Embossed coloured papers, known as *brocade papers*, were made chiefly at Augsburg in the 18th century, and popular later were paste papers for which dyed paste was worked into patterns by hand or block. See also *dutch gilt paper, Rizzi paper*. See A. Haemerle & O. Kirsch, 'Buntpapier', Munich, 1961.

Decoy Press: the publishing imprint chosen by Joseph Thorp, publicist and typographer, for the occasional illustrated pieces he issued about 1919. They were printed for him at the *Curwen Press*, q.v., to which he was a printing consultant. Thorp encouraged the directors of Curwen Press to employ artists such as Lovat Fraser and Edward Bawden on designing company brochures, publicity material and the like for the firm's customers.

dedication: in the 16th and 17th centuries, an inscription by the author in which he commended his book to the favour or patronage of a nobleman or eminent person. In modern practice an inscription of a less fulsome nature in which the author records his esteem for a person. The dedication is traditionally printed on the recto of the leaf following the title leaf. See F. B. Williams, Jr., 'Index of dedications and commendatory verses in English books before 1641', Bibliographical Society, 1962. See also *impensis*, *patron*.

dedication copy: a copy of a book given by its author to the dedicatee. It is also an *association copy*, q.v.

deep-etch half-tone: a half-tone plate from which the highlight dots of the screen have been removed from areas which are to appear as plain white paper on the printed sheet. The process is suitable for black and white wash drawings. An alternative is to paint out the highlight areas of the negative with photopaque before printing down instead of routing away the unwanted dots afterwards. Also known as *drop-out half-tone*.

deep-etch lettering: line lettering on a half-tone background. Black lettering on a white ground is attached in register as an overlay to the half-tone copy. This simplifies photography which calls for two negatives to be made: a screened one from continuous tone copy and a line one from the lettering. A contact positive of the former is adhered to the non-emulsion side of the half-tone negative. The combination is then exposed to a pre-sensitized metal plate for etching. Also known as *drop-out lettering* and *out-printing*.

deep-etch process: a method of making a *photolitho-graphic plate*, q.v., by photomechanical means. It was devised by Julius Bekk in 1930 for making a sub-surface image (0·008 mm). Also known as *positive reversal process*.

deep gold: the best quality leaf, used for lettering and tooling on hand bound books, as distinct from the cheaper *pale gold* leaf which is used for edge gilding.

deeply-etched half-tone: a half-tone plate in which the spaces between the dots have been etched to extra depth, but without removing the highlights. This gives finer detail to the highlight areas when printing on rough paper.

deerskin: the grey leather of deer or doeskin used by medieval monastic binders to cover wooden book boards. It was for this purpose that about the year 850 Geoffroi Martel, count of Anjou, reserved a tenth of the skins from deer killed on his lands for the bindery of an abbey he founded at Saintes. Deerskin was later superseded by calf, sheep or goatskin. See also *cheveril, forel bindings*.

definitive edition: the final authoritative edition of an author's complete writings.

deflaker: a pulping machine for the final defibring of wet slush, of which the Hydrapulper and Vokes rotor are among several models. See also *slushing*.

Degener, Friedrich Otto: see *Liberty press, platen press*.

delamination: 1. the separation from its base support of a photopolymer printing plate.
2. the separation of the plies in a multi-ply paper or board.
3. the splitting of coating from a weak base paper which may occur when a web of coated stock reaches the printing nip of a blanket-to-blanket web-offset press, i.e. before it is heat dried. See also *blistering*.

dele: the symbol *ɚ* representing the letter d, the initial letter of the Latin 'deleatur', delete. This is used marginally when correcting proofs to indicate that a word or words scored through with a line must be deleted.

Delegates: the governors of the *Oxford University Press*, q.v., being persons appointed by the Vice-Chancellor and Proctors of the University for a period of years.
In 1584 the University appointed a delegacy to consider the question of printing and allowed a printer to establish himself in the city and call himself 'Printer to the University'. The first acquisition of printing equipment was a fount of greek matrices, bought in 1619, and by 1652 the University owned sufficient matrices to warrant their housing in a special room called the 'printing-house' (Domus Universitatis Publica).
The committee of Delegates of the Press was first appointed in 1653 to select texts for printing and publishing by Oxford master printers in the name of the University, but the present University Press is perhaps best regarded as descending from a venture of John Fell, Bishop of Oxford, who undertook in 1669, with three partners, to lease the University's right, granted by Royal Charters of 1632–6, to print all manner of books. Fell and his partners were granted the use of University premises and the equipment from the 'printing-house'. Fell made further purchases and under his will the printing business and all the equipment and plant became the property of the University. This was in 1691 since which date the Delegates have controlled it.
The Delegates, who give their services free, are responsible to the University for the successful conduct

132

and development of the Press and they direct its policy. They appoint the principal officers, control finance and supervise the selection and production of the learned and educational books chosen for publication. See also *Oxford imprints*.

deliciae: a word used in 14th century Italy for manuscript collections of inscriptions copied from monuments.

delivery: the disposal of sheets immediately after they have been printed. There was originally no special equipment, even on cylinder machines, for delivering the sheets, and they were taken by hand from the cylinder. (See *delivery flies*.) Mechanical delivery from impression cylinders was introduced in 1834 by Isaac Adams of Rochester, U.S.A., and is now standard on cylinder and automatic platen machines though in different forms. Apart from speed the object is to prevent the newly printed surface from coming into contact with parts of the press and smearing. Modern delivery arrangements work with movable grippers, entirely without tapes, and such equipment is usual on offset machines and intaglio machines for sheet work. On these presses delivery is often combined with high feeders. Modern two-revolution machines may have feeding equipment supplied as a separate apparatus connected to the press after removing the usual delivery table.
The increased running speeds of modern printing presses may necessitate the use of a second delivery pile to which the pressman can switch while the first is being removed. This is known as *double delivery*. See also *collecting drum*.

delivery flies: the delivery tapes of a printing press along which the printed sheet, impression side uppermost, is conveyed to the delivery table. Before the automatic flyer was invented by R. Hoe in 1846 the boy who removed the sheets was called a *fly*.
In *extended delivery* extra long tapes allow several successively printed sheets to be in simultaneous process of delivery. This allows the ink to dry off slightly before reaching the pile, and lessens set-off troubles. See also *printer's devil, shoo flies*.

(With GU)

de luxe edition: an edition of a work printed on higher-grade paper than the standard edition, often from specially cast type, and usually expensively bound. The lavish use of illustrations is a feature of French books of this type.

demand publishing: the supplying to individual demand of a copy of a rare or out of print book. The book is first microfilmed and prints are made by using photocopying machines of the Xerox type. In the 1960s University Microfilms of Ann Arbor, Mich.

acquired in 1962 by Xerox Ltd, began a project to microfilm all STC books for photocopying 'on demand' by libraries and scholars. These are comparatively cheap to produce and make good working copies. See also *microform publishing*.

demonym: a pseudonym for which a quality or qualification is used e.g. 'First Nighter', 'Theatre-goer', etc.

demotic: a form of Egyptian writing used by the people (as its name implies) as distinct from the priestly hieratic (of which it was a cursive derivative, and which it later superseded), and the stone-cut hieroglyphics used for monumetal inscriptions. Demotic script belongs to the era 700 BC–AD 476 and is the middle script on the Rosetta Stone. See also *letters – forms and styles*.

demy: a former standard size of printing paper, 17½ in. by 22½ in.

demy octavo: see *American book sizes*, *British book sizes*.

dendritic growths: small discolorations in a sheet of paper caused by the oxidation of minute particles of copper or brass present in it. The metal may not have been removed from the rags, or may have entered the stuff if this has been beaten with bronze roll bars. With the passage of time irregular fern-like designs radiate from the particles, sometimes for as much as ¼ in.

Denham, Henry, fl.1559–91: a London printer and official of the Stationers' Company, remembered now as the printer of the first edition of the New Testament in Welsh, 1567, and the second edition of Holinshed's 'Chronicles'.

densitometer: an instrument used for measuring the density of a photographic layer by the process worker who requires to know the density (or degree of blackness) of a photographic image. There are also instruments for measuring the density of an opaque surface (print) before setting the camera and screen for half-tone exposure. a reflection densitometer is used for this. Measuring the optical density of ink films during the run is done with a similar instrument. See also *grey scale*.

density: the density of a developed photographic plate (or film) determined by measuring on a logarithmic scale the amount of light which will penetrate it.

dentelle bindings: the manner of decorating book covers believed to have been devised in the 18th century by the Frenchman *Padeloup* 'le jeune'. He

used broad borders having an effect of lace edging tooled on the covers. Dentelles were later used to embellish *doublures*, q.v. See also *Derome bindings*.

deposit copies: see *statutory copies*.

depth of strike: the depth from face to base of the *counter*, of a type character.

De Ricci, Seymour: see *Ricci, Seymour de*.

Derome bindings: the bindings of *Jacques Antoine Derome* (1696–1760) and his third son *Nicolas Denis* (1731–c. 88), known as 'le jeune', who were the most important members of a Parisian family which in the course of a century included sixteen master binders. Both father and son made mosaic bindings, while the latter is particularly associated with pointillé-tooled dentelle borders, some of which featured a bird and were known as 'dentelle à l'oiseau' (although other binders used this style). For an illustration see *bookbinding*.

De Roos, S. H.: see *Roos, S. H. de*.

descenders: the portion of lower-case letters below the base line, i.e. g, j, p, q, y. Depending on the design and size, when setting to measures of twenty-one or more picas a face with short descenders will have its appearance and effect improved if longer descenders are used, the whole type being cast on longer bodies. Cf. *ascenders*.

descumming: in powderless etching (see *Dow etching machine*), the use of various chemicals to remove grease, oxides, deposits of resist and other contaminants from the non-printing areas of a plate before it is etched. Without this the non-image areas of the plate will not accept the etch.

desensitization: the treatment of a lithographic plate after an image has been transferred to it by applying a solution of nitric acid and gum arabic (for stone); or gum arabic, chromic acid and phosphoric acid (for zinc); or gum arabic and phosphoric acid (for aluminium). This solution, called an *etch*, desensitizes the non-image areas, removes stray traces of grease from them, and increases the moisture-retaining capacity of the plate.

Design & Industries Association: founded in London in 1915 with the basic tenets of sound design, technical excellence and economic production. Ten printers were among the 200 founder members. All were aware of and spurred by Germany's lead in most branches of industrial art, including printing, and sought to rival it.

designation marks: letters corresponding to the initial letters of the title of a book which are occasionally printed near the signature letter of each section and help the binder to identify the particular title. See also *signature*.

Designer Bookbinders: the name given to the former *Guild of Contemporary Bookbinders*, q.v., after its reorganization in 1968. Its aims are 'to promote and exhibit the art of the hand-bound book and to seek to exert a progressive influence on the design and technique of bookbinding'. From 1971 the work of members has been exhibited in England and America.

desk copies: copies of a textbook given by the publisher to lecturers in higher education establishments with the aim of increasing sales to students if the book is prescribed or recommended. Also known as *inspection copies*.

De Thou, Jacques Auguste, 1553–1617: a French historian, statesman, Royal librarian, and bibliophile who in 1583 inherited his father's library of rare books. (His father had been a friend of *Grolier* q.v.). While many of the books were simply bound in morocco with a coat of arms on the front panel and a monogram in the compartments formed by the bands on the spine, others were in the celebrated *fanfare style*, q.v. De Thou had copies of books pulled on paper specially made for him, and it is not surprising to learn that his library was one of the glories of Paris. By the time of his death he possessed about 1,000 manuscripts and 8,000 books.

After an interim period (1617–43) in which the library was administered by Pierre and Jacques Dupuy it passed to *Jacques De Thou*, jun., the French Consul at The Hague, who greatly enriched it. On his death in 1677 the collection went to *Jacques Auguste De Thou*, abbé de Souillac, but due to the demands of creditors it was sold in 1679, most of the books being bought by the Marquis de Menars.

Other subsequent owners were Cardinal de Rohan (from 1706) and his nephew the Prince de Soubise (until 1787). Between January and May 1789 the library was dispersed in a series of sales.

De Tournes, Jean: see *Tournes, Jean de*.

Detterer, Ernst Frederick, d. 1947: an American who studied calligraphy with *Edward Johnston*, q.v. In 1913 he returned to Chicago where he had considerable influence as a designer and teacher of calligraphy and printing while at the Art Institute (1921–31). He was later custodian of the John M. Wing Foundation at the Newberry Library.

Deutsche Gesellschaft für Forschung im Graphischen Gewerbe EV: see *FOGRA*.

Deutsches Museum der Schriftgiesserei: see *Sabon*.

devanagari: or *nagari*, the type mostly but not solely used for printing Indian Sanskrit literature as well as works in the modern languages Bihari and Hindi.

Sanskrit. From 1200 BC or earlier, Classical Sanskrit was the language of kings, priests, and Hindu scripture, science, and philosophy. Its form was fixed by Panini's grammar, the 'Astadhyayi' (4th or 3rd century BC), a systematic analysis in 4,000 aphoristic rules (*Sutras*) based on earlier works. Sanskrit was not a 'dead' language; it absorbed words from other sources and remained a language of culture.

At the time of Panini Sanskrit was written in a syllabary known as *Ashokan Brahmi*. The concurrent and simpler vernacular *Prakrit* (i.e. unrefined) was used in several regional forms, but by the 5th century AD Prakrit was superseded in Northern India by Sanskrit for coins, inscriptions, and literature. The *nagari* script, used from about the 7th century, derived from Brahmi via Gupta and Siddhamatrka scripts. It was and is written from left to right in a syllabary of 48 signs, 14 for initial vowel diphthongs and 34 for consonantal groups, all modified according to position in a word.

What may be the first published translation of a Sanskrit text into a European language was a Dutch version of Bhartrihari's 'Satakas' appended to Abraham Roger's 'De opendeure . . .', Leyden, 1651. In the late-18th and 19th centuries European studies in the Sanskrit language by Charles Wilkins and William Jones in Calcutta, followed by the von Schlegels and Franz Bopp in Germany, led to the extensive publication of grammars and texts (in or with translation) in Europe and India.

Hindustani. The modern *lingua franca* of Northern India has two literary forms: *Urdu*, used chiefly by Muslims, written and printed in the Persian-Arabic script, and *Hindi*, written and printed in *devanagari*, with simpler current hands for daily use (*Kaithi* and *Mahajani*).

The East India Company required its officials in both England and Calcutta to learn Indian languages. This called for books to study them. In London T. Cadell issued George Hadley's 'Grammatical remarks on . . . the Indostan language commonly called Moors' (i.e. Urdu) in 1772, and John Fergusson's 'Dictionary of the Hindostan language' in 1773. At that time, and until the early 19th century, the official language in British India was Persian. Sanskrit had no place in public life.

In Calcutta Dr Charles Wilkins set up a press for the Company in 1778 for printing works in oriental languages. (See also *Bengali printing and typography*) The first Persian literary work printed anywhere in India was published here in 1781. This was F. Balfour's edition of 'Inshā-i-Harkaran' printed with type cut and cast by Wilkins. It was described by Balfour in the preface as '. . . a perfect imitation of the Taleek . . .' although later critics considered 'neither the shapes of the letters nor the ligatures' were wholly satisfactory. Wilkins's type and copies of it were used by others in Calcutta.

The development of Urdu and Hindi prose in the early 19th century owed much to J. H. B. Gilchrist and his British and Indian colleagues at Fort William College, Calcutta. His own works, from the presses of several British printers active in the city, included a dictionary 1786–90; a grammar, 1796; and a 'Hindee story teller . . . in roman, persian and nagree characters', 1802. His edition of Aesop appeared in 1803 as 'Oriental fabulist . . . translated from English into Hindustani, Bongla and Sunkrit' (sic). He also encouraged local *pundits* to write, notably Sri Lalu Lal whose 'Rajviti', 1809, and 'Prem Sagar', 1810, both printed in devanagari, were examples.

Lithography was used in 1827 for 'Anwari Sohili', a paraphrase in Persian by Hussein Kashify of Pilpay's Fables, Bombay Native Education Society; in 1830 at Cawnpore, in 1832 at Lucknow, and in 1837 at Delhi and Lahore. In 1840 the lithographic printing of Urdu newspapers began at Delhi and, being found less troublesome and costly than acquiring and setting type in persian-arabic, was soon adopted elsewhere. Even today the local-language newspapers of India and Pakistan are first written out by hand and then printed by lithography.

Historical note on devanagari type

1. *In India.* In addition to making type for bengali and persian-arabic Wilkins cut a fount of devanagari. A notable use of it was for William Jones's edition of Kalidasa's 'Ritusamhara' (The seasons), the first book ever printed in the Sanskrit language, Calcutta, 1792. In 1800 the nearby Serampore Press had Panchanan Karmakar's nagari type, used in 1804 for Carey's edition of the 'Hitopadesa'. In 1806 Manohar Karmakar completed a superior fount of 1,000 character combinations, used in 1808 for Colebrooke's edition of the Sanskrit dictionary Amara Sinha's 'Cosha, or dictionary of the Sungskrita language', for a New Testament in Sanskrit, and in 1811 for a Sanskrit Pentateuch.

There was also an Indian owned press in Calcutta capable of good work, that of Babu Ram, who published Colebrooke's Sanskrit dictionary of synonyms 'Hemacandra' in 1807.

2. *In Europe.* The earliest of several unsuccessful attempts to cut a fount of nagari was ordered by Maffeo Barberini (Pope Urban VIII, 1623–44) for the *Congregatio de Propaganda Fide*, q.v. It lay neglected for a century until Constantino Ruggieri, printer to the Congregatio, attempted with the help of Cassiano Beligatti to correct and complete it. The result appeared in Antonio Giorgi's 'Alphabetum

tibetanum', Rome, 1759. Beligatti later reworked the type, and his primary alphabet was shown in 'Alphabetum brammhanicum . . . ', edited by Amaduzzi, Rome, 1771. Although used to print translations of the Paternoster and Ave Maria the types were too simple for printing an original Sanskrit text.

The first Sanskrit grammar to be published anywhere was 'Sidharubam seu grammatica Sanscrdamica . . .', by Paulinus a Sancto Bartholomeo, 1790, followed in 1791 by his 'Alphabeta indica . . . ', both printed by the Congregatio and showing the basic syllabary.

In London William Kirkpatrick of the East India Company commissioned the Jackson Foundry to cut a fount of devanagari for his projected Persian, Arabic, and English grammar and dictionary. The first part, issued in 1785, had no Sanskrit words, and the work was not completed. However, a Jackson specimen sheet of *c*. 1784 showed 'Deo Nagri' characters.

In 1786 Dr Charles Wilkins was obliged by ill-health to return to England. He made the first direct rendering into English of a Sanskrit text: this was the 3rd century AD Vaishnava creed, the 'Bhagavad-Gita', London, 1785, and the Company paid for publication. He followed it with a translation of the 'Hitopadesa', Bath, 1787. At his house in Bath he worked on a fount of devanagari type. In the preface to his Sanskrit grammar, which he began printing in 1795, Wilkins writes that he 'cut letters in steel, made matrices and moulds and cast from them a fount of type of the devanagari character all with my own hands'. Before the book was finished fire destroyed his workshop, though the punches were saved. Ten years later the Company persuaded him to resume work. His was the first fount of nagari type in Europe of which systematic use could be made. The Caslon foundry cast it in commercial quantities in English (14 point) size. It was used for Wilkins's 'Grammar of the Sanskrita language', London, Bulmer, 1808; for Alexander Hamilton's edition of the 'Hitopadesa', 1810; and also for Bopp's 'Nalus, Maha-Bharata episodium', 1819. Although this type is now of only historical interest it was the sole fount available in Europe until 1821. Thus in Germany, as an alternative to buying it, Othmar Frank's 'Chrestomathia Sanskrita . . .', Munich, 1821/2, was one of several works printed by lithography. After setting the non-Indian portions of the text in roman type a pull was taken. The Sanskrit words called for were then entered by hand in spaces left on the printed sheet and the whole was transferred to stone.

In France, following the acquisition of the Pons collection of Sanskrit MSS in 1729, the Royal Library in Paris became Europe's main centre of Sanskrit studies. It was here, in 1820, that August Wilhelm von Schlegel, professor of Sanskrit at the Bonn Academia Rhenana, commissioned a fount of nagari

135

type. The result was Vibert's excellent 20-point size of 1821, first shown in a pamphlet 'Specimen novae typographiae Indicae . . . litterarum figuras ad elegantissimorium codicum Bibliothecae Regiae Parisiensio exemplaria delineavit . . . Aug. Guil. Schlegel . . . Lutetiae Parisiorum ex officina Georgii Crapelet, MDCCCXXI'. Vibert cut the punches and J-B Lion Lettern cast the type. Schlegel gave Europe the first nagari type to remain in use until the present day, personally setting the type for his edition of the 'Bhagavad-Gita', Bonn, 1823. In 1825 Delafond of Paris cut a 16-point size.

At Bopp's instigation the Akademie der Wissenschaft in Berlin acquired Schlegel's matrices and equipment for its newly established oriental printing office in 1821. Here Bopp supervised the cutting of a smaller fount of nagari to be used for textual notes. They were used in Bopp's edition of 'Ardschuna's Reise zu Indra's Himmel . . .', Berlin, 1824. In 1825 the Société Asiatique in Paris bought the Schlegel and Bopp founts, using them in Antoine Chézy's Sanskrit/French edition of the 'Sakuntala', Dondey-Dupré, 1830. By mid-century the founts were acquired by Brill of Leyden who issued a specimen 'De Sanskrit Drukletters' in 1851. Thus Schlegel's type spread through Europe. The Vibert and Delafond punches are now in the *Cabinet des Poinçons*, q.v.

In the present century founts of nagari have been made for hotmetal composition and photosetting. Some years ago *Adrian Frutiger*, q.v., was invited by the Indian National Institute of Design to visit India. There he sought to establish the fundamental shapes of devanagari and recommend simplifications which would further the spread of literacy. As a result Frutiger, in collaboration with Mahendra Patel, designed a devanagari type for Monotype.

For a specimen see Appendix A.

device: a trade-mark or design introduced by a printer or publisher on the title-page or at the end of the text to distinguish his productions. Their use dates from the 15th century at which time the printer was usually the publisher of his books and early devices passed from one printer to another often with only slight modification. The orb and cross was the basis of several 15th-century marks.

The earliest known device is the twin shields of Fust and Schöffer who first printed it in their 'Biblia latina' of 1462 (GKW 4204). The Vienna copy of the Mainz Psalter, 1457, is the only one of this work extant to bear the device and it is assumed that this was stamped in by hand at a later date. The Fust and Schöffer shields were adopted by Gerhard Leeu (Antwerp), Peter Drach (Speyer), Johann Veldener (Lyons), Bernhard Richel (Basle), and Wolfgang Stöckel (Leipzig) with only slight variations. See also *Aldine device*.

In 1539 François I of France issued a decree forbidding printers and booksellers to make use of a device which had been originated by another printer.

As the craft of printing became independent it was the publisher who retained the trade-mark. After 1700 their use became rarer, but was revived towards the end of the last century by printers as well as publishers. See also *canting mark, colophon.*

devil: see *printer's devil.*

De Vinne, Theodore Low, 1828–1914: a distinguished American printer whose work was careful and skilled if not always inspired. He is also known for his writings on the craft especially 'The Invention of Printing', Hart, 1876. De Vinne was a co-founder in 1884 of the *Grolier Club*, q.v., and printed its first publication, a reprint of the Star Chamber Decree of 1637.

About 1860 he encouraged New York printing-house owners to form a union known as 'Typothetae': such groups from several cities merged as 'United Typothetae' in 1887 with De Vinne as first president.

In 1894 De Vinne commissioned the cutting by L.B. Benton of the first fount of his Century family of type, intended for printing the *Century Magazine*. De Vinne's design shows the influence of the modern face types then popular but it is without the hairlines of the true modern face. The range has been extended through the years and, being easy to read even in small sizes, has been widely used for school books.

When he retired in 1908 the family firm of magazine and book printers 'The De Vinne Press' was managed by his son. It closed in 1923. See M. Koenig, 'De Vinne and the De Vinne Press', *LQ* 1971 1–24.

De Westfalia, Johannes, fl.1473–96: a printer, also known as *John of Paderborn* (where he was born), who was trained in Italy (at Padua?). In 1473 he brought types to Alost where, in association with Thierry Martens, he set up the second printing press in Belgium (Caxton's Bruges press being the presumed first). In this year and the next they printed four known books: by Dionysius, Augustinus, Petrus Hispanus and Aeneas Sylvius (Pope Pius II).

In 1474 De Westfalia printed at Louvain, remaining there until 1501, becoming one of the most important printers in the Netherlands. He published an edition of Justinian's 'Institutiones', 1475, in the colophon of which was a small woodcut self-portrait. He specialized in classical and humanist authors, the writings of Cicero, Gerson, Juvenal, Quintilian and Virgil being among the nearly 200 works he produced.

In 1481, trading as *John van Acon* (Aachen) he exported books to London, and in 1483, as *Johannes de Aquisgrano* (Aachen) he supplied books to Thomas Hunt of Oxford. Some were products of his own press.

Conradus de Paderborn, who in 1473 was printing

Fust and Schöffer   *Nicolaus Jenson, succs*   *Aldus Manutius*

Johann Froben   *Lucantonio Giunta*   *Erhard Ratdolt*

Christopher Plantin   *William Caxton*   *Bernhard C. Breitkopf*

Firmin Didot   *William Morris*   *Joaquim Ibarra*

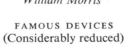

FAMOUS DEVICES
(Considerably reduced)

in Padua, also established a press in Louvain. He may have been a relative.

The entry form *De Westfalia, Johannes*, is that used in the BMC. In other works he appears as *John of Westphalia* or *Johannes de Paderborn*. See also *Thierry Martens*.

De Worde, Wynkyn: see *Worde, Wynkyn de*.

diacritical marks: signs used to denote the different sounds or values of a letter. See also *accents*.

diaeresis: two dots placed over the second of two vowels to show that it must be pronounced, e.g. coöperate (co-operate).

Dialogus creaturarum moralisatus: a popular collection of fables in which animals, plants and rocks were given the power of speech. It is known from the famous edition printed by Gerard Leeu at Gouda in 1480 which had over a hundred small woodcuts. There were several other editions before 1490, including one in French printed at Lyons in 1483. The authorship of the fables is uncertain but has been attributed to Nicolaus Pergamenus and also to Maynus de Mayneriis.

diamond: the name for a former size of type, about 4½-point.

diapered: 1. said of the gold- or blind-tooled cover of a book on which the decoration consists of a panel divided by a small uniform geometric pattern, e.g. a diamond. Each compartment of the pattern may bear a design or be left blank.

2. said of cloth for book covers which has a grained pattern of diamonds or squares: the style was first popular about 1840.

3. the uniformly patterned background for pictorial scenes in illuminated manuscripts. Their extensive use dates from the later 13th century.

Diatyp: a semi-automatic daylight operated table-top photosetting machine made by H. Berthold AG. of Berlin. Development from 1952 resulted in first showing in 1958. There have been subsequent improvements. The Diatyp is particularly suitable for in-plant printing and such jobbing work as catalogues, continuous stationery, labels, letterheads, etc.

No fewer than 250 type designs are available. Each fount is carried on a glass disc, a single disc holding 195 negative characters in 12D size. Dial control gives a size range from 4½- to 38-point. There is also provision for stripping in special sorts. The film is contained in a cassette and positioning automatically follows each exposure. The end product can be a right or wrong reading film positive or negative or a right reading paper positive.

138

The same firm's *Diatronic* machine is a semi-electronically controlled photosetter for quantity composition, with keyboard, computer, memory and exposure complex combined in one unit. Development began in 1964 and the first model was shown in 1967. It is suitable for all book, newspaper and periodical work.

The Diatronic is a direct-input machine, i.e. not tape controlled. Characters are stored in the memory before exposure. After the release command the line is spaced out and exposed character by character. The use of sheet-film instead of the usual roll facilitates direct complicated setting without extra make-up work. Justification is automatic. The end product of the system is a right or wrong reading positive film or a right reading papercopy.

diazo paper: paper coated with a light-sensitive dye. It is used as a method of obtaining a proof of a sheet of imposed negatives or positives so that corrections or imposition can be checked before an offet printing plate is made. See also *Ozalid paper, presensitized plates*.

Dibden, Thomas Frognall, 1776–1847: a famous English bibliographer who, when librarian to Lord Spencer, did much to improve the Althorp collection. Of his numerous writings 'Bibliomania', 1809, an edition of Ames's and Herbert's 'The typographical antiquities of Great Britain', 1810–19, and 'The bibliographical decameron', 1817, deserve mention.

It was after the sale in 1812 of a copy of Boccaccio's 'Il Decamerone', printed by Valdarfer, Venice, 1474, for the sum of £2,260 (at the Roxburghe sale) that Dibdin proposed an association of bibliophiles to be known as the *Roxburghe Club*, q.v.

diced: covers of a book on which the decoration is an ungilded field of diamonds or squares. To make it the leather could either be scored in a rolling press before covering or be impressed with a hand tool when finishing the book. Examples are found on russia leather covers of the 18th century and on calf of the early 19th century.

dichromate process: see *chromate process*.

Dickinson, John, 1782–1869: the inventor of a *cylinder machine*, q.v., for making endless lengths of paper. His patent (No. 3191 of 1809) describes how the mould wire revolves in a trough of stuff. In the earlier model of Joseph Bramah the stuff had been allowed to drop on the mould wheel from a cistern. See J. Evans, 'The endless web', Cape, 1955.

dictation of copy: there has been much bibliographical speculation as to whether writers of books in scriptoria, as well as early printers, worked from dictated copy.

This, it has been held, would account for errors otherwise unexplainable. One of the earliest extant codices, the 4th century *Codex Sinaiticus*, q.v., which was written by three scribes, has standards of spelling and phonetic errors peculiar to each of the three which could not have resulted from the direct copying of the original text, *ergo*, it must have been dictated.

Working methods of the 15th century professional scriptorium, described under *manuscript book writing*, q.v., show no evidence that they included dictation. However, there was a long medieval tradition of reading aloud, even when alone, as by monks in their separate carrels and indeed by people generally. Personal reading, particularly for pleasure, was little practised from the 12th to 14th century: ideas were transmitted orally and the entertaining *chansons de geste* and *romans d'aventure* were declaimed and sometimes composed by the travelling jongleurs and minstrels of Europe. Later manuscripts of them were often written in cramped script with many contractions. The reader continued to interpret the text through an auditory memory of spoken sounds rather than his visual memory of written signs. When texts were multiplied professionally the same aural tradition caused the orthographical inconsistencies found in copies of a text, particularly when an English scribe was copying from a French original. Copying from a defective copy would lead to further errors. There are, however, paintings in manuscripts showing a saint apparently dictating his text to two copyists (e.g. the Troyes Missal, BN Lat. 818).

In the case of printing it has been thought that setting by a compositor, without sight of copy, could explain many of the curious errors found in certain 16th and 17th century books, and Conrad Zeltner, in his 'Theatrum virorum eruditorum', Nuremberg, 1720, mentions the custom of employing a reader, or *agnostes*, to dictate. Writing in his 'Introduction to bibliography', O.U.P., 1927, R. B. McKerrow discusses the probability of this and concludes 'My own belief . . . is that dictation was never customary but that it may sometimes have been resorted to'.

The dictes or sayengis of the philosophres: the first dated book printed in England, issued by *Caxton*, q.v., in November 1477. Its long and curious history goes back to the apocryphal Persian king Bonium, supposed during his travels to have collected maxims and sayings of wise men in India, ancient Greece and Rome. Various versions were known in Europe through Arabic adaptations, notable being the 'Mukhtar al-hikām', written about 1053 in Cairo or Damascus by the Syro-Egyptian amir al-Mubashshir ibn Fatik al-Qu'id. For this he drew on Arabic translations of Greek philosophical works (the 'Nawadir al-falasifa' ?) made by the Nestorian Hunayn ibn Ishaq of Hira (809–73).

Prior to 1250 Mubashshir's text had been translated into Spanish as 'Los Bocados de oro, el qual fizo Bonium, Rey de Persia' (Mouthfuls of gold), well known from manuscript copies (editio princeps by M. Ungut and S. Polonus, Seville, 1495). Before 1300 a Latin translation of the Bocados, attributed to Giovanni da Procida and known as 'Liber philosophorum moralium antiquorum', was widely copied: (editio princeps Naples, 1854).

At the request of Charles VI of France Guillaume de Tignonville, provost of Paris, (d. 1414) made an abridged translation into French of Procida as 'Les Dicts moraulx des philosophes' of which more than forty manuscripts, in variant readings, have been traced. *Colard Mansion*, q.v., printed the editio princeps at Bruges *c.* 1475 (GKW 8319), without naming the author.

There are three English versions of Tignonville surviving in thirteen known MSS. One was completed in 1450 by Stephen (Stebin) Scrope; a second, and better, made before 1460 by an anonymous translator survives in a unique copy, until 1961 owned by Lord Tollemache of Helmingham Hall; the third was made about 1473 by Caxton's friend and patron Anthony Woodville, Earl Rivers (beheaded in 1478), who commissioned him to print it. Rivers named the author as Jehan de Teonville. This folio volume of 156 pages was sufficiently popular for Caxton to reprint it *c.* 1470 and *c.* 1489.

(The Bocados-Procida-Tignonville sequence is set out by C. F. Bühler in his 'The dicts and sayings of the philosophers', EETS o.s. 211 1941, but in Michaud's 'Biographie universelle', vol 41 1843, it is stated that Tignonville based his adaptation on the Latin 'De dictis et factis memorabilibus philosophorum' attributed to William of Malmesbury who died in 1143.) A facsimile reprint of 'Dictes' was published in London in 1877, repr. in 1974 in London and New York.

dictionary: 1. a reference book on any subject where items are arranged in alphabetical order and are much shorter than in an *encyclopaedia*, q.v.

2. a book explaining the words of a language, usually in the form of an alphabetically arranged sequence which includes the orthography, pronunciation, and meaning of each entry word. Some dictionaries include the etymology of words.

The dictionary traces its beginnings to the *glossary*, q.v., and Johannes de Garlandia was one of the first writers to use the word 'dictionarius'; this was for a collection of Latin vocables arranged by subject, *c.* 1225, though there were many earlier Greek and Latin works in dictionary form.

Not until the 17th century were dictionaries compiled giving explanations in English of English words and they were often limited to difficult (hard) words. (See *English spelling by printers*). In 1623

Henry Cockeram's 'The English dictionarie' was published by N. Butter, the first to have this title. Nathan Bailey's etymological dictionary of 1721, Samuel Johnson's of 1755, and John Walker's of 1791 are among the landmarks of English lexicography.

The most famous English dictionary, the 'Oxford English dictionary' (O.E.D.), was conceived at a meeting of the Philological Society in 1857. It was to be on an historical basis so that the changes in form and meaning which any given word had undergone since its appearance in the English language could be traced. In 1879 the Clarendon Press arranged to finance the editing of the work under J. A. H. Murray (thus the dictionary was sometimes called 'Murray's dictionary'). Publication began in 1884, letter Z not being reached until 1928. The work is under constant revision and the publication of a three-volume supplement began in 1972.

Noah Webster (1758–1843) was an ardent American nationalist who wrote grammars, readers, spelling books and dictionaries. His 'A grammatical institute of the English language', 1783, subsequently reissued as 'The American spelling book', preceded his 'Dissertations on the English language', 1789, in which he proposed reforms in American spelling, e.g. *center, color, theater* and so on. These were presented in his 'Dictionary of the English language', 1806, and finally established in his 'An American dictionary of the English language', New York, Converse, 2 vols, 1828. It became, and remains to this day, the standard dictionary for most Americans. It was praised for the clarity of its definitions, all of which Webster wrote, and he included many words in current speech not in other dictionaries. Printers were quick to adopt his new spellings, thereby giving them currency. After Webster's death the rights to his dictionary were acquired by the brothers Charles and George Merriam, printers. As the rights did not include the sole use of Webster's name many cheap and often plagiarized 'Webster's' dictionaries were printed in America.

Merriams' first revision appeared in 1847. They and their successors claim that only *Merriam-Webster* dictionaries, constantly revised, are true descendants of Noah's original. However, for many years an excellent rival in America was the 'Standard dictionary', first published in 1893/4 in two illustrated volumes by Isaac Kaufman Funk and Adam Willis Wagnalls. See also *concordance, encyclopaedia, index, lexicon, vocabulary.*

dictio probatoria: the first word or two on the second leaf of a medieval manuscript, used as a means of identification and help in establishing the date or place of origin. See also *incipit.*

Didot: an important French family of typefounders,

printers and publishers. The earliest recorded connection with the book trades was the admission in 1697 of *Marie-Anne Didot* into the Parisian guild of booksellers (on the death of her husband Denis?), but the first member of note was *François* (1689–1757), son of *Denis Didot*, who was apprenticed to André Pralard, printer-publisher. François began working in Paris as a bookseller and printer in 1713. He published the novels and other writings of his friend abbé Prévost, and issued his own translations of Greek classics.

François-Ambroise (1730–1804), the eldest of his eleven children, began publishing in 1753, printing in 1757, and added a foundry to the business. He improved typefounding methods (see *Didot point*), introduced wove paper (papier vélin) to the trade in 1780, substituted metal formes for wooden in 1785, and devised a press on which a whole forme could be impressed with one pull. In 1784 he showed a modern face roman in a fine edition of Tasso's 'Gerusalemme liberata', noting that the type for it had been cut by his nineteen year old son *Firmin* in 1783. In 1795 his former apprentice punchcutter Waflard cut an improved version. The care and attention given to his printed texts secured him in 1783 Louis XVI's commission to print an elegant series of French classics for the education of the Dauphin.

Pierre-François (1732–93), second son of François, worked independently as a publisher (1753), printer (1755) and papermaker, buying the Essonnes mill in 1789. He had three sons. *Henri* (1765–1852) was famous as a punchcutter and inventor in 1819 of a mould for casting a hundred letters at a time with one intake of metal. This was used in 1823 for his $2\frac{1}{2}$-point type which he appropriately named 'microscopique'. It was used by his brother to print the Maxims of Rochefoucault and of Horace. The second son, *St Léger* (1767–1829), managed the Essonnes papermill where he was associated with his foreman Louis Robert in the development of papermaking on an endless wire web. They made their first specimen in 1799. Shortly after this the work continued in England (see *Fourdrinier*). A third son, known as *Didot le jeune*, worked as a typefounder.

Pierre (1761–1853) (dit *l'aîné*) and Firmin (1764–1836) were the sons of François-Ambroise whose business they inherited and shared. *Pierre* became the most eminent printer of his day, being granted premises in the Louvre whence came in 1798 a folio edition of Virgil in his elegant illustrated series of *éditions du Louvre* of French and Latin classics. Two hundred and fifty copies of Virgil were pulled, some on vellum. He also issued the monumental 'Voyage en Egypte' of Denon and a long series of French classics. He commissioned his father's former apprentice Vibert to cut or improve types for his use. About 1818 he bought from the Beaumarchais family some 3,000 steel punches and as many matrices of twenty-two Baskerville types but did not use them.

Firmin, second son of François-Ambroise, worked as a printer, type designer and founder. In 1783 he cut the first true modern face roman, used by his father in 1784. In 1795 he sought to combine into a unit type for printing logarithmic tables, coining the word *stéréotypie* for his method and patenting it in 1797. This enabled him to print cheap editions of standard French, English and Italian literary works. In 1812 he was invited to reform the type of the Imprimerie Impériale. His series of modern face, shown in a specimen of 1819, remained the standard type used by most French printers throughout the 19th century.

The last important member of this remarkable family was *Ambroise-Firmin* (1790–1876), son of Firmin. Following a visit to England in 1814 he introduced the Stanhope press in France. As an active Hellenophile he set up at Chios in 1821 the first book-printing press in what is now modern Greece. With his brother *Hyacinthe* (1794–1880) he organized the business in 1827 as *Firmin-Didot frères* with departments for papermaking, ink making, typefounding, printing and publishing. For the greater part of the 19th century their firm 'embodied the honour and glory of the printing profession in France'. Eventually much of their material was acquired by *Deberny and Peignot*, q.v. For a specimen Didot roman see *letters forms and styles*.

Didot point: the Continental unit of measurement for type established by François-Ambroise Didot in 1775. He based his work on the Fournier point of 1737. One Didot point equals 0·343mm. See also *cicéro, millimétrique, point*.

die: an intaglio engraved stamp used for impressing a design.

Diehl, Edith, d. 1953: an American craft bookbinder and teacher of binding. About 1905 she received instruction in Belgium, France and England (from Cobden-Sanderson, and Sangorski and Sutcliffe). She then opened a bindery in New York. Her 'Bookbinding: its background and technique', 2 vols, New York, Rinehart, 1946 is still an authoritative work on the subject.

Digby, Sir Kenelm, 1603–65: the donor to the Bodleian Library in 1634 of a valuable collection of over 200 vellum manuscripts, mostly from English medieval scriptoria. Digby also had a fine library at his Paris house, part of it being brought to London after his death and part passing to the Bibliothèque Nationale where it remains.

digester: a vessel in which wood, esparto or rags are boiled with chemicals in the first stage of papermaking. Digesters can be stationary, revolving, spherical, upright or horizontal. Cf. *boiler*.

Digiset photosetting machine: a photosetter devised by Dr Rudolph Hell of Kiel and announced in 1965. It is designed to work with Dr Hell's Digicon computer or the Siemens 3003 and 4004 computers. It can also be used as a direct tape-controlled photosetter. Over 6,000 characters a second can be set in sizes from 4- to 18-point. The image is created on the line grid of a high definition cathode ray tube of such brightness that a photographic image can be made on paper or film (70 to 140mm wide). See also *CRT photosetting*.

digit: 1. any numeral between 0 and 9.

2. the printer's symbol (☞. This type ornament has a long history, the printed outline of a hand being used as a paragraph mark by, among other early printers, Huss at Lyons in 1484 in the edition of Paulus Florentinus's 'Breviarum totius juris canonici' he printed with Johannes Schabeler. As with other typographic conventions this was taken from scribal practice, carefully drawn hands pointing to a new paragraph being found in early 12th century (Spanish) manuscripts. It is also known as a *fist, hand,* or *index*.

Dijck, Christoffel van, 1601–c. 69: of Amsterdam who worked as a freelance punchcutter for several foundries before establishing in 1648 what became the leading Dutch typefoundry of the 17th century. His types were used in England, Thomas Marshall buying several founts on behalf of Oxford University about 1670, while Richard Bentley bought van Dijck roman and italic types for Cambridge University where they were in use from 1697 onwards.

In 1673 his foundry was acquired by Daniel Elzevier whose widow issued a specimen sheet of the stock in 1681. Some of the punches were subsequently in the possession of Enschedé of Haarlem by whom, says Updike, the romans were melted down in 1808; the van Dijck Sephardic hebrew is, however, still used.

No original van Dijck specimen sheet is known to survive. When Monotype's Series 203, roman and italic, was cut under the guidance of Jan van Krimpen in 1935 the roman was adapted from type used in Vondel's translation of Ovid's 'Metamorphoses', 1671, the italic being based upon a surviving size of van Dijck's italic at Enschedé's.

Dioscorides: see *Vienna Dioscorides*.

diplomatic: the science of seeking to establish the authenticity of old writings, documents, charters, etc. See also *heuristic, paleography*.

diplomatic edition: an edition of a work which exactly

reproduces the *text* of an original manuscript in the author's own hand. The text is run on without regard to the line and page endings of the original (cf. *facsimile reprint*). It may be accompanied by an editor's commentary, notes or translation. Use of the term is limited to manuscripts which pre-date the invention of printing.

An example is the reproduction of the holograph copy of Giovanni Boccaccio's 'Decameron' which he transcribed about 1370 (now MS. Hamilton 90, Staatsbibliothek, Berlin) and which Johns Hopkins University Press published in 1974.

diptych: two tablets, hinged to open like a book. They were usually of ebony or boxwood, adorned with carved ivory, gold or jewels, and with writing on their waxed inner surfaces. They were used by Roman consuls who gave them to other officials to mark the assumption of office and often bore an image of the donor or of the reigning Caesar. The most lavishly embellished were made in Constantinople during the period 506–41. See R. Delbrück, 'Die Consular-diptychen', Berlin, 1929.

direct edition: an edition of a text for which the author provides the publisher with error-free camera-ready copy produced on an electric typewriter. Lines are unjustified. This means of publishing cheaply a book which it could be uneconomic to produce by routine printing methods was formerly limited to theses and in-house work, but in 1977, to cite one example, the London publisher Routledge issued in this form Jeffares' 'W. B. Yeats: the critical heritage': only the title-page and part of the prelims were printed from type.

direct-entry photosetting: the preparation of camera-ready copy for printing from photopolymer plates on letterpress machines. Systems have a keyboard, a video display terminal, a magnetic tape store and a photosetting unit. The several makes available include the Compugraphic Universal, the Linocomp, and the Quadritek 1200. They offer a wide range of type face designs, sizes and line lengths.

direct half-tone: a half-tone for which the negative is made by using a contact or variable density screen in the camera as an alternative to exposing through the usual ruled glass screen. Better definition and detail are claimed though the resulting range of tones is less.

direct-impression typesetting: see *direct edition*. See also *reprographic printing*.

direction line: the line on which *catchwords* were printed, q.v., and now used if the abbreviated title

142

of a book follows the signature mark. See also *designation marks*.

direct mail selling: 1. the supplying of books by post from publishers to retail customers. It is most successful for books where there is a limited but clearly defined market, e.g. law and medicine, in which fields it has been practised throughout publishing history. Also known as *direct selling*.

2. Certain new publishing firms established in Britain in the 1960s used direct mail order selling in their search for a new book-buying public. To ensure that their sales publicity for books would be on target these publishers used the services of list-brokers who kept registers of business firms (unconnected with the book trade) willing to hire their specialized mailing lists. Thus the publisher of a gardening book might pay a broker to despatch leaflets about it to addresses on a seed firm's list. List-broking services can, of course, be used by all publishers whether they sell direct to customers or through bookshops. See also *book clubs*.

director: an alternative name for *guide letters*, q.v.

directory: 1. a book giving instructions for the order of Divine Service.

2. a book which lists persons or business houses, either by trade, residence, or alphabetically by name. The oldest directory in Europe appeared in London in 1595.

direct printing: printing in which the inked impression is made directly from forme to paper, as in letterpress, and is not offset on to it.

direct rotary printing: lithographic printing in a rotary machine (sheet or reel fed) on the direct principle, i.e. not by offset.

dirty proofs: proofs with many printing errors.

disc inker: an inking system for platen machines. Inking is done by a round disc which revolves about a central axis. Its introduction is credited to William Congreve who devised a circular revolving inking table for his two-cylinder press in 1820.

Discotype: an experimental photosetter of the 1920s. Letters were arranged marginally around a glass disc which revolved to bring a required character in front of a lens for exposure. For a development of the principle see *Photon*.

display: printed matter sometimes hand-set to which prominence is given by size or position, as distinct from continuous reading matter, e.g. prelims, part and chapter titles, headings, title-pages, advertisements, etc.

display photosetters: see *photolettering machines*.

display type: larger type faces designed especially for headings, advertisements, etc. In bookwork sizes above 14-point are regarded as display type. See also *cockroach, inline letters, outline letters, sand letters, woodletter type*.

distribute: the returning of individual letters and spaces into their correct places in the case, or for melting, after a job has been printed. Usually abbreviated as *dis*. See also *baked, foul case, kill, standing type*.

distributing machine: a machine for distributing type. During the experimental days of type-composing machines there were also several models of distributing machine. Each piece of type had its special nick combination which, during distribution, guided the unit to its correct place. The best known of such machines were Green & Burr's built in 1880 and Dow's built in 1886: the former dispersed 12,000 types an hour, the latter is said to have reached a capacity of 40,000 an hour.   (GU)

distribution imprint: a statement on the back of a title-page or the last page of a book to indicate the branches or representatives through which the publisher's books are distributed.

distributor rollers: rollers on a printing press which receive ink from the duct roller, roll it to the correct consistency on the ink slab and transfer it to the forme-inking rollers. They can be made of metal, of rubber, or of composition on a metal core.

Some rollers have a rubber covered steel stock over which a polyurethane skin is cast. The rubber base reduces heat build up, and the outer skin can be removed and replaced by remoulding.

There are also rollers cast from polysulphide rubber. These are suitable for use with both oil based and water reducible inks. See also *inking system*.

Ditchling Press: see *St Dominic's Press*.

Diurnal: 1. a book containing the day-hours (except matins).

2. a newspaper published daily.

divinity calf: bindings in plain dark brown calfskin, usually with bevelled boards, blind tooled with single lines which terminate in Oxford corners: the style is often a feature of theological works. See also *Yapp*.

divinity circuit: see *circuit edges*.

division of words: the division of words at the end of a line of type is done according to generally accepted rules and recommendations set out in house-style manuals. The main principle is that a word should be divided after a vowel, turning over the consonant, unless two consonants occur together, when the break should come between them.

doctor blade: 1. a thin steel blade used to scrape superfluous ink from a photogravure cylinder during running. A correctly ground doctor blade is perfectly straight, has an even bevel, and is uniformly sharp. Machine grinding now achieves these desiderata better than the hand grinding formerly practised. Plastic and bakelized cotton are modern alternatives to steel.

2. a flexible steel blade used to keep clean the steam-heated rollers which smooth the damp web of paper when in the Fourdrinier. Similar blades are also fitted to calender and other rolls over which paper is passed during manufacture.

Dodsley, Robert, 1703–64: the leading 18th-century London publisher of belles-lettres. He published for Pope, Johnson, Goldsmith and Gray, and is also remembered as the founder of *The Annual Register*, 1759, which continues today.

Doesborgh, Jan van, fl.1508–30: a printer of Antwerp, important as being one of the early Dutch printers to produce books specially for the English market; this branch of the Dutch trade having been first systematically developed by *Leeu*, q.v. Whereas Leeu had mostly used Caxton's editions for his reprints (a Jason, 'Chronicles of England', etc.) Doesborgh appears to have printed some fifteen original English works. Among them were a 'Robin Hood', 'Euryalus and Lucretia', 'Life of Virgilius', 'Tyll Howleglas', and 'The Wonderful Shape'.

Dolet, Etienne, 1509–46: a French man of letters, passionate disciple of Cicero and Plato, advocate of liberty, and admirer of Luther. About 1532 he was imprisoned in Toulouse for his beliefs. On his release he went to Lyons, working as corrector and press supervisor for Sébastien Gryphius. In 1538 he began printing independently. His first book was neither the expected selection of Latin poets nor a work of philosophy, but 'Cato christianus', a religious work later condemned as heretical. This was followed by Latin classics, an unexpurgated edition of 'Pantagruel', works on medicine and orthography and a succession of theological treatises in French, all with elegant typography and layout. He was given a licence by François I to print any work the monarch might choose.

His later publications, which included Calvin's 'Institution chrétienne' and Olivétan's French trans-

143

lation of the Bible, convinced the authorities that he was a heretic. As such he was denounced by the Sorbonne and publicly tortured, strangled, and burned with his books in Paris in 1546. See R. C. Christie, 'Etienne Dolet, the martyr of the Renaissance', 1880.

dolphin: see *Aldine device*.

The Dolphin: an American journal of the making of books, issued irregularly by the Limited Editions Club of New York. Four volumes appeared between 1935 and 1941.

Its form was a small folio cased book, and among writers whose work was included were George Macy, Lehmann-Haupt, Pollard, Koch, Hofer, Goudy and Winship, thus giving the journal an international interest. A reprint was issued in 1970.

Domesday characters: special letters for the contractions used in the Domesday Book, charters, and other Anglo-Saxon-Norman records. They were cut in wood until *c.* 1712 when Robert Andrews cut them as types for Mrs Elstob. A later and better version made by Joseph Jackson under the supervision of Abraham Farley was used by George Nichols for his folio facsimile of the Domesday Book, 2 vols, 1773–83. Vincent Figgins cut and cast founts in 1800 and 1805 for Eyre and Strahan, the King's Printers.

Such contractions as þ (pro = for) may still be seen in modern legal works.

donat: a term used in 14th century England and elsewhere for any grammar textbook: thus William Langland writes in 'Piers Plowman' of 'learning a donat'. It derives from the two Latin grammars of *Aelius Donatus*, a 4th century Roman scholar and teacher of St Jerome, which were popular in Europe for over a thousand years. The better known was 'De octo partibus orationis' or 'Ars minor', for beginners, written in the form of questions and answers: the 'Ars major' was for advanced pupils. The 'Ars minor' was one of the earliest texts to be printed (by Gutenberg, *c.* 1453?, surviving only in fragments) and there were more than 200 editions in the 15th century alone. Probably for cheapness some printed editions were copied on wood as blockbooks, though inevitably few are extant.

In England Donatus was replaced after 1540 by Lyly's grammar, established by Henry VIII's proclamation as the official textbook for use in all grammar schools. Not until 1868 was it superseded at Eton. See K. Haebler, 'Xylographische Donate', *Gutenberg Jahrbuch*, 1928. See also *Costeriana, Cracow fragments, Primer*.

Donkin, Bryan, 1768–1855: an inventor who was responsible for the practical development by 1803 of the *Fourdrinier* machine, q.v. He based his work on a machine devised in 1798 by Nicolas-Louis Robert of the Didot papermill at Essonnes, France. A model of this had been brought to England by John Gamble, patented by him, and shown to the brothers Fourdrinier. It was they who engaged Donkin to experiment with the model. The first machine was built at Frogmore Mills, Herts, *c.* 1803.

Donkin, who was associated with Richard Bacon in the invention in 1813 of a composition inking roller using glue and treacle, also invented the first (though unsuccessful) rotary printing press in 1813, and attempted a method of casting type by machine.

doreur sur cuir: a gilder of leather or finisher. From 1581 onwards French binders (relieurs) and finishers (doreurs) were organised as separate guilds and the distinction is still maintained. Consequently from the 17th century onwards French books tooled with the same tools by the same finisher may have been bound in different shops. 'It is probable, however, that many of the larger French binding shops had their own finishing tools and employed their own doreurs' (Nixon).

dorse: the back or verso of a manuscript or parchment sheet.

dos à dos: back to back, i.e. two books bound as one with a shared lower board in the middle and the fore-edges of one adjacent to the spine of the other. A typical pair of books linked in this way was the New Testament and the Prayer Book with Psalms, probably since they were needed together in Church.

This curious style was known to Berthelet who referred to it in a bill in 1542 (Nixon), but their main vogue in England was 1600–40. The usage of this term is English: in France such books are known as *reliures jumelles*.

dot-etching: see *retouching* (2).

dotting wheels: small hand-tools of varying design used by graphic artists when engraving metal plates.

double: 1. words or lines repeated in error when composing.

2. a prefix to former standard paper-size names. The double of any paper size is ascertained by multiplying the lesser of the two dimensions by two, e.g. crown, 15 in. by 20 in.; double crown, 20 in. by 30 in. See also *paper sizes*.

doublé: see *doublures*.

double case: see *case*.

double character: a double type; a diphthong or ligature of two letters on one type-body.　(ML)

double column: matter set to half the width of a normal page line with an em or more space or a rule between the columns, e.g., as in a dictionary having two columns per page. Sometimes referred to as *half-measure*.

Double Crown Club: a dining club, founded in 1924 by Hubert Foss, Holbrook Jackson, and Oliver Simon, among whose members were the most distinguished printers, typographers, book designers, and bibliophiles of the time. Dinners were held in various London restaurants where papers were read and discussed. As can be imagined the printed announcements and menus for these occasions were varied and elegant. The club is still active. See J. Moran, 'The Double Crown Club', 1974.

double dagger (or **double obelisk**): the printer's sign ‡. See also *reference marks*.

double delivery: see *delivery*.

double edition: 2,500 copies of a book. The term is associated with a regulation of the *Stationers' Company*, q.v., dated 1587, which prescribed the number of copies which were to be printed from one setting of the type: an edition was usually 1,250 to 1,500 copies. Double editions were not usual.

double-ending: running a half-width web of paper through a non-perfecting press and then turning the web by means of turner bars so that the web can be perfected by passing it through the press again, adjacent to the first pass, or by passing it through a second unit. See also *drum cylinder press*.

double pica: the name of a former size of type, about 22-point; now superseded by 24-point.

double quotes: see *punctuation marks*.

double rule: brass rule having two lines of different thickness, compared with a *parallel rule* which has two lines of the same thickness.　(ML)

double setting: the re-setting of part of a book after some of the type has been distributed. This is made necessary when more copies are needed than were originally planned. Cf. *reimposition*.

double sized: paper which has been well sized in the beater, and is then passed through a tub of animal size.

double-spread: two facing pages on which matter is

continued directly across as if they were one page. When printing an illustration in this way two blocks must be used unless the spread comes in the middle of a signature. Cf. *conjugate leaves*, *opening*.

double title-page: a book having a left-hand and a right-hand title-page. One may be a series title-page the other being particular to each title in the series.

double-tone ink: a combination of a normal letter-press ink and an oil-soluble dye of different colour. Such inks are used to print half-tones with a gravure effect. After printing in the normal way overtones later appear on the print; they are caused by the dye spreading as a halo round the dots which form the image. The result is affected by drying speed as well as the tone and finish of the paper.

doublures: decorative linings of watered silk, vellum or tooled leather fitted to the inside face of the boards of a hand-bound book. This binding feature may have been conceived by Muslim craftsmen at Herat whence a surviving binding made *c.* 1407 has dark red leather doublures with gold roll-tooled borders. The cover has blind-stamped medallions outlined in gold (British Library, Or.2773). The art was brought to perfection in Persia where morocco doublures of

Tooling a doublure (with a roll)
The leather joint between the book and its cover is also visible.

great delicacy were made in the mid-15th century. Examples have large central medallions and corner pieces of finely cut leather fretwork of gilt vine arabesques positioned over a ground of coloured silk or paper to give emphasis and contrast. Moorish craftsmen working in Spain before 1500 made bindings with doublures tooled in blind and gold in the *mudéjar* style of knotted ropework.

The Bibliothèque Nationale has two of the earliest known purely European bindings with gold-tooled morocco doublures. They were made in Milan when under French rule (1515–22): one is on a manuscript volume of Guineforte degli Bargigi's commentary on Dante's 'Inferno', given to François I about 1520; the second, on an Aldine edition of Catherine of Siena's letters, 1500, was presented to his sister Marguerite de Valois, prior to 1521. In Venice in the mid-16th century Muslim craftsmen made doublures of pierced leather over silk, finished with a combination of brushed and tooled gold.

Doublures are still a feature of some fine binding, and if simpler than their predecessors they require skill of a high order. See also *Sutherland bindings*.

Douce, Francis, 1757–1834: an antiquarian and bibliophile who bequeathed his important collection of books and manuscripts to the Bodelian Library.

Doves Bindery: see *Cobden-Sanderson*.

Doves Press: a private press founded at Hammersmith, London, in 1900 by *Thomas James Cobden-Sanderson* who was advised by *Sir Emery Walker*, qq.v. Two types used in Venice in 1476, one by Jenson and the other by Rubeus, served as models for the Doves Press proprietary type. The orginals were redrawn by Percy Tiffin, an employee of Walker, under Cobden-Sanderson's supervision, and the punches were cut by *E. P. Prince*, q.v.

The most important publication was the Doves Bible in five volumes which appeared in 1903. The Bible was hand-set by J. H. Mason. Initials drawn by Graily Hewitt or Edward Johnston were the sole decorative feature of Doves Press books which were unillustrated. They were, in their stark simplicity, in complete contrast to those of his friend and neighbour William Morris and thereby had a greater influence on fine book production in western Europe.

A catalogue of books printed by the press was the last book to appear. After 1908 Cobden-Sanderson worked alone, and the final assertion of his independence came in 1917 when he threw the printing type (to which Walker laid claim) into the Thames. The matrices and punches had been similarly despatched sometime previously. See R. MacLean, 'Cobden-Sanderson and the Doves Press', Wormerveer, 1964.

Dow, Alexander: the Bostonian inventor of an ingenious typesetting machine, 1885–6. It had an automatic spacing mechanism which in the course of setting registered the width of types set, and at the end of the line divided the remaining empty space by the number of inter-word spaces, registering the correct spacing between the words. Another feature was a machine attached to it for quick distribution.

(GU)

Dowelex plates: an electro-photographic plate making

process which was developed in America in 1965 by the Dow Chemical Co., based on the RCA Electrofax process. The purpose is to cut out the film negative stage of plate making by exposing photosensitive magnesium and zinc plates in a process camera.

Dow etching machine: an American machine or bath for etching photoengraved plates announced in 1953 by the Dow Chemical Co., since when there have been modifications to the machine and the chemicals used in it.

Early models were intended for flat magnesium alloy plates. Briefly, a series of paddles revolving in an enclosed tank projected nitric acid over the plate as it was rotated and also moved laterally. Undercutting, a usual problem in line work, was obviated by adding certain chemicals to the acid, the effect being to deposit a protective coating on the side walls. Gelatine, a component of the etchant, had a controlling effect on the coating, causing a greater depth in small non-printing areas.

In 1963 the Dow Chemical Co's. new formulae using more stable chemicals were introduced into Britain. They give a minimal loss of tone. Newer etching machines use sprays instead of paddles to apply the etchant, an advantage of this being that it is no longer necessary to maintain a constant level of emulsion in the tank. It is now possible to etch curved plates by using, for example, the 'Lithotex' rotary etching attachment to the standard powderless etcher. A fine-grain zinc, *microzinc*, has been developed in America as an alternative to magnesium.

down time: the time during which a manned printing press is not running. The machine man may be making ready, correcting a fault or washing up. The press may only be running for as little as 40% of his working day.

drag: when the end of a sheet printed on a cylinder press does not print clear and sharp, because of not being held close to the cylinder, it is said to drag.

(ML)

dragon's blood: a dark-red powdered resin which is dusted against the sides of etched lines in line-blockmaking. After heating the plate this powder becomes acid resisting and prevents undercutting the lines when the plates are re-dipped in the etching bath to deepen those lines of the design which require it. The use of dragon's blood has been superseded by *powderless etching*, q.v.

drawn in: in bookbinding, when the glued and frayed slips are drawn through holes pierced in the boards and hammered down, the attached boards are said to be 'drawn in' or 'drawn on'.

drawn lithography: lithographic printing from a stone or grained plate on which an original has been copied by a *lithographic artist*, q.v.

drawn on: 1. a paper cover which is attached to a book by gluing it to the back. If the end-papers are pasted down it is said to be *drawn on solid*.
2. in hand binding *drawn on* and *drawn in*, q.v., denote the same process.

draw out: a printing fault caused when the roller pulls out a loose type.

draw sheet: the sheet which is drawn over the make-ready on a letterpress printing machine cylinder. See also *dressing the cylinder*.

dressed forme: see *forme*.

dressers: various tools used for the trimming, cutting and planing of cast types, stereos, blocks, etc., it being important that these should all have true and precise surfaces and dimensions. Also known as *trimmers*. (GU)

dressing: 1. the fitting of furniture between and around the pages in a chase prior to locking up the forme.
2. to fit an illustration block into type set up for text so that they can be printed together.

Dressing the forme

dressing block: see *planer*.

dressing the cylinder: the fitting of several sheets of paper to a printing cylinder which is the first stage in preparing it for use. A ground sheet is pasted and fitted

so that it dries smooth and tight. Further sheets and a final manila draw-sheet are then fitted: each must lie flat and be free from bulges, the whole operation requiring great care. See also *make-ready*.

driers: compounds of cobalt, lead or manganese usually dispersed in an oil or resinous medium, which are added to printing inks to shorten the drying time, and often to modify the printed impression in some way.

drill: a coarse cotton cloth used by bookbinders.

driography: printing from plates on which the non-image areas have been made ink-resistant without the use of water. Printing is then done on a lithographic press with the dampers lifted off the plate and with special inks.

drive: another name for *strike*, q.v.

drive out: 1. said of type which occupies much lateral space.
2. an instruction to the compositor that wide spaces are to be inserted between words. Cf. *keep in*.

drolleries: small humorous drawings used to enliven the margins of illuminated manuscripts. They were popular in 13th-century France, whence they spread elsewhere, especially to Italy. See L. C. Randall, 'Images in the margins of gothic manuscripts', Berkeley U.P., 1967.

drop: to unlock a forme and remove the chase and furniture after printing, the type being either distributed or tied up and stored.

drop fingers: metal strips which assist the sheet of paper in its passage from the feedboard to the impression cylinder.

drop folios: page numbers when printed at the foot of each page.

drop in: when a block is used to print a design common to a number of books published in series, e.g, on decorated title-pages, the wording particular to each is set up in type and *dropped in* a space left in the block for this purpose.

drop initial: the initial capital letter at the beginning of a chapter, approximately aligned at the top with the cap line of the first line of text and ranging at the foot over two or more lines.

Dropmore Press: a private press in London founded in 1945 by Lord Kemsley with the aim of producing, by experiment and new techniques, fine books of uncommon literary merit. Some of the equipment of the defunct Corvinus Press was taken over. The press was disbanded about 1956.

Many of the books were designed by Robert Harling. Most were set by Monotype, the galleys being adjusted or even re-set by hand if necessary. This reduced costs but not at the expense of quality. Editions were usually of from 300 to 500 copies and rarely exceeded 1,000.

The most important and splendid works issued were 'The royal philatelic collection' by Sir John Wilson, 1952, and 'The Holkham bible picture book' with commentary by W. O. Hassall, 1954.

drop-out half-tone: synonymous with *deep-etch half-tone*, q.v.

drop-out lettering: synonymous with *deep-etch lettering*, q.v.

dropped head: the headline or title of a chapter which is set lower than the first line of text on a full page of text. Chapter headings and the headings of each separate item of prelims should be dropped to a uniform height throughout the book. In pamphlets published without a title-page the title may appear as a dropped head on the first page of text. See also *margins.*

dropped letter: when the forme on a hand-press was being inked the heavy leather balls could cause a loose type to be jerked out. Careless replacement by a wrong letter may account for minor textual differences between copies pulled from the same setting up of type. Such errors were common in the 16th century.

drop roller: a roller used to convey ink in the inking system of a printing press (or moisture in the damping system of a litho press) from the slowly revolving duct roller to the rapidly moving distributor rollers. The drop roller, which is on free bearings, comes into alternate contact with both revolving systems, adapting itself to the speed of each. See also *ink roller*, *inking system.*

drum cylinder press: 1. a flatbed press of the continuous revolution type. An early model was that of R. Hoe, 1830. The circumference of the cylinder measured double the length of the type bed. The sheet, on its supporting blanket, occupied about half the circumference, and after impression was complete the cylinder continued its revolution without touching the returning bed.

2. a web offset press with a large drum-type impression cylinder around which are grouped four plate and four blanket cylinders. The latter separately and serially offset an impression in four colours on the moving web; all on one side of the paper. After travelling round the drum paper is led through a heated dryer. If the reverse is to be printed on the same machine only half the maximum web width will have been fed into it so that, after drying turner bars are used to turn the web prior to running it through the machine again adjacent to the first pass. This is known as *double-ending.*

Alternatively, for long runs, the full width of the drum is utilized and a second drum unit is used for perfecting.

It is claimed that drum presses require little elaborate equipment to maintain register, and that cheaper paper, with fewer web breaks, can be used than with *blanket-to-blanket presses*, q.v. Also known as a *satellite press* or *sun and satellite format.*

dry-coated paper: a variety of coated paper developed in 1955 at the Battelle Memorial Institute, Columbus, Ohio. Briefly, an electrically charged dust-cloud of coating material is deposited on a web of paper by strong electrostatic fields.

dry end: the section of a papermaking machine where paper is dried by winding it over a series of steam-heated cylinders, and is subsequently finished by calender rolls for reeling on to a shell or spindle. The operator of this section of the Fourdrinier, who is responsible for the moisture content of the paper, is the *drierman.* Cf. *wet end.*

dry flong: see *flong.*

drying cylinders: hollow steam-heated cylinders of highly polished cast iron. They are part of the papermaking machine. The moving web of paper is held against the cylinders by dryer felts made of cotton, asbestos, or synthetic fibres. When it reaches the cylinders the proportion of water to paper in the web is roughly two to one.

The cylinders, which may be up to 150 cm in diameter, are used in series and may number from six to sixty-five on a big machine. An intermediate calender stack may be built in the machine before the last set of drying cylinders to improve the surface of the paper while it is still damp.

A possible alternative to the above was devised in the late 1960s by the Canadian P & P Research Institute. Instead of the battery of steam-heated cylinders the drier has a large cylinder with reduced pressure inside it. As the partly dry paper is carried round the cylinder it passes two high-temperature gas streams.

drying tunnel: in papermaking, an insulated enclosure in which evenly pressured warm air is blown by a series of jets across a moving web of coated paper.

According to the design of the tunnel paper may be supported by a woven mesh, a rod conveyor system, or jets of air.

This is quicker than the now obsolescent *festoon drying* method by which loops of paper were suspended from sticks on a trackway in a room where warm air dried them at a rate of ninety metres a minute. See also *Bramah*.

dry offset: see *indirect letterpress*.

dry paper: a term used at the Oxford University Press 'to distinguish machine-finished printing papers from India papers' (Batey). Such paper is not wetted before being printed because damping would take the gloss off; nor do the sheets require glazing or rolling after printing. . . .' (Hart).

dry plate: a photographic negative (and transparent positive) material consisting of a silver bromide gelatine emulsion, poured on a glass base-plate. As distinct from the *wet plate*, a dry plate can be kept in a dry state without losing its sensitivity which, in addition, is greater than that of the former. The whole development of modern photography is based on the dry plate or on film produced on this principle. It was discovered in 1871 by *Maddox*, q.v.   (GU)

dry-point: 1. an engraving process in which a design is hand-cut directly on to a burnished copper plate (more rarely zinc) with a steel or diamond point, no acid being used. A ground is used when first tracing the design with a needle and then washed off. Ink is applied and after removing the surplus the lines are deepened as required; their main characteristic is a softened edge due to the burr raised by the point as it is drawn through the metal. After rolling ink over the plate the surplus is wiped off with a rag and the palm of the hand; the ink retained by the burr softens the printed image. Dry-point, which can be combined with *aquatint*, q.v., is not suitable for long runs as the burr wears down. When dry-point is used for retouching etched plates the burr must be removed so that the lines have a greater likeness to the etched ones.

2. a print taken from such a plate.   (With GU)

dry pressing: to press out indentations made by type when printing, so that the printed sheet is perfectly smooth on the back.   (ML)

dry (relief) offset: see *indirect letterpress*.

dry transfer lettering: see *transfer lettering*.

dryworker: an employee of a hand-made papermaking establishment who takes *packs* of paper, q.v., to the pressing room. About twelve packs will have been loaded on a truck by the layerman prior to this. The packs are pressed, opened, pressed, opened again and pressed a third time. They are then taken away for loft drying and the dryworkers lay the sheets on canvas (which is now preferred to the former practice of hanging the sheets on hessian ropes).

Dubuisson, Pierre-Paul, fl.1746–62: a skilled Parisian binder who used engraved plaques in a press to stamp gilded designs on covers instead of building up with small hand-tools the dentelle borders he favoured. Examples are to be seen on numerous copies of the 'Almanach royale'. From 1758–62 he was appointed royal binder.

Ducali bindings: bindings made for the edicts, decrees and governors' commissions issued by the Doges of Venice. They were a combination of European and oriental styles and belong to the era 1473–1600.

The decrees were written on vellum, illuminated and lavishly bound prior to presentation by the Doge. On a typical example the boards were covered with morocco and had a deeply recessed central compartment and corners. These were gilded and enamelled or lacquered. Gold-painted arabesques and painted flowers enhanced the decoration.

Several styles were used through the years, probably, it has been suggested, because 'the newly appointed official was expected to pay for the cost of binding his commission' (Nixon).

duck: a strong linen or cotton cloth used in binding.

duck-foot quotes: a form of inverted commas used on the Continent viz. « ». Also known as *guillemets*. They were first used in 1546 by Guillaume Le Bé. While French printers use the form of quotes shown above, German and Swiss practice is » «.

duct: the trough or container from which ink is metered out to the inking system of a printing machine. See also *fountain*.

duct roller: a roller which conveys ink from the duct to the *distributor rollers*, q.v.

duernio: a gathering of four leaves, i.e. two sheets folded once.

dues: copies of a title or titles which are temporarily out of stock, binding, or reprinting when the publisher is making up a bokseller's order. The publisher records these (formerly in the *dues book*) for supply when copies become available. A bookseller may request dues to be supplied when available or may want temporarily out of stock titles cancelled. See also *publishers' abbreviated answers*.

Duff, Edward Gordon, 1863–1924: an English bibliographer, many of whose important researches into early printing and the book trade were published by the Bibliographical Society, London. He also wrote 'Early printed books', 1893, and 'Fifteenth-century English books', 1917.

dummy: a prototype of a proposed book, either bound or not, made up of the same weight of paper and number of leaves which the book is expected to need. The dummy is to show the bulk and page size of the book. From it the size of the binder's brasses can be calculated and it is also used in planning the layout of the jacket. Also known as *bulking dummy, mock-up,* or *size copy.*

dumpbin: a portable free-standing display container for the self-service of paperbacks in a bookshop, newsagents, supermarket or elsewhere. The containers are supplied at low cost by publishers' publicity departments complete with supporting printed identification material (*header cards*). A stand may be filled with multiple copies of a single title, or titles in a series, set out in forward-facing rows with additional copies behind them. Thus a bin showing twelve titles may hold up to sixty paperbacks in all.

Dun Emer Press: the name by which the *Cuala Press,* q.v., was first known. It was founded in 1902 by Elizabeth Yeats, sister of the poet, at Dundrum in Ireland. She was at first advised by Emery Walker. Eleven books were issued under the Dun Emer Press imprint, the first being 'In the seven woods', 1903. See L. Miller, 'The Dun Emer Press, later the Cuala Press', Dublin, 1973.

Dunlap Society: a New York book club founded in 1885 for the reprinting of early American literature, especially plays. It was named after John Dunlap, printer of the Declaration of Independence.   (DW)

duodecimo: see *twelvemo.*

Duodo bindings: Parisian bindings made for Pietro Duodo, Venetian ambassador to Henry IV of France, 1594–97. They were characterized by delicate oval leaf and floral motifs, with an armorial panel on the upper cover and the motto 'Expectata non eludet' on the lower.

duotone: an illustration process in which the image is printed in two colours, e.g. black and dark green or dark blue. Two negatives are made from a monochrome original, one for the darker shade with the greater detail, the other for the lighter flat tint. There are other methods. Also known as *duplex half-tone.* See also *double-tone ink.*

duplex press: a *perfector press,* q.v.

150

Dupré, Jean, fl.1484–97: an important printer of Lyons. From 1484–5 he worked at Salins, from 1487–95 at Lyons, and in 1497 at Avignon. His first appearance at Lyons was in collaboration with Nicolaus Philippi in an illustrated French edition of St Jerome's 'Vitas patrum', 1486/7. It was the first French book to have decorative initial capitals printed with the text. Dupré, or Du Pré's known output of some forty editions included grammars, law books, theology and works in Latin and French. The first roman fount used in Lyons was cut by him for an edition of Juvenal's 'Satires', 1490. He supplied other printers with type and woodcuts.

His most important publication was the folio 'La Mer des hystoires', 1491, for which he copied some of the illustrative material of Le Rouge's Paris edition of 1488–89 but added some remarkable initials and borders which were inspired by, rather than copied from, the earlier book. ('En fait d'illustration, il ne sait que copier.' (Brun))

In the imprints to some of his books he styles himself *Iohannes de Prato.*

Dupré, Jean, fl.1481–1504: an important Parisian printer whose first great work was the Paris Missal of 1481; it was the first printed Missal and probably the earliest book illustrated with woodcuts to appear in that city. He specialized in the printing of Books of Hours, Breviaries and Missals, illustrated with cuts from wood or copper blocks, and in 1482–3 was commissioned to visit Chartres to print a Breviary and Missal.

In 1483 he issued a translation of Boccaccio's 'De casibus virorum illustrium' with the title 'De la ruine des nobles hommes et femmes'; this was the first illustrated book written in French to be published in Paris. The identical blocks were used by Pynson for Lydgate's translation into English of the same work, 'Falle of princis', 1494.

Dupré's true surname was Larcher, and although he is thought to have known his contemporary *Jean Dupré* of Lyons the two were not related.

Dürer, Albrecht, 1471–1528: the Nuremberg painter and artist-draughtsman whose designs for woodcuts illustrate many famous books, e.g. Apocalypse, 1498; the 'Passio Christi', 1511; and 'Divae Parthenices Mariae historia' printed in 1511 by Hieronymus Hölzel. After his apprenticeship to Wolgemut, 1486–90, he visited Basle and Strasbourg, important centres of book production, and worked in both places. The cutting of the blocks was done for him. Dürer's copper engravings and woodcuts were known throughout Europe, and were widely copied and even forged. See also *bookplates, woodcut.* See W. Kurth, 'The complete woodcuts of Albrecht Dürer', 1927, repr. Dover, 1963.

Durham Cassiodorus: a mid-8th-century English manuscript, less carefully illuminated than many of its contemporaries. This version of the 'Commentary on the Psalms' (Cassiodorus) was written by several scribes. The book is now in Durham Cathedral.

Durrow, Book of: a Latin text of the Gospels, written in the late 7th century, of either Irish or Northumbrian origin, most probably the latter. It is decorated in a then new and vigorously native style. The figures of saints are little more than barbaric symbols, but the intricate geometric patterns, based on a cross, panels and borders, the work of skilled artists, derive in all probability from late Roman art in Britain as seen in mosaics, and in part from contemporary Anglo-Saxon and Irish metalwork and enamelwork, with traces of Coptic influence. Yellow, green and red were the only colours used. The work is now in Trinity College, Dublin.

Du Seuil, Augustin, 1673–1746: a leading Parisian binder who was noted for his brilliant and richly gilded mosaic bindings. He married into the Padeloup family and worked for a time with Antoine-Michel Padeloup. See also *à la Duseuil.*

dust cover, dust jacket, dust wrapper: see *jacket.*

dutch gilt paper: decorative printed paper popular throughout the 18th century as an alternative to marbled paper for end-papers, and for covering children's books, chapbooks, pamphlets, and other small publications. In the early 18th century these papers were made in Augsburg and Nuremberg in Germany and Bassano in Italy, the name 'dutch' probably deriving from the route of their importation into England. Although mainly imported a certain B. Moore of London had a 'manufactory' for producing them in 1763.

In making them an engraved roller or wooden block impressed a pattern on a sheet of paper coated with size. Before it dried gold dust was applied and colours were dabbed or stencilled on. Some kinds had floral and leaf patterns, often resembling brocade, and were printed in gold on coloured paper. In other examples designs printed from woodblocks were in solid gold with the pattern faintly embossed. Children's alphabets printed in gold on coloured paper were also made. Also known as *dutch flowered paper.*

dutch leaf: an alloy of copper and zinc which after being beaten into leaf form is used in tooling as an imitation of gold leaf. It quickly discolours and is seldom used. Also known as *dutch gold.*

dutch mordant: an etching fluid made up of potassium chlorate and hydrochloric acid for use in aquatint and hard- or soft-ground etching.

dutch paper: at one time limited to Van Gelder's hand-made paper but now descriptive of any deckle-edged paper produced in Holland.

Du Tour, Henri: see *Keere, Hendrik van den.*

dwell: the brief moment of contact between paper and type during which an impression is made. The term is particular to a hand or platen press. Cf. *kiss impression.*

Dwiggins, William Addison, 1880–1956: a distinguished American calligrapher, book designer and type designer who studied under *Frederic Goudy,* q.v., and at one time was associated with the Harvard and Yale University presses. Of his type designs made for Mergenthaler Linotype the sanserif Metro, late 1920s; the modern face Electra, 1935; the popular Caledonia, 1939; his book types Eldorado, 1951, and the posthumous Falcon, 1961, are notable. For a specimen of Caledonia see Appendix A.

For over thirty years he designed the books of A. A. Knopf Inc., and was also commissioned by the Limited Editions Club. Under his personal imprint 'The Society of Calligraphers' he issued several pamphlets on calligraphy and printing. His achievements won him the gold medal of the American Institute of Graphic Arts in 1929 and an Honorary Master of Arts degree from Harvard in 1947. See D. Agner, 'The books of WAD, a bibliography . . .', Baton Rouge, Press of the Nightowl, 1974.

Dycril relief plates: proprietary (Du Pont) plates made of a light-sensitive plastic material, hardened by ultra-violet light, bonded to a metal support of either rigid aluminium for flatbed plates, segmented plates for rotary printing, or thin steel for wrap-around plates.

The printing down of high-contrast negatives of text and illustrations, both line and half-tone, is done in a vacuum frame. Exposure to ultra-violet light polymerizes (i.e. hardens) the image areas: the unexposed non-image areas being removed by pressure-washing. The finished plate has a relief image suitable for long runs, and it can be stereotyped. See also *indirect letterpress.*

dyeline print: see *diazo paper.*

151

E

Eadwine Psalter: a copy of the 9th-century Carolingian *Utrecht Psalter*, q.v. This example of Canterbury Romanesque illumination was written at Christ Church about 1147 (suggests Dodwell) by the scribe Eadwine. Three or more artists added the illuminations, being influenced in their style by the Hildesheim Psalter of the St Albans school.

The slender figures are elongated, with craning necks and solemn mien, but without the lightness and animation of the Utrecht original. Other differences include the use of bright colours, the painting of large decorative initials in the text and the addition of illustrations to the commentary on four of the psalms: there is also a full-page portrait of Eadwine, which marks a new development in 12th-century art. The manuscript is now in Trinity College Library, Cambridge.

Early English Text Society: a society founded in 1864 by F. J. Furnivall with the aim of making widely available to subscribing members printed and reprinted editions of surviving literature written in Early and Middle English. Some 350 volumes have been issued to date, distribution being effected by the Oxford University Press.

early impression: said of a print from an engraving; it is considered more valuable than a later impression when the plate has become worn. (ML)

easer: a substance added to printing ink to modify it for some purpose. This may be to make it more fluid, or affect its speed of drying, colour, paper penetrating properties or liability to set-off. Varnishes or oils can be used as easers for ink reduction.

East Anglian School: the leading late 13th- and early 14th-century school of illumination in England flourished at its best in the monasteries of Ely, Peterborough, Bury, Norwich and Gorleston during the years 1300–25. The art here achieved its greatest technical perfection and final development before the secularizing influence of lay work for lay patrons presaged the decline of the early 15th century.

The most important survivals are Psalters. The basic decorative feature of their pages was a large, irregular band of gold, blue or lake, often framing the text. Armorial shields and portrait medallions were set along the band which was elsewhere embellished with leaves of several kinds (not all in natural colours), wild flowers (usually correctly coloured), grotesques, drolleries and small allegorical scenes. There was an increased use of gold and purple.

Briefly, emphasis was more on profusely ornamented borders than narrative miniatures. The Beatus page of the Psalters was often filled with Biblical scenes and the Jesse Tree, becoming the most important single page. The influence of this school spread, via Belgium, to 14th-century Cologne. See also *Arundel, Gorleston, Luttrell,* and *Ormesby Psalters.*

East, Thomas, fl.1565–1607: a London printer, noteworthy for several important books he printed. Between *c.* 1567 and *c.* 1572 he was in partnership with Henry Middleton. East issued several books of voyages and travels, including an edition of John Mandeville, 1568, and also a popular nautical handbook, Bourne's 'A regiment for the sea', 1580.

He also printed one or two medical works including one each on the waters of Bath and Buxton written by John Jones, 1572. In 1579 he printed for Gabriel Cawood John Lyly's famous 'Euphues', and in 1581 the second edition of Spenser's 'Shepheards calendar' for John Harrison II. His edition of 'De proprietatibus rerum' (Bartholomeus) of 1582 was one of the more carefully printed books of this time.

In 1588 he printed William Byrd's 'Psalmes, sonets and songs of sadnes and pietie' being assigned the latter's patent. This was followed by other musical works.

Echternach MSS.: the name given to a series of Northumbrian manuscripts written in the 8th century of which the most famous is the *Willibrord Gospels* now in the Bibliothèque Nationale, Paris. This work, probably done by the artists of the *Book of Durrow,* q.v., was formerly at Echternach in Luxembourg where it was taken by St Willibrord.

Ecole de Lure: an annual 'international graphic arts retreat' initiated in 1953 by *Maximilien Vox,* q.v., at Lurs-en-Provence, France. Typographers, graphic artists and others assembled there to discuss problems and developments of common interest.

écrasé leather: split sheepskin which before polishing has been mechanically crushed to give it a grained effect.

edge-rolled: said of the board edges of a leather-bound book which have been tooled with a fillet.

edges: see *bleed, burnished, circuit, cropped, cut edges, edge-rolled, foot, fore-edge, gilt edges, gilt top, goffered, gutters* (1), *marbling, opened, tail* (1 and 2), *thumb index, top edge gilt, trimmed, uncut, unopened, witness* (2), *Yapp.*

edge trimmer: 1. a machine which has a disc carrying three cutters. Used for trimming the edges of blocks, stereotypes, etc. Simple hand-tools (trimmers) can be used as an alternative. Also called a *Bowler.*

2. a machine for trimming the edges of books as the last stage of machine binding prior to pasting and casing. Early models were the Latham of 1865 and the Mercer of 1900. Modern automatic three-knife machines can trim sixty or more books a minute.

Edinburgh Bibliographical Society: founded in 1890. Its objects are the discussion and elucidation of questions connected with books, manuscript or printed, especially Scottish; the promotion and encouragement of bibliographical studies; the exhibition of rare or remarkable books; and the printing of bibliographical works, in particular in a series of transactions.

editing and proofing terminal: a self-contained machine which has a video display unit (VDU), a CRT display console (i.e. TV screen), and a TTS keyboard. It is designed to be the primary means of editing and proofreading text prior to typesetting. It interfaces with standard paper tape systems and with a wide range of typesetting computer equipment and programmes (either hot-metal or photosetting systems). Six-level paper tape can be used for both input and output: it then serves, after correction and editing, for input to subsequent typesetting equipment.

The video screen, 8½ in. by 11 in., displays copy as it is inputted. Some 2,000 characters in a mono-spaced 14-point serifed fount can be accommodated: they are presented in 25 lines of adjustable length from, ideally, 40 up to 80 characters. A cursor is used to identify the text material to be modified.

The machine can be used for on-line or off-line operation. Typical of such models is the Harris-Intertype 1100. See also *text string.*

edition: the whole number of copies of a work printed from the same setting of type (or from stereos or electros of that type) and issued at any time. An edition may consist of a number of impressions if the matter is not altered to any appreciable extent.

See also *abridged edition, acting edition, authorized edition, collected edition, Colonial edition, definitive edition, de luxe edition, diplomatic, direct edition, édition de tête, editio princeps, expurgated edition, facsimile, facsimile reprint, fine paper copy, first edition, hard-cover edition, impression, issue, large paper edition, library edition, limited edition, new edition, paperback, pirated edition, plant-free reprint, re-issue, reprint, revised edition, school edition, simplified edition, soft-back edition, special edition, state, trade edition, unauthorized edition, variorum edition.*

edition binding: the machine binding in cased form of substantial quantities of a title for supply by a publisher to the trade. Not all copies of an edition will be cased at one time, or even by one binding firm. Synonymous with *publisher's binding.*

Before about 1830, when machine-made lettered cloth cases came into use, it was the bookseller who bought stocks of sheets from the printer, binding them up as required. In the 17th century this was normally in unlettered calf. By 1800 the 'common manner' was 'sewed' or 'in boards': leather was 'extra'. See also *chipboard, original boards.*

edition cost: the binder's charge to a publisher for the dummy bindings and sample cases he submits for approval. For big binding runs the charge may be waived.

édition de tête: special copies of a French *édition de luxe* with plates, usually of an erotic nature, thought unsuitable for the latter and omitted from it.

editio princeps: the first printed edition of a work which previously circulated in manuscript form. The term applies particularly to classical texts first printed in the 15th and early 16th centuries.

editor: one who arranges for publication the writing of another author or others. His work may be the preparation of a manuscript for the printer (i.e. a *copy editor*), the annotation of a text, ensuring the accuracy of it, or merely the selection of material. The editor of a *series*, q.v., is required to ensure that all volumes in it are presented in a uniform style. Cf. *compiler.*

Educational Publishers Council: developed from the PA Educational Books Group to represent the interests of publishers of school books. Members send travelling exhibitions to teachers' conferences as one of their activities. The EPC provides a forum for negotiations with the Schools Council and HM Inspectorate of Schools. It is now incorporated in the Educational Books division of the PA.

Edwards of Halifax: a distinguished Yorkshire family of binders and booksellers. *William Edwards* (1723–1808) founded the Halifax firm by 1755. He was noted for *fore-edge paintings* and *Etruscan bindings*, qq.v. He also used vellum to cover books, and he decorated these with painted portraits or scenes. To make them durable he had the idea of using pearl ash to make the vellum transparent, and the painting was done underneath. Patent No. 1462 was taken out by his son *James* in 1785 for 'my said new invention of Embellishing books bound in vellum, by making drawings on the vellum which are not liable to be defaced but by destroying the vellum itself. . . . Copper plates may also be impressed so as to have a similar effect.' Evidence of his career suggests that James was a businessman rather than a craftsman, and as books so made were produced in Halifax at a time when James was elsewhere it is not unlikely that his father invented the process.

In 1783 William Edwards bought the libraries of several deceased bibliophiles. Realizing that the handsomely bound books would sell better in London he opened a bookshop in Pall Mall in 1785 with his sons *James* (1756–1816) and *John* (1758–*c.* 91) as managers. The shop flourished, rapidly becoming 'the resort of the gay morning loungers of both sexes'.

James achieved a certain notoriety among bibliophiles by his purchase of the Bedford Missal in 1786 for 203 guineas; he kept it until 1815. He travelled widely, buying books and libraries in Germany, France and Italy, to be sold, apparently at great profit, in Pall Mall. At the same time he made his father's binding styles known abroad, thus the French bibliophile Antoine Renouard (1765–1853) owned several volumes with Edwards's fore-edge paintings, and Pierre Didot (1761–1853) printed in Paris the 'Book of Common Prayer', 1791, to be 'sold by W. Edwards & Sons, Halifax'. Between 1788 and 1797 the name of Edwards appears as a publisher's imprint, thus in 1791 Bodoni printed at Parma an edition of 'Castle of Otranto' by Walpole for 'J. Edwards, Bookseller, of London'. Copies of both these works were bound in Etruscan calf with fore-edge paintings. James retired in 1804 and sold his famous library in 1815: curiously enough no fore-edge painted bindings were listed in the sale catalogue.

The search of John Edwards for the fine volumes for sale in the Pall Mall shop led him principally to Paris (where he died). In their catalogue of French books, 1791, the brothers listed books formerly owned by Diane de Poitiers.

Another son, *Thomas Edwards* (1762–1834), succeeded to his father's business in 1808, acquiring also the vellum patent from James and a valuable collection of books. It is probable that Thomas and his father were the only practising binders in the family. He remained in Halifax. After trying without success to dispose of his stock of finely bound books in 1820 and 1821 he auctioned much of it in Manchester and retired in 1826.

William's youngest son was *Richard Edwards* (1768–1827) who opened a bookshop in Bond Street, London. He specialized in the sale of the then popular illustrated book, and published in his own name. In 1797 he commissioned an edition of Young's 'Night thoughts' illustrated by William Blake. Of the 537 designs Blake prepared forty-three were used. After closing his shop Richard lived in Malta, later moving to France where he died at St Omer. See also *Frye*.

e.g.: an abbreviation for the Latin 'exempli gratia', i.e. for example.

Egenolff, Christian, 1502–55: the first regular printer of Frankfurt where, after studying in Mainz University and working in Strasbourg, he established a press and foundry in 1530. It is probable that he also cut punches. He engaged the Nuremberg engraver Hans Sebald Beham (1500–50), a follower of Dürer. An early book from his press was a Lutheran Bible with illustrations by Beham. By the time of his death he had issued 420 works. Among them was Philipp Melanchthon's 'Latin grammar', 1540, which ran through several reprints and was published in English, French and Italian editions. Egenolff's Fraktur type was used throughout Germany.

After a quarrel between his son and sons-in-law in 1572 the printing business was continued until 1700 under the name *Egenolffs Erben*. The foundry was separated and in 1572 passed via his granddaughter *Judith* to the Lyons typefounder *Jacques Sabon*, q.v., under whose name the subsequent history of the firm will be found.

Egerton, Francis Henry, eighth Earl of Bridgewater, 1756–1829: a wealthy bibliophile who bequeathed to the British Museum a collection of about sixty-seven volumes of manuscripts and ninety-six charters together with a fund for the purchase of more. (The collection is still known by the family name; the fund by the title.) As a result of this financial provision the Egerton MSS number more than 2,000.

Egerton, Sir Thomas (later Viscount Brackley), 1540–1617: the founder of one of the oldest private libraries in Britain. This was begun in 1600 and much enlarged by his son, the first Earl of Bridgewater, after whom the library was ultimately known. In 1917 a large portion of the archives, manuscripts and family papers was bought by *Henry E. Huntington*, q.v., for his library in San Marino, California. See also *Ellesmere Chaucer*.

egghead paperback: the popular name for an academic or semi-academic non-fiction work published as a *paperback*, q.v. It usually applies to the higher-priced paperback editions issued by the original hard-back publisher.

eggshell finish: coated paper or board which has a smooth but not glossy finish.

egyptian: a term first used for a type face by William Caslon IV in 1816 when he applied it to the first English sanserif face. This was not a popular face and later sanserif types were given such names as doric, gothic, and grotesque by different founders. Figgins, in 1832, was the first founder to use the name *sanserif* for types which are still so named.

The name egyptian now describes a group of display types having heavy slab-serifs and little contrast in the thickness of stroke. The first slab-serif alphabet was shown in the specimen book of Vincent Figgins, 1815. He listed it as *antique*. Other founders used this name for their slab-serif founts until Thorowgood, in his 1821 specimen book, gave it the name *egyptian*. Modern examples are Beton, Cairo, Karnak, Luxor, Playbill, Rockwell, etcetera.

Ehmcke, Fritz Helmut, 1878–1965: a German graphic artist and type-designer who founded the Steglitzer Werkstatt in Berlin in 1900. He was partnered by *F. W. Kleukens*, q.v., and G. Belwe. They planned to print beautiful books in the spirit of Morris and his followers, but the only book they issued was an edition of Elizabeth Browning's 'Sonnets', 1903. Ehmcke designed several types for various foundries, including D. Stempel. Many of them were used for the publications of the *Rupprecht-Presse*, q.v., which Ehmcke founded at Mainz in 1914.

eighteenmo: a book made up from printed sheets which have been folded to form sections of eighteen leaves, thus having thirty-six pages per section. Written 18mo. Also called *octodecimo*.

Einhorn Presse: the private press of the German artist and book designer Melchior Lechter (b. 1865) founded in Berlin in 1909. His early books, influenced in design by William Morris and Art Nouveau, were printed under his supervision by the bookprinting firm of Otto von Holten for whom Lechter designed numerous layouts, initial letters, ornamentation and covers for books not associated with his own imprint (for example a ten-volume edition of Shakespeare, in German, published by Bondi, 1908–18).

The somewhat exotic Einhorn-Presse books, few in number, included copies printed in gold and coloured inks, pulled on vellum, and enclosed in covers of gilded metal embellished with enamel, amethysts and elaborate bosses and clasps. A work so treated was an edition in 1922 of Thomas à Kempis. See W. Raub, 'Melchior Lechter als Buchkünstler', 1969.

ELBS: see *English Language Book Society*.

electio librorum: the periodic formal meeting of warden and fellows of a medieval college at which books loaned from special collections were returned, checked and distributed anew. The collections were not part of the college library. The term *electio* described the actual meeting, the distribution of books, and the bundle of them returned or taken away by a fellow. Loans were recorded on vellum rolls known as *electiones librorum*.

During the 14th–16th century the loan collections were often larger than the library proper. Fellows were expected to give books when they left the college or died, and to replace any they lost. See F. M. Powicke, 'Medieval books of Merton College', O.U.P., 1931.

electric etching: a method of etching copper blocks electrically to disintegrate the metal on those parts of the plate not protected to resist it. This is an alternative to using acid or other chemicals.

electricity in paper: see *static electricity*.

electro: *electrotype*.

Electrofax: the trade name of an electrophotographic printing process for the rapid direct copying of printed matter. It was announced by RCA in 1954, and is based on the use of zinc oxide in a resin binder coated on paper, used once only, and bearing the finished copy. See also *Xerography*.

electronic colour scanner: see *electronic scanning machine*.

electronic engraving machine: a machine for the automatic production of line or half-tone printing plates by using the principle that rapidly varying light intensities can be converted into positively related movements of an electronically controlled cutting or burning stylus. These machines produce a metal or plastic plate ready for printing, without the use of camera, darkroom processing, chemicals or etching. Models, varying in scope, include the American Fairchild *Scan-a-Graver*, the Swiss *Elgrama*, the French *Luxographe*, and the German *Klischograph*, qq.v. See also *electronic scanning machine*.

electronic linecasting keyboard: an American device, announced in 1969, for speeding up output on existing Lintotype and Intertype machines. A typewriter-style keyboard is fitted in place of keybars, cams, triggers and rubber rolls. By using solid-state circuits character keys activate solenoids which result in the release of matrices.

electronic scanning machine: a machine having a scanning unit and a linked computer for producing a balanced set of colour separation negatives or continuous tone positives for plate making. Methods vary according to the make of the machine and nature of the copy. This may be a flat colour print or a design, a transparency, or three uncorrected separation negatives. Basically, when a spot of strong light is transmitted through a transparency, or on to flat copy, the light is split into three beams which energize three photo-electric cells. These send signals to the computer which calculates the tonal density required on each of the set of separation negatives. Signals from the computer control the amount of light from four lamps positioned below four frames, each containing an unexposed negative or photographic plate. As copy is scanned, line by line, the plates are progressively and simultaneously exposed. Routine developing and processing follow. Only limited hand correction of the plates is needed. See also *electronic engraving machine, Scan plates*.

electrostatic printing: 1. printing without ink, pressure, or rollers, being based on photoconductivity. This includes methods of printing on irregular surfaces, e.g. corrugated board, or even metal.

2. printing devised for computer data, facsimile signals, and images transmitted by wire or radio.

3. the use of surfaces which in the dark are electrical insulators able to retain an electric charge but become conductors when exposed to light. Examples are *Electrofax* and *Xerography*, qq.v.

electrotype: or *electro*, a duplicate relief printing plate made by depositing a shell of copper on a mould of an original forme. Prior to 1945 beeswax, resin and turpentine were standard matrix material. Mould and forme were dusted with graphite and pressed together in a cold press. Electrodeposition of copper followed.

This method has been superseded by others using moulds of lead, thermoplastics and such well-known proprietary materials as Vinylite and Tenaplate. In a typical process the forme is cleaned, covered with a sheet of vinyl, a moulding pack and a felt blanket. They are heated and held together at great pressure in a hydraulic press in which they remain until chilled and set. The resulting mould is washed and made conductive by spraying it with silver nitrate solution. It is then put in an electrochemical plating bath where a copper shell is 'grown' on the face. The shell is removed by flexing the mould.

To make a printing plate the shell is tinplated on the back and then filled with a molten lead alloy backing metal in a casting box. When cool, levelling, planing, trimming, slabbing, routing, bevelling, mounting, and proofing follow. For long runs electros can be nickel or chrome faced.

Lead-moulded electros, being less subject to shrinkage than other materials, are suitable for the reproduction of fine-screen half-tones and for process colour plates which require close register. They are less satisfactory for reproducing type matter owing to the great pressure used in making them.

An alternative to lead backing is liquid plastic which sets hard. Thermoplastic bonded to an aluminium base is also used.

elephant face: *fat-face type*, q.v.

elephant folio: a former book size, 14 in. by 23 in. approx.

Elephant hide: the proprietary name of a fabricated parchment made in Germany. It is used for edition binding, being strong, flexible, colour-fast, and with good abrasion resistance. It can be printed, embossed, or gold blocked with excellent results, and is made in many colours.

Elgrama: an *electronic engraving machine*, q.v., made by Elgrama AG of Zurich, for making half-tone, colour process blocks, line blocks and combined blocks. The plate can be of copper, zinc, brass or a plastic foil. The original is not interpreted into dots, as in normal half-tone, but in parallel lines varying in thickness with the density of the original. The lines, which run at an angle of about 45° across the plate, are so fine and close that when printed they are no more visible to the unaided eye than screen dots. The single-line screen is available in eleven half-tone rulings and two line rulings for line work. Enlargement and reduction are possible.

As with other machines, the original to be scanned and plate to be engraved are carried on a revolving shaft. The cutting head uses a V-shaped cutter.

Multi-colour plates are made from separation prints (previously obtained from four colour-corrected negatives) by scanning from different angles. This obviates *moiré*, q.v.

elhi books: a collective acronym used in the American educational book publishing trade for elementary and high-school textbooks.

ELK: *electronic linecasting keyboard*, q.v.

Ellesmere Chaucer: an illustrated manuscript of the Canterbury Tales completed prior to 1410 (Chaucer died in 1400). In addition to paintings of twenty-three of the pilgrims seventy of the pages have elaborately decorated borders with pen ornamentation in red or purple within the lines of text. This lavish treatment of a secular manuscript in English made at a time when the rich preferred to read in French was unusual, but it is not known who commissioned it.

The Ellesmere Chaucer is the earliest version to make clear the relationship between the portraits of the 'Prologue' and the tales of the pilgrims. The unknown patron-compiler devised a tale order consistent with the foregoing and had the beginning of each tale illustrated with a portrait of the teller. Although the Ellesmere MS. is the usual basis of Chaucer's text later scholars, notably F. J. Furnivall, revised the order to eliminate what were considered to be geographical inconsistencies.

Early in the 15th century the MS. may have belonged to the de Vere family, earls of Oxford. There were other owners before it passed to the Egerton family, earls of Bridgewater in the 17th century. It eventually descended to George Leveson Gower, created earl of Ellesmere in 1846. On the death of the third earl in 1914 the library, including the Chaucer, was sold at Sothebys in 1916, passing to the *Huntington Library*, q.v.

A collotype facsimile was published in Manchester in 1911. See H. C. Schultz, 'The Ellesmere manuscript of Chaucer's Canterbury Tales', San Marino, 1966.

Elliott, Thomas, d. 1763: one of the two London binders recorded as working for *Robert Harley*, q.v., and his son Edward between 1720 and 1726. From the diary of their librarian *Humfrey Wanley*, q.v., it seems that Elliott frequently overcharged and was also rebuked for 'employing his Men about my Lord's Work' instead of doing it himself. He succeeded in business Mrs Richard Steel, the widow of one of Samuel Mearne's apprentices.

ellipsis: an omission of a word or words. This is shown typographically by a group of three interspaced full points, or four if the omitted matter ends a sentence. Cf. *leaders*.

Elrod caster: a mould machine for casting leads and rule in lengths from 1- to 36-point thick. Larger sizes are cored to reduce weight and save metal. The moulds consist of rectangular steel units with a duct in the shape of the lead or rule. Molten metal is pressed through the mould by means of a pump which at each piston stroke feeds in a standard amount of metal. Before this cools a second pump stroke impels fresh metal forward to fuse with the first. While still in the mould the cast line passes a cooler; it then moves to a cutter which can be set

to cut lengths of from 6 to 144 ems of 12-point. See also *Ludlow caster*.

Elston Press: founded in 1900 by Clarke Conwell at New Rochelle, New York. He was one of several men in Europe and America influenced by the dictum of Morris that '. . . a work of utility might be also a work of art, if we cared to make it so'. The first of Conwell's twenty beautifully executed books, issued before his press closed in 1904, was Browning's 'Sonnets from the Portuguese', 1900, printed in a type of his own design. For reprinting two essays by Morris in 1902 he used Caslon type. Editions varied from 120 to 485 copies. See *PBSA* 70 1976 429.

(With DW)

Elyot, Sir Thomas, *c.* 1490–1546: a diplomatist, humanist, translator and author who wrote all his books in English. He is remembered for his call to the governing class to equip itself for its task by education in politics, ethics and law. This was published by Berthelet in 1531 as 'The Boke named the Governour'. The second edition of 1537 was more important, permanently influencing the English language and prose style by his adaptations of Latin words to express ideas 'where unto we lacke a name in englisshe'. Most of his borrowings survive in the vocabulary of English prose just as does his use of the Latin sentence pattern.

Also of note was his English–Latin dictionary which Berthelet printed in 1538.

Elzevir (or **Elsevier**): a famous Dutch family of booksellers, printers and publishers, active from about 1585 to 1712. The originator was *Louis Elzevir* (1546–1617) who about 1565 left his native Louvain for Antwerp where he briefly worked with Plantin before settling in Leyden in 1580 as a binder and bookseller. He was granted premises in the University in 1587 and in 1592 published his first book, an edition of Eutropius. He did not print, but published for himself and the University. The considerable expansion of the business into one of Europe's largest publishing concerns began after his death. His sons and their families had branches in The Hague, Utrecht, and Amsterdam.

Printing at Leyden was begun in 1618 by *Isaac* (1596–1651), grandson of Louis, but it was *Bonaventura* (1583–1652) and his nephew *Abraham* (1592–1652) who expanded the family business, initiating in 1629 their famed pocket editions of Latin classics and French literature, a series which continued until 1665. The aim was to ensure a wide circulation of accurate texts for everyday use. The books were given engraved title-pages, narrow margins and solid setting: of them the Caesar of 1635 has been considered the best. An influencing factor in the original decision to publish in such small format may have been the cessation of paper imports from France, due to war, at a time when there were few Dutch paper mills. The distinctive face used in these books, cut by Christoffel van Dijck, had a great influence, and derivations of both face and format were revived in France during the 19th century by Perrin, Lemerre and Beaudoire. For their other books they used types from Egenolff of Frankfurt.

The Amsterdam branch, established in 1638 by *Louis III* (1604–70) began printing in 1640. From 1655 until his retirement in 1664 he was partnered by *Daniel* (1626–80), son of Bonaventura, who came from Leyden. Daniel is remembered for his fine Dutch New Testament. In 1673 he bought the Dijck foundry. After his death his types and matrices were sold, ultimately passing to Enschedé of Haarlem.

The Elzevirs sold books throughout Europe and would print special editions for a particular country; thus, for example, 2,000 copies of Grotius 'De veritate religionis', 1675, for a London publisher.

The last member of the family in the business was *Abraham* (1653–1712) who was active in Leyden. His office and foundry were sold in 1713. See D. W. Davies, 'The world of the Elzevirs, 1580–1712'. The Hague. Nijhoff, 1954.

em: 1. the square of the body of any size of type, and the unit of measurement for the size of type in use. See *body-em.*

2. the standard of typographic measurement, for which a 12-point em is the basis. This equals 0·166 in. and there are approximately six 12-point ems in one inch. This unit is used for computing the area of a printed page no matter what size of type is used for setting the text; thus if the area is twenty ems wide and thirty ems deep the width is 240-point and the depth 360-point. Synonymous with *pica* (2). See also *em quad, en.*

emblem book: a variety of illustrated book used for meditation and popular in Europe during the 16th and 17th centuries. The emblem was a woodcut or engraving, the meaning of the moral lesson represented pictorially being interpreted by a motto, epigram, verse or prose explanation. To some extent emblems were a revival of the medieval love of allegory and symbolism typified several centuries earlier by such works as the 'Hortus deliciarum', written and illuminated by Herrad de Landsperg, Abbess of Hohenburg (1167–95) which was burnt at Strasbourg in 1870 (though copies of some of the miniatures were made), and by the symbolism of the heretical Catharists of the same era.

The first anthology of emblems, printed at Augsburg in 1531 by Heinrich Steiner, was the 'Emblematum liber' which the Italian Andrea Alciati compiled in part from Latin translations of Greek epigrams; the illustrations were by Jörg Breu who worked for many Augsburg printers.

The first to be published in England was 'A choice of emblemes and other devises' by Geoffrey Whitney, 1586, but more important as literature was Francis Quarles's 'Emblemes', 1635, with copper engravings adapted from those in two Jesuitical works 'Typus mundi . . .', 1627, and Hugo's 'Pia desideria . . .', 1629, both printed in Antwerp.

In the late 1960s the Scolar Press Ltd published facsimile reprints of some sixty of the more important English and Continental emblem books. See R. Freeman, 'English emblem books', 1948.

embossed bindings: covers of leather or cloth which, before being attached to a book, had a design impressed on the sides and spine. This was done with a heated die and counter die held in a *fly embossing press,* q.v. Any lettering or gilt filleting was added by hand after fitting the cover to the book.

Some of the designs were inspired by Gothic architecture (see *architectural bindings*) while others had an all-over formal or pictorial pattern of flowers and leaves, a style known at the time as *arabesque,* q.v. To some extent they can be considered as successors to the *blind-stamped panels,* q.v., of earlier centuries.

English, French and German publishers of Bibles, prayer books and the then fashionable annuals began commissioning these bindings in the 1820s. The embossed bindings in morocco made by the London firm Remnant & Edmonds originated about 1824 when Remnant was asked to fit books with some embossed covers brought from France. A silversmith, Eley, in collaboration with James Barritt (later proprietor of the Wholesale Bible Warehouse), was commissioned to cut dies for use on Remnant's Bibles. Barritt supplied embossed covers to other binders. See E. Jamieson, 'English embossed bindings, 1825–1850', C.U.P., 1972.

embossing: relief printing or stamping in which dies are used to raise letters or a design above the surface of paper, cloth or leather. See also *Braille.*

embossing plate: a plate cut or etched below its surface for producing a raised design on the surface of a sheet. (ML)

embossing press: a machine used largely in bookbinderies for impressing book-cover designs. (ML)

embroidered bindings: bindings covered with velvet, silk or canvas bearing designs worked in gold or silver thread and coloured silks. They were sometimes enriched by the addition of small pearls or sequins and gold or silver clasps. They are also known as *needlework bindings* or *textile bindings.*

The main period when they were made in England, France and Italy was during the 16th and 17th centuries. The embroidery was sometimes domestic and done by court ladies, but most embroidered bindings were supplied by trade binders who would position over the boards a canvas stitched by paid needleworkers. Bibles, prayer books and works for personal devotion were the books most often chosen for covering in this way. For an illustration see *bookbinding*. See C. Davenport, 'English embroidered bookbindings', The English Bookman's Library, London, 1899.

emerald: a former size of type common in England, larger than nonpareil and smaller than minion, about 6½-point. Formerly known as *minionette*.   (ML)

emptying the stick: lifting the lines of types from the composing stick to the galley.   (ML)

em quad: the unit of spacing material, being a type body cast less than type height. It is always the square of the size of type it accompanies, e.g. an em quad of 10-point type is 10 by 10 points. Em quads are used to indent paragraphs and may follow a full stop. They are also cast in units of two or three. The popular name for an em quad is *mutton*.

en: half the printer's unit of square measure, i.e. half an em. See also *cast-up, en quad*.

enamelled bindings: see *champlevé, cloisonné*.

enamel process: copying on a fish-glue layer containing dichromate. The method (also known as the *hot top enamel process*) is used for making copper half-tone blocks and for a number of other reproduction processes.

enchiridion: a manual or handbook of devotions. The most famous work to include the word in the title is perhaps 'Enchiridion der kleine Catechismus für die gemeine Pfarher vnd Prediger, Gemehrt vnd gebessert, durch Mart. Luther', Wittenberg, 1529.

encyclopaedia: a work of reference containing a summary of human knowledge arranged, usually alphabetically, according to some plan. Such works trace their origins at least as far as Pliny, AD 23–79. See S. H. Steinberg's article 'Encyclopaedias' in *Signature*, 12 1951, 3–22.

end a break: an instruction to the compositor that the last line of a take of copy is to be filled with quad spacing after setting the last word. Cf. *end even*. See also *break-line, run on*.

end even: an instruction to the compositor that the last word of a take of copy is to end a line, i.e. there will not be any space after it. Cf. *end a break*. See also *break-line, run on*.

end-leaves: see *end-papers*.

end-matter: an alternative name for *subsidiaries*, q.v.

end-papers: the leaves of paper added by the binder at the front and end of a book to cover the insides of the boards. They serve together with the linings to reinforce the joints and to add finish to a hand-bound book: in machine binding the end-papers secure the book in its case. The simplest form, and as used in publishers' binding, is a four-page sheet of cartridge paper tipped in the bindery to the first and last leaf of a book. The outer leaf of each end-paper is known as the *paste-down* or *board paper*, and the conjugate leaf as the *fly-leaf*. The paper should be strong and suitable for pasting. An off-white shade tones well with the average run of book papers. It is essential that the grain direction should be from head to tail otherwise severe warping of the boards is likely to occur.

Coloured end-papers are frequently used but with some risk of discoloration. End-papers are sometimes printed with reference matter, a map, or a decorative pattern (an obstacle to rebinding). Fancy papers with figured or marbled designs give a finish to the book but may require lining, especially if the reverse side of the paper is unsightly.

Elaborations are to mount the end-paper to a folded four-page of blank paper similar to the text, the additional leaves thereby created also being known as *fly leaves*; to add a strip of coloured cloth to the joints known as *cloth joints*, q.v.; to add a guard at the back which wraps round the first section and thus the end-paper becomes sewn in but without the sewing appearing in the joints. End-papers which are mounted in any way are known as *made end-papers*.   (LK)

In cheap work the lining papers may be part of the first and last sections. Thus if a book has eight sixteen-page sections page 1 is pasted to the inner front cover as a lining and is conjugate with the leaf carrying pages 15 and 16 of text. At the end of the book page 128 is pasted direct to the inner rear cover. Pages 2 and 127 may or may not carry text or other matter. Such books cannot be rebound. See also *doublures, marbling, scratted paper*.

end stacking: the storing of reeled paper in a warehouse by placing reels one on the end of another in vertical piles which may reach 30′ high. Floor space is saved.

Endter, Georg: a Nuremberg craftsman who established a bindery in 1590. Under his son *Wolfgang* (d. 1659) the business was extended to include typefounding, printing and publishing, becoming the most famous Nuremberg house of the 17th century. Notable was the 'Kurfürstenbibel' of 1641 which included copper engravings by Joachim von Sandrart and others. In 1658 *Michael Endter* issued the popular instruction manual 'Orbis sensualium pictus' of Johann Comenius (1592–1670). This illustrated work which included a chapter of printing terms with Latin and German equivalents was frequently reprinted, translated and imitated. J. Kirby's Latin-English version of 1659 had the title 'Commenius's visible word'. In 1666 the Endters issued a polyglot edition in German, Latin, French, and Italian. (See K. Pilz, 'Die Ausgaben des "Orbis sensualium pictus",' Nuremberg, 1967.)

In 1717 their foreman Johann Ernesti (1664–1723) acquired the business, issuing in 1721 'Die woleingerichtete Buchdruckerey', a manual on printing which included type specimens.

Engelmann, Gottfried, 1738–1839: of Mulhouse. Having studied the technique of lithography in Munich he established the first important lithographic printing office in France in 1814 and a second in Paris in 1816. His work soon gained him an international reputation. In late 1836 he perfected the first successful method of *chromolithography*, q.v. This was developed by his son *Jean* (1815–75) who for some time had the only chromolithographic establishment in Paris.

engine-sized: paper which has been sized by the addition of rosin or starch to the pulp, either in the beater or at a later stage prior to the stuff flowing on the machine wire. The use of rosin was conceived in 1806 by the German chemist Moritz Friedrich Illig of Darmstadt. Engine-sized paper is not as strong as *tub-sized*, q.v., being less resistant to penetration by the oil of printing ink or atmospheric moisture. It can be improved after the sheet has been formed by *surface sizing*, q.v.

Abbreviated as *ES*. See also *animal sized*.

English (or **english**): 1. the former name for a size of type, now standardized as 14-point. Thus in specimen books we read 'english arabic' and 'english greek' for 14-point sizes of founts in those languages.

2. prior to 1800, the name for all black-letter type faces used in England. Thus a 14-point black-letter was referred to as 'English-English'.

English bookbinders: see *Adams, Bartlett, Baumgarten, Bedford, Berthelet, Bohn, Caumont, Chapman, Cobden-Sanderson, Cockerell, Designer Bookbinders, Edwards, Elliott, Frye, Godfrey, Gosden, Guild of Women-Binders, Hayday, Holl, Kalthoeber, Leighton, Lewis, McLeish, Matthewman, Mearne, Middleton, Nott, Payne, Powell, Prideaux, Pye, Reynes, Rivière, Sangorski and Sutcliffe, Sauty, Settle, Spierinck, Staggemeier, Sutherland, Walther, Weir, Zaehnsdorf.*

160

Although several scholars have published their researches on particular periods of English binding history a single definitive survey of English master binders is still to be written. Many craftsmen of the 16th to 18th century are known only by the distinctive tools they used, from the place where they worked, or from the patron who commissioned them, hence the use of such designations as 'Half-stamp binder', 'Hanway binder', 'Initial binder', 'Naval binder', 'Queen's binder A', and 'Settle binder' to describe them. For notes on these and others see the series of illustrated articles by Howard M. Nixon published in *The Book Collector*, 1952–1977, and as a collected edition by the Scolar Press in 1978.

The English Catalogue of Books: an annual cumulated edition of the lists of books issued in the United Kingdom which were given weekly in *The Publishers' Circular*, q.v. This famous trade bibliography of authors, titles and subjects, arranged in one alphabetical sequence, began in 1801. Issues from 1801–1951 were reprinted by the Kraus Reprint Corporation of New York. From 1950 the function of the 'English Catalogue' was superseded by the *British National Bibliography*, q.v.

English finish: a book paper which is calendered to give greater smoothness than *antique* or machine finish, qq.v. It is suitable for half-tones up to 110-line screen and also for gravure. If given a high finish between calendering cylinders it emerges as *supercalendered*, q.v.

English Grolier: see *Wotton*.

English Language Book Society: the publishing imprint for a series of British textbooks, many prescribed by universities and colleges in developing African and Asian countries. The books are publishers' identical reprints of their full standard editions but by virtue of a government subsidy retail at prices between a third and a half of the original. They are not on public sale in Britain being supplied through trade channels to overseas booksellers. Since the scheme began in 1961 some twenty million copies of 700 titles had been printed by early 1978. ELBS editions display a special device on title-pages and covers.

English spelling by printers: prior to 1430 Latin and French were the languages of English legal and royal chancery documents. Thereafter they were increasingly written in English. Concurrently, a new merchant class and the spread of education led to a demand for books and documents in English which were produced by trained professional scribes (see *manuscript book writing*). Lay scriptoria in London stabilized written English to some extent by observing agreed scribal rules and fixed conventions, but the first London printers and their foreign compositors lacked scribal training and spelled inconsistently. In this they were far behind the scholar-printers of France, Germany and Italy who had the advantage of printing in Latin with its regularized orthography. Thus while Caxton was concerned with printing intelligible English and enriching the language he used variant spellings, for example *had, hadde, sayd, saide* occur on one page. Not only were there no rules but methods of justifying type were crude and longer or shorter spellings helped to fit words in a line.

Spelling reform began in the mid-16th century. Among printer pioneers of it were John Allde and also *Richard Field*, q.v., who improved the English of Harington's translation of 'Orlando Furioso', 1591 (cf. the MS. in the British Library). Also of note was Richard Mulcaster whose alphabetical list of recommended spellings 'The first part of the elementarie', 1582, was the precursor of later English-English dictionaries with the authority such works implied.

On a more popular level was Edmund Coote's 'English schole-maister', 1596, which gave the spelling of 1,400 hard words. It had twenty-five editions by 1636 and fifty-four by 1737. More ambitious was Robert Cawdrey's 'Table alphabeticall of English wordes', 1604, which had 3,000 words.

In long books, set by several compositors, spelling variations particular to each man are found: the Bible of 1611 is among examples. By the early 17th century printers had begun to fix their spelling much as we know it.

Many printers and publishers set out their spelling preferences in *style of the house* manuals, q.v. See also *dictionary, Elyot*.

English Stock: publications of which the *Stationers' Company*, q.v., held sole rights to print and sell. Almanacs and prognostications, ABC primers, catechisms, psalters and psalms in metre were included. The rights were secured in perpetuity in a patent granted in 1603 by James I to the Company. It then had over a hundred members. In the same year members put up £9,000 to finance the English Stock. Turnover was considerable, in some years exceeding £5,000. Six Stock-keepers were elected who managed the Stock under the supervision of the Master, Wardens and Court, an arrangement which continues to the present. A Liveryman may still be invited to invest money in the Stock: dividends are small.

engraved face: a display type having as its essential feature a pattern of ruled lines or hatching. It may or may not have an outline. An early type of this kind was Figgins' Phantom, 1843, while another example is Stephenson Blake's Spartan Shaded, c. 1902.

engraver's proof: a careful impression of an engraving, made on fine paper with good ink, furnished by the engraver to show the excellence of his work; usually better than later impressions by the printer.   (ML)

See also *proof before letters.*

engraving: 1. any metal plate or wooden block on the surface of which a design or lettering has been cut with a graver or etched.

2. a print taken from such a plate. See also *burin, copper engraving, steel engraving, stipple engraving, woodcut, wood engraving*.

enlarged edition: see *revised edition*.

enlumine: an obsolete term for 'to illuminate'. See also *illumination*.

en quad: half an *em quad*, q.v. The popular name for an en quad is *nut*.

Enschedé: the most famous Dutch type-founding and printing concern. Established in Haarlem, 1703, by *Izaac Enschedé* (1681–1761), it has, since 1771, traded under the name Johannes Enschedé en Zonen.

The punchcutter *Johann Michael Fleischman* (1701–68) cut music types for the firm in 1760, In addition to much other work of note. Their Lutetia type, cut 1923–27, and Romulus, 1931–35, are well known in Britain; they were designed by *Jan van Krimpen*, q.v.

Harry Carter has written a detailed history of the firm in *Signature*, 4 1947 29–50.

Entered at Stationers' Hall: see *Stationers' Register*.

entrelac initials: decorated initials used at the beginning of chapters in which the letter forms part of an interlaced design or tracery.

The 16th-century French printer Geofroy Tory was noted for his examples.

entrelacs: interlacing ribbons or strapwork. They derive from Islamic arabesques and early printed examples decorate the 'Historia Romana' of Appianus issued by Ratdolt at Augsburg in 1477.

As a feature of book covers they have embellished the work of most great French binders since the 16th century, notable being those made about 1545 for Grolier and François I by the so-called Entrelac bindery of Paris.

ephemeris (pl. **ephemerides**): 1. an almanac or calendar.

2. an obsolete term for a diary; its origin in this sense goes back at least to the 4th century BC.

3. a title-word of many 17th- and 18th-century periodicals.

4. an astronomical almanac giving the daily positions of stars and other heavenly bodies.

epigraph: a short sentence or quotation printed as

part of the prelims, solus on a recto page following the dedication page, or placed at the beginning of each chapter of a book to indicate the main theme or idea in it.

epistles: letters which because of their elegant style are regarded as a form of literary composition such as, for example, the collections made by Cicero, Pliny, Libanius and their contemporaries, while on a different level are the collections of model letters used by the clerical staffs of Roman emperors. There were fictitious letters from mythological persons, from philosophers to monarchs and so on.

Manuals of letters gave guidance in the Middle Ages and by the 10th century they had become a fashionable branch of rhetoric which was to develop in Rome and Bologna. Petrarch's collections inspired later humanists and anthologies or manuals of different kinds of letters were written in Italy, France and Germany. Most important were the epistles of Erasmus whose first collection was issued in an unauthorized edition by Schöffer at Mainz in 1520. His second collection was first printed, also without the author's approval, by Siberch at Cambridge in 1521. It was dedicated to Robert Fisher, English pupil of Erasmus. The approved, extended and rededicated edition was issued by Froben in Basle as the 'Opus de conscribendis epistolis' in 1522. It was reprinted eighty times before 1600 and inspired a generation of imitators including Angel Day whose 'English secretarie' appeared in two parts, 1586 and 1592.

epitome: a condensed version or summary of a work in which only the essential matter of the original is retained. Synonymous with *compendium*.

eponymous press: descriptive of an early printing press to which, because of their common typographical affinities, a group of incunabula issued without identifiable imprints are assigned by bibliographers. A famous example is the press in Mainz which in the 1450s printed the 36-line Bible, a Sibyllenbuch fragment, an Indulgence, and the Turkish calendar, even though these are generally associated with *Gutenberg*, q.v.

Eragny Press: a private press founded in 1894 by Lucien Pissarro (eldest son of Camille Pissarro) who settled at Hammersmith, London, from the Normandy village of Eragny. His first book was 'The queen of the fishes', 1894. The first sixteen books were printed by the *Vale Press*, q.v., Vale type being used.

In 1903 he employed E. P. Prince to cut a type of his own design which Pissarro named Brook. For illustrations he effectively developed the art of wood engraving in colour. In all stages of book production, from printing to binding, he was assisted only by his wife Esther in making the octavo volumes he issued.

162

The press closed in 1914, having issued thirty-two books. Pissarro also designed type for the Kunera, later *Zilverdistel Press*, q.v. See L. Pissarro, 'Notes on the Eragny Press', (Privately published) C.U.P., 1957.

Erasmus, Desiderius, 1466–1536: see *Aldus, epistles, Froben, Gryphius, paper-book, Poggio.*

erotica: works treating of sexual passion in a manner calculated to stimulate the reader. (See also *pornography*.) These are not a 20th century phenomenon and as long ago as the 17th century there were proceedings against publishers and booksellers who issued them. Notable was the case against John Coxe, translator, Joseph Streater, printer and Benjamin Crayle, bookseller who '. . . with the intention of debauching and corrupting young men and others . . . maliciously and scandalously uttered published and offered for sale, a certain most pernicious, wicked and vicious book entitled 'The School of Venus or the Ladies delight Reduced into Rules of Practice . . .' The book was Coxe's translation of Millot and L'Ange's 'L'escole des filles', 1655, Englished as 'The school of Venus', 1680, repr. Panther Books, 1972. See R. Thompson, 'Two early editions of Restoration erotica', *The Library*, xxxii 1977 45–8.

erratum (pl. **errata**): an author's or printer's error, only discovered after the book has been printed. In the 15th century a line of type which had been omitted might be stamped by hand in the foot margin of a page, and the omission of a word or two might be made good with a pen in the printing office. An extensive textual omission would be separately run off and inserted after the leaf it was designed to correct. Both at this time and later a small strip or *cancel*, q.v., would be pasted over an incorrect word. This was uncommon after 1700.

The inclusion in a book of a printed list of errors, or *errata slip*, is found in the 15th century, e.g. in 'Corona florida medicinae' of Antonius Gazius, Venice, 1491, which has a list headed 'Principaliores impressorum errores'. Similar lists in 16th and 17th century books were headed 'Faultes', 'Ad Lectorem', or 'Corrigenda', and the reader was advised to consult the list and ink-in the corrections himself. A prefatory note in which author or printer excused or explained the faults was not unknown, thus the reader of John Florio's translation of Montaigne's 'Essays', 1691, is offered six folio pages of errors and told 'if any thinke he could do better, let him trie; then will he better thinke of what is done'.

In the 18th and 19th centuries small errata slips were inserted in the prelims of a book much as they are today.

Erwin screen: a half-tone screen which may be used when printing on uncoated stock. It is formed in irregular particles, as distinct from the ruled lines of the standard screen, these giving the print a fine stone-like texture. See also *screen*.

ES: an abbreviation for *engine-sized*, q.v.

esparto: a long, rough grass with fine, soft fibres. It grows in southern Spain and North Africa and is used for papermaking. Its suitability for this purpose was discovered by Thomas Routledge of Eynsham Mills, Oxford, who exhibited sheets made from it in the 1851 Exhibition. Commercial production followed ten years later when he patented his process. Esparto bulks well and is used for featherweight, antique, and general book papers, and for body paper for certain grades of coated stock.

In Britain the production of esparto papers has been particularly associated with the Scottish paper-making industry, but in recent years eucalyptus fibre from Brazil and West Africa has increasingly replaced esparto.

Espinosa, Antonio de, fl.1550–75: a typefounder of Seville who in 1551 emigrated to Mexico to work for *Pablos*, q.v. Espinosa later set up his own press.

Essex House Press: a private press founded in London in 1898 by *Charles Robert Ashbee* and later moved to Chipping Campden, Glos. He sought to perpetuate the traditions established by the *Kelmscott Press*, q.v., and bought printing presses from the latter. In 1901 Ashbee designed the Endeavour type, cut by E. P. Prince, and in the same year added a bindery to his premises for individual orders. Between c. 1907 and 1910 the press was directed by A. K. Coomaraswamy.

Some ninety books were issued before the press closed in 1910, many having coloured title-pages and initials, but none being outstanding typographically.

Essling, François-Victor, Prince d', 1799-1863: a Parisian bibliophile who collected early printed books and Livres d'Heures. His library was sold in 1847.

His son, *Victor Massena* (1836–1910), is remembered for his studies on the early Venetian woodcut published as 'Les livres à figures vénitiens de la fin du XVe siècle et du commencement du XVIe', 3 vols, Florence, 1907–14. This, and his work on the printed Missals of Venice, are used by present-day bibliographers and rare-book cataloguers.

Estienne: a famous family of Parisian printers, known also by the latinized form *Stephanus*. The business began in 1502, a year after *Henri Estienne* married the widow of Jean Higman, to whom he had presumably served his apprenticeship. Many of the hundred or more books he issued included Tory's woodcut initials and decorative material. On his death in 1520 his widow took for her third husband *Simon de Colines*,

q.v., who trained her second son *Robert* (1503–59) as a printer. In 1526 Robert took over the business. He married the daughter of *Jodocus Badius*, q.v.

Robert Estienne, Royal Printer in Hebrew, Latin and Greek to François I, was one of the great scholar-printer-publishers. It was he, de Colines, and their like, whose enthusiasm for classical scholarship led them to attract thinkers, philosophers and men of letters as their associates and collaborators in selecting and editing texts to be published. Of his household his son wrote: 'Robert eut chez lui une sorte de décemvirat littéraire . . .; originaires de diverses contrées . . . ils se servirent entre eux de la langue latine. Mon frère et moi n'eussions jamais osé nous servir d'une autre langue devant notre père'.

The careful editing of the classical texts, dictionaries, and translations issued by Robert Estienne was matched by fine presswork done under his close supervision. He was one of the first printers to use the new Garamont roman type, notably in an edition of the 'Isagoge' by Jacques Dubois, 1531.

In the same year he issued a great Latin thesaurus, to be followed by a series of di-glot dictionaries. It was he who introduced verse division in Bible setting. In 1540 he issued a fine folio Bible in Hebrew, Chaldaic and Latin, with vellum copies. Between 1542 and 1547 he issued five priced catalogues of his publications, probably the first of their kind, excepting broadsides, to be issued anywhere. Works were arranged under Hebrew, Greek, and Latin, sub-divided into grammars, dictionaries, and texts. For his Greek New Testament, 3rd ed., 1550, fifteen manuscript versions were collated. (See also *grecs du roi*, *greek type*.)

From 1550 until his death he worked in Geneva, embracing Calvinism. He was succeeded there by his eldest son *Henry* II (d. 1598) who maintained the scholastic traditions. He edited and published several classics and in 1572 a Greek thesaurus. Important, too, was his 'Historia' of Thucydides, 1588.

Estienne's second son, *Robert* II, was Royal Printer between 1564 and 1571, while his third son *François* printed for some time in Paris and Geneva.

The Estiennes were among those who, between the second and seventh decades of the 16th century, created typographic standards of book printing for generations to emulate and none to excel. It was only later, when the intellectual climate which inspired close scholar-printer associations gave way to tight secular and religious control over what was printed, that the publisher assumed responsibility for copy. Then the printer became a commissioned, if sturdily independent craftsman, usually without the guidance or interest to create fine printing. See E. Armstrong, 'Robert Estienne, Royal Printer', C.U.P., 1954.

estimating: the calculation of the likely total cost of publishing a book, following which the selling price is determined. Factors to consider include composition, blocks, paper, machining, corrections, size of edition, binding, jacket, permissions and promotion. See also *cast off*, *cast-up*.

et al: an abbreviation for the Latin *et alii*, 'and others'. It is found in bibliographies after the first of more than three names.

etching: 1. the treatment of surfaces with substances which have a chemical effect on them, either by dissolving the material as in block etching, photogravure etching, art graphic etching, etcetera, or by setting up reacting products which give the surface different properties as in lithographic etching on zinc or aluminium. See also *block*, *lithography*, *photoengraving*, *photogravure*.

2. *Art graphic etching*. The basis of all etching methods properly so named is the treatment with acid of a metal plate on which certain parts of the surface are protected by the application of a ground. According to the manner of applying the ground and the artist's method of etching the processes have been given different names. The chief methods in use are *hard ground etching*, *soft ground etching* and *aquatint*.

As with certain other art graphic processes *hard ground etching* is ascribed to the Augsburg artist and armourer Daniel Hopfer (*c.* 1470–1536); his most famous work appears in the 'Sachsenpiegel', 1516, but about 1510 he had made prints from etched iron plates as a cheaper alternative to copper. The earliest dated etching is a single leaf by Urs Graf, 1513, now in Basle Museum: from 1515–18 Albrecht Dürer furthered the new art, but it was Rembrandt (1606–69) who worked with the greatest mastery.

A cleaned and polished plate of copper or zinc is warmed. A quantity of ground (a mixture of wax, asphalt and hartshorn) is evenly distributed with a dabber or roller until it forms a thin film over the whole surface. While still hot it is smoked over a wax taper or something similar. On the grounded plate a tracing of the drawing to be reproduced is laid and the two are lightly rolled through a press; the result is an image of the drawing in grey lines on a black ground. Going over these lines with a round polished needle exposes the metal at the point of contact. Before etching commences the back and edges of the plate must be given a protecting coat of varnish. Repeated dippings of the plate in an acid bath, with a trial pull after each immersion, are needed to etch the lines to the required depth. The finest lines are etched first, and after removing the plate from the bath and drying it, these lines are varnished over. This etching by stages continues until the darkest lines have been etched sufficiently.

Soft ground etching was introduced in the later 18th century to facilitate the reproduction of pencil or crayon textures; etchings by Cotman are, perhaps, the best known in this medium. The copper plate is heated and given a thin coating of soft ground consisting of ordinary hard ground mixed with axle grease or tallow. As this remains soft after cooling a hand support or bridge must be used when drawing.

A sheet of tissue or other slightly grained paper is carefully stretched across the soft ground; on this the drawing is made with a pencil, chalk or a small stick. Tones can be produced by pressing the thumb on the paper, or alternatively a piece of gauze or other fabric can be used. The ground adheres firmly to those parts of the tissue-paper pressed on to it by the pencil, so that on removal of the paper the metal under the ground is exposed. Etching is usually done in one immersion. Such etchings have heavier lines than hard ground etchings, and, of course, are characterized by their soft tones. For *aquatint* see separate entry.

3. a print taken from the plates described in (2) above. (GU)

etching machine: an apparatus for etching plates (see *photoengraving*) by means of an etching fluid kept in continuous motion. The etching machine was invented by Louis Edward Levy of Philadelphia about 1900.

Etchomatic: the trade name of a machine for the automatic etching of gravure cylinders. It was invented by the Detroit Gravure Corporation of America who sold the rights to the British firm Crosfield Electronics Ltd. The machine uses ferric chloride as an etchant and automatic control gives quicker and more consistent results than older etching methods.

etch proof: see *reproduction proof*.

ethiopic type: type used to print *Amharic*. Since the 14th century this has been the principal (and is now the official) language of Ethiopia. It is a modified version of the old South Semitic script *Ge'ez* which, as a spoken language, died out in the mid-14th century and survives only as the liturgical language of the Ethiopian church.

Amharic script, written from left to right, is not based on a simple alphabet of consonants and vowels comparable to the twenty-six roman letters. It has thirty-three basic consonant characters in each of which the vowel *a* is implied. There are forty-five additional characters representing certain consonants followed by the sound *w*. Consonant characters must be modified by adding strokes to and/or altering the shape of the main form in order to give other vowel values. This makes for a complicated type case since each of the thirty-three basic characters takes seven variations to denote the full range of syllables, i.e. consonants plus vowel sounds. Numerals, punctuation and other signs are additional.

The first appearance in print of the Amharic alphabet occurs in the woodcut specimen by Erhard Reuwich in Breydenbach's 'Peregrinatio in terram Sanctam', Mainz, 1486. Jerusalem, one of the places visited in the pilgrimage, had an Ethiopian monastery. Breydenbach, following contemporary usage, referred to the Ethiopians as 'Indians', it being thought that India had a western part in Africa, namely the remote and isolated kingdom of Ethiopia. Ethiopian pilgrims to Rome had the use of the small church Santo Stefano dei Mori. Pilgrims to this church attracted the attention of Johannes Potken, a Cologne priest and linguist living in Rome. Assisted by Thomas Waldo Samuel, an Ethiopian pilgrim, Potken published at his own expense a 'Psalterium aethiopicum', printed in movable type by Marcellus Silber, Rome, 1513. Potken incorrectly described the language as Chaldaic. The names of the punchcutter and typefounder are not known. On returning to Cologne in 1515–16 Potken took his type with him and it is next seen in the polyglot 'Psalterium in quator linguis hebraea, graeca, chaldea, latina', printed by his relative Johannes Soter in 1518. In 1522 a page was added showing the Ethiopic alphabet, Lord's Prayer and Ave Maria in Ethiopic and Latin. Potken died in 1524, his type passing to Soter who made little use of it.

Johannes Froben of Basle used a new fount of ethiopic for the 'Chaldaica grammatica' of Sebastian Münster which he published in 1527. The first showing of ethiopic in France was in a work of Postellus, 1538, but a wood block was used instead of type, as in the famous writing manual of Palatino, Rome, 1540. In 1548–9 a New Testament in ethiopic type was published by Tesfaye Sejon of Santo Stefano and others under the joint patronage of the Pope and the Emperor of Ethiopia. It was printed by Valerius Doricus as was Vittori's Ethiopic grammar of 1552. The type used in both may have been commissioned by Marcellus Cervinus. The European interest in Ethiopia then current may have come from a view that the doctrine of that long isolated Christian kingdom in the mountains of East Africa was likely to resemble its original uncorrupted state. During the latter half of the 16th century ethiopic type is to be seen in a few linguistic studies including a fount cut by Andreas Hindenberg for the Berlin printer Thurneysser; the woodblock text in Victor Caietanus's 'Paradigmata . . .', Paris, 1596; and the engraved specimen in Johannes de Bry's 'Alphabeta . . .', Frankfurt, 1596.

From Leyden came a fount probably cut by Jodocus Hondius in 1593 and cast there by Thomas de Vechter. It was used for the second edition of Justus Scaliger's great work 'De emendatione temporum' printed by the Raphelengius press heirs in 1598. The compositor and corrector was Jan Theumisz, later of Leyden University. The Scaliger type was recut and cast by Pierre de la Rovière when he printed the third edition of this work at Geneva in 1629. The fount owned by

Thomas Erpenius (1584–1624) had a remarkably long history subsequent on its passing to the Elzevir family in 1625.

The Jesuit community in Ethiopia, active there up to 1633, sent drawings of ethiopic characters to Rome where Achilles Venerius cut them for the *Congregatio de Propaganda Fide*, q.v. They were the smallest then available, but those sent to Ethiopia were not used. In Rome they were used for some linguistic works including Jacob Wemmer's 'Lexicon aethiopicum', 1638.

Two German students at Leyden University, both interested in Eastern languages are important in this brief chronicle of printing in ethiopic type. They were George Nissel (1622–62) and Theodorus Petraeus (c. 1625–72) for whom in 1654 the printers Daniel and Johannes Elzevir issued the Epistles of St Paul, St John and St Jude in Arabic, Ethiopic and Latin using their Erpenius type. In 1655 Nissel set up his own press and bought an ethiopic fount from Johannes Elzevir, using it until 1661 to print a series of liturgical books. When Nissels died Petraeus used the type once, in Amsterdam in 1668. After his death the type was bought by a Hamburg printer but the matrices and punches of the Great Primer size (18-point) were given in 1686 by the Burgomaster of Amsterdam to Oxford University Press where they are still usable.

However, the first use in England of ethiopic type occurred in Brian Walton's introduction to oriental languages printed in a new fount in 1655 by Thomas Roycroft, to be followed by the Polyglot Bible in 1657 which included Potken's Ethiopic Psalter and New Testament from the 1548–9 edition. The same type was used by Roycroft in 1661 for Hiob Ludolf's 'Lexicon aethiopicum-latinum' and Edmund Castell's heptaglot 'Lexicon' of 1669 which complemented the Polyglot. The types subsequently passed to Robert Andrews who about 1683 had succeeded to the Moxon foundry. The typefounder Nicholas Nicholls showed an ethiopic in his specimen of 1665.

Hiob (Job) Ludolf (1624–1704), referred to above, of Frankfurt, was an important linguist who specialized in Ethiopic (Ge'ez) and Amharic. Among his studies published in Frankfurt were a history of Ethiopia printed by Balthasar Wustius in 1681, (and reprinted in 1691) who used both old types and a new fount cut and cast by Johann Adolf Schmidt of the Egenolff foundry; an Amharic lexicon and grammar, printed by Martin Jacquet in 1698; and a revised edition of the Potken Psalter in 1701. The Jacquet type may have been acquired by Johann Andrea who used it in 1707 to print Hartmann's 'Grammatica aethiopica'. For much of this century there was little interest in Ethiopian studies, though William Caslon II had by 1766 a particularly clear ethiopic type.

In the 19th century the Bible Society of London reprinted the Ludolf 'Psalter', 1815, in a type which Dr Fry had acquired from earlier founders, but the

Gospels they printed in 1826 showed the Ludolf fount of 1701. Oxford University Press issued the Ethiopic texts of Richard Laurence in the Erpenius fount between 1819 and 1838. The catalogue of Ethiopic manuscripts in the British Library, compiled by the German August Dillmann (1823–94), was published in 1847. For his catalogue of the Bodleian collection, 1848, the Erpenius types were used, the most enduring of all founts. By 1851 he was publishing Ethiopic works in Germany, continuing to do so until at least 1866.

Ethiopians consider that a well designed type for setting Amharic should have the calligraphic qualities of traditional Ethiopian hand-writing. Although serviceable most ethiopic type cut before 1851 fell short of this ideal. In that year the Imprimerie Nationale in Paris had a fount cut by Marcellin Legrand. It was based on the writing of Ethiopian scribes. The 14D size of 1851 was followed in 1852 by smaller sizes. They were used for the 'Catalogue raisonnée' of Antoine d'Abbadie, 1859, in which he gave the first known, if inaccurate, history of ethiopic types in Europe.

In the present century the firm of E. J. Brill, Leyden, has become a leading printer of Ethiopic works (as of other oriental languages). Notable have been Enno Littmann's 'Bibliotheca Abessinica', 1905–11, and other works by the same scholar. In 1955 Linotype designed and cut their first fount of ethiopic for use by the Artistic Printing Press, Addis Ababa, first seen in a St John's Gospel. Later the Ethiopian State Printing Press (Berhanena Selam) acquired three Monophoto machines for its educational book publishing programme.

This entry is based on H. F. Wijnman's 'An outline of the development of Ethiopian typography in Europe', Brill, 1961, to whom acknowledgement is hereby made. See also Appendix A.

Etruscan bindings: calfskin bindings decorated with patterns adapted from Etruscan vases and other classical ornaments. The style was used by William Edwards of Halifax in the 18th century. His method was to brush acid on the calf, thus burning the design into the skin. Tree-calf panels were occasionally set within Etruscan borders. See also *Edwards of Halifax*.

eucalyptus fibre: now increasingly used in papermaking as a substitute for *esparto*, q.v.

Evans, Charles, 1851–1935: compiler of the 'American bibliography', a projected chronological dictionary of all books, pamphlets and periodicals printed in the United States between 1639 and 1820. When he died he was half-way through the alphabet for 1799. An appendix for 1799–1800 was completed by C. K. Shipton, Worcester, Mass., 1955. Evans was an organiser of the American Library Association in 1876.

Ève bindings: books bound in the workshops of the Frenchmen *Nicolas Ève*, fl.1578–81 and his son or nephew *Clovis*, fl.1584–1634, who were Court binders and booksellers to successive kings of France. Their typical designs had a field powdered (*semé*) with fleurs-de-lis and, occasionally, a centre-piece of the Crucifixion or royal arms. Some examples were in the *fanfare* style, q.v. A remarkable series of nine macabre bindings, attributed to Clovis, was made for Henri III or members of his 'Compagniè des confrères de la mort'. Some were tooled in silver with a field of skulls, crossbones and tears. For an illustration see H. M. Nixon, 'Sixteenth-century gold-tooled bindings in the Pierpont Morgan Library', NY, 1971, p214.

even folios: the verso or left-hand pages of openings, numbered 2, 4, 6, etc.

even s. caps: an abbreviation for *even small capitals* or *even smalls* which, when written on copy, indicates to the printer that a large capital is not to be used as in *caps and smalls*, q.v., but that words are to be set in letterspaced small capitals on the type size body. Further abbreviated as *even s.c.* The instruction to the compositor for inter-character spacing is *even smalls 1- or 2-unit letterspaced.*

excelsior: a size of type, one-half the size of brevier, or about 4-point. (ML)

excerpts: quotations or passages selected from books: they may not be reprinted without permission from the publishers of the originals.

exemplaires de chapelle: 1. see *copy money*.
2. in the French book trade, copies of a limited edition pulled off in excess of the number announced in the 'justification du tirage'.

exemplar: an official copy of a scholastic text made by a stationer under the direct control of a medieval university. See also *manuscript-book writing*.

Exercitium super Pater Noster: a Netherlands block book and one of the earliest known. The original text may have been written by Henri van den Bogaerde (1382–1469) of the *Fratres Vitae Communis*, q.v. The first edition, c. 1430–40, was chiroxylographic, with a text written in Flemish under the large printed woodcuts of which there were probably ten. The only known copy of the first edition (Paris, BN) has eight.

The second edition with Flemish and Latin woodcut text had new copies of the original illustrations and there was a German edition, c. 1470.

ex libris: 1. a Latin phrase meaning 'out of the books', used on a *bookplate*, q.v., before the name of the owner. Between the late 12th and 14th century it

166

was customary for the custodians of monastic library books to enter in them an inscription of ownership. Such inscriptions were written either on a flyleaf or on the first page of text.

Among formulae used were 'Hic est liber . . .', 'Iste liber est de almario ecclesie . . .', 'Liber de claustro Roffensi' (Rochester), etcetera.

An alternative in some monastic libraries was to identify a book by recording its donor, e.g. 'Psalterium Radulphi', or by the formula 'Hunc librum dedit . . .', or the words 'Ex dono . . .'. See also *anathema*.

2. the modern term used on the Continent for a bookplate.

exotic types: such non-roman founts as *arabic*, *bengali*, *cyrillic*, *devanagari*, *ethiopic*, *hebrew*, qq.v.

expandable cloth: a variety of cloth, notably that made under the trade name of *Bookflex*, woven with a crinkled cross-thread especially for lining up the backs of books. The cloth will expand with the book during *rounding* and *backing*, qq.v. See also *Steamset*. (LK)

expanded type: display type with a flattened oblong appearance. A modern example is Stephenson Blake's Chisel Expanded series. Also known as *extended type*.

'Expectata non eludet': see *Duodo bindings*.

explicit: the last words of the text of an early printed book which sometimes stated the title, but more often the place and date of a book's publication and the printer's name. The word is contracted from the Latin 'Explicitus est liber', i.e. 'it is unrolled to the end', a phrase which originated when the form of a manuscript was a roll or *volumen*, q.v. The word *colophon* (1), q.v., is an alternative. See also *incipit*.

expressed folio: see *blind folio*.

expurgated edition: an edition of a book from which parts which might be thought objectionable, usually on moral grounds, have been omitted. See also *Bowdlerized*.

extended: synonymous with *expanded type*, q.v.

extended delivery: see *delivery flies*.

extender: a transparent or semi-opaque chemical which is added in powder form to printing ink either to vary the colour strength or improve working properties. Aluminium hydrate and aluminium silicate are examples.

extension cover: a paper cover which extends beyond the outer edges of the pages of a booklet or pamphlet, compared with a cover which is *trimmed flush*. (ML)

extra bound: a book bound by hand, the boards laced on by cords, a tight or hollow back, a morocco cover, all edges gilt and special attention given to the endpapers, headbands and finishing details, especially an abundance of gold tooling.

extra calf: said of an extra-bound book covered in specially selected high-grade calf instead of morocco.

extra cloth: used for bookbindings, in plain finish and a variety of patterns; the cloth is well covered with colour, concealing the weave and giving a solid colour effect. (ML)

extracts: lengthy quotations set within the main text of a work. They are sometimes set in smaller type and/or indented one em on the left or indented both left and right. Alternatively extracts may be set in the same size as the text and full out, but preceded and followed by extra space and within quotes.

extra illustrated: see *Grangerized*.

extruders: the collective term for *ascenders* and *descenders*, qq.v.

Exultet roll: an illustrated manuscript roll bearing the words and music chanted at the Catholic ceremony of lighting the paschal candle on Easter eve in token of Christ's resurrection. The name derives from the opening words 'Exultet iam angelica turba caelorum'.

Many of these rolls were produced by the Beneventan monks of southern Italy, notably at Monte Cassino, where the custom began of writing the hymn on sheets of vellum which were laced together to form a roll about a foot wide by twenty or so in length. The roll was wound about an umbilicus. The illustrations were upside down in relation to the text, thus when the roll was unfurled as chanting proceeded it was allowed to hang over the reading desk so that the pictures were seen correctly by the congregation.

Extant examples belong to the period 900–1200.

F

Fabriano: an Italian hand-made paper. It was in Fabriano that Italy's first papermill was established prior to 1283.

Fabroleen: a cheaper variety of *linson*, q.v.

face: 1. the printing surface of any type character.
2. the series or family name for types with common characteristics, thus *modern face, old face,* qq.v.

facet: the bevelled edge on a block or other printing plate.

facet edge: the impression left on paper by the edge of a printing plate when copperplate printing.

facetiae: see *jest book*.

fac initial: see *factotum*.

facsimile edition: in its modern sense an exact copy of a book made either photographically or by an offset process. Used to avoid setting up new type when republishing an out-of-print book.

In an earlier sense a facsimile edition was published to make widely available copies of a work which existed only as a rare manuscript or incunabulum. One of the earliest facsimile editions was Plantin's reproduction in 1626 of the 6th-century 'Martyrologium Hieronymianum' which he engraved on copper plates. Cf. *period printing*.

facsimile half-tones: highlight half-tones, when the half-tone screen is eliminated from the highlights. They are used to reproduce pencil, crayon, or charcoal drawings. (ML)

facsimile reprint: a reprint for which the type, decoration and layout of the earlier printed original are faithfully copied. Before mechanical composition the relatively unchanging conditions in printing workshops made the reprinting of texts in this way an easy matter. The printer only had to follow copy. For his well-known facsimile reprints of Caxton's texts, however, William Blades specially cast type to reproduce the original. Cf. *facsimile style*.

facsimile style: the use of layout and typographical treatment appropriate to an earlier period without closely copying a particular book printed during it.

factotum: a printer's ornament having a space in the centre of which any letter of the alphabet may be inserted. It is then used for printing an initial capital letter at the beginning of a chapter. Especially applied to early printed books. See also *guide letters*.

Fairbank, Alfred, 1895–   : from 1920–22 a student of calligraphy and illuminating under *Graily Hewitt*, q.v. He designed and supervised the production of the Royal Air Force Books of Remembrance containing 150,000 names, the work of a team of scribes and illuminators.

Fairbank has had great influence in England and America in popularising the teaching of italic handwriting and in 1932 published 'A handwriting manual'. In 1952 he was responsible for the establishment of the *Society for Italic Handwriting*, q.v.

With Berthold Wolpe he collaborated to write 'Renaissance handwriting: an anthology of italic scripts', 1960.

In 1951 Fairbank was awarded the CBE for his services to calligraphy. See A. S. Osley, ed. 'Calligraphy and palaeography: essays presented to Alfred Fairbank', Faber, 1965.

fair calf: an alternative name for *law calf*, q.v.

fair dealing: see *Copyright Act*.

Faithfull, Emily, 1835–95: an active worker for the emancipation of women who gave practical form to her aims in 1860 when she established her Victoria Press in London. Initially she engaged fifteen female compositors, trained by men, and worked on contract printing. She ignored trade opposition to the employment of women.

In 1862 she was appointed 'Printer and publisher in ordinary' to Queen Victoria, and a year later issued the first number of her *Victoria Magazine* which continued until 1880. She published numerous tracts, many by women writers. In 1867 her interest in the printing business was sold to her associate W. W. Head, Miss Faithfull using the Victoria Press imprint at a separate publishing office. See W. E. Fredeman, 'Emily Faithfull and the Victoria Press', *The Library*, 5th ser., xxix 1974 139–164.

false bands: strips of leather, card or board which are glued to a hollow-backed book before fitting the leather cover. This simulates the appearance of a flexibly sewn book. The process is known as *under-banding*. Cf. *raised bands*.

family: a group of printing types in *series*, q.v., with common characteristics in design but of different weights. Thus the Times family which includes Times Bold, Times Roman, Times Titling, Times Extended Titling, and others. Cf. *fount*.

fan binding: a decorative style for de luxe bindings made in France and Italy, mostly during the later 17th century. In France it was known as *à l'éventail*. The central design on the board was a fully opened fan, built up from numerous small tools to give a delicate lace-like effect. Quarters of a fan were tooled in the four outer corners of the board. In the following century the style influenced Scottish binders. For an illustration see under *bookbinding*.

The Fanfare: a printing office established in London in 1925 by Charles Hobson to support his advertising agency. The few books issued in limited editions included a collection of poetry by Robert Bridges for which composition and machining were closely supervised by Stanley Morison and Frederic Warde.

Ernest Ingham, who had been employed as printer, moved to the London Press Exchange in 1926 when the latter bought the Fanfare. See also *Cloister Press*.

fanfare: a style of book cover decoration developed and practised in France from about 1570 to 1640. The main features are interlacing ribbons forming compartments of various shapes, with emphasis given to a central compartment. This interlacing ribbon is bounded by a double line on one side and a single on the other. As fully developed naturalistic floral and foliage ornaments, made with small hand tools, often azured, fill all the compartments except the central one and almost completely cover the sides.

The name *fanfare* derives from a copy of 'Les Fanfares et corvées abbadesques des Roule-Bontemps', printed in 1613, which the bibliophile Charles Nodier acquired in 1829 and gave to his friend Thouvenin to be bound. *Thouvenin*, q.v., based his decoration on the style attributed to the Ève's workshop. It was from this 19th century plagiarism that the 17th century bindings became known retrospectively as *à la fanfare*. For an illustration see *bookbinding*.

Fann Street Foundry: a famous London typefoundry

successively associated with *Thorne, Thorowgood,* Besley and *Reed*, qq.v.

Fanti, Sigismondo, fl.1514–35: of Ferrara, a nobleman who was interested in architecture and mathematics. In 1514 he published in Venice the earliest printed writing manual, 'Theorica et pratica . . .', in which he illustrated the geometrical principles of capital letters. The title-page describes him as 'Professoris de modo scribendi'.

Faques, William, fl.1504–08: a printer of Normandy who settled in London, and by 1504 was King's Printer, the first holder of the office. His output was modest, some eight works being known: one was an illustrated Psalter, 1504 (STC 16257).

In 1509 his printing material was in use by *Richard Faques*, a presumed relative. He did not, however, inherit the royal privilege, which passed to *Richard Pynson*, q.v. Some twenty-five works are attributed to him, among them being John Skelton's 'Goodly garlande,' 1523.

Nothing is known of him after 1530 in which year he printed 'Myrroure of Our Lady' at the request of the Abbess of Syon. In it his name appears as *Fawkes*.

fascicule: a single number of a work published in instalments. Also called *fascicle* or *fasciculus*.

fashion boards: simple body boards lined on one side with a good rag cartridge paper, and with a thin paper on the other to prevent warping. They are used by artists when preparing originals for blocks. See also *not*.

fat-face type: display types having letters with vertical strokes nearly half as thick as the letters are high, vertical shading and unbracketed or only slightly bracketed serifs. Fat-face types as fully developed date from 1805 and were probably the design of Robert Thorne. Their origin is often disputed, it being claimed that certain display letters of William Cottrell, *c*. 1766, were prototypes, while other claims are made for the founders Bower and Bacon about 1810. Types of this kind were much used by printers of broadside ballads.

Modern versions are many and include Falstaff and Ultra Bodoni. There is a tendency to describe these last, which have much thicker main strokes than, for example, Fry's Canon fat-face, as *elephant faces*. For a specimen see Appendix A.

fat matter: printing copy which can be set easily since it includes much space, e.g. in a novel which is mostly dialogue. This is distinct from difficult copy, which is known as *lean matter*.

faults in printing: see *printing faults*.

Favil Press: a private press founded in London by P. A. L. C. Sainsbury in 1920, whose partner, C. A. Birnstingl, bought it in 1922. In addition to jobbing work the press issued books, mostly of poetry, including works by Osbert, Edith and Sacheverell Sitwell. It was later commercialized, the imprint being found up to 1961. See also *Cayme Press*.

Fawcett, Samuel: a Lancashire engraver who worked with *Karl Klič* on the *photogravure* process.

feathering: 1. a fault in printing caused by using an ink containing too much solvent or an unsuitable paper. The feathered effect is visible when ink spreads beyond the printed impression via the fibres of the paper.
2. the thinning down of the overlapping edges of a join in two pieces of paper. This is done by a book-binder when restoring a volume. He is careful to choose paper of similar texture to the original and may need to tone down the colour of the new piece.

featherweight paper: descriptive of *antique wove* or *laid paper* made to a bulk basis of 32, or in metric terms, volume 23. It is the highest bulk usually obtainable. One hundred sheets of featherweight antique wove in substance of 100 g/m^2 will produce a bulk of 23 mm. Other substances are pro-rata.

Featherweight papers have a characteristic rough, fluffy surface which can cause problems on offset litho printing machines, and most publishers prefer to use lower bulk antique woves. See also *fluffing*.

fecit: a Latin word meaning 'he has made it', frequently added to an artist's name on a drawing or engraving. (ML)

Federigo da Montefeltro, Duke of Urbino, 1422–82: from 1444 until his death a *condottiero* or professional captain of a private army hired by kings and popes. In 1474 he was created KG by Edward IV. His court was a leading centre of Renaissance culture and included a great library. It was rich in Latin, Greek and Hebrew texts and he strove to acquire the complete works of the writers represented. He eschewed printed books and employed more than thirty scribes to prepare fine manuscripts which were often illuminated and sumptuously bound in crimson velvet with silver clasps.

He commissioned *Vespasiano da Bisticci*, q.v., to collect for him and to supervise about 1475/8 the preparation of his finest treasure, the great Urbino Bible (now Vat.Lat.1–2). The artist Attavante (1452–1517) was among those who worked on this apotheosis of Florentine illumination. When complete the work was covered in gold brocade, richly plated with silver.

After many years in the family possession the Urbino library was acquired by the Vatican in 1658.

170

Fëdorov, Ivan, fl.1563–83: the first printer in Russia to sign and date a book. This was in 1564 when, with *Pëtr Timofeev Mstislavec*, he issued from his press in Moscow the 'Apostol' (Acts and Epistles of the Apostles). He used a cyrillic type which he may have brought from Poland, and illustrated the book with a German woodcut of St Luke. The next book was 'Casovnik', 1565. Soon after this the two left Moscow, taking most of their equipment, and worked in Zabloudov, Lithuania. Fëdorov alone was printing in Lvov in 1572, and later in Ostrog where in 1580/81 he issued a complete Bible of 627 pages, using six different types (two each large and small greek, slavonic and large slavonic). The types were used for nearly a century after his death.

Fëdorov's successor in Moscow was *Andronik Neveja*, fl.1588–97. Not until 1634, when V. Bourcev wrote and printed an ABC, was a non-liturgical book printed in Russia. He issued a second edition of 6,000 copies in 1649.

From its inception printing in Russia was an instrument of state and church, used by Ivan the Terrible for administrative control. Until the 18th century, however, a considerable production of hand-written books of all kinds continued.

Mention should be made of a group of four books which appeared between 1556 and 1563. They were the Gospels, reprinted twice; the Psalter; and Carême's 'Triodion'. The dates are only conjectural since the books were without date or printer's name. Russian bibliographers have tentatively assigned them to *Marusha Nefediev* and *Vasjuk Nikivorov* who would thus be Russia's first printers. See also *cyrillic*.

feed board: the platform on a printing machine on to which single sheets of paper are passed from the stock pile and from which they pass to the impression cylinder.

feeder: an apparatus for feeding and positioning paper sheets in printing presses, and in paper processing machines of various kinds. Feeding was formerly done entirely by hand but gradually technical means were devised, at first for moving the sheet forward and adjusting it, while the sheets in the pile were still separated by hand. From this 'semi-automatic' feeding, which still exists in some machines, modern entirely automatic feeders have developed. One of the first practicable feeders for cylinder presses was built in 1896 by the Swede Lagerman, who also built a platen press in 1902 with wholly automatic feeding and delivery (Lagerman press). Modern machines are often constructed with built-in feeders of various kinds but large presses are usually supplied without feeders which are manufactured and fitted as separate units. There are many such feeders differing mainly in the manner of separating the sheets from the pile.

Some employ friction, suction or blowing arrangements to release sheets singly from the *pile feeder* to the grippers and transporting bands which convey them to the press. There are also *stream feeders* of various makes in which sheets slide forward in a continuous overlapping stream.

Modern feeders are equipped with automatic stopping devices such as mechanical detectors, photo-electric cells or micro-circuit breakers. If sheets fail to reach the lays correctly these devices stop the feeder and release pressure in the printing machine.

In large machines the feeder is installed as a separate floor-standing unit with automatic hoisting and re-loading so that piles can be changed without stopping the press. (With GU)

feeding: the insertion of a sheet of paper into the printing press. This was formerly done by hand, and pinning devices were used to obtain register. Hand-feeding still survives, but pins have been replaced by feed guides or *lays* along which the front edge and one side edge of the sheet are placed.

In the platen press paper is fed by hand or machine directly on to the platen; the lays supporting the front edge are adjusted and the sheet grippers fixed. The side lay consists of a pin fixed to the tympan.

In cylinder and other presses feeding proceeds automatically from a feeding table the lower edge of which is flush with the cylinder. High-speed machines are often equipped with pre grippers which turn or revolve between the feeding table and the cylinder and can accelerate the sheet in a short time from its motionless state to the speed of the cylinder.

In American offset machines the front edge of the sheet rests against non-adjustable front lays and, after being adjusted to the side lay, is gripped by revolving crown wheels and led to the cylinder grippers at a speed slightly greater than the periphery speed of the cylinder. There the edge of the paper strikes against guides before the grippers close. The sheet is adjusted in this direction solely by altering the position of the printing plate.

In high-speed sheet-fed rotary presses the diameter of the cylinder is so small that almost the whole of its circumference is filled by the printing surface; for this reason a sheet must be ready to be taken by the grippers almost as soon as the previous sheet has left the feeding table. This is facilitated by stream-feeding or other devices. Cf. *delivery*. See also *rotary press*. (With GU)

feeding edge: see *gripper edge*.

feet: the base on which a type stands, being formed by a separating groove cut in it by the dresser. Type not standing squarely is said to be 'off its feet'.

Although modern machines cast type with an ungrooved base this is still called the 'feet' *not* 'foot'.

Feierabend, Sigmund, 1528–90: a woodcutter and type-cutter from Heidelberg who married into a wealthy family of Frankfurt where he established himself in 1560, at first working for the printers Zöpfel and Rasch before becoming the leading printer of his day. By way of repayment for debt he took over the press of Peter Schmidt who continued to work for him for many years. When Schmidt died his widow said that Feierabend had stripped her husband of everything but his shirt. As he developed Feierabend formed a consortium with other printers and soon controlled most of the Frankfurt book trade.

He was the printer of a fine illustrated German Bible in 1560, and of 'Eygentliche Beschreibung aller Stände auf Erden' illustrated by *Jost Amman*, q.v., in 1568. This book included the frequently reproduced cuts of printing trade workshops, though inaccuracies in the depictions have been noted. From his press Feierabend published simultaneously the writings of Innocent IV and Lutheran tracts.

Feierabend's use of the Neudörffer Fraktur led to its extensive adoption by other German printers. See also *Theodore de Bry*.

Feliciano, Felice, 1433–*c*. 79: of Verona. From about 1458 he was a manuscript copyist. He was a disciple of Ciriaco d'Ancona and made similar collections of lapidary inscriptions. About 1460 he wrote a treatise intended for use by stone cutters on the construction of roman capitals (Cod.Vat.6852). This was reprinted by the Officina Bodoni in 1960. His most important work was a lavishly illuminated collection of classical inscriptions completed in 1465, now in the Biblioteca Estense, Modena (Cod.a.L.5.15), with plain copies in Paris and Princeton. In the drawings of the monuments Feliciano's fanciful restorations differed from those in Ciriaco's factual representations.

About 1465 he was employed as scribe and rubrisher by Giovanni Marcanova, a wealthy antiquary. Ten years later he collaborated with the printer Severino of Ferrara before opening his own press in 1476 at Pojano in association with Innocente Zileta. In the same year they issued Petrarch's 'Libro degli uomini famosi' with Feliciano's woodcuts. See also *humanistic scripts*. See C. Mitchell, 'Felice Feliciano, Antiquarius', *Proc. Brit. Academy*, 1961.

Fell types: the collection of punches and matrices of greek, roman and oriental founts purchased by Dr John Fell (1625–86) and bequeathed by him to the Oxford University Press in 1686.

In 1669 Fell formed an association with others to improve the printing done by the University. An early step was the sending of Thomas Marshall to Holland to buy types. This was in 1670 and 1672 and Marshall bought founts from Abraham van Dijck and Jacques Vallet. Other types came from Moxon and from Peter de Walpergen, a Dutch punchcutter who Fell invited to Oxford where he died in 1703. The collection included work of the great French punchcutters Garamont, Granjon and Haultin as well as Van Dijck.

Important works completed during Fell's lifetime were a Bible and a Greek New Testament, both published in 1675, and a Cyprian of 1682.

For many years the types were not in use, but they were revived in 1863 by Henry Latham who had a fount of small pica roman cast. C. H. O. Daniel (1845–1919) used them from 1876 for his private press at Worcester. Still later Robert Bridges used them for his Yattendon Hymnal, 1895–99. See S. Morison, 'John Fell, the University Press . . .', O.U.P., 1967.

felt finish: a finish given to sheets of paper by drying them on a special marking felt positioned over the cylinder.

felting: the binding together of fibres in paper pulp while on the moving wire of the Fourdrinier.

felts: pieces of coarse woven wool or cotton (not felted in spite of the name) in which sheets of waterleaf were couched while still wet. On the Fourdrinier endless felts of several kinds, which vary according to the kind of paper being made, are used to convey and dry the newly formed paper.

felt side: the upper side of a sheet of paper as it is formed on the wire. It is smoother than the under, or wire, side. See also *twin-wire paper*.

fere-humanistica: the name given to a group of types deriving from the 14th century Italian book script developed by Petrarch and Poggio Bracciolini from earlier Latin hands. It was a simplified and legible round gothic script.

Between 1460 and 1485 it was cut and cast as a type face being used in Italy, Germany and elsewhere (in England by Rood at Oxford). It was without the serifs of roman or the hair-lines and feet of gothic and was used by Günther Zainer, Ulrich Zel, Johann Mentelin and Peter Schöffer.

In the present century revivals based on it have included the Troy of Morris, the Distel of the Zilver Distel Press, and the Ashendene Press Subiaco.

In Germany it was known as *gotico-antiqua* and in France as *lettre de somme*. See also *letters – forms and styles*.

Ferrara Bible: the name given to the first printed version of an anonymous translation into Castilian Spanish of the Pentateuch. Because of archaisms in the language it has been attributed by some to the pen of David Kimhi (1160–1235). The text has been the basis of subsequent Spanish translations of the O.T.

The work was printed at Ferrara in 1553 by Abraham ibn Usque. The single edition of 802 double-column pages comprised de luxe and small paper copies, each with dedication and colophon in two versions. One dedication is to the fourth Duke of Ferrara whose privilege to publish the work in that city would be necessary. It is signed Duarte Pinel and Jeronimo de Vargas. The alternative version is to Doña Gracia Nasi, a wealthy Jewish lady who is presumed to have financed publication. Here the signatories are Yom Tob Atias and Abraham Usque. The Spanish Atias and Portuguese Usque families may have changed their names to Vargas and Pinel because of the Inquisition.

The variant forms of name occur in the two versions of the colophon, but careless make-up has resulted in inconsistencies in marrying the colophon to its correct dedication. See S. Rypins, 'The Ferrara Bible at press'. *The Library*, 5th ser., x 1955 244–69.

festoon drying: see *drying tunnel*.

Festschrift: a German word ('the term providentially has no English equivalent' *TLS*) now used by British publishers for a volume of essays written in honour of a scholar of repute. The essays are related to the subject in which the scholar has won his renown, and are often published to mark a birthday or retirement. The titles of French collections often begin with the words 'Mélanges offerts à . . .'.

Feyerabend, Sigismund: see *Feierabend, Sigmund*.

fiction series: cheap reprints of fiction issued in uniform cloth covers, a style belonging to the years 1830–90. See also *three-decker novel, yellow-backs*.

Field, Richard, 1561–1624: a London printer, born at Stratford. He was bound to George Bishop but served as an apprentice to *Thomas Vautroullier*, q.v., marrying the latter's widow in 1588 and continuing the business. He held various offices in the Stationers' Company. During his busy working life he printed nearly three hundred books and worked for over forty publishers. He was the printer of Shakespeare's first published work 'Venus and Adonis', 1593; his 'Lucrece', 1594; and Harington's translation of 'Orlando furioso', 1591.

In 1626 the stock of Field's business was assigned to an ex-apprentice, George Miller.

Figgins, Vincent, 1766–1844: a London typefounder who in 1782 was apprenticed to Joseph Jackson, establishing his own business in 1792. One of his first commissions was the cutting of a two-line english roman for Thomas Bensley, and in 1796 a series of greek capitals for Oxford University. Also of note were his learned and oriental founts. His specimen book of 1815 showed under the name *antique* the first-known *egyptian* fount.

In 1836 he was succeeded by his two sons *Vincent II* and *James*, followed by other direct descendants until 1907 when the firm was reconstituted by R. H. Stevens, later trading as Stevens, Shanks & Sons. See 'Vincent Figgins type specimens, 1801 and 1815', reproduced in facsimile and with notes by Berthold Wolpe, Printing Historical Society, 1967. See also Appendix A.

figure: 1. an illustration on a page of text with which it is printed from a forme imposed together with type. Cf. *plate*.
2. see *numerals*.

filler: a *tail-piece*, q.v.

fillers: *loading*, q.v.

fillet: a roll-tool used by the finisher for impressing straight lines on the covers of a book; also the line so made. Small lines across the spine are done with a *pallet*, q.v. Curved lines are tooled with *gouges*, q.v., although small fillets can be used for slightly curving lines.
There may be one or more lines cut on the edge of the fillet, and a small notch is cut in the edge to facilitate the making of neat corner joins. The fillet has a long handle which rests against the shoulder. Illustrated under *doublures*, q.v.

filling in: a faulty impression caused when type characters or the spaces between the dots of a half-tone fill with ink. This may be due to using an unsuitable ink or too much of it; the forme being too high or the rollers incorrectly set; or a paper which fluffs.
Clogging or *choking* are alternative names for filling in.

filling-in guards: see *compensation guards*.

film advance: the photosetting equivalent of *leading*, q.v., i.e. the provision of space between lines of characters. Also known as *interline space*.

film make-up: the preparation of photoset matter for proofing and platemaking. Only one of several methods is described here.
The equipment used includes an illuminated glass-topped frame, a display photosetter, film galleys, a vacuum frame, and a diazo proofing machine.
The assembly of image-carrying film is done on self-adhesive transparent transfer sheets. Point-size graphs are used to assist positioning. After taping the graph to the frame it is marked up to show the layout of page area, running heads, and so forth. Pasted up galleys may be provided as a guide. Corrections can be added during make-up. Proofing is done by contact copying the film image on to a light-sensitive paper which is developed by ammonia vapour. See also *photosetting*.

filmsetting: see *photosetting*.

final size: the size of an illustration as it will be printed. This may be a reduction or an enlargement of the original art work submitted to the blockmaker. See also *same size*.

fine etching: the giving of correct emphasis to the middle tones and high lights of a half-tone plate, after its first dipping in an acid bath, by staging out the darker tones so that only those parts of the plate which require it are affected by the acid. See also *staging out*.

fine-grain morocco: a very durable morocco with a fine natural grain brought out by hand.

Finé, Oronce, 1494–1555: the first French Royal Mathematician. He was also an artist. In addition to the usual diagrams necessary to explain the texts of his 'Protomathesis', 1532; 'Arithmetica', 1535; and Euclid, 1536, he designed engraved title-pages, borders and elegant initial alphabets for them, bringing to French book design the influence of the Italian Renaissance as interpreted by artists in Basle.
His printers, all outstanding craftsmen, were Estienne, Morrhé, Vascosan and Collines: for the latter Finé designed an elaborate full-page frame with allegorical figures for a series of scientific works.

fine paper copy: a copy of a book printed on better paper than the ordinary edition, usually hand-made.

fine rule: one of hairline thickness.

fine whites: unprinted offcuts which result when paper is trimmed by the papermaker, printer or binder. See also *broke, recycled paper*.

finish: the surface given to paper during manufacture. Factors affecting this are ingredients, sizing and calendering. See also *paper finishes and varieties*.

finisher: 1. an alternative but little used name for a *serif*, q.v.
2. the craftsman employed in *finishing*, q.v.

finishing: the lettering and decoration of a hand-bound book. This is done by the finisher who uses brass tools in wooden handles (sometimes designing his own), a burnisher, gouges (for curves), fillets and pallets (for lines), rolls, flowers and letters. In modern hand bookbinding very few engraved tools are used and the decoration is achieved by inlaying or onlaying leathers of contrasting colours. The term finishing is not applied to *cased books*, q.v. For an illustration see *gilt edges*.

In his 'Bookbinding then and now' (Faber, 1959) Lionel Darley writes that finishing 'remains the essential trade practice which from time to time, through the hand and eye of some dedicated workman, is mysteriously exalted to an art'. For an illustration see *tooling*.

2. finishing also refers to the hand or machine processing of printed matter. In bookwork this includes cutting, folding, machine binding and jacketing.

Fiol, Szwajpolt: see *cyrillic*.

first edition: all copies of a book as first printed and issued. Repeated printings from the same type, plates or stereos without major textual alterations are still part of the first edition. A second edition implies re-set type, or changes of format or text. See also *edition, first impression,*

First Edition Club: a club founded in 1922 by A. J. A. Symons and Max Judge with the objects of promoting the study of book collecting and bibliography, issuing books unlikely to be sponsored by other publishers, inspiring by example an improvement in the standard of book production, and arranging exhibitions.

Among publications of note were 'Bibliography of the principal modern presses' by G. S. Tomkinson, and 'Book clubs and printing societies of Great Britain and Ireland' by H. Williams. These productions showed care and taste, for which the Curwen Press was largely responsible.

The club, which was incorporated in 1927, failed in 1932.

first gluing: see *gluing-up*.

first impression: all copies of a book resulting from the first printing of type or plates. Minor corrections may be made for a second or subsequent impression. See also *first edition, issue*.

first lining: see *lining*.

First Novel Award: an annual house dinner in honour of the author of what is considered to be the most promising first novel of the year. It was instituted in 1954 by the Authors' Club, Whitehall Court, London. Under the club's rules only male authors are eligible, and a panel of members makes a preliminary selection from novels submitted by publishers; the final choice is then made by a distinguished author. The first award was to David Unwin for his 'The Governor's Wife.'

fish-glue enamel: a dichromated colloid used as a

photoengraving resist for half-tone blockmaking. Powderless etching and electronically engraved plates have largely replaced it. Cf. *cold enamel*.

Fishenden, Richard Bertram, 1880–1956: for many years Britain's leading authority on printing and the graphic arts as interpreted by printing processes. As a youth he studied process engraving technique, then in its infancy, and in 1902 he began lecturing in the Manchester College of Technology, remaining as head of the printing department until 1921. In this year he joined Stephenson Blake, the letter founders, leaving in 1931 to join Lorilleux and Bolton, ink-makers. In 1942 he was appointed technical editor of the 'King Penguin' books, and a year later was adviser to Spicers, the papermakers. These two posts were held concurrently.

It was, however, as the editor of *Penrose Annual* from 1935 to 1956 that he was known throughout Europe and America. Under his direction this volume, recording all aspects of printing, developed into a work of considerable authority.

Fisher, George: binder to the *Gregynog Press*, q.v.

fist: see *digit* (2).

fit, fitting: the degree of proximity between adjacent type characters.

fl.: see *floruit dates*.

flare the balls: to hold *ink balls*, q.v., over a piece of burning paper to make them tacky.

flash drying: a method of drying the printed web of paper on a high-speed rotary press. Immediately after impression the paper speeds past a source of intense heat (up to 480°C). The volatile thinner or solvent in the ink instantly evaporates, flashing into flame and leaving a hard dry image on the web. The passage of the paper is so quick that it is unaffected by the heat.

flat: any flat printing plate.

flat back: a binding style in which the rounding of the back is omitted. The *spine*, q.v., is thus flat, and narrower than it would be if rounded. Also known as *square back*.

flatbed: any press which prints from flat formes carried on a bed.

flatbed cylinder press: a printing machine having a flat bed on which the forme is placed and carried to and fro under the impression cylinder. See also *letterpress machines*.

flatbed rotary: a widely used term for a reel-fed or *web-fed flatbed machine*, q.v. The term 'flatbed rotary' is misleading since 'rotary' implies printing from a moulded or curved plate carried on a cylinder, not from a forme carried on a bed.

flatbed web press: a machine for printing from a flat forme on to an endless roll of paper. The press was introduced in 1891 and intended for small newspapers.

flat copy: an original for platemaking, e.g. a drawing, painting, photograph, or transparency in monochrome or colour.

flat proofs: prints made from the separate plates used in colour printing.

flat pull: see *rough pull*.

flat stiching: stitching a pamphlet or book by means of wire or linen thread in such a way that it passes from the side right through the whole book (which must have a flat back). See also *stabbing*. (GU)

flat tint plate: zinc plate, shaped as required, for printing a flat tint.

Fleischman, Johann Michael, 1701–68: a Nuremburg punchcutter. The fount of roman and italic he cut in 1735 for the Wetstein foundry of Amsterdam passed with the latter's stock to the Enschedé family in 1743. The precision and clarity of Fleischman's types made them popular and led to his long association with Enschedé en Zonen. Of particular importance was the music type he completed in 1760.

fleurons: see *flowers*.

Fleuron Society: a publishing society formed in 1922 by Holbrook Jackson, Francis Meynell, Bernard Newdigate, Stanley Morison and Oliver Simon. It was planned to produce one book a year to show that a machine-set book could rival a private press book set and pulled by hand. After its third meeting the Society was dissolved.

Morison and Simon then founded the periodical *The Fleuron: a journal of typography*, publishing it from the office of The Fleuron at St Stephen's House, Westminster, the former London office of the defunct *Cloister Press*, q.v.

Numbers 1–4 (1923–25) were edited by Simon and printed by the Curwen press: numbers 5–7 (1926, 1928, 1930) were edited by Morison and printed and published by C.U.P. Publication then ceased, but the authority of the essays on the history and theory of typography, matched by careful setting and machining gave *The Fleuron* an internationally recognised status. A reprint of the series was published in America

in 1970, and a one-volume anthology was published in Toronto and London in 1973.

Flexiback: the trade name of a *thermoplastic binder*, q.v., made by the Book Machinery Co. of London.

Briefly, folded and collated sections are fed into the machine which in one operation produces a completely lined book, thus avoiding the usual separate stages of sewing, nipping, back gluing and lining. The adhesive used is a polyvinyl cold emulsion synthetic glue.

flexible binding: a binding style in which boards are omitted. Such volumes are usually covered in real or imitation leather on to which the end-papers are pasted direct. The leather may be slightly stiffened by first pasting on to it a stout paper or very thin card. Cf. *flexible sewing*.

flexible glue: a bookbinding glue which contains a hygroscopic additive to prevent it from drying out completely. It is used for gluing-up the back of a book after sewing.

flexible sewing: the oldest and strongest method of sewing the sections of a book on to raised bands or cords. The stitching thread passes around each cord: greater strength results, and the book can be opened flat at any page unless the book is thick, small, or on stiffish paper. See also *raised bands, sunken flexible*.

flexicover: a tough cloth or proprietary fibrous material used without boards to cover books. The result is more durable than paper-backing but less so than casing in boards.

flexography: printing from relief-image rubber plates on a reel-fed rotary press. The term was used about 1952 by the Mosstype Corporation of New York for their development of the *aniline printing* process. Instead of the cheap inks made from aniline dyes dissolved in alcohol, used during the first thirty years of this century for paper-bag and similar packaging material, improved inks made from pigments, resins and solvents of various kinds and combinations have transformed the potentialities of the process to include book printing and by the 1970s it was extensively used for paperback production.

flier: an advertiser's small handbill inserted at random into a book at some point before sale.

flimsy: the sheets of thin, tough and semi-transparent bond paper used for planning in the layout department.

Flinsch, Heinrich: of Frankfurt. In 1859 he acquired the typefoundry which had been established in 1827 by Friedrich Dresler and Karl Rost-Fingerle. Under his son *Heinrich II* the firm developed considerably until by 1867 it was turning out 2½ million types a week, and by 1882 ninety-two casting machines were in use. The artistic quality of the products was low: quantity was everything. However, about 1900 *Edgar Flinsch*, grandson of Heinrich I, increased and improved the firm's range of proprietary types by commissioning young designers such as F. H. Ehmcke and Lucian Bernhard.

When the business was sold to Georg Hartman of the *Bauersche Giesserei*, q.v., 145,000 punches and 420,000 matrices were transferred to the new owner.

floating accents: see *accents*.

floating fleurons: decorative panels in which small ornaments are used to build up a design for printing as an embellishment to a chapter heading, etc.

floating the forme: the filling with plaster of any spaces below the level of type shoulders or hollow quads. This is done before pouring melted wax on to a forme of type to make a mould for electrotyping.

flong: the material used for moulds in *stereotyping*. There are two kinds – wet and dry. *Wet flong* consists of alternate layers of blotting paper and tissue paper pasted and rolled together into a unit with a blotting paper base and a tissue face. The flong is placed tissue side down on the forme and beaten into it. The flong-bearing forme is next dried in a hot press. *Dry flong*, which has now superseded wet flong, is made in the same way but dried before use leaving a moisture content varying from 5 to 25% according to the class of work for which it is required. Sheets of it are placed on the forme which is passed under a heavy roller or through a hydraulic moulding press to force it into the type.

When making curved stereos the flong is bent to a semi-circular shape and placed, impression side inwards, in an *autoplate machine* for casting.

By facing dry flong with a polyvinyl emulsion it will give high-quality results from fine-screen and process colour work. See *stereotype*.

Florence Press: founded at Letchworth in 1908 with the aim of producing cheaply fine books in large editions. In 1909 E. P. Prince cut the Florence type designed by Herbert Percy Horne for the press. Chatto & Windus were the trade publishers and distributors. The press is now defunct.

Florentine woodcuts: a group of artists and craftsmen working in Florence between 1492 and 1508 produced what are often considered the finest of early book illustrations. The five hundred or so cuts appeared on chapbooks, sermons, and ephemeral texts, written in Italian, and mostly badly printed on poor paper. Their unique quality was a finely executed combination, on the same cut, of black on white and white on black technique. Examples survive in the Tracts of Savonarola, printed by Antonio Miscomini, 1494–6.

Their prototype was contained in a lost edition of about 1492 of 'Fior di Virtù', Societas Colubris, 1498. See P. Kristeller, 'Early Florentine woodcuts', Kegan Paul, 1897.

floret: a binder's tool used to impress a flower or leaf design. See also *flowers*.

floriated: said of a border, initial, or book cover which is decorated with small flower or leaf ornaments. Initials floriated with acanthus leaves date from the 12th century, and these developed in the following century into *historiated letters*, q.v. See also *blooming letters*.

florilegium: 1. a Latin word, anglicized as *florilegy*, for an anthology of the 'flowers' of literature. Florilegia of classical writers were used by later writers as sources of quotations, the 'Florilegium Gallicum' being a well-known example. It contained prose and verse. Among compilations of the kind issued by early English printers was De Worde's 'Floure of the Commaundmentes', 1505; a later example was Udall's 'Floures for Latine spekynge . . . gathered oute of Terence', 1533. See also *garland*.

2. a picture book of flowers of horticultural rather than botanical interest. One of the first to be printed was 'De historia Stirpium . . .', Basle, 1542, written by Leonard Fuchs, after whom the flower fuschia is named. It had fine woodcut illustrations from drawings by Albrecht Meyer, to be coloured after purchase. Others followed and the peak of popularity was reached in the 17th century, but their appeal continued as, for example, with Redouté's famous 'Choix des plus belles fleurs', 1827–33, and its numerous successors. See also *Weiditz*.

floruit dates: the approximate dates when a person flourished in the capacity for which he was famous; used when exact dates are not known. Abbreviated as *fl.*

flow box: the container from which pulp flows on to the moving wire of a *Fourdrinier*, q.v. The old type, also called a *breast box*, was a copper-lined steel tank in which the fluid stock was maintained at a pre-set depth to ensure it would flow through the slice opening at a velocity approximately equal to that of the moving wire which received it. The slice was a flat steel or copper plate with a similar plate mounted above it, above there being an adjustable orifice between them so that pulp distribution could be controlled.

For machines with wire speeds in excess of 1,500 feet a minute this type of flow box proved uneconomic and led to the introduction of the *pressure headbox*, also known as a *stock inlet*. Designs vary but the most commonly used comprises a closed box lined with stainless steel. A cushion of compressed air is maintained over the stock in the the box, pressure being adjusted so that stock is discharged or projected on to the wire at the desired speed although the actual depth of stock is only a few inches.

flowers: type ornaments used to embellish page borders, chapter headings, tail-pieces, title-pages, and generally to enliven printed matter.

Probably the earliest use of the decorative printing types known as flowers was in Dominico Capranica's 'Arte de ben morire' printed by Giovanni and Alberto Aluise at Verona in 1478 (Hain 4398). In addition to forming a page-border they were set up with lines of display type.

Basic designs, popular since the early 16th century, have been the acorn, vine leaf, and arabesque. They may be traced to the Venetian pattern-books of arabesques and other decorative material, deriving from the Near East, used by metal-workers, engravers, weavers, painters and bookbinders. Venetian binders used small stamps, known as *piccoli ferri*, bearing motifs adapted from the pattern-books, and it seems that early punchcutters copied these for casting on type-bodies. With the simple leaf, tendril, acorn or arabesque as a unit, printers either set them singly or built up elaborate patterns to fill as much of a page as they wished. Of early printers Aldus, Ratdolt, Giolito, de Tournes, Tory and Granjon made extensive use of flowers, while later, P-S. Fournier was an inspired cutter of new designs.

Flowers have been particularly popular in the present century, and the number of flower matrices available from Monotype and Linotype together with the decorative units of the major European foundries must total several thousands, and new designs continue to be made. Notable examples have been commissioned by the Curwen Press and the Fanfare Press, among others, for their exclusive use.

Flowers are variously known as *fleurons*, *florets*, *printers' flowers*, and, in Germany, as *Röslein*.

For much of my information I am indebted to John Ryders's 'A suite of fleurons', Phoenix House, 1956. See also *Aldine leaves*, *arabesque*, *floating fleurons*, *ornaments*.

Monotype Borders

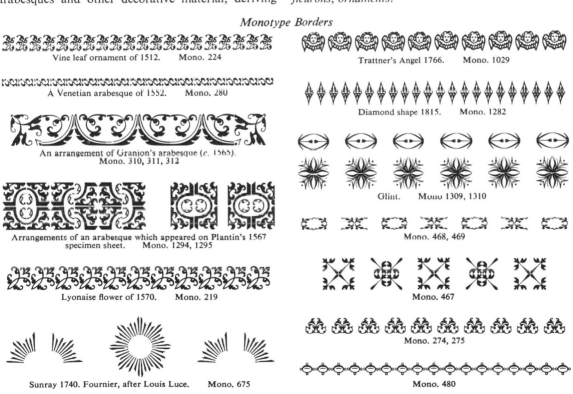

Vine leaf ornament of 1512.   Mono. 224

A Venetian arabesque of 1552.   Mono. 280

An arrangement of Granjon's arabesque (c. 1565).
Mono. 310, 311, 312

Arrangements of an arabesque which appeared on Plantin's 1567
specimen sheet.   Mono. 1294, 1295

Lyonaise flower of 1570.   Mono. 219

Sunray 1740. Fournier, after Louis Luce.   Mono. 675

Trattner's Angel 1766.   Mono. 1029

Diamond shape 1815.   Mono. 1282

Glint.   Mono 1309, 1310

Mono. 468, 469

Mono. 467

Mono. 274, 275

Mono. 480

Fournier flowers 1736–67.   Mono. 475, 476

Linotype Borders

Matrix No. 15

Matrix No. 141

Matrix No. 142

Matrix No. 109

Matrices Nos. 141, 109, 142

Matrix No. 131

Matrix No. 124

Matrix No. 200

Matrices Nos. 146, 148, 147

Matrices Nos. 125, 127, 126

Matrix No. 197

Slide No. 1267A

Slide No. 1283A

Slide No. 1312A

Matrix No. 317   Matrices Nos. 280, 281

Typefoundry Amsterdam

Stephenson Blake

Stempel

Bauer

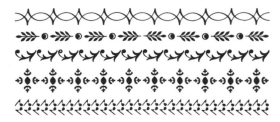

Curwen Press Borders

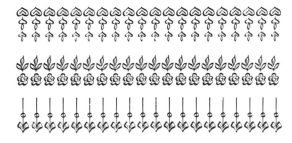

Edward Bawden   Harry Carter

Edward Bawden   Edward Bawden

Reiner Borders (Simson Shand)

fluffing: the release of fibres which rub off the surface of paper as it passes through a press. The fibres adhere to type, necessitating frequent wash-ups. While the fault occurs in both letterpress and litho work it is more serious in the latter particularly when press speeds are increased.

The tendency to fluff may be reduced by *surface sizing*, q.v. Better bonding of the fibres, while maintaining bulk, also helps to minimize fluffing.

flush and hang: synonymous with *hanging paragraph*, q.v.

flush boards: a method of binding in which boards are glued to the paste-downs and the book then receives a paper cover which in turn is glued to the boards. The book, boards and cover are *cut flush*. An alternative name is *stiffened and cut flush*.   (LK)

flush paragraphs: paragraphs in which the first word is not indented but set flush with the vertical line of the text.

flush work: binding styles in which the cover is applied before cutting and cut with the book. Thus in the finished book the edges of the cover are level with the edges of the book. (LK)

fly: see *delivery flies*.

flye: the name given by 16th century mariners to the *wind-rose*, q.v., which formed the inner circle of the Italian and Portuguese pictorial charts and tide-tables then in use. The north was always indicated by the fleur-de-lis and the name flye may be a corruption of this.

fly embossing press: a very large heavy press, built in the basement of a bindery, for the blocking at one strike of the complete design for a panel-stamped cover. Two operators were needed and the leather was embossed before attaching. Such presses were introduced in England and France in the late 1820s. See also *blind-stamped panels*, *embossed bindings*.

Flying Fame Press: a private press founded in 1912 by Claud Lovat Fraser, Holbrook Jackson and Ralph Hodgson with the aim of publishing in chapbook and broadside form original prose and verse, with illustrations. The press continued until the First World War.

flying paster: see *rotary press*.

fly leaf: see *end-papers*.

flyswing: a very thin skiver leather widely used for title labels on cloth- and leather-bound books: after mounting the leather label the normal procedure is to letter in gold. (LK)

fly-title: 1. a leaf indicating the beginning of a distinct portion of a book. An anthology of plays will usually have a fly-title for each.

2. an alternative name in England for *bastard title*, *half-title*.

FOGRA: the acronym for Deutsche Gesellschaft für Forschung im Graphischen Gewerbe EV, which is the West German research institute for graphic arts.

Fogra plates: half-tone printing plates made of Perlon (nylon), developed by the Deutsche Gesellschaft für Forschung im Graphischen Gewerbe.

Sheets of nylon are sensitized on both sides in a dichromate solution in acetone. When exposed to a screen negative the nylon is hardened. The plate is developed in an alcohol solution which etches both sides, one with a relief image for printing, the other being a make-ready.

foil: see *blocking foils*.

Folchart Psalter: a 9th-century Carolingian manuscript notable for the finely decorated initials which embellish its pages, made for Folchardus, a monk of St Gall.

folded and collated copies: the usually folded and collated copies of a work sent to the publisher for approval of printing before binding commences. Also known as *advance sheets*. Books are often sold in bulk in this form, e.g. to American publishers for casing in the U.S.A.

folding: the folding of flat printed sheets to book size. The number of pages in the folded sheet is always a multiple of four (i.e. two leaves) hence, when the sheet is subsequently opened and sewn through the last fold, all leaves are secured. The thickness of the paper is the principal element in determining the number of pages in a folded sheet as sheets which are too thick or too thin do not make a satisfactory section for binding. Printer's formes and binder's folding machines are largely standardized and as a result folded sheets are usually of 8, 16 or 32 pages, 12- or 24-page sheets being exceptional. The flat printed sheet may contain as many as 128 pages but folding machines convert such sheets into either eight individual 16-page folded sections or four sections each of 32 pages. Printed sheets of 64 pages or 32 pages are much used and slit and folded into lesser sheets by folding machines.

The printing size will be determined by the size of paper available and the machines on which the work will be printed and folded, the larger sizes being economic only for long runs. The various folding machines show great diversity in the pattern of the folds they produce hence it is essential that the sheets should be printed to the precise imposition demanded by the machine on which they will be folded. The procedure is made simple in trade practice by the use of *Book Impositions 1975*, q.v.

In general terms, anything which can be folded by machine can be folded by hand, but work which is being printed for hand-folding is normally printed in small-size sheets or alternatively cut by guillotine into its component sections before folding. (LK)
See also *folding machines*.

folding chases: a pair of chases used to lock up large many-page formes.

folding in gangs: folding in a machine which takes a large sheet and folds several sections at one operation. As it passes through the machine the sheet is folded, cut into sections, the heads are slit, and the sections are delivered singly or inset.

folding machine: a machine for folding printed sheets for bookbinding. The first is thought to have been invented by Black of Edinburgh in 1850. He built a machine for hand-feeding based on the blade or knife and roller method of making the fold. An automatic folding machine for newspaper work was invented in America by Walter Scott. It was added to the *Bullock press*, q.v. in 1869. In extensive use in Europe were the Dexter folders brought from America in 1898. They folded two and then four 16-page sections simultaneously. Present-day machines are based on one of two principles: knife-folding or buckle-folding, and the two may be combined in a single machine.

In the knife-folder a blunt-edged knife is set parallel with and above the slot formed by two rollers. The rollers are continuously revolving so that when a

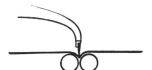

Principle of knife-folding

sheet of paper is placed over the rollers and the knife descends the paper is caught between the rollers and carried away by them, a fold being made where the the knife made contact.

In practice sheets are fed one at a time either by hand or mechanical feeders (see *feeder*) and carried by moving tapes beneath the knife where they are mechanically positioned for folding. The knife having descended, the sheet, now with one fold in it, is carried by rollers and tapes to a second unit of knife and rollers where a second fold is made, and so on for the third and maybe fourth fold, the folded sheets being delivered into a stacker from which they are removed by hand. If any knife unit is at right-angles to the previous knife unit a fold at right-angles to the previous fold is made, but if the machine is constructed with the folding units parallel to preceding folds then parallel folds are made. If it is desired to slit the sheet into individual sections during folding, the sheet, when passing from one folding unit to the next, will travel through rotary slitters and the resulting portions will be conveyed to individual folding units. Thus a sheet printed with 64 pages can be slit into four parts producing four individual 16-page folded sections. Machines are normally provided with perforators which will perforate the bolts, thus avoiding creasing.

Buckle-folders work on an entirely different principle. The sheet is fed end on between a pair of continuously revolving rollers and the leading edge is guided between two closely spaced plates, the plane of the plates being at 45° to the plane of feeding. The plates

are fitted with internal adjustable stops and when the leading edge of the sheet comes in contact with these stops further forward movement is arrested. The latter half of the sheet, however, is still being propelled forward by the rollers and, the sheet being already bent at 45°, buckles at the point of entry to the plates. The buckle is gripped between the lower of the aforementioned rollers and a third roller in contact with it and the buckle passes between these rollers, thus forming a fold. The portion of the sheet between the plates is by this action immediately

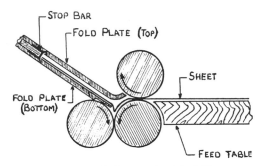

Principle of plate- or buckle-folding

withdrawn, leaving the mechanism clear for the next sheet. The sheet continues to be propelled by rollers and the folded edge may be deflected into a second and following that a third plate and additional folds parallel to the first thus made.

Such machines frequently incorporate knife-folding units, the knives being used to make folds at right-angles to the parallel bucklefolds. As with knife-folding machines, perforators and slitters are incorporated for use at varying stages of folding.

In general it may be said that buckle-folders may be run at a rather higher speed than knife-folders, but knife-folders are usually favoured by bookbinders as they are better adapted for dealing with a great diversity of papers. The simplest form of folding machine is one constructed to make one fold only but the largest knife-machines will fold a flat sheet of 128 pages and from it produce four 32-page folded sections, each of four folds. Buckle-folders, by means of the use of or the by-passing of a large number of plates and knives, in their most complex forms will produce almost any series of folds, but in general such machines are more used for the production of publicity matter than book work. (LK)

folding plate: an illustration on a page larger than those of the text it is to accompany so that it must be given one or more folds before insertion.

fold out: see *thrown out*.

folds: see *folding*.

fold sealing: see *thread sealing*.

fold to paper: an instruction to the folding department that the printed sheets are to be folded so that the edges of the leaves and the bolts are all level in the folded sheets. Cf. *fold to print*.   (LK)

fold to print: an instruction to the folding department that sheets are to be folded in register, i.e. the edges of the printed areas are to be placed exactly over one another before the fold is made.

Folger, Henry Clay, 1857–1930: a New York biblio-phile who spent some forty years assembling a library of 20,000 volumes of Shakespeariana, early Eliza-bethan English literature and various editions of Shakespeare's works including fifty First Folios. He bequeathed his collection to the nation, and it is now kept in a special building in Washington, D.C.

foliation: the forerunner of pagination; only the recto sides of leaves in manuscripts or early printed books being numbered, usually in roman numerals. Leaf numerals were printed as early as 1470, Johannes da Spira of Venice being the first printer to do this. See also *pagination*.

folio: 1. the book size resulting from folding a sheet with one fold, thus giving pages half the size of the sheet. To define fully the size the paper size must also be stated, e.g. *Crown folio*. In practice double-size paper folded twice, or quad-size paper folded three times would be used, thus producing the requisite folio size but in sections convenient for binding. Abbreviated as *Fo.*, or *fo.*
2. a leaf of paper or parchment numbered only on the front.
3. the number of a page (this is a loose usage of the term). See also *blind folio*, *drop folios*.

follow copy: an instruction to the compositor indi-cating that the spelling and punctuation of a manu-script are to be followed, even if unorthodox, in preference to the *style of the house*, q.v.

font: an early form of *fount*, q.v. The term survives in the U.S.A.

foolscap: a former standard size of printing paper, $13\frac{1}{2}$ in. $\times$ 17 in.

foot: 1. the margin at the bottom of a page; also the bottom edge of a book.
2. the terminal point or finishing stroke on the ascenders and descenders of 15th century black-letter type. Cf. *feet*.

footline: the last line of a page, particularly that containing folio or signature mark.

footnotes: short notes, printed at the foot of a page, to which the attention of the reader is drawn by textual reference marks. Footnotes should be set in type two sizes smaller than that used for the text.

footstick: a wedge of wood or metal placed along the foot of pages when locking them up and secured in the chase by quoins. See also *sidestick*.

fore-edge (pronounced *forage*): the outer edge of a book parallel to the back. Synonymous with *foredge*.

fore-edge margin: the outer margin of a page, parallel to the *backs*, q.v.

fore-edge painting: painted decoration on the edges of the leaves of a book is of two kinds: 1. intended to show when the book is closed. This form is found on medieval manuscripts, as on a Psalter written and decorated near Paris about 1250 which has edges painted in red and blue with gold fleurs-de-lis (BN Mss. lat. 10434), and the style has been in occasional use ever since.
2. the almost exclusively English practice of painting a water colour on the fanned out fore-edge of a book. When the painting is dry the edges are gilded or marbled in the usual way so that the closed book shows no trace of the painting.

The earliest known example, unsigned but dated 1649, is in the Pierpont Morgan Library. Also in New York is a Bible of 1651 on which the fore-edge painting of the Leigh arms is signed by the binder 'Lewis fecit. Anno Dom. 1653'. The binding is in Mearne's cottage style, but the connection between Lewis and Mearne is not known. Various London binders of the late 17th century made or commissioned these bindings. In the early 18th century John Brindley produced bindings with armorial fore-edges for Queen Caroline.

It was William Edwards of Halifax, however, who about 1750 pioneered the taste for painted landscapes on fore-edges; hitherto, floral scrolls and armorial bearings had been subjects. These were at first worked in monochrome – brown or grey – but later in a full range of colours. Portraits were also included, often flanking a landscape. Subjects depicted included country seats and ruined castles. The types of books most frequently embellished were Bibles and prayer books, the classics, travel books and poetry.

There are also double paintings, one scene made with the leaves fanned over to the right, and a second painted with them fanned to the left. This idea may have originated early in the present century, for the truth is that most of all known fore-edge paintings have been done since 1890 and they are still being added to old books. Among the most competent artists to produce them have been Joseph C. Clarke, Miss B. Currie of Rivière and Kenneth Hobson, followed by a number of anonymous artists commissioned by the London antiquarian book trade. The addition of fore-edge paintings has meant saleability for many dull morocco bindings of Victorian England, and has even enhanced the value, or rather price, of genuine Edwards bindings originally sold without them. See C. A. Weber, '1001 fore-edge paintings'. Waterville, Maine, 1949. See also *Bozérian, Edwards of Halifax, Etruscan bindings, Pillone.*

forel bindings: early English bindings in which oak boards were covered with roughly dressed unsplit sheepskin. They were made by monks in the 8th and 9th centuries.

fore-stay: the frontal wooden support for the carriage assembly of a hand-printing press. The rear of the carriage was secured to the *cheeks*, q.v.

foreword: introductory and often laudatory remarks to a work or about its author written by someone other than the author. The foreword will not be changed for successive editions. Cf. *preface* and *introduction.*

format: 1. an imprecise indication of the size of a book, being based on the number of times the printed sheets have been folded. See also *American book sizes, British book sizes, folio, quarto, octavo.*
2. the general appearance or style of a book, i.e. size, shape, quality of paper, type-face and binding. This is a loose usage, known in America as the 'get up' of a book.

forme: type matter and blocks assembled into pages and locked up in a chase ready for printing. The impression taken from it is a signature. A 'naked forme' consists of pages of type secured by page-cord; a 'dressed forme' is one of pages of type with furniture between and around them and the page-cord removed. See also *foundry forme.*

former: the enlarged model of a letter or other character used for making a steel punch with a pantographic cutter. Does not apply to hand punchcutting.

forme roller: see *inking system.*

Formschneider: the German term for a block-cutter. Before printing from movable type was invented the craft of block-cutting was well established in Germany, notably in such towns as Ulm and Augsburg where the cutters were organized into guilds. Due to a dispute between the new printers of the mid-15th century and the older cutters over the right to pub-

lish illustrations in books it was decided that while printers might publish illustrated works the actual cutting of the blocks they used must be done by an approved Formschneider. This may account for the technical superiority of the cuts in German incunabula over many of those printed elsewhere.

One of the most accomplished of these craftsmen was *Jost de Negker* (*c.*1485–1544) who in 1508 was invited by Maximilian I to leave his native Antwerp and settle in Augsburg. Here he cut blocks of illustrations by Hans Burgkmair and Hans Schäufelein for the 'Theuerdank', 1517. See also *Florentine woodcuts, woodcut.*

42-line Bible: see *Bible printing, Gutenberg, Mazarine Bible.*

forwarding: properly, the processes involved in the binding by hand of a book subsequent to cutting and up to the point of fitting on its cover or case: loosely, the stages (including covering) prior to decoration, lettering, and other finishing work, Cf. *finishing.*

forwarding sucker: a rubber suction device which assists in passing sheets of paper singly on to the feed board of a printing machine.

foul case: a compositor's case in which types have been distributed into wrong compartments.

Foulis, Robert, 1707–76: one of Scotland's best known printers of the 18th century. From 1740–41, when he had a bookselling business in Glasgow, the title pages of his own publications bore the inscription 'Printed for Robert Foulis', but from 1742–76 the inscription was 'Printed by Robert Foulis'. In 1743 he was appointed University Printer. His brother *Andrew* (1712–75) joined him in 1744. Mostly they published reprints of standard authors, plainly printed with no extraneous ornament, and soon established a reputation for their carefully edited editions of Greek and Latin classics. For these they used the types of *Alexander Wilson*, q.v. Their editions of Horace, 1744, and Homer, 1756–58, are considered among the finest and most accurate ever printed.

After 1776 the firm was continued by Robert's son *Andrew* who interested himself in *stereotype*, q.v. The business closed in 1795. See P. Gaskell, 'A bibliography of the Foulis Press', Hart-Davis, 1964.

foul proof: a proof having many faults marked in it.

founder's type: type cast by a typefounder for hand composition as distinct from that cast on Linotype, Monotype, Intertype or Ludlow machines. See also *fount scheme, typecasting.*

foundry clump: a length of type-high metal used at

sides and ends of a forme when making a stereotype or electrotype.

foundry forme: type, blocks, formes or other relief printing surfaces prepared for duplicate printing-plate making. See also *electrotype, stereotype*.

foundry proof: a proof pulled before a forme is sent to the foundry. It accompanies the *foundry forme*.

fount: 1. a complete array of type characters designed and made up as a set. It normally includes upper and lower case, numerals, punctuation marks, accents, ligatures, etc. A *type family* includes founts of roman, sloped roman, italic, bold, condensed, sanserif and sometimes greek, cyrillic, etc.

2. a complete set of matrices in the magazine of a composing machine.

fountain: the trough or container from which *damping solution* is conveyed sequentially via a fountain roller, an oscillating feed roller and a chromed distributing roller to two cotton-sleeved rubber rollers (known as *plate dampers*) which apply the solution to the non-image areas of a lithographic plate on a sheet-fed press. There are other methods of conveying moisture to the plate but all require careful setting of the various rollers to achieve optimum damping. (See diagram under *offset press*).

On web-offset machines a separately-powered fountain roller is used and there are various proprietary wetting systems, some using an alcohol-water mix.

fountain solution: see *damping solution*.

fount scheme: the assembly of mixed type of one design supplied by the typefounder to the printer. The serviceable number of each character varies from country to country according to the language of it. The whole is known as a *bill of type* or *bill of fount*. In his 'Typographia', 1824, J. Johnson stated that letter founders call 3,000 lower-case 'm' a *bill*.

Fouquet, Jean, *c.* 1420–80: of Tours. A leading 15th century French miniature painter, noted for his handling of architectural details. An early masterpiece was the Hours of Étienne of Chevalier, painted *c.* 1452–56, now in the Musée Condé at Chantilly, and another important work from his atelier was the 'Antiquités judaïques', originally commissioned from another artist by the duc de Berry. From a copy of Boccaccio's 'Des cas de nobles hommes et femmes', 1458, we can study his fondness for painting crowds and processions, and his interest in perspective which he introduced from Italy to France after studying in Rome. In the contemporaneous 'Grandes chroniques de France', probably made for Charles VII, there

are detailed panoramas of Paris (now in the Bibliothèque Nationale).

It has been said that true manuscript painting in France reached its apotheosis with Fouquet and merged into panel painting, a development which he influenced. See P. Wescher, 'Jean Fouquet and his times', Basle, 1947.

four-colour process: see *colour separation*.

Fourdrinier: the standard papermaking machine, invented in France by *Nicolas-Louis Robert* before 1798, and subsequently developed in England by *Bryan Donkin*, qq.v., on behalf of *Henry* and *Sealy Fourdrinier* after whom it is still named. They set up an experimental machine at Frogmore, Herts. in 1799, but it was not perfected until 1806. During the years of experiment Didot (the first sponsor of Robert) came to England to supervise the work of Donkin. Most of the British patents, at first held by Didot's English associate, *John Gamble*, were bought by the Fourdriniers in 1804. In 1806 they patented an improved wire cloth (Pat. No. 1951). Due to defects in their patent rights, however, the Fourdriniers and Gamble went bankrupt in 1810. Later they continued activity, patenting various improvements, but never enjoyed the financial rewards their invention merited. Sealy died in 1847, Henry in 1854. The first Fourdrinier in America was set up by Donkin in 1827, and by 1851 his firm had set up eighty-three in Britain, forty-six in Germany, twenty-three in France, twenty-two in Scandinavia, fourteen in Italy and south Europe, two in America and one in India.

The Fourdrinier machine was the first on which it was possible to make a continuous roll of paper, and its principles are used today. The fluid pulp is kept in a tank from which it flows on to a moving meshed wire belt. In moving, the pulp is strained, and by agitation the fibres are shaken into a web. This passes under a dandy roll, suction boxes, heated drying rolls, airhoods and a calender unit to be wound on a reel, re-wound and cut as required. A big news-print machine is designed to run at up to 2,000 feet (609 m) a minute and produce 100,000 tons a year. See R. H. Clapperton, 'The paper-making machine: its invention, evolution and development', Pergamon, 1967. See also *papermaking, Whittingham*.

Fournier, Jean Claude, d. 1729: for over twenty years manager of the Le Bé foundry in Paris. The elder of his sons, *Jean Pierre* (1706–83), known as *l'aîné*, was a punchcutter and typefounder. He bought the Le Bé foundry in 1730. It was, however, his youngest brother *Pierre-Simon* (1712–68), known as *le jeune*, who began typefounding in 1736 and brought great fame to the family name. In 1766 he claimed to be the first in France to have carried out as part of one business type designing, punchcutting, striking and justifying the matrices, the making of moulds and typecasting; very much, in fact, what his contemporary Caslon was doing in London.

He was noted for his vignettes, music types, an elegant roman, many alphabets of decorated capitals, a profusion of type flowers, probably inspired by engravings of Cochin, and then known as *vignettes de fonte*. He showed these flowers, elegantly grouped, in his 'Modèles des caractères de l'imprimerie', 1742. His work was without peer in Europe, and the éclat of early 18th century fine printing in France owed much to his types. (See Appendix A.)

About 1737 Pierre-Simon proposed a standard of measurement for type based on an ideal unit which he called the 'typographical point' (0·0137 in.). To encourage its acceptance by the trade he printed a scale on paper (which due to dimensional instability could never be precise), and he made a metal gauge which he called a 'prototype'. In its revised and final form his point system was described in his 'Manuel typographique', 2 vols, 1764–66: the first was a manual on typecutting and founding, the second a specimen which included over a hundred alphabets. He printed this work himself on a temporary press he was allowed by special licence to set up (it being in excess of the permitted number of presses in Paris). After completion the press was dismantled.

On his death the business was continued for some time by his elder son *Simon-Pierre* (1750– after 1789)

The Fournier point was superseded in France in 1775 by the *Didot point*, q.v.

The modern Fournier type of the Monotype Corporation appeared in 1925 as Series 185. Barbou, a Fournier type re-cut by Monotype, was the face Stanley Morison had intended to be cut. This appeared in 1926 as Series 178. (See his 'Tally of types', C.U.P., 1953.) See A. Hutt, 'Fournier: the compleat typographer', Muller, 1972.

four-up: the processing in book production of four 16-page sections as a unit. Separation is done after gathering, gluing-up and adhering the cover. This is suitable for long runs of paperbacks. See also *two-up*.

foxed: said of book pages discoloured by damp which has affected impurities in the paper. See also *bleaching paper*.

William Foyle Poetry Prize: established in 1949; an annual award of £250 made by the famous London bookselling firm. Recipients have included John Betjeman, Richard Church, Edith Sitwell, and Dylan Thomas.

fractions: see *split fractions*.

Fraktur: 1. the German name for *black letter*, q.v.
2. a German black-letter type-face believed to have

184

originated in Augsburg, c. 1510, from designs by Leonhard Wagner based on the 15th-century lettre bâtarde. The first book to be printed in this type was the Prayer-Book of Maximilian I, dated 1513. It was, however, Neudörffer's design of 1522 which became traditional.

Fraktur types rapidly replaced roman in Germany where in the late 16th century foreign words set in roman appeared in pages of black-letter text much as italic is used today to distinguish an occasional foreign word in an English text. Several attempts were made to popularize roman, unsuccessfully in the 18th century, for scientific literature in the 19th, and finally, by decree, in 1941. See K. Bauer, 'Leonhard Wagner, der Schöpfer der Fraktur', Frankfurt, 1936. See also *letters – forms and styles*.

frame: the cabinet containing cases of type, galley units, drawers, cupboards, bins for spacing, and a place for the operator to work at. More flexible frames,

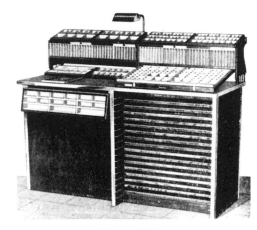

A typical frame

based on unit systems of construction, were introduced in the 1920s to increase efficiency and output. See also *hand composition*.

Francesco da Bologna, fl.1499–1518: or *Francesco Griffo*, a goldsmith of Bologna and one of the first independent punchcutters in Italy. He is particularly remembered for his association with *Aldus*, q.v., for whom he cut the first known italic type, c. 1499. The fount was of lower-case letters only. A second version was used at Fano by Gershom Soncino. A third was used in the books he printed himself in 1516.

No less important was the first roman type he cut for Aldus which the latter used in 16-point size for Cardinal Bembo's 'De Aetna' in 1495. His recutting of this face about 1499 was the inspiration for roman types designed during the next three centuries by

Garamont, Granjon, Van Dijck, Jannon, and *Caslon,* qq.v. In 1929 it was revived by the Monotype Corporation as Bembo, Series 270.

In 1516 he set up a press at Bologna, issuing some six Italian and Latin books, all in small format, before he died in 1518. See also *Petrucci.*

Frankfurt Fair: a trade fair held at Frankfurt-am-Main, originally each Lent and Michaelmas. Writing of it in 1574 Henri Estienne II described it as 'la nouvelle Athènes' where a prince could equip an army. Though the fairs had been important long before printing was invented for the next two centuries the bigger printer-publishers from France, Holland, Italy and Switzerland joined their German counterparts in developing Frankfurt as the centre of European book trade. Records for 1569 show that eighty-seven of them attended that year's fairs, seventeen from Frankfurt itself, five from Geneva, four from Lyons, three from Venice and so on, doubtless each with commissions from others. An indication of the scale of individual participation is given in a letter dated 10 October 1534 from Christopher Froschauer to Joachim Vadian telling him that 2,000 copies of the first edition of the latter's 'Epitome trium terrae partium' will be on sale at Frankfurt. Unsold books could be warehoused in Frankfurt for a later fair.

Although separate lists of books for sale had been issued for many years, notable being those of Georg Willer of Augsburg from 1564, the first official catalogue was that printed in 1590 by Peter Schmidt: they continued to appear until the 18th century. Of the 22,000 or so works catalogued between 1564 and 1600 14,724 were published by 117 German firms from 61 towns, 6,112 were from other countries, and 1,014 were unlocated. Plantin or his relative Moretus regularly came to the fair to settle accounts. English buyers were frequent purchasers, and we learn from one of them, James Allestrye in 1653, that 'it is a very usual thing for the booksellers of Germany to send the titles of their books to be put in the catalogue before they are printed, so that at present they are not to be had', a practice not unknown 300 years later.

It was at Frankfurt, too, that typefounders came to buy matrices and sell type. Engravers of wood and copper sought commissions, as did translators, proof correctors and authors.

For many years Catholic and Protestant books were sold alike, but when in 1579 Rudolf II established a censorship of books exhibited Protestant publishers moved to the more tolerant town of Leipzig. The Thirty Years War (1618–48) caused social dislocation which almost brought the fair to a standstill. Another factor furthering its decline was the growth of a public which preferred to read in the vernacular, and the barter system by which books in Latin had been freely traded at Frankfurt diminished. During the second half of the 17th century the British and French book trades began to develop their national catalogues of books on sale and the journey to Frankfurt became unnecessary. By this time the trade for German language books centred on Leipzig where German booksellers were joined by those from Holland, Poland and Russia.

The Frankfurt book fair took a on new lease of life when it opened on 18 September 1949 under the auspices of the publishers and booksellers of Hesse. Since 1950 it has been organised by the West German Publishers and Booksellers Association, speedily becoming a vast annual display of books from many countries with strong British representation. It is a favoured meeting place for publishers anxious to dispose of rights and to arrange the syndicated publication of expensive illustrated books. See also *Leipzig Fair.*

Franklin, Benjamin, 1706–90: one of the most eminent Americans who was a printer, publisher, author, scientist and statesman. His printing career began when he was apprenticed to his brother James, a Boston printer. The first imprint to bear his name was an issue of the weekly newspaper *New England Courier,* 4 February 1723, which his brother, the owner, had been forbidden to print. The new imprint was a subterfuge which continued until 1726, though Benjamin had left Boston in 1723 for Philadelphia where he printed for Samuel Keimer. In 1724 he sailed for England to buy printing equipment to establish his own workshop, but his letters of credit from the Governor of Boston proved valueless.

In London he began working with Samuel Palmer, later as a compositor and pressman with John Watts, but by 1728 he was back in Philadelphia where he entered into a short partnership with Hugh Meredith, a fellow printer. Their first known work was the completion for Keimer of the third edition of Sewell's 'History of Quakers'. The partnership ended in 1730.

Franklin's reputation as a printer developed with his publication of the *Pennsylvania Gazette* and a series of pamphlets known as the 'Poor Richard' almanacs, of which the first appeared in 1732 and the last in 1757 (for 1758). Although the authorship was attributed by Franklin to the late Richard Saunders, Franklin compiled most of the contents. These collections of aphorisms were enormously popular and were printed in editions of 10,000 copies.

In 1730 Franklin became official printer to the state of Pennsylvania. His printing of Richardson's 'Pamela' in 1744 was the first novel to be printed in America. He considered his edition of Cicero's 'Cato major', 1744, as his finest work, but it was not, as he claimed in the preface, the 'First Translation of a *classic* in this *Western World*', since in 1735 he had published Cato's 'Moral distichs', similarly 'Englished' by James Logan.

In 1731 he founded the Library Company of Philadelphia which, by making books widely available, was the precursor of later book clubs.

In 1748 he took into partnership his Scottish employee David Hall, and this association lasted until 1766, Franklin meanwhile being less active as a printer. Ten years later, when in Paris as representative of the colonies, Franklin had a private press at his home in Passy where he printed about forty items.

His interest was lifelong, and even his Will began 'I, Benjamin Franklin, Printer . . .'. He corresponded with Baskerville, Bodoni, F. A. Didot, the Fourniers and other printers and founders. He was also an admirer of Caslon whose types he used.

Franklin was active in furthering the establishment of printing offices in several towns and instigated the erection of the first copperplate printing press in America. In 1785 he erected a type-foundry in Philadelphia which was active for a few years. Both the hand-press then in general use and later platen presses were named after him. See C. W. Miller, 'Benjamin Franklin's Philadelphia printing, 1728–66: a descriptive bibliography', Am. Phil. Soc., 1974.

Miles Franklin Award: an annual award of $A1,250 established under the will of the Australian writer Miss Miles Franklin who died in 1954. It is given for 'the novel of the year which is of the highest literary merit and which must present Australian life in any of its phases'.

Fratres Vitae Communis: *Brethren of the Common Life*, a religious order founded at Deventer by Gerard Groote about 1374. They formed a group of priests, clerks and laymen which aimed at promoting religious observance by education without withdrawing from secular society. Members devoted their time to teaching and book production, the copying of religious texts spreading their influence as far as Rome. Thomas à Kempis was a pupil as was Gerard Mercator. At the time of their foundation the brethren were known as 'Devotio moderna'.

The brethren had the only printing press at work in Brussels during the 15th century, the first book to be issued being Jean Gerson's 'Opuscula', 1475. They are also thought to be the printers of St Jerome's 'Vitas patrum', *c.* 1476, and are generally credited with having printed about thirty works by 1485, many of them theological and liturgical tracts.

Fredericksen, C. W., 1823–97: an American businessman and book collector who after assembling an important Shakespearian library turned to early 19th century poetry and especially Shelley.

free hand: the irregular and more quickly written form of *set hand* which was widely used in England from the 12th–16th century. See also *set hand*.

186

French bookbinders: see *Badier, Bauzonnet, Bonet, Boyet, Bozérian, Bradel, Cretté, Creuzevault, Cuzin, Derome, Dubuisson, Du Seuil, Ève, Gruel, Le Gascon, Legrain, Michel, Monnier, Padeloup, Picques, Purgold, Roffet, Ruette, Thouvenin, Trautz.*

french calf: calfskins used to cover the nap rollers of a lithographic printing machine.

French Cape Levant: a handsome morocco leather of the finest quality made from the skin of a large Cape goat. This is said to have a Levant grain which is larger than the small pin-head grain of ordinary morocco. It was extensively used by French masterbinders with beautiful results.

french dash: a *swelled rule*, q.v.

french fillet: a combination of fine double-line and single-line tooling used as an outer frame on the boards of French bindings from the early 16th century onwards. Similar three-line tooling, which gave the effect of strapwork, was used to surround mosaic inlays and also to form compartments subsequently filled with small tooled motifs as in *à la fanfare*, q.v.

french fold: said of a sheet printed on one side only and then folded into a section with bolts uncut; the insides are blank. See also *orihon*.

french folio: thin, smooth, sized paper, thicker than tissue, used by pressmen for overlays and underlays in make-ready. (ML)

french furniture: large, hollow metal *quads*, q.v.

french groove: synonymous with *french joint*, q.v.

french headcaps: see *headcap*.

French illumination: in the 11th and 12th centuries illumination flourished in such centres as Chartres, Clairvaux, Limoges, Lyons and Paris. Perhaps the most important single feature was the decorated initial since the illustration of texts was restricted in extent and treatment.

Paris was the great centre of 13th-century French Gothic, much work being done in lay workshops, with more emphasis on fine craftsmanship than innovation. By the 14th century a secular iconography replaced the religious, largely due to the patronage of such wealthy noblemen as the *duc de Berry*, q.v., and the growing popularity of fables, romances, and chronicles. The illuminators, freed from tradition, largely abandoned symbolism for poetic naturalism. The most beautiful Books of Hours of the Middle Ages were made in France for castles, not churches or monasteries; of these the 'Breviaire de Belleville' made in the atelier of *Jean Pucelle* (fl.1320–50) q.v., was the first to depict the months with separate scenes, and with these the development of French landscape art may be said to have begun.

In the 15th century Italian and Flemish influences were important, the latter largely due to artists brought together by the Dukes of Burgundy. See also *Channel School, illumination*.

French imprint dates: there is a difficulty in dating precisely Parisian books of the early 16th century since, for many printers, a new year began at Easter. It was not until 1567 that Charles IX's decree of 1563, fixing January 1st as the advent of the new year, was generally accepted.

french joints: in binding if the boards are set away from the joints a space is left into which the covering material is pressed, forming a gully. This is of parti-

French joint

cular advantage with heavy boards and thick covering material such as buckram, which need this assistance to make a free-hinging joint. Synonymous with *grooved joints, sunk joints*. (LK)

french morocco: split sheepskin grained to resemble morocco.

french nick: an incision on the back of a type-body, i.e. on the lateral surface bordering the upper edge of the type-face. (GU)

french rule: a straight length of brass or type-metal rule which is divided in the middle by a diamond-shaped ornament.

french sewing: 1. the normal method of machine sewing, i.e. without tapes.

2. in *hand-sewing*, q.v., a method of sewing a book without the usual frame, the sections being sewn at the edge of the binder's bench. The needle enters the first gathering at the kettle-stitch point and emerges at one or two points along the back. Loops are left for the needle to pass through when sewing the next gathering. The thread is now tightened and tied. As sewing proceeds the thread is connected to the previous section at these points. The first and last gatherings are tightly laced to the upper and lower covers. This results in a back without bands, and was the method used by the Copts, Greeks and Persians and in the early 16th century by the French.

french shell: a variety of marbled paper used in France in the 18th century. See also *marbling*.

friar: a white patch left on a forme due to imperfect inking. Cf. *monk*.

Friburger, Michael: see *Gering, Ulrich*.

Friedenspreis des deutschen Buchhandels: established in 1950, being an annual award of ten thousand marks made to a writer of any nationality who is considered to have contributed by his work and way of life to peace and freedom amongst men. The award is sponsored by the West German book trade and is presented at the annual Frankfurt Fair. Past winners have included Schweitzer, Burchhardt, and Thornton Wilder.

frisket: a thin rectangular iron frame covered with brown paper and attached by a hinge to the upper part of the *tympan*, q.v. It is used to hold the sheet to the tympan and lift it off the forme after printing. The centre part of the brown paper is cut away over the printing area, the remainder preventing the chase and furniture soiling the sheet.

Froben, Johann, 1460–1527: born at Hammelburg in Bavaria. After studying in Basle he began printing there in 1491, issuing some law books and a small Latin Bible. He was a pupil and sometime partner of *Johannes Amerbach*, q.v., and at one time of Johann Petri. Froben printed mostly works in Latin, Greek and Hebrew becoming one of the greatest printers of his time. He took into partnership Wolfgang Lachner (1465–1518) whose daughter he married.

He employed scholars to edit and correct the classical and humanistic texts he produced, notable among them being Beatus Rhenanus and, from 1514, Desiderius Erasmus whose Latin translation for the first printed edition of the Greek New Testament, 'Novum instrumentum', 1516, was to influence such later translators as Luther and Tyndale: Erasmus was also employed and paid as a press corrector. He printed several works by Luther to whom he wrote in 1519 that he had sent them for sale to Brabant, England, France, Italy and Spain.

Froben was quick to use roman and italic types, the latter particularly for quotations, a custom he may have originated. His hebrew type was in the Ashkenazi style with its gothic emphasis. To embellish his finely printed books Froben commissioned Urs Graf and, after 1516 the Holbein brothers to design borders, initials and other engraved decorations. He sold type to printers in other European countries. When Froben died his business traditions were continued by his son *Hieronymous* (1501–65) and grandson *Ambrosius* (1537–95).

front delivery: the delivery from a cylinder press of the printed sheet in such a way that it is brought forward in the direction of the cylinder motion with the impression side uppermost. This serves the dual purpose of facilitating constant supervision of the sheets and easy assembling of the pile. Front delivery is usual in two-revolution presses, but less so in stop-cylinder presses where the working of the machine presents construction difficulties if this is to be arranged.

front matter: 1. in British publishing, an alternative name for *preliminary matter*, q.v.

2. in the U.S.A., a heading at the beginning of editorial notes and comments which precede the first article in an academic serial. The term gained currency in the mid-1950s.

frontispiece: an illustration facing the title-page, either printed with the prelims or separately pasted and guarded into a book.

Froschauer, Christopher, fl.1521–64: a German printer born at Neuburg in Bavaria who in 1519 was granted citizenship of Zurich where he became the leading printer. He placed his press at the service of Ulrich Zwingli whose writings, and those of other Reformers, he printed. His house was the centre of an influential circle of thinkers, very similar to the Froben-Erasmus house in Basle.

Froschauer's first known publications (1521) were translations into German by Leo Jud of two Erasmus works. In 1529 he issued Zwingli's German Bible, the first complete version in that language. Before his death he printed at least twenty-seven editions of the whole Bible and fifteen N.T.s in German, Latin and English. He printed the 1550 edition of Coverdale's Bible and was for long credited with the 1535 edition, having used similar type with the Hans Beham woodcuts in other books, but modern scholars now assign the work to Soter and Cervicornus of Marburg.

Froschauer's thirty-five page catalogue of 1543 offered 110 works in German and 106 in Latin. He printed the first volume of Gesner's 'Bibliotheca universalis', 1545, and an important writing book 'Libellus valde doctus' by Urban Wyss in 1549.

His nephews *Eustace* and *Christopher II* (d. 1585) continued the business after 1564. Notable were their series of official almanacs issued until 1580. The firm continues to this day, being now known as the Orell Füssli Verlag. See J. Staedtke, 'Anfänge und erste Blütezeit des Zürcher Buchdrucks', Zurich, 1965.

frothing: a possible trouble which may arise when coating paper. It results in minute unsurfaced dots on the finished sheet.

frotton printing: a method of taking an impression from type by rubbing the verso of a leaf laid upon it. This method was used before the invention of the press.

Frutiger, Adrian, b. 1928: an internationally known typographer of Swiss origin and training. He learned wood engraving while an apprentice printer but it was his study of calligraphy in the Zurich School of Fine Arts which led to his career as a type and print designer. In 1952 he was appointed artistic director to *Deberny and Peignot*, q.v. Two years later he began there the creation of the sanserif family *Univers* which ensured his fame. It was first shown in 1957 and has been licensed to several manufacturers in Europe and America (for a specimen see Appendix A).

Other designs include President, 1954; the shaded sloped Phoebus, 1953; the heavy script Ondine, 1954; the classical roman Méridien, 1957; the Apollo series for Monophoto setting, 1964; and OCR-B for Monotype, 1968. See also *devanagari*.

Fry, Joseph, 1728–87: a doctor of Bristol where in 1764 he established a typefoundry in partnership with a printer, William Pine (1739–1803), and with Isaac Moore as manager. In 1768 they moved to London. To cater for current fashion they cut a series of types modelled on Baskerville's, and from the printing press attached to their business they issued a Bible under the imprint of Moore, also like Baskerville's. After Moore's retirement from the partnership in 1776, Fry, catering for a changed fashion, reproduced the Caslon letter thereby provoking the latter to issue a public protest in 1785. In 1782 Pine withdrew to Bristol where he continued to print until 1803.

Fry's sons *Henry* and *Edmund* (d. 1835) joined the business in 1782, in which year they acquired a range of oriental and greek matrices from the James foundry. Edmund Fry, also a doctor of medicine, became the dominant partner and developed the business into one of the first rank, with a clientele extending to colonial America. He took into partnerhip Isaac Steele, their type specimens carrying both names until 1816. In 1788 Fry built new premises in London, the Type Street Foundry (in 1816 renamed Polyglot Letter Foundry). Henry Fry remained at the earlier premises with the printing office, known as the Cicero Press, where he printed John Bell's edition of Shakespeare in 1785–88.

In 1799 Dr Fry published his 'Pantographia: containing accurate copies of all the known alphabets of the world . . .', on which he had worked for sixteen years. When he retired in 1828 the stock was sold to *William Thorowgood*, q.v.

Frye, Bartholomew: an emigrant from Osnabrück to Halifax in Yorkshire where contemporary records show him to have been working as a bookbinder between 1809 (when he was a Freemason) and 1818. He also worked in Manchester and Liverpool.

In Halifax he may have been associated with William Edwards and he was certainly skilled in the various Edwards styles. Among his eleven known bindings are a copy of the Bible, printed in 1811 by Whittingham for Reeves, now in Halifax Public Library. It bears Frye's ticket and has an attractive fore-edge painting of a cathedral. There was a fine two-volume set of Aesop in the former Abbey collection.

Frye also used painted panels of transparent vellum which he inserted into morocco-covered boards. The combination of the two skins was probably to counteract the tendency to warp of vellum used alone. See also *Edwards of Halifax*.

Fugger: the name of a German family of merchants and bankers to emperors and popes. They had agents in Antwerp, Constantinople, London, Paris, Rome and elsewhere whose 'News-letters, 1568–1604' provide an interesting comment on Elizabethan England (ed. by V. von Klarwill, Bodley Head, 1926).

Several members of the family were book collectors, notable being *Raimund von Fugger* (1489–1535) whose 15,000 volumes are now in the Österreichische Nationalbibliothek, Vienna. His son *Johann Jakob* (1516–75), also a bibliophile, bought the library of *Hartmann Schedel*, q.v., the whole collection passing in 1571 via Albert V of Bavaria to what is now the Bavarian State Library, Munich. Other members of the family to have important libraries were *Ulrich* (1526–84), *Marcus* (1529–97), and *Philip Edward* (1546–1618).

Ulrich, while still a young man, commissioned bindings when studying at Bologna and Bourges. Later, in Augsburg, he set up a private bindery, probably bringing craftsmen from Geneva. Moving to Heidelberg in 1567 he gave his library to the Elector Palatine whose collection developed as one of the greatest libraries of the German renaissance. In 1623 its 7,000 books and manuscripts were taken as reparations to the Vatican where most of them remain: 822 manuscripts were returned to Heidelberg in 1816.

Philip Edward's library of 14,000 volumes by 17,000 writers (short works being bound up together as was then the custom) was bought by the Emperor Ferdinand III in 1655 and taken by rafts and boats to Vienna where the books and their catalogue are now in the Nationalbibliothek.

Fugger, Wolfgang, fl.1551: a Nuremberg printer remembered for his writing manual of 1553 which outlined the geometric construction of roman capitals. A facsimile was published by the Lion and Unicorn Press in 1958, repr. O.U.P., 1960.

full bound: a book wholly covered in one material, usually leather; thus *full calf, full morocco*, etcetera. If in cloth, the term *full cloth* can be used. Cf. *half-bound, quarter bound*.

full colour: the rich black effect of a printed page which results when ample ink has been used on suitably chosen stock, as distinct from the light grey effect when only little is used. (The choice of type face is another factor.) See also *tonal colour*.

full edition: the edition of a work which contains the author's complete text. The term is only used after an abridged, shortened, simplified or otherwise modified edition of the original has been published.

full face: see *full on the body*.

full gilt: a book having all its edges gilded.

full on the body: a fount of capitals designed to cover the maximum area of the body. It must, in hot metal, allow a *bevel*, q.v. See also *titling alphabet*.

full out: said of matter which begins flush with the margin. Cf. *indented*.

full point: a full stop.

furnish: the collective term for all the ingredients used together in any single variety of paper, vegetable fibre, chemical wood, rag, loading, etc.

furniture: lengths of wood, plastic or metal used in a forme for making margins or filling large blank areas on a page. They are made to standard point widths and lengths and are less than type height. Duralumin is often used for lightness, and metal has largely superseded wooden furniture. See also *skeleton*.

fusible: a relief (positive) image, cast in type metal in a hand-mould, made from a brass or phosphor-bronze matrix plate engraved with a letter or other character (in reverse).

This relief master letter is electroplated with nickel and copper to form the negative electro (character in reverse) which is trued up to provide the type matrix.

The foregoing is a stage in the preparation of a new type-face, or when making italic or script forms.

fusile types: an 18th-century expression for types made from molten lead poured into a mould.

Fust, Johann, fl.1450–66: a merchant of Mainz who, between 1450 and 1455, advanced money to *Gutenberg*, q.v., to develop his invention of printing. Fust later took over the business and entered into partnership with *Peter Schöffer*, q.v. Together they issued in 1457 the famous and beautiful Mainz Psalter of which the red and blue initials were the first successful attempt at colour printing. The initials were constructed in two interlocking pieces which were separately inked and then fitted together in the page of text, the whole being printed at one pull. This was also the first printed book to contain a colophon giving printer, place of printing, and date. The considerable time the printing of the Psalter must have taken, and the previous association of Fust with Gutenberg, justify the assumption that the latter must have worked on the preparatory stages. There were two issues: the first has 143 leaves. In the second, for which part of the type was re-set, the text was extended to include the Vigils of the Dead: it has 175 leaves. Ten copies of the Psalter are known, the finest now being in Vienna (of which a reproduction was published at Stuttgart in 1969). There being no title-page the work is catalogued as 'Psalterium Romanum cum canticis, hymnis', i.e. a psalter of the Roman rite. It had blank spaces for the manuscript insertion of differences necessary to adapt a copy to the usage of a particular diocese, thus the British Museum copy, the *Psalterium Moguntinum*, is for the usage of Mainz.

The 48-line Bible the partners issued in 1462 was the first printed Bible to bear a date and to have their device in all copies.

Fust died from the plague when on a visit to Paris in 1466 where he had probably gone to arrange for the sale of his publications. See Sir Irvine Masson, 'The Mainz Psalters and Canon Missae, 1457–1459', Bibliographical Society, 1954.

G

galley: 1. an open-ended tray, formerly of wood but now of steel, on which the compositor places type matter line by line as he proceeds. Type on the galley can be corrected more conveniently and cheaply than elsewhere. Type is transferred from the galley to the imposing stone by a *slice*, which is a flat board with a handle.

2. a long sheet, or *slip*, of paper bearing a proof of unpaged type composition. A subsequent intermediate stage between galley proof and page proof is *page on galley* for which the type has been divided into pages but is still not imposed. This stage is not customary unless the setting is difficult.

The earliest proof sheets of which fragments survive were pulled in Germany about 1458, but galley proofs as now used were an early 19th century innovation in both England and America. See G. D. Hargreaves, 'Correcting in the slip: the development of galley proofs', *The Library*, 5th ser., x 1971 295–331, and J. B. Jones, 'Galley proofs in America', *Proof*, 4 1975 153–64.

Galley Club: a London club, revived in 1955 from a former club of this name, for the study of all aspects of book production. It is open to persons employed or interested in the various relevant trades (printing, blockmaking, papermaking and binding, as well as publishers, typographers, jacket designers and artists), and exists to promote social contact between those engaged in book production.

galley press: a small press on which proofs are pulled on long slips of paper known as *galleys*.

galley proof: see *galley* (2).

Gally press: a platen machine built by an American, J. Merrit Gally, in 1869. It was the first large printing press to have a cylindrical inking device and to have lateral motion of the vertical bed and platen. It was imported into Europe about 1880 by Schelter & Giesecke of Leipzig who named it Phoenix. See also *platen press*.

Gamble, John: the man who in 1801 introduced into England the French prototype of what developed as the *Fourdrinier*, q.v. See also *Didot*.

Garamond: the form of name used by most non-French writers, and by some in France, for the Parisian punchcutter, his types and derivations of them. In both contemporary contractual documents and the imprints of books he co-published with Jean Barbé his name appears as *Garamont*. See next entry.

Garamont, Claude, *c.* 1500–61: a Parisian type designer, punchcutter and founder, influenced in his early years by *Tory*, and apprenticed to *Augereau*, qq.v.

The development of Garamont's roman, which he began cutting about 1530, can be linked with the Griffo fount used by Aldus in Bembo's 'De Actna' of 1495 and has affinities with the type used by de Colines to print Bochatel's pamphlet 'Le Sacre et coronnement de la Royne' in 1531. De Colines used it also for Terentianus Maurus's 'De literis Horati', 1531. The earliest book printed in Garamont's new type was 'In linguam Gallicam Isagoge' by Jacques Dubois (*dit* Sylvius), Robert Estienne, 1531, in which it appeared in three sizes (36-, 16½-, 12-point approx.). Garamont's type was more elegant and refined than any other, and his introduction of 36-point capitals led to their use with lower case for the interior of displayed words on title-pages as an alternative to all cap. setting. There were re-cuttings and further founts until 1560.

Garamont, who was one of the first independent typefounders in France, initiated the designing of roman and italic as part of one family, and he pioneered the setting of upper case italics on title-pages. Several leading booksellers and printers were among his customers for types and matrices, as was Plantin, and for nearly two centuries his roman and its derivatives were used in France, England, Holland and Italy. Between 1543 and 1560 he trained at least four apprentices as typefounders, but not as punch-cutters.

After his death the stock was sold. *Guillaume Le Bé*, q.v., since 1551 his business associate and subsequent executor, acquired material, and Plantin also bought some. Plantin showed Garamont's founts in his specimens of 1567 and 1585. Surprisingly none of the original punches and matrices of Garamont's famous roman and italic survives in France, the best collection being in the Plantin-Moretus Museum at Antwerp.

Many proprietary types known as Garamond roman have been made in the 20th century: they are partly based on the roman of *Jean Jannon*, q.v. See also *grecs du roi*. For a specimen of a Garamond roman see Appendix A.

garland: a popular anthology of songs, tales, lyrics and short literary pieces. Garlands, usually of eight pages, were cheaply printed, sometimes with a wood-cut title page, and were sold by chapmen, particularly in England in the 17th century. See also *florilegium*.

garter: the band or ring which secured the *hose*, q.v., on a hand press.

Gascon: see *Le Gascon*.

gathering: 1. assembling in their correct order for binding the folded sections of a book. This can be done by hand (when a revolving table with the sections piled in sequence helps) or on a large mechanical gatherer as is used for *edition binding*, q.v. Gathered sections are then collected and knocked up. An early mechanical gatherer was patented by John Mercer in 1897 (Pat. 3834).

2. another name for a *section*, *signature* or *quire*, qq.v.

Gatling gun: an apparatus having a large cylinder into which are inserted a number of tubes of varying diameter for the simultaneous casting in each of a composition *inking roller*, q.v. There may be as many as thirty small tubes or as few as four large ones into which the hot composition is forced upwards from the bottom, thereby expelling air bubbles. The first Rowe Gatling system to be set up in England was for Parsons, Fletcher & Co., of London, about 1897.

The name derives from a now obsolete machine gun with clustered barrels invented in 1862 by the American Richard Gatling.

Ged, William, 1690–1749: of Edinburgh. The pioneer in Britain of *stereotype*. By 1727 he devised a method of casting printing plates from plaster of paris moulds of pages of type, calling his process 'block printing'. Printers and typefounders of the time sought to hinder the development of his invention.

In 1729 he went to London, having entered into partnership with William Fenner, stationer and Thomas James, letter-founder. In 1731 they obtained from Cambridge University a licence to print Bibles and Prayer Books by the new method. In 1732 work on a Prayer Book was in hand at Cambridge but not, at least, to Fenner's satisfaction. A year later Ged returned to Edinburgh and Fenner died shortly after. A book of Common Prayer printed at Cambridge by Fenner in 1733 may include in its first portion sheets printed from stereo plates, the remainder being im-

192

pressed from formes of type. Lowndes 'Bibliographers manual' lists the item: 'Book of Common Prayer. Stereotyped by William Ged by permission from the University of Cambridge. 1735. 12mo'.

Back in Edinburgh Ged printed an edition of Sallust in 1739. He refused invitations to go to Holland or sell his invention to Dutch printers and died embittered and impoverished. For the subsequent history of his process and its commercial adaptation see *stereotype*. See J. Carter, 'William Ged and the invention of stereotype', *The Library*, 5th ser., xv 1960 162–192.

Gehenna Press: a private press imprint established by the distinguished American sculptor, wood engraver and artist Leonard Baskin of Northampton, Mass. His limited editions, mostly of poetry, had illustrations as their main purpose and were commercially machined for him. Notable have been a selection of Wilfred Owen's poems with drawings by Ben Shahn, 1956, and a suite of his own drawings for 'The Iliad', Chicago U.P., 1962. About 1972 Baskin moved to Devon in England.

gel: the gelation or drying of printing ink on paper; this is by oxidation, evaporation and penetration.

gem: the name of a former size of type, about 4-point.

Gemini, Thomas, *c.* 1500–70: or *Geminus*, an engraver, instrument maker and printer of London. His real surname was Lambrit or Lambert and he was born near Lille in Belgium. He printed maps, and in a work on mensuration which he issued in 1556 under the title 'Tectonicon' he claimed he could supply the instruments described. He was the friend, if not the tutor, of Humphrey Cole who made remarkably accurate astrolabes, theodolites, etc.

Gemini is remembered for two works. The first, printed by John Hereford in 1545, was 'Compendiosa totius anatomiae delineatio', which was an abridgement by Gemini of Vesalius's 'De humani corporis fabrica' and 'Epitome', printed at Basle by *Oporinus*, q.v. Gemini engraved a suite of forty copper plates, based on the original woodcuts, and they are considered to be the first copper engravings of importance to appear in an English book. The same plates were used for Nicholas Udall's translation of the work which N. Hill issued in 1553.

The second important work was George Lily's copperplate map of the British Isles which Gemini printed in 1555, making slight changes to the original plate which had been printed in Rome in 1546. See Geoffrey Keynes, 'The Anatomy of Thomas Geminus', *Annals R. Coll. Surgeons*, 1959.

Gerardus de Lisa, fl.1471–94: an important bookseller-printer of Treviso, Venice and Udine. Classical texts, divinity, philosophy and Italian belles-lettres formed the bulk of the ninety or so texts he printed. They were more distinctive and elegant than the work of many of his contemporaries. Notable were the editio princeps of Brunetto Latini's 'Il Tesoro', 1474, and the Nicolaus Perottus 'Rudimenta grammaticae', 1476.

He died in 1499 at Aquileia.

Gering, Ulrich, d. 1510: of Beromünster, and the proto-typographer of Paris. In 1461 he entered Basle university, returning to Beromünster about 1467 where, according to an 18th century tradition, he learned printing at the press set up by Helyas Helye, a canon of the cathedral who had engaged a former Mainz printer, Hans Müller, to operate it. In 1470 Gering, with his two assistants Martin Crantz, probably of Beromünster, and Michael Friburger of Colmar took punches and moulds to Paris where they set up the first printing press in France 'au collège de Sorbonne'. They did so at the invitation of *Johann Heynlin*, q.v., and Guillaume Fichet.

The first book issued was the 'Epistolae' of the Italian humanist Gasparino Barzizza, edited by Heynlin. The work was undated but is known to have been issued in late 1470. This quarto of 118 leaves was printed in a roman type resembling that used by Helyas Helye, probably in an edition of 100 copies, the first pages of each being illuminated. It was followed in early 1471 by the same author's 'Orthographia'. By the end of 1472 they had printed some twenty-two works, all in Latin, mostly classics, and intended for scholars and students.

In 1473 Gering and his two associates, now independent of their sponsors, moved the press to the rue Saint-Jacques at the sign of the 'Soleil d'or' from which their Latin Bible of 1476 was the first to be printed in France. Here they began to use gothic type and chose works of wider appeal than formerly. They were granted letters of naturalization in February 1475 but later in the same year Crantz and Friburger may have returned to Germany since only Gering is named in colophons. From 1494 until 1509 he had Berthold Rembolt as a partner, the latter continuing the business until 1519. Their Paris Psalter of 1494 was particularly noteworthy, being well printed in a fine black letter fount now described as *textura quadrata*.

Gesamtkatalog der Wiegendrucke: an author catalogue of incunabula which gives the location of all copies of a work when fewer than ten are believed to exist. Publication of this German work began in Leipzig in 1925; volume 8, part 1 was issued in 1940 and the project is not completed. Abbreviated as *GKDW* or *GKW*.

Gesellschaft der Bibliophilen: the principal bibliophilic society in Germany, founded in 1899 at the instigation of Fedor von Zobeltitz (1857–1934). It is the oldest of its kind in Germany. Zobeltitz was concerned at the lack of organized and informed interest in rare and beautiful books and worked hard to remedy this. In 1897 he issued 'Zeitschrift für Bücherfreunde' as a means of stimulating a wider knowledge of books.

In 1930 the society began publishing 'Imprimatur', a journal for bibliophiles and typophiles. Associated with the project until 1955 was the Gesellschaft der Bücherfreunde zu Hamburg. Since 1957 publication has been from Frankfurt.

Gesellschaft für Typenkunde: a society formed in Leipzig in 1907 to publish facsimiles of all typographical and decorative material used in European printing offices during the 15th century. Over two thousand plates were issued before World War II.

Gesner, Conrad, 1516–65: of Zurich, a professor of physics, naturalist and doctor of medicine. After studying at Bourges and Paris he returned to Switzerland for a formidably busy life. Among his numerous writings were an enlarged edition of Phavorinus' Latin-Greek dictionary, Basle, Petri, 1537; and 'Bibliotheca universalis', 3 vols, Zurich, Froschauer, 1545–49 (with appendix, 1555), which was an immense biobibliographical dictionary of Latin, Greek and Hebrew writers and books. It was the first major work of this kind.

His encyclopaedic illustrated 'Historia animalium', 4 vols, 1551–8 (with a fifth issued in 1587 after his death), was compiled with the assistance of correspondents in many countries. It has been described as representing the beginning of modern zoology. See H. Fischer, 'Conrad Gesner as bibliographer and encyclopaedist', *The Library*, 5th ser., xxi 1966 269–81.

Gesta Romanorum: a collection of anecdotal moral tales, intended for preachers. It was first written down in Latin prose during the later 13th or early 14th century. Myths, legends of saints, romances of chivalry and oriental tales were the basis of the stories. When translated into English about 1420 it was known as 'Deeds of the Romans' being first printed by Wynkyn de Worde, *c.* 1510. It was still current reading in the early 18th century and was popular throughout Europe. The editio princeps of the Latin version is attributed to Ulrich Zel, *c.* 1473.

get in: 1. to set copy in less space than estimated. Also to set type very close or use thin spacing so that matter will fit within required limits.

2. to add chapter headings, footnotes, formulae or tabular matter to a galley of type matter. A catch line is added to the head of the galley. The operation of getting in is done prior to page make-up.

get up: an Americanism for the *format* of a book, i.e. design, printing and binding.

ghost: 1. a printing fault seen on one area of a sheet when a badly set roller has left there the faint impression of a line of type or part of a block from another area of the same forme.

2. an edition of a book which, while being listed in library catalogues and elsewhere, never existed. An example is the supposedly unique edition in the Huntington Library of Bernard Richel's 'Missale Constantiense' which is actually his short 'Missale Basiliense' of 1481 and in no way unique.

The term 'ghost' is not applied to a work for the former existence of which evidence is available even though all copies of it may have perished.

ghosting: a printing fault which may occur in multi-colour letterpress or offset litho work. It appears as variations in ink transfer or in gloss. As the liquid ink of the first impression is converted by oxidation into a solid film on the paper an active gas is given off. In stacking sheets to dry this gas may be absorbed by the unprinted sides so that when this plain side comes to be printed the rate of ink drying will be affected.

Reducers, driers, resinated pigments, humidity and size of stack are among factors which need to be considered as possible causes of the fault.

Ghotan, Bartholomaeus: a German printer who first worked in Magdeburg and Lübeck, moving to Stockholm in 1486 where he printed five works of which a Missal for Strängnäs, 1487, was the most important. In 1493 he went to Russia to establish a printing press but is said to have been robbed there of all he possessed and he finally drowned in Russia some time before 1496. (GU)

giggering: polishing a blind impression on a leather binding by rubbing a short tool in it.

gilder's tip: see *tip*.

gilding rolls: in bookbinding, brass rolls faced with ornamental designs, used for gold tooling. (ML)

Gill, Eric, 1882–1940: an English craftsman, engraver, type designer, sculptor and philosopher whose influence on contemporary book production has been profound and world wide. As a young man he studied lettering under *Edward Johnston*, q.v., at London's Central School of Arts and Crafts. Gill carried this teaching on into stone lettering. Between 1905 and 1909 he designed and engraved title-pages and initials for the Cranach Press of Kessler of whom he said '. . . it was largely by his encouragement and financial support that I took up the engraving of letters on wood . . . and this led to pictorial engraving'. Gill subsequently did a considerable body of work for the *Golden Cockerel Press*, q.v.

His most famous type, Perpetua, which is in use

throughout the world, was designed and cut between 1925 and 1928. Perpetua became a family – light, medium, bold, titling – as did his other equally well-known design Gill Sans, commissioned by Monotype whose technicians made certain modifications to his original drawings before showing a titling fount in 1928 and a lower-case in 1933.

In 1930 Gill's daughter Joanna married René Hague, and the Hague & Gill printing office was established at Pigotts, Bucks. Gill disclaimed the title 'private' for their venture. In the same year he designed the Joanna type for the press (roman and lower-case italic) describing it as 'an attempt to design a book-face free from all fancy business'. It was cut by H. W. Caslon Ltd. Because of economic difficulties Messrs J. M. Dent acquired the fount in 1936 and commissioned matrices from Monotype in 1937. In 1940 the firm of Hague & Gill Ltd was a public company. After it closed in 1952 all sizes of Joanna, including those hitherto reserved for Hague & Gill, passed to Dent. In 1958 Monotype made them generally available.

In 1934 Gill designed a special type, which he named Bunyan, for the printing on the family press of Sterne's 'Sentimental journey' for the Limited Editions Club of New York, 1936. This alphabet was the basis of Linotype's Pilgrim face which appeared in 1953. In 1954 The Monotype Corporation acquired from Gill's widow the entire collection of drawings, rubbings, proofs and sketches for lettering in the roman and some other alphabets (some 2,500 items) which Gill left when he died: they are now in the St Bride Printing Library, London.

See E. R. Gill, 'Bibliography of Eric Gill', Cassell, 1953, and R. Harling, 'The letter forms and type designs of Eric Gill', Svenssen, 1976. See also *Hebrew printing before 1600* and Appendix A.

gilt after rounding: synonymous with *gilt solid*, q.v.

gilt edges: book edges which have been covered with gold leaf. For this binding process the trimmed book is put in a simple screw press (see illustration) where the edges are shaved in order to obtain as smooth a surface as possible. The surface is then primed with paste and Armenian bole and polished with paper shavings or something similar. A diluted solution of albumen or gelatine is spread on as a medium, and then the gold leaf is applied (laying on). After a short period for drying glazing is done with a burnisher, if necessary at first through waxed paper and then directly on the edges. Different qualities of paper call for slight variations of treatment. It is usual to dust the sheets with talcum to prevent them sticking together. Abbreviated as *g.e.*

When gilding is wanted on the edges of cased books the work is done by automatic machines using reel-fed gold foil.

For varieties of gilt edges see under *bookbinding styles and binding features*. (GU)

Edge gilding in a hand-press with extended support. On the table are burnishers, gold cushion, press lever, etc.

gilt solid: said of edges which have been gilded after the book has been rounded: special semicircular burnishers are required. This process is only used for expensive hand-finished bindings. The highly burnished edges have a solid metallic appearance which not everyone finds attractive. Occasionally only the

Burnishing 'gilt solid' edges

fore-edge is treated in this way, the top and bottom edges being gilt normally.

Also known as *gilt after rounding*.

gilt top: a book having only the top gilded. Abbreviated as *g.t.*, *g.t.e.*, or *t.e.g.*

Giolito, Gabriel, fl.1539–78: the most influential of an important family of Venetian publisher-printers who was associated with the development and use of flowers, head-pieces, and decorated title-pages. Many of his books were printed in italics, and reprints of Ariosto, Boccaccio, Dante, and Petrarch, together with translated classics and works in Spanish were among the 850 or so he issued.

Giolito was a patron of letters, especially of the professional writers known as 'i poligrafi'. He was summoned before the Inquisition in 1558, after which he stopped publishing novelle and plays, concentrating on devotional works.

Giornale della Libreria: since 1881, the official bibliography of the Italian book trade, prepared by the Associazione Italiana degli Editori, Milan. It is based on publishers' announcements, and also gives domestic and foreign book-trade news.

girdle book: a book which had a leather cover almost like a bag, enabling monks and clergy to carry and protect their breviaries. The leather cover extended beyond the limits of the book itself and could either be fixed to the girdle or gathered into a knot for carrying by hand. (Illustrated under bookbinding.) They were common in the later Middle Ages, particularly in Germany.

girts: two leather straps encircling a barrel (or windlass) underneath the *plank*, q.v., of a hand printing press. The straps were attached to the *rounce*, q.v., the turning of which caused the forme to be moved under the platen for an impression to be made.

Giunta: a famous Italian family of printers and publishers, of Florentine origin, who had businesses in Venice and Florence until the middle of the 16th century; there were also branches or agents in London, Lyons, Rome and Salamanca. The printer's mark of the Giunta family, a Florentine lily, is reproduced under *device*, q.v.

Filippo Giunta (1450–1517) established the Florentine business from which, advised by a corpus of scholars and men of letters, he issued Greek and Latin classics printed on his own press and those of others. He was succeeded by his son *Bernard*.

Lucantonio (1457–1538), brother of Filippo, established the Venetian business in 1489, similarly printing himself and commissioning others, notable among them being *Johannes da Spira*, q.v. He was noted for an edition of the Bible in Italian illustrated with nearly 400 woodcuts. He was succeeded by his son *Thomas*, but eventually this branch of the family amassed sufficient wealth to sell their publishing interests and engage on the still more profitable activity of marine insurance.

Jacques (1486–1546) learned printing in Venice with his uncle Lucantonio before founding a branch in Lyons in 1520. He specialized in law, medicine, and theology, commissioning more than twenty printers. He was head of the Lyons publishers guild, and had agents in Italy, Germany and Spain. See A. M. Bandini, 'Juntarum typographiae annales', Lucca, 1791, repr. 1965.

Giustiniani, Marco Antonio: a Venetian humanist who founded a press for printing Hebrew books for which he used Le Bé type. His sometime foreman *Cornelius Adelkind*, q.v., printed a fine Babylonian Talmud for him, 1546–51. Two years later his stock of Hebrew books was ordered by Papal decree to be burned. In 1554, however, he published jointly with *Daniel Bomberg*, q.v., the Midrash Rabbah.

GKDW or **GKW:** the abbreviation for '*Gesamtkatalog der Wiegendrucke*', q.v.

GL: a bibliographer's abbreviation, used in catalogues and lists, to indicate that a foreign book, not German, Scandinavian, or Dutch, is printed in *gothic letter*. Cf. *BL*.

glair: an adhesive mixture of egg white (albumen) and vinegar, a thin coating of which is applied to a book cover before blocking or tooling in gold leaf. It causes the gold to adhere permanently to the book when a heated tool or die stamp is impressed upon it.

glassine: a glossy transparent paper made from very clean chemical wood pulps, heavily supercalendered, and occasionally used for book jackets.

glazed morocco: goatskin which has been flattened and polished by calendering.

glazed roller: a lithographic roller particularly suitable for short-run colour work as it can be quickly washed for re-use. A *nap roller*, q.v., is given several coats of hard-drying ink, each being allowed to dry before applying the next.

gloss: 1. a word of explanation inserted in the margin or text of a book in order to clarify a foreign or difficult passage, e.g. an edition of the Iliad set with an interlinear English translation may be referred to as 'with glosses'. In strict usage a gloss is not synonymous with a free translation; the former is a word by

word rendering into a second language, preserving the order of the first.

2. the light reflectance of paper. The machine finishing of paper by pressure under rolls imparts a slight gloss. Gloss can be measured by various instruments. Cf. *smoothness*.

glossary: an alphabetically arranged sequence of unfamiliar, little used, or technical terms together with explanations of them. It is thus to be distinguished from a *dictionary*, q.v., which embraces all the words of a language.

Glossographers or glossators, as compilers of glossaries are known, were active in Greece in the 4th century BC. Somewhat later the law books of Justinian attracted writers of alphabetically arranged *glossae nomicae*. These were cumulated in the 12th century as the *Glossa ordinaria*.

Bilingual glossaries, e.g. of Greek explanations to Latin texts, date back to the 6th century AD, as do interpretations into non-classical languages. Biblical and medico-botanical glossaries continued to be written until the 14th century.

In England, early manuscripts were glossed either in Latin or Anglo-Saxon, and the glossaries of several manuscripts in a monastic library would be brought together as a *glossarium*. Such a compilation is the 'Corpus Glossary', which was probably written about 725 and is now in Corpus Christi College, Cambridge. It contains an alphabetical sequence of over 2,000 words or *lemmata*. See also *concordance, encyclopaedia, index, lexicon, vocabulary*.

gloss finishing: the giving of a protective transparent covering of varnish, lacquer or film to a printed sheet. In addition to increasing the durability of book jackets and paperback covers the gloss causes the colours to appear stronger, thereby adding to the sales potential of a book. See also *lamination, varnishing*.

gloss ink: a printing ink consisting of a synthetic resin base and drying oils. Such inks dry quickly, without penetration, and are suitable for use on coated papers of low absorbency in both letterpress and lithographic printing.

glue: see *adhesives*.

gluing-up: a stage in the binding of a book after sewing, nipping, and cutting, but prior to rounding and backing. The object is to cause glue to penetrate to a limited degree between the sections, thereby strengthening the effect of sewing. The hand method is now largely superseded by special gluing-up machines. It is important that gluing-up, rounding, and backing all be completed before the glue sets hard. See also *pasting*.

glyph: a pictorial symbol intended to surmount language barriers by conveying a universally recognisable meaning, e.g. a broken wine glass to denote 'fragile'.

g/m²: grammes per square metre. See also *paper substance*.

goatskin: see *morocco, Turkey*.

Goddard, Mary Katharine, fl.1777: a famous woman printer of America. It was she who in 1777 printed on her press the official copies of the Declaration of Independence authenticated with the signatures of subscribing members of Congress. One was sent to each of the thirteen United States. The imprint on the broadside reads: 'Baltimore, in Maryland: Printed by Mary Katharine Goddard'. Congress was then in session in Baltimore.

She also had a bindery, described as 'a complete and elegant Bookbinding Room', a book and stationery store and a publishing business. In the *Maryland Journal*, which she took over from her brother William and published from 1775–84, she invited subscribers to pay cash or in 'country produce'. She listed this as including, among other items, tanned sheepskins, linen and cotton rags. The last were for her brother's papermill.

It should be mentioned that the first copy of the Declaration to be printed was from the Philadelphia press of John Dunlap in 1776. This did not include members' signatures as signing took place subsequently.

The Library of Congress has kindly confirmed that Katharine, and not Katherine as used by some authorities, is correct. See also *Honig paper*.

Godfray, Thomas, fl.1510–32: a London printer, considered the first in England to receive an exclusive right to print a book. This was 'The history of King Boccus', printed 'at the coste and charge of Dan Robert Saltwode, monk of saynt Austens of Canterbury', 1510. His only dated book was the first complete edition of Chaucer's works (excluding the Ploughman's tale) edited by William Thynne and published in 1532.

Godfrey, Garrett, fl.1502–39: a native of the Low Countries who in 1502 established himself at Cambridge as stationer and binder. He used roll tools of birds, animals and foliage as well as panel stamps of the royal arms. More than two hundred of his bindings are known.

Goes, Hugo: possibly the son of the Antwerp printer Matthias van der Goes (fl.1483–97) and one of the first provincial printers in England, setting up his press in the Steengate, York. He is known to have used one of Caxton's types, obtained via Wynkyn de

Worde, to print the York 'Directorium sacerdotium' in 1509/10. See W. and E. Sessions, 'Printing in York from the 1490s to the present day', Sessions Book Trust, 1976.

Goff, Frederick: the compiler of 'Incunabula in American libraries: a third census of fifteenth-century books recorded in North American collections', N.Y., Bibliographical Society of America, 1964.

This basic reference work extended the scope and usefulness of the 'Second census', 1940, of *Margaret Bingham Stillwell*, q.v., by adding 11,956 copies of incunabula to the 35,232 she listed. Copies held in certain libraries in Canada, Mexico and Puerto Rico were included. A supplement to Goff was published by the BSA in 1972. This raised the number of titles to 12,923 and of copies to 50,688.

goffered edges: the gilt edges of a book which have been decorated by the finisher who uses heated tools to indent a small repeating pattern in them. The style was popular in the 16th and 17th centuries. Also called *chased edges* or *gauffered edges*.

gold: the traditional material for illuminating manuscripts and decorating bookbindings. From the 4th century, when first used for manuscripts, powdered gold suspended in a medium (white of egg or gum arabic) was used for writing (see *codex aureus*) or to embellish the page. About the 12th century a method was found of laying gold in leaf form over glue or glair, a subsequent technique being to lay it on a raised surface of gesso. See also *illumination*.

gold bindings: book bindings of which the boards were overlaid with panels of thinly beaten gold, richly chased and often inlaid with silver, enamel or jewels. These superb examples of the medieval goldsmith's art (as distinct from the binder's) were made as early as the 7th century for wealthy monasteries or churches to enclose books for altar use.

gold blocking: the stamping of a design on a book cover by using a heated die or block in a press, and gold leaf. Cf *gold tooling*.

gold-blocking press: a bookbinding machine for press gilding. In principle the press consists of two smooth plates which can be brought together. A die is fixed to the upper one and the book cover rests on the lower plate, in most cases on a matrix (counter punch) built up of millboard. The upper plate is heated by gas or electricity, the temperature being controlled by a thermostat. Both plates are exchangeable so that a die or matrix setting can be preserved for future use.

In the *hand-press* commonly used the lower plate moves towards the fixed upper plate, pressure being applied by a knee-joint construction.

There are *machine presses* of various design and both hand and machine presses can be adapted for the automatic laying of foil from reels. Entirely automatic presses are made which feed the covers (cases) from a magazine and impress lettering or a design as they pass through.

The first commercially successful attempt at mechanically blocking gold on bookcloth was made by John Young, a finisher employed by *Archibald Leighton*, q.v. It resulted from his experiments with a second-hand arming press to which adjustments had been made. It was used for the first book in the world to be published with gold blocked lettering (within a simple shield frame surmounted by a peer's coronet) on the cloth-covered spine. The book was volume II of Moore's 'Life and works of Lord Byron', issued by John Murray in February 1832 in an edition of 5,000 copies. For volume I, published a month earlier, a label printed in gold was pasted on the cloth spine. The blocked version was repeated on all subsequent volumes in the set.

The first die-stamping and gilding press made for bookbinding was built in 1832 by Thomas de la Rue in London. An improved model was built in 1857 by Karl Krause of Leipzig. See also *embossed bindings.*

Golden Cockerel Press: a private press founded in 1920 at Waltham St Lawrence, Berks, by Harold M. Taylor. It started as a 'cooperative society for the printing and publishing of books . . . produced by members without the help of paid labour', and in 1921 advertised in the T.L.S. for 'one or two interested people, without family or other ties, having craft aptitude, adventurous inclination and a readiness for hard work . . .'

In 1924 Robert Gibbings joined the press. The aim was to make finely produced books available to a wide public at reasonable prices. Such eminent artists as Eric Gill, Robert Gibbings, Osbert Lancaster, the Nash brothers, and Blair Hughes-Stanton were commissioned to illustrate them. The press was acquired in 1933 by Christopher Sandford of the Boar's Head Press, who at various times was assisted by Owen Rutter, Francis Newberry and Michael Samuelson. He sold his interest in 1959. See 'Chanticleer: a bibliography of the Golden Cockerel Press, April 1921–August 1936,' 1943; 'Pertelote . . . being a bibliography. October 1936–April 1943; and 'Cockalorum . . . being a bibliography, June 1943–December 1948. 1950'. A combined reprint was issued in 1975, and a continuation in 1976.

Golden Hind Press: an American private press begun in 1927 by Arthur Rushmore and his wife and named after Drake's flagship.

The Rushmores planned the books, mostly poetry, and composed the type, for many of which printing off and binding were done commercially. Publishing

and distribution were done by Harper and Brothers, Rushmore's employer, under the Golden Hind imprint.

They used Lutetia type from Enschedé and also Bruce Rogers' Centaur, and for their personal pleasure would print off copies on an old hand-press.

By 1955, when work ceased, they had produced nearly 200 books and pamphlets.

Golden Legend: see *Legenda aurea.*

gold knife: a flat blade, sharpened on both sides, used by bookbinders for cutting gold leaf. (ML)

gold leaf: the traditional material used on books for spine lettering, edge gilding and gold tooling. For beauty and durability of impression it has not been superseded by any of the cheaper substitutes found today. The thickness of leaf used by binders is four millionths of an inch, and its preparation is a highly skilled craft. Pure gold is melted with small amounts of silver and copper and cast into bars of $\frac{3}{4}$-carat silver and copper with $23\frac{1}{4}$-carat gold. The bars are rolled into ribbons which are cut into 2 in. squares. These are interleaved with 4 in. squares of Montgolfier paper. A pile of about two hundred layers is made and encased with two bands of parchment, the whole being known as a *cutch.* The pile is handbeaten until the gold pieces are extended to 4 in. squares. The gold is quartered and placed between vellum squares, a pile of eight hundred skins and leaves being formed. A second beating is given in a *shoder.* After another quartering of the gold the pieces are interleaved with gold-beater's skin to form a *mould* and beaten for four hours. The resulting gold leaves are made up into rouged tissue-paper books, twenty-five pieces per book. One ounce of gold will make about 250 sq. ft. of leaf.

The gold-beater's skins used for the mould are made from ox intestines, Frederick Puckridge and Nephew being the only firm in Britain to prepare them. A mould contains eleven hundred skins.

While much leaf is made in the traditional way described, a mechanical hammer has been devised to eliminate hand-beating, and a method has been found to produce gold in roll form with the same consistency as the leaf but without beating.

The British firm of G. M. Whiley Ltd, using hand and mechanical methods, produces most of the gold leaf used by bookbinders. See also *skewings.*

gold size: see *bronzing size.*

Goldschmidt, Ernst Philip, 1887–1954: a scholarly antiquarian bookseller, born in Vienna, who from 1924 had his business in Bond Street, London.

He will be remembered for his work on (and financial support of) the *'Gesamtkatalog der Wiegendrucke'*, q.v., also for his writings on the Renaissance book, notably 'Gothic and Renaissance bookbindings' which is one of the seminal works on bookbinding history.

gold tooling: the pressing of a design, with heated tools applied by hand, upon gold leaf which is laid on the cover of a book. The cover is first marked up with the main lines of the design, coated with glair, then the gold leaf is laid on, and finally the impression is made. In some cases a blind impression is first made before coating with glair to achieve a clearer result when executing intricate patterns. In recent times imitation gold leaf (80% copper with 20% zinc) or foil is often used: this carries its own adhesive for which heat is also required, but glair is not necessary; while primarily used for machine blocking, its disadvantages are a lack of sharpness and a tendency to tarnish quickly, so that it is best avoided for hand tooling.

Historical note. Gold tooling was introduced from the East into Europe about the mid-15th century. It probably came first direct from the Levant to Venice where leather gilders from Turkey and Persia worked. In their technique, of which examples from the early 14th century survive (e.g. on a Koran written and bound in Persia in 1338 AD) the design was first blind-stamped before applying liquid gold with a brush. From Morocco gold tooling was introduced into Spain and thence to Naples where one of the earliest known examples was on a manuscript translation of Strabo's 'Geographia' presented by the Governor of Padua to King René of Anjou in 1459. The use of Islamic motifs for the decoration points to Muslim craftsmen (the book was later rebound but the original covers were preserved). Twenty years later Baldessare Scariglia of Naples made gold tooled bindings on red morocco for Ferdinand I of Aragon. (See *Islamic bookbinding*).

In France early gold tooling began about 1507, the date of a manuscript bound for Louis XII, now in the Bibliothèque Nationale.

In England gold tooling was probably first used in 1519, but not regularly before 1529 between which date and 1558 some five workshops were producing it. (See H. M. Nixon, 'Early English gold-tooled bookbindings'. *In* 'Studi di bibliografia e di storia in onore di Tammaro de Marinis', Verona, 1964, Vol. III, 283–308.)

Prix Goncourt: since 1903, a French literary prize awarded annually by the Académie Goncourt in Paris. It is given for the most remarkable imaginative work written during the previous year by a young French writer, and the announcement of the winner marks the beginning of the publishing 'season'.

The Académie was founded by an endowment bequeathed by the novelist Edmond de Goncourt (1822–96).

good: said of composed type which, after printing off, may be required for further use and is not to be distributed. See also *blocked up, dead matter, kill, live matter, standing type.*

Goodhue, Bertram Grosvenor, 1869–1924: an American architect who was also a type designer. In 1894 he designed the Merrymount face for Updike's Merrymount Press. The *Cheltenham old style* fount for which he interpreted in 1896 the design of Ingalls Kimball of the Cheltenham Press, New York, was made available to the trade by ATF in 1902 and by Mergenthaler Linotype in 1906. It was popular in both America and Europe where it was cut and cast under various names, e.g. *Titus Antiqua*, AG für Schriftgiesserei u. Maschinenbau, Offenbach; *Roosevelt*, Flinsch, Frankfurt-am-Main; *Style*, Haag, Hanover; and *Toscana*, Klinkhardt, Leipzig.

Goodhue also designed covers for publishers' bindings. An example is on Cadell's translation of 'The Rubayat of Omar Khayam', N.Y., John Lane, 1900. The ribbed-cloth boards and spine have floral and fruit motifs with thick 'orientalized' lettering.

Gordon press: see *platen press.*

Gorleston Psalter: an early 14th century English Psalter in Latin, probably written by or for Augustinian friars of Norfolk. This example of East Anglian illumination is notable for the finely drawn grotesque creatures and agricultural scenes which fill the margins, for its delicacy and light colours. It is also an early manuscript to be decorated with heraldic devices. The work includes a whole page Crucifixion scene added later (*c.* 1325).

The Psalter is now in the British Library.

Gosden, Thomas, 1780–1840: a London bookseller, bookbinder and sportsman. Books on angling and sports were his speciality and for the covers he used emblematic tools of fish, animals or birds as appropriate. Thus, for example, on a binding for John Latham's 'History of birds' the tools were based on Bewick's engravings.

gothic: 1. book hands evolved in northern Europe in and after the 12th century. They are described under *letters – forms and styles,* q.v.

2. black-letter printing types in use in 15th century Europe. It may be convenient to classify them in four main groups: (a) for printing *liturgical and biblical texts* until well into the 16th century printers used types which were narrow, tall and without curves, e.g. the 42-line Bible and the Mainz Psalter. Regional names for these types were *Textura* or *Missalschrift* in Germany, *text* or *black letter*, in England, and *lettre de forme* in France (which term had been used for a

comparable script in an inventory of the library of Charles V of France, c. 1411).

(b) for *legal and classical texts* in the later 15th century less formal types were used with rounder more open letters, no serifs, occasionally an open 'a' and descenders. Examples are Schöffer's 'Durandus', 1459, and the Mainz 'Catholicon', 1460. They were used by Caxton in England and Vérard in France. Regional names were *Goticoantiqua* in Germany, *lettre de somme* in France, and *fere-humanistica* in Italy.

(c) for *vernacular texts* various cursive types generically known as *bastardas* were used. They were less formal than (a) and (b) and in some examples had pointed descenders and looped ascenders. Regional names were *Fraktur* and *Schwabacher* in Germany, *lettre bâtarde* in France, and, inaccurately, *secretary* in England.

(d) for *classical texts* group (b) was superseded in Germany by a round type, or *rotunda*, deriving from the Italian script *littera Bolognese*. When this was introduced into Germany from Venice, about 1470, it was dubbed *litterae Venetae*. Ratdolt favoured this type. In England it was known as *round text* and was occasionally used by de Worde, Lettou and Pynson, but it was never popular.

It may be added as a footnote to the foregoing that the early 15th century calligrapher Johann van der Hagen of Bodenwerder am Weser used on a specimen of his writing the names *textus, bastardus, fracturarum* and *rotundus* for book hands after which later printing types with similar characteristics became known.

3. a loose term for modern sanserif types.

Gothic illumination: the Gothic era of manuscript painting in England, particularly in East Anglia during the 13th and 14th centuries, was characterized by a softening of the 12th-century Romanesque style. Basically, the latter was the art of draughtsmen, 13th-century Gothic that of painters. Thus pattern and flow of line were superseded in importance by modelling of form, greater naturalism and range of colour. French Gothic influenced English art and their interdependence caused the name Channel School to be given to work done in southern England and northern France.

Complete Bibles and Apocalypses were the favourite works, and the Jesse Tree with the Virgin and Child, or Christ alone, was often depicted. Characteristic features were the use of gold, lake and blue as main colours, historiated initials and diapered backgrounds. Gold-edged bands of colour led from historiated initials up or down the margin and along the top or bottom of the page. Scrolls and dragons enlivened earlier borders; leaves, grotesques, birds, drolleries and heraldic shields being introduced later. Centres were Canterbury, Rochester. Peterborough, Salisbury, York and St Albans.

In later Gothic art much attention was paid to small-scale background detail and in the early 15th century lightly drawn borders of buds, leaves and flowers are typical. By the end of this century the delicate tinted grisaille drawings popular in France began to appear in England. In general continental work influenced English illumination until the 16th century when the printed book eclipsed the written and painted manuscript.

gótico-mudéjar: a style of bookbinding done in Catalonia from the 13th to 15th century. The lines of the design were drawn on dampened leather with a blunt tool and formed compartments for the main decoration which was made by impressing small stamps of real or imaginary birds, flowers, fishes or other emblems. No gold was used. Cf. *mudéjar bindings*.

Gottlieb, Theodore, d. 1929: an Austrian librarian remembered for his research into the history of bookbinding. Notable was his publication 'Bücheinbände . . . aus der K. K. Hofbibliothek', Wien, 1910.

gouache: opaque water-colour for which the pigments are mixed with white lead, bone ash or chalk. Gouache colours were used for the illumination of manuscripts, particularly in the 14th and 15th centuries.

Goudy, Frederic W., 1865–1947: a renowned American type designer, and founder in 1903 of the Village Press, Park Ridge, Illinois, which was later moved to Marlborough, New York. He also established the journal 'Ars Typograhica' in 1918.

Probably his first attempt at design was a series of letters he made for the Chicago brewery Pabst. These were redrawn for typecutting in 1902. With his other privately commissioned types they were later brought out by the Lanston Monotype Company. Among the more important of his many types are Village, 1903; Forum roman capitals, 1911; Kennerley, 1911–24; the Goudy Old Style family, from 1915 and Goudy Modern, 1918.

See his 'The Alphabet' *and* 'Elements of lettering', revised ed. 1942; 'A half-century of type design and typography, 1895–1945', 2 vols, New York, 1947; also *Monotype Newsletter*, 77 1965 in which his types are shown, described and dated. (See Appendix A.)

gouge: a brass finishing tool for impressing curved lines on book covers.

Grabhorn Press: an American private press founded in 1919 by Robert and Edwin Grabhorn of San Francisco. Much of their hand-done work was for other publishers and book clubs in California. Bibliographies of Grabhorn books were issued in 1941 and 1956; reprinted together in 1975.

Gradual: a book containing the Song of Ascents, i.e., the antiphon between the Epistle and the Gospel sung at the foot of the altar steps in services of the Roman Catholic Church.

Graesse, Johann Georg Theodor, 1814–85: a German librarian and bibliographer. In 1843 he was appointed librarian to the Elector of Saxony. He is remembered for his history of world literature, 1837–59, and more widely for his bibliography 'Trésor de livres rares et précieux', 7 vols, Dresden, 1859–69.

Grafton, Richard, 1507–73: a London printer and associate of *Edward Whitchurch*, q.v. See also *Bible printing in England*.

grain direction: the direction in which the majority of fibres lie in a sheet of paper. After the pulp flows on to the moving web of a papermaking machine the fibres tend to lie parallel with one another in the direction of movement. On damping with adhesives, paper swells to a greater degree across the grain than in the grain direction, and it is of importance in bookbinding for this and other reasons that the paper used for the text should be made so that the grain direction runs from head to tail in the finished book. The terms *grain direction* and *machine direction* are synonymous.

grained leather: tanned skin on which the natural grain has been worked up to raise and accentuate it. The grain side is that on which the hair grows. Cork-covered boards are used. Graining is also artificially produced by stamping the skin with engraved metal plates.

graining: the roughening of a lithographic plate so that it will retain moisture, give better adherence of the image, and, according to the depth of grain, increase plate life. Fine grain is necessary for fine lines and dot definition free from distortion: for large solid areas or other work without fine detail coarse grain will suffice. The less grain on a plate the greater the care needed to control the ink/water balance.

Graining can be done chemically or mechanically. *Chemical graining.* For zinc plates immersion in a bath of sulphuric acid and hydrogen peroxide is used. For aluminium the chemicals used are a solution of nitric-sulphuric acid and sodium hydroxide often combined with electrically anodizing the plate. *Mechanical graining.* This is done in a graining machine. A smooth plate is placed in a trough and covered with a double layer of glass, porcelain or steel marbles (the latter are better since they last longer and give a finer grain). An abrasive is added, either aluminium oxide, carborundum, crushed quartz or pumice powder. Water acts as a lubricant. Mechanical agitation gives the required surface. Rinsing and

drying conclude the process. *Sand blasting.* In this dry process compressed air blasts sand on the plate. *Brush graining.* A fine abrasive powder is sprinkled on a moistened plate. In passing over it rotating wire brushes give a fine uniform grain. Nylon brushes are also used for especially fine grain.

graining boards: wooden boards or copper plates with a regular or irregular pattern cut on the surface. They are impressed on bookbinding leather as, for example, when making *diced calf*, q.v. Graining also partly conceals any minor surface blemishes on the skin. See also *boarded leather, straight-grain morocco*.

For graining *book cloth*, q.v., used for cases, an embossing machine came into use from about 1830 to impress a permanent relief pattern on it. The cloth was fed between either a pair of flat engraved plates or a pair of engraved cylinders (one of each pair being positive and one negative, and one of each being heated).

Grandjean de Fouchy, Philippe, 1666–1714: a Parisian punchcutter whose youthful attempt at improving the design of capital letters led to his appointment at the Imprimerie Royale. It was here that he cut the punches for the famous *romain du roi* type, q.v., which made his reputation.

Grange Press: a private printing press established near Darlington about 1768 by George Allan who issued numerous books and pamphlets on the history and antiquities of Durham.

Grangerized: any book in which blank leaves are left for the addition by the purchaser of illustrations to his taste. The term derives from James Granger, (1723–76), copies of whose 'Biographical history of England', 5 vols, 1769–74, were bound up with blank leaves in this way although the idea had been used in the 17th century, notably by Ferrar of Cambridge.

Granjon, Robert, fl.1545–89: a renowned type designer, punchcutter, justifier, printer and publisher who worked in Paris; in Lyons (1557–62) where he married the daughter of *Bernard Salomon*, q.v.; and in Rome (c. 1578–89) where he was invited by Pope Gregory XIII to cut types for the Typographia Vaticana, founded in 1559, and re-established in the Vatican in 1587 by Sixtus V. For this and for the Stamperia Orientale Medicea he cut several oriental founts to be used for printing works of religious propaganda. One of his arabic types was used as a model by Caslon when making arabic punches and matrices for the SPCK, completed by 1724.

Granjon is remembered for his cursive type known as *civilité*, q.v., and for his roman and italic founts which were widely used in Europe including, via

Dutch founders, Oxford and Cambridge, until the 19th century.

It was probably he who first cast as type units the various basic motifs known as *flowers*, q.v., which made up the designs of former woodcut borders and headpieces. He had a long association with Plantin in Antwerp where his civilité, greek, and syriac founts were used in the Polyglot Bible of 1569–72.

Graphic Arts Technical Foundation: the name chosen in 1963 for the former *Lithographic Technical Foundation*, q.v.

graver: a steel tool used for incising designs in wood blocks or metal plates, or for adding detail to etched plates.

gravure: see *photogravure*.

gravure à la poupée: see *colour printing*.

Gravure Research Inc.: an American research organization, founded in 1947, through the cooperation of member firms. There is a staff of scientists and engineers.

Gravure Technical Association: founded in 1949 by American gravure printers who hoped through meetings and conventions to standardize business practice. These standards affect etching, inks, proofing and machining, and are designed to ensure uniformity of reproduction quality throughout the United States.

great primer: the name for a former size of type, now standardized as 18-point. Early printers often referred to this size as *Bible Text* from its use in Bibles.

Great Totham Press: a private press founded in 1830 at Great Totham Hall, near Witham, Essex, by Charles Clark (1806–80). In addition to printing his own poetry he also issued broadsides and reprints of tracts. The press appears to have closed in 1862.

grecs du roi: a cursive greek type cut and cast at the instigation of François I of France by Claude Garamont who was commissioned to do so in 1540. It was based on the script of Angelos Vergetios, a Cretan calligrapher employed as copyist and curator of the king's Greek manuscripts, who acted as an adviser. The three sizes cut featured a large number of ligatured letters and contractions. Robert Estienne, who supervised the cutting, printed his pamphlet 'Alphabetum graecum' as a specimen in 1543 and he used it in a majestic edition of Eusebius' 'Historia ecclesiastica', Paris, 1544. Recuttings of the type were made in 1546, 1550 and 1691.

The grecs du roi, just as other greek types in use at the time, were based on Byzantine methods of writing

and pronunciation, not classical Greek. Hence the reproduction in type of the numerous contractions and ligatures traditionally used to increase speed in writing. This made the type difficult to set and the printed result difficult to read. One Oxford greek fount needed 354 matrices. Many contractions were eliminated from types by the end of the 17th century, but the slope of Byzantine Greek script continued. See also *greek type*.

Greek binding style: a distinctive forwarding technique, producing projecting head- and tailcaps, which is found on early Greek bindings. Gatherings were sewn to each other, the needle passing from one to its neighbour as the stitches were drawn inside the central fold. This gave a smooth back to which was glued a strip of cloth big enough to extend to the outer side of the boards. Head and tailbands were sewn to the body of the book by a long stitch through each gathering, being then fastened into grooves made in the top and bottom edges of the boards. Thus the book when covered had an unorthodox shape since the spine was as much as 10 mm. higher than the sides. The grooved wooden boards, covered with goatskin, were flush with the page edges. Braided leather clasps were fastened to bone or metal pegs on the fore-edge of one board. Rectangular fore-edge flaps are also found.

In general the style derived from Coptic and early North African techniques. It was used in Russia from the 11th to 15th century for theological works, and in the 16th century the style had a certain vogue in France, Germany and Italy where classical Greek texts were sometimes bound in this way.

greek type: in the 15th century the study of Greek classics as an integral part of humanism was based on Latin translations. These were the first to be printed, orginating, as had the translations, in Italy. North of the Alps the printing of orginal Greek texts was comparatively rare before 1500. When a quotation in Greek was called for early printers left blank spaces for words to be hand written.

An alternative, from about 1465, was the use of those roman letters which had an identical shape (but not meaning) to greek, to which were added a few simply cut greek letters.

In *Italy* Sweynheym used an upright greek lowercase type in the Lactantius he printed at Subiaco in 1465: it was without accents or breathings which were added by hand. Jenson's minuscule fount with accents, in use from 1471, was clearer and had few ligatures and contractions: a quotation in his Aulus Gellius, 1472, may be the first full page printed in greek type. The first continuous Greek text ever printed, an edition of the 'Batrachomyomachia' with an interlinear Latin prose version, was issued by Thomas Ferrandus at Brescia about 1474

(BMC.VII.lii) in a type copied from Jenson's. Another complete Greek text came from Milan in 1476 when Dionysius Paravisinus and the printer Demetrius Cretensis (or Damilas) issued a Lascaris grammar. The type, designed and probably cast by Demetrius, was the first to have upper case letters. It was used in Milan by others including Accursius for his Latin-Greek dictionary, *c.* 1480, and also in Florence for the editio princeps of Homer printed by Bernardus Nerlius in 1488. De Alopa used greek type in the 1490s, printing at Florence in 1494 an edition of the 'Anthologia Graeca' set entirely in capital letters.

Printers in greek type in *Venice* included the Cretans Alexander and Laonicus who in their edition of the 'Batrachomyomachia', 1486, used a complicated fount of some 1,300 sorts, but it was the splendid folios of Callierges and Blastus, who from 1495 printed with type and accents cast in one piece, as well as the convenient series of octavo classics begun in the same year when Aldus issued the Lascaris 'Erotemata' which fully established printing. with greek type. Aldine types were based on the cursive script of contemporary scholars instead of the book hands which had inspired earlier type designers. Results were serviceable but complex to use, with many ligatures. Victor Scholderer wrote that the Aldine 'greek type systematically violates the first principles of type design and its success was a disaster from which greek printing did not recover for generations'. In *Rome* Antonio Blado and his associates were commissioned to print Vatican Library Greek texts for Cardinal Marcello Cervini at the latter's expense. Notable was the editio princeps of Eustathius on Homer, 1542–50, for which two founts of greek based on the calligraphy of different scribes were prepared by the printers Onorio and Sofianòs.

The first printer in *France* to use some greek type was Antoine Lambillion in the edition of Virgil he issued at Lyons in 1492, preceding its early use in Paris in the Perottus 'Cornucopiae', 1496. Not until 1507 did a French printer set an entire book in greek type. This was a reprint of part of the Aldine Theocritus issued by Gilles de Gourmont who was also the first outside Italy to print Greek text-books. His earliest texts were edited by François Tissard, later ones by Jerome Alexander. In 1512 Gilles cut a revised fount in which letters and accents were integrated. Simon de Colines sponsored, and may have designed, an improved fount in 1528, but of much greater influence and widespread use were Garamont's *grecs du roi*, q.v., described by Proctor as ' . . . by far the best of its kind that has ever been cut . . .' and by Krimpen as ' . . . a miscarriage (when) seen and judged as a printing type'. Haultin's greek founts of the mid-16th century and Granjon's made for Plantin in the 1560s, all of note, were in use until the end of the 18th century. By 1550 France was the leading producer of finely printed Greek texts: they came from many

presses including those of Badius, de Colines, Augereau, Wechel, and the Estiennes, reaching a peak with the monumental 'Thesaurus graecae linguae' printed in 1572 by Henri Estienne II after being in the press for eleven years.

In *Germany* Schöffer used occasional greek letters in his edition of Cicero's 'De officiis', 1465, which was the first classic printed there, and primitive types were used for quotations by Koberger in an edition of Virgil, 1492, and by the Marschalk-Schenck press at Erfurt in 1499. Early in the next century Anshelm, printer in several towns, issued works in Greek, but it is probable that books imported from Italy supplied German classicists with their texts during the incunabula period.

In *Spain* the first use of greek type was in an edition of the Perottus 'Rudimenta grammaticae' printed by Johannes de Salsburga and Paulus Hurus, Barcelona, 1475. In the next century De Brocar used a specially designed greek type in the Complutensian Polyglot Bible, 1514–17.

In *Switzerland* Amerbach of Basle included quotations in greek type in the 'Epistolae' of Filelfo about 1486, but Froben was from 1516 the most important Swiss printer in greek type: in this year he issued the Erasmus Greek Testament. He sold types to printers in France and Germany. Oporinus, also of Basle, printed in greek.

Any demand for original Greek texts in the *Netherlands* during the 15th century was probably met by importations from over-productive Italian presses for it is not to be supposed that there was no interest in the classics. The only printer in *Holland* to use greek type was Pafraet of Deventer, noted for school editions of the classics, who did so in 1488 when he issued a 'Conjugationes verborum graecae' and De Villa Dei's 'Doctrinale'. In *Belgium* the first greek was in Martens's 'Doctrinale' Pt. II, Alost, 1491. While working in Louvain Martens printed quarto editions of Greek textbooks between 1516–29 as did his successor Rescius until 1545. In time the typefounders of Amsterdam rivalled the French excellence of greek types and supplied them to the main centres of printing. Notable were the founts of Heinrich Wetstein, of J. A. Schmidt, of Blaeu and of J. M. Fleischman.

In *England* a few woodcut greek letters were used by de Worde in 1509 but it was Siberch at Cambridge who used the first greek type. In 1521 he set two words in it on the title-page of his second book and four lines in a translation of Lucian's 'Dipsades'. Not until 1543 when Wolfe printed an edition of St Chrysostom was a whole text set in greek: his type was of Basle origin. Sir Henry Savile's eight volume folio edition of Chrysostom was printed in a type resembling the *grecs du roi* by Bradwood for John Norton, 1610–12, after which some of the matrices were given to Oxford University which since 1585 had begun to develop the printing of Greek works. The first English printer to specialize in classics in greek type was George Bishop from 1590.

For nearly 150 years after this English printers used imported types of Dutch or French origin, all in complicated founts of from 350 to 770 sorts. The first to break with this tradition was Alexander Wilson whose greek was used with great effect by the Foulis brothers in their four-volume folio edition of Homer's works, Glasgow, 1756–8. The clear non-ligatured Double Pica fount (22-point) shows a Dutch influence attributed to Heinrich Wetstein's type of 1698 onwards. In 1758 Oxford University Press commissioned a Great Primer greek from Baskerville, using it for a New Testament in 1763. However, the cramped letters set no fashion, being described as unlike any known greek. About 1806 Cambridge University commissioned Richard Austin to cut a fount of English (14-point) greek based on sketches by Richard Porson (1759–1808). Caslon and Catherwood made the matrices. It was first used in 1810 for an edition of Aeschylus. Figgins and Fry were two firms producing type in the clear and readable Porson style. Monotype Porson, issued in 1958, is a refined version of the manuscript original. Pickering's Greek Testament of 1826 showed a fount of Diamond ($4\frac{1}{2}$-point) greek cut by Caslon, and the same publisher's Homer, 1831, has been described as a masterpiece.

In the present century several German presses commissioned or used new greek founts which broke away from earlier calligraphic traditions. Notable were the types cut by Louis Hoell in 1922 for the Flinsch foundry and used in the same year by the Bremer Presse, the Tischendorf-Type of the Officina Serpentis, cut and cast by Schelter & Giesecke, and E. R. Weiss's fount for the Marées Gesellschaft.

In England new types included a fount designed by Selwyn Image for Macmillan and Proctor's Otter inspired by the Complutensian Polyglot fount. Punches for the latter were cut by E. P. Prince and type was cast by Miller & Richard in 1903. Its first showing in Aeschylus's 'Oresteia', 1904, revealed it as too large for text setting. More successful was Scholderer's New Hellenic, based on a Venetian face used by Rubeus in 1492, and cut in 1927 by Monotype (which firm by 1965 offered twenty-four series of greek, adding three of Univers greek in 1970). Of note, too, is van Krimpen's upright Antigone, a simple clear fount used from 1937 for all school editions of Homer printed in Holland, and also available from Monotype. 'As for the shape of Greek type', wrote Krimpen in 1957, 'we are still in a mess, and it seems improbable that the relative uniformity characteristic of roman will ever be reached in Greek'.

It may be added to this survey that in his *New-England Courant* of 4 February 1723 James Franklin wrote 'We should have obliged the World with a Greek scrap or two, but the Printer has no Types, and

therefore we intreat the candid Reader not to impute the defect to our Ignorance . . .' Not until 1821 was a Greek book printed in what is now modern Greece: the type used was a Didot fount. See also Appendix A.

Kate Greenaway Medal: from 1955, an annual award made by the Library Association to the illustrator of an outstanding picture book for children. Recipients must be British subjects domiciled in the U.K.

Green Paper: an official British Government publication issued in green paper covers presenting a topic of public interest to stimulate comment which might contribute to the formulation of government policy. The first was issued in 1967.

Green, Samuel, fl.1649–1702: the first printer in what became the United States of America. From his press at Cambridge, Mass. he began by issuing calendars, broadsides and minor pieces. In 1660 he was joined by Marmaduke Johnson and together they issued John Eliot's translation into Algonquin of the New Testament in 1661, followed by the Old in 1663. See also *Bible printing in America*.

Gregynog Press: a private press founded in 1922 within the cultural centre set up by Gwendoline and Margaret Davies near Newtown, Wales. They commissioned a succession of controllers, namely Robert Maynard, William MacCance, Loyd Haberly and James Wardrop. The first book was issued in 1923; the last in 1940 when the press closed.

The aim of the press was 'to introduce and encourage fine printing in Wales'. The use of wood engravings was a tradition soon begun, work being contributed by such artists as Reynolds Stone, David Jones and Blair Hughes-Stanton whose illustrations for an edition of 'Comus', 1931, are well known. Among types for texts were Kennerley, Bembo and Poliphilus, the latter being particularly suitable for setting in Welsh. Books were printed on a slow-running Victoria platen press.

There was no unifying 'house style', format, illustrations and bindings being varied as thought appropriate to a book's subject. They were never economic, and had no local influence on printing. From 1925 the head binder was George Fisher (1879–1970), an apprentice of Rivière. His best finishing was done on the series of special levant morocco bindings fitted on fifteen to thirty copies of some forty limited editions. They were notable for the simple tooling on highly polished leather, and until 1939 were designed by Maynard and Horace Bray. In complete contrast were the complex designs which MacCance and Stanton made for Fisher to interpret in the 1930s. When the press closed the bindery continued under Fisher until 1945.

The Gregynog estate was willed to the University

of Wales which in 1974 set up a fellowship, the holder being expected to produce a fine hand-printed edition of a specified book on equipment at Gregynog. The first Fellow was Michael Hutchins. In 1978 the University restarted the press. See T. Jones, 'The Gregynog Press', Oxford, 1954.

Grenville, Thomas, 1755–1846: an English book collector whose library of some 20,000 volumes included a 42-line Bible, a Mainz Psalter of 1457, the Aldus Virgil of 1501 and 1505, the letters of Columbus and Vespucci, and an important collection of Italian and Spanish romance poems. He is said to have spent £54,000 on buying his books, for which he sought the most perfect copies, and a further £56,000 on having them bound. He bequeathed his books to the British Museum where they are housed in a room named after him.

grey scale: a means of achieving even density when developing a photographic image (of importance, *inter alia*, in photosetting). A row of numbered squares of graded density is exposed at the beginning of a roll or section of film. The user can arrest development of the film when the required density is reached. Also known as *step wedge*. Automatic film processors, now mostly used, are kept constant by using factory-exposed strips.

griffin: a fabulous creature, part eagle and part lion, seen in German woodcuts of printing shops where a griffin segreant is depicted holding a pair of ink balls.
    Whether the link between the griffin and printing is coincidental or symbolic is obscured by conjecture and legend. Discussing this use H. W. Davies in 'Devices of the early printers, 1457–1560', 1935, says ' . . . Centaurs are from ancient legend; Griffins from Assyria . . . The printers seem to have chosen these various creatures rather as emblems or symbols of pride, self-confidence, not to say boastfulness, as watchers over their owners' interests, as protection against the envious . . .'
    The griffin has often been used in printers' marks; the printer Jakob Bellaert of Haarlem used the griffin as his device from 1483 onwards. He was the first to do so. Among other printers to adopt a griffin were the Gryphius family of Lyons and the Viennese brothers Alantsee (fl.1505–51) who used two griffins segreant. (The Viennese printer Johann Singriener (1510–46) used two lions rampant, each with one ink ball.)

Griffits, Thomas E., 1883–1957: of London. A lithographic printer whose reputation as a craftsman and teacher was world wide. He will be remembered for his three books 'The technique of colour printing by lithography', 1941; 'Colour printing', 1948; and 'The rudiments of lithography', 1956, all published by Faber and Faber.

Griffo, Francesco: see *Francesco da Bologna*.

Grimaldi, Giovanni Battista, 1524?–*c.* 1611: member of a Genoese patrician family and younger son of Cardinal Geronimo Grimaldi. In Rome in 1543 he met Claudio Tolomei, humanist secretary of Pier Luigi Farnese (1503–47) who was Pope Paul III's son. He commissioned Tolomei to form a collection of works intended to complete his education. They numbered about two hundred.
    The books were bound by Roman craftsmen between 1544 and 1548 in red morocco for works written in Italian and olive or brown morocco for the classics. Their decoration included a cameo or medallion device, invented by Tolomei, depicting Apollo driving the chariot of the sun towards Mount Parnassus on the summit of which Pegasus is standing. After impression on the cover the medallion was painted, with some details touched with gold and silver. Anthony Hobson has shown that Apollo in the device represents Grimaldi as a patron of poets, while the chariot's course through the sky, 'straight and not crooked' in the words of the Greek motto (in hand-tooled lettering bordering the medallion) symbolises the humanist concept of 'The ascent to Parnassus', i.e. the acquisition of *virtù*, and thus fame, through study. Two versions of the medallion were used, vertical for folios and horizontal for smaller formats. Because the books were planned as a complete collection there would not be later additions in the same bindings.
    Ultimately the books were divided between the descendants of Grimaldi's eldest son, who lived in the kingdom of Naples, and of his second son who lived in Genoa. The former group was probably sold soon after 1682; the latter remained largely intact until the death of the last Genoese Grimaldi in 1826.
    The origin of the books, of which some 145 are known to survive, was rapidly forgotten. For a time they were referred to as *Canevari bindings* after J–J. Techener in his 'Histoire de la bibliophilie', 1861, had proposed the Genoese doctor Demetrio Canevari (1559–1625) as the first owner of the collection. This claim was generally accepted until convincingly demolished by Giuseppe Fumagalli in 1903. G. D. Hobson discovered the vital clue linking the books with the humanist circle around the Farnese family, but was misled into attributing their ownership to Pier Luigi Farnese (see his 'Maioli, Canevari, and others', 1926). Subsequently Tammaro de Marinis found an Apollo-stamped binding on a book printed in 1548, after the death of Farnese, and scholars began to refer to them as *Apollo and Pegasus bindings*.
    Finally Anthony Hobson submitted the collection to a fresh examination and analysis in 1970/1, and

205

was able to prove its identity with the libary referred to in Tolomei's correspondence with Grimaldi as printed in the former's 'Delle lettere libri sette', Venice, Giolito, 1547 (BM.1085.m2).

See A. R. A. Hobson, 'Apollo and Pegasus: an enquiry into the formation and dispersal of a Renaissance library', Amsterdam, Philo Books, 1973.

grinding: see *stone grinding*.

gripper edge: the edge which is caught by the grippers as a sheet of paper is fed into a cylinder press.

grippers: on job presses, the iron fingers attached to the platen to secure the sheet and take it off the type after impression; on cylinder machines, short curved metal fingers attached to an operating rod which grip the sheet and carry it around the impression. In high speed sheet machines there are pre-grippers for carrying the sheet from the feeding table to the revolving cylinder. See also *feeder*.   (ML & GU)

grisaille: a painting technique first seen in 14th century French manuscripts and used in France, the Netherlands and Italy through most of the 15th century. Painting is in a flat bluish-grey monochrome with highlights in white, gold and touches of red as the only colours used on it. In France it was known as *camaïeu gris*. In Italy it was to develop as *chiaroscuro*, q.v.

Grolier Club: a New York club for bibliophiles founded in 1884 by, among others, *Theodore de Vinne* and *Robert Hoe*, qq.v. In addition to such activities as exhibitions for promoting the graphic arts a number of bibliographical works have been published, perhaps the best-known of these being 'One hundred books famous in English literature', 1902, and 'Grolier 75', 1959. They are offered for sale to the public.

The Club has also published a Gazette, 1st series, 1921–29; 2nd series, 1931–49; and the current series 1966–   . These contain records of the various exhibitions.

Grolier, Jean, vicomte d'Aguisy, 1479–1565: one of the most famous French bibliophiles, remembered particularly for the bindings he commissioned for the (mostly) Italian books he collected, of which roughly 610 survive. He was the friend and patron of Aldus and other Italian humanists.

His collection began with a group of bindings made by Italian craftsmen, probably at Milan where he lived for a time. The main decorative feature of most of these is an impression of a classical scene with figures blocked from a metal die or plaquette, either in blind or painted on gesso. It was thought that these bindings, of which twenty-seven are known, were made for his father Etienne, but in 'Festschrift

Ernst Kyriss', Stuttgart, 1961, Jacques Guignard suggests that they were in fact made for Jean Grolier between *c.* 1510 and 1516. There is then a gap between these Italian bindings and his earliest Parisian bindings which date from *c.* 1535. J. Guignard suggests that in the interval he commissioned velvet covers which perished and required rebinding in leather.

It is probable that *Claude de Picques*, q.v., was his binder from 1538–48, preceded for a year or two by the so-called Fleur-de-lis binder.

After 1548 his bindings are attributed to an unknown workshop tentatively styled by historians as the Cupid's Bow binder (an example is illustrated under *bookbinding*, q.v.). His last binder, of the 1560s, is also unknown. At no time, however, did Grolier restrict himself entirely to any one atelier.

In a very general way the various styles of decoration on his books may be classed in six broad groups: 1. the Italian plaquettes; 2. arabesque fleurons, made in several shops prior to *c.* 1538, some with a corner tool of a fleur-de-lis; 3. the de Picques atelier, mostly morocco, simple rectilinear interlaced strapwork, plain or coloured, and a central lozenge with solid tools; 4. the same atelier, more emphasis on curved interlaced strapwork with azure (hatched) tools, notably the shamrock stamp; 5. the Cupid's Bow atelier, mostly on brown calf, more elaborate interlacing ribbons often painted in several colours, and the use of open, hatched, and solid tools; 6. the last binder, less emphasis on strapwork and more on the decoration of corners and central cartouches, mostly azured tools.

Grolier favoured plain gilt edges at a time when gauffering was fashionable, and a vellum paste-down as part of the end-leaves. About 1538 he began to have an inscription of ownership stamped on the upper cover and a motto on the lower (they had been written inside in earlier books). Beginning with the de Picques bindings the ownership inscription reads IO. GROLIERII ET AMICORVM, implying that they were for his use and also his friends. Occasionally the ownership inscription appears on the spine which was otherwise plain. The fleur-de-lis and other tooling found on many of the spines was probably added in the early 17th century.

The most useful conspectus of Grolier bindings, with photographs of 128 of them, is (H. M. Nixon's) 'Bookbindings from the library of Jean Grolier', British Library, 1965. It is the catalogue of a commemorative exhibition held in October of that year.

groove: the channel which runs set-wise across the bottom surface of a shank of type, i.e. between the feet.

grooved boards: boards with their back edges grooved. This was originally done to allow the upper board to be pierced and is found in Egyptian papyrus bindings.

The practice spread to Europe via Greece where it continued in occasional use until the 17th century for Greek books.

grooved joints: see *french joints*.

grotesque: 1. a decorative graphic style in which distorted animal and human forms are combined with floral and foliate elements to form strange and fanciful patterns. The word was first used in Italy to describe the late Roman murals found in buildings erected at the time of Nero (AD 37–68). The Italian term *grottesca* (from *grotta*, a crypt), translated as *grotesque*, was widely used in France and England from the mid-17th century to describe this art form.

The name is given retrospectively to the often humorous marginal decorations found in French and Flemish manuscripts of the 13th and 14th centuries, and especially in English Psalters of the same period where the style was fully developed by the East Anglian school of painters. See also *bestiary*.

2. a name given to 19th century sanserif display types. They were for a time superseded in the present century by display sanscrifs such as Futura, Gill, Granby and Vogue: these were simpler and more geometric. Since 1942 revivals of hand-cut 19th century grotesques have come into use. Also known as *grots*.

ground: see *etching*.

Gruel, Pierre-Paul, fl.1832–48: the founder of a famous Parisian bookbinding business which successive generations carried on into the present century. Its initial prosperity began with the considerable demand in Paris for lavishly tooled bindings by a clientele which rarely read the books they enclosed.

Léon Gruel, (b. 1841) was the best known craftsman of the family. He was the author of 'Manuel historique et bibliographique de l'amateur de reliures', 2 vols, Paris, 1887–1905. The firm later traded as *Gruel-Engelmann*.

Gryphius, Sébastien, fl.1522–56: born at Reutlingen in Germany in 1491. After serving as an apprentice printer in Venice he settled in Lyons in 1522, probably at first as a sales agent for his Venetian publisher friends. He opened his printing business in 1528.

He first printed legal works in gothic types, then acquired roman and italic founts and issued cheap 12mo and 16mo editions of Latin classics, hoping to replace the trade in France of the Venetian Aldines. He also published Latin translations of Greek classics and the work of humanist scholars, notably Erasmus. A friend of the leading scholars and writers of Lyons, he was typical of many European scholar-printers, receptive to new ideas and willing to risk publishing them.

He is believed to have had his own bindery, covering his small format classics (13 cm high) in brown calf or crimson morocco bindings. They had tightly glued backs. Edges were gilded and goffered, the boards being decorated by patterns of broad interlacing strapwork. This strapwork, within gold tooled outlines, was emphasised by thickly applied lacquer colours. They were probably made by Italian craftsmen employed in his bindery.

Among his more important publications was the 'Commentaria linguae latinae', 1536–38, assisted by a fellow printer and former corrector Etienne Dolet. His folio Bible of 1550 was also a fine production.

On his death the business was continued by his heirs until 1564. In 1566 it passed to his illegitimate son *Antoine* who was active until 1593. His brother *François* printed in Paris from 1532–45.

The famous Lyons printer *Jean de Tournes*, q.v., was an apprentice of Gryphius.

Guardian Fiction Prize: an annual award of 200 guineas made by the British newspaper to a British or Commonwealth writer whose work shows originality and promise. It was announced in 1965 and the first recipient was the Australian Clive Barry for his second novel 'Crumb borne' published by Faber.

guarding: the inserting into a book of two separate plates which have been first glued to a narrow strip of paper or linen. The four-page unit they thus become is either wrapped around or inserted within a section when gathering. Single plates can be similarly guarded. Cf. *hooked*.

guards: narrow strips of linen or paper to which the inner margins of single plates are pasted prior to sewing them with the sections of a book. Four-page plate units are also strengthened in this way before sewing. A pair of leaves to be positioned around a section is guarded on its inner side; an inner pair of leaves is guarded on the outside, the sewing thread passing through the centre of the guard. The operation is known as *guarding* or *guarding-in*. See also *compensation guards*, *continuous guard*, *hinged*, *hooked*, *inserted after binding*, *meeting guards*, *plating*, *thrown out*.

guide book: a book containing information for travellers, tourists, museum or exhibition visitors, etc. An early printed work of this kind was 'Mirabilia Romae', a guide to the churches of Rome for the use of pilgrims. Some twenty editions from various presses appeared between 1475 and 1500.

Of world renown is the extensive series begun in 1832 by Karl Baedeker of Coblenz. The first volume in it was for the Rhine journey from Mainz to Coblenz. These authoritative guide books are still issued and are continually revised.

guide letters: small letters inserted in blank spaces

left by a scribe at the beginning of a chapter or paragraph for the subsequent insertion by an artist of illuminated, historiated or rubricated capitals after the work had been written. This feature of manuscript writing was continued in those early printed books which were to be hand-decorated after printing. See also *corpora*, *factotum*, *illumination*, *initial letters*, *versals*.

Guild of Contemporary Bookbinders: founded in 1951 as 'The Hampstead Guild of Scribes and Bookbinders'. While originally centred in Hampstead, London, the time came when no member lived there, and as the calligraphic element also dwindled the name was changed in 1955.

Edgar Mansfield, Bernard Middleton and Arthur Johnson were the instigators of the new Guild. Between 1955 and 1967 exhibitions of members' bindings were sent to Europe and America. In 1968 the Guild was reorganized as *Designer Bookbinders*, q.v.

Guild of Women-Binders: an association of women bookbinders formed in 1898 by Frank Karslake (1851–1920), founder of *Book Auction Records*, q.v. The women had previously worked in small groups in various parts of Britain, many binding in their own homes 'aided by no mechanical devices whatever', and they continued to work individually after the formation of the Guild. They had a showroom at 61 Charing Cross Road, London, and advertised 'Beautiful books in artistic bindings, suitable for Wedding Presents, Birthday Presents, Christmas Presents, etc., always on view'.

The Guild was closely associated with the *Hampstead Bindery*, q.v., and the two were awarded a silver medal for work they showed at the Paris exhibition of 1900. Shortly after this the Guild was dissolved, probably after the last of their joint sales of bindings in 1904. See G. E. Anstruther, 'The bookbindings of tomorrow', 1902.

guillemets: see *duck-foot quotes*.

guillotine: a machine for the simultaneous cutting of a large number of sheets, either flat or folded and

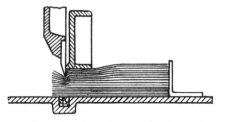

Diagram of a guillotine showing knife in the cutting beam in front of the press beam, cutting stick let into the table, and back gauge

stitched. The usual paper guillotine is a single-edge cutter in which a heavy blade slides between vertical runners and is intended for comparatively large edge lengths, while for trimming books there are special three-edge cutters.

Three-edge cutters, designed for cutting the three edges of a book, are of two types: three-edge machines and three-cutter machines. The three-edge machine, which is the older, is built like a single-edge cutter

Three-cutter guillotine

but the table revolves and the press beam is replaced by a pressing plate the size of the book. The table can be turned into three fixed positions in which the book is cut in turn at the fore-edge, tail, and head.

The three-cutter machine, built by August Fomm, Leipzig, in 1908, operates with a stationary table and three cutters, the book being cut simultaneously at the head and tail by two parallel cutters and immediately after at the fore-edge by a third cutter (see illustration).

Modern *electronic guillotines* are those in which movements are actuated by a series of relays and contactors brought into operation through the medium of a number of thyratrons, tubes and a photo-electric eye unit. All operations are mechanical, being set in motion by push-buttons or the tripping of micro-switches which control the electronic circuit and thus the cutter.

A guide rail at the front of the machine carries the photoelectric cell and its lens. Interruption of the light beam between the two sends an electrical impulse to various tubes and thence to various circuits. One of these leads to the electro-magnetic clutch which activates the knife and clamp. Another circuit operates the back-fence motor.

Ease of operation, with greater accuracy and safety, are among advantages claimed for electronic guillotines.

Guillotines came into use in the 1830s, when Thirault built a model with a fixed blade in 1837. In 1844 and 1852 Guillaume Massiquot patented machines very similar to those in use today. Since the middle of the 19th century considerable improvements were made by August Fomm and Karl Krause of Leipzig, and Furnival in England. The American Oswego and Seybold machines should be noted. See also *programming*.

guinea edge: the pattern tooled on a book edge by a fillet which impresses a design like the grooved edge of a guinea.

Günther, Albert: a firm of craftsmen bookbinders established in Vienna early in the 19th century and still producing work done with the same careful attention to forwarding and finishing. Examples are to be found in the Vatican, royal libraries and in the national collections of many countries. The Treaties of the Congress of Vienna, 1815, and the Austrian State Treaty, 1955 were bound by the Günther bindery.

The firm is now fully mechanised and does edition binding for many European publishers including British. The present craftsman-director is Kurt Kierger who designed the griffin for the case of this book.

Gutenberg, Johann, *c.* 1399–1468: the reputed inventor of printing from movable type. He was born at Mainz as Johann Gensfleisch zum Gutenberg where his uncle was master of the archiepiscopal mint. As a result of disputes between craftsmen's guilds and patrician families, of which Gutenberg's was one, he moved to Strasbourg in 1428. He remained there until 1444. In 1438 he was working with Hans Riff, Andreas Dritzehn and Andreas Heilmann as partners in a secret project. When Dritzehn died in 1438 his bothers unsuccessfully sought to take his place in the partnership. A lawsuit followed in 1439, the two documents of which reveal that Gutenberg borrowed large sums of money, bought quantities of lead, and was in possession of a press built for him by Konrad Saspach for taking multiple impressions for 'Formen' (which could mean blocks). It is uncertain if his invention of separately cast letters had then been made.

By 1448 he was again in Mainz where he met a wealthy lawyer, *Johann Fust*, q.v., who in 1449 or 1450 lent him 800 rhein.Gulden for completing work on his 'apparatus'. For this loan Gutenberg pledged his tools and equipment. Two years later Fust lent a second 800 Gulden and undertook to pay the cost of rent, materials and assistants' wages on the understanding that Gutenberg would work for their mutual benefit. The work may have been the 42-line Bible which appeared not later than 1456, inevitably after many years of gestation, and possibly, too, part of the Mainz Psalter, dated 1457, published from the office of Fust and Schöffer. (See *Mazarine Bible*.)

In 1455 Fust sought the return of his loan which with interest at 6% amounted to 2026 Gulden. As Gutenberg was unable to repay it legal proceedings began, nicely timed it would seem, to prevent him from becoming independent of Fust should the Bible be a success. One of the documents in this lawsuit, Ulrich Helmasperger's notarial instrument, survives

Fragment of the 'Sibyllenbuch', c. 1454 (Reduced)

in Göttingen University Library and constitutes one of our principal sources for Gutenberg's biography. The verdict of the case is not on record, but it is probable that Fust, who may or may not have been a schemer, took over all Gutenberg's books and equipment and also invited Gutenberg's foreman Peter Schöffer to continue the business with him.

How Gutenberg next occupied himself is unclear. In 1465 he was given an appointment at the court of Adolf of Nassau, Archbishop of Mainz. He presumably retained the printing equipment he owned prior to his association with Fust and is known to have acquired more with the help of Dr Konrad Humery to whom it was returned by the Archbishop when Gutenberg died on 3 February 1468.

No printed work extant bears Gutenberg's name but in addition to the 42-line Bible and possibly a 36-line Bible some smaller works, which must for various reasons be dated prior to 1456 when the break with Fust occurred, are often ascribed to him. These include part of the Sibyllenbuch of *c.* 1454 and some Donatus grammars in a similar but larger type than that of the Bible; at least one of three broadside astrological calendars prepared for 1448, 1456 and 1457; the 31-line indulgence of Nicholas V to those willing to give money to help the king of Cyprus against the Turks, printed in a bastarda letter and dated by hand 1454; and the *Türkenkalender*, 1454, q.v. It should not, however, be overlooked that as six presses were used simultaneously to print the 42-line Bible many workmen would be in a position to attempt the surreptitious printing of small pieces. The 'Catholicon' of Joannes Balbus de Janua, dated Mainz 1460, is often ascribed to Gutenberg's second

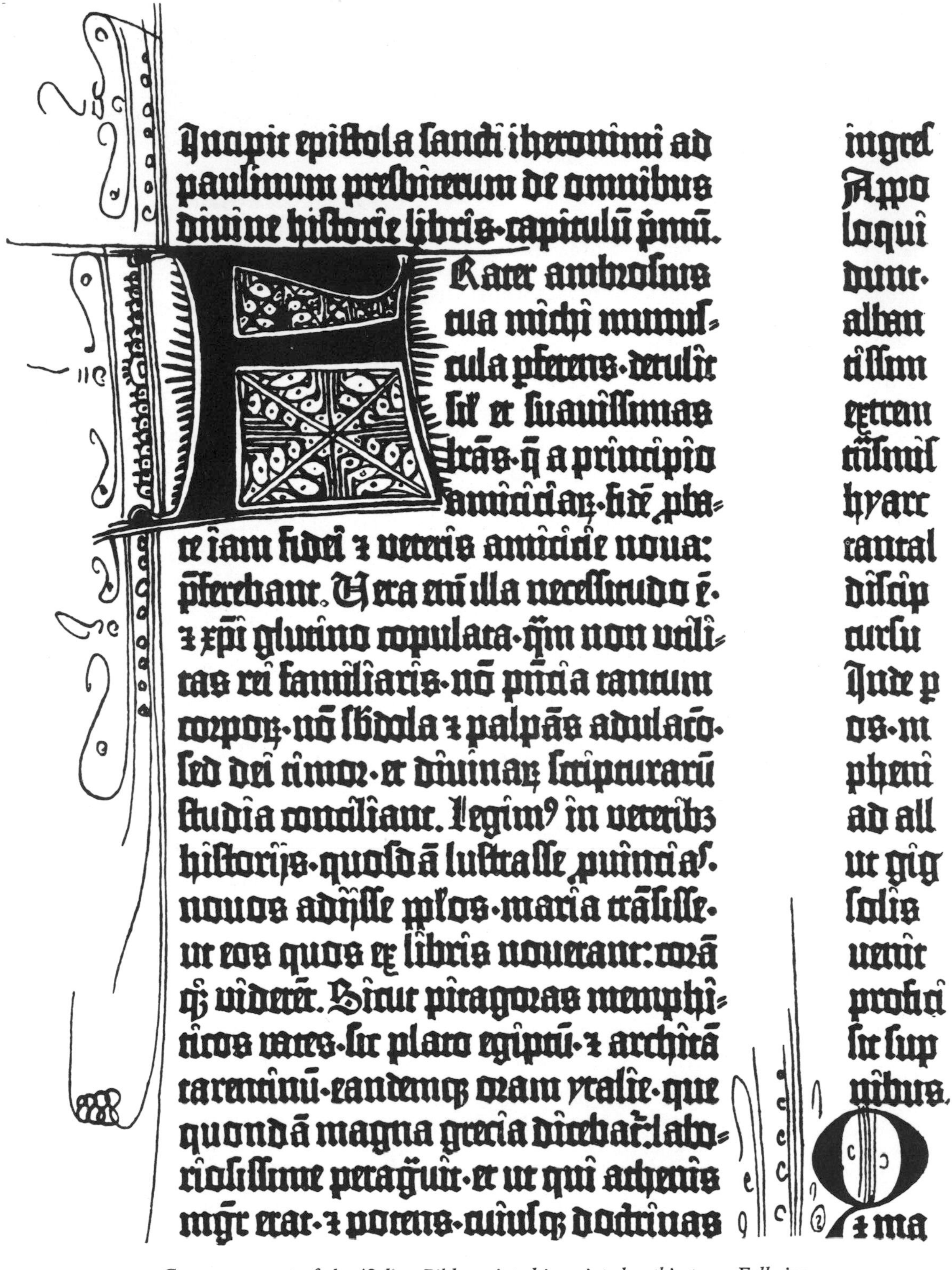

Incipit epistola sancti iheronimi ad
paulinum presbiterum de omnibus
diuine historie libris. capitulū pmū.

Rater ambrosius
tua michi munus-
cula pferens. detulit
sit et suauissimas
lras. q a principio
amicicias. fide pba-
te iam fidei z veteris amicicie noua:
pferebant. Uera eni illa necessitudo e
z xpi glutino copulata. qm non utili-
tas rei familiaris. no psia tantum
corpoz. no subdola z palpans adulaco-
sed dei timor. et diuinaz scripturaru
studia conciliant. legim9 in veterib3
historijs. quosda lustrasse puincias.
nouos adiisse ppłos. maria tralisse.
ut eos quos ex libris nouerant: cora
q viderent. Sicut piragoras memphi-
ticos vates. sic plato egiptū z architā
tarentinū. eandemq oram ytalie. que
quonda magna grecia dicebat: labo-
riosissime peraguit. et ut qui athenis
mgr erat. z potens. cuiusq doctrinas

ingred
Apo
loqui
dunt.
alban
tissim
extreu
tumul
hyatc
cantal
discip
ursu
Inde p
os. m
pheu
ad all
ut gig
solis
uenit
profici
sir sup
nibus.
Q
z ma

Commencement of the 42-line Bible, printed in pointed gothic type. Full size press though many German scholars attribute it to that of Peter Schöffer. See also *Bible printing, Brito, Costeriana, Cracow fragments, Kefer, Mazarine Bible, Pfister, printing – historical survey, Schöffer, Waldvoghel, Zel.*

Gutenberg Museum: established in 1900 in Mainz. Since 1920 it has been developed by Professor *Aloys Ruppel*, q.v., as the leading centre for Gutenberg and early typographic studies. It is also the editorial office of the authoritative *Gutenberg Jahrbuch*, (from 1926).

Guthlac Roll: a roll of vellum on which were drawn a series of tinted roundels depicting the life of St Guthlac of Crowland, Lincs. They were probably intended as designs for stained glass or enamels. The roll, which is nine feet long, may have been made at Crowland *c.* 1196, or a little later. It was formerly in the Harley collection and is now in the British Library.

gutter: 1. spacing material in a forme between the *margins* of two adjacent pages, q.v.

2. in a pair of facing pages in a book the space comprising the two facing back margins is sometimes called the *gutter*.

gutting: 1. the practice of reviewing a book, not by critically appraising it, but by disclosing the main lines of the book and its plot, i.e. by 'tearing the guts' out of it. Publishers naturally deplore this practice.

2. a colloquialism for the judicious selection by a publisher of such felicitous phrases from reviews of a book as are likely, when printed on the jacket or in advertisements, to further the sale of it. An inspired copywriter's skilled substitution of 'leaders' for rude or offensive words can transform even the unkindest of notices into fulsome and useful praise.

Guyot, François, fl.1539–70: a Parisian who worked in Antwerp as a punchcutter, justifier of strikes, and typefounder. Types of his design were used for nearly two centuries in Germany, Spain, Austria, Goa and England (where some were used in the Bible of 1611 and Shakespeare's First Folio of 1623). He was one of the first to begin what later developed as a family of type by cutting a roman with companion italic. Between 1558 and 1570 Guyot executed orders for Plantin.

Towards the end of his life Guyot and his family stayed in the house of the London printer *John Day*, q.v., an association recorded in the Aliens Register for 1568. One of his sons, Gabriel, also a typefounder, worked in England from 1576 to 1588, a period when all typefounding in England was done by aliens. He later worked in Rotterdam.

H

Haas: a family of typefounders in Basle where *Johann Wilhelm Haas* acquired the foundry orginally owned by Jean Exertier (d. 1607) and subsequently by Genath. His son *Wilhelm* snr (1741–1800) took over the business in 1764, adding to it in 1770 the foundry which Cyriakus Pistorius had established a century earlier. He considerably developed casting techniques and in 1772 invented a strengthened hand-press with an iron frame, counterweight, hose, spindle and platen which, being larger than previous platens, enabled a sheet to be impressed at a single pull. This major step towards an all-metal press is illustrated under *hand-press*, q.v.

His son *Wilhelm* jnr (1766–1838) made an improved model in 1784 and another in 1789.

In 1780 the elder Wilhelm collaborated with August Preuschen of Karlsruhe on a method of setting map names in type.

The firm continues as Haas'sche Schriftgiesserei A.G. See also *Deberny & Peignot*.

Hadego: a Dutch display-photosetter introduced in 1948 by H. J. A. de Goeij. Plastic matrices, each with a white character on a black background, are composed and justified by hand in a special stick. Lines are then photographed. Cf. *Ludlow.*

Haebler, Konrad, 1857–1946: a prominent German bibliographer remembered for his research work and writings on the incunabula and type history of Spain, Italy, and Portugal, also for his contribution to the *Gesamtkatalog der Wiegendrucke*, q.v.

Among his studies were the 'Typenrepertorium der Wiegendrucke', 6 vols, Halle and Leipzig, 1905–24, and 'Handbuch der Inkunabelkunde', 1925, in addition to writings on bookbinding.

The 'Typenrepertorium' was intended as an aid to identifying type used in 15th century books by showing facsimiles of an upper case 'M' for gothic and 'Qu' for roman letters since the designs of these were the most peculiar to one printer.

Hafod Press: a private printing press established in 1803 at Hafod House near Aberystwyth by Thomas Johnes. His plan was to translate and publish the early French romances of which he had manuscripts in his library, and he bought printing equipment the better to supervise the scholarly work. He employed James Henderson, a Scot, to operate the press. Apart from minor pieces the first work to appear was the 'Chronicles' of Froissart, issued in four volumes, 1803–5. The edition was of 300 quarto and 25 folio sets. The maps and illustrations were separately printed in London by John White who retailed the complete work. The Johnes translation survives today in the Everyman Library edition.

In spite of a disastrous fire in 1807 which destroyed his library Johnes was able to complete and publish his translation of the 'Chronicles' of Monstrelet in four volumes, 1808, with a fifth volume of plates. The last work of the press was Froissart's 'Memoriae', 1810. Johnes died in 1816.

While typographically unadventurous his books were carefully printed. His real achievement was in making available lively translations of writings largely unknown.

Hain, Ludwig, 1781–1836: the compiler of '*Repertorium bibliographicum ad annum 1500*', q.v.

hair-line rule: the thinnest of printers' *rules*, q.v.

hair-lines: the thin strokes of a type-face.

hair-spaces: the thinnest spacing material, cast less than type height, and used between letters. Hair-spaces vary in thickness, according to body size, from eight to twelve to the em.

Hakluyt Society: a society founded in London in 1846 for the printing of 'rare and valuable voyages, travels, naval expeditions and other valuable records'. It is named after the geographer and traveller Richard Hakluyt, 1553–1616. Publication began in 1847 with 'Observations on his voyage into the South Sea in 1593' by Sir John Hawkins, and by 1974 some 300 works had been issued. They are listed in D. B. Quinn's 'The Hakluyt handbook', 2 vols, 1974. The Society now publishes from the British Library.

half-bound: a book having the back and corners covered in one material, the sides in another. It is customary for only the top edge to be gilded; more frequently, all edges are stained.

Half-bindings were made in the late 15th century. Those made in Italy for the Pillone family had morocco spines with blind fillet tooling and plain wooden sides. In the German renaissance leather spines and paper sides were used.

It is probable that the great vogue in the 19th century for half-bound books was due to the realisation by the newly risen moneyed class which commissioned them that the effect on the shelves of a gentleman's library was the same as that of full-bound books at less cost.

half-cloth: a half-bound book with cloth-covered spine and corners and paper-covered boards. The title on the spine is often on a printed label and as they soil quickly some publishers tip a spare label inside the book.

half-diamond indention: a manner of setting type when successive lines are indented at both ends, each one being shorter than the preceding line. Also known as *in pendentive* setting.

half-leather: a half-bound book having leather as the covering material for the spine and corners with cloth or paper sides.

The use in England of half-calf dates from the early 18th century; half-morocco probably towards the end of it. For a note on the use of half-leather bindings in Italy see *Pillone*.

half-line drawing: a block made by exposing a line drawing through a half-line screen. The printed result is lighter in tone than the original.

half-measure: see *double column*.

half see safe: an expression used by a bookseller when ordering copies of a book from a publisher to indicate that while all copies will be paid for the publisher may be asked to take back half the quantity and offer the bookseller another title in lieu. Cf. *see safe*. See also *terms*.

half sheet: literally, a sheet half the size of the normal. For example, a book is being printed in 32-page sheets but there is a 16-page oddment to complete; then the latter will constitute a *half sheet*. The same term would be used for an 8-page oddment when printing sheets of 16 pages. In both cases it would be convenient for the printer to use the full-size paper but impose the sheet for *work and turn*, q.v., and subsequently cut in half. (LK)

half-sheet work: an alternative name for *work and turn*, q.v.

half-stuff: the wet pulp to which the raw materials of

paper are reduced in the potcher before being mixed with other ingredients and beaten. See also *stuff*.

half-title: the title of a book as printed on the leaf preceding the title-page. The use of such a page dates from the latter half of the 17th century, though a blank leaf had from earlier times been included in books to protect title-pages. Also known as *bastard title* or *fly-title*.

half-tone block: a letterpress relief printing plate prepared by the *half-tone process*, q.v., which after mounting to type height is used to reproduce in monochrome or colour an original consisting of graduated (i.e. continuous) tones. Cf. *line block*.

half-tone paper: any coated, high machine finished or super-calendered stock of good colour and with a smooth surface.

half-tone process: the preparation of copper, magnesium or zinc plates for reproducing continuous tone originals in print. Suitable originals include photo-

Meisenbach's first half-tone, patent dated May 9th, 1882

graphs, transparencies, paintings, wash drawings, charcoal or crayon sketches, and water colours.

An essential step is to break down the continuous tones of the original image into a pattern of small dots, *equally spaced but of varying size*, which cover the whole printing area. To do this a negative is made by photographing the original through a ruled glass *screen*, q.v., positioned between the lens of a camera and the plate inside it.

Stated simply, when the negative has been developed and printed down on to a copper printing plate (in a manner roughly similar to that used for line work) the light tones of the original will appear as minute dots, widely separated. For the darker tones the dots are bigger and thus appear closer. As it is these relief dots which take up ink the printed result simulates the tones of the original. A half-tone print is thus something of an optical illusion and compromise since while the dots are unnoticeable when viewed

Squared-up half-tone

Cut out half-tone

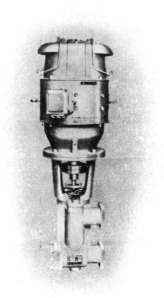

Soft vignetted half-tone

Hard vignetted half-tone

at normal reading distance a magnifying glass will reveal them. Reproduction quality is proportionate to the quality of the original, careful exposure of it, closeness of the screen ruling, fine etching, and the characteristics of the paper.

For powderless etching copper, magnesium or zinc plates can be used (see *Dow etching machine*). See also *electronic engraving machine, photoengraving*.

Historical note. Contributions to the development of the half-tone process were made by *Fox Talbot*, q.v., in the mid-19th century, by F. von Egloffstein in 1865, by *Sir Joseph Swan*, q.v., in 1879, but most notably by *Georg Meisenbach*, q.v., who made the method practicable and is generally held to have invented it. In 1881 he made his first half-tones, some of which survive, and in 1882 he and von Schmädel patented their half-tone method the procedure of which was as follows. A negative made from a transparent positive was put in contact with a line screen and photographed. After half the required exposure time the screen was turned 90° and exposure completed. The negative was transferred to a zinc plate, developed and etched with acid.

News of the method spread, and other people made improvements. In 1883 *Carl Angerer*, q.v., made a screen negative direct from an original picture, but still used a single-line screen which required turning during exposure. Among American experimenters were S. H. Horgan, *Frederick Ives*, q.v., and von Nemethy of Chicago to whom is credited the invention in 1888 of the squared screen still used. This was brought to perfection by *Max Levy*, q.v.

In the 1960s electronic engraving machines transformed half-tone platemaking by eliminating screen, camera, darkroom, etching and chemicals. Such

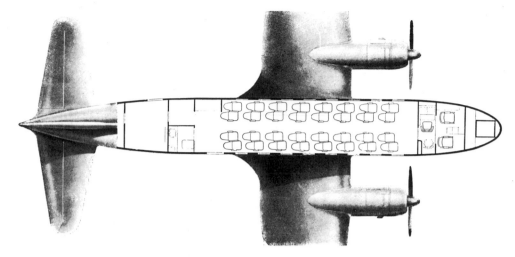

Combined line and half-tone block

Deep-etched half-tone

plates can no longer be termed photoengravings but either *electro-mechanical engravings* or *electronic engravings*. See also *bumping up, contact screen, direct half-tone, fine etching, screen process work, staging out*.

half-tone screen: see *screen* (1).

half uncial: the alphabet of mixed uncial and cursive letters used in Europe as a book hand from the 6th to 12th century. The original half-uncial formed the basis of several national book hands, e.g. Irish, Merovingian, Lombardic. The Irish half-uncial was introduced to England at Lindisfarne in 634 where it developed independently and later influenced Carolingian minuscule letters. See also *letters – forms and styles*.

Halkett, Samuel, 1814–71: librarian of the Faculty of Advocates, Edinburgh. For many years he collected material for a dictionary of anonymous English works: on his death the manuscript was continued and more than doubled by *John Laing* (1809–80), librarian of New College, Edinburgh. His daughter, *Catherine Laing*, finally edited the work which was published as 'A dictionary of the anonymous and pseudonymous literature of Great Britain', 4 vols, Paterson, 1882–8. It quickly became a standard work. A revised edition by James Kennedy, W. A. Smith and Λ. F. Johnson was published in 7 volumes by Oliver & Boyd, 1926–32; with a continuation as volume 8, 1956, and a ninth volume in 1962.

Halliwell, James Orchard, 1820–89: antiquarian, book collector and Shakespearian scholar. He was a generous donor to institutional libraries, notably the Chetham Library in Manchester, which received several thousand ballads, poems and broadsides; the Smithsonian Institution in Washington, which received documents on aspects of economic history; Edinburgh University, which received Shakespeariana; and the town of Penzance, where his donations over many years earned him its freedom.

After marrying the daughter of *Sir Thomas Phillipps*, q.v., (who never spoke to either of them again) he changed his name to Halliwell-Phillipps.

Hammer, Victor, 1882–1967: a Viennese artist-craftsman whose skills included calligraphy, type-design and printing. In the late 1920s he set up a

215

private press in Florence with the name Stamperia del Santuccio. His editions were small, hand-set, and printed on Italian handmade paper. First to be issued was an edition of Milton's 'Samson Agonistes', 1931. When he moved to Aurora, New York in 1939 he continued the imprint until 1967. Other imprints used by him and his family were Wells College Press (1941–49), Anvil Press (1949–) and Hammer Press.

His types, some of which he both designed and cut, include a series of uncials. The first appeared in 1924 as Hammer-Unziale; the last was America Uncial, 1953. His Andromaque, cast for him by Deberny and Peignot in 1960, is too mannered for easy reading.

Hammersmith Workshops: see *St Dominic's Press*.

Hampstead Bindery: a workshop of craftsmen binders established at the instigation of Frank Karslake, antiquarian bookseller, about the turn of the century. Its most prominent worker was *Alfred de Sauty*, q.v. In 1898 and 1900 exhibitions were held jointly with the *Guild of Women-Binders*, q.v.

Han, Ulrich, fl.1467–78: a printer who left his native Ingolstadt for Vienna where, it is claimed (*Gutenberg-Jahrbuch*, 1933), he printed in 1462 (making him the first printer there). He then went to Rome. From his press came what is claimed to be the first book in Italy illustrated by woodcuts, the 'Meditationes vitae Christi' by Cardinal Johannes de Turrecremata, 1467, and *c.* 1468 Bonaventura's 'Legenda maior S. Francisci' which was the first book printed in the Italian language. With the advice of Johannes Campanus he issued classical and humanistic works. Two Roman Missals from Han appeared in 1475 and 1476.

Hancock, William: see *caoutchouc binding*.

hand: see *digit* (2).

Hand and Flower Press: a press founded at Aldington, Kent in 1939 by Erica Marx who designed books printed for her by commercial firms. Her first publication was 'The turn of the screw' by Henry James, 1940. Some forty or so works had appeared under this imprint by 1963, mostly plays or poetry.

hand-binding: successive stages in the hand-binding of books, after *sewing*, are grouped under two heads: *forwarding*, which includes gluing the sections, rounding and backing, and covering with leather; finally, *finishing*, qq.v., which includes lettering and any embellishment. See also *bookbinding methods and processes*.

handbook: a comprehensive book of information or instruction of a size which can conveniently be carried. The word often occurs as part of the title.

hand-coloured illustrations: the hand-colouring of copper engravings dates from the early 18th century. The work was mostly done in workshops where women and even children, engaged by the artist of the original, produced between two and three hundred plates a week.

In the 19th century coloured lithographs of botanical, zoological, landscape and costume subjects were made in the same way. (See *Ackermann*.)

Hand-colouring in the 20th century, as distinct from the re-touching by hand of machine-printed colour work, is mostly limited to small, costly editions, particularly in France, though in Britain the Curwen Press and the Folio Society, to name but two, have issued editions so illustrated and at modest prices. See also *illumination*, *pochoir*.

hand composition: type-setting by hand proceeds today as in the early days of printing. The compositor's tools are a composing stick, a composing rule, a steel scale, a galley, a bodkin and tweezers. His material consists of types, rules, ornaments, quads, leads, quoins, furniture and a chase.

Types are removed by hand from a case in which each character has its own compartment. Cases are kept in wood or metal cabinets which also serve as work-tables for the compositor, and are mostly set up in rows to form an alley in which he works; he usually stands. Cases were formerly used in pairs, an upper and a lower, and those containing the particular type required were put in position on the cabinet, being supported there by a frame and bracket. As hand composition is now mainly used for display work a single double-case, the California job case (see illustration), is usual. *The lay of the case* (arrangement of the characters in it) is not standardized in Britain, but the size is, i.e. $32\frac{1}{2}$ by $14\frac{1}{2}$ by $1\frac{1}{2}$ or $1\frac{3}{4}$ in. (in U.S.A. 32 by 16 by $1\frac{1}{2}$ in.).

The manuscript to be set is held in a copyholder; it should be near but above the case for ease of access to the latter. The letters selected are put in a *composing stick*, q.v., which is made of steel, in various lengths; some are calibrated in 12-point ems and ens. The stick has a fixed side and a sliding one by means of which the stick is adjusted and secured to the proper measure. If uncalibrated, a steel type-scale can be used: this is marked in various point ems (1, 5, 6, 8, 10, and 12) and inches. The final stage in preparing the stick for use is the fitting to it of a brass setting rule. These pieces of brass vary in length, are type high, and about three points thick: at one end is a projecting lip. The composing stick is held in the left hand, and the types are picked singly out of the case with the right hand and placed next to each other in the stick, word by word and line by line. Thick spaces, i.e. a blank type equal to a third of the body in width, are placed between words as they are set. In order that the type should slide easily and not catch in

A compositor at work.

He stands before the case (1) with the copyholder (2) on his left. The composing stick (3) is in his left hand. On the bench to the right of the case are a galley (4) with furniture (5) and tweezers and bodkin (6). Also visible are a roll of page cord and a sponge for damping (7). In the background are cases in their cabinet (8), quoin shelves (9), and slip galleys (10)

previous lines, the setting rule acts as a partition, and by its protruding lip can easily be lifted when the line is completed, and be placed in front of it for the setting of a fresh line.

It is very seldom that a line is filled by a word. If there is no room for one or two letters in the last word space is made for them by removing the thick spaces and inserting thinner ones; the compositor begins this at the right-hand edge. Alternatively, he may decide to remove the partly completed last word and spread out the remainder in order to fill the measure; he then starts on the left and increases the intervals with one or more thin spaces. A further solution is the division by hyphen of the last word. His craftsmanship is revealed by the apparent evenness of the setting, resulting from well-positioned spacing; quick decisions and an eye for the shape of letters are also required of him. Each line should be read and corrected as soon as composed. When the composing stick is full (which means a varying number of completed lines, according to the body) the matter is lifted out of it and placed on the galley where the number of lines required for a page is made up and

checked by a page gauge. The completed page is tied up with page-cord and can now be moved as a firm unit (unsuccessful attempts have been made to tie and untie a page by machine). Before making up the matter into pages it is usual to set it up in long slips and pull *galley proofs* for reading and correcting (see *proof, proof corrections*). Any blocks are inserted during the making up. A headline and footline are placed above and below the matter and in one of these the page number is placed.

On the iron imposing surface the pages are imposed in the order proper for their correct sequence on the printed and folded sheet. A metal chase is now fitted round the pages, furniture and quoins are put between them and the chase (*dressing the forme*), and the whole is tightened by locking the quoins: it is now known as a *forme*.

When printing is completed, the matter which is not to be left standing or used for making stereos should be cleaned and distributed, i.e. the types, furniture, leads and spaces returned to the case or bins. (See also *washing up*.)

From an aesthetic viewpoint hand composition is

217

preferable to mechanical, and even the latter must be finished off by hand, but most people, including many printers, would have difficulty in determining which of two well-printed pages had been hand-set and which by machine. See also *composing*, *margins*.

(With GU)

hand-folding: the folding of sheets into sections by hand instead of by machine. See also *folding*.

hand-letters: brass letters, mounted in wooden handles, which are used by the finisher for adding lettering to the cover of a hand-bound book. See also *binder's brass*, *pallet*.

hand-made paper: fine-quality grain-free paper made by dipping a mould into rag rag pulp and skilfully shaking it until a sheet is formed. Wet sheets are pressed between felts (see *post*). On removal from the post they are further dried in a *pack*, q.v. At this stage the paper is known as *waterleaf*. Tub-sizing and loft drying follow.

Finishes vary according to final treatment. *Rough surface* is paper which has been dried in warm air without a second pressing. *Medium surface* (or *NOT*) is paper which is not given a second pressing between felts after removal from the post and first pressing. Instead, the surface is smoothed by a second pressing without felts and dried on a heated cylinder. *Hot pressed* (or *HP*) refers to very smooth-surface sheets made by glazing medium surface paper, interleaved with zinc plates, and pressing the pile between steel rolls.

By the mid-1970s only two British firms were producing hand-made paper commercially: Inveresk's St Cuthbert's Mill and Barcham Green's Hayle Mill. Such paper is still used for artists' prints and water-colour painting, for limited edition printing, and also for repairing books calling for this high-quality material. See J. B. Green, 'Papermaking by hand', Phillips, 1953. See also *Arches*, *coucher*, *dryworker*, *felts*, *Honig*, *layerman*, *papermaking*, *pilcher*, *rag paper*, *slice boy*, *upper end boy*, *Van Gelder*, *Whatman paper*.

hand-matrix: a matrix for slug-casting machines (accents, fractions, etc.) which is not placed in the matrix magazine but kept in a special hand-matrix case for selection and positioning in the assembler box. On being distributed these matrices slide through a groove to the hand-matrix assembler for removal by the compositor to the hand-matrix case. Linotype and Intertype hand-matrices are called *pi characters*.

hand-press: 1. a printing press in which the forme is inked, the paper is fed and removed, and the pressure is applied by hand. There are various transitional stages from the hand-press to the printing machine in which one or more of these actions are performed

218

automatically or partly mechanically. (a) *The hand-press for printing books* dates back to Gutenberg's day, but the presses used at that time for printing books differed very little from the wine- or cheese-presses of old. Gutenberg's first press was built in accordance with his instructions by Konrad Saspach, a turner,

From 'Dance of Death', printed by M. Huss, Lyons 1499 (Reduced)

but no description of it survives. The oldest known illustration of a printing press is reproduced here from 'Dance of Death', printed in Lyons in 1499. The interior of the Jodocus Badius printing shop, *c.* 1520, is more realistic.

Pressure was applied by means of a screw which was turned by a lever and pressed a platen against the forme lying on the bed. The bed rested on a carriage assembly in such a way that it could be drawn in and out under the platen. When the bed was pulled out

The Badius printing press, from a 16th-century woodcut

the printer could lay the forme on it and then do the inking with two ink balls.

The sheet of paper to be printed was laid on the tympan, the frisket was closed, and then the tympan with the frisket and paper was laid over the forme

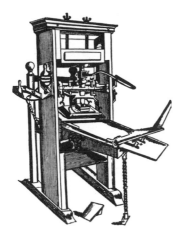

Blaeu printing press. From 'Mechanick Exercises' by Joseph Moxon, 1683

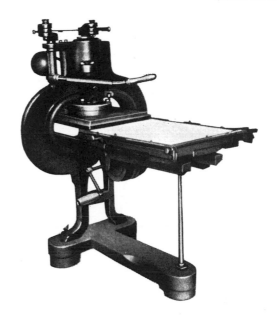

The Stanhope press, as developed by 1830

Usually half a quire of paper (a 'layer') was placed in the tympan at a time, and as impressions were taken, the top sheet was removed. Wooden presses were retained, with some minor improvements, until the early 19th century, though in 1792 Haas of Basle invented a strengthened press with several metal components which foreshadowed the all-metal press of *Stanhope*, q.v. See also *Albion press, bellows press, Blaeu, carriage, cheeks, coffin, fore-stay, frisket, garter, girts, hose, ink ball, joiner's press, letterpress machines, plank, platen press, rounce, tympan, winter.*

The press of Wilhelm Haas, sen., Basle, 1772

(see illustration). The bed was drawn in under the platen and the impression made. The object of the tympan was to distribute the pressure of the platen evenly over the forme, that of the frisket to protect the margins of the paper from coming into contact with the forme and being soiled. The oldest hand-presses were built entirely of wood (hence the name *joiner's press*) and the pressure obtainable was so small that large formes had to be printed in stages by drawing the bed gradually under the platen, which often had a surface only one half or one third the size.

George Clymer's Columbian press, 1817

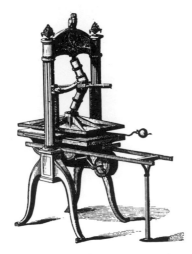

The Hagar press, showing the toggle joint

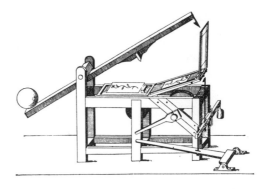

Rubber press, from Senefelder's handbook of 1818

(*b*) *The hand-press for lithographic printing.* From the days of *Senefelder*, q.v., two principles for applying pressure have been used. As a lithographic stone or plate has a practically level surface without differences in height the pressure per unit of surface would be insufficient, if an attempt were made, as in the platen press, to print a large surface at one time. Instead pressure is applied only to one narrow strip at a time: this can be done in a rolling press of the copperplate

variety, or in a scraper press which has a blade placed on edge under which the stone or plate is moved forward. For more modern rubber presses see *transfer press*.

(*c*) *The hand-press for copperplate printing* is described under *copperplate printing press*, q.v.

2. in *bookbinding* hand-operated presses are used to secure books or apply pressure at several stages of forwarding and finishing. For their designs and functions see *arming press*, *backing*, *gilt edges*, *gold blocking press*, *guillotine*, *lying press*, *nipping up*, *standing press*.

hand-roller: a roller used with a hand-press for inking type. See also *ink ball*.

hand-set: type matter which has been composed letter by letter in a stick.

hand-sewing: the sewing of books by hand. The work is done in a sewing frame which is a simple device consisting of a board with two vertical screws and the nuts for them: a crossbar rests on the nuts. Between the bar and the front edge of the base-board hemp or flax cords (or tape) are fitted, fastened by sewing hooks, and stretched by raising the bar. (See illustration.)

The book to be sewn, made up of folded sections, lies on the left of the sewing frame, the last section of the book being on top. One section at a time is laid with its back to the cords and sewn through the back fold in such a way that the threads lie like stitches, a few cm. in length, in the middle double page of the sheet, going out and round for each stitch. Formerly the cords lay entirely outside the back of the book (see *raised bands*), but now sawing-in is usual, which means that before being sewn the book is given grooves ($\frac{1}{32}$ in. deep) to make room for the cords. Cutting is done in a small press. If sewing is done on three cords, five cuts are made, the outer two being for the knotted sewing threads which link one section to the next (kettle-stitches). In addition, the three

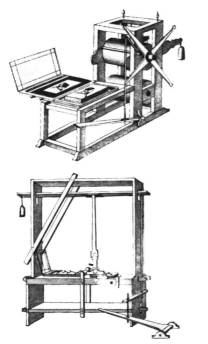

Senefelder's first hand-presses. Top, a primitive copperplate press. Below, a gallows press

middle cuts are usually filed with a three-edge file. The first and last sections of a book are sewn 'all along' to give strength, i.e. the threads run from one kettle-stitch through the middle spread to the nearest cord, out and round the latter, and back into the same

Hand-sewing

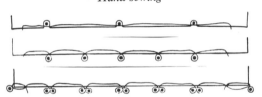

Top to bottom, Sunk cords; Raised bands; Double raised bands

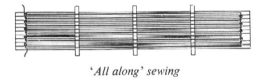

'All along' sewing

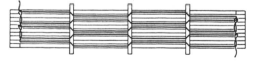

'Two sheets on'

section, and so on to the second kettle-stitch, where the thread is fastened into a knot before being led into the next section. In heavy books with thick sections each is sewn all along; for books with thin sections *two sheets on*, q.v., may be used, which means that two sections are sewn simultaneously with

stitches entering alternately the first and the second. By this means the sewing threads in the sections run alternately to the right and the left from each stitch, and the back of the book will not be unduly thick.

To find easily the middle spread of a section when sewing, a 'sewing heart' is sometimes used to mark it; this is a piece of cardboard cut with a flap. Linen thread is usually used for sewing and the needle is like a large-eyed darning needle. Several books of the same size and with the same arrangement of stitches can be sewn one above the other in the same frame. They then form a span which is divided into separate books by 'cutting off', care being taken to allow two inches of tape or cord to project from the side of each book. (GU)

See also *bookbinding methods and processes*.

hanging figures: the numerals of certain type-designs which range within the limits of the *extruders*, q.v. E.g. the Caslon figures 3, 4, 5, 6, 7, 8, 9, as distinct from the 1, 2, and 0 of the same face. Old-face types usually have hanging figures, though in some faces alternative *ranging figures*, q.v., are available (e.g. Plantin).

hanging paragraph: a paragraph with the first line set to full width, the remaining lines in it being indented one or more ems from the left margin. See also *in pendentive*.

Hansard, Luke, 1752–1828: Printer to the House of Commons. After his apprenticeship in Norwich he entered the employ of a Mr Hughs, the then Printer to the House, becoming a partner in 1774. From that time until his death he printed the Parliamentary Journals. He was succeeded in business and in the official appointment by two of his sons *James* and *Luke Graves*.

His eldest son, *Thomas Curson*, (1776–1833), is remembered for his 'Typographia: an historical sketch of the origin and progress of the art of printing', 1825. This was a thorough practical manual in addition to being a history. More important was his compilation 'Hansard's parliamentary history from the Conquest to 1803', and from 1806 'Hansard's debates', a series which still continues. A reprint of 'Typographia' was published in 1967.

hard copy: 1. in *photosetting*, a reading 'proof' produced at the keyboard unit of a photosetter simultaneously with the perforated tape which operates the photographic unit. The operator uses hard copy for checking work in progress, for house corrections, and for checking accuracy before merging lengths of correction tape.

2. in *computer-assisted typesetting*, a typewritten print-out for reading produced at the keyboard of a computer-assisted typesetting system simultaneously with the punched tape for the computer unit.

3. an enlarged copy of a microfilmed image. It is usually on paper, being known as a *print out*.
Cf. *soft copy*.

hard-cover edition: an edition of a book which is cased in boards. Often, and with equal imprecision, known as *hardback edition*. Either term implies the availability of cheaper copies in paper-covered or limp-cover form. Cf. *softback edition*.

hard-grain morocco: goatskin finished with a deep pin-head grain by hand-boarding. The leather is very supple.

hard-ground etching: see *etching*.

hard packing: thin card or stiff paper used to cover the cylinder of a printing machine so as to obtain a sharp impression, with little indentation, when printing on to smooth, hard paper.

hard sized: paper which contains the maximum of size. Cf. *double sized*.

Harleian Society: a society founded in 1869 for the printing of 'heraldic visitations of counties, and any manuscripts relating to genealogy, family history and heraldry'.

Harley, Sir Robert, 1579–1656: the first member of the Harley family to assemble (at Brampton Bryan) 'an extraordinary library of manuscript and printed books, which had been collected from one descent to another'. In 1644 the castle was besieged and burned, the library of books valued at £200 being destroyed. The family library was re-developed by his grandson, the first Earl of Oxford. See next entry.

Harley, Robert, first Earl of Oxford, 1661–1724: the founder, in 1705, of the famous Harleian collection. Within twenty years he had assembled over 40,000 books and 6,000 manuscripts, many finely illuminated. Subjects were English history, early theology (especially the Eastern Church), and the classics.

His son Edward (1689–1741) added to the collection. At his death it numbered 50,000 printed books, 14,236 charters and rolls, and 7,639 manuscripts. Large sums were spent on binding, for which Thomas Elliott and Christopher Chapman were employed; they used mostly red morocco supplied by the Earl, on which an ornate centre-piece and a broad border, or a narrow roll border were tooled.

The skilful development of the library was largely due to *Humfrey Wanley*, q.v., who from 1708–26 was the Harleian librarian-collector. It is from his diary we learn that Elliott and Chapman were rival binders, not partners as was long supposed.

The manuscripts were purchased for the British Museum in 1753. The printed books had already been sold and dispersed.

Harrild, Robert: a London printer who after 1832 developed his family business as a leading manufacturer and supplier of printing equipment. He is recorded as having invented an inking roller about 1810, better known in its improved seamless form of 1842, and as the inventor of the *Paragon* platen press.

Thomas Harrison Memorial Award: a series of prizes awarded to students of craft bookbinding. In 1955 a fund was launched in London to finance a memorial, in the form of an annual award, to Thomas Harrison (1876–1955). He was an influential craftsman-binder who after working with several London firms, gained a considerable reputation for his free-lance work. He lectured to trade audiences in London and elsewhere, and in 1946 his services to bookbinding were recognised by the award of the OBE.

The first memorial award was made in 1957. In 1975 sponsorship was assumed by *Designer Bookbinders*, q.v.

Harris press: an American automatic platen press built and manufactured by the brothers Alfred and Charles Harris in 1890–1, for the production and sale of which the Harris Automatic Press Co. was formed in 1895. Alfred Harris also built a litho-offset press, the first fully satisfactory one being supplied to the currency printing works in Pittsburgh, 1906. In 1909 the Harris offset press was given a pile feeder. The Premier and Potter Press Manuf. Co. and other undertakings were incorporated in the company, and in 1927 the name was changed to the Harris-Seybold Potter Co., now the Harris Intertype Corporation with works in Britain and the U.S.A.

Hartz, Sem: a Dutch type designer, engraver of stamps and banknotes, and punchcutter known in Britain for his Emergo, 1948, for Enschedé, Mole Foliate for Stephenson Blake, and Juliana, 1958, commissioned by Linotype for book work. Juliana is a condensed face with long descenders. Its companion italic, based on the same matrix width, has a pleasant calligraphic quality. Both are shown in Appendix A.

Harvey, Michael, b. 1932: a British letter designer and lecturer who after training as an engineering draughtsman was inspired to pursue his craft by Eric Gill's 'Autobiography'. This led to instruction in letter cutting with Joseph Cribb, Gill's first assistant, and from 1955 to 1961 to work as a monumental letter-cutter with *Reynolds Stone*, q.v. Harvey has produced lettered book jackets for several British publishers and his book 'Lettering design: form and skill in the design and use of letters', Bodley Head, 1975, is a basic practical manual on the subject.

hatched tooling: see *azured tooling*.

Hattersley, Robert: the inventor of a composing machine which was used by several provincial newspaper offices in England. It appeared in 1859. Depression of keys released type stacked in grooves into a short line for justification. Distribution was by hand.

Haultin, Pierre, fl.1549–87: an eminent Calvinist punchcutter, typefounder and printer of Paris, Lyons and La Rochelle particularly noted for his Protestant Bibles, Testaments and Psalters.

He was long thought to have been the inventor in 1525 of a method of printing music by a single impression, cutting punches for each note with a portion of stave attached. This attribution by Fournier to Haultin was challenged by F. Lesure in 'Die Musik in Geschichte und Gegenwart', Kassel, 1956. Music types of this kind were first used by *Pierre Attaignant*, q.v., about 1527, and he may have made them.

Haultin's printing types were known throughout Europe and were sold in London by his nephew *Hierosme* (Jérôme) from about 1574–86. Day, Vautroullier and Waldegrave used them, and it was to a fount of Haultin roman that O'Kearney added Irish characters when preparing the Irish catechism of 1571. In 1587 Jérôme began printing at La Rochelle whence Pierre had moved his Paris press.

Some writers give the family name as *Hautin*.

Hausleiter process: see *offset reproduction*.

Hawthornden Prize: the prize established in 1919 by Alice Warrender as an annual non-competitive award of £100 and a medal to an English writer under 41 years of age for the best work of imaginative literature, prose or verse. Administered by the *Society of Authors*, q.v.

Hayday, James, c. 1796–1872: a fashionable bookbinder of London whose styles were competent imitations rather than original conceptions. A feature of his work was all-along sewing with silk thread and tight backs covered with *Turkey leather*, q.v.

Haye MSS: three medieval treatises, 'L'Arbre des Batailles', 'L'Ordre de Chevalerie' and 'Le Gouvernement des Princes', translated into Scots by Gilbert of the Haye for the Earl of Orkney. The considerable importance of the manuscript derives principally from the binding, of which it is the earliest surviving Scottish example. It was the work of Patrick Lowes whose stamped inscription on the cover 'Patricius Lowes me ligavit' makes the book doubly unique as the first-known British binding made before 1500 to bear the binder's full name.

Lowes used no fewer than thirty-three stamps, apparently made in Cologne, arranging them in a pattern deriving from Cologne or Erfurt. The principal stamps bear the Tudor rose, rosettes and the twelve Apostles with their emblems, mostly within frames made by a four-line fillet. The translation is dated 1456 but the binding was not made before 1480; it 'may well be ten or fifteen years later' (G. D. Hobson).

The book is now in the National Library of Scotland.

Hayward, John, 1905–65: scholar, critic and anthologist, widely known in Europe and America as editor of *The Book Collector*, q.v.

head: the margin at the top of a page. See also *heading*, *margin*.

headband: 1. a narrow band made up of coloured silk or linen threads wound about a short length of hemp, catgut, cane, leather, board or rolled paper. This is tied to the sections of a book by passing the thread round the *kettle-stitch*, q.v., at about every fifth turn. It lies close to the spine after the cover is fitted and remains visible. Sometimes the headband was also sewn to the boards for greater strength, but nowadays only in very high class work is the headband handmade and sewn round the kettle stitches. A headband may also be placed at the foot as well as the top of a book.

Headbands of one form or another appear to have been known in Europe from the time of the *Stonyhurst Gospel*, q.v. In medieval bindings they were sewn in before the edges of the book were trimmed: the 16th century practice was to sew after trimming. Since the early 17th century separately made headbands were stuck on with glue which saved time without diminishing the visual appeal of the result. Cheapest of all are rolls of striped cotton, cut up, glued and wound round a core of paper or string. This method is widely practised in Asian hand-binderies today. See also *bottomband*, *headcap*.

2. a decorative printed or engraved band used as a *head-piece*, q.v.

head box: see *flow box*.

headcap: the fold of leather at the head and tail of the spine of a hand-bound book, set or shaped by tapping with a hammer. When fitting the glued leather cover to the body a piece of hemp is put inside the turn-in at the head and tail of the spine. This is done whether *headbands*, q.v., are used or not: if they are, they are left visible.

header card: a card with prominent lettering to draw attention to books displayed in a *dumpbin*, q.v., over which it is placed.

heading: see *chapter heading, cross-heads, dropped head, shoulder-heads, side-heads.*

headline: a line of type and quads set in the margin above the text area of a page. It may give the book title, chapter title, subject of a page or the page number. Also known as *page head.*

Practice varies but often the book title is on the left-hand page openings with chapter title opposite. In books where detailed guidance can be useful the chapter title may be given on even-numbered pages with a brief reference to page subject opposite. Such headlines are known as *running heads, running titles,* or *topical heads.* If running heads are placed at the bottom of pages they are known as *running feet.* See also *skeleton.*

head margin: the margin above the first line of the text area on a page.

head-piece: decoration printed in the blank space above the beginning of a chapter. It may be a *printer's ornament,* q.v., a pattern built up with printer's *flowers,* q.v., or a small copperplate etching or engraving designed by a professional illustrator.

Copperplate head- and tail-pieces (*culs de lampe*) reached their peak of delicacy in the 18th century French designs of Boucher, Moreau, Choffard, Gravelot and others. See also *Bewick, tail-piece, vignette.*

heat-set inks: inks designed to dry quickly and facilitate faster printing. Ingredients vary but usually contain a concentrated pigment, synthetic resins, and a volatile petroleum oil. These are combined to form a thermoplastic fluid. The printed web of paper is heated to vaporize the oil and then quickly cooled to harden the plastic residue on the sheet.

heavy type: synonymous, in popular usage, with *bold face,* q.v.

Heber, Richard, 1774–1833: a wealthy bibliophile and founder in 1824 of the Athenaeum Club in London. His library of about 146,800 volumes was stored in his eight houses in England and on the Continent. Of special importance were the works on English poetry and the classics. He bought at all auctions and even purchased whole libraries.

His collection was sold from 1834–7, the British Museum and the Bodleian Library being among buyers.

Hebrew printing before 1600: the invention of the printing press did not find Jews indifferent to its potential. Their culture called for the daily study and discussion in the home of sacred texts and commentaries on them, and printing, regarded by Jews as holy work, meant that cheap and accurate copies could be multiplied for wide distribution. Jewish printing was required to show and maintain the differences in language and script between the handwriting of the original biblical texts and the rabbinical commentaries on them. Even so there was controversy at Salonika in 1515 as to whether a printed text was as sacred as a manuscript version of it.

There was also a demand from Gentile scholars for books in Hebrew, a language officially studied by the 'homo trilinguis' at the universities of Basle, Bologna, Louvain, Paris, Rome, and Salamanca, the better to understand the Bible. Nor were Jews regarded as the essential interpreters of their heritage, and the growing interest in Hebrew theology and philosophy occurred when they were being vigorously persecuted and exiled from centres of Hebrew studies in Spain, Portugal, Germany and Switzerland.

In the early incunabula period, before printing spread from Germany, Jews were not accepted as apprentices to printers, and only south of the Alps, in Italy, could they learn the craft and work with less difficulty. It was the wealthy Jewish communities in Spain, Portugal and Italy who sponsored the earliest presses. That they were never numerous can be deduced from the fact that of the entire total of some 35,000 incunabula editions of which copies survive, wholly or in part, only about 200 were printed with Hebrew type, and only half are complete. They were produced in some twenty-two Hebrew printing shops of which twelve were in Italy, nine in Spain and Portugal, and one in Constantinople. It is assumed that all complete copies of other works perished as a result of daily use, Christian censorship, or public book burnings such as that of the Talmud in Rome in 1553 and other Italian towns.

In *Italy* the first printers may have been Obadiah ben Moses and two associates working in Rome between *c.* 1469 and 1473. They could there have learned the craft from *Sweynheym* and *Pannartz,* qq.v. The three are credited with between eight and ten undated folio works having a common square type, size, and typographic features, but are named in the colophon of only one, a commentary on the Pentateuch by Moses ben Nachman. Another work, probably theirs, was the Maimonides Mishnah Torah. The only Hebrew press in Rome during the 16th century to be officially licensed by the Pope was that of Elijah Levita who issued three of his grammatical works from it in 1518.

In February 1475 Abraham ben Isaac ben Garton completed the printing of Rashi's commentary on the Pentateuch at Reggio di Calabria. He used an elegant square type based on a reed-written script. This was the first printed Hebrew book to identify in a colophon the printer, place and date. In July of the same year Meschullam Cusi and his sons completed an edition of Jacob ben Asher's 'Arba'a turim' at Piove di Sacco. The type had marked contrasts between bold and fine strokes, and was derived from a German quill-written angular script.

At Mantua the physician Abraham ben Solomon Conat set up a press where he employed Abraham Jedidiah of Cologne and Jacob Levi to print Levi ben Gerson's commentary on the Pentateuch. Conat commissioned a fine italian-rabbinic type based on his own Italo-German cursive writing. The press issued part one of the 'Arba'a turim' in 1476. In 1477 the Tehillim (Psalms) with David Kimhi's commentary was printed at Bologna by Joseph Mordecai in a similar type. In 1477 Abraham ben Hayyim dei Tintori began printing at Ferrara with Conat's equipment. He completed Conat's 'Arba'a turim' and also Finzi's astronomical tables, 1477. In Bologna he was commissioned by Joseph Caravita to print Isaac ben Aaron's edition of the Pentateuch with Rashi's commentary, 1482. The text was printed in a large new square letter type of Sephardic style: the commentary in Conat's smaller cursive. This edition fixed the layout for later printers. Abraham also worked as press corrector for others, notably in 1488, Joseph Soncino who was the most active of all Jewish printers in Italy before 1500. (See *Soncino*.)

The leading printer of Hebrew books in Italy during the 16th century was the Christian *Daniel Bomberg*, q.v., of Venice. Blado of Rome used his fine chancery italic to print Leone Ebreo's influential philosophical work 'Dialoghi d'amore' in 1535, which was followed by many editions and translations. Another Italian printer of Hebrew was Marcantonio Giustiniani of Venice for whom Le Bé cut types in 1544/5.

In *Spain and Portugal* Rashi's Pentateuch was the first Hebrew book to be printed, being issued by Solomon ben Moses al-Kabiz at Guadalajara in 1476. The elegant square cursive Sephardic type was based on a reed-written alphabet and cut by Piedro da Guadalajara. Solomon was active until about 1482.

Eliezer ibn Alantansi was a physician who owned a printing shop at Hijar (Spain) from which came some of the most beautiful Hebrew incunabula. Noteworthy were the vellum copies of his Rashi Pentateuch, printed in square and rabbinic hebrew type in 1490. The white on black initials and ornaments filled with birds, animals and tendrils show Islamic influence. They were engraved in wood by Alfonso Fernandez of Cordoba, a Valencian typecutter. The same type, border and initials were used in a slightly larger size at Lisbon by Rabbi Eliezer Toledano from 1488–92. He issued a fine Perush ha-Torah, Lisbon, 1488, (where it was the first book to be printed), and a Pentateuch in 1491. Another Jewish printer in Portugal was Samuel Dortas who printed the Proverbs at Leiria in 1492 and the Prophets in 1494.

When the expulsion of Jews from Spain in 1492 and from Portugal in 1498 ended for a time printing there by Jews there was a migration of Jewish printers with their equipment to Muslim Turkey. While working in Constantinople as general printers they were allowed to issue Jewish books, Jacob ben Asher's 'Arba'a turim', printed by the Spanish refugee David ibn Nahmias and his son Samuel in 1493, being the first book published in Turkey. His business there continued until the early 16th century. Early in the 16th century Portuguese Jewish refugees set up at Fez the first printing press on the African continent. They were active between 1516 and 1522, using type of Lisbon origin. Hebrew printing at Salonika began in 1512.

In *Germany* woodcut Hebrew letters were used for a few words in Petrus Niger's 'Tractatus contra perfidos Judaeos', printed by Conrad Fyner in 1475. Johann Petri of Nuremberg and Thomas Anshelm of Pforzheim, both in 1506, were the earliest printers north of the Alps to use cast hebrew type: Anshelm cut three founts. Large numbers of Hebrew grammars and primers were printed in southern Germany in the early 16th century. Those from the Würtemberg press of Paul Fagius were closely supervised by Elijah Levita who had worked with Bomberg in Venice. Two early founts of hebrew type were used by Öglin of Augsburg from 1514. The complete Jewish ritual was published by Thomas Murner at Frankfurt in 1512. The first Pentateuch printed in Germany was issued in 1530 at Oels in Silesia by Hayyim Schwartz who later moved to Frankfurt where he printed the Rashi commentary in 1533.

German humanists and Reformers studied the scriptures in the original Greek and Hebrew in attempts to find the literal sense of the Bible without the allegorical flummery of the medieval church. This led the Reformers to accord more authority to the Bible than to the Pope, and to a demand for the publication of original texts as well as for vernacular versions based upon them. The first complete German Bible was the work of Ulrich Zwingli, assisted in his independent translation of the O.T. by the Jew Leo Jud. It was published by Froschauer in 1529. Luther's German Bible, for which he was assisted in his translation of the O.T. by Melanchthon, was completed in 1532.

In *France* woodcut Hebrew words appeared in the 1488 edition of Breydenbach's 'Peregrinations', while in Paris Gilles de Gourmont was the first printer to use hebrew type. He issued an 'Alphabetum hebraicum et graecum' about 1507, and a Hebrew grammar in 1508. His first types were imperfect, but in 1519 he made better punches and matrices. The new type was used in 1520 for Moses Kimhi's 'Liber viarum linguae sanctae' which was the first book in France printed wholly in hebrew. Among other printers were Wechel, Gryphius, and Estienne whose decorated edition of the Hebrew O.T. in four quarto volumes, 1539–44, was of note. The leading supplier of hebrew type to printers in France and Italy was *Le Bé*, q.v.

The *Netherlands* printer Johannes de Westfalia printed from woodcut blocks the passages of Hebrew text in the 'Epistola' of Paulus de Middelburgo, Louvain, 1488, and T. Marten's 'Grammar' of 1528 showed an early hebrew type. The Plantin Polyglot Bible of 1569–72 included the Hebrew O.T. The Le Bé type used, cut under the direction of Robert Estienne, was superior to all its predecessors.

In *Bohemia* Prague developed from 1512 as a centre of Hebrew printing. It was the first town north of the Alps where Jews were allowed to print. Types used were based on German gothic hebrew scripts. (See also *Kohen*.) It was here that Gershom Cohen ben Salomon printed the first illustrated Haggadah, *c*. 1520. Jewish printing in *Poland* began at Cracow in 1534.

In *Switzerland* Basle developed as the leading European centre of Hebrew scholarship. It was here that the German Protestant Sebastian Münster (1489–1552) wrote many of his works on Hebrew grammar. Most important was his diglot Hebrew-Latin Bible, the first to be prepared by a Christian. Froben was the leading printer of Hebrew books, employing Christian compositors and correctors. His hebrew type was supplied by Peter Schöffer II, a friend of Münster. Froben published the Hebrew Psalms in 1516. An edition of the Talmud, printed by his son Ambrosius in 1580, was the work of Jewish compositors and correctors whose right to live and work in Basle had received special approval. One of them was the Italian Israel Sifroni.

In *England* no Hebrew work was printed in the 15th century. Wynkyn de Worde used crudely cut wooden blocks for a few Hebrew words in Wakefield's 'Oration on three languages' (Arabic, Chaldaic, Hebrew), 1524. In 1573 John Day was obliged to use words cut in wood because hebrew type was not available, and it was not until 1591/2 that a book printed in England showed any extensive use of it. This was J. D. Rhys's 'Cambrobritannicae Cymrae caeue linguae institutiones', printed by T. Orwin (STC 20966). The type resembled that used by Froben some years earlier.

This survey of Hebrew printing before 1600 is necessarily brief. During the 16th century about 4,000 Hebrew works are known. Religious texts and commentaries upon them formed 80%: grammars, dictionaries and philosophy being an important part of the remainder.

Note on modern Israeli typography.

Harry Carter and *Eric Gill*, qq.v., designed types for the Jerusalem publisher, book and type designer Maurice Spitzer. Carter's 12-point Bezalel was based on a 15th century Sephardic original. Gill's modern hebrew of 1937, cast by Spitzer, has been described as 'a hybrid attempt to implant the system of roman

capitals into meruba (square script) which is governed by entirely different laws'. Only the display size is occasionally used today.

Of mid-20th century types in general use for printing Hebrew and Yiddish books the Ha-Zevi family designed by Zevi Hausmann and Maurice Spitzer for the Jerusalem Type Foundry has been very successful. It is a quasi-sanserif, pruned of the decorative additions of its predecessors, and is available in several weights and sizes from 6- to 48-point, plus an outline display fount. Ismar David's fount, named after him, is available from Intertype and has two display sizes for hand-setting. It was cut by the Spanish engraver Alfonso Ayuso. Zvi Narkis's fount for Linotype, Franziska Baruch's Schocken for Monotype, and Z. Korngold's Koren for Deberny are among others.

Hebrew is still an alphabet of capitals, written from right to left, and the only 20th century approach to an italic was the Rabat of Spitzer, Rothschild and Lippmann, inspired by a North African cursive script: it has remained experimental. See Appendix A.

See D. W. Amram, 'The making of Hebrew books in Italy', Philadelphia, 1909, and A. Freimann, 'Thesaurus typographiae hebraicae', 1924–31. See also *Adelkind, Ashkenazi, Bible printing in England, colophon, Ferrara Bible, Reuchlin*.

Heidelberg: the name of automatic printing machines made by what was until 1967 the Schnellpressenfabrik A.G. of Heidelberg in Germany: the name was then changed to Heidelberger Druckmaschinen A.G. The firm was founded by Andreas Hamm and began making presses in 1850; in 1914 they built their first automatic machine.

Heidelberg machines, which include a vast range of single and multi-colour offset models, continually updated, are in world-wide use.

height to paper: the overall height of type and plate printing surfaces in letterpress work. This is standardized in Britain as 0·918 in. (23·317 mm.) from feet to face.

W. H. Heinemann Awards: see *Royal Society of Literature Award*.

heliogravure: 1. a method of reproducing line drawings by *process work*, q.v. It resulted from experiments by Paul Pretsch, *c*. 1854, and involved the preparation of an image-carrying silvered copper plate. It was also used for developing the original plates of maps by Emil Mariot of Graz in 1867.

2. the terms heliogravure and *photogravure*, q.v., are loosely used to refer to the latter process.

hell-box: a receptacle for broken or discarded type. See also *batter, bow*.

Hempel quoin: a patent steel quoin used for locking up type in the chase. It was invented by Henry A. Hempel about 1878. Two wedge-shaped units, with toothed inner sides, are operated by a key which pushes the wedges outwards, thereby creating pressure between type and chase.

heraldic colours: the standard colours (or *tinctures*) used in heraldry are occasionally printed in monochrome when the expense of colour reproduction is not warranted. Hatching is used to distinguish the various colours and a standard system is in use

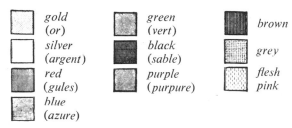

Heraldic tinctures and metals
(With Norman-French names in parentheses)

throughout most of the world: this is said to have been first employed for Langrius's armorial chart of the Duchy of Brabant, 1600, and popularized by the Jesuit Silvester de Petra Sancta for the book 'Tesserae gentilitiae', Rome, 1638. (With GU)

herbal: a book giving the names and descriptions of plants in general. Herbals are believed to date from the 4th century BC (Theophrastus); and a noteworthy early example is the *Vienna Dioscorides*, q.v.

An early printed herbal was the 'Herbarius' printed by Johannes Philippus de Lignamine, Rome, *c.* 1483, of unknown origin but probably based on a 2nd-century AD work of Apuleius Platonicus. The first printed illustrated herbal was 'Herbarius Moguntinus' which Peter Schöffer issued in 1484; his 'Gart der Gesundheit', probably compiled by Johann Wonnecken von Cube, appearing in 1485. In England Rycharde Banckes's 'Here begynnyth a new mater, the whiche sheweth and treateth of ye vertues & proprytes of herbes, the whiche is called an Herball' was printed in London in 1525.

Better known was the enormous compilation of John Gerard whose 'Herball' of 1597 in its corrected revision by Thomas Johnson of 1598 included over 2,700 blocks. See A. Arber, 'Herbals, their origin and evolution', 2nd ed., C.U.P., 1938. See also *florilegium*.

Herbert, William, third Earl of Pembroke, 1580–1630: an English statesman deserving mention here for his purchase in 1629 of the 242 Greek manuscripts from the Venetian Barocci library. At this time Pembroke was Chancellor of Oxford University and it was to the Bodleian Library there that he gave most of the collection. The twenty-four items he retained were later bought by Oliver Cromwell who gave them to the Bodleian in 1654.

Hercolani, Giulantonio, fl.1571–77: of Bologna, where he was a Doctor of Law. He is remembered for his writing manual 'Essemplare utile di tutte le sorte de l're cancellaresche correntissime . . .', 1574. This was a technical innovation in that he used copperplate engravings instead of wood blocks for his copy-book, thereby achieving greater contrast between thick and thin strokes. However, this meant that the writing quill could not so easily be used to copy them: they were more suitable as models for engravers.

Hereford world map: a famous map of the world preserved in Hereford Cathedral where it was used as an altar piece. It was made in the 13th century by Richard of Haldingham who may have copied a Roman original. The map, contained within a circle over four feet diameter, is drawn in ink with touches of colour for rivers and seas. Around it are drawings of the Day of Judgement, Julius Caesar and a miscellany of real and imaginary fauna. See G. R. Crone, 'The Hereford world map', 1948.

Heremberck, Jacques, fl.1488–92: a German printer, also known as *Jacobus of Herrenberg*, who settled in Lyons where he was until 1492 the associate of *Michel Topié*, q.v. In 1488 they published an adaptation and translation by Nicole Le Huen of Bernhard von Breydenbach's 'Peregrinatio in terram Sanctam' with illustrations freely adapted from the drawings of Erhard Reuwich which had appeared as woodcuts in the Mainz edition of 1486. The seven copper engravings, which included a folding panorama of Venice five feet wide, were the first in this medium to be used in a French book. There were also fifteen woodcuts. Le Huen, who had made a similar journey, added material where his itinerary differed from Breydenbach's.

In 1490 they issued Raoul Le Fèvre's 'Le Recueil des histoires troyennes' with numerous capitals, borders and woodcuts in an earlier Flemish style, and an unsigned and undated translation of Aesop's 'Fables' is attributed to their press: it had somewhat crude cuts, probably of German origin.

Herford, John, fl.1526–48: the owner of the second printing press at St Albans where he worked under the patronage of Richard Stevenage, the Abbot. He printed a Breviary, *c.* 1526, John Lydgate's 'Lyfe and passion of Seint Albon', 1534, and five other small works. His alleged association with a tract held to be heretical led in 1539 to his confrontation with Thomas Cromwell. The Abbey was suppressed in the same year and Herford later printed in London.

The edition of 'Compendiosa totius anatomiae delineatio' (by *Gemini*, q.v.) which he printed in 1545 was the first book in England to have an engraved title-page. He may have died in 1548 since in 1549 his widow was printing. See also *Schoolmaster of St Albans*.

Hermann, Caspar: a German-American printer who introduced *offset printing*, q.v., into Europe in 1907. In 1908 he patented the first practical offset press for perfecting the paper. He subsequently made several inventions used in lithographic printing.   (GU)

Herwagen, Johannes: a printer of Basle, remembered for the editio princeps of the works of Archimedes which he published in 1544, and for Johannes Herold's edition of Bede's works, issued in eight volumes in 1563.

Hess, Andreas: the first printer in Hungary who came from Rome to establish a press at Buda in 1472. Among his few works was 'Chronicles of the Hungarians', 1473.

heures, livre d': see *Book of Hours*.

heuristic: the search for and location of manuscripts. See also *diplomatic*.

Hewitt, William Graily, 1864–1952: an outstanding calligrapher and gilder. He was a pupil of *Edward Johnston*, q.v., whom he succeeded in 1901 at the Central School of Arts and Crafts in London. During the thirty years he taught there he revived the art of manuscript illumination. One of his pupils was *Alfred Fairbank*, q.v. Hewitt also designed the calligraphic Treyford type for the Corvinus Press.

Heynlin, Johann: or *Johannes de Lapide*, was born at Stein in the Duchy of Baden. After studying at Leipzig from 1448–50 he went to Paris in 1454, holding various offices at the Sorbonne and teaching theology. He spent 1464–7 at Basle University before returning to Paris in 1467 when he appears to have begun planning with his friend Guillaume Fichet, doctor of theology, to establish what was to be the first press in France. During the winter 1469/70 Heynlin visited Basle and Beromünster where he recruited *Ulrich Gering*, q.v., and his associate printers Crantz and Friburger. Heylin's position as 'prieur' of the Sorbonne, 1470–1, and Fichet's as librarian favoured the carrying out of their plan.

Money to set up the press and buy stocks of paper appears to have come from Fichet's rich patron Cardinal Jean Rolin to whom he dedicated his 'Rhetorica' of 1471, using the words '. . . à vous qui depuis dix ans jusqu'à ce jour m'avez constamment

subventionné de la manière la plus large . . .' It was to encourage patronage that Fichet included personal dedications in copies printed on vellum and embellished by limners before sending them to kings, princes, bishops and the Pope. Heynlin's particular patron was Jean II, brother-in-law of Louis XI, who visited the press in 1471 and was the dedicatee of the 'Speculum vitae humanae' printed in 1472.

Although none of the books printed gave the precise location the press appears to have been set up in rooms within the cloister of Saint-Benoit belonging to the Sorbonne but outside the control of the *Socii*. Both Heynlin and Fichet recognised the opportunity the press gave to establish accurate texts. If Fichet managed the business side of the enterprise it was Heynlin who amended texts, divided them into chapters and often corrected with pen and ink errors found on the sheets as an alternative to resetting the type. It was Heynlin also who chose and prepared the first four works to be printed, anticipating their use by students and a wider educated class. The first work sponsored by Fichet, Bessarion's 'Orationes', 1471, was a call to the Crusade against the Turks. This was followed by his own 'Rhetorica'. Fichet saw both books through the press and it was he who sponsored the only incunable edition (in Latin) of Plato's 'Epistolae', in 1472. Some time later he left for Rome to enter the service of Sixtus IV.

When Heynlin became a doctor of theology in 1472 he invited a friend, Erhard Windsberg, to edit and correct for the press so that he could devote himself to teaching. Among his pupils to achieve fame were Rudolf Agricola, *Johannes Amerbach*, q.v., and Johann Reuchlin. In 1474 Heynlin left Paris to live and teach in Basle and Tübingen. In 1487 he became a Carthusian monk. When he died in 1496 he left 300 volumes to what is now Basle University Library but no manuscript exemplar of the works he edited and printed in Paris has been found among them.

Hibbert Press: a private printing press established at Kentish Town, London, by *Julian Hibbert* (d. 1834). He is remembered for two books he issued, 'Orpheus Umnoi', 1827 (extracted from Hermann's edition of the Orphica), which he printed in uncial letters as an experiment, and 'Peri deicidaimoniac', 1828 (Plutarch and Theophrastus on Superstition).

Hiberno-Saxon illumination: the origins of Celtic illumination are obscure since examples survive only in such fully mature works as the *Book of Durrow*, *Book of Kells*, and *Lindisfarne Gospels*, qq.v. These 7th- and 8th-century manuscripts of the Gospels were made in Christian monasteries of northern Ireland or Northumbria whence the art of illuminating was brought by Irish monks. There was usually a whole-page representation of the Evangelists, one before each Gospel. The initial and first few works of the text were illuminated and there were some full pages based on cruciform patterns. Gold and silver were rarely used, and never extensively. Drawings were not in perspective; typical designs had an all-over effect of continuous pattern, mostly strapwork, with convoluting lacertine animals.

The influence in Europe of Celtic and Anglo-Saxon illumination was wide and profound; monks emigrated and established monasteries which became important centres of learning (e.g. at Bobbio in Italy, 613; at St Gall in Switzerland, c. 612; Salzburg in 739; Echternach in 698).

With the arrival in England of the Danish hordes little illuminating was done in the 9th century. In 954 Aethelwold founded a monastery at Abingdon, later moving to Winchester where his patronage of painting led to the *Winchester School*, q.v., and a new flowering of art.

From 970–1070 there was a noteworthy series of manuscripts illustrated by lively outline drawings or sketches, done in brown ink, and positioned on the page close to the text they illustrated: colour washes were sometimes added. In style and treatment the hunchbacked figures with curiously protruding necks and tapering legs derive from the *Utrecht Psalter*, q.v. An example of this style is the Malmesbury Prudentius, c. 1040, now in Cambridge University Library. See also *illumination*.

hickeys: specks of dirt or hardened ink which leave spots of irregular shape on a printed sheet.

hic nullus est defectus: Latin words, meaning that 'nothing is omitted here', sometimes found in manuscripts and early printed books where a blank page occurs, to inform the reader of this fact.

Before the days of galley proofs, later to be paged, it was customary to divide the author's manuscript of a lengthy book between several presses (not necessarily within one workshop) and the exact calculation of how much matter would make up a page was not always achieved. Hence the occasional need for a page cramped with corrections, the insertion of an extra leaf within a quire, or the inscription noted above.

The words *hic deficit* in a manuscript or early printed book indicated a gap in the exemplar or that the script could not be deciphered by scribe or printer.

hieratic: a cursive form of *hieroglyphics*, q.v., used principally by religious scribes in ancient Egypt for writing texts on papyrus. It was originally written in vertical columns but later in horizontal lines from right to left and continued in use until the 3rd century AD.

hieratica: 1. the finest quality of papyrus used in Rome at the time of Pliny, AD 23–79. Under Augustus Caesar its name was changed to 'Augusta'.

2. the trade name for a certain quality of paper.

hieroglyphics: literally, 'holy stone-writing,' being the form of communicating thought by pictorial symbols used in Egypt from 3000 BC. The meaning of the symbols was discovered by Champollion in 1799 when he deciphered the Rosetta Stone on which was a parallel text in hieroglyphics, *demotic script*, q.v., and Greek. See also *letters – forms and styles*.

With the development of Egyptology in 19th century Europe hieroglyphic sorts were needed by the printer of research papers. In Germany a fount was cut in 1843 from drawings by Richard Lepsius. In France one was designed in 1842 by E. E. Devéria and J.–J. Dubois for the Imprimerie Nationale where, between 1842 and 1852, Delafond and Ramé jnr engraved 3,325 punches for an 18D size. A 12D size, reduced from the above, was made in 1873.

In England hieroglyphics were shown in a broadside specimen of type for sixty-seven languages issued by W. M. Watts of London in 1851: the designer was not named. Punches for an improved fount were cut by W. J. Bilton from drawings by Mr and Mrs de G. Davis. Matrices were cast by R. P. Bannerman & Son and the type was used for an Egyptian grammar (O.U.P.) in 1926. The fount had the advantage of aligning well within lines of text in roman, and the most complicated inscriptions could be set by combining them.

High House Press: the private press established by James E. Masters at Shaftesbury, Dorset, in 1924. He issued poetry by Lyly, Milton, Shenstone, Suckling and others, usually in editions of between 100 and 200 copies which he bound himself. When the press closed on the death of the owner in 1943 it had been moved to Westbury, near Bristol.

See S. Matthewman, 'The High House Press: a short history and appreciation', 1930.

high mill finish: calendered paper with a surface intermediate between MF and super-calendered paper.

high quads: spaces cast nearly type high. Used in plaster stereotyping.

Higonnet-Moyroud photocomposing machine: see *Photon*.

Hildesheim Psalter: a 12th-century manuscript from the Abbey of St Albans. Notable are the numerous figures, often ugly, and complicated initials in which the animals seem to derive from bestiaries of the period.

hinged: plates or other separate sheets to be inserted in a book which have been given a narrow fold on their inner edges; they will thus lie flat and turn easily when bound.

hinges: channels lying between the two halves of the end-papers where the body of a book is fixed to the covers. See also *joints*.

Hinman, Charlton: the inventor of a *collating machine*, q.v.

historiated letters: initial capital letters embellished with detailed drawings illustrating an incident in the text they introduce. English examples are found in 11th to 13th century manuscripts. See also *illumination, rubricator, versals*.

Historische Kommission des Börsenvereins des deutschen Buchhandels: an independent group of bibliographers, booksellers, librarians and publishers formed in Leipzig in 1876 to establish a historical record of the part played by the printed book in the economic, literary and social history of Germany from the time of Gutenberg. It was funded by the *Börsenverein der Deutschen Buchhändler*, q.v.

A library was assembled to support research. Publications of major importance were J. Goldfriedrich's 'Geschichte des deutschen Buchhandels', 4 vols, 1886–1913, and the journal *Archiv für Geschichte des deutschen Buchhandels*, 1878–98, with a final volume in 1930.

In 1953 the Kommission was revived in Frankfurt a. M., and a new library was formed. At the same time the research programme was extended to include the place and history of authorship and reading. In 1956 publication began of *Archiv für Geschichte des Buchwesens*, now the leading bibliographical journal in West Germany.

Hoe: an important American firm of printing machine manufacturers which traces its origins to the arrival in New York in 1803 of *Robert Hoe* (1784–1833) a Leicestershire carpenter. In 1805, partnered by Matthew Smith whose daughter he married, he built furniture. After Smith died Hoe formed a partnership with his brother-in-law Peter Smith, inventor in 1822 of the Smith press, and together they built platen and flat-bed presses. When Smith died in 1825 Hoe acquired the rights for Samuel Rust's press, 1829. Hoe's combination of the Smith and Rust machines was marketed as the *Washington press*. The firm, now R. Hoe & Co., developed considerably when presses of the Napier type were built in an improved form.

It was Richard March Hoe (1812–86) who built the first true rotary newspaper printing press. In this, his 'Type Revolving Machine', patented 1845,

ordinary type was used with wedge-shaped leads, directly justified on a cylinder of large diameter, being secured to it by tapering column rules. Paper was sheet-fed by boys, being taken from the feed-board by automatic grippers and pressed on to the large forme cylinder by from four to ten impression cylinders, each having its own feeder (illustrated under *letterpress machines*). It was first used in 1847 to print the *Philadelphia Public Ledger*. Type-revolving presses were popular for newspaper work (including from 1848 Applegath's for *The Times*) and were made until 1876 when they were superseded by the Hoe web-perfecting press of 1871. The firm continued to pioneer improved printing machines of various kinds among which a 4- to 6-colour offset sheet press should be mentioned.

Robert Hoe IV (1833–1909) who directed the firm for some years was also a bibliophile. He 'gathered together one of the greatest collections of books in the United States, cosmopolitan in flavor, rich in manuscripts, early printed books, fine bindings, classics of world literature . . .', (vide E. Wolf and J. Fleming, 'Rosenbach', 1961). His library was dispersed by auction in 1911 and 1912, the great collectors Huntington (more than a million dollars worth), Morgan, and Mrs McCormick buying extensively.

Hoernen, Arnold ther, fl.1470–82: the second printer in Cologne where he learned his craft with *Ulrich Zel*, q.v., before setting up on his own in 1470. He was the second printer there. He is remembered as the first to print leaf numbers (in arabic): this was in his edition of Rolewinck's 'Sermo in festo . . .', 1470 (also known as 'Sermo ad populum'). He was also an early printer of woodcut illustrations: this was in Rolewinck's 'Fasciculus temporum', 1474. Latin classics and several works of Thomas Aquinas were among his output.

hog: a revolving agitator fitted at the bottom of a papermaking vat so that fibres cannot settle. This helps to maintain consistency and thus the quality of the hand-made sheet.

Hogarth Press: originally a private press set up in 1917 by Leonard and Virginia Woolf at their house in Richmond, Surrey. Early works, some of which they printed and bound in coloured paper covers, were by T. S. Eliot, K. Mansfield, E. M. Forster, Maxim Gorky, and, of course, their own early writings. Their original press is preserved at Sissinghurst, Kent.

Until 1923 they sold their limited editions on a subscription basis; thereafter they sold through bookshops and within ten years the press was a successful commercial publishing business.

Hogenberg, Franz, 1540–90: a Flemish map engraver,

born at Malines. In the late 1560s he worked in England with his brother *Remigius*, his engravings appearing in Jugge's 'Bishops' Bible of 1568. In Antwerp he engraved the plates for Abraham Ortelius's 'Theatrum orbis terrarum', 1570, and he also worked for Plantin.

After 1570 he moved to Cologne where he collaborated with Georg Braun (1541–1622), Georg Höfnagel (1542–1600) and others on the plates for 'Civitates orbis terrarum', 1572–1618, a beautifully illustrated work in six volumes issued without a general title. Among its six hundred views and plans was one of London, probably based on a copper engraved map by an unknown craftsman (Anthony van den Wyngaerde?) made between 1553 and 1559: of this two of some twenty original plates survive and are in the London Museum, but no prints are known.

Hogenberg's sons *Johann* (fl.1594–1614) and *Abraham* (d. *c*. 1653) were also engravers of copper plates for title pages and illustrations.

Holbein, Hans, 1497–1543: the great portrait painter who worked for a time at Basle where he designed small woodcut decorations and title-page borders for Froben and other publishers. He employed a craftsman-cutter for the blocks (Ger. Formschneider).

Probably his best-known book illustrations appear in 'Les Simulachres et historiées faces de la mort', a series of forty-one small cuts, one per page, with a Bible quotation in Latin and a French verse under each. The blocks were cut by Hans Lützelburger, a man of rare talent, and the book was printed by Gaspar and Melchior Treschel at Lyons in 1538.

From Holbein's 'Dance of Death', drawn in 1523–26, and cut by Lützelburger. The work was printed at Lyons in 1538 by Gaspar and Melchior Treschel. Reproduced here in original size

Holbein's work was widely copied and imitated by other printers.

holdout: resistance by the surface of highly glazed coated paper to the drying of ink. The gloss reduces porosity and absorption.

Hole, William, fl.1607–24: one of the earliest English engravers of music on copper. An example of his work is 'Parthenia', subtitled 'the maydenhead of the first musicke that ever was printed for the virginalls' which he engraved in 1612–13. He was mainly a portrait engraver.

holiday: said of any area on a paste-covered surface which is left uncoated in the pasting unit, e.g. on a lining paper.

holing out: the boring of holes through the boards of a book which is being hand-bound: this is done prior to lacing.

Holkham Bible Picture Book: a manuscript containing 'a pictorial representation of the Creation and Fall, . . . the story of Christ, interspersed with aprocryphal incidents, and finally the signs of the end of the world and the Last Judgement' (Hassall). The work had no contemporary title, the present one being suggested by M. R. James in 1922. It consists of 231 pictures on forty-two leaves, all but two being illustrated, and was probably made in London for a wealthy Dominican patron between 1326 and 1331.

It appears that the draughtsman was the first to work on the book. His strokes are vigorous, accurate and observant, ranging from gross caricature to great beauty. The colourist was less successful, on occasion masking the delicacy of the drawing or misinterpreting the meaning. No gold was used. After the colourist came the scribe who added an explanatory text in Anglo-Norman, using a large 14th century hand.

The book is now in the British Library (MS. Add. 47680) but easier to consult is the Dropmore Press reproduction of 1954, with commentary by Dr W. O. Hassall, on which this entry is based.

Holl, John: a bookbinder of Worcester where he worked in the late 18th century. He is remembered for his use of silk as a covering material for some of his bindings. The silk was glued to very thin card before being fitted to the boards. Books were then tooled and lettered in gold. Occasional use of silk was made by other craftsmen binders prior to the introduction of *book cloth*, q.v., but it was more costly than leather and less durable.

holland: a plain-woven linen fabric known after the country of its first manufacture. Occasionally used for book covers with lettering stamped in ink rather than gold.

Hollander: the standard beating machine, of which there are several kinds, used by the paper manufacturer to reduce half-stuff to pulp. The machine was invented in Holland, probably about 1673 (by Jacob Honingh of Zaandijk?), and is basically an oblong vat, lined with tiles, and having a central divider called a mid-feather, around which the stuff is circulated and forced between a revolving beater-roller and ridged, fixed bed plate.

Its use speeded up papermaking, and was the critical factor in the amount of paper a mill could produce. With one hundredweight of rags at each filling one Hollander would produce six hundredweight of pulp a day.

It was first used in England in the mid-18th century and somewhat later in America where it is called a *beater*. See Voorn Henk, 'On the invention of the Hollander beater', *Paper Maker* **25** 2 1956.

Hollar, Wenzel, 1607–77: a Bohemian engraver who was a prolific etcher and copperplate engraver. He worked in Frankfurt, Strasbourg and Cologne until 1637 when, after meeting the Earl of Arundel, he came to London and introduced the art of etching. He did title-pages and illustrations for several publishers, but his collections of women's fashions are perhaps best known today.

Holle, Lienhart, fl.1482: a blockcutter of Ulm who began printing about 1482. In this year he printed Ptolemy's 'Cosmographia', edited by Nicolaus Germanus, with thirty-two woodcut maps. The type was a fine clear text, almost roman. For 'Das Buch der Weisheit', printed in 1483, he used what is considered the precursor of the later *Schwabacher*, q.v. A year later he was forced to flee from creditors and his press was acquired by Johann Reger who also issued 'Cosmographia', 1486.

Hollis, Thomas, 1720–74: an English republican who sought to further his concept of liberty by presenting collections of books to libraries in Europe and America. Thus between 1758 and 1765 he gave over four hundred to the city of Berne, and several thousand to Harvard Library to which he bequeathed a fund of £500 from which books are still bought.

Since he believed that finely bound books would be more acceptable to their recipients he employed Matthewman and Montagu, two London binders, for the task. He commissioned Giovanni Battista Cipriani to design a suite of appropriate emblematic tools: typical of those stamped on the boards were figures of Britannia, Liberty, as well as the cockerel, the owl, etc. After fire destroyed Matthewman's premises in 1764 replacement tools were engraved by the medallist Pingo.

hollow back: the type of back in a book which, when the book is open, has a hollow space between the spine covering material and the sewn back. Cf. *tight back*. (LK)

hollow quads: large quads cast with hollow channels to make them lighter and save metal.

hollows: flattened tubes of strong, pliable brown paper, used to support the spine of a book during tooling and to allow it to be opened easily. They are made by

Folded hollow

cutting a piece of paper three times as wide as the back and giving it two lengthwise folds. The top two leaves are glued together. After the back of the book has been glued, lined, and rubbed down, the third leaf of the hollow is glued to it. More linings may be needed if the book is heavy. Hollows are necessary for *drawn-in* work, q.v. False raised bands, if wanted, are pasted across the upper two layers of the hollow before covering. There are other methods. French bookbinders began to use hollows about 1770 and their English counterparts about 1800. Cf. *tight back*. See also *lining up, Oxford hollow, recessed cords*.

holograph: a work written wholly in the author's handwriting.

holster book: a pocket book used for memoranda, so called from its unusually long and narrow shape resulting from folding the sheet along the length. Such books were used in the 15th century for accounts, but others which survive were used as *commonplace books*, q.v. The usual language was English.

Winifred Holtby Memorial Bequest: an award of £100 administered by the Royal Society of Literature for the best regional novel of the year written by an author of British or Irish nationality or citizen of the Commonwealth. Miss Holtby (1898–1935) was a Yorkshire novelist.

Holtrop, John William: Librarian of the Royal Library, The Hague, and author of 'Monuments typographiques des Pays-Bas au quinzième siècle', La Haye, in parts from 1856–68. The work was a pioneer attempt to make an inventory of types used in a particular area. The accompanying lithographed reproductions were by E. Spanier.

Hondius, Jodocus, 1563–*c.* 1612: born *Josse de Hondt*, the leading Dutch map engraver and publisher of his day who worked in Ghent and Amsterdam before moving to London in 1583. Here he married the sister of his co-worker *Pieter van den Keere*, q.v., and the latter assisted him in engraving maps. The work of Hondius is seen in an edition of Waghenaer's 'Mariner's mirrour', London, 1588, and in a map of Drake's and Cavendish's world voyages. In 1592 he engraved maps on gores for pasting on to wooden globes.

About 1593 Jodocus and Pieter returned to Amsterdam but continued to work for London map publishers including, from 1605, *John Speed*, q.v. Hondius engraved and published a writing manual showing the fine italic hand he used for map lettering. After buying the plates and stock of *Mercator*, q.v., he issued an edition of the latter's 'Atlas' in 1606, adding thirty-six new maps.

He engraved most of the maps for Speed's folio atlas 'Theatre of the Empire of Great Britaine', 1611–12: later editions included a small one known as 'Miniature Speed', engraved by Pieter Keere.

When Jodocus died his sons *Jodocus II* (1595–1629) and *Henricus* (1597–1657) inherited the business. In 1633 Henricus was joined by *Jan (Joannes) Jansson*, q.v. They published a revised Mercator-Hondius atlas as 'Atlas Novus' in 3 vols, 1637. Jansson married the sister of Henricus and, after managing the business from 1638, acquired it in 1657. It eventually passed to *Peter Schenck* (1645–*c.* 1730) and *Gerard Valck* (1626–1720), both engravers.

Honig paper: high-quality paper made by the Dutch firm of J. Honig en Zonen of Zaandyk. In America copies of the Declaration of Independence which in 1776 Congress ordered to be distributed to official bodies were printed upon it.

Honoré, fl.*c.* 1288–1318: a miniaturist and illuminator of Paris. No signed work of his is known but among manuscripts attributed to him are the 'Decretum' of Gratian, *c.* 1288, now in Tours Library; a Breviary, probably made prior to 1296 for Philippe IV of France; and a copy of 'La Somme le Roy', not later than 1295, in the British Library. His elegant, subtle and precise style can be considered from reproductions in Dr E. G. Millar's 'The Parisian miniaturist Honoré', Faber, 1959.

hooked: said of single-leaf illustrations printed on slightly wider paper than the text pages they are to accompany. This allows for an inner marginal fold, or hinge, which fits round the back of the section to which the plate belongs. Alternatively, the plate can be folded round an inner pair of pages, nearer the relevant text. See also *guards*.

hook in: to set words, for which there is no room when setting a line of type to a given measure, within a bracket on the line below.

hooks: an obsolete term for printers' *brackets*, q.v.

Horae: see *Book of Hours*.

horn book: a form of child's primer in use in England from the 15th–18th century. The earliest examples were made from 'wainscot' (thin panels of oak) and had a label bearing the alphabet, simple spelling, numbers and the Lord's Prayer pasted on the wood and covered with a thin transparent veneer of cattle horn. A wooden handle was fixed to the frame. In later examples the back of the panel was covered with morocco or roan stamped with an ornamental device. Other, but rare, examples were made entirely of cow-hide with a window cut in the upper portion. See B. Folmsbee, 'A little history of the horn-book', Stevens, 1965. See also *battledore, criss cross row*.

Hortulus animae: or 'Garden of the soul'; an anthology of personal devotions, Catholic in tone, popular in pre-Reformation Germany where printed editions of the 'Seelenwurzgarten', as it was known, date from that of Schönsperger, Augsburg, 1484. Continental editions for the English market included the Hours of the Virgin and the Seven Psalms, the work as a whole resembling a *Primer*, q.v.

The edition of Hortulus translated about 1530 by George Joye and Martin Bucer in Antwerp, where it was printed for the English market, was anti-Catholic in its commentaries, the graces to be said before meals being distinctly Lutheran. See also *Primer*.

hose: the wooden sleeve enclosing the screw (spindle) which raises and lowers the platen of a hand-printing press. The hose, which enables the spindle to be turned without turning the platen, is secured to the spindle by a ring or *garter*. See also *hand-press*.

hot-melt adhesives: tough, flexible adhesives which are a combination of vinyl resins, waxes, and plasticisers. They are much used in paperback binderies where their big advantage over animal glues is that they bond and set immediately (1 to 15 seconds), thus obviating the drying, stacking and pressing stages of production. They are, however, costly, and require special machinery on which the hot melt can be applied at temperatures between 135° and 175°C. If overheated the hot melt becomes useless and the machine has to be prepared anew.

In some machines two shots are used. The first applies a PVA primer which holds the roughened cut sheets, then a coating of hot melt bonds the cover. Infra-red drying sets the primer and pre-heats the backs. The machine produces 200 books a minute.

The use of a one-shot machine is cheaper since the PVA applicator and infra-red dryer are not needed, but more roughening is necessary, and the result is not so good since the books will not stay open flat.

hot metal composition: composition involving the use of a Monotype caster, a Linotype slug-caster or comparable apparatus which casts fresh type for each job, after which it is re-melted. Cf. *cold composition*.

hot-pressed: paper glazed by heated metal plates; limited to the finest qualities. Abbreviated as *HP*.

hot-rolled: paper glazed by steam-heated calenders.

hot-top enamel process: see *enamel process*.

hot type: type cast from molten metal, either as single characters or slugs. Cf. *cold type*.

Hours: see *Book of Hours*.

Hours of Catherine of Cleves: a Book of Hours, probably made at Utrecht c. 1435 for Catherine, daughter of the Duke of Cleves. The two parts which survive are in the Pierpont Morgan Library, New York. A reproduction was published in 1966.

It is remarkable for the treatment of the borders which surround the miniatures. Instead of the traditional floral border painted to the same scale as the inner miniature the artist has painted still-life forms on a much larger scale. By this trompe-l'oeil effect the border appears nearer to the viewer than the miniature.

L. M. Delaissé has described this major work as 'a key to the understanding of later panel painting in Holland'.

Hours Press: a private press started in 1928 by Nancy Cunard at La Chapelle, Normandy. In 1930 it was moved to Paris.

The books issued in editions of from one to five hundred copies were mostly hand-set and printed on hand-made paper. Although only two dozen titles appeared they were by an astonishingly distinguished group of writers including Havelock Ellis, George Moore, Roy Campbell, Richard Aldington, Samuel Beckett, Ezra Pound, Robert Graves and Norman Douglas. Production ceased in 1931. See N. Cunard, 'Those were the hours', Southern Illinois U.P., 1969.

house corrections: alterations made to proofs or script by the publisher or printer, as distinct from those made by the author.

house style: see *style of the house*.

Howard, Thomas, second Earl of Arundel, 1585–1646: the assembler of an important collection of State Papers, charters, registers and early literary works, as well as Latin, Greek and French manuscripts. Notable additions were the *Arundel Psalter*, q.v., and the library of the Nuremberg bibliophile, Bilibald Pirckheimer (1470–1530), which Howard acquired in 1636.

In 1666 Henry Howard, grandson of Thomas, disposed of the library. Half the manuscripts he gave to the College of Arms; the books and the other half were given to the Royal Society which was accommodated in Arundel House. The printed books were ultimately sold, partly by Quaritch in 1870, and partly by Sotheby in 1925.

Hoym, Karl Heinrich, Graf von, 1694–1736: a German diplomatist and bibliophile who between 1717 and 1729, when ambassador to France, formed a library notable for the fine bindings by such masters as Boyet, Du Seuil and Padeloup. The collection was auctioned in 1738.

H.P.: see *hot-pressed*.

Hubbard, Elbert, 1856–1915: the founder of the *Roycroft Press*, q.v.

Huber colour press: one of the earliest machines to employ two formes and two cylinders for colour printing. It was made in 1885 by Huber and Hodgman of Taunton, Mass., makers of various machines on the two-revolution principle.

Huebner, William C.: an American inventor and builder of several machines used in the graphic art industry including, about 1939, a photosetter.

Hullmandel, Charles, 1789–1850: a London printer and publisher whose name is particularly associated with the development in England of colour lithography (see *lithotint*).

humanistic scripts: humanism began in Italy in the later 14th century as a revival of the literary heritage of ancient Rome. The pioneer scholars of this movement included Petrarch (1304–74), Salutati (1330–1406), Niccoli (1363–1437), and Bracciolini (1380–1459), all of Florence. Their endeavours inspired a generation of scholars and the results remain today.

The classical texts which they copied or had copied were generally written in Carolingian minuscule. Considering the style of script appropriate for the purpose they revived it, using the name *lettera antiqua* to describe it. From these beginnings there developed the 'general calligraphic form (used) by a numerous body of professional scribes towards the middle of the fifteenth century' (Morison). The influence of the script was to spread throughout Italy and beyond.

234

The scholastic *lettera antiqua* became the medium for the writing of sumptuous manuscripts, illuminated and rubricated, made for such princely patrons as the Medici, Estes, Sforzas and the Neapolitan kings. The great Florentine bookseller Vespasiano da Bisticci employed, among others, the professional copyists Sigismondo, Sinibaldi, Mennio of Sorento, Antonio di Mario, and Gherardo del Ciriago. All wrote in what we may consider a disciplined humanistic roman script, or *lettera antiqua formata*. For plain scholastic texts, as distinct from the foregoing, the form of lettera antiqua was cursive, and often written by the scholar himself on vellum or paper. Small, quickly written, and often ligatured, it may be considered for ease of terminology, a humanistic italic script or *lettera antiqua corsiva*. *Niccoli*, q.v., was the first to bring diagonal connecting strokes to an adaptation of the Carolingian minuscule.

The influence of classical inscriptions on stone or marble had been in some measure transmitted by a group of scholars and epigraphers of Verona and Padua. Wardrop suggests that in compiling these Greek and Roman inscriptions copyists insinuated into the cursive hand they used forms alien to the strictly Latin tradition. A notable example was the writing of Ciriaco d'Ancona (*c.* 1390–1455), a merchant who travelled widely in Greece and Asia Minor collecting inscriptions. To him and his disciple *Felice Feliciano*, q.v., Wardrop assigns the development of ligatures used by the north Italian scribes, and the use of classical roman capitals. The conventions of these capitals led, from about 1465, to the use in calligraphy of clear serifs and rounded, more carefully formed letters. In the 16th century this developed script was known as *lettera antiqua tonda*, q.v.

It might be added by way of a footnote that among early scholars in England to use humanistic cursive was Petrus Carmelianus of Brescia who came in 1480. Others were the various Latin secretaries employed by Henry VIII. Sir John Cheke (1514–57) and Roger Ascham (1515–68) were early humanists, the latter as tutor to Elizabeth I and Edward VI, teaching both to write 'a fair hand'. Cheke, Ascham, and Bartholomew Dodington (1536–95) made Cambridge the leading English centre of humanism.

The early roman types of the printers Rusch, da Spira, and Jenson were related in appearance to the *lettera antiqua formata* as it had been used in the carefully made humanistic manuscript texts. For the development as a type of the quicker cursive scripts see *cursive*.

See R. Weiss, 'Humanism in England during the fifteenth century', 2nd ed. O.U.P., 1957; A. Fairbank and B. Wolpe, 'Renaissance handwriting: an anthology of italic scripts', Faber, 1960; and J. Wardrop, 'The script of humanism', O.U.P., 1963. See also *adversaria, antiqua, Aurispa, calligraphy, Leto, Poggio, Sanvito, writing manuals*.

humidified: said of paper which has been artificially matured to influence its working properties. See also *conditioning*.

Humphrey, Duke of Gloucester, 1391–1447: an English statesman and scholar who employed agents in Italy to obtain books for him. Subjects included medicine, science, theology, and Latin and Greek poetry. He also commissioned translations into Latin of Greek writings on politics, and employed Italian humanist scribes in his household.

Between 1439 and 1446 he donated about three hundred manuscripts to Oxford University where, about 1487, they were housed in the new divinity school. Only two or three works now remain in the Bodleian as most of them were destroyed or scattered in 1550 when Edward VI ordered the reformation of the University: a few are in the Bibliothèque Nationale, Paris, and in three Oxford colleges.

Hungarian leather: see *tawing*.

Hunter, Dard, 1883–1966: born in Steubenville, Ohio. He studied in Vienna where he designed several books for a Viennese publisher before going to London in 1911. There he acquired a considerable knowledge of papermaking in addition to working as a commercial artist. He subsequently returned to America to become the leading authority on papermaking and a writer on the subject. See Dard Hunter, 'My life with paper', New York, Knopf, 1958.

Huntington, Henry E., 1850–1927: one of the wealthiest of American bibliophiles of whose library in California it is claimed there are as many books printed before 1640 as are in the British Library. He bought extensively in Europe. Included in his library are 5,400 incunabula, 20,000 English first editions, twenty-five Caxtons, Shakespeare folios, some 55,000 Americana, etc.

Huntington, Robert, 1637–1701: an orientalist from whom the Bodleian acquired some 680 Oriental manuscripts, including Coptic Gospels, which he had brought back from the Nitrian Convents of Egypt in 1678.

Hupp, Otto, 1859–1949: a German craftsman, engraver, and type-cutter. He made some beautiful typefaces for Genzsch & Heyse, e.g., Neudeutsch, 1899; Gebr. Klingspor, e.g. Liturgisch, 1906, and others. He was greatly interested in a revival of German printing, and did important research into Gutenberg's history and that of other early printers. (With GU)

Huss, Martinus, fl.1478–81: a German printer, born

235

in Bottwar near Marbach, who after working at Toulouse in 1476 settled in Lyons in 1478, at first partnered by Johannes Siber. In this year he issued the first illustrated book in France. This was a translation of 'Speculum humanae salvationis' made into French by an Augustinian monk, Julien Macho, with the title 'Le Mirouer de la rédemption'. In this he used 257 of the woodcuts which had appeared in the German version 'Spiegel der menschlichen Behältniss', Basle, Bernhard Richel, 1476. This popular work was reprinted in 1478, and later by his kinsman *Mathias Huss*, who succeeded him in 1482.

Mathias introduced new types, first seen in a reprint of the 'Mirouer', 1482, with cuts from the two earlier editions. He collaborated with Petrus Ungarus and Johann Schabeler until 1484, afterwards working alone. When he ceased printing in 1500 or 1501 he had issued about seventy works. His list included further reprints of the 'Mirouer', Voragine's 'Legenda aurea' and Bartholomaeus' 'De proprietatibus rerum', these and others being translated into French. The famous depiction of a printing press, which he issued in a 1499 edition of 'La Grant danse macabre', is reproduced under *hand-press*, q.v. Unlike many of his cuts, which were plagiarised, this may have been commissioned by him.

Huth, Henry, 1815–78: a banker and bibliophile who from 1855 began to develop his library. By the time of his death he had such rarities as a Mazarine Bible,

block books, a Coverdale Bible, 1535, Caxtons, Aldines, etc.

The library was increased in importance by his son, *Alfred Henry Huth* (1850–1910), who bequeathed fifty items from the collection to the British Museum: among those chosen were twelve illuminated manuscripts, first-edition quartos of some Shakespeare plays, and important early printed German and Spanish works. Much of the library was auctioned in 1911 and 1912, realizing about £300,000. The majority of the treasures went to American collections.

hydrapulper: a machine for separating the fibres of wood pulp. It is a bowl-shaped tank with a rotating blade which swirls sheets of pulp in water until the fibre clusters break up and are suspended in the water. This stage precedes *beating*, q.v. See also *laps*.

hydraulic press: a powerful standing press the platen of which is operated by water at very high pressure. Such presses are used both in printing works and binderies wherever great pressure is needed. In *edition binding* they have been superseded by the *pneumatic press*, q.v.   (LK)

hygrometer: an instrument, of which there are several models, used in paper conditioning plants and elsewhere, to check the moisture content of paper.

Hypnerotomachia Poliphili: see *Colonna, Francesco*.

I

IARIGAI: see *International Association of Research Institutes for the Graphic Arts.*

Ibarra, Joaquim, 1725–85: a distinguished printer of Madrid, and Court printer to Carlos III, who had a great influence on raising the standards of printing, not only in Spain, but in Europe generally. His edition of Sallust with parallel Latin and Spanish texts, 1772, and his 'Don Quixote', 4 vols, 1780, are considered his finest works.

IBBY: see *International Board on Books for Young People.*

ibid: an abbreviation for the Latin 'ibidem', i.e. in the same place. In footnotes and bibliographies, after an author and title have been referred to once the word *ibid* may be sufficient guide to succeeding references to the same author and title. Cf. *id., loc. cit., op. cit.*

IBIS: the *International Book Information Service,* q.v.

IBIS Mailing Services Ltd.; the re-named *International Book Information Service,* q.v.

IBM 72 Composer: an International Business Machines electric typewriter suitable for preparing copy to be photographed for lithographic reproduction. It has a fixed carriage. Characters are carried on a 'golf ball' head which gives the required impression by moving against the paper. The result closely resembles a printed page, being precise and even. Contributing to this is the unusual method of justification. Copy is typed twice. As the first typing proceeds the machine calculates the space left in a line and then adds the units of word spacing necessary for justification during the second typing.

By changing the golf ball a range of over forty founts in sizes from 7- to 12-point is available, with light, medium, bold and italic faces.

IBM Executive typewriter: a type bar electric typewriter produced for normal secretarial work. All characters are accommodated on a range of two to five unit widths and the result is, therefore, much more satisfactory than that obtained from a conventional typewriter. It is widely used for in-plant and technical composition.

Ibrahim Müteferrika, fl.1729–45: a Hungarian Calvinist or Unitarian who after capture by the Turks about 1693 converted to Islam and entered the Sultan's service as a Müteferrika or personal attendant. About 1727 he obtained permission to set up in Istanbul a press for the printing of non-religious books in Turkish. There had been earlier presses in Istanbul (that of Nachmias in 1493, the Soncino Hebrew press in the 16th century, etcetera) but not one for printing in Turkish. In 1728 Ibrahim issued his first book 'Lughat-i-Vanquli' which was a Turkish translation of al-Jahari's Arabic dictionary, to be followed between then and 1734, and after 1740, by some sixteen works on geography, history and science. Maps and diagrams were included in some of them but pictorial representations only in one or two, and of these unmutilated surviving copies are rare. Editions were small.

The fount of arabic type used to print works in Turkish influenced a generation of printers in Egypt and Syria through the 19th century; Ibrahim also used the first roman type cut and cast in Turkey.

ICBA: see *International Community of Booksellers Associations.*

Icograda: the acronym of the *International Council of Graphic Design Associations,* q.v.

id.: an abbreviation for the Latin 'idem', i.e. the same person. In footnotes and bibliographies this may be used for subsequent references to an author previously named. Cf. *ibid.*

ideogram: a symbolic mark which indicates an idea or a concept, e.g. happiness, warmth, misery, cold. (The Chinese can communicate by means of ideograms with other Chinese whose speech is unintelligible.) See also *isotype.*

idiot tape: tape for insertion into a photosetting machine on which hyphenation and justification instructions have not been coded and must be determined by the front-end computer on the photosetter.

i.e.: an abbreviation for the Latin 'id est' ('that is').

ILAB: the initials of the *International League of Antiquarian Booksellers*, q.v.

Illig, Moritz Friedrich: the reputed discoverer, about 1806, that resin added at the pulp stage would make paper non-absorbent. See also *engine-sized*.

illuminated: 1. said of books or manuscripts having letters, initial words, or borders painted in gold or silver as well as colours. Illuminated initials were a development of *versals*, q.v. See also *rubricator*.

2. a slang term for the glosses in a Greek or Latin text which has an interlinear translation.

illumination: the decoration of a manuscript or incunabulum with gold or silver as well as colours, the result being a compound of illustration and ornament.

Until the 14th century illuminating was mostly done by monks for religious houses, and while the exchanging or giving of books between monasteries had influenced work done in various centres, a continuity of tradition in the choice and treatment of subject was inevitable. From this time, however, groups of artists travelling a country or established in city workshops were commissioned by wealthy nobles and other lay patrons. Several artists worked on one manuscript and were paid on piece-rates, the patron specifying the number of initials and scenes he required.

A design was first drawn and sized with a mixture of clay, gypsum or lime, to be followed by an adhesive such as egg-white; gold or silver was laid on and burnished, finally colours were applied, their traditional association with certain subjects being a guide to the artist. The eight colours mostly employed (yellow, red, blue, green, white, black, rose, purple) were made from mineral earths or plants, e.g. yellow from turmeric roots, white from burnt bones, purple from turnsole or shellfish (murex), red from minium, black from sloe berries, green from copper, etc.

Precise directions for making colours were written by the 12th-century monk Theophilus Presbyter in his 'Schedula diversarum artium', where he warns that ingredients must be varied according to the quality of the parchment, and that a good craftsman must devise his own recipes. The first English printed book on the preparation of colours for illuminating was issued by Richard Tottill in 1573 (STC 24252).

Earliest surviving examples of the art are fragments of papyrus rolls, and notable is an 'Iliad' on vellum, now in Milan, dating from the 3rd–5th century, of which about sixty pictures remain.

From the 6th–11th century the purpose of illumination was to tell a story or compose a pattern, thus backgrounds carefully drawn from nature had no place, and we see figures with green or blue hair and red skies. Symbols often interpreted a subject; thus an angel was associated with St Matthew, a lion with Mark, an ox with Luke, and an eagle with John, walls for the heavenly city, and a gaping-mouthed whale for the entrance of hell, etc. See also *model-books*.

In the mid-11th and 12th centuries, in Western Europe, outline figure drawings within a system of frames, owing something to the art of glass staining, became important. Gold or purely ornamental backgrounds were usual.

By the 13th century Byzantine influence spread to such German scriptoria as Echternach, Fulda, Salzburg, Regensburg, Cologne, and Hildesheim. In France, however, Gothic art developed in historiated initials, a greater realism in ornament, architectural details, and costume. In this great change the scriptoria of Paris led the way.

In Europe generally, from the 14th century onwards, great attention was paid to faces, which were almost portraits. Actual buildings and nature scenes were painted with great fidelity, and backgrounds were often crowded with happenings not connected with the subject of the work being illustrated.

For notes on schools, artists and periods see *Aubert, Byzantine illumination, Canterbury school, Carolingian illumination, Channel school, Crivelli, Fouquet, French-Gothic-, Hiberno-Saxon illumination, Honoré, Islamic-, Italian illumination, Marmion, Mozarabic-, Mughal illumination, Northumbrian school, Ottonian-, Persian illumination, Pucelle, Romanesque illumination, St Alban's-, Salisbury-, Salzburg school, Scheere, Spanish illumination, Turkish manuscript painting, Winchester School.*

For short notes on individual manuscripts see *Ambrosian Iliad, Anglo-Saxon Chronicle, Arundel Psalter, Ashburnham Pentateuch, Athelstan Psalter, Augustine Gospels, Bedford, (John), Benedictional of St Aethelwold, Berry, Carmelite Missal, Cathach Psalter, Cerne, Book of, Codex Alexandrinus, -Amiatinus, -Argenteus, -Bezae, -Laudianus, -Rescriptus Aphraëmi, -Rossanensis, -Sinaiticus, Conradin Bible, Cura Pastoralis, Durham Cassiodorus, Durrow, Book of, Echternach MSS, Ellesmere Chaucer, Exultet roll, Folchart Psalter, Gorleston Psalter, Guthlac Roll, Haye MSS, Hildesheim Psalter, Holkham Bible Picture Book, Hours of Catherine of Cleves, Kells, Book of, Lambeth Bible, Laurentian Codex, Lindisfarne Gospels, Luttrel Psalter, Minnesängerhandschriften, Ormesby Psalter, Psalter of Alphonso, Queen Mary Psalter, Rohan Book of Hours, Roman Virgil, Sacramentary of Robert of Jumièges, St Chad Gospels, St Gall Gospels, St Omer Psalter, Sherborne Missal, Stonyhurst Gospel, Tickhill Psalter, Utrecht Psalter, Vatican Virgil, Vienna Dioscorides, Winchester Bible.*

See also *acanthus, armarian, babewynes, banderole, bestiary, calligraphy, camaïeu gris, chamber lye, chrysographer, cista librorum, codex aureus, cumdach, drolleries, factotum, floriated, gold, gouache, grisaille, guide letters, historiated letters, inhabited scroll, initial letters, Jesse tree, khoran, lacertine animals, lapis lazuli, limner, lunellarium, mosaic gold, murex, pecia, phylactery, putto, rubricator, scriptorium, shell gold, turnsole, umbilicus, untouched, white vine.*

illustrated: descriptive of a book which includes reproductions of photographed originals. These may be paintings, photographs, drawings, objects, lettering, maps or anything which is not text, though formulae, tables and graphs are not normally considered as illustrations.

In sales-promotion literature not all publishers quantify illustrations, e.g. 'With 200 illustrations in black and white and 15 in colour', which is un-ambiguous, resorting instead to such coy imprecisions as *abundantly-, brightly-, candidly-, copiously-, extensively-, fully-, generously-, handsomely-, heavily-, highly-, lavishly-, magnificently-, profusely-, richly-, sensitively-, and stunningly illustrated*; all found in publishers' lists.

illustration of books: from the second millennium BC to the invention of printing the written word has been supplemented or made clearer by some form of picture (see *illumination*). Illustrations in the first printed books were made from wooden blocks (see *block book, woodcut*). About the end of the 15th century printing from engraved metal plates developed, and by the late 16th had superseded the woodcut. *Etching* and *copper engraving*, qq.v., were all important in the 17th and 18th centuries.

Lithography, q.v., invented in 1798, offered a new medium for the book illustrator, and proved very suitable for colour work. The somewhat inflexible and impersonal nature of the photographic reproduction processes which dominated the 19th century was followed early in the present century by a revival of craftsmanship in which wood engravers and auto-lithographers created their designs directly on the printing medium.

In the 20th century the purpose of illustration has sometimes been deflected from its role of interpreting a writer's text as in the French *livres de peintres*, q.v. Notable was Ambroise Vollard who commissioned artists and then added texts to their designs.

Among skilled and original artists whose work has appeared in 20th century *British* books mention should be made of Edward Ardizzone, Edward Bawden, John Buckland-Wright, John Farleigh, David Gentleman, Barnett Freedman, Robert Gibbings, Eric Gill, David Hockney, Blair Hughes-Stanton, Lynton Lamb, Clare Leighton, Mervyn Peake, John Piper, Eric Ravilious, Reynolds Stone and Rex Whistler. In *America* book illustrators are fewer as artists have done most of their work for magazines and other media. Notable for their book illustrations are W. A. Dwiggins, McKnight Kauffer, Rockwell

Kent, Allen Lewis, Henry Pitz, Howard Pyle, Boardman Robinson, Rudolph Ruzicka and Edward Wilson. See also *aquatint, collotype, drypoint, half-tone, line engraving, lithography, mezzotint, photogravure, pochoir, steel engraving, wood engraving.*

image: the subject to be reproduced as an illustration by a printing process.

image process: the generic term for printing from copy prepared without the use of metal type, i.e. by IBM typewriter, photosetting, etc.

imbrication: a style of book-cover decoration in which the design includes a pattern of overlapping leaves or scales.

imitation art paper: a heavily loaded uncoated paper which is highly glazed on a supercalender. Its surface does not compare with a true coated paper. Due to the high production cost and the availability of good quality cheap coated printings, imitation art is now largely extinct. See also *water finish.*

imitation leather: paper, cloth or other substances finished and embossed to simulate leather. See also *leather.*

imitation morocco: any imitation of morocco leather.

(LK)

imitation parchment: a pure or part-mechanical wood paper. It is strong, transparent, and fairly grease and water resistant, these qualities being imparted by prolonged wet beating of the pulp. Not to be confused with *parchment substitute* which is hand-made.

imitation russia: see *American russia.*

imitation watermark: a watermark made by pressing paper between a male die and a flat piece of polished steel. The watermark is thereby embossed on the under side of the sheet, the top being quite smooth. See also *impressed watermark, watermark.*

impensis: a Latin word meaning 'at the expense of'. Up to the end of the 17th century it often appears in printed works followed by the name of the patron, publisher, or other person who financed publication.

imperfections: 1. a bookbinding term used (anomalously) for good sheets required to complete an order for binding. Faulty or damaged sheets are known as *bad sheets.*

2. copies of books which contain printing or binding faults. The publisher usually exchanges or perfects such books when returned by a bookseller or member of the public and pays all expenses including postage.

Copies are not returned for the insertion of corrigenda or errata slips since these are not connected with defective make-up.

Imperial Letter Foundry: see *Austin, Richard.*

imposing surface: the iron surface on which a forme is imposed. It was formerly made of stone. See *imposition.*

imposing to quire: the arranging of pages in the chase so that when printed the work can be made up by insetting one folded sheet inside another.

imposition: the arranging of pages of type in a chase in a particular sequence (known as the *imposition scheme*) so that when folded the printed pages will be in consecutive order. Furniture is added and the whole is locked up into a forme. Imposition is done in close liaison with the folding department, where it must suit the particular folding machine used by the binder. See also *Book Impositions, 1975, come and go, folding, skeleton, tack marks.*

Imposition also refers to the appearance of the margins on a pair of facing pages. Normally the printer submits for approval a margin or imposition sheet before completing page proofs.

impressed watermark: the design left on sheets of paper by a rubber stereo placed against paper at the press rolls. This is an alternative to the genuine watermark and is of no security value as it can be put into a sheet at any time after manufacture. Also called *press mark.* See also *dandy roll, imitation watermark, watermark.*

impression: 1. all copies of a book printed at one time from one setting of type (however achieved), or from original plates, or from stereos and electros made of either. It also results when the original Monotype composition tape is re-run through the caster, and when a photographic reproduction of an earlier impression is made. Thus an *edition*, q.v., may be issued unaltered in several impressions, though publishers' former practice of printing on the title-leaf verso of novels such details as '14th impression, July 1952', '15th impression, September 1952', while indicating that one set of plates had been re-run, was intended as a sales stimulant and not a bibliographical record.

The term has a long history, thus William Bullein in the preface of his 'Gouernement of healthe', 1558, promises that corrections to it will be made 'At the next impression . . .' In the printing trade an impression is also referred to as a *printing*, and one subsequent to the first as a *reprinting*. Cf. *issue.*

2. the pressure applied to an image-bearing surface by a cylinder or platen to obtain a reproduction of the image. See also *make-ready.*

impression cylinder: the cylinder around which paper is carried during its contact with type, plates or an offset roller.

impressor regius: the Latin equivalent of *Imprimeur du roi* or *Queen's Printer*, qq.v.

imprimatur: the Latin for 'let it be printed'. Originally a statement appearing in early printed books to show that permission to print the work had been granted by an authority empowered to do so, but now confined to texts officially approved by a bishop of the Roman Catholic church as being free of doctrinal or moral error.

See also *cum licentia, licence leaf, nihil obstat, privilege.*

Imprimerie Royale du Louvre: established in 1640 at the instigation of Richelieu for Louis XIII as a royal printing house. Workmen were brought from Holland, and the first director was *Sébastien Cramoisy*, q.v. The first book published was 'De imitatione Christi', 1640. The eight-volume Vulgate Bible, 1642, was among the finest of the hundred or so titles which appeared during the first ten years. Many were folio volumes and had a certain monumental impressiveness which was admired, envied and imitated. It was to make the work of the royal printing house more distinctive that Louis XIV in 1692 ordered the cutting of special types for its exclusive use, e.g. *romain du roi*, q.v. Fine printing by the Imprimerie has been a continuing feature of French de luxe book production in addition to other official printing.

Through the years changes of government in France have meant changes of name for the press, but since 1871 it has been known as *Imprimerie Nationale.* See Bernard, 'Histoire de l'Imprimerie Royale du Louvre', Paris, 1867. See also *Cabinet des Poinçons, Congregatio de Propaganda Fide, Luce.*

Imprimeur du roi: the former French equivalent for our present *Queen's Printer*, q.v. The office was created by Charles VIII who bestowed the title on Pierre Le Rouge in 1488. Last to receive it was A. F. Didot in 1829.

Imprimeurs et libraires parisiens du XVIe siècle: an important bio-bibliographical dictionary catalogue of the Parisian book trade in the 16th century. The first volume was issued in 1964. The work is an extension of the unpublished and published material amassed during a lifetime's research by the Parisian printer-publisher *Philippe Renouard* (1862–1934), remembered for his studies of Colines, 1894, and Badius, 1903.

The editing of the first volume, Abada-Avril, was coordinated by Mme Veyrin-Forrer and Mlle Moreau. Volume II, Baaleu-Banville, appeared in 1970 (dated 1969).

'The Imprint': a periodical established in January 1913 by Gerard Meynell, Edward Johnston (who designed the sanserif type used throughout London Transport), and *J. H. Mason*, q.v. Its aim was to raise the standard of printing.

Meynell and Mason designed a new type-face for this journal, now Monotype series 101, which is widely used today. The ninth and last issue of *The Imprint* appeared in 1913.

imprint: 1. printer's. The name of the printer and place of printing which the law requires shall identify every printed paper or book which, at the time it is printed, is meant to be published (*vide* 'Newspapers, Printers, and Reading Rooms Repeal Act, 1869'). This usually appears on the back of the title-page, or on the last printed page of a book. The first book to have imprint and title together on the title-page was the 'Calendario' of Johannes Regiomontanus, printed at Venice in 1476 by Erhard Ratdolt and his associates.

2. publisher's. The name of the publisher which with place and date of publication is usually printed on the title leaf.

imprint date: the publication date as stated on the title-leaf.

impulse outlet: in the context of this book, a rack or display stand of paperbacks placed, for example, in a barber's saloon, a greengrocery or a supermarket, where people will buy on impulse a book they might not have troubled to obtain from a bookseller. This is merchandising, not bookselling in the usual sense of the word, and is known in the U.S.A. by the inelegant term *rack-jobbing distribution*.

in boards: said of a book which is cut after the boards have been attached. The book is taken from the sewer, end-papered, glued up, rounded and backed, and the boards are laced on. It is pressed and cut with a plough.

in boards extra: an 'in boards' binding with edges gilt solid.

incipit: the Latin for 'it begins'. The words 'hic incipit' and the first words of the text are the means of entitling and identifying manuscripts and also incunabula published without a title-page. For these introductory words majuscule letters or a distinguishing colour were used. An alternative is the *initia*, q.v. See also *explicit*, *label title*, *title-page*, *titulus*.

incunable (pl. **incunables**): the English form of *incunabulum*, q.v.

incunabulum (pl. **incunabula**): a book printed before 1500, i.e. in the infancy of printing. The limit of 1500 for the term incunabulum may derive from the earliest known catalogue of them: this was an appendix to Johann Saubert's 'Historia bibliothecae Noribergensis . . . catalogus librorum proximis ab inventione annis usque ad a. Chr. 1500 editorum', 1643. The word derives from the Latin 'cunae' = cradle, it being said that Philippe Labbé (1607–67), a Parisian bibliographer, was the first to apply the term 'incunabula' to the early art of printing, not to the books themselves. In 1653 he issued a list of incunabula in the Royal Library, Paris. The first attempt to make a list of all known incunabula was by Cornelius à Beughem, a bookseller of Emmerich-am-Rhein, in his 'Incunabula typographiae', 1688. The last of these early attempts to catalogue known incunabula was Michel Maittaire's chronological list 'Annales typographici', 5 vols, 1719–41.

The German term 'Der Wiegendruck' came into use towards the end of the 19th century, largely because the word 'Inkunabel' had acquired a wider connotation, e.g. 'Inkunabel der Lithographie', 'Inkunabel des Kupferstichs', etc. See also *Brunet*, *Goff*, *Graesse*, *Haebler*, *Hain*, *Panzer*, *Proctor*, *Stillwell*, and *Gesamtkatalog der Wiegendrucke*.

incut notes: see *marginal notes*.

indented: a line of type set in from the margin, e.g. the first line of a paragraph. See also *hanging paragraph*, *in pendentive*, *run out and indented*.

indention: the setting of a line of type to a narrower measure, e.g. the first line of a paragraph or a list of items. An em quad indention is normal for the average 24 em line. Subdivisions are indented as follows: 1, 2, 3, a, b, c, i, ii, iii, e.g.

    1. Useful Arts
      (a) Engineering
        (i)   Steam
        (ii) Electrical
        (iii) Hydraulic
      (b) Agriculture
        (i)   Farming
        (ii) Gardening
        (iii) Forestry
        (iv) Animal Husbandry
    2. Fine Arts
      (a) Music
        (i)   Orchestral
        (ii) Operatic   etc.

See also *in pendentive*.

Independent Publishers Guild: formed in London in 1962 to represent the interests of its member companies who produce and publish books under their own imprints and who are independent of any other group or consortium. Meetings, seminars and conferences are held at which ideas and information on matters of mutual concern are exchanged.

index: 1. a former standard size of board, $25\frac{1}{2}$in. by $30\frac{1}{2}$in.

2. see *digit* (2)

3. an alphabetical list, usually at the end of a book, giving names of persons, places or subjects mentioned in the text and the numbers of the pages or sections where they occur. (Pl *indexes* or *indices*, the latter for scientific works only.)

An extensive index may be set in *run-on style*, e.g.

> sacred books: Apocalypse 21, Bible 32, Book of Hours 40, Koran 136, Talmud 201

or alternatively in *indented style*, e.g.

> sacred books: Apocalypse 21
> Bible 32
> Book of Hours 40
> Koran 136
> Talmud 201

The provision of an index to a work of non-fiction should be considered an essential part of it, though many are published without, and many indexes are inadequate. There is now a *Society of Indexers*, q.v., in Britain which will recommend competent indexers, and the Library Association has given encouragement to the compilation of better indexes by making an annual award, the *Wheatley Medal*, for the best of the year. This is named after Henry Wheatley, a noted indexer in the early part of this century. There is also a British Standard 'Recommendations for the pre-paration of indexes for books, periodicals and other publications' (BS 3700:1976) which should be con-sulted when preparing an index. There is a comparable indexing society in America.

Index librorum prohibitorum: the official list, published by the Roman Catholic Church, of books which were not to be read or possessed by Roman Catholics without authorization, or which could be read only in approved expurgated editions (the passages to be deleted being listed in the 'Index expurgatorius').

The practice of prohibiting the reading of books inimical to the views of the prohibiting authority dates back at least to the time of St Paul when the Christian settlement at Ephesus (near Izmir, Turkey) collected and publicly burnt all the superstitious books they could find. Similar burnings of Jewish books took place in the 16th and 20th centuries in Italy and Germany.

Pope Gelasius issued in 496 a decree proscribing the reading of a number of apocryphal and heretical books. With the advent of printing the fears of authorities increased. In 1485 the Bishop of Mainz began ecclesiastical censorship prior to the printing of German versions of Greek and Latin texts. In England Henry VIII forbade the reading of certain books in 1526.

The first *Roman Index*, printed by *Blado*, q.v., was published under Paul IV in 1559, its severity being mitigated by a Holy Office decree of the same year ('Moderatio Indicis librorum prohibitorum'). The 1564 list of forbidden books, drawn up after the Council of Trent, was revised in 1897 at the instigation of Pope Leo XIII; about 1,000 titles were dropped and the rules were modified. The last edition of the Index, issued in 1948, was continued by supplements until 1961. In 1966 the Vatican announced that no more would be published.

Index Translationum: an international bibliography of translations which since 1949 has been published annually by Unesco. It continues the work of the same name published from 1932 to 1940 by the League of Nations. About fifty countries are represented and the translations are set out by country of publication. Subdivision within each country is by alphabetical arrangement within the ten sections of the Universal Decimal Classification. An author index lists all writers whose works have been translated during the period covered by any particular Index.

india paper: originally (1768) a soft absorbent paper, cream or buff in colour, imported from China and used for proofing engravings, but later, a thin opaque paper made in England from hemp or rag (substance about 7 lb demy or $25g/m^2$). Cheaper kinds can be made from chemically treated wood pulp. Sometimes known as *Bible paper*.

What may have been the first book in England issued on the thin paper now known as 'india' was an edition of Tate and Brady's 'New version of the Psalms', printed by Charles Whittingham the elder in 1795/6. See also *Oxford india paper*.

indirect letterpress: letterpress printing on the offset principle, using curved or flexible right-reading relief plates from which the image is transferred to paper by an offset blanket. A sheet-fed offset machine can be used by removing the damping system, and the plate is inked as for normal letterpress.

Alternative names have been given to this process, namely *letterset* (from 'letterpress' and 'offset'), *dry offset* (which gives no hint of the letterpress element) and *indirect relief*.

inedited: 1. a work published without editorial changes; such a work may contain indelicate passages.

2. unpublished works, especially letters or memoirs of a dead writer.

inferior figures: small letters or figures printed at the foot of larger letters as in chemical formulae, H_2SO_4, etc., and cast partly below the base line. Cf. *superior figures*.

infra: the Latin for 'below'. Used as *vide infra* in the text of a book to refer to matter appearing subsequently. Cf. *vide supra*.

infra-red drying: the drying by means of infra-red rays of a printed paper web running on a high-speed press. This alternative to drying by heated cylinders uses the principle that the maximum evaporation of ink solvent from the surface of a paper web can be achieved by molecular agitation within the solvent. Such agitation can be induced by infra-red rays of predetermined wavelength. Factors affecting the process are the colour of the ink, and whether its base is alcohol or water. As further radiation is impeded if the layer of evaporated ink is not quickly removed, a strong jet of cold air is used to blow it away.

The speed at which a rotary press will print may be limited by the speed at which the printed web can be dried, and this alternative to heat-drying offers an opportunity to run the press at a higher speed.

inhabited scroll: an arabesque pattern of foliage in which figures appear. This was an early feature of illuminated manuscripts. In pre-Conquest England the Anglo-Saxon artist drew birds or beasts on a scroll formed from an acanthus leaf: the inclusion of human figures was a later addition.

initia: literally, beginnings. A name given to the first words or sentence of the first and last pages of a manuscript; used as an alternative to the *incipit*, q.v., to identify works written or printed before the title-page was introduced.

As the first and last pages of a manuscript were liable to damage the initia of the second and penultimate, or of all four (i.e. *dictio probatoria* or *initia foliorum*), were used, a custom said to have originated in Paris. See also *titulus*.

initial letters: 1. *manuscript*. The use of decorated initials in manuscripts dates from the earliest times. Developing from *versals*, q.v., initials of the 10th century were embellished with drawings of animals; colours, gold and silver were in use by the 8th century. Interlaced foliage, which often extended the length and foot of a page, was also a feature of 10th–11th-century initials.

2. *incunabula*. Initials were at first entered by a rubrisher after the sheets were printed. Decorative coloured initials were used by Schöffer in 1457. Zainer and Ratdolt were pioneers of woodcut initials. The Holbein-Froben alphabets, the entrelacs of Tory and the later copper engravings of France were other developments of the printed initial.

3. *modern printed*. Large capital letters, sometimes decorated, are used at the beginning of a work or chapter. Ideally an initial should range with the top and bottom of so many lines of type, it should 'fit'; there being no extra space above or beneath. Alternatively an initial may 'stand' on the first line of type and extend above. A variation of either of the foregoing is the initial which extends slightly into the margin.

See also *blooming letters, cock up, drop initial, guide letters, historiated initials, illumination, vignette* (2).

ink: this consists basically of a finely ground pigment, which may be a plant dye, a mineral or an earth, contained in a medium (or vehicle) to make it fluid. Its manufacture consists mainly of two processes, the production of the vehicle (e.g. boiling the oil) and the admixture and grinding of the pigment which is done in *ink-grinding* mills, q.v. As well as the pigment and vehicle printing ink contains other ingredients to give it special properties. Such ingredients include driers, resin, wax, oils, etc. Black ink is made from carbon black, and the medium is normally linseed oil.

Printing inks are divided into main categories according to the process for which they are intended. In each category a division can be made into *black* and *coloured* ink and into different classes according to the quality. Thus *letterpress inks*, black (ornamental printing ink, half-tone ink, jobbing ink, rotary printing ink) or coloured (trichromatic ink, rotary printing ink, special ink); *newspaper inks; lithographic printing inks* (offset ink, litho ink, collotype ink); *photogravure inks*, either actual photogravure ink or copperplate ink and die stamping ink; and special inks of various kinds, e.g. carbonizing ink.

Printing ink can also be divided according to the way in which it dries. Litho and ordinary letterpress inks dry by oxidation and partly by penetration and evaporation; newspaper ink by absorption; aniline and photogravure printing inks by evaporation. Modern inks have been perfected which dry on contact with the paper, principally for use on rapid reel-fed rotary presses, but also for sheet work. There are *heat-set inks* which dry by passing the paper web through a heating chamber at a temperature of about 300°C (infra-red rays are also used for heating); *cold-set inks* which are solid at room temperatures and in using which the ink boxes, inkers and forme cylinders must be heated, while the paper is conveyed after printing over a cooling cylinder; and *steam-set inks* which consist of artificial resin dissolved in a hygroscopic solvent, e.g. ethylene glucol, the web being passed through a steam chamber where the small quantity of water absorbed by the layer of ink causes the artificial resin to be deposited in a solid form. Another type of *quick-drying ink* is combined with a vehicle which would solidify at room temperature if this were not prevented by the admixture of certain substances. The admixtures are absorbed by the paper with the result that the impression dries quickly.

The consistency of ink is important. Ink is said to be *thin* when it is easily set in motion, and *stiff* when it offers comparatively strong resistance to changes in form. *Long* ink is viscous and can be drawn out into threads: the opposite is a *short* ink. With regard to printing varnishes a distinction is made between weak, medium and strong or rigid varnish, the last being a varnish which is consistent and at the same time often viscous. For printed matter which is to be glazed *varnishable ink* must be used, and for most purposes ink must be non-fading, i.e. fast colour.   (GU)

See E. A. Apps, 'Ink technology for printers and students', Hill, 1963; and R. F. Bowles, *ed.* 'Printing ink manual', Heffner, 1961. See also *collotype-, double-tone-, gloss-, heat-set-, job-, metallic-, offset-, wet printing process inks; easer, extender, ink coverage, lampblack.*

Inkatron: the trade name of an ink monitor for checking ink density. It is made by Crosfield Electronics of Britain. Changes in density occurring on printed sheets during running off are detected by a photo-tube in a scanning head. Variations from a pre-set norm cause the photo-tube to actuate an electrical control on the inking rollers and set off the automatic return of colour to normal.

ink ball: a circular pad made by covering a filling of cotton, wool, or horsehair with a tightly stretched

Ink balls

piece of sheepskin or (in France particularly) dogskin. The inner core was a turned wooden stock of which one end formed the handle. These heavy and ponderous pads, used in pairs, were the means of inking type until the invention of the *inking roller*, q.v. The latter reduced ink consumption by as much as half.

244

Ink was taken up on one of the balls, and then, by holding a ball in each hand, one above the other, the ink was worked by rubbing and rotating until both had an even film. The ink was then dabbed, rolled and beaten on to the forme. By chance, about 1800, it was found that a compound of glue and treacle (as then used for transferring designs to ceramics) applied to the balls gave a better surface for the ink. These composition balls, with a cover of canvas instead of leather, were, according to Hansard, the invention of Benjamin Foster, a printer of Weybridge. They led to the composition roller. See also *chamber lye.*

ink blocking: the blocking of titles, etc., on book covers in black or coloured inks. An unheated press and quick-drying binder's inks are used.

ink consumption: the quantity of ink consumed in printing a work. This depends on the nature of the printed matter, the properties of the paper and ink, and the size of the work and number of copies run off. As a guide for calculating the consumption of ink the following approximate figures can be given, representing the consumption in kilogrammes per 1,000 impressions for one square metre (10,000 sq. cm.) of printing surface. The figures in the table (except those for four-colour work) refer to black ink in letterpress. For example, if 3,000 copies of an illustrated catalogue are to be printed on glazed stock, with 320 pages each having a type area of 11 × 18cm., the type area will be 320 × 11 × 18cm. = 6·3 sq. m. The consumption of ink will be 3 × 6·3 × the figure in the table for glazed stock, i.e. 0·9. The consumption of ink will thus be 17kg.

For coloured ink in general the figures should be increased by about 25%, for chrome yellow by about 45%, and for opaque white by 65%. Double-tone ink should be calculated at a 15% higher consumption; metallic colours (gold and silver) at 100–125%. In superimposing several colours a smaller quantity is required for those printed last. In mixed work which can be classified under different headings in the table each kind is calculated separately. The figures can also be used for offset printing but should be reduced by 25%.

Paper quality (see notes)	1	2	3	4
Spaced matter	0·7	0·5	0·4	0·35
Ordinary letterpress	1·1	0·7	0·6	0·5
Illustrated catalogues	1·8	1·3	0·9	0·8
Heavy tabular work and forms	2·7	2·0	1·4	1·2
White-faced letters	5·5	4·0	2·8	2·5
Whole plates	9·3	6·7	4·6	4·2
Four-colour reproduction:				
yellow			2·8	1·7
black			1·8	1·1
red			2·2	1·3
blue			2·2	1·3

Notes

1. Thick unsized paper, blotting paper, unglazed soft pamphlet covers, antique paper, engraving paper, etc.

2. Dull printing paper, bond paper, sulphite (MG), pamphlet covers, etc.

3. Glazed printing paper, manila, rag paper, Bristol and higher quality boards.

4. Coated stock (matt or glazed), label chromo paper, highly glazed Bristol, millboard, etc.   (GU)

ink coverage: the area which can be satisfactorily printed with a known amount of printing ink. By custom of the trade ink is sold by weight not volume. As ingredients vary, so will the same weight of different inks vary in volume and cover differing areas of paper. Paper surface also affects the amount needed, rough-surfaced or heavily coated papers requiring more ink to print a given area than smooth stock. See also *full colour*.

ink distributing rollers: rollers which receive ink from the *ink duct* and progressively break it down until it reaches the *ink plate* or *slab* as an overall even film. *Inking rollers*, or *inkers*, then transfer the ink from plate to forme. Also known as *ink pyramid*, *ink train* or *roller train*.

ink duct: see *duct*. An alternative name, now less used, is *fountain*.

inkers: see *inking roller*, *inking system*.

ink fly: a problem with high-speed machine operation when ink flies off the rollers in the form of a mist. The addition of certain chemical compounds to ink was found by PIRA to reduce mist. It may be further reduced by using jets of low-pressure air to blow the ink particles back to the rollers which produced them.

ink fountain: see *duct*.

ink grinding: mixing and distributing ink pigments in an oil or resin medium (the *vehicle*) in order to obtain ink of correct consistency for printing. Grinding is done in both ink factories and printing works, in each case by similarly constructed grinding mills. Final grinding is done on the printing machine by the *ink distributing rollers*, q.v. See also *pugging machine*. (GU)

ink-horn terms: a pejorative appellation used in 16th century England for the decorative 'aureate' language of such 14th and 15th century writers as Gower, Lydgate and Hoccleve. Thus Thomas Wilson in 'Arte of rhetorique', 1553, '. . . never affect any straunge ynkhorne termes . . .'

Ink grinding-mill

inking roller: a cylindrical device for inking type on the forme. The early history of attempts to replace the heavy *ink balls* used since the 15th century is unclear, but William Nicholson described 'colouring cylinders' in his patent specification of 1790. This was visionary rather than practical. Earl Stanhope was among several men who attempted to perfect a workable inking roller. Silk, skin and canvas were used to cover a wooden cylinder, but the seam formed by stitching prevented even inking. In 1803 Bulmer's 'Shakspeare Printing Office' issued a specimen of which the title-page reads 'Specimens of typography, without the use of balls, executed at the printing press lately invented by Earl Stanhope. The printing press made by Mr Robert Walker . . ., the Inking Roller made by Mr Charles Fairbone, of New Street, Fetter Lane'. In the Suhl press, made in Saxony by Friedrich König in 1803, the ink was distributed by a system of rollers, one being covered with leather.

Efficient inking rollers were, however, essential to the successful development of the mechanical press. By 1809 the composition balls of Benjamin Foster were known in the trade, and it would be logical to apply the covering substance to rollers. In 1818 Edward Cowper (the partner of Applegath) made the first composition roller for hand use. Trade prejudice was against them for a time. Bryan Donkin is also associated with the introduction of the new roller. General trade acceptance began with their manufacture by Robert Harrild & Sons who had been marketing composition ink balls since 1810. Harrild's method was to cast in a brass or iron tube a heated mixture of glue and treacle, with a canvas-covered stock as core. This worked fairly well but adequate surface

245

stability was not achieved until gelatine was added to the ingredients at the suggestion of Thomas de la Rue in 1854. Successful commercial development followed about 1860. Even so roller surfaces were affected by press and storage room humidity, and the formula was improved by adding carefully controlled amounts of glycerine which acted as a plasticizer. Certain chemicals are nowadays added to make the composition infusible, i.e. one which will not melt on a high-speed press.

Improved casting of rollers resulted from the machinery devised by the Americans Samuel Bingham and James Rowe. It combined a steam-heated cooking kettle, air pressure, and a *Gatling gun*, q.v.

Composition inking rollers continue to be satisfactory for large slow-running presses but for fast machines synthetic rubber rollers are widely used. They resist shrinkage and swelling and can be accurately ground after processing without impairing the surface. Nor do they heat up at high speeds. A disadvantage is the difficulty of cleaning them when changing from dark to light ink on the press. Surface treatment of the rubber by giving it a thin veneer of polyurethane lessens this.

In the 1950s the Avon Rubber Company of America introduced cast polyurethane inking rollers which were found to be stable, to have adequate tack, to resist abrasion and to be easily cleanable. They are also more durable than composition, especially when cast as a coating over a rubber base. Similar treatment improves the surface of nitrile rubber rollers used on modern offset presses. See also *Bottcher rollers*, *disc inker*, *distributor rollers*, *drop roller*, *inking system*, *nap roller*, *roller*, *Stanhope press*.

inking system: the arrangement in printing machines for the automatic inking up of printing formes. Friedrich König, the inventor of the modern letterpress machine, also indicated the basic principles of most inking systems now in use in letterpress and lithographic machines. Only intaglio machines have any major difference.

The inking system of a letterpress machine must perform three functions: feeding the ink, distributing it and inking up the forme. Feeding can be done from an open ink box with a duct roller, or by means of a pump in which the ink is pressed out over the distributor rollers (note the difference from an inking system in which the ink is pumped from a bigger container into an ordinary duct roller system), or by spraying. Distribution is done by rollers which either operate against a round disc which turns slightly between each inking (*disc inker*), or against a table moving to and fro (*table ink distribution*), or against a cylinder with a diameter larger than that of the rollers (*cylinder inking arrangement*). From these the ink is conveyed to a varying number of *forme rollers* which ink up the forme.

246

In König's first press (1803) a pumping device was used for supplying the ink, a piston driven by the machine squeezing ink out of a container through a narrow slot in its base, whence the stream of ink was carried via a steel roller to a leather-covered distributor

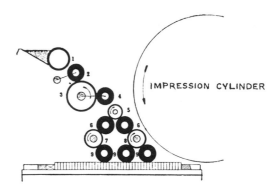

IMPRESSION CYLINDER

Inker on a Heidelberg cylinder press
1. *duct roller*, 2. *lifter roller*, 3–8. *distribution rollers* (5 *and* 6 *reciprocate laterally to break down the ink structure*), 9. *forme rollers*

roller. From this the ink was transferred to an iron roller and thence to a fairly large forme roller which inked the forme twice during its movement to and fro. In a later model the distributor roller was provided with a heating arrangement to keep the ink pliable, and the single forme roller was replaced by two rollers in mutual contact which thus revolved in opposite directions. They were raised and lowered alternately, so that the forme was inked up by one when moving forward and by the other when returning. In 1825 König built the first *duct roller system*: an open ink container has a *duct* blade and a cylindrical duct roller at the bottom which, in revolving, draws the ink through an adjustable slit between the roller and the blade. This allows the quantity of ink to be carried both for the inking system as a whole and from one

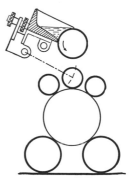

Diagram showing, from top, ink duct, duct blade and roller, with distribution rollers below

edge of the forme to the other. The duct roller makes only part of a revolution for each inking up. The ink is transferred from the duct roller to the distributor rollers by means of a drop roller. The use of the drop roller, which is brought into alternate contact with the duct roller and the first distributor roller (being moved by friction with whichever roller it is in contact at any moment), solved the problem of transferring ink from the slowly revolving duct roller to the rapidly revolving distributor rollers, the peripheral speed of which must

platen presses. On most modern machines there are cylinder inking systems; on two-revolution letterpress machines mostly table ink distributors. In letterpress machines both the distributor and forme rollers are made of composition or rubber, while distributing cylinders are usually made of copperplated or plastic coated steel. In older machines the rollers revolved only by friction with the surfaces with which they were in contact, ultimately with the printing forme. In modern machines the distributor rollers and some-

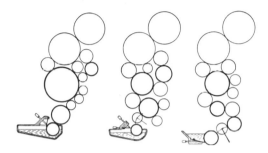

Diagrams of inking systems for rotary presses. Left, *English-American model with continuous feeding by duct and transfer rollers (film inking system).* Right, *Swiss-German models with drop roller and, in one case, bathing duct roller*

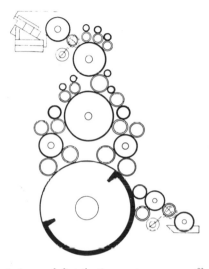

Ink metering and distribution system on an offset press, characterized by its large number of distributor rollers. The damping unit, lower right, is much simpler

adapt itself to the movement of the printing forme in accordance with the rule that all surfaces which are in contact must have the same speed. In some later models, especially on rapid rotary presses, the duct feeding principle is carried out differently, i.e., the drop roller is replaced by a screw spindle which feeds the ink to the distributors.

H. A. Wise Wood (U.S.A.) patented a construction for a *film inking system* in which the surplus ink is scraped off the duct roller by an adjustable blade. A rapidly revolving *transfer roller* lies at a minimum distance from the slowly moving duct roller, and the distance between them is so adjusted that the ink film, but not the duct roller itself, comes in contact with the transfer roller. There is also a *duct blade* on the duct roller which collects remains of ink, paper fluff, etc., that would otherwise accumulate in the ink duct. In several modern rotary machines König's original principle of feeding ink by a pump has been reverted to. Hoe & Co. were the first to build a pump inking system consisting of several pumps which force the ink out through individual mouthpieces quite close to the first distributor roller. The width of the mouthpieces is adjusted to the column width of the printing forme. Hoe also experimented with *spraying inking systems* in which, on the injector principle, outflowing air pressure carries the ink with it, very finely distributed, to the distributor rollers.

Disc inking arrangements are only used on small

times the forme rollers also are mechanically operated, with the exception of a few heavy rollers and riders. In addition, one or more of the distributor rollers moves laterally. See also *roller train*.

Lithographic presses, i.e. stone printing and offset machines, have inking systems similar in basic principle to letterpress machines. Stone printing machines are usually stop-cylinder presses with table ink distribution, while offset machines are purely rotary presses with cylinder inkers. Lithographic machines also have a damping unit designed on the same basis. The rollers in these presses must be of waterproof material, special composition, rubber, or leather. The distributors are mostly rubber or glazed rollers, while the forme rollers are nap or rubber. (See *glazed roller*, *nap roller*).

Collotype presses are built in all essential respects like stone printing presses, but composition or leather nap rollers are also generally used as forme rollers.

Intaglio presses are inked up on a totally different principle, and the hardest problem is not the inking up of the forme but the removal of superfluous ink from the blank areas. The construction of the inking system is very closely connected with the construction

247

and working of the rest of the machine. See also *copperplate printing press, photogravure printing press.*
(GU)

inking up: the provision on lithographic stones or plates of a layer of ink for further treatment of the surface. For example, transferred or copied plates must, by means of washing and renewed rolling, be given a layer of ink to protect the image prior to etching. A plate which is to be stored after printing must have the drying printing ink replaced by transfer ink: this is done by inking up or rolling. (GU)

ink-jet printing: or *non-impact ink jet printing*, a revolutionary *word processing* technique, q.v., researched and developed in America by IBM who announced it in 1976. Copy prepared on magnetic code cards by an IBM typewriter is fed into a special IBM Word Processing Printer where an electrically charged spray of ink drops, directed at the paper to be printed, is deflected and manipulated by a charged field of opposite polarity so as to form the droplets into characters (letters, numerals, etc.) on the sheet. In Britain its potential for general printing was considered at a PIRA conference in 1977.

inkless printing: see *electrostatic printing.*

ink makers: early printers made their own ink, as did many printers until the mid-18th century. But as long ago as 1522 one Guillaume de Launay was in business in Paris as an ink supplier to printers. Plantin supplied ink, and the bigger printers may have employed men solely on its preparation.

The first specialist ink-making firm in Europe to survive to the present day was established in 1754. The present firm of Mander-Kidd traces its origins to 1773. See C. H. Bloy, 'A history of printing ink, balls and rollers', Adams & Mackay, 1967.

ink penetration: the penetration rate of ink into paper. This is higher during the moment of impression than after it. On high-speed web-fed presses less ink is transferred from the printing surface and there is less penetration of the paper on contact, but unless there is rapid absorption soon after there is a risk of smudge and set-off in subsequent stages (e.g. second printing, re-reeling, folding).

ink receptivity: the degree to which paper will absorb printing ink. This can be measured. See *paper-testing* (3).

ink slice: a spatulate tool for use in grinding, mixing, and transferring ink to the duct and rollers. (GU)

ink spread: a feature of offset printing which occurs during the transfer of ink from plate to paper via the

248

rubber blanket. Thus, for example, printed half-tone dots occupy a larger area than the dots of the plate. The amount of spread varies, the highlights being less affected than the dark tones.

ink, standards for: see *British Standard letterpress inks.*

ink table: the flat surface across which an ink roller is moved until it bears an evenly distributed film of ink. The roller is then ready for inking up type on a hand-press. The table may be of iron or plate glass.

ink tack: see *tack.*

ink transfer: the amount of ink transferred to paper depends on the thickness of ink film on the forme or plate. The amount rises to a maximum as the film is increased but then decreases if the film is further thickened.

Other factors affecting ink transfer are the degree of *tack*, q.v., the roughness of the paper and its humidity.

inlaid bindings: see *inlaying.*

inlaying: 1. the technique of decorating a book cover by insetting strips or pieces of leather differing in texture or colour from the background. After a design has been marked on the cover selected areas are cut out and pieces of corresponding shape and thickness are fitted in the empty spaces, being secured with paste. There is often gold tooling round the inlays to give a neater finish and enhance the effect. This technique, known in France as 'incrustation', has been used in Europe since the mid-16th century. Cf. *on-laying.* See also *mosaic bindings.*

2. the setting of a leaf or plate into a larger page by cutting out of portion of the latter and pasting the leaf over the gap.

inline letters: display and jobbing letters in which hand-tooling of the main strokes results in a white line forming their central part when printed. The effect is one of blackness relieved by white, and is thus distinguishable from *outline letters*, q.v. An early example was for the title line of John Bell's *The World* which he published from 1787.

in metal: a book (or other work) is said to be 'in metal' when the copy has been set up in type and the type has been made up into a forme ready for printing.

inner forme: see *sheet work.*

inner margin: see *backs.*

in pendentive: type setting in which successive lines are set in decreasing width. The first line (or two) is set to the full measure, subsequent lines are indented left and right of a central axis so that the last line of a page or paragraph is occupied by a single word. The effect is of a triangle resting on its apex. Examples are to be found in 16th-century French books. See also *hanging paragraph*.

in-plant printing: see *direct-impression typesetting*, *reprographic printing*.

in-plant proofing: the correcting of proofs by the printer's reader. The term is limited to jobs which are not subsequently sent to the client for further checking.

in print: a trade phrase referring to books obtainable from the publisher as distinct from those *reprinting* or *out of print*, qq.v.

in quires: unbound printed sheets, especially in the flat. The term is also loosely used of sheets which have been processed up to the point of folding and gathering. It is gradually losing ground in favour of the term *in sheets* with which it is synonymous. See also *quire*, *sheet stock*. (LK)

Insel-Verlag: founded in Leipzig in 1902 under the direction of Rudolf von Pöllnitz. After his death in 1904 control of the firm passed to Anton Kippenberg and *Carl Ernst Poeschel*, q.v., whose firm Poeschel & Trepte printed the books.

The origins of the firm began with *Die Insel*, a periodical first published in 1899 by Otto Bierbaum, a novelist and poet. This and a series of books were published on commission until 1902. The first Insel book was Heinrich Vogeler's poems, written and designed by the author. The Insel-Verlag began by issuing the writings of young authors, mostly in limited editions, and a group of artists, later to be identified with good book production in Germany were, at various times, associated with the firm. They included Gotthard de Beauclair, Peter Behrens, Otto Eckmann, Heinrich Vogeler and Emil Weiss, as well as the Englishmen Eric Gill, Emery Walker and Edward Johnston. In 1918 the firm acquired the *Janus-Presse*, q.v.

The Insel-Verlag's international reputation rests on the *Insel-Bücherei*, a series of low-priced illustrated books published in printed paper-covered boards. This began in 1912, and within fifty years included 800 titles. Also of note was the two-volume facsimile edition of the 42-line Bible, Leipzig, 1913–14, completed in 1923 by Schwenke's introductory volume.

insert: 1. essentially, a folded section placed into another folded section so that the subsequent sewing passes through the back folds of both sections. The insert may be of four pages only or multiples of four pages and may be placed in the centre of the host sections, on the outside, or, more rarely, in an intermediate position. The method is of considerable value in binding for the incorporation of plates as an alternative to tipping in the plates with paste. A systematic use of inserting is in the folding of 32-page sections, many folding machines achieving this by slitting the printed sheet into 16-page units and then inserting one unit into another if desired, thus producing 16-page sections or 32-page sections at will. In such 32-page work the outer 16 pages bear the signature mark, e.g. B, and the inner 16 pages will then bear the signature B*.

Where inserted plates are on the outside of the host section they are sometimes termed *outserts* or *wrap rounds*.

More than one insert can be added to a folded section but, to produce a satisfactory binding, sections must not be too thick.

2. attempts have been made to reserve the term *inset* for the above and use *insert* to indicate slips, bookmarks and the like (usually bearing advertisement matter) thrown between the leaves after binding. These, however, are generally referred to as *loose inserts* or *throw ins* to avoid ambiguity. The term *inset* is synonymous with *insert*. (LK)

inserted after binding: bulky maps, plans and the like which have many folds have to be tipped into a book after binding as they interfere with edge cutting. *Compensation guards*, q.v., may be required to prevent the book from gaping. See also *nibbed*. (LK)

inset: 1. a small map or diagram, enclosed by lines of rule and printed within the area of a larger one.
2. see *insert* (1).

in sheets: see *in quires*.

insides: the eighteen quires inside a ream of paper, the top and bottom quires being known as *outsides*. Insides are all 'good' sheets and a full ream is charged extra.

in slip: said of matter in galleys before making up into pages.

inspection copies: copies of a book given to teachers and others whose approval could lead to steady sales. Such pump priming includes the giving of academic books to lecturers in the hope that recommendation for university courses will follow. Also known as *desk copies*. See also *lead-in titles*, *reading copies*.

Institute of Printing: established in London in 1961 to further the 'science and art of printing and bookbinding'; to set standards for professional examinations; to hold conferences and meetings; to publish papers; to assist in establishing chairs and faculties of printing technology at any university; to lay down standards of education, training and experience appropriate for the admission of persons to the various grades of members of the Institute. Address: 8 Lonsdale Gardens, Tunbridge Wells.

Institute of Reprographic Technology: established in London in 1960 to unify and improve graphic techniques. Address: 52 Carnaby Street, London W1V 1PF. See also *National Reprographic Centre for documentation, reprographic printing*.

Institut voor Grafische Techniek: the Dutch printing research organization, founded in 1938.

Insular hand: the name given to the Hiberno-Saxon scripts used in the British Isles and in the continental Irish and Anglo-Saxon missionary foundations during the 7th and 9th centuries for writing and copying biblical, liturgical, patristic and other Latin texts. The several forms of *half-uncial* used, q.v., were varied according to the purpose and importance of the work being copied. The *Book of Kells*, and the *Echternach* and *Lindisfarne Gospels*, qq.v., show the scripts in their most formal and developed state.

intaglio: printing from a metal plate, usually copper, on which the image areas of the surface are incised by gravers or etched by acid. The plate is then inked and wiped, leaving ink only in the engraved parts. It is then placed with a damp sheet of paper on the bed of a press, layers of felt are added, and all pass through the press. The thickness of the layer of ink transferred to the paper is proportionate to the depth of the incised or etched recesses. As distinct from planographic and letterpress printing intaglio plates leave a layer of ink on the paper which can often be felt. Intaglio is the principle of *aquatint*, *dry-point*, *line engraving*, *mezzotint* and *photogravure*, qq.v. The first book to have illustrations produced by an intaglio process was 'Il monte sancto di Dio', Florence, 1477.

integrated mill: a papermill in which mechanical grinding or chemical digestion are done as well as making pulp into paper. See also *laps*.

interlaying: the placing of a sheet or sheets of paper between a printing plate and its block or mount. This varies from below the pressure on different parts of the plate. See also *make-ready*.

interleaved: 1. a book having blank leaves between the printed pages for the entering by hand of notes.
2. a book having thin tissues inserted to prevent the illustrations and text from rubbing. These protecting leaves may be pasted to the inner margins of the plates or be left loose. They are known as *tissued plates*.

3. a plate to the inner margin of which is pasted a thin leaf bearing a descriptive caption. A leaf of Cellophane is a modern variation of this. Known as *interleaved plates*.

interlinear matter: explanatory notes, or translation, set in small type between the lines of text they accompany. See also *gloss* (1).

interline spacing: see *film advance*.

International Association of Research Institutes for the Graphic Arts: established in Finland in 1965. Founder members were the research institutes of Britain (PIRA), Germany (FOGRA), Sweden, Holland and Denmark, a list soon extended to include other countries in Europe as well as Canada and the U.S.A.

The objects of the association are to promote international co-operation on research, thus avoiding duplicated effort, and by means of biennial conferences to exchange information on an agreed aspect of graphic industry, science and technology. Ink drying, print quality, half-tone printing and paper printability have been among topics discussed.

The acronym for the association is *IARIGAI*.

International Board on Books for Young People: or *IBBY*, an association proposed by Mrs Jella Lepman to the authors, booksellers, librarians and publishers she invited to attend a children's book congress in Munich in 1951. They shared a concern for the improvement of children's literature. Headquarters are in Zurich.

A periodical *Bookbird* was started in 1957 to record international children's book work. Until 1962 it was mimeographed; subsequently printed.

The Board marks Hans Christian Andersen's birthday, 2 April 1805, by an International Children's Book Day: the first was in 1967. The famous writer is also commemorated by the biennial award of the Hans Christian Andersen Medals, first made by the Board in 1956 to Britain's Eleanor Farjeon and Edward Ardizzone. Awards are based on collective works.

After an absence of some years Britain rejoined the Board in 1973, thereby becoming eligible to submit a children's author and illustrator for the medals and, in 1974, to sponsor an International Children's Book Day.

International Book Information Service Ltd: or *IBIS*, a company formed in London in 1971 when the Book Development Council's overseas book promotion mailing list and its home market academic-trade counterpart, which was originated in 1967 by Longmans, Associated Book Publishers, O.U.P. and C.U.P. as the *University Mailing Service*, were amalgamated. Both had developed highly sophisticated mailing lists for the distribution of publishers' publicity for forth-

250

coming books. The result was a subject-coded computerized mailing list of some 350,000 names and addresses. Publicity takes the form of printed cards, one per title, leaflets and jackets.

IBIS is now known as *IBIS Mailing Services Ltd.* Its subsidiary company *IBIS Mailing Ltd.* prints and distributes *Publishers Information Record Cards*, q.v., and since 1972 has operated *Orders Clearing*, q.v. Address: London Colney, St Albans, Herts.

International Bureau of the Federation of Master Printers: a body founded in 1929 to further the economic and technical interests of the employers' organizations affiliated to it. These aims are achieved in such ways as the collation of wages and working conditions agreements, the dissemination of information about the industry, the investigation of new methods and materials, and the international exchange of sons of master printers with a view to broadening their experience. Conferences are held, and a council of administration conducts the regular business of the Bureau.

International Community of Booksellers Associations: or *ICBA*, an organization founded in 1956 to provide a regular basis of co-operation among national organizations representing the bookselling trade. The training of young assistants, the analysis of book distribution costs, price maintenance and related matters were the principal subjects for co-operative discussion. Representatives of Associations in the following countries joined the Community as founder members: Austria, Belgium, Denmark, Great Britain & Ireland, France, Italy, Netherlands, Sweden, Switzerland and West Germany.

International Copyright Information Centre: set up in 1971 by Unesco to help publishers in developing countries to secure rights to books published elsewhere. The headquarters in Paris acts as a clearing house for requests for copyright clearance and offers of copyright concessions or facilities. See also *Stockholm Protocol, 1967*.

International Council of Graphic Design Associations: a body which at its Zurich Congress in 1964 urged its members to seek the international unification within the metric system of typographic measurements, including height to paper, this to be done in close cooperation with the appropriate sections of the printing industry and national bureaux of standards. The Council is known by the acronym *Icograda*.

International Graphical Federation: inaugurated in 1949 as an international federation of printing trade unions, and established on a free trade-union basis to protect and further the occupational, economic and idealistic interests of print workers. Membership is open to trade unions of workers in three groups: letterpress; bookbinding and paper and board conversion; and lithography, offset, photogravure, process engraving and photography. Present members are from Europe, Asia, Africa and Australia, but Communist countries and the Americas are not represented. Periodic conferences are held, and special importance is attached to the exchange of information and experience on health and welfare problems of the printing-trade worker. Headquarters are in Berne.

International League of Antiquarian Booksellers: founded in 1942, a trade association of booksellers in thirteen countries whose members deal principally in books which are no longer in print.

The League has published a directory giving the specialities of each of the members, and other reference works are published. An annual conference is held, usually in a European capital. The name is abbreviated as *ILAB*.

international paper sizes: see *paper sizes*.

International Publishers Association: or *IPA*, founded at the International Congress of Publishers, Paris, 1896. Some thirty national associations are now members. They hold conferences at three- or four-yearly intervals and meet at working sessions in between to discuss such matters as international copyright, public lending right and the attempts of governments to control publishing.

International Rights Information Service: or *IRIS*, from January 1978, a monthly journal published in New York by R. R. Bowker, listing titles for which publishers hold rights for sale. Each title is briefly described and the rights available for it are specified.

The complete journal is available in subject parts which can be subscribed separately, i.e. arts and humanities, children's books, fiction, general non-fiction, scientific and medical, and technical.

International Standard Book Number: or *ISBN*. This is a unique code number for identifying a book, and eliminates the need to quote author, title, edition and publisher in all transactions. The *Standard Book Numbering System* in the U.K. was researched by Professor Gordon Foster of Trinity College, Dublin, on behalf of W. H. Smith & Son and the Publishers Association, with J. Whitaker & Sons, publishers of *The Bookseller*. Impetus was given to its adoption by the increasing use of computers in order processing and stock control. The first practical steps were taken by the SBN Agency Ltd, set up by Whitaker with the co-operation of the PA and BNB, and its use in Britain began in 1967, soon followed by Canada and the U.S.A.

For book identification the letters SBN are followed

by a nine-digit number divided into three parts. The first is the *publisher identifier* which may be from two to seven digits: the bigger the publisher's title output the fewer the digits used to identify him. The second part is the *title number* which identifies the particular title, volume, or edition (so precisely that different numbers are given to cased and paperback editions of one title). Title numbers can be from six down to one digit, this being determined by the number of digits in the preceding publisher identifier. The combined total of the two is always eight digits. The third and last part of an SBN is always a single digit known as the *check digit* which is calculated on a modulus of 11 with weights down to 2, using X in lieu of 10 where 10 would occur as a check digit. This is a necessary device to ensure that the computer will not accept errors in transcription or transposition which would lead to the supply of a wrong book. As an example, the number given to the first edition of this Glossary was SBN 04 655001 1.

Modifications to the foregoing were made in 1969 when, after discussions with booktrade organizations in the U.S.A. and meetings of the International Standards Organization, it was decided and agreed how the British-originated scheme could be adapted for general use. The scheme was re-named *International Book Numbering System*, the prefix *SBN* becoming *ISBN*. The original nine-digit number was extended to ten by including a *group identifier* to show the geographical, language, national or other convenient group. For example, the group identifier for Britain, U.S.A., Canada and Australia is 0 (zero) and all earlier numbers given to British books now have this 0 in front of them. Thus the number for the first edition of this Glossary became ISBN 0 04 655001 1. A special group identifier, 92, is used for intergovernmental organizations, thus ISBN 92 3 is Unesco's reference. A complete list of ISBNs is given in *British Books in Print*, q.v.

The ISBN of a book should be printed on the verso of the title-leaf, on the jacket if there is one, or on some other prominent position on the outside. Numbers are often stated in publishers' advertising material (though not as frequently as book-ordering librarians would like), and are given on printed catalogue cards, e.g. BNB and Library of Congress.

Prior to the setting up of an international agency to assume responsibility for the system and to allot group identifiers the British Standards Institution operated it. National bodies allot publisher identifiers. In Britain this is done by J. Whitaker & Sons Ltd, the Council of the British National Bibliography, and the Publishers Association, who jointly formed the SBN Agency Ltd. Members of the PA allot their own title numbers; other publishers have numbers assigned to their titles by the agency. In the U.S.A. R. R. Bowker & Co. assigns numbers. For the method of constructing an ISBN see BS 4762:1971.

International Typographical Union: see *Association Typographique Internationale*.

Intertype: a leading firm of composing machine manufacturers which originated in America. In 1911 Herman Ridder, then of the Associated Press and American Publishers Association together with W. S. Scudder resolved to develop a new line composing and casting machine. Following a search of existing patents a prospectus was issued under the name of the International Typesetting Machine Company of New York (whence *Intertype*) to interest investors. A factory was built in Brooklyn and in November 1912 the prototype was completed and demonstrated. In March 1913 the first tool-made Intertype was installed for the New York *Journal of Commerce*. In 1914 the Intertype appeared on the market and rapidly achieved sales both in America and Europe.

The operating principle is essentially the same as that of the Linotype and similar matrices are used: the end product, too, is a single-line slug. Various details differ, frequently being simplified. Without diminishing the ease of operation which typified the first machines numerous improvements introduced through the years have ensured a world-wide demand for later models. The Intertype range of linecasting machines fills the needs of all printers using hot-metal line composition. Standardized design permits the interchange between different models of major items of

Intertype model with side magazine

equipment and the fitting of improvements to earlier machines.

There are two complementary groups of machines: single distributor and double distributor. *Single distributor machines* compose matrices from one main magazine or one main and one side magazine at one time. They are ideal for setting straight matter calling for roman with bold or roman with italic and small capitals and may be tape operated. In the early 1970s the range of single distributor machines included (1) the single-magazine *Model V*, suitable for newspaper or book work with extensive setting in the same type face and type size. Easy removal of the magazine made possible a quick change of face or size. (2) The versatile text and display *Model C*. This can be equipped with up to four 90-channel main magazines (with complete matrix founts up to and including normal 18-point) and a side unit comprising up to four 34-channel side magazines (with capitals or lower case alphabets, numerals, and punctuation). (3) The *Monarch*, specially designed for the continuous high-speed production of straight text matter from tape, and available with or without keyboard, and with a double-stack galley for more than 24in. of slugs.

Double distributor machines, when equipped with side magazines, can compose matrices from up to four magazines in one line giving the full range of roman, italic, bold, bold italic and small capitals (a maximum of thirteen alphabets). The range includes (1) *Model F* for such text and mixed display work as advertisements, multi-alphabet setting, catalogues, school and technical books. (2) *Model G* for setting extra display faces up to 30-point, full face, as well as text faces from main magazines, making it suitable for newspaper and periodical headline and display work. See also *teletypesetting*.

Intertype Fotosetter: the first commercially available photosetting machine, working mainly on the same principle of circulating matrices as the Intertype slug-casting machines. Briefly, keyboard operation released matrices known as *Fotomats*. Each carried a photographic negative character embedded in its side, but in other respects looked like the standard toothed Intertype matrix. Lines in measures from 4 to 42 ems were made up of characters exposed separately on to a roll of film or photographic paper. Corrections could be stripped in.

With the development of the *Fototronic* range, the Fotosetter, which came into use in 1947, and its immediate successor the *Fotomatic*, were superseded although many remained in field use.

Intertype Fototronic: the name given to the range of photosetting systems developed, made and marketed by Harris-Intertype Corporation. The original model, announced in Britain in 1965, had two units. The first included a standard electric typewriter and a digital computer. Its product was a coded 8-level tape and a print out. The tape was then fed into a separate photographic unit which also included a digital computer. Two type discs were used, each of 240 characters. As the coded tape was interpreted characters on the rotating disc were exposed via a plasma jet light source on to a roll of film at the rate of twenty a second, the equivalent of twenty-two newspaper lines a minute.

Continuing development led to more sophisticated models which in the early 1970s included the *Fototronic 1200* system. This comprises Master and Satellite keyboards and a photographic unit, or non-justifying keyboards feeding the photographic unit via a computer. Input to the photo unit is an 8-level justified tape: the output can be film or photographic paper in measures from 18 to 51 ems. After exposure (at one millionth of a second) this is automatically cut on signal and can be removed for processing in an integral darkroom (or booth) without interrupting the work. A special feature of the *1200* system is the instant availability on command of 1,200 characters in nineteen type sizes from 5- to 72-point. They are carried on discs, each containing two 120-character founts with extra locations for storing accents or special sorts: the turret holds five discs. Other facilities include full mixing of type faces, weights and sizes, kerning, letter spacing, all in one line with a common base alignment.

Intertype Fototronic 1200 system. Type discs

253

The *Fototronic 600* is a low cost medium speed (50 single column lines per minute) photosetter using 6-level justified or unjustified TTS tape. Characters are set on film or photographic paper from a disc containing six founts, each of 120 characters in sizes from 5- to 24-point. The *Fototronic TxT* is a high speed electronic photosetter with inbuilt computer using 6-level TTS justified or unjustified paper tape, 8-level justified paper tape, or 9-channel magnetic tape. Character capacity and production speeds can be varied according to need from 90 to 150 single column lines per minute.

The *Fototronic CRT* system is a high speed third generation electronic photocomposing machine utilizing a cathode ray tube display device and magnetic tape input. The system will set type in sizes from 4- to 144-point at speeds in characters per second determined by the size being set, thus, for example, 7-point type can be generated at a rate of 1,000–1,500 cps. Up to 4,000 characters are accessible at any one time: they are stored in digital form and in a variety of sizes and formats, this storage capacity being supplemented by electronic manipulation to enlarge, reduce, expand or otherwise vary the basic character. Output is right or wrong-reading film or paper. The system offers considerable advantages for high speed low cost composition for newspapers, periodicals, directories, dictionaries and encyclopaedias and other material stored or processed by computers.

The *Harris 1100* editing and proofing display terminal is a self-contained CRT video text-editing and proofing system utilizing 6-level TTS tape for input and output, and permitting the addition, deletion or alteration of characters and words through the use of a keyed cursor for the identification of data to be modified. As copy is inputted it is instantly displayed on the video screen in characters generated in a 14-point monospaced fount with serifs. A 63-key keyboard for entering alphanumeric data anywhere on the screen has keys for controlling typesetting commands. The video terminal output of corrected tape complete with copy identification and typographic function commands is then ready for computer processing (hyphenation, justification and formatting) or for direct insertion into typesetting equipment capable of handling blind-keyboarded tape. See also *computer-assisted typesetting*.

introduction: a declaration by the author of his viewpoint or an outline of his subject matter. While normally part of the *prelims*, q.v., it is not uncommon to find the introduction forming the first chapter. In either case it is part of the work and is not always changed for successive editions (as the preface may be). While some authorities claim synonymity for the terms *foreword* and *introduction* the two are demonstrably different in purpose. See also *foreword, preface*.

introductory titles: see *lead-in titles*.

in usum Delphini: see *ad usum Delphini*.

in usum scholarum: Latin words sometimes found on the title-pages of Greek and Latin classics printed in England during the 18th century to indicate that the edition was 'for the use of schools'.

in usum tyronum: 'for the use of beginners'. See preceding entry.

Inverform: a British system for the speeding up of sheet formation on a papermaking machine. Briefly, the wire of a Fourdrinier has a matching endless woven wire mounted immediately above it. After the stock has flowed on to the bottom wire it is pressed or nipped between the two wires. In moving along the wires pass between various water-extracting appliances. This speeds up sheet formation and means that a shorter wire is needed.

inverted commas: " " in Britain. In Germany and Austria they are set thus ,, ". See also *duck-foot quotes, primes*.

invert half-tone: in gravure work, a method of continuous tone for which a film positive is made with a half-tone screen in the camera. Exposure of this to carbon tissue without pre-screening results, after etching into a copper plate or cylinder, in a half-tone with *cells* of various sizes (but uniform depth) instead of *relief dots*. If line work is involved it must be separately exposed to the tissue after pre-screening it.

iodized collodion process: a process invented by Scott Archer in 1851 used in photographic reproduction. It is now known as the *wet-plate process*, and is based on the sensitivity to light of iodized silver when nitrate of silver is present.

Irish bindings: the important era for bookbinding in Ireland was the 18th century; before 1700 little elaborate work had been done. Books were mostly bound for institutions or for presentation rather than for bibliophiles, and the Parliamentary Journals bound from about 1740 for the Parliament House in Dublin represent the finest examples of Irish binding. The crimson morocco volumes had as their main features a cottage-roof pattern, and a central inlaid panel or a lozenge of fawn leather, ornamented with natural forms extending over the whole cover. The treatment of these features varied, as did the tooling, from year to year, no two volumes being alike (unless one year's records exceeded one volume).

The 149 volumes of Journals were burned during the political disturbances of 1922, but a series of rubbings taken by Sir Edward Sullivan is kept in the National Library, Dublin. See M. Craig, 'Irish bookbindings, 1600–1800', Cassell, 1954.

Irish Book Lover: founded in 1909 by John Crone as a literary and bibliographical periodical, important for its new poetry, articles on Irish printing and book reviews. Crone remained editor until 1924, being succeeded by Seamus O'Casaide until 1930, and *Colm O Lochlainn*, q.v., until 1957 when publication ceased.

In 1971 the Irish University issued the complete series as a twelve-volume reprint.

Irish half-uncial: a book hand developed in Ireland about AD 600. It was derived from Roman cursive and uncial letters, differing from the latter by having new forms of b, d, g, m, r, and s. The *Book of Kells*, q.v., is the finest manuscript in this script, which indirectly became the basis for our lower-case roman letters. See also *Carolingian script*.

Irish type and printing: type used for printing Irish characters is based on the two forms of manuscript letter used by Irish scribes about the end of the 9th century. These were the half-uncial or round, and the pointed. The latter influenced the earliest Irish type which in authentic form was used in Antwerp about 1611: the influence of the rounder half-uncial was more apparent on type designed in the 19th century.

From the 16th to 18th century most books in Irish were printed in England or on the Continent. The first printer in Ireland was an Englishman, Humphrey Powell, who was given £20 by the Privy Council towards the expense of transferring his press from London to Dublin. He was active until 1566. He issued a Prayer Book in 1551.

Another early printer in Dublin was Séon (John) Francke. In 1570 John O'Kearney, treasurer of St Patrick's, received from Queen Elizabeth I a sum of money for providing the necessary punches and matrices for printing in Irish. The type, cut in London, was a mixture of roman, italic and eight Irish characters. It was used, as intended by the donor, for a Catechism printed, probably by his nephew William, in 1571 (STC 18793). The same fount was used by Francke for the first edition (500 copies) of William O'Donnell's translation into Irish Gaelic (Erse) of the New Testament, printed at Dublin in 1602 (STC 2958), and remained in use until about 1650.

A rather better type was used by exiled Irish monks living in Belgium where they established a press at Antwerp about 1611. In 1616 this was moved to Louvain where it was in operation until 1728. The type they used was adapted from Irish manuscripts and later served as a model in London for the Irish type commissioned by Robert Boyle from John Moxon in 1680. Boyle sponsored the printing of a second edition, revised by Reilly, of the N.T. in 1681, accompanied by Bishop William Bedel's translation

of the O.T. in 1685. This was the first complete Bible printed in Irish type, the printer being Robert Everingham of London. In 1690 the whole Bible was printed in roman type for use in Scotland.

Moxon's type was widely used from 1681 until 1820 when it was superseded by Dr Edmund Fry's of 1818. However, about 1787 Stephen Parker, a Dublin founder, offered for sale his 'complete font of beautiful Irish characters'. They were used by the printer George Bonham for the 'Transactions of the Royal Irish Academy', Vol II, 1789, and continued in use by Bonham and other printers until about 1810.

Fry's type marked a change from an angular to a round letter form and was popular until about 1870. Towards the end of the century a type cut for the Figgins foundry of London became a standard type for many years.

It should be mentioned that from 1735 Catholics in Ireland began printing books in roman type, and this has continued in use for certain classes of book.

See Séan Jennett, 'Irish types: 1571–1958'. *British Printer*, 1958, 50–5; and E. W. Lynam, 'The Irish character in print, 1571–1923', facsimile edition, revised by A. MacLochlainn, Irish U.P., 1970.

ISBN: see *International Standard Book Number*.

Islamic bookbinding: it is probable that by the beginning of the 7th century the codex form of bound book was used in what became the Moslem world. It would be known from books made in Egypt, Syria and Mesopotamia. There was already a flourishing leather industry in South Arabia with an export trade of finely finished skins including the white and yellow striped Cordovan leather of Sana'a and the morocco leather of At-Taif where (states Arnold) excellent bindings were produced by the 10th century. Morocco leather was also made in Egypt and by the early 13th century quantities were exported.

The Arabs retained the classical form of book for literary texts, of almost square shape, until the use of papyrus ceased in the mid-10th century. They took over the artistic traditions of the peoples they conquered, and it may be assumed that in Egypt Coptic craftsmen, whose binding was highly developed, worked for Muslim patrons and instructed Muslim craftsmen. Having absorbed the skills, the Muslims refined them and spread them in the countries they conquered or with which they traded. They used the Coptic technique of sewing the leaves with chain-stitch, affixing a strip of fabric to the backs before gluing on the cover, and they adopted the tooling on the covers of rectangles set within each other, parallel to the edges, about a large central ornament. They took over the classical practice of using decorative patterns for front and rear boards. Thongs were inserted in the boards to close the book.

Bookbinding became an esteemed craft in the

expanding Muslim empire, particularly in Syria, Egypt, North Africa and Spain where 'Malaga was above all a treasure-house of exquisite leatherwork' (Arnold). Unfortunately little other than a few copies of the Koran has survived from the famous Muslim libraries which existed by the 13th century: they mostly came from Egypt and North Africa.

In Tunisian bindings of the 9th century the leather of the lower cover was extended on three sides to form rigid flaps. The effect was like a box, the upper board acting as a lid. Triangular fore-edge flaps, extending from the cover to enclose the book, rather like a purse or wallet, are found in Islamic books from the 12th century.

Some surviving Tunisian leather covers of the 11th century have embossed decoration. An outline of the design was laid on the wooden board with pieces of glue-soaked cord over which the leather was then pressed and moulded. Tooling in blind round the raised outline followed.

In Egypt boards were made of cedarwood or of papyrus pulp covered with leather. If left uncovered, the cedarwood was often decorated with inlays of ivory, bone or wood arranged in mosaic patterns showing Coptic influence. Egyptian Tulunid bindings (9th and 10th centuries) now in Cairo, show the use of a single sheet of parchment to form an end-paper, with one half pasted down and the free half bearing the conclusion of the Koranic text. From the late 10th century papyrus and parchment were replaced by paper end-papers. These were often decorated with geometrical patterns in black and colour, either stamped with a wooden block or built up from small dies. Also in the 10th century cut out patterns of paper were pasted as a filigree on to a doublure of differently coloured paper. Occasionally a Kufic inscription would be cut out and applied in this way.

Experts believe that a Koran written in 1286 at Marrakesh (where it is preserved) may be the earliest known example of tooling with heated irons on gold leaf. The morocco cover bears a design of interlaced strapwork about a central eight-pointed star which derives ultimately from the Coptic pattern of two interlaced squares. The use of gold tooling in Persia may date from the first half of the 14th century. In early examples it is not possible to determine whether or not the decorative points and lines were first tooled in blind and then painted with liquid gold as had been done on Coptic bindings made in Egypt in the 7th century.

From Moslem Persia the earliest extant bindings are those made for Mongol princes in the early 14th century. The boards have geometrical ornamentation without gold. An early 15th century binding, made in 1407, has on the front board, 'a piece of perforated leather cut into an intricate pattern and superimposed on a ground of blue and gold' (Arnold). On the first Timurid bindings made in Herat patterns of leaves

256

and flowers or geometrical designs were used, often in blind. Whole patterns were often stamped from large metal blocks, while another technique was the embossing of designs with matrices of toughened camel hide. On other covers of the same period elaborate gold tooling was done. Animals and birds were popular motifs. A large almond-shaped shield, filled with tendrils or plaited ribbons, was the principal motif on many Islamic bindings from the 14th century onwards.

The introduction of filigree cut-out work is attributed to Qiwām-al-Din of Tabriz who between c. 1430–50 worked in the Baysunqur atelier at Herat. The use of moulds for stamping large pictorial designs had also developed at Herat by 1446.

Persian doublures became very elaborate, often with delicate filigree work of hair-thin leather set on a coloured ground. Dyed leathers, mostly black, blue, crimson or green were used for covers. Thin strips of different colours were set in border patterns and often gilded, or thin strips of gilded leather were set in panels depressed in the boards.

Covers on which paint was applied directly to the leather were made in Persia in the 15th century, but the paint tended to crack and flake off. This led to the use of pasteboards and papier mâché for boards, the surface being overlaid with gesso or other filler as a ground for a miniaturist's scenes painted with water colours, the theme of the picture often, but not always, being suggested by the text of the book. The painting was then given several coats of lacquer, liquid gold and silver (depicting water) and mother of pearl dust (depicting rocks) being carried on the final layer. Such bindings continue to be made.

See Sir T. W. Arnold and A. Grohmann, 'The Islamic book: a contribution to its art and history from the VII-XVII century', Paris, Pegasus Press, 1929; F. Sarre, 'Islamische Bucheinbände', Berlin, 1923; E. Gratzl, 'Islamische Bucheinbände', Leipzig, 1924.

Islamic illumination: the Arabs had no graphic art traditions so in the early centuries of the new faith they employed craftsmen from the areas they conquered, some of whom may have been converted to Islam. The influence of Christian art came via the Nestorian and Jacobite churches. Other influences were Sasanian sculpture and metalwork, and Manichaean religious paintings.

Translations into Arabic of Greek medicine and science were widely copied and illustrated from the mid-8th century, but it was the work of scribes, gilders and bookbinders who wrote and embellished copies of the *Koran* which was most esteemed and received religious sanction. The work of painters did not. The custom of writing the Koran in letters of liquid gold, which began about the 8th century, seems to have come from the east, and is first found in Jewish literature (Arnold). The use of the blue ground for the gold, a favourite Muslim combination, may derive from Pharonic Egypt.

Unlike Christianity, Islam never used pictorial representations of religious imagery for the furtherance of its message, it being considered that for a man to fashion with his hands a form to which God had given life was an attempt at assimilation with God. The sayings of the Holy Prophet assembled by later writers (the Hadith) forbade the imitation of human and animal forms and instructed the artist to confine himself to plant and abstract motifs. These sayings include 'Those who make pictures will be punished on Resurrection Day; it will be said to them 'Give life to what you have created', and 'On Resurrection Day God will consider image makers as the men most deserving of punishment'. The puritanical interpretation of such passages resulted in a strict prohibition of all figural representation, but the more tolerant held that only the setting up of images to be worshipped was proscribed. The iconoclasm officially decreed by Caliph Yazid II in 721 was principally directed against dissident Christian factions.

Nonetheless representational paintings of high quality were made in Turkey, Persia and Mughal India. It is thought that many such portrait albums and murals, often the work of Christian artists, only survive because they were kept in the private apartments of a Sultan or Shah, their existence being unsuspected by the public.

The earliest surviving representations of the Holy Prophet date from the 14th century, and they were never numerous: many have been defaced by zealots. From the 16th century onwards it was usual to veil his face or leave it uncompleted. However, even in the 20th century European publishers risk giving considerable offence and having their books banned in Muslim lands when they publish books containing alleged depictions of the Holy Prophet.

See Sir Thomas Arnold, 'Painting in Islam', O.U.P., 1928; and R. Pinder-Wilson, 'Paintings from Islamic lands', Cassirer, 1969. See also *arabesque, Mughal illumination, Persian illumination, Turkish illumination*.

isolario: a book of directions for sailing between islands, particularly of the Mediterranean. See also *portolano*.

isotype: a technique for presenting statistical information by means of *pictograms* or *ideograms*, qq.v., which substitute symbols for numerals-cum-words.

issue: part of an edition, being copies of a book made up largely from sheets run off for the first printing but differing from that printing by having, for example, a new title-page, matter added as an appendix or correction, or with matter transposed. The term 'issue' is used after copies of the work without any of these changes have been published. Bibliographers then speak of a 'first issue' and 'second issue' of the 'first edition'.

In 1960 the first edition of this Glossary was published simultaneously in London and New York. There were differences in the title and contents pages of copies prepared for the American market: this constituted a *separate issue*, not a *second issue*, since publication was simultaneous.

The term, which is not concerned with *binding variants*, q.v., is less precisely used in the book trade. Cf. *new edition*. See also *impression, state*.

Itala of Quedlinburg: part of a pre-Vulgate Old Testament in Latin written in a square uncial script, probably in Rome, and surviving on five parchment leaves. They contain portions of Samuel and Kings. Four of the leaves have scenes of figures and landscape details painted in colours and gold. An interesting feature is that where the colours have been rubbed away there are instructions to the artist, written in a cursive script. The date assigned by scholars to the work, late 4th–early 5th century, makes it the earliest extant illuminated manuscript of western Christianity. It is now in the Berlin State Library.

Italian illumination: the pilgrimage to Italy brought foreign monks to Bobbio and Monte Cassino where, from the late 9th century, manuscript painting developed. Irish, Carolingian, Byzantine and eventually Islamic influences were brought and absorbed there. Greek artist-monks were particularly active. Other early centres were at Benevento, Rome and Palermo. In the 11th century *Exultet rolls*, q.v., decorated with line drawings, were widely circulated. As early as the 12th century the affinity between manuscript and panel painting had been established, and this quality, seen in larger brush strokes and shapes, was to be the mark of much Italian book illumination until it ceased. Also typical was the extensive use of pink and blue to paint thick leaf ornamentation which in the scriptoria of other countries would be painted much smaller and in natural green.

The Gothic style of the 13th century survives at its most splendid in a group of large choir books made in Bologna, which was also a centre for decorated legal codices. In the 14th century choir books with large historiated initials are characteristic. Niccolò di Giacomo (*c.* 1330–*c.* 1402) led an active workshop at Bologna. His vividly coloured crowd scenes decorated many secular works, and he had considerable influence on north Italian artists.

Bright colours, particularly yellow, were characteristic of Florentine miniature painting during the 14th century. The art of Cimabue and Giotto influenced many painters. Here, too, large scale painting in folio choir books was preferred to the minute detail appropriate to a Book of Hours. By this time a fully developed national art of painting flourished in Venice, Milan, Florence, Naples and Siena where the great Simone Martini (*c.* 1283–1344) had his atelier. In Renaissance illumination emphasis was on decoration rather than illustration. There were numerous wealthy patrons, most famous being the Medici family of Florence. Francesco d'Antonio, Zanobi Strozzi, and Attavante are three better known miniaturists, the latter working for the Duke of Urbino and the kings of Hungary and Portugal. Another princely patron was Borso d'Este of Ferrara for whom, between 1455–62, Taddeo Crivelli and others painted the thousand miniatures in the sumptuous Bible now at Modena.

The illumination of choir books and psalters continued in Italy until well into the 16th century, returning to the devotional but by now artificial style of the Middle Ages. See M. Salmi, 'Italian manuscript miniatures', Collins, 1957. See also *Conradin Bible*, *Federigo da Montefeltro*.

italic: cursive type of which the prototype was cut about 1499 by Griffo for *Aldus Manutius*, q.v. Letters sloped to the right and the cursive quality was emphasised by its somewhat cramped appearance and numerous tied letters. They derived from informal sloped humanistic scripts. Manutius only commissioned lower-case letters, using small roman capitals with them. Italic capitals were first used in Vienna by Singrenius about 1524, and another early printer to use them was Gryphius of Lyons in 1537. Italic type was used in England by Wynkyn de Worde in 1528.

The Manutius type was widely copied by other printers anxious to share the market for cheap small editions of the classics, but several less cramped designs superseded the original (see *Arrighi*). Although originally used for setting complete texts the practice diminished through the years, and by the 19th century, when italics designed on the over-refined principles of modern face were made, their thin wiry quality was found unsuitable for continuous reading.

Present day use of italics, which are cut to accompany most text romans, continues for textual emphasis and display. When preparing copy for the printer a straight line is ruled under words to be set in italics: if bold-face italic is wanted a wavy line is drawn under the straight one. See also *letters – forms and styles*.

Ives, Frederic Eugene, 1856–1937: of Philadelphia, a technician and inventor, in 1886, of an improved screen for half-tone plate making. He positioned two ruled glass screens at right angles, face to face, and sealed them into a unit. He also made the first three-colour blocks for letterpress work in 1881, and perfected the chromoscope and the working out of various methods of reproducing in colour. In Philadelphia 28 July is called 'Ives' Day'.

ivory boards: see *boards*.

J

jacket: 1. the paper protecting cover in which most cased books are sold in the U.K. and the U.S.A. Copies of Heath's 'Keepsake', 1833, are held to be the first book for which a paper protecting jacket was provided by the publisher. It was printed on paper folded over the head and foot of the boards as well as round the sides, and carried an advertisement on the area covering the rear board. However, it was not until the 1880s that the provision of jackets became at all common. In the late 1890s the front inner flaps were used for *blurbs*, q.v., relative to the book they enclosed.

Jacket designing and printing have now become a highly skilled and costly part of book production frequently involving a graphic artist, photography, and lithography. The jacket is an important factor in sales promotion. (See *advance jackets*.)

Also known as *book jacket, dust cover, dust jacket*. Cf. *wrapper*. See G. T. Tanselle, 'Book-jackets, blurbs, and bibliographers', *The Library*, 5th ser., xxvi 2 1971.

2. a transparent plastic carrier with a sleeve or pocket made to hold flat strips of microfilm, microfiche, etc.

jacketing machine: a machine introduced to the binding trade in the late 1950s, prior to which jackets were fitted to books by hand. The machine mechanically lifts the cover boards and while they are raised folds the jacket round the case much as the case-making machine turns in glued cloth.

Jackson, Joseph, 1733–92: a brilliant London type-cutter and founder who after being apprenticed to Caslon's Chiswell Street foundry and serving until 1763 as an armourer at sea, worked for a time with his co-apprentice Thomas Cottrell before setting up his own business sometime before 1765. His specimen sheet of 1773 was remarkable for its showing of hebrew, persian-arabic and bengali type. He also cut types for a facsimile of the Domesday Book published by John Nichols in 1783, for Dr C. G. Woide's folio facsimile of the N.T. portion of the Codex Alexandrinus which Nichols issued in 1786, and for Dr Kipling's facsimile of the Codex Bezae which was published at Cambridge a year after his death.

In 1782 he took as his apprentice and later manager *Vincent Figgins*, q.v., who completed the two-line english roman which Jackson began about 1789 for Bensley to use in the Macklin Bible, 1800.

The Jackson business was bought by William Caslon III in 1792.

jaconet: a cotton fabric, glazed on one side, used as a lining for the spines of books. See also *mull*.

Jaggard, William, d.1623: an Elizabethan printer who about 1604 acquired the printing house in Barbican, London, founded in the 1560s by John Charlewood (d. 1593). On completing his apprenticeship to Henry Denham in 1591 he worked as a bookseller from 1594 to 1608. He was appointed printer to the City of London in 1610.

Jaggard mostly printed for others. He went blind about 1612 and about that time was assisted by his son *Isaac* (b. 1595).

William Jaggard is important for his part in the publication of Shakespeare's First Folio of 1623. The colophon includes his name as one of the four at whose charge the work was produced. The title-page gives the names of Isaac Jaggard and Edward Blount as printers; the latter was a bookseller. The selling price of bound copies was £1.

William Jaggard had been the printer, albeit anonymously, of an earlier attempt at a collection of Shakespeare's plays in association with his friend Thomas Pavier: this was in 1619 when ten genuine or faked Shakespearian reprints of published plays were published.

James, Thomas, *c.* 1689–1738: a London typefounder who established his business in 1710, initially with stocks of Dutch matrices. He and his son John eventually acquired the punches and matrices of the 17th century London founders Thomas Grover, Robert Andrews and Joseph Moxon.

When John James died in 1772 Edward Rowe Mores bought the stock and prepared a specimen book, issued in 1782 after his death. Part of the stock of matrices was then purchased by *Joseph Fry*, q.v., via whom it later went to Stephenson, Blake & Co. of Sheffield. See also *William Ged*.

Jänecke: a famous Hanover firm of ink-makers whose

a

b

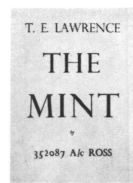

c

d

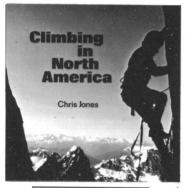

e

f

g

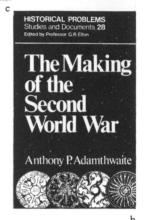

h

i

j

k

l

a. *Aubrey Beardsley* (1909) (*Dent*)

b. *Typography in one colour* (*Faber*)

c. *Typography in two colours* (*Cape*)

d. *Typography in two colours by Stanley Morison, one of the yellow paper series* (*Gollancz*)

e. *Artist lettering by Hans Tisdall* (*Cape*)

f. *Artist design by Barnett Freedman in three-colour lithography from artist's own separations* (*Faber*)

g. *Artist lettering by Sexauer-Effert* (*German*)

h. *Reverse block in one colour* (*Allen & Unwin*)

i. *Photographic* (*Geri Davis, U.S.A.*)

j. *Photographic* (*Bergström and Boyle*)

k. *Artist design by Charles Mozley in three-colour photo-lithography* (*Bodley Head*)

l. *Line block with typography in two colours* (*U.S.A.*)

ink was used by the Ashendene, Essex House, and Kelmscott presses.

Jannon, Jean, 1580–1658: born in Geneva. He worked as a punchcutter, typefounder and printer in Sedan, France. In his specimen of 1621 appeared the roman fount later known as Caractères de l'Université, for which he based his designs on the 16th century types of Augereau, Garamont, and Granjon. Some matrices of Jannon's fount survive in the Imprimerie Nationale, Paris, where they were thought by French authorities to have been cut by Garamont. Thus when the Monotype Corporation revived the Caractères de l'Université in 1922 they reasonably enough gave the name Garamond to the series. It was in 1926 that Mrs Beatrice Warde discovered the 1621 specimen sheet and made the correct attribution of the design to Jannon. (See Appendix A.)

Jansenist bindings: late 17th century French bindings of austere design with little or no ornamentation on the outside of the cover but with richly tooled doublures. They were named after Cornelius Jansen, Bishop of Ypres.

Janson, Anton, 1620–87: a Dutch typefounder, trained in Amsterdam by *Christoffel van Dijck*, q.v. He later worked in Frankfurt, and from 1656 in Leipzig where he established the first independent typefoundry in 1659. Janson's roman, with a strong Dutch influence, was popular in Germany. Punches formerly believed to be his work were acquired by the Ehrhardt foundry of Leipzig about 1710. Matrices of them passed in 1919 to Stempel of Frankfurt: they have been identified by Harry Carter and George Buday as the work of *Nicholas Kis*, q.v., a Hungarian punchcutter who worked in Amsterdam from 1680–89.

Linotype's revival of Janson appeared in America in 1934: the Monotype version, 1938, was named Ehrhardt.

Jansson, Joannes, *c.* 1596–1664: a Dutch printer and publisher noted for his finely printed atlases. He married into the family of *Jodocus Hondius*, q.v., and after 1638 took charge of the latter's business, continuing to publish atlases and reprints of John Speed's maps.

Janus-Presse: the first German private press devoted to the production of finely made books. It was established in 1907 at Leipzig by *Carl Ernst Poeschel* and *Walter Tiemann*, qq.v., who together composed and printed five books on Zanders fine Büttenpapier. Their first book was Goethe's 'Römische Elegien', 1907, in an edition of 150 copies, bound in parchment by Carl Sonntag, jnr.

After 1918 the business affairs of the press were taken over by the firm of Insel-Verlag, but the two men remained responsible for design and typography. The press closed in 1923.

Japanese paper: a thin, tough and highly absorbent paper of silky texture used for artists' proofs. It is made from the inner bark of various trees cultivated in Japan, particularly the mulberry. See also *china paper*.

Japanese vellum: a thick, hand-made paper made in Japan. It has a pleasing ivory colour but if much handled by frequent reading the pages of books acquire a furry or flannel-like texture. There are European copies, one of which is marketed as *Japon*.

Jarry, Nicolas, fl.1633–53: one of the last great French calligraphers who copied mostly on vellum the small books of devotion which were fashionable among the circle of Louis XIV. Some were finely bound, probably by *Le Gascon*, q.v.

Jenson, Nicolaus, 1420–80: a punchcutter-printer of Venice whose work inspired generations of printers, especially in the 19th century English revival of fine printing. He was born at Sommevoire near Troyes in France, probably studied his craft at Mainz, and in 1470 established himself in Venice where he perfected the roman type face. (For a specimen see *letters – forms and styles*.)

Shortly after 1473, with the help of German capital, he formed a company known as 'Nicolaus Jenson et Socii'. Jenson issued more than seventy works in the decade of his activity, mostly Latin and Greek classics. Of these his edition of Pliny's 'Historia naturalis', 1472, is considered a monument of Renaissance printing. Many of his books were illuminated and decorated, and in some cases special vellum copies were impressed. See also *venetian types*.

Jesse tree: a theme chosen by medieval illuminators in which scriptural personages were shown springing from the loins of Jesse. (*Vide* Isaiah xi 1 'And there shall come forth a rod out of the stem of Jesse, and a branch shall grow out of his roots'.) The tree symbolized the continuity of lineage from David to Christ.

jest book: a collection of short humorous anecdotes or prose tales. Cuckolded husbands and erring priests figured in many, and some were based on actual events.

Jests had a long history of oral transmission and their sources were forgotten before manuscript collections were made. Many famous tales originated in the Muslim world (e.g. those of Ashab of Medina; 8th century, and Nasreddin Hodja, 14th century), reaching Europe via Spain and Italy. An early compilation of eastern tales was the 'Disciplina clericalis' of Petrus Alfonsi (Spain, early 12th century) which inspired later writers in France and Italy. Translations and adaptations passed from country to country.

In England Caxton printed some 'Fables of Poge the Florentyn' which, with some of the Alfonsi tales, he added at the end of his Aesop, 1484. 'Poge' was Poggio Bracciolini whose Latin 'Facetiae', widely circulated in manuscript, was printed in nineteen editions between 1470 and 1500. In making his English translation from a French version Caxton omitted the concomitant crudities of the original.

Wynkyn de Worde printed 'A mery jest of the frier and the boye' (STC 14522). Next was 'A C mery talys' (i.e. 'A hundred merry tales'), printed about 1526 by John Rastell who may have compiled it. Rastell's work was followed by 'The jests of Scoggin' by Andrew Borde, c. 1560?, and many others up to 1739 when the well-known 'Joe Miller's jests: or, the wit's vade-mecum' was published, to be reprinted with additions by other hands until the 19th century.

Jest books remained common reading in Europe for several centuries, but their ephemeral nature has meant that few copies of earlier editions have survived. See J. Wardroper, 'Jest upon jest', Routledge, 1970.

jetté en moule: see *Costeriana*.

jewelled bindings: covers of gold, silver, or silver-gilt, often encrusted with semi-precious stones surrounding a central ivory plaque, were made in Europe to enclose service books for the church from about the 6th century onwards. Such books were carried in procession and kept in the church sacristy, not in the monastic library. The use of the costliest materials to enclose the Gospels was an act of piety, not ostentation, and even the colours of the gems were symbolic, each associated with a mystical meaning. However, St Jerome, among others, condemned such lavishness when he said 'Gemmis codices vestiuntur et nudus ante fores emoritur Christus'.

Only slightly less costly were codices bound in coloured leathers with jewelled and gold ornamentation around a central portrait of the Emperor in 6th century Byzantium. Inevitably these books were plundered and stripped of their jewels when churches or monasteries were sacked, so survivals are rare. Sometimes an early carved ivory plaque would be inset in a later cover: those from 4th century consular diptychs were so used in the 9th century. St Gall and Metz were important centres where ivory was sculpted in the 9th and 10th centuries for use on book covers. In general, the making of gold and jewelled covers for church use diminished towards the end of the 13th century, but later examples were made for royal and noble patrons often with silver substituting for gold.

Quite different in purpose and technique were the

leather bindings with inset jewels made in the early 20th century. They were nearly all the work of the London binders *Sangorski and Sutcliffe*, q.v. Jewels were set in metal cups with a small base plate. The plates were pasted to the millboard, the bases being hidden by the leather of the cover which was cut so that only the jewel and the rim of its cup could be seen. For an illustration see *bookbinding*. See M. W. Elkind, 'Jewelled bindings, 1900–39', *Book Collector*, 24 Autumn 1975 401–16 and 25 Winter 1976 549–51. See also *champlevé, cloisonné*.

Jewish leather-cutting: an alternative name given to the *Lederschnitt* (cuir-ciselé) binding technique simply because in the 14th and 15th centuries German Jewish craftsmen were the principal workers in it. Their ornamentation often included grotesques.

Notable was Meir Jaffé of Ulm, master bookbinder and copyist, to whom some fifteen surviving examples are attributed. An official decree of 1468 invited 'Meyerlein, Juden von Ulm' to come to Nuremberg to bind a manuscript Pentateuch in this style. The binding, now in the Bavarian State Library (Cod. Hebr.212) is signed in Hebrew. Other bindings which may be his are in the Bamberg State Library. See also *Lederschnittbände*.

jobbing printing: display and commercial printing other than bookwork, periodical and newspaper work.

The term formerly meant any item of printed matter that could be worked off complete on a single sheet of paper or card and included handbills, trade cards, menus, invitation cards and the like. These items were normally set by a specialist compositor who was sometimes known in the trade as an 'art comp.' See also *publicity faces*.

jobbing types: types used for *jobbing printing*, q.v.

job inks: inks used for most book work and general printing; black pigment forms 25% of the weight, gums and oil forming the balance.

jogger: a machine for *knocking up* paper, q.v.

John of Lancaster, Duke of Bedford: see *Bedford, John of Lancaster, Duke of*.

John of Westphalia: see *De Westfalia, Johannes*.

Johnson, John: the author of a major manual on the history and art of printing, 'Typographia', 2 vols, London, 1824, a work of over twelve hundred pages. He was also associated with the *Lee Priory Press*, q.v. 'Typographia' was reprinted in 1967.

Johnston, Edward, 1872–1944: a teacher of calligraphy (Royal College of Art, 1920–35) whose influence on calligraphers and typographers was profound and widespread (particularly in Britain and Germany). This was partly due to his awareness of the fundamental principle that writing and printing are interdependent parts of a whole, and his ability to demonstrate and teach this. No less influential were his pupils Eric Gill and William Graily Hewitt, while Jan Tschichold admits to having studied Johnston's teachings as outlined in his 'Writing and illuminating, and lettering' (1906), Pitman, 1945.

The original broadsheet examples of Johnston's writing, published in 1916 by Douglas Pepler at Hammersmith, are now collectors' items. See P. Johnston, 'Edward Johnston', Faber, 1959, and E. Johnston, 'Formal penmanship', edited by H. Child, Lund Humphries, 1971.

joiner's press: the name given to the early printing presses which were made entirely of wood.

joint author: one who collaborates in the writing of a book with one or more associates. The part for which each is responsible is not always indicated.

joint publication: see *conger*.

joints: the parts on either side of a book about which the boards hinge; the abutments formed for the boards in *rounding* and *backing*, q.v.   (LK)
See also *cloth joints*, *french joints*.

Jones, George W., 1860–1942: a master printer, first employed as works manager of the Leicester printing firm Raithby, Lawrence & Co., where, as a means of improving technical and artistic standards he pioneered classes for young printers. He developed the idea by founding *The British Typographia* in 1887 as an association for others who shared his enthusiasm. Lectures and practical demonstrations were held in England and Scotland. The official journal, enthusiastically sponsored by his employers who also printed it, was first published in 1888 with the title *The British Printer*, q.v.

He later set up his own business in premises at The Sign of the Dolphin, Gough Square, London. His work was considered to be of the highest quality by the American H. L. Bullen who wrote 'George W. Jones is the best all-round printer that Great Britain has ever produced': not a view shared widely in Britain.

He was a friend of the punchcutter *Edward Prince*, q.v., who about 1914 cut for him both the Dolphin type, designed by E. Shanks inspired by the Jenson roman, and Venezia, issued commercially by Linotype in a recut version in 1928. The face is a compact, clear fount, well suited to close-set book work. Jones used Linotype Granjon to great effect in 1934 to print a fine edition of 'Canterbury Tales' for the Limited Editions Club of New York.

Jones, Owen, 1809–74: an architect, artist and lithographic printer of London who was one of the first printers to realise the possibilities lithography offered for colour and facsimile work. Important productions of the printing office he set up included an illustrated record of the Spanish Alhambra, 1836–46, various chromolithographed 'gift-books', his 'Illuminated books of the Middle Ages', 2 vols, 1844–9, and the 'Grammar of ornament', 1856, which included a hundred folio plates.

Jordan: a pulp-beating and refining machine used in making certain grades of paper; a cone fitted with blades revolves in an outer casing similarly fitted. It was invented in 1859 by Jordan of Hartford, Conn., U.S.A.

Joshua Roll: originally, a vellum roll bearing drawings in brown ink, occasionally tinted, depicting the life of Joshua. Whence it came is unknown, it having been suggested that it is a 10th century copy of a 5th century Alexandrian Greek original. Some of the scenes form a continuous frieze, others are self-contained. Short Greek extracts from the Book of Joshua appear among the scenes: they are written in a 10th century minuscule.

In 1571 it was owned by Ulrich von Fugger of Augsburg, passing by way of the Palatinate Library in Heidelberg to the Vatican (Palat.Gr.431). In 1902 the thirty-five foot roll was cut into pieces and put in an album.

journeyman: one who has completed his apprenticeship.

journey orders: orders collected from booksellers by publishers' travelling sales representatives.

journey terms: terms given by a publisher to a bookseller who has placed a re-order for a stock title with the publisher's traveller. Journey terms should not be confused with *subscription terms*, q.v., which are given on orders for a book before publication. See also *terms* (1).

Jugge, Richard, fl.1547–77: a London printer, said to have been educated at Eton and King's College. In 1552 he had a privilege to print the New Testament. In 1568, at which time he held with John Cawood the Bible patent, he issued the folio Bishops' Bible with copperplate illustrations. A curious feature of it was the printing of the N.T. on thicker paper than the Old since it was likely to be more used. After Cawood's death in 1572 the undertaking appears to have been too much for him, and the Stationers' Company

263

limited him to the printing of quarto editions of the Bible. On his death the Bible and Testament patents passed to Christopher Barker.

justification: 1. the spacing of words to a given width of line, done by the compositor when setting up type, or by machine as on the Monotype. The words will thus align at the right. In the early days of printing a compositor would often contract or modify spelling to simplify justification, a practice of the still earlier times when books were handwritten. See also *ragged right, spacebands*.

Justification in *computer-assisted typesetting*, q.v., has its own terminology, thus *hyphenless*, which indicates spacing between words and/or characters only; *discretionary*, indicates a code which can be interpreted as a hyphen at a meaningful line ending or be ignored within a line; *logic*, a routine by which the computer analyzes each word that must be divided, and inserts a hyphen at a point within the word, based on pre-determined parameters; *exception dictionary*, which is a file of words with permissible hyphenation points differing from those specified by the logic rules.

2. the levelling and squaring up by the typefounder or a specialist matrix maker of a *strike*, q.v. This highly skilled work is necessary to ensure that the face of a type character is at the correct depth and is even and regular; in short, that the design of the punchcutter will, after the further stage of casting type, be correctly aligned with and properly spaced from its fellows when impressed on paper.

justified left: see *ragged right*.

Justowriter: an American machine for typewriter type composition. Two electrically-driven units are used, each having a typewriter keyboard. As words are typed on paper on the first machine a tape is punched with a code for each character and the spacing needed to justify each line. When this tape is run through the second machine automatic interpretation of the punched code produces automatically typed and justified lines. The type can be any one of several type-faces fitted by the manufacturer. The finished and corrected page can be reproduced by photo-offset or gravure. This process is classed as *near-print*, q.v.

A modified Justowriter will produce tape for the *Justotext* photosetting unit introduced in 1969.

jute board: a light but strong binding board.

K

Kalinga Prize: an award of £1,000 made on behalf of Unesco to a writer whose work has contributed to the popularization of science. Recipients have included Bertrand Russell, Julian Huxley and the Indian writer Jagjit Singh.

Kalthoeber, Christian Samuel, fl.1780–1813: a German bookbinder working in London. In 1781 he succeeded to the business of *Baumgarten*, q.v., from whom he had learned his craft. Kalthoeber was an outstanding craftsman and was responsible for the introduction of a number of new binding styles. He was Beckford's first English binder.

After his business failed in 1808 Kalthoeber worked for the comte de *Caumont*, q.v.

Kastenbein, Karl: of Kassel. The man who in 1869 patented the first mechanical type composing machine to be used by a London newspaper (*The Times*, from 1872 to 1908). The actual inventor was a Parisian typesetter with whom Kastenbein had shared a garret. On the machine, which was developed for practical use in *The Times* office, there was a bank of eighty-four keys. Type was stored in vertical tubes from which characters were released in response to the tapping of the keyboard and guided to an assembly point. Here they were removed for justification. There was also a distributing machine, pedal-powered, as was the setter.

keep down: an instruction to the compositor to use capitals sparingly, Cf. *keep up*.

keep in: 1. said of type which does not take up much lateral space.

2. an instruction to the compositor that narrow spaces are to be inserted between words. Cf. *drive out*.

keep out: to use unnecessarily wide interword spacing so that matter makes as many lines as possible. See also *fat matter, lean matter*.

keepsake: a variety of illustrated *annual*, q.v., popular in France, America and England where the first to be entitled 'The keepsake', published by Charles Heath, was issued regularly between 1829 and 1857.

Lady Blessington edited this from 1841–50, to be followed by her niece Margaret Power from 1851–7. Editions were about 15,000 copies.

Such books were very fashionable among the upper middle classes who did not require any profound text but expected illustrations by the best artists: hence the occasional appearance in many of fine steel engravings from drawings by Turner. Silk covers made the books attractive Christmas gifts. See A. Renier, 'Friendship's offering', Private Libraries Association, 1964.

keep standing: an instruction to the printer to hold type after running off for a possible reprinting. The printer charges a rental for holding it. See also *dead matter, distribute, standing type*.

keep up: in setting type, an instruction to the compositor to use capital letters to begin each word of the title of any book mentioned in the text of a work, though usually internal articles, prepositions and conjunctions are *kept down*, thus 'The Tale of Four Men Stranded on an Island'. Also known as *all up* setting.

Modern practice, as seen in the publications of the British Library, the British National Bibliography and elsewhere, is to capitalize proper names only, printing the above example as 'The tale of four men stranded on an island'. This is neater, saves space, and is found by many to be quicker to read. Also known as *all down* setting.

In French practice only the first word following the initial article (other than proper names) is capitalized, e.g. 'L'Apparition du livre'. In Italian printing only the initial article is capitalized, e.g. 'La vedova sceltra'. In German all nouns begin with a capital.

Keere, Hendrik van den, c. 1540–80: of Ghent, where his grandfather bought the Lambrecht foundry in 1553 and where his father (also *Hendrik*) was a printer. Hendrik worked as a punchcutter, founder, binder and bookseller, becoming one of the most accomplished craftsmen of his day. Of importance were his fine roman types, with large x-height, which influenced other Dutch designers for many years. He cut nine founts. His gothics, of which he cut twelve, continued in use until the early 19th century. He also cut seven music types of which the six-line pica single-impression characters were notable. The civilité type he cut in 1570 and named 'mediaan geschreven' was less successful.

Van den Keere started working for Plantin in 1568, and after the death of Tavernier and Guyot in 1570 he did all Plantin's punchcutting, matrix making and casting. Forty sets of his punches and matrices survive in the Plantin Museum. Other matrices were sold to his foreman de Vechter who settled in Lyons.

He was also known as *Henri du Tour*. His son *Pieter* (1571–1646) went to London in 1584 and joined *Jodocus Hondius*, q.v., who married his sister. While in England Pieter's work included the engraved maps for Norden's 'Speculum Britanniae', 1592. After returning to Amsterdam, probably in 1593, he continued to work with Hondius and later *Jansson*, q.v., as well as for English publishers. Notable were his engraved maps for the 'Prospect of the most famous parts of the world' which Speed published in 1646.

Kefer (or **Keffer**), **Heinrich**, fl.1455–73?: an associate of Johann Gutenberg. It was suggested in *Gutenberg Jahrbuch*, 1950 that Kefer may have settled in Mainz about 1459 and there printed the 36-line Bible (see, however, *Pfister*) and that he later went to Nuremberg where Sensenschmidt had established the first press in 1470. Together they issued in 1473 the 'Pantheologia' of Rainerius de Pisis.

Kells, Book of: an important example of Hiberno-Saxon art, written and painted at either the Columbian monastery of Iona or the Abbey of Kells in Ireland, and probably in the late 8th or early 9th century. The 340 surviving folia contain an incomplete Latin text of the Gospels, written in a combination of uncial and round half-uncial scripts, the version being the Irish recension of the Vulgate.

The ornamentation includes leaf and plant forms, zoomorphic forms, interlaced strapwork patterns and curious barbaric figures. The use of lapis lazuli blue, the unusual square punctuation marks, and the introduction of vine foliage as a new element in Celtic art all suggest a later date for its composition than the 7th–8th century once assigned. No gold was used. Since 1661 the work has been in Trinity College, Dublin. See 'The book of Kells: reproductions from the manuscript . . .', Thames & Hudson, 1974.

Kelmscott Press: the private press founded at Hammersmith, London, in 1891 by William Morris in close association with *Emery Walker*, q.v. They turned for their inspiration to the roman types of the 15th century and woodcut title-pages. Work was based on the double page opening as a unit. The fifty or so books to leave the press during the eight years of its existence had a great influence on other private press owners in England, Germany and America. The

266

quality of materials used, with the care and attention given to detail make them a fine achievement. They were costly, collected by eager bibliophiles, and usually over-subscribed before publication.

The special types cut for Morris by *E. P. Prince*, q.v., were the Golden, 1890, based on types of Jenson and Rubeus; the gothic Troy, 1891; and the Chaucer of 1892 which was a re-cutting in a smaller size of the Troy. See H. H. Sparling, 'The Kelmscott Press and William Morris', Macmillan, 1924, repr. Dawsons, 1975; and 'William Morris: ornamentations and illustrations from the Kelmscott Chaucer', Dover, 1973, in which 100 pages are shown.

kerfs: two shallow grooves sawn into the back of the gathered sections of a book, about ¼in. from the top and bottom. The loops of the *kettle-stitches*, q.v., fit into them.

kerned letters: type faces in which part of the letter projects beyond the body, e.g. an italic *f* which is kerned on both sides.

Kerned type

Kerver, Thielman, fl.1497–1522: a German printer and publisher of devotional books who worked in Paris. He printed many Books of Hours, some with woodcuts by Tory, others copied from those of Pigouchet and Vostre in their Horae. His attractive woodcut device was of two unicorns under a tree.

Kessler, Harry, Graf von: see *Cranach-Presse*.

kettle-stitch: in flexible sewing, the linking or catch-up stitch at the head and tail of each section. See also *hand-sewing*, *kerfs*.

key: 1. in colour printing, the block, plate or stone used to fix position and register.

2. a binder's tool used to secure the bands when hand sewing.

keyboard: the bank of keys on a typesetter.

keyboard layout: see *QWERTY keyboard*.

keying: 1. tapping off copy on a typesetter to produce

either a perforated spool of paper or tape from which individual types are cast, as in *Monotype*, or to release matrices from which a slug is cast, as in *Linotype*, qq.v.

2. entering numbers sequentially in the margins of a typescript to indicate where illustrations are to be positioned. The copy for illustrations and their captions must be correspondingly numbered.

khoran: literally 'tabernacle', being an ornate head-piece with a geometric pattern in gold and colours, featured in the concordance tables and title-pages of Armenian Gospel manuscripts.

kier: the papermaking boiler in which raw materials are cooked under steam pressure.

kill: to distribute type for a job when no longer required. See also *dead matter*, *live matter*.

King Athelstan's Psalter: see *Athelstan Psalter*.

Kingsford, Florence, 1871–1949: a pupil of *Edward Johnston*, q.v., and an outstanding illuminator of the present century. She embellished some sixty books, notable among them being the Ashendene Press edition of 'The song of songs', 1902.

In 1907 she married Sir Sydney Cockerell.

King's Gold Medal for Poetry: see *Queen's Gold Medal for Poetry*.

King's Printer: see *Queen's Printer*.

Kippenberg, Anton, 1874–1950: from 1905 the director of the *Insel-Verlag*, q.v. He was also famous as a Goethe scholar and writer.

kipskin: a skin midway between calf and cowhide, sometimes used for bookbinding.

Kis, Nicholas: a Hungarian punchcutter and printer who learned his craft in Amsterdam about 1680, probably from Dirk Voskens. It was in that city that he printed a fine Hungarian Bible in 1685. For a time he also worked in England where a two-line italic attributed to him was bought by Oxford University Press in 1695. See also *Janson* and Appendix A.

kiss impression: one in which the ink is deposited on the paper by the lightest possible surface contact and is not impressed into it. This technique is required when printing on coated papers. It is also the principle when printing from rubber plates, and means that less ink is used and that there is less wear on the press. Presses built specially for printing from rubber plates can be of lighter construction. See also *dwell*.

Kleukens, Friedrich Wilhelm, 1878–1956: a German graphic arts teacher and type-designer who directed the Ernst Ludwig-Presse at Darmstadt from 1907–14. He designed four special types for the press (obtainable from Bauersche Giesserei and D. Stempel). From 1914 his brother *Christian Heinrich Kleukens* (1880–1954) directed the press before founding the Kleukens-Presse in 1919, and the Mainzer-Presse in 1929. The latter also wrote several books on printing and typography.

Klič, Karl, 1841–1926: the inventor of modern doctor-blade photogravure. From 1875–78 he evolved an etching process with the transfer of carbon tissue, Klíčotype, intended for producing letterpress blocks; but which developed into what we now call *photogravure*, q.v. The first photogravure reproductions were printed by Pisani, a Viennese copperplate printer, but Klič kept the process secret until it was made public in 1886 without his permission. In 1890 he made a thorough study of calico printing at Neunkirchen (Austria) and of the *doctor blade* already used for such work. By 1894, by the introduction of the cross-line screen and using carbon tissue, invented by Sir Joseph Swan, he succeeded in combining photogravure and doctor-blade printing in the process now known by the name *intaglio printing*. By that time he had removed to England where the Rembrandt Intaglio Printing Co. was established at Lancaster under his direction. Even then he preserved the secret of producing these 'Rembrandt Prints' which were first issued in 1895. Colour printing of great technical perfection was also produced. In 1906 Klič returned to Vienna. His name is also spelled *Klietsch*. (GU)

Klingspor, Karl, 1869–1950: a distinguished German typefounder of Offenbach am Main. His firm traces its origins to the Rudhard'sche Giesserei, founded in 1842, which Klingspor's father bought for him in 1891. His first type, cut by Heinz König, was a Schwabacher. The next, by Otto Eckmann, appeared in 1900. In 1906 the firm traded as Gebr. Klingspor, continuing do to so until its acquisition by Stempel AG in the 1950s.

Karl Klingspor commissioned several gifted designers whose work was to win European acclaim. Notable were *Walter Tiemann*, q.v., who designed his first type in 1909; *Rudolph Koch*, q.v., who designed several faces after his first in 1910; *Otto Hupp* and *Emil Weiss*, qq.v.

In 1953 the Klingspor Museum was opened in Offenbach to further the art of modern book design. Among collections to be seen there is one of bindings by *Ignatz Wiemeler*, q.v.

Klischograph: a German electronic photoengraving machine which produces a plastic, zinc, copper or magnesium half-tone plate. The original to be reproduced is placed face down on a glass plate, a blank plastic printing plate (face up) is fitted above it, and the two are clamped. An optical device (or scanner) under the table is used to scan the original, light reflected from the picture being picked up by two photoelectric cells. These transmit impulses through amplifiers to the engraving head above the plastic plate, and hence to the V-shaped engraving needle which digs dots of a size and depth varying in relation to the brightness of the original. The engraving head is stationary and the plastic plate and original are reciprocated under it, scanning being done diagonally. As each line is completed the scanner returns into position for the next line. The machine will also engrave the back of the plate for removing highlight areas. The Klischograph, also known in Britain as the *Clichograph*, was devised by Dr Rudolph Hell of Kiel in 1953.

There is a Klischograph for making separate colour blocks for three- and four-colour printing. Scanning and engraving are done as on the standard model, but colour filters are used to separate the image into primary colours. The fine point of light which scans the original image is picked up by two photoelectric cells. The first of these transmits, via an amplifier, information about the primary colour: the second controls the electrical operation for colour correction. These impulses control the engraving needle fixed above the rotating engraving table. Models are continually updated.

knife folding: see *folding machine*.

Knight, Charles, 1791–1873: a London bookseller and publisher who believed that cheaply produced books could further mass education. In 1838 he patented a method of colour printing in which four relief blocks of wood or metal were rotated and impressed in turn on to a sheet of paper. Thus each print was built up and finished before another copy was begun. The method lapsed after 1847, in which year it was used for Knight's 'Old England's worthies'.

knocking copy: a colloquialism for uncomplimentary phrases in a book review which are extracted from their context and used in advertisements for the same book with the intention of provoking sales: 'An odious book' (*Daily Telegraph*), 'A sickening book' (*Sunday Times*), and 'A superb pity' (*New Statesman*) are quoted examples. Cf. *gutting*.

knocking up: the adjustment on one or two edges of a pile of printed or unprinted sheets so that they can be cut squarely, or used for some purpose requiring squared-up sheets. Thin paper is often knocked up in a jogger, particularly between printing and cutting.
(GU)

R. A. Knox Prize: an award made on the recommendation of the tutorial committee of Trinity College, Oxford, for meritorious performance in one of the Honours schools for Literae Humaniores, History, Theology, English literature or Modern languages. It was announced in 1960.

Koberger, Anton, 1440–1513: a printer and entrepreneur of Nuremberg. He began printing about 1470, his first dated book being Alcinous's 'Disciplinarum Platonis epitome', 1472. He printed Bibles, philosophical and theological works. By 1509 he had twenty-four presses, yet so extensive was his business that he had to commission other printers. He also had a bindery for completing books sold locally (exporting was in sheets). He was one of the most enterprising publishers of the day with sales outlets in Budapest, Cologne, Frankfurt, Lyons, Paris, Vienna and Warsaw.

His best known productions included the 'Schatzbehalter' of 1491 with whole-page cuts by *Wolgemut*, q.v., and the 'Liber chronicarum', 1493, of *Hartmann Schedel*, q.v., (also known as 'Die Weltchronik' and 'Nuremberg Chronicle'): the presswork of this outline of geography and history was not of a very high standard and many of the blocks were repeated. They were also copied by *Schönsperger*, q.v., for his Augsburg edition of 1496. The Apocalypse, printed by Koberger in Latin and German editions in 1498, was also important since it included woodcuts attributed to Dürer. See A. Wilson, 'The making of the Nuremberg Chronicle', Amsterdam, 1977. See also *woodcut*.

Koch, Rudolph, 1876–1934: born in Nuremberg. He was an artist-craftsman whose interest in calligraphy and type designing dated from 1906 in which year he joined *Klingspor*, q.v., for whom he created some twenty type faces, gothic and roman. All his founts derived from written hands. Of his gothics the Deutsche Schrift, 1910, was notable; many showed the influence of the 'Jugendstil'. His early romans were perhaps too mannered to win trade acceptance in England (e.g. his Antiqua, 1922). Other types included Maximilian, 1914; the heavy capitals Neuland, 1922–3; and the sanserif Kabel (Cable), 1926–9. He also designed booklets, bookcovers, posters, hand-lettered texts in broadside form, and a fine edition of the four Gospels, Klingspor, 1926.

Concurrently with his Klingspor appointment Koch was a type designer and teacher at the School of Lettering in the Offenbach Arts and Crafts College where the many talented pupils he attracted were known as the 'Offenbacher Schreiber': *Berthold Wolpe*, q.v., was one of them. See also *Beauclair, The Dolphin*.

His son *Paul Koch*, also a typographer and teacher of note, had a workshop at Haus Fürsteneck in

Frankfurt-am-Main: his pupils included *Will Carter* and *Hermann Zapf*, qq.v.

Kodak Colour Proofing System: a patented system for making pre-press proofs with consistency, speed and simplicity from half-tone positive separations by exposing in sequence four light-sensitive matrices consisting of pigmented polymers (black, magenta, yellow and cyan) and transferring them in succession and in register on to coated paper stock with heat and pressure. Between each transfer the transferred polymer must be hardened with an overall flash exposure to prevent back transfer. A modified proofing press is used to make these transfers.

The half-tone positives are exposed on to the four light-sensitive matrices, and as the matrices are balanced for speed all can be exposed at one time.

The black matrix is placed on the register pins of the press cylinder and the press is set in forward motion. As the matrix passes across the heated platen the unexposed areas are softened and transferred to the paper which is held on the bed of the press. As the cylinder is reversed in travel a high-intensity pulsed xenon light source is automatically turned on. This hardens the transferred polymer so that the next colour will trap it. The same procedure is followed for the other three colours.

Kodak Photomechanical Transfer System (PMT): a quick and economical method of producing: 1. top quality screened prints for paste-up; 2. reflex proofs by contact (in room light) from paste-up originals; 3. enlarged or reduced copy line work without the need for intermediate film negatives.

The four basic materials used are: 1. PMT Negative Paper for screen and line camera use; 2. PMT Reflex Paper for contact proofs; 3. PMT Receiver Paper to receive the transferred image; 4. PMT Activator for processing in a diffusion transfer processor. They make it possible, and for the first time, to produce a screened positive print from an original continuous tone photograph without having to make an intermediate film negative.

Procedure is by three simple stages: 1. expose the Kodak PMT Negative Paper through a contact screen (up to 120 lines per inch ruling) to the continuous tone black and white print in the camera; 2. after exposure feed the PMT Negative Paper together with a sheet of PMT Receiver Paper into a diffusion transfer processor; 3. thirty seconds later peel away the two papers to yield a screen positive print having a full half-tone scale and free from filled-in shadows and burned out highlights.

The process can also be used to prepare sized-up linework and quick page-proofs from original copy.

The Kodak PMT System, introduced in the early 1970s, offers the advantage of working from completed full-page paste-up and the elimination of intermediate film negatives, giving shorter production time and lower material costs. No matter how the PMT System is used only one film negative is required, namely the one used to make the final plate.

Kodalith MP System: introduced in the early 1970s as the first system to be designed exclusively for mechanized processing and offering as its main advantages compatibility (no product intermix problems), speed (higher film speeds and faster through-put times), and stable chemistry (from a new liquid developer and replenisher to maintain a constant activity and minimize stand-by losses).

Initially three new films were introduced: 1. *Kodalith MP Ortho Film* which gives superb dot quality and enhanced dot etching characteristics, and has an emulsion speed sufficiently fast to enable the film to be used not only as a normal camera speed film, but also as a lateral reversal film; 2. *Kodalith MP High Speed Duplicating Film*, a fast film combining the qualities of the current High Speed Duplicating Film with MP compatibility; 3. *Kodalith MP Contact Film* offering dot for dot characteristics with MP compatibility.

With no intermix problems a 100% load of any one of the films or any intermix of them can be processed without introducing any control restrictions.

Koebau: the trade name of Schnellpressenfabrik König & Bauer AG of Würzburg, the printing machine business established in 1817 by Friedrich König and Friedrich Andreas Bauer. See *König*.

Koelhoff, Johann, fl.1472–93: an early printer of Cologne, remembered as having been the first to print *signatures*, q.v. His early types were cut in the Venetian manner of Wendelin da Spira and it is probable that Koelhoff learned his craft in Venice before going to Cologne. His fame rests on the 'Cologne Chronicle' which he began in 1499. Over seventy of his publications are in the British Library. He was succeeded by his son of the same name who worked in Cologne until 1502. See also *Ulrich Zel*.

Koenig: an alternative spelling of *König*, q.v., and the form used in his English patents.

Kohen, Gershom, d. 1594: an important early printer of Hebrew works in Prague where his family business continued, with minor interruptions, from 1526 to 1784. With his brother *Jerome* he printed the first illustrated Passover 'Haggadah' in 1526 with sixty woodcuts, mostly by Hayyim Shahor. In 1527 Kohen obtained a privilege as sole printer of Hebrew in Bohemia. With his sons *Solomon* and *Mordecai* (d. 1592) the family issued many editions of prayer books and Pentateuchs. They had an agent in Cracow and in 1535 sold books at *Frankfurt Fair*, q.v. Their exclusive right to print Hebrew books was renewed until the early 1600s, but books imported by Christian printers in Italy diminished its effectiveness.

In 1784 the firm merged with the rival printing business of *Jacob Bak* (d. 1618), another German Jewish printer whose descendants were still active.

König, Friedrich, 1774–1833: the inventor of the cylinder press. In 1803 König began construction of what might be called an automatic hand-press in Wolfgang Kummer's workshop at Suhl. It performed automatically the inking up, running the bed, printing, and return of the bed. It was made of wood and iron. In 1806 König went to London and in 1807 began a partnership with *Thomas Bensley*, q.v., and others to finance the patenting and development of König's inventions. The first of these (patented 1810) was an all-iron steam-powered platen press which was completed in 1811. As with the Suhler press of 1803 this had an automatic inker, the fluid being forced from an ink-box on to a leather-covered roller. The only manual task was laying on and taking off the sheets of paper, and König claimed that the first part of any book to be printed by machine, as distinct from a hand-press, was sheet (H) of the *New Annual Register* for 1810 in an edition of 3,000 copies worked off in April 1811.

The second (1811) and third patents (1813) were for a cylinder press in operation in 1812; sheets G and H of Clarkson's 'Life of Penn', vol. 1, were the first ever printed on a powered cylinder machine (at 800 iph). A double machine consisting of two single presses built symmetrically round a central inking system was ordered by J. Walter, owner of *The Times* and first used for the issue of 29 November 1814.

König began his collaboration with F. A. Bauer (1790–1860) in 1810, a German mechanic living in London. They introduced tape feeding and delivery among other improvements, and in 1814 patented a perfector press, installed in 1816 in the premises of Bensley where it was used to print books at the rate of 900–1,000 perfected sheets an hour. This, of course, obviated the need for a second press. König's partner Bauer reported that the second edition of Elliotson's translation of Blumenbach's 'Institutions of physiology' was the first book wholly printed by a machine. König continued to improve the register, inking, and speeds of his machines.

Bauer later alleged that Bensley, having secured the controlling share of the partnership, hindered sale of the machines to other printers to benefit his own business (the machine was later referred to as 'Bensley's'). Other press makers, notably Cowper who brought out his perfector in 1819, based their models on König's machines without acknowledgement. König and Bauer had many detractors who accused them of having plagiarized the never-realised ideas of William Nicholson.

In 1817 König entered into sole partnership with Bauer (see *Koebau*). He then returned to Germany while Bauer remained in London to complete the first successful single-cylinder two-revolution press. In Würzburg, after initial difficulties, the firm was firmly established. When König died he was succeeded by Bauer and subsequently by his sons *Friedrich II* and *Wilhelm König*. See 'The first printing machines . . .', Leipzig, Brockhaus, 1851. See also illustrations under *letterpress machines*.

Koran: or *Quran*, the sacred book of Islam, being the word of God as made known to his Prophet Mohammed by the angel Gabriel. These revelations, which began about AD 610, cover a period of twenty years and are the foundation of the Islamic faith.

While probably written or dictated during Mohammed's lifetime the present arrangement of its 114 *suras*, or chapters, is of later date. The first complete written version is attributed to Mohammed's secretary, Zayid ibn Thābit. A later recension was made in 651 by Zayid and three others during the reign of 'Othmān, and this is still the standard text. Copies were sent to the main cities of the caliphate and the work of preparing them grew into an esteemed and important craft. Sumptuous examples, illuminated in gold and colours were made, the finest being Persian. The earliest dated complete Koran (AD 784) is now in Cairo. Modern oriental editions are usually hand-written and then lithographed.

Copies of an Arabic edition printed about 1520 by Paganino de Paganini do not survive, if they ever existed (it being claimed that all were burned by Papal decree) and the editio princeps is considered to be Abraham Hinckelmann's edition printed at Hamburg by Schultz-Schiller in 1694. For Gustave Flügel's edition 'Corani textus arabicus', printed in red and black by Friedrich Nies at Leipzig in 1834 a somewhat heavy type was specially cut. The first *official* version printed from type was issued by the Egyptian Government in 1925.

The first European translation, albeit somewhat inaccurate, was one into Latin commissioned about 1143 by Petrus Venerabilis, Abbot of Cluny. It was the work of Robert of Chester and Herbert of Dalmatia. The editio princeps of this, with prefaces by Luther Melancthon, was published in three volumes by Theodore Bibliander at Basle in 1543. Two better Latin translations were Lodovico Maraccio's 'Alcorani textus universus', Padua, 1698, which also had an Arabic text and commentary, and that of Adrian Reland entitled 'De religione Mohammedica', Utrecht, 1705. For the Muslim, however, a translation into another language is no longer truly a Koran since only Arabic script can reproduce the language in which the word of God was revealed to the Prophet Mohammed.

An English Koran was published in 1649. This was

a translation by Alexander Ross of Du Ryer's French version of the Arabic text, but the best known and first of several direct translations into English was George Sale's, printed by C. Ackers for J. Wilcox in 1734. See also *Arabic calligraphy, arabic type, Islamic illumination, Persian illumination.*

Krause, Jakob, 1531–86: the most famous German bookbinder, born at Zwickau where he was apprenticed. After working briefly in Paris he settled in Augsburg where he worked for Antonius Flander, a Venetian master binder of Flemish origin. In 1561 he was independent.

From 1566–85 he worked in Dresden as court binder to Augustus, Elector of Saxony in whose library, now the State Library, over a thousand Krause bindings survived until World War II. His work was remarkable for its technical excellence, precision of gold tooling and finishing detail, though the elaborate and often heavy decoration may seem excessive to non-German eyes. Many of his books had painted or goffered fore-edges. For an illustration see *bookbinding.* See Ilsa Schunke, 'Leben und Werk Jakob Krauses', Leipzig, Insel-Verlag, 1943.

Krause, Karl: a German precision-instrument maker who in 1855 established a business in Leipzig which is still active. The firm has made several contributions to the development of machines for the graphic industries. In 1857 a new gilding press was introduced, in 1858 a new guillotine and in 1877 a three-bladed *guillotine,* q.v. In the 1920s the firm brought out a *step-and-repeat machine,* q.v.   (GU)

Krimpen, Jan van, 1892–1958: a famous type-designer who in 1925 became artistic adviser to the Dutch printing firm Enschedé en Zonen. Types of his known in Britain are Lutetia, Romulus, Antigone, Romanée, Spectrum and Cancelleresca: they were cut by P. H. Rädisch. (For a specimen of Spectrum see Appendix A.)

Van Krimpen also designed a face for the Oxford University Press. He was also well known for his designs for books and postage stamps. See J. Dreyfus, 'The work of J. van Krimpen', Sylvan Press, 1952, and J. van Krimpen, 'On designing and devising type', Sylvan Press, 1957.

Kunera Press: (or *Kunera-Pers*), the name to which J. F. van Royen changed his *Zilverdistel Press,* q.v., in 1923.

L

labels: paper, or other material separate from that used for covering a book, on which the author's name and title are printed or engraved and glued to the spine or front board. Such labels in England belong to the era 1760–1830, and were usual on books sold in boards, but their use has not entirely ceased.

On another style of label the title was printed in large type as a vertical strip on one of the otherwise blank leaves of the first or last section of a book. To be used it had to be cut out and pasted on the spine so that the lettering ran from bottom to top. These *vertical title labels* were occasionally used in England during the last half of the 17th century. See also *flyswing, lettering on the spine, panel*.

label title: the name given to the first form of title-page in early printed books (1470–1550). Title and author's name were printed on an otherwise blank protecting leaf at the beginning of a book. The earliest extant example is a Papal Bull printed at Mainz in 1463, probably by Schöffer; a second is the 'Sermo ad populum' of Rolewinck printed in 1470 by Arnold ter Hoernen. The first English label title was printed by Machlinia for the 'Treatise of the pestilence', c. 1489.

Label titles were sometimes printed from wooden blocks, thus the addition of an illustration was easy: an example is seen in the 'Testament' of Lydgate printed in 1515 by Pynson. See also *incipit, title page*.

Laboratory Press: an American school press founded in 1923 at the Carnegie Institute of Technology in Pittsburgh by Porter Garnett. It published reprints of rare books, keepsakes, etc., great attention being paid to the faithful reproduction of the originals. Work was done by students on a hand press, and the standard was very high. Garnett remained with the press until 1935. In 1963 the press had a brief revival under the name New Laboratory Press. See W. Leuba, 'A Porter Garnett list', *The Black Art*, 3 1964–5.

lace bindings: a style of book-cover decoration devised in the 18th century by Parisian craftsmen. Elaborate tooling of a broad lace-like border covered most of the cover, with a small space in the centre for an armorial shield. The finest examples were made by Pierre-Paul

Dubuisson and the Deromes. Also known as *dentelle bindings*.

lace borders: lace-like borders occasionally found in 19th century French books as a frame for an illustration. The paper is pierced as in a paper doily.

laced on: said of boards which are held to the book by the cords on to which the sections have been sewn. The cords, with their ends splayed and moistened with paste, pass through holes pierced in the boards. The ends are hammered flat. See also *holding out*.

lacertine animals: a name for the elongated animal forms used from the 8th century as part of the ornamentation in manuscript illustration. The bodies of animals formed involved patterns and terminated in the head of a lion, dog or lizard, etc.

lacing in: attaching boards to a hand-sewn book prior to fitting on a leather cover. See also *slips*.

lacquered bindings: 15th to 19th century Persian, Turkish and Indian bindings decorated with a painted miniature on one or both boards, and without a fold-over flap. The craft is particularly associated with Persia where an early lacquer-painted binding was made at Herat about 1483. It was on leather from which the paint later cracked and flaked off. About 1540 pasteboard edged with leather was used. The board was sized, given several coats of lacquer, dried and polished. A design in gold and colours was then painted on it, followed when dry by a final protective coating of lacquer. See also *Persian illumination*.

laid paper: paper which shows a series of ribbed lines when held up to light, the vertical or *chain lines* being about 25 mm. apart and the horizontal or *laid lines* being close together. This effect is caused by the weave of the *dandy roll*, q.v., in machine-made papers or by the wires of the *mould* in hand-made papers. (Cf. *wove paper*.) To obtain a good impression on laid paper care should be taken that the narrow lines run across the page, the wide lines down it. See also *water lines, wire-mark*.

Laing, John, 1809–80: the Edinburgh librarian who

compiled jointly with *Samuel Halkett*, q.v., 'A dictionary of the anonymous and pseudonymous literature of Great Britain', 1882–8.

Lair, Johann, 1476–1554: the printer of Siegburg near Cologne who worked in England as *John Siberch*, q.v.

Lambeth Bible: a mid-12th century manuscript of the Bible which has been in Lambeth Palace Library since 1610. It is in two volumes of which the text of the first is completed by the second volume of another Bible. The missing original second volume, now in Maidstone Museum, has been badly mutilated.

The first volume, written in Romanesque script, has six large illuminated pages as well as decorated and historiated initials. The style of illumination owes much to the Bury Bible of *c.* 1130–40, decorated by the secular artist Master Hugo, which showed strong Byzantine influences. Pastel shades are used in the Lambeth Bible, blue, mauve, and brown being the dominant colours. The figures are drawn with an emphasis on linear pattern. See C. R. Dodwell, 'The great Lambeth Bible', Faber, 1959.

Lambinet, Pierre, *c.* 1742–1813: a Belgian historian of printing whose important 'Recherches historiques . . . sur l'origine de l'imprimerie' was published at Brussels in 1799, with an enlarged edition, Paris, 1810.

Lambrecht, Joos, fl.1536–53: a poet, engraver, punchcutter, type-founder and printer of Ghent. He cut four roman types, the use of which he tried to popularize locally for printing works in Dutch. His types were also sold in England.

In 1553 he sold his presses and foundry to *Pieter van den Keere* whose grandson *Hendrik II*, q.v., later inherited sets of matrices. Lambrecht afterwards moved to Germany where he died in 1556.

lambskin: a smooth-finished leather used for binding; it is similar to calf but less durable.

lamination: in the context of this book, the adhering of a transparent film to printed paper. This will enhance the appearance and increase the durability of book jackets and paperback covers.

The work is done on a machine fitted with a device to unwind a reel of cellulose acetate film (*c.* 0·0008in. thick), a coating head which applies to the film a layer of transparent adhesive (solvent-based such as industrial spirit of trichloroethylene), and a drying tunnel where hot air evaporates excess solvents in the adhesive.

After the adhesive-bearing film emerges from the tunnel, still in a tacky state, it is married to the printed paper as they pass through nipping rollers (which may be hot or cold). Some machines have a heated laminating drum instead of a drying tunnel.

The suitability of inks and paper for such jobs must be established by preliminary testing. Another factor which may affect the result is the anti set-off spray used during printing; any residue on the sheet will prevent perfect adhesion. Cf. *nitrocellulose lacquering, varnishing*.

lampblack: pure carbon, and the most important ingredient of black printing *ink*, q.v. From the time of Gutenberg, to whom the suitability for printing of an oil-based black pigment may reasonably be attributed, until the end of the 18th century, printers made their own ink from jealously-guarded recipes. Properties required of all inks were (and are) ready transferability to the paper surface (and retention by it) without penetrating the underside of the sheet, adherance to the paper, good, non-fading colour and rapid drying.

Carbon black could be obtained by burning resinous wood or pitch in an enclosed space (e.g. a tent) and collected by scraping from the surface. Residual tar was removed by burning it with spirits of wine. The ink was made in the 'Lamp Black house'. Old linseed oil was clarified of fatty matter by boiling brown bread crusts and onions in it, which at the same time increased viscosity and promoted drying. After cooling, the black was added.

An interesting selection of old ink recipes is given in C. H. Bloy's 'A history of printing ink . . .', Adams & Mackay, 1967.

Modern ink making is a matter of chemical technology. Lampblack for the best black inks is obtained by burning natural gas with a restricted air supply. The carbon so formed collects in iron channels from which it is removed by scraping. Cheaper blacks are made by burning oil in a furnace. There is also some use of organic lampblack obtained by carbonising animal bones.

landscape format: see *oblong*.

Lanston, Tolbert, 1844–1913: the inventor of the *Monotype* typesetting and casting machines, q.v. Lanston was born at Troy, Ohio, U.S.A., and was originally a lawyer. He took out his first patent in 1885, being sponsored by J. M. Dove, and an early model was shown at the Columbian World Fair, 1893. Production began in 1894 in Philadelphia where Sellers & Co. built the machines. John Bancroft of this firm was in charge, and by 1899 had considerably improved technical details, giving the machine the basis of its subsequent form.

To seek capital four Monotype machines were shipped to London in 1897. While crossing the Atlantic the Earl of Dunraven learned of the machine and later formed a syndicate to secure British rights for £220,000. In the same year the Lanston Monotype Corporation was founded with a capital of £550,000. The name was changed to The Monotype Corporation in 1931, and in 1975 to Monotype International for world-wide operations.

A detailed history is given in *The Monotype Recorder*, 1949.

lapidary: a treatise on the magical and medical properties which precious stones were thought to have, beliefs handed down from pagan times. Such works were popular in medieval Europe, notable being the 'Liber lapidum', a late 11th century poem composed by Marbode, bishop of Rennes. See J. Evans and M. S. Serjeant, 'Medieval lapidaries', EETS, 1933.

lapis lazuli: the ultramarine pigment used in manuscript painting, for which purpose it was known in 7th century Byzantium if not earlier. In Europe in the late 12th century an improved quality was made. Finely powdered lapis lazuli, resin, gum mastic, wax and linseed oil were made into a paste. After being kept for some days the paste was clarified in a warm alkaline solution and the pure ultramarine floated on the surface for collection.

laps: thick sheets of semi-dry wood pulp supplied by a pulping mill to a papermaker. Wood pulp is sent from Scandinavia to Britain in this form. See also *hydrapulper, integrated mill*.

large paper edition: a special or de luxe edition of a book, having large fore-edge and foot margins, and sometimes numbered or autographed. Printing is done from the same setting of type as for the standard edition. In the 18th century the classics were often issued in this form. For some titles two editions were prepared, the type being re-set for the large paper edition, the cheaper edition being somewhat cramped.

'When care has been taken to adapt the size of the type to the size of the page it seems absurd to print the book upon a larger size. The margins which suit the original book are quite wrong for a larger one.' Thus Emery Walker in 1929, who added that the custom 'may have originated in consequence of a former habit of binders to cut the margins off when rebinding a book'. Large paper copies became a means of inducing purchasers to buy what they supposed was a more exclusive product than the standard edition.

Larousse, Pierre, 1817–75: the founder in 1856 of the Parisian publishing house known throughout the world for its encyclopaedic dictionaries. The most popular of these, 'Le Petit Larousse illustré', was first published in 1906 and by 1922 had already reached the 185th revised edition. Just as the name *Kodak*

has become synonymous in many countries for any camera, so *Larousse* is widely applied in French-speaking countries for any illustrated dictionary.

laser: the acronym for 'light amplification by the stimulated emission of radiation', i.e. light with an intensely focused parallel beam transmitted with a low use of energy. Lasers are used *inter alia* in photogravure and photosetting: thus the *Lasercomp*, announced in 1977, in which pasted-up pages are scanned by a red laser beam, followed by the transfer of the scanned image to a printing surface by means of a blue beam.

Latin abbreviations: the monks' tradition of abbreviating certain nouns and verbs when writing Latin and Greek texts was continued by printers of books in the 15th and 16th centuries. Usage varied, being dictated by custom and not rule, but the following list gives a selection of the commonest Latin non-legal abbreviations: it is reprinted from R. B. McKerrow's 'An introduction to bibliography for literary students', O.U.P., 1928, by courtesy of the Clarendon Press.

aliqñ–aliquando	.n.—enim
alr—aliter	nr̃—noster
añ—ante	nr̃is—nostris
aplice—apostolice	oẽs—omnes
aploᴏ̨—apostolorum	oĩm—omnium
bñ—bene	or̃o—oratio
cãm—causam	orõñ—orationem
corpibus—corporibus	pñtes—praesentes
dc̃m—dictum	pp—propter
dño—domino	pr̃—pater
dñs—dominus	pr̃is—patris
ds̃—Deus	p̃t—potest
ẽ—est	qđ—quod
eẽ—esse	qm̃—quoniam
eẽt—esset	rõ—ratio
em̃—enim	r̃furr̃ctõem—
ẽt—etiam	resurrectionem
etem̃—etenim	.f.—scilicet
fr̃em—fratrem	fc̃us—sanctus
ġ—ergo	fñia—sententia
gr̃a—gratia	fp—semper
hẽant̃—habeantur	fpm̃—spiritum
hẽat—habeat	fpũs—spiritus
.i.—id est	f̃te—sancte
igr̃, igr, ġ—igitur	tm̃—tantum
ip̃ius—ipsius	tñ—tamen
ip̃oᴏ̨—ipsorum	tp̃a—tempora
ir (perhaps for ir̃)—ire	tpe—tempore
lr̃as, lr̃is—litteras, litteris	tp̃s—tempus
mõ—modo	uñ—unde
mr̃is—matris	xp̃s—Christus

Latin place names: see Appendix B. See also R. A. Peddie, 'Place names in imprints: an index to the

Latin and other forms used on title pages', Grafton, 1932; repr. Detroit, Gale, 1968.

Laurentian Codex: an 11th-century codex of the works of Sophocles, Apollonius Rhodius, and Aeschylus, found in the 15th century by Aurispa for his patron Niccolò de' Niccoli. It is now in the Biblioteca Mediceo-Laurenziana, Florence.

Laurentii, Nicolaus, fl.1477–86: a printer of Breslau who went to Florence where he worked with Johannes Petri of Mainz, and also at the Dominican house of St Jacobum de Ripoli. He is remembered as having been the first printer to include illustrations from copperplates in a book: the work was Antonio Bettini's 'Monte santo di' Dio', 1477 (GKW 2204). Other examples were used in the first illustrated edition of Dante's 'La divina commedia', 1481 (GKW 7966), which had nineteen copperplate engravings by Baccio Baldini after drawings made by Sandro Boticelli for an earlier manuscript version.

law calf: tanned, uncoloured calfskin, which in the 19th century was often used in England for the covers of law books. Also called *fair calf*.

law sheep: sheepskin used as in *law calf*, q.v.

lay edges: the two edges of a sheet which are placed flush with the side and front lay gauges on a printing machine. This ensures the sheet will be removed properly by the grippers and have uniform margins when printed. The front edge is the *gripper edge* and the side edge the side *lay*. See also *feeding*.

layerman: the craftsman who takes the still moist sheets of *leaf* (2) from the *post*, qq.v. He places them in piles of about 230 sheets on a felt-covered zinc plate and lightly presses the pile under a second plate. The pile is opened and re-assembled several times, the process taking several days. See also *slice boy*.

layer-on: the machine room employee who fed sheets into a printing press. Women were often employed, and their speed affected the press speed. With the introduction of quicker two-revolution presses in the early 19th century men replaced women as layers-on. Mechanical feeding subsequently replaced both.

laying on: placing gold leaf on a surface to be gilded. In gilding by hand pieces of cut leaf are transferred from the gold cushion with a piece of cotton wool and pressed on the leather. Gold leaf on reels is transferred directly from them. In edge gilding leaf is taken from the cushion by means of a gilder's tip, a simple wooden frame over which threads or a network of threads are stretched, or 'on a piece of paper previously greased by drawing it over the head' (Zaehnsdorf). See also *gilt edges, gold leaf*.

laying press: see *lying press*.

laying the fount: putting type into the case when a new fount is acquired by the printer.

lay of the case: the arrangement of letters etc. in the compositor's case. By custom, the usage of John Johnson, William Savage and John Southward (all 19th century printers) has influenced present-day standardization in Britain.

layout: 1. the preparation of copy for setting up in type, indicating the face and size of type to be used, the position of blocks, etc. Evidence of the early practice of marking up a manuscript to show the printer the desired position of illustration blocks survives in the Nuremberg Stadtbibliothek where the 'copy' for the German version of Schedel's 'Liber chronicarum', printed by Anton Koberger in 1493 is now kept. See also *copy fitting, margins*.
2. a sketch or outline which gives the general appearance of a printed page. This is made on sheets of paper ruled in 12-point squares. See also *mechanical*.

lay sheet: the sheet of glass or other transparent material on which the negatives or positives of text and illustrations are assembled preparatory to printing down a photo-offset plate.

lay stool: large boards supported on stools. They were put conveniently near a pressman to hold printed and unprinted sheets.

l.c.: see *lower case*.

leaded: type which is set with leads between the lines. Cf. *set solid*. See also *white out*.

leaders: interspaced full points used in groups of two or three to direct the eye across a page as in a table of contents. The use of leaders can be avoided by setting contents pages to a narrower measure than text pages or by generous interlinear leading. Cf. *ellipsis*.

leading: the insertion of *leads*, q.v.

lead-in titles: a feature of a book club's advertising campaign, being back-list titles offered through the post at very low prices, or free, as introductions to potential or new members, or as dividends or bonuses to existing members. Also known as *introductory titles*.

lead moulding: a process of making electros of half-tone printing surfaces in which lead is used instead of wax. A sheet of soft lead is forced into the forme under great pressure and a mould obtained. A copper shell is deposited on this.

leads: thin strips of lead of varying thickness used to separate lines of type. Thicknesses are 1-point, 1½-point (thin), 2-point, and 3-point (thick). An alternative way to increase the space between lines without using leads is to employ type cast on bodies larger than normal, e.g. 10-point on 12-point, known as *long-bodied type*. See also *reglets*.

leaf: 1. *gold leaf*, q.v.

2. newly formed sheets of paper before they are dried and finished.

3. each of the folios which result when a sheet of paper is folded. Each side of a leaf is a page. In the late 16th century the term leaf denoted a whole printed sheet; furthermore, a particular printer was occasionally accorded the right to print the first leaf of a book for which another printer held the right to print the remainder.

4. a small leaf and stalk cast as a printer's *flower*, q.v. Its inspiration was the vine leaf cut as a punctuation mark in classical Roman stone inscriptions. It was later used by manuscript painters. When, in the earlier 16th century, printed decoration replaced the hand-done embellishments added to 15th century printed pages, the leaf was cast as a type. It was used to indicate paragraphs and also to decorate title-pages, as, for example, by Ratdolt at Venice in 1512. See also *Aldine leaves*.

lean matter: see *fat matter*.

leather: skin from any of several animals prepared as a material for covering books: goat, calf, sheep, pig, and seal are mostly used. See references under *bookbinding materials*.

leatherette: a bookbinding fabric made of a strong MG base paper which is coated and embossed or printed and embossed to simulate grained leather. Colours and finishes are many. Cf. *linson*.

leather joints: inner leather hinges which reinforce the end-paper hinges of a heavy hand-bound book, giving additional strength.

leather preservation: leather bindings can be preserved by gently wiping with a cloth wrung out of a weak soap solution, a little methylated spirit being dabbed on any traces of varnish. Cotton wool is then used to apply a preservative solution made up of hexane, lanolin, cedarwood oil, and beeswax. The preparation should soak in for a day, after which the book should be polished with a soft brush.

A method of protecting leather against atmospheric deterioration was evolved by R. F. Innes and published in 1933. It involves the introduction of potassium lactate during manufacture, and leather so made may be stamped 'Guaranteed to resist PIRA test'. The British Library laboratory reports favourably on such leather and it is commercially available. See also *mildew*. See B. C. Middleton, 'The restoration of leather bindings', Chicago, 1972.

Le Bé, Guillaume, 1515–98: of Troyes, the first of a famous Parisian family of punchcutters, matrix makers and typefounders. After some years with Estienne, from whom he learned his craft and cut a Sephardic cursive hebrew for use in the latter's Hebrew Bible, 24 parts, 1539–44, he worked in Venice between 1545 and 1550 cutting inter alia two founts of hebrew for Marc Antonio Giustiniani and six for Meir Parenzo. He then went to Rome, not opening his business in Paris until 1552. He specialized in the cutting of oriental and hebrew types of which he is credited with some twenty founts. Some of the latter were used in the Polyglot Bible of Plantin to whom Le Bé sold strikes and matrices. He also cut music type for Robert Ballard whose family printed most French music for nearly two centuries.

His son of the same name (*c.* 1565–1636) added printing and bookselling to the business. He bought punches from several contemporary cutters.

Guillaume III, grandson of the founder, continued the business until his death in 1685, after which it was managed by Claude Fauré until 1707, being subsequently entrusted to Jean-Claude Fournier until 1729, both on behalf of the Le Bé family. It was then managed by Jean-Pièrre Fournier. The foundry was destroyed in the Revolution, probably only two founts of hebrew, now with Deberny and Peignot, surviving. Le Bé's hebrew types were copied in Italy until the 19th century, and influenced the Nebiolo foundry's hebrew of the 20th. See S. Morison, 'L' Inventaire de la fonderie Le Bé', Paris, 1957.

Le Blon, Jacques Christophe: see *colour printing*.

lectionary: (or *legenda*), the portion of a breviary containing the lessons, i.e. readings from the Scriptures, lives of saints, and homilies appropriate to each day of the liturgical year. The work was written and circulated in manuscript versions, notable being the 'Legenda aurea' of Jacobus de Voragine (1230–98) which was one of Caxton's sources for his 'Golden legend' of 1483.

lectori: a note 'to the reader' in the form of a preface.

Lederschnittbände: the German name for bindings made in the *cuir ciselé* or cut-leather manner. Characteristics were thick dark leather with a geometrically divided surface decorated with groups of plant or grotesque animal forms. These designs were outlined in the flat with a pointed tool on the dampened leather (they are not, in fact, cut); then the background areas were stippled with punched dots or small circles causing the main design to stand out in relief.

Lederschnitt bindings belong to the era 1370–1500, and most surviving examples were made in Germany and Austria in the later 15th century. They were also made in Hungary and Spain where the patterns of interlaced strapwork on stippled backgrounds were probably the work of Moorish or Jewish craftsmen.

This form of decoration and style of binding were suitable for large books and declined as the development of printing made smaller books possible. See M. Bollert, 'Lederschnittbände des XIV Jahrhunderts', 1925. See also *Jewish leather-cutting*.

Lee Priory Press: a private press established in 1813 by Sir Samuel Egerton Brydges (1762–1837) at Ickham near Canterbury, with *John Johnson*, q.v., (later famous as the author of 'Typographia', 1824) and John Warwick as printers. Brydges edited some of the minor Elizabethan literature he issued, many items being reprints of little known poetry. The press closed in early 1823.

Leeu, Gerard, fl.1477–93: the first printer at Gouda in Holland. He specialized in the printing of books on religion and chivalry, mostly illustrated, and destined for a wealthy merchant class. His best-known work was a collection of animal fables 'Dialogus creaturarum moralisatus', 1480, illustrated with 121 simple but effective woodcuts. The work was very popular and widely copied. Leeu issued seven editions in Dutch, French and Latin, all with the same cuts.

In 1484 he began printing in Antwerp where in 1491 he printed what was probably the first illustrated poster to advertise a book (Melusine). It was in a book he printed here in 1492 that he began the typographic distinction between i and j, u and v: this was in an edition of 'Dyalogus between Salomon and Marcolphus'. Of his considerable output seven books were printed for the English trade, and it was while he was reprinting Caxton's 'Cronycles of the londe of Englōd' of 1480 that he was stabbed to death by a workman. This was in 1493 and a colophonic epitaph in the book reads '. . . a man of grete wysedom in all manner of kunnyng, which nowe is come from lyfe unto the deth, which is grete harme for many of poure man . . .' The workman was *Henric van Symmen*, q.v., nicknamed Lettersteker.

After his death Leeu's illustration blocks were acquired by *Thierry Martens*, q.v.

legal deposit: see *statutory copies*.

Le Gascon, fl.1620–50: a leading Parisian bookbinder whose identity has not been accurately established, but who may have worked within the Royal Library. He favoured a simplified style of fillet frames with large fleurons in the corners, usually tooled in red morocco of an exclusive colour. His spinal lettering was particularly fine. Some 350 bindings attributed to him are in the Bibliothèque Nationale, Paris. Many bear the coat of arms of Loménie de Brienne. Le Gascon is also associated, perhaps inaccurately, with *pointillé* bindings, q.v., but there is no pointillé on the examples referred to above.

legend: correctly, the name for the descriptive matter printed below an illustration. The custom of printing and publishing establishments is to prefer the term *caption*, q.v.

Legenda: a book of sermons, lessons from the Bible, and hagiographies for use at Divine Service.

Legenda aurea: a collection of lives of the saints, written between 1263 and 1272 by Archbishop Jacobus de Voragine. The work was widely copied (and translated) in manuscript form, and later engaged the attention of many well-known early printers in England, France, Germany, Holland and Spain. In England Caxton (1483) and Wynkyn de Worde (1493) printed editions, both using the same woodcuts (STC 24873–24880). In France Nicolaus Philippi and Marcus Reinhart issued the first printed editions at Lyons in 1478; another edition (in French) with similar woodcuts was printed in 1483 by Mathias Huss and Petrus Ungarius. In Germany Günther Zainer issued the editio princeps at Augsburg in 1471 ('Der Heyligen Leben'). This was illustrated with 258 woodcuts.

Legge, Henry Bilson, fl.1790–1800: a bookbinder of Boston. His work was unusual in American binding of the time for the materials used (tree calf, red morocco, marbled end-papers), technique (onlays, sprinkled edges) and decoration (including a distinctive engraved tool of a bird perched on a floriated urn), though his spinal lettering was somewhat uneven. See H. D. French, 'Bound in Boston by Henry B. Legg', *Studies in Bibliography*, 17 1964 135–9.

legibility: the cumulative effect on the human eye of printed matter. This depends on the size, shape and degree of density of letters, their distance from one another, the space between words, the length of lines and the width of interlinear spacing. Colour, paper quality, and light also affect legibility, as do the sight, proficiency in reading and intellectual level of the reader. In France and Germany doctors, teachers and psychologists have studied the problem since the end of the 19th century. Important results have been achieved in America (Luckiesh, 'Reading as a visual task', New York, 1945) and Britain (Burt, 'A psychological study of typography', 1959).

Scientists recommend not more than thirteen words to a line, with type varying between 9- and 12-point according to the measure and page size, matt white paper and ink of good density. Balanced margins, clear type without dazzle or eye-catching affectations in its design are among other desiderata. See also H. Spencer, 'The visible word', Lund Humphries, 1969.

Legrain, Pierre, 1889–1929: the pioneer of 20th century luxury bookbinding in France. He began binding towards the end of the First World War, being encouraged to do so by his wealthy patron the couturier Jacques Doucet. By reviving the method of sewing without raised bands he was able to plan as one unit his design for the upper cover, spine and lower cover. Gone were the floral mosaics and panels of stylized tooling from past centuries. Instead Legrain created abstract patterns interpreted in leather of contrasting colours and textures. He sought particularly to develop to its logical conclusion the theory of *Jean-Marius Michel*, q.v., that the covers of a book should be in harmony with its contents. Earlier binders had chosen an incident or other feature of the text as a motif for tooling. This was a form of illustration. Thus on a copy of Lacordaire's 'Vie de saint Dominique' instead of tooling a monk's habit he used black and pale grey morocco and a large silver disc to interpret the spirit of the work. The choice of lettering also received careful treatment.

In 1965 the Librairie Blaizot of Paris published an illustrated catalogue of more than 1,200 of Legrain's binding designs.

In the 1940s his son-in-law Jacques Anthoine-Legrain continued the same binding traditions.

Leighton, Archibald, 1742–99: of Glasgow, who established a bookbinding business in London in 1764. His eldest son, also *Archibald* (1784–1841), pioneered the use of book cloth in the late 1820s, embossed cloth to simulate morocco in the 1830s, and gold blocking on cloth.

Other members of this family had binderies in Victorian London, while *John Leighton* (1822–1912) became famous from 1845 for his binding designs. Over elaborate though many of them now seem they showed considerable inventiveness. See S. Pantazzi, 'John Leighton, 1822–1912', *Connoisseur*, April 1963.

Leighton, George, 1826–95: an apprentice of George Baxter who set himself up as a colour printer in 1843. From 1858 until 1884 he was printer and publisher of the *Illustrated London News*.

278

Leipzig Fair: from the late 16th century onwards the book fairs of Leipzig developed in importance just as the town became the centre of the German book trade. The first catalogue of books shown at the fair was published in 1594 by Henning Gross. By 1765 the rival Frankfurt Fair had lost much of its trade, and visitors came from all parts of Europe to Leipzig. By the 19th century the Cantate Fair was the main event of the publishing trade in Germany. Leipzig book fairs have been held since 1945, forming part of a general trade fair at which British firms are represented. See also *Frankfurt Fair*.

Le Monnier bindings: see *Monnier bindings*.

Lenox, James, 1800–80: one of the most famous American book-collectors who appears to have acquired the major portion of his library between 1840 and 1880. He was the most active Bible collector of his age and bought the first 42-line Gutenberg Bible to be imported to America. His vast collection is now in New York Public Library.

Le Preux, Poncet, fl.1498–1559: one of the earliest major Parisian booksellers who did an extensive trade in imported books which he supplied to other book-sellers. On some of the books he commissioned from publisher-printers he had his own printer's mark to identify them. He was related by marriage to *Philippe Pigouchet* and *Pierre Attaingnant*, qq.v.

Le Rouge, Pierre, fl.1478–99: member of a French family of calligraphers and illuminators. He printed in Chablis and Paris where from 1484–87 he worked for Marchant and probably Jean Dupré.

In 1488 he was appointed Imprimeur du Roi, and in this year and 1489 he issued what was to prove his most important publication, a superbly illustrated folio edition of 'La Mer des hystoires' in two volumes. The text was based on the editio princeps of 'Rudimentum nouitiorum' by Lucas Brandis, Lübeck, 1475. Le Rouge included 200 woodcuts (some repeated), large initial capitals with figures and calligraphic flourishes and floriated border pieces with grotesques strongly reminiscent of illuminated manuscripts. It was one of the most beautiful early French books.

He also printed for other Parisian publishers, and notable was an edition of 'L'art de bien mourir', 1492, for *Antoine Vérard*, q.v.

Others in the family who printed were *Jean*, who worked with Pierre at Chablis in 1483 before going to Troyes, and *Guillaume*, son of Pierre, who worked at Troyes and Chablis where he issued a beautifully illustrated edition of 'Les Expositions des évangiles' in 1489, before succeeding his father in Paris from 1493 to 1517.

Le Roy, Guillaume, fl.1473–88: of Liège, and the first

printer of Lyons where he worked the press of *Barthélemy Buyer*, q.v. His first dated book was the 'Compendium breve' of Cardinal Lothaire, 1473. He also issued the first book in French to be published in Lyons, the 'Légende dorée', 1476. Notable too, were, Pasquier Bonhomme's 'Grandes chroniques', and an early book on surgery by Guy de Chauliac, 1478.

After 1480 he printed for himself and about this time he illustrated his books with the work of local artists as an alternative to importing or copying foreign cuts. His blocks were probably cut by the makers of playing cards. He issued many French 'romans de chevalerie'.

For his first books Le Roy used a heavy lettre de forme based on early Dutch type; later, after Buyer visited Venice where he met Jenson, he used a venetian gothic. For books in French he had an elegant bastarda resembling that of *Colard Mansion*, q.v.

Le Sueur, Vincent and Pierre, jun.: the best known of a French family of wood engravers who, in the early 18th century were renowned for their head- and tail-pieces. In general, however, wood engraving in France was then a dying art.

Lethaby, William, 1857–1931: an architect and also first principal of London's Central School of Arts and Crafts which opened in 1896. He was a friend of William Morris and Emery Walker who shared his belief in the need for craft education by craftsmen-teachers.

Lethaby's aim of raising the level of book production was furthered by the team of dedicated men he recruited as instructors. They included Douglas Cockerell (bookbinding), Edward Johnston (lettering) and J. H. Mason (typography) who pioneered minimum inter-word spacing. Pupils were mainly apprentices engaged in the book trades but included also Eric Gill and Anna Simons (from Germany). In 1913 some of the staff combined to write *The Imprint*, q.v.

The work of the school was unnoticed by Britain's printing trade but in America, and more especially Germany it was soon recognized, leading to a higher standard of book production than was to appear in Britain for several decades. See G. Rubens, 'William Lethaby: his life and work . . .', Architectural Press, 1976.

Leto, Pomponio, 1428–97: a classical scholar and teacher of Rome who founded the Roman Academy about 1460. The marginally annotated texts which he edited and transcribed were widely imitated and copied, extending his influence on humanistic hand-writing and book scripts.

letra de Tortis: the Spanish name for *lettre de somme*,

q.v., and so called after the Venetian printer Battista de Tortis who used it in the 1490s for law books. See also *fere-humanistica*.

letter: 1. a single type.
2. a group name, e.g. roman letter, black letter, etc.

lettera antiqua tonda: a name first used by *Tagliente*, q.v., in his handwriting manual of 1524 for the round humanist script developed by copyists in the later 15th century. Each letter, and not a whole word, was the scribe's unit, ascenders were short, giving an effect on the page not unlike print.

lettera cancellaresca corsiva: see *cursive*.

lettera cancellaresca formata: see *cursive*.

lettera rotunda: a round gothic script used in the scriptoria of 13th-century Italy. See also *black letter*.

letter assembly: a composite name for the several methods of originating reading matter in print.

lettera Venetae: the name given by German printers (*c.* 1485–90) to the rotunda or round gothic types of Italian origin.

Lettergieterij Amsterdam: see *Typefoundry Amsterdam*.

lettering on the spine: wording necessary to identify a book as it stands on a shelf. This is usually the author's name, title, volume number when relevant, and on cased books the publisher's name.

In medieval times when books were either laid on shelves, chained, or kept in cupboards there was no lettering on the spine which was invisible during storage. Any external identification was ink written on the bottom edges of the leaves, the fore-edge, or on a tag of vellum. When, due to the increase in their number in a library, the practice of shelving books upright began, still with fore-edges outward, it was the custom to write the title on the fore-edge.

On many books bound in the earlier 16th century (e.g. Grolier bindings) the title was lettered in gold on the front board. The tooling of gold letters on the spine is found on Italian bindings from 1535. The wording ran up the spine. Gilt lettering across the second panel of the spine began in Italy about 1560 and the practice became standard, spreading via France to England by 1604. On some books bound in the 16th century, and indeed later, there is a marked contrast between the elegance and precision of designs tooled on the covers and that of the lettering for which each letter was separately stamped. Thus Wanley who noted ('Diary', 3 Dec 1722) the 'vicious' lettering on bindings done for Harley by *Elliott*, q.v. Titles were often clumsily abbreviated, had arbitrary word divisions, and were badly aligned. They may have been done by less skilled workmen who did not first mark up the leather. This practice did not cease until the 18th century when printing type set up in a holder was used in Germany as early as 1708, and in England by about 1780. Lettering pallets of brass letters were probably contemporary with the latter date.

As an alternative to lettering directly on the book thinly pared morocco *lettering pieces* pasted on the spine can be dated from 1680. These became a decorative feature in their own right when pieces of contrasting colours for author, title and volume number were used in France from the 1720s, as well as using up binder's off-cuts. Lettering pieces are not necessarily contemporary with the bindings on which they appear, often being affixed later particularly when it became necessary to identify on library shelves the unlettered books of earlier periods.

When the lettering on the spine or jacket of a book cannot conveniently be set across it, the alternative is to set it downward or upward, but as anyone visiting a bookshop will know to their irritation British publishers cannot agree which. The Publishers Association and Booksellers Association recommended in 1948 that spinal lettering should run from head to foot of the spine, so that the title can easily be read when the book lies flat, face upward. This reversed their 1926 recommendation that 'when the volume stands on the shelf the lettering reads from bottom to top'. The dilemma continues.

Lettering on the spine of gramophone record sleeves is always from top to bottom.

letterpress: 1. the text of a book, including the line illustrations, but not any 'plates'.

2. printing done from raised types or blocks as distinct from intaglio or lithographic plates. A feature of letterpress printing is its crispness due to pressure on the type tending to concentrate the ink at the edges of the letters. See also *letterpress machines*.

letterpress binding: the binding of printed books which are to be read as distinct from *stationery binding* which is the binding of those to be written in, e.g. ledgers, account books and so on. See also *vellum binding trade*.

letterpress inks: see *extender, ink consumption, ink coverage, ink fly, ink grinding, inking roller, inking system, ink table, tack, viscosity*.

letterpress inks, standards for: see *British Standard letterpress inks*.

letterpress machines: printing presses in which the impression is taken from raised types or blocks, i.e. relief printing. The earliest letterpress machines were

280

platen presses, q.v., and their somewhat simple construction was not much changed until the 19th century. In 1803–4 König constructed an entirely automatic platen press known as the Suhler press (after the Thuringian town of Suhl, where it was made

Suhler press, 1803

in Kummer's mechanical workshop). It was not successful, and only in 1810 did a practical working platen press, having automatic inking and printing, make its appearance.

Long before the platen press was perfected the *cylinder press* was invented; the first, constructed and

König's cylinder machine of 1812

patented in 1811 by König, was a *stop-cylinder press*. It was completed in December 1812. Here the forme moved to and fro on a flat bed underneath a cylinder which made a one-third revolution while printing from the forme in its forward movement. On the return of the forme the cylinder was stationary, without coming into contact with it, this interval being used for feeding the paper. The sheets were held tightly against the cylinder by a tape frame. The *inking system*, q.v., consisted of an ink pump, grinding rollers, and forme rollers. Capacity was 800 sheets an hour. Two years later a double press was ready, and it was first used for printing *The Times* on 29 November 1814. This press had two cylinders placed symmetrically round an inking device, the forme being printed during its forward movement against one of the cylinders, and during its receding movement against the other. Both cylinders had a feed and distribution table. Sheets were guided by tapes running on reels. Capacity was 1,100 sheets an hour. In 1814 König patented a *two-revolution machine*, i.e. a press in which the cylinder was in continuous motion, but in which printing took place only during every second revolution. In 1815–16 König constructed the first *perfecting machine*, and in this the inking rollers were solid cast cylinders instead of the leather rollers used previously. To secure the sheets during printing David Napier & Son introduced grippers. In early cylinder presses the bed on which the forme rested was moved to and fro by a toothed wheel in gear with a journal bearing on one side of a frame under the bed.

In 1845 the Maschinenfabrik of Augsburg introduced the *crank motion*. Here, on the under-side of the bed are two rails resting against two or more pairs of wheels which run on rails at the bottom of the press (see illustration). The bed is set in its forward and reverse motion by a connecting rod. In modern models the large wheel construction is replaced by a gliding movement in which the bed bottom rails glide against the supporting rails; in larger presses,

however, steel rollers are introduced between the rails to reduce friction. To act as brakes to the movements of the bed and give a smooth motion adjustable *buffers* are usually fitted in cylinder presses.

In relation to the movement of the cylinder and its

Press with crank motion, about 1900

size in proportion to the forme, we distinguish between *stop-cylinder presses*, q.v., in which the cylinder completes one revolution during the forward movement of the bed, remaining motionless during the return, and *two-revolution presses*, q.v., with a continuously rotating cylinder which at every second revolution makes an empty movement, the cylinder being raised above the forme. In addition,

Hoe's rotary sheet press of 1846

there are *single-revolution presses*, also having a continuously running cylinder, but with a diameter twice that of the two-revolution press. Printing is done during the first half of the revolution, the bed returning to its original position during the second half. The Heidelberg press bed has an accelerated return movement, thereby increasing the cylinder capacity for printing, and by maintaining the same peripheral speed the time required to complete a revolution is reduced.

Rocking-cylinder machines have a cylinder which either accompanies the bed in its forward motion, being then raised and swung back to its original position, or else it accompanies the bed all the time, effecting printing in both directions.

There were early experiments to substitute a rotary motion for the to and fro motion of the bed. In 1846 Richard Hoe of New York patented a *rotary sheet*

Applegath & Cowper's rotary sheet press of 1848

press which had ordinary types on large forme cylinders. In 1848 Applegath and Cowper of London built a similar press with a vertical cylinder. Both were used for newspaper printing.

Rotary printing from curved formes was made possible by the development of *stereotyping*, q.v., and the first to adapt it for printing on a continuous roll of paper was William Bullock who, in 1863, patented a rotary press which in its final workable form was completed in 1865.

Presses for the simultaneous printing of both sides of the paper, known as *perfectors*, were, as stated previously, first constructed by König: their most extensive use is in rotary press printing on roll paper, thus enabling folding and cutting to be combined direct with the printing press. There are now letterpress machines with linked binding units, using proprietary photopolymer printing plates mounted on twin endless polyester belts to print up to 40,000 complete hardcover books a day.

Multi-colour presses are designed for the simultaneous printing of the several colours of a colour print. Among early models may be mentioned the Congreve press. Modern multi-colour letterpress machines, having separate formes for each colour,

are usually built as two or more single-colour presses coupled together. The Miehle two-colour two-revolution machine had two printing cylinders and an intermediate ferry cylinder to carry the sheet from one to the other. By combining a two-revolution press with a rotary feed two colour printing was possible. This method was known in America as the *Upham system*, and in Germany as the *Beckmann system*. See E. Hutchings, 'Printing by letterpress', 3 vols, Heinemann, 1964.

letterpress platemaking: see *electronic engraving machine*, *photoengraving*.

letterpress plates: most *line plates* are produced on fine-grain micro-zinc or lighter magnesium alloy of thickness varying according to purpose: thus 161 gauge for flatbed plates or rigid curved segments for rotary letterpress, 21 gauge for flexible wraparound plates, and 23 or 26 gauge for dry offset.

For *half-tone plates* coarse screen work on zinc or magnesium and fine-screen work in black and white on fine-grain micro-zinc are usual.

Letterpress U.S.A.: a country of origin imprint adopted in 1955 by American letterpress firms as an approved variant of the legend 'Printed in USA' which was previously required by Federal law to identify printing done in America, and to distinguish it from imported material. Litho firms used the form 'Lithographed in USA'.

letterset: see *indirect letterpress*.

letters—forms and styles: in writing the forms of letters partly depend on the implement (stylus, reed,

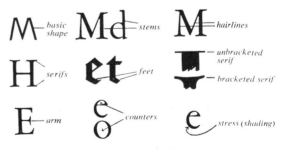

Main parts of a letter

quill, pen), the liquid, and the way the implement is held and moved forward. The history of letters may be divided into the era of the manuscript and the post-Gutenberg era of the printed book. The development of the letter can be traced from the earliest stages of *picture writing* and *ideographic writing* to the *phonetic writing* of our time. An example of picture writing is the earlier form of the Egyptian *hieroglyphs*

(Gk. *hieros*, sacred; *gluphikos*, carve) which were conventional simplifications of pictures representing, at first, concrete ideas. Hieroglyphic writing is thought to have originated prior to 3,000 BC. Two forms of it developed: the *hieratic* of the priests and

Hieroglyphics. 'Cleopatra', after a cartouche on the Philae obelisk; read from top to bottom and right to left

the *demotic* of the people, qq.v. Hieroglyphs were usually written on papyrus which continued in use until AD 300 (and in the Papal Court still later) when parchment became more and more a substitute for it. Writing on papyrus was done on rolls from 20 to 40cm. wide and sometimes 9 to 18 metres long. The Latin name for a book in this form was *volumen* (= a roll). Among other writing tools the *calamus* (a reed) was used. Chinese writing is an example of *ideographic* writing for which several signs which separately have different meanings are combined to denote an idea. About 1500 BC Egyptian hieroglyphs developed a phonetic tendency in which each sign also represented a phonetic sound. Later, the Phoen-

ACAMBMYOY

Greek writing, 6th century BC

icians applied this principle to their language. Through this medium the alphabet came to Greece about 900 BC where it was adapted to Greek linguistic usage. The Greeks introduced vowels and later, the western custom of writing from left to right. The Greek alphabet quickly became useful for both commerce and the spread of culture, being taken by colonists to Italy. There the Greek alphabet became the prototype of the Roman. Centuries later it was borrowed in part by Cyril and Methodius to represent the sounds of the Slavonic group of languages and thus it forms an essential part of Cyrillic.

Roman square capitals. About the time of Christ's birth the Roman or Latin alphabet had developed into one of capitals only, now known as Roman square capitals. They were first used for inscriptions

carved in stone. Letters were characterized by a severe monumental beauty which has never been surpassed. The letter shapes have been preserved in their original form up to the present, and served as a basis for later developed variants of scripts and

ABCDEFG HIKLMNOP QRSTVXYZ

Redrawn capitals based on the Trajan letters of AD 113

printing types. The Romans adapted the Greek signs for their own phonetic requirements. Some of the letters which lacked corresponding Latin sound values were removed, and certain additions were made. An important form of square capitals was

Pompeian mural writing

employed at Pompeii (destroyed in AD 79) where the letters were made with a flat brush – *Pompeian mural writing*. Here writing received the linear shapes characteristic of broad nib or flat brush technique which remains one of the features of later development. When the writing tool is held at an angle of 45° to the line of writing some of the stems and curves become accentuated, while others become fine. This

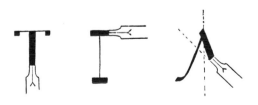

Broad pen strokes

283

writing technique also influenced the cutting of letters on stone.

Rustic capitals. The writing which came into use for books from about the 2nd century AD, and in which the writings of the classic authors were first recorded, is known as rustic capitals. The writing tool was a reed with its rather flat nib held parallel

Rustic capitals, AD 200

to the line, an unusual position for writing. The result was an alphabet with fine upward stems and bold horizontal lines. Rustic capitals, named, it is suggested, from the rustic simplicity of their character, form a narrow, often exaggerated writing which is difficult to read. They continued in occasional use for titles or headings right up to the Middle Ages.

Roman current writing. This was a running script developed in daily use from Roman capitals. When writing rapidly short-cuts were resorted to, and simplified forms adopted. The pointed stylus served

Development of Roman current script from capitals to small letters, from c. 50 BC to AD 350

Roman current script, c. AD 400

A B C D E F G

Two-line system

a b c d e f g

Four-line system

as a writing tool, and the surface was a waxed tablet; both contributed to a delicate outline which in time became extremely difficult to decipher. Towards the Fall of the Roman Empire current writing developed into an easy, elegant hand, and in it were created the original forms of the small letters – minuscules on a 4-line basis, in contradistinction to the 2-line capitals, or majuscules.

Uncials. About the 4th century AD, there arose a conventional script for books, especially those of the

Uncials

Christian Church, the so-called uncials. Uncials contain several of the minuscules formed in the current script, but these are here based on the 2-line principle. Attention is drawn to new forms of D, E, H, M and Q. Factors contributing to the greater evenness and calligraphic quality of uncials were the introduction of parchment which had a better writing surface than papyrus, and the substitution of the quill for the reed. Uncials were influenced in their shape by Byzantine art.

Half-uncials. By the Fall of the Roman Empire a more extreme form of uncials had developed, the

Half-uncials, 6th century

so-called half-uncials or semi-uncials, which consisted mostly of minuscule forms. The script is based on four-lines, and may be regarded as a transition stage to the later Roman minuscules. During the 6th–12th century the use of uncials spread throughout Europe, receiving certain national modifications in each country. Of importance is the Irish script in which the famous *Book of Kells*, q.v., is written.

Carolingian script. At the same time as the half-uncial there were national forms of writing used partly in official hands, and partly in everyday

Irish majuscules, 8th–9th century

scripts. These national forms were to a certain extent developments of the Roman cursive, but owing to frequent peculiarities, writing became in time less legible. The first to bring about an effective reform in the art was the Emperor Charlemagne, who at the

Carolingian script, c. 1100

close of the 8th century called an English scholar, Alcuin of York, to his Court to improve, *inter alia,* the standard of writing in the Carolingian domains. From Tours, where Alcuin became Abbot in the Monastery of St Martin, influences spread for remodelling the art of writing, which turned out to be of essential significance for its later development.

On the basis of the half-uncial and the national scripts was worked out the Carolingian minuscule, and this is the prototype of our common alphabet. The Carolingian script reached all the civilized West, and owing to its clarity and beauty became a noble means of expression for the writer. When the Gothic era began about the 11th century Carolingian script was somewhat adapted to harmonize with the new conceptions: Gothic scripts and later type-faces may therefore be regarded as converting Carolingian script into Gothic.

Gothic scripts. After a long period of development, during which several transitional forms were created, the Gothic style in France, Germany and England produced about the 14th century a conventional script, in France called *lettre de forme,* in Germany *Textur,* and in England *black letter.* Black letter is characterized by its intense blackness, acute angles,

Black letter

and the absence of curves. Instead of serifs the main strokes conclude in short 'feet' set at an angle. The script was made very cramped and narrow; the powerful colour and the stiff shapes forming a distinct surface ornament, a plaited pattern, which gave the name *textus* (= plaited). Although the unusually short vertical strokes allow the lines to be closely written, legibility tends to be reduced in consequence. An alphabet of initial letters, majuscules (in print: capitals), was introduced, based in the first place on uncials, the Gothic counterparts of which were often somewhat difficult to read. Black letter, as the earlier uncials, was the special script adopted by the Church. With the exception of Italy and Spain it was in general European use throughout the Middle Ages; it was moreover the basis of the type-faces of the mid-15th century. In Italy the Gothic style did not flourish: in the art of writing there, however, the form of letters received the impress of the Gothic spirit, but the strict angular forms of black letter were not popular. Instead was developed the *rotunda* or

Rotunda

round Gothic script, which in its main features reflects the style of the period, yet in details preserves Romanesque features. Rotunda is characterized by the richness of its curves; it is broad and not cramped, and its forms retain the outlines of Carolingian script. Rotunda also spread to regions north of the Alps, and was extensively used in the Middle Ages, and later adapted as a type for printing. Erhardt Ratdolt, for example, produced exquisite examples of type based on rotunda.

Several forms of Gothic script developed parallel with the conventional variants. In France the *lettre bâtarde* had a particular vogue. Whereas black letter and the various related scripts were firstly dedicated

Lettre bâtarde

285

to Latin and the solemn writings of the Church, various forms of *Bastarda* were employed for vernacular texts. Bastarda is a current form of Gothic script written in a dashing, rapid fashion. Calligraphic details often present themselves (e.g. *d* in the lettre bâtarde); the elegant curves also give an easy flow to the outline, but Gothic blackness and heaviness are still noticeable.

A form of writing in Germany corresponding to the lettre bâtarde was the *Schwabacher* script, which

Schwabacher

in spite of its rustic and less elegant appearance nevertheless points towards a transition to the characteristic *German type*. Schwabacher introduces curved strokes to the Gothic form; especially characteristic is the *g*, the upper part of which protrudes to the right. The German *Fraktur* (Latin fractus = broken) is a particularly Teutonic form of Gothic script, influenced by the Renaissance, which made its appearance in several versions at the beginning of the 16th century. The first printed version was in a Prayer Book ('Liber Horarum . . .') issued by Martin Schönsperger in 1513 for the Emperor Maximilian; another example was cut by Hieronymus Andreae in 1522 after designs by Johann Neudörffer, and this became traditional. Fraktur types were used extensively in the Scandinavian and Baltic countries until the end of the 19th century, and in Germany and Switzerland they have not been entirely superseded by roman. Characteristic of this type are the interchanging curves and angles, and the small flourishing ornaments to many of the vertical strokes (Ger. Schnörkel). During the German Baroque era Fraktur tended to develop

an excessive turgidity and blackness. About 1800 a modified, more readable type was introduced by Unger, and this later influenced the Weiss-Fraktur. Walter Tiemann and Rudolf Koch are among those who have designed modern Frakturs.

J. F. Unger's Fraktur, 1793

Roman type. The Renaissance humanists readopted the Carolingian script, believing this to be more in keeping with the classical spirit than Gothic. This script when cut as type was subsequently known as *roman.* The difference between the earlier Carolingian

Roman script, 1520

and the new roman was not great. Roman capitals were accepted as initial letters, and thus we find in the 15th-century script the direct prototype of our present printing types. On the basis of the Italian *cancellaresca corsiva* used in government offices and the Papal chancery from the end of the 14th century, a roman cursive (*italic*) was formed. In 1500 it was

Roman cursive as a book hand,
Venice, 1521

GEOR·

P hillyrides Chiron, Amythaonius'q; Melampus·
S æuit et in lucem ſtygiis emuſſa tenebris
P allida Tiſiphone, morbos agit ante, metum'q;,
I n'q; dies auidum ſurgens caput altius effert,
B alatu pecorum, et crebris mugitibus amnes,
A rentes'q; ſonant ripæ, colles'q; ſupini·
I am'q; cæteruatim dat ſtragem, atq; aggerat ipſis
I n ſtabulis, turpi dilapſa cadauera tabo,
D onec humo tegere, ac foueis abſcondere diſcunt.
N am neq; erat coriis uſus, nec uiſcera quiſquam,
A ut undis abolere pote ſt, aut uincere flamma·
N ec tondere quidem morbo, illuuie'q; pereſa
V ellera, nec telas poſſunt attingere putres,
V erum etiam inuiſos ſiquis tentarat amictus,

Virgil, printed in italic by Aldus Manutius, 1501

cut as a type-face for Aldus Manutius of Venice. It was at first intended for the printing of complete books, and it was only during the 16th century that it was combined with vertical type to be used as an alternative with the latter. Roman cursive is also the basis of our present *handwriting*. Roman cursive was initially closely allied to the forms of Renaissance script then in vogue, but under the influence of copperplate engraving and, later, lithography, it became more and more impersonal and artificial.

English copperplate writing, 18th century

15th-century roman. The earliest form of roman printing types is regarded as a special group, known as *venetian*, and differs slightly from later groups. Type-faces of this group have a rustic and powerful form, clearly reflecting the calligraphic nature of their prototype. The first types, whether gothic or roman, represented an attempt to imitate the hand-written manuscripts they now replaced. Adolf Rusch of Strasbourg, Wendelin da Spira and Nicolaus Jenson, both of Venice, are the pioneers of the 15th-

A : Deo optimo & Immortali auſpice' :-

A abcdeeʄgghiklmnopqrsſtuxx
xyxyzʒ & ʒ

Coſi ua il ſtato human : Chi queſta ſera Finiſce'
il corſo ſuo, chi diman naſce'. Sol
virtu doma Morte' horrida
, e, altera .

Ludo. Vice timus Rome' in Parhione'
ſcribeba T.

· ANN · MDXXII ·

Deo, & Virtuti' omnia debent ,

From the writing book of Ludovico degli Arrighi, 1522

Ommodū ad te dederā lit
nane Dionyſius fuerit: eg
ſé: ſed totū remiſiſſé ſi ueniſſet
ſic in tuis litteris quas Arpini acc
uellé. Ego uolebā auté uel cupie
plane cū i formianum ueniſſ&
ſolebā: at ille perpauca locutus
ſceré ſe rebus ſuis impeditū nob

From Cicero, 'Epistolae ad Brutum'. Jenson, 1470

century roman type-face. Many consider Jenson's types are still unsurpassed for beauty and legibility.

Old face. Soon after the end of the 15th century roman type underwent a change in the direction of

287

greater sharpness and easier, more elegant forms. The beginning of this development is noticeable in the types of Aldus Manutius, but it was brought to perfection by Claude Garamont. Old-face types preserved the alternating thick and fine strokes and the slanting distribution of the centres of gravity of the curves as occurring in the manuscript. Serifs are bracketed, but more flexible and finer than in the roman of the 15th century. During the 18th and 19th centuries, with certain interruptions, old face still retained its popularity, and is now the type form most used in western countries. Bembo, Garamond, Granjon and Weiss roman are among popular versions used.

Transitional faces. During the 18th century, roman type became more geometric in design, and the forms of the letters more severe and sharp. By way of transition to this stage are various type-faces which cannot easily be assigned to any particular group. William Caslon's types represent an art which most closely approaches the old face or medieval roman. These types, cut about 1720, were broad and had a marked difference between thick and thin strokes. A more geometric character is obvious in the types of John Baskerville, cut in the middle of the 18th century. His types are broad and give an impression of serenity and dignity. It would seem that these, rather than Caslon's, were to be regarded as the direct precursors of the new form of letter that made its appearance at the end of the century.

Modern faces. In 18th-century France, as in England, there was a tendency to a more geometric type with a pronounced vertical construction. Early examples were Philippe Grandjean's *romain du roi*, q.v., dating from 1702, some of Fournier's types cut towards the mid-century and types cut in 1732 by J. M. Fleischman for the Dutch firm Enschedé. A

Bei uns in Deutfchland befteht n
bei jeder Gelegenheit in allem un
ift auch der Grund dafür, daß De
dertelang das Exerzierfeld für fre

Fleischman's roman cut for Enschedé of Haarlem,
c. 1760

fully developed modern-face roman was cut in 1784 by F. A. Didot, but it was Giambattista Bodoni who, at the end of the 18th century, brought perfection to the face. Characteristics are contrasting thick and thin strokes, serifs at right-angles, and curves thickened in the centre. Modern face was popular throughout Europe during the 19th century.

Contemporary faces. Revivals of classic old, transitional and modern faces are used today. But since

1900 entirely new faces, showing mainly old-face influences, have been designed by typographers in Europe and America. Notable are *Times New Roman* designed by Stanley Morison; Eric Gill's *Perpetua*;

ABCDEFGHIJKLMNOPQR
STUVWXYZabcdefghijklmno
pqrſstuvwxyzſtßäöü1234567890

Didot roman, about 1800

Frederic Goudy's *Goudy Modern*; W. A. Dwiggins's *Electra*, a narrow elegant type designed for Linotype; Jan van Krimpen's *Lutetia*, and Walter Tracy's *Europa*. Other types have been designed specially for photosetting.

Jobbing and display types. Social changes during the 19th century brought about a demand for types with mass appeal, and it was in 1810 that Robert Thorne produced the first actual jobbing type, a *bold-face roman*. In 1815 appeared the first of several *egyptians*, a heavy type with thick strokes and slab-serifs. In the 1830s sanserif types had a vogue which never died, and modern sanserifs include *Futura* by Paul Renner, *Kabel* by Rudolph Koch, *Gill sans* by Eric Gill, and Adrian Frutiger's *Univers*.

Towards the end of the 19th century advertising and general commercial printing saw employed in their service an astonishing collection of script types, fat-face types and similar unfortunate fantasies which are now forgotten. See Appendix A for type specimens. (GU)

See also *accents, bastarda, Beneventan, black letter, book hand, calligraphy, Carolingian script, codex aureus, Court hand, cuneiform script, cursive, demotic, fere-humanistica, free hand, gothic, half-uncial, hieratic, humanistic, Insular hand, Irish half-uncial, italic, lettera antiqua tonda, lettera rotunda, Merovingian, neo-caroline, roman, rustic capitals, scrittura umanistica, serif, set hand, square capitals, text hand, textus, transfer lettering, uncials.*

letterspacing: the inserting of thin spaces between the letters of words set in small capitals to improve appearance and increase legibility. They are also used on either side of certain roman capitals, e.g. between those letters which occupy most of the width of their shanks. Lower-case words do not need letterspacing but occasionally this is done, e.g. when text is set by the side of an illustration; also for emphasis, e.g. in German texts as an alternative for italic.

Lettou, John, fl.1480–3: an immigrant printer who may have learned his craft in Rome before setting up a press in London in 1480. His was the first shop in the city, but it may not have been a financial success for after printing two works in two years he joined *William de Machlinia*, q.v., in 1482. The small type he used enabled him to try two-column setting. This was its first use in England as was his use of quire signatures.

lettre bâtarde: the form of *bastarda*, q.v., used by French printers from about 1484–1500. The sloping, light, pointed characters were influenced by Italian chancery hands and the legal scripts used in northern France. Also known as *Textur*. See also *Fraktur*.

lettre de forme: a formal northern pointed black letter being narrow, tall and almost without curves. It was used in the 42-line Bible and the Mainz Psalter, etc. See also *letters – forms and styles*.

lettre de somme: the name used in France for a simplified round gothic type, known elsewhere as *rotunda*, and based on the script known as *fere-humanistica*, q.v. It is said to have been so named after its use in the popular 'Summae theologicae' of Thomas Aquinas, Schöffer, Mainz, 1467. It was used by Gering in Paris after 1473 and in Lyons by Buyer in 1477. Thereafter its popularity waned, being superseded by *lettre bâtarde*.

lettres françaises d'art de main: another name for *lettres de civilité*. See *civilité*.

lettres tourneures: a name used in France for *lombards*, q.v.

levant: a good-quality morocco with a large open grain; it is given a high polish and used for book covers. See also *French Cape Levant*.

level stock: a term descriptive of a bookseller's basic stock, e.g. guide books, series of classics, dictionaries, standard reference books, established novelists, poets and so forth. The range varies with the degree of specialization in a particular shop.

lever press: any printing press in which the impression is made by the moving of a lever, but the term is mostly applied to the type of presses used for proofing, etc., in which the lever is pulled down.   (ML)

levigator: a heavy steel disc which is rotated by hand over a lithographic stone to prepare the surface; sand and water are used as an abrasive. See also *graining*, *stone grinding*.

Levy, Benjamin, b. 1786: born in New York. He was the first important Jewish printer in the U.S.A. and, between 1822–41, one of the most active publishers in New Orleans. He issued legal, political and literary works. For a bibliography of 109 of them see B. W. Korn, 'Benjamin Levy', *PBSA* 54 1960 243–64. (DW)

Levy, Max: of Philadelphia, who with his brother Louis perfected the Ives half-tone glass screen in 1888, making finer lines with a ruling machine, etching them in the glass, and filling them with black resin. In 1900 Louis Levy invented an *etching machine*, q.v.

Lewis, Charles, 1786–1836: a leading London bookbinder, noted for his fine craftsmanship. He was the son of *Johann Ludwig*, a German immigrant. Charles Lewis opened a shop in the West End in 1817, and within three years was employing twenty journeymen with *Francis Bedford*, q.v., as his sometime foreman.

He favoured a simple binding style with fillet frames on the spine and sides and leaf tools in the corners. The decoration of his doublures was more elaborate. Beckford of Fonthill was one of his important clients.

lexicon: a dictionary of Greek, Hebrew, Arabic and certain other literary languages. In this sense the word was used by the Humanists, e.g. 'Lexicon graeco-latinum', 1532. The word was later used for subjects as distinct from languages, e.g. Kirchner's 'Lexikon des Buchwesens', 1952–6. See also *dictionary*, *encyclopaedia*, *glossary*, *onomasticon*, *vocabulary*.

Leypoldt, Frederick, 1835–84: a German settler in New York where he arrived in 1854. Moving to Philadelphia in 1859 he set up as a bookseller, specializing in imported English, French and German books. Aware of the absence of bibliographical tools for the trade he began his monthly *Literary Bulletin* in 1868 with a cumulation in 1870 as 'The American catalogue of books for 1869'. His *The Trade Circular and Literary Bulletin*, 1871, renamed *Publishers' Weekly* in 1873, is still published (without the apostrophe). He intended it as a practical and educative trade journal. In 1879 he sold the title to *R. R. Bowker*, q.v. His publishing activites overextended his finances and he died penniless.

libel: or written defamation, is anything published in printing or writing calculated to expose a person to hatred, ridicule or contempt. This includes such illustrative matter as prints, drawings or caricatures. Qualified privilege exists for certain publications.

Authors, printers, publishers, booksellers and librarians should be aware of their liabilities under the Defamation Act of 1952, one of which is the obligation placed upon a publisher to prove that any alleged defamatory words were written by the author without malice. See J. C. C. Gatley, 'Gatley on libel and slander', 7th ed., Sweet & Maxwell, 1974.

liber: the bark of a tree, which at one time was used for writing upon. It later denoted a roll of papyrus, and in medieval times a book in codex form.

Liberty press: see *platen press.*

librarius: in medieval times, principally a seller of books on commission on behalf of authors. Cf. *stationer.*

library: 1. a collection of books for lending, reading or study and, by extension, the room or building, public or private, in which they are kept.

2. a collective noun used by publishers, originally in Victorian England, for books published in series. The Bohn Library, the Railway Library and the Parlour Library were examples, while in the present century Dent's Everyman's Library is one which continues the usage.

Library Association Carnegie Medal: see *Carnegie Medal.*

Library Association Kate Greenaway Medal: see *Kate Greenaway Medal.*

Library Binding Institute: since 1935, an American trade association of commercial library binders with headquarters in Boston. In 1967 there were fifty-eight member firms.

The LBI which has issued standards for both rebinding and prebinding, has an extensive programme for protecting librarians' interests. This includes the inspection of binding plant, the testing of materials, and the insistence that member firms shall certify on invoices that work has been done to LBI standards.

library edition: 1. an edition of a book having strengthened joints and covers.

2. the binding, more elegant than that of the trade edition, in which a set of volumes is sometimes issued by a publisher.

Library Licence: an agreement among the Publishers Association, the Booksellers Association and the Library Association, reached in 1929. It was adapted in 1957 to fit the requirements of the Restrictive Trade Practices Act, 1956, and is now an authorized relaxation of the Net Book Agreement, 1957, administered by the PA. By its provisions public libraries and certain other libraries which do not 'unreasonably withhold' the free use of their books from the public may, if they comply with the conditions of the agreement, receive discounts of up to 10% on copies of new net books. The Licence is now issued to the bookseller empowered to grant discount to a named library (which receives a copy).

licence leaf: a separate leaf at the beginning of a book on which the *imprimatur,* q.v., was formerly printed.

Liédet, Loyset, fl.1461–78: a Flemish illuminator of Bruges and Hesdin. His atelier was commissioned by such patrons as Philip, Duke of Burgundy to produce Books of Hours, romances and other works popular with the laity. Liédet's attention and skill were devoted to landscapes, architectural details and costumes, crowd scenes and brilliant colouring marking his work. He worked with or for Jean Wauquelin, Simon Marmion and David Aubert at various times and his output was considerable.

lifted matter: type matter transposed from one job for use in another. (ML)

ligator: the Latin word for 'bookbinder'.

ligature: two or more letters joined together and often cast on one body, e.g. fi, fl, ffl. See also *logotype.*

light face: the opposite of *bold face,* q.v. Many type families are made in varying weights, light, medium, bold, extra bold; medium being the normal book weight.

lightweight paper: thin tough paper of a substance ranging from 20 to 50 g/m², or 80 g/m² and below for coated paper. Its high printing opacity is achieved by using a combination of clay or chalk with titanium dioxide. While giving good surface smoothness the high proportion of fillers tends to produce a sheet lacking stiffness. This may be compensated by surface sizing or adding binders. Such papers have a relatively low moisture content.

In spite of its flimsy appearance lightweight paper can be run on web-offset presses at up to 32,000 iph without tears. Its tensile strength ranges from 1kg/cm for 20 g/m² to 3kg/cm for 50 g/m² paper. The manufacturer also gives special attention to reeling and cutting.

On sheet-fed presses problems of curl may be experienced, particularly if printing large areas of solid black near the sheet edge on a litho press. Extra care in knocking up the sheets before backing is needed. Air blowers assist both feeding and delivery. By minimizing ink weight while slightly increasing pressure there is less tendency to show through. Heatset drying is practicable. See also *Bible paper.*

Limbourg brothers, fl.1400–16: three brothers, Pol, Jan and Hermann, who illuminated manuscripts for various wealthy patrons. Their most famous work was the sumptuous 'Très riches heures', made for the *duc de Berry,* q.v., and now in the Musée Condé, Chantilly.

limitation notice: a statement appearing in limited editions indicating how many copies have been printed and usually bearing a hand-written serial number in each.

limited edition: an edition confined to a specific number of copies, and one which will not be reprinted in the same form. Copies of a limited edition are usually numbered. See also *limitation notice, out of series, overs* (2).

Limited Editions Club: a New York club for discriminating book collectors, formed in 1929 under the direction of George Macy with the aim of publishing fine books for exclusive supply to a maximum of 1,500 members. The publishing programme called for a book a month. Macy (d. 1956) invited the world's leading artists, typographers and printers to produce editions of the classics notable for fine composition and fine presswork, presented in a tall format uncommon in Europe.

The British Library has a collection of Club books designed, illustrated, or printed in Britain. They include work by Eric Gill, Arthur Rackham, Oliver Simon, Sir Francis Meynell, Barnett Freedman, Edward Ardizonne, Lynton Lamb, Hans Schmoller, the Curwen Press and Oxford University Press.

limner: one who embellished manuscripts in gold or colours.

limp binding: a style of binding books with thin flexible covers made without boards. See also *Yapp*.

limp flush: see *covering* (3).

Linasec: a system developed in the 1960s by the Compugraphic Corporation of Reading, U.S.A., for the conversion of unjustified typewriter tape into six-hole teletypesetting tape for the operation of line-casting machines. Unjustified typing is much quicker than tapping off copy on a composing keyboard. When the tape is fed into the Linasec computer it quickly produces a TTS tape with justification codes. The Linasec is used with high-speed Linotypes and Intertypes.

Lindisfarne Gospels: a Latin text of the Gospels written on 258 leaves in Insular majuscule script about AD 700 with Anglo-Saxon glosses added in the 10th century. At that time a colophon was inserted stating that the original was written by Bishop Eadfrith of Lindisfarne who died in 721. It is generally considered as the finest example of early English illumination.

The detailed geometrical patterns on a cruciform axis are a development in style of the larger scale backgrounds seen in the *Book of Durrow*, q.v., but the curious interlacing which distorts the birds and animals is new to Northumbrian art and shows a Byzantine influence. Another innovation was the use of gold. The extravagantly patterned capitals are also noteworthy.

The work, which is also known as the *Gospels of St Cuthbert*, is now in the British Library (Cotton Nero D IV). See T. D. Kendrick and others, 'Evangelium quattuor Codex Lindisfarnensis', Olten, 1960.

lineal type: see *sanserif*.

line and half-tone fit up: see *combined line and half-tone*.

linear flow diagram: a sequence of instructions or information presented diagrammatically. A common method is to link with rule a number of rectangles, each containing wording to indicate the successive steps of a course of action.

line block: a letterpress relief printing plate, mounted to type height, and used to reproduce in monochrome or colour an original consisting of lines or solid areas without any gradation of tone. Cf. *half-tone block*.

Originals suitable for line work include artists' drawings done in waterproof black drawing ink on Bristol board or well-sized white paper, and crayon drawings on lithographic chalk transfer paper. Tints to add texture and shading can be applied direct to artwork from self-adhering acetate film: they give the artist more control of the result than by leaving the addition of *mechanical tints*, q.v., to the process engraver. Line plates are also suitable for reproducing music and prints of type matter.

As a first step the original is photographed in a process camera to obtain a negative of it. A plate of polished copper (for fine work) or zinc (whence the popular name *zinco*) is put in a *whirler*, q.v., to receive a coating of dichromate and albumen. This acts as a photo-sensitive soluble acid resist. When dry, plate and negative are held in a *vacuum frame*, q.v., and exposed (known as *printing down*). The effect of light passing through the clear (or image) parts of the negative is to harden the coating into insolubility. The non-image areas remain soluble and must be reduced in depth by etching so that they will not be inked.

Before etching begins the plate is inked up and washed in warm water to remove the unwanted soluble coating. The image remains inked. The plate is then warmed and dusted with powdered bitumen. Heating causes this to melt on the design, forming an acid resist. The plate is then put in an etching bath for a quick immersion in nitric acid, leaving the image outlined in bright metal.

To prevent any of the image being undercut during

Reproduction of a line drawing on a line block

The same drawing after the addition of mechanical tints

Line block made from an original drawing

Reverse line block from the same drawing

Line block greyed back with mechanical positive tint

Reversed line block with mechanical negative tint

the removal of the non-image areas the plate is dusted with *dragon's blood*, q.v. This collects against the lines of the design and is fused to it by heating the plate. The action is repeated by brushing more dragon's blood until the shoulders of the design are protected by a hard ridge of resin. Etching is done in stages, with dusting between each, until a sufficient depth has been reached. The plate is then scrubbed in a hot alkaline solution. A trial proof is made. Finishing stages include routing large open areas, the hand-engraving of details, bevelling and mounting.

The laborious and lengthy etching process described above has been superseded by the use of photopolymer plates, electronic engraving, and powderless etching, the last being quick, automatic, and giving a clean vertical edge. See also references under *photo-engraving*.

lined characters: letters and numerals which have a lateral stroke through them. The effect when assembled in words is a continuous line running through. They were used in legal printing to show alterations and erasures. Caslon showed a fount as 'small pica erased'.

line engraving: an intaglio printing process for reproducing drawings. The design is transferred on to a copper plate into which the lines are cut with a scorper or graver; no acid is used. Printing is direct from the inked plate, but if thousands of copies are required a transfer print is made on a zinc litho plate. Line engravings cannot be printed with type.

line gauge: the printer's rule. This is calibrated in picas and is 72 picas in length.

linen faced: originally, the name for paper lined on one or both sides with linen to strengthen it. It was used for cheap book covers, the top side being printed. It is now known as *cloth-faced* or *cloth lined*.

linen finish: paper or bookcloth embossed to resemble coarsely woven linen. (LK)

linen paper: originally, paper made from pure linen rags but now applied to paper which has been passed through embossing rolls or between plates to imitate the original, i.e. *linen finish*.

liners: pieces of thin strong paper pasted to the boards of a book which is being bound in full leather. A single-width piece of paper is glued and applied to one side of the board only. A double-width sheet is next glued and pressed on both sides of the board. The double thickness will cause the first side to curve on drying, and this concave side forms the inner board. This will be pulled flat by the leather which covers the book. End-papers, added last, are part of this skilled balancing of materials. As a check to

later warping the grain direction of the lining paper must be vertical.

line work: a drawing for reproduction made up of black lines on a white ground. Mechanical tints are used for shaded areas. See also *Ben Day tints*.

lining, lining up: the giving of strength and firmness to the back of a book by gluing a strip of mull to it after sewing and nipping. The mull should extend to $\frac{1}{4}$in. from the head and tail of the book and project $1\frac{1}{4}$in. on either side for affixing to the end-papers, and this is known as *first lining*. It is then covered with a strip of brown paper the full size of the back, known as *second* lining. Flexible glue is used. See also *one on and two off*, *Oxford hollow*.

lining figures: synonymous with *ranging figures*, q.v.

lining papers: see *end-papers*.

lining-up table: see *register table*.

linocut: a relief printing block in which the design is cut with a knife and gouges into a linoleum surface. The medium is best suited to bold designs with few isolated lines.

Linofilm: the name given to the initial range of photosetting machines designed and built by the Mergenthaler Linotype Company of New York where the prototype was demonstrated in 1954. Its first European showing was in 1958. The system had four basic units: an electric typewriter keyboard with associated controls, a photographic unit, a corrector and a composer. It bore no resemblance in either method of construction or operation to the hot-metal Linotype.

Various developments of the basic model have been (1) the *Linofilm Super-Quick*, operating automatically from 6-channel punched paper-tape produced on any standard perforator with TTS coding. Characters are carried on four glass grids, each with 184–192, or roughly equivalent to 90 duplexed matrices for mixed composition. Output is right or wrong reading positive on film, photopaper, or stabilization paper. Type size range is 6- to 72-point. (2) the *Linofilm VIP*, or variable input photosetter, which will accept 6–7 or 8-channel tapes and give mixed setting in one line from six 96 character founts. While any 6-channel perforator may be used as a keyboard, special boards with programmed instruction keys may be fitted, thereby reducing the input keystrokes needed for format changes.

Linoscreen: a video editing terminal for proofing, editing and correcting paper tape or magnetic cassette input. It consists of a *video display unit*, q.v., with a built-in mini-computer and can be used as a stand-alone terminal, or in the on-line mode when it is interfaced to the central processor of a *Linotron* photosetting system using magnetic disc storage.

Linotron: the first photosetter using an optical master image grid with cathode ray tube write-out on to film or paper to become commercially viable. Devel-oped from the Purdy-McIntosh photosetter, which was originally manufactured by K. S. Paul, it was renamed the Linotron 505 when the new company Linotype-Paul was created in 1967. The later *Linotron 505C Phototypesetting System* incorporates a front-end mini-computer in place of the original control unit. This computer can be loaded with compre-hensive typesetting and pagination programmes.

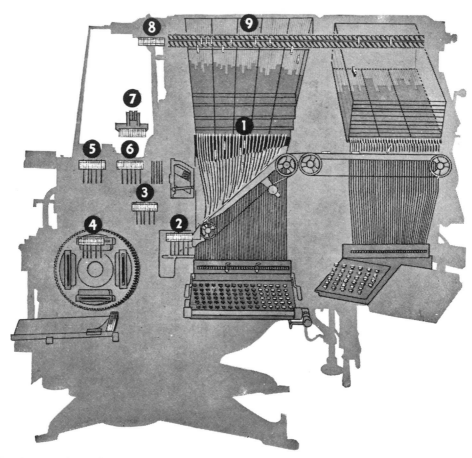

This diagram shows the path taken by the matrices as they circulate through the Linotype machine

1. *Matrices leaving the magazine in order required by the operator, having been released by the depression of keybuttons.* 2. *Matrices and spacebands in process of assembling in line formation.* 3. *Completely assembled matrices being transferred to the first elevator, after being released from the assembler by the operator (who now proceeds to set the line to follow).* 4. *Matrix line in front of the mould for justification and casting.* 5. *The matrix line after casting being carried upward for its transfer to the second elevator.* 6. *The matrix line is transferred to the second elevator ready for raising to the distributing mechanism. At this point the spacebands are separated from the matrix line and transferred to the spaceband box ready for use again.* 7. *The matrix line (now free of spacebands) being lifted to the level of the distributor bar suspended over the magazine.* 8. *Matrices being separated into single units again so as to be engaged by rotating screws, which propel them along the distributor bar.* 9. *Matrices passing along the dis-tributor bar until released by their combination of teeth, which causes them to fall into their original channels ready for reassembling into new matrix lines.*

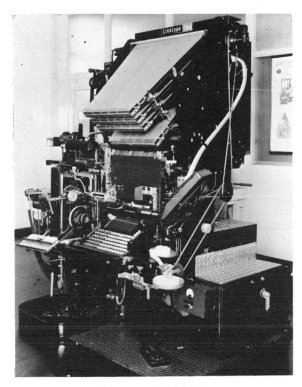

Linotype, Model 794

The *composing mechanism* has a keyboard, each key being connected with its channel in the magazine. Matrices are made of brass and vary in thickness according to type width. The type character is stamped into the edge of the matrix body. In two-letter (duplex) matrices the character is usually

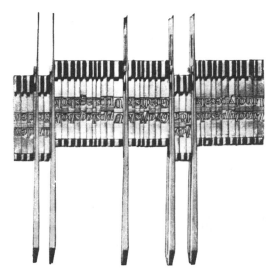

Line of duplex matrices ready for casting; some are in position for italics. Note the long spacebands. The slug will be cast from the dies forming a complete line

Special justifying and non-justifying keyboards have been designed for this system. Non-justified input can be used to produce text, display, tables, multi-column pages and mathematical formulae.

The system can be expanded by adding magnetic tape units and magnetic disc files to achieve text storage and correction, pagination and automatic classification. No stripping of corrections is necessary. Digital storage was introduced in the *Linotron 606* of the late 1970s, i.e. the image of a letter (character) is stored in the form of magnetic impulses in a computer.

Linotype: a machine for setting matrices and casting type in continuous lines known as *slugs*. It was invented by Ottmar Mergenthaler and demonstrated in New York in 1886. After further experimenting the machine was given the outward appearance it still has. Regular manufacture began in 1890, and in 1891 the first Linotypes appeared in Britain. They are now made in West Germany, Italy, Britain and America and used world-wide.

The machine, which required but one operator, has three main parts: the *composing machine*, in which matrices are assembled in lines; the *casting mechanism*, in which lines are justified and cast as slugs; and the *distributing mechanism*, which returns the matrices, after casting, to the matrix magazine.

stamped in two different faces, e.g. roman and italic or bold. The matrix magazines are positioned vertically over the keyboard.

As copy is tapped off released matrices slide from the magazine towards a revolving belt which conveys them to the *assembly box*: this is the composing stick of the Linotype which is set to the required measure. Between each word the compositor strikes a spacing key which discharges steel spacebands from a separate magazine. When the matrix line almost fills the assembler box the operator must judge whether the words already set will fill the measure or how an over-long word shall be divided. The matrix line is then mechanically transferred to the casting mechanism.

The *casting mechanism* has an elevator which receives the matrix line and places it between two vice jaws, an air-cooled mould wheel which has four moulds, a metal-containing pot with a plunger, an ejector and trimming knives.

In operation, the line of matrices in the vice is tightened and positioned against one of the four mould wheels. The plunger then forces a stream of metal into the mould where the line is cast.

After casting, an ejector blade pushes the slug from the mould to trimming knives which reduce it

295

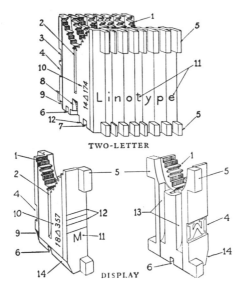

TWO-LETTER

DISPLAY

Parts of the Linotype matrix

1. *Tooth combination.* 2. *Separator slot.* 3. *Normal character position.* 4. *Italic position.* 5. *Lugs (ears).* 6. *Body distinguishing notch.* 7. *Bridge notch.* 8. *Channel cut out in matrices for certain models.* 9. *Safety bevelling.* 10. *Fount reference number. Point size indicated before diamond (not triangle), type-face identification number after.* 11. *Character stamped in the side of the matrix enabling the compositor to read the matrix line before sending it to be cast.* 12. *Lines incised in the base of duplex matrices or on the side of display matrices to indicate whether a matrix of another fount is unintentionally mixed in the magazine.* 13. *Channels cut in big matrices to make them lighter.* 14. *Chamfer on big matrices to facilitate distribution.*

to accurate body dimensions before it comes to rest in the galley.

Meanwhile, other devices have passed the line of matrices to the *distributing mechanism* which, according to the combination of teeth on their edges, returns each matrix to its proper channel in the magazine.

From the simple machine with one magazine models with up to eight were developed. By 1898 mixed composition machines were built to enable type from several magazines to be mixed: the first had two adjacent magazines and two keyboards. In 1906 this was reconstructed with one keyboard, and by 1914 a four-magazine machine for mixed composition was built. Updated, improved and enlarged models have continued to appear.

The tape-operated *Elektron*, shown in Europe in 1962, has a straight line matrix delivery eliminating the elevator of earlier models. Thus matrices can be assembled continuously. The *Elektron* II is for manual operation and can have up to four magazines with manual or hydraulic justification.

296

Linotypes were at one time associated in the public mind with newspaper work only but the machines are now widely used for bookwork (though correction is dearer). This has led the makers to add several book faces to their already extensive range e.g. Jubilee, Juliana, Pilgrim, etc. See Appendix A. See also *Mergenthaler*, *teletypesetting*, *type metal*.

linson: as *Linson*, the trade name of a British non-woven bookbinding material first made in 1936 by R. &. W. Watson Ltd and their subsidiary The Grange Fibre Company Ltd at Watson's mill at Linwood, Scotland. (The name derives from *Lin*wood and Wat*son*.) Not until 1945, when bookcloth was scarce and costly, was linson generally used by edition binders. Basically, the product is a very strong paper made from manilla pulp dyed to the colour required, and treated to have good folding properties and abrasion resistance. The paper is then embossed, a variety of designs being available.

Linson is available in rolls or sheets in a wide range of colours, designs and finishes. It is washable, very hard-wearing, can be printed by letterpress or litho, and is increasingly substituted for cloth, being much cheaper.

Under such proprietary names as *Excelin*, *Fabroleen*, *Linmaster*, and *Milskin* the firm markets non-woven fibre materials of several qualities and strengths, each suitable for a particular type of binding.

linters: the fibres obtained by shaving cotton seeds. They are then compressed into thick sheets in which form they are supplied to papermills for making good quality printing and writing papers. Cf. *laps*.

linting: a fault which may occur with certain grades of uncoated litho papers from the surface of which fibres work loose and collect on the offset blanket. On high speed presses this can lead to serious loss of printed image.

Lion and Unicorn Press: the printing press of the Royal College of Art, London, where it is an integral part of the School of Graphic Design. Experimental book production by students began in 1953, and in 1955 it was decided to invite annual subscriptions for a series of three books a year. Text composition is done commercially; display, make-up, printing and binding being done at the College.

Some of the books have subsequently been published commercially, notable being Juan de Yciar's 'Arte subtilissima', issued in 1958 by the College and in 1960 by Oxford University Press.

The choice of paper, methods of illustration and varied binding styles have resulted in an interesting presentation of unfamiliar texts.

literal: a mistake in setting type which does not involve more than a letter-for-letter correction, such as a transposition, or a comma for a full point. It includes turned sorts, wrong founts and battered letters.

literary agent: an intermediary between author and publisher who will advise a writer on the suitability of his manuscript, offer it to a publisher most likely to accept it, negotiate the contract, arrange the sale of subsidiary rights and collect royalties. His fee for these services is a commission on earnings. Although some authors, often after having been nursed to success, dispense with their agent, and other writers prefer the friendliness of direct dealings with a publisher, there are advantages in having an expert attend to the business side of authorship.

Agents were a long time in coming. For centuries after Caxton an author sold his work outright to a printer-publisher in return for either a negligible sum or a few printed copies. Or he sought a patron to sponsor publication. The powerful *Stationers' Company*, q.v., protected the rights of printer-publishers but not authors.

By the 19th century some writers were helped in their dealings with publishers by solicitors or accountants. *John Forster*, friend of Dickens, acted on his behalf in a similar way and without fee. Across the Atlantic *Henry Stevens* (1819–86) in addition to selling rare books assisted British authors who feared the piracy of their writings in America. But although not the first to act in this capacity, it was not until the Glaswegian *Alexander Pollock Watt* (1834–1914) opened his office in London about 1878 that the idea of literary agency developed. Watt's extensive list of writers included Doyle, Haggard, Hardy and Kipling. Until 1900 he was unrivalled; thereafter the increasing number of writers wanting such help as he gave encouraged others to set up agencies, notable being *James Brand Pinker* (1863–1923) whose list included Bennett, Conrad, James, and Wells. The American *Curtis Brown* came to London in 1898, later setting up what is now the leading international agency. See J. Hepburn, 'The author's empty purse and the rise of the literary agent', O.U.P., 1968.

literary awards and prizes: rewards to writers whose work has been judged, by those appointed to decide, to meet the donor's conditions for giving them. Prizes now current range from medals, assistance to needy writers and travel grants, to large sums of money far removed from the laurel crown bestowed on classical poets. But big advances on royalties given for an unpublished manuscript which lavish publicity will turn into a bestseller when published are viewed with scepticism, and certain other prizes are seen as no more than a device to stimulate sales, especially if the award is made at a big public luncheon or dinner, or, as in France, to launch the 'season'. Wider approval attaches to commemorative awards demonstrably given in recognition of creative ability to the author of a book unmindful of a prize when he wrote it, when no financial gain accrues to the donor, and when the judges' decision is seen as neither arbitrary nor capricious.

The selection listed below includes some which have lapsed. For current prizes see the latest editions of 'Cassell's directory of publishing' and 'Literary and library prizes', N.Y., Bowker.

See also *Hans Christian Andersen Medals, Australian Children's Book Award, Benson Medal, David Berry Prize, Besterman Medal, James Tait Black Memorial Prizes, Bollingen Prize, Booker Prize, Bowater Awards, Caldecott Medal, Campe Prize, Carnegie Medal, Chambers Awards, Cholmondeley Awards, Collins Religious Book Award, Rose Mary Crawshay Prize, Cromer Greek Prize, Crompton Bequest, First Novel Award, William Foyle Poetry Prize, Miles Franklin Award, Friedenpreis des deutschen Buchhandels, Prix Goncourt, Kate Greenaway Medal, Guardian Fiction Prize, Hawthornden Prize, Winifred Holtby Memorial Bequest, McColvin Medal, Katherine Mansfield Prize, Somerset Maugham Trust Fund, Moomba Award for Australian Literature, National Book League Award, Newbery Medal, Newdigate Prize Foundation, Frederic Niven Literary Award, Nobel Prize for Literature, Pulitzer Prizes, Queen's Gold Medal for Poetry, Regina Medal, Royal Society of Literature Award, Saltire Award, Schlegel-Tieck Prize, W. H. Smith Prize, Swiney Prize, Tom-Gallon Trust, Whitbread Literary Awards.*

lithograph: an impression from a lithographic forme (stone or plate).

lithographer: the printing craftsman who prepares plates for lithographic printing and controls the press while impressions are taken from them.

lithographic artist: a commercially employed craftsman who copies an original by direct drawing on to stone or grained plates for *auto lithography*, q.v. He is thus distinguished from an *autolithographer*, who is an independent artist creating as he works an original drawing directly on the surface from which printing will be done. See also *Plastocowell*.

lithographic copy: when letterpress printers have installed presses for litho work they often find it convenient to commission plates from a trade house as an alternative to setting up their own processing department. Unlike letterpress printing, in which type and any accompanying blocks are movable units in the forme, permitting last minute changes or adjustments, a litho plate is complete and fixed, and although a trade house may submit a trial proof plate before the final printing plate, in general type matter (preferably filmset but otherwise proofed on repro paper) and same-size photographic originals must be carefully planned and positioned before photography for plate making begins. For colour work the platemaker should be consulted before finished originals are made. Among other things he will require to know the make of press to be used, the type and size of plate wanted, the ink specification and the colour sequence.

Proofing should be done on the paper to be used for the main run.

lithographic paper: for the printing of artists' lithographs the best quality paper is made from rag, the next from esparto with a high machine finish or a super-calendered surface.

For offset lithography a much wider range of papers can be used. When ordering paper for lithographic work the papermaker should be told in detail the conditions in which it will be used. The printer should store it at pressroom temperature and humidity, ensure that it is carefully trimmed and handled, and that when on the machine the grain direction runs down the length of the sheet.

lithographic plates: plates for lithographic printing are of many kinds. For descriptions of some of them see *albumen process, anodized aluminium plates, bimetallic lithographic plates, lithography, multimetal plates, offset reproduction, pre-coated plates, pre-sensitised plates, wipe-on plates.*

lithographic press: a lithographic cylinder machine. Outwardly it does not differ much from a stop-cylinder press as used for bookwork. Feeding and delivery are done in the same way, and the movement of the bed with the printing stone is, on the whole, the same. In addition to the inking device (table

The lithographic press of Georg Sigl, 1851

inking rollers), however, the machine is fitted with a damping unit on the same principle. The inking rollers and damping unit are usually situated on either side of the cylinder. As it may be necessary to ink up the stone several times during printing the press is

298

so equipped that the cylinder can be kept stationary while the stone moves to and fro under the inkers for $\frac{1}{2}$ (as is usual in stop-cylinder printing), $1\frac{1}{2}$, or $2\frac{1}{2}$ revolutions.

The bed on which the stone rests can be raised or

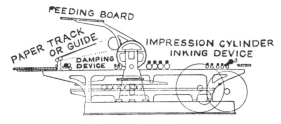

Diagram of a litho press

lowered according to the thickness of the stone so that the printing surface is in the position required for correct peripheral speed relationship. Leather or rubber rollers are used for inking up, glazed rollers for ink mixing, and rough or smooth rollers against the stone. The damping rollers and damping table are cloth-covered. Litho machines can be used for printing from plates.

An English patent for a lithographic press was taken out in 1845 by George Scholefield (No. 10,924) which had an image cylinder of stone, zinc or other material. The press built by Sigl in Vienna (see illustration under *lithography*) gave 1,000 impressions an hour and was the first of several powered machines for the trade, but they did not come into general use before the 1880s. See also *offset press.* (With GU)

lithographic rollers: see *compostion-, glazed-, nap roller.*

Lithographic Technical Foundation: an American organization, founded in 1942 'for conducting research and education for better lithography'. This non-profit-making body is supported by contributions from the trade and membership is international. A valuable service to members and others is the periodic publication of *Research Progress* as well as books on the subject.

In 1963 the name was changed to *Graphic Arts Technical Foundation.*

lithographic transfer: see *transfer.*

lithography: originally, printing from a stone slab. The idea was conceived in Munich by Aloysius Senefelder in 1796 when he discovered the possibility of drawing on stone and then relief-engraving it to a printing surface. By chance he made an inscription on limestone and had the idea of treating the stone with acid to raise the script. He later found it was not necessary to raise the printing surface, but that the essential point was to make a greasy image surrounded with a water-attracting surface. Thus only the image would take up greasy ink and be transferred to paper. In this way he discovered the principle of 'chemical printing', i.e. actual lithography. (The term 'lithography' was first used in 1804). In 1797 he built the first lithographic hand-press with grinders, in 1798 he experimented in stone engraving and lithographic transfers, in 1799 in crayon drawing, and during the first years of the 19th century his process spread to most European countries. In 1818 he published a 'Complete handbook of stone printing' with a description of all his discoveries and inventions.

In 1805 Senefelder found that in addition to stone it was possible to lithograph on suitably prepared metal plates, and in 1818 he made an attempt to replace the expensive natural stone by artificial products. It was soon evident that the only entirely satisfactory stones were those obtained from Solnhofen in Bavaria, and the price of these increased as the demand for them grew.

About the year 1800 lithography was introduced into France by Nidermayer, a resident of Strasbourg, and in 1805 Andreas Dallarmi started a lithographic printing works in Rome. The method reached the U.S.A. in 1828 through Barnett and Doolittle. At an early date Senefelder came into association with distinguished artists who made drawings directly on his stones, e.g. Strixner and Piloty. (See *autolithography*.)

In France the process was taken up with enthusiasm by artists, and since about 1815 France has been a home of artistic lithography. Lithography was used to a great extent by the political cartoonists who played so large a part in French society during that time. The most outstanding of them was probably Daumier (1808–79). Among German lithographers of the 19th century Adolf Menzel (1815–1905) is most important. The Spaniard Goya (1746–1828) was one of the first artists of considerable importance who also produced work in lithography. See also *autolithography, drawn lithography, music printing, stone engraving, stone printing, transfer*.

Chromolithography, or colour lithography, was probably practised successfully from the beginning. The term occurs for the first time in connection with a French patent taken out in 1837 by Gottfried Engelmann for stone engraving in colour with the individual colours of a crayon drawing. During the whole of the 19th century chromolithography remained the principal means of making coloured reproductions, and has survived with the same working methods until the present day, although here, as in all other spheres of graphic art, photographic process work predominates. See also *photolitho-offset, offset reproduction*.

Lithographic printing was first done in a hand-press, with Senefelder's construction as a prototype, and it was not until 1851 that Georg Sigl built a cylinder machine for lithographic printing. For printing on tin a stone printing press on the offset principle was built by Barclay in 1875, but it was not until 1904 that Rubel perfected a method of offset lithography on paper. This is now the chief process used.

Modern lithographic offset printing is mostly done in rotary presses. This was facilitated by abandoning stone as the printing material and substituting zinc or aluminium plates, though other metals are also used. While stone has a surface in itself suitable for lithographic work, metal plates must undergo preparatory treatment to make them capable of holding the inked image and absorbing water. As the adhesion of ink or moisture is a phenomenon connected with surface, an increase of surface is achieved on a plate by *graining*, q.v., by which means the smooth metal surface is given a fine-grained structure. When the inked image has been transferred to the plate, the latter is desensitized with chemicals which cause deposits insoluble in water, and still finer grain on the empty spaces of the plate which thereby increase their capacity to absorb water. Before the plate is put in the printing press it is gummed with a solution of gum arabic and allowed to dry. The layer of gum held on the plate by the grained surface is not dissolved when moistened by water, but absorbs it, forming a swollen, grease-resisting layer. If corrections on the plate are necessary, both the layer of gum and the surface coating obtained by the 'etching' must be removed by 'counter-etching' for the surface to be receptive to thick ink. With reference to stainless steel and other materials for printing plates see *offset reproduction*. See also *albumen process, bimetallic lithographic plates, deep-etch process, planographic printing*.

See I. Faux, 'Modern lithography', Macdonald & Evans, 1973. (GU)

lithopone: a combined precipitate of zinc sulphide and barium sulphate used as a filler to increase the opacity and brightness of the paper being made.

lithotint: a method of printing illustrations from lithographic stones with resinous washes of varying tone densities. The process was patented by Charles Hullmandel in London in 1840. In 1841 he printed J. D. Harding's 'The park and the forest' in this way. The process was little used.

The name lithotint is also given to what are properly called *tinted lithographs*, q.v.

Litos: the first *teleordering system*, q.v.

littera or **litera:** used as was *lettera*, q.v., by Italian writing masters to identify scripts.

Little Britain: a London street between Aldersgate and Smithfield associated in the later 17th and early 18th centuries with the publishing and selling of books in foreign languages. It is named after the Dukes of Brittany who had a residence there.

Little Gidding bindings: a series of early 17th century bindings made by members of the Anglican community which Nicholas Ferrar and his family founded at Little Gidding, Hunts. The works bound were albums of Biblical texts cut from printed editions to which the Ferrars added numerous illustrations and gave the name 'Harmonies'. It is probable that Katharine Moody, daughter of a Cambridge binder, taught the community how to bind. Volumes were bound in gold-tooled morocco, vellum or velvet. The velvet was gold-tooled, and no embroidered bindings were produced at Little Gidding as used to be believed. The original group was disbanded in 1649.

live matter: a forme of type which awaits printing, stereotyping or electrotyping. Cf. *blocked up, dead matter*.

Livre d'Heures: see *Book of Hours*.

livres à vignettes: books having copperplate vignetted illustrations as their raison d'être. They had a great vogue in 18th century France where an edition of Molière, 1734, led the fashion. François Joullain and Laurent Cars etched and engraved the plates by François Boucher. Notable also was the work of the Cochin family and François Gravelot.

livres cochons: French slang for illustrated *erotica*, q.v.

livres de peintres: limited editions of French books featuring etchings, lithographs, wood engravings or other hand-produced plates designed and printed (or supervised) by well-known artists, any text being subordinate. Paris is the centre of this trade and Chagall, Dufy, Matisse and Picasso are among those who have contributed to them.

The form of publication is normally *en feuilles* for subsequent binding. They are intended for rich connoisseur collectors, who alone can afford them, and are issued in a hierarchy of exclusivity identifiable by the price, the sequence of printing pulls or impressions, the number of plates, any extra sets and, not least, the paper. This last is clearly of particular importance and its nature is set out in the *justification du tirage* as, for example, so many copies on japon impérial, japon nacré, pur fil Vidalon, vélin d'Arches, vélin du Marais, vélin Murier d'Annam de Rives, vélin supérieur Alfana, vélin Hollande Pannekoek, papier d'Auvergne, vergé de Monteuil, vergé Lafuma-Navarre, to list but a few exotica. See N. Rauch, 'Les Peintres et le livre, 1857–1957',

Geneva, 1957; 'The artist and the book', Boston, Museum of Fine Arts, 1960; and W. J. Strachan, 'The artist and the book in France', Owen, 1969.

loading: chalk, clay or similar minerals added to stuff in the beater, or flowed into stock before it goes through the flow box of the Fourdrinier. Loading fills spaces between fibres and acts as a pulp extender. Loaded paper has a smooth opaque finish and a good printing surface. See also *art paper*.

loc. cit.: an abbreviation for the Latin 'loco citato', i.e. at the place cited in a previous reference. Cf. *op. cit.*

locking up: adjusting quoins between imposed type and the sides of the chase to secure the forme for printing.

Locking up a forme

The forme secured in its chase

lock-up table: any of several varieties of imposing surface specially equipped for the accurate imposition of formes for colour registration. A beam with sliding gauges, T-squares, or a gridded visor are among fittings used to achieve precision.

loft dried: said of hand-made paper which has been dried by hanging the sheets on hessian ropes in a loft, the air temperature and moisture content being controlled. See also *air dried, back mark* (1), *relative humidity*.

logography: a method of casting several letters as a unit, or *logotype*, first patented by Henry Johnson of London in 1780. He had a fount of 3,500 words and syllables, his view being that to cast such word endings as -ing, -ity, -ment, -ton, etc., would save time. The idea could not be fully developed since compositors of the day equated saved time with diminished earnings.

logotype: a word or several letters cast on one body. See also *ligature, logography, slug*.

lombardic: in the context of 15th century printing, a majuscule type in the style of the Lombardic or Beneventan uncial manuscript hand current in Italy until about the 13th century, and thereafter (when it had ceased to be used as a text hand) widely used in Europe as a design for decorative capitals in rubrication. Many 15th century printers used red inked lombardic type in liturgical works for rubrics within the line. This may have been cast like any other type. Metal-cast, metal-cut, or woodcut initial capitals in lombard style were also in general use.

Specimen alphabets may conveniently be examined in an 18th century Dutch copy reproduced in Updike's 'Printing types', 1922, in which they are called 'Gothise Monnikke Letteren'. In Stower's 'Printers' grammar', 1808, they appear as 'Anglo-Norman, or lettres tourneures'. Goudy's somewhat stylized fount of lombardic was designed in 1929 and made available by Monotype in 1933.

The British Library kindly supplied part of this note.

London Book Fair: an annual book exhibition held in a London hotel. It originated in 1971 as *SPEX* (Specialist Publishers Exhibition), being a one-day exhibition for librarians. The name was changed in 1975 when, in addition to specialist publishers, several medium-sized general firms participated. The common aim of the 140 exhibitors was to bring to public notice books not widely on display in bookshops.

London Chappel of Private Press Printers: begun in 1962 by a group of private press owners for the sole purpose of printing for pleasure and experiment. Members met monthly at Monotype House for discussions on problems of mutual interest and to exchange specimens of work. By 1965 there were twenty-five press owning members.

In America there have long been many similar chappels.

long-bodied type: type cast on bodies larger than normal, e.g. 10-point on 12-point. This increases the space between lines without using *leads*, q.v.

long descenders: the letters g, j, p, q and y made with descenders of extra length. They are obtainable as alternative characters on such proprietary faces as Linotype Caledonia and Times Roman, with their italics.

long primer: the former name for a size of type, about 10-point.

long ream: 500 or 516 sheets of paper.

long s: a lower-case s, printed f. It differs from a lower-case f in that the horizontal cross-stroke projects only to the left. Until 1749 the long s was used by all English printers. In that year, exceptionally, Ames discarded it in his 'Typographical antiquities', but it was not generally discarded until after the publication of John Bell's 'Shakespeare', 1785, in the Prolegomena of which he abandoned the long s, giving his reasons in a prefatory note.

look through: an expression for appraising the quality of paper when a sheet is examined against light; being a means of determining whether the paper is laid or wove, and if the texture is marred by impurities. See also *opacity, salle*.

Lotter, Melchior, fl.1491–1536: a printer of Leipzig. He was a friend of Luther, and when anti-Reformation edicts made it unwise for him to print in Leipzig he opened premises in Wittenberg in 1519, installing his son *Melchior II* as manager. It was here that the Lotters printed the first edition of Luther's New Testament in 1522 for the publishers Lucas Cranach and Christian Döring. There were fourteen reprints in Wittenberg within two years. A second son *Michael* joined them in 1523. The Lotters, who were wealthy and important, worked almost solely on the proliferation of Luther's works. See also *Hans Lufft*.

lower case: the compositor's type-case in which small letters are kept, and also the letters themselves. The abbreviation *l.c.* is used as a proof correction mark to indicate that a capital letter is to be changed to a small. See also *case*.

Lowndes, William Thomas, c. 1798–1843: a London bookseller who in 1820 began his major work 'The bibliographer's manual', published in four volumes by William Pickering in 1834. It was an alphabetically arranged annotated list of all books published in Britain from the time of Caxton. Collations of rare books and current values of the 50,000 titles listed were included.

When Pickering sold the copyright of the 'Manual' to *H. G. Bohn*, q.v., Lowndes entered the latter's employ. Here he compiled the 'Guinea catalogue', a mammoth achievement containing descriptions of some 300,000 works. This appeared in 1841 as a work of nearly 2,000 pages. See also *Robert Watt*.

Luce, Louis-René, 1695–1774: a distinguished French punchcutter who began working for the Imprimerie Royale *c.* 1726. He succeeded his father-in-law Alexandre as royal punchcutter *c.* 1738. The gros-romain type he cut in 1732 was among those studied by Fournier le jeune when designing his own gros-romain some years later.

His 'Essai d'une nouvelle typographie', Paris, 1771, includes the only showing of his *types poétiques*, cut in 1732, and displays specimens of his other types and an extensive range of flowers. The book also gives his principles of letter designing. On his death the collection of flowers and border pieces was acquired by the Imprimerie Royale and is now in the *Cabinet des Poinçons*, q.v.

Lucidarius: a 12th century work attributed to Honorius Augustodunensis written in the form of a dialogue between master and pupil as a method of instructing lesser clergy and the laity in Christian doctrine. It was widely used in translation. Printed versions began with Anton Sorg's of 1479, the German text being illustrated by woodcuts. There were others in France, Germany and Italy. Wynkyn de Worde printed an English translation from a French version about 1505: it had the title 'Here begynneth a lytell treatyse called the lucydarye'.

Ludlow caster: a semi-mechanical typecasting machine in which brass matrices are set by hand in a stick,

Ludlow matrices for different sizes of type

spaced, and cast in solid lines or slugs. The product is used for display work and jobbing printing. When a stick has been made up it is locked in position on top of the caster. The machine automatically places the mould against the line of matrices, casts, trims and ejects the slug to the galley in about four seconds. The machine also has a repeat arrangement which casts one line of matrices without interruption until stopped.

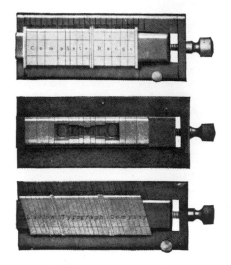

Ludlow composing sticks

Ludlow slug

The Ludlow Typograph Company was founded in Chicago in 1906 to develop a typecasting machine invented by Washington I. Ludlow. This differed from the present system which dates from 1911. Ludlow Industries (UK) Ltd, as the firm is known in Britain, manufactures matrices for most alphabets including exotics and has commissioned proprietary founts of display type.

Lufft, Hans, 1495–1584: from 1530–72 the leading printer-publisher of Wittenberg where he had six presses. Where he learned his craft is not known, but his first book appeared in 1523. He was an active supporter of the Reformation and succeeded the *Lotter* family, q.v., as the chief publisher of Luther's works.

Lufft's output included forty-four printings of the folio German Bible, first issued in 1534, to a total of 88,000 copies. He used beautiful woodcut borders and initials designed by such artists as Lucas Cranach and Virgil Solis, and commissioned scholar-editors to prepare texts for printing. See W. Mejer, 'Der Buchdrucker Hans Lufft zu Wittenberg', 2nd ed., Leipzig, Hiersemann, 1923.

Lumitype: see *Photon*.

lunellarium: a knife with a semicircular end used for the preparatory scraping of a parchment, sharpening a scribe's quill, erasing mistakes, and steadying the parchment while writing. Scenes in illuminated manuscripts occasionally show a scribe at work, often with a lunellarium on his desk or held in the left hand.

Luthersche Giesserei: see *Sabon*.

Luttrell Psalter: a Psalter of the East Anglian School, written in Latin about 1340 for Sir Geoffrey Louterell of Lincolnshire. Grotesque beasts and monkeys (babewyns) are the main decorative feature, with agricultural scenes, games and sports, and incidents from the lives of saints. The work is in the British Library (Add.MS.42130).

Luxographe: an electronic engraving machine introduced by Jean Mincel et Cie, Paris, for making plastic half-tone plates. The original is mounted on a cylinder and scanned. Correlated with the movement of the electronic scanner is a heated needle which burns half-tone screen dots into a plastic foil. Cut-out half-tones can also be made.

The machine is very similar to the Fairchild *Scan-a-Graver*, q.v., with which it was incorporated in 1955.

lye: an alkaline preparation, traditionally wood ash and quicklime in solution, used for cleaning type after use. See also *chamber lye, washing up.*

lying press: a movable horizontal press which lies on the binder's bench, or on trestles, and is used for holding or clamping books during several binding operations. 'Usually ungrammatically called a *laying press*' (Cockerell).

Lyonese style: or *reliure lyonnaise*, the name given without documentary evidence of a Lyonese origin to a style of cover decoration used in France from the mid-16th century on what may be termed demi-luxe bindings. Many of the books so covered were printed in Lyons.

The style was inspired by the entrelac designs made by contemporary master binders in Paris. On a typical example a complete design for corners and centrepiece was stamped on covers of fawn calf, then paint, lacquer or coloured waxes were applied to the interlaced strapwork.

An alternative was to use a large lozenge-shaped ornament on the centre of each cover and large corner ornaments, the ground being covered with small ornaments or dots. See next entry.

Lyons bindings: bindings made in Lyons, specifically during the 16th century when a large number of unnamed binders worked there. Many were employed making undecorated leather covers for works as they

came from the presses, and there were customers for Books of House and octavo classics, either plain or decorated in the painted strapwork with tooling styles then current in Paris; but there was no brilliant series of de luxe bindings of the quality found in Paris, and none of the great French binders is known to have worked there. Many books, printed in Lyons, which may be assumed to have been bound there, show no distinctive style; the tools and designs used are found on books bound elsewhere in France.

The great collector Grolier, born in Lyons, commissioned Parisian binders, but from the collection assembled in Lyons by a contemporary, Benoît Le Court, E. P. Goldschmidt has suggested a Lyons origin for the bindings. Most were very simply decorated on good quality calf, with wooden or pasted-paper boards and raised bands, having blind or gilded fillets and simple tooling. There were none of the mosaic bindings long supposed to have been traditional in 16th century Lyons. See previous entry.

Lyons printing: during the first hundred years in which printing was practised in France it was inevitable that Lyons should be second only to Paris in its development. Then a prosperous commercial town on the confluence of two navigable rivers, it was the French centre of international commerce where merchants from Italy, Switzerland and Germany could trade unrestrictedly with their French counterparts at the four annual fairs it was then privileged to hold.

Although without a university Lyons was a centre of humanism and the gateway into France for the ideas of humanist scholars and their printed works, works which local printers did not hesitate to copy or imitate. It was also on the route by which books were sent from France and its neighbours into Spain.

A merchant, *Barthélemy Buyer*, established the first press in Lyons, with *Guillaume Le Roy*, qq.v., as his printer. The first dated book appeared in 1473.

Early printers found a considerable demand for popular law books, medical works, romances and poetry, all in French, as distinct from the academic works in Latin then being printed in Paris. There was a large public for Italian poetry, in the original as well as translated, and a ready market for broadsheets of occasional verses in French which marked such happenings as a royal visit, an earthquake, or even a comet.

Woodcuts were popular, and the Italian printers who settled in Lyons brought with them the influence of the Florentine and Venetian illustrated book. This was seen in the features and groupings of figures. As an alternative to bringing blocks from Germany, Italy, or Paris, cuts were copied locally by 'tailleurs d'histoires' as the anonymous craftsmen were known. Their early work had some of the crude stiffness of playing cards, but later woodcuts were simple, realistic and expressive without, however, equalling the originality and elegance of the best Parisian work.

By the end of the 15th century only a minority of those printing in Lyons were of French birth, several Germans and Swiss having joined the Italians who settled there.

By the mid-16th century the reputation of Lyons printers was at its zenith, a reputation achieved by a rare combination of the quality of paper, the elegance of type faces and layout and the editorial care of scholar-printers. By this time, too, illustrators had developed a distinctly French style. Copper engraving became popular, mostly for title pages and head-pieces. Such books were never so harmoniously integrated as those illustrated solely with woodcuts.

The decline of printing in Lyons was hastened by the disruptive effect of the wars of 1562 and 1572, by a preoccupation with commerce, and by the concentration of monarchial power in Paris. By the 17th century Lyons was no more than a provincial capital and never regained its importance and prosperity as a printing centre.

For notes on Lyons printers see *Jodocus Badius, Jean de Tournes, Étienne Dolet, Jean Dupré, Robert Granjon, Sébastien Gryphius, Jacques Heremberck, Martinus Huss, Johann Neumeister, Guillaume Rouillé, Michel Topié.*

M

McColvin Medal: an annual award established by the Library Association in 1971 for an outstanding reference book such as an annual, atlas, dictionary, directory or encyclopaedia. It is named after Lionel McColvin, (1896–1976), a former Librarian of Westminster.

McCreery, John, 1768–1832: an Irishman, apprenticed in the 1780s to a Liverpool printer before setting up his own press there about 1791. Works printed by him included Roscoe's 'Life of Lorenzo de' Medici', 1796; Currie's edition of Robert Burns, 1800; his own poem 'The Press', 1803; and Roscoe's 'Pontificate of Leo X', 1805. He moved to London in 1806.

He produced 'firm, workmanlike printing' and was much concerned with the quality of the paper, ink and type he used. Cadell and Davies and Longmans were among the publishers for whom he printed, yet his business scarcely flourished and he retired in 1828, his premises in Tooks' Court passing to *Charles Whittingham*, jnr, q.v.

Macé, Robert II, fl.1522–57: the bookbinder-bookseller of Caen to whom Christopher Plantin was apprenticed. Macé was the son of the first printer in Normandy to use movable types.

machine: a generic name for all power-driven printing presses, i.e. neither lever nor treadle operated. The first press to which the term can be applied was König's *Suhl* of 1803 and its English successor patented in 1811. However, the word 'press' continues to be used throughout the printing industry for all machines which print.

The operator of a printing machine is still known in the U.S.A. as a *pressman* as in hand-press days: in Britain the preferred name is *machine-minder* or *machine-manager*.

machine-binding processes: briefly, and each by a separate machine, these are bundling, affixing endpapers to first and last sections, gathering, sewing, nipping, trimming, gluing, rounding and backing, lining, casing-in and pressing. Linked machines are used in bigger binderies particularly for long runs or paperbacks.

machine clothing: the collective term for the wire, press felts and drier felts on a papermaking machine.

machine-coated paper: see *coater, imitation art paper*.

machine direction: synonymous with *grain direction*, q.v.

machine finish: or *MF*, paper made fairly smooth but not glossy by receiving the normal finish of a papermaking machine. This completes its process by passing the paper through stacks of polished chilled iron calender rolls, some of which may be steam-heated. MF paper is suitable for normal bookwork consisting of text and line illustrations.

machine glazed: or *MG*, paper with a glazed surface on one side and a rough surface on the other.

machine lay edges: see *lay edges*.

machine-made paper: the continuous web of paper made on a *Fourdrinier* or *cylinder machine*, qq.v.

machine minder: the operator of any automatic printing machine. Cf. *pressman*.

machine proof: a proof taken when corrections marked on the galley proof and page proof have been made and the forme is on the printing machine. The machine proof affords the last opportunity to correct mistakes before printing the book. Also known as *press revise*.

machine ruling: see *ruling machine*.

machine-sewing: sewing the sections of a book by mechanical means; a necessary feature of modern commercial publishing. The bookbinding machine sews the sections of a book together, and at the same time the inner leaves of each folded sheet are sewn to the outer ones through the back fold.

The origin of the sewing machine is attributed to Philip Watt of London, 1832, but the first practicable thread-sewing machine was invented by David Smyth, U.S.A. (patented 1871), and his machine inspired the brothers Brehmer of Leipzig. Prior to 1928 the Smyth machine worked with a curved needle, the size of which determined the length of the stitches; modern high-speed machines (from sixty to ninety sections a minute) all work with straight needles. The Brehmer and Smyth semi-automatic machines appeared at the end of the 1920s, and in 1945 the latter was equipped with an automatic feeder.

The basic principle of machine-sewing is that one needle does not go along the section, taking its thread with it, but a series of needles operate, each with its kettle-stitches. Linen thread should be used, but cotton often is.

Part of a Brehmer sewing machine

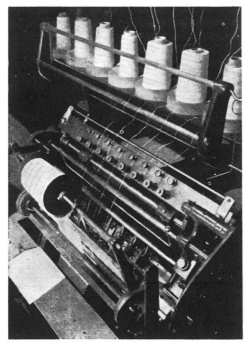

Sewing on a web of gauze which is carried over the backs of gathered sections and secured to them by the moving needles

In the usual type of machine one section after another is laid by hand on a feeding arm which brings the fresh section to the part of the book already sewn. As the illustration shows, the feeding arm forms a saddle with a pronounced ridge over which the half-open section is so placed that the back fold is just above the edge of the saddle. This has a row of holes through which piercers rise to enter the section.

A Brehmer machine, equipped for the semi-automatic separation of a rack of sewn books

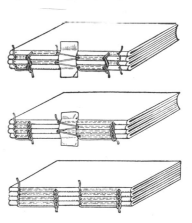

*Top, off-and-on stitch on tapes
Middle, ordinary stitch on tapes
Bottom, ordinary french stitch*

Immediately after, needles descend from above the machine, each with thread attached, and pass through the holes already pierced. The thread is now gripped by the side-needles of the feeding beam (arm) and drawn double for a few centimetres along the back fold to the hook-needles coming from above. The hook-needle grips the loop of the thread, and draws it up through the paper and also through the corresponding loop in the preceding section. (The Swiss factory Martini has introduced a screw-shaped hook-needle with a view to simplifying the construction of the sewing machine.) Then the feeding arm goes out to bring in the next section, and so the work proceeds.

Sewing with thread alone is called *ordinary french*

stitch. In most machines sewing can be done on gauze or tape fed from reels right across the back of the book. The sewing is done in the same way, but the thread passes through the cloth and through or over the tape. Some machines work with an *off-and-on*

Rear view of Gutberlet sewing machine, showing the splits inserted between books. Note the cutting groove

stitch which is suitable for books on thin paper and corresponds to the 'two sheets on' method on hand-sewing. Whereas ordinary sewing is done by two needles for each stitch, the off-and-on stitch requires three working in combination, the threads being drawn alternately to one or other of the outer needles (see illustration). In the *staggered stitch* method the needle changes its position for each section, so that

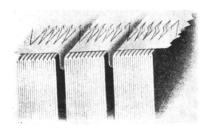

Sewing on a gauze strip of which an uncut fold is dropped after each book. After separation, this extra strip of cloth is used to secure the body of the book to the boards

the threads form a zig-zag pattern across the tapes and are thus better secured to the back of the book. Thread can also be sewn over or under the material in other ways.

In ordinary french stitch the books are sewn to

The operator at the sewing machine

each other until the machine is filled, when the books forming a span are taken out and separated by cutting, a process carried out automatically on some models or by a second operator on others. In sewing on gauze or tapes the width of the cloth for each book must be greater than the width of the back. This can be effected by inserting a split after each book, i.e. a wooden strip of a suitable width, usually with a metal gutter to facilitate cutting. In order to allow the sewn book to be moved forward with the necessary thread corresponding to the width of the split, a free stroke is made after each book.

In Britain, sewing through gauze is seldom practised, and the use of tapes is dying out due to improvements in back-lining techniques which make them superfluous. (GU)

See also *bookbinding methods and processes*.

machining: the actual process of printing; running the forme through the machine so that the paper receives the impression from it. See also *presswork*.

Machlinia, William de, fl.1482–90: of Mechlin in Flanders, and an early printer of London where he was briefly in partnership with *John Lettou*, q.v. They issued five law books, one being Sir Thomas Little-ton's popular Norman-French treatise 'Tenores novelli', c. 1482. This was frequently reprinted by others.

Independently Machlinia is credited with about thirty books, some only extant in fragments, and also with having printed the first English book to have a title-page. This was in an edition of the first medical work to be printed in England 'A litil boke the whiche traytied . . . for the pestilence', *c.* 1485, originally written by Johannes Jacobi *c.* 1357.

After 1490 his printing material was acquired by *Richard Pynson*, q.v.

mackle: a printing fault seen as a blurred or double impression. This is caused by a shifting of the paper while the impression is being made.   (ML)

McLaughlin press: a moulding unit used in making an *electrotype*, q.v. In it a cleaned, level forme and a sheet of plastic are heated, subjected to great pressure, cooled and separated. The plastic mould is then removed for spraying to make it conductive.

McLeish, Charles, 1859–1949: a binder of Edinburgh where he was apprenticed to Andrew Grieve before going to London in 1890. Until 1893 he worked for Rivière & Son and then moved to the *Doves Bindery*, q.v., as a finisher. In 1909 he left to set up a business with his son Charles, and it was here that subsequent 'Doves Bindery' books were finished until 1921 when the Press closed. In 1920 George McLeish joined the firm which was then extended to include bookselling. It closed in 1958.

made end-paper: see *end-papers*.

made-up proofs: synonymous with *page proofs*, q.v.

magazine: the matrix storage bank of a *Linotype*, q.v.

magenta masking method: a proprietary process for making colour-separation negatives. It involves positioning two magenta-dyed colour correcting masks in the screen holder of a camera to modify light reflected from an original or transmitted by a transparency.

Maggs Bros: a leading London firm of antiquarian booksellers, specializing in manuscripts, incunabula, early illustrated books and first editions.

It was about 1850 when Uriah Maggs and his father left the village of Midsomer Norton, in Somerset, for London. After the failure of several ventures Uriah Maggs decided in 1853 to take up bookselling with his own library as the nucleus of his stock. After trading from his home he opened a shop in Paddington in 1855. In 1894 Uriah retired, leaving the business in the hands of his sons Benjamin and Henry. In 1901 the firm, now known as Maggs Bros, moved to the Strand. Catalogues were a regular feature. When Henry died in 1906 two other sons of

the founder became partners in the firm, Charles and Ernest. In 1918 new premises were taken in Conduit Street, to be vacated in 1938 for the present Berkeley Square home. Ernest Maggs died in 1955.

The most important transaction of the firm was the negotiation in 1933 of the purchase from the Russian Government of the *Codex Sinaiticus*, q.v.

magister almarii: literally, the 'master' of book presses in a medieval monastery, an official subordinate to the precentor.

magnesium plates: photoengraving plates used in *powderless etching*, q.v.

Magnus, Albert, fl.1669–86: the most important 17th century bookbinder of Amsterdam, where his family were booksellers. For his comparatively small output he made elaborately tooled boards; delicate roll tool borders of birds in vine foliage being a motif he often used. His masterpieces covered Elzevier Bibles, of which there is an example in the British Library. See 'Bookbindings by Albert Magnus', Amsterdam, 1967.

Mahieu, Thomas: see *Maioli bindings*.

mail-coach copies: copies of newly-published books which, in the early 19th century, were sent by mail coach from London (or other place of publication) to provincial booksellers. Customers paid an extra charge for this quick supply of the latest novels.

Mainz Psalter: see *Johann Fust*.

Maioli bindings: the styles of binding done by Parisian craftsmen for the French book-collector Thomas Mahieu, secretary to Catherine de Medici. (His name is latinized as *Maiolus*.) They belong to the period 1550–65. Styles varied, some having dotted and gilded backgrounds for designs of curved strapwork and arabesques; ornaments were in outline or azured. They were often lavishly decorated with coloured inlays on a gilded ground. The upper cover bore the words THO MAIOLI ET AMICORUM.

majuscule: an upper-case or capital letter. Cf. *minuscule*.

make even: to extend a line of type to full measure by adding spaces. The compositor may be instructed to *make even* or *end even* when setting the last line of a 'take' of copy, thereby leaving no break in the text when setting is resumed.

make-ready: 1. *Letterpress.* The skilled treatment of a forme of type, by which the machine-minder obtains the best impressions from type and blocks by patching up with paper, or cutting away on the impression cylinder or platen bed; also by underlaying or interlaying the blocks and stereos. The amount and position of make-ready are determined by a trial pull. With ferrous metal-backed stereos magnetized

Make-ready on a cylinder press

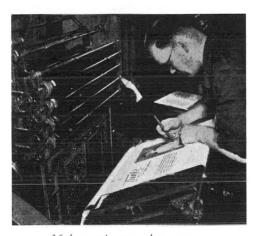

Make ready on a platen press

cylinders can be used as an alternative to extensive make-ready. See also *dressing the cylinder, interlaying, mechanical overlay, overlaying, pre-press work, underlaying.*

2. *Lithography.* The fitting of new blankets on the press. This involves piercing holes along the edges and adjusting gripper bars, fitting thin-paper underpacking where necessary and cleaning the surface. Some blanket making firms supply blankets for web-fed machines with pre-mounted grippers.

make-up: 1. the arranging by the compositor of type matter (including running heads, footnotes, and blocks) into pages and securing them with page-

cord. They are then ready for locking in the chase. See also *dressing* (1).

2. a list of the contents of a book in edition binding supplied by the publisher to instruct the binder, but only necessary where many plates, plans, etc., and other complications are involved. Hence *make-up copy*, i.e., a set of folded sheets and plates put in the correct order as a pattern. (LK)

Malermi Bible: an Italian translation of the Vulgate made by Niccolò Malermi and first printed in Venice by Wendelin da Spira in 1471. More famous, however, is the illustrated folio edition published by Lucantonio Giunta in 1490: this was printed by Giovanni Ragazzo and was remarkable for its 383 small column-width woodcuts. Some of these lively scenes, by two unknown designers, were small adaptations of the cuts in Quentell's Cologne Bible of *c.* 1478. The layout and woodcuts influenced other Venetian printers.

There was another edition, for which the illustrations were reinterpreted in a more classical style, printed in 1493 by Guilelmus Anima Mia at Tridentino.

Malin, Charles, 1883–1955: a Parisian punchcutter, who in 1926 cut the punches for Eric Gill's Perpetua type. They were cut in upper- and lower-case 12-point Didot, and were later brought to England for the Monotype Corporation. Malin subsequently cut some sizes of capitals for use as titling founts (Monotype Series 258).

He was commissioned by Stanley Morison to re-cut the italic of Arrighi's 'La Operina', 1522. The work was supervised by Frederic Warde, and the types (for hand composition) were first used in 1926. The Monotype fount for machine composition appeared in 1929 under the name 'Arrighi'. He later engraved the Dante type of *Giovanni Mardersteig*, q.v. which was first used in 1954 at the *Officina Bodoni*, q.v., and is now available in Britain from the Monotype Corporation.

Mall Press: a private printing press established in London in 1916/7 by Emery Walker and Bruce Rogers. They produced only one book, this being a translation of Albrecht Dürer's 'On the just shaping of letters' set in Centaur type. It was commissioned by the Grolier Club of New York.

Malone Society: a society founded in 1906 to publish 'faithful reprints of old plays, mostly Tudor, and of documents illustrative of the drama and the stage'. From 1907–39 W. W. Greg was general editor.

manière: a manual of instruction, and as here described, one for learning French, written in the form of dialogues about everyday events. Such books were popular in England where printed manières preceded printed French grammars (of which the first to appear was probably Alexander Barclay's, printed by Copland in 1521 (STC 1386); much more important was John Palsgrave's 'Les clarcissement de la langue françoyse', a work of over a thousand pages, printed by Pynson and Hawkins in 1530 (STC 19166).)

An early publication attributed to Caxton, c. 1480, was an untitled French-English vocabulary in the style of a *manière de langage*. This was a phrase book with parallel columns of French and English suitable for commercial travellers and others visiting France. Because of the linguistic and typographical errors in the work the attribution to Caxton as translator has been doubted.

A similar book of instruction was the earliest medieval phrase book 'Le Livre des mestiers' (A book of crafts and trades) intended for use in schools.

manière anglaise: see *colour printing*.

manière criblée: an early method of engraving, using dots. An example may be seen in 'Horologium devotionis', printed by Ulrich Zel at Cologne, c. 1490. See also *criblé initials*.

manila: a very strong vegetable fibre paper made from hemp, rope, jute, sulphite, sulphate, or mechanical wood pulp. It is sometimes used for covering brochures or similar publications. See also *boards*.

Mann, George: of Leeds, who with his partner Charles Pollard was a pioneer of lithographic printing machines. Their first, delivered in 1873, was a powered flatbed known as the Imperial Climax, and within ten years they had sold 452, many to printers in North America, Australia and New Zealand.

Mann patented several improvements, notably a 'take-off apparatus' in 1878, a 'damping apparatus' in 1881, and a double-cylinder flatbed in 1892. As were most other offset litho machines of the day it was described as 'for printing on either tin or paper', an extra £10 being charged for adaptation for paper. Due to production difficulties, however, the company went bankrupt in 1901.

It was reconstituted in 1903 by George Whichmann, a London entrepreneur, partnered by Arthur Evans, a talented draughtsman. It was Evans who developed the all-rotary printing machine which was to make George Mann & Company famous. He based his work on an unsuccessful prototype designed by the American J. S. Morris. In 1906 Evans designed the first commercially successful rotary offset press specifically for printing on paper. The plate cylinder carried two plates, the blanket cylinder two blankets, with a two-revolution common impression cylinder carrying the sheet round twice to receive an impression from each blanket in turn. There had been earlier

offset presses, e.g. the Pelaz and Huguenet, 1869–70, Robert Barclay's of 1875, but these had all been for printing on tin, while the American Ira Rubel's was described by Evans as 'crude both mechanically and lithographically'. Within twenty-five years George Mann & Co. had sold more than 2,000 machines. In 1913 their quad crown rotary was used to print in fifteen colours.

However, after many prosperous years international trade difficulties led to a second bankruptcy in 1931, and reconstruction by fresh backers in 1932. New machines, the stream-fed Fast Three single-colour and Fast Five two-colour presses, soon re-established the firm's reputation.

In 1947 the firm was acquired by the Vickers engineering group, introducing new machines in the 1950s. In 1965 Mann's former rival R. W. Crabtree & Sons, also of Leeds, was added to what became the Printing Machinery Group. Others absorbed were Dawson, Payne and Elliott (of Wharfedale press fame), Waite & Saville (printing-plate makers), and the Cundall Folding Machine Company of Luton. Further rationalisation to meet world-wide foreign competition led in 1969 and 1970 to the formation of Crabtree-Mann, Leeds, currently, with 1,500 employees, the largest British manufacturer of sheet-fed offset presses and specializing in high-speed unit-type multi-colour presses (i.e. without a common impression cylinder): sheet sizes are 965 × 1270mm.

Manresa Press: a private printing press set up at the novice house of the Jesuit Fathers, Roehampton. Historical works printed included Helen Foley's 'Records of the English Province of the Society of Jesus', 1877–83, and John Morris's series 'The troubles of our Catholic forefathers', 1872–7. They were of little typographical merit.

Mansfield, Edgar, b. 1907: a leading British bookbinder whose work has had considerable influence on modern British bookbinding and is represented in several public and private collections. He was born in London but educated in New Zealand where his father settled in 1911. After teaching abstract art and design Mansfield returned to London in 1934, continuing his studies of design and crafts, including bookbinding, under William Matthews. Between 1948 and 1964 he taught bookbinding at the London College of Printing. He was also one of the founders of the *Guild of Contemporary Bookbinders*, q.v.

His work as a painter and sculptor, with its emphasis on space, colour and form, is paralleled in his binding designs. He now lives in New Zealand. See 'Modern design in bookbinding: the work of Edgar Mansfield', Owen, 1966.

Katherine Mansfield Prize: a triennial award of c. £100 each made to a French and a British writer of a short story of less than 1,000 words. The award, announced in 1957, is made by the French Riviera town of Menton where the famous short-story writer frequently stayed. It is administered by the French and English centres of International PEN.

Mansion, Colard, *c.* 1425–84: a scribe who by 1450 was one of the leading calligraphers of Bruges. It would be as a purveyor of manuscripts that he began an association with *Caxton*, q.v., and at the latter's suggestion that he learned to print (taught by Veldener in Cologne?) before working in Caxton's shop in 1475 'probably as a junior partner' (Painter): as a middle-aged man with his own business he would not have been offered a lesser role. In the absence of records evidence of their association rests on their similar editorial methods, the use of translations, a common style of page layout and of type used. Both used unjustified setting until 1479 (Mansion) and 1480 (Caxton).

After printing for Caxton Mansion worked on his own towards the end of 1474 when he issued Petrus de Alliaco's 'Le Jardin de dévotion'. His first signed and dated book was 'De la ruine des nobles hommes et femmes', 1476, which was a French translation of Boccaccio's 'De casibus virorum illustrium'. Some copies had nine separately printed copperplate engravings pasted in: the first use in bookwork.

Following a further twenty-two editions, mostly of French works, he was ruined by his financially unprofitable French prose version of Ovid's 'Metamorphoses', 1484, illustrated with large woodcuts. He left Bruges and is not known to have printed elsewhere.

Manuale: a small book containing the forms used when administering the sacraments.

manuscript: a work written by hand. The term comes from the Latin for this, viz.: 'codex manu scriptus', and denotes either a book written before the invention of printing or the written or typed work which an author submits for publication.

manuscript book writing: from the 6th century to the mid-15th European books were multipled according to certain common practices which evolved through the years, though there were regional differences.

The monastic book. Until the 13th century monastic scribes were the principal producers of books. In addition to agriculture, weaving and prayer, their rules enjoined intellectual work and part of their daily activity was the copying out of service books and similar works. Indeed, for some time after the invention of printing monks continued to write the books they needed. They were written in Latin which was for centuries the *lingua franca* for religion and learning in Europe. Latin, inherited from classical times, was stable and fixed at a time when the regional dialects of such countries as England, Germany and France had not been moulded into generally understood languages. The use of Latin was a big advantage in that books, and the learning they recorded, could be sent from one country to another and be sure of readers, much as with English books today.

The discovery that sheepskin could be prepared as a surface for writing upon with a pen and ink was of particular importance since it was more durable than the earlier papyrus. This reputedly occurred in the 3rd century AD at Pergamum in Asia Minor, whence the name *parchment* by which it is still known.

Writing was done in the *scriptorium*, q.v. The first task was the preparation of vellum or parchment for which animal skins were soaked for some days in a lime solution and stretched on a frame to dry. They were then scraped with a knife to achieve a uniform thickness, followed by smoothing and glazing with pumice stone. Powdered chalk was rubbed in to add whiteness. The finest skins were uterine vellum from which very thin leaves were made: they were used for *Books of Hours*, q.v.

Prior to writing the scribe might fold but not cut a skin, marking out the page areas by pricking through the thickness of the quire to ensure register (to borrow a later printer's term). Foliation may have been done at this stage. Then the skin was laid out flat for copying. When writing was completed the skin resembled a sheet of paper printed from a forme of type. An uncut example of such a skin survives in the library of Durham Cathedral. Both sides of the skin were written upon.

However, it was more common for the scribe to fold and cut the skin into a number of bifolia, assemble them flesh sides facing, hair sides opposite hair sides, into quires, and begin writing. The quire or quaternion of eight leaves, and thus sixteen pages, was his basic unit. Up to the 12th century many European manuscripts were assembled in tens (quinternions).

Having formed a quire the scribe would next rule lines to guide his writing. Marginal holes were pricked with an awl or a pair of compasses, and then lines were made across each page. Prior to the 12th century they would be done with a stylus, from the 12th–15th century a plummet of lead was used, while during the 15th century ink lines are found. Ruling with a stylus or plummet made grooves, usually on the hair side, and ridges, usually on the flesh side.

The scribe wrote with a quill. His ink was contained in a small pot or horn. In writing he would take one leaf of his quire and complete the recto, and then turn it to write the verso. While the first side was drying he would sharpen quills with his *lunellarium*, q.v., mix ink, or prepare more pieces of skin. Neither sand nor chalk appear to have been used to blot the ink. This, in any case, would have diminished the good rich black which was so esteemed. As a guide to re-assembling the sheets in their quires the scribe would add a signature mark in the bottom recto margins. This mark would be a letter, numeral, or symbol. It was usual for only the first half of a quire to be signed. A scribe would often write a catchword at the foot of the last page of each quire, this word being the first word of text which began the next quire. It may be wondered why signatures and connecting catchwords were needed if, as pictures in many manuscripts show, scribes wrote in bound volumes, but in 'The English library before 1700', Athlone Press, G. S. Ivy suggests convincingly that this practice was very unlikely, and that the bound blank books of vellum sold by London stationers in the 14th century were solely for the keeping of accounts.

Scholars have sometimes considered if dictation was practised; that is, if a reader dictated the text to a group of four or six monks who wrote it simultaneously. This is an attractive theory at first sight, but scrutiny leads us to reject it. Men would not all write at the same speed; in order to fit the text into the space available they would need to see what they had to produce, and there would be interruptions at varying times to sharpen pens. There might also be difficulties of hearing, leading to mistakes. There was the rule of silence. So it is now generally accepted that each copyist was given a limited portion of a text – a quire – and made many copies of it. (See, however, *dictation of copy*.)

As each quire was completed a corrector would compare it with the original. The final stage, done by an artist monk, was the embellishment of the manuscript. His work would vary in extent from the adding of incipits, initials, chapter headings and simple border lines in red (see *rubricator*) to painting whole pages in gold and colours (see *illumination*). Before painting began directions to the artist were entered on the manuscript by the overseer of a scriptorium. The painting of a really important service book might take up to two years to complete and would be the work of a team of artist monks.

Sewing on thongs of leather and enclosing the book with undecorated leather covers were features of most monastic bindings, but an important service book might be given a cover of thin gold panels inlaid with ivory and set with jewels. Such books were very costly and were kept in the Sacristy with the church gold and silver vessels.

The university book. Religious books were not the only ones to be made. From the 13th century, when universities developed as centres of learning in Bologna, Rome, Florence, Padua, Paris and Oxford, there arose an urgent need for the quick production of scholastic texts, together with commentaries on and glossaries of them. To make them lay scriptoria headed by *stationarii* were established under the direct control of a university. This control included the purchase of

writing materials, the copying, binding and lending of books.

University regulations obliged a tutor to submit his disputation or text so that within a fixed time an official copy, or *exemplar*, could be made from it by the stationer. The text was written out on as many sections, called *peciae*, as were needed to contain it, corrected by university officials (*correctores peciarium*), numbered and assembled. By dividing the exemplar among a number of scribes, giving one or more peciae to each, the book could be duplicated fairly rapidly. Scribes were paid according to the number of peciae they copied, and were instructed how many words were to fill a line, and how many lines a page. This was necessary if all copies of the work were to be uniform when the separate peciae were made up into books. The disposition on the page of text and blank areas was usually well balanced. The wide margins on the outer sides and foot of a two-page opening were available for annotations or glosses unless the book was to be decorated, and this was not usual for academic books.

The stationer was forbidden to lend his official copies outside the university for illegal copying for his personal profit, nor could he refuse to sell or hire his books to students. It was in this way that authoritative texts were made and circulated, and officials known as *peciarii* were appointed to supervise stationers and control their work.

Other early books. In medieval times romances, chronicles and lives of saints were communicated by wandering minstrels who often composed what they recited. Other minstrels were retained in the courts of kings and nobles. Before the end of the 12th century the writing down of such works, dedicated to or commissioned by a patron, led to a demand among the rich for copies. The Norman poet Wace, c. 1100–84, said he wrote only for the moneyed class since they alone could afford books, thus

> 'Ki unt les rentes e le argent
> Kar pur eus sunt li livre fait'
> *Roman de Rou, c.* 1160

The 14th century in Europe was marked by the emergence of an educated and literate class of lawyers, merchants, officials and others who began to collect books and wanted scholastic texts, books of devotion and works of a more general kind. The latter included grammars, herbals, bestiaries and almanacs as well as such favourites as 'Song of Roland', 'Romain de la rose' and similar romances. In England English replaced French as the principal vernacular, though French continued to be used in the royal court until about 1430. In the 15th century there was a considerable production of manuscript books in English unrelated to the needs of monasteries and universities, and it was to meet these demands that independent scriptoria were established in the bigger towns where scribes organized themselves into guilds with fixed charges for work. The need for the quick production of many books affected their appearance. The big folios used in churches were unwieldy for home use so books were made smaller and written in smaller script on thinner skins, often with two columns to each page. Bindings, too, were lighter. With the growth from the later 14th century of copying by secular professional scribes working in lay scriptoria the conventions of writing tended to become regularized and fixed. In English manuscripts either one or a group of points denoted a pause, and both prose and verse were written in lines of full measure. A regional rather than a national form of the English language was usual.

Such activity marked the beginning of publishing, and books were offered for sale from bookstalls. That prior to printing the production of manuscript books was extensive is proved by the survival of more handwritten copies of such popular works as 'Canterbury tales' than of Caxton's printed editions. An idea of the quantity of books which might be commissioned is given by a manuscript now in Leyden University on which is an order to a stationer for 200 handwritten copies of the Penitential Psalms and 400 small prayer books: that was in 1437. Similarly in 1441, after entrants for a poetry competition in Florence had read their works in public, 200 copies of the collected poems were copied out for public sale within a fortnight.

When printing began in the mid-15th century the earliest craftsmen were at pains to make their books resemble the handwritten books of previous centuries. The same proportions of text to surrounding margins, the same use of contractions and abbreviations, and the inclusion of hand-painted initial capitals continued for a time the manuscript traditions. Almost the only change in layout was the innovation during the later 15th century of the title-page which replaced the *incipit*, q.v. Even so, and particularly in Italy, there was a moneyed aristocracy which continued to commission superb handwritten books until the turn of the century.

In Germany Gutenberg and Schöffer made vellum copies, it being suggested by Ruppel that as many as thirty-five copies of the 42-line Bible may have been pulled on vellum, calling for some 5,700 skins. Not only was vellum more suitable than paper for the limner's art but there was probably a belief that paper would not be as durable.

In Paris, too, when printing began in 1470 the skilled scribes and limners did not immediately lapse into unemployment. Many men from scriptoria found work with or as printers or correctors of texts, while others were engaged to complete printed books by the addition of manuscript leaves. Richly illuminated vellum copies of printed books were pulled for wealthy patrons, including Charles VIII and his court, who required them to be unique. Production methods varied: in some books the woodcut illustrations were overlaid with gesso as a base for painting, in others the colophon or imprint and any woodcuts were scraped away for the same purpose, alternatively the blocks in a forme were covered with paper so that no impression was left on the sheet when the text was printed off. Notable were the publications of *Antoine Vérard*, q.v., purveyor of both manuscript and printed books.

Paradoxically, printed books were issued which faithfully copied the initials, vineleaf borders and illustrations from manuscripts made a hundred years earlier, while a few manuscripts survive with illustrations based on those in printed books. Not until the beginning of the 16th century did the Parisian printed book achieve the homogeneity found much earlier in those of Lyons.

Manutius: see *Aldus Manutius*.

map making by machine: an automated map-making machine was shown by Oxford University Press in 1964. It was jointly conceived by D. P. Bickmore of the Press and R. Boyle of Dobbie McInnes (Electronics) Ltd.

Stated briefly, it is a device for storing the data compiled for the making of a map on magnetic tape and punched cards: such continuous details as rivers and railways are stored as a stream of coordinates on tape, with place names and conventional symbols on cards. Then by selecting the stored information he requires a cartographer can use a moving 'light pen' to 'draw' automatically a map with all its features and data on film or films for monochrome or multi-colour reproduction. This is done quickly and without needing the skilled draughtsmanship of manual drawing, although programming the machine to produce the correct output is still a skilled task. See also: T. A. Margerison, 'Computer-aided map-making', *Endeavour*, 1977 139-42.

mappae mundi: maps made by medieval scholars to depict the world. They date from the 8th-15th century and were often drawn to illustrate religious texts, the maps giving moral as well as geographical meanings, thus the east, origin of light, was indicated by a cross. A famous mappa mundi was the *Hereford World map*, q.v.

map printing: before the invention of *lithography*, q.v., most maps were printed from engraved copper plates (see *copper engraving*). Inevitably, in view of its importance through 1,300 years, the 'Cosmographia' of Claudius Ptolemaeus was the first book published with printed maps. They were the first engraved maps in and of the world. The book was printed at Bologna by Dominicus de Lapis in 1477 (mis-dated 1462 in the colophon), in an edition of 500 copies. The twenty-six maps were engraved on copper plates by *Taddeo Crivelli*, q.v., who was commissioned in 1474 to make them. The edition printed by Bernard Sylvanus in Venice, 1511, was unusual in that the maps were *printed* in two colours, red and black: the *hand* colouring of maps by artists paid by the publisher was not superseded until the 19th century.

In Germany the earliest important maps were the thirty-two woodcuts which *Holle*, q.v., cut and printed for his edition of Ptolemy, Ulm, 1482. By the end of the 16th century European publishers had issued at least thirty-six editions of Ptolemy. Many had additional maps, notable being that printed by Johannes Schott of Strasbourg, 1513, with twenty contemporary woodcut maps prepared by *Waldseemüller*, q.v. It was in Germany at the beginning of the 16th century that Erhard Etzlaub made the first known road map, 'Der Rom Weg': it covered an area from Paris to Cracow and from Denmark to Naples, and was engraved on wood, long the usual medium in Germany.

In England the earliest important maps printed from engraved plates were those of *Christopher Saxton*, q.v., whose series of county maps of England and Wales was issued between 1574 and 1579 when they were published together as an atlas. They were based on his own surveys. A cartographer rarely made his own plates, and Saxton's were engraved partly by Augustine Ryther and partly by Flemish refugees in England. In the next century the county maps of *John Speed*, q.v., are renowned. Most were engraved by *Hondius*, q.v. By this time maps had become minor works of art, embellished with coats of arms, cartouches, views and town plans, collections of them being preceded by brilliantly designed and engraved title-pages. (See also *John Cary*.)

In the Netherlands the cartographers, engravers and printers of charts and maps were unsurpassed through the 16th and 17th centuries. The best known include *Blaeu*, Danckerts, Frisius, *Hondius*, *Mercator* and *Ortelius*, qq.v. In Antwerp Plantin did a considerable business in the sale of maps and supplied them to England, France and Germany. In Amsterdam the Dutch publisher Jan Thesing (or Tessing) had a shop in which he printed works in *cyrillic*, q.v. Peter the Great granted him a licence to print maps and in 1699 he issued the first map printed in cyrillic characters.

In Colonial America the Bostonian John Foster printed the first map made there: it was of New England and taken from a woodcut. Somewhat later, *Franklin*, q.v., also printed woodcut maps, notably of Maryland and Pennsylvania in 1733. In 1755 the Franklin press issued Lewis Evans's 'Map of the Middle British colonies in America', engraved by James Turner.

Today all reproduction processes can be used for the printing of maps, but lithography is the most popular. It is sometimes done in combination with copperplate engraving, photo-litho or auto-litho.

Letterpress map printing from line blocks in black and colours is often used for small maps. Reproductions of maps are also made from originals drawn on paper or on transparent material (Astrafoil, Kodatrace, Plastocowell, etc.). Place names are typeset and embodied in the original map as a tracing impression or patched in from type proofs. Letterpress can be photographed on to the sensitized material. For school wall-maps with little detail drawing is done directly on the (offset) plate. See L. Bagrow, 'History of cartography', 2nd ed. by R. A. Skelton, Watts, 1964; D. Woodward, 'Five centuries of map printing', Chicago, 1975, and 'The bibliography of cartography', Library of Congress, 5 vols, Boston, Hall, 1973.

map views: a descriptive term for the 16th and 17th century maps of towns in which buildings are shown pictorially by conventionalized representation, rather like a bird's-eye view. They resemble the artistic panoramic views of the period, but differ in that a horizontal scale is attempted. See also *Hogenberg*.

maquette binding: a sample case submitted to the publisher for approval in advance of *edition binding*, q.v.

marbled calf: calfskin which has been stained with dilute acid so that a pattern resembling marble results. The acid is harmful to the leather and affects the durability of any book so bound unless the leather is very thoroughly washed after staining. The style was used in France in the 16th century and in England from about 1655. See also *tree-marbled calf*.

marbles: glass, porcelain or steel marbles used for *graining*, q.v. They vary in diameter from 127mm. to 380mm. Other conditions being constant, small marbles give finer grain, and small steel marbles give the finest deep grain.

marbling: decorating book edges or sheets of paper by the transfer to them of colours floating on the surface of a gum solution. This solution is a size, preferably made from carragheen moss or gum tragacanth boiled in water. Strained size is poured in a shallow trough. Specially prepared water-colours mixed with ox-gall are floated on the surface and combed or twisted into patterns. Meanwhile the book edges or sheets are sponged with concentrated alum water as a mordant for the colours. After drying for ten minutes the books are held tightly closed while the edges are touched down on to the surface of the size, or if it be a sheet of paper this is gently laid down. Colours transfer at once, any dirty size being washed off with water.

Oil-colours can be used for marbling, but do not allow for such fine control or produce the clean sharp lines of water colours. There are also imitation marbled papers printed lithographically, but they lack the freshness of the genuine product.

Historical note. The art of marbling is of obscure origin. It was practised in Japan *c.* AD 800, and marbled end-papers were used by the Persians from the 15th

Marbling the edges in a bath prepared for the 'splash' pattern

century. Turkish marbled paper of about 1586 is preserved in the Bibliothèque Nationale, and it was used in Holland as early as 1598.

Writing of it about 1622 in his 'Sylva sylvarum', published in 1627, Francis Bacon states 'The Turks have a pretty art of chambletting paper which is not in use with us. They take divers oyled colours and put them severally upon water and stir the water lightly and then wet their paper (being of some thickness) with it and the paper will be waved and veined like chamblett or marble' (spelling modernized).

The Parisian bookbinder Macé Ruette (fl.1598-1644) is credited with its first production in France about 1610. The earliest dated English binding to include some is of 1655. It was imported from Holland as the best kinds continued to be through most of the 18th century. Among those in England who made marbled paper were Messrs Portbury & Smith about 1763, and Richard Dymott, a London master binder active between 1766 and 1772, who also marbled leather.

An early manual to describe the process was 'Ars vitraria experimentalis' by the German Johannes Kunckel, 1674, while a well-known account is C. W. Woolnough's 'The whole art of marbling', 1853.

British marbled papers are currently among the best being used by craftsmen binders in several parts of the world. Many are made by S. M. Cockerell of Riversdale who offers 150 coded designs. His chief marbler is William Chapman. When in 1960 swatches

of Cockerell's marbled papers were shown to a seventy year old master binder in Paris he said 'on doit s'agenouiller devant un tel travail' ('one should kneel before such work').

Marchant, Guy, fl.1483-1508: a French priest who became a distinguished Parisian printer. The woodcuts used in his several editions of the well-known 'Danse macabre', from 1485, have been considered the finest to appear in France during the 15th century. Also of importance was his editio princeps of 'Compost et kalendrier des bergiers', 1491, with two enlarged editions in 1493, followed by others. Marchant's blocks, and copies made for Vérard, illustrated the edition printed by Nicholas Le Rouge at Troyes in 1529. This popular work was printed in England by Pynson in 1506 with the title 'Kalendar of shepherdes' (STC 22408), and with Vérard's blocks by de Worde in 1508, and by Notary in 1518.

Mardersteig, Giovanni, 1892-1977: the inspired founder and proprietor of the *Officina Bodoni*, q.v. His interest in printing and publishing began while a student in Germany and in 1917 he joined the Kurt Wolff Verlag of Leipzig. Here he was concerned with building up a list of books on modern art. When the firm moved to Munich in 1919 he was co-editor of a lavishly illustrated review of art and literature, the bi-annual 'Genius', printed by Drugulin and published by Wolff.

When he came to set up his own hand-press and bindery it was almost as a disciple of Bodoni, hence the name of his press. Apart from his work as a printer Mardersteig is known in Britain for the Fontana type he designed in 1936 for William Collins at whose Glasgow press he worked for a year. It was based on a type cut about 1760 by Alexander Wilson and used by Foulis. His Dante series, cut by Charles Malin, was first used in 1954 for a work of Boccaccio, and is available from Monotype. (Shown at Appendix A.) See J. Ryder, 'The Officina Bodoni', *Private Library*, 4 1972. See also *Albatross Library*.

marginal notes: notes printed in the side margin of a page opposite the portion of text to which they refer. They are set in a distinguishing type. See also *cut-in side notes, shoulder-notes.*

margins: the four blank borders which in traditional bookwork enclose and give emphasis to the type area of a page. According to their position on the page the four margins are known as *inner* or gutter, *head* or top, *fore-edge* or outer, and *tail* or foot. By limiting eye movement at the ends of a line margins are thought to aid legibility, and by combining to create an optically satisfying balance between blank and printed areas they set off the latter much as a picture is set off by its mount.

315

The importance of space surrounding a text and of regular marginal proportions throughout a book was recognized and established before the mid-4th century (e.g. Codex Sinaiticus). Subsequently, the large fore-edge and tail margins left by medieval scribes provided space for the embellishment in gold and colours of an altar Bible, or for the later addition of a scholar's commentary on a classical text. Both traditions were continued when printing began. Gutenberg's Bible was merely the first of many printed books in which marginal decoration was added after purchase, and a centrally positioned Latin text would be accompanied on three sides of the page by a commentary or translation set in a different size of type. Margins also permitted a book to be trimmed when rebinding without loss of text.

In spite of the high cost of paper 16th century printers, particularly in France and Switzerland, established the generous margins still held to be consistent with good book work. Yet wide margins are uneconomical; thus in a book of the limited edition class only 40% of the page may be used for text area, increasing in cheaper books to 60% and even more for directories and similar quick-reference works where very narrow margins are unlikely to trouble users.

The book designer's working unit is a double-page spread (or *opening*). In outlining the margins on a layout sheet traditional proportions may be followed: they are in the ratio of $1\frac{1}{2}$ for inner margin, 2 for head, 3 for fore-edge, and 4 or $4\frac{1}{2}$ for the tail. The inner margin is always determined first. Its width may need increasing if the planned book will be bulky or printed on heavy paper. Nor must the intended binding method be overlooked as unsewn and saddle-stitched styles will affect the inner margin size. After *copy fitting*, q.v., minor adjustments to margins may be needed.

Particular parts of a book also call for adjustments to margins. Thus while the head and tail margins of a *title-page* will be the same as those on text pages the inner may be slightly increased and the fore-edge proportionately altered. *Headlines* of more than two words are included by some designers as part of the text area. Similarly *hanging shoulder notes* are treated typographically as coming within the text and not as marginal intrusions. *Dropped folios*, however, are inserted in the tail margin (or *white line*) as are *signature* marks. In paperbacks of traditional pocket size the inner and fore-edge margins are often equal. See also *gutter, large paper edition, sinkage.*

Marguerite de France, 1553–1615: the wife of Henry IV of France and a great bibliophile. Her collection included items from the duc de Berry's library. She employed Nicolas and Clovis Eve to bind for her, and it was at one time believed that books they lettered with the inscription 'Expectata non eludet' were made for her. They were mostly of red, green or

316

yellow morocco and had a semé of emblematic tools on the upper cover and spine. Some fifty are known. It is now thought that they were made for Pietro Duodo, Venetian ambassador to France about 1600.

Marian Primer: see *Book of Common Prayer, 1549.*

maril: marbled inlaid leather. See also *Smith, Philip.*

Mario, Antonio di, fl.1417–56: a Florentine scribe who was employed to copy out manuscripts in the new humanistic minuscule for such patrons as Niccolò Niccoli and Cosimo de' Medici. His script was modelled on that of his contemporary Giovanni Aretino. Forty-one manuscripts signed by Mario are known, all in Latin. In one of them, made for an English scholar, was the Ciceronian passage later chosen by Caslon for his specimen sheet of 1734.

Marion Press: one of the earliest private presses concerned with fine printing to be established in America. It was started at Jamaica, Long Island, in 1896 by *Frank Hopkins* (b. 1863) who had learned his craft at the De Vinne Press.

marked proof: the proof supplied to the author for correction. It bears on it the corrections and queries of the printer's reader. See also *author's proof.*

marking up: a binder's term to describe the dividing of the spine into equal parts, and indicating the position of the cords.

Marmion, Simon, *c.* 1425–89: a Flemish miniature painter whose outstanding work was the 'Grandes Chroniques de France', now in the Leningrad Library. It was probably painted between 1445–60 for Philip the Good, Duke of Burgundy. It is notable for its portraits of Plantagenet kings, paintings of the siege of Calais and the battle of Courtrai, as well as for the clever groupings of figures.

Marschalk, Nicolaus, fl.1499–1525: of Thuringia; a Greek scholar, poet, and patron of printing. After first commissioning at Erfurt the printer Wolfgang Schenk he started his own private press with a roman type similar to that used at Cambridge by *Siberch,* q.v. Marschalk moved to Wittenberg in 1502 where his was the first press, and to Rostock in 1507, taking his equipment with him. Many of his books were illustrated. Among the pressmen he employed were Henricus Sertorius at Erfurt and Hermannus Trebelius at Wittenberg.

Martens, Thierry, 1446/7–1534: an important humanist printer who, in association with *De Westfalia,* q.v., began printing at his native Alost in 1473, using a type acquired from the Venetian typecutter Bartholomaeus Cremonensis. The next year he worked alone and is then not heard of until 1486–92, still at Alost, where he issued the first Greek book printed in Belgium in 1491. Between 1493–97 he printed at Antwerp; in Louvain 1498–1501, issuing a Sarum Breviary in 1499. He was at Antwerp from 1502–11, returning to Louvain from 1512–29 where he printed the first edition of More's 'Utopia' in 1516.

Martens devoted himself to Greek and Latin studies, notably works by Erasmus and Rudolphus Agricola. His small Greek quarto textbooks included Homer, Euripides, Plutarch and Plato. He had editorial assistance from the scholar-printer *Rutger Rescius*, q.v.

Martin, William, d. 1815: a typefounder who may have learned his craft in Baskerville's foundry before coming to London about 1786. Shortly after this he was established in a foundry attached to the Shakspeare Printing Office of John Boydell and George Nicol. The types he cut were based on the roman faces of Didot, Bodoni and Baskerville.

Martineau, Louis, fl.1484: an early printer of Paris and Tours and an associate of Antoine Caillaut. He was the first in Paris to identify his work with a *device*, q.v., taking as his design the arms of Paris. A similar device used by Caillaut depicted Saint Anthony. They printed many Books of Hours: of one of these which had copperplate borders to the text after the manner of *Jean Dupré*, q.v., Christian wrote in 'Débuts de l'imprimerie en France', 1894, '. . . on avait gravé des bordures sur cuivre et en relief tirées avec le texte sur la presse typographique'.

Mason, John Henry, 1875–1951: a scholar-printer and teacher of London, and an important influence in raising the standard of printing craft education in the early 20th century. He began his career in 1891 as an apprentice compositor at the Ballantyne Press, remaining there until 1900 when fire destroyed the business. To equip himself for his life as a printer Mason began quite early an in-depth study of classical and modern European and Oriental languages. In 1910 Mason was engaged by *Cobden-Sanderson*, q.v., as chief compositor for his Doves Press. Here he met *Emery Walker*, q.v., and under the influence of the two came to appreciate the beauty of disciplined unadorned typography. Mason set the type for the great Doves Bible, completed in 1905.

From 1905 until 1941 Mason was associated with the Central School of Arts and Crafts, until 1909 as a part-time teacher of printing, thereafter as Head of the Printing Department. His intention was that his teaching would 'carry the practice and ideals of the best of the private presses into the general printing trade' (Owens). This undoubtedly happened.

Elsewhere Mason visited Weimar to advise Kessler of the *Cranach-Presse*, q.v., and supervised the setting of the folio 'Hamlet' of 1929.

In 1936 Mason was one of the first ten recipients of the RDI, awarded to designers who consistently produced work of a high aesthetic standard: it was a fitting tribute. See L. T. Owens, 'J. H. Mason, 1875–1951, scholar-printer', Muller, Ars Typographia Library, 1976. See also *The Imprint*.

Massey coater: a high speed paper-coating machine, patented in 1933 by the American printer Peter Massey. It was developed in America by Consolidated Papers Inc., and in Britain by a separate firm. The Massey (or *print roll coater*) can be linked in tandem with the papermaking machine or be built as an 'off-machine' unit. Clay and starch are the coating materials and they were initially applied to cheap mechanical pulp papers: better qualities are now made. The coater has two large rubber rolls which form a nip, thus coating both sides of the nearly-dry web as it passes between them. These applicator rolls are fed with an even film of coating by a series of metering rolls.

Master Bookbinders Alliance of London: the trade association of master bookbinders in the London district. The Alliance began in 1891 as the Bookbinding Section of the London Chamber of Commerce. In 1910 it was decided to form a Master Bookbinders Association, but the Section still continued and for some time dealt with labour matters. Gradually the Association undertook all the work and in 1939 became an Alliance of the BFMP, now BPIF. See E. Howe and J. Child, 'The Society of London Bookbinders, 1780–1951', Sylvan Press, 1952.

mathematical setting: the setting up in type of the signs, symbols, letters and figures which mathematical notation comprises. This is often done on a Monotype keyboard, cast, and made up by hand.

An author must pay special attention to the presentation of formulae in his copy. Typed copy may lead to errors because the ordinary typewriter cannot produce figures and signs in a sufficient variety of sizes or positions. Carefully written copy allows more flexibility for expressing notation. Whatever method is used, the manuscript should be read by a copy-preparer who will mark up the size, position and spacing of the notation. This helps the compositor but he, too, needs to understand something of mathematical conventions if errors are to be avoided.

Since many special sorts are required for advanced mathematical formulae setting is normally done in one of half a dozen type-faces of which Monotype Modern Series 7 is often used. It is provided with over 600 special sorts. Special matrix-case arrangements are used and additional Monotype equipment will be needed by the book printer who wishes to accept such work. See also *Linotron*.

The printer having only occasional demands for such setting may find the production of type-set formulae very costly. This has led to the use of *pro-printing*, q.v. See T. W. Chaundy, 'The printing of mathematics', O.U.P., 1954.

matrix: 1. a metal die from which a single type is cast, either as a unit or as part of a solid slug. In the 15th century matrices may have been made of lead, struck with copper punches (wooden punches may also have been used). As the need for a more durable metal was perceived, copper was used for the matrix and brass or steel for the punch. See also *justification* (2), *punch*, *strike*.

2. the impression in papier-mâché or plastic taken from a forme of type for stereotyping.

matt art: a clay-coated printing paper with a dull finish. See also *art paper*.

matter: type, either set up for use or standing. Also copy to be set is sometimes called 'matter'. See also *dead-*, *fat-*, *lean-*, *live-*, *open-*, *solid matter*, *standing type*.

Matthewman, John: an 18th century London binder remembered particularly for work commissioned by *Thomas Hollis*, q.v.

Matthews, William, 1898–1977: a leading British craftsman binder who after studying under Peter McLeish, Noel Rooke and Graily Hewitt at London's Central School of Arts and Crafts gained practical experience with the binding firm W. T. Morrells of London before starting his own bindery in 1926. As an instructor for nearly fifty years 'he linked the past securely to the future by teaching his considerable skills to a large proportion of the next generation of English bookbinders' (Middleton). His pupuls included Anthony Cains, Bryan Maggs, Edgar Mansfield and Desmond Yardley.

His work, represented in major public and private collections, is 'marked by a sober dignity, and his bindings for pleasure display a rich and joyful charm enhanced by the sparkle created by his hand-cut tools' (Middleton). Matthews favoured oasis morocco, the hand-stained end-papers of Morris Marbles of Oxford, and often doublures and end leaves of morocco, silk or vellum. He did his own edge gilding.

In 1976 he was awarded the City and Guilds Institute of London insignia, the first binder so honoured.

Somerset Maugham Trust Fund: annual awards of about £1,000 made to British subjects under thirty-five years of age for a literary work, in English, which shows originality and promise. The prize is to enable the winners to travel, thus enriching their experience and extending the influence of modern English literature. Authors may submit their own works to the Society of Authors in London.

Maybury binding: the name given by Remploy Ltd to their method of re-binding library books. It was begun commercially in 1950. After removing the original case and lining material the back of the sections is sheared off leaving the book as a pile of single leaves. New end-papers are positioned and the pile is then held in a clamp on an Ehlermann Quick III machine where cold pvc is applied to the back as the leaves are fanned across a roll. While the adhesive is still wet a lining strip of pre-shrunk (and thus expandable) calico is fitted across the back and rubbed down, thereby bonding the pages into a unit.

With heavily loaded art papers the adhesive is not absorbed and lies on the surface, tending to peel off when the book is handled. The process is therefore used for fiction or non-fiction with only a few plates.

The name Maybury is not registered, but is in practice used only by Remploy who kindly supplied this note. See also *adhesive binding*.

Mazarine Bible: a name given to the 42-line Bible of *Gutenberg*, q.v., after the Parisian bookseller Guillaume François de Bure (1731–82) published his 'Bibliographie instructive', 1763–82. In this he recorded his discovery in 1760 of an inscription in the copy of the Bible owned by Cardinal Mazarin (1602–61). The inscription, at the end of volume two, was a note by Heinrich Cremer, vicar of St Stephen's, Mainz, stating that on 24 August 1456 he completed the rubrication and binding of it. As the Bible was undated this note was important since after estimating the time for the vicar's work on 643 leaves a printing date of about 1454 could be conjectured (assuming that he acquired his copy on publication and began rubrication soon after).

At one time Giulio Mazarini, cardinal, statesman and bibliophile, had some 40,000 books in the care of his librarian *Gabriel Naudé*, q.v.; many were transferred to the Collège des Quatre-Nations, founded in 1688 after his death. This is now part of the Bibliothèque Mazarine, Paris.

Of the original edition of the Bible forty-eight exist of which fewer than half are perfect. Fourteen are in the U.S.A. See D. A. Randall, 'Changing the Gutenberg census', *PBSA* 56 1962 137–74.

mean line: the imaginary line to which are aligned the top of lower case letters without ascenders, i.e. a c e i m n o r s u v w x z. Cf. *base line*, *cap line*.

Mearne, Samuel, 1624–83: from 1660 Bookbinder to King Charles II, Stationer from 1674, and Bookseller from 1675; the last combined warrant including his son Charles (1657/8–86). Mearne was apprenticed to a bookbinder between 1637 and 1646. By 1653 he had his own business in Little Britain, but it is doubtful if after the royal appointment he personally bound books in the bindery attached to his bookshop. He employed talented craftsmen led by Suckerman.

Bindings made for the King were in two main styles: the first, usually in brown or red turkey leather, had fine parallel lines very close to the edges of the boards and an inner rectangle, equidistant from the edges, in the centre of the panels. The royal cipher between palm leaves was placed at the four corners of this rectangle, and also on the spine. The effect was of restraint and good taste.

More lavish were the formal patterns of tooling covering both boards and with painted fore-edges. Many had black-painted outlines of the 'cottage-roof' design. Most of his best work was on Bibles and prayer books for the royal chapels and the court.

One of Mearne's duties was to seek out illicit presses on behalf of the Stationers' Company of which he was twice Master. When Charles Mearne died his elder brother Samuel II was appointed Royal Bookbinder until 1688. He died in 1700. See H. M. Nixon, 'English Restoration bookbindings: Samuel Mearne and his contemporaries', British Library, 1974.

measure: the width, expressed in so many 12-point ems, of a full line of composed type with spacing (or of a slug).

mechanical: the final layout of artwork, captions and text matter pasted in position on a piece of illustration board, marked up and sent to the printer. See also *layout, montage.*

mechanical overlay: a means of overlaying by one of several proprietary methods. In one, an impression is made on chalk-coated paper. The coating on the non-inked parts is etched off, leaving the inked design in relief.

mechanical tints: ruled or dotted celluloid sheets used to add texture, shading or detail to artwork. Now superseded by photographic masters of various types of tint from which negative or positive contacts are made on stripping film. See also *Ben Day tints, Zip-a-tone.*

mechanical wood: or *furnish*, soft wood logs ground to pulp by a revolving stone cylinder, all the impurities remaining in the pulp. It is then strengthened with sulphate pulp and is used in the manufacture of newsprint. For some letterpress and gravure work its printing quality is superior to chemical wood pulps, however it is of poorer colour and strength and

deteriorates more readily on exposure to light, becoming brown and brittle. Cf. *chemical pulp.*

Mediaan: the Belgian unit of type measurement in which 12-point equals 0·1649in. or 4·18mm.

medical and pharmaceutical symbols:

ℨ	dram	℥	ounce
ℳ	drop	O	pint
C	gallon	℞	recipe
gr.	grain	℈	scruple
ℳ	minim	fs	semi-
aa	of each	S	signa

Medici, Cosimo de, 1389–1464: an Italian merchant, scholar, bibliophile and patron of libraries. In 1433 he founded the San Giorgio Maggiore Library, Venice, and in 1441 he gave 400 of the classical manuscripts he had inherited from Niccolò de' Niccoli to the newly built library of San Marco Convent, Florence. He employed *Bisticci*, q.v., to copy books for Fiesole Abbey Library. A second 400 Niccoli manuscripts were added to his personal library. The Fiesole, Medici, and San Marco collections are now in the Biblioteca Mediceo-Laurenziana, Florence. See also *Poggio.*

Medina, José Toribio: see *Toribio-Medina, José.*

medium: 1. a former size of printing paper, 18in. by 23in.

2. the liquid, usually linseed oil, in which the pigment of a printing ink is dispersed and via which it leaves an impression on paper.

3. an alternative name for a *Ben Day tint*, q.v.

4. the weight of type-face midway between light and bold. Normally used for the body of a book.

meeting guards: V-shaped guards of paper to which folds of sections are sewn when it is desired that a book of narrow-margined pages shall open quite flat. The open side of each guard is then folded, the pile of sections pressed, marked up, sawn in and sewn by the *all along* method, q.v.

Meisenbach, Georg, 1841–1912: the inventor of *half-tone* reproduction, q.v. From 1873 he worked in Munich, first as a copperplate engraver, and later on experiments for making printing blocks by means of photography. In 1881 he produced his first serviceable half-tone blocks in the printing house he had established with J. von Schmädel in 1878, and in 1882 he was granted British and German patents for his method. In 1884 The Meisenbach Co. Ltd was formed in London, the management including J. W. Swan, who had also experimented with this process. The Munich business passed into the hands of Meisen-

319

bach's son August, and was amalgamated in 1892 with a Berlin firm under the name of Meisenbach, Riffarth & Co.

membrane: a skin parchment.

mending: inserting a corrected piece in a printing plate.

menologium: a calendar of saints' days of the Greek Church in which the lives of the saints are arranged in the order of the calendar. Menologia were written during the 11th and 12th centuries and were based on Simeon Metaphrastes' 'Lives of the saints' written during the reign of Basileios II (976–1025) for whom the most important extant example was made. More than four hundred pages survive, each with a miniature. Eight artists contributed to the book. Their work appears on lavish gold backgrounds with calm figures in carefully drawn robes, each scene within an ornamental frame. This menologium is in the Vatican Library (Cod.Gr.1613). There is a portion of a similar work in the British Library (Add.MS.11870).

Mentelin, Johann, fl.1458–78: born at Schlettstadt in Alsace. He was the first printer of Strasbourg where he issued the 49-line Latin Bible in 1460 (GKW 4203), and the first Bible printed in German, 1466. He was a pioneer in Germany of the roman letter which he used in 1477 for the first printed edition of Eschenbach's 'Parzival', and was one of the earliest printers known to have issued advertisements of his books. 'Parzival' was unillustrated, decoration being limited to initial capitals drawn in red ink and ending in marginal flourishes.

Mercator, Gerard, 1512–94: born Gerhard Kremer, a native of Rupelmonde and a pupil of the Brethren of the Common Life. He was an instrument maker, cartographer and engraver, and had been a pupil of the great Gemma Frisius (1508–55), mathematician and cartographer.

About 1537 he established his business as globe and map maker in Louvain, moving in 1552 to Duisberg where he achieved his greatest fame and eventually died. Notable were his maps of Europe, 1554, England, 1564 and the well-known seamen's map in eighteen sheets based on his projection, 1569. His major work was the great *atlas*, q.v., of which the first part appeared in 1585. The work was completed in 1595, a year after his death. In 1604 the plates passed to *Jodocus Hondius*, q.v., whose family continued for some years to publish it under Mercator's name. For many years Mercator's maps and globes were distributed in Europe by Plantin, his principal supplier of paper.

Mercator attached considerable importance to calligraphy of which he was a teacher, and in 1540 issued his 'Literarum latinarum' on the use of cursive script. For his maps he used a clear but compact italic script, engraved on copper: this was admired and copied by other cartographers. See A. S. Osley, 'Mercator', Faber, 1969.

Mercurius Librarius: see *Term catalogues.*

Mergenthaler, Ottmar, 1854–99: a native of Hachtel near Stuttgart who emigrated to Washington, D.C. when eighteen, working as a watchmaker. Later he went to Baltimore where he met a certain Charles Moore and his partner James Clephane who had invented a 'Typewriter'.

Mergenthaler interested himself in the problem of mechanical typesetting, and the result was his invention in 1884 of what was developed as the *Linotype* typesetting machine, q.v. A redesigned model built in the following year, was sufficiently satisfactory for a trial on 3 July 1886 in the office of the *New York Tribune*. It was named the *Blower* since circulating matrices were assembled by a blast of compressed air.

Merovingian: a cursive script developed in Gaul as the national form of the Roman half-uncial. It was used from about 625 as the official script for charters and other documents issued from the Merovingian chanceries of the Frankish kings in Gaul and remained in use through the 8th century. The principal scriptorium was at Luxeuil. Features were elongated ascenders thickened at the heads, many ligatured letters and a backward slant to them. The result is compressed and not easy to read as may be judged from its use as a book-hand in the best-known exemplar of it, the Luxeuil Lectionary, now in Paris (BN.Lat.9427).

Merrymount Press: see *Updike.*

metal: see *type metal.*

metallic inks: printing inks which produce an effect of gold, silver, copper or bronze. For good results they must be used on coated stock, otherwise an underprinting in a coloured ink is first made from the same block to act as a size for the metal.

metallography: 1. metal-lithography, a printing process similar to lithography in which metal plates are used instead of stone (O.E.D.). See *lithography.*

2. the name given to the process of making a cast metal plate from a mould. Such plates are held to have been used in Holland as relief plates for printing in the early 15th century; they thus preceded the invention of printing from movable type. (After *Library Association Record*, 1931, 153–62.) Also known as *jetté en moule.*

meteorological symbols: the following symbols for

recording weather were approved by the International Meteorological Organization at Warsaw, 1935.

- ◯ air, pure (abnormal visibility)
- ◠ aurora borealis
- ◠ dew
- ❟ drizzle
- ↪ duststorm
- ≡ fog
- ⊟ fog, frost
- ≣ fog, ground
- ≈ fog, shallow
- ∿ frost, glazed
- ⊔ frost, hoar
- ↲ gale
- ▲ hail
- △ hail, small
- ⋏ hail, soft
- ∞ haze
- ◿ ice, grains of
- ⟷ ice needles and crystals
- ⟨ lightning, distant (i.e. thunder inaudible)
- ⟨ lightning, sheet
- ⋃ lunar corona
- ▽ lunar halo
- ▷◁ mirage
- ══ mist
- • rain
- ▽ rain, shower of
- ◠ rainbow
- ▼ rime, hard
- ∨ rime, soft
- ↪ sandstorm
- ⚹ sleet
- ⚹ sleet shower
- ✳ snow
- ⊹ snow, drifting (high up)
- ⊹ snow, drifting (near ground)
- ✳ snow shower
- ✳⊹ snowstorm
- ⊕ solar corona
- ⊕ solar halo
- ☉ sunshine
- ⏃ thunder; also thunder and lightning
- 0 (after symbol) light*
- 2 (after symbol) heavy*

( ) enclose symbols when phenomena pass near but not over observing station.

* Used as superior figures, thus ▲² means heavy hail.

metering-bar coater: a small-diameter chromium plated rod which revolves against the direction in which a freshly coated web of paper is moving. The rod smooths the coating. See *Champflex coater*.

metrication: a term used in Britain during the early 1970s for the conversion of imperial units of measurement into metric terms and the adoption of new standardized (SI) units.

The Weights and Measures Act, 1963, established the legality of the metric system for use in trade, it being hoped that by 1975 all industries would have changed to it. Since 1901 the basis of the metric system has been the metre, kilogramme and second (MKS) to which in 1950 was added a standard unit for electromagnetic measurement (the ampere), giving the MKSA system. In 1954 this was expanded and rationalized into the Système International d'Unités, or SI units, comprising metre, kilogramme, second, ampere, degree Kelvin (temperature) and candele (light) with their multiples and divisions.

Of interest to the printing and kindred trades are the following SI units:

length	metre (m), millimetre (mm)
area	square metre (m²), square millimetre (mm²)
weight	kilogramme (kg), gramme (g), grammes per square metre (g/m²) (formerly gsm), pence per kilogramme (p/kg)
temperature	degree Celsius (°C), widely known as 'centigrade'.

The complicated task of converting to metric units the countless measurements given in imperial units in the first edition of this book has not been attempted, not least because the latter will be familiar for some years to come and will continue in use in the U.S.A. Metrication in Britain does not yet extend to the point/pica system of measuring type and lettering even though paper, plates and blocks may be expressed metrically.

See 'Changing to the metric system: conversion factors, symbols and definitions', HMSO, 1965, and 'Going metric with the printing industry', BPIF, 1971. See also *British book sizes*, *paper sizes*, *paper substance*.

metric conversion table: the numbers in the centre column are the key to the two-way table below; e.g. 10 inches = 254 millimetres and 10 millimetres = ·3937 of an inch.

The figure in the central column can be read as either the metric or the British measure. For example: 1 millimetre = ·03937 inch; or 1 inch = 25·400 millimetres.

millimetres		inches
3·175		$\frac{1}{8}$
6·350		$\frac{1}{4}$
12·700		$\frac{1}{2}$
15·875		$\frac{5}{8}$
19·050		$\frac{3}{4}$

millimetres		inches
25·400	1	·03937
50·800	2	·07874
76·200	3	·11811
101·600	4	·15748
127·000	5	·19685
152·400	6	·23622
177·800	7	·27559
203·200	8	·31496
228·600	9	·35433
254·000	10	·39370
279·400	11	·43307
304·800	12	·47244
381·000	15	·59055
508·000	20	·78740
762·000	30	1·18110
1016·000	40	1·57480

millimetres		inches
1270·000	50	1·96850
1905·000	75	2·95275
2540·000	100	3·93700
	200	7·87400
	300	11·81100
	400	15·74800
	500	19·68500
	1000	39·37000

metres		feet
0·305	1	3·281
0·610	2	6·562
0·914	3	9·843
1·219	4	13·123
1·524	5	16·404
1·829	6	19·685
2·134	7	22·966
2·438	8	26·247
2·743	9	29·528
3·048	10	32·808
4·572	15	49·213
6·096	20	65·617
15·240	50	164·042
22·860	75	246·063
30·480	100	328·084
152·400	500	1640·420

Meynell, Sir Francis, 1891–1975: one of Britain's leading book designers and advertising typographers. In 1923 he founded the *Nonesuch Press*, q.v., having previously managed the Pelican Press, an establishment noted for a limited output of fine printing between 1916 and 1923. It was under this imprint that Francis Meynell issued 'Typography', 1923, which was both a notable type-specimen book and an essay on book production.

In 1954 the Limited Editions Club of New York awarded him their Aldus Statuette; the citation for this, written by Bruce Rogers, described Meynell as 'the father of fine book making in England'. See F. Meynell, 'My lives', Bodley Head, 1971. See also *Romney Street Press*.

Meynell, Gerard: a partner and director of the Westminster Press which in the first years of the present century was noted for fine printing. In 1913 he established *The Imprint*, q.v.

mezzotint: 1. an intaglio illustration process for reproducing tones as distinct from lines. A copper plate is given a pitted surface by passing a steel-toothed rocking tool (see *cradle*) over the whole of it. (If used in this state the whole printed sheet would be black.) The surface is now scraped with a knife and a scraping iron to remove all recesses save those required to

print. Those areas which are to appear white are scraped quite smooth and burnished. Printing is done on dampened paper in a copperplate press.

The invention of mezzotint is ascribed to Ludwig von Siegen in 1642, but it was the influence of his friend Prince Rupert of Bavaria that made it better known, especially to the Dutchmen Wallerant Vaillant (1623–77) and Abraham Blooteling (1640–90) who developed it.

It was Prince Rupert who introduced mezzotint into England where William Sherwin produced the first-known dated print from a mezzotint plate in 1669. The process had its greatest vogue from 1670–1750. In England the finest work was done by such craftsmen as John Smith (1652–1742), James MacArdell (1729–65), John Raphael Smith (1752–1812) and Valentine Green (1739–1813): they reproduced paintings by Gainsborough, Rembrandt, Reynolds and Romney.

(With GU)

2. the print taken from a mezzotint plate.

MF: the abbreviation for *machine finish*, q.v.

MG: the abbreviation for *machine-glazed* paper.

Michaelisbrüder: the German name for the *Brothers of the Common Life*, q.v.

Michel, Jean-Marius, 1821–90: a famous Parisian binder who from 1839 worked as a gilder in the atelier of *Pierre-Paul Gruel*, q.v. In 1849 he opened his own premises and was commissioned to gild books for Capé, Chambolle, Cuzin and Duru. In 1876 he and his son *Henri-François* (1846–1925) opened joint premises as binder-gilders, trading as 'Marius Michel'.

The father's work, while technically perfect, was largely traditional but the son was more enterprising: he used curved stamps and fillets instead of small dies to work exotic leaf and flower forms, also attempting to relate cover decoration to a book's contents. Both made superb mosaic bindings.

They also wrote on bookbinding, notable being 'Essai sur la décoration extérieure des livres', 1878; 'La Reliure française', 2 vols, 1880; and 'L'Ornement des reliures modernes', 1889.

microform publishing: the publication on roll film or microfiche of copy which has been reduced by microphotography to a size which is not eye-legible. Microphotography was invented in 1853 by J. B. Dancer of Manchester. One of his experiments was to reduce 560 pages to microdots on an area $9·5 \times 9·5$mm, though not for 100 years was commercial use made of it for reducing books. In 1964 the NCR Company produced a micro-Bible by PCMI. It had 1245 pages on an area $38·1 \times 31·7$mm (a reduction of 150 to 1).

Publishing a work in microform, subsequent to full-size printing, is termed *retrospective microform pub-*

lishing. Where microform replaces or is simultaneous with full-size publication it is termed *original microform publishing*, and the end product is described (by some) as a *microbook*.

Roll film, 35mm or 16mm, has long been used for microfilming files of newspapers and journals. For books the *microfiche* is increasingly used. This is a strip of film carrying multiple micro-images arranged in a grid pattern. If a work cannot be contained on a single carrier any additional fiche needed is called a *trailer microfiche*. The two standard sizes of fiche are 105 × 148mm/A6, and 75 × 125mm which approximates a 5in × 3in. filing card. The first permits a reduction ratio of 24:1 or 48:1 and a frame capacity, excluding title area, of 98 images arranged in 14 columns of 7 pages. *Ultrafiche* has a reduction ratio of 105:1. An eye-legible title strip identifies every microfiche.

Commercial development of microfiche publishing began in America following governmental use of several million a year. In Britain librarians and the book trade took note of this form of publishing following the appearance on high-reduction microfiche of *Books in English*, q.v.

Less costly to produce is the master fiche in 105 × 148mm size. Advantages are quick and cheap duplication, durability, compact storage, economical postal transmission and easy regeneration as hard copy. By 1976 one British firm alone was putting up to five million pages on microfiche every month.

The British world of business and industry was quick to adopt microfiche publishing for parts catalogues, trade lists, inventories and the like. For them ease of consultation and updating were the desiderata. The book trade, having different needs, followed more slowly. Suitable material for fiche includes out of print or other on-demand titles produced in small quantities (a few hundred), theses, illustrations or lengthy appendixes to a book which the expense of normal publication would preclude, updated matter to supplement a reference work (fiche being kept in a pocket inside the cover), runs of periodicals, and publishers' complete catalogues.

Microform publishing is already big business in America where, for example, libraries can subscribe to current periodicals on fiche instead of printed paper copies. In Britain in 1974 the Scolar Press issued a microfiche edition of its 365 volume 'English linguistics, 1500–1800' series of facsimile reprints to sell for about a third of the original cost. By the mid-1970s there were 200 micropublishers worldwide.

There are several unresolved problems. One is copyright in areas not covered by existing legislation. Another is the absence of a generally acceptable projection viewer or 'reader', essential for scanning, manufacturers having produced equipment without sufficient research into users' requirements. Better quality control and the inclusion of systematically accurate cataloguing data are also needed. It is here that the needs of commerce and scholarship diverge, and microfiche publishing seems unlikely to supersede printed books until user convenience and the personal pleasure of owning them prove unacceptably costly. See BS 4187:1973. See also *National Reprographic Centre for documentation, reprographic printing*.

microwave drying: the drying of a web of printed paper moving at up to 275 metres a minute by using a series of units which discharge high-speed microwaves into the print. Little moisture is lost from the paper and there is no risk of scorching it. Ink solvents are removed by scraper bars in an extraction hood. Similar drying units can be linked to adhesive binding machines. Cf. *radiation curing*.

micro-zinc plates: plates of micro-crystalline zinc alloy, developed in America as an alternative to magnesium plates for photoengraving.

Middle Hill Press: the private press set up at his house in Broadway, Worcestershire by *Sir Thomas Phillipps*, q.v.

Middleton, Bernard, b. 1924: one of Britain's leading craftsman bookbinders and book restorers. He worked successively at the British Library, the Royal College of Art, and Zaehnsdorf Ltd before establishing his own craft bindery in 1953. Middleton has written articles on bookbinding for trade journals, and his 'History of English craft bookbinding technique', Hafner, 1963, is of major importance. It has been described as 'the first attempt to chart the history of bookbinding in all its technical aspects'. His excellently illustrated 'The restoration of leather bindings', Chicago, ALA, 1972, is also of note. His work has been acquired by several major collectors and shown in the exhibitions of *Designer Bookbinders*, q.v. See D. A. Harrop, 'Bernard Chester Middleton', *Book Collector*, Autumn 1977.

mid-feather: the central partition in a *Hollander*, q.v., around which the half-stuff circulates.

Miehle, Robert, d. 1932: the originator, in 1887, of the modern two-cylinder press which is particularly suitable for process work. Among the many well-known Miehle presses made in the Chicago business he founded is the *Miehle Vertical*, first built in 1921, which is an entirely automatic stop-cylinder machine with a vertically placed forme. During impression, cylinder and bed are carried in opposite directions. The cylinder revolves on the printing stroke only, a gap in the cylinder clearing the forme when the cylinder is tripped.

Feeding, using a system of combers and blowers, may be by stream or single sheets. In the chain delivery mechanism the pile builds up on a standard stack board which, when full, can be replaced without interrupting delivery.

Miehle presses, which are used throughout the world, include two-revolution, two-colour, stop cylinder, and high speed models. See also *cylinder press*.

Mierdman, Steven, fl.1543–53: a Netherlands printer recorded as having worked in Antwerp from 1543, in which year he married the sister of *Matthew Crom*, q.v., until about 1546. He printed Reformation tracts.

He was probably the printer of certain books in English long attributed from their imprints to Richard Jugge, Gwalter Lynne, John Day and other English printers. From about 1548–53 he worked in London, after which he returned to Antwerp, but some of his ornamental material seems to have been sold to *Cawood* and *Jugge*, qq.v. See C. Clair, 'On the printing of certain Reformation books', *The Library*, 5th ser., xviii 1963 275–87.

mildew: a growth caused by micro-organisms whose spores become moulds in a moist, warm atmosphere, deriving food from the material on which they form, e.g. the bindings and pages of books. During growth they produce organic acids damaging to leather or paper. Every part of a book must be treated with a suitable inhibitor. The best preventives are cleanliness, sunlight, dry circulating air and temperatures below 20°C. Cedarwood oil and clove oil or saddle soap, applied with a clean linen pad, are recommended for leather bindings. (With ML)

See also *leather preservation*.

Miliani, Pietro, 1744–1817: the founder of a famous Italian firm of hand-made papermakers of Fabriano. He was the first papermaker in Italy to use a *Hollander*, q.v. Successive members of the family directed the business until the present century.

millboards: strong boards of good quality used in England since the early 18th century for the covers of hand-bound books. They are occasionally used for cased books if dimensional stability is important. Ingredients include rope, fibre refuse and wood pulp, and they are now usually made in sheets from layers formed on a cylindrical mould as it revolves in a vat of pulp. Each layer is couched as it comes from the cylinder and is carried into a press. The upper roll of this press is the making or forming roll. As the first layer is caught up by the nip of the press it adheres to the revolving roll: subsequent layers accumulate on the roll until the desired number of plies has been built up. A board which is to have a finished thickness of $\frac{1}{4}$in. will be pressed from a pile of plies $1\frac{1}{2}$in. thick. The boards are carefully dried before they are *milled*

324

(hence the name) between heavy squeezing rolls which flatten and smooth them.

Hand-made boards for bookbinding are now rare.

mill brand: in the paper trade, the trade-mark and brand name belonging to the manufacturer and so identified, as distinguished from a private jobber's brand where the goods bear the jobber's identification but not the manufacturer's. (ML)

mille: the unit of 1,000 sheets in which form British papermakers and printers have agreed paper shall be sold. Packing is in parcels of 1,000, 500, 250, or 100 sheets. See also *centum, mill ream, outsides, printer's ream, quire, ream, retree*.

Miller, William, d. 1843: a foreman in the Glasgow typefoundry of *Alexander Wilson*, q.v. In 1807 he set up his own business in Edinburgh very much as a rival concern. He was able to sell type to London printers much cheaper than that sold by London founders, principally because of the low wages paid to his journeymen. About 1810 he commissioned *Richard Austin*, q.v., to cut the modern type face for him which is now, as revived by Linotype and Monotype, known as Scotch Roman.

In 1832 he took *Walter Richard* as a partner, and after 1838 the firm traded as Miller & Richard. In 1849 they acquired a Bruce typecaster, being one of the earliest British firms to do so. They also supplied *The Times* with a specially hardened type.

The famous Old Style face cut by their employee Phemister had a considerable vogue both in Britain and America.

Miller, William Henry, 1789–1848: a book collector who began his library at Britwell Court, Bucks., with purchases in 1834 from the Heber collection. It was enriched by his successors *Samuel Christy* (d. 1889) and *Wakefield Christy* (d. 1898) who both took the name *Christie Miller*. Their library included works by England's first printers and was rich in early English and Scottish literature.

The collection was dispersed in a series of sales at Sotheby's, mainly between 1916 and 1927, for more than £500,000, many of the books being acquired for the Huntington and Folger libraries in America. A two-volume catalogue listing 14,000 items formerly in the Britwell Library was issued by Quaritch in 1933.

mill-finished: see *machine finish*.

Mill House Press: a small private press established by Robert Gathorne-Hardy (1902–73) and Kyre Leng at Stanford Dingley, Berks. Using original Baskerville type they produced small editions of occasional verse by Gathorne-Hardy and such friends as Siegfried Sassoon ('Common chords', 1950).

millimétrique: the designation of founts of roman and italic type cut by Firmin Didot between 1812 and 1814 for the Imprimerie Nationale, Paris. In 1811 Napoleon had instructed him to re-cut certain Imprimerie types, and the substitution of metric measurements for the earlier Didot point system was one of his proposals: his basis was a point of 0·4mm. The new system of measurement and the project to replace the whole range of types were abandoned after 1814.

mill ream: 472 sheets of hand-made or mould-made paper, good or retree, i.e. 18 'inside' quires of 24 sheets, and 2 'outside' quires of 20 sheets. See also *mille, perfect, printer's ream, quire, ream.*

miniature: a picture painted in a manuscript. If touches of gold or silver are added it is said to be illuminated. See also *minium, illumination.*

Miniature Press: a private press established in 1935 at Richmond, Surrey, by John Ryder. He works for his own pleasure and that of his friends.

minion: the name for a former size of type, now standardized as 7-point. The name may have originated in France where it was first used in the 17th century.

minium: red lead (ground cinnabar), mixed with water and egg-white, and used for rubrics in Egyptian papyri and for embellishing manuscripts.

The Latin *miniare* originally meant to colour with minium, thus to draw a picture with it in a manuscript, and in subsequent usage, as *miniature*, the finished picture.

Minnesängerhandschriften: the name for collections of 12th- and 13th-century German lyrics, originally written on single leaves, or on a few leaves, and brought together in the 13th and 14th centuries, probably for some patron as an act of preservation. About twenty such collections survive, some only in fragments, but the largest, best-known and most beautiful is the 'Grosse Heidelberger Liederhandschrift', also known as the 'Manessische Liederhandschrift' after Rüdeger Manesse (*c.* 1252–1304) and his son Johann, both of Zurich.

Lyrics by 140 poets, written in Middle-High-German, survive on some 430 parchment leaves. There are 138 full-page illustrations, believed to be the work of four limners. They mostly depict knights (the poets) and ladies in stylized scenes of chivalry, often of considerable tenderness. Some show interesting details of games and sports (e.g. chess, falconry, fishing), while others show musical instruments. Clear shades of blue, red and mauve are mostly used for the clothing; gold is used on armorial shields, and also in a very natural way to suggest the metal of weapons, jewellery, and the collars and cuffs of clothing.

The whole-page illustrations are bounded by simple narrow bands of gold and colours, with the name of the knight added in red at the head of the page.

The manuscript was in Zurich in the 14th century; it subsequently belonged to Ulrich von Fugger, and in 1584 it passed to the Bibliotheca Palatina. In 1657 it was sold to the Royal Library in Paris where it remained until 1888 when the German Government sponsored the purchase by a Strasbourg bookseller of 166 French manuscripts from the Ashburnham Library (they had been stolen from French libraries by Barrois and Libri). Twenty-three of these manuscripts were exchanged for the Manessische Liederhandschrift which was restored to Heidelberg University Library, (Cod.Pal.lat.848).

Francis Minns Memorial: from 1971 an annual award of money to the designer considered by the selectors for the N.B.L. British Book Design and Production Exhibition to have earned special recognition. The Memorial was created to perpetuate the memory of Francis Minns, book designer and teacher, who died in 1971. The first recipient was Sebastian Carter. Others have been Berthold Wolpe, 1972; Gerald Cinamon, 1973; Hans Schmoller, 1974, and Dr Herbert Spencer, 1975.

mint: a second-hand book trade term for a book in immaculate condition: as new.

minuscule: a lower-case or small letter. Cf. *majuscule.*

miracle bindings: see *Chudov bindings.*

miscellaneous binder: a trade binder of single books to an individual customer's order. See also *craft bookbinding.*

misprint: a printing error resulting from careless reading and proofing of copy.

Missal: a book containing the Mass services for the year. Early examples were handwritten and illuminated. The term is also used for any illuminated prayer book or *Book of Hours*, q.v.

missal caps: decorative capitals printed with black-letter type.

Missale plenarium: a term used in the 12th century for a complete Roman Missal. Prior to this no single manuscript had contained the whole Missal. From the end of the 7th century the name Missal had been given to the *Sacramentary* which included the Collects, Secrets, Prefaces, Canons and Post-communions. Other volumes contained the Gospels, Lessons,

325

Epistles and choral portions of the Mass. As the practice of including all parts in one volume became general the word 'plenarium' was dropped.

Every diocese had its own Missal, and many churches in a diocese had uses of their own. A local usage would often be added in the form of marginal notes or at the end of the volume.

Missals were usually large and costly and it became customary, particularly in Germany and Switzerland, to have shortened versions containing the text of the Masses for Sundays and the principal feast days. Such abridgements were called *Missale speciale*.

Missale speciale Constantiense: an early printed Missal of which four copies are known. They are in the Bavarian State Library, Munich; the Pierpoint Morgan Library, New York; the Zentralbibliothek, Zurich; and the Stadtbibliothek, Augsburg.

The book is printed on 192 folio leaves in a type which is an adaptation of an early form of the smaller of the two large types used in the Mainz Psalter of 1457. The place of printing, printer and date have been matters for conjecture, and thus pleasurable controversy, since 1898 when Otto Hupp (1859–1949) published his conclusion that the Missal was printed by Gutenberg and pre-dated the 42-line Bible. Equally undetermined was the date of a 'Missale abbreviatum', printed from the same press, and surviving in one known copy now at the Benedictine monastery of St Paul in Carinthia.

However, the date of printing was finally established as 1473 by Dr Stevenson who compared the watermarks in the Missale paper with those in numerous other books. He located the press at Basle and swept away the misleading appellation 'Constantiense' by showing that the book was intended for general use in the upper Rhine area. As printer he tentatively suggested Johann Meister, a sometime associate of Wenssler and later of Köllicker, both of Basle.

For a brilliant exposition of his research see A. Stevenson, 'The problem of the Missale speciale', Bibliographical Society, 1967.

missing copy: such items as an index or appendix to a book which may not be written when a publisher sends a typescript and his specification to the printer for an estimate of costs. Allowance must be made for copy which is to follow. See also *signature*.

mitred: 1. the leather corners of a bound book when folded so that the inside line of joint is at an angle of 45° from the top and side edges of the book.
2. the ends of rules which are bevelled so that in forming the right-angle joints of frames they will fit flush. See also *Oxford corners*.

mixed composition: said of matter which in its setting calls for various type-founts, e.g. a single paragraph

with words in bold-face or italic type among the main portion which is set in roman. See also *fat matter*.

mock-up: see *dummy*.

model: a specification in verbal or mathematical terms used as a means of studying the behaviour and relationships of complex systems, as in economics and industry. Flow diagrams, organizational charts and mathematical formulae may be involved, requiring special hand-setting by the printer. See also *technical book illustration*.

model-books: the precursor of the artists' handbooks of the 15th century, being books of outline sketches to guide medieval artists in basing their iconography on long established conservative tradition. The representations of figures, animals and plants were less observations than conventional formulae and often, in later copying, only costumes would be updated.

The earliest model-book to survive is that of the Limoges monk Adémar de Chabannes who died in 1034. It contains drawings of single figures, set at random on the page, and suitable for such frequently copied works as Aesop, the New Testament and Prudentius; it is now in Leyden University.

Through the years model-books were used by sculptors, metal-workers and illuminators of manuscripts. Notable was the compilation of Villard de Honnecourt of *c.* 1230 which was an early attempt to emphasise the geometrical foundation of subjects depicted.

By the later 14th century artists were much less restricted to conventional interpretations when illuminating manuscripts, particularly when working for lay patrons. Even so, preliminary sketches were usually made either marginally or as underdrawings in the actual space to be painted. Nor were sketcher and painter always the same man. Pattern books for craftsmen in metal, plaster and stone continued in use much longer. See also *Amman, arabesque*.

Model Copyright Law, 1964: the result of a conference held at Geneva by former colonial African states resentful of the limitations imposed on them by the *Berne Convention*, q.v. It was taken as the basis for legislation in several countries including Kenya, Malta, Uganda and Zambia. These governments claimed the right to reprint without permission or payment any work written by their nationals which might be needed for educational purposes. After a similar meeting held in Delhi in 1967 Malaysia and other Far Eastern states enacted legislation on similar lines. The needs of developing countries were more generally met in the 1971 revisions of the Berne and Universal Copyright Conventions (see *Paris Texts, 1971*), although a new African 'Model' was adopted at Abidjan (Ivory Coast) in 1973. See also *Stockholm Protocol.*

modern face: type having contrasting thick vertical and thin horizontal strokes, unbracketed serifs set at right angles and curves thickened in the centre: the effect is of marked vertical emphasis. Examples, which include Bodoni, De Vinne, Didot and Walbaum, are available from most founders.

As type, the style originated in France in the late 17th century for the *romain du roi Louis XIV*, q.v., but the centrally thickened vertical strokes and hairline serifs were pre-figured in certain marginal capitals seen in the *Winchester Bible*, q.v.

Grandjean's royal fount was followed by Fournier's types of 1745, Didot's of 1784, and most notably by Bodoni's of 1790. In England the Didot type inspired a fount cut in 1788 by Richard Austin for John Bell whose finalized design appeared in 1792. Most modern-face types have a somewhat chilly elegance and print well on smooth rather than antique papers. See also *letters – forms and styles* and Appendix A.

Moholy-Nagy, László, 1895–1946: Hungarian teacher of and writer on typography who was successively associated with the Bauhausverlag of Leipzig (est. 1923), where he was among pioneers of what was often referred to as the 'New Typography' in Germany, and later with the Chicago Institute of Design where he led American book designers away from classicism in layout. He was also a considerable artist and photographer.

moiré: an imperfection, noticed when printing coloured half-tones, which is seen as a mechanical pattern of dots. This can be minimized by photographing each colour at a separate angle or by using screens ruled at varying angles for each exposure. See also *half-tone screen.*

moisture content: see *relative humidity.*

moke: a nickname common in early 18th century pressrooms for a compositor. Cf. *pig.*

monastic bindings: the name now given to the diapered leather covers of manuscript volumes which were common in most North European monasteries up to the 15th century. Each square or diamond was filled with a small stamped design. No gold was used. An alternative name is *antique bindings.*

monastic book writing: the principal copyists of manuscripts in the Middle Ages were monks working under the direction of the precentor. He was in charge of the monastic scriptorium and often had delegated to him the selection of works to be produced. The duties of the monks, which all were taught to perform,

included the preparation of ink, parchment and binding materials, all issued by the precentor. They copied not only Bibles and service books for use in the choir and refectory, but also original work and chronicles. By the late 10th century, in England, Bibles were supplied to other religious houses and to churches: to meet this demand lay copyists were often employed. All copyists were carefully trained in the style of script current at the time. By the 12th century this script (Carolingian minuscule) was so uniform and exact in England and France that identification of origin is often difficult, though by the 13th century regional differences began to appear.

The more important altar books were decorated (see *illumination*). Binding was in thick parchment or leather-covered boards except for the major items which were ornamented with gems and precious metals. See also *aumbry, magister almarii, manuscript book writing.*

monk: an ink blot or splash on a printed sheet. The term originated in the days when *ink balls*, q.v., were used to ink the formes. Cf. *black, friar.*

Monnier bindings: the binding style associated principally with the Frenchman *Louis François Monnier* (fl.1737–76) and his son *Jean Charles Henri* (fl.1757–80), who in 1757 was binder to the duc d'Orléans. Features of their work were inlaid mosaics of Chinese landscapes, brilliantly coloured birds, and allegorical scenes. For the backgrounds they used cream, red and green morocco. The Monnier family were binders from 1623–c. 1800.

monogram: 'two or more letters . . . interwoven' (O.E.D.). However, F. W. Goudy considered a monogram to be a single character which signifies the letters that compose it, e.g. &, in which one letter (e) forms part of the other (t). He wrote that 'a monogram is thereby distinct from a *cipher* which is an interwoven combination of two or more separate letters, each entire and not part of any other.'

monograph: a treatise on a single subject.

Monoline: a typesetting machine invented by the American Wilbur Scudder in 1893. It was simple and relatively cheap, but failed to establish a market. Production ceased in 1910.

Monophoto Filmsetter: the function of a 'Monophoto' filmsetter is to project character images directly on to photosensitized film or paper, and to compose those characters automatically into justified lines of text matter, all according to the control by a perforated programme tape. The mechanisms for matrix selection and presentation are those used for the composition caster.

The film matrix case of the *Mark 3* contains 272 film matrices arranged in 16 rows of 17 matrices each, all of which are separate and interchangeable. With some exceptions one set of matrices will cover all sizes from 8- to 24-point, though for 6- and 7-point a second set is needed.

An important feature of the machine is its departure from conventional justification methods in favour of combined spacing linked with proportional justification, where one increment of coarse justification is equal to one unit of set.

On the *Mark 4* model the matrix case has 340 matrices and a re-designed air system. A different programme-tape coding system is used, requiring a keyboard able to address separately each of 340 matrix positions. The machine is capable of setting the special signs in mathematics, chemical and scientific composition, or foreign languages.

On the *Mark 5* the capacity for handling complex work and the flexibility of operation have been extended by the introduction of a system of line spacing for line feeds in either a forward or a reverse direction. A range from $\frac{1}{2}$- to $31\frac{1}{2}$-point in $\frac{1}{2}$-point increments can be coded into the programme tape at a keyboard fitted with a shift control. Other modifications include safeguards for excluding dust and simplifying cleaning.

Monophoto 400 Filmsetter: introduced in 1973, is an 11cps unit designed to be used with a Monotype pneumatic keyboard or a Monotype electronic perforator. The 400 matrices, stacked 20 × 20 in a matrix case, are separate and interchangeable to give maximum flexibility. More than 200 faces are available plus many thousands of special characters. Special features for complex typesetting include reverse set feed (as well as reverse film feed), variable alignment, double exposure, etc. Most kinds of film and paper with lith or stabilization emulsions can be used, and the film can be in sheet or roll form.

Monophoto 600 Filmsetter: introduced in 1970, a 30cps machine carrying a fount made up from 397 standard matrices and 200 special pi matrices to provide a maximum of 597 characters at any one time. It will produce justified text from 6- to 28-point in direct reading form, on film or paper, from an 8-level programmed input control tape perforated at a special keyboard or generated by a general-purpose computer.

Film matrices are arranged around the perimeter of four discs, each carrying 100 matrices, which are rotated for the selection of individual matrix positions and aligned in the path of flash-discharge tubes, one for each disc. Superimposed on the optical arrangement is a subsidiary pi matrix facility which employs a rotating magazine of 35mm slides; the magazine

328

contains 100 individual matrices, each of which can carry two character images.

Monophoto 600 Tape Perforator: a tape perforator consisting of a keyswitch array with a display panel, a free-standing console and an 8-channel punch which

A 'Monotype' composition caster

A 'Monotype' high-speed composition mould

A set of stop-pins, one of which has just risen (C), control the forward movement of the matrix case (D). Lateral movement of the matrix case is controlled by another set of pins (not shown here).
Each pin corresponds to one of a combination of holes in the perforated paper tape (E)

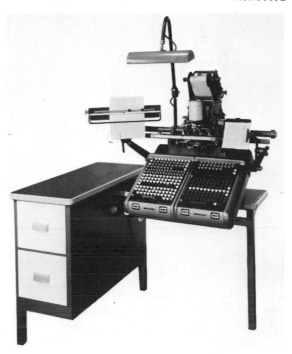

A 'Monotype' pneumatic keyboard

is mounted on the console. There are two keybanks, each with 18 rows of 12 keys, giving 416 character keys with four space bars. Each keybank has a shift key which can induce an alternative response from each of the 208 keys in that bank to produce a total of 832 key codes and four space bars.

Type size is selected from a row of eight switches on the display panel within the range of 6- to 14-point on normal composition and from 16- to 28-point on large composition. Other switches determine unit adding and justified letterspacing.

Monotype: the registered trade mark of The Monotype Corporation Limited of Salfords, Redhill, Surrey, manufacturers of type composing and casting machines. (For a historical note see *Lanston.*) The machines comprise two separate units: the *keyboard* and the *caster*, each with its own operator.

The keyboard has two banks of keys representing seven complete sets of alphabetic characters as well as figures, punctuation signs, spaces and justification keys. Usually the left-hand bank is used for roman

and small capitals, and the right-hand bank for italic and bold face. The position of keys for letters of the alphabet corresponds to the QWERTY (or universal) arrangement used on typewriters.

When the keyboard operator taps the keys according to an author's copy mechanisms are set in motion which cause combinations of perforations, corresponding to each character key, to be made in a paper tape by punches, operated by pistons raised by compressed air.

Synchronised with the movement of the punch is the mechanism for registering the widths of characters and spaces. For this, levers operate to allow a controlled movement of an indicator on the em scale to show the amount of space remaining to complete a line. When the line is nearly finished, this mechanism indicates on an automatically revolved justifying scale (a kind of ready-reckoner) which two justification keys must be depressed so that, when cast, all spaces between words will be sufficiently increased to extend the line of type to the required length. After each line is set the depression of a reversing key restores the registration mechanism to its starting position ready for the composition of the next line.

To speed up production of paper tape and relieve

329

The width of every character and space is registered through rotations of the unit wheel and recorded by a visible pointer (A) moving along the em scale. On the justifying scale an indicator (B) notes the number of spaces which the operator taps between words

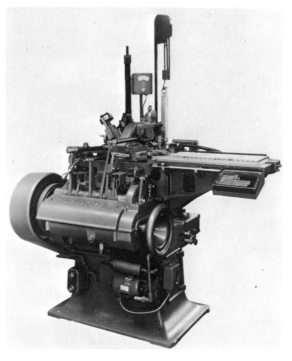

A 'Monotype' Super caster

The matrix case containing up to 272 separate matrices and space blanks. These are arranged in 16 rows with 17 matrices to each row

A 'Monotype' electronic perforator

the keyboard operator of end-of-line procedures involved in justification, a Monotype *electronic* perforator may be used. This comprises a desk-mounted keybutton display unit, a free-standing computer console for feeding information into the electronic calculators, and a 31-channel electronic paper punch, positioned on the console. The keys of this perforator are arranged in two banks, with one key per character. The operation of keys triggers an advanced electronic system for the generation of codes and activation of the tape punch. Justification is completed automatically, and is effected by a single keystroke which also re-sets the machine in readiness for the next line. After each line is set, the depression of a reversing key restores the registration mechanism to its starting position ready for the composition of the next line. On completion of keyboarding the perforated paper tape is transferred by hand to the air tower of the composition caster.

The Monotype composition caster produces a separate character for each type required, in a wide range of styles and sizes from 4¼-point to 14-point (or 24-point if a special attachment is fitted). Types are cast in rapid succession and are automatically assembled into words, and lines of words, evenly spaced to occupy a predetermined width. The machine responds to instructions coded on the paper tape, producing metal types of the letters 'signalled' at the keyboard. The tape passes over air vents on the caster in the opposite direction to that in which it travelled on the keyboard, so that the justifying signal which the operator perforated at the end of the line is the first perforation to pass over the air vents on the caster. It adjusts the mechanism to cast spaces of appropriate width.

The mechanical movements of the caster are governed by a series of cams driven on a single shaft by a small motor, while the accurate selection and positioning for casting from the required matrix is controlled by the perforated paper tape. During each revolution of the caster the tape advances ⅛in. Compressed air, passed through the perforations, causes selected stop pins to rise in the path of a system of levers that move the matrix case (containing up to 272 matrices), thus arresting their motion to site a particular matrix over the mould orifice. This matrix is pushed down firmly on to the mould while molten metal is forced into the cavity from below. The metal solidifies in the water-cooled mould and the newly formed type is ejected into a channel where types accumulate to form a line. The complete line is pushed on to a galley to be assembled with previous and subsequent lines.

Supplementary mechanisms are available to facilitate a particular aspect or class of work, e.g. mathematics or chemical formulae.

For casting display type up to 72-point, also leads, rules and borders, furniture, plate-mounting material,

etc., a Monotype *Super caster* is used. This is not a composing machine. Each piece of the product is cast separately, automatically ejected from the casting cavity, and delivered in finished form on to a galley.

Monotype Lasercomp: demonstrated in 1977. This is a photosetter having a laser light source with a 1,000 lines per inch resolution. It offers type sizes from 4- to 256-point, and a maximum 58 picas line length.

Monophotolettering Machine Mark 2: a machine designed both to complement a Monophoto filmsetter and be a general purpose unit for all kinds of jobbing printing as well as certain specialized types of work such as cartography, TV titling, posters and display cards. The machine photographs manually selected individual characters direct on to film or paper.

Monotype Studio-lettering Machine: an enlarger-style unit incorporating a semi-automatic composition process. It is intended for art studios, advertising agencies, typesetters and general printers, and provides facilities for the composition of copy, in body sizes from 3mm to 125mm on light-sensitive paper or film. It must be operated in darkroom conditions.

montage: an assembly of portions of several photographs or drawings to form an original. The separate parts are cut out and assembled like a jig-saw puzzle, care being taken to avoid overlapping edges which would cause shadows. See also *mechanical*.

Montague Press: a private press founded in 1911 by *Carl Purington Rollins*, q.v., at Montague, Mass. It was here that Bruce Rogers' distinguished Centaur type was first used for a limited edition of De Guerin's 'The Centaur'.

Montgolfier, Jean: a Frenchman who according to legend was captured when on the second Crusade and sent to work in a papermill in Damascus. He is supposed to have returned to France where he set up a papermill at Vidalon in 1157. No documentary proof of this has been found.

Whenever established, the Montgolfier family owned a papermill at Vidalon from the 17th century. The two brothers *Joseph* (b. 1740) and *Jacques* (b. 1745) worked there before making the aeronautical discoveries which made them famous.

Moomba Award for Australian Literature: a sum of £500 awarded annually to the writer of a work judged to be an outstanding contribution to Australian literature. The first award, made in early 1964, was to Geoffrey Serle for his 'The golden age', Melbourne U.P., 1963.

331

Moon: an embossed type-face invented by Dr William Moon of Brighton about 1850, for the printing of books to be read by blind persons whose affliction comes in later life. It is based on the roman alphabet and employs simple lines and curves. Cf. *Braille*.

Moore, John, Bishop of Ely, 1646–1714: an eminent bibliophile whose collection of 29,000 books and some 1,800 manuscripts was bought by George I who gave it to Cambridge University in 1715. Dibdin described Moore as 'the father of black-letter collectors in this country'.

mordant: 1. an adhesive for fixing gold leaf.
2. any fluid used to etch lines on a printing plate.

Mores, Edward Rowe, 1730–78: a scholar and antiquarian, remembered for his 'Dissertation on typographical founders and founderies', 1778. In 1772 he bought 'all the curious parts of that immense collection of punches, matrices, and types which had been accumulating from the days of Wynkyn de Worde to those of John James', a London typefounder. The collection was dispersed by sale in 1782.

moresques: a term used in Europe during the later Middle Ages to describe the interlaced patterns made on pottery, leatherwork and architecture by Arabs (Moors) working in North Africa and Spain. As interpreted and developed in the Italian Renaissance they were known as *arabesques*, q.v.

Moretus, Joannes, 1543–1610: the latinized name used by Jan Moerentorf, the son-in-law and successor to Plantin's press in 1589, prior to which he had managed the shop and accounts. Under his control fewer humanistic texts were produced, being superseded by liturgical and religious books, many by Jesuit writers. He was followed by his sons *Balthasar* (1574–1641) and *Jan* (1576–1618).

Balthasar was much concerned with maintaining Plantin's standards of presentation. Between 1608 and 1640 he commissioned Rubens to design frontispieces. He also built the library which still exists and generally improved the premises.

Descendants of the first Moretus carried on the business until 1867 when it closed. For its subsequent history see *Plantin Moretus Museum*. See also *Plantin*.

Morgan, John Pierpont, 1837–1913: an American financier, important here for the magnificent library of books and illuminated MSS. he assembled in New York. His son, *J. P. Morgan*, jun., (1867–1943), added to the collection and dedicated it to the public. See 'Early printed books and major acquisitions, 1924–74', N.Y., 1974.

Morison, Stanley, 1889–1967: probably the most distinguished British scholar-typographer of this century. He was successively associated with *The Imprint*, 1913; the Pelican Press, 1918–21; and the Cloister Press in Manchester, 1921. In 1923 he was appointed typographical adviser to both the Monotype Corporation and Cambridge University Press. It was he who devised the then unusual styling for the publications of Victor Gollancz in the early thirties.

He was typographical adviser to *The Times* from 1929–60. Within three years of his appointment he had completely re-styled the typography of the paper, and his Times New Roman type is now used in many parts of the world for books, newspapers and periodicals, though no longer for *The Times*.

Morison's considerable literary output included contributions to *The Fleuron* and the *Monotype Recorder*, his 'Four centuries of fine printing', 1924; the writing of most of the five-volume history of *The Times*; and his posthumous 'Politics and script'.

See *Signature*, 3, 1947; also 'A handlist of the writings of Stanley Morison', compiled by John Carter, (Privately published) C.U.P., 1950; the continuation for 1950–59 compiled by P. M. Handover, in *Motif*, 3 1959, and T. Appleton's cumulation, 1977.

His collection of 4,000 books is in Cambridge University Library.

morocco: properly, sumach-tanned goatskin which has been hand-boarded to bring up the grain, glazed and polished. It is used for good quality bookbinding. The name comes from the goatskins stained red with a dye obtained from the kermes insect prior to tawing with alum which were first produced by the Arabs of North Africa, particularly in Libya and Morocco, whence they were exported to Spain by at least the 11th century. Later, similar leather was made in the Levant, but this was tanned in sumach. The product was known in Europe as Turkish morocco (a patent misnomer) and in England as Turkey leather or simply *turkey*.

But although all moroccos are goatskins, all goatskins which have been used for binding are not moroccos. Vegetable-tanned goatskins were used for *Coptic bookbindings*, q.v. Locally tanned goatskins were plentiful in northern Italy where binders used them from the end of the 15th century. They were not moroccos. Such distinctions have, however, largely disappeared in modern leather-trade usage.

It was the exotic orange, green, blue and deep red skins of the Islamic world imported via Turkey to Venice and from the Balearic Islands to Naples in the early 16th century which made morocco known and immediately fashionable in Italy. After 1536 goatskins were used in France. They were eventually finished locally, a method of doing so being patented in Paris about 1675 and in England by 1710. In England Turkish goatskins were used from the 16th century and not until about 1721 was leather from Morocco used at all extensively, notable being the skins imported from Fez via Gibraltar for Lord Harley. Smooth-grained goatskin continued in general use for less important bindings.

For varieties of morocco see *assisted-, cross-grained-, crushed Levant, fine-grain, French Cape Levant, french morocco, glazed, grained leather, hard-grain-, imitation leather, levant, Niger-, oasis goat, Persian-, pin seal-, straight-grain-, Turkey leather.* Cf. *calf.*

Morris, William, 1834–96: English poet, craftsman, socialist. In 1891 he started the *Kelmscott Press,* q.v., at Hammersmith, London, seeking to return to the style of the earliest printers and to break away from Victorian commercialism. The basic concepts of printing which he proclaimed were that the unit of book design should be the opening (two facing pages), and that type, imposition, paper, ink and impression were interdependent. Morris had a tremendous influence on book design and production in England, Germany and America. His principles inspired work done in the many private presses which were started as a result, and stimulated the improvement of standards in the wider field of commercial publishing; but his own books were costly and limited in number, while the richly inked gothic type and wooden blocks made their pages too heavy for easy reading.

To make Morris, his friends, their work and ideals better known the *William Morris Society* was established in London in 1955. Lectures, visits and exhibitions are arranged, and a further function of the Society is to keep readily available to the public his literary works as well as his wall-papers and textiles. See P. Needham, 'William Morris and the art of the book', N.Y., Pierpoint Library, 1976.

mortise: 1. a space cut out of a printing plate in order to insert type or another plate.

2. the cutting away of metal from the non-printing area at the sides of a type to permit closer setting.

mosaic bindings: book covers decorated by *inlaying* or *onlaying,* qq.v., pieces of leather of contrasting colour or texture in a regular or irregular pattern.

The technique of applying contrasting leathers to book covers had been practised in England and France from the 16th century, the decoration being based on formal geometrical designs with a centrally-placed oval, square or rectangle on the front board as a background for arms or a monogram, and elsewhere, the adding of geometrical shapes. But about 1716 a new conception of the mosaic style appeared on a group of bindings made for the Regent of France. Although unsigned they have been attributed by Michon to Augustin Du Seuil who later worked with Antoine Michel Padeloup. Leaves and flowers in onlays of coloured leathers were freely disposed

about a central cartouche. Tooling was typified by the extensive use of straight and curved fillets, with less emphasis on small dies. Other leading Parisian binders associated with this highly skilled work were Louis François Monnier and his son Jean Charles Henri, and Jacques Antoine Derome and his son Nicolas Denis. The most exotic of these mosaic bindings were made in the Monnier workshops: some had scenes in Chinese style, with pagodas, trees and even people in Chinese costume, all in contrasting leathers. Historians are inclined to consider them interesting curios rather than bindings.

Excellent mosaic bindings were made in the 19th century for rich collectors. Notable were the successful copies of earlier styles made in the 1850s by Georges Trautz, and the entirely modern floral and leaf compositions made in the 1890s by the younger Marius Michel. Both were French. In England Francis Bedford, Rivière and Zaehnsdorf made examples.

In the present century the mosaic technique has almost entirely replaced the use of gold tooling with engraved tools. See L. M. Michon, 'Les Reliures mosaïquées du XVIIIe siècle', Paris, 1956.

mosaic gold: or 'aurium musicum', an imitation gold made from bisulphide of tin and mercury used from the 13th century by illuminators as a cheap substitute for powdered gold.

Mosher Press: established as a publishing imprint in 1891 at Portland, Maine, by *Thomas Bird Mosher* (1852–1923), a retired seaman turned publisher. From 1894 to 1914 he published as 'gift books' a series of anthologies called 'The Bibelot'. The books he published were small, usually 12mo, printed mostly on Van Gelder paper, and prettily tricked out with decorative title pages, slip cases and limitation notices. They were made to be sold cheaply, which his critics claimed could only be done because he pirated English texts by authors who had failed to register them in Washington. Andrew Lang, Francis Thompson, Robert Louis Stevenson and Robert Bridges were but a few of those affected. The British trade referred to him as the 'Portland Pirate'.

Mosher argued with reason that what he printed was unknown in America since others were unaware of it or considered it unprofitable to publish, and he certainly extended the reputation there of the writers he chose. By 1923 he had issued some 800 editions. After his death Flora Lamb ran the Press for his widow until 1938. In 1941 it was sold to a Boston bookshop. See B. L. Hatch and R. Nash, 'A checklist . . .', Amherst, University of Massachusetts Press, 1967.

mother set: a set of printing plates, e.g. of a standard reference work, kept for the purpose of electrotyping further sets.

Motif: from 1958, a journal of the visual arts edited by Ruari McLean and James Shand and published in cased form three times a year by the latter's Shenval Press, London. Although it ceased publication with Vol. 13 it remains important as a record of the book illustration and graphic art then being done, and as an example of the highest production standards.

mottled calf: calfskin, used for book covers, which has been given an irregular pattern by dabbing it with sponges dipped in acid or coloured dyes.

mottling: a fault in printing seen as an uneven impression and caused, especially in flat and solid areas on the sheet, by using too much pressure, an unsuitable paper, or an unsuitable ink.

mould: 1. the wire cloth and its surrounding frame on which pulp is shaken into a sheet of paper. See also *hand-made paper*, *papermaking*.
2. generally, any container in which molten metal is poured to solidify into a required shape. In *type-casting*, q.v., the mould consists of a casting box with a matrix inside it (Intertype, Linotype, Monotype and comparable machines have special casting moulds). In *stereotyping*, q.v., an impression of a forme is taken in plaster or papier mâché: this, after drying, becomes the mould.
3. see *mildew*.

mould machine: a cylinder machine used for the making of liners, duplicator papers or *mould-made paper*, q.v.

mould-made paper: a manufactured simulation of *hand-made paper*, q.v. Best quality mould-made papers have a high rag content with minimal evidence of *machine direction*, q.v., achieved by forming lengths of paper on a slow-moving special web. Tearing the dried and finished ribbon into sheets gives them deckle edges of true hand-made paper.

mount: see *block mounting*.

movable type: type cast as single-letter units. The term is usually limited to foundry type, set up by hand in a composing stick. See also *printing – historical survey*, *typecasting*.

Moxon, Joseph, 1627–91: an hydrographer, instrument maker, author and printer, who added a typefoundry to his London business in 1659. He may previously have worked in Holland for a time. In 1669 he issued his 'Proves of several sorts of letters cast by Joseph Moxon'. This folio sheet shows eleven founts and is the first typefounder's full *specimen sheet*, q.v., known in England. In another work, 'Regulae Trium Ordinum . . .', 1677, he outlined his rules for the geo-

334

metrical proportion of letters and figures, but his fame rests on 'Mechanick exercises', begun in 1677 as a series of monthly parts. Volume II of this work, 1683–84, was devoted to all aspects of printing and letter-founding, being the first comprehensive manual on the subject in any language, and the first to name letter forms. A scholarly reprint prepared by H. Davis and H. Carter was published by O.U.P. in 1958.

Mozarabic illumination: the distinctive style of manuscript painting developed in the Christian monasteries of Spain between the 9th and 11th century, at which time the country was under Muslim rule. (Mozarabic is derived from *Musta 'rib* which means 'arabized', i.e. a Christian convert to Islam.)

The chief survivals of the art are some twenty manuscript copies of the commentary by Beatus of Liébana on the Apocalypse of St John, written about 776. The commentary was largely a compilation of writings by earlier writers including the 4th century African theologian Tyconius. The style of painting is typified by ornamental lettering and geometrical shapes, often in vivid reds, yellows and blues; with severe figures in strangely mystical scenes rendered as patterns set against bands of strong colours which formed the backgrounds. The treatment and motifs showed classical, Islamic and primitive Visigothic influences.

There are examples in the British Library and in the John Rylands Library, Manchester (Lat. MS.8).

MS.: manuscript. **MSS:** manuscripts.

mudéjar bindings: Spanish bindings of Cordovan leather done from the 13th–15th century. The main design was a blind-tooled pattern of double outline interlacings, or strapwork, with stamped strips of cords or knots, dots, curves, and rings as part of the subsidiary or background design. The Moorish inhabitants of Christian Spain were known as mudéjares. They were allowed religious freedom and to practise their crafts, of which bookbinding was one. See also *gótico-mudéjar*.

Mughal illumination: painting done for the Muslim court at Delhi in the 16th and 17th centuries.

Babar (1483–1530) came from Persia to found the Mughal empire in 1526. His son Humayun (1508–56) founded a court library and brought Persian painters of the Safavi court at Tabriz, notable being Mir Sayed Ali and Abdussamad.

Manuscript painting achieved its finest flowering during the reign of Akbar (1542–1605) who ruled from 1556. Akbar maintained a large staff of calligraphers, painters and bookbinders, the majority of whom were Hindus from the courts of Indian princes. They worked under the supervision of Persian artists.

There was also a workshop for making paper and paint.

Important works made for Akbar were the 'Hamza-anama' (painted between 1567 and 1582) which was a series of Persian romances, Firdausi's 'Shahnama' of the same period, and the 'Akbarnama' of Abu el Fazl, chronicling the emperor's reign and completed by 1602. The illustrations to this last are now scattered throughout collections in Europe and America. Akbar also had many Indian classics translated into Persian.

One of the major Islamic works prepared for Akbar was the 'Jami-ut-tavarikh' written by the Persian scholar Rashiduddin Fazlullah (1247–1318). This was a history of the Asian Mongols of whom the best known was Jenghiz Khan. The copy which Akbar had made was known as the 'Kitabi Changez-nama' and is now in Tehran. It has 98 full-page miniatures painted over a period of many years by more than thirty artists. Basavan was perhaps the most important of them. Not surprisingly the pictures document the life of the Indian epoch in which they were painted and not the simple roughness of the Mongols.

Although early Islamic painting in India owed its origins to Persia, whence came the first artists, by the end of the 16th century a style had been evolved in which Persian, Turkish, European and Indian influences were present. The European influence was brought to Delhi via Goa by Jesuit missionaries. Architectural perspective, shading and landscape details from Italian and Flemish woodcuts were introduced as European elements in Mughal painting, but it was the Indian influence which created the style we know as Mughal and which differentiated it from Persian. Dasvanth and Basavan were the leading Hindu painters at Akbar's court.

His son Jehangir (ruled 1605–27) continued his father's patronage of painting. The best-known artists working for him were Mohammed Nadir of Samarkand, noted for his portraits, and Manohar (son of Basavan) noted for his birds and animals. About this time artists painted separate pictures which were later collected and bound in albums.

During the reign of Shah Jehan (ruled 1628–58) the patronage of painting, particularly of portraits, extended outside court cirles. His successor Aurangzeb (1659–1707) was an orthodox Muslim and no supporter of artists. Thereafter manuscript painting in Muslim India declined in importance. See P. Brown, 'Indian painting under the Mughals', O.U.P., 1914.

mull: a coarse variety of muslin which forms the first lining of a case-bound book. It is glued to the back of the book, and in the course of binding adheres to the case in which it is largely responsible for holding the book. Abbreviated from the Hindi *mulmull*; it is also known as *scrim*. See also *jaconet*.

muller: a cone-shaped lump of stone or marble used to give fine texture to a lithographic stone. Fine sand is sprinkled over the stone and then the muller, held in both hands, is rotated over the surface. See also *levigator*.

Müller, Johannes, 1436–76: see *Regiomontanus, Johannes.*

multi-metal plates: lithographic printing plates made of two or more materials.

1. *Relief plates.* These carry a raised copper image on a stainless steel or other water-retaining base plate. They are made by either negative- or positive-working processes. See *bimetallic lithographic plates.* An American development is the diazo plastic-coated bimetallic plate which is very stable.

2. *Recessed plates.* A steel base carries the copper image layer over which is deposited a chromium water-retaining surface. While only suitable for the *deep-etch process*, q.v., they give good results for long-run colour work on high quality web-offset presses. These are trimetallic plates (e.g. *Nuchrome*). They are described under *bimetallic lithographic plates*, q.v.

multiple rule: a rule in which two or more strips of brass or type metal are mounted on the same body.

muniments: the title-deeds or charters recording privileges belonging to a family, society or corporation.

Munsell, Albert: a teacher of Boston, Mass., who in 1899 began research on a system for noting colour. This was subsequently adopted by the American National Bureau of Standards. See also *colour systems.*

Munsell, Joel, 1808–80: a printer, publisher and bookseller of Albany, N.Y. Apart from his business he was a historian of printing and papermaking, amassing an important collection of books and over 10,000 newspapers which are now in New York State Library.

The use of imported Caslon types and good paper, with careful presswork, marked many of his books (of which he printed over 2,000 titles) as better than the general level of New York printing in the 19th century. He used as his device the Aldine dolphin and anchor with the motto 'Aldi discipulus Albaniensis'.

murex: a purple dye obtained from the shellfish murex, and probably in use since 1600 BC. The particular shade obtained from *murex brandaris* and *murex trunculus* has been variously known as Royal, Phoenician and Tyrian purple, the last from the town in Lebanon where, as in other Mediterranean coastal regions, huge dumps of broken shells remain to this day.

In Byzantine manuscripts murex was used to stain the background prior to writing in gold. There was also use of *turnsole* for this purpose.

Museo Bodoniano: opened in 1963 in the Palazzo della Pilotta, Parma, in which Bodoni had his printing office on an upper floor and his foundry on the ground floor. It is a repository for Bodoni's 70,000 punches, moulds, matrices, proof sheets, personal papers and an extensive but still incomplete collection, transferred from the Biblioteca Palatina, of the books and miscellaneous pieces he printed.

Dr Angelo Ciavarella was appointed first director of the museum and of the institute for typographical studies and training which was established at the same time. See also *Officina Bodoni*.

music engraving: for engraving music, metal plates are used, formerly of pewter, but now a cheaper alloy of tin and lead. The plates are planed and the

A finished plate

A music engraver at work

staves are made with a five-pointed scorer. The scoring must be repeated until the lines are sufficiently deep. After laying out the manuscript, the notes and any words are drawn on the plate with a needle and, guided by this work (which is in reverse), the letters and signs are punched in. The depth of punching may vary and any unevenness thus caused on the back of the plate is removed by lightly hammering. Key signs, brackets, rests, etc., are on punches, but bars, slurs and crescendos are usually hand-cut. The music engraver's case contains about 150 punches. Burrs on the front of the plates are removed with a scraper and a smoothing plane.

When engraving has been completed, an impression is taken for proof reading by colouring the plate (usually grey), and printing it in a small hand-press. This gives a white script on a coloured ground. Corrections to the plates are made by flattening from the back the places where errors occur and then

336

engraving the correct notes. In order to identify on the back these places, the music engraver uses a pair of proof-reading marking callipers with which he measures and scores the distance from the edge of the plate. When the plate is ready, positive impressions can be obtained by making prints on the intaglio principle, i.e., by inking the entire surface, wiping off the surplus and allowing ink to remain only in the engraved depressions.

However, a plate of soft metal is not suitable for printing a large edition and for this the music must be transferred to printing surfaces of other kinds. There are various methods. By a transfer, when using suitable ink and paper, lithographic printing plates for offset printing can be made. Impressions can also

Music case and tools

be taken for copying directly on prepared printing plates, or reproducing photographically. See also *Hole, William, music printing*.

music printing: there are three main methods now in use for printing music: it can be set up in type with special sorts and printed by letterpress, it can be drawn on paper for photography and platemaking, or it can be produced by *music engraving*, q.v., in which the actual printing is usually done by lithography.

Because of its place in church ritual music printing was attempted in the 15th century. The earliest printers left spaces in the text for the insertion by hand of lines and music notes; this was done in the Mainz Psalter of 1457. Another method was to print the lines and insert the notes by hand. Notes printed from movable types on hand-drawn stave-lines occur in the 'Collectorium super Magnificat' of Jean Charlier de Gerson, printed at Esslingen in 1473 by Conrad Fyner; the notation was in roman style with square symbols printed from quads.

A Graduale, probably printed at Constance or Augsburg in 1473, of which the only known complete copy is in the British Library, has gothic-style notation with symbols like four-pointed stars and the vertical strokes of gothic letters: the stave lines are printed.

In Italy musical notation was first printed in Ulrich Han's 'Missale Romanum', 1476. He printed the staves in red, and with a second impression, the notes in black. Theodorus Francus of Würzburg used specially designed type when he printed the first specimen in Italy of secular music in the 'Grammatica' of Franciscus Niger, Venice, 1480. This had no staves, which were first printed in Italy by Petrucci.

Georg Reyser of Würzburg was the first in Germany to use movable type for liturgical music in plain-song notation: this was in his 'Missale Moguntinense' of 1482. Staves and notes were printed separately. A mask was used for the first impression, the forme being inked in red for rubrics and staves. For the second impression, when letterpress and two sizes of notes were printed in black, quads replaced the rubrics and the blocks used for the staves. Another method was to use wooden blocks for music, an example being 'Opusculum musices' by Nicolaus Burtius, printed at Bologna by Ugo Rugerius in 1487.

In England R. Higden's 'Polychronicon', printed in 1495 by Wynkyn de Worde, contained the earliest example of music printing: this was eight notes built up from quads and rules.

The Venetian printer Ottaviano Petrucci invented in 1498 the printing from movable type of figured or measured music: this first appeared in his 'Harmonice musices odhecaton A', 1501, a collection of secular songs for several voices. He carefully made three impressions in register to complete the music. Two impressions were also needed for the music type

Music printed by Ottaviano Petrucci, Venice 1504. He printed from movable types on previously printed staves

cut by the younger Peter Schöffer, used by 1535 for measured music. Music printing in a single impression was probably first accomplished in Paris by *Attaingnant*, q.v., in 1527. The music types used, long attributed to *Haultin*, q.v., included parts of the stave on either side of the note in addition to the note itself. The use in London by *John Rastell*, q.v., of single-impression music type has been tentatively dated to 1520, which if correct, would pre-date the Parisian.

The German Valentin Bapst of Leipzig is thought to have experimented with complete lines of music (like a Linotype slug), cast from sand, chalk, or wood matrices in which the staves were first impressed in the mould and then the notation and signs were punched in the casting. The somewhat uneven result may be seen in his 'Psalmen und geistliche Lieder', 1547. About 1560 Guillaume Le Bé cut types with oval and tied notes for printing keyboard instrument music. Between 1530 and 1640 printing from movable type was the general practice.

Music printed from engraved copper plates appeared first in Rome in 1586 in 'Diletto spirituale', an anthology of canzonetti printed by Simon Verovio, although it has been suggested that Petrus Sambonettus of Siena used such plates in 1515. In England

337

'Parthenia', an anthology of virginal music by Byrd, Bull, and Gibbons, engraved by William Hole, 1612–13, was printed from copper plates. By the end of this century music printing from engraved or punched metal plates was usual. The leading music engraver of the time was Thomas Cross (fl.1683–1733) who stressed the superiority of engraved over punched plates with the words 'Beware of ye nonsensical puncht ones'. The engraved copper plates of Verovio were improved upon in 1724 when W. Croft used pewter plates on which notation was struck with punches.

Movable types for printing music of a precision and clarity to rival that done from engraved or punched plates were devised at Haarlem by Jacques-François Rosart in 1749–50, and by Immanuel Breitkopf of Leipzig by 1754. Breitkopf's improvement consisted of each type taking up only part of a single music line, with or without a note, so that the most complicated score could be set, even if somewhat laboriously. His punchcutter was Johann Schmidt who had come from The Hague. Fournier le Jeune was similarly engaged in devising music types in 1755/6, and the Fleischman music type for Enschedé was completed in 1760. The Swedish King's Printer Henric Fougt came to London in 1767 and registered a patent (No. 888) to print music from the movable types he had completed in 1763. After publishing music in London he returned to Sweden in 1770, selling his equipment and types to Robert Faulkener.

In the 19th century lithography became the leading method of printing music. Its inventor, Senefelder, communicated his process to a minor German composer, Gleissner, who helped him to start a music printing office. This was in 1796. Towards the end of the century, and after several improvements had been made to the method of printing, Gleissner and Senefelder were invited to set up their press in the premises of Philippe André, music publisher of Offenbach. In 1800 Senefelder and André introduced the new process in England where a press was set up in London. The successor of André was Georg Johann Vollweiler who printed music from stone at the Polyautographic Press c. 1806. The first British firm to use lithography in a large way was Augener & Co., 1853. Punched pewter plates were still made but only as originals for lithographic printing.

Later attempts were made to improve the method of printing from type, including the use of continuous steel rule for the staves and divided heads of notes. Notable was the progress made in this direction by William Clowes II (1807–83). The music publisher Joseph Alfred Novello established a printing business in 1847 in which movable types were used, but by the turn of the century the firm used the cheaper method of engraving.

In 1913 Linotype brought out a method of type-

Modern musical notation

setting music script in vertical lines on a typesetting machine. Photosetters for music printing have also been constructed. See also *Hole, Musicwriter*.

Musicwriter: an American machine resembling a typewriter which provides an alternative method to setting music by hand from type or engraving it on metal plates. The operator types music on paper which is either plain or pre-printed with staves. With the exception of long slurs the machine can print all notation, signs and instructions. A once-through acetate-based ribbon gives a crisp black impression for reproduction. Corrections are made by pasting white paper over the error and retyping. The copy is then photographed and a litho or letterpress plate is prepared for subsequent printing.

mutton: see *em quad*.

Mychell, John, fl.1546–56: a London printer who in 1549 became the first to print in Canterbury. His thirteen or fourteen books included a Psalter, other theological works and the 'Breviat Cronicle'.

Myllar, Androw: a citizen of Edinburgh who held jointly with *Walter Chepman*, q.v., the first licence to print in Scotland. Myllar had learned the craft of printing at Rouen and brought French workmen with him to Edinburgh.

The granting of the licence in 1507 was probably a result of James IV's desire to have the newly compiled Aberdeen Breviary adopted throughout Scottish churches instead of the *Sarum use*, q.v. As Myllar's name does not appear in the Breviary, and Chepman is not known to have issued any works subsequently, it is probable that Myllar, the manager of the press, died while the Breviary was being printed. See W. Beattie, 'The Chepman and Myllar prints', Edingburgh, 1950; and T. Rae, 'Andrew Myllar: a short study of Scotland's first printer', Greenock, Signet Press, 1958.

N

nagari type: see *devanagari*.

naked forme: see *forme*.

Napier, David, 1785–1873: a Scottish engineer who in 1819 began making printing presses in London. He is credited with the introduction of *grippers*, q.v., for securing a sheet before and during impression: this was featured in his 'Nay Peer' perfecting press, 1824. In 1830 he introduced a machine with two cylinders for double feeding. It could print on one side only up to 2,400 sheets an hour and was manually operated by crank and flywheel. Large numbers were exported to America where a steam-powered model was built in New York in 1835.

nap roller: the best quality lithographic roller. It has a wooden stock covered with layers of flannel which form a packing for the outer cover of french calf. This is sewn with the flesh or nap side outermost. It is then oiled to make it waterproof and supple before rolling it in varnish to give a smooth texture to the skin. See also *glazed roller*.

Narrenschiff, Das: or 'The Ship of Fools' (Lat. 'Stultifera navis'), a satire on contemporary weaknesses and vices written by Sebastian Brant (1458–1521) and first printed in Basle in 1494 by Bergmann von Olpe. It had considerable influence on pre-Reformation literature and thought, the original German text being quickly translated into Dutch, Latin and French. The Basle edition was illustrated by 114 woodcuts, believed by some to be wholly or partly the work of Albrecht Dürer who was then aged twenty-four: others suggest they were the work of artists active in the Bergmann shop. Peter Wagner at Nuremberg and Johann Schönsperger at Augsburg issued pirated editions in 1494, and the work was soon popular.

Two adaptations into English were printed in 1509. Alexander Barclay's 'Ship of Folys', a verse rendering largely based on the Latin translation of Jacob Locher, Basle, 1497, was printed by Pynson who used re-cut copies of the original Basle woodcuts (STC 3545). Henry Watson's 'Shyppe of Fooles', a prose version adapted from Jehan Drouyn's French paraphrase, Lyons, 1499, was printed by Wynkyn de Worde (STC 3547).

The first translation into English of the German text of 1494 was made by Edwin Zeydel and published by Columbia University Press in 1944. A facsimile of this edition, with all the woodcuts, was issued by Dover Publications Inc. in 1962.

narrow copy: a book with a board width less than two-thirds of its height. Cf. *tall copy*.

Nash Papyrus: the oldest known Biblical fragment. It may date to the late Maccabean period (1st century BC) and contains the Hebrew text of the Ten Commandments and the Shema (Deut.) written in square Hebrew-Aramaic letters. It was acquired in Egypt by W. L. Nash in 1902 and is now in Cambridge University Library (Or.233).

National Association of Paper Merchants: the organization covering the British paper and board merchanting trade.

Until 1803 there was no permanent organization of the trade though in the 18th century regional groups of papermakers had met to discuss common problems. Thus in 1799 William Balston was chairman of the Master Paper Makers of Kent and also of the Master Paper Makers of England, who met in London. The Kent group represented more than thirty-seven manufacturers, the national group represented eighty. Their meetings were usually to deal with wage demands. The first union of paperworkers was established in 1800, though clubs and combinations of journeymen were active prior to this. The papermakers had petitioned for an Act against workmen's combinations. It proved ineffectual, so in 1801 the Society of Master Paper Makers of the Counties of Kent and Surrey was formed to resist the worker's demands. June 1803 saw the formation of the United Society of Master Paper Makers of Great Britain, representing 120 firms, with Balston as chairman.

All through the 19th century co-ordinated activity among papermakers was limited to combating taxation and resisting wage demands. It was not until the turn of the century that the need was felt to establish trade customs and organization. In 1903 the Association of Wholesale Stationers and Paper Merchants was formed for this purpose, and in 1906, in conjunction with the Paper Makers' Association, the first set of trade customs governing the sale of British paper was issued. In the next decade several local Associations were formed or developed, e.g. in Birmingham, Bradford, Leeds, Manchester and Scotland. After 1918, when the Paper Makers' Association had been renamed the British Paper and Board Makers' Association, it was decided to form a national association of merchants to regulate the buying and selling of paper: this resulted in 1920 in the National Association of Wholesale Stationers and Paper Merchants. The scope of the Association was increased to include all merchants of paper and board, and the name National Association of Paper Merchants (NAPM) was adopted in 1930.

The objects of the NAPM are to take all possible action to safeguard and promote the interests of the paper-distributing trade, to negotiate with the Government and also other trade associations, and to deal with wage and labour matters.

National Book Committee: a body formed in New York in 1954 to further public interest in books. Its initial aims were the increasing of personal reading so that it develops into a lifetime habit, the extension of public library service, and the stimulation of an adequate flow overseas of those American books which will contribute to a clearer understanding of American policies, life and thought.

National Book Committee: formed in London in 1975 by the Association of Mail Order Publishers, Booksellers Association, Library Association, Periodical Publishers Association, Publishers Association, Society of Authors and the National Book League (which administers the committee). Its aim is the coordination of action and research in the interests of the printed word in book or serious magazine form, particularly in the relationship with the Government and public bodies.

National Book League: an independent and non-profit making organization, developed in 1944 out of the *National Book Council* which was founded in 1925 on the initiative of Sir Stanley Unwin. Membership is open to all. It exists to stimulate a wider interest in reading and literature, and to further this aim holds and circulates excellent book exhibitions and issues authoritative subject reading lists, regularly updated. The League's address is 7 Albemarle Street, London W1X 4BB.

National Book League Award: announced in 1964, being the sum of £2,500 given to a British author over sixty-five years as a 'mark of gratitude' for past achievements. Selection of an author is not oftener than once in three years. The first recipient, in 1964, was John Masefield.

National Book Trade Provident Society: founded in 1902 as an association existing to help members of the bookselling and publishing trades, also their dependants, by giving financial assistance when needed. In addition to donations from firms and individuals funds derive from members' dues.

In 1961 the name was changed to *National Book Trade Provident Institution* upon amalgamation with the *Booksellers' Provident Institution*, formed in 1837, and the *Booksellers' Provident Retreat*. See also *Book Trade Benevolent Society*.

National Paper Museum: opened in 1963 at St Mary Cray as a permanent display of historic papermaking equipment, samples of paper, and books on the subject. The project was sponsored by the British Paper & Board Makers Association. The Museum was later moved to the North Western Science & Industry Museum in Manchester.

National Reprographic Centre for documentation: or *NRCd*, the British national centre for reprography, established at the Hatfield Polytechnic in 1967, with financial support from the Department of Education and Science. NRCd is concerned with the whole field of reprography and in particular with micrographic systems and techniques. It provides an information and advisory service to subscribers, evaluates equipment, runs courses and seminars, and publishes the quarterly *NRCd Bulletin* which in 1974 continued as *Reprographics Quarterly*. Address: Hatfield Polytechnic, Hatfield AL10 8AU.

natural tint: a description for paper of a light cream colour.

nature printing: making impressions on paper of plants, leaves, ferns, etc. As practised in the late 15th century a lightly oiled leaf or plant was uniformly blackened over a flame, placed between two sheets of paper and rubbed. This left a lifelike impression of the veins and fibres.

The most successful of subsequent attempts to take multiple impressions from a single natural specimen for use in botanical book illustration was developed in Vienna in 1852 by Louis Auer and Andrew Worring of the Imperial Printing House. Their method was to press plants into a plate of soft lead and make an electrotype of the resulting impression. The process was quick and gave a print of astonishing fidelity.

In 1853 the process was brought from Vienna to England by Henry Bradbury who had seen Auer's work, and was then patented by the printers William Bradbury and Frederick Evans. They used it to prepare large folio volumes of prints in 1854 and 1856 and later for smaller books of wider appeal.

For a succinct illustrated account of the history of nature printing see R. Cave and G. Wakeman, 'Typographia naturalis', Wymondham, Brewhouse Press, 1967.

Naudé, Gabriel, 1600–53: a French doctor and humanist who worked as librarian to Cardinals Bagui, Berberini and Richelieu before achieving his greatest fame as librarian to Cardinal Mazarin.

near-print: a general term for substitute printing processes. Typewriter-composition and offset printing form the basis of such techniques. The *Justowriter*, q.v., is an example. See also *typewriter composing machine*.

Nebiolo, Giovanni: the purchaser in 1878 of a small typefoundry in Turin. It developed into one of Europe's largest printing machinery factories. Among machines known in Britain is a reduced-stop cylinder press which because of its patented system of sector gears permits a bigger cylinder to be used. It has only two forme rollers. See also *Nebitype*.

Nebitype: a machine for casting display matter in slugs from hand-set matrices, developed in Italy by an associate firm of the Società Nebiolo of Turin. The machine was first shown in 1958.

neck: the part of a type character which is between the shoulder and the face; commonly called *bevel*.

needlework bindings: see *embroidered bindings*.

Neobar, Conrad, d. 1540: born in Cologne. A printer who in 1538 became a French subject and was appointed first King's Printer in Greek to François I. He was able to issue only a few works before his death. The first was a commentary on Aristotle's 'Rhetoric'.

neo-caroline: an alternative name for 15th century scripts based on Caroline minuscule.

net: said of the price of any book which is not subject to a retail discount or reduction. See also *Net Book Agreement, 1957 net net, non-net books*.

Net Book Agreement, 1957: an agreement between publishers that the net prices they fix for their books shall be the prices at which those books are sold to the public, and that they will not permit them to be sold at less than the net price. The 1901 Net Book Agreement, now replaced, was based on the right of the Publishers Association to act on behalf of its publisher members in ensuring that the conditions of supply of net books were observed.

The 1957 agreement was made necessary when the Restrictive Trade Practices Act of 1956 banned *collective* measures for the maintenance of resale prices. This meant that publishers, having stated their conditions of sale, could only take *individual* action against any offender selling their books at less than the net prices in breach of those conditions. A publisher can enforce the condition of sale right down the line of distribution, as, for example, in the case of books bought by a bookseller from a wholesaler.

The text of the 1957 Agreement is reproduced here by permission of the Publishers Association:

We, the undersigned several firms of publishers, being desirous that in so far as we publish books at net prices (as to which each publisher is free to make his own decisions), those net prices shall normally be the prices at which such books are sold to the public as hereinafter defined, and in order to avoid disorganization in the book trade and to ensure that the public may be informed of and able uniformly to take advantage of the conditions under which net books may be sold at less than the net prices, hereby agree to adopt and each of us does hereby adopt the following standard sale conditions for the net books published by us within the United Kingdom:

Standard Conditions of Sale of Net Books

(i) Except as provided in clauses (ii) and (iv) hereof and except as we may otherwise direct net books shall not be sold or offered for sale or caused or permitted to be sold or offered for sale to the public at less than the net published prices.

(ii) A net book may be sold or offered for sale to the public at less than the net published price if

(a) it has been held in stock by the bookseller for a period of more than twelve months from the date of the latest purchase by him of any copy thereof and

(b) it has been offered to the publisher at cost price or at the proposed reduced price whichever shall be the lower and such offer has been refused by the publisher.

(iii) A net book may be sold or offered for sale to the public at less than the net published price if it is second hand and six months have elapsed since its date of publication.

(iv) A net book may be sold at a discount to such libraries, book agents (including Service Unit libraries), quantity buyers and institutions as are from time to time authorized by the Council of The Publishers Association of such amount and on such conditions as are laid down in the instrument of authorization. Such amount and conditions shall not initially be less or less favourable than those prevailing at the date of this Agreement.

(v) For the purposes of clause (i) hereof a book shall be considered as sold at less than the net published price if the bookseller

(a) offers or gives any consideration in cash to any purchaser except under licence from the Council of The Publishers Association or

(b) offers or gives any consideration in kind (e.g. card indexing, stamping, reinforced bindings, etc., at less than the actual cost thereof to the bookseller).

(vi) For the purposes of this Agreement and of these Standard Conditions:

Net book shall mean a book, pamphlet, map or other similar printed matter published at a net price.
Net price and *net published* price shall mean the price fixed from time to time by the publisher below which the net book shall not be sold to the public.

Public shall be deemed to include schools, libraries, institutions and other non-trading bodies.

Person shall include any company, firm, corporation, club, institution, organization, association or other body.

(vii) The above conditions shall apply to all sales executed in the United Kingdom and the Republic of Ireland whether effected by wholesaler or retailer when the publisher's immediate trade customer, whether wholesaler or retailer, or the wholesaler's immediate trade customer, is in the United Kingdom or the Republic of Ireland.

We the undersigned several firms of publishers further agree to appoint and each of us does hereby appoint the Council of The Publishers Association to act as our agent in the collection of information concerning breaches of contract by persons selling or offering for sale net books, and in keeping each individual publisher informed of breaches in respect of such net books as are published by him and we further hereby undertake and agree that we will each enforce our contractual rights and our rights under the Restrictive Trade Practices Act 1956 if called upon to do so by the Council of The Publishers Association and provided that we shall be indemnified by The Publishers Association if so requested by us in respect of any costs of such action incurred by us or by the Council of The Publishers Association on our behalf.

(Here will follow the names and addresses of the signatory publishers.)

net net: an indication that a book so marked or described is sold to all at the published price, and that the publisher does not allow any discount. The use of this term is confined almost exclusively to reference works published at the lowest possible sum for the

benefit of the trade, and not normally resold by its members.

Neudörffer, Johann 1497–1563: a writing master of Nuremberg whose 'Fundament', 1519, which was a collection of models of Fraktur script, was the first German writing book to be published. More important was his 'Ein gute Ordnung', 1538, for which engraved copper plates were used. Of the various Fraktur types cut in Germany between 1513 and 1524 it was the designs of Neudörffer, as cut by Hieronymus Andreae in 1522, which became traditional.

His son *Johann* (1543–81) and grandson *Anton* (fl.1598–1628) were also prominent calligraphers, while his pupil Wolfgang Fugger produced a writing book 'Schreibbüchlein' in 1553. See W. Doede, 'Schön schreiben, eine Kunst: Johann Neudörffer und seine Schule im 16. und 17. Jahrhundert', Munich, Prestel Verlag, 1957.

Neumeister, Johann, fl.1470–98: a German printer who lived in Mainz and was at one time considered to have been an associate of Johann Gutenberg. Whether true or not he established the first printing press at Foligno, sponsored by Emiliano Orfini, where he is known to have printed three books, one being the editio princeps of Dante's 'La Divina commedia', 1472. After imprisonment for debt he returned to Mainz where he probably printed Torquemada's 'Meditationes', 1479, next to be heard of in Albi where in 1481 he issued another edition of Torquemada with the same plates.

Continuing his wanderings (typical of printers of the time) he settled in Lyons where his first book was Jacques Theramo's 'Le Procès de Belial'. Other Lyons publications included a Missal, 1487, printed with types resembling the first Mainz founts. By 1498 he was destitute and his material passed to a one-time associate, *Michel Topié*, q.v. Neumeister died in 1507 or 1508.

Newbery Medal: since 1921, an annual award administered by the American Library Association for 'the most distinguished book for children' written by a citizen of, or resident in, the United States. It is named after *John Newbery* (1713–67) who, from 1745, included publishing and the sale of patent medicines among his enterprises. His premises were in St Paul's Churchyard, London.

He was one of the first to make books for children an important part of a publishing business. He planned books to be read for pleasure with less emphasis on the improvement of moral tone. Probably the best-known title was 'Little Goody Two-shoes', 1765. Children were advised on the title-page of the 1768 edition to 'See the Original Manuscript in the *Vatican* at *Rome*, and the *Cuts* by *Michael Angelo*'. See B. M. Miller, *ed.* 'Newbery medal books, 1922–1955',

Boston, 1955; and L. Kingman, *ed.* 'Newbery and Caldecott medal books, 1956–1975', 2 vols, Boston, 1965 and 1976.

Newdigate, Bernard, 1869–1944: a British scholar-printer, influential in raising standards of commercial book production. In 1890 he learned printing in his father's business, the Art & Book Company of Leamington. In 1904 the printing side was renamed *Arden Press*, q.v. About this time Newdigate was commissioned by Wilfrid Meynell to design several liturgical works for Burns, Oates Ltd.

From 1920 he made his reputation by his work at the *Shakespeare Head Press*, q.v. Newdigate was an active supporter of the Double Crown Club and *The Fleuron*, while his literary work included notes on book production for *The London Mercury*, 1920–37, and the writing, editing and design of 'The art of the book', Studio Ltd, 1914 and 1938. See J. Thorp, 'B. H. Newdigate: scholar-printer, 1869–1944', Blackwell, 1950.

Newdigate Prize Foundation: a trust established by Sir Roger Newdigate (1719–1806) for the annual award of £50 for verse written by a member of Oxford University.

new edition: an edition of a book in which fresh material has been added and existing material revised. Also known as *revised edition*. Cf. *issue*.

nib: the small projection on the end of a composing rule by which the compositor takes the rule from between the lines after setting. (ML)

nibbed: a term used where folded maps and the like are trimmed to provide a wide tongue which is tipped to the text of a book. This permits free opening of the map. The tongue is termed a *nib*. (LK)

Niccoli, Niccolò, 1363–1437: an Italian humanist who expended considerable time and money assembling a library of eight hundred or so classical texts, many of which had been considered lost for centuries. Cicero's orations and the works of Quintilian were but two. Niccoli encouraged the copying of texts and himself copied many. Stanley Morison considered him 'more responsible than any of his contemporaries for the trend taken by humanistic calligraphy'. His letters were joined by thin connecting strokes and suggest later italics. See also *Poggio*.

Nicholson, William, *c.* 1755–1815: a London inventor for details of whose innovations see *inking roller*, *printing press*, *stereotype*.

nick: a groove on the body or shank of type cast as an aid to placing it the right way up in the composing stick and in identifying the fount. The single Monotype nick is simply to distinguish the front of the type from the back.

nickel-electro: when making electros of half-tones a lead mould is sometimes used. For long runs a nickel shell is deposited on this and then a final layer of copper. Cf. *nickel-faced electro*.

nickel-faced electro: the copper surface of an electro which is made more durable by coating it with nickel. Cf. *nickel-electro*.

nickel plating: the protective surface coating of nickel given to blocks, stereos and other printing formes by nickel plating in a galvanic bath.

Nicol, George, 1765–1833: bookseller to George III. In 1786 he conceived the idea of a sumptuously illustrated folio edition of Shakespeare. The project began by the commissioning from thirty-three artists of 167 pictures to form a gallery. Stipple engravings were made of these as illustrations for the books. In 1786 he engaged William Martin of Birmingham as punchcutter of transitional-style types.

The next stage in his plan was the sponsorship with John and Josiah Boydell as joint publishers in the setting up in 1790 of *William Bulmer*, q.v., as printer of the Shakspeare Printing-Office. The first fascicle of Shakespeare was issued in 1791: the last in 1804, although the title-pages of the nine bound volumes were dated 1802.

Niepce, Joseph Nicéphore, 1765–1833: a French landowner and inventor who was a pioneer of photography. He used asphalt as a light-sensitive substance and was the first to produce permanent photographs by means of a camera, 1822.

As the exposure time was too protracted, he combined with L. J. M. Daguerre, q.v., in improving the method. After the death of Niepce the latter discovered a quicker method of photography, using copper plates, 1837. (GU)

See 'Hommage à Niepce', (catalogue), Paris, Bibliothèque Nationale, 1967. See also *daguerreotype*.

Niger morocco: a tough but flexible goatskin, dyed in various shades of red, or sometimes green, and used for fine bookbinding. It has a fine grain, brought out by hand, and is given a soft finish. A product of Nigeria.

nihil obstat: words meaning 'nothing hinders' which occasionally appear on the verso of the title-pages of Roman Catholic books as an indication that they are free of doctrinal or moral error and have received a Catholic censor's approval. See also *imprimatur*.

nipping: see *smashing*.

nipping up: a stage in hand-binding, prior to covering, in which nippers are used to give shape to the bands. After drawing the pasted cover over the book the

Nipping up bands

leather is nipped up over the bands before being stretched and smoothed down on the boards.

nitrocellulose lacquering: an alternative to *varnishing*, q.v., used when it is desired to give printed matter a better appearance than the latter without the expense of *lamination*, q.v. The lacquer dries quickly, has improved adhesion and gives a more flexible result.

Work to be lacquered is often sent by the printer to a trade varnisher who is equipped to process the highly inflammable materials used.

Frederick Niven Literary Award: an award of £50 made for the most outstanding novel by a Scottish author. It is made every three years in memory of Frederick Niven who died in 1944.

Nobel Prize for Literature: the prize founded by Alfred Bernhard Nobel in 1900 and awarded annually by the Swedish Academy, Stockholm, to 'the person who shall have produced in the field of literature the most distinguished work of an idealistic tendency'.

nom-de-plume: a pen-name; assumed by an author who wishes to conceal his identity.

Nonesuch Press: the publishing house established in 1923 by Miss Mendel, David Garnett and *Sir Francis Meynell*, q.v., with the aim of adapting mechanical methods to the production of finely made books which were to be sold at modest cost through normal trade channels. Sir Francis prepared the designs and layout of each work.

After a period of inactivity during the war the Press re-started in 1953 with the production of the

Nonesuch Shakespeare, in four volumes, while in the 1960s the 'Cygnet' series of finely-made editions of children's classics was begun: the last was issued in 1968.

non-net books: copies of a work, usually a text-book sold in bulk to schools, on the sale of which a bookseller may, at his personal discretion, allow a discount. The publisher does not usually indicate a sale price in non-net books. See also *Net Book Agreement*, 1957, *terms*.

nonpareil: the name for a former size of type, now replaced by 6-point. The designation, used by Jean de Tournes of Lyons in 1547, and by his contemporaries, later spread throughout Europe. It is still used for a 6-point lead.

Non-Parliamentary papers: papers issued by Government Departments covering their activities.

non-woven binding materials: the generic name for several proprietary alternatives to *book cloth*, q.v. Examples are Glindura and *Linson*, q.v. See also *vinyl binding materials*.

Norden, John, *c*. 1548–1625: an Elizabethan cartographer remembered now for his uncompleted series of county maps 'Speculum Britanniae', Part I, 1593, and maps of Tudor London. He was probably the first to enter the main roads of counties on maps.

Northumbrian School: a name given to the style of illumination characteristic of manuscripts originating in northern England during the era 650–850. It was here that monks from Ireland, England and elsewhere gathered, their various influences being traceable in the development of manuscript painting.

Features are interlaced strapwork, at first largely geometric and probably deriving from Roman mosaics and sculpture, but later less disciplined and with the animal forms found in Anglo-Saxon jewellery of the period. A cruciform was often the basic design.

The finest surviving examples are the *Book of Durrow*, *Book of Kells*, *Echternach MSS.*, and *Lindisfarne Gospels*, qq.v.

Norton, Bonham, 1565–1635: son of *William Norton*, q.v. He shared the patent for common law books, and in 1613 was appointed King's Printer for Latin, Greek, and Hebrew. He also engaged in disreputable schemes to secure from the King's Bible Printer, Robert Barker, the valuable patent for the Authorized Version of 1611. This he achieved, and with his partner John Bill, moved the King's Printing House from Barker's premises to Printing House Square (subsequently the site of *The Times* office). Barker repurchased his share of the patent in 1629 but shortly afterwards published the 'Wicked' Bible which included the injunction 'Thou shalt commit adultery' (Exodus xx.14). This was the ruin of Barker. The unprincipled Norton died in prison.

Norton, John, fl.1587–1612: a nephew of *William Norton*, q.v. John was a London bookseller-publisher who was sometime Master of the Stationers' Company and Queen's Printer for Latin, Greek and Hebrew texts. He is remembered as the printer of John Gerard's famous 'Herball' of 1597, illustrated with the 1,800 woodcuts used in the 'Icones plantarum' of Tabernaemontanus, Frankfurt, 1590, and with a text largely based on a translation of Rembert Dodoens 'Stirpium historiae pemptades' of 1583. Norton brought the blocks from Frankfurt.

About 1602 he was commissioned by Sir Henry Savile to print at Eton his magnificent edition in eight volumes of St Chrysostom's works. This was ultimately done in Norton's name by Bradwood of the Eliot's Court Press in London, 1610–13, with greek types probably bought by Norton in Frankfurt or from Moretus in Antwerp.

Norton also sold books from a shop in Edinburgh from 1587–96, importing some of his stock from Germany, this being cheaper than doing so from London.

Norton, William, 1527–93: a bookseller of St Paul's churchyard who held office several times in the Stationers' Company. He was an original freeman and thrice Master. He commissioned others to print for him and was apparently very successful since he died a rich man. He had a share in a patent for grammars, and with four partners published a Bible in 1575.

not: properly, *not glazed*. This is a finish in high-quality rag papers, and is midway between *rough*, which is without finish, and *hot pressed*, which is a smooth plate-glazed finish. Papers finished in all three ways are used in *fashion boards*, q.v.

Notary, Julian, fl 1496–1520: a French printer working in London. Of the forty-eight or so books attributed to him a Sarum Missal printed in 1498 for Wynkyn de Worde is the most important. In this he was partnered by Jean Barbier. It was the first Missal printed in England. While mostly a printer of service books he also issued 'The Golden Legend' in 1504, 'Chronicle of England' in 1515, and 'Kalender of Shepardes', *c.* 1518.

notes: references too long to be treated as *footnotes*, q.v. They may follow a chapter or appear at the end of a book, and are sometimes set in a smaller size of type than the text.

Nott, William, fl.1669–89: a London publisher, stationer and bookseller, referred to in Pepys' diary (March 1668/9) as a 'famous bookbinder'. King Charles II, Catherine of Braganza and Lord Chancellor Clarendon commissioned or owned work from his bindery. Red turkey goat, pointillé outlines, drawer-handle tools and fanfare panels were common to several Restoration binders. Those grouped by binding historians (Hobson, Nixon) as the work of Queen's Binder A could have come from Nott's bindery.

novel: 1. a fictitious prose narrative sufficiently long to fill one or more volumes. See also *category fiction, character book, three-decker novel, yellow backs*.

2. as *Novels*, the constitutions or decrees of Justinian issued *c.* 534 as supplements to his 'Corpus Juris Civilis'.

novel distributor: in the early 19th century London book trade, an intermediary between publishers and circulating libraries. The unlabelled paper wrapper in which publishers distributed their books was not strong enough for library use. The novel distributor bought books in sheet form, enclosed them in boards, affixed title labels, and sold them to libraries. As several distributors were simultaneously handling the same impression of a book there was no uniformity in binding style.

The need for novel distributors gradually diminished after the introduction of bookcloth and gold lettering at the end of the 1820s, although cloth covers did not become standard for fiction until the late 1850s. See J. Carter, 'Binding variants in English publishing, 1820–1900', Constable, 1932.

novella: a short prose narrative, usually dealing with one situation, generally of a surprising or unusual nature.

NRCd: see *National Reprographic Centre for documentation*.

number book: see *serial*.

numbered copy: a copy of a book issued in a *limited edition*, q.v., which has a notice, usually in the colophon, of the total number of copies of the work printed and an individual copy number inserted by hand. The custom of numbering books in this way is said to have been originated by Bodoni.

The practice of numbering separately each copy of a work may also be used as a security measure for restricted official publications. See also *limitation notice, out of series, overs*.

numerals: when preparing copy for the printer the following rules for setting out linked numerals are offered for guidance:

first	second	examples
(a) Less than 100	use all	3–10, 71–72
(b) 100 or multiple	use all	100–104, 600–613
(c) More than 100 but under 110	use changed part only	107–8, 1002–3
(d) More than 109 (in multiples of 100)	use last 2, or 3 if needed	321–25, 415–532, 1536–38

See also *arabic numerals*, *dates*, *hanging figures*, *ranging figures*, *roman numerals*, *split fractions*.

nut quad: see *en quad*.

N.V. Lettergieterij Amsterdam Voorheen N. Tetterode: the Dutch name of the *Typefoundry Amsterdam*, q.v.

Nyloprint: a polymer process-engraving plate with a hard surface unaffected by glycol-based inks and requiring no preconditioning. It also holds a finer and stronger dot image than earlier polymer plates. It was announced in 1966.

Nypels, Charles, 1895–1952: a Dutch typographer who was a pupil of *Roos*, q.v. He designed books for various publishers and also for the *First Edition Club*, q.v.

O

oasis goat: 1. leather for book covers, obtained from goats found in the Cape of Good Hope region.

2. the trade name for a second-quality Niger morocco tanned in sumach and dyed.

o.b.a.: the papermakers' abbreviation for *optical bleaching agents*, q.v.

obelisk: or *obelus*, the printer's reference mark †, or *dagger*. See also *reference marks*.

obituary roll: see *bead-roll*.

oblong: a book which is wider than it is high. Hence oblong quarto, oblong folio. Synonymous with *landscape*.

obscene publication: under the Obscene Publications Act, 1959, an article is deemed to be obscene 'if its effect is, it taken as a whole, such as to tend to deprave and corrupt persons who are likely, having regard to all relevant circumstances, to read, see or hear the matter contained or embodied in it'.

The issuing of such a work is a common law misdemeanour triable on indictment. In prosecutions the jury must read the publication said to be obscene and form their own opinions. Cf. *erotica*, *pornography*.

OCR: *optical character recognition*, q.v.

Octateuch: a volume containing the first eight books of the Bible. Many were copied in Constantinople from the 9th–12th century, and they were illustrated with drawings based on earlier Greek or Jewish originals. Few survive.

octavo: written 8vo. The book size resulting from folding a sheet of paper with three right-angle folds, thus giving pages one-eighth the size of the sheet and forming a 16-page section. To define fully, the paper size must also be stated, e.g. Crown 8vo. If for binding purposes a 32-page section were required, paper of double size would be used and given four folds. See *British book sizes*. (LK)

octodecimo: see *eighteenmo*.

odd: in papermaking, sheets that are not according to regular or standard sizes, weights, finishes, colours, etc. (ML)

Oeglin, Erhard, fl.1491–1518: of Reutlingen. A printer of Augsburg and Basle, in his early years as an associate of others. He was the first printer in Germany of figured music from movable type. He issued an edition of Petrus Tritonius' 'Melopoiae' at Augsburg in 1507, and a four-part song book in 1512. He used two impressions as did *Petrucci*, q.v. For some of his non-musical publications Oeglin included woodcuts by Hans Burgkmair.

off: a forme is 'off' when all the sheets required have been printed, and it is ready to be taken off the press. (ML)

off-cut: waste portions of paper, boards, cloth etc., resulting from trimming stock to the size required: if the off-cuts are of usable size they may serve for other jobs. (LK)

Officina Arbuteana: see *Strawberry Hill Press*.

Officina Bodoni: the famous Italian private press founded in 1922 at Montagnola di Lugano. It was granted an exclusive licence to use some of the matrices of Bodoni, kept in the Biblioteca Palatina of Parma. The leader of the press was *Giovanni Mardersteig*, q.v., who stated in 1929 'A book consists of five elements: the text, the type, the ink, the paper, and the binding. To create a unity from these five elements in such a way that the result is not a passing product of fashion, but assumes the validity of permanent value – that is our desire.'

The first work to appear was 'Orphei tragedia' of Angelo Poliziano, 1923, to be followed by editions of Shelley, Goethe, Shakespeare, Dante, Browning, Seneca and Plato, all in their original languages. The books were printed on hand-made paper, either Fabriano or Du Marais.

In 1927 the press moved to Verona for its most ambitious project: this was an edition of Gabriele d'Annunzio's works in forty-nine volumes, sponsored by the Italian Government. It was completed in 1936.

Mardersteig later set up the Stamperia Valdonega

in Verona where trade editions of machine-set and machine-printed books are produced in close collaboration with the Officina Bodoni. See 'Officina Bodoni, Verona: catalogue of books printed on the hand-press, MCMXXIII-MCLIV', British Museum, 1954.

Officina Serpentis: a private press founded in 1911 by Eduard Wilhelm Tieffenbach (1883–1948) in Berlin. He had the aim of reviving the former high traditions of hand-printing, with hand-coloured initials, etc. The press issued many works by Martin Luther in addition to classics.

off its feet: see *feet.*

off-machine coating unit: see *coater.*

off-print: a separately printed copy of an article or paper which has appeared in a larger publication. It may or may not be enclosed in a cover. Also known as a *separate* or an *overprint*, and by the printer as a *run-on.* A contributor to academic journals will usually receive a number of off-prints of his article, sometimes in lieu of payment.

What may have been the first off-print in the history of publishing was the separate edition of Michelangelo's life from Vasari's 'Vite', 2nd ed., Florence, Giunti, 1568. This was given a special title and dedication in which Vasari explained that there were many readers who only wanted this portion which was on pp. 717–796 of the complete work.

offset blanket: a number of laminated plies of finely woven cotton which support a top surface of rubber. The basic function of this lithographic blanket is to transfer an inked image from a printing plate on to paper (or any other material in non-book work). To do this well blankets must be dimensionally stable and of uniform thickness, sufficiently resilient to leave a perfect impression on surfaces which are not microscopically even yet have sufficient hardness to resist the action of solvents and heat-set inks. They should have a minimal tendency to attract deposits of paper fluff and ink.

The fitting to the cylinder of an offset blanket is a matter for care and skill. Some firms now supply blankets for web-fed presses with pre-mounted grippers.

Proper cleaning, storage and resting of blankets will all contribute to better working and longer life. See also *offset printing.*

offset cartridge: a good quality paper made from esparto, sulphite or soda pulp with clay or titanium dioxide loading. It has a smooth non-fluffing surface and is suitable for offset litho work.

offset ink: mineral oil based ink for lithographic

printing is ground very finely, free from water-soluble particles and contains hydrocarbon resin as a pigment binder. The ink must be insensitive to sulphur since this is an ingredient of rubber printing rollers. High pigment concentration is required for offset ink as rubber rollers do not transfer to the paper all the ink they take up from the plate. Drying is mainly by absorption into the substrate.

offset letterpress: see *indirect letterpress.*

offset lithography: printing in which the inked impression from a lithographic plate is received upon a rubber surface (see *blanket*), from which it is transferred to the printing paper.

offset press: this usually means a machine for lithographic offset printing, although presses have been constructed for intaglio or letterpress work on the offset principle. The first offset presses were built for printing from stone on to tin, but about the time the idea was adapted for printing on paper metal plates for the printing surface came into common use,

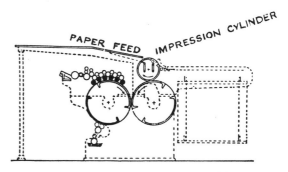

Offset press, George Mann, 1906

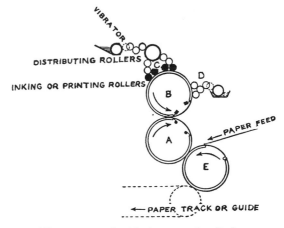

'Potter system' with three equal cylinders

facilitating rotary printing. Offset presses for printing from stone fell into disuse, and attention was concentrated on presses to print from plates curved around cylinders. Where printing from flat lithographic plates or stones occurs now, in offset work, is for proof printing, or printing on glass or some special

substance. In 1905 Rubel set up an offset machine at the Eastern Lithographic Co., New York, and imported a model into England in 1906. His machine was built according to the 'American' system by which three cylinders of equal size make a complete revolution for each impression. The model was built

Single-colour press on the two-cylinder system

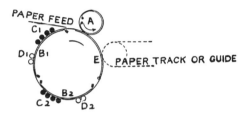

Two-colour machine on the two-cylinder system

A—rubber cylinder. B—plate cylinder. C—inkers (C1 and C2, rise and fall alternately). D—damping device. E—portion of the cylinder bearing the paper which serves as an impression cylinder

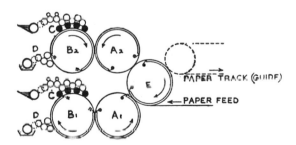

Two-colour machine (Crabtree)

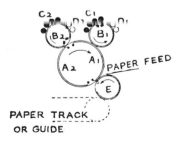

Two-colour machine with two plate cylinders, but only one rubber cylinder

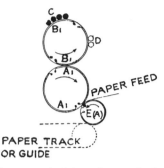

Sheet perfector with joint plate cylinder and joint rubber cylinder

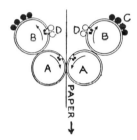

Reel-fed perfector. The two rubber cylinders serve as counter-pressure cylinders to one another

and sold all over the world by the Premier & Potter Printing Press Co.

In England the *George Mann* Co. q.v., patented in 1906 the offset machine shown in the diagram. It embodied the two-revolution system, the paper-carrying cylinder making two turns for each impression. In 1912 L. & M brought out an offset press in which both the rubber and paper cylinders made two revolutions while the plate cylinder was making one. Machines based on the Potter system were made by Waite & Saville Ltd, in 1909, and by Furnival & Co, in 1912.

Caspar Hermann of Baltimore invented an offset press with an automatic feeder in 1904; he went to Germany where he introduced offset printing in 1907. He patented a two-cylinder offset press and later an offset perfecting machine. The manufacture of offset machines was taken up by several German firms but progress was interrupted by the 1914–18 war, and it was not until the late 1920s that German makers widely adopted the 'American' system which is now the main one used for modern machines. All modern offset presses have a chain delivery.

Different principles for the construction of two-colour or multicolour machines are shown in the accompanying diagrams. For such machines, too, the 'American' system predominates, but in combining two three-cylinder machines they can be given a joint paper cylinder, the result being a five-cylinder machine; or the two machines can be entirely separated which necessitates a transferring cylinder between them or seven cylinders in all. The Crabtree and Roland machines are of the former type, as is the Planeta Super-Quinta, although the positioning of the cylinders and many other details vary.

Offset proof-printing machines (hand-presses) are usually constructed with a rubber cylinder which rolls over a flat printing plate (inked by hand or mechanically) and then over the paper. In addition to proof printing, such presses are used for direct transfers or for producing reversed proofs on transfer paper. See L. Lawson, 'Offset lithography', Vista, 1963.   (GU)

offset printing: a planographic printing process in which the forme and sheet have no direct contact. The impression of printing plates is taken up by a rubber sheet or roller and from this transferred to the printing paper. Owing to the resilience of the rubber this indirect process gives sharp impressions even on unglazed paper. Generally the term offset is associated with lithography, though book printing can be done in this way, and attempts at intaglio-offset have been made.

offset reproduction: for reproducing text matter type is set, made up into pages and a reading proof pulled. After correction, a perfect impression of the type is photographed and the negative placed with others, both of text and any accompanying illustrations, on a 'lay-sheet'. The assembled negatives are exposed to a sensitized grained metal plate. This is developed and placed on the cylinder of the offset press. The foregoing is for big printings: otherwise the text of an already printed copy is photographed.

For reproducing line drawings photo-litho paper which was copied and transferred was long in use, but for screen process work there was at first no better expedient than to produce ordinary printers' blocks and make transfers from them to the offset plates. By about 1920 it was realized that for first-class offset reproductions direct copying (without a transfer of the screen image to the printing plate) was necessary, and improved retouching methods (corresponding to tone etching in making half-tone blocks) were needed. The former was facilitated by the step-and-repeat machines then appearing in the U.S.A.; the latter has been done in many ways. An early practical method was that of Müller (about 1925) by which screen negatives exposed in a special way in the camera could be retouched with graphite, by painting, and scraping, prior to copying on the printing

350

plate. The Chromorecta process invented by H. Schupp of Dresden in 1927 forms the basis of most modern methods of offset reproduction: it consists, briefly, in producing from a half-tone negative, by exposure in the camera, a screen transparency with cone-shaped dots in the bed which can be etched down by chemical means to the desired size without losing the covering power. The Hausleiter processes (F. H. Hausleiter, Munich, 1927) and Beka offset retouching methods (Bekk & Kaulen, Cologne) serve the same purpose, the latter also making it possible to strengthen the screen point. In all these methods the principal work is done on the screen transparency from which negatives are produced, if necessary, by contact copying or in an enlarging apparatus.

Offset plates were formerly made exclusively by copying negatives on chrome albumen (see *albumen process*); latterly, a partial change has occurred in favour of positive copying, especially in connection with the deep etching of the image in the printing plate. Such copying is generally done on chromate glue by various methods (Manultief, Bekatief), after which the image revealed on developing is etched to a certain depth before being inked in (see *deep-etch process*). Instead of the usual zinc or aluminium plates, bimetallic plates are used now for offset printing (for large editions), the copying and treatment of plates being done in such a way that an image is obtained in ink-attracting metal on a base of another metal to which the ink is less able to adhere. These methods include Alkuprint (copper surface and aluminium base) and the Pax method which also permits etching the copied screen point on the printing plate. Modern processes of this kind use a combination of copper and stainless steel (Aller), or of copper and chrome (Coates Bros).   (GU)

Old English (or **English**): a black-letter type having angular emphasis. See *Appendix A*.

old face: a roman type which is descended from a French modification (by Jenson) of the venetian letter. The prototype was cut in 1495 by Francesco Griffo for Aldus Manutius who first used it when printing Pietro Bembo's tract 'De Aetna ad Angelum Chabrielem liber', 1495. In its re-cut and perfected form Aldus first used it for the famous 'Hypneroto-machia Poliphili' of Francesco Colonna in 1499. The use of old face spread to other European countries, and of particular importance was the version cut by Claude Garamont from 1530–40. In England William Caslon cut his well-known version from 1720–26. Old face is distinguishable from the later *transitional* and *modern faces*, qq.v., by its oblique stress. See *Appendix A*.

In recent years there has been a revival of old faces, a well-known example being Monotype Bembo (1930).

Most old-face types print well on antique papers. See also *letters – forms and styles*.

old style: 1. the somewhat lighter and more regularized versions of *old face* which, in the 19th century, were cut as modern adaptations of the latter. Extruders were shorter and letters narrower than old face, while having a more calligraphic quality than the generally cold, engraved modern face.

A famous example is that cut by Alexander Phemister for the Edinburgh foundry of Miller and Richard. Cast about 1860, it is still used extensively in Europe. (It must be stated that this is not a class of types as are old face, transitional, or modern.)

2. the American term for *old face*, q.v.

olivined edges: book edges stained olive green: a Victorian bookseller's term.

O Lochlainn, Colm: historian, university lecturer and printer of Dublin where he opened his Sign of the Three Candles Press in 1926 ('Three candles that light up every darkness: truth, nature, knowledge'). His extensive range of commercial printing, all of high standard, has included centenary volumes for various societies, a series of officially sponsored pamphlets on Irish arts and folklore, books in Irish-Gaelic, and occasional limited editions. His output exemplifies his precept that 'the creative printer must turn his back on the over-decorated book, and strive in austerity, by use of good classical type faces, to produce a satisfying and elegant book'. Between 1928 and 1957 he produced *The Irish book lover*, a small bibliographical journal. He was also Head of the Dublin School of Printing.

As a type designer his work included, in 1932, the extended range of Hammerschrift Unzial (Klingspor) to fit it for printing modern Irish, to which he gave the name Baoithín, and the Colum Cille series for Monotype which he described as 'a new readable Gaelic type'. The cutting of the punches, which included a cursive or italic, took ten years to complete and was supervised by Stanley Morison.

omnibus book: a one-volume edition of books or papers previously published separately.

one on and two off: said of a *hollow*, q.v., having one width of paper glued to the back of a book. The remainder of the piece forms a double fold (i.e. two layers) glued together as a support for the spine. For heavy books *two on and two off* may be necessary; for this a double layer of paper is glued to the back, and a double layer to the spine.

one-way half-tone: see *single-line halftone*.

onlaying: the technique of decorating a book cover by applying to it very thin pieces of leather of contrasting colour or texture. The book is first covered with calf or morocco of the finest unblemished quality, the outlines of a design then being traced upon it. Next, thinly pared pieces of leather, corresponding in shape to the parts of the design, are positioned and fixed with a little flour paste. After drying, the book is pressed prior to tooling which on contemporary work is given less prominence than formerly. Cf. *inlaying* (1). See also *mosaic bindings*.

on-machine coating unit: see *coater*.

onomasticon: an alphabetically arranged lexicon of proper names as, for example, those occurring in classical geography, history and mythology.

on sale or return: terms allowed by a publisher to a bookseller when a condition of supplying copies of a book is that the bookseller may return for credit those unsold. 'On sale' books are usually charged by the publisher but payment is not due until they are sold or until the end of a specified period. See also *terms* (1).

ooze leather: calfskins or split sheepskins prepared to give them a suede or velvet finish on the flesh side; sometimes used for covering slim volumes of poetry, belles-lettres, etc.

o.p.: the abbreviation for *out of print*, q.v.

opacity: a term applied to printing papers to describe the degree to which light will pass through a sheet. This is an important factor, especially in thin papers, as show through may occur if the sheet is not sufficiently opaque.

When the fibres of paper are closely packed, with little air space, light can pass through the sheet more easily than through a sheet made from free-beaten stock which has greater internal air space. Mineral loading also improves opacity. Esparto papers have good printing opacity.

The opacity of paper can be roughly measured by comparing different sheets, or by using a number of sheets to blacken out a light of standard intensity, but for accurate measurement such instruments as the Hilgar-Patra opacimeter or the simpler Eel opacimeter can be used. See also *show through, strike through*.

op. cit.: an abbreviation for the Latin 'opere citato', i.e. in the work (previously) cited.

open back: another name for *hollow back*, q.v.

opened: said of the edges of a book which have been hand-cut with a paper-knife, usually by the purchaser. Cf. *uncut*.

351

opening: any two facing pages. Cf. *conjugate leaves*, *double-spread*.

open letters: display and jobbing type, usually known as *outline letters*, q.v.

open matter: type generously leaded. Cf. *set solid*.

opisthograph: a manuscript or parchment bearing writing on both sides of the leaf. Also applied to block books bearing printing on both sides of the sheet. Cf. *anopisthographic printing*.

Oporinus, Johannes, 1507–68: a scholar-printer of Basle. In 1538, while professor of Greek there, he set up a printing office in association with Thomas Platter, Balthazar Rusch and Robert Winter. In 1542 he resigned his professorship and worked alone. He issued more than 800 publications including classics, the Koran, the writings of Luther, and the great thirteen-volume 'Church history of the Magdeburg Centuriators' by Matthias Flacius. To achieve this enormous output he commissioned other printers yet was himself commissioned by the publishers Feierabend, Froschauer and Herwagen.

Of special interest was his printing of the foundation of anatomical study of Andreas Vesalius 'De humani corporis fabrica', 1543. This large folio included some remarkable woodcuts which may have been designed in Venice and a dramatic engraved title-page showing Vesalius dissecting before a crowd of onlookers. The chapter initials show putti in various medical antics. The work was abridged, copied, imitated, and frequently reprinted. For details of the first English edition see *Gemini*.

optical bleaching agents: fluorescent dyestuffs added to paper pulp to make it look whiter when viewed under certain lighting. In spite of the name these dyestuffs do not bleach the pulp; their effect is to increase the amount of visible light rays reflected from the surface of the sheet due to absorption of invisible ultra-violet light which is re-emitted as visible light. See also *titanium dioxide pigments*.

optical character recognition: or *OCR*, the scanning of type copy in a word processing machine which converts the characters into impulses to activate a computer.

The various systems available include the *Dataflow 3800* which, instead of reading the actual characters, 'reads' a miniature bar code which appears under each as it is typed on a standard IBM Selectric typewriter. Output can be via an associated TTS conversion unit which produces tape for the typesetter.

The *Scan-data* system is among several on which copy, including encoded typographic commands, can be prepared in a publisher's office. A fine-typed copy

is made and sent to a trade house with a Scan-data installation. This can 'read' a variety of normal founts, thereby extending the range of work for which OCR gives an acceptable result from directories to simple bookwork. The magnetic input tape emerging from the Scan-data is fed into a Photon 713, a Linotron 505C, or the RCA Videocomp, all of which will give positives for platemaking.

It was claimed that David Divine's children's story 'The three red flares', Macdonald, 1970, was the first book in Britain commercially produced by this method.

In the late 1970s the British book trade considered the use of OCR for the adding of ISBNs to books, jackets, labels and stock cards. As an alternative to a bar code two eye-readable OCR type designs were appraised, known as OCR–A, and OCR–B. The first is already used for stock control in the United States, and elsewhere. The non-bookwork type OCR–B of *Adrian Frutiger*, q.v., shown in 1968, was made to accord with a recommendation of the European Computer Manufacturers Association (ECMA) which sought, for OCR systems, a fount having 'character shapes which are as distinguishable (by a computer) as possible without undue sacrifice of their acceptability by the public as a general purpose type fount'. A sample of A and B is shown below.

OCR A 1234567890 X

OCR B 1234567890 X

optic centre: the point on a page which appears central to the eye but which measurement will reveal is slightly higher than the geometric centre, a fact of importance to graphic designers.

Orders Clearing: started in 1955 at the request of the BA by *Book Centre*, q.v., following the liquidation in 1955 of Simpkin Marshall, the book trade wholesalers, but passed in 1972 to *IBIS Mailing Ltd* to operate. It exists for the cheap and quick processing of trade orders. Payment is by vouchers purchased in advance. Any bookseller in the U.K. or overseas can send his orders to publishers in one envelope addressed to Orders Clearing for sorting and forwarding to the publishers concerned.

ordinal: 1. a book of rules for a religious house or college.
　2. a book giving the service used at ordinations.

oriental leaf: a mixture of bronze and brass, carried on foil, for use as an alternative to gold in cheap casing work.

oriental type: see *exotic types*.

original boards: a term used to describe copies of novels published between (roughly) 1770–1830 which have survived into the 20th century in their original paper-covered boards with paper labels. As many first purchasers would subsequently have them bound in full or half leather survivors in sound clean condition are now collectors' items. When the manufacture of bookcloth enabled the publisher to offer a permanent binding on first publication paper-covered boards were abandoned.

orihon: a long strip of paper on which a manuscript was written in short columns across the width of the sheet with margins between them. The strip or roll was then folded to page size, the margins giving the effect of a closed fan. The term also describes a book made up of a continuous sheet, or of small single sheets, folded but uncut: such a book is held together by cords laced through holes pierced down one side. This form, still found in China and Japan, arises from the use there of extra thin paper which can only be printed on one side. See also *french fold.*

Oriole Press: the name Joseph Ishill (d. 1966) gave in 1926 to the private press he had begun at his home in New Jersey ten years earlier. For his considerable output of occasional pieces and books (including works by Havelock Ellis, Peter Kropotkin and Stephan Zweig) he used hand setting and a hand-press. Some of his work was illustrated. A measure of his enthusiasm for his craft was his custom of giving rather than selling his books.

'With the passing of the Oriole Press went one of the finest of all amateur printers, which in the modesty and probity of its work is unlikely to be equalled.' (R. Cave, 'The private press'). See M. C. Brown, 'Joseph Ishill and the Oriole Press', Berkeley Heights, N.J., 1960.

Ormesby Psalter: one of the finest examples of the East Anglian school of manuscript illumination, begun in Norfolk or Suffolk in the later years of the 13th century. As the work passed from owner to owner each commissioned the decoration of a few pages; thus some show heraldic arms, others fabulous beasts and birds, while narrative border scenes are also found. The important Beatus page was completed about 1320 for the Foliot family. Some time later the still unfinished work passed to Robert of Ormesby who presented it to Norwich Cathedral. It is now in the Bodleian Library (MS. *Douce* 366).

ornament: a generic term for the various kinds of decoration which compositors may use with type, e.g. *arabesques, borders, flowers, head-pieces, rules,* qq.v. See also *printer's ornaments.*

ornithomorphic letter: in an illuminated manuscript, a decorated initial capital of which the outline is represented by a real or imaginary bird painted in gold and colours. In Europe they date from 8th century Merovingian art up to the 12th century, but they were also used elsewhere, notably in Cilicia where, in Armenian illuminated Gospels, a line of ornithomorphs would begin each text.

Ortelius, Abraham, 1527–98: born Abraham Wortels, a cartographer and map publisher of Antwerp. His career began about 1547 as a map painter, buying his stock of outlines at the Frankfurt Fairs, and not publishing his own maps until about 1564.

He is remembered for his great atlas 'Theatrum orbis terrarum', 1570, for which the seventy maps, the work of many cartographers, were mostly engraved by *Hogenberg,* q.v. It was printed by Gilles Coppens van Diest, probably on paper supplied by Plantin with whom Ortelius had a long and close business friendship. There were enlarged editions until 1612. The first English edition, subtitled 'The theatre of the whole world', and with maps printed in Antwerp by the Officina Plantiniana, was issued by J. Norton in 1606 (1608?)

o.s.: *out of stock,* q.v.

Ostertag, Leonhard: a leading Munich bookbinder of the late 16th century who worked for Philipp Fugger and Duke Albert V. His styles varied but many books bore the coat of arms or supralibros of the owner.

Ostwald colour system: see *colour systems.*

Ottonian illumination: in the 10th century German illuminators at the time of Otto I were particularly active, Reichenau, Echternach, Fulda and Cologne being important centres. Byzantine, Carolingian, and early Christian artistic influences are traceable in the work of the various scriptoria.

Whole pages were decorated in heavy, rich colours, with strongly drawn figures and formal symbolic scenes, showing little movement, set against a sombre gold or purple background. It was not unusual to include an illuminated dedication in which the patron of the work is shown receiving it from the scribe or artist. See P. Block, 'Die Ottonische Kölner Maler-schule', Düsseldorf, 1967–71.

out: copy which is accidently omitted in composition.

outer forme: see *sheet work.*

outer margin: see *fore-edge.*

outline half-tone: a half-tone illustration in which the background and any unessential parts have been removed by routing or etching away the metal of the block. Also known as *cut out* or *deep-etch half-tone*. See also *block*. (GU)

outline letters: display and jobbing work letters in which the centre of the strokes is recessed and thus beyond the reach of the inkers. The effect on the eye when such letters are printed is one of white areas rather than black. Gill's Shadow Titling is an example. Cf. *inline letters, shaded letters*.

out of print: said of a book which is not only unobtainable from the publisher but which is not likely to be reprinted. Abbreviated as OP. Cf. *out of stock*. See also *publishers' abbreviated answers*.

out of register: see *register* (1).

out of series: a term applied to the un-numbered copies of a limited edition which have been printed and bound up as *overs*, q.v.

out of stock: said of a book of which the publisher is temporarily without copies, waiting for the binder or other supplier to deliver. Abbreviated as OS. Cf. *out of print*.

outprinting: see *deep-etch lettering*.

outright sale of copyright: a little used form of publishing contract whereby for a single cash payment an author cedes all rights in a book to the publisher of it. See also *publishers' agreements*.

outsert, outset: see *insert*.

outside rights: see *subsidiary rights*.

outsides: sheets of hand-made paper which are found, when sorting in the salle, to have torn edges, iron-mould, creases or a broken surface. When reams of paper are made up outsides are marked XXX. (Cf. *retree*). When a mill ream consisted of 472 sheets there were eighteen quires of good paper plus a top and bottom quire of XXX to each.

overcasting: see *oversewing*.

overlaying: a method of increasing pressure on the solids or dark tones of a printing plate, and decreasing it on the lighter tones or highlights, by placing appropriately shaped pieces of paper on the tympan. See also *make-ready, mechanical overlay*.

over matter: set-up type which cannot be printed due to lack of space.

overprint: see *off-print*.

overprinting: 1. in blockmaking, the superimposing of one negative over another on the coated metal plate before developing.

2. the adding of booksellers' addresses to prospectuses of books or other publicity material; space on the prospectus having been left blank at the time of the original printing.

over-running: the re-adjusting of a paragraph of set-up type made necessary when corrections affecting the length of a line in it are made. Words from the end of one line of type are inserted at the beginning of the next; the remaining lines in the paragraph are adjusted until the matter fits.

overs: 1. extra sheets issued from the paper warehouse to the printing room to allow for make-ready, spoils etc.

2. sheets or copies of a work printed in excess of a specified number, as with limited editions, copies of which are numbered serially. Overs will be printed to make up spoiled copies, for reviewing purposes, or for presentation; they will not be numbered.

oversewing: the manner of stitching employed in a book consisting of separate leaves or plates. (The same style of stitch is used for the edges of blankets.) While strength is given to a book sewn in this way it cannot be opened flat. Also called *overcasting* or *whipstitching*.

overstocks: quantities of titles held by booksellers and publishers for which a steady public demand has ceased. Booksellers may order more copies of a particular title than the market can bear to obtain better terms from the publisher; or the latter may have over-estimated the sales potential of a title. Possible solutions suggested by the 1948 Book Trade Committee included the controlled sale of overstocks by means of a National Sales Week; the easing of terms for minimum quantities; uniformity of terms offered by all publishers on books falling into the same classification, and their expression in terms of percentages.

Ovid Press: a private hand-press founded in London by John Rodker in 1919. Before it closed in 1920 eight works were issued: authors and artists represented were T. S. Eliot, Ezra Pound and E. Wadsworth.

own ends: synonymous with *self ends*, q.v.

Oxford Bibliographical Society: a society founded in 1922 with the general aim of furthering an interest in all matters pertaining to the book by holding lectures, exhibitions and publishing papers.

Oxford corners: right-angles formed outside a printed

frame (e.g. on a title-page) where the lines meet and project. See also mitred (2).

Oxford corners

Oxford hollow: a flattened paper tube which is attached to the back of a book on one side and on the other is attached to the cover (spine), leaving a true hollow opening in between so that when the book is opened the back opens up independently of the spine. It is not suitable for machine methods, but many cased books have a hollow which is sometimes mis-called an Oxford hollow, and which gives the same effect as an Oxford hollow, although the linings on the back of the sections and the inner side of the spine are not joined at the shoulders as in true Oxford hollow style.

The O.U.P., who have supplied this note, state 'presumably the word Oxford was used to describe this kind of binding because undoubtedly the old Oxford bindery was the first to use it, particularly for leather-bound Bibles. It is properly applied only to a leather-bound book and is a style which is now used by most leather binders in place of what are known as flexible-sewn books where the leather cover is attached to the back.'

Oxford imprints: 1. *Oxford at the Clarendon Press.* Used from 1713 on books printed at Oxford for which the University, through the Delegates to the Press, assumes a particular responsibility. Profit is not a necessary factor when issuing such works, and they are never remaindered. See also *Sheldonian Theatre.*

2. *London: Oxford University Press.* Not until 1883 was the office of 'Publisher to the University of Oxford' set up to publish in London books for which a less particular responsibility was assumed by the Delegates, and to publish books for such other bodies as the British Museum and the Bibliographical Society. Successive holders of the office have been Henry Frowde, 1883–1913; Sir Humphrey Milford, 1913–45; Geoffrey Cumberlege, 1945–56; and Sir John Brown from 1956. The name of the office holder no longer appears on the title-page or distribution imprint, and in 1974 the Oxford and London publishing departments were integrated at Oxford. The distribution warehouse remained at Neasden in London.

Oxford india paper: a thin tough opaque paper developed in 1875 by Thomas Brittain & Sons of Hanley from their 'pottery tissue' for exclusive supply to the Oxford University Press. In the same year it was used to print 250,000 copies of the Bible which sold out within a few weeks.

The University's Wolvercote Mill began making india paper at the same time but ceased before 1890, Brittains continuing their exclusive supply. The Press sold the paper to printers in London and overseas. Paper of similar substance is made elsewhere.

It was said that the furnish of Oxford india paper was kept secret even from the workmen. As made at Oxford it was of two kinds: demy 9 lb. and demy 6 lb. See also *Combe, T.*

Oxford rule: two parallel rules, one fine and one thick.

Oxford University Press: from the 13th century Oxford stationers (i.e. makers, sellers and hirers of books) were regarded as servants of the University, enjoying its support and protection but also to some extent under its control (see also *manuscript book writing*), and the first printers in Oxford may have had official encouragement. Printing began when 'Expositio sancti Ieronimi in simbolum apostolorum' by T. Rufinus, Bishop of Aquileia, was printed in a type of Cologne origin. The work is dated '1468' but this is assumed to have been an error for '1478'. The printer is not named in the colophon, but the book is ascribed to Theodoric Rood of Cologne, then resident in Oxford. It was followed by sixteen works, Rood first being named in an imprint of 1481. Not until 1585 was a printer licensed and subsidized by the University. Mr Charles Batey kindly supplied this list of official printers:

Oxford Printers

Theodoric Rood	1478–85
Thomas Hunt	1485
John Scolar	1517–8
Charles Kyrfoth	1519

Printers to the University

Joseph Barnes	1585–1617
William Wrench	1617
John Lichfield	1617–35
James Short	1618–24
William Turner	1624–40
Leonard Lichfield I	1635–57
Henry Hall	1642–81
Leonard Lichfield II	1657–86
Leonard Lichfield III	1689–1749
John Basket	1715–42
Thomas Basket	1742–62
William Jackson	1754–91
Joshua Cooke	1775–1814
Samuel Collingwood	1792–1841
Joseph Parker	1805–50
Thomas Combe	1838–72
Edward Pickard Hall	1839–83
Horace Hart	1883–1915
Frederick Hall	1915–25
John Johnson	1925–46
Charles Batey	1946–58
Vivian Ridler	1958–78
Eric J. Buckley	1978–

See N. Barker, 'The Oxford University Press and the spread of learning: an illustrated history, 1478–1978',

O.U.P., 1978; and P. Sutcliffe, 'The Oxford University Press: an informal history', O.U.P., 1978. See also *Carter, H., Clarendon, Delegates, Fell types, Oxford imprints, Sheldonian Theatre*.

Ozalid paper: the trade name of a paper coated with diazo compounds, used among other purposes for photocopying and by the lithographic plate maker. Diazo compounds provide an alternative to dichromated colloid coatings since the action of light makes them sufficiently resinous to act as the image area of lithographic plates.

P

PA: see *Publishers Association*.

Pablos, Juan: born *Giovanni Paoli*, an Italian printer of Brescia in Lombardy, who in 1539 was sent with a quantity of equipment and his pressman, Gil Barbero, to set up a press in Mexico on behalf of *Cromberger*, q.v. The first dated work printed there was 'Manual de Adultos', 1540. From 1548 until his death in 1561 Pablos owned the press. He issued many theological works, his finest (and last) being 'Manuale sacramentorum secundum usum ecclesiae Mexicanae', 1560. He was succeeded by his son-in-law Pedro Ocharte.

An interesting item of typographical minutiae is that the title-page decoration of 'Dialectica resolutio cum textu Aristotelio' which Pablo printed in Mexico in 1554 is almost identical with that used in London by Edward Whitchurch on the title-page of his Prayer Book of 1549. The initials E. W. appear on both. The same block was copied or adapted by Tottell in 1554, by Jugge in 1562, and for a Mexican tract of 1638: a period of ninety years and a separation of three thousand miles.

Pablos had a large collection of roman and gothic types as well as ornaments made by his assistant *Espinosa*, q.v., who joined him in 1551 as punchcutter and founder.

Pacioli, Luca: a 15th century friar and mathematician who was a protegé of Ludovico de' Medici and is remembered for his book 'De divina proportione', printed at Venice by Paganinus de Paganinis in 1509. To the Italian text of his rules for the mathematical proportion of the arts Pacioli added letters of the alphabet, probably based on the theories of Leonardo da Vinci with whom he had worked in Milan.

pack: a pile of about 234 sheets of still-moist paper which is formed by the layerman on a felt-covered zinc plate. This stage of hand-made papermaking follows the pressing of a *post* of paper, q.v. If the paper is very thin the layerman will be assisted by a *slice boy*, q.v.

The pack will be pressed and parted and reassembled, the process taking several days.

packing: paper, rubber, or other material placed on the impression cylinder of a press to give adequate overall pressure for printing. Known as *dressing the cylinder*. See also *hard packing*.

padded sides: a term applied to a leather binding in which cotton-wool has been inserted between the leather and the boards. (LK)

Padeloup, Antoine, d. *c.*1666: the first of a Parisian family of binders which through the years included twelve practising craftsmen. His atelier has not been identified and it is possible that he worked in close association with the printer-publisher Pierre Rocolet (fl.1618–62) who between 1638 and 1662 owned a bindery. Certainly some of the tools and pointillé-fanfare designs used by his grandson Antoine-Michel appeared on books printed and bound sixty years previously in or for the Rocolet establishment.

Antoine-Michel Padeloup began work about 1707, set up his own bindery in 1712, employing several binders and gilders in it and owning a considerable stock of tools, many of them historic. Styles varied, but all were impeccably executed, especially the mosaics of coloured leathers and elaborate doublures. Padeloup used pointillé and dentelle tooling with elegant restraint, and many examples signed 'Padeloup le jeune' are known. He was Relieur du Roi, 1733–58.

His son *Jean* (1716–58) emulated his father in whose shop he worked. He was binder to the King of Portugal.

Paderborn, Johannes de: see *De Westfalia, Johannes*.

page: either side of a *leaf*, q.v.

page-cord: waterproof cord used to secure type-matter after it has been made up into pages. The cord is removed prior to locking up the pages in the chase. See also *Quick-S*.

page gauge: a measure to determine the length of the page of a work, commonly a piece of reglet, a lead, or rule notched to show the proper length, and used by the make-up hand to keep pages of a book of uniform length. (ML)

Gertrude Page Fund: a fund established by the late

Gertrude Page to assist authors and journalists in times of temporary need, particularly when this is due to illness. Grants, which never exceed £30, are made by the Society of Authors. The fund is now incorporated into the Authors' Contingency Fund.

page head: see *headline*.

page papers: sheets of heavy paper or card upon which tied-up pages are placed for storage instead of keeping them on galleys. (ML)

page proofs: proofs of type which has been paginated and locked up in a chase, the secondary stage in proofing. When galley proofs are returned to the printer the corrections indicated by the reader and author are dealt with and then, normally, the type is made up into pages and page proofs are pulled for further correction or approval. Also known as *made-up proofs*.

pagination: a sequence of numbers used to identify the pages of a book. Pagination was not in common use until the mid-16th century, prior to which only the recto of each leaf had been numbered, i.e. *foliated*.

In music published during the 18th century, especially by John Walsh, double, triple and even quadruple pagination occurs, indicating the use in later editions of plates from former ones. See also *blind folio, foliation, preliminary matter*.

painted edges: see *fore-edge painting*.

Palatino, Giovanbattista, fl.1538–75: of Rossano in Calabria. A successful and popular writing master of Rome. The main script he showed in his manual 'Libro nuovo d'imparare a scrivere', Rome, 1540, with later editions in 1545 and 1566 was the *cancellaresca formata*. While beautifully made it was so angular and compressed that it was no longer a practical current script, being lettering rather than handwriting. See also *Arrighi*.

pale gold: see *deep gold*.

paleography: the skilled study of ancient writing in which the date of a manuscript can be established by examining the manner in which the characters on it were made.

The word appears to have gained currency with the publication in Paris of Bernard de Montfaucon's 'Palaeographia graeca', 1708, which was the first book on the history of Greek writing.

palimpsest: a parchment from which the original writing has been erased (but is still faintly visible) in order to write on it a second time. Also known as *codex rescriptus*.

358

palladium: a white metal which when beaten into leaf form is used for book decoration and edge gilding. It is very costly, and suitable either alone or with gold for the finest work as it does not tarnish quickly as silver does. Cf. *gold leaf*.

pallet: 1. a wooden storage device on which sheets of paper are stacked. It resembles a shallow box with open ends. The ends are used when, with a fork-lift truck, stacks of paper are to be lifted and moved from the warehouse to the machine-room. Cf. *stillage*.

2. finishing tools for impressing straight lines on spines. They can be patterned, and are made of brass within a size range of $\frac{1}{16}$ in. to 2in.

3. a small hand-tool in which letters are placed by the finisher prior to heating them and impressing either the cover of a book or a *panel*, q.v., which is then stuck on it. See also *palleted*.

palleted: said of a binding which is signed by the binder, usually in gold letters, at the foot of the inside front board. A stamp or pallet bearing the complete name is used, e.g. *Bound by Sangorski & Sutcliffe, London*. The term does not include gummed tickets, often used as an alternative. See also *signed bindings*.

pallet knife: a thin flexible knife used for mixing printing ink and for scraping surplus ink from cylinders.

Palmart, Lambert, fl.1475: a printer of Flemish origin who worked at Valencia in Spain. The first work known to be his was 'Bellum Jugurthinium' of Sallustius Crispus, 1475, though he may have printed a volume of Fenollar's poems 'Obres o trobes en lahors de la Verge Maria' in 1474. (A Synodal and five other pieces, issued about 1473 by an unidentified printer at Segovia, represent the first known printing from movable types in Spain.) Palmart used coarse roman type for the first five books he issued, gothic for the remaining ten. He died in 1490.

pamphlet: a short piece of polemical writing, intended for wide circulation, printed and issued as an unbound publication, with either stapled or sewn pages; it may or may not have a paper cover. In his introduction to 'British pamphleteers' (Allan Wingate, 1948) the editor George Orwell wrote: 'Probably a true pamphlet will always be somewhere between 500 and 10,000 words, and it is written because there is something that one wants to say *now* . . . in essence it is always a protest. The great function of the pamphlet is to act as a sort of footnote or marginal comment on official history' (adapted with permission of the publisher).

The most famous collection of pamphlets, now in the British Library, covers the period 1640–61, and was assembled by George Thomason (d. 1666), a

London bookseller. It has 22,000 items and includes Milton's defence of the freedom of the press (Areopagitica), 1644.

pandect: 1. a complete treatise or digest of a subject.

2. as *Pandects*, the digest or collection of legal opinions which Justinian ordered to be compiled and to which he gave the force of law in 533.

panel: 1. a rectangular space, often enclosed by a frame, on the spine of a book. There may be several panels, in one of which the title may be lettered, in another the author's name, the panels being separated by raised bands. A panel of one, two or three lines or *fillets* may also be tooled on the covers of a book, positioned near the edges to form a frame for any other design tooled on them. The panels may be either gilt or plain. See also *frame, labels, pallet*.

2. the list of books 'by the same author' facing the title-page. As this is included more for bibliographical than advertising purposes titles which are out of print or issued by other publishers may be given.

panel back: the spine of a hand-bound book on which decorated panels are tooled between the raised bands.

panel stamp: an engraved metal block used in a blocking press to stamp with one application of pressure a complete design on the covers of a book. The leather is first moistened and then an engraved plaque is positioned over it and pressed. For a historical note see *blind-stamped panels*. See also *butter stamp, embossed bindings*.

Pannartz, Arnold: see *Sweynheym, Conrad*.

pantograph: an instrument for the copying of a design, either the same size, reduced or enlarged. See also *Benton, L. B.*

Pantone: a seldom used planographic printing process devised by Ronald Trist and introduced to the trade about 1927 by the Sun Engraving Company. A chromium-faced steel plate was used and by means of a pyro-tanning process an image was obtained directly on the plate by exposure with a fine screen in a camera. Non-image areas were treated with mercury. Curved or flat plates could be used in rotary or flatbed machines for long runs on any cheap rough-surfaced paper.

Panzer, Georg Wolfgang Franz, 1729–1804: a German theologian of Nuremberg remembered for his bibliographical recording of early printing. Most important was the 'Annales typographici ab artis inventae origine ad annum MD (ad annum MDXXXVI continuati)', 11 vols, Nuremberg, 1793–1803, in which he grouped under place, date and printer his descriptions of incunabula. He published a similar work limited to books printed in German before 1526, entitled 'Annalen der ältesten deutschen Literatur', 1788–1805. His researches may be considered to have prepared the way for the compilers of the *Gesamtkatalog der Wiegendrucke*, q.v.

Panzer's personal library is now part of the Landesbibliothek, Stuttgart.

paper: a substance consisting essentially of cellulose fibres interwoven into a compact web, made by chemical and mechanical processes from rags, straw, wood, bark and other fibrous material, into thin sheets or strips. (After Funk & Wagnalls Dictionary.)

paperback: in the British trade a paperback is considered to be a book of 96 or more pages with a printed paper cover adhered to the back; anything less is a *pamphlet* or *brochure*, qq.v. It may be (i) an original work first issued as a paperback, (ii) a work issued simultaneously in hard-cover and paperback form, (iii) a paperback reprint of an earlier hard-cover edition. However, implied by the term 'paperback' is a low selling price, and it is the huge quantity of a title printed, not its enclosure in paper covers instead of a case, which makes this possible and calls for the mass-marketing technique of widespread sales from non-traditional bookselling outlets.

To reduce the production cost per copy big printing runs using rubber plates on reel-fed rotary machines, small type, narrow margins, cheap paper, a fairly standard size (18·5cm), adhesive binding, paper covers trimmed flush with the pages, and a low royalty are usual. In Britain a run of 35,000 copies is an economic minimum for a paperback.

A precursor of the mid-20th century paperback was the German Tauchnitz Verlag series of English and American reprints begun in 1841. By 1939 over 8,000 titles had been issued in somewhat austere paper covers. Paperbacks as now known began in Britain in 1935 when the first ten titles in Allen Lane's Penguin series appeared, all fiction. To create a new and bigger reading public they were retailed (at 6d each) in Woolworth's stores, not bookshops. In two years *seven million* Penguins had been sold, all reprints of other publishers' cased editions. They were slug-set, printed from flat stereo plates on perfecting machines, sewn and wrappered. The same firm started Pelican books in 1937 to publish serious works, many being specially commissioned originals. The expansion of the paperback market and the ready acceptance of the cheap format were boosted by wartime paper restrictions which limited normal book production at a time when there was a big demand for reading matter.

By 1965 some thirty British publishers of paperbacks were issuing about a hundred million books a year. Some firms issue only reprints of books first published by other houses, but others issue paper-back reprints of their own backlists and may set up a separate publishing imprint for the purpose. Production methods of Penguins and similar series have become· specialized and streamlined. Slug setting, once preferred for speed and low cost, has been replaced by TTS perforators, photo-setters and computerized units. Moulds are made of set-up type and then rubber or plastic plates are made: rubber gives longer runs, but plastic plates carry a cleaner image of type and line illustrations. Reel-fed presses can produce about 15,000 sections an hour (of 64, 96, or 128 pages). Sections are imposed for two-up binding (known as 'coming and going' or 'fore and aft' imposition).

Present day paperbacks usually have covers printed offset in four or five colours. It is economical to print them four up on a medium-sized offset press. For runs over 30,000 they may be printed eight up on a double-demy machine. Covers may be put out to specialist litho firms, similarly the varnishing or lamination which enhances and protects many paper-backs may be done outside.

Mechanical adhesive binders of the Sheridan or Martini type are usual. Bundled sections are brought to the machine on trolleys and then put in hoppers. After automatic collation on a conveyor belt at the gathering end of the binder sections pass as complete books to have the backs sawn and roughened. Rollers now apply one or two shots of hot or cold adhesive. Covers are fed in and drawn round the books. The books are still two-up so a circular or band saw cuts them into singles. A three-knife edge trimmer completes the process. Machine speeds are about 10,000 books an hour.

Another impressive machine, introduced in the late 1960s, has a series of linked units giving an uninterrupted flow sequence from printed sheets to stacked paperbacks at a net production rate of up to 9,000 books an hour. Flat printed sheets pass through a folder, gatherer, adhesive binder with back chopper and a trimmer, to a counter stacker where finished books are machine-counted and stacked in whatever number has been pre-set. Electronic control of all units is from a central panel on which warning lights, actuated by safety devices on the several machines in tandem, indicate faults during running. (See also *shrink wrapping*.)

The name 'egghead paperback' or 'quality paper-back' is now used to refer to academic literature in this form. This has proved a means of extending the availability and sale of university text-books, particularly when exported to the emergent countries of Africa and Asia. Sponsors of paperbacks in this group include the bigger publishing houses as well as university presses in Britain and America. (See also *English Language Book Society*.) For eggheads the paper is often better than that used for general

360

paperbacks (woodfree or esparto grades), the size larger, the sections sewn, and the price range higher. Very often the sheets for the cased and paperback editions are the same, especially when both appear under one imprint.

Also practised is the simultaneous publication of a work in cased and paperback form, not necessarily by the same publisher. A book first issued in hard covers by one firm which is subsequently published as a paperback by another is known as a *take-over*.

Germany, France and Switzerland are among the many countries which in post-war years have successfully followed the Penguin example, but the United States is now the world's biggest producer of mass-appeal reprints with minimum print runs of between 100,000 and 200,000 copies and individual sales of up to three million. The competition to secure paperback rights is so keen that an author may be paid $500,000 for a book of which not a word has been written. Cf. *paper covers*. See also *impulse outlet*.

paper boards: a style of cased binding in which paper is used instead of cloth to cover the boards. Cf. *paper covers*.

paper-book: a form of *commonplace book*, q.v., in which, some four centuries ago, pupils of grammar schools in particular wrote vocabularies of words and phrases, anecdotes, lists of people and places, notes on natural history and so on. The result was a personal core of knowledge to be memorized as a form of self education, and was seen as an alternative to learning by heart from oral repetition.

In England the making of paper-books began in the early 16th century. Juan Vives and Erasmus, in England at the time, recommended the practice. Another visitor, Commenius, noted in 1641 that stenography was often used for these personal compilations.

paper covers: a style of binding without boards used for ordinary books sewn in sections (not mass-produced paperbacks). The stiff paper cover, which is stuck to the back, is often varnished or laminated for strength and protection. It may overlap by extending beyond the edges to form *squares*, q.v., or be trimmed or folded over so that the cover is flush with the edges. At one time most French books were published in paper covers.

The binding style with paper covers pasted down on to thin boards, cut flush head and tail, is known as *stiffened paper covers*. See F. L. Schick, 'The paper-bound book in America', Bowker, 1958.

paper durability: the degree to which paper retains its original qualities when subjected to the strains of continuous use. Factors affecting this include purity of ingredients, degree of beating and the finish. See also *paper-testing*.

paper finishes and varieties: see *air dried, animal sized, antique laid, Arches paper, art paper, azure, Batchelor, calendered paper, cameo coated paper, cartridge paper, china paper, chromo-paper, Cobb's paper, crash, cylinder dried, deckle edge, double sized, eggshell finish, engine-sized, English finish, featherweight paper, felt finish, french folio, gloss finishing, half-tone paper, hand-made, hard sized, high mill finish, hot-pressed, hot-rolled, imitation art paper, india paper, Japanese paper, Japanese vellum, laid paper, linen-faced, linen finish, lithographic paper, loft dried, machine dried, machine finish, manila, matt art, mechanical wood, mill brand, mould-made paper, not, odd, offset cartridge, Oxford india paper, plated paper, plate finish, rag paper, ribbed paper, smoothness, Spilman, stock sizes, strongfold papers, sulphate pulp, sulphite pulp, super-calendered paper, text* (2), *tub-sized, twin-wire paper, Van Gelder paper, vat paper, water finish, waterleaf, wet strength, Whatman paper, wood free, wood pulp, wove paper.* See H. Osborn, *ed.*, 'Paper finishing', Benn, 1972.

papermaking: *Historical note.* The craft of making paper, excluding *papyrus*, q.v., was reputedly discovered in China about AD 104 by Ts'ai Louen, director of the Imperial workshops. It was made from mulberry and bamboo bark, probably with other vegetable fibres. It is assumed that pulped fibres were spread on a woven or plaited cloth and left to dry. Two centuries later trays consisting of closely laid bamboo strips made into matting by hairs or silken threads which joined them at regular intervals were used. The matting was laid on a groundwork of stronger bamboo rods and was dipped into a vat of pulp. On removal, water was allowed to run off and the layer of paper was allowed to dry, the flexible matting being rolled away from it. Papermaking was introduced into the Islamic world by Chinese artisans among the prisoners taken by Ziyad at the battle of Atlakh, AD 751. It was first made at Samarkand. Chicago's Oriental Institute has a dated paper manuscript of 252 AH/AD 864. The craft spread to Damascus, Cairo and the Maghreb by the 10th century and then the Moors brought it to Europe where in 1085 rag paper is said to have been made at Jativa in Spain. An Arabic treatise on bookmaking, ascribed to the Tunisian ruler al-Mu'izz ibn Bādis (AD 1007–61), but probably 'ghosted', has a chapter on papermaking. In the 12th century papermaking began at Catalonia, and a mill established at Capellades in 1238 is still operative. The first mill in Italy was at Fabriano prior to 1283, in France at Troyes in 1338, in Germany at Nuremberg in 1389, in Switzerland in 1411, in England *c.* 1490, and in Austria in 1498. Paper was not made in Holland until the late 16th century, nor in Russia before 1556.

In spite of its early manufacture in England prior to 1600 most paper used for printing was imported, but during the late 17th century there was a big influx of French Huguenot refugees many of whom established papermills in Kent, Hampshire and Somerset where rags and clear water were abundant. Their improved manufacturing methods resulted in sufficient fine quality paper being available to meet two-thirds of the country's needs. A protective tariff and restrictions on the export of rags helped, and the import of foreign paper diminished. Henri de Portal of Bordeaux (d. 1747), Nicholas Dupin, and Gérard de Vaux were among the more important refugee papermakers. Further impetus to the British industry, and protection for some years, came with the incorporation in 1686 of the *Company of White Papermakers*, q.v., which claimed for its members a monopoly on the making of all printing paper.

The complete process of making paper by hand is shown in this copper engraving from Georg Böckler's 'Theatrum machinarum novum', Cologne, 1662

Technique. European paper was at first made as described above, but the material consisted almost exclusively of linen rags. These were converted into pulp after removing any buttons and hooks, sorting and washing, by steeping them in water, i.e. subjecting them to a process of fermentation which dissolved some of the particles and loosened the fibres. After steeping, the rags were disintegrated into a fibrous pulp by pounding them in mortars. The pulp was transferred to the paper vat or trough being here diluted with water to a thin gruel which was passed through strainers made of flat iron wires stretched as a foundation over a wooden frame. Here the sheet formed.

At the end of the 13th century methods improved, especially in Italy which then became the leading centre for paper. Hand pounding in mortars was replaced by a machine in which iron-shod stamping rods beat the rags in a line of oak mortars. The rods were raised by gears or cams driven by a water-wheel. Forty pairs of rods could make a hundredweight (*c.* 50kg) of pulp in a day. Moulding trays were made of drawn iron wires. (See *wove paper.*) Due to the altered methods of manufacture paper changed in character to some extent. Prior to the 14th century paper was long-fibred, rough and yellowish: subsequently it was markedly short-fibred, thin and flexible. The newly-formed sheet of wet paper was *couched* on a woollen felt, i.e. it was firmly pressed on to the cloth so that it adhered to it, freeing the mould for re-use. The couched sheet was covered by another felt, and this continued until a pile (or *post*) of alternating felt and paper resulted. This was pressed in a screw press which removed some of the water. The sheets were then taken out, assembled in a fresh pile and pressed again, after which they were hung up to dry in a loft. To make them non-porous to ink the dried sheets were then sized by steeping them in a solution of starch, replaced since the 14th century by animal glue, mostly made in the papermill's own sizing kitchen. After further pressing and drying the paper was glazed with a glazing stone. Water-powered glazing hammers were introduced about 1540, and glazing in a calender in the 18th century in Holland. There, probably about 1673, one of the greatest aids to modern papermaking was invented, the *Hollander*, q.v. See also *rag paper.*

Technical note. Ingredients of present-day papers, which vary according to their intended use, include rags, esparto grass, eucalyptus fibre, wood pulp, china clay, chalk, starch, size, dyes and water. Paper is made by boiling, beating, draining and pressing the materials. Originally laboriously made by hand, it is now made almost universally by machine.

The modern treatment of rags is largely mechanized. Rags are sorted and cut and dust is removed before boiling. After *scouring* (boiling under pressure with alkali) various impurities dissolve and can be removed by washing. In a 'half-stuff Hollander' the rag pulp is ground into *half-stuff*, q.v., and is then bleached with chloride of lime in the same machine (in former times paper was bleached in the sun). After thorough washing the half-stuff is ready to be worked up into paper pulp; this is done in the same way whether the basic material is half-stuff of rags or pulp made from wood. The paper pulp is ground in a Hollander of the type already described, combined, if necessary, or at times entirely replaced by centrifugal-type machines and grinding mills. Fibrous material of different kinds is mixed in fixed proportions. Waste paper is often added, finely ground in crushing or grinding mills. In some cases the fibrous materials are separately broken and then put in a mixing Hollander. When treating paper pulp loading agents, size and colouring materials are also added. Treatment in the Hollander can be so controlled that 'long fibre' or 'short fibre' pulp results.

Properties of paper depend largely on the loading agents in addition to the fibre material and the degree of treatment. These agents consist of certain mineral substances (chiefly china clay) which affect the opacity of paper, its suitability for printing, etc. Sizing is done in the pulp, i.e. in the paper pulp Hollander, by adding aluminium sulphate (alum) and resin soap, as well as by the size press. In the Delthirna method resin, dissolved in caustic soda, and aluminium sulphate are added to the pulp, when the sulphate precipitates the resin from the soda solution on to the paper fibres. In the Bewoid method (of Bruno Wieger, Brunswick) resin and water is run into the stuff chest with the alum and not in the beater. Other substances are also employed as sizing material.

Hand-made paper, q.v., is still made by the traditional method of dipping a mould into rag pulp and skilfully shaking it until a sheet is formed. The mould is a rectangular wooden frame over which is fastened a wire cloth (laid or wove); on this a loose wooden deckle rests and it is this which determines the size and thickness of the sheet to be formed, and also gives the sheet its distinctive *deckle edge*, q.v. When the deckle has been removed the sheet is couched as previously described. Pressing is generally done in a hydraulic press at about two tons per sq. inch.

Machine-made paper. The standard papermaking machine was invented by a Frenchman, *Nicolas-Louis Robert*, who took out his first patent for a long wire cloth machine in 1799. This was improved by the Englishman, *Bryan Donkin*, q.v. and the brothers Henry and Sealy Fourdrinier, after whom the machine was later called the *Fourdrinier*, q.v. In 1821 another Englishman, Crompton, added steam cylinders for drying the paper. In 1805 *Joseph Bramah* invented the *cylinder machine*, qq.v., which was considerably improved upon in 1809 by John Dickinson and is now used chiefly for making boards.

Briefly, machine-made paper is manufactured as follows. From the Hollander, in which the pulp has been beaten, sized, and coloured at a pulp concentration of 3 to 6%, it is drawn off (further diluted in drawing off to a pulp content of 2 to 3%) into *mixing chests*. From these the pulp is pumped to the sand trap, a broad channel, the bottom of which is furnished with sloped baffles behind which heavy impurities collect and are removed. Centrifuges are also used for this purpose. The pulp is allowed to pass slowly through the sand trap, being diluted by recovered water from the machine to a concentration of about $\frac{1}{2}$ to 1%. The pulp next passes through the strainer, usually a slotted drum. The drum vibrates as it revolves, the clean pulp going through the slots, while clumps of fibre remain outside to be washed away. The pulp, now clear of impurities, is ready to enter the paper machine via the *flow box* (also called *breast box*). The diluted pulp flows out of the breast box over the breast board (of leather or rubber) on to the endless moving wire which is the main feature of the Fourdrinier. The pulp must be spread evenly on the wire. Moving rubber deckle straps at either side keep the pulp on the wire. In moving, the pulp is strained, and by lateral agitation the fibres are shaken into a web; water pours through the mesh in large quantities, along the numerous tube rolls which support the wire, into save-all trays. As this water contains valuable paper material it is led back and used for the diluting referred to above. After passing the tube rolls the wire is supported by a number of vacuum boxes, each connected with a suction pump. The object of these is to remove water which has not run off earlier. Between two such boxes a light *dandy roll*, q.v., of metal cloth revolves on a fixed axle over the wire. As the web of paper passes underneath, the dandy roll closes the surface of the web and impresses any watermark desired.

After the last suction box the wire with the paper is conveyed through the couching press round the lower roller of which the returning empty wire is guided. The upper couching roller is covered with thick absorbent felt. After being couched in this press the web is sufficiently firm to move on independently to the first press. (Pressing by the couching press is often replaced by suction with a suction couch roll.) In the successive presses through which the web next passes it is guided by widely spaced woollen felts between pairs of rollers, of which the upper roller is usually of granite, or granite composition, and the lower is usually covered with rubber. After leaving the third press the dryness of the paper is between 55 and 65%, and further drying is done by passing the web over a number of steam-heated cast-iron cylinders. The paper is guided round between twenty and thirty such cylinders, pressed hard against them by thick felts.

Developments were announced in 1967 for alternatives to the horizontal Fourdrinier just described. A feature common to the several versions was the simultaneous removal of water from both sides of the web of paper as it formed. The first machine in commercial use was erected for the Canadian International Paper Company in 1968. This was the *Verti-Forma* in which the paper is formed between the nip of two converging endless wires.

There is also the *Papriformer*, developed at the Canadian Pulp and Paper Research Institute and manufactured under licence in Canada and Sweden. This can make paper at up to 5,000ft. per minute as against the modern Fourdrinier's maximum of 3,000ft. There are two wire mesh screens, each moving over a series of rollers. Stock flows in where they meet at the point of nip. The sandwich of wire-pulp-wire then passes round two large mesh cylinders placed one above the other. While this is taking place a combination of low-pressure suction and high-pressure blowing from within the cylinders removes much of the moisture. The newly formed web of paper is then led off for further drying by high temperature gas streams. (See also *Inverform*.)

After drying the web next passes through the finishing section, i.e. stacks of calender rolls, and finally round a water-cooled cylinder (to get rid of static electricity). It is now ready for winding on drums or reels.

It is still not ready for delivery, however. Even if it is to be used in reel form it has to be re-wound in order to obtain reels that are sufficiently even and firm. At the same time it is usually cut into narrower widths by revolving knives. Certain grades are *tub-sized* at this stage by passing the web through a solution of animal glue and then pressing and drying it. The *glazing* of the web is done by passing it through a calender separate from the Fourdrinier calender already referred to. This is a vertical stack of alternately finely polished steel and compressed fibrous rolls in which only one of the rolls is power-driven, the others rotating by friction with the paper which is thus polished. The web may be cut into sheets in machines so constructed that several webs are cut simultaneously. Hand-made paper, cut into sheets, is also glazed either in a calender or in a *plate glazer* in which the sheets, laid between metal plates or glazed boards, are pressed between steel rolls.

Special finishing is needed for the production of *art paper* (also known as *coated or enamelled paper*). The web is coated on one side (or both) with a composition of mineral salts (kaolin, gypsum, barium sulphate) and a binding material (casein, etc.). This is done on machines which evenly coat the surface of the paper. Coated paper is dried in a drying chamber and glazed in a calender. A high degree of glazing can be obtained by polishing the surface.

For offset paper in particular some mills give the paper a certain relative degree of moisture in a conditioning machine.

Paper that is cut to size is sorted, counted and

363

packed in wrappers; if necessary also between wooden boards. (Partly GU)

See also *back-tenter, backwater, beating, bleaching, bowls, breaker, broke, calender, chemical wood pulp, clearing the stuff, coating machine, conditioning, contraries, couch, counter-mark, dead, deflaker, digester, doctor blade (2), dry end, drying cylinders, drying tunnel, esparto, felt side, felting, finish, furnish, grain direction, hog, Hollander, impressed watermark, Jordan, kier, leaf (2), loading, look through, machine clothing, midfeather, mould (1), opacity, pallet (1), paper substance, pond, pope roll, post, potcher, pulp, rag cutter, relative humidity, retention, salle, sheeter, size, slice, stillage, stock, stuff, text (2), tranchefile, vatman, watermark, well closed, wet end, wire, wire-mark.*

paper permanence: the degree of stability which paper can be expected to possess. This resistance to chemical change depends on the presence or absence of resin (which oxidizes in light and air) and the quality of the papermaking fibre.

Generally speaking, all-rag paper should retain its colour and quality indefinitely. Paper having an alpha-cellulose content of over 90% is similarly stable; bleached sulphite paper with an alpha-cellulose content of less than 85% will be less so.

A high residual acidity or excess of resin will increase the tendency of paper to discolour and become brittle as the years pass. See also *paper-testing*.

paper printability: the fitness for purpose of paper which is to be printed. It must be strong enough to withstand the strains of machining. The relative humidity of the printing room atmosphere and the moisture content of paper affect its dimensional stability, register control, speed of drying and tendency to generate static electricity.

Other desiderata are such paper-surface qualities as resistance to plucking and fluffing, smoothness, compressibility, firmness and ink absorbency. Uniformity in the paper quality and even tension in the reels are also important.

Paper Publications Society: a Dutch society formed at the instigation of E. J. Labarre (1884–1965) to publish researches into the history of paper. It is a non-profit making venture supported by the sale of its publications to scholars and libraries in many parts of the world.

The first work to be issued was E. Heawood's 'Watermarks: mainly of the 17th and 18th centuries', Hilversum, 1950; but the most important has been 'Monumenta chartae papyriceae historiam illustrantia', 5 vols, Hilversum, 1951–7. In 1966 the Society announced a facsimile of the original text and plates of Briquet's 'Les Filigranes' with annotations, corrigenda and addenda.

364

The address of the Society is Nieuwe Prinsengracht, Amsterdam.

paper quality control: the maintenance during its manufacture of whatever physical and chemical properties it is intended a paper shall have. It is essential that the purchaser should be able to rely on the maker's specification since the smooth running of printing presses and binding machines will be affected by even slight changes in sizing or coating. Quality control is achieved by sampling and testing paper at all stages, including the raw ingredients, the additives, the operation of the Fourdrinier and finishing units, and concluding with a series of evaluation tests to check the properties which the finished paper should have.

paper sizes: the German DIN A series of paper sizes is widely used in many European countries. DIN stands for Deutsche Industrie Normen, a body comparable with the British Standards Institution. The A distinguishes this size from others known as B and C which apply to related poster and envelope sizes.

The main features of the DIN A series are that they apply to all types of paper, and that the proportions of a sheet remain constant when it is cut or folded in half across the long side. The letter A is always accompanied by a figure indicating the relation of a particular paper size to the basic size A0 which is 1 square metre. Thus half A0 is A1, half A1 is A2, and so on. For larger dimensions the A is preceded by a figure, thus 2A is twice the size of A0.

In 1959 the DIN A series was accepted as a national standard for paper and board by the British Standards Institution and published as BS 3176:1959. In Britain the scale of dimensions is known as *International Standard Paper Sizes* about which the BPIF published a useful booklet.

The following table shows seven *trimmed* sizes in the ISO or DIN A series which correspond most nearly to former British sizes from double quad demy to demy 8vo.

	Millimetres	Inches (approx.)	Demy sizes
2A	1189×1682	$46\frac{13}{16} \times 66\frac{3}{16}$	45×70
A0	841×1189	$33\frac{1}{8} \times 46\frac{13}{16}$	35×45
A1	594×841	$23\frac{3}{8} \times 33\frac{1}{8}$	$22\frac{1}{2} \times 35$
A2	420×594	$16\frac{1}{2} \times 23\frac{3}{8}$	$17\frac{1}{2} \times 22\frac{1}{2}$
A3	297×420	$11\frac{11}{16} \times 16\frac{1}{2}$	$11\frac{1}{4} \times 17\frac{1}{2}$
A4	210×297	$8\frac{1}{4} \times 11\frac{11}{16}$	$8\frac{3}{4} \times 11\frac{1}{4}$
A5	148×210	$5\frac{13}{16} \times 8\frac{1}{4}$	$5\frac{5}{8} \times 8\frac{3}{4}$

(Continental practice is to state the smaller dimension first.)

In America the prevailing practice is to specify the size of paper by inches and by its weight per ream rather than by name. The following are the ordinary sizes of book papers in the U.S.A.:

22 in. by 32 in.		33 in. by 44 in.	
24	36	33	46
25	38	34	44
26	39	35	45
26	40	36	48
28	42	38	50
28	44	41	51
29	52	42	56
30½	41	44	56
32	44	44	64

paper substance: British authorities express paper substance in pounds per ream of 500 sheets, or in grammes per square metre (g/m^2). Although known for many years the g/m^2 was not extensively used by British printers until the 1970s despite its advantage of expressing paper weight (substance) in a basic figure which does not change whatever the size of paper or number of sheets. Thus if a ream of crown and one of quad demy are quoted as $85 \ g/m^2$ it is apparent that their substance is the same, but from their former respective weights of *c.* 18 lb. and *c.* 95 lb. the fact that the reams have the same substance is only revealed by consulting a table of equivalent weights.

The adoption of g/m^2 by the British trade followed the replacement of inches by millimetres for linear measurement. See also *metrication*.

paper testing: for the various purposes for which paper is used different properties are required, and many testing methods have been devised for ascertaining whether they are present or not. The development of methods for testing paper began in the latter half of the 19th century.

Methods of testing paper may be divided into three main groups: 1. testing the composition; 2. mechanical testing; 3. physical testing.

1. *Composition.* The first category consists mainly of *fibre analysis*. By de-fibring the paper the exposed fibres can be examined under a microscope. By adding various solutions different colour effects can be produced in fibres of different kinds, such as sulphite, sulphate, mechanical wood, straw and rag. The proportion of different fibres can be established by comparison with standard samples or by counting them. The *sizing content* can be ascertained by extracting the paper with a solvent, after which the solvent is evaporated and the residue weighed. The content of various *impregnating materials* can be established in a similar manner. The *ash content*, i.e. the proportion of incombustible inorganic matter, is determined by incineration and weighing the residue. The *copper number* is a measure of the content of reducing agents (oxycellulose and hydrocellulose).

2. *Mechanical testing.* In all mechanical and physical testing of paper it is very important that the tests should be carried out at a certain relative humidity and temperature, for paper is a hygroscopic substance which alters in its degree of moisture according to the relative humidity of the surrounding air. At the same time most of its mechanical and physical properties change. Since the end of the 19th century a relative humidity of 65% and a temperature of 20°C have been accepted as a standard for paper-testing. Recently, in view of the fact that this humidity is higher than that at which paper is generally used, a relative atmospheric humidity of 50% has begun to be used in some tests, especially those relating to the printing properties of the paper. Mechanical testing includes, above all, the determination of *substance*, i.e. the weight of the paper per square metre, and *thickness*.

The Danish Arkass Profile Tester will measure and record on a moving chart variations as small as one micron in thickness along and across a web of paper.

For determining the *strength* of paper there are many methods and instruments. These tests have been standardized is most countries but no international standard methods are as yet in existence. The most general tests are to determine *tensile strength*. This is usually expressed as the *breaking length* of the paper and is defined as the length of the web of an arbitrary, but constant, width and weight which, when suspended from one end, breaks due to its own weight. In determining the tensile strength the *stretch* at the breaking point is also obtained, this being indicated in percentage and constituting a certain measure of the plasticity of the paper. The *bursting strength* is determined in a Schopper-Dalen apparatus, or a Mullen apparatus (with the paper clamped over a circular diaphragm of thin rubber and pressure applied from below until the paper bursts). This is indicated in lb. per sq. in. and known as a Mullen number. For some kinds of paper the determination of the *folding resistance* is of great importance. The paper is folded many times in a special apparatus (e.g. Schopper) until it breaks at the fold, when the folding number can be read off by the counting device: different values will be obtained by folding with the grain direction or across it. Other mechanical tests determine elasticity and tearing properties.

3. *Physical testing.* Physical tests of paper vary greatly according to its intended use. There are many tests for printing paper. The *moisture content* is found by weighing the paper before and after drying. It is important to determine the *stretch* and *shrinkage* of paper for lithographic printing. The *degree of sizing* is determined in many ways. The *absorbent capacity* (or *ink receptivity*) is important because paper must quickly absorb the oil in the ink. Absorbency is tested using the K & N test for which ink of a standard tint and viscosity is wiped on a sample of paper. After

two minutes the excess is wiped off and the density of the inked area measured.

The *optical properties* of paper are of importance in the graphic industries. *Opacity*, *transparency*, *whiteness*, *colour* and *gloss* are determined by various instruments, often with photoelectric cells. For all printing paper the *glazing* is important. This is determined by Bekk's or Bendtsen's apparatus. The latter is more modern. Both are based on the principle that the higher the glaze the less air can pass between the surface of the paper and a polished metal surface or edge.

Very occasionally it is impossible to determine the suitability of paper for printing by using the above methods. In such cases a printing test must be made in unvarying external conditions. The result can be expressed in figures by using optical gauging methods. The tendency of paper to fluff often causes trouble in printing works, and attempts have been made to introduce methods for testing this, but none can be considered quite satisfactory. The sandy particles in paper are often a drawback owing to too rapid wear and tear of blocks and cylinders for intaglio printing. Their content can be easily and reliably determined by putting the paper under pressure on a polished glass plate in an apparatus constructed by Bekk, when the scratches made on the glass by the sandy particles can be examined and counted under a microscope. The determination of the durability and discoloration of paper also enters into the physical tests. See also *Beta Ray substance gauge*, *coverage*, *cushion*, *smoothness*.

(GU)

paper weight: see *paper substance*.

paper wrappered: said of a book enclosed in *paper covers*, q.v.

papier mâché: a greyish substance made from paper pulp which is used for taking moulds for stereotypes. These are taken in its soft state; when hard, the papier mâché moulds may be stored indefinitely prior to stereotyping, a precaution publishers frequently take when they authorize the distribution of a book's type. See also *flong*.

Papillon, Jean Michel, 1698–1776: the most distinguished of a French family of wood engravers, who was renowned for the delicacy of his floral head- and tail-pieces. His 'Traité . . . de la gravure en bois', Paris, 1766, was an early history of wood engraving. See also *Barbou*.

papyrotype: a photolithographic method of printing illustrations devised in 1873 by a Captain Abney. The picture is first printed on a sensitized gelatine film and then transferred to a zinc plate or lithographic stone.

(After OED)

papyrus: a giant rush from which the ancient Egyptians made sheets of writing material. Thin strips of stalk were placed side by side, and a second layer was added at right-angles to the first. After soaking in water, pressing, drying and polishing, the surface was ready for use. Papyrus was exported from Egypt to Phoenicia as early as the 11th century BC and was used in Greece and Rome from the 4th century BC; its last use in Europe was for Papal Bulls, *c.* 1051. Writing ink was probably a mixture of copperas and carbon. See N. Lewis, 'Papyrus in classical antiquity', O.U.P., 1974. See also *capsa*, *hieratica*, *rotulus*.

Greek papyrus roll

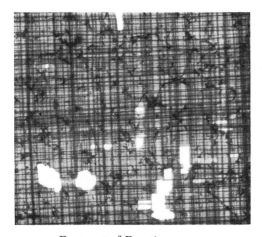

Fragment of Egyptian papyrus

paragon: the name for a former size of type, about 20-point. The name, used in Holland as long ago as 1563, may have been an allusion to the beauty of the face rather than the size of the shank bearing it. Also known as *two-line long primer*.

paragraph: the printer's sign ¶ used as a *reference mark*, q.v.

parallel: the printer's sign ‖ used as a *reference mark*, q.v.

parallel folding: see *folding*.

paraprint process: a papermaking process, no longer used, in which a coating of clay-starch composition was given to the underside of the sheet to separate it from the wire during making and also to increase the surface receptivity to printing ink.

parchment: the flesh split skin of a sheep or goat, and sometimes of other animals, which is scraped, dressed with lime and pumice, and prepared for writing upon. It is not tanned. If required for painting upon it may be given a coating of size.

Skin rolls were used in Egypt from *c.* 1500 BC, and also by Jews for synagogue rolls. Herodotus wrote that when papyrus was scarce the Ionians used coarse skins of sheep and goats for writing upon. That they were found to be more durable and readily available than papyrus may have led to their eventual substitution for it. It was, however, in the reign of Eumenes II (197–159 BC) at Pergamum in Asia Minor that methods were found for preparing smoother close-textured skins. Pergamum became the main centre for the finest skins for writing upon, and by the 2nd or 3rd century AD 'pergamena' (whence 'parchment') was the accepted name for the product. Ink was a solution of soot in olive oil or gum arabic.

Writing in 'The Alexandrian Library', 1952, E. A. Parsons comments that the distinction (in English) between *parchment* and *vellum* seems unsolvable, and suggests that usage favours the former as a general term, the latter for refinements of the product. He quotes 'Vulgaria uiri doctissimi', Guil. Hormani, 1519: 'That stouffe that we wrythe vpon: and is made of beestis skynnes: is somtyme called parchement, somtyme velem, somtyme abortyue, somtyme mem braan. Parchement: of the cyte where it was first made. Velem: bycause it is made of caluys skynne. Abortyue: bycause the beest was scant parfecte. Membraan: bycause it was pulled of by hyldynge fro the beestis lymmes.' See R. Reed, 'Ancient skins, parchments and leathers', Seminar P., 1973, and his 'The nature and making of parchment', Elemete, 1977.

parentheses: the punctuation mark or ornament ( ). Known to the printer as *parens*. An early use of printed parentheses occurs in the Barzizius 'Epistolae', Paris, 1470, which was the first book printed in France.

paring: thinning and chamfering the edges of leather to provide a neat turn-in over the boards in hand-binding. (LK)

Paris, Matthew, fl.1217–59: a monk of St Albans where in 1235 he was appointed historiographer to the Abbey. His great work was the 'Chronica majora' for which he revised the work of earlier scribes and wrote the years 1235–59, the year of his death. The first printed edition of this was issued by Archbishop Parker in 1571. Witty marginal drawings in the manner of cartoons were a distinctive feature of his manuscripts, which included the popular Apocalypse, and he trained pupils in his atelier.

Francis Walsingham (*c.* 1530–90) wrote of him 'He wrote down fully in his books the deeds of great men in Church and State, with sundry and marvellous chances and events, whereby he bequeathed to posterity a marvellous knowledge of the past. . . . Moreover he was so subtle a workman in gold and silver and other metals, in carving and in painting (illuminating) that he is believed to have left no equal in this world of the West.' See also *St Albans School*.

Paris Texts, 1971: the revised texts resulting from meetings held in Paris in July 1971 to revise both the Berne and Universal Copyright Conventions. The revised conventions preserve the concept of international copyright while recognizing realistically the needs of developing countries who sought the compulsory licensing to them of translations and reprints.

One recommendation was to reduce from seven years the period following first publication of a work before developing countries could translate and publish it in their national languages for schools and universities. For local languages the period would be one year. For languages in general use (English, French, Spanish) the period would be three.

The texts were embodied as an Appendix to the Paris Act, 1971, of the Berne Convention, and incorporated in the Revised U.C.C. of 1971.

Parker, Matthew, 1504–75, Archbishop of Canterbury: a scholar and prelate whose important library of historical and ecclesiastical printed books and manuscripts is now at Corpus Christi College, Cambridge. Parker spent much money in efforts to secure for posterity manuscripts from former monastic libraries and he employed agents at home and abroad.

At Lambeth Palace he installed 'limners, writers and bookbinders' and he had many old books completed by inserting manuscript transcriptions from others. He also sponsored the publication of ancient chronicles and Anglo-Saxon histories in addition to such works as the Bishops' Bible.

He commissioned *John Day*, q.v., to print Aelfric's Anglo-Saxon homily, edited as 'A testimonie of antiquitie' in 1567. This was the first book to be printed in Anglo-Saxon characters: these were probably cut and cast by one of Day's foreign workmen.

Parliamentary papers: House of Lords and Commons

Acts and Bills (e.g. Order Papers), also reports of Select Committees.

Parlour press: see *bellows press.*

partial remainders: quantities of books offered at low prices by certain publishers to selected booksellers which they permit the latter to sell to the public at less than the published price, although the books, so far as other booksellers are concerned, are still net books. This practice is condemned by the Councils of the Publishers Association and the Booksellers Association.

parts of a book: in order of gathering within the covers these are half-title, frontispiece, title-page, printer's imprint and copyright note, dedication, preface, acknowledgements, table of contents, list of illustrations, introduction, errata, text pages, appendices, author's notes, glossary, bibliography, index, colophon. On examination it will be found that publishers vary the order slightly. See also preliminary pages.

parts of type: *type* has the following main parts: *face, body, beard, shoulder, bowl, counter, pin-mark, nick, groove and feet, serif,* qq.v. The minutiae of a type-face are described in 'Type for print' by D. Thomas, Whitaker, 1939, and in other manuals. See also British Standard: Typeface nomenclature, BS 2961:1967.

passim: a Latin word printed after a subject in an index, or in a footnote after the name of an author or of a book, to indicate that references to a subject or topic are *scattered throughout* the book and occur too frequently or briefly for precise page references to be given.

pass sheet: a specimen pull, taken so that the colour and general suitability of ink for the paper can be judged by the printer before running off an impression. See also *proof.*

pasteboards: sheets of paper, printed or not, pasted together to a thickness considered suitable for the cover linings of books. Their use in England is thought to date from the early 16th century. In the 18th century pasteboards were gradually superseded by *millboards,* q.v.

Boards made of pulped paper shavings were often made into boards by binders. Although known as pasteboards, pulpboard would have been a more accurate term.

paste-downs: the halves of end-papers which are pasted on to the boards of a book. (An alternative name is *board paper.*) The free halves form fly-leaves.

paste-grain: split sheepskin hardened by coating it with paste and given a highly polished surface.

368

paste in: see *tipped in.*

paste on: a plate or similar component of a book which is affixed by pasting all over. Cf. *tipped in.*

(LK)

paste-over cancel: see *cancel.*

paste-up: a layout of a number of pages made in the publisher's office to show the position of illustrations, captions and text prior to sending copy to the printer.

pasting: in hand bookbinding, the application with a brush of paste to surfaces which require sticking together, e.g. end-papers, hollows, linings of marbled papers and the sides of books in the half-binding style. Edition binders use pasting machines which are either separate units or built into other machines, e.g. casing-in machines, the paster consisting of a cylinder to which paste is fed from a container or by transfer cylinders.

pasting down: to cover the inside boards of a book by pasting one half of a double-leaf end-paper to each. In hand binding the body of the book is secured to the boards by *lacing on,* and pasting down the end-paper is necessary to give a neat finish. With cased books the pasted end-papers serve additionally to secure the body of the book in its case. The action is also called *pasting up.* See also *doublures, end-papers.*

PATRA: see *PIRA.*

patron: a sponsor. From the early days of printing until the reign of George III (as in the still earlier times of handwritten works) a wealthy or titled patron often sponsored the printing of a work and, on occasion, commissioned the writing of it. The patron was the dedicatee, it being hoped that preferment or money would be the form of acknowledgement. English literature of the 16th and early 17th centuries could not have flourished without patronage, an author's receipts from printer-publishers being modest. See also *dedication, impensis, subscription works.*

Payne, David: see *Wharfedale machine.*

Payne, Roger, 1738–97: an English master binder, born at Windsor, and apprenticed to the Eton bookseller Joseph Pote. Roger and his brother Thomas appear to have moved to London about 1766 when Roger worked first as a bookseller before setting up his bindery.

For some of the books he bound Payne used russia leather or straight-grain morocco in blue, red or green, embellished with a combination of blind and gold tooling. He used small, well-cut tools to build up patterns of acorns, vine leaves and leaf sprays, but 'the assertion that he cut his own tools is almost certainly untrue' (Nixon). Typical designs on covers and spine had ornamental corners filled with stamped honeysuckle flowers and backgrounds of dots or circles. Goffered edges and green headbands were features of some.

Much of his work was done for Lord Spencer and Clayton Cracherode, two bibliophiles whose collections are now in the John Rylands Library (including the Aeschylus Payne bound in 1795) and in the British Library respectively.

It was his habit to send customers invoices describing in detail how his work had been done, such as 'Em-bordered with ERMINE expressive of the High Rank of the Noble Patroness of the Designs. The other Parts finished in the most elegant Taste with small Tools Gold Borders.'

For a time he worked in association with his brother Thomas and with Richard, or David Weir (or Wier) whose wife worked for them as a restorer. In his later years Payne worked for a time as finisher with John McKinlay whose well-known bindery in Bow Street, Covent Garden, was the stable of many celebrated craftsmen, e.g. *Walther*, q.v. See illustration under *bookbinding*.

PCMI: photo chromic micro image. See *Books in English, microform publishing.*

pearl: the name of a former size of type, approximately 5-point.

Pear Tree Press: a private printing press founded in Essex in 1899 by James Guthrie and moved to Flansham in 1907. Mr Guthrie was influenced by William Blake and he specialized in the use of intaglio plates, doing the etching and printing (in two or more colours) by hand. His most important production was Blake's 'Songs of innocence', 1937, of which all copies differed in colouring. For some of his books he substituted calligraphy for type. Editions were as few as twelve copies. His last book appeared in 1951 and he died the next year. See 'James Guthrie and the Pear Tree Press', *Private Library*, 1 1976.

peasant bindings: a name given to the crudely tooled and painted vellum bindings made in Germany, Holland and Hungary during the 17th century for Bibles and devotional books intended for rural family use. Central panels on the boards were decorated with religious scenes painted directly on the vellum; alternatively, simple coloured engravings on paper were pasted on.

peau de truie: the French word for *pigskin*, though English antiquarian booksellers sometimes use it in their catalogues, presumably to invest with glamour an otherwise dull binding.

peccary: the skin of a wild pig found in the Americas. It is occasionally used for fine book covers.

pecia: the medieval tanner's term for one sheepskin. After a skin had been trimmed and stretched in a frame the largest possible parallelogram was cut from it. This was folded to give either four pages in folio or eight in quarto and the word pecia was used to describe it. A pecia was the unit on which payment for copying done by a medieval scribe was calculated.

A university would prescribe a standard for a particular class of book, thus in Bologna in the 13th century a pecia for the copying of a law folio consisted of a skin folded twice. This gave eight pages on which were written two columns, each of sixty lines, with thirty-two letters per line. Uneven copying resulted in blank spaces, and it was customary to write 'nihil deficit' to confirm that nothing was missing. When continuing peciae of four leaves were being copied into units of more than four leaves a marginal inscription such as 'incipit .2. pecia' marked the point of continuation. See also *manuscript book writing*.

peciarii: officials appointed by medieval universities to supervise the stationarii and periodically examine their stock of texts. See also *manuscript book writing*.

peculiars: type characters for the non-standard accent-bearing letters, e.g. those required when setting phonetics, or texts in Scandinavian, Slavic, Turkish and certain other languages. (See *accents*.)

A selection of these is given here:

Å B̆ Č Ḍ Ê F̌ Ğ Ḥ Î Ḳ Ł M̌ N̲ Ō R̠ Ṣ Ť Ů V̌ W̆ Ý Ż

peg: a small wooden stand used by a punchcutter. A magnifying glass is fastened above it.

Peisenberg, Heinrich, fl.1572: an eminent Munich bookbinder. He was for a time court binder to Duke Albert V. For humbler patrons he used blind-stamped pigskin.

Pelican Press: the imprint of a small typesetting business begun in London in 1916 by Francis Meynell. Machining was done by the Victoria House Printing & Publishing Company and the *Herald* newspaper, owners of Pelican. In 1919 *Stanley Morison*, q.v., joined the firm as typographical director. Types in use at the beginning included Caslon, Kennerley, Forum and Cloister; later Plantin and Imprint were added. An important collection of *flowers*, q.v., was acquired and were 'scattered everywhere – to surround advertisements, for the borders of books, even to enclose political manifestos' (Meynell). They were shown in an elegant specimen book, 'Typography', 1923.

With Meynell as typographer the press became an important influence in raising the standard of commercial printing design, but in 1924 he left to develop the *Nonesuch Press*, q.v., which he had founded in 1923, and Pelican appears to have closed about 1931.

Pellechet, Marie, 1840–1900: a French bibliographer whose major work 'Catalogue général des incunables des bibliothèques publiques de France', Paris, 1897–1909, was incomplete when she died. In 1950 a reproduction on microfilm of her unpublished later volumes was made in New York.

Pelletan, Édouard: a distinguished French book designer and publisher of the 20th century, much of whose work was printed by the Imprimerie Nationale. His theory of book design was set out in his 'Première lettre' and 'Deuxième lettre aux bibliophiles', 1896. This was that a good text was the first essential of a book, that the typography of a book should be in harmony with the author's thoughts, illustrations interpret a text and decorate a page and that woodcuts do this most harmoniously. He also said that fine books should not be made only for the rich.

pelt ball: see *ink ball*.

penalty copy: copy which is difficult to set and thus costs more. Examples are elaborate chemical formulae and copy with extensive passages in an exotic foreign language. See also *fat matter*.

Pendred, John, *c.* 1742–93: a London printer and publisher remembered for his directory of the book trade, 'The London and country printers, booksellers and stationers vade mecum', 1785, which was '. . . the earliest directory of any trade in this or, as far as I have been able to discover, any other country' (G. Pollard in his introduction to a new edition, 1955).

Penitential: a book of Church canons relating to penance.

penny history: see *chapbook*.

The Penrose Annual: the leading British review of the graphic arts. It was founded by William Gamble of the London printing firm A. & W. Penrose & Co. to arouse interest in new process-engraving techniques, hence its first publication with the title 'Process work year book', subtitled in a cartouche 'Penrose's annual for 1895'. With the 1936 issue it became 'The Penrose annual'.

Since 1897 the annual has been printed by Lund Humphries & Co. of Bradford, and from 1909 until 1973 they also published it. In that year 'Penrose', renamed 'Penrose graphic arts international annual', was sold to Northwood Publications, a division of the Thomson organization.

This lavish glossy, with illustrations produced by all three major processes, has an international reputation. Notable through the years have been articles on technical innovations written well ahead of their practical breakthrough in the trade, and 'Penrose' is recognised as an authoritative report of progress in printing plus articles on a general graphic theme, the whole impeccably printed and produced.

When Gamble died in 1933 he was succeeded as editor by *R. B. Fishenden*, q.v. Subsequent editors have included Allan Delafons and, from 1964–73, Herbert Spencer. The 1977–78 volume was issued as 'Penrose' Vol 70, 1977–78, with 'International review of the graphic arts' as a subtitle.

Pentateuch: the first five books of the Old Testament, known to Jews as the *Torah* (i.e. the law of Moses). See also *Hebrew printing before 1600, Septuagint, Talmud*.

Peregrine Press: the private press established by Henry Evans, a San Francisco bookseller. He bought a hand-press in 1949 and subsequently printed a number of small editions, mostly with woodcut illustrations.

perfect: in edition binding the printed sheets are said to be *perfect* as soon as some of all the sheets (and plates) have been printed. At that point perfect copies are ready for binding. (LK)

perfect binding: see *adhesive binding*.

perfect copy: 1. a complete set of folded sheets (and plates) ready for binding. The term is used in the sense that the printed matter is complete.

2. a bound or cased book in saleable condition. (LK)

perfecting: printing the second side of a sheet or web of paper. Also known as *backing up*. In letterpress the usual ways of doing this are described under *sheet work* and *work and turn*, qq.v. However, the production of long-run bookwork can be speeded up by simultaneously printing both sides in a sheet-fed *perfector press* which has two type beds, two impression cylinders (which rotate inwards towards each other), automatic feed, and extended pile delivery. An alternative is to use two linked printing units. They are known as the *first couple* and the *second couple*, and it is the latter which backs up the paper. As the gap between the two units is too small to permit effective drying of the printed impression on the first side of the paper before it enters the second couple special inks and arrangements to prevent set-off are needed.

Sheet-fed offset perfecting machines which print, *inter alia*, from litho plates bearing photoset matter, are suitable for long runs of paperbacks. An efficient continuous feeder fitted with fault detectors and, after impression, a rapid jogging and stacking system to remove work are integrated adjuncts. See also *blanket-to-blanket press*.

perfector press: see previous entry. Perfector presses for flatbed letterpress are no longer manufactured though many are still in use.

PERI: see *Platemakers Educational & Research Institute*.

period: a full stop marking the end of a sentence. See *punctuation marks*.

period printing: 1. the production of a book in a typographical style which in all respects resembles that of an earlier period. The text may be by a living author, his subject being thought by the publisher to benefit from a contrived 'historical' presentation. This is quite distinct from a *facsimile edition*, q.v.

2. the reproduction of a book in the style of the original edition.

peripheral speed relationship: when a printing cylinder rolls on a flat surface (as in a cylinder machine) or against another cylinder surface (as in a rotary machine) both surfaces must have the same speed along the line of contact (periphery) for a good impression to result. Packing, forme, offset blankets and underlay, etc., must be adjusted with this in mind. An incorrect peripheral speed relationship may cause a lack of sharpness in the impression and undue wear of the forme. (GU)

periplus (pl. **periploi**): a coastal *pilot book* giving an account of a sea voyage. The earliest surviving periplus is that of Scylax, dating from the 4th century BC. It describes the harbours and landmarks westwards from the Nile delta. Early periploi may have been accompanied by charts though none survives. Later coast pilots gave descriptions of the route a voyage was to take, tides, bearings, sailing directions and a wind-rose.

There was an anonymous Greek periplus of the Erythrean Sea, made in the 1st century AD, and famous for being the first to suggest the existence of coasts and islands beyond India, e.g. *Thin* or China. The English called a pilot book a *rutter*. See also *portolano*, *wind-rose*.

permissions copy: a copy of a book which contains quoted copyright material. It is sent on publication to the owner of the copyright as evidence that the quotation is as was agreed when permission to use it was granted. Also known as a *voucher copy*.

Perpetua Press: a small private press set up by David Bland (1911–70) and Vivian Ridler at Cotham, Bristol. One of their few productions, 'Old nursery rhymes',

was chosen by the First Edition Club as one of the fifty best books of 1935. In 1937 David Bland began a distinguished career with Faber & Faber who published his important 'History of book illustration' in 1958 (2nd ed. 1969). Vivian Ridler, appointed Printer to Oxford University Press in 1958, later used the name Perpetua Press on occasional pieces printed at his home.

Persian bindings: see *Islamic bookbinding*, *Safavid bindings*.

Persian illumination: the basic conception of manuscript painting in Persia was the creation of a beautiful design; its inspiration was poetry, which was often mystical, and its sponsors were rulers, princes and their entourages. It thus differed fundamentally from its European counterpart where manuscript painting developed in the service of the Church, artists seeking to create representations of spiritual power, wisdom and piety as objects of and for adoration. Persian religious paintings are few, and are simply illustrations of holy writ. Such paintings were (and are) condemned by Muslim theologians as irreligious. Calligraphy, however, was highly esteemed, and beautifully written copies of the Koran, with lavish borders of repeated ornaments in gold and lapis lazuli, afforded their creators a satisfaction comparable to that felt by a monastic scribe in Europe.

Earliest surviving Persian manuscripts date from the 11th century, and are the work of scribes and artists commissioned by patrons of the Turkish Seljuk empire (Mesopotamia, Persia and Asia Minor). One of them is Abu Mansur Muwaffak's fundamentals of pharmacology completed in 1056, now in Vienna (Cod.A.F.340).

The fully developed Persian style of painting was formed before the end of the 14th century. To generalize, its characteristics were an emphasis on beauty and the abundance of nature, with an absence of perspective and of light and shade. Artists created patterns of contrasting colours, controlling the subservient parts of a design to form a harmonious whole. Paintings of a single figure were rare, partly due to the absence of religious conceptions. Early work shows the Hellenistic influence of Mesopotamian art. There were also elements deriving from 7th century Sasanian metalwork and rock sculpture, notably hunting scenes and military costumes. The Mongol conquest brought Chinese influences seen in the depiction of landscapes with mountain tops and clouds, the flame halo, the dragon, and trees, though these Chinese conventions were differently used.

The *Timurid School* was the first of importance, although its style was a natural development of 14th century art, and was substantially in existence before Timur's invasions of 1386 and 1393. Centres were at Shiraz, Tabriz and Herat where Baysunqur (1399–

1433) had an atelier which included forty scribes. He is remembered for his revision in 1426 of Firdawsi's 'Shah-namah' (written in 1010) of which many copies were made during succeeding centuries. Another work frequently copied was Nizami's 'Khamsa' (five poems) written prior to 1200.

Herat became the leading centre of painting under Hussain Mirza (ruled 1468–1506). The most famous court painter was Bihzad (fl.1480–1524) whose influence was to extend to the early Mughal court of India where he was esteemed as a painter of battle scenes. Late 15th century Persian miniatures are marked by elaborate composition, a wealth of carefully painted ornamentation seen in carpets and architectural details, and an emphasis on decoration, always elegant and finished. Figures were more varied in type and shown in court scenes of great luxury. Although as court painter Bihzad must have painted many important manuscripts present-day scholars do not accept as his all those bearing his purported signature.

In 1510 Shah Ismail founded the Safawi dynasty which ruled Persia for over two centuries. Bihzad came to Tabriz and in 1522 was appointed director of the *Safavid School* of court painters, scribes, illuminators and other book-making craftsmen. In the first half of this century Persian miniature painting reached its peak: the finest pigments were used for scenes of luxurious court life, drinking parties, hunting, all crowded with richly-dressed people set in gardens or noble apartments. New techniques included the sprinkling of the paper with gold, marginal figures in gold, and the painting of miniatures on book covers which were then lacquered. The unusual elongated turban is a recognizable Safawi feature. One of the most important works of the century is generally held to be the 'Khamsa' of Nizami, copied by the scribe Shah Mahmud between 1539 and 1543, and now in the British Library (Or.2265).

After about 1560 Persian manuscript painters were generally less lavish in the use of costly materials, and their drawing was more mechanical. Some were active elsewhere, notably at Constantinople and at the court of the Indian Emperor Humayum where they influenced the Mughal school of painting.

In 1600, under Shah Abbas (1587–1629), the Persian capital was moved to Isfahan. The book arts were practised independently of court patronage, and the decline which had begun in the later 16th century continued, though miniatures not intended as book illustrations were extensively produced. Books were still written, however, until about 1815 when printing was introduced into Persia.

Materials. The paper used for Persian manuscripts was made from coarse rags and had a somewhat uneven surface. It was sized either with egg white or a starch solution and then burnished with mother of pearl or a crystal egg. An alternative way may have been to wax and polish it.

Only mineral colours were used since they had to be opaque and vegetable dyes are transparent. A mineral was ground to a fine powder, sieved, and mixed with a binding medium. At different periods albumen, glue and gum arabic were used as binders, the latter probably with an admixture of insect wax.

In Pope's 'Survey of Persian art' (O.U.P.) we learn that the brush used for fine work was 'made from hair cut from the throat of a white kitten, two months old, and painters bred cats expressly to obtain the best possible quality'. The hairs were bound in such a way that the tip of the brush consisted of a single hair.

The gold used in Persia was of two kinds – yellow and green, and each was used in two states – raw or cooked: the former was dull the latter bright. The method of preparing it in leaf form – by beating the metal between pieces of skin – has not changed through the centuries (see *gold leaf*). For use in manuscript illumination a leaf of gold and some powdered dry glue were pounded until blended into a paste. This was put in water and shaken until the glue dissolved. After being allowed to stand the particles of gold settled and the fluid was poured off. After mixing with pure saffron and dried glue the gold was ready for use. An alternative to glue was honey in which the leaf of gold was worked by hand until it was blended.

When a lustrous effect was wanted the gold was polished with jasper or cornelian, the burnisher being passed across the forehead whence the natural grease acted as a lubricant. This process was called cooking. The alternative was to leave it dull or raw. For this a sheet of tissue paper was laid over the gold before polishing. A greenish tint could be given to the gold by adding silver during preparation. See L. Binyon and others, 'Persian miniature painting', O.U.P., 1933.

Persian morocco: a soft goatskin used for the finest book covers. Persian goat and Persian sheep are trade names for goat- and sheepskins tanned in India. The skin is not durable.

Petrucci, Ottaviano, 1466–1539: a printer of Fossombrone and Venice who also established a papermill which operated until the 19th century. In 1498 he received a privilege for music printing from the Senate in Venice where, *c.* 1500, he established the first press devoted to music publishing. To Petrucci is attributed the invention of printing music in measured notation. (Han of Ingolstadt, the first printer of music from movable types, had printed roman choral notation. See *music printing*.)

The first work from his new press was a collection 'Harmonice musices adhecaton', 1501, for which he first printed the staves, then the notation, then the text, initials and page numbers, but more important were his editions of 'Frottole', 1504–8. In 1504 he introduced the printing of polyphonic music in separate part books for choral use. Other publications were lute songs and Missals.

By 1514 Petrucci had returned to Fossombrone with Francesco da Bologna, typefounder, as partner. However Venice remained the centre of music publishing in Italy, Ottaviano and Girolamo Scotto being the principal successors of Petrucci. See C. Sartori, 'Bibliografia delle opere musicale stampate da Ottaviano Petrucci', Florence, 1948.

pewter plates: see *music engraving, music printing*.

Peypus, Friedrich: a printer of Nuremberg where prior to setting up his own business in 1512 he worked at a privately owned press in the house of Ulrich Pinder. In 1524 Peypus issued a fine edition of Luther's N.T., and in 1529 the first systematic German orthography 'Lautbuchlein deutscher Orthographie'. He was a friend of several leading humanists and often accepted commissions from patrons to print works of their choice.

Pfister, Albrecht, fl.1459–64: the first printer of Bamberg, remembered for his use of the 36-line Bible type. This Bible, 1459/60, has been attributed to his press on such circumstantial evidence as the paper used and the typical Bamberg style of binding on surviving copies. About 1460, if not earlier, Pfister used the same type in the same state, but somewhat worn, as that of the Bible, but his known work was less competently printed and in the Scholderer 'Festschrift', Mainz, 1970, G. D. Painter postulates a Gutenbergian association for the Bible.

The first book more confidently attributed to Pfister is the undated Ackermann von Böhmen, *c.* 1459, which could be the first book to contain woodcuts. Of the nine or so works he issued Ulrich Boner's 'Der Edelstein', 1461, was the earliest *dated* book written in German and the earliest dated book with illustrations (an example is shown under *woodcut*, q.v.). The single surviving copy is in Wolfenbüttel. See G. Zedler, 'Die Bamberger Pfisterdrucke und die 36-zeilige Bibel', Mainz, 1911.

Pforzheimer, Carl H., 1879–1957: a New York banker and bibliophile whose library has, within the general framework of English and American literature, eight special collections of which 'Shelley and his Circle' is the outstanding feature. It is one of the three major collections of Shelley in the world (the others being in the Bodleian and the British Library), and a catalogue has been published. There is a large amount of manuscript material of Shelley and his wife, Byron, Hunt, Hogg, Peacock, Trelawny and Mary Godwin, and there are also first editions of the works, later editions, and studies.

pharmacopoeia: a book listing drugs, with an indication of their preparation and prescription, and in precise usage, those to be employed by doctors and chemists with the approval of a city, state, or national medical authority.

Origins of such compilations can be traced to the 1st century when a popular collection was made by Scribonius Largus, *c.* AD 47. What is often claimed to be the first pharmacopoeia was the 'Aqarabadin-i-Kabir' which Sabur bin Sahl of the famous medical school and hospital at Jundi-Shapur (now Shahabad) in Persia completed in 869. It was adopted throughout the eastern Caliphate and much of the Islamic world.

A well-known book of prescriptions based on Arabic materia medica was the 'Antidotarium' of Ibn Serapion (d. 945). It was enlarged by Nicolas of Salerno about 1140 as 'Antidotaria magna', being printed by Jenson of Venice in 1471. Also noteworthy was the first printed edition of 'Nuovo ricettario', Florence, 1498, compiled by the city's College of Doctors. After 1573 it was adopted throughout Tuscany as 'Ricettario Fiorentino', and was 'official' in that its use was obligatory.

By the end of the 16th century many towns had official pharmacopoeia such as the 'Pharmacorum conficiendorum ratio, vulgo vocant dispensatorium' which Valerius Cordus (1515–44) compiled for the city of Nuremberg. It was printed by Johann Petreius in 1546 and was the first to be published in Germany.

The first to appear in England was the College of Physicians' 'Pharmacopoeia Londinensis' of which two editions were published in 1618. As the title indicates, the work was written in Latin, but Nicholas Culpeper (1616–54) made a reputedly bad translation into English, issued in 1649. Scotland had the 'Pharmacopoeia Edinburgensis', the first of its fifteen editions appearing in 1699, the last in 1841.

The first 'Dublin Pharmacopoeia' came out in 1807, and the last edition in 1850.

In 1858 the General Medical Council of the U.K. was instructed by Section 54 of its establishment Act to compile a book of medicines and compounds, with the manner of their preparation, to be called 'British Pharmacopoeia': the exclusive rights to print, publish and sell it were given by the Act of 1862. Other pharmacopoeias existing in the U.K. at that time were replaced. After more than a hundred years the Medicines Act of 1968 transferred responsibility for preparing and publishing the 'British Pharmacopoeia' (BP) from the GMC to the Medicines Commission. The 12th edition, published by HMSO in 1973 for the Health Ministers, was the work of a new British Pharmacopoeia Commission advised by various committees and panels (and, as an aside, was judged one of the best designed and produced books of that year).

Since 1907 the Pharmaceutical Society has published the 'British Pharmaceutical Codex, (10th ed. 1973). This gives information on drugs, other pharmaceutical substances and formulated products, and provides standards of identity and purity for a range of substances either not included in the BP or omitted from successive editions of it. Codex standards are recognised in Britain by the Medicines Act, 1968.

Phemister, Alexander, fl.1860–94: an Edinburgh punchcutter who cut for Miller and Richard the 'old style' types first shown in 1860. In 1861 he went to America (where he died) cutting the Franklin Old Style types for the Boston Dickinson Foundry.

Philip the Good, Duke of Burgundy, 1396–1467: one of the greatest bibliophiles and patrons of learning of his day. He would admit only the finest manuscripts to his collection and employed such scribes and illuminators as Jehan Miélot, Jean Wauquelin, *Loyset Liédet,* and *Rogier van der Weyden,* qq.v., while *Colard Mansion,* q.v., was engaged as a supplier.

At the time of his death Philip left 3,211 MSS in Paris, Dijon, and the Low Countries. His son Charles the Bold (1433–77) added to the collection and it was later bequeathed to Philip's granddaughter. After her death in 1482 the manuscripts were partly dispersed, but about 540 volumes subsequently formed the basis of the Royal Library, Brussels. The Dijon group are in the Bibliothèque Nationale.

Phillipps, Sir Thomas, 1792–1872: a wealthy bibliophile of Broadway in Worcestershire who devoted his life to assembling what was at one time the largest private collection of manuscripts in Europe (*c.* 60,000). His aim was to preserve for posterity as many unpublished works as possible.

About 1822 Phillipps set up the *Middle Hill Press* to print catalogues of his collection and works of antiquarian interest. Much of the collection has been dispersed at a series of sales which began in 1886 and still (1978) continues. See A. N. L. Munby, 'Phillipps studies', C.U.P., 1951–60. See also *Halliwell.*

Philobiblon: see *Bury, Richard de.*

photocomposing: see *photosetting.*

photodisplay setters: see *photolettering machines.*

photoengraving: the preparation of a relief printing surface on a plate of metal or synthetic material by one of several methods employing photographic, chemical, and mechanical means. The process is used for the reproduction by letterpress of an original image. When the plate is finished and mounted to type height (23·317 mm) it is known as a *block.*

Photoengraving is also known as *letterpress platemaking, process engraving* or, more accurately in view of the means used, as *photomechanical engraving.* The craftsmen involved are the *camera operator* and the

process engraver who is often referred to as a *blockmaker* or *photoengraver.*

The original copy for reproduction may be a photograph, transparency, painting, ink drawing, pencil sketch, print, water colour, print of type matter, music, an actual object, or a combination of these. It is the nature of copy which determines whether the plate shall be made as a *half-tone block* or *line block,* qq.v. Reproduction of either may be in monochrome or colour.

The lengthy and highly skilled work of photoengraving was done in a trade establishment separate from the printer's until the advent of photopolymer plates, electronic engraving, and powderless plate etching machines, operating automatically, led larger printing concerns to instal equipment for making their own plates. See F. G. Wallis & R. V. Cannon, 'Letterpress platemaking', Pergamon, 1969.

See also *Ben Day tints, block mounting, buffing, burnisher, burr, camera, cliché, cold enamel, Collobloc, colour scanner, colour separation, composite block, contact screen, continuous tone, copper plates, cut, dark-room camera, deep-etched half-tone, Dycril relief plates, edge trimmer, electronic engraving machine, electronic scanning machine, electrotype, Elgrama, enamel process, etching machine, facet, fine etching, fish-glue enamel, flat tint plate, graver, Ives, Klischograph, Luxographe, magnesium plates, Meisenbach, moiré, nickel-electro, nickel plating, outline half-tone, photopolymer printing plates, pierced, plastic plates, printing down, proofing chromo, relief block, resist, retouching, reversal developing, reversing, rough etch, router, Scan-a-Graver, Scanatron, scan plates, screen, screen process work, single-line half-tone, staging out, stereotype, thermoplastic plates, undercutting, vacuum frame, vertical camera, whirler, Zip-a-tone.*

photography: the production of an image by the action of light on substances affected by it. This is usually done by exposing an emulsion-coated film in a camera and then developing and fixing it for the subsequent production of positives on light-sensitive paper. See also *camera, photoengraving.* See H. Gernsheim, 'History of photography . . . up to 1914', O.U.P., 1955.

photogravure: an intaglio process for the making by photographic means of an image on an etched copper surface from which it can be printed on to another surface, usually paper.

Historical note. Following several experiments by *Nicéphore Niepce,* who made the world's first permanent photograph from nature in 1826, other inventors worked on methods which led to photogravure printing. Briefly, they included *Mungo Ponton* (1802–80) who in 1839 discovered the sensitivity to light of dichromate of potassium; *Fox Talbot* (1800–77) who used dichromate and gelatine in his phytoglyphic engraving process, patented in 1852; *Louis Poitevin*

(1819–82) who applied the foregoing to the production of permanent prints (as well as to photolithography) by adding carbon dust to dichromated gelatine in 1855; *Sir Joseph Swan* (1828–1914) who in 1864 patented a carbon tissue on which was a film of gelatine and finely powdered carbon and used it in 1866 to reproduce a painting in an edition of 1,000 copies; and *Karl Klíč* (1841–1926), a Bohemian who had an engraving establishment in Vienna and, basing his work on the above-noted discoveries of Talbot and Swan, invented the *photogravure process* in 1879. He took a polished copper plate coated with resin dust to which he fused it by heating. He then printed a sheet of carbon tissue under a diapositive and transferred it to the plate. Washing with water removed the soluble portions of the carbon. After etching the plate with perchloride of iron in several baths of decreasing strength and cleaning off the gelatine he found the plate was etched to different depths, varying with the tones of the original; the shadows, being deepest, held most ink.

An essential item was the *doctor blade*, q.v., to remove surplus ink from the plate. This had been foreseen in 1785 when a certain Thomas Bell used a moving knife to scrape away, or duct, excess ink from the engraved copper cylinder of his wallpaper printing press.

Photogravure in Britain began in 1883 when T. & R. Annan of Glasgow used it (with flat plates). Printing from a rotary cylinder press followed the invention by Klíč in 1890 of a cross-line screen, and in 1895 he founded the Rembrandt Intaglio Printing Company in Lancaster in association with *Samuel Fawcett* as foreman. The first British periodical to be printed by the new method was the *Illustrated London News* of 12 October 1912.

Summary of practical photogravure. The image (type or picture) to be reproduced is photographed to obtain a negative from which a document print (a continuous tone positive) is then made. This calls for skilled work by photographer and retoucher who often use photo-electric density meters to maintain uniform quality. The positive is then printed on a sheet of pigmented gelatine-coated sensitized carbon tissue. After exposure the tissue is mounted on the copper cylinder and developed by rotation in hot water. It is varnished in any areas which are not to be etched, fanned dry, and etched with ferric chloride.

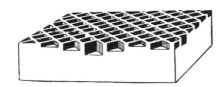

The intaglio screen divides the surface of the cylinder into small cells which hold the ink

Screen. Fundamental to the printing process is the division of the picture etched in the cylinder into a number of small cells which hold the ink. There must be screen walls over the whole etched surface. There are several types of screen in use (see *screen*). The screen is first copied on the carbon tissue by exposure in a vacuum frame, after which the glass bearing positive pictures and text is superimposed on the screened tissue and a second exposure is made.

Planning. The assembled positives which will make up a printed sheet are mounted on a glass plate under which is a marked up plan of the layout. Margins outside the image area are covered with black tape which will ultimately make an unexposed border on the carbon tissue (the unhardened gelatine under this border will then adhere more easily to the cylinder).

Exposure. The glass plate is put on the bed of a vacuum frame, the screened and coated carbon tissue is fitted to it, and an exposure is made. Possible light sources include arc lamps, mercury vapour lamps, pulsed xenon and fluorescent tubes. Each has its special merits. Exposure is controlled by a photometer.

Mounting. The prepared carbon has to be transferred to the printing surface. This is done by damping the gelatine layer with alcohol and water sufficiently for it to adhere, but damping must be restricted to prevent dimensional change in the tissue. On revolving the cylinder a rubber roller presses the tissue against its surface, water being flowed in at the point of contact. Following transfer, the carbon tissue on the cylinder is soaked in methylated spirit before development takes place in a bath of water. The backing paper is peeled off, leaving the gelatine resist in relief on the copper surface. After removing all soluble gelatine the remaining gelatine relief is soaked with spirit and dried. Among other methods of mounting is one in which direct copying on a prepared cylinder replaces carbon tissue transfer.

Etching. Before etching begins all parts of the cylinder surface which are not to be etched are covered with an acid-resist. Etching is done with ferric chloride solution in separate baths of varying strengths. Etching is followed by washing in cold water, then in diluted acid, and finally the relief is removed with chalk and water and the resist with benzol. For printing large editions it is usual to chromium plate the cylinder, after which it is ready for the press from which proofing and printing will be done. In the mid-1970s laser technology was used to speed up the etching of copper gravure cells.

Photogravure work is identifiable by the fine screen network which is faintly discernible in the finished print and in the lack of sharpness of accompanying type. See G. C. Wensley, 'Photogravure process', Benn, 1964. See also *Colloplas, colour gravure, Etchomatic, Uniprint.*

photogravure printing ink: thin volatile ink which dries by the evaporation of a solvent in it. Ingredients, which vary according to purpose, include bitumen or resins, e.g. dammar, hartshorn, albertol or gilsonite asphalt, in a solution of one or more inert volatile solvents such as zylol or toluol, with the addition of the soft pigment. The solvents are costly so equipment is used to recover up to 80%. There are also fire and health hazards for which special plant must be installed to diminish.

photogravure printing press: machines for gravure printing are built to work with sheets or reels of paper. Printing is mostly from a cylinder. Arrangements for feeding paper are similar to those for letterpress and offset printing (see *feeding, printing press, rotary press*). The printing mechanism, however, is built on a different principle. In photogravure the whole plate is covered with thinly flowing ink, the surplus being removed by the doctor blade. The inking arrangement can often be simplified by allowing the cylinder to revolve in a trough of ink. Above the trough is the doctor blade. As the cylinder is usually removed for the transfer to it of the image and for etching, the bearings must be constructed with this in view. In reel-fed machines the paper course is pressed against the plate cylinder by another cylinder. Sometimes the impression is made through an intermediate roller but in any case the impression cylinder is rubber coated. In sheet presses the printing cylinder supporting the sheet must have a circumference equal to or exactly double the size of the plate cylinder. The latter is more usual when working with entire copper cylinders, the plate cylinder then being inked and scraped twice for each impression. In presses for built-in copper plates cylinders double the size are used to avoid any excessive bending of the plate.

In reel-fed presses it is desirable to increase the speed of printing as much as possible. Gravure ink dries by evaporation and ways have been tried to accelerate this so that the paper course can be introduced quickly into subsequent printing stages, or into folders or guillotines. It was formerly usual to conduct the paper across rotating steam-heated drying drums. Heating, however, was detrimental to the paper, due both to changes in size and dust from the dry paper fluffing the forme. There was the additional risk of static electricity arising in the paper with a danger of sparks igniting the inflammable vapours in the ink. Cool air drying, developed by Fuykers & Walber of Düsseldorf, was more successful, especially since 1934 when it was combined with a device for the recovery of the solvent from the ink.

In some modern high-speed presses working with extremely volatile solvents, practically the whole press is enclosed and the inking system forms an enclosed container limited above by the plate cylinder, on one side by the doctor blade, and on the other by a spring lid. Only the narrow strip of cylinder required for

376

printing is to be found outside the enclosed container.

The doctor blade consists of a thin spring blade which rests at a certain pressure against the cylinder surface. In the knife-holder of the press the blade is strengthened by a thicker supporting blade. Many different types of doctor blade have been tried; one patent is an endless blade which wipes the cylinder, travels on, is cleaned, honed, lubricated and comes round again to continue the operation. Different means of adjusting the blade to the cylinder have been tried, including hydraulic, but in every case the blade is set at an angle to the cylinder, the ink forming a lubricating film which is imperative if scratches on the plate cylinder are to be avoided.   (GU)

photolettering machines: keyboard operated machines, of which there are several proprietary models, for precision display composition. No lead type is involved. Basic to most models are characters on film strips, glass discs, or type plates, and an optical system for projecting in sizes which can range from 6- to 216-point. Curved, linear, slanted or distorted setting is possible, and images can be expanded or contracted within the x-height. The output is in the form of bromides or film. Also known as *display photosetters* and *photodisplay setters*.

photolitho-offset: printing from photolitho plates in which the image is first taken on a rubber blanket from which it passes to the paper. Such work has a softness which in the lighter tones given to line drawings is an advantage, but lacks the crispness and contrast obtained by impressing type and blocks as in letterpress. See E. Chambers, 'Photolitho-offset', Benn, 1967. See also *blanket, offset press, offset reproduction*.

photolithographic plate: a fine-grained metal plate which is prepared for lithographic printing by either of two processes known as (1) the *albumen process*, or (2) the *deep-etch process*.

In (1) the plate is coated with a colloid solution of dichromate and egg albumen to make it light-sensitive. It is placed in contact with a photographic negative in a printing frame, and after exposure to light is covered with a waterproof developing ink and immersed in water to develop. The light-affected parts of the plate, i.e. the open or transparent parts of the negative, retain the ink and resist developing. The non-image areas are desensitized and, after gumming, the plate is ready for printing.

In (2) a photographic positive is used, as distinct from the negative of (1), and the surface of the plate is very slightly etched (in spite of the name deep-etch) to produce a more durable printing surface. The processes above described are known as *printing down* or *printing to metal*.

photolithography: in the widest sense of the term,

planographic printing combining photography and lithography for the reproduction of illustrations or text. For line work a negative of the subject is made without a screen; for photographs or wash-drawings a screen is used; for reproducing complete books the pages are dismembered and photographed. In each case the negative is copied on to a *photolithographic plate* from which printing is done by *offset reproduction*, q.v.

photo-mechanical reproduction: see *photoengraving*.

Photon: a company which has specialized in the development of electronic photosetting equipment for both printing and computer industries. The first Photon machine was invented by two Frenchmen (and first called the *Lumitype*). Initial research was sponsored in America by the Graphic Arts Research Foundation of Cambridge, Mass. The first machine developed by Photon was the *200*. This was introduced in 1950 and gained acceptance particularly in American letterpress newspaper plants for the production of display advertisements. A keyboard is directly connected to the photographic unit. The machine has its types on a revolving glass matrix disc about eight inches in diameter. On each disc there are eight rows of characters arranged in concentric circles. There is only a single character of each family and style. Each circle contains two full founts arranged in a semi-circle. Thus one matrix disc contains sixteen founts or some 1400 basic characters plus border flowers. The disc rotates constantly, sweeping every character past the photographing position. A stroboscopic lamp passes light through the selected character on the disc into an optical system; this in turn projects the light in the form of a type character on the sensitized film. The type image is stopped on the film since the duration of the light flash is only a few micro seconds (eight characters can be photographed per second). Any character on the disc may be projected on to the film in twelve different point sizes. This means there are 192 normal founts under the operator's control. Furthermore any family, size, or style available at the keyboard may be placed in any single line being composed. Not only can type styles be mixed within a line but point sizes and families may also be mixed without interfering with justification or alignment.

In 1964 the *Photon 713* was introduced and was soon widely adopted as a newspaper photosetter. This was probably helped by the rapid increase about the same time of web offset printing for newspapers. Solid state electronics were used instead of the relay circuitry of the Photon 200 with an expected rise in reliability. The Photon 713 has a photo-matrix drum instead of a disc. The principle of shooting light through a poised image was retained and output speeds of 70,000 characters per hour were achieved.

The Photon 713 is driven by either paper tape or magnetic tape so that the machine will accept the output from a number of keyboards.

The Photon 713 developed through the years into eight models differing in speed or typographic flexibility. A minimum configuration of four type styles in two sizes to a maximum of eight type styles in eight sizes is available. Speeds range from 70,000 to 360,000 characters per hour. Models were also developed with the facility of justifying text, thus obviating the need for justifying keyboards or a separate computer. The development of incorporating small computers into photosetters came from this innovation.

The *Photon Zip 900* was also introduced in 1964. Originally developed under a contract with the U.S. Library of Medicine, the Photon Zip became the first ultra high-speed photosetter (over two million characters per hour). Before being superseded by CRT machines the Photon Zip was installed in fourteen locations for the speedy production of telephone directories, spare parts lists and similar computer-based information.

In 1970 Photon announced an agreement with Autologic Inc. to market their CRT photosetter, now named the *Photon 7000 CRT*. This is a true CRT photosetter with characters for setting held digitally in core store or on a magnetic disc. Twenty 100-character type styles are available for setting in a size range of 5- to 72-point. Output speed depends on means of input and character size. When driven by magnetic tape 3,000 8-point characters can be set in one second.

In 1971 Photon launched another new range of machines, the *Pacesetter*. The glass matrix, similar to the original Photon disc, has 112 characters per type style. The Pacesetter is of modular design which means that the basic model, with four type styles and four point sizes, can be built up to eight type styles and sixteen point sizes from 5- to 72-point. This expansion of the specification can be arranged when the Pacemaster is ordered or in the customer's plant subsequent to delivery and installation. The Pacesetter uses a new principle called *optical leverage* by which the character is positioned before being sized. This allows a very simple optical system to produce the same number of characters per second irrespective of size. The disc spins in the machine and each of the four circles of characters has its own xenon flash tube. After character exposure the image is positioned correctly in the line by two mirrors. The image passes through a sizing lens and is projected on to the photographic emulsion on film or paper. Hyphenless justification and tabular attachments are standard equipment.

All Photon machines produce photographic positives which may be used for lithography, photogravure, or to make letterpress blocks.

photopolymer printing plates: relief plates made of plastic materials to which the image they carry is transferred by photochemical means. There are many proprietary plates (e.g. Collobloc, Dycril, Fogra, Nyloprint). Some can be used for either flatbed or rotary printing; most give long runs of high quality, and all can be used for half-tone or line work. See also *photoengraving*.

photosetting: selecting according to copy letters, numerals or symbols carried on transparent matrices, or in digital form, and photographing them on to film or paper for subsequent reproduction by a printing process. No metal type is involved.

From several experiments early in this century the first systems to be developed commercially were the Intertype *Fotosetter*, Monotype's *Monophoto*, Linotype's *Linofilm*, the *Photon*, the *ATF Typesetter* and the Dutch *Hadego*. Such machines as the *Videocomp 500* gave output on paper, film, stabilization paper, photosensitive paper, plate or microfilm and microfiche.

Several machines were introduced for display setting, notably Monotype's *Photoletterer* and Crosfield's *Diatype*, as well as simpler small display-setting devices which produced processed film without darkroom work: Stephenson Blake's *Letterphot* and the Vari Typer *Headliner* are examples.

As these machines are continually being improved and updated to include new technical developments any detailed consideration here of their capacities would soon be out of date. Technicians should see the useful comparative 'CIS analysis of phototype setting systems', Composition Information Services Inc., Chicago, 1974 or later, which gives details of thirty-five systems made by fifteen major companies in Europe and the U.S.A.

See A. Bluhm, 'Photosetting', Pergamon, 1968. See also *computer-assisted typesetting*, *CRT photosetting*, *film make-up*, *optical character recognition*, *pre-correction*, *typewriter composing machine*, *video display unit*.

phylactery: a narrow band or scroll on which was inscribed a name or a speech. They are occasionally seen in medieval illuminated manuscripts where they are drawn as if issuing from the mouths of characters, or they may be held in the hand.

Their use has not entirely died out and they now appear as 'balloons' coming from the mouths of characters in cartoons or comics.

physiologie: the French term for a collection of humorous or satirical character sketches of the kind popular in the 1830s. An early example was Balzac's 'Physiologie du mariage', 1829. Some were issued in yellow covers, and many were illustrated by such

famous artists as Daumier and Gavarni. See also *character book*.

Physiologus: a collection of Christian allegorical descriptions of real or imaginary natural forms (e.g. beasts, birds, fish, rocks) intended for moral instruction. The anonymous original Greek Physiologus of the 2nd century AD (written in Alexandria ?) and translations and adaptations of it remained popular through the Middle Ages in England, France, and Germany.

In England such books were called *bestiaries* of which the earliest surviving native example is in the British Library (*Arundel* MS.157). It dates from the late 13th century, but there were probably earlier ones now lost.

phytoglyphy: the name given by Henry Bradbury to the process of *nature printing*, q.v., which he learned in Vienna and for which he took an English patent in 1853.

Pianotype: the name of the composing machine invented by *Young-Delcambre*, q.v.

pi box: the container on a composing machine for storing matrices of special sorts of a fount of type. They are hand-set. On photosetters there may be a special pi control for exposing such *pi characters* as fractions, arrows, brackets, stars, foreign accents and the like.

pica: 1. the name for a former size of type, now 12-point. The name may derive from the use in 15th-century England of types of this size for *Pye-books*, (1), q.v. or merely from the piebald effect of the printed page.

2. a unit of measure, e.g. for the width and depth of text on a page. A pica is 0·166in. (Pica rhymes with Leica.) Synonymous with *em* (2).

pick brush: a brush used for cleaning formes of type. A 'pick' is a blob of ink adhering to type.

Pickering, William, 1796–1854: a Londoner who in 1820 set up as a bookseller and began publishing in the same year, issuing a volume of Horace as the first of his Diamond Classics. They were printed in the minute type of that name (4½-point) by Charles Corrall and were thus not easy to read. Baxter's 'Poetical fragments', 1821, printed by S. & R. Bentley was notable as an early book to be without full points on the title-page and to be the first trade edition of a book to be issued in a glazed calico binding with a printed title-label on the spine. Five hundred copies were so covered by R. E. Lawson.

A notable production was an edition of Bacon's works in seventeen volumes, 1825–34, the first eleven printed by Thomas White the rest by *Charles Whittingham II*, q.v., who began printing for Pickering in 1828. Between 1828–54 Pickering used several adaptations of the Aldine device, most with the inscription 'Aldi Discip. Anglus'.

In 1825 Pickering began his series of 'Oxford English Classics', including among the forty-four titles Gibbon's 'Decline and fall'. Another successful series was the 'Aldine Poets', begun in 1830 with the works of Burns, and continuing until 1844 by which time fifty-three volumes had appeared. All were available in either blue cloth or full morocco by *James Hayday*, q.v. As Pickering priced his editions less than those of other publishers he encountered opposition from them, apparently overcoming it by public support for his products.

In 1840 Pickering and Whittingham began what amounted to a revival of interest in Caslon's old face roman, long neglected by printers. After 1844 they extended its use from title-pages and heading display to whole texts. A simple title-page with as few words and styles of type on it as possible was typical of Pickering's publications. For his books with woodcut decoration Mary Byfield cut the blocks, sometimes based on 16th century originals.

His considerable output included in addition to the foregoing Lowndes's 'Bibliographer's manual', in parts, 4 vols, 1834; several liturgical works and folio reprints of various versions of the Prayer Book, all now sought by collectors. See G. Keynes, 'William Pickering, publisher, a memoir and a check-list of his publications', 2nd ed. Galahad Press, 1969.

picking: the removal during printing of coating from coated stock or fibres from uncoated stock. Picking occurs when the strength of paper is less than the stress in the ink film as forme (or plate) and paper separate. Instruments are available to measure the picking strength of ink and the surface strength of paper. When these factors are determined and considered in relation to each other the fastest safe printing speed can be ascertained.

Efforts to reduce picking have included lengthening the fibres of the paper stock, reducing the ash content, and giving the sheet a smoother surface. This last can be assisted by *surface sizing*, q.v. Thinning the ink to avoid picking may lead to *powdering*, q.v.

picking list: a list of titles given to a publisher's or wholesaler's warehouseman to 'look out' a customer's order.

Picques, Claude de, fl.1538–75: a Parisian bookseller and binder who bound books for *Grolier*, q.v., from *c.* 1538–48. After the death of Etienne Roffet in 1547 much of his work was done for Henri II, Diane de Poitiers, and their entourage. The entwined initials HD appeared on many of the books he bound for the King. On some, interlaced strapwork surrounded a central cartouche bearing the royal arms, the cartouche obviously inspired by the engravings of ornamental sculpture found on contemporary title-pages, and the various tools he used deriving from oriental sources via Francesco Pellegrini's embroidery pattern book published in Paris in 1530.

PICS: see *Publishers Information Cards*.

pictogram: a symbolic mark for an object, e.g. a bed, cutlery, a house or a telephone so that irrespective of language and without any words information can be presented and understood. Pictograms, in the form of logos, are widely used in hotel guides, travel books, and so on. See also *isotype*.

pie: composed type which has spilled and been indiscriminately mixed.

pierced: a block from which a portion of the surface has been removed for the insertion there of type. See also *drop in*.

pig: a nickname common in early 18th century composing rooms for a pressman. Cf. *moke*.

pigment: colouring matter. For printing *ink*, q.v., finely ground particles of insoluble pigment are evenly dispersed in a medium.

Pigouchet, Philippe, fl.1488–1526: a Parisian printer-publisher who is remembered for the *Books of Hours*, q.v., which he printed for Simon Vostre: the first for Paris use, appeared in 1491; the finest, for Rome, in 1498. These were small books (*c.* 5¼in. × 4in.) suitable for personal devotions, and printed in gothic type often on vellum. The decoration, based on the two-page opening, continued the tradition of earlier illuminated manuscript copies. Floriated and historiated borders with criblé backgrounds extended to page edges. Much of Pigouchet's work was imitated by Thielmann Kerver who also worked in Paris as a printer of Books of Hours.

Note. The floruit date 1488–1526 comes from E. G. Duff's 'Century of the English book trade', 1905; however, in 'Le Livre français', 1948, R. Brun gives the years when Pigouchet was active as 'de 1488 à 1512 environ'. He is not known for his Horae after 1505.

pigskin: a strong, distinctively-grained leather used for covering heavy books which may also be given wooden boards. Decoration is most satisfactory when blind stamped, and alum-tawed pigskin was much used for *blind-stamped panel* bindings, q.v. See also *peau de truie, peccary*.

pilcher: a wad of three or four felts sewn together which is placed on top of a *post*, q.v., before pressing wet hand-made paper.

pile: a pile of paper placed on a transfer platform, feeder or delivery table. *Pile feeder* and *pile delivery* are the names for apparatus which conveys sheets to the press from the pile of paper, or delivers them when printed from the press to a pile. *Pile reversers* are used for turning a whole pile of paper upside down, e.g. for *perfecting*, q.v.   (GU)

piling: a fault in offset lithography which occurs when coating particles from coated stock or mineral particles from uncoated stock accumulate on the blanket. Abrasion of the printing plate results.

Correction lies with the papermaker rather than the pressman. Paper should be well bonded and be given a coating which is not too water soluble.

pillar: a good-quality paper made in Normandy between *c.* 1610 and 1680, and in only one size, 12½in. by 16in. A pillar was the watermark.

Pillone, Odorico, 1503–94: an Italian jurist and book collector of Belluno. He is important for the library he inherited and developed, notable for its bindings. Some sixty books, printed in Italy between 1474 and 1502, were in the half-bound style with blind-tooled morocco spine and wooden sides. Slightly later were bindings in full morocco over wooden boards with bosses and clasps. These were probably bought by or made for *Antonio Pillone* (1464–1533), the soldier-statesman father of Odorico. There was also a group of German blind-stamped bindings, all pre-1550, forty-three in pigskin over boards.

Many of the later books, printed between 1575 and 1591, were covered in vellum decorated with ink and wash scenes of landscapes with figures extending almost to the edges of the boards. They were the work of Cesare Vecellio (a cousin and pupil of Titian) and others. About 1580 Pillone appears to have commissioned Vecellio to paint the fore-edges of his books with portraits, interior scenes, or floral motifs. (They were not disappearing paintings in the manner of *Edwards of Halifax*, q.v.) It will be remembered that until the end of the 16th century books faced outwards on the shelves and that the titles were lettered in ink on the fore-edges.

In 1874 Odorico's descendants sold the library, many of the painted bindings being bought by Sir Thomas Brooke who included them in the catalogue of his library issued in 1891. His heirs sold them in 1957 when Pierre Berès of Paris bought 171 Pillone bindings. Three were stolen en route to Paris. Berès issued a beautiful catalogue of the exhibition he held of them in the same year.

pilot: an atlas of maritime charts. Notable was the work of the 17th century publisher John Sellar and his colleagues Fisher and Thornton. See C. Verner, 'A Carto-bibliographical study of *The English Pilot*', University of Virginia Press, 1960. See also *periplus*.

pinax (pl. **pinakes**): a Greek word (now rarely used) for a board or tablet on which was written a list, catalogue, or index. The term originated with Kallimachos, librarian of the Alexandrian Library, *c.* 260–240 BC, who made an annotated catalogue in 120 volumes of the works in the library. How the entries were arranged is now a matter for conjecture since no evidence survives, but the *pinakes* laid the foundation for the first critical study of Greek literature.

Pinelli, Gian Vicenzio, 1538–1601: a famous Italian book-collector who established in Padua a library at which the bibliophiles of the day held meetings. After his death Pinelli's library suffered a curious fate. Nearly 300 manuscripts were confiscated for the St Mark's Library, Venice, while most of the remaining works were loaded in three ships bound for Naples (his birthplace). Pirates seized one ship, and the contents of the other two were bought by Cardinal Borromeo for his Ambrosiana Library in Milan. A small residue of the original collection had been kept in Padua by Pinelli's relatives. Successive generations developed this once more into an important library. On the death of Maffeo Pinelli the collection was brought to London by James Edwards and auctioned in 1789 and 1790 for £9,356.

pinholes: 1. small holes in a sheet of paper made by short pins or *points* attached to the sides of a tympan frame on a hand press. When the sheet is laid on the tympan prior to printing, and the frisket is folded over to secure it, the pins make holes in it. When, after being allowed to dry out, the sheet is turned to print the back, register is ensured by easing the pinholes on the pins.

The use by the earliest printers of a hinged tympan frame to carry pins has not been confirmed by evidence, the hinged tympan not being known before the first quarter of the 16th century. But the use of pins began with the 42-line Bible for which it is thought that as many as ten were positioned, four at the top of the leaf, four at the bottom, and two on the outer margin. By 1474 Schöffer had already changed from four to two, and he stopped using them in early 1477. Caxton used four in his earliest works. The number of pinholes can thus be a help in deciding at what stage in his career an early printer issued an undated work.

Several books on printing, from Moxon onwards, describe the use of points and give a diagram of them. In a folio the pinholes may be seen in the fold, near the top and bottom of the leaves. In octavos they were made in what, after folding, became the outer edge and were often trimmed off. In quartos the pin-holes would be made in the top edge of a folded sheet and would disappear during trimming.

2. small holes which occur in paper when *shiners*, q.v., or similar solid contraries drop out during calendering.

pin-mark: a round depression in the side of a shank of typefounder's type made by the pin which ejects the type from the mould.

pin seal: the fine-grained skin of the young seal used for costly bindings.

pin seal morocco: goatskin hand-grained to resemble *pin seal*, q.v.

pinxit: a Latin word meaning 'he painted it'. It is found after the artist's name on coloured engravings and elsewhere, often shortened to 'pinx.'.

Pipe Roll Society: a society founded in 1883 for the printing of Pipe Rolls, charters and national manuscripts prior to 1200. (The Pipe, or Great, Roll was the document commenced in 1131 on which were entered in a large set hand the accounts due to the King from his lands and services.)

PIRA: the abbreviated name of the Paper & Board, Printing & Packaging Industries Research Association which was formed in 1967 by the merger of the Printing, Packaging & Allied Trades Research Association (PATRA) with the British Paper & Board Industry Research Association.

pirated edition: an edition of a work published without the permission of the copyright owner. Cf. *authorized edition*.

PIRA test: see *leather preservation*.

Pirckheimer, Bilibald: 1470–1530: a wealthy citizen and *Rat* of Nuremberg. He appears to have begun book-collecting when studying in Padua, 1490–97, and his books included much Latin and Italian literature. He returned to Nuremberg where his library came to be the most important in Germany and was made available to scholars. About 1501 he met *Albrecht Dürer*, q.v., and Conrad Celtes, while his house became a literary and artistic centre. Dürer designed at least two bookplates for Pirckheimer, one for quarto and one for folio volumes. Pirckheimer translated and published several Greek and Latin authors including Ptolemy's 'Geographia', Strasbourg, 1522.

His library survived him intact for about a hundred years but in 1636 was sold to *Thomas Howard*, Earl of Arundel, q.v. It passed in turn to his nephew, Henry Howard, Duke of Norfolk, who gave part of his uncle's library to the newly formed Royal Society and part to the College of Arms. The manuscripts in it were sold to the British Museum in 1830, while the non-scientific volumes (including the Pirckheimer books) were sold to Bernard Quaritch in 1870 and have since been dispersed.

Pissarro, Lucien, 1863–1944: see *Eragny Press*.

Pistorius, Cyriakus, *c.* 1629–*c.* 1690: a famous typefounder of Basle, whose business was taken over in 1692 by his son *Johannes* (1664–1730), and in 1770 by *Wilhelm Haas*, q.v.

Pitt Press: a building erected for Cambridge University Press in 1831 with the surplus subscriptions for the statue of the younger Pitt, a Cambridge student, erected in Hanover Square.

plagiarism: the copying of another person's writings and publishing the material copied as original matter.

planer: a slab of hard wood used to level the type in a chase by placing it on the surface and tapping it with a mallet.

planetary signs: see *astronomical symbols*.

planing machine: a machine for adjusting flat stereotype plates to an exact thickness.

plank: the heavy piece of hardwood (often mahogany) to which the *coffin* and *stone*, qq.v., of a hand-printing press were fixed. The plank rested on rails fitted to the carriage, the whole (i.e. forme, stone, coffin, and plank) being drawn under the platen by turning the *rounce*, q.v.

Plannck, Stephan, fl.1480–1500: of Passau. About 1480 he began printing in Rome, probably acquiring the press of *Ulrich Han*, q.v. Plannck (whose name is sometimes given as Planke) became a leading printer of Rome. He issued a magnificent Missale Romanum in 1496 and about three hundred mostly small works before 1500. He printed books on astronomy and mathematics, notable being John Sherwood's 'Ludo arithmomachiae', *c.* 1482.

planographic printing: printing from level surfaces prepared so that the parts to be printed accept ink from the rollers while the non-image areas reject it. The image areas are greasy, the rest moist, utilizing the mutual repulsion of grease and water (the principle of lithography).

Printing is by the even pressure of a hand-roller or

cylinder over the flat plate, or by offsetting the image from a curved plate on to a rubber roller and thence to the paper. Even colour is a characteristic of planographic printing. Also known as *surface printing*. See also *lithography*, *photolithography*.

plant-free reprint: an impression taken from standing type or plates after recovering initial costs. In explaining this term Longman, one of Britain's oldest publishing houses, stated 'we use the expression "plant" to cover all the initial costs of printing a book, i.e. composition, illustrations, making of blocks, making of moulds, casting of plates. Usually everything except the making of plates is charged to the first printing which is run from type. We charge the casting of plates and the insertion therein of the blocks to the second printing. On the third printing there are none of these charges to be met, since they have all been paid and plates exist: this is what we call a "plant-free reprint".'

Plantin, Christopher, *c.*1520–89: bookbinder, printer and publisher, born near Tours in France. After apprenticeship at Caen to the royal printer Robert Macé II he stayed briefly in Paris before moving in 1548 to Antwerp, then Europe's leading centre of publishing, learning and commerce. Before setting up as a printer in 1555 Plantin worked as a leather-box maker and binder, being one of several French and Italian craftsmen to pioneer gold tooling and inlaid binding techniques in the Low Countries. Until 1562 he continued to bind books for a few important clients; thereafter he provided materials for the twenty or so binders he employed. They worked in a simple style on brown calf, with gilt edges, a double fillet frame on the boards, and small gilt corner fleurons. Other printer-publishers in Antwerp issued editions in similar bindings.

His first printed book was an edition of Giovanni Bruto's 'La institutione di una fanciulla nata nobilmente' with parallel Italian and French texts, 1555. In time he became one of the most notable printers in Europe and had the valuable monopoly for supplying liturgical books to Spain and its colonies. Of importance was his Polyglot Bible (or *Biblia regia*) in eight volumes, 1569–72, commissioned and partly financed by Philip II of Spain for whom thirteen sets were printed on vellum. The general issue of twelve hundred sets was printed on paper.

Other works from the twenty-one presses he owned by the late 1560s included dictionaries, scientific writings and Waghenaer's famous 'Spieghel de Zeevaerdt', Leyden, 1584–5. He printed in all 1,500 works: a prodigious number for a 16th century business. He also supplied paper and other printing materials.

When Plantin began printing, woodcut book illustrations were the norm, but from 1570 his increas-

ing use of copperplate illustrations led to their general adoption in the Low Countries and France. His principal designers and engravers included Pierre and François Huys, Pierre van der Borcht, Abraham de Bruyn, Martin de Vos and the Wiericx brothers (see also *Rubens*). He continued, however, to use woodcuts for tail-pieces, devices and initial capitals. Of the latter he used nineteen sets, outclassing in design and workmanship those of other printers. They included the roman, greek and hebrew grotesque initials, cut 1570–73, used in the Polyglot Bible. Plantin had sixty-eight versions of his device, a hand holding a compass with the legend 'Labore et Constantia' on a ribbon (one is illustrated under *device*, q.v.)

Plantin never owned a foundry, buying and selling strikes or matrices on his regular visits to Frankfurt Fair. Strikes were finished for him at Antwerp or Ghent and cast by local founders, probably from metal he supplied. Among punchcutters represented in his vast stock of types were Granjon, Guyot, Haultin, Le Bé, Keere and Sabon.

The old face type which Monotype issued in 1913 as Plantin, series 110, was based on a Grosse Mediane Romaine by Robert Granjon. Plantin may not have owned the original matrices, but in 1567 he used some of the characters to modify a Garamond roman. Monotype Plantin is a somewhat heavy face with a large x-height and thick serifs. It is excellent for letterpress on coated stock. See C. Clair, 'Christopher Plantin', Cassell, 1960; W. Godenne, 'Les Reliures de Plantin', Bruxelles, 1965; and L. Voet, 'The golden compasses . . .', 2 vols, Amsterdam, van Gendt, 1969–73. See also *Moretus*, *Plantin-Moretus Museum*, *specimen sheet*.

Plantin-Moretus Museum: the museum established in the printing house of Christopher Plantin and his successors the Moretus family.

The last dated work of the Plantin press was issued in 1866 by which time the Moretus family had more important business interests. Rather than disperse the unique material assembled through the centuries it was decided to preserve it as a museum and in 1876 it was acquired by the city of Antwerp. The first curator was Max Rooses (d. 1914). In addition to the printing material and archives there is a library of 20,000 volumes plus manuscripts and drawings.

plaquette: a small tablet of bronze or lead, circular or oval in shape, bearing on one side a design in relief of a classical or religious subject. They were made by casting in a mould and were fashionable in Italy as ornaments for boxes, sword pommels, and caps between roughly 1450–1550, the best being made in Rome.

Among other collectors the French bibliophile Jean Grolier had a group of ornamented bindings stamped directly on the leather by dies used for plaquettes: they were then painted. They are believed to be of Milanese workmanship of the period 1510–13. See also *cameo bindings, Grimaldi*.

plaster-moulding process: the preparation of stereos by pressing a film of moist plaster on to a forme or block; a skilled operation which gives results of great detail. The mould of plaster is then prepared for casting.

plastic binding: see *spirex binding*.

plastic plates: printing stereos made from any of several plastic materials. They should be 12-point thick. Advantages are lightness and good resistance to chemical deterioration by inks and cleaning solvents. The printing image is less liable to damage by rough use and long runs than in metal plates. See also *thermoplastic plates*.

Plastocowell: a reproduction process developed by W. S. Cowell Ltd, of Ipswich. The artist makes his drawing or painting in Photopake (a retouching paste) on a transparent grained plastic film. The paste contains fine opaque particles, and the concentration of these in any given area affects the strength of the tint. One sheet is made for each colour.

The plastic sheet is laid on a sensitized zinc plate, whereupon exposure to light prints the image on the metal which can be used for a lithographic forme or a letterpress line block in the usual way.

The absence of a photographic screen is a distinct advantage over normal photo-litho methods, and the elimination of hand-retouching is both more economical and, from the artist's viewpoint, more aesthetically satisfying. Various drawing techniques are employed and the possibilities are limited only by the artist's skill and understanding of the medium.

plate: 1. an electro or stereo of set-up type.
2. wood, metal, rubber, or plastic bearing an image to be printed.
3. a full-page book illustration, printed separately from the text, and often on different paper. Cf. *figure*.
4. a photographic plate; whole, $8\frac{1}{2}$in. by $6\frac{1}{2}$in.; half, $6\frac{1}{2}$in. by $4\frac{3}{4}$in. See also *interleaved* (2) and (3).

plate-boring machine: a machine for reducing curved stereotype plates to a required thickness. The boring machine may be intended solely for boring, or may comprise a complete finishing machine which also cools the plates. See also *casting box, router*.

plate cylinder: the cylinder to which *plate* (2), q.v., is fixed for printing.

plate-dogs: bevelled clips for holding blocks, stereos, etc., firmly in position on the plate cylinder of a rotary press. The clips slide in grooves.

plated paper: paper made of new and old rags, together with clay: it has good printing qualities for copper engravings, etchings, and photogravures, but is not strong. It is usually unsized, and there is often a considerable difference between the two sides of the sheet. (ML)

plate finish (or **plate glazed**): the smooth surface given to sheets of paper by interleaving them with polished copper or zinc plates and then pressing them between chilled iron rollers.

plate folder: synonymous with *buckle folder*. See *folding machine*.

Platemakers Educational & Research Institute: an American research organization founded in 1945 when it was known as Photoengravers Research. In 1959 a laboratory was opened at Park Forest, Illinois. Recognizing that the trend in printing industries is away from platemaking for one process exclusively, the name of the institute was changed in 1968. Thereafter its research programme and facilities were expanded to permit studies of problems faced by platemakers dealing with all printing processes. These have included the one-bite powderless deep etching of combination half-tone and line images on copper, colour proofing, and the production of intermediate colour transparencies. This last involves the creation of colour positive or negative images of customers' copy in correct relative size and position, with density ranges adjusted to fit the characteristics of the printing process. This has been named the *PERI Intertron system*.

Other work has been the establishment of formulae to correlate ink tack with ink film thickness, and the study of variations between the transfer characteristics of oil-based proofing inks and heat-set production press inks.

plate mark: a line depressed into the paper by the edges of an intaglio engraved plate during printing.

platen press: the earliest hand-printing presses and their many improved successors were platen presses, since they had a heavy flat plate, or *platen*, which was lowered and pressed against a horizontal type forme. Modern platen presses are non-cylinder machines in which the forme of type is held on a flat bed (which may be sloping or standing vertically). They have inkers which, in small American presses, are in the form of rotating discs, while European models usually have cylindrical inkers, their movements being automatically connected with the motion of the platen. Printing is done on a platen which is a square steel slab covered with sheets of paper over which a final sheet is stretched. This packing and its enclosing frame, known as the tympan, serve to equalize pressure. Sheets of paper to be printed are fed singly

Liberty press, 1857

and held to the tympan by guide pins or frisket fingers. Mechanical action then moves the flat surface of the paper-bearing platen into contact with the forme and an impression is made.

Small presses may be actuated by a hand lever (table presses) or, if floor standing, by a treadle (treadle presses), but these are no longer common. Some powered machines have hand-feeding, which may be necessary for some of the multiple jobs done on them,

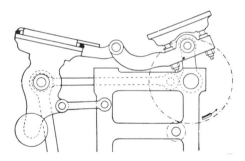

Diagram of the Liberty press

but the popular *Heidelberg* and *Thompson-British Automatic Platen* and similar machines have automatic feed and delivery, locking register devices, geared inkers, automatic wash-up and anti-set-off arrangements.

Historical note. The first attempt to make a platen *machine* (i.e. neither treadle nor hand operated) was made at Suhl by Friedrich König in 1804. It was unsaleable. In 1810 he and his partner Bauer patented in London a steam-driven platen press with automatic inkers, tympan and frisket mechanism. It was used experimentally by Bensley in 1811 to print a sheet of the *Annual Register*, the first part of any book,

384

claimed Bauer, to be printed by a *machine*. It was not developed.

Through the years others in America, Germany and Britain devised platen machines. Isaac Adams of Boston made his first powered bed and platen

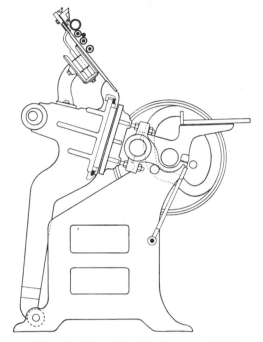

The principle of the Gordon press, 1856

machine in 1830, to be improved in 1836. For some years it was widely used for book printing.

The *Liberty* press of Friedrich Otto Degener of Hanover was patented in the U.S.A. in 1857. In it the bed and platen swung towards each other on a

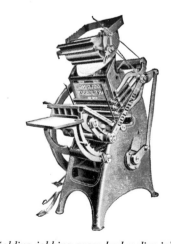

The Golding jobbing press had a disc inker, 1874

common axle, like a hinge. George Phineas Gordon of New York began making jobbing platen presses about 1850, (*Yankee Job, Alligator*). His most successful press was the treadle operated *Franklin* of 1856 (to which the name *Gordon* was usually given). It

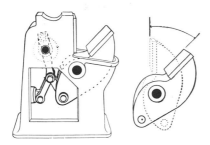

The knee-lever and platen motion of a Heidelberg

had a revolving disc inker and achieved impression when bed and platen were in a nearly vertical position (see diagram). By the end of the 19th century several firms offered presses on the Gordon principle. In England it was made from 1867 by H. S. Cropper & Co. and named the *Minerva*. The *Craftsman Automaton* for half-tone work was made by Chandler & Price who in 1901 acquired the Gordon business.

The *Gally*, or *Universal* press, invented in New York by J. M. Gally in 1869, was the first to be fitted with fountain, distributor and forme rollers. It had a stationary bed and a platen which rolled to a vertical position and then glided forward so that immediately before impression the platen was parallel to the bed and moving perpendicularly towards it. A successor to it was the *Victoria*, imported into Germany by Schelter and Giesecke of Leipzig who renamed it *Phoenix*.

The movement of the platen and its pressure against the forme can be effected in various ways; the knee-lever motion of the Heidelberg is shown in the diagram. It is common to utilize a crank movement in connection with a friction-coupled flywheel as in the Victoria.

To secure an even motion free from vibration, and accurate impression, both platen and bed must be well proportioned: in large machines the latter is cast with the floor stand. (With GU)

plating: 1. a printers' term for the preparation of stereotype or electrotype plates from set-up type.

2. see *guarding*.

plenarium: see *Missale plenarium*.

Pleydenwurff, Wilhelm, fl.1491–95: an artist of Nuremberg. He was the stepson of Michael Wolgemut with whom he was associated in designing the 1,809 illustrations for Schedel's 'Die Weltchronik', 1493.

Plomer, Henry Robert, 1856–1928: an Assistant Keeper at the British Museum, who made valuable researches into the history of printing in England during the 16th century. Many of his writings were published by the Bibliographical Society in *The Library*, or as separate monographs.

Important was 'A dictionary of booksellers and printers who were at work in England from 1641 to 1667', 1907 (supplement, 1668–1725, 1922); and 'Wynkyn de Worde and his contemporaries', Grafton, 1925.

plough: a hand-machine used to cut the edges of a book. While still used for the edge-trimming of hand-bound books, elsewhere the quicker, but possibly less accurate *guillotine*, q.v., is used.

PLR: see *Public Lending Right*.

plucking: a printing fault which is caused by the ink plucking the surface of the paper and leaving irregular white patches in printed areas. The main causes of this are either too stiff an ink, or the surface fibres of the paper being too loosely bonded. See also *featherweight paper*.

pneumatic press: a press in which compressed air is used to apply pressure. Such presses are used for several purposes in mechanized binderies. Unless extreme pressure is called for they are speedier and cleaner than *hydraulic presses*, q.v. (LK)

pochoir: the French name for a hand-coloured illustration process used in its essentials as long ago as the early 15th century to print playing cards and occasionally woodcuts in books. It was revived by the French in the late 19th century and by Curwen Press in the 1920s, but the hand work involved makes it too costly for modern book production.

The foundation was a monochrome outline of the design printed by letterpress or lithography. As many as twenty to thirty celluloid stencils were cut out for the various parts of the design, and special brushes with gouache and watercolours were used for colouring. Fresh and brilliant results were obtained.

pocket edition: a small octavo edition, usually not larger than foolscap octavo: $6\frac{3}{4}$in. by $4\frac{1}{4}$in.

Poeschel, Carl Ernst, 1874–1944: a printer and sometime publisher of Leipzig. He entered his father's printing firm Poeschel & Trepte, founded in 1870, and devoted himself to reviving in Germany the art of fine book-printing much as did Morris in England. He had various roman types of former days re-cut for his use, many by his friend Walter Tiemann.

In 1905 he took over, as a joint venture with Anton Kippenberg, the Insel-Verlag, which was noted for its fine typography and well-produced low-priced editions. In 1907 he founded the *Janus-Presse*, q.v.

Poet Laureate: a title and pension bestowed by the Sovereign upon an eminent poet who is expected to compose commemorative poems for national occasions. The first to receive a warrant from the King formally granting him the Office of Poet Laureate was John Dryden in 1668, though Ben Johnson, Sir William Davenant, and other former poets had styled themselves and been known by this title. The prototype for such an office is found in the *versificator regis* of the 13th century and the court minstrels of still earlier times. Holders of the office have been:

John Dryden	1668–88
Thomas Shadwell	1688–92
Nahum Tate	1692–1715
Nicholas Rowe	1715–18
Laurence Eusden	1718–30
Colley Cibber	1730–57
William Whitehead	1757–85
Thomas Wharton	1785–90
Henry James Pye	1790–1813
Robert Southey	1813–43
William Wordsworth	1843–50
Alfred Tennyson	1850–92
Alfred Austin	1896–1913
Robert Bridges	1913–30
John Masefield	1930–67
Cecil Day Lewis	1968–72
John Betjeman	1972–

Poetry Book Society: a body established in 1954, under the auspices of the Arts Council of Great Britain, to bring to the notice of its members 'the best English poetry being written today'. The annual subscription is used as a deposit against which members receive newly published volumes of poetry.

Poggio, 1380–1459: properly *Poggio Bracciolini*, but known by his first name as was the custom of the time. He was a scholar, scribe and notary whose searches for ancient manuscripts led to the recovery of many long-neglected classical texts. At St Gall he found the entire works of Quintilian; elsewhere he found hitherto unknown works by Cicero, Lucretius, Petronius, Plutarch, and Vitruvius. His 'instinct seemed to lead him unerringly to his target like a pig to truffles . . . his haul was prodigious' (Plumb. 'Penguin book of the Renaissance'). He came to England but found nothing of interest in the libraries he visited.

About 1400 Poggio worked in Florence, moving to Rome in 1403 as *scriptor apostolicus*. He copied some manuscripts himself, for others employing copyists, and sent the results to Florence for rubricating and binding. The patrons for whom copies were made

included Niccolò (*c.* 1364–1437) who was also a copier of texts in a fine *lettera corsiva* script, and Cosimo de' Medici (1389–1446) who was his patron, as of other humanists.

One result of his discoveries was that between 1447 and 1471 the popes Nicholas V and Sixtus IV secured the rarest MSS for the foundation of the Vatican Library: notable were the Greek classics, obtained after the fall of Constantinople, on which teams of copyists were to labour for years.

Another of Poggio's enduring contributions was his use of a formal book hand based on Carolingian originals. This was the *littera antiqua formata* which later served as an exemplar for the earliest roman types. A copy of Cicero's 'Epist. ad Atticum' which Poggio signed and dated in 1408 shows this script: it is now in Berlin, Staatsbibliothek (MS. Hamilton 166).

Still more important was the recognition of works by Cicero, Plutarch and Quintilian as basic guide books to educational reform, at first by Italian humanists in the 15th century, and by Erasmus, Vives and others north of the Alps a century later.

Poggio's 'Liber facetiarum' (facetiae), a collection of 273 coarsely humorous stories, was first made public in 1451. Translations of a French version of some of the stories were included by Caxton in his edition of Aesop, 1484. See 'Two Renaissance book hunters: the letters of Poggius Bracciolini to Nicolaus de Niccolis', Trans. by P. W. Gordan, Columbia U.P., 1974.

point: the unit for measuring type, approximately seventy-two points equalling one linear inch. Former type size names such as nonpareil, brevier, pica, have as their equivalents 6-, 8-, and 12-point.

The Parisian typefounder *Fournier*, q.v., gave the name *point* to the unit of measurement he introduced in 1742. One point equalled 0·0136 in. Another Parisian, *Didot*, q.v., began about 1784 to cast type on bodies which were multiples of a unit he called a *metre*. This was later known as the *Didot point*, of which one equalled 0·0148in. His scale of measurements was generally used by French founders from the early 19th century and later by German founders.

The American point system, with a unit of 0·0138in., was originated about 1872 by the Chicago typefoundry of Merder, Luce & Co. Their system was generally adopted by American founders in 1886 and by British in 1898. See also *body* (2), *cicero*, *height to paper*, *line gauge*, *long-bodied type*, *Mediaan*, *millimétrique*, *parts of type*, *type sizes*.

point holes: see *pinholes*.

pointillé: dotted tooling, a decorative style which originated in France about 1630 and was used by many French binders, notably Florimond Badier and

Macé Ruette. Spirals and the outlines of flowers were done in minute gold dots, giving an effect of lightness to the whole design.

point moulding: making a stereotype mould by passing the forme of type and moulding material under a heavy steel cylinder which gives concentrated pressure at the point of contact, not over the whole forme at one instant. See also *stereotype*.

points: short pins in the sides of a tympan which pierce the sheets to ensure the pages will be in register when they are backed up.

Poitevin, Alphonse Louis, 1813–82: the French inventor, in 1855, of *carbon tissue*, q.v., the use of which was developed by J. W. Swan between 1862 and 1864.

Polain, Marie-Louis, 1866–1933: of Liège; a bibliographer who worked in France as a cataloguer of several private collections and is remembered for a list of 4,000 incunabula located in Belgian libraries, Brussels, 1932. Polain continued the catalogue of incunabula in French libraries begun by *Pellechet*, q.v.

polaires: leather satchels used by 6th century Irish monks for carrying books. They were usually undecorated but sometimes bore a design stamped in relief. Illustrated under *bookbinding*.

Polidori Press: a private press established near Regent's Park, London, about 1840, by Gaetano Polidori. He was head of the London firm which in 1796 published an Italian translation of 'Paradise Lost'. The first work issued was Polidori's Italian translation of Milton's works, 3 vols, 1840. He also printed early verses written by his grandchildren Dante Gabriel and Christina Rossetti (1843 and 1847). The press appears to have ceased activity about 1850, and Polidori died in 1854.

poligrafi: as 'i poligrafi', professional writers in Italy who in the 16th century were adept in assembling popular literary anthologies, and in writing to order on any topic, sometimes by paraphrasing earlier writers. Some were printers or were employed by them to feed the presses during slack periods. Noteworthy was Lodovico Dolce (1505–68) fifty of whose works are listed in the British Library catalogue. He worked for *Giolito*, q.v.

polished calf: calfskin which is given a high finish for use in fine bookbinding.

Pollard, Alfred William, 1859–1944: Keeper of the Department of Printed Books, British Museum 1919–24, and Secretary of the Bibliographical Society from 1893 to 1944 who contributed important studies to our knowledge of early printed books. Many of his writings were published by the Society in *The Library*; other studies appeared as 'Fine books', Putnam, 1912, and 'Early illustrated books', Kegan Paul, 1917. See also *Short-title catalogue*.

polyautography: the name by which *lithography*, q.v., was known in early 19th-century England.

polychromatic printing: the name given by William Savage to the *chiaroscuro* process, q.v., which he revived in the 19th century.

polyglot edition: a book, or series of books, giving versions of one text in several languages. For purposes of comparison the text may be set in columns across two facing pages. The Bible is the text which has been most frequently treated in this way, and Aldus planned a version in Hebrew, Greek and Latin, issuing verses from Genesis as a specimen between 1498 and 1501. Next came the 'Psalterium quadrilingue' of Paulus Porro, Genoa, 1516. The first complete printed polyglot Bible was the 'Biblia polyglotta Complutensis', printed 1514–17 by Arnao Guillen de Brocar at Alcalá de Henares (Complutum) for Cardinal Ximines, but not published until 1522. Plantin's polyglot Bible had texts in Hebrew, Greek, Latin, Chaldaic, and Syriac; it appeared 1569–72. The Paris polyglot of 1645, sponsored by Michel Le Jay, added Arabic and Samaritan to Plantin's text. It was printed by Antoine Vitré who began work on the first of its ten volumes in 1628.

Brian Walton (1600–61) was the editor of the great London polyglot issued as 'Biblia sacra polyglotta', 1654–7. It was printed by Thomas Roycroft and had fine engraved title-pages by Wenzel Hollar. The orientalist Edward Pococke (1604–91) was the principal adviser and scholar who prepared the text. A supplementary 'Lexicon' by Edmund Castell was issued in 1669. Walton's Bible interested Oliver Cromwell, and by his permission paper for printing it was imported duty free. The Protector was thanked in the preface, but after the Restoration the two-line passage was cancelled in unsold copies, words more appropriate to the times being substituted. Hence the distinction between 'Republican' and 'Loyal' copies, the latter being more numerous.

polyptych: a codex consisting of more than three hinged waxed leaves.

polyurethane roller: see *inking roller*.

polyvinyl alcohol enamel: a photoengraving resist used for coating zinc or copper half-tone plates.

pond: the box at the 'wet end' of a papermaking machine in which the pulp is contained until it is flowed on to the moving wire to be formed into paper.

Pontifical: a book containing the ceremonies and offices to be performed by bishops.

Ponton, Mungo, 1802–80: an Edinburgh scientist who invented a cheap and simple method of preparing paper for photographic work without the use of a silver salt. He made the discovery that the action of light renders potassium dichromate insoluble: this meant that unexposed portions of a plate could be washed away with water and was fundamental to subsequent photo-mechanical reproduction processes.

pope roll: a moving roller at the 'dry end' of a Fourdrinier where the paper is reeled. Also called *drum reel-up*.

pornography: originally, a term restricted to descriptions of harlotry, but now extended to include all books having as their principal object the titillation of the sensualist. Such works are described as *obscene* when they have a tendency to corrupt and deprave people whose minds are open to such influences. The literary merits of many pornographic books are often slight, but large private collections have been made notably in France and Germany: that in the British Library is inaccessible to those unable to satisfy the authorities that they need to consult it for scholarly research. See also *erotica*.

portas: a medieval Breviary written on thin vellum and of small size so that it could be carried conveniently by a travelling friar. By extension the name was given to small manuals of philosophy and other subjects.

The word is also found as *portace*, *portiforium*, and *porthors*; thus Chaucer's 'Shipman's tale', line 135, 'By God and by this Porthors I yow swere'.

portolano: a development of the *periplus*, q.v. A portolano, made by and for seamen, was a projectionless plane sea chart with an equidistant latitude scale but no longitudinal markings. It showed the outlines of coasts and indicated wind directions by loxodromes or rhumb lines, the point of their intersection being a *wind rose*, q.v. Some charts had simple colouring, with place names written at right angles to the landward side of the coastline.

One of the earliest to survive, from about 1295, is in the BN, Paris, while an early dated portolano was that of Petrus Vesconte of Genoa who was a professional map-maker. It was dated 1311. By the late 14th century they sometimes included drawings of harbours and showed trade routes; some, too, were in atlas form.

Most surviving examples belong to the 14th and 15th centuries and are on parchment or vellum. They originated in Italy, Spain and Portugal and were charts of the Mediterranean: later they were made for other areas. They also lost their utilitarian simplicity and became lavish works of art to decorate the rooms of wealthy landsmen.

Portolani were also known as *compass charts*, *rhumb charts*, *sea charts* or *ruttier books*. For a list of the better known portolano makers see R. V. Tooley, 'Maps and map-makers', 6th ed., Batsford, 1978.

positive reversal process: see *deep-etch process*.

post: a pile of wet sheets of paper, interleaved with felts, formed on the couch by the coucher when he removes them from the mould in hand-papermaking. He may be assisted by an *upper end boy*, q.v. The post, usually of six quires, is then covered with a final layer of felts (called a *pilcher*) and pressed. For subsequent treatment see *pack*.

posthumous: said of a work which is first published after the author's death.

pot cassé: the line drawing of an urn pierced by a drill (Fr. *toret*) which, with the words NON PLUS, was used from 1524 by *Geofroy Tory*, q.v., as his symbolic device. Its meaning is explained in his 'Champ Fleury', 1529. The symbol also formed part of his designs for tooled book covers (Tory did not bind books himself), graceful arabesques flowing from and around it to fill the panels. Tory used ten versions of his device, and later Parisian booksellers adopted it, notably O. Mallard.

potcher: a modified form of *breaker*, q.v. It is a machine fitted with a washing drum in which rags and also esparto, after being boiled in a separate machine, are washed for some hours and are then broken by the machine's beater roll. Preliminary chemical bleaching can also be done here. The resulting *half-stuff* is put in a draining pit where it is left for a week to soften. It is then ready for putting in the *beater*, q.v. See also *deflaker*, *Hollander*.

pouncing: 1. the final stage in the preparation of parchment in which it is well rubbed with powdered chalk or resin (gum Sandarach) to give it whiteness and smoothness for writing upon.

2. the rubbing of tracing paper with pumice powder to roughen the surface slightly. This is done when the faintly greasy surface of paper will not properly accept the ink of pen drawings.

powdered: the effect obtained on a book cover when small tools are impressed in regular rows over it.

Early examples were made for François I and Henri IV, the fleur-de-lis or an initial being usual motifs. Also known as *semis* or *semé*. See also *repetition bindings*.

powdering: a printing fault in which the vehicle and pigment separate after printing, leaving the latter loosely on the surface of the paper. The cause may be an unduly mobile ink or an over-absorbent paper.

powderless etching: a quick and automatic etching method for giving copper, magnesium or zinc line and half-tone plates a clean relief image by a single acid bite. The traditional powdered acid resist (*dragon's blood*, q.v.) is not used.

This alternative technique employs a powderless etching machine of which there are several proprietary models. Common to most are a stainless-steel or plastic tank fitted with a series of speed-controlled jets or paddles, a rotatable plate-holder, a pump to keep the etching chemicals mixed, a heating and cooling system, a piped water supply, and a control panel. The various chemicals used, some of which etch while others protect the image sidewall from undercutting, are chosen according to the metal of the plate.

The machine operates by spraying etching fluid from an angle of about 90° against the rotating plate. This disintegrates the surface of the non-image areas and, as etching proceeds, cuts down the shoulders of the image.

Although quick, a successful etch depends on skilfully controlling the factors which produce it, i.e. chemicals, temperature, paddle speed or jet force, and time. See also *Dow etching machine*, *photo-engraving*.

Powell, Roger, b. 1896; an outstanding British book-binder. Not until 1930 did his serious study of book-binding begin: in that year he attended the Central School of Arts and Crafts in London. A year later he set up a bindery at Welwyn Garden City, and in 1935 became a partner of Douglas Cockerell at Letchworth. Between 1943 and 1956 he taught binding at the Royal College of Art.

In 1947 he opened his own workshop at Petersfield in Hampshire where his former pupil, Peter Waters, joined him in partnership. The principal activity of the workshop has always been the restoration and rebinding of books and manuscripts for libraries. Notable examples of his skill in this work include the Book of Kells and the Book of Durrow. His fine bindings are in major collections and libraries. See D. A. Harrop, 'Craft binders at work III: Roger Powell', *Book Collector*, Winter 1973, 479–486.

prebinding: the giving by a library trade supplier of a strong binding as an alternative to the publisher's case. This is done on new books in bulk before libraries receive, process and use them. Thus the term is distinguishable from *rebinding* which, in library usage, refers to the recovering of used books.

Books are made more durable by oversewing the sections, reinforcing end-papers with cloth hinges prior to sewing (not gluing) them to the book, strengthening the corners, and bonding a plastic film to the cloth covering material. Although the work is largely mechanical hand operations are also used. See also *Library Binding Institute*.

pre-coated plates: factory-coated litho plates which are insensitive to light and can be stored without difficulty. When required for use a liquid sensitizing solution is washed over the plate and dried. It is then ready for exposure.

precon: a tape which has been pre-conditioned by encoding whatever formatting instructions are needed for a particular job specification, e.g. justified, paragraph indented, flush right, tight set copy. The use of precons minimizes keyboarding and speeds up computerized composition. See also *computer-assisted typesetting*.

pre-correction: in photosetting, the operating procedures carried out before a punched tape is fed into the photo unit.

preface: the author's personal remarks to the reader which sometimes conclude with a paragraph of acknowledgements. It is usual to write a new preface to successive editions, outlining the extent of changes and additions. Previous prefaces may or may not be included, if so they should follow the latest. Cf. *foreword*, *introduction*. See also *lectori*.

preliminary pages: *front matter*, *prelims*, or *preliminaries*; the pages of a book which precede the text (or body) of it. The practice of publishers varies in what is included as well as in the sequence of presentation. The following order is fairly common: half-title, frontispiece, title-page, imprint and copyright notice and ISBN, dedication, contents, list of illustrations, foreword, preface, acknowledgements, introduction (if not part of the first chapter), and corrigenda.

When preliminary matter is set up after the text has been composed it is given separate pagination in lower case roman numerals.

For fuller lists of the constitution of prelims see O. Simon, 'Introduction to typography', rev. ed. Faber, 1963, and J. Butcher, 'Copy-editing', C.U.P., 1975. See also *parts of a book*, *subsidiaries*.

pre-press colour proofing: the use of one of several proprietary systems to produce for clients a set of four-colour offset-litho proofs. They offer an alternative to trial runs of plates on a proofing press.

pre-press work: any of several techniques used in the composing room to prepare the forme with greater precision. This saves time on the press, reduces possible machine trouble, and leads to better printing.

Mechanical quoins, saw-trimmers for the accurate cutting of slugs and blocks, thickness gauges for type and slugs which are accurate to a thousandth of an inch, block levellers for planing wood and metal mounts, block and plate gauges, a make-up gauge for registering plates on their mounts, and a trolley for the careful moving of the forme are among the many items of equipment used: but it is the pride and skill of the composing room staff which make these aids of value. Also called *pre-make-ready*. See also *make-ready*.

preprint: 1. the production by such proprietary methods as Xerox of a few copies of a manuscript for use within a publishing office. This makes possible the circulation to a number of specialists of copies for reading, criticism and correction.

2. the printing and publishing of a portion of a work prior to the publication of the whole. Cf. *off-print*, *separate*.

pre-proofing: the preparation of a finished proof from a set of negative or positive colour separations before making printing plates.

pre-sensitized plates: factory-coated light-sensitive plates for lithography. They are sold ready for exposure. Diazo and photopolymer resins are the surface substances.

press: see *printing press*.

pressboards: see *millboards*.

press books: books published by *private presses*, q.v.

press-clipping bureau: an organization which, for a fee, collects reviews and notices of a book or its author from periodic literature.

pressing unit: a stage in modern mechanical binding in which freshly-cased books are flowed down a channel. At each of six stations by the sides of this channel the book is momentarily gripped along its joints by heated jaws and quickly released. The final pressing is between flat plates. The pioneer model of this machine, which saves the lengthy pressing of cased books in a standing press, was made by the Smyth-Horne Company.

pressman: in Britain, the operator of a hand-printing

press: in the U.S.A. the operator of *any* press or machine which prints. Cf. *machine minder*.

pressmark: usually a letter followed by an arabic number used either to indicate the shelf location of a book in a press or cupboard, or to refer to a catalogue entry. In the later Middle Ages, when books were often laid flat on reading desks, a location pressmark might be affixed to a corner of the cover, protected by a strip of horn held in position by nails; elsewhere the pressmark might be entered on the first page of text.

press number: the number assigned to a printing press in an office which had several presses. It was a means of identifying the work run off from each. The number of a press was put on each forme 'in a white line (i.e. a *direction line*, q.v.) at the bottom of a page, about four ems from the fore-edge' (Savage). The practice in England was fairly common in the 17th and 18th centuries. See K. Povey, 'A century of press-figures', *The Library*, 5th ser., xiv 4 1959.

press proofs: the final corrected proofs of a work. Usually a set of page proofs with the author's, publisher's, and printer's final corrections or approval.

press revise: an extra proof from the corrected type when ready for machining. The machine-man generally sends a press revise to the machine reviser (at the printer's) who finally passes for press. Also known as *machine revise*.

presswork: the printing off on paper of matter set up in type, and in modern usage, the care and attention devoted to this as revealed by the quality of the result. Presswork includes the preparation of the impression cylinder for even printing and the control of ink-flow during the running of the press. An alternative name, inapplicable to work done on hand-presses, is *machining*.

Pretsch, Paul, 1808–73: a Viennese who prior to 1853 was employed in the State Printing House. He later worked in London where he invented various methods of process work based on the sensitivity to light of a compound of dichromate and gelatine or glue. (GU)

Prideaux, Sarah Treverbian, 1853–1933: a craftswoman binder working in London between 1884 and 1904. She learned her skill with T. J. Cobden-Sanderson, Zaehnsdorf, and the Paris firm Gruel. For the bindings she made for wealthy collectors she used the finest leathers with tooling of large floral and leaf scrollwork surrounded by ruled borders which often contained dots or small circles. She is also remembered for her writings on the history of bookbinding. See also *Katharine Adams*.

prima: the page of printer's copy on which a new slip or galley proof begins. The first word of the slip proof is marked on the copy.

primary binding: the binding style used for a book when it is first published. Cf. *secondary binding*.

Primer: also *primer*, the medieval devotional Book of Hours, *Horae Beatae Mariae Virginis*, which had its origin and existence until the 13th century as part of the Psalter. Thereafter the portion containing the Hours of the Virgin was often written as a separate book. In the 13th century this book was known in England by its Latin name *primarium*, later being Anglicized as primmer, prymer, or primer. The reason for using the word *primer* for such books is uncertain. It may have been from Prime, the first of the Hours, or because, as the Bishop of Rochester suggested in 1539, primers were 'the first books in which the tender youth was instructed'. Primers were written in Latin, and also in French during the Norman period. Towards the end of the 14th century primers appeared with devotions in English, but the Hours were not translated until about 1535.

The basic structure of a medieval primer was a calendar of saints, an almanac for finding the dates of movable feasts, the Little Office, the seven penitential psalms, the fifteen gradual psalms, the Litany of saints, the Office of the dead, and the Commendation of souls. Since intended for the laity, although based on Church usage, its content was never strictly prescribed and there were simpler primers for the instruction of younger children. After 1514 these often included the alphabet. The Latin primer was extensively used by literate people for their private devotions in 14th and 15th century England.

Prior to 1523 the text of Biblical passages was always printed in Latin, and not until that year was the Lord's Prayer printed in English (by de Worde). The first printed Book of Hours to have an English title and be designated 'Primer' was that of Regnault, Paris, 1527. Like its predecessors it was of the Catholic faith and much of the text was in Latin.

The complete primer in English was among books which people were forbidden by a royal proclamation to possess. One had been printed by 1529, probably in Antwerp, but no copy is known to survive. The earliest extant printed primer in English was issued by de Keyser in Antwerp in 1530 under the title 'Ortulus anime . . . or the englische primers . . .', believed to be the work of George Joye, a collaborator of Tyndale. Joye's reformed Lutheran primer, the first to be issued in London, was printed by John Byddell for William Marshall, *c.* 1534 (STC 15986). The text owed much to the *Hortulus animae*, q.v.

In 1536 the basic instruction of children in their mother tongue was officially enjoined upon clergy. As a help to the English trade the considerable import from Paris and Rouen of primers for the English market was forbidden in 1538. The primer of Henry VIII, Grafton, 1545, (STC 16034) was intended by the King to supersede all others and to be used for instructing those unfamiliar with Latin. Other primers were issued after Henry's death, but by 1549, when the *Book of Common Prayer*, q.v., was available and widely accepted, primers diminished in importance until they were finally abolished by the Commonwealth in 1651. Thereafter the word primer was limited to a 'first' book of instruction in any subject, a usage which has never ceased. See C. C. Butterworth, 'The English primers . . .', Philadelphia, University of Pennsylvania Press, 1953.

primes: „ '', used in Germany as an alternative to *duck-foot quotes*, q.v.

Prince, Edward P., 1847–1923: a London punch-cutter and typefounder of considerable skill and patience. His work was in great demand by the whole private press movement, and types cut by him were used by the Ashendene, Doves, Eragny, Essex House, Florence, Kelmscott and Riccardi Presses as well as by similar presses in America, Germany and Holland. See F. C. Avis, 'Edward Philip Prince, type punch-cutter', Avis, 1967.

Prince Society: founded in Boston in 1856 with the object of publishing rare works existing in manuscript or print relating to America. It was named after *Thomas Prince*, b. 1687, a collector of materials on New England. In 1874 the Society became the first incorporated book club in America. All publications were issued in small quarto format.   (DW)

Print: an American graphic arts periodical published since 1940 by William E. Rudge Inc. of New York. There were no issues between 1945–8. One of its main themes was the recognition and improvement of American book design and craftsmanship. After Vol. VII, when publication became bi-monthly, the scope of the periodical was extended to include all graphic processes as well as direct-mail, cinema and television.

print: 1. to transfer an inked image from blocks, type or plates to paper. See also *near-print*, *printing*.

2. the sheet of paper after a transfer has been made. The term is particularly associated with transfers from surfaces bearing artists' drawings, etchings, lithographs and the like.

print convertors: mechanisms for performing such post-impression functions as folding, bundling, cutting, slitting, perforating, gumming, varnishing, numbering, collating, insetting, saddle-stitching and thread stitching printed sheets.

While many of these jobs are done on separate machines it is possible to fit some units in line with the printing machine as, for example, a dryer, folder and sheeter attached to a web-offset press. Cf. *warehouse work*.

printed edges: matter printed on the cut edges of books. When the printing is in aid of quick reference to the contents the fore-edge only is used, but advertisements (e.g. on directories) are printed on any of the cut edges. Printing is done from rubber type. (LK)

printer's devil: a humorous term of obscure origin for a printer's apprentice. Joseph Moxon wrote in 1683 that the boys who removed finished sheets from the tympan 'commonly black and Daub themselves, whence the Workmen do Jocosely call them *Devils*; and sometimes *Spirits* and sometimes *Flies*'.

printer's flowers: see *flowers*.

printer's mark: see *device*.

printer's ornaments: letterpress blocks, mostly of wood but also of metal, bearing designs cut in relief by an engraver for printing together with the text of a book. Such ornaments were particularly popular as decorative head- and tail-pieces in 18th century England, though used before and since.

The printer *Samuel Richardson*, q.v., to name but one, had over a hundred designs, and their use in books not identified by his name as printer has led to the attribution to his press of some 500 works. Ornaments, while occasionally imitated or copied, were usually the property of one printer. As they were not stereotyped the progressive deterioration of the blocks by cracking indicates the sequence of use.

Wood and metal ornaments were exported to Colonial America where the same designs were used by several printers. See E. C. Reilly, 'A dictionary of printers' ornaments and illustrations', Charlottesville, 1976, which reproduces over 2,000 ornaments in books, pamphlets and broadsides printed in the American colonies, and lists each imprint in which they appeared by place, printer, date and reference number.

The term printer's ornaments should not be applied (though often is) to printer's *flowers*, q.v., which are cast as type and usually sold to any printer. Nor does it apply to engraved copperplate head-pieces which are printed in a rolling press independently of the text they embellish. See also *Bewick*, *head-piece*, *Papillon*, *wood engraving*.

printer's ream: formerly 516 sheets of paper, the sixteen sheets extra to the standard ream of 500 being the number traditionally issued to the book printer for *overs*, q.v. Modern practice is for publishers to order paper by the tonne and so many sheets, making their own allowance for overs. See also *centum, mille, mill ream, quire, ream*.

printing: 1. the taking of an impression on paper from inked type, plates, blocks or cylinders. The different methods used for producing and inking the printing surface, and for transferring the image upon it to paper, are primarily classified as *letterpress*, *intaglio*, and *planographic printing*.

A forme made on the *letterpress* principle has all its printing elements at the same height in relation to

Letterpress printing, from raised elements

the inking rollers and to the surface on which printing is done, while the non-printing areas of the forme are sunk below the plane of the printing elements (see diagram).

Intaglio printing works on the opposite principle, the image to be printed being sunk or recessed below the surface of the plate. Intaglio is the principle of

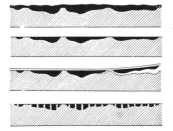

Inked photogravure plate, intaglio printing

The same with surplus ink removed

Ink relief on the impression

For technical reasons the deeply laid image is divided into small cells

etching, line engraving, dry-point, mezzotint, aquatint and photogravaure.

Planographic printing is done from surfaces having image and non-image areas on the same level. It is

Planographic printing

based on the antipathy between grease and water and includes lithography and collotype.

2. see *impression* (1).

printing down: a stage in the preparation of a letterpress printing plate for reproducing an original image. The original is photographed to obtain a negative of it. This is then put in a *printing down frame* and exposed to a sensitized metal plate. Exposure is

Enlargement of type when printed; top row, letterpress with thin ink on hard paper; middle, offset on matt paper; bottom, doctor-blade photogravure

by light from an iodized-quartz or pulsed xenon lamp which in passing through the negative causes an acid-resisting image of it to form on the plate.

It is usual to expose together a batch of negatives from several jobs, positioning them on a glass supporting plate with the emulsion side in contact with the sensitized metal. See also *photoengraving, photolithographic plate, process engraving, vacuum frame*.

printing faults: see *back-edge curl, bad colour, black, bottoming, creasing, crystallization, double, draw out, dropped letter, feathering, filling in, fluffing, friar, ghosting, hickeys, holdout, linting, mackle, moiré, monk, mottling, piling, plucking, powdering, rivers, scumming, set-off, show through, slur, squabble, sticking, strike through, trapping, wet pick, wipe.*

Printing Historical Society: founded in London in 1964 'to encourage the study of and to foster interest in the history of printing, to encourage the preservation of printing machinery, records, and equipment of historical value, and to produce publications in connection with these aims'.

The Society publishes a *Newsletter* and a *Journal*, the latter contains 'authoritative articles on aspects of the history of printing techniques and materials, of individual printers, and of the organization of the trade that are of current interest . . .'

Address: St Bride Printing Library, Bride Lane, Fleet Street, London EC4Y 8EE.

printing – historical survey: the printing of text from wooden blocks was done in the Far East as long ago as the 8th century, the first known block-printing on paper being the million copies of Chinese Buddhist texts ordered by the Empress Shotoku to be printed for distribution in Japan in AD 770, and we learn of printing with separate types in China by the 11th century. There are extant specimens of printing done in Korea by means of type, and some of those types dating from the 15th century have been preserved. No connection between Asiatic and European printing at this time has been established.

In Europe the craft of printing began in the mid-15th century. Its invention is claimed, without proof, for *Johann Gutenberg*, q.v., of Mainz, who apparently in the thirties of this century was occupied with the problem of printing by means of type. When judging the achievement ascribed to Gutenberg we must bear in mind that the joining of separate letters into words is older, being used in the Middle Ages, for example, to punch legends on coins, seals, etc. There are also printed woodcuts dating from the early 15th century. Gutenberg's great achievement was to solve the problem of making a large number of uniform types through the invention of the mould (see *typecasting*), which he may have brought to its final form. It was an advantage for Gutenberg that he was a master goldsmith, and that he had been closely connected with the minting of coins. The methods and tools he used derived from metal working. The printing press used at the time of Gutenberg remained basically unchanged for centuries. Gutenberg, apparently, also invented a printing ink of a consistency differing from that used for the printing of woodcuts. In addition, there was a problem of a more artistic nature to be solved, namely the division of the current script into separate characters. Gutenberg endeavoured to imitate this as far as possible. He was thus obliged to use a larger number of types than are now employed, not only abbreviations and ligatures but also two variants of each type employed depending on what letter preceded it in the text. The number of types for the 42-line Bible was no less than 290. This complicated type system was soon abandoned, and its use is a criterion of the printing done by Gutenberg and his followers. In 1455 or 1456 his printing press was acquired by Johann Fust and Peter Schöffer who continued working in Mainz. Printing spread next to Bamberg, where the 36-line Bible may have been printed about 1459. In 1461 a calendar was printed for the astronomical position of Vienna; whether actually in Vienna is uncertain, but it was not printed in Mainz. In Cologne, Strasbourg and Basle there were printing presses in operation in the mid-sixties of the century. Somewhat later important centres of printing developed in Nuremberg, Augsburg, and Lübeck. See also *Cracow fragments, Kefer*.

The new craft soon reached Italy whence a surviving fragment of an Italian prayer-book shows that a printing press must have existed in northern Italy about 1462. The earliest dated book, an edition of Lactantius, 1465, was issued by the Germans Sweynheym and Pannartz at Subiaco near Rome. In Venice the first press was established by Johannes da

Spira in 1469. The city soon became the most important centre of printing, where such men as Jenson, Erhard Ratdolt, and Manutius worked.

The date when printing began in Holland is uncertain. There exists a small amount of printed matter of Dutch origin, mostly Latin grammars, the typography of which is most primitive. These so-called *Costeriana* are all undated, and attempts made to connect them with Laurens Coster of Haarlem, or at least to a very early period, have not proved convincing. The earliest Dutch printing datable with certainty is of 1470, in which year also the first press was set up in Paris. Early printing in Spain appears to have begun with a Synodal issued about 1473 (see *Palmart*).

England's first printer was *William Caxton*, q.v., whose earliest work done in London was a letter of indulgence which must have been printed before 13 December 1476.

From Lübeck printing equipment was taken by Johann Snell to Denmark (1482) and Sweden (1483). Other dates (about which, as in the preceding, authorities differ) are 1468 Switzerland, 1473 Belgium and Austria-Hungary, 1487 Portugal, 1494 Bulgaria, 1508 Scotland and Roumania, 1551 Ireland, 1553 Russia, 1718 Wales (although the first book printed in Welsh, 'Yny Lhyvyr hwnny traethir', was dated 1546), 1821 Greece, 1885 Albania.

Books of the earliest period of printing, i.e. up to 1500, are called *incunabula*, q.v.

The initial benefit of printing in Europe in the 16th century was the wide availability of relatively accurate texts in large quantities of identical copies. Manuscript versions had been marred by scribal errors in copying. A further benefit was the stimulus printed books gave to literacy and learning, leading to personal study in place of oral teaching. Colet, Erasmus, More and Vives were among proponents of the 'new learning' who saw printing as an essential adjunct to the educational reforms they advocated to meet contemporary social needs and changes. Printing also facilitated the wide and speedy dissemination of radical ideas inimical to church or state authority, witness Luther's challenge to the Pope nailed to Wittenberg church door in 1517, to be speedily translated from Latin into German and printed. In this form it influenced the Reformation in Germany and France: the power of the press was established.

During the first half of the 16th century Italy, France and South Germany were the foremost European centres of the new art; in Augsburg and Nuremberg especially book production was of very high standard. Such prominent artists as Dürer, Holbein, and Cranach developed the ornamentation of books, and decorated title-page borders and woodcut initials were characteristic of the period. Great interest was also taken in type-design, and in the early 16th century the German Fraktur type came

into use, to be extensively employed in all German-speaking countries. Basle also developed as a centre of fine printing. In Italy the achievements of Aldus Manutius impressed their stamp on the whole of the next century. Owing to Italian influence, the gothic character of the type hitherto prevailing in France and Spain was replaced by roman and italic, the latter created by Manutius. The first half of the 16th century is rightly called the golden age of printing, not only because of the high artistic quality of the work, but also considering the printers' social position in the community; many among them were learned and cultured men, and their offices became centres of scholarship. This applied to Manutius of Venice and Froben of Basle, with both of whom Erasmus worked for a number of years as editor and proof reader, and also to the Estienne family of Paris. In the later 16th century the Low Countries took the lead, especially through Christopher Plantin of Antwerp. He pioneered the extensive use of copperplate illustrations, a prototype for the 17th century. Printing in 17th-century Holland was led by the Elzevir family, who, helped by their bookselling organization, created greater demand for their products. Their elegant and cheap duo-decimo volumes, printed in a distinct, if somewhat monotonous type, had a great vogue. In other respects the main feature of 17th-century printing is its pomposity and heaviness, while the numerous copperplate illustrations and large-size format are unable to gloss over the often mediocre typography.

In the 18th century France led in the art of printing as in culture generally. Illustrations and other decorative features took first place in book production. About the mid-century the baroque style with its heaviness gave way to the easier elegance of the rococo. Vignettes and head- and tail-pieces enjoyed a vogue. A reaction emphasizing the purely typographical side of the book began in the mid-century with John Baskerville of Birmingham whose works were almost devoid of decorative elements. Instead, great attention was paid to type, balanced composition, presswork, and the quality of the paper. Baskerville's new roman type, later developed by Bodoni and Didot, was widely employed elsewhere, especially in France. A corresponding modernization of the Fraktur was attempted in Germany by Unger and Breitkopf. In Italy Giambattista Bodoni of Parma was one of the most skilled printers of the 18th century, if not of all time, and the most typical representative of a strict classicism in the art of printing.

The 19th century was characterized by the great technical inventions, above all by the cylinder press of König, 1812. Graphic techniques were also revolutionized through lithography, steel engraving, wood engraving, and process work. Another feature was the number of new type-faces that made their

394

appearance, particularly in England, during the early decades of the century, finding popularity also in other countries. Technical progress, however, had nothing to show in a corresponding general excellence of fine printing (Bulmer, Bentley, and Pickering excepted). Type-forms as well as typography were not based on definite artistic rules. A reaction to this degeneration and lack of principle began in the nineties with the work of William Morris, and later in Germany with that of Karl Klingspor and his circle. Prototypes were sought from the golden age of printing, and this tendency, at first historical in scope, laid the foundation for the higher standard of printing now a feature of our century.   (With GU)

Printing Industry Research Association: the name by which the *Printing, Packaging and Allied Trades Research Association*, q.v., was known when established in November 1930. It was renamed in 1947.

Printing, Packaging and Allied Trades Research Association: a body founded in 1930 to help its members by conducting research into problems which they submit, to issue reports of these researches and to circulate abstracts of technical information taken from some 250 journals published all over the world.

An elected Council represents all branches of the printing and allied trades. From members' subscriptions (varied according to the size of the firm and the facilities required) and an annual grant from the Department of Scientific and Industrial Research a laboratory staffed by qualified scientists is maintained at Leatherhead. There is a library, which includes an information service, where the monthly 'Printing Abstracts' (free to members) is prepared. Liaison visits between the Association and its members are a further valuable activity. For details of the Association after 1967 see under *PIRA*.

printing press: a mechanical arrangement for taking impressions from an inked forme on paper or some other material. According to the principle of printing adopted a distinction is made between presses for intaglio, lithographic, and letterpress printing. Printing presses may also be divided into the following main types according to the manner of applying the paper to the forme: *platen* presses, in which the paper is pressed by a flat surface on to the flat forme; the *rubber* press, in which the forme is also flat, but the pressure at any given moment is exerted only on a narrow strip of the paper by means of a rubber blade which is moved over the paper as it rests on the forme; the *cylinder* press, in which the paper is pressed on the forme by a cylinder which rolls over it; and the *rotary* press, in which both the surfaces pressing on each other consist of cylinders between which the paper is conveyed in sheets or an endless web.

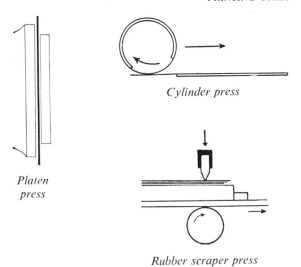

Platen press

Cylinder press

Rubber scraper press

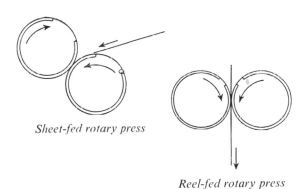

Sheet-fed rotary press

Reel-fed rotary press

The earliest printing machines were hand-presses in which the inking of the forme, the feeding and extracting of the paper, and the application of pressure were done by hand. They were built of wood. The first iron press was made in Basle by Haas, q.v., in 1772. In England, Stanhope's first iron press was made *c.* 1803. The lever principle proper appeared first on Dingler's Washington press of 1820. The idea of a mechanical press (in which cylinder printing was also conceived) came from William Nicholson of London in 1790, but its successful development was not until 1810 when Friedrich König, with the financial backing of Bensley, built a mechanical platen press. König's cylinder machine was installed in 1812; with Andreas Bauer he experimented on a two-revolution machine in 1814–17, but the modern model was developed by Robert Miehle in 1883.

In the U.S.A. successful attempts have been made to employ a wholly different principle, it being unnecessary for the forme to have contact with the sheet. The ink is transferred by means of electrical fields of force, under the influence of which the ink can be made to jump to the paper. (See *Xerography*).

See also *Albion-, Applegath, Blaeu, Cameron System, Campbell-, cylinder-, hand-, joiner's-, Mann, Miehle-, platen-, rotary-, Stanhope press, letterpress machines, wraparound press.* (GU)

printing processes: for descriptions of the three basic processes see *intaglio, planographic, relief printing*. See also *image process*.

printing vocabulary: the earliest list of printing terms used in the sense they have today may be that in 'Of the interchangeable course, or variety of things in the whole world', London, 1594, pp. 21–2. This was a translation by Robert Ashley of Loys Le Roy's 'De la vicissitude ou variété des choses en l'univers', Paris, 1579. The following are given: (type) casting, characters, counter-punches, justifying the matrices; (composing) case, chase, compositor, forme, furniture, gather the sheets, proof, sorts; (press) bar of the press, platen, spindle. See Becker, 'Un Humaniste au XVIe siècle, Loys le Roy', Paris, 1896.

print-out: see *hard copy*.

print roll coater: see *Massey coater*.

Private Libraries Association: 'an international society of book collectors' with headquarters in London. The Association's annual compilation 'Private press books', since 1957, is a useful and essential review of the work of presses in America, Britain, and elsewhere.

privately printed: said of books issued from a private press or for private distribution.

The first such book in England is said to be 'De antiquitate Britannicae ecclesiae Cantuariensis, cum Archiepiscopis eiusdem 70', printed at Lambeth Palace in 1572 by John Day for Matthew Parker, Archbishop of Canterbury.

privately published: a work published at the expense of the author. It may, however, be offered for public sale, e.g. 'A world bibliography of bibliographies', by T. Besterman. Published by the author, 1947. Printed by the Oxford University Press. See also *vanity publisher*.

private press: a small printing house which issues for public sale limited editions of books which have been carefully made on the premises. Similar but even smaller presses are operated on a club basis by groups of amateurs working in their homes, the results being given to members and friends. Publishers may also style themselves 'Press' and issue limited editions of books they have not printed. Non-printing trade business houses often print on their premises works

for internal circulation only. Thus no concise all-embracing definition of a private press is possible.

Writing to the *Monotype Recorder* in 1933 Eric Gill stated 'a "private" press prints solely what it chooses to print, whereas a "public" press prints what its customers demand of it. The distinction has nothing to do with the use of machinery or with questions of the artistic quality of the product'.

Private presses are almost as old as printing itself. One of the earliest was that of the wealthy Nuremberg physician Ulrich Pinder who installed one in his house and employed *Friedrich Peypus*, q.v., to print the ten works he issued from it. Notable was the illustrated 'Garten des Rosenkranzes', 1505. Pinder, as others of his kind, set up the press because he wanted to see particular texts in print; the artistic presentation of those texts, if any, was incidental. See R. Cave, 'The private press', Faber, 1971.

The selection of presses referred to below includes some no longer active. See *Appledore, Arden, Argonaut, Ark, Ashendene, Asphodel, Association of Little Presses, Bampton, Beaumont, Beldornie, Blakeney, Boar's Head, Bremer, Caradoc, Cayme, Cloister, Cranach, Cuala, Daniel, Darlington, Decoy, Doves, Dropmore, Dun Emer, Einhorn, Elston, Eragny, Essex House, Fanfare, Favil, Florence, Flying Fame, Gehenna, Golden Cockerel, Golden Hind, Grabhorn, Grange, Great Totham, Gregynog, Hafod, Hammer, Hand and Flower, Hibbert, High House, Hogarth, Hours, Janus, Kelmscott, Laboratory, Lee Priory, Mall, Marion, Marprelate, Merrymount, Middle Hill, Miniature, Montague, Mosher, Nonesuch, Officina Serpentis, Oriole, Ovid, Pear Tree, Pelican, Peregrine, Perpetua, Polidori, Rampant Lions, Raven, Riccardi, Riverside, Rochester, Romney Street, Roycroft, Rupprecht, St Dominics, Sale Hill, Samurai, Stanbrook Abbey, Strawberry Hill, Temple Sheen, Three Candles, Three Mountains, Trajanus, Trevecca, Trovillion, Unicorn, Vale, Village, Vine, Westminster, Zilverdistel.*

privilege: a licence according the sole right to print and sell books granted by Letters Patent from an authority. The first recorded privilege to a printer was given in 1469 when the Signoria in Venice granted *Johannes da Spira*, q.v., an exclusive patent to print in Venice and district for five years. This is noted in his edition of Pliny's 'Naturalis historiae', 1469. However, he died in 1470 and was succeeded by his brother, apparently with the lapse of the privilege as *Jenson*, q.v., began printing in Venice in that year.

At the time of its inception in England in the 16th century a privilege was valid for a specified period and class of books, e.g. law, music, ballads, psalms; the title pages of such works often bearing the words 'cum privilegio'. Of interest is the privilege granted in 1575 to William Byrd and Thomas Tallis who held jointly a monopoly for twenty-one years for the 'printinge of all musicke bookes'. Dissatisfaction, pirating and lawsuits resulted from these monopolies, and the only privileged presses today are Oxford University Press, Cambridge University Press, and Eyre & Spottiswoode (the Queen's Printer) who alone may print the Authorized Version of the Bible and the Book of Common Prayer. (See *Bible printing in England*.) See also *imprimatur, nihil obstat, Queen's Printer, Star-chamber, Stationers' Company, Vérard.*

prizes: see *literary awards and prizes.*

process block: the printing plate prepared by *process engraving*, q.v.

process embossing: see *embossing.*

process engraving: see *photoengraving.*

Processionale: a book containing the hymns, psalms and litanies used during the processions in a church or cathedral.

process work: a general term for the preparation of a printing surface by the use at some stage of photographic, chemical and mechanical means. This includes *photoengraving, photogravure* and *photolithography*, qq.v.

Proctor, Robert George Collier, 1868–1903: the author of the 'Index to the early printed books in the British Museum . . . to 1500, with notes of those in the Bodleian Library', 1898–1903. This four-volume work lists some 10,000 items under country, town, and press. The numbers Proctor assigned to the books are still used to identify them. The work became the foundation of the British Museum 'Catalogue of books printed in the XVth century now in the British Museum', 1908, begun by A. W. Pollard. Proctor, who worked in the British Museum from 1893 until his accidental death in 1903, made the study of incunabula his life-work, adding a great contribution to our knowledge of early printing in Augsburg, Venice, and in the Greek language. See also *greek type.*

production press: any press on which a job will be printed as distinct from one on which it was proofed. Some of the bigger *proof presses*, q.v., can be used as production machines for short runs, usually at slower speeds.

proem: an obsolete term for a *preface*, q.v. Also spelled *proheme.*

profit-sharing agreement: a contract sometimes made between an author and a publisher whereby the latter recovers from receipts of sale all production and advertising costs for a book before the author receives any payment; subsequent profits from further

sales are halved. It may thus be several years before either party benefits. See also *publishers' agreements.*

prognostications: tables of astrological or other forecasts, usually compiled for one year, and often forming part of an *almanac*, q.v. They were often political in emphasis. Early ones printed in England were translations (e.g. de Worde's of 1497 and Pynson's of *c.* 1500), Andrew Borde's of 1545, known only from its title-page, being the earliest extant of English origin.

Prognostications were very popular since the significance of comets and eclipses as portents of natural disasters, famines, and the deaths of rulers was widely believed in Elizabethan England, and it is not surprising that some six hundred books of this kind were issued before 1600. Thus in Shakespeare's 'King Lear' we read 'These late eclipses in the sun and moon portend no good to us' (I.ii.98).

programming: pre-setting the controls of a machine so that they will automatically set in motion a desired sequence of movements. An example is an electronic *guillotine*, q.v., which is programmed to make a series of cuts.

progressive proofs: proofs made in colour printing as a guide to shade and registration. Each colour is shown separately and imposed on the preceding ones. Also called *progressives.*

promotion copies: copies of a forthcoming book given to sales representatives to show to the trade. They may also be 'placed' with potential bulk buyers for retail chains of shops, particularly when an anticipated bestseller is being launched. They thus differ from *inspection copies*, q.v., which are normally academic or school textbooks, given after publication. Also known as *reading copies.*

proof: 1. in *letterpress*, an impression taken from composed type for checking and correction only, not to show the appearance of the finished work. In bookwork several proofs may be taken: (i) *first proof*, a preliminary galley, corrected by the printer's reader and returned to the compositor; (ii) *galley* or *slip proof*, the corrected galley, again checked by the reader and sent to the publisher for the author; (iii) *page proof*, pulled after making the type into pages, and sometimes used instead of (ii) for correction by the author, or sent to the author after corrections he marked on (ii) have been made by the printer; (iv) the returned author's proof, i.e. *marked proof*, is again read by the printer's reader to ensure the *style of the house*, q.v., has been followed (if this is the desired style), to check illustrations, imprint, etc.

The reader signs the proof. If he marks it *show*

revise, a further proof must be submitted; *clean proof* means that a clean proof is wanted. The final instruction *press* is marked by the publisher.

If the foregoing sequence delays production it also contributes to its accuracy and quality.

2. in *photosetting*, a photostat of matter on film. See *film make-up*.

3. in *computer-assisted typesetting*, with a general purpose computer, a *print-out* in readable form of the information stored in the resulting perforated tape. As the print-out is in capital letters and includes input codes for format, paragraphing, etc., it is less easy for an untrained reader to correct. See also *author's corrections, author's proof, corrigenda, editing and proofing terminal, erratum, foundry proof, galley, house corrections, in-plant proofing, literal, machine proof, optical character recognition, pass sheet, press revise, prima, pull, reader's box, reproduction proof, rough proof, video display unit*.

proof before letters: the last proof or *state*, q.v., to be made of an artist's plate. It awaits titling, numbering and signing. When these details have been added by the artist a subsequent pull is called a *proof after letters*.

proof corrections: additions or corrections to a proof made marginally in ink. Recognized symbols are used. (See BS 5261C: 1976, reproduced as Appendix C.) A certain amount of correcting is allowed for in the printer's estimate to the publisher; corrections in excess of this are charged separately, the latter particularly referring to an author's alterations to his text after setting.

proofing chromo: a superfine coated paper used by process engravers for block proofing. Also known as *B.P. chromo*.

proof presses: printing presses specially designed for proofing. The numerous models available vary from small hand-inked and operated presses for jobbing work, simple cylinder machines without grippers for proofing on galleys, pre-make-ready presses in which overlays can be fitted, to elaborate and costly power-operated precision machines which approach as closely as possible production press standards of accuracy and strength. These last, fitted with ink ducts and deliveries, will take large formes and can be used as short-run production machines.

Well known among the many proprietary makes are the American *Vandercook* presses. Introduced to the trade in 1970 was their four-colour offset proof press. One large cylinder holds four plates; another the four blankets. The grippers of the impression cylinder hold the sheet for all four revolutions, on each of which a separate colour is picked up with automatic registration. Cf. *production press*.

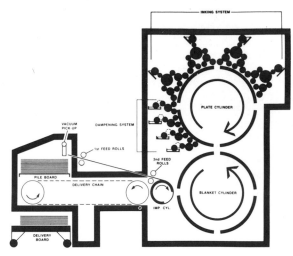

Diagram of 4-colour offset proof press

pro-printing: the reproduction of printed matter without the use of letterpress type: duplicators or small office litho machines are used, litho plates being prepared by photography from typewritten copy, or stencils by direct typing. See also *direct edition*.

prospectus: a publishers' sales device, being a descriptive leaflet outlining the plan of a work to be published. It usually contains a specimen page and illustration, and often a table of contents.

The first printed prospectus of a book was issued by Johann Mentelin at Strasbourg in 1469.

prototypographer: the first printer of a particular place. The term is usually applied only to 15th century first printers.

provenance: an indication of a book's previous ownership. A special binding, a bookplate, or an inscription of ownership may point to the collections, libraries, or sale-rooms through which a particular copy has passed.

prover and transferrer: the craftsman in a lithographic printing establishment whose work is gumming and inking plates, transferring outlines from key plates to other plates, and printing proofs.

Provincial Guild of Printers' Readers: an organization founded in 1923 which works for the welfare and professional betterment of the printer's reader. The Guild operates in all parts of the country through honorary district secretaries who are in turn responsible to a national council meeting annually in London. A quarterly journal *The Printer's Reader* is published, examinations are held, and certificates of ability are awarded.

Prudentius, Aurelius Clemens, 348–405: a poet of the early Latin church whose 'Psychomachia' was a popular subject for copying by 9th to 12th-century scribes in England, France and Germany. The Malmesbury Prudentius, now in Cambridge University Library, is the finest surviving English example of this poem about the struggle between the Virtues and Vices for possession of the soul. It was illustrated by lively outline sketches drawn in coloured inks, deriving in style from the *Utrecht Psalter*, q.v., (the latter was drawn in brown ink only).

The editio princeps was printed at Lyons by Pierre Mareschal about 1497: it had the title 'De conflictu virtutum et vitiorum'.

Psalter: the Book of Psalms, either for devotional or liturgical use.

Psalterium Moguntinum: see *Johann Fust*.

Psalter of Alphonso: an illuminated Psalter commissioned about 1284 by Edward I as a gift to his son Alphonso who died in the same year. The work was completed after his death by a second and inferior artist. Bands of colour fill up blanks after each verse, while narrow frame borders lead from some of the initials; the *drolleries*, q.v., birds and animals which embellish the borders are most delicately drawn.

The work is also known as the *Tenison Psalter*, being once owned by Archbishop Tenison (d. 1715): it is now in the British Library.

Psalter of Queen Mary: see *The Queen Mary Psalter*.

pseudepigraphia: a collective term for writings or books falsely or erroneously ascribed to someone not the author.

pseudonymous: said of a book written and published under an assumed name. See also *demonym*.

publication date: 1. the date announced by a publisher before which no copies of a book should be sold to the public.

2. the year of publication which, except in the case of juvenile and certain school books, should always be shown in a book. It is usual to print the date of first publication where different from that of the current edition and also, in the case of a technical or scientific work, to indicate whether it is a re-issue or revised edition.

publicity faces: an American term for jobbing types and also display sizes of book types, all being suitable for advertisements, publicity catalogues and so on.

Public Lending Right: the authors' right to be paid for the use the public makes of copyright works that are borrowed from, or available for reference in libraries. This was considered in the British Parliament in 1976 after nearly twenty-five years of campaigning, notably by the *Society of Authors*, q.v.

The scheme envisaged the setting-up of a PLR Registry to administer the scheme. Single authors or their heirs wishing to benefit from it would be required to register their eligible works. Payments to authors were to be calculated on sampling returns from seventy-two public library service outlets, and would be made from government funds.

publisher: a person or a company in business to issue for sale to the public through booksellers books, periodicals, music, maps, etc. In the 16th century London trade the licence to print a work was assigned to a printer who was, by implication, the publisher of it, though sometimes in association with sponsors. Later in the same century bookseller-publishers became more influential and commissioned printers to work for them. Publishing as a business separate from bookselling dates from the early 19th century. See F. A. Mumby & I. Norrie, 'Publishing and bookselling', 5th ed., Cape, 1974; and Sir Stanley Unwin, 'The truth about publishing', 8th ed., George Allen & Unwin, 1976.

The Publisher and Bookseller: between 1928 and 1933 the title of *The Bookseller*, q.v.

publishers' abbreviated answers: the code approved by the Publishers Association in 1953 for reporting the non-supply of a book.

OP	Title discontinued.
TOP	Temporarily out of print. No reprint in hand.
RP/6m	Reprint in hand: expected in (e.g.) about six months.
RP/Jan.	Reprint in hand: expected in (e.g.) January.
NE/ND	New edition in preparation: no date can be given.
NE/6m	New edition in preparation: expected in about (e.g.) six months.
B/Jan.	Binding: expected in (e.g.) January.
B/12 Jan.	Binding: will be ready on (e.g.) January 12th.
B/ND	Binding: no date can be given.
NK	Not known, or not ours.
NP	Not yet published. (This replaces NO, which should not be used.)
OO/USA	Out of stock but on order from (e.g.) U.S.A.
OTO/USA	Only to order from (e.g.) U.S.A.

(OS (out of stock), NO (not out), and an unqualified RP (reprinting) and B (binding) *should not be used*.)

In 1971 a standard code of numbers instead of letters (themselves slightly changed from the above) was proposed by publishers for use in mechanized invoicing, viz.:

0	Not known	NK
1	On order to follow shortly	O/O
2	Binding (date)	Bdg (date)
3	Reprinting (date)	RP (date)
4	Not yet published	NYP
5	New edition in preparation	NEIP
6	Reprint under consideration	RP/UC
7	Out of print: title discontinued	OP
8	On order abroad	OO/Abroad

A similar code was devised by West German publishers.

publishers' agent: a term relevant to the British book trade of the early 19th century for an entrepreneur or link-man between publishers. He would arrange for them to share marketing costs and send advance copies or sheets of their forthcoming books across the Atlantic to American reprinting houses. A notable London agent was John Miller who between 1817 and 1822 was sending some fifty titles a year to *Mathew Carey*, q.v., of Philadelphia.

The agent would also collect in England such bulk new and second-hand books as were required and despatch them to clients in America, bringing back American publications for the London trade.

publishers' agreements: contracts between authors and publishers to establish the basis on which an author's writings shall be published and sold; while these vary in detail they are, in the main, usually within the framework of the following, qq.v.: *royalties*, a *profit-sharing agreement*, a *commission agreement*, or an *outright sale of copyright*. See also *literary agent*, *subsidiary rights*.

The Publishers Association: or *PA*, the representative body for the British book publishing trade, founded in 1896. Membership is open to any publisher in the United Kingdom whose business, or an appreciable part of it, is the publication of books. The Association affords book publishers the means of dealing collectively with the many problems that face them which are not otherwise susceptible of resolution. It regulates conditions of employment within the trade and supplies its members with information and advice on technical, legal and economic aspects of publishing. The Association also represents publishers *vis-à-vis* the Government, local authorities, public and trade bodies, foreign publishers' associations, and the International Publishers Association.

Its original object was to maintain the retail prices of net books, and while this remains one of its activities, the Association is now largely engaged in assisting its members to secure a greater and more efficient distribution of their books. To this end the Association's activities are carried out by its permanent staff and by elected and nominated representatives to various divisions.

The Association's address is 19 Bedford Square, London WC1B 3HJ.

See R. J. L. Kingsford, 'The Publishers Association 1896–1946, with an epilogue', C.U.P., 1970. See also *Book Development Council, Booksellers Association, British Publishers Market Agreement, Educational Publishers Council, Net Book Agreement, Society of Authors*.

publisher's binding: the binding, usually cased, in which a publisher supplies books to the trade. Synonymous with *edition binding*, q.v. See also *bookbinding*.

The Publishers' Circular and Booksellers' Record: a weekly book-trade paper which includes an author and title list of new British books; some Government publications are mentioned, but not musical scores. It was first issued fortnightly in 1837 by Sampson Low, who from 1845 also issued annual lists. From 1853 he gave these the title 'The British Catalogue of Books'. This title was merged with 'The London Catalogue' in 1860.

After 1864 the two then appeared as 'The English Catalogue of Books': the first volume with the new name covered the years 1835–63 and included 'importations of original American works, and Continental English books'; American books are not mentioned after 1901.

In 1959 the title was changed to *British Books* and subsequently to *The Publisher*.

publisher's cloth: the cloth casing which since the late 1820s has been the usual covering material for edition-bound books. See also *edition binding*.

publisher's device: see *device*.

publisher's dummy: see *dummy*.

Publishers Information Cards: printed cards, 125mm × 75mm, issued by PIC Services Ltd to give information about forthcoming books. Each card describes one book. Details, which include author's qualifications, intended readership, chapter contents and price are prepared by **PIC Services Ltd** for presentation in an objective and uniform style from information supplied by publishers who choose to use the scheme and pay for entries. Cards are supplied to libraries and booksellers in Britain and are also used for sales publicity overseas. This standardization offers advantages when preparing book orders, and the cards are easier to store on file than the many sizes used for publishers' trade lists.

PIC Services Ltd uses a basic U.K. mailing list and a list of key libraries overseas (excluding U.S.A.) prepared by the *Book Development Council*, q.v. The service began in 1968; for its subsequent history see *International Book Information Services*.

Publishers Information Record Cards: or *PIRCs*, a standardized business record card for book trade use. Each publisher's card indicates location of departments, telephone numbers, agencies, warehousing arrangements and terms structure. Cards are easy to update and IBIS Information Services will print and distribute them on behalf of publishers.

publisher's reader: one who, for a fee, reads, judges, criticizes and reports on typescripts submitted to a publisher.

publisher's series: titles which a publisher issues in a uniform style of binding and which are often, but not necessarily, related by subject.

Publishers Special Accounts House: a non-profitmaking company which began operating in London in 1965 under the auspices of Book Centre Ltd to service the many small accounts of its publisher members. Stocks of books were carried. Booksellers used special order-invoice forms and received single monthly accounts. The aim was a quicker and cheaper supply of small orders to booksellers, but due to lack of support the scheme closed in 1970. See also *Standard Account Numbers*.

The Publishers' Weekly: the principal journal for the whole American book trade, founded in 1872 by *Frederick Leypoldt*, q.v. The weekly author list gives new U.S. non-government publications, and there is a monthly title index. Extensive information is given about new books and sales campaigns. In addition to the main author list, which is partly annotated, there is a subsidiary list of paperbacks, pamphlets and minor pieces. Special Spring and Fall numbers are of particular interest to overseas subscribers.

publishing and bookselling organizations: see *American Book Trade Association, American Company of Booksellers, Antiquarian Booksellers Association, Association of American Publishers Inc., Association of Publishers' Educational Representatives, Australian National Book Council, Book Centre, Book Clubs Group, Book Development Council, Book Publishers Representatives Association, Booksellers Association, Booksellers Association Charter Scheme, Booksellers Association Service House, Booksellers Clearing House, Booksellers Order and Distribution (BORD), Booksellers Order Distribution (BOD), Book Tokens Ltd, Book Trade Benevolent Society, Börsenverein der Deutschen Buchhändler zu Leipzig, Borsenverein deutsche Verleger-und-Buchhändlerverbände, British Publishers Guild, British Publishers Market Agreement, Clique, Educational Publishers Council, English Language Book Society (ELBS), Frankfurt Fair, Galley Club, International Board on Books for Young People, International Book Information Service (IBIS), International Community of Booksellers Associations, International Copyright Information Centre, International League of Antiquarian Booksellers, International Publishers Association, International Standard Book Number (ISBN), Library Licence, National Book Committee, National Book League, National Book Trade Provident Society, Net Book Agreement, Orders Clearing, Publisher Information Record Cards, Publishers Association, Publishers Information Cards, Quantity Book-buying Scheme, School Bookshop Association, Society of Authors, Society of Young Publishers.*

publishing and bookselling terminology: see *abridged edition, acting edition, adaptation, addendum, advance copies, advance jackets, advertisements, All rights reserved, American book sizes, ana, annuals, anthology, appendix, artwork, atlas, authorized edition, author's proof, beauty, belles-lettres, bestseller, birthday book, blad, block quotation, blurb, bogus, book, book club, book form, bookhandler, book proof, bound book, Bowdlerized, British book sizes, brochure, browse, caption, car stock, cased books, category fiction, character book, chrestomathy, circular, classics, close out, co-edition work, coffee-table book, collected edition, colonial editions, composite book, concordance, condensed book, conger, co-publishing, copy editor, copyright notice, courtesy terms, crowner, definitive edition, de luxe edition, demand publishing, desk copies, dictionary, direct-mail selling, directory, distribution imprint, dues, dummy, dumpbin, edition, edition binding, edition cost, egghead paperback, elhi books, emblem book, encyclopaedia, epistles, epitome, expurgated edition, extracts, facsimile edition, Festschrift, fiction series, flier, florilegium, format, front matter, get up, glossary, Grangerized, guide book, gutting, half see safe, handbook, hard-cover edition, header card, herbal, house corrections, illustrated, imperfections, imprimatur, imprint, impulse outlet, inedited, in print, insert, inspection copies, interleaved, introduction, issue, jacket, jest book, journey terms, keepsake, knocking copy, large paper edition, lead-in titles, legend, level stock, lexicon, libel, library edition, limitation notice, literary agent, literary awards, mail-coach copies, maquette binding, missing copy, net, net net, new edition, non-net books, novel, novel distributor, numbered copy, omnibus book, on sale or return, out of print, out of stock, outright sale of copyright, overprinting (2), overs, overstocks, pamphlet, panel (2), paperback, paper covers, partial remainders, paste-up,* *perfect copy, permissions copy, pharmacopoeia, picking list, pirated edition, plant-free reprint, pocket edition, prebinding, Primer, privately published, profit-sharing agreement, prospectus, publication date, publishers' abbreviated answers, publishers' agreements, publishers' series, puff, quality paperback, railway libraries, reading copies, remainders, reprint, republication, retail bookseller, return on full credit, returns, review copies, revised edition, royalties, rums, school edition, see safe, self ends, serial, serial rights, share-books, shelfliner, shrink wrapping, simplified edition, slip case, softback edition, songster, special edition, sponsoring editor, starting charge, statutory copies, stockholding book wholesaler, streamer, stuffer, style of the house, subject books, subject series, subscribing a book, subscription terms, subscription works, subsidiary rights, supplement, take-over, technical book illustration, teleordering system, terms, textbook, thesaurus, thickness copy, total publication, toy books, trade books, trade edition, trade sales, trade terms, traveller's samples, tummy band, uniform edition, vanity publisher, vertical house, visualizer, volume rights, voucher copy, warehouse copies, wholesale bookseller.*

Pucelle, Jean, fl.1319–28: a Parisian manuscript painter who perfected, if he did not originate, the form of grisaille known as *camaïeu-gris* in which black ink drawings are given only a few touches of colour. An important example of his work is the Belleville Breviary, completed about 1325, and interesting for its marginal notes of payments made to the men who made it. There is also the charming Breviary of Jeanne d'Evreux, completed about the same time, and given by Jeanne to Charles V in 1371. It is now in The Cloisters, New York. See K. Morand, 'Jean Pucelle', O.U.P., 1962.

puff: exaggerated praise for a book, written by the author or a copy-writer, for use in advertisements or on book jackets. For pre-publication publicity a *preliminary puff* is supplied to travellers.

The term was used in the 17th century, and still is. See also *blurb, gutting.*

pugging machine: a machine for softening and mixing the ingredients of printing ink. After pugging the mixture is sent to the grinding mill.

pugillaria: the Roman table book. From two to eight wax-covered leaves of ivory, wood or metal, bearing writing done with a stylus, were fastened together with leather thongs or rings. Covers were of parchment or skin, and later of wood. See also *diptych.*

Pulitzer Prizes: a series of literary prizes awarded annually since 1917, in the U.S.A., for the best drama,

novel, and (since 1921) poetry written by American authors. Historical works, biographies, and journalistic work also qualify for special prizes.

Funds derive from an endowment provided by Joseph Pulitzer (1847–1911), a newspaper magnate and philanthropist. See 'The Pulitzer prizes: a history . . .', N.Y., 1974.

pull: an impression of type. The term originates with the action in the early presses when, after an impression had been made, the bed was pulled out and the platen raised. See also *proof.*

pulling: the removal of the cover, boards, end papers, tapes, and any lining material which, with the softening of old glue and cutting of sewing threads, are necessary stages in the preparation of a book for re-binding.

pulp: the wet mixture of various ingredients which flows on to the web of a papermaking machine, or is taken up in a hand-mould, to be formed into paper.

pulp board: see *boards.*

pulp water: an alternative name for *backwater*, q.v.

pumice stone: a light volcanic rock used for smoothing parchment prior to writing upon it, or when preparing it for re-use. This action is known as *pouncing*. See also *palimpsest.*

punch: a piece of steel on which is engraved a type character. It is then hardened and used as a die to strike the matrices from which type is cast. See also *justification* (2), *matrix* (1), *strike.*

punchcutter: the craftsman whose work was fundamental to printing from its beginnings in the 15th century and for centuries after, since it was only when he had engraved a *punch*, q.v., that a matrix could be struck and type cast. The technical skill, artistic sense, and patience needed for punchcutting are akin to the qualities of a goldsmith, engraver of seals, or die-sinker. The tools used are the same or similar: gravers, files, oil-stones, various gauges, a magnifying glass, and a small bench. Thus we are not surprised that Gutenberg should be recorded in 1436 as having employed the goldsmith Hans Dünne 'for that which pertains to printing', or that among early punchcutters of note were Francesco Griffo, goldsmith of Bologna; Dominic Cennini, goldsmith of Florence; and Lautizio, goldsmith and sealcutter of Perugia. Later came Dijck who had been a goldsmith and the great Caslon who was apprenticed to an armourer as an ornamental engraver.

Punchcutters were independent craftsmen who usually sold their work in the form of *strikes* which were unfinished matrices of copper struck with the punches. The printer-purchaser would have them justified or dressed prior to casting from them. There were also punchcutters who cast types and printed, Jenson and Joos Lambrecht being early ones to do so. In England John Day cut and cast type for the works he printed.

By the early 16th century there were independent foundries in Germany (Hollar, Sabon) and Paris (Le Bé). Matrices and types sold by these foundries at the Frankfurt and Rouen trade fairs were taken to many countries including England and Scotland. England's first independent foundry may have been that of *Benjamin Sympson*, q.v.

Caslon was probably the first in England to set up an establishment where type was designed and cut (in conditions of great secrecy), and where matrices were made and type cast and sold in founts of several sizes. As his trade grew the importation of foreign types diminished and he in turn was a considerable exporter to Colonial America.

For notes on punchcutters see *Augereau, Austin, Bodoni, Buell, Carter, H., Carter, M., Caslon, Cottrell, Didot, Dijck, Figgins, Fleischman, Fournier, Francesco da Bologna, Fry, Garamont, Grandjean, Granjon, Gryphius, Guyot, Hartz, Haultin, Hupp, Jannon, Jenson, Kis, Lambrecht, Le Bé, Luce, Malin, Martin, Phemister, Prince, Sabon, Sanlecque, Tavernier, Trattner, Walpergen.* See also *specimen sheet.*

punchcutting machine: a machine which uses the pantograph principle to guide a borer which cuts in steel a reduction of an enlarged template of each letter or character. Without this machine, which was invented in 1884 by the American Lynn Boyd Benton of Milwaukee, mechanical typesetters, with their need for profuse supplies of matrices, could not have been developed. The first model was used by Ottmar Mergenthaler for the *Linotype*, q.v. In 1910 an improved model was introduced by Grant and Legros.

punctuation marks: listed alphabetically, and also under alternative names where applicable, are punctuation marks in common English use:

'	apostrophe
[ ]	brackets
:	colon
,	comma
–	dash
" "	double quotes
!	exclamation mark
.	full stop
-	hyphen
?	interrogation mark
"	inverted commas
( )	parentheses (parens)
.	period
.	point
?	question mark
" "	quotation marks (quotes)
;	semi-colon
' '	single quotes
[ ]	square brackets

See also *duck-foot quotes, guillemets, primes.*

pure: see *wood-free.*

Purgold, L. G., fl.1805–30: a well-known Parisian binder of considerable technical excellence who made the straight line, or fillet, his principal decorative motif. His business passed to his former apprentice *Antoine Bauzonnet* who married his widow, and subsequently to *Georges Trautz*, qq.v. who married his daughter.

putto: a small winged boy. The word derives from the Latin *putus*, which means 'little man', and the plural form *putti* is given to the plump unclad *amorini* which originated in pre-Christian art. It was, however, the work of Donatello which led to their popularity in Italian Renaissance art. By the mid-14th century drawings of putti enlivened the margins of Naples manuscripts, a practice followed in most Italian scriptoria for the next two centuries.

put to bed: see *bed.*

Pye-book: 1. briefly, the Directorium of the Roman Church which determines the appropriate office to be used when a movable holy day coincides with a fixed holy day.

2. a term used in 18th-century England for an alphabetical index to a collection of rolls or records.

Pye, Sybil, 1879–1958: an English bookbinder important for her evolution of a bold personal style expressed in inlays of narrow strips of coloured leather arranged in parallel columns across the upper and lower covers. The cubist effect was unlike anything done before or since. Gold decoration was independent of the mosaic.

She lived at Limpsfield in Surrey where her father was a friend of Cobden-Sanderson, Douglas Cockerell, and Charles Ricketts. She taught herself from Cockerell's 'Bookbinding and the care of books', 1901, and began binding in 1906 using some tools given to her by Ricketts as well as others of her own design. In 1913 she recorded her first inlaid binding, continuing with this style for the rest of her life. She designed all her own bindings.

Her binding tools are now in London's V. & A. Museum, but more important are her three note-books given to the Royal College of Art Library by her nephew David Pye. They contain a presumably complete dated record of her work with photographs, brief descriptions, exhibitions at which shown, and the name of the purchasers. The last entry is dated 1954.

She has been described as 'a most modest and unpretentious person with a deep devotion to her craft and a total absence of any hint of display'.

Pynson Printers: a New York printing firm founded in 1923 by Elmer Adler (1884–1961), a wealthy bibliophile, with the aim of producing fine books for commercial publishers (e.g. Random House). Adler also founded the graphic arts journal *The Colophon* in 1930. The firm closed in 1940.

Pynson, Richard, fl.1490–1528: a printer of Norman birth who worked at Rouen before coming to London where he began by printing legal works for John Russhe. About 1490 he took over the business of William de Machlinia. Pynson quickly became the most important printer of the day and was the second holder of the office of King's Printer (1508). In 1509 he introduced roman types into England, importing them from Paris: the first works in which he used them were 'Sermo Fratris Hieronymi de Ferraria' and a speech by Petrus Gryphus of Pisa, both in 1509. Other printing included lives of the saints, illustrated by crude cuts, as well as law books and Whittinton's popular grammars. The custom of enclosing the matter on title-pages with ornamental borders was typical of his work.

His most important publications were John Lydgate's translation of Boccaccio's 'Falles of princes', 1494, in an edition of *c.* 600 copies; a Sarum Missal, 1500, for Cardinal Morton; and Lord Berners's translation of Jean Froissart's 'Chronicles', 1523–5. He printed in 1521 Henry VIII's 'Assertio septem sacramentorum' which earned for the English Crown the title *Fidei defensor* (Defender of the Faith).

On his retirement in 1528 Robert Redman acquired the business. Pynson died in 1530.

Q

qq.v.: see *q.v.*

quad: a prefix to former standard paper-size names to denote a sheet four times the single and twice the double area, e.g. demy, 17½ in. by 22½ in.; double demy, 22½ in. by 35 in.; quad demy, 35 in. by 45 in.; double quad demy, 45 in. by 70 in.

quadrata: square capitals.

quads: blank types cast less than type height, in standard point sizes, and used as inter-word spacing material. Usual sizes are en, em, 2-em, 3-em, and 4-em quads. The word quad is shortened from *quadrat*, which term, however, is never used in full. See also *high quads*, *hollow quads*, *spaces*.

quality paperback: a preferable term for what is often called an *egghead paperback*. See *paperback*.

Quantity Book-Buying Scheme: an arrangement jointly initiated in 1937 by the Publishers Association and the Booksellers Association whereby a bookseller was, as an exception to the *Net Book Agreement*, q.v., allowed to give a discount on the net price of a book where a large quantity of a specific net book was ordered.

This was simplified in 1951, and amended and extended in 1954 to cover large single orders for net books of an aggregate value of £250 or more, regardless of the number of copies of any one title contained in the order. The prime condition to be fulfilled before the Publishers Association will issue to the bookseller a licence for the granting of discount is that the books must be required for gift or presentation in connection with the purchaser's business, or for philanthropic or propaganda purposes. The provision of a library, whether recreational or educational, for use by the purchaser's own employees, free of charge, would qualify. Discount is never more than 10% but may be less.

Quaritch, Bernard, 1819–99: one of the most famous antiquarian booksellers of Europe. He was born at Worbis in Saxony and in 1834 was apprenticed to a bookseller in Nordhausen, moving to Berlin in 1839. In 1842 he left Berlin for London, working there for Henry G. Bohn, at that time the leading secondhand bookseller. He became a British citizen. During 1844 he went for a time to Theophile Barrois, a noted French bookseller, but the next year found him back with Bohn.

It was in October 1847 that he founded his own business at 16 Castle Street, Leicester Square. His personality and developing reputation attracted the patronage of such famous people as W. E. Gladstone, Mr Disraeli, Lord Dufferin and Edward Fitzgerald (whose translation of the 'Rubaiyat' was first published by Quaritch in 1859). His first (broadsheet) catalogue appeared in 1847.

In 1858 his book-buying ventures started in earnest. He acquired his first Mazarine Bible for £596 and sold it to Lord Lindsay; he bought back this same copy in 1887 for £2,650 and sold it to Lord Carysfort; in 1923 it went to America for £9,500. No fewer then seven copies of this book passed through the hands of Bernard Quaritch or his son Alfred.

In 1860 the business was transferred to 15 Piccadilly. Patrons received here included the Earls of Kimberley, Northbrook, Derby and Crawford; the Dukes of Devonshire and Somerset, Sir Henry Irving, Ellen Terry, Henry Huth, John Ruskin and Sir Richard Burton. He continued to buy on a princely scale whenever a library was auctioned. At the Henry Perkins sale in 1873 Bernard Quaritch spent £10,775. His catalogue of 1874 listed most of the items acquired from the Perkins collection. No such catalogue of valuable books and manuscripts, classified and accompanied by a complete index, had ever before been attempted by any bookseller. It had 1,889 pages and listed 23,000 items. At three sales between 1880 and 1884 Quaritch's purchases amounted to over £97,000; the £3,900 he paid in 1884 for the Syston Park library copy of the Mazarine Bible was, up to that time, the highest price ever paid at a public auction for a printed book.

The acquisition of rare books and manuscripts in such quantities made Quaritch, in the last twenty years of the 19th century, the holder of the chief book treasures for sale in the European market. His last great catalogue, completed in 1888, listed 38,552 items, while its index, published in 1892, contained over 100,000 entries.

Quaritch was associated with William Morris for whom he published a series of translations of the Icelandic Sagas in 1891 ('The Saga Library'); he also published four of the Kelmscott Press books in 1892 and 1894.

In 1878 Quaritch founded the society known as *Ye Sette of Odd Volumes*, q.v.

On the death of the founder the business was directed by his son *Alfred* who had entered the firm in 1889. He was particularly active in America and assisted in the formation of a number of great collections there: he bought for J. P. Morgan, H. C. Folger, H. E. Huntington, and R. Hoe. Alfred Quaritch died in 1913.

In 1907 the firm moved to 11 Grafton Street, transferring in 1971 to its present address 5 Lower John Street, W1R 4AU, where it remains one of the world's leading booksellers. Its most recent notable sale was a copy of the Gutenberg Bible for $2,400,000.

quarter-bound: a book bound with either leather spine and cloth sides, or cloth spine and paper sides. Cf. *half-bound*.

While this style is usually found on books which have been bound by hand, publishers' edition binding can be quarter bound, though two runs through the casemaker may be necessary. See also *siding*.

quartern book: every thirteenth book which the hand binder traditionally bound without charge (analogous to the baker's dozen). In 18th- and early 19th-century England the class of work to which this custom applied was limited to copies of one title all delivered to the binder at the same time.

quarto: written 4to. The book size resulting from folding a sheet with two folds at right-angles, thus giving pages one quarter the size of the sheet. To define fully the size, the paper size must also be stated, e.g. Crown 4to. In practice a double-size sheet would be used to produce in three folds a 16-page section for binding, or a quad-size sheet folded four times to produce 32-page sections for binding. See *British book sizes*. (LK)

quarto galley: a galley about 21cm. by 30cm., or wide enough to take quarto pages.

quaternion: a gathering made up from four sheets, folded once, in which form some bound manuscripts and early printed books were assembled; thus the 1st and 8th, 2nd and 7th, 3rd and 6th, 4th and 5th were conjugate leaves. Hence *ternion* (three sheets), *quinternion* (five sheets) and *sextern* (six sheets).

Quedlinburg Itala: see *Itala of Quedlinburg*.

The Queen Mary Psalter: an early 14th century English Psalter in Latin, probably written for Edward II. It is illustrated by miniatures of Christ's life and those of the saints as well as by 223 tinted drawings based on the Old Testament for which only light colouring was used. The fabulous beasts and birds which appear in contemporary Psalters are here absent. Decorations at the foot of pages include grotesques, scenes of people, and show traces of French influence.

The Psalter, now in the British Library, is named after Queen Mary I who acquired it in 1553.

Queen's Gold Medal for Poetry: an award established in 1933 by King George V (when it was known as the King's Gold Medal for Poetry), and offered once in three years for a volume of poetry in English by a British subject, published in the British Commonwealth. It is administered by the Poet Laureate, advised by a committee.

Queen's Printer: 1. at the time of its creation by Henry VII in 1504, the person appointed by royal licence to be the sole printer of official proclamations and certain specified classes of books, e.g. Bibles, Testaments, Greek and Latin grammars. A royal licence giving a printer the sole right to print a book or even a class of books was a form of privilege and a protection against piracy by others of the copy of his text.

The books reserved to the holder of the Office of Queen's (or King's) Printer, who was paid a salary, were those for which the Crown claimed the privilege since the text was regarded as its property. The office could be bought, as for example, by Christopher Barker in 1577, and it could also be assigned, as was done by Barker's son Robert in 1634.

The present Queen's Printer is the firm of Eyre & Spottiswoode. See also *Bible printing in England*, *privilege*.

2. the civil servant who, as Controller of the Stationery Office, is granted Letters Patent by the Queen appointing him the copyright holder of British Government documents. The Stationery Office is not concerned with Bible printing.

Quentell, Heinrich, fl.1478–1501: a native of Strasbourg who worked in Cologne as a printer, at first of theological works. His most important publication was a translation of the Bible into two German dialects, issued separately about 1478, and now referred to as the *Cologne Bible*. Both had elaborate borders to some of the pages as well as over a hundred woodcuts. For many years the illustrations were to influence other Bible illustrators and printers.

His son *Peter* (fl.1520–46) developed the business into one of the leading establishments of Cologne. His extensive publishing activities led him to commission such other printers as Hieronymous Fuchs.

Peter's son *Johann* continued to print until his death in 1551.

query: the symbol ?, used by the printer's reader in proof margins when the author is required to check some detail.

quick-drying inks: printing inks to which driers have been added to speed up the conversion of the varnish in the ink into a solid film.

Quick-S: the proprietary name of a mechanical alternative to *page-cord*, q.v. It consists of four pieces of zinc alloy which form a frame about a page or any other piece of setting where page-cord would otherwise be used. Each piece or section is extendible and self-adjusting, tension being maintained by recessed coil-springs. Corner fitting is by pegs and holes.

Quick-S, a Norwegian invention, is available in England in pica units; elsewhere in cicero sizes. It permits quicker and safer handling of type, easier correction and quicker lock-up, finer register for colour-proofing, and safer storage of type. Quick-S becomes part of the forme and is not removed until the type is distributed.

quick-set inks: printing inks in which the vehicle contains both a thin mineral oil and a stout varnish. When printed, the thin oil is quickly absorbed into the paper, leaving the pigment and varnish on the surface. The sheets can be handled sooner than if normal linseed oil-based inks have been used. As the final setting of the varnish is slower, the surface remains receptive longer to subsequent printings in multi-colour work.

quinternion: a gathering made up of five sheets. See also *quaternion*.

quire: 1. twenty-four sheets of paper (and one 'outside'); the twentieth of a ream. See also *cording quires, insides, mille, mill ream, outsides, printer's ream, ream, retree*.

2. a *gathering, section,* or *signature,* qq.v., particularly when unfolded. A quire was originally a gathering of four sheets forming eight leaves or sixteen pages after one fold had been made. It was thus synonymous with *quaternion.* The low-Latin word *quaternum* was shortened to 'quair' or 'quaer'. In the days of parchment books quires of four sheets would make a gathering convenient for sewing; when the use of paper spread it was possible to use from five to seven sheets without forming too thick a gathering for the binder. Thus the original association of quire with four became obscured. See also *in quires.*

quirewise: the manner of gathering the leaves of a

booklet by folding them and placing them one in another. They are then stitched. See *insert* (1).

quoins: metal or wooden wedges which are placed between the outer furniture and the sides of the chase in order to lock the type and blocks in it during printing. Metal quoins, of which there are various patent designs, are adjusted with a key until the required tension is attained.

The 'Speed' quoin operates on its whole length, and its adjustment can be read. (Challenge Mach. Co., U.S.A.)

At first wedges were used for this purpose, later wedge quoins and French quoins of different designs, but now screw quoins, or combined screw and wedge quoins, are most used. Quoins are also used inside a forme when it is desirable that some parts should be movable in relation to others, e.g. in colour printing.

Iron quoins were introduced in 1863 by Hippolyte Marinoni of Paris. See also *Hempel quoin, Wickersham quoins.* (GU)

quotation marks: or *quotes;* the inverted comma, singly or in pairs, is used in Britain and America to indicate a quotation. Continental practice is described under *duck-foot quotes* and *primes,* qq.v. See also *punctuation marks.*

quotations: 1. written or spoken words from elsewhere included by an author in his text. Such passages may be enclosed between *quotation marks,* q.v., and set within the text. This is usual for short prose extracts of up to five lines.

Longer quotations, or *block quotations,* may be made more noticeable to the reader by separating them from the text with space, indention, beginning on a fresh line, and the use of a smaller type. They are not enclosed within quotes and are said to be *broken off* or *set off.*

2. an obsolete term for marginal notes.

3. printers' spacing material, cast with hollowed centres, used to *white out,* q.v.

quotes: see *punctuation marks, quotations.*

quousque tandem abutere: see *specimen sheet.*

q.v.: an abbreviation for the Latin 'quod vide', i.e.

'which see'. The abbreviation for the plural form 'quae vide' is *qq.v.*

QWERTY keyboard: said of the layout of letters and numerals common to the keyboards of most typewriters, composing machines, display photosetters, VDT-based equipment and OCR devices used in the English-speaking world. It was devised by the American printer Christopher L. Sholes (1819–90), inventor of the modern typewriter, who found that by separating the letters most frequently found together in English orthography (e.g. *ing*, *th*, *qu*) the likelihood of key-jamming at the printing point was reduced. When, after many experiments subsidized by James Densmore, his first perfected typewriter was introduced in 1874, it was made and marketed by Remington. The keyboard arrangement was long known as 'universal', and not until the 1970s did the appellation QWERTY achieve currency in printing trade literature.

Modified and alternative layouts have been developed to speed up keyboarding (e.g. the DVORAK, the MALTRON, and the Palantype), but the original continues to be generally used throughout the world in spite of differing orthographies.

R

rack-jobbing distribution: see *impulse outlet.*

racks: lengths of stout cord running in parallel between two facing walls in a pressroom, high above the working area. In hand-press days batches of printed sheets were hung on them to dry out the water used to dampen the paper prior to impression. After the introduction of machine presses heated drying rooms were used.

radiation curing: drying a web of printed paper under a unit fitted with infra-red or ultra-violet heaters. See also *microwave drying.*

radio frequency drying: see *microwave drying.*

rag cutter: a machine with blades and prongs which reduces rags to small pieces.

ragged right: type which is set flush to the left-hand margin but is not justified and thus, while evenly spaced, has lines of uneven length as, for example, in poetry setting. Conversely, type can be set flush at the right and be *ragged left* though this is rarely seen in bookwork.

Ragged setting may be more troublesome than straight setting since it has its own rules, such as the avoidance of hyphenated line endings and ensuring that two consecutive lines are not of the same length. Also known as *justified left* or *unjustified setting.*

rag paper: the finest quality paper, made from linen or rag pulp. This has been used in Europe since the 12th century.

The collection and grading of rags was a well-organized trade, thus we read in a memorandum of 1696 addressed to John Locke, Commissioner for Trade: 'The Raggs of England are not soe well preserved or gathered as in other Countryes, where all people are more carefull of them than our Country people are of their Feathers, which is the Reason that a Tonn of French Raggs will make neare double the Vallue of Paper than a Tonn of English Raggs will, as was tryed about 15 yeares since.'

In *The Spectator*, 1 May 1712, Joseph Addison wrote: 'It is pleasant enough to consider the Changes that a Linnen Fragment undergoes . . . The finest Pieces of Holland, when worn to Tatters, assume a new Whiteness more beautiful than their first, and often return in the Shape of Letters to their Native Country. A Lady's Shift may be metamorphosed into Billets doux, and come into her Possession a second time. A Beau may peruse his Cravat after it is worn out with greater Pleasure and Advantage than ever he did in a Glass. In a Word, a Piece of Cloth, after having officiated for some Years as a Towel or a Napkin, may by this Means be raised from a Dunghill, and become the most Valuable Piece of Furniture in a Prince's Cabinet.'

It should be added that woven rag for hand-made paper has now been replaced by cotton linters and other textile fibre pulps which are first processed in specialist mills. See also *papermaking.*

railway libraries: a term used in England after 1848 for single volume reprints of English and American novels, issued in small type on cheap paper, and retailing for a shilling. It was found that they would sell well on railway station bookstalls. In 1848 William Henry Smith opened his first bookstall at Euston Station in London, and eventually had an extensive network of such outlets, giving great impetus to the publishing of cheap reprints.

raised bands: ridges on the spine of a book where the leather of the cover is nipped up over the cords to which the sections have been secured by *flexible sewing*, q.v. When the book has not been sewn on raised cords the bands may be built up with thin strips of card or board, the leather being nipped up as at first described. See also *false bands, nipping up, underbanding.*

raised initial: a display capital letter usually set at the beginning of a chapter. It aligns at the foot with the first line of text, and ranges above it. Also known as a *stickup initial.* See also *initial letters.*

Ramage, Adam, fl.1795–1850: a Scottish joiner who in 1795 emigrated to America. In Philadelphia he began making wooden hand printing presses (after 1820 with an iron bed and platen) as well as bookbinding and paper-cutting machines. He is credited with having made some 1,250 'Ramage' presses, though his name was given generically to similar presses made by others. Their light construction made them popular with pioneers in the spread of printing in the United States.

Ramage called his iron hand-press the *Philadelphia*, but it was renamed the *Bronstrup* by his successor in business, Frederick Bronstrup, who continued to manufacture them until 1875.

Rampant Lions Press: a printing office at Cambridge established by Will Carter, a calligrapher, letter-cutter and printer. His press has been described as 'one of the very few in this country where books are planned, set up and printed by a single pair of hands'. The first book he issued was one of poems by Robert Nichols entitled 'A Spanish triptych', 1936.

Carter has designed books for publishers, cut inscriptions in wood and stone and designed the display type Klang, shown by Monotype in 1955 (see Appendix A). In association with David Kindersley, a letter-cutter and sculptor, Carter designed the Monotype series 603, Octavian, first shown in 1962.

Rampant Lions Press has been a commercial concern since 1959. See A. Tarling, 'Will Carter, printer', Galahad Press, 1968.

random: the sloping work-top of a composing frame. Also known as *bank*.

ranging figures (or **lining figures**): the numerals of modern type-faces which all extend from the base line to the cap line. E.g. the Times Roman figures 1, 2, 3, 4, 5, 6, 7, 8, 9, 0. Cf. *hanging figures*. John Bell pioneered ranging figures but they were cast slightly below the cap line.

Ransom, Will, d. 1955: an American authority on printing, remembered for his 'Private presses and their books', 1929, and for his association with *Goudy*, q.v., in establishing the Village Press. Ransom's considerable collection of books on printing is now in the Newberry Library, Chicago.

Raphelengius, Franciscus: fl.1595–1600: a teacher of Latin and Greek at Cambridge who then went to Leyden to teach Hebrew and become official printer to the university. He managed the Leyden branch of Plantin's office and married one of his daughters. See also *arabic type*.

Rashi, *c.* 1040–1105: the Rabbi Solomon ben Isaac of Troyes. His commentary on the Pentateuch, with the Biblical text, was the first dated Hebrew book to be printed. See also *Bomberg, Hebrew printing before 1600*.

Rastell, John, *c.* 1475–1536: a Londoner who employed himself variously before adding printer-

publishing to his activities. This may have been as early as 1510 when an edition of his brother-in-law Sir Thomas More's translation of 'The lyfe of Johan Picus' is thought to be from his press. He may have learned printing in France, a country he frequently visited, but in London he probably worked as editor and publisher, employing others to work his press.

About 1515 he obtained from France a fount of secretary type, using it to print legal works of which one of the first was Fitzherbert's 'La Grande abbrège-ment de le ley', 1516, in three folio volumes. More than half the thirty-five publications he issued were law books.

Rastell was a minor Tudor dramatist, both writing and publishing his play 'A new interlude . . .', which was remarkable for the inclusion of a song for which text and music were printed together by one impression. The type was cast from matrices struck twice: first with a punch bearing a segment of staff, over which a punch bearing notation was then struck. The work was undated, but if, as scholars are inclined to believe, it was printed about 1520, it would pre-date the invention of single-impression music printing in 1528 by *Attaingnant*, q.v. The type may have originated in northern France, though no example of music printed there with it is known.

He is remembered for his adaptation of Robert Fabyan's 'Chronicles' to which he gave the title 'The pastyme of people; the cronycles of divers realmys', 1529; it included full-page woodcuts of English kings.

He became involved in religious controversy, converting to Protestantism, and died in prison in 1536. The business then passed to his son *William* (*c.* 1508–65) who was a practising lawyer and later a judge. He printed between 1529–34, issuing some thirty books. However, after selling his press, he continued to edit works for publication, notable being his uncle Sir Thomas More's complete works, issued in 1557. Because of his Catholic beliefs he twice exiled himself to Louvain where he died. See A. Hyatt King, 'The significance of John Rastell in early music printing', *The Library*, 5th ser., xxvi 3 1971.

Ratdolt, Erhard, *c.* 1447–*c.* 1527: a distinguished and enterprising German printer and type-cutter who from 1476–86 worked in Venice, and from 1486 in his native Augsburg where the same year he issued the first known specimen sheet. It had ten sizes of gothic letter, three of roman and a greek. At first he worked with Peter Löslein (probably as editor and proof reader) and Bernhard Maler (as designer of border decorations). Their names appear on the first nearly complete *title-page*, q.v., printed in two colours in 1476.

Ratdolt printed numerous Missals and Breviaries for such places as Melk, Passau, Regensburg and Salzburg. He devoted much care to the ornamentation of his books, using *entrelac initials*, q.v., and elegant woodcuts. In the editio princeps of Euclid's 'Elementa geometriae', 1482, he included over 400 of what were the first printed geometrical diagrams (whether from wood or curved rule has not been determined). In the vellum dedication copy for the Doge he used gold ink, made by substituting gold dust for lampblack. The 'Obsequiale Augustense', of 1487 had a dedicatory woodcut in colour. See G. R. Redgrave, 'Erhard Ratdolt and his work at Venice', Bibliographical Society, 1894.

Raven Press: a private press set up in 1931 at Harrow Weald, London by Robert Maynard and Horace Bray, two wood engravers who had worked together at the *Gregynog Press*, q.v. Notable among the four books they issued were Shakespeare's 'Venus and Adonis' and Milton's 'Samson Agonistes'. Bray appears to have left before 1937, and no work was done after 1940. In 1944 Maynard used the name Raven Press for his greeting-card business. He was also a consultant designer to several publishers. His business closed in 1965 and he died a year later. See J. A. Dearden, 'The Raven Press', *The Private Library*, 4 1973.

reader's box: the room in a printing office used for proof-reading. There may be several readers with attendant copy-boys, ideally separated by partitions or screens into boxes. Rooms should have good lighting and be reasonably quiet, but in 19th century England, and sometimes today, they were often little more than dim and airless cupboards.

reading copies: gratis copies of a forthcoming book supplied by the publisher as part of his sales promotion to selected booksellers. Although supplied in advance of publication they are sometimes part of the edition run and are in the same binding as trade copies. Cf. *advance copies, desk copies*.

ream: originally twenty quires or 480 sheets of paper. Reams of book paper are now standardized at 500 sheets. The word may be a curious survival of the Arabic origin of the paper trade in the Western world, coming from *rizmah*, meaning a bundle of rags, and by extension a fixed quantity of paper (Spanish *resma*, Latin *risma*, and French *rame*). See also *long ream, mill ream, mille, printers' ream, quire, short ream*.

re-backed: said of a book having the spine re-covered in a style or material approximating the old. Cf. *backed*.

recension: a revised version of a text: the term implies critical editing.

receptivity: see *ink receptivity*.

recessed cords: cords of hemp or flax which lie in grooves sawn across the gathered sections of a book. Sawing is done in a *lying press*, q.v. In the sewing frame the thread is passed over the cord, not round it (see diagram under *hand-sewing*), the sections being secured at head and foot by kettle stitches. The result is a smooth flat back.

The style was used in France from the late 16th- to mid-17th century, in England until about 1710, and was later popularized by Nicholas Derome. The excess of glue used at that time gave a hard smooth back which cracked with repeated opening. This led to the use of a *hollow back*, q.v., introduced in France by 1772, and in England a little later.

The method is still in occasional use for hand-bound work and for heavy morocco or pigskin books. *Sawn-in sewing*, as the style is known, is much quicker to do than *flexible sewing*, q.v., on raised cords.

recess printing: processes in which the ink for printing is contained in recesses in the printing plate or cylinder, e.g. *photogravure*, q.v.

recto: 1. a bibliographer's term for the upper side of a leaf of parchment or paper whether written or printed upon or not. Cf. *verso*.

2. the right-hand pages of a book, bearing uneven numbers.

recycled paper: paper made from waste, i.e. from a furnish which includes *fine whites* and *broke*, qq.v. For cheaper grades furnish includes lightly printed waste, tinted papers and mechanical waste. In book publishing the best recycled grades have been found suitable for printing fiction.

Redman, Robert, fl.1525–40: a London printer of lawbooks, and in 1525 an edition of 'Magna Carta'. He took Pynson's premises in Fleet Street on the latter's death and also used his device.

red under gilt edges: book edges which have been sprayed with a red dye before gilding: a feature of better-quality devotional bookbinding.

Reed, Talbot Baines, 1852–93: a London typefounder and man of varied interests. He wrote serial stories for *Boys Own Paper*, reviewed books for *The Leeds Mercury*, was the first secretary of The Bibliographical Society in 1892, and wrote the first major history of typefounding in England 'History of the old English letter foundries', 1887, of which a revised edition appeared in 1952. Reed also managed the family typefounding business, the Fann Street Foundry, which cast for Morris his Chaucer, Golden and Troy types. See S. Morison, 'Talbot Baines Reed: author, bibliographer, typefounder', (Privately published) C.U.P., 1960.

reel-fed: synonymous with *web-fed*, q.v.

reel gold: a somewhat misleading binding-trade term used for continuous rolls of imitation gold, i.e. bronze. In short, a *blocking foil*, q.v.

reel stand: see *rotary press*.

The Reference Catalogue of Current Literature: the original name of the British book trade bibliography published by J. Whitaker & Sons. The first edition, 1874, consisted of 135 publishers' catalogues of uniform size, bound in two volumes, with a separate index of 35,000 entries. The work continued in this form, at three- or four-year intervals, until 1932. From 1936–40 it appeared at two-year intervals, and was increased in scope by giving fuller bibliographical details of each book. The 1957 edition (issued 1958) records the books in print in Britain at the end of 1956. The listing of all works in print makes the catalogue unique among book-trade tools; and its useful features include an annotated list of publishers, a directory of directors, and the listing of works issued in publishers' series (in Vol. II. Titles).

From 1965 publication continued as *British Books in Print*, q.v.

reference marks: signs inserted in the text of a work to direct the attention of the reader to footnotes. In order of use these are:

*   asterisk, or star
†   dagger
‡   double dagger
§   section
‖   parallel
¶   paragraph

If more are needed they are printed in pairs. *Superior figures*, q.v., are preferable since they clearly indicate the order of the notes.

references: 1. words used in the text of a work to direct the reader to another part of it, e.g. *see above*, *see below*, or their Latin equivalents *vide supra*, *vide infra*.

2. Latin abbreviations used in footnotes and bibliographies to refer the reader to other writers, authorities, sources quoted, books referred to or particular pages in those works. Examples are *ibid.*, *id.*, *loc. cit.*, *s.v.*, *qq.v.*

3. see *reference marks*.

reflex printing: a means of reproducing documents or books without setting up type. The principle was discovered by Albrecht Beyer about 1839. Among

412

several applications subsequently patented is the *Typon process*, q.v.

Regemorter, Berthe van, 1879–1964: born at Malmis. A Belgian bookbinder remembered for her published researches into the history of forwarding techniques from Coptic times.

Regina Medal: since 1959, an annual award made by the American Catholic Library Association to a person in the literary world judged to have made a lifetime contribution to children's literature. The first recipient was Eleanor Farjeon.

Regiomontanus, Johannes, 1436–76: a German scientist and printer of Königsberg (after which city he changed his birth name of Johannes Müller). After living in Vienna and Hungary he settled in Nuremberg where, financed by a patron, he established a printing press, a workshop and an observatory. He issued a few astronomical works written by himself and his friends, notable being George Purbach's 'Theoricae planetarum novae', c. 1472. His printing acitivities were really an adjunct to his more important work as an astronomer.

It was in an edition of his 'Calendarium', Venice, 1476, that Erhard Ratdolt printed an early example of the modern title-page.

register: 1. the precise superimposing of the separate plates in an illustration printed in two or more colours. Careless work is said to be 'out of register'. See also *lock-up table*.

2. the exact correspondence in position of the printed area on the two sides of a leaf. See also *cut to register*, *pinholes*, *points*.

3. a *signet*, q.v.

4. a list of signatures appearing at the end of early printed books as a guide to the binder. They were mostly used in Italy c. 1470–1600, the first being in the 'Epistolae Hieronymi', printed by Sixtus Riessinger, Rome, 1470, though examples do occur in English books. The list was usually headed *registrum foliorum* or *registrum chartarum*, and the first word of each signature would be given as an alternative to a letter.

register sheet: the sheet used to obtain correct register or position of the printed page. See also *shining*.

register table: a table with an opaque-glass top and a white-washed interior under it fitted with lights. This is used in the gravure planning department to position negatives or positives and any accompanying type matter on a layout sheet. It is also used for register work in colour printing and for other purposes.

Also known as *lining up table* or *shining-up table*.

registrum chartarum: see *register* (4).

registrum foliorum: see *register* (4).

reglets: strips of oil-soaked wood used as inter-linear spacing material, ¾ in. high and from 6- to 18-point thick. (6-point and 12-point are known as nonpareil and pica reglet respectively.) See also *clumps*.

reimposition: the rearrangement of pages in a forme made necessary when it is desired to add additional text to matter already arranged in pages or to use a different folding machine. Cf. *double setting*.

Reiner, Imre, 1900– : an eminent graphic artist and typographer, born in Hungary, now a Swiss citizen, known for the imaginative and technically advanced wood engravings with which he illustrated books as well as for his writings on typography. Types designed by him include Corvinus, 1929–35 (for Bauersche Giesserei) and several script faces for display work such as Matura, 1938, and Mercurius, 1957 (for Monotype).

reinforced binding: a strengthened binding, i.e. at the joints, for public library use.

reinforced signatures: signatures which have had cambric pasted around or in the fold for the purpose of strengthening the paper and binding; this is often done on the first and last signatures of a book because of the extra strain at those points. (ML)

re-issue: 1. a new impression of a work, usually from standing type or plates.
2. said of what should properly, if type is re-set, be termed a new edition, e.g. 'Re-issued in the Malvern Library' or 'Re-issued in pocket form'.

relative humidity: the percentage of moisture in the atmosphere compared with the amount which would be present were the atmosphere fully saturated with water vapour at the same temperature. Saturated air has an RH factor of 100%: in press rooms it may vary from 30% to 80%.
Like all fibres of organic origin paper is hygroscopic and absorbs or emits water to adjust its moisture content to that of the air in which it is stored. As this affects its weight and printing properties its RH must be known: it is measured by reading a sword hygrometer inserted in a stack or roll of paper. The RH factor varies with different fibres but remains constant for the same kind of fibre or pulp, i.e. for the same specification of paper.

RH of the air	Corresponding water content of equal weights of a cellulose fibre
30%	5%
40%	6%
50%	7%
60%	8·5%
70%	10%
80%	13%

Changes in the water content of a fibre affect its dimensions. The fibre diameter swells as its moisture content increases, and this stretches the paper. Other properties are also affected. The absorption and emission of water require a certain time, the former less than the latter. It is the edges of stored paper which will first be exposed to changes in humidity. If the air is damper than the paper the edges will tend to buckle: drier air may cause undulations in the middle of the pile. (See also *conditioning*.) Paper conditioning is more effective if the pressroom is also air conditioned. In offset establishments, where attention must be paid to the moisture transmissible to the paper direct from the damped plates (by way of the rubber blanket), an RH of approximately 60% has proved suitable for register purposes. In other printing offices and paper-handling concerns a lower moisture content may be better.

Normally, if sheet stock in the printer's paper warehouse is kept in the maker's waterproof wrapping humidity control there will not be essential, but paper should be taken to the pressroom to stand some time before use, and must be kept wrapped. With reeled stock the wrapping should be removed when the reel is put on the press to prevent the edge distortion referred to above.

When ordering paper the printer should give the average temperature and RH figures of his pressroom as well as stating the process for which it will be used. See also *static electricity*. (With GU)

relief block: a line or half-tone printing plate mounted to type height for letterpress printing. See also *photoengraving*.

relief printing: printing from surfaces which are raised to a standard height (see *type height*) so that ink is deposited only on the image which is to be transferred to paper. Relief printing, also known as *letterpress printing*, includes printing from hand and machine-set type or slugs, linocuts, woodcuts, wood engravings, photoengraved plates and stereos or electros of them.

remainder binding: see *remainders*.

remainders: copies of a book which has ceased to sell well and of which the publisher has large stocks. Disposal is by selling the remainder of the stock, or unbound folded and collated copies, or unfolded sheets to a remainder dealer who then markets them to the trade (folded and collated copies being bound up in a cheap *remainder binding*). American practice is to pulp unbound remaindered stock.

A remaindered work is not necessarily a poor one: it may have been priced too high, or the edition may have been too large, or a subject have lost its topicality. It is not unknown (though never admitted in respectable circles) for a publisher, on finding a demand for a book at its reduced price, to print further copies for sale as a *remaindered edition* in jackets bearing the original price or even an artificially enhanced price.

In Britain, a publisher planning to remainder a title will insert an announcement in *The Bookseller*, traditionally a few weeks in advance. See also *terms*.

The practice of remaindering books was considerably developed by James Lackington (1746–1815) of the 'Temple of the Muses' bookshop in London. In the 19th century certain London dealers came to specialize in this branch of bookselling. See also *trade sales*.

remboîté: a term descriptive of a book which, after the original case or binding has been removed, is rebound in the covers taken from another book. A remboîtage may be created (a) to place an important text which has been unsuitably rebound in what appear to be its original covers, or (b) to put what is deemed a more suitable or less damaged text in a valuable binding. In both instances the intent is normally fraudulent.

removes: quotations or notes set at the foot of a page and in a smaller type than that of the text. Thus a book set in 12-point may have notes set in 10-point.

Renner, Paul, 1878–1956: a German artist and type designer whose sanserif series Futura was cut between 1928 and 1957 for the Bauersche Giesserei. Other types were designed for the Stempel and Berthold companies. He was an influential teacher of typography at the graphic art school he founded in Munich with Emil Preetorius in 1911, while his 'Die Kunst der Typographie', 1940, was one of several important manuals on the subject.

Repertorium bibliographicum ad annum 1500: originally, an alphabetically arranged author list of 16,311 incunabula based on the collection in what is now the Bavarian State Library, Munich. This was compiled by Ludwig F. T. Hain (1781–1836), and published by J. F. Cotta, 4 vols, Stuttgart, 1826–38.

An English bibliographer, *Walter Arthur Copinger* (1847–1910), published a supplement, 3 vols, 1895–1902, in which he corrected 7,000 entries and described a further 6,619 incunabula. An index to Hain was prepared by Konrad Burger, 1891, and a further

1,921 incunabula were described in Dietrich Reichling's series of appendices, Munich, 1905–14.

A reprint of the 'Repertorium' was published in Milan, 1948.

repetition bindings: a term descriptive of bindings having as the principal decorative feature on the boards rows of small outline tools, sometimes with onlays of contrasting leather and bearing an initial or motif tooled in each small compartment. The style was popular in England and France in the 18th century. They are sometimes known as *all-over pattern* bindings.

Replika process: the trade name for a method of photolitho facsimile printing practised by Percy Lund, Humphries & Co. of Bradford. The main use is for printing out-of-print books when standing type is not available; corrections can be made before photographing the original and it is especially economical when this includes tabular work, symbols, etc. By keeping, to the publisher's order, the photographic negatives of the reprints the firm can make further issues at any time without bulky storage problems. A further use of the process is its adaptation to the reproduction of line illustrations, typescript catalogues, brochures, etc. When preparing the manuscript for tabular matter an outline of the framework is drawn and photo-printed on to carbon-backed typing paper. The figures are typed in. After correction, the typed sheets may need to go to the composing department for the addition of pagination, prelims, etc. The book or booklet is then ready for photographing and machining. An advantage is that the typescript to be reproduced can either be prepared by the printer or in the customer's office, thus eliminating post-printing proofing and reading.

repped: see *ribbed paper*.

reprint: 1. a reproduction in print of any matter already printed.

2. a reissue of a work using the same type or plates employed in the original, with the text unchanged except for the correction of minor errors.

3. printed matter used as copy to be set up and printed again.

reproduction camera: see *camera*.

reproduction proof: a carefully pulled proof, showing all details of the type, used for reproduction purposes.

reprographic printing: the printing on its own premises of material required for the furtherance of its business by any organisation not part of the printing trade, and employing for this purpose staff who are not members of a printing trade union. Users of *reprography*, as it is also known, include large industrial firms, ministries, municipalities, and airlines. Typical work produced includes publicity leaflets, technical manuals, sales catalogues, spare parts lists, minutes of meetings, and stationery. Advantages are that the user has more control over the result, time is saved, and there is greater security.

Electric typewriters, electrostatic cameras, electrostatic presensitized plates and simple processors are among equipment used. Reproduction is on small offset-litho machines, which print from thin easily fitted plates of aluminium. The microfilm storage of copy facilitates single-copy or short run reprints.

Also known as *in-plant printing*. See also *Institute of Reprographic Technology, National Reprographic Centre for documentation, near-print*.

republication: a reprint of a book without corrections.

Resch, Conrad, fl.1516–26: a Parisian publisher, born in Basle. He was a devotee of the German Reformation and published the first translation into French of Martin Luther's tracts. His printing was done by Pierre Vidoue and Simon Dubois. The title pages of his books have woodcut borders in the Basle style (with cherubs, garlands, cornucopiae, etc.), some of them being the work of Urs Graf. In 1526 Resch returned to Basle and his shop passed to Chrestien Wechel.

Rescius, Rutger: a scholar-printer, protégé of Erasmus, and professor of Greek in the Collegium Trilingue, Louvain. He was a sometime associate of *Thierry Martens*, q.v., whose business he continued from 1529 to 1545 when he died. He issued several Greek text-books, sometimes in partnership with Johannes Sturmius, and in 1540 Mercator's famous 'Literarum latinarum . . .'

resin: see *size*.

resist: a coating of glue, enamel, or shellac, given to a plate when etching to protect non-printing areas from acid corrosion. See also *cold enamel, fish-glue enamel, polyvinyl alcohol enamel*.

Restoration bindings: English bindings, made by various craftsmen at the time of the restoration of the English monarchy, 1660. The best known are those done in the workshop of *Samuel Mearne*, q.v., the Court binder. Mottled calf covers were popular. See also *sombre bindings, Turkey leather*.

retail bookseller: one whose main business is to sell books to the public at the full net published price. In addition to private individuals the term 'public' embraces schools, public libraries, university libraries and institutions wherever situated, and officials of such bodies. See also *terms* (1 and 2).

retention: the percentage of loading remaining in the sheet as it forms on the wire. Factors affecting this are the other ingredients of the stock, the amount of beating and the speed of the Fourdrinier. Cf. *backwater*.

retouching: 1. the skilled treatment of an original photograph prior to making a block. Process black and white are applied by brush in order to accentuate the high lights, deepen the dark tones and cover any unwanted parts; if the latter are at all extensive an airbrush is used.

2. the hand-correcting of colour separations in the photoengraving and photolithographic processes. This is known in America as *dot-etching*. See also *offset reproduction*.

retransfer: an impression taken from a lithographic surface, usually in special ink and on special paper, for the sole purpose of duplicating this original lithographic image on to another lithographic surface. It is thus distinguishable from a *lithographic transfer* which is a surfaced paper bearing an inked image taken from any impression on a *non*-lithographic surface and then transferred to a lithographic plate. Cf. *transfer*.

retree: the papermaker's term for the slightly damaged sheets of several reams of paper. Damage is limited to slight specks and minor defects. Outsides or broken sheets are marked XXX; 10% less than good are marked XX. Quires of retree are often sold separately with the latter marking.

retree copy: a copy of a limited edition book made up from spare sheets of which some may show uneven inking or discolorations. Such copies are, if offered for sale, *out of series*, q.v. See also *overs* (2).

retroussage: the passing of a fine muslin rag across the etched or engraved surface of a copper printing plate to draw out ink from the recesses so that it will spread over surrounding areas. This treatment of a hand-inked plate is done to soften the outlines of the image or to enrich dark tones.   (GU)

retting: in papermaking the partial disintegration of fibres by soaking them in water.

return on full credit: said of books supplied to a bookseller of which unsold copies may be returned to the publisher who will supply other titles to the same value.

returns: books which have been supplied to a bookseller on sale or consignment which are returned unsold to the publisher. Also copies ordered 'firm'

415

which do not sell, for which the bookseller seeks an agreement to return unsold stock.

Reuchlin, Johann, 1455–1522: a German humanist, scholar and teacher of Hebrew who sponsored the cutting of the first hebrew types cast in Germany. They were the work of one of his printers, Thomas Anshelm of Hagenau. Anshelm cut three founts.

Reuchlin studied the Hebrew Bible as a grammarian, believing his philological method was the only way to a true understanding of God's word. Among his important works were the first Hebrew grammars written by a Christian, 'De rudimentis Hebraicae linguae', 1506, and 'De accentibus et orthographia linguae Hebraicae', 1518. He considered the Cabbala to be the earliest philosophical document and issued his 'Capnia, seu de verbo mirifico', 1494, and 'De arte cabbalistica', 1517.

reversal developing: developing so that the material exposed in the camera shows a positive image on completing the process instead of a negative one. First developing proceeds as for an ordinary negative, a negative silver picture appearing. Instead of fixing it the developed plate is put in a bleaching bath which dissolves the silver reduced by the developer, but leaves the silver bromide unchanged. The plate is again exposed to light and developed, only the silver bromide left after the first developing being blackened. A positive picture is thus obtained. The process is used in colour photography, amateur film photography and for making duplicate negatives.

Reversal developing is used in process work, e.g. in copying positive originals or photographic positives on litho plates. (GU)

reverse aquatint: see *aquatint*.

reversed calf: synonymous with *rough calf*, q.v.

reversed lettering: in letterpress, white lettering on a black background. A pull is made from set-up type, photographed, and a reverse plate made by the photoengraver. Drawn lettering may be treated in the same way. If clear lettering on a half-tone background is wanted two negatives are made, a line and a half-tone. An ink albumen print of the lettering is made from the line negative. The plate is re-coated with dichromated fish glue and the half-tone negative is exposed to it. After developing the half-tone the ink image of lettering is removed with benzole.

reversing: a photoengraving term for reversing black to white or left to right. If an image on a letterpress plate is to be transferred to an offset plate it must be reversed for the impression in the offset press to appear correctly. A reversing apparatus is used to do this. (GU)

416

review copies: copies of a book in its final form sent to reviewers before publication date. They are thus not quite the same as *advance copies*, q.v.

revise: a proof embodying corrections made by the author and/or reader of an earlier proof.

revised edition: an edition of a work bearing changes to the text as previously published. The new matter may be embodied in the text or added as a supplement, and the changes may have been made by someone other than the original author. A revised edition is sometimes, if less precisely, described by the publisher as an *enlarged edition* or a *new edition*.

It is helpful to purchasers, particularly of academic, scientific and technical titles, if the changes between the revised edition and the one which preceded it are fully explained in a preface or introduction. Cf. *re-issue*.

Reynes, John, fl.1510–44: the first English binder of note, who was bookseller and binder to Henry VII and Henry VIII. He was a native of Holland and set up premises in London as a stationer, being active in all branches of the trade. A fine example of his work, on brown calf-covered boards had a centre panel on each, with the royal arms, gilded, stamped on the upper cover and the Tudor rose on the lower. The edges were gilded. It can be dated between 1521 and 1524.

Reynes used a signed roll tool of a thistle, bee, falcon and hound among foliage, impressed in blind to form a frame, and he had five different pairs of panels. Many of his bindings survive.

RFD: radio frequency drying. See *microwave drying*.

RH: see *relative humidity*.

Rhenanus, Beatus, 1485–1547: a book collector, Greek scholar, editor and press corrector remembered for his close association first with Henri Estienne in Paris, and later with Erasmus and Froben in Basle in which city he prepared editions of Eusebius, Livy, Pliny, Seneca and Tacitus. His searches for texts to edit for subsequent printing took him to monasteries in Alsace and the Upper Rhine. Most of his personal library is preserved in his native Sélestat in Alsace.

rhumb chart: another name for a *portolano*, q.v., which had rhumb lines drawn from a central point in the directions of the compass or winds. These lines assisted pilots in setting a course between harbours. See also *wind rose*.

John Llewelyn Rhys Memorial Prize: a prize established in 1921 by J. L. Rhys as an annual award to a British man or woman under 30 for a memorable work, either 'in achievement or promise', published for the first time in the previous year.

ribbed paper: wove paper which during making is given a ribbed effect similar to that of laid paper by pressing before the web is dry. Currently rarely seen, but is to be found in some books printed in the 1840s. Also known as *repped*.

Riccardi Press: the name used since 1909 for the publications of the Medici Society, London. Herbert P. Horne, who founded the press, designed the Riccardi type in 1909, E. P. Prince cut the punches, and printing was done by the Chiswick Press.

The imprint continued to be used until about 1933.

Ricci, Seymour de, 1881–1942: a scholar and bibliographer who evolved an entirely new type of bibliographical study, the enumeration of all known examples of a given book. His first work of this kind was the 'Census of Caxtons', Bibliographical Society, 1909; similarly in 1911 he listed all known examples of Gutenberg's printing in 'Catalogue raisonné des premieres impressions de Mayence', Gutenberg Gesellschaft. His sixth edition of Henry Cohen's 'Guide de l'amateur de livres à vignettes du XVIIIe siècle, Paris, 1870, appeared as 'Guide de l'amateur de livres à gravures du 18e siècle', Paris, 1912, and is known as *Cohen-Ricci* by bibliographers and librarians. A supplement to this by Reynaud was published in Geneva in 1954.

Ricci's 'The book collector's guide', 1921, listed over 2,000 first editions of authors from Chaucer to Swinburne. He gave the Sanders Lecture for 1929, published as 'English collectors of books and MSS., 1530–1930', C.U.P., 1930. Supplements to his 'Census . . .' (see above) were published in America in 1962 and 1963.

Richard, Thomas: a monk of Tavistock Abbey, Devon, where he operated the second monastic press in England. The first book he issued was a translation by John Watts, made about 1410, of the 'Consolation of philosophy' by Boethius. This was in 1525, and the colophon bears the arms of Robert Langdon who probably advised the printer. No second book from his press is known though his type may have been used in the neighbourhood for a few years. See also *Schoolmaster of St Albans*.

Richardson, Samuel, 1689–1761: an important London printer and sometime novelist. In 1706 he was apprenticed to the printer John Wilde (d. 1720) whose daughter he married prior to setting up his own business about 1721. During his well-organized and successful working life he bound no fewer than twenty-four apprentices, nine of whom became master-printers. He held several offices in the Stationers' Company and was Master in 1754.

Works produced from his nine presses included newspapers, the *Transactions* of the Royal Society, the first printed edition (in twenty-six volumes) of the *Journals* of the House of Commons, as well as from 1737 to 1761, bills and reports.

He joined publishing and bookselling *congers*, q.v., and owned valuable copyrights. Poets, playwrights and clergy were among authors who asked him to print their works, often on a commission basis.

In later life he wrote and published three very successful novels, 'Pamela', 1740, 'Clarissa', 1748, and 'Sir Charles Grandison', 1753/4. Two of his wretched journeymen stole sheets of this last as they came from the press and sold them to Dublin booksellers who promptly reprinted them without payment to Richardson.

See W. M. Sale, 'Samuel Richardson: master printer', N.Y., Cornell U.P., 1950, See also *printers' ornaments*.

Richel, Bernhard, fl.1474–82: an important printer of Basle. He issued the first dated book printed there, the 'Sachsenspiegel' of 1474, and also the city's first illustrated book, the 'Spiegel des menschlichen Behältnisses', 1476, in which the woodcuts appear to derive from earlier blockbooks. The same blocks were used in 1478 when Martin Huss printed the work with the title 'Mirouer de la Rédemption'.

Richel worked for a time in association with Michael Wenssler. After his death Richel's wife and son-in-law Nicolaus Kessler continued the business.

Richenbach, Johann, fl. *c.* 1467–85: a binder of Geislingen of whose output over forty bindings are recorded. He was one of the first binders known to have used roll tools. Also noteworthy were his large panel stamps for impressing a complete design. In the frame-like border of the panel he lettered the title and author of the work plus his own name as binder.

Ricketts, Charles, 1866–1931: founder of the *Vale Press*, q.v. He was also interested in edition-bindings. A meeting with Oscar Wilde in 1889 resulted in a commission to design the binding for 'Dorian Gray', 1891, followed by other works published by Osgood and McIlvaine and later John Lane. Pastel-coloured paper boards, calligraphic titling on the front boards and spine and small floral ornaments typify some of his designs which were in the spirit of the fashionable Art Nouveau movement. His occasionally elaborate covers, such as those for Wilde's 'A house of pomegranates', 1891, were unfavourably criticized, and for 'The sphinx', 1894, and 'De profundis', 1905, he returned to Rossetti's simpler style, symbolic and sparse, which had been his original inspiration. The best of his binding designs were linear, owing nothing to Art Nouveau.

In the 1900s Ricketts designed occasional edition-bindings until the 1920s. See also *Pye, Rossetti*.

Ripoli Press: see *Apud Sanctum Jacobum de Ripoli*.

Rittenhouse, William, 1654–1708: a German paper-maker (born *Wilhelm Rittinghausen*) from Mülheim who, in 1690, built on behalf of *William Bradford*, q.v., and Samuel Carpenter the first American paper-mill: this was at Germantown, Pa.

Rittenhouse and his family appear later to have assumed full control of the business which established the supremacy of Pennsylvania as a papermaking centre.

Rituale: a book containing the form and order to be used at religious services.

rivers: unsightly white channels flowing down a page between adjacent words on successive lines of type. They occur when interword spacing is too wide.

Riverside Press: an American private press founded in 1888 by Henry Houghton in Cambridge, Mass., as a subsidiary of the publishing firm Houghton, Mifflin of Boston. D. B. Updike was an employee of the press for two years, having previously worked in the publishing house. In 1896 *Bruce Rogers*, q.v., was appointed director of the press which, until it closed in 1911, issued limited editions of some sixty books. See R. Nash, 'Notes on the R. press . . .', *Gutenberg Jahrbuch*, 1960.

Rivière, Robert, 1808–82: a London bookbinder of Huguenot descent who was commissioned by Queen Victoria and leading bibliophiles. In 1829 he set up a bookselling and binding business in Bath, the move to London taking place about 1840. Here his business expanded to become the leading bookbinding firm of his day.

Lavishly tooled bindings with onlaid covers and doublures were typical of the firm's work. The finishing was often brilliant though the excessive gold tooling on some books totally obscured the fine morocco underneath.

A son-in-law continued the business until 1939 when the binding tools were acquired by Bayntun of Bath. See also *Cosway bindings*.

roan: thin sheepskin tanned in sumach, dyed and finished with a smooth or embossed grain for use in bookbinding, often as a substitute for morocco. It is not as durable. See also *skiver*.

Robert, Nicolas-Louis, 1761–1828: the pioneer inventor of the papermaking machine. While working as an overseer in the Didot papermill at Essonnes, near his birthplace of Paris, he tried to evolve a papermaking machine. After some years, assisted by the mill-owner, *St Léger Didot*, he accomplished this, and in 1798 made the model of a machine for which he was awarded a State grant in order to construct a demonstration model for the Conservatoire des Arts, Paris. In 1799 he patented his invention, an endless wire machine: couch rolls were added by Perrier in 1801.

Robert sold his patent to Didot, who persuaded an English relative, John Gamble, to interest an English papermaker in a scheme for building the machine in England. (No French capital for this project was available.) Gamble approached the London stationery firm Walker, Bloxam & Fourdrinier whose leading partners were the brothers Henry and Sealy Fourdrinier. Gamble himself took out the first English patents in 1801 and 1803. For the subsequent development of the machine see under *Bryan Donkin* and *Fourdrinier*. (With GU)

Rochel paper: a high-quality printing paper imported into England from the Angoumois during the 16th and 17th centuries.

Rochester Press: a private printing press established in 1858 by Edwin Roffe, a steel engraver, at Somers Town, London. He issued small editions of several volumes of miscellaneous diaries, notes and reminiscences. 'He was evidently a true bibliomaniac, and his notes upon his favourite books are full of the unction with which the real book-lover dilates upon his cherished treasures.' (B. Dobell.)

He appears to have ceased printing about 1876. The curious may examine examples of his work in the British Library.

rocker: see *cradle*.

rocking-cylinder press: a cylinder machine in which the cylinder revolves in one direction during the forward movement of the bed, reversing and swinging back to its original position during the return of the bed. Some rocking-cylinder machines are so constructed that printing is done during both movements; in this case the press must have double feeding and delivery arrangements for the paper. See also *letterpress machines*. (GU)

Rodker, John, d. 1956: see *Ovid Press*.

Roffet, Pierre, d. 1533: the leading Parisian binder from about 1510 until his death, and one of the two official binders to the Sorbonne. From a document dated 1523 we learn of the sale by the heir of *Simon Vostre*, q.v., to Pierre Roffet of the former's binding equipment and books both bound and in sheets.

He was succeeded by his publisher-binder son

Etienne (fl.1533–47), known as 'Le Faucheur', who was the first 'relieur du roi', an office created by François I. The title occurs in Roffet's imprints between 1539 and 1547. His publications included royal edicts on coinage, and it is possible that the craftsmen who engraved reproductions of coins for these works also made binding tools. The latter were very fine and were copied by other binders.

On the royal books Roffet's tooling usually consisted of small compartments filled with curved fillets and floral tools, repetitions of the royal cipher and fleurs-de-lis, all within a fillet border frame.

Etienne Roffet has been identified by the late L. Michon as the binder, about 1535, of the important 'Évangéliaire de François I', to be followed by a group of 175 similar bindings. Michon also attributed to Roffet a binding on Grolier's copy of Vida's 'Oeuvres', 1536, but this has been doubted by later authorities.

The two-volume Estienne folio Bible (1538–40) which Roffet bound for François I may show the first use of morocco for a royal binding. The artistic possibilities of this alternative to calf were quickly appreciated by other Parisian binders.

After his death Roffet's widow Nicole Pléau published with *Pierre Haultin*, q.v., a final book on coinage.

Rogers, Bruce, 1870–1957: a distinguished American printer and typographer. After graduating from Purdue University in 1890 he tried newspaper illustrating, then designed a title-page for the magazine *Modern Art* in 1893. The first book he designed was a volume of poems by G. W. Russell (A. E.) issued by *Mosher*, q.v., in 1895, but his typographic career really began with the red and blue printed title-page, headpieces and initials of vines, with glosses in red which Rogers designed for Gruelle's 'Notes: critical and biographical: collection of W. T. Walters', Bowles, 1895. The decoration was clearly inspired by William Morris to whom Bowles sent proof sheets for comment. Between 1896 and 1911 Rogers directed the *Riverside Press*, q.v.

On visits to England Rogers worked between 1917 and 1919 at the Cambridge University Press, from 1929 to 1931 with *Emery Walker*, q.v., and later at the Oxford University Press on the Lectern Bible of 1935. His World Folio Bible is considered the finest produced in America.

Notable types designed by him are Montaigne, 1901, and the widely used Centaur, 1915, which is a refinement of the former: both are based on Jenson's roman of 1470. Centaur was first cut by Robert Wiebking of Chicago, then by Monotype in 1929 and used in the Lectern Bible (shown in Appendix A).

Rogers was widely recognized as an outstanding book designer. In his address to the Roxburghe Club of San Francisco, 15 May 1933, Edwin Grabhorn said 'It was Bruce Rogers' books that have influenced American and English printers more than any other recent single force.' See also *British Letter Foundry*, *Mall Press*.

Rohan Book of Hours: a masterpiece of French book illumination made *c.* 1418–25 for Yolande of Aragon, Queen of Sicily. In 1416 she bought the famous Belles Heures from the duc de Berry's estate and this may have been a model for some of the work done by the unknown artists Yolande employed in her atelier. The Master of the Rohan Hours excelled in composition but paid scant attention to natural or architectural perspective. Figures were printed in tense attitudes, complexions were chalky, bodies emaciated, and the background skies were of dark blue sprinkled with angels or small gold clouds. An extensive use of deep blue paint is a feature of many scenes, while most impressive is the serenity and compassion with which the heavenly Father has been portrayed.

About 1434 the book was acquired by the Vicomte de Rohan who caused his arms to be added, hence the name. It is now in the Bibliothèque Nationale, Paris (Lat.9471). See L. Porcher. 'The Rohan Book of Hours', Faber, 1959.

roll: 1. a manuscript written on a sheet of parchment or vellum which is kept rolled, not folded. Official records of a Court or Government were often so preserved.

2. a binder's revolving tool for impressing either a line (fillet) or a repeating pattern. The tool is a brass wheel, *c.* 3in.–5in. diameter, with a long handle which rests on the shoulder during use.

Rolls appear to have originated in Europe about the mid-15th century for impressing one or more continuous lines on book covers. One of the earliest binders known to have used them was the German *Johann Richenbach* (fl.1467–85), q.v. About 1500 they occur with motifs based on the small dies previously used for hand stamping. In the early 16th century Parisian binders introduced roll tools with patterns of flowers and leaves, geometrical compartments, armorial bearings, and even border features copied from illuminated manuscripts.

3. the design impressed by (2) above.

roller: a roller for inking up the printing forme, or for rolling ink to its correct consistency and distributing it to other rollers which ink the forme. See *distributor-*, *glazed-*, *ink-*, *nap roller*, *inkers*.

In letterpress work hand-rollers are used in connection with small proof presses, the composition roller being held between a fork-like tool. Narrow 'line-inking rollers' can be used for inking up single lines.

In the inking device of printing machines rollers of greater length are used, with consequently greater need for durability and strength of the core and composition. A distinction is made between *distributing rollers* that roll the ink to correct consistency, carry and distribute it evenly, and *forme rollers* which rest against the forme. The former are made entirely of metal, or are cast in the same way as forme rollers which have a rubber or composition surface and an iron core. Cast composition rollers are of particular importance owing to the elasticity and absorbent capacity of their surface. This is, however, very sensitive to changes of moisture and temperature and has little mechanical strength, and troubles occur. In rapid rotary presses high temperatures may cause the rollers to melt or buckle, so rubber is preferable. The latter, unlike composition, is not capable of keeping the forme clean and giving a first-class reproduction of illustrations. Experiments have been made in Holland and U.S.A. to combine the two by having a rubber roller which is given a thin gelatine coating; this is easily renewed. (GU)

In the 1950s the Avon Rubber Co. introduced polyurethane rollers which were found to be stable, to have adequate tack, to resist cutting, and to be easily cleaned. They are also more durable than composition and gelatine rollers, especially when cast on a rubber base. In the 1970s Teflon cylinder sleeves were introduced.

Modern offset rollers are made from nitrile rubber which resists penetration by the ink vehicle as it dries on them. Surface treatment of the rubber, after grinding, reduces the tendency of the ink to adhere and permits its easier removal. See also *Bottcher rollers, roller train.*

roller basil: the skin of the Welsh sheep tanned in an extract of oak bark and glazed.

roller train: on letterpress and lithographic machines, the series of rollers through which stiff-bodied ink fed continuously from the reservoir is progressively broken down to the correct consistency for a printing job, and is evenly spread to cover the full width of the forme roller. Also referred to as a *cluster* and as *distributor rollers.*

roller washing: rollers in a printing machine must have the ink on them removed after printing, and often during it, by *washing up*, q.v. (preferably with photogen in the case of composition rollers). In rotary presses, and especially in offset machines with their complicated inking systems, washing is mostly done mechanically by attachments to the machine which consist in principle of a rubber blade which is brought into contact with one of the metal ink distributing drums, wiping off the ink and a solvent solution which has first been sprayed on. The inking system is allowed to revolve while this is being done. Simpler apparatus can be used for washing rollers when they are off the machine. (GU)

rolling press: see *copperplate printing press.*

Rollins, Carl Purington, 1880–1960: lecturer and writer on the graphic arts. He was an early member of the Boston *Society of Printers*, q.v. In 1918 he was appointed Printer to Yale University Press which he completely reorganized and improved. See also *Montague Press.*

romain du roi: a type face with precise condensed letters having thin, unbracketed serifs, cut by *Philippe Grandjean*, q.v., for use under royal monopoly in the French *Imprimerie Royale*, q.v. To make the type distinctive a lateral trait or spur was added at the x-height of the lower case l; this calligraphic tradition marked later types cut for the Imprimerie as a deterrent to piracy.

In 1693 the Académie des Sciences ordered a study of craft techniques including printing. A committee was set up to study, *inter alia*, the proportions of letters established by Dürer, Fanti, Pacioli and Tory. They prepared drawings of roman letters on a grid of 2,304 squares. Final designs were engraved on copperplates by Simonneau between 1695 and 1718. Some of the early plates were 'used by Grandjean for the first size of his new type which he engraved between 1694 and 1699' (Jammes). He did not make identical copies. His work was influenced also by the calligraphy of Jarry and certain types of Garamont and Granjon. Grandjean published his first specimen in 1700, but did not live to complete the entire project. Work on the series was continued by his pupil Jean Alexandre and the latter's son in law *Louis Luce*, q.v., who finished it in 1745.

The first book printed in the new Grandjean type was a splendid folio edition of 'Médailles sur les principaux evénéments du règne de Louis-le-Grand', 1702.

Types from Grandjean's punches marked a departure from the Jenson-Griffo-Garamont tradition and led to the types with sharper contrast between thick and thin strokes created by Fournier, Didot and Bodoni, later referred to as *modern face*, q.v.

See A. Jammes, 'Académisme et typographie: the making of the romain du roi', *Jnl. Printing Historical Society*, 1 1965 71–95.

roman: the formal Latin alphabet of majuscule and minuscule type as distinct from black letter or gothic. The inspiration for the majuscule or upper-case letters was the alphabet as seen in the stone-cut inscriptions on tombs and monuments of ancient Rome. Interest in them was revived in the 15th century by the antiquary Felice Feliciano and others who brought geometry to their aid in establishing principles of proportionate letter design. The minuscule or lower-case letters were adaptations of the non-cursive book hands used in 15th century Italy.

The essential factor in successfully combining the two as a fount of type was the degree of harmony and unity the punchcutter could create between the contrast and chiselled precision of inscriptional capitals and the even thickness of scribal writing with its inherent qualities of flow, roundness and terminal thickness left by the pen. In refining the latter serifs were added to the upright strokes.

The earliest form of roman type was that used by Sweynheym and Pannartz at Subiaco, c. 1464. This was markedly calligraphic in style and has been called 'gotico-antiqua'. Somewhat less so were the venetian types of Wendelin da Spira, 1469, and Nicolaus Jenson, 1470. They led to the Aldine roman of 1495, which in Griffo's refined version of 1499 represented the perfected old-face type. With the European diffusion from Italy of texts in Latin the use of roman spread between 1510–30 when the great printer-publishers Amerbach, Badius, Estienne, Froben and Vascosan, to name but a few, employed it effectively. In Italy it was also adopted for books written in Italian although gothic-rotunda is seen in liturgical works until the end of the 16th century.

In France roman letters were used for the first work printed there in 1470 but not until 1527, and as a result of the sponsorship of François 1 and the inspiration of Geofroy Tory, was roman used for vernacular printing, eventually replacing the traditional but less elegant textura and bâtarde even though the latter continued in use for legal and some theological books in French. The poorer printers of cheap almanacs and chapbooks bought discarded founts of bâtarde from their richer brethren, able to afford the new types of Garamont and Granjon, using them until replacement was necessary. Not until the second half of the 16th century was roman supreme in France.

In Germany the first roman types were those used by Adolf Rusch for his edition of Hrabanus Maurus, Strasbourg, 1467. They had minuscules rounded to be consistent with the capitals and had serifs, in both respects differing from the Sweynheym of 1464. But no more than a dozen founts of roman were seen in Germany before 1480, the several forms of gothic and its later derivations Schwabacher and Fraktur being used for all works in the national languages of Germany, Austria and the Low Countries, although roman was used in the latter for printing Latin and French texts. Even Luther, whose early writings had been printed at Wittenberg in roman, realized that gothic must be substituted if the masses he wrote for were to read them.

In Slavic-speaking countries cyrillic types, first used in 1491, based on 9th century Greek scripts, took the place of both roman and gothic. In Spain Lambert Palmart, whose Fenollar of 1474 was printed in roman, had few followers other than Brocar until the 1540s when the 'letra antigua', as it was known, is seen again.

In England the first work set wholly in roman type was the 'Oratio in pace nuperrime composita' of Richard Pace, printed in 1518 by Richard Pynson who had, however, made occasional use of it from 1509. Black letter and roman continued in parallel use, according to purpose, until well into the 17th century. Not until 1560 was a Bible in English printed in roman and that had been done in Geneva. English printers used roman founts of Continental design, mostly Dutch and French, until the 18th century when the excellent type of Caslon (1720s), Alexander Wilson (1740s) and Baskerville (1760s) and their competent successors made further importation unnecessary. See also *italic, modern face, old face, old style, transitional.*

roman à clef: a novel in which characters are based on real persons but with their names changed.

Romanesque illumination: the art of the manuscript painter in 12th-century England was characterized by dignity and severity, suggesting the remoteness of the Almighty. A favourite subject was Christ on a rainbow, symbolic of His power; the Virgin and Child were also introduced.

Very large initials of coiled stems and leaf motifs were carefully drawn and painted in brilliant colours against a gold background. The solemn figures were curiously elongated or contorted, the swirling draperies which clad them tending to divide the body into oval shapes. Naturalism was often subordinated to rhythmic pattern, and the symbolism owed much to Byzantine art. The use of highly burnished gold for large background surfaces is also characteristic of Romanesque illumination.

It was during this era that complete Bibles and Psalters were widely produced, an outstanding example of the former being the Winchester Bible. Popular also were *bestiaries*, q.v. See also *Canterbury School, Salisbury School, Winchester School.*

roman notation: the method of recording dates in the colophons or on the title-pages of some early printed books, e.g.

M iiiiC iiiiXX Viij

i.e. $1,000 + 4 \times 100 + 4 \times 20 + 8 = 1488$

roman numerals: forms of these are: I = 1, II = 2, III = 3, IV = 4, V = 5, VI = 6, VII = 7, VIII = 8, IX = 9, X = 10, XI = 11, etc., L = 50, C = 100, D or I⊃ = 500, DC or I⊃C = 600, CM or DCCCC or I⊃CCCC = 900, M or CI⊃ = 1,000. XL = 40, XLIV = 44, LX = 60, LXIV = 64, XCIX = 99. Thus MCMLXXIX = 1979.

Roman Virgil: a manuscript of 309 parchment leaves, illustrated by nineteen miniatures from the Georgics, Eclogues and Aeneid. The leaves are almost square, c. 13in., and the text is in very large rustic capitals.

It was made about the 5th century. Bright colours were used for the illustrations which, in general, are somewhat crude and vivid.

It has been in the Vatican since 1475 (Cod. Vat. Lat. 3867). See also *Vatican Virgil*.

Romney Street Press: a hand-printing press founded by Francis Meynell in 1915 at 67 Romney Street, Westminster. The aims were to publish books, pamphlets and single sheets of poetry. Only two works, in editions of fifty copies each, appear to have been issued for sale before 1918. See also *Meynell, Nonesuch Press, Pelican Press*.

ronde: a script type-design based on a French manuscript hand and having the appearance of upright handwriting.

Rood, Theodoric, fl.1478–86: of Cologne, and the presumed first printer to work at Oxford where three books without a printer's name were issued between 1478 and 1481 when Rood's name first appeared as the printer of a commentary on Aristotle's 'De Anima'. In 1483 he entered into partnership with an official stationer of the University, Thomas Hunte: together they issued in 1485 a translation into Latin by Franceso Griffolini (d. 1460) of the letters of Phalaridis, a popular work of which forty editions by various European printers were published before 1500.

Some seventeen works were issued at Oxford between 1478 and 1486. The first three were printed in a type brought from Cologne: other types were used for the books printed after 1481 and they are also thought to have come from Cologne.

After 1486, when Rood and Hunte issued the 'Liber festivalis', there appears to have been no printing at Oxford until 1518. See *Oxford University Press*.

Roos, Sjoerd H. de, 1877–1962: one of Holland's leading type designers. Among his faces known in England are Egmont, 1933, and De Roos Roman, 1947, both made for the Amsterdam Typefoundry where De Roos was engaged as a typographer from 1907 to 1941. Other founts of importance included Hollandsche Mediaeval, 1912, widely used for hand and machine composition. A lighter version, Erasmus Mediaeval, was issued in 1923. His bold Grotius fount appeared in 1925. (See Appendix A.)

In 1927 he founded the *Heuvel Press* at Hilversum, this being the second modern private press in Holland. It was closed in 1935. In his first production, 1928, he showed the Meidoorn type he had created for the press. It was an archaic fount with overtones of 15th century Venice. The 'Stichting de Roos' continued fine book production after his death. See A. M. Stols, 'Het werk van S. H. de Roos', Amsterdam, 1942.

Rosart, Jacques-François, 1714–77: a Belgian punch-

422

cutter and typefounder active from 1740 in Haarlem and from 1759–68 in Brussels. He is remembered for a range of text types and for his contribution to music printing from cast type. His first attempt called for two impressions, but about 1764 he successfully made a single-impression fount, showing a specimen in his 'Épreuves', 1768. See C. Enschedé, 'Fonderies de caractères et leurs matériel dans le Pays-Bas du XVe au XIXe siècle', Haarlem, 1908.

Rosenbach, Abraham S. Wolf, 1876–1952: a scholar, bibliophile and antiquarian bookseller who was a partner with his elder brother in the Rosenbach Company of Philadelphia and New York. During the 1920s his activities on behalf of American collectors brought him to the more important European book sales for such acquisitions as Shakespeare Folios, a Gutenberg Bible from Melk, illuminated manuscripts, the rarest incunabula and first editions of English literature. During the years Dr Rosenbach assembled the major collection of Shakespeariana which in 1952 was bought by *Dr Martin Bodmer*, q.v. See E. Wolf & J. F. Fleming, 'Rosenbach', Weidenfeld, 1961.

Rosenbach, Johann, fl.1490–1530: an early printer of Barcelona whence he came from Heidelberg. He printed in several towns, his work being characterized by woodcut borders and illustrations, and best known for the letter in which Columbus described his crossing of the Atlantic.

Rosenwald, Lessing J. b. 1891: a contemporary American bibliophile whose major collection of about 2,000 illustrated books of all periods was presented to the Library of Congress in 1943. For the term of the donor's life, however, the books are housed in his library at Jenkintown, Penn. Notable among the 400 or so incunables are works printed by Gutenberg, Fust and Schöffer, Jenson, Zainer, Caxton, Sorg and Verard; also here are the Laurentii 'Monte Santo di Dio', 1477, the Morgiani and Petri 'Epistolae et evangalia', Florence, 1495, and the Plannck edition of Turrecremata's 'Meditationes', Rome, 1484. Notable bindings include three Groliers, a Grimaldi, and examples of 'à la fanfare'.

rosin: the main agent in *engine-sized* papers, q.v. Rosin for this purpose is the residue left after turpentine has been extracted from the resin tapped from pine trees. It is also obtained from *tall oil*, a by-product from chemical woodpulp manufacture. See also *size* (2).

Röslein: the German name for printers' ornaments or flowers.

Rospigliosi bindery: an Italian bindery where an unknown craftsman worked from the 1640s until the 1680s to produce elaborately tooled bindings for several Popes and princes, and also for Queen Christina of Sweden who lived for a time in Italy. Cardinal Giulio Rospigliosi (later Pope Clement, 1667–9) commissioned some of the finest examples, and it is after him that A. R. A. Hobson named the bindery.

Foliage scroll borders, putti, elaborate corner fleuron pieces, with a central escutcheon of the owner's arms are typical.

Rossetti, Dante Gabriel, 1828–82: the poet and painter who interested himself in edition-binding design from about 1861 to 1880. His asymmetrical patterns of Japanese simplicity with none of the traditional emphasis on the rectangularity of the boards was a foretaste of the Art Nouveau movement which began in England in the 1880s. Typical designs were isolated groups of small circles, screen-like blocks of small circles with floral sprigs superimposed, or large emblematic discs near the edges of the boards. As his correspondence with publishers and binder (Burn) shows Rossetti concerned himself in detail with the colour of end-papers and cloth. Most of the editions were of poetry. See also *Ricketts*. See G. Barber, 'Rossetti, Ricketts, and some English publishers' bindings of the nineties', *The Library*, 5th ser., xxv 1970.

rotary press: a machine for printing from a revolving cylindrical forme to which paper is usually fed from a reel. If printing is done on sheets the term *sheet-fed rotary* is used. Modern presses for intaglio and lithographic offset printing are always built on the rotary principle; for letterpress work rotary presses are mainly used for newspapers, periodicals and paperbacks, printing being done from cylindrical stereos. Sometimes printing is done from the original flat forme on an endless web of paper, a *flat-bed web press*.

For early forms of letterpress rotary machines see *letterpress machine*. The Bullock press (1865) and the Walter press (1868) were the first reel-fed rotary machines used to any great extent, especially for newspapers. Early rotary presses were not equipped with folders and the web was cut into sheets either before or after printing, as in the press of Josiah Warren, a typefounder and printer who also experimented with stereotyping.

A modern letterpress rotary machine consists of one or more units in which the actual printing is done; a *folder* in which the printed matter is cut from the continuous web and folded; arrangements for conditioning the paper reels and controlling their speed; a number of conducting rollers for guiding the web through the press; and sometimes circular knives for cutting the web longitudinally. Their mutual position varies and is often adapted to the premises in which the press is installed. Small presses, on the contrary,

are fairly standardized. A typical press is shown in the illustration.

Rotary presses may be over 45 metres long, but should then be regarded as a series of machines built

Bullock's rotary press of 1865, *from a contemporary illustration*

tandem-fashion from which the printed matter is taken out at various points. While theoretically an unlimited number of pages can be printed at a time, the upper limit is determined by the folder. When premises are sufficiently lofty the press is then built on three decks. The lowest is for conditioning the paper reels and controlling their speed; on the middle one the printing units and folders are placed; while the top deck contains guiding rollers, cutting devices and, when required, gumming apparatus. In this way the main

Small rotary press

deck, where the most highly skilled work of operating the press, distributing ink, etc., is carried out, is free from transporting paper and finished matter.

Paper is fed into a rotary press from a *reel stand*. On presses other than composite machines the reel stand consists of a simple storage device at one end of the press in which the reel is conditioned after being secured to an iron axle. In presses working on the deck principle, in which the units are placed one above the other, lifts for the reels are used. Composite machines have stands on the lowest deck either for two reels or three. Axles are not used, the reels being suspended on dowels, one of which is conical and smooth and the other cylindrical and provided with expanding spurs which penetrate into the cardboard wrapper of the reel. The two-reel and three-reel stands

Rotary press with unit and reel stand on several decks

can be moved a few cm. in the transverse direction of the press to regulate the width of the margin: this is done by a motor operated by push-buttons. A special kind of reel stand, known as a *flying paster*, enables a reel to be changed at full speed or only slightly slower: this expensive device is only of profit in the case of large newspaper printing.

The paper reel in a rotary press cannot be used up to the innermost layer. The remnants of the reel can be preserved by re-winding in a special machine.

To regulate the tension in the web each reel is provided with a brake. In its simplest form a reel

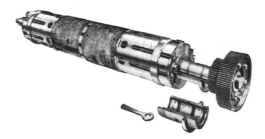

Plate cylinder

brake is a steel band fixed round the reel of paper and fastened to a wire rope loaded with weights, or it consists of a hand-operated band- or shoe-brake working against the axle which supports the reel during printing. Opinions differ as to the advantages of brakes being on the reel or on the axle: Continental manufacturers favour the former, British and American users the latter. The degree of tension required on

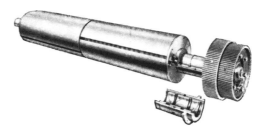

Impression cylinder

the web is estimated by the pressman. Immediately after starting up, the brakes on the different reels are adjusted, after which constant tension is automatically kept until the reel is finished.

The printing unit is adapted for perfecting the web at one operation. It is composed of two pairs of cylinders, each with its own inking device and drive. In modern composite machines the two pairs of cylinders and the inkers are placed symmetrically (see illustration). One of the cylinders in each pair carries the printing forme (stereotype plates) and is known as the *plate* or *forme cylinder*, the other is the *impression cylinder*. The forme cylinder has a fixed ring in the middle, movable rings at the ends (each embracing half of the circumference), and loose plate-clips in grooves for securing the plates. In the longitudinal direction of the cylinder supporting strips are fixed which prevent the sheets from sliding along the cir-

Printing unit of a composite press

cumference. A method of increasing the durability of the plates and fastenings, and thereby the maximum speed of the press, was tried by Goss who built a Unitube press for plates embracing the whole circumference of the cylinder.

The impression cylinder is usually made of heavy steel with a tympan clamp for fastening the packing. In recent presses, however, impression cylinders are made of special cast iron with the durability of steel but better able to moderate the vibration. The impression cylinder is on roller bearings resting on eccentric bushes, by turning which it can be moved nearer to or farther from the forme cylinder in order to regulate the depth of the impression. There is usually an indicator at each bearing of the impression cylinder to indicate its position in relation to the forme cylinder.

Presses for colour work vary in design; two colours can be printed on the same impression cylinder, but as a rule separate units are preferred for each colour with register adjustment by hand or photo-electric means.

There are various electric safety devices on the units for stopping the press in the event of a web breaking. This can be done from top speed in a few seconds, and is necessary in view of the risk of the paper winding itself round cylinders and inkers and breaking the bearings or even bending the axles.

Although letterpress work is most generally associated with rotary printing on reels, lithographic offset and intaglio work can also be done. The delivery of the paper through the press, the arrangement and driving of the units, folders, etc., are mainly the same as for rotary letterpress printing but with the differences inherent in the nature of the printing processes (see *drum cylinder press, intaglio, offset press, offset printing, satellite press, signature rotary*).   (GU)

rotary printing: printing from a plate fitted to the surface of a revolving cylinder. Rotary printing is used for intaglio, lithographic, and letterpress work, and for printing on sheets or paper reels; as a rule the term refers to the latter (see *rotary press*).

The whole object of rotary printing is a high output. For various reasons (durability of plates, quality of paper, etc.) the presses cannot be worked at any speed desired. Arrangements must therefore be made for working at a maximum speed as long as possible, and for seeing that interruptions are reduced to a minimum. Careful interlay, devices for changing the reels without stopping the machine, steps for reducing the unavoidable breaks of paper, and proper care of the paper during transport and storage are steps in this direction.

In rotary printing both sides of the paper are impressed in quick succession without an opportunity for drying. As the paper passes into the second pair of cylinders some ink from the first printing is deposited on the packing of the impression cylinder. If the impression of type, screen dots, etc., in subsequent copies of these pages does not strike the ink on the packing with perfect accuracy, part of the ink returns to the clean paper quite close to the type or dot and appears as a shadow. The defect is due to jolts in the web from paper reels which are not quite round. This can be counteracted by careful handling of the paper. Another method is to use a *set-off reel*. A special web is conducted between the web to be printed and the packing on the second pair of cylinders, and then the set-off reel is wound up again: it can be passed through the press in this way several dozen times. A packing is made in America which is said not to absorb any ink so that displacement is totally eliminated. Its surface is covered with very small glass beads, about 8,000 per sq. cm. Quick-set inks which dry on surface contact with the paper offer fresh possibilities.   (GU)

rotogravure: printing from photogravure cylinders on a web-fed rotary press. See also *intaglio, photogravure*.

rotogravure paper: the main requirements are for smoothness and, when colour work is being reproduced, whiteness and a certain degree of absorbency. Esparto is one of the best papers for gravure, but good results are possible on super-calendered and imitation arts.

rotulus: a manuscript roll of papyrus or membrane. Writing was done on one side only. One of the oldest extant, the Prisse Papyrus, dates from about 2000 BC. It is seven metres long, and between 140 and 150mm. for the page height, written in hieratic script, thirteen lines per page. It contains the maxims of Ptahhotep and the precepts of Kagemni. The work is in the Bibliothèque Nationale. See also *papyrus*.

rotunda: the round black letter or gothic type-face of the 15th century. It is typified by a marked contrast between thick and thin strokes and curved forms of c d e, etc. For an example see *letters – forms and styles*.

rough calf: calfskin used for binding with the flesh side of the skin outward. It may be dyed. It was much used from the 16th to the 18th century on large folios. Also known as *reversed calf*.

rough etch: or *flat etch*, the first etching of a descummed half-tone plate in a machine containing ferric chloride (for copper) or dilute nitric acid (for zinc). The result is to reduce dot size. This will give contrast and good printing depth. Rough etching is followed by *fine etching*, q.v.

rough gilt: uncut edges are occasionally gilded before sewing, fore-edge first. When this is specified the overlap paper is trimmed, but sufficient short sheets are left as binding proof. (Thus Beckford of Fonthill instructed his binder, Lewis, '. . . gilt leaves to be kept large and roughish . . .'). The finish is left dull. The book must be interleaved with thick paper to give a solid working surface.

The head may be cut in the plough and gilded after attaching the boards. It will be burnished. Cf. *antique gold edges.*

rough proof (or **pull**): 1. a first or galley proof which has not been read or corrected by the printer's reader before it is sent to the publisher.

2. a proof taken on rough paper without underlay or overlay. Also called a *flat pull*. See *make-ready.*

Rouillé, Guillaume, fl.1544–89: a French printer who after his apprenticeship in Venice with Gabriel Giolito began printing in Lyons in 1544. He specialized in the printing of translations from the classics and also legal works, being to some extent a rival of his contemporary *Jean de Tournes*, q.v., whose work he often plagiarized and whose woodcuts (by Salomon) he had copied.

rounce: the handle at the side of early printing presses used to turn a roller to which were affixed the ends of two leather straps. The other ends of the straps were secured to the sliding carriage bearing the forme. Turning the rounce thus drew the carriage under and out of the press. Some authorities define rounce as including both the handle and the roller. See also *girts.*

rounding: the process of giving a book back a convex shape, after first gluing, and before casing. This is done by machine or by the forwarder who uses a round-headed hammer. In Britain and America books

Rounding

are rounded and backed to provide joints (see diagram under *backing*). In most European countries it is customary to round the book only without joints. See also *backing.*

426

router: a machine with a rotating cutter for working metal or wood. Such machines are used when preparing blocks and stereos to follow the outlines of an image with accuracy and, for example, to cut away superfluous parts of a half-tone; also, when preparing line blocks, the mechanical routing of the metal can be a partial substitute for deep etching. John Royale's radial-arm router, the type most used, was invented in 1874.

Several types of router are used when making stereos, and there are also routers for removing the jet after casting. See also *blockmaking, planing machine, stereotype.*

Rowfant Club: a club for bibliophiles, established in Cleveland, Ohio, in 1895. Activities have included the publishing of books for members.

Roxburghe binding: a quarter-binding with red flint-paper or cloth covered boards and a narrow strip of reddish-brown or green skiver on the spine. The style was used for the publications of the *Roxburghe Club*, q.v., from its inception until well into the 20th century, and was also used by others, among them *Pickering*, q.v. The original quarter-bindings were probably intended to be of a temporary nature until the owner could commission a swagger binding by a master craftsman: certainly the leather on many original volumes now in public collections is faded and crumbly. After 1876 large folio volumes were issued in the somewhat more substantial half-bound style.

Roxburghe Club: a club formed in London in 1812 after the sale of the third Duke of Roxburghe's library, by prominent bibliophiles who met in St Alban's Tavern (Dibdin, Lord Spencer, and others). The club's purpose was the printing or reprinting of rare works, tracts, etc., for the benefit of the thirty-one (later forty) members. See N. Barker, 'The publications of the Roxburghe Club', C.U.P., 1964.

Roxburghe, John Ker, third Duke of, 1740–1804: a bibliophile who inherited and developed a library so rich in rarities that no one today could hope to assemble its equal. In this note it is only possible to outline its main groups: the manuscripts and printed editions of the Arthurian and other romances, numerous works printed by Caxton, de Worde, Pynson, and an extensive collection of Elizabethan and Jacobean drama. Many books were bound specially for him.

At the sale by auction in 1812 the Roxburghe collection realized £23,341. See also *Roxburghe Club.*

royal: a former size of printing paper, 25in. by 20in. See *paper sizes.*

Royal Literary Fund: a fund established in 1788 as the 'Literary Fund' by the Rev. David Williams. It was incorporated in 1818, and in 1842 became the Royal Literary Fund, Stationers' Hall, London. Grants are made to authors who are British nationals or foreigners resident in the U.K. whose work is of approved literary merit.

Royal Society of Literature Award: established through a bequest by the late publisher W. H. Heinemann. There are usually two prizes of £200 or £300 awarded annually for works in any branch of literature, originally written in English, judged by the Royal Society to be of real literary worth and of a kind unlikely to command big sales. Works may be submitted by publishers, not authors. The Society also administers other prizes. Address: Hyde Park Gardens, London W2A 2LT.

royalties: regular payments made by a publisher to an author for the right of publishing and selling his work. Payment is made out of the difference between production costs and the publisher's net profit, and the amount is usually a mutually agreed percentage of the published price and paid only on copies sold.

Prior to the last quarter of the 19th century it was usual for a writer to sell his book to a publisher for a single payment or to do so on a profit-sharing basis. One of the earliest royalty agreements was that made with Disraeli for his novel 'Lothair' which Longmans published in 1870.

The Publishers Association issues a 'Guide to royalty agreements'. See also *publishers' agreements*.

Roycroft Press: a private press and bindery founded in 1893 by Elbert Hubbard (1856–1915) at East Aurora, NY State. Hubbard was inspired by a visit to Morris at Hammersmith to set up a community of craftsmen which included printers.

Between 1894 and 1909 his 'Little journeys' series appeared monthly and were so popular that printing was done on machine presses. Roycroft books were considered by some to be vulgar, and in 1903 the poet Yeats described them as 'eccentric, restless and thoroughly decadent'. Hubbard was drowned in the sinking of the Lusitania, 7 May 1915.

Royen, J. F. van: see *Zilverdistel Press*.

R-printer: see *Rusch*.

Ruano, Ferdinando, fl.1541–60: a Spanish scribe employed for some twenty years in the Vatican Library where he made a catalogue of the books under the direction of the librarian Cardinal Cervini.

In his manual 'Sette alphabeti', Rome, 1554, Ruano advocated the writing of chancery script on geometrical principles, accompanying each specimen of his 'lettera de' brevi' with a detailed drawing and description of how it was to be done: this was des-

cribed by Morison ('Politics and script') as the highest and final absurdity.

rubber stereo: a stereo made by pressing a rubber plate against a heated matrix in a moulding press. The heat vulcanizes the rubber and thus makes the impression permanent.

rubbing-off chest: in the blocking shops of late 19th century trade binderies, a wooden chest topped with a grill upon which surplus gold was cleaned off blocked cases. The contents were sent annually to a refiner who returned a gold ingot to the bindery. See also *skewings*.

Rubel, Ira W.: a New York lithographer who commercially developed *offset printing* on paper in 1904. It is said the discovery was made when a rubber cloth was accidentally used to cover the cylinder of a lithographic press. Due to the operator's negligence an impression was made on the rubber cloth, and when the next sheet of paper went through the press there was a good impression on the back of it. The first offset press built on the 'American' system was constructed according to Rubel's direction. See also *offset printing*. (GU)

Rubens, Peter Paul, 1577–1640: painter and sometime book-illustrator of Antwerp where he worked mostly for Moretus of the Plantin office. The association began in 1612 when he designed a frontispiece and six vignettes for the 'Opticorum libri sex philosophis . . .' of d'Aguillon, 1613. His designs were usually classical interpretations of allegorical or symbolical figures relating to a book's subject.

The last work by Rubens was for 'Opere omnia' by Juste Lipse, 1637; thereafter he gave *grisailles* or suggested designs for Erasmus Quellin to execute. Engravers who transferred Rubens' drawings to copper included Theodoor and Cornelis Galle: they were paid four or five times as much as the artist.

rub-off lettering: see *transfer lettering*.

rubric: 1. the heading of a chapter, section or other division of a book, printed in red ink. The text is printed in black.

2. a direction for the conducting of Divine Service: often printed in red ink.

rubricator: an artist employed by early printers to inscribe decorative initial letters, often in red ink, at the beginning of chapters. Spaces for these were left blank when printing the text, with possibly the insertion of a *guide letter*, q.v. This was the continuation of a practice common to manuscript book writing. Also known as a *rubrisher*.

During the 15th and early 16th centuries Latin was

427

read universally, and most books were written in it. This led to an export trade in books from the various centres of printing. Books were sent in sheets packed in barrels, and rubrication was done after the book was assembled by the receiving bookseller. See also *illumination, untouched.*

rubric posts: wooden posts found outside booksellers' shops in 17th and 18th century England. They were used as a form of advertisement to display title-pages, of which extra copies were always pulled; a fact which may account for the detailed address of the bookseller being printed on them.

ruby: the name for a former size of type, approximately 5½-point.

Ruette, Macé, 1584–1644: from 1606 a Parisian master binder and bookseller who in 1634 succeeded Clovis Eve as Court binder. He appears to have ceased binding by 1638.

It was for a series of Elzevier 16mo books, bound between 1620 and 1634 for the collector Habert de Montmort (1600–79) that Macé Ruette developed *pointillé* tooling, q.v. In general his most elegant work was done on small books: for quarto volumes he created mosaic panels of contrasting moroccos, entirely filling the compartments on spines and boards with pointillé tooling, though such profusion, if skilled, obscured the natural beauty of the leather. The introduction, about 1622, of marbled end-papers is attributed to him.

Antoine Ruette, fl.1644–69, succeeded his father as 'relieur ordinaire du Roi' about 1644. He was also a publisher, but although his bindings were numerous his styles were often derivative and of only secondary quality. See G. D. Hobson, 'Les Reliures à la fanfare', 1935, where their work is described and illustrated.

rule: strips of brass or type metal, type high, cast in point sizes and to various lengths. See also *brass rule, column-face rule, french rule, hair-line rule, mitred* (2), *multiple rule, Oxford corners, Oxford rule, setting rule, swelled rules.*

rule-curving machine: a machine for curving lead or brass rule. A strip is placed between a concave and a convex steel block; pressure is applied. Interchangeable blocks for different degrees of curve are used.

(GU)

ruling machine: a machine devised by John Tetlow in 1770 for the mechanical ruling of music and ledger paper. This had formerly been ruled by hand.

rums: a slang term, used by 18th-century London booksellers, for a large assortment of unsaleable books. The suggested explanation that 'rums' were barrels of

428

such books shipped to Jamaica in exchange for rum cannot be confirmed. See also *barrels.*

run: a machinist's term for the number of impressions taken from a forme at one time.

run-in sheets: the sheets of paper passed through a press at the beginning of a run and rejected by the pressman as spoils until he considers ink colour and quality of impression to be satisfactory.

runners: small figures printed for reference purposes in page margins, e.g. in school texts of plays, or in long poems.

running heads: see *headline.*

running stationer: a chapman. See *chapbook.*

run on: 1. an indication to the printer that a new paragraph is not to be made. This instruction is marked in copy and proofs by a line joining the end of one piece of matter to the beginning of the next. See also *break-line, end a break, end even.*

2. the printer's term for an *offprint,* q.v.

run on chapters: chapters which do not begin on a fresh page but which are set on the same page as the conclusion of the preceding chapter. A style found in cheap bookwork.

run out and indented: type with the first line set to full measure; the next and succeeding lines of the same paragraph are indented.

run round: said of an illustration set in a page of text which has been indented to allow for it.

run up: the beginning of a press run, between starting the machine and the point when it produces results of the desired print quality. The adjustments needed on a high-speed web-offset machine during this period can lead to a spoiled paper factor of 10%. See also *run-in sheets.*

run-up spine: said of the spine of a book when part of the decoration tooled on it consists of twin lines running up the edge of the two joints and across the spine, thus forming panels. A two-line roll and pallet are used.

Ruppel, Aloys, 1882–1977: of Mainz, where until 1967 he was director of the Gutenberg Museum, editor since its inception in 1925 of the *Gutenberg-Jahrbuch,* and the world's leading scholar of Gutenberg's work.

Ruppel, Berthold, fl.1455–88: of Hanau. In 1455 he was an assistant of Gutenberg. When he left Mainz is uncertain, but he is regarded as the first printer to set up a press in Switzerland. This was at Basle, whither he took Gutenbergian types or matrices about 1468. Early books associated with his name, all undated, include a folio Biblia Latina (GKW 4207), 'Moralia in Job' (Hain 7926), and 'Postilla super evangelia' (Hain 10384). He collaborated with Michael Wenssler and Bernhard Richel in printing an edition of Panormitanus's 'Super libros Decretalium', 1477. One of his latest books was the 'Sermones Meffreth' of 1488. He died about 1494.

Rupprecht-Presse: a private printing press founded in Munich in 1914 by *Fritz Helmut Ehmcke*, q.v. In 1922 the press became part of the Beck'sche Verlagsbuchhandlung. Poetry, philosophy and belles-lettres were the principal publications, all printed in types designed by Ehmcke.

Rusch, Adolf, fl.1466–89: of Ingweiden in Germany. He was a lettercutter, printer, publisher and paper merchant of Strasbourg where he worked with *Johann Mentelin*, q.v., later marrying his daughter and taking over the business in 1478. He was the first printer in Germany to use a recognizably roman type. This was about 1467 when he used it in an edition of the encyclopaedia 'Opus de universo' by Rabanus Maurus. It was the curious capital letter 'R' of this type which led to his long being known as the 'R-printer' of books not identifiable by his name, since he neither signed nor dated them.

About 1471 he issued 'Vitae parallelae', which was a Latin edition of Plutarch's 'Lives' (Hain 13124), and in 1480 he printed for Koberger a Latin Bible in four volumes.

russia cowhide: an inferior russia leather in which cowhide is used and given a straight grain. A process for tanning various leathers and impregnating them with russian oil so that they resembled the genuine material was devised in England in 1691 by John Tyzack.

Also known as *American russia*.

russia leather: a reddish brown leather made from calf and used for binding. The skin is impregnated with birch-tar oil which leaves it aromatic. It originated in Russia. Its great popularity in England as a material for book covers was between 1730 and 1840 but it is not often employed today as it tends to dry out and disintegrate.

In the 17th and 18th centuries it was the custom to score the leather in blind with a pattern of crossed diagonal lines (diced). This was done in one of two ways, on the piece in a calendering machine, or by hand tooling the cover. In the late 18th or early 19th century *John Bohn*, q.v., invented graining plates which were used to dice the leather after covering. It was

necessary to soak, beat and work paste into the leather before use.

Russian printing: for a note on early printing in Russia see *cyrillic, Fëdorov*.

rustic capitals: the roman alphabet as adapted from *square capitals*, q.v., by early Roman scribes, and used as a book hand from the 1st to 6th century. Its essential quality was calligraphic and less formal than square capitals. Letters had serifs, and could be written quickly, resulting in a narrow condensed effect on the page. In the 9th century scribes in the service of Charles the Great used rustic capitals for colophonic inscriptions.

The script was also known as *scriptura actuaria*. Illustrated under *letters – forms and styles*.

Ruthven, John: an Edinburgh printer who in 1813 patented an iron hand-press with the novel feature of a stationary bed over which a suspended platen was moved laterally into position and lowered for impression. In addition to the full-size model it was made in a scaled-down version known as the *Scottish table-press*.

In America his press influenced the press of *Adam Ramage*, q.v.

Rutland: the trade name of a fine-quality sheepskin used in binding.

ruttier book: a book of sailing directions. The name derives from the French 'Routier de la mer' published at the beginning of the 16th century. In the late 15th century and throughout the 16th ruttier books gave sailing directions between ports on trade routes. Some had simple drawings of landmarks. After 1544 charts were added.

In England the name was corrupted to *rutter book* as in Copland's translation of Pierre Garcie's work which appeared as 'The rutter of the sea . . .', *c.* 1555 (STC 11552). See also *mappae mundi*.

Ruzicka, Rudolph, 1883–   : a Bohemian who in 1894 emigrated to Chicago where he studied wood engraving. He worked as a book illustrator and typographer. In 1939 he designed the Fairfield roman and in 1951 the newspaper face Primer, both for Mergenthaler Linotype. The Grolier Club of New York held an exhibition of his work in 1948, the catalogue documenting his many achievements.

Ryland, William Wynne, 1732–83: Royal engraver to George III. After working in Paris with Roubillac he brought to London the art of *stipple engraving*, q.v., later made famous by Francesco Bartolozzi. Ryland was hanged for forging banknotes.

S

Sabin, Joseph, 1821–81: a bibliophile, publisher and antiquarian of New York and Philadelphia. He wrote 'A bibliography of bibliography' in 1877, followed by his monumental compilation 'Bibliotheca Americana, a bibliography of books relating to America from its discovery to the present time', 29 vols, New York, Bibliographical Society of America, 1868–1936. The first thirteen volumes were issued in his lifetime, Wilberforce Eames and R. W. G. Vail continuing and completing the work. In 1974 an author-title index was published.

The first volume of L. S. Thompson's thoroughly revised edition was issued in New York in 1974 as 'The new Sabin . . .'.

Sabon, Jacques (Jakob), d. 1580: a French typecutter and founder, born at Lyons. He may have been related to *Sulpice Sabon* who printed there between 1535 and 1549. He is recorded as managing the Egenolff foundry at Frankfurt in 1555 and in 1563 was employed in Antwerp by Plantin to finish some of Garamont's punches and make matrices. He then returned to Frankfurt where his marriage into the family of *Christian Egenolff,* q.v., in 1571 brought him control of the latter's foundry a year later. When Sabon died his widow married another typefounder, *Konrad Berner* (d. 1606). Their grand-daughter married *John Luther* in 1626 who then controlled the foundry and whose family were in business until 1780.

The firm traded as the *Egenolff-Berner-Luthersche Schriftgiesserei,* and was situated from 1616 until it closed in 1810 at 'The Sign of the Old Frog' in Frankfurt. It was one of the most important foundries in Europe: the Elzevirs were among their clients, and their types were sold in America. Towards the end of the 18th century much of the firm's material was acquired by *Unger,* q.v. In 1900 what remained was taken over by the city of Frankfurt and in 1940 it was opened as the *Deutsches Museum der Schriftgiesserei,* only to be destroyed by bombing in 1944.

The Egenolff specimen sheet of 1592, issued by Konrad Berner, was the first to give designers' names: it included founts by Garamont, Granjon and Haultin. The name of Sabon is perpetuated as the name of a type face designed by *Jan Tschichold,* q.v.

Sacramentary: a *Missal,* q.v., without Epistles and Gospels.

Sacramentary of Robert of Jumièges: a famous Missal (properly, Sacramentary) lavishly illuminated by artists of the *Winchester School,* q.v., probably between 1013–17, though whether at Winchester, Ely, or Peterborough has not been established. Before his banishment from England, Abbot Robert of Jumièges was Bishop of London (1044–50) and Archbishop of Canterbury (1055).

The work is illustrated with thirteen scenes from the New Testament and lives of the Saints; these are enclosed in the elaborate borders typical of the School. Since 1791 the Sacramentary has been in the Municipal Library of Rouen.

saddle: a mount of metal or plastic which may be required to bring a photopolymer printing plate up to impression height if, for example, lead stereos and photopolymer plates are used together. Plates can be mounted to saddles by either adhesive or mechanical means.

saddle-stitched: a method of stitching brochures and pamphlets by placing them open astride a saddle-shaped support and stitching through the back. Simple machinery exists to do this, but for big outputs there are larger installations: sheets are cut into four page sections and put unfolded on the machine which has sixteen stations. They are then automatically collated, saddle-stitched, folded and trimmed at speeds up to 4,500 an hour. Also known as *binding quirewise* or *insetting.*

Safavid bindings: 16th-century Persian bindings. Patterns were either contained in medallions or filled the whole cover, flowers, birds and arabesques being usual motifs. The designs were impressed from large engraved plates of copper or steel. While pressing the design and gilding were normally combined in one operation, the leather was sometimes gilded before being pressed with the heated die. Such bindings had doublures often excelling in the splendour of their decoration that on the outer cover; delicate filigrees of leather or gold paper were placed on backgrounds of various coloured leathers. Persian bindings mostly had a protecting flap which formed part of the back cover and extended round the fore-edge to lie on the front cover. See also *Islamic bookbinding*.

St Aethelwold, Benedictional of: see *Benedictional of St Aethelwold*.

St Albans School: an important 13th century school of English manuscript illumination. By 1236 *Matthew Paris*, q.v., royal historiographer, was head scribe. He revived tinted outline drawings, avoiding the lavish use of bold colours. His draperies were notable for their soft, natural folds.

The *Apocalypse*, q.v., was a favourite work for copying at St Albans.

St Albans, Schoolmaster of: see *Schoolmaster of St Albans*.

St Bride Printing Library: an important technical library in Britain for the printing and allied trades. Until 1958 it was directed by W. Turner Berry, Esq., who supplied this note.

The collections of William Blades, Talbot Baines Reed, and works purchased with money donated by J. Passmore Edwards formed the nucleus of the stock of the library which was opened in 1895 by Sir Walter Besant. The 40,000 volumes and pamphlets cover in scope all branches of typographical history, inventions, general histories of printing, private presses, famous printers, publishing, binding, etc. There is a valuable collection of type specimens and of historic printing equipment. In 1970 a museum of printing and type-founding equipment was opened.

Address: Bride Lane, Fleet Street, London EC4Y 8EE.

St Chad Gospels: an 8th-century manuscript, written by an Irish monk, characterized by the simple severity of its pen drawings, the figures represented being almost symbols. The work is now in Lichfield Cathedral.

St Dominic's Press: the name chosen by Hilary Douglas Pepler (1878–1951) for the hand press he set up at Ditchling, Sussex. He had been closely associated with *Eric Gill* and *Edward Johnston*, qq.v., in the Hampshire House Workshops at Hammersmith, under which imprint as publishers three books were issued. In 1915 Pepler moved to Ditchling, where Gill was already living, and set up a hand press to continue his ideal of earning a living by hand craftsmanship. As can be imagined, wood engravings by Gill were included in some of the simple books issued, an example being a Book of Hours published in 1923. Pepler also did jobbing work. The last book produced by Pepler was 'The hand press', 1934, which he wrote and printed for the Society of Typographic Arts, Chicago.

The name was later changed to Ditchling Press Ltd and operated as a commercial printing business.

St Gall Gospels: a 5th-century (or later) manuscript of the pre-Vulgate Gospels written either in Ireland or at the monastery of St Gall in an unserifed uncial script.

Two Irish monks, Gall and Columban, left Bangor c. 590. They journeyed through France and Germany until c. 613, when Columban founded Bobbio monastery in Italy, and Gall founded St Gall on the Steinbach in Switzerland. Both places were centres of illumination.

Saint Jean: the patron saint of French printers. He appears twice in the calendar, as *Saint Jean Porte Latine* on 6 May, and as *Saint Jean l'Evangéliste* on 27 December. The Parisian printers marked both days with a mass in the church of St André-des-Arts, a right first granted to the scriveners, illuminators and binders in 1401. A further link was in the many Books of Hours published in Paris towards the end of the 15th century in which there was often a cut showing the martyrdom of Saint Jean being boiled in oil, the main ingredient of printing ink.

During the 16th century Parisian journeymen organized themselves as a body exclusive of master printers. The monks of the Order of St Jean de Latran gave them the use of a chapel, not only for worship but as a regular meeting place. The use of the word *chapel*, q.v., for the association of printers within a workshop or the branch of a printing union may derive from this. French workmen also used the expression 'prendre son saint Jean' which meant to pick up tools and leave the place of employment.

After the Revolution French 'chapelles' were successively replaced by 'secours mutuels', 'sociétés typographiques', and 'syndicats', but however known French printers always maintained their tightly controlled tribal independence.

Centuries later the brothers Henri and Jules Desclée revived the association of the saint with printing when they gave the name 'Société de Saint Jean l'Evangéliste' to the press they founded at Tournai in 1882 for the printing of liturgical books.

St Omer Psalter: an early 14th-century Psalter of Norfolk origin, completed, however, in the 15th century. The principal decorative feature is a series of marginal miniatures of domestic animals and scenes of rural life. The work is now in the British Library.

St Stephen's Parliamentary Press: opened in 1961 on the site of the former Stationery Office printing works which bombing destroyed in 1940. For the first time all Parliamentary printing of the Stationery Office (for

431

which responsibility was assumed in 1834) can be done under one roof.

sale by candle: an auction sale at which a candle was lit when bidding began and continued until an inch had burned. The last and highest bidder before the flame died was the purchaser, a happening sometimes accelerated by a well-directed cough. Such sales were known in the 14th century, particularly in France and Italy, as a means of disposing of an estate or chattels to disputatious heirs, and they are mentioned in Pepys's 'Diary' as occurring in London in the 1660s. Inevitably when books formed part of an estate they would be included, and there was a famous sale by candle at Naples in 1608 when the library of Giovanni Pinelli (1538–1601) was auctioned *en bloc* in the presence of a judge but not of the books which were in a nearby villa. They were bought by the agent of Cardinal Federico Borromeo for the Ambrosiana Library he had founded in 1603.

There were variations of this method of auctioning books but sales by candle were discontinued after the later 17th century. See also *book auction.*

Sale Hill Press: a private printing press founded in 1904 by G. A. Hammond of Sheffield, but later moved to London. Until it closed in 1909 this handpress was used for very small editions of privately circulated works.

Salisbury School: an important centre of illumination in the mid-13th century was Salisbury. Work was typified by the deep emotion shown in the faces (e.g. the tenderness of the Madonna and the agony of Christ); by the use of white hatching on garments; by the delicacy and strength of line; and by the rippling draperies. An example may be seen in the John Rylands Library, Manchester.

Sallando, Pierantonio, *c.* 1460–*c.* 1540: a scriptor and writing master of Bologna University where there was an active and influential school of calligraphy from the 13th century onwards.

Several of his manuscripts are now in the Bodleian Library, while finer than these is the Bentivoglio Hours in the Victoria and Albert Museum, London.

salle: a well-lighted room in a papermill where the paper is examined sheet by sheet, sorted, counted and put up in reams. See also *look through, opacity, outsides, retree.*

Salomon, Bernard, fl.1545–61: an artist and woodcutter of Lyons where he worked with the printer *Jean de Tournes,* q.v., for whom he designed arabesques, flowers and blocks. Their long association began with a scientific book, 'Paraphrase de l'astrolabe' by Focard, printed in 1546.

His finest work appeared in an edition of the Bible, 1553; in 'La Métamorphose d'Ovide figurée', 1557; and the Lyons edition of Alciati's 'Emblemata libellus', 1560.

A feature of Salomon's work was its careful detail and small scale (the Ovid volume was only 6¼in. high).

In 1963 Sir Francis Meynell revived a suite of 105 Salomon woodcuts for the edition of the Bible published by his *Nonesuch Press,* q.v.

Saltire Award: an annual award, established in 1956 but first made in 1957, of an inscribed silver quaich, for an outstanding contribution to Scottish literature. The award is made by the Saltire Society of Edinburgh for a book published in the preceding year from the following categories: history and biography, poetry, drama, fiction and belles-lettres.

Salutati, Coluccio, 1330–1406: a Florentine humanist who was one of the first to experiment with Carolingian script. In its revived form it became known as *lettera (or littera) antiqua.* About 1400 Salutati employed *Poggio,* q.v., to copy books for him in this script, his 'De Verecundia' probably being the first datable example of humanistic script.

Salzburg School: from the 8th to the 12th century the Benedictine Monastery at Salzburg was an important centre of German illumination. A notable early work was the Cuthbert Gospels, *c.* 770. This was written by St Cuthbert, but whether in England or Salzburg is not known. The miniatures are similar in style to Canterbury work, with a strong Byzantine influence.

The two finest works of the 12th century are the 'Admonter Riesenbibel' and the Antiphony of St Peter. The latter is decorated with fourteen whole-page illuminations in gold and colours, and over four hundred initials drawn in ink on coloured grounds. The works noted above are in the Österreichische Nationalbibliothek, Vienna.

Salzburg continued to be a centre of illumination until the end of the 15th century, the emphasis being more on secular work and even including grammars of Donatus.

same size: an instruction to the blockmaker that illustrations submitted as copy are to be reproduced without reduction or enlargement. Abbreviated as S/S. See also *final size.*

Samurai Press: a press founded at Ranworth, Norfolk, by F. M. Browne, H. Monro, and others in 1907, but in the same year moved to Cranleigh, Surrey, where A. K. Sabin, of the *Temple Sheen Press,* q.v., managed its affairs. Among the small editions issued by the press before it closed in 1909, mostly of poetry, was one by Drinkwater.

Reproduction in two-colour half-tone of a painting, 'Siberian Tigers' by W. Kuhnert
(Below) Enlargement of the yellow and blue screen dots which build up the picture
See *two-colour reproduction*

COLOUR PRINTING

Reproduction in four colours printed in letterpress on coated stock. Photograph from Söderberg,'Garden Flowers'.
The picture is built up of screen dots in yellow, red (magenta), blue (cyan), and black
as shown (enlarged) in the panel below

Half-tone printed in duplex ink on coated stock, 150-*line screen*

The same block printed in ordinary ink

Printed on coated stock with a 175-line screen. By combining a black plate with a tint block a monochrome effect is obtained, but it is much richer and better toned than that obtainable by single-colour half-tone

Enlargement of the screen dots on which the above picture is based

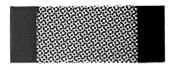

The sensitized layer under the colour screen is influenced (blackened) as shown below when the incident light is

| red | yellowish green | blue-violet | yellow | blue-green | blue-red | white | (black) | grey |

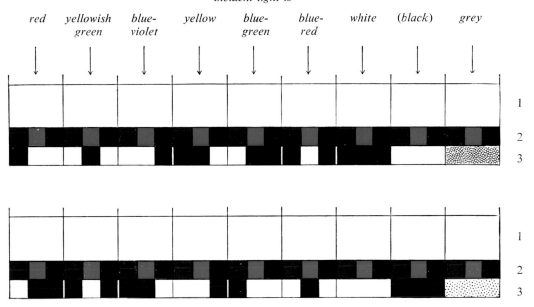

The lower illustration shows how a negative image is converted into a positive. In transmitting a white light, only such rays penetrate in the respective parts as correspond to the tone of the original light

The principle of the three-colour screen
1—glass or film base   2—colour screen   3—photographic film

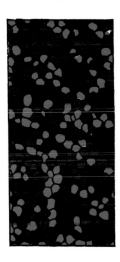

Colour screen in Lumière's autochrome plates and in the earliest Agfa material

Colour screen of the Dufaycolor process

*Original picture (= completed
reproduction)*

*Blue filter absorbs yellow (green+yellow+red)
light causing yellow parts of picture to appear black*

*In the top row the original coloured picture is repre-
sented, then its appearance through the blue, green,
and red filters. As the eye is much less sensitive to
blue than to the rest of the spectrum, the blue filter
appears very dark. For the same reason the yellow
printing, which only absorbs blue and reflects the
other colours, appears very light*

*Positive image obtained from the negative exposed
through a blue filter*

Yellow and magenta plates superimposed

The above printed in yellow (minus blue)

*Green filter absorbs magenta (blue+red) light; red
parts of picture appear black*

*Red filter absorbs cyan light
(blue+green)*

*The same exposed through a green
filter*

*The same exposed through a red
filter*

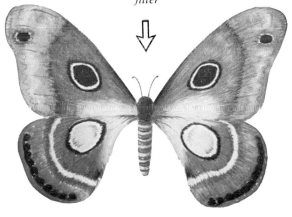

*The above printed in 'red'
(magenta=minus green)*

*The above printed in 'blue'
(cyan = minus red)*

Made by photographic three-colour analysis of a natural subject, three-colour block printed in letterpress on art paper

Enlargement of the colour elements which build up the reproduction above

sand letters: the name given to large display letters made in sizes from 6 to 18 line pica (now 72- to 192-point). They were cast from patterns impressed in an open box of moist sand. The practice ceased in the early 19th century following James Jackson's method of casting from a large mould and matrix. See also *woodletter type.*

sandwich dressing: a variety of cylinder dressing for letterpress machines. A typical combination would be a manilla top sheet, a middle sheet of acetate and a plastic blanket. See also *dressing the cylinder.*

Sangorski and Sutcliffe: a leading British firm of craftsmen binders. It was founded in 1901 by *Francis Sangorski* (1875–1912) and *George Sutcliffe* (1878–1943) who in 1897 had studied under *Douglas Cockerell,* q.v., at London's Central School of Arts and Crafts and in 1899 spent a year in his Denmark Street bindery.

The two men quickly established a reputation for swagger bindings, using jewels for some, and they found a ready market for a succession of elaborately bound copies of the Rubáiyát of Omar Khayyám, culminating in one with over a thousand pearls and stones.

The firm bound the Coronation Bible in 1953, to a design by Lynton Lamb, interpreted by Stanley Bray, and is still generally considered to be Britain's leading firm for fine bindings.

Sanlecque, Jacques de, 1558–1648: a Parisian punch-cutter who was a pupil of Le Bé before setting up his business in 1596. He and his son of the same name specialized in the cutting of oriental types, notable being his syriac and samaritan cut for the private press of Savary de Brèves at Rome. The punches were back in Paris by 1619 and types from some of them were used for part of Le Jay's 'Bible polyglotte' printed by Antoine Vitré, 1628–45. They are now in the *Cabinet des Poinçons,* q.v.

That the family business had been successful for many years may be gathered from a letter written in 1779 by the widow of the last Sanlecque (d. 1778) to Benjamin Franklin. She wrote 'I am the proprietress of a foundry which I dare assure you is the finest in Europe'. On her death in 1784 the typographic foundry, now in a decline, passed to Maurice Joly who sold it to Henri Haener of Nancy in 1786: the latter also acquired part of the J. P. Fournier foundry when he died in 1786.

sanserif: type without serifs. At different times in their history such types have been known as *condensed, doric, gothic, grotesque* and *monoline,* the name sanserif being first used by Vincent Figgins in his specimen book of 1832. In recent years they have also been referred to as *lineal type* since ideally they are based on the purity of linear pattern.

Among scores of modern examples are Airport, Futura, Gill, Helvetica, Mercator, Nobel, Univers and Vogue. With exceptions, they are most suitable for display work and attempts to set a whole text in sanserif are rarely successful since the reader is subconsciously hindered by the absence of any connecting strokes between letters, a function of serifs. See also *grotesque, serif,* and Appendix A.

Sanskrit: see *devanagari.*

Sanvito, Bartolomeo, 1435–c. 1518: a scholar of Padua. He worked in Rome as a transcriber of texts for several wealthy patrons. Of the forty or so of his manuscript books which survive in public collections a Eusebius, 1478, and the epigraphic inscriptions of Fra Giovanni Giocondo are in the British Library (Royal 14.C.3 and Stowe MS.1016). Notable were his pages written in capitals, often in gold and colours.

In his 'The script of humanism' Wardrop invites speculation on a possible connection between Sanvito's script and the Aldine italic. Sanvito was a 'friend of the Aldine academicians . . .'.

sarsanet: a lining material made of stiffened cotton.

Sarum use: the Book of Hours and the Missal as used in the diocese of Salisbury from the 11th century to the Reformation. The Hours began as a medieval modification of the Roman rite used at Salisbury Cathedral. By the mid-15th century it was common to most of England. The first printed edition was that of Caxton, 1487. The first Sarum Missal printed in England was that printed by Julian Notary for Wynkyn de Worde in 1498 (Caxton's of 1487 had been printed in Paris). Other editions of this popular work were printed by Pynson. Copies for those able to afford them were pulled on vellum.

satellite press: see *drum cylinder press.*

Sauer: an important family of printers and type-founders in Colonial America. The founder of the business, *Christopher I* (1694–1758), settled in Germantown, Pa., in 1724. In 1738 he established a press to make more effective his religious propaganda among the local German colony. Most important was the Sauer Bible, 1743; this was a 12,000-copy edition of Luther's translation.

Christopher II (1722–84) expanded the business, and in 1771 he added a typefoundry with German matrices and moulds. In a copy of his religious periodical 'Ein geistliches Magazien' (est. 1764) he claimed that it was 'Gedruckt mit der ersten Schrift die jemals in Amerika gegossen worden', i.e. printed from the first types to be cast in America. He cast black-face types. His two employees Justus Fox and Jacob Bay (or Bey) later set up their own premises and one of them probably cast the first commercially successful roman letter to be made in America. (It was not until 1781 that the roman face designed, cut, and cast in 1769 by *Abel Buell* of Killingworth, Conn., was made in quantity.) In the war of Independence Sauer's property was auctioned and he ended his days as a bookbinder.

Christopher III (1754–99) took over the firm in 1774, expanding it still further, and adding an ink mill to the premises.

Sauty, Alfred de: a London bookbinder who worked at Rivière's before establishing his own bindery in the late 1890s. About 1908 he emigrated to Chicago where, in 1923, he directed the bindery of R. R. Donnelly. His work was of considerable skill as indicated, for example, by the lavish onlay binding of 'The floure and the leafe' (Kelmscott Press) now in the British Library (C.68.g10).

Savage, William, 1770–1843: of Howden in Yorkshire where he began bookselling and printing in 1790. He moved to London in 1797, working for a time as superintendent of the Royal Institution's printing office. About 1803 he decided to set up his own business and concentrate on fine colour printing. His efforts failed and were later abandoned: they may be judged in his 'Practical hints on decorative printing, with illustrations engraved on wood and printed in colours at the Type Press', 1822. Hansard was sharply critical of the work since the quality of the result bore no relation to the labour. Of one plate for which twenty-nine blocks were made and thirty tints were worked he wrote 'I think this picture-print of "Mercy" a monstrous abortion – it is horrible – its only merit is in the patience and difficulty with which it was gestated and brought to parturition.'

In 1832 Savage published a book on the making of printing inks, and in 1841 his 'Dictionary of the art of printing'. It is by the latter that he is remembered today. A reprint was published in 1967.

Savile, Sir Henry, 1549–1622: a scholar of Oxford where in 1619 he founded two lectureships (in geometry and astronomy). It was for the use of Readers here that Savile gave an important collection of Latin and Greek astronomical and mathematical manuscripts as well as printed books on the sciences. He encouraged professors to enrich this library by donating additions. One holder of the Chair of Astronomy was Sir Christopher Wren (1661–73) who left a collection of works on geometry and astronomy.

In 1607 Savile sponsored the printing of his edition of the Greek text of St Chrysostom's works. This was issued in eight volumes, printed at Eton for John Norton, 1610–12(13).

434

The administration of the Savile library was taken over by the Bodleian in 1884. See also *greek type*.

sawn-in back: see *hand-sewing, recessed cords*.

Saxton, Christopher, fl.1570–96: the principal English cartographer of his day whose maps were engraved by Augustine Ryther, Reynolds and others. His most famous work was 'Britannia Insularum', 1583, on twenty-one sheets; these were widely copied.

SBN: see *International Standard Book Number*.

SC: the abbreviation for *super-calendered paper*, q.v.

sc.: an abbreviation for the Latin 'scilicet', i.e. namely.

scabbards: a term known in the 16th century for thin wooden boards used in bookbinding. At the end of the century the Stationers' Company forbade their use for prayer books.

Scan-a-Graver: an *electronic engraving machine*, q.v., made by the Fairchild Camera & Instrument Corporation, U.S.A., and introduced in 1948. Original models produced an engraved half-tone plate (a *Scan-plate*) of cellulose acetate ready for printing or for duplicating as a stereo. Subsequent models included one for both line and half-tone work and offered a choice of screen from 24 to 48 lines per cm. Scan-plates can be set up with type for letterpress formes or be fitted to the cylinders of rotary machines.

Machines have a revolving shaft on the lathe principle and both the original to be scanned and the plate to be engraved are carried on it. A pinpoint beam of light is directed on the original. Light reflected back to a photoelectric cell causes impulses to be transmitted via amplifiers to an electrically heated stylus. The pyramidal point of the stylus thrusts into the plastic plate, burning a square hole of a depth proportionate to the tonal densities of the original (shallow for shadows, deep for highlights). As the scanning and engraving heads move laterally over the revolving shaft the engraved plate is given a cross-ruled screen effect.

The more versatile *Scan-a-Sizer*, first made in 1955, has only one cylinder and this carries the blank plate. Copy for scanning is held flat in a vacuum frame. This machine will either enlarge or reduce the original.

Scanatron: a British *electronic scanning machine*, q.v., for making a set of colour-corrected positives from a continuous tone negative. Final screen negatives for printing down to metal are then made from the positives. Etching follows.

scanner: see *colour scanner*.

scanning head: see *electronic engraving machine*.

scan plates: the name approved by the Federation of Master Process Engravers, London, for any plate made on an *electronic engraving machine*, q.v.

Schäufelein, Hans Leonhard, fl.1505–38: a German book illustrator whose early style suggests his tuition by Dürer. He worked mostly for publishers in Augsburg, but also in Basle, Hagenau, and Nördlingen. His twenty woodcuts for the 'Theuerdank', printed by Schönsperger in 1517; illustrations for Luther's 'Neue Testament', 1522; and for translations of the classics published by Heinrich Steiner, are among his best works.

Schedel, Hartmann, 1440–1514: a Nuremberg physician and bibliophile remembered for his great history of the world as seen from Nuremberg the 'Liber Cronicarum' (Nuremberg Chronicle). This was printed by *Anton Koberger*, q.v., in two editions, both in 1493. The Latin version (Hain 14508) appeared in July. The German translation of it by Georg Alt was issued in December as 'Die Weltchronik' (Hain 14510). The work is famous for the 1,809 woodcut illustrations designed by Michael Wolgemut (or Wohlgemuth) and Wilhelm Pleydenwurff which made it the most lavishly illustrated German book of the period. There were, however, only 645 blocks, many being repeated. Also of interest is the survival in Nuremberg City Library of the layouts of the German edition, probably the earliest surviving designs of any book.

Schedel's personal library, which included 300 manuscripts and many incunabula, is in the Bavarian State Library.

Scheere, Herman, fl.1400–20: a painter and illuminator who came probably from the Low Countries to work in England where he had a large workshop with many assistants. Several manuscripts bearing his name or attributable on stylistic grounds survive in public collections, notable being the Bedford Hours and Psalter (BM.Add.MS.42131) which contains over 300 delicately modelled portrait heads within medallions; a Book of Hours now in the Austrian Abbey of Altenburg; and the Beaufort Hours, also in the British Library, which includes a particularly fine Annunciation unmatched in any other English work of the period. His use of the acanthus scroll and rich border ornament mark an innovation in English painting.

Scheide, William Taylor: an American bibliophile who with his son *John Hinsdale* and grandson *William Hurd* developed at Titusville, Pa. what is now named the *Scheide Library*, since 1965 at Princeton University. Among its innumerable and rare books are the Gutenberg Bible, the only copy in America of the Mainz Psalter of 1457, and one of the 1459 edition, both on vellum. It is notable for its fine collection of Bibles. See *Princeton University Library Chronicle*, xxxvii 2 1976.

schematic: in technical book illustration, a simple outline drawing of part of a machine or process showing its working principle.

Schlegel-Tieck Prize: announced in 1964 as an annual award of £300 made by the Society of Authors and the Translators' Association for the best English translation, commissioned by a British publisher, of a 20th century German work previously published in the German Federal Republic.

Schöffer, Peter, fl.1449–1502: the associate of *Johann Fust*, q.v. About 1450 he was working in Paris as a calligrapher. A few years later he came to Mainz and worked as a foreman for *Gutenberg*, q.v. When the lawyer Fust acquired Gutenberg's printing equipment in 1455/6 he employed Schöffer who in addition to proving an accomplished printer designed and cast type for him. The first book the two issued was the *Mainz Psalter* of 1457, q.v., although some preparatory work on this may have been done in Gutenberg's workshop. Other works issued jointly included the Latin Bible of 1462, editions in 1465 and 1466 of Cicero's 'De officiis', and the 'Liber sextus decretalium', 1465, for Boniface VIII.

That Schöffer did not marry Fust's daughter Christina until late 1466 or early 1467, and not before, is inferred from Fust's reference to him in the Cicero of 1466 as 'puer meus' which indubitably means 'my employee' and not 'my son-in law' as is sometimes supposed.

At the time of Fust's death, probably in October 1466, the pair had printed about twenty-five works, subsequently Schöffer printed some 130 books and seventy-five broadsides, intended largely for an academic and official public. The books, mostly in Latin, included the famous illustrated 'Hortus sanitatis', in German, issued in 1485, missals, psalters, and canon law. His broadsides and pamphlets, of a political and quasi-official kind, may be considered the precursors of later news-sheets. The last book known to have been printed by him was a Mainz Psalter in December 1502.

Peter Schöffer was the first international bookseller-printer and built up a considerable business through depots and selling agents as far afield as Paris, Lübeck and Basle. He was probably the first printer to trade at the *Frankfurt Fair*, q.v.

He was succeeded in 1503 by his son *Johann* (c. 1468–1531) whose extensive list included works by Erasmus and other humanists in addition to editiones principes of Latin classics and liturgical books done on commission for various towns. In the preface to an edition of Livy which Schöffer printed in 1523 he stated that printing was invented by Johann Gutenberg in Mainz in 1450 and later improved by Fust and his own father.

The younger brother of Johann, *Peter II* (fl. 1510–47) was important as a punchcutter and typefounder. He printed variously in Mainz (where he issued a pioneer example of organ music in 1512), in Worms, 1513–29, where about 1526 he printed the first edition (8vo) of Tyndale's New Testament and may have completed the 4to edition begun by Quentell in Cologne (of which no copies survive). He then moved to Strasbourg in 1529 where between 1533 and 1536 he printed much music in association with Matthias Apiarius (who at Strasbourg and later at Berne used Schöffer's titling types). When in Venice in 1541/2 he used a new italic with sloped capitals, later to be used by other printers as far afield as England. He cut founts of hebrew and greek, probably two alphabets of roman titling letters, had a music fount which required two impressions, and may have supplied punches and type to Froben. He died in Basle in 1547.

Ivo Schöffer (fl.1531–56), probably a son of Peter II, continued the original Mainz business. He was a distinguished citizen, did much official printing, and founded Mainz University Press. See H. Lehmann-Haupt, 'Peter Schoeffer of Gernsheim and Mainz', N.Y., Hart, 1950.

Scholderer, Victor, 1880–1971: a scholar who in 1904 joined the Department of Printed Books at the British Museum. A major contribution to his international reputation as an authority on the history of the printed book was the great folio 'Catalogue of books printed in the XVth century now in the British Museum'. Nine volumes had been published by the time of his death.

Some of his numerous articles and reviews on bibliography concerned printing in greek type of which his own fount, New Hellenic, was cut by Monotype in 1927.

scholium: a short marginal note by a grammarian or professional writer explaining an adjacent text or interpreting or criticizing the author's treatment of his theme. Usage of the term is limited to works written before 1450. In some manuscripts the scholium would be a note by the owner of the codex, or a quotation from an earlier scholar's writings. See also *adversaria, gloss.*

Schön, Erhard, *c.* 1491–1542: a German woodcut designer and pupil of Dürer. From 1514–40 he was commissioned by most printers in his native Nuremberg. Notable were his illustrations for the New Testament printed by Peypus in 1524 (which included the work of others).

Schönsperger, Johann, fl.1481–1524: an important printer of Augsburg. He issued many books with woodcut illustrations and printed several works notable in German literary history ('Sachsenspiegel', 1482; 'Narrenschiff', 1494; 'Die Weltchronik', 1496; 'Theuerdank', 1517).

He attracted the attention of Maximilian I, and it was in his service that one of the first of several examples of *Fraktur* type, q.v., was used. Its design, based on court hand, was the work of Vincenz Rockner, head of Maximilian's chancery, and it was cut by Hieronymus Andreae.

School Bookshop Association: a limited company established in London in 1976 representing educational authorities, publishers, booksellers, teachers and the NBL. There is a full-time School Bookshop Officer, and the SBA took over publication of *School Bookshop News*, which for its first four issues had been financed by Penguin Books.

By the mid-1970s some four to five thousand British schools had set up bookshops to develop reading and book *owning* habits among children. It was the need for advice and assistance in starting new ones and in making older ones more effective that led to the forming of the SBA. Funds for administration came from publishers, from schools with shops, and from booksellers. The Association has a president and a council. Address: 7 Albemarle Street, London W1X 4BB.

school edition: an edition of a book printed from the original plates but usually in a different format or style of binding and annotated. See also *in usum scholarum, Primer.*

Schoolmaster of St. Albans, fl.*c.* 1480–86: the nameless printer who set up a press at St Albans. This may have been in the monastery or in the town, the arms of both being the same. In 1480 he printed the 'Nova rhetorica' compiled by the humanist Lorenzo di Savona while at Cambridge. He later printed the 'Book of St Albans' for which he used coloured inks for the sections on heraldry and field sports.

In all copies of eight works from his press survive. It is thought that he used Caxton's second type and that some connection may have existed between the two printers. See also *John Herford, Thomas Richard.*

Schwabacher: a later form of *bastarda*, q.v., used in Germany and Switzerland from *c.* 1480 until 1540 for vernacular printing. Schöffer's 'Hortus sanitatis', Mainz, 1485, is printed in this type. See also *letters – forms and styles.*

Scinzenzeler, Ulrich, fl.1477–1500: a German printer working in Milan, remembered as the printer of the first illustrated book in that city (Hain 7159). He was at one time partnered by Leonhard Pachel, and was commissioned by other publishers. He issued independently theological and legal books, also several works in Italian and Greek, and a well-known work by Rhazes on children's diseases in 1481.

scorcher: the machine which heats and curves stereo matrices for use on rotary presses.

scoring: the making of a crease in paper or card so that it will not be damaged by folding.

Scot, John, fl.1552–71: a printer of St Andrews and Edinburgh. Very few of his publications survive, due partly to their ephemeral or controversial nature. For printing a Catholic tract by Winzet in 1562, Scot was imprisoned and lost his stock and press.

Scottish bindings: two distinctive styles of decoration were used by Edinburgh binders during the years 1725–75, mostly on the covers of Bibles. On one group the central motif on the board was a large wheel resembling a fully opened fan with quarters of the fan as corner pieces. The inspiration for this pattern can be traced to the European 'fan' bindings of the previous century (illustrated under *bookbinding*, q.v.) though on these the wheel was smaller.

For an alternative design, often referred to as a 'herring bone', the central motif was a long stem with flattened leaves arranged in pairs on either side of it. The rest of the panel was filled with floral or foliate tools. In other examples there is a central wheel combined with sprigs of the leaf pattern in the four corners. End-leaves were mostly of *dutch gilt paper*, q.v.

There were probably several craftsmen making these bindings, but their names have not been traced.

See M. J. Sommerlad, 'Scottish wheel and herringbone bindings in the Bodleian Library', Oxford Bibliographical Society, 1967, in which twenty-eight are shown. See also *Haye MSS*.

Scottish early printing and publishing: prior to 1508 printing for the Scottish trade was done in England or on the Continent, but in 1507 James IV approved the setting up by *Androw Myllar* and *Walter Chepman*, qq.v., of a press in Edinburgh, and he forbade anyone to send manuscripts out of the country for printing if the books were intended for subsequent sale in Scotland. Myllar and Chepman appear to have printed about eleven small tracts and the Aberdeen Breviary between 1508 and 1510.

The second Scottish printer was *Thomas Davidson*, fl.1532–42, of Edinburgh, who was the first to use roman type in a Scottish book, and who is remembered chiefly for 'The hystory and croniklis of Scotland' (Hector Boece), *c.* 1532.

The first English Bible printed in Scotland was issued between 1576 and 1579 by *Thomas Bassandyne*, q.v. The first Glasgow printer was George Anderson whose earliest work 'The Protestation of the General Assemblie of the Church of Scotland' appeared in 1638.

Until *Alexander Wilson*, q.v., established a foundry at Glasgow in the 1740s type used by Scottish printers was mostly bought in England: he was able to reverse the flow by selling type cheaply in London. See also *Foulis, Vautroullier*.

Scottish Text Society: a society founded in 1882 'for the purpose of publishing works illustrative of the Scottish language, literature and history prior to the Union'.

scraperboard: a coated board used by artists preparing illustrations (original drawings or photos in line) for reproduction by a variety of processes. Much used in commercial artwork.

scratted paper: a 17th century form of marbled paper, made by splashing small blobs of colour on to a sheet and used for end papers.

screamer: a composing-room term for an exclamation mark.

screen: 1. *half-tone*, q.v. Until the late 1960s the glass cross-line half-tone screen was used in process work for converting 'genuine' half-tones into 'false' half-tones which consist of dots of uniform density but varying size which are usually too small to be distinguishable by the eye alone. These screens have been superseded by flexible *contact screens*, q.v., of which three kinds are in use: *negative-dot magenta* for making half-tone negatives from monochrome originals; *positive-dot magenta* for making half-tone positives by projection or contact; *grey screens* for monochrome half-tone negatives and direct-screen colour separation negatives. All give improved definition though the closeness of the ruled lines affects this, e.g. 50–65 lines per inch for newsprint, 120–150 for coated stock. See also *Erwin, Ives, Levy, Meisenbach, moiré, single-line half-tone, Swan, Talbot*.

2. *photogravure*, q.v. A screen for printing-in the network for doctor-blade gravure or intaglio. The expensive glass screens of former days have been superseded by flexible contact screens. The ruling is usually about 175 lines per inch. See *screen ruling*.

screen process work: 1. the reproduction of half-tones by means of exposure through a screen in a camera. This is the basis of the half-tone process and modern offset reproduction.

2. the contact printing of a half-tone negative on to a film by means of a screen with vignetted dots. This gives a screen transparency which can be used for

Details in the picture made up of screen dots of varying size

offset printing. See also *contact screen, deep-etch process, half-tone process.*

screen ruling: metric half-tone rulings are based on the number of lines per centimetre: former British rulings on lines per inch. Both are given here (conversion factor 2·5)

    (a) lines per cm.

              20 30 34 40 48 54 60 70 80

    (b) lines per inch

              50 75 85 100 120 135 150 175 200

scribal copy: a manuscript written by a copyist as distinct from that written or dictated by the author. See also *scriptorium.*

scribe: a writer of manuscripts. The term is particularly associated with the professional multipliers of texts before printing was invented. See also *manuscript book writing.*

scrim: see *mull.*

script: type faces designed to suggest handwriting. Early examples were the French *civilité* q.v., and the Kanzleischriften used by German printers in the 1540s.

    Examples of more recent script types, widely used in display and jobbing work, are given in Appendix A.

scriptorium: the room in a monastery in which manuscripts were copied; the form varied, in some cases being a large room, in others a room divided into small cells or carrells by partitions. An armarius was responsible for administering the strict rules which governed conduct in these workrooms. Artificial light was excluded to minimize the risk of fire, and absolute silence prevailed, a system of gestures being used for communication. See also *illumination, manuscript book writing.*

scriptura actuaria: see *rustic capitals.*

scrittura umanistica: Carolingian minuscule as revived in the 15th century by Italian renaissance scholars. See also *humanistic.*

scroll: a roll of parchment or paper, usually handwritten.

scumming: a fault in lithographic printing in which greasy ink adheres to the non-image areas of the plate. Causes are the use of a badly desensitized plate, excessive driers, and certain pigments in the ink.

seal: the skin of the Newfoundland seal prepared for bookbinding, usually for limp covers. It is a handsome, hard-wearing, flexible leather with a distinctive bold grain. See also *Alaska seal, pin seal, seal grain leather.*

seal grain leather: split sheepskin grained to resemble seal.

secondary binding: a difference in the *publisher's binding*, q.v., between copies of the same printing of a work may occur when the sales potentiality of a book cannot be foreseen, and the publisher deems it better for the sheets to be bound up in batches, a process which may be spread over a period of years. The colour or material first used may no longer be available, or the spinal lettering may be altered. While such binding variants are secondary bindings, it is necessary to establish which was first put on sale before applying the term. *Remainder bindings* are not secondary bindings. Cf. *primary bindings*.

second couple: see *perfecting*.

secretary: a term loosely and inaccurately applied to English gothic bastard types.

Properly, secretary describes a script fully developed by 1550 as a ceremonious hand for writing in English, and it so appears in John Baildon's writing book of 1571. Its chief characteristics were a strong vertical emphasis, an absence of connecting strokes, and a contrast in thickness between main and subsidiary strokes. However, in 1637 the writing master Billingsley wrote of the great variety of secretary hands then in use of which the sloped 'fast hand' was intended for quick writing, and the 'set hand' for engrossing documents.

As a printing type it roughly corresponds to the French *civilité*, q.v., which was used in Edinburgh in 1571. In England comparable script types were used in the late 16th and 17th centuries for printing various forms, notices and official documents rather than for books.

section: 1. the reference mark § inserted in the text of a work to direct the attention of the reader to a footnote. This conjoined 's' symbol was used by 12th-century scribes as a paragraph mark.

2. a folded printed sheet, inclusive of *plates* and *inserts*, if any, and thus ready for *gathering* and *sewing*, qq.v. The term is not entirely synonymous with *signature*, q.v., as a signature does not become a section until plates and the like have been added to it, should they be needed.   (LK)

see copy: a proof mark indicating an omission too long to be written on the proof. The copy is attached and the omission indicated for the compositor's guidance. Also a mark indicating to the author that the reader is unsure about something on the copy.

see safe: said of books bought by a bookseller from a publisher, and paid for, but with the understanding that at some future date the publisher may be asked to exchange the bookseller's surplus for copies of another title. Cf. *half see safe*. See also *terms*.

Selden, John, 1584–1654: a jurist, parliamentarian, and Oriental scholar who assembled a library of works on theology, law, history, Hebrew literature and studies, as well as an important array of Oriental manuscripts. Some 8,000 items from his collection passed to the Bodleian Library in 1659.

selectasine: a colour printing process in which a single silk screen is used for all the colours.

self ends: end-papers of the same stock as is used for the text of a book and part of the first and last sections of it. Also known as *own ends*.

self wrapper: the cover of a pamphlet when formed by the first and last leaves of it, i.e. an integral part of the printed text sheet(s). It is usually printed. See also *wrapper*.

semé (or **semis**): see *powdered*.

semi-uncial: see *half-uncial*.

semi-yapp: protective covers which turn over a little beyond the edges of a book. This style is a compromise between *limp* and *Yapp* bindings, qq.v.

Senefelder, Aloysius, 1771–1834: the inventor of *lithography*, q.v. His father was an actor in Munich, and in his youth Aloysius wrote some comedies. As he had difficulty in getting his plays printed he tried to do the work himself. He made various experiments, including engraving and etching on copper, and printed his works on a primitive copperplate press. In trying to find a cheaper material for the plates he also tried pieces of limestone slate. According to his own statement he happened to write a laundry bill on a polished stone which was at hand, and the writing was done with a mixture of ink which he used as an etching base on his plates. Later, the idea occurred to him of using script on the stone for printing purposes, and when he etched this with spirit of nitre he obtained a printing surface with raised script which lent itself to inking in and printing. This was the origin of *stone printing* (1796), although done at first on the principle of relief printing. The inking up of the low image in relief, without affecting the intermediate surfaces, gave Senefelder trouble, and he found that for this purpose he had to use a flat board on which the ink had been ground with an ink-ball. By chance, however, he discovered that it was not necessary to etch the stone in relief, but that a usable printing image could be obtained by damping the stone with diluted etching liquid, after inscribing

439

it, and inking it in before it dried. He found that the limestone from Solnhofen was the most suitable material, and this has remained the only one for practical use in actual stone printing.

Senefelder soon discovered that a copperplate press was unsuitable for stone printing, and in 1796 he built a rod or cross-beam press which was improved in the next year and became the model for the lithographic hand-press still in use. (For an illustration see *hand-press*.) In 1798 he experimented with methods of stone engraving and transferring (including a kind of anastatic printing), in 1799 with autographic printing and crayon drawing, and in 1805 with lithographic printing from zinc. The Elector of Bavaria gave him support, and in 1799 granted him a privilege for all lithographic printing; but when his first attempts to keep the process secret failed he was obliged, in order to raise money, to instruct others in the craft. Philipp André, a music publisher of Offenbach, offered Senefelder 2,000 florins to establish a press for him and train workmen in its use. André also brought Senefelder to London to secure British patents (granted in 1801), the first book in England to show specimens being printed in 1803. He was not long in England.

In 1809 Senefelder obtained an appointment as inspector at the Kataster Printing Works in Munich and thus had a fixed income. He continued his experiments, and in 1813 invented a substitute for the heavy stone in the form of a substance which was spread on paper or cloth. In 1817 he built an automatic inking, damping and printing stone press, and in 1826 he announced the invention of an original printing process in which the surface consisted of small ink reservoirs placed close together; this did not require inking between each impression (mosaic printing).

Senefelder seems to have envisaged most of the developments and possibilities of his invention. In 1818 he published his manual on the subject 'Vollständiges Lehrbuch der Steindruckerei' (in German, simultaneously by Thienemann of Munich and Gerold of Vienna; an English translation published by Ackermann appeared in 1819, and in the same year a French translation was issued by Treuttel & Wärtz of Strasbourg). The illustrations to the various editions were the work of nationals of each country.

(With GU)

Sensenschmidt, Johann, fl.1470–91: the founder of the first printing press in Nuremberg. He worked at first with Heinrich Kefer (or Keffer), an associate of Gutenberg. Their first joint work was the 'Pantheologia' of Rainerius de Pisis, 1473.

From 1481 Sensenschmidt worked in Bamberg, both alone and with Heinrich Petzensteiner, where he issued many liturgical works.

separate: an article reprinted from a periodical and issued separately. Also known as an *off-print*.

Septuagint: a translation into colloquial Greek of the Pentateuch and the Apocrypha, made in Alexandria about 270 BC.

According to legend seventy Jewish scribes in as many separate cells were given the task, and by divine inspiration produced seventy identical versions. See also *Hebrew printing before* 1600.

sequela: a Latin term, generally limited in its usage to pre-16th century writings, for a literary work which, while complete in itself, continues an earlier work.

Serampore Press: see *Bengali printing and typography*.

serial: a book published in parts which appear at regular intervals. This may precede publication in *book form*, q.v. Publication in instalments was known in the early 16th century as, for example, the *responsa* of Isaac ben Sheshet Perfet which at Constantinople in 1546 were printed weekly in sections for sale to subscribers. In England, the method of publishing whereby books were sold in consecutively numbered parts, or fascicules, issued monthly or weekly, developed in the 18th century. They were known as *number books*. Each part consisted of two or more folded sheets stitched together within blue paper covers. The title-page for the whole book would either be issued and dated at the time of the first part, or with the last some weeks or months later.

Another form of serial publication was popularized by Robert Walker, an enterprising newspaper publisher of 18th century London. He printed newspapers for particular provincial areas, with local items in each, as, for example, the *Shropshire Journal* of 1737–39. But they all included a supplement from one of his religious books. Public reaction to serial publication was not always favourable as the following extract from a letter printed in the *Grub Street Journal* of 1724 shows: '. . . I take notice of the strange Madness of publishing Books by piecemeal, at six or twelve Pennyworth a Week. . . . The Bible can't escape. I bought the other Day, three Pennyworth of the Gospel, made easy and familiar to Porters, Carmen, and Chimney-Sweepers.'

Nonetheless, in the 19th century the publication of fiction in serial form contributed greatly to the spread of the reading habit among classes of non-buyers of bound books, and Tagore's epitaph on this practice merits quotation: 'He who will may swallow at a mouthfull the whole of Chandrashekhar or Bishabriksha, but the process of longing and anticipating, month after month, of spreading over long intervals the concentrated joy of each short reading, revolving every instalment over and over in the mind while watching and waiting for the next, the combination of satisfaction with unsatisfied craving, of burning curiosity with its appeasement; these long-drawn-out delights of going through the original serial none will ever taste again.' ('My reminiscences', 1917).

Serial publication is still used for heavily promoted encyclopaedias of popular appeal, and occasionally for more scholarly works (e.g. 'Encyclopaedia of Islam', Leyden, 1960–). See R. M. Wiles, 'Serial publication in England before 1750', C.U.P., 1957.

serial rights: the author's or publisher's right to arrange for a book to be published in serial form in a newspaper or magazine.

series: 1. a set of type founts based on one design and graded in size. Thus the type in which this book is set is named Monotype Times New Roman, Series 327. It is available in composition founts ranging from 4¾-point to 14-point, and in display sizes from 14- to 72-point for hand-setting. See also *family*, *fount*.

2. see *fiction-*, *publisher's-*, *subject series*.

serif: the short finishing stroke set across or projecting from the end of a letter stem. There are several varieties of serif; those on old-face types are *bracketed* and curve from the stroke to a point; on modern faces they are flat *hair-lines* set at right angles to the main strokes of letters; most egyptian faces have thick *slab* serifs, while such types as Clarendon have *slab bracketed*. *Latin* serifs slope towards but do not curve into the main stroke, Chisel is an example; while types such as Albertus are said to have *bluntly sheared* serifs. (See Appendix A.)

Of all the foregoing the serifs of old face are more patently part of the basic letter design and less of an addition to it. Cf. *sanserif*.

Service books: see *Antiphonary, Book of Common Prayer, Book of Hours, Breviary, Collectarium, directory* (1), *enchiridion, Exultet roll, Gradual, Legenda, Manuale, Missal, Missale plenarium, Penitential, Pentateuch, Pontifical, Portas, Primer, Processionale, Psalter, Pye-book* (1), *Rituale, Sacramentary, Sarum use, Totum, Troper.*

set: 1. the width of a type body.

2. a figure used to indicate the comparative width of a Monotype type design. 12-point, 10½ set is narrower generally than 12-point, 12 set.

3. to compose type.

set flush: matter set up without any indented lines.

set hand: the individual and formal style of hand-writing used by each of the various Courts, or departments, in medieval England. This ensured a degree of uniformity within the Court. Cf. *free hand*.

set-off: 1. a printing fault caused by the transference of ink from the freshly inked impression on a printed sheet to the underside of the next sheet to be laid upon it in the pile. This can be avoided by printing with quick-set inks or by using an anti-set-off spray. An alternative to the use of spray powders is the ultra-violet curing of printed sheets. The press requires modification and specially formulated solvent-free inks are used. Drying is quicker and the press remains cleaner.

2. see *quotations* (1).

set-off reel: a paper reel with a set-off sheet, used in reel-fed rotary machines to prevent ink from the first forme setting off on the packing of the impression cylinder. The set-off sheet is wound off its reel at the same speed as the printing paper, passing between the latter and the packing of the cylinder, being then wound up automatically. One set-off reel can be used many times.   (GU)

set solid: matter set without leads between lines. Cf. *leaded*.

setting rule: a thin strip of brass, type high, about three points thick, and made in various lengths. It is placed in the composing stick before setting the first line; a nib projecting at one end enables it to be removed when a line is completed and placed in position for the setting of the next. Illustrated under *composing stick*, q.v.

Settle, Elkanah, fl.1704–25: an eccentric London versifier and playwright who about 1700 conceived the idea of enshrining volumes of his verse in elaborately tooled bindings for despatch to wealthy or titled families. The arms of those who received them had first been stamped on the boards and he hoped that the innocent intoxication of seeing them so displayed would induce patronage. Whether Settle made or only commissioned the bindings has not been recorded. More than a hundred survive, some being in the British Library.

sewing: fastening the sections of a book together by means of thread. This may be done by hand or machine and in various styles (see references below). Determining factors are paper substance, number of sections, type of binding, size of the book and the use to be made of it. Cf. *adhesive binding*. See also *all along, chain stitch, flexible sewing, french sewing, hand-sewing, kettle-stitch, machine sewing, overcasting, saddle-stitch, side-stitch, stitching, two-sheets on, whipstitching.*

sewing frame: see *hand-sewing*.

sewing thread: the thread used for sewing books by hand or machine. Silk or linen (for hand-sewing), cotton or linen (for machine sewing) are usual though there is some use of synthetics. The thickness of the thread is important as if one too thick is chosen it will cause swelling at the back and make rounding difficult. Thread thickens the back by the sum of its caliper in each section, e.g. if a book of thirty sections is stitched with 0·22mm. caliper thread the book will have a swell of 6·6mm. The swell is reduced during *smashing*, q.v., or it can be lessened by sewing with thinner thread.

sewn flexible: see *flexible sewing*.

sextern: a gathering of six sheets, folded once, in which form some bound manuscripts and early printed books were bound. See also *quaternion*.

sexto-decimo: see *sixteenmo*.

Sforziada: an account in verse of the life of Duke Francesco Sforza (ruled 1450–66) of Milan, written by his friend Joannes Simoneta. An Italian translation of the original Latin was printed by Zarotto in Milan in 1490. Splendid vellum copies are in the British Library and the Bibliothèque Nationale, Paris, but the finest, illuminated and signed by the artist-priest Giampetrino da Birago, is in Warsaw.

sgraffito: a woodcut technique in which the design appears in white on a black or red ground. Ratdolt of Augsburg printed examples. See also *woodcut*.

shaded letters: display and jobbing work letters in which a white line running at one side of the main strokes gives the effect of shadow caused by a light. Cf. *inline letters*, *outline letters*.

Shakespeare Folios: the first four collected editions of Shakespeare's comedies, histories and tragedies. The *First Folio*, 1623, gives in the imprint the names Isaac Jaggard and Edward Blount. Isaac was the son of William Jaggard, one of the publishing syndicate; Edward Blount, a bookseller, was another. The 908 page double-column work preserved the text of at least seventeen plays which might otherwise have been lost. Eighteen of the total thirty-six had appeared in quarto editions before 1623.

The *Second Folio*, 1632, was printed by Thomas Cotes for Robert Allot and others. It was a reprint of F1 with certain corrections. The *Third Folio*, 1663, printed for Philip Chetwinde, had further corrections and new errors. A second impression of it in 1664 was the first to include 'Pericles' and the six spurious plays. The *Fourth Folio*, 1685, printed for H. Herring-

man and others, was a reprint of F3 with more corrections and errors. Of the four Folios only the First is considered to have any textual authority.

Shakespeare Head Press: the publishing imprint adopted by Arthur Henry Bullen in 1904 for the business he established at Stratford. His intention was to publish a scholarly edition of Shakespeare's works printed and bound in the playwright's native town. This he did in ten volumes in a series entitled 'Stratford Town Shakespeare', completed in 1907. Bullen was an eminent Elizabethan scholar and issued other works of the period in limited editions until his death in 1920.

The press was then acquired by Basil Blackwell of Oxford, and others, who appointed *Bernard Newdigate*, q.v., as typographer. The latter chose Books X–XV of Ovid's 'Metamorphoses' for the first limited edition, issued in 1924. In 1930 the press was moved to Oxford. Under Newdigate's direction the standard of trade book production from this printing firm was immediately improved, surpassing that of many private presses. Notable were editions of Austen, the Brontës, Chaucer, Jonson, Milton and Trollope. Books were printed for other publishers, sometimes in limited editions with special copies pulled on vellum and with wood engravings by contemporary artist-craftsmen.

After a post-war period of inactivity Blackwells revived the imprint in 1975 for a limited edition of Beerbohm's 'Zuleika Dobson'.

Shand, James, 1905–67: the son of a Glasgow printer. After studying at the London School of Printing he worked at the Oxford University Press until 1930 when he established the *Shenval Press* imprint. He and his family acquired a printing business at Hertford which traded as Simson Shand Ltd.

Shand cared nothing for so-called 'de luxe' and 'limited' edition books. His aim was to produce well designed and printed trade books and in this he was successful for some thirty years. In addition to contributing to graphic arts journals he was printer-publisher of *Motif*, and for some years, of *Book Collector*, qq.v.

sharebooks: books published and distributed jointly by a *conger*, q.v.

sheepskin: prepared sheepskins were used in England for bookbinding from about 1400; the boards they covered were usually of oak. That they were not durable, and thus unsuitable, was apparently recognised by the Stationers' Company which in 1557 fined Richard Tottel a shilling 'for byndynge of bokes in shepes lether contrarie to our ordenaunces'.

As now understood in the trade sheepskin is a leather of poor wearing quality often grained to resemble morocco. For varieties of sheepskin see *Alaska seal*, *basil*, *calf-finish lambskin*, *flyswing*, *lambskin*, *paste-grain*, *roan*, *roller basil*, *Rutland*, *seal grain leather*, *skivers*, *Smyrna morocco*, *vellum*.

sheet: any single piece of paper, either plain or printed.

sheeter: a machine for cutting a roll of paper into sheets. An inline sheeter can be attached to the infeed section of a printing press. Paper is fed from a single roll of required width, cut, and fed into the press.

sheet fed: a printing press into which sheets are fed singly. See *feeding*.

In the 1960s the Harris Intertype Corporation of America devised a web-feed for sheet-fed presses whereby in a continuing sequence a reel of paper is positioned, cut into sheets, and fed to the front guides for printing. This is claimed to save paper by eliminating jogging and trimming, to save handling, to avoid stoppages due to double feeding, and to give steadier running. Cf. *web fed*.

sheet stock: unbound printed sheets held in stock pending binding. Such stock is normally held by the printer or binder on behalf of the publisher. Synonymous with *quire stock*. See also *in quires*.   (LK)

sheet work: book printing in which one forme is used for one side of the paper and another forme for backing up. This is essential when printing on a perfector press. The forme for the first side printed bears the signature mark and is known as the *outer forme* and the backing up is printed from the *inner forme*. Also known as *work and back*. Cf. *work and turn*.

Sheldonian Theatre: a building 'where public ceremonies might take place' erected at the expense of Gilbert Sheldon, Archbishop of Canterbury, which he formally presented to Oxford University on its completion in 1669. At the instigation of *John Fell*, then Vice-Chancellor, special provision was made in it for a printing room. It was he who secured types and ornaments and, by 1672, a staff of twenty French compositors and pressmen, also a Dutch typefounder, Herman Hermansen. Books published from 1669 bore the imprint *OXONII. E Theatro Sheldoniano*, or the English form '*at the theater*' (sic). This imprint continued in occasional use until 1783 though Hawksmoor's new printing house, completed in 1713, was in operation.

However, in 1710 *Uffenbach*, q.v., wrote 'In the theatre (or rather under it) very few books are printed, as it is thought this might damage the building. The far-famed printing office, therefore, is housed in a small edifice not far from the theatre'. See also *Fell types*.

shelf back: the spine of a book.

shelfliner: a package made of folded cardboard. It is put on a bookshop shelf to hold a selection of forward-facing paperbacks. The coloured front edge of the liner, bearing the publisher's name and any display copy, together with the books on display, attract customers to an otherwise unremarkable shelf of books showing spines only.

shell gold: matt gold used for the gilding of a manuscript. It is applied with a brush or quill, and when dry is lightly burnished. The name derives from its sometime preparation in mussel shells.

Sherborne Missal: a work made about 1400 for Sherborne Abbey, Dorset, by John Siferwas, illuminator, and John Whas, scribe. It is now considered one of the last great examples of English illumination. While having ornamentation typical of the *East Anglian School*, q.v., the frame or page border was here more prominent. Siferwas included portrait medallions, birds, black- or red-winged angels, and figures standing in architectural niches. It is now owned by the Duke of Northumberland.

shifting tympan: an impression surface which shifts automatically. Also called *travelling tympan*.   (ML)

shiners: mineral impurities in a sheet of paper seen as shining specks on the surface.

shining: the holding up to light of printed sheets, when folding to ensure they are in register.

shining-up table: see *register table*.

Ship of Fools: see *Narrenschiff, Das*.

shoes: small silver or brass sheaths fitted to the corners of large hand-bound books.

Shoestring Press: a private printing press operating in Whitstable where it was founded in 1956 by Ben Sands for the occasional issue of limited editions of illustrated books, poetry, etcetera. Coloured linocuts enlivened many.

shoo flies: the mechanism on a printing cylinder which raises the front edge of a printed sheet so that it passes over the edge of the stripper fingers and on to the delivery tapes.

shooting stick: a tool of metal or hardened wood used to secure wooden quoins against the sides of a chase when tightening the forme.

shoot plane: a process engraver's tool for trimming the edges of blocks.

443

short ream: 480 sheets of paper.

Short-Title Catalogue: the standard British reference guide to early printed books. It was compiled by A. W. Pollard and G. R. Redgrave, and published in 1926 by the Bibliographical Society as 'A short-title catalogue of books printed in England, Scotland and Ireland, and of English books printed abroad, 1475–1640'. It is an author list, with appropriate group headings for some anonymous works, of books held in certain British libraries and, if rare, elsewhere. Every entry is numbered, and these numbers, preceded by the letters STC, are used in catalogues and lists. STC was reprinted in 1946 and 1950. Users were handicapped by the lack of an index until 1950 when one by Paul Morrison was published by the University of Virginia Bibliographical Society. In 1976 the Bibliographical Society in London issued the second of a two-volume major revision of STC.

A continuation of the original STC is D. Wing's 'Short-title catalogue of books printed in England, Scotland, Ireland, Wales and British America and of English books printed in other countries, 1641–1700', 3 vols, New York, Columbia University Press, 1945–51. This author catalogue has entries for anonymous works made mostly under the first word of the title not an article; others are under group headings. Locations are given. The work is referred to as *Wing*. See A. F. Allison & V. F. Goldsmith, 'Titles of English books, vol. I, 1475–1640', Dawson, 1976, which is a key to STC-Wing.

shoulder: the platform of a shank of type from which the face rises, i.e. the non-printing area surrounding the face.

shoulder-heads: headings to mark the second division of text within a chapter, subsidiary to *cross-heads*, q.v. They are set in caps., large or small, or in italics, and are flush to the left-hand margin, often being separated by a line of leading from the first line of the paragraph they head. See also *side-heads*.

shoulder-notes: marginal notes at the top outer corners of pages.

shoulders: the name given in etching a line plate to the steps of metal allowed to remain until the final bath.

show copies: synonymous with *promotion copies* but not with *inspection copies*, qq.v.

show side: the side of a material which is to show in the finished article, the other side being hidden, for instance, by pasting. Used especially of book cloths.

show through: a fault in which the printed impression on one side of a leaf is visible through the paper when reading the other side; caused by using ink and paper which are not suited to each other.

shrink wrapping: a method of packing such printed products as periodicals and paperbacks by sealing them in a plastic film.

As finished copies are delivered from a stitching or adhesive binding unit they are mechanically aligned, counted, and stacked in piles for conveying to the wrapping unit. Each pile is here automatically address-labelled, held under pressure, and fed into the wrapping station where it is enclosed in a tough sleeve of plastic film. This is heat-sealed and shrunk to fit the packet tightly and completely. It emerges ready for despatch. Bookshops use shrink wrapping to protect costly books from finger marking by casual browsers.

Siberch, John, 1476–1554: a bookseller, printer and bookbinder, born Johann Lair of Siegburg near Cologne, who described himself as 'primus utriusque linguae in Anglia impressor'. In 1520 he came to England where, encouraged and supported by Richard Croke, Henry Bullock and other humanist scholars, he set up with a university-chest loan what is regarded as the origin of the *Cambridge University Press*, q.v. He brought with him a fount of roman type attributed to Peter Schöffer II and also a cursive minuscule greek, both probably cast for him by Froben who had matrices for them and would be known to him from their mutual friend Erasmus. He later used a fount of textura.

His first work was an oration of Henry Bullock, printed in February 1521, followed by five other works in the same year. Fourteen items have been identified with certainty as having been printed by him of which two were broadsides and some survive only as fragments. Nothing printed by him is known after 1523 when he may have left Cambridge, and until 1583 nothing else is recorded as having been printed there. Siberch may have returned to Antwerp, where his printing materials were dispersed, eventually returning to Siegburg where he was ordained as a priest and where he died.

See E. P. Goldschmidt, 'The first Cambridge press in its European setting', C.U.P., 1955; and O. Treptow, 'Johann Lair von Siegburg', 1964. (English version, C.U.P., 1970). See also *Birckmann, epistles*.

sic: Latin for 'thus'. Used between brackets after quoting a work which was wrongly spelled or mis-used in the original. It is usually set in italics, and as it is not an abbreviation is not followed by a full point. A Continental alternative is the exclamation mark !

side-heads: headings to mark the third division of text within a chapter, subsidiary to *shoulder-heads*, q.v. They are set in caps., large and small, in bold or in italics, at the beginning of a paragraph with the matter running on.

side lay: see *lay edges*.

side marks: the fixed marks on a printing machine to which sheets are placed, or laid, to ensure uniformity of margins. See also *lay edges*.

side notes: see *marginal notes*.

siderography: see *steel engraving*.

sides: the front and rear boards of a book.

side sorts: the less frequently used characters of a fount, e.g. j, q, z, etc., kept in the small boxes at the side of the case. (ML)

sidestick: a long wedge of wood or metal placed along the length of pages when locking them up, and secured in position in the chase by quoins. See also *footstick*.

side-stitch: to bind a pamphlet by wiring or sewing the sheets together sideways. (ML)

siding: a term for fitting and gluing to the boards the paper or cloth sides of a half- or quarter-bound book.

Siegen, Ludwig, von, 1609–80: the inventor in 1642 of *mezzotint*, q.v.

Siferwas, John, fl.1396–1407: a Dominican friar who may have been the head of an English atelier in which manuscripts were painted. Only two works associated with him are now known. One is the *Sherborne Missal*, q.v., and the other is the Lovel Lectionary, painted before 1408, now in the British Library (*Harley* 7026). Siferwas is remarkable for the great attention he paid to facial expression.

sig.: an abbreviation of *signature*, q.v.

Sigismondo de' Sigismondi, d. 1525: a major scribe of the Italian Renaissance who worked for such patrons as Matthias Corvinus, Lorenzo de' Medici and the dukes of Ferrara. Many of the twenty or so of his manuscripts which survive date from the period 1481–1522 and include six illuminated Horae. He worked in Carpi and Ferrara.

signature: a small capital letter or numeral usually placed by the compositor in the white line (tail margin) immediately below the text of the first page of each section of a book. Letters or numerals are assigned in sequence and serve three purposes prior to pub-

lication of the book. The *compositor* and *machine manager* find it easier to identify a forme by its *signature mark* than by page numbers; the *warehouseman* is guided by them when folding sheets to form sections; and the *machine binding operator* follows the sequence when laying out sections in the stations of an insetting or gathering machine for subsequent stitching.

If letters are used as signature marks either I or J, U or V, and W are omitted; this derives from the custom in manuscripts and incunabula of using the twenty-three letter Latin alphabet in which I and J, U and V, were alternative forms of but two letters, and there was no W. If one run of the alphabet is insufficient it is commenced again but doubled, thus AA, BB, or if necessary trebled, thus AAA, BBB. In speech these signatures are dubbed *two* A, *three* A, etc.

When, as often happens, copy for the preliminaries is to be given to the printer after that for the text, he will assign B to the first page of text. Preliminary matter is reckoned as A but the letter is not printed. Should the prelims exceed one section italic lower case letters may be used to identify them.

If the book is printed without the title as a *running headline* it is important (to the binder) to add to the signature mark initials indicating the title, e.g. B-GL.B., to ensure identification. Similarly, it may be essential to add the volume number.

The term signature is not synonymous with *sheet* since a sheet as printed may contain more than one signature (see *folding*), and in the case of a *half-sheet*, q.v., be a signature of fewer pages. Nor, to the purist, is signature synonymous with *section*, which is the binder's unit, since in some books sections are given black-step *collation marks* instead of letters, and thus have not been *signed*. And if, for any reason, the publisher does not wish signatures to disfigure the pages, the printer will place marks to fall at the extreme head and foot of untrimmed sections for removal when the edges of the assembled book are trimmed.

Signature marks are of importance to the librarian. In bibliographical collation it is usual to account for each leaf of books printed prior to the 18th century by giving a register of signatures. Superior figures added to the signature marks show how many leaves each gathering contains.

Signatures were first printed, instead of being entered by hand after printing the sheets, by Johann Koelhoff in Johannes Nider's 'Praeceptorium divinae legis', Cologne, 1472. See also *designation marks*, *gathering*, *imposing scheme*, *quire*, *section*.

signature rotary: any web-fed rotary letterpress machine on which rubber or plastic plates are used for long runs of bookwork.

signature title: or *catch title*, the abbreviated indication of author and/or title printed in the signature line of the first page of each section of a lengthy book. The term *catch title* is attributed to C. T. Jacobi of the Chiswick Press, but signature titles were first printed in books issued by *Torresano* of Venice, q.v.

signed bindings: bookbindings bearing the name of the binder. The name may be stamped in gold (see also *palleted*), appearing either at the foot of the spine or on the leather turn-in at the foot of the paste-down. Alternatively a small paper ticket with the printed or engraved name may be glued at the head or foot of the front or rear paste-down.

Three mid-17th century Badier bindings signed in gold on the leather are the earliest known French examples. The name in gold at the foot of the spine occurs on early 19th century French books; examples by Roger Payne are in Eton College Library. Palleted names with letters in gold have been used since the late 18th century. These unobtrusively positioned names are analogous to a printer's imprint. As occasionally found on *panel-stamp* bindings of earlier centuries, q.v., the binder's name was an integral part of the cover design, and these are not signed bindings as here defined. See also *Haye MSS, Richenbach*.

signet: a silk ribbon secured at the head of a book for use as a page-marker. Signets were frequently used by 16th century French binders and were often enriched with precious stones. A Roman Catholic service book may be fitted with several differently coloured signets to assist easy reference to the sequence of the Mass. Also known as *register*, q.v.

Silber, Eucharius, fl.1480–1510: a German who established an early press in Rome where he became a leading printer. He published many original works, some in Italian, and issued a fine Roman Missal in 1488. The business was continued from 1510 until 1527 by Marcellus Silber.

silurian: paper flecked with minute particles of fibre of various colours.

Simon, Oliver, 1895–1956: one of Britain's leading typographers who began his career in 1920 when he studied printing under Harold Curwen of the *Curwen Press*, q.v. Simon was later Chairman of this firm, the work issued being of the highest standard.

At one time Oliver Simon edited *The Fleuron*, and later *Signature*; both journals dealt with typography and the graphic arts.

Simon's 'Introduction to typography', Faber, 1945, issued as a Pelican Book in 1954, and his 'Printer and playground', 1956, are both of note.

Simons, Anna, 1871–1951: of München-Gladbach. In 1901 she studied lettering with *Edward Johnston*, q.v., and after returning to Germany had considerable influence in leading type design away from the tra-

ditional gothic. For many years she was associated with the *Bremer-Presse*, q.v., adding titles and initial capitals by hand to most of the limited editions issued.

simplified edition: an adaptation of a published work which has been made easier than the original for a particular age group or class of reader to understand. This is usually achieved by substituting words graded according to difficulty or based on a word list, by shortening the story, and by adding footnotes or a glossary.

Since 1945 an extensive business has developed in editions of English fiction and classics of literature skilfully and systematically simplified for use by those learning English as a second language. Cf. *abridged edition*.

sine nota: a Latin term used in catalogues of incunabula for books issued without an imprint identifying printer and place of printing. Abbreviated as *s.n.*

single-line half-tone: a half-tone plate in the making of which a screen bearing parallel lines of uniform width is used as an alternative to the normal glass screen bearing lines ruled at right-angles. See also *screen*.

single quotes: see *punctuation marks*.

single-revolution machine: a cylinder machine in which the cylinder rotates at a constant speed and in such a way that during the first half-rotation the bed moves forward and the impression is made, while the bed returns during the second half-rotation. There are, however, single-revolution presses with varying speeds for the bed and/or cylinder, e.g. the Heidelberg cylinder.   (GU)

See also *letterpress machines*.

Singleton, Hugh, fl.1548–88: a Protestant printer of London. He issued notably five tracts of John Foxe, the martyrologist, Coverdale's translations, and Spenser's 'Shepheardes Calendar', 1579. In 1584 he was official printer to the City of London but employed a deputy to print for him. He died *c.* 1593.

sinkage: the amount of space, measured in picas, between the top of the type page and the first line of a chapter. The amount should be the same for all chapters in a book as well as for such other parts of it as preface, bibliography, etc. See also *dropped head, margins*.

sixteenmo: written 16mo. A book size resulting from folding a sheet of paper with four right-angle folds, thus giving a page size one-sixteenth the size of the sheet and forming a 32-page section. To define fully the size the paper size also must be stated, e.g. Crown 16mo. Also known as *decimo-sexto* or *sexto-decimo*. (LK)

sixty-fourmo: written 64mo. A book size resulting from (notionally) folding a sheet of paper with six right-angle folds, thus giving a page size one sixty-fourth of the sheet. In practice paper cannot conveniently be folded more than four times, thus a quarter sheet folded four times would be used. From Crown paper the resulting page size would be $2\frac{1}{2}$in. × $1\frac{7}{8}$in., viz. Crown 64mo. (LK)

size: 1. a glutinous substance made by boiling the hide and bones of animals. It is thus purer than *glue* which is made by boiling the hide, bones, and occasionally other parts of animals.

2. animal glue, casein, gelatine, rosin, starch, synthetics or waxes used in papermaking to assist fibre bonding, improve printability and make the paper surface resistant to liquids and atmospheric moisture. The sizing agent can be added to paper stock in the beater (see *engine sized*) or be applied to the surface of the sheet after it has been formed (see *surface sizing*).

size copy: see *dummy*.

size of books: see *book sizes*.

size of paper: see *paper sizes*.

size press: a unit in papermaking for *surface sizing*, q.v.

size water: an alternative name for *backwater*, q.v.

skeleton: the frame of *furniture*, q.v., which forms the margins of pages when they are in the chase. Prior to the mid-17th century the headlines of a book, which consisted of the running title extended to full measure of the line by quads and spaces, remained in position in the skeleton after type was distributed and subsequent pages were imposed. Thereafter, with the need to speed up the printing of bigger editions, two formes, an inner and an outer, became standard practice, each with its skeleton and set of headlines.

skewings: a term used for waste gold leaf arising in the course of gold blocking and sent to gold refiners for recovery of the gold. (LK) See also *rubbing-off chest*.

Constance Lindsay Skinner Award: an annual award made by the American Women's National Book Association for an outstanding contribution by a woman to the world of books.

skiver: the outer half of a split sheepskin, tanned with sumach, and often finished to resemble superior leathers. It is not durable. The use in England of skivers for binding dates from 1768 when William Powers of Coventry announced his new method of splitting and dividing sheep pelts so that the upper (grain) part could be used for cheaper bookbinding. See also *roan*.

slab serifs: square serifs of almost the same thickness as the strokes on which they are placed. See also *egyptian*.

slabbing: the process of rolling and hammering an electro or stereo after casting in order to obtain a level surface.

slice: 1. in papermaking, a long flat plate, set vertically, by which the depth and even distribution of pulp are controlled as it flows on to the moving wire belt from the head-box.

2. see *ink slice*.

3. see *galley*.

slice boy: the layerman's assistant in a hand-made papermaking establishment. The removal of still moist sheets of very thin paper after pressure in the *post*, q.v., calls for care and skill. The layerman strips the top sheet off the post and lays it on a felt-covered zinc plate where a *pack* of about 230 sheets will be built up. As the next sheet is laid the boy steadies it on to the pile with a smooth wooden slice. He then holds the slice in position ready to assist in the laying of the next and subsequent sheets. See also *layerman*.

slip case: a box to contain a book, or set of books, with one side open so that the spine of the book is visible. Its function is to protect the edges from soiling until purchased. See also *solander*.

slip proof: see *galley*.

slips: the loose ends of the cords which, after sewing,

Fraying the slips

extend at the sides of a book. They must be frayed with a bodkin, leaving them soft and pliable, before attaching the boards.

slip sheeting: the placing of rough paper as interleaving between freshly printed sheets to prevent *set-off*, q.v.

Sloane, Sir Hans, 1660–1753: an Irish scientist and physician whose large scientific collections and library of 50,000 books on botany, medicine and natural history were available to scholars. On his death the whole was offered to the nation, authority to purchase it being granted by an Act of 1753. The Sloane, Harleian and Cottonian libraries were the three foundation collections of the British Museum when it opened in 1759. See G. R. de Beer, 'Sir Hans Sloane and the British Museum', O.U.P., 1953.

sloped type: type which is inclined to the right of a vertical axis but does not have the calligraphic features which typify all italics designed prior to the 1920s. When compared with the normal roman of the same family a *sloped roman* shows modifications in the balance of such curved strokes as C G O and Q and a slight lengthening of the base strokes of B D E and L.

The first version of the italic cut by Lanston Monotype to accompany Eric Gill's Perpetua roman of 1929 was an approach to a sloped roman book type (notably the non-descending f). Other examples are Gill Sans, Rockwell, Romulus and Gill's Pilgrim which, while listed in specimen books as italic, could be termed *sloped roman*. Also known as *inclined type*. See S. Morison, 'Towards an ideal italic', *The Fleuron*, V 1926 93–129, in which he argues in favour of 'sloped roman' treatment for italics used with roman.

slug: a line of type cast as a unit in an Intertype or Linotype slug-casting machine.

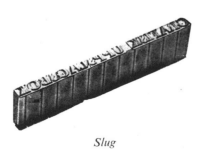

Slug

slur: a letterpress-machine printing fault in which irregular movement between paper and forme causes half-tone dots to be distorted, or letters to show a double impression. The cause may be an incorrectly packed cylinder, faulty make-ready, or a mechanical

defect. On a platen machine the frisket should be examined, the quoins be readjusted, or the paper may need conditioning.

slurry: see *stuff*.

slushing: the mechanical action of breaking down the raw materials of paper in water in a *breaker*, q.v.

small capitals: capital letters set smaller than the upper-case letters of the fount to which they belong, e.g. ZEKI; indicated in manuscripts and proofs by two lines underneath the letters concerned.

small pica: the former name for a size of type, now standardized as 11-point.

smashing: the pressing of a book in a machine, after sewing, to compress the pages and expel air from between them. An early machine for this purpose was the rolling press of William Burn for which he received the Royal Society of Arts medal in 1827, but it was not popular among operatives since fewer were needed.

Smashing is also known as *nipping*.

Smith, George D., d. 1920: a New York bookseller and buying agent for Folger, Huntington and other great American collectors. Although it has been said that 'he was concerned with books as commodities and not a whit as literature or history' in the years prior to his death he was the unquestioned king of the rare book trade in America.

Smith, Philip, b. 1928: a British craftsman binder and teacher of the craft who has an international reputation. He studied under *Roger Powell*, and in 1957 became an assistant to *Sydney Cockerell*, qq.v. His work is in public and private collections in Europe and the Americas.

Of the craft he wrote (1971) 'Artistically it is no longer considered sufficient to cover the sides of books with arbitrary decorative patterns, or simply to evoke the title by mere illustrative means. The springboard for the artist-binder is the author's text which gives the book its *raison d'être*. When the significance of the text has been considered in depth and its essence embodied in an open-ended visual image capable of valid interpretation, then may the book become a total and unique work of art.'

His innovatory feathered onlay and maril techniques are combined with blind stamping to create abstract conceptions which are brilliant, remarkable and unique.

Smith, Richard, 1590–1673: an early English bibliophile whose library of about 20,000 volumes was renowned in his day. It was particularly rich in

English history. A movement to buy it by public subscription was started after his death, but as this failed it passed to the London bookseller Richard Chiswell who sold it by auction in 1682. Prices paid were not high and we learn that a Latin Psalter written on vellum in 1383 went for 2/10d; Higden's 'Polychronicon' written on vellum, 2/6d; Caxton's 'Game of chess', 1474, 13/2d, and his 'Mirrour of the world', 1480, for 5/–.

W. H. Smith Prize: an annual award of £2,500 for an outstanding contribution to English literature, announced in 1959 by W. H. Smith & Son, the London firm of booksellers and newsagents. It was stated that books must have been originally written in English by a Commonwealth author, and have been published in the United Kingdom during the two years prior to the award.

Smith's Trade News: from 1926 to 1974, a weekly journal published by W. H. Smith & Son covering the trades relative to the firm's business, i.e. newspapers, periodicals, toys, stationery and books. Special articles on the book trade, children's books, paperbacks and bestseller lists were included.

smoke: an experimental proof from a smoke-blackened punch: taken before a matrix is made.

smooth calf: an untooled calf binding.

smoothing press: two unfelted rolls placed before the first drying cylinder of a Fourdrinier. They remove felt marks and improve the surface as the web of paper passes between them.

smoothness: the even, blemish-free surface of paper with any irregularities no more than 1/100 to 1/200in. apart. It is affected by the fibres and loading used, and by surface treatment during manufacture. The smoothness of finished paper can be measured by instruments, e.g. an 8-power lens and a low angle surface light or on a Bendtsen smoothness tester. Cf. *gloss*. See also *paper-testing*.

smooth washed: ungrained bookcloth. The cloth most used by trade binders in the 19th century was finished with a mechanically grained surface. They referred to that which was not as 'smooth washed'.

smooting: a slang description for a printer who worked for two employers at the same time without informing them.

Smyrna morocco: sheepskin grained to represent morocco.

Smyth, David McConnel: an Irishman who emigrated to America in 1856. He was a pioneer constructor of bookbinding machinery, notably a sewing machine about 1856, first used in England in 1878 by Burns. In 1878 he invented the first wire-stitching machine and founded a business which now, as Smyth-Horne, has world-wide sales for its regularly improved mechanical binders.

s.n.: see *sine nota*.

Snel, Johann: a printer of Lübeck whence he was invited in 1482 to Denmark to print a Breviary for the diocese of Odense, the first book printed in Denmark. In 1483 he went to Stockholm where, in addition to a large Missale Upsalense, he printed a small collection of fables 'Dialogus creaturarum moralisatus', the first dated book printed in Sweden. He issued other minor items there before returning to Lübeck where he then worked for Hans von Ghetelen. (GU)

Société de la Reliure Originale: a society founded in Paris in 1946. Its aim is 'to develop a knowledge of, and a taste for fine binding; to stimulate public interest in it; and to encourage binders to evolve a personal style. It seeks to do this by holding exhibitions, giving prizes and publishing specialized books and articles.' Members include bibliophiles, booksellers and a limited number of bookbinders chosen because they are creative artists. See also *Designer Bookbinders*.

Société des Bibliophiles et Iconophiles de Belgique: founded in 1910 in Brussels to further the interests of book collectors by holding occasional exhibitions and publishing a journal 'Le Livre et l'estampe' to review important European book sales.

Société des Gens de Lettres: established in Paris in 1837 to protect the interests of authors. Its British equivalent is *The Society of Authors*, q.v.

Society for Italic Handwriting: founded in London in 1952 by the *Society of Scribes & Illuminators*, q.v., at the instigation of *Alfred Fairbank*, q.v. The Society has done much to arouse an interest in italic script by developing a cursive book hand which, because of its joined letters, is functional as well as beautiful. The Society's international membership includes many schoolteachers in England and America. Their enthusiasm has had considerable influence on the teaching of writing in a number of schools.

The Society of Antiquarian Booksellers' Employees: a society founded in London in 1951. Its aims are social, educational and benevolent. Membership is open to all men and women, other than principals, employed in the antiquarian book trade. The Society is popularly known as the *Bibliomites*.

The Society of Authors: founded in 1884 by Sir Walter Besant, novelist and historian. The aim was to defend the rights and protect the interests of authors by reforming copyright in Britain and elsewhere.

Prominent authors gave their immediate support and with the publication of *The Author* from May 1890 the Society increased its membership and gained recognition as the representative organization for authors, playwrights and composers. The Society also administers several literary awards and prizes as noted elsewhere in this glossary.

Members, of whom there are now some 4,000, are advised in regard to contracts, offered legal aid in any part of the world, and benefit from campaigns conducted on their behalf for copyright protection, theatrical agreements, obscenity law reform and tax concessions. Most recent has been a lengthy campaign to establish a balance between the rights of an author to a fair return for his work and the needs of society for reasonable access to its intellectual and artistic heritage, epitomized in the concept of *Public Lending Right* for which attempts to introduce legislation began in the 1970s. Address: 84 Drayton Gardens, London SW10 9SD.

Society of Bookmen: a society of authors, publishers, critics, librarians, booksellers, etc., founded in 1921 by Sir Hugh Walpole. Membership is limited and is by election. The Society's object is the advancement of the knowledge and appreciation of good literature. The Society meets monthly for dinner and formal but outspoken discussion of some important topical problem in the creation and distribution of books. The proceedings are not reported unless by permission of the members and the speaker. The Society has considerable influence and has, among other things initiated the National Book Council (now the National Book League), the Joint Advisory Committee of the PA and BA, and several trade working parties.

Society of Calligraphers: formed about 1906 by *Edward Johnston*, q.v., for the advancement of lettering. *Eric Gill*, *Graily Hewitt* and *Anna Simons*, qq.v., were among members. The Society was short-lived, but throughout their careers the ex-members had considerable influence in England and Germany.

Society of Indexers: formed in London in 1957 with the aims of improving the standard of indexing and securing a measure of uniformity in technique. It was planned to issue occasional papers and notes on the subject, and to establish a panel of indexers, specializing in various fields, for the assistance of authors,

publishers and others. Advice will be given on the qualifications and remuneration of indexers. A journal, *The Indexer*, is published.

Membership of the Society is open to bona-fide indexers, librarians, cataloguers, archivists and others interested in promoting its objects. See also *American Society of Indexers*. There are similar societies in Australia and Canada.

Society of Printers: founded in 1905 in Boston, Mass., for the study and advancement of the art of printing. Through the years this has been achieved by means of lectures, exhibitions, support for such educational projects as a printing course at Harvard, and the publication of monographs on printing history.

Bruce Rogers, D. Berkeley Updike, and Henry Lewis Johnson were among the founders, with W. A. Dwiggins and Carl Purington Rollins as early members of note. Distinguished foreign speakers at the Society's meetings have included T. J. Cobden-Sanderson (1907), Alfred W. Pollard (1909), E. P. Goldschmidt (1933), Giovanni Mardersteig (1936), Walter Gropius (1939), Beatrice Warde (1942) and James Wardrop (1949 and 1953). See R. Nash, 'Printing as an art', Cambridge, Mass., Harvard U.P. 1955.

Society of Scribes and Illuminators: formed in London in 1921 for the 're-establishment of a tradition of craftsmanship in the production of manuscripts, books and documents'. Candidates for craft membership have to submit original specimens of work on which the committee vote but lay membership is open to all those who wish to forward the aims of the Society. There are many members in America where there is considerable interest in calligraphy and related crafts. Lectures and exhibitions are sponsored. Address: c/o Federation of British Craft Societies, 6 Queen St, London WC1. See also *Society for Italic Handwriting*.

Society of Typographic Designers: founded in London in 1928 as the *British Typographers' Guild* by Vincent Steer and a number of leading typographers and compositors. Their aim was the promotion of the highest standards in all branches of the typographic arts. Steer was the author of 'Printing design and layout', 1934.

Membership was restricted to those who submitted an approved typographic layout. When the name of the Guild was changed in the 1950s graphic designers without specifically typographical qualifications were admitted to membership.

Society of Women Employed in Bookbinding: formed in London in 1874 with the aim of protecting the interests of women working in the trade. From members' fees and subscriptions sick and unemploy-

450

ment benefits were paid. The Society was not a force in trade disputes. In 1850 out of a total of 11,029 bookbinding trade operatives 4,154 were women or girls (Parliamentary Papers). They were taught folding, stitching, and sewing. A general complaint was that apprentices, who earned 1/6d a week, were taught only one process so that employment elsewhere was difficult.

In the first union of bookbinders, founded in 1779 and known as The Friends, women were not admitted to membership.

The Society of Young Publishers: since 1949, an unofficial body which holds monthly meetings of its members at the National Book League, London, with a view to improving the knowledge about book publishing and kindred matters of those younger people in publishing who are likely to be the publishing executives of the future.

soda pulp: chemical wood digested in caustic soda. See *chemical wood pulp.*

softback edition: an edition of a book published in covers of pliable thin card, often varnished or laminated, or else of cloth adhered to thin card or lining paper. Such books are trimmed flush. This may be a cheap alternative to a hard-cover edition of the same printing, issued simultaneously. Cf. *wrapper.*

soft-copy: a micro-image as enlarged on the screen of a reader. Cf. *hard copy.*

soft-ground etching: see *etching.*

soft-sized: cheap mechanical wood paper such as newsprint (also used for mass-market paperbacks) which has little filler (clay) and little or no size added to the beater.

solander: a box made in the form of a book, suitable for storing loose plates or maps. It was devised by Daniel Charles Solander (1736–82), a Keeper at the British Museum, 'originally for the preservation of botanical specimens' (Nixon).

solid gilt: see *gilt solid.*

solid matter: see *set solid.*

sombre bindings: bindings of blind-tooled black turkey, black velvet, or black cloth with black-stained edges and restrained ornamentation. Large numbers of Bibles and prayer books were covered in this way in late 17th century England. They are rare after 1730.

The term survives in antiquarian sale catalogues, probably to create interest in somewhat dull bindings.

Soncino: a family of Jewish moneylenders who left Speyer in Germany as exiles in 1454, settling at Soncino near Cremona in Italy, thereafter calling themselves Soncino. About 1480 the head of the family Dr Israel Nathan ben Solomon Soncino (d. *c.* 1492) founded a printing business. His sons Moses (d. 1493) and Joshua Solomon managed the press (only the latter being named in imprints). His first two books, the Talmudic treatises Berakhot, 1483, and Betzah, 1484, were followed by works on moral philosophy, the Mahazor, 1485/6, and the first complete vowelled Hebrew Bible in 1488. Joseph moved to Naples in 1489 where he issued his major work, the Mishnah, in 1492. He died in 1493 having printed some forty works. In some he used the fine woodcut borders with scrollwork and animals which had appeared in the Aesop printed at Naples by Francesco del Tuppo in 1485.

It was his nephew *Gershom ben Moses Soncino,* also called Menzlein, who in continuing the business became the best known of the family. His first work was Moses de Coucy's 'Book of precepts', Soncino, 1488, followed by sixteen more incunabula and over a hundred works in the 16th century, all notable for their scholarly editing. He worked in several Italian towns, notably at Brescia, where he printed an octavo edition of the complete Hebrew Bible in 1944. He was the first to use woodcut illustrations in a Hebrew book (as distinct from ornaments) and to issue secular Hebrew literature. The types he used were based on the Sephardic Hebrew alphabet. He also cut the first *arabic type,* q.v.

After 1500 he printed non-Hebrew books in Greek, Latin and Italian, being the first Jewish printer to do so. In the imprints he used the names Geronimo, Girolamo and Hieronymous. He used an italic cut by Griffo. Gershom's non-Hebrew books were scarcely less excellent than those of his contemporary Aldus and represented a triumph over the hostile, jealous and even dangerous Christian environment in which Jews lived. His occasional patrons included the Tiepolos of Venice, the Borgia of Fano, and the Sforza at Pesaro.

Finally, as thousands of others from France, the Iberian peninsula and Italy before him, he fled after the sack of Rome in 1527 to Turkey, going first to Salonika where his son Moses had set up a press in 1521, and then to Constantinople in 1530. Here he died in 1534, another son, Eliezer, continuing the press until 1547. The latter issued a polyglot Pentateuch in Hebrew, Chaldee, Persian and Arabic in 1546. It was the first edition to include Persian and Arabic texts (printed in hebrew type). Gershom ben Eliezer, who printed two books at Cairo in 1557 and 1562, was the last known member of the family to print.

See G. Manzoni, 'Annali tipografici dei Soncini', Bologna, 1883–6, repr. 1970. See also *Hebrew printing before 1600*.

songster: a collection of ballads and poems published in *broadside* or *chapbook* form and intended for singing to tunes with which the public was familiar (and so did not require printed notation). Songsters were cheap and popular.

In America the earliest listed was issued in Philadelphia in 1734 (see I. Lowens, 'A bibliography of songsters printed in America before 1821', Charlottesville, 1976). In England the principal publisher was *John Pitts* (1765–1844) of Seven Dials, London. Many of his sheets had such subtitles as '. . . being a choice collection of the newest songs, now singing at all public places of amusement and in the most convivial assemblies'. (See L. Shepherd, 'John Pitts, ballad printer . . .', Private Libraries Association, 1969.)

Among important collections of songsters are that of W. N. H. Harding in Chicago, and the Baring-Gould collection in the British Library.

sophisticated: said of an incomplete copy of a book which has been made complete by replacing a missing leaf or leaves with a leaf or leaves taken from another copy of the same edition, or with a carefully made facsimile reprint.

Sörensen, Christian, 1818–61: see *typesetting machine*.

sorts: specific letters as distinct from complete founts of type. Also applied to matrices on a typesetter.

Sotheby & Co.: the senior firm of book auctioneers in London. It was in the 17th century that dealers discovered by degrees that consignments of books imported from the Continent could be disposed of more expeditiously and equally well by the auction method than by ordinary retail outlets, or even by exhibition and tender. (See *book auction*.) For some years, however, they were only a by-product of a dealer's business and it was not untill 1744 that Samuel Baker of Russell Street, Covent Garden (the DNB states York Street, Covent Garden), held the first of a continuous series of sales of books, manuscripts and prints which constitute him the first professional book or art auctioneer and entitle his firm, since known as Sotheby's to claim the senior status in that business in London. Baker did not take a partner until he was joined by George Leigh in 1767 (DNB dates this event 1774). Baker died in 1778 and his nephew, *John Sotheby* (1740–1807), joined Leigh in partnership about this time. He was the first of three generations of Sothebys who between them carried on the firm for nearly 100 years.

John Sotheby's nephew, *Samuel Sotheby* (1771–1842), directed the firm after Leigh's death in 1815.

Both he and his son *Samuel Leigh Sotheby* (1805–61), who also entered the firm, were authorities on typographical history. Thirty-six folio volumes of their writings are in the British Library, while the sales catalogues they issued became of great importance to librarians and bibliographers everywhere.

At the time of his death in 1861 S. L. Sotheby was in partnership with John Wilkinson (1803–94). The latter was joined in 1864 by Edward Gross Hodge whose son, Tom Hodge, was left as sole partner in 1909, the point from which the modern history of the firm begins.

Hodge sold the business to a group of friends. They were Montagu Barlow, who secured a seat in Parliament in 1910, entered the Cabinet as Minister of Labour in 1922–23, and retired from Sotheby's in 1928; Geoffrey D. Hobson, a scholar and leading expert on bookbindings, who died in 1949; and Felix Warre, who successfully controlled the finances of Sotheby's, and died in 1953.

The business the 1909 syndicate had acquired conducted the sale of almost every British library of importance to come in the market for at least two generations, as well as such foreign collections as those of Talleyrand and Napoleon I. Within a few years they had three sales which realized over £1,000,000: the Huth Library (sold 1911–22 for £278,498); the Britwell Library (sold 1916–27 for £650,000); and the Yates Thompson manuscripts (sold 1919–21 for £135,349).

After the Great War the firm developed their handling of art sales, and within twenty years books were accounting for no more than 10% of the annual turnover.

Since the Second World War fewer great libraries have come up for disposal, but mention should be made of the Dyson Perrins illustrated books which realized £148,000 including £22,000 for only one of the two volumes of a Gutenberg Bible.

I am indebted to Messrs Sotheby for this note.

spacebands: the interword spacing material of the Linotype machine, being steel wedges mechanically inserted between the matrices when in the assembler box. After the line is set the justification block forces the wedges between the matrices until they occupy the full measure. Also used on Intertype machines.

spaces: type less than type height, cast in point sizes, and used as interword spacing material. They are cast smaller than an em quad, usual sizes being 3-em, 4-em, and 5-em space, i.e. a third, quarter or fifth of an em. See also *hair-spaces*.

spacing: the aesthetically satisfying distribution of printed matter on a printed page or pair of pages. It relates to the distance between letters, words, lines and any illustrative or decorative matter. See also *leads, letterspacing, rivers, white out.*

spacing material: see *hair-spaces* (interletter), *spaces* and *quads* (interword), *leads*, *clumps* and *reglets* (interlinear), *quotations* and *furniture* (for whiting out pages having only a few lines of type). Type metal, wood, duralumin, lead and plastic are among some of the materials which may be used.

Spalding Club: a club founded in Aberdeen in 1839 'for the printing of the historical, ecclesiastical, genealogical, typographical and literary remains of the north-eastern counties of Scotland'. It ceased activity in 1871 but was reconstituted in 1886 as the New Spalding Club issuing, among other works, the first county bibliography to be published in Scotland.

Spanish calf: a light calf on which brilliant colour effects can be produced by staining.

Spanish illumination: the Spanish contribution to Renaissance illumination schools was slight, Christian influences being modified by the Islamic avoidance of natural forms.

Widely copied, however, from the 9th–12th century, especially in French Benedictine houses, was the important Spanish work 'Commentaria in Apocalypsin' written by Bishop Beatus of Liebana, *c.* 776.

special edition: an issue of a standard work with added notes, illustrations, or an appendix. The term is of little bibliographic significance.

special sorts: types required for mixed composition or matter which is not straight composition. See also *accents, astronomical symbols, botanical symbols, chessmen, cross, Domesday characters, glyph, medical symbols, meteorological symbols, peculiars, punctuation marks, split fractions.*

specifications: the instructions sent to a printer with a typescript relating to size, type, paper, specimen page, etc., required.

specimen page: printed pages, usually four and including a chapter opening with any sub-headings, submitted by the printer to show the proposed style of setting.

specimen sheet: a broadside sheet on which printers displayed the range of founts, alphabets, ornaments, etc., available in their presses; typefounders issued similar sheets. Their use has not ceased and modern printers and founders issue *specimen books* to make known the range of types available.

Fust and Schöffer probably originated the idea when, in 1469, they issued a broadside advertisement of their books bearing the words 'hec est littera psalterij' as a specimen of their Psalter type. An early Continental example of a sheet devoted solely to specimens of type was printed by Erhard Ratdolt in 1486; on it were shown ten sizes of black letter, three of roman, and one of greek. The Berner sheet of 1592 was the first to give to founts the names of their cutters. The earliest English example is that of Nicholas Nichols dated 1665 which showed arabic, ethiopic and hebrew, but William Caslon's of 1734 is probably the most famous.

The first specimen *book* known to have been issued by a printer is that of Christopher Plantin, 1567. The first in England was Dr John Fell's of 1693 (it was reprinted in 1970, see *Walpergen*). The first such book in America was issued in 1809 by Binny and Ronaldson of Philadelphia: their 1816 edition was reprinted in 1975.

A surprising number of 18th century printers in England and elsewhere used as a text for display the passage from Cicero's Catiline oration '*Quousque tandem abutere, Catilina, patientia nostra? . . .*', a custom begun by Caslon in 1734. 'The old type founders usually printed their specimens of type in Latin as that language contains fewer tailed letters than English and consequently the printed page has an evener effect', Emery Walker, 1922. See also *Bowyer.*

Speculum humanae salvationis: a pictorial Harmony of Old and New Testament scenes intended for lower ranks of clergy in their teaching. The text, in irregular Latin verse, has been attributed to the Carthusian monk Ludolf of Saxony (*c.* 1314–77), and has been dated about 1325. The work was similar in scope and intention to the *Biblia pauperum*, q.v. A manuscript version of *c.* 1440 preceded the first block book version for which the text was printed from movable type, some pages having an illustration printed by hand rubbing over the block. Printing was on one side of the paper. There were fifty-eight blocks, each showing two scenes framed by adjoining arches. There were two editions with Dutch text, and two with Latin of which one, unusually, had twenty pages of xylographic text cut separately from the illustrations. Neither of the editions gave the name of the printer, place of printing, or a date, but a study of the paper has led scholars to assign the work to Brussels, *c.* 1466–71. Some scholars attribute the designs for the woodcuts to the atelier of Rogier van der Weyden in that city.

The blocks, which were later used by *Veldener*, q.v., also inspired sculptors, enamellers and tapestry weavers, notably those working for Rheims Cathedral.

Speed, John, 1552–1629: the first English publisher of a printed general atlas, 'Prospect of the most famous parts of the world', 1627; and now particularly remembered for his 'Theatre of the Empire of Great Britaine', 1611.

Spencer, Charles, third Earl of Sunderland, 1674–1722: a statesman and bibliophile who began to found his library at Althorp when only nineteen. He was a sale-room rival of *Harley*, q.v.

It was *George John Spencer* (1758–1834), however, who made the library the most splendid of his age. In 1807 he retired from public life to devote his attention to book-collecting. From 1805 his librarian was Thomas Frognall Dibdin (1776–1847), one of the most famous English bibliographers.

The Althorp library included fifty-seven Caxtons, Manutius and Elzevir collections, first printed editions of the classics, and 108 books printed on vellum. The library remained at Althorp until 1892 when it was bought by Mrs H. A. Rylands for £250,000; with it she established the John Rylands Library in Manchester.

Spierinck, Nicholas, fl.1514–34: a Dutchman who about 1505 established a business as stationer and bookbinder in Cambridge. He used various roll tools, probably engraved by Continental craftsmen: these included a lion and griffin. More than three hundred of his bindings survive, including six chained bindings. Some panel-stamped bindings he made bore his full name. He died about 1545.

spike: see *bodkin*.

Spilman, Sir John, fl.1580–1626: a German paper-maker who, *c.* 1588, had a papermill at Dartford, Kent. He was granted a monopoly in 1589. Paper continued to be made in this mill until 1739.

spine: the portion of the outer cover of a book which protects and encloses the *back*, q.v., and is usually lettered with the title, author's and publisher's name. See also *flat backs, lettering on the spine*.

spinner: a bookshop display stand, being a number of wire racks arranged in layers on a central steel column around which they can be revolved. Each pocket in a layer holds up to six outward-facing paperbacks. Counter spinners hold up to 72: larger floor-standing units up to 288. Cf. *dumpbin*.

Spira, Johannes da: a goldsmith of Mainz, and the first printer of Venice where he established a press in 1469. In this year he issued two editions of Cicero's 'Epistolae ad familiares' and Pliny's 'Historia naturalis'. For these editions he used an early genuine roman type. See also *privilege*.

He died in 1470 and was succeeded by his brother *Wendelin* (Lat. Vindelinus) who first completed an edition of St Augustine's 'De civitate Dei' begun by his brother. He issued classical texts including the first edition of Petrarch in 1470, the first edition of the *Malermi Bible*, q.v., and several law books, the latter in gothic type. *Catchwords*, q.v., were first printed by Wendelin da Spira: this was in an edition of Tacitus, 1471.

Spiral Press: a small printing office established in New York by Joseph Blumenthal in 1926. He soon gained a reputation for carefully designed work of high standard and was commissioned by academic bodies, bibliophiles, book clubs and specialist publishers. After the press closed in 1971 the founder turned his attention to writing on the history of printing (for titles see Appendix D).

Blumenthal also designed type for his press. Notable was Emerson, cut by Louis Hoell, and issued by Monotype, 1936–39.

spirex binding: a means of securing a number of leaves without using glue or thread. A spiral wire, often plastic coated, is run through holes punched in their inner margins. A form of this was invented in 1924 by the German Staab, developed in France, and brought to England where the binding firm Burn & Co. bought the patent in 1927. An alternative is the use of plastic combs, introduced to the English book trade from France in 1935, but a tendency to tear the pages when these are numerous makes the style unsuitable for general bookwork. See also *twin-wire binder*.

splash manner: a method used in lithography for obtaining a grained tone on a smooth surface by scraping an ink-filled brush across a sieve held in the hand. See *autolithography*.

split boards: boards for use as book covers made of a thin strawboard and a millboard pasted into a unit, but with an unpasted marginal border on one side. After pressing and drying out the split marginal border is used for the insertion of sewing tapes. There are other types of split board. See also *boards* (1).

split-duct printing: simultaneous printing in two or more colours from one forme on a single-colour press. This involves the division of the ink duct into sections, with a different colour in each, and ensuring they do not mix on the rollers where, if not prevented, the lateral oscillation of the distributors would cause colour spoilage during the run.

split fractions: type for setting fractions, cast in two parts. One sort bears the upper figure, the lower figure and the dividing line being cast on the other. Fractions may be set diagonally (3/4) or horizontally ($\frac{3}{4}$).

spoils: sheets bearing imperfections, either as received from the papermaker or after they have been printed. It is to allow for spoilage that *overs* are issued to the printer.

sponsoring editor: a member of a publisher's staff who develops and implements the firm's publishing programme. This calls for literary judgement, editorial skill, and an ability to initiate and supervise projects from manuscript to bound copies. It is he who corresponds with an author on matters concerning his manuscript. Also known as an *acquisition editor* or *desk editor*. See also *copy editor, editor*.

spray lithography: a means of obtaining delicate grained tones on a smooth surface by spraying it with litho ink from an airbrush. See also *autolithography, splash manner*.

sprinkled calf: calfskins, used for book covers, having a speckled surface made by sprinkling acid on it. This was sometimes done in the 17th century, but the work was not durable as the acid rotted the skins. Cf. *marbled calf*.

sprinkled edges: the cut edges of a book which have been sprinkled with coloured ink to make the soiling of usage less noticeable. This alternative to gilding has been a feature of bookbinding from the 16th century to the present day.

squabble: a printing fault which occurs when one or more letters in a line are pushed into an adjacent line.

square back: synonymous with *flat back*, q.v.

square capitals: the alphabet as adapted from the Roman lapidary capitals and used as a book hand from the 3rd–5th century. The thick letters were finished with wide square serifs instead of being sharply pointed as were those cut in stone. Square capitals were also known as *capitales quadrata*. See also *letters – forms and styles*.

squared up: an illustration printed within right-angled corners as distinct from illustrations of irregular shape. Cf. *vignette* (1).

square folding: the method of folding a printed sheet in which the second fold is at right-angles to the first, the third to the second, etc. See also *folding*.

squares: the margins of the cover of a book which extend beyond the pages and protect them. When a book is cased equal margins of cover are formed on the three edges, Cf. *cut flush*.

squash: said of ink which spreads beyond the area of contact between type and paper.

S/S: *same size*, q.v.

stab: a journeyman on the establishment of a printing firm, paid weekly not hourly. The *stab rate* was paid for a week's work which in the late 19th century meant fifty hours. The setting of music, greek and hebrew type, equations and tabular matter called for extra skill, and specially trained compositors were paid on the *stab-piece* system, the 'piece' being a bonus for work done in excess of an agreed daily norm.

Non-stab craftsmen, or *piece hands*, were paid so much per 1,000 ens. The rate included time spent on distributing type to case after machining.

In England the concept of paying journeymen according to a precisely graded scale which took into minute account the nature of copy and size of type to be set was first regularized in 1785 at a meeting in London of Master Printers. The basic rate was 4½d per 1,000 ens of English (14-pt) and Brevier (8-pt); 5d per 1,000 was the rate for bilingual dictionaries. By 1810 the rate for 8-point without interlinear spacing had risen to 6d.

stabbing: 1. mechanically stapling a closed section or pamphlet near the back edge. Two staples may be used. This is cheap but not satisfactory since the pamphlet cannot be opened flat. See also *wire stiching*.

2. to make a hole with an awl, bodkin or needle in the side of a section prior to stitching. In England in the 16th century this method was used for small books sold in plain paper covers. As it was much quicker and cheaper than sewing in a frame the Stationers' Company in 1586 prescribed the maximum number of pages which were to be bound up in this way.

stacking tray: a tray made of battens of wood used in printing presses without pile feeders to receive the printed sheets from the press. Such trays are provided with raised edges at two opposite ends so that they can be stacked in piles to form shelves.

(With GU)

Staggemeier, L.: the partner of Samuel Welcher in a London bindery from about 1791–1810. They then worked independently. Their names suggest a German origin. Some of their work reproduced French styles of the 18th century.

staging out: the first step in the fine etching of a half-tone plate. The darker tones of the plate are painted with an acid-resisting ink so that the dots forming the middle tones and highlights can be further etched as required. See also *fine etching*.

stained calf: calf that has been stained brown (only).

stained edges: see *coloured tops*.

stake: a small anvil used by a typefounder when hammering punches into a piece of copper. The result is known as a *strike*, q.v.

stamp: the compositor's term for a single type: thus 'picking up stamps', i.e. composing.

Stamperia Orientale Medicea: the printing office established in Rome in 1584 by Cardinal Ferdinand de' Medici. Pope Gregory XIII had appointed him protector of the patriarchates of Antioch, Alexandria and Ethiopia, and the purpose of the press was to propagate the Gospels overseas. This was not the first venture from Rome of oriental printing since in 1513 Marcellus Silber had printed Potken's translation into Ge'ez of a Psalter.

To direct his press Ferdinand appointed the oriental scholar Giovanni Battista Raimondi (1536–1614). The Vatican printer Domenico Basa had in 1585 acquired a large (14D) arabic type from Granjon. He sold it to Raimondi who engaged Granjon to extend the range and to cut a smaller arabic fount (8D size) for his interlinear folio edition of the Gospels, ('Evangelium Sanctum') illustrated with fine woodcuts, and printed in 1590/1, followed by Ibn al-Hadjib's 'Kaflyah' (Arabic grammar) in 1592, Avicenna's 'Canon', 1593, Euclid's 'Elements of geometry', 1594, and the 'Geography' of al-Idris.

After the Cardinal became Grand Duke of Tuscany Raimondi bought the press in 1596, issuing books under the imprint *Typographia Linguarum Externarum*. A fine Graduale printed in black and red, with musical notation, dated 1614, may have been his last production. The press closed in that year but its aims were later revived by the *Congregatio de Propaganda Fide*, q.v. The Raimondi types were briefly looted by Napoleon and located in Paris, but most were returned after 1815 to Florence where they remain. Some are still in Paris.

Stamperia Reale: see *Bodoni*.

Stamperia Valdonega: see *Officina Bodoni*.

Stamperia Vaticana: the name given in 1610 to the official printing office of the Roman Catholic Church. This was upon the merger of the former *Tipografia Camerale* and the *Typographia Apostolica Vaticana*, qq.v. The first specimen book, issued in 1628, of the types 'esistenti nella Stampa Vaticana, & Camerale' included founts by Granjon among the roman, exotic and music types shown. The unique dedication copy of it, for Cardinal Francesco Barberini, was pulled on satin, and is now in the Houghton collection at Harvard. A facsimile edited by H. D. L. Vervliet was published in Amsterdam in 1967.

In 1910 the Stamperia was amalgamated with the Typographia Polyglotta to form the *Tipografia Poliglotta Vaticana*. See also *Congregatio de Propaganda Fide*.

stamping mill: a water-driven machine in which a series of heavy wooden hammers, each weighing about 150 lb., pound rags in a trough of water until they become pulp. The stamping mill may have originated in Valencia in the 12th century and machines several hundred years old still operate in isolated papermills.

Stanbrook Abbey Press: begun in 1876 and thus one of the oldest active private presses in Europe. It is run by the Benedictines of Stanbrook, Worcester, an enclosed order of nuns, and was founded to print liturgical books and similar productions for internal use. The first nuns were instructed by a professional printer, thereafter the craft in all its aspects was handed on from generation to generation by the nuns themselves.

In 1907 Sir Sydney Cockerell brought Emery Walker and St John Hornby to Stanbrook and new life was infused into the printing shop. In 1955, after a period of decline, Robert Gibbings helped to restore standards, but the outstanding reputation of the press rests on the combined work of Jan van Krimpen and Dame Hildelith Cumming; he the brilliant Dutch typographer who visited the Press in 1957, and she the resident perceptive pupil who, listening to him and observing how he looked at print, caught as it were in an instant the full nature of letterpress printing.

The era from 1957 has been the most productive in the history of the Press. Siegfried Sassoon's poems 'The path to peace', 1960, marks an elevation in style, perception in layout, and fastidiousness of impression which place the press in the forefront of modern printing.

Other notable productions have been 'Rituale Abbatum', 1963; 'Unless the grain die', 1961; 'Patriarch tree' (poems by Raissa Maritain), 1965; and Siegfried Sassoon's 'Something about myself', 1966.

Type founts used have included Perpetua, Romanée, Romulus and Spectrum. George Percival and Rigby Graham have added binding quality to some of the publications, and the lettering and gilding of Margaret Adams has added its special virtue. See 'The Stanbrook Abbey Press: ninety-two years of its history', 1970. See also *Katharine Adams*.   (FGBH)

Standard Account Numbers: formulated in London in 1971 on the initiative of the Publishers Association as a scheme for international account numbers to be used by the publishing trade and for any centralized computer ordering system which may evolve. Abbreviated as *SANs*.

Standard Book Number: see *International Standard Book Number*.

standard work: a work which ranks as an authority or as an exemplar of reference.

standing formes: see *standing type*.

standing press: a large hand-operated vertical press standing on the floor and principally used by binders. Pressure is applied by a platen which is screwed down

Pressing cased books in a standing press

by the aid of a crow-bar. A smaller model of such presses is also used and is known as a *bench press*. A modern alternative to a standing press is the *pressing unit*, q.v. See also *building-in machine, lying press*.

(LK)

standing type: type which has been printed and which, instead of being distributed, is kept in store by the printer (but at the publisher's expense) for reprints. Also known as *live matter* or *standing formes*. See also *keep standing*.

The rules of the Stationers' Company forbade the keeping of standing type except for such works as

ABCs, primers, almanacs, etc., and even for these the formes were to be distributed once a year. This, of course, was to create employment. Cf. *dead matter*.

Stanhope press: the first all-iron printing press in England. It was designed by Charles, third Earl Stanhope about 1800 and built by his engineer Robert Walker for William Bulmer's 'Shakspeare Printing Office'. It had a compound lever action and a large platen so that a whole sheet could be printed at one impression. The design was improved in 1807.

Earl Stanhope also proposed an improved layout of the compositor's case, and he was largely responsible for the commercial development of *stereotype*, q.v. For an illustration of the press see *hand-press*.

Star-chamber: the Court of the Star-chamber, an offshoot of the Privy Council, issued a decree in 1586 which empowered the Archbishop of Canterbury and the Bishop of London (as principal members of the Court of High Commission) to determine the number of presses, master printers and apprentices in London, Oxford and Cambridge (the only places in England where presses were allowed). Names for approval were submitted by the Court of the Stationers' Company. The Star-chamber, which in effect established Government control of printing and bookselling, was abolished in 1641. See also *privilege, Stationers' Company*.

star signature: see *insert*.

start: a binding fault in which one section has been thrown forward from the others, much weakening the binding. This may occur when rounding, particularly in books with a large number of sections, and is caused by uneven hammering.

starting charge: the sum included in an edition binding estimate for setting up machinery to do the job. This covers folding and sewing, trimming, forwarding, casemaking, blocking and casing-in units.

state: 1. part of an edition; being certain copies of a book differing from other copies of the same printing by alterations in the make-up or type setting made either during the printing of the sheets or at any subsequent stage before first publication. Such alterations may be additions, corrections, deletions or transpositions.

The custom during the 16th and 17th centuries of allowing authors to visit the pressroom while their works were being printed, and to make insertions or deletions, was often the cause of 'states' in books. See also *issue*.

2. a trial impression taken by an artist before a plate is finished or the inking is perfect. See also *progressive proofs, proof before letters*.

static electricity: a phenomenon occurring in paper. In the paper warehouse this may be due to circumstances connected with its manufacture, such as evaporation, friction against the cylinder and the felt during the shrinkage which takes place when drying, or its passage through the machine glazer or calenders, etc. It also occurs when the paper is on the printing press or other machines where it is handled. The electricity causes the sheets of paper to adhere to each other or to machine parts and may be very troublesome. The drier the paper the more easily it retains any electricity generated by its handling, so that moistening the air in the warehouse and storing the paper under carefully controlled conditions in an atmosphere of 65 to 70% relative humidity are helpful. The latter tends to be expensive due to the special equipment required.

There exist methods to free the paper course from static electricity in the paper machine or printing press by conducting it through electric fields or by having earthed netting or trailing wires by the paper course. The principle here is that if the air round the paper web is ionized the current in the paper will be neutralized. See also *relative humidity*.   (GU)

stationer: the earliest non-monastic producer and lender of books by way of trade. Stationers, known in medieval times by the latinized form *stationarii*, were men licensed by English and Continental universities to organize the copying and distribution of approved texts. They also arranged for binding and repair. There is a reference in a Memorandum Roll of 1262 to Reginaldum *stacionarium* Oxoniensem.

Early sellers of books from fixed stalls in London were also known as stationers, and William de Southflete is remembered as a *stacionarius* who in 1311 sold parchment and bound books. Such men were independent of university control. In 1379 the stations round the High Cross in Cheapside were leased to tradesmen, and the stalls round St Paul's were long associated with stationers who were dealers employing craftsmen in the different book trades (parchminers, scriveners, limners and binders). See also *Latin abbreviations*, *librarius*, *manuscript book writing*, *Stationers' Company*.

Stationers' Company: the authority established in 1557 by a Royal Charter from Queen Mary to regulate and organize printing and the book trade in England. It was created a livery company in 1560. Members were the booksellers, printers and bookbinders of London (i.e. the 'stationers' as the word was then used).

In the 14th century stationers had accepted commissions and coordinated book production by parchminers, scriveners and limners. Scribes who drafted legal documents formed a guild in 1373 (Writers of Court Hand, or Scriveners). On 12 July 1403 the 'Writers of Text Letter those commonly called scriveners and other good folks citizens of London who were wont to bind and sell books' petitioned the Lord Mayor to form them into a guild. This was done in 1404 and officiating wardens had power to enforce their ordinances in the courts.

When scriveners were succeeded by printers, who often disposed of printed sheets to stationers to bind and sell, the stationers became the more numerous and powerful body, and their guild was known as the Guild or Company of Stationers. Members were required to enter in the clerk's book details of every book or copy they claimed as their property.

After 1557 this practice continued in the Register in which all works other than Bibles, almanacs and certain other privileged books were to be entered. This was not always done, nor was entry in the Register necessarily more than a printer's claim to the rights of printing or publishing a work, thus entry cannot be accepted as evidence of publication date in the case of undated books.

The Stationers' Company drew up strict rules to control all aspects of the book trade, and searchers ensured their observance. This practice continued until at least 1677. Until the passing of the Copyright Act of 1842 printing trade apprentices were obliged to serve a member of the Company, and the number of apprentices an establishment might employ was limited. See C. Blagden, 'The Stationers' Company', George Allen & Unwin, 1960. See also *English Stock*, *privilege*, *Star-chamber*.

Stationers' Company's Library: opened at Stationers' Hall, London in 1978 for persons interested in the history of the papermaking, printing, bookbinding, publishing, bookselling and newspaper trades from the 15th to 20th century. There is also unique material on the history and records of the Company. Enquiries to the Clerk, Stationers' Hall, London, EC4.

Stationers Register: the register begun in 1557 by the Stationers' Company as a record of a printer's right to print, not as a record of what had been printed by members of the Company.

Entries took the following forms: books entered before they were written, e.g. translations; books entered before printing was begun so that copyright was assured; books entered while printing was proceeding; books entered long after publication. The King's Printer did not usually enter his official publications and there were other books published but never entered since non-members of the Company had no right to entry.

Prior to the Copyright Act of 1911 it was common to include on the verso of a book's title leaf the statement 'Entered at Stationers' Hall'. See also *Edward Arber*.

stationery binding: see *vellum binding trade.*

stations: in machine bookbinding, the places on a collating machine where piles of folded sections are put to await gathering. Each station may have a micromatic detecting device so that if a section is not properly removed the whole machine will stop.

Statute book: a book containing the laws made by the legislative body of a nation or state.

statutory copies: copies of any published work which publishers are required by law to supply free, within one month of publication, to the British Library and, if requested within twelve months, to the Bodleian Library, Oxford, the University Library, Cambridge, the National Library of Scotland in Edinburgh and the Library of Trinity College, Dublin, Eire. The National Library of Wales comes in a slightly different category and there are restrictions on publishers' liability. Under the National Library of Wales (Delivery of Books) Regulations, 1924, publishers were not required to deliver to the Library a copy of certain classes of books except where these were of particular Welsh or Celtic interest. Two of these classes were 1. where the number of copies in the published edition does not exceed 400 and the published price of each volume exceeds £5, and 2. where the number of copies does not exceed 600 and the published price exceeds £10. An Amendment Regulation published in 1956 raised the price limits to £10 and £20 respectively. See the Copyright Act, 1911, Section 15.

An alternative name is *deposit copies.*

Forerunners of statutory copies date from the Ordonnance de Montpellier of 1537 by which printers and booksellers were required to give a copy of every new book to the library which François I assembled at Blois, and Sir Thomas Bodley's arrangement in 1610 for the presentation to his library of a copy of every book printed by members of the Stationers' Company. See R. C. B. Partridge, 'History of the legal deposit of books in the British Empire', Library Association, 1938.

STC: the abbreviation for 'A Short-title catalogue of books printed in England, Scotland, and Ireland and of English books printed abroad, 1475–1640', by A. W. Pollard and G. R. Redgrave, London, Bibliographical Society, 1926. The Society commissioned a revised edition for publication in the mid-1970s.

Steamset: the trade name for a protected process in publishers' bookbinding, announced in 1956 by G. & J. Kitcat Ltd of London, whereby the back of the book is lined with an *expandable cloth*, prior to *rounding* and *backing*, qq.v. The lining and the adhesive on the back are softened by the application of steam, the rounding and backing being performed while the components are in the softened state. Full rounding with good joint formation together with durability and free opening are claimed for the process.　　　　　　　　　　　　　　　　(LK)

steel engraving: a print from an engraved steel plate. Most steel engravings are characterized by a certain stiffness even though done with extraordinarily fine lines.

Claims have been made that artistic steel engraving was used first in France as early as 1792 by Nicollet and Tardieu, but credit for its commercial exploitation is claimed for Charles Heath of London and Jacob Perkins of Massachusetts who collaborated in 1819. Their prime concern was to make forgery-proof banknotes. Perkins also perfected a method of transferring engravings from a steel original to duplicate steel plates. This is known as *siderography* and was used in the 1830s for bookplates and title-pages.

The most famous artist to show an interest in the new steel engraving technique was Turner. Several topographical works with his illustrations were published between 1824 and 1835. Books illustrated in this way were produced until the 1880s, the work of making the plates being speeded up by ruling machines and pantographs. It was also found that copper plates could be made more durable by steel-facing them.

Stempel, David, 1869–1927: a typefounder who learned his craft in Offenbach before opening in Frankfurt a foundry for casting spacing material in 1895. This developed into the typefounding business which today trades as *Schriftgiesserei D Stempel AG.* In 1898 Stempel took into partnership his brother-in-law *Wilhelm Cunz* (d. 1951). Since 1900 the firm has had the sole right in Germany to make Linotype matrices.

Financial holdings in various typefoundries in Offenbach, Leipzig, Vienna, Basle and Budapest during the period 1898–1920 furthered Stempel's ambition to become one of the largest foundries in Europe. From Drugulin of Leipzig, in particular, he obtained punches and matrices of a major collection of oriental founts. The *Klingspor* business, q.v., was added in 1956.

Famous typographers associated with the firm have included Gustav Mori, whose writings on printing history were published by Stempel between 1909 and 1945, Gotthard de Beauclair and Rudolf Wolf. Types have been commissioned from such well known designers as Warren Chappell, F. H. Ehmcke, F. W. Kleukens, Rudolph Koch, Paul Renner and Hermann Zapf. The popular sanserif face designed in 1956 for Haas of Münchenstein under the name Neue Haas-Grotesk was adopted by the Stempel foundry who renamed it Helvetica. It was subsequently made by Linotype in Britain and America.

In 1951 Stempel established the *Trajanus-Presse*, q.v.

stencil process: see *pochoir*.

step-and-repeat machine: an apparatus for multiple copying (on offset plates, etc.) with devices for the precise adjustment of each copy. These machines are intended especially for reproduction in colour, in which the printing plates for yellow, red, etc., must be precisely superimposed in printing.

Stephanus: the latinized name of the Parisian printing family *Estienne*, q.v.

Stephenson Blake & Co.: a typefounding firm of Sheffield, established in 1818 by James Blake, John Stephenson, and William Garnett. In 1819 they acquired the foundry of William Caslon IV, transferring the plant to Sheffield. The original trading name, Blake Garnett & Co., was changed to Blake and Stephenson in 1830, and to its present form in 1841. London premises were opened in 1865. In 1905 the firm bought the foundry of Sir Charles Reed & Sons Ltd, in this way acquiring types from the foundries of Dr Edmund Fry and William Thorowgood.

From 1907 a separate works was operated for the manufacture of furniture and other composing room equipment. In 1937 the firm acquired the goodwill of the typefoundry business of H. W. Caslon & Co. Ltd, and some of the matrices and punches, and in 1951 some of the proprietary types of Miller & Richard.

The range of display types marketed by Stephenson Blake & Co. is known and used all over the world: included are Chisel, Playbill, Windsor, Verona, Fry's Ornamented, Elongated Roman, Keyboard, and Marina Script. See R. S. Hutchings, 'Type founders for 150 years: a history of Stephenson Blake', 1973.

stereotype (or **stereo**): a printing plate made by taking an impression from set-up type or another plate in a mould of plaster of Paris, papier mâché or flong. Stereotype metal (an alloy of tin, antimony and lead) is then poured into the matrix, as the impression bearing mould is known, the surface of the resulting stereo being made more durable by nickelling. English stereos are usually 12-point thick; American are 10-point.

Historical note. The stereotype process, which saves wearing the original type and re-setting it for reprints, resulted from the work of several experimenters. The Nuremberg book 'Kunst-und-Werk-Schul', 1690, outlined a method of casting plates from paper matrices. Gabriel Valleyre of Paris tried copper plates taken from a cast of type. The date of this is not known but the late 17th century has been

Beating the flong

Both sides of a matrix. Upper, the face, showing the impression. Below, the obverse, packed out with card

conjectured. *Johann Müller* of Leyden (d. 1710) is believed to have invented stereotype plates about 1701. The earliest book extant printed from them is a Syriac-Latin Testament of 1708: others may be a Syriac lexicon of 1709, a quarto and folio Dutch Bible, 1711 and 1718, and a Greek New Testament, 1716. Müller was for a time the partner of the Leyden bookseller Samuel Luchtmans and their names appeared together in the imprints of certain books. A plate thought to have been made by the Müller process survives in the British Library.

Next in time were the attempts of *William Ged* which are described under his name.

In 1779 Alexander Tilloch and Andrew Foulis experimented with plates from type, independent of Ged's work, and patented in 1784 their process for making from plaster of paris moulds 'plates for letterpress printing'. They issued Xenophon's 'Annabasis' in 1783.

The name 'stereotype' was given about 1794 by Firmin Didot of Paris who experimented with the Ged and Müller processes.

Earl Stanhope, with the approval of its inventor, perfected Tilloch's process between 1800 and 1802, aided by a London printer, Andrew Wilson. They used a plaster mould from which a single plate could be cast. Charles Brightly of Bungay published in 1809 an account of his method of making stereotypes, closely following Stanhope's system. By 1820 there were at least twelve establishments in London for the casting of stereotype plates.

Charles Genoux of Lyons invented the papier mâché mould in 1829 from which multiple castings were possible.

The idea of fitting curved stereos to printing cylinders dates from William Nicholson's attempts in 1816. In 1857 the Italian James Dellagana successfully made printing plates from a papier mâché mould of a page of *The Times*. With the curved casting box he patented in 1861 he made plates to fit the printing cylinder of a rotary press. By this time stereotype was fully accepted by the printing trade. See also *autoplate machine, Bruce, clichage, electrotype, flong, papier mâché, plate-boring machine, point moulding, scorcher.* (GU)

stereotype metal: an alloy of tin, antimony, and lead for casting stereos. Lead is the main ingredient, about 80%. Tin makes the alloy tough and improves the sharpness of the cast. Antimony gives further hardness and also counteracts contraction in solidifying, so that the plate is as faithful a casting of the matrix as possible. Antimony by itself expands when it solidifies, whereas the other two metals contract. Correctly constituted stereo metal remains stable when solidifying. (GU)

stet: a word meaning 'let it stand' which is written marginally in proofs to cancel a previously marked correction. Dots are written under the word or words concerned. Archaic spelling in an author's typescript may be similarly marked.

stick: see *composing stick*.

sticking: sheets of paper may, stick together either before or after printing. The former is due to incorrect storage of the paper or to cutting the sheets with a blunt knife which forces the edges into a solid pack. Sticking after printing is due to ink remaining wet on the paper, especially hard-surface papers.

Static electricity, q.v., is also a possible cause of sticking.

stickup initial: see *raised initial*.

stiffened and cut flush: see *flush boards*.

stigmatypy: the printing of a design or portrait built up from small type-units. (GU)

stillage: a low platform on which paper is stored in the warehouse. It is made of battens of wood strengthened by metal angle-bars. Advantages from its use are that damp floors do not affect the paper, air circulates around it, and the stillage and paper can be moved by hand truck or a fork-lift truck. Cf. *pallet*.

Stillwell, Margaret Bingham: an American librarian and bibliographer responsible in the 1920s for recording details of American-owned incunabula on behalf of the Kommission für den *Gesamtkatalog der Wiegendrucke*, q.v. Also important is her 'Incunabula in American libraries', New York, 1940, published by the Bibliographical Society of America. This gives details of over 35,000 incunabula in public and private collections and is a standard bibliographical tool. See also *Goff*.

In 1972 the Bibliographical Society of America published her monograph 'The beginning of the world of books, 1450-1470', a scholarly charting of the early years of printing.

stilted covers: said of a book bound in extra large covers so that it will appear uniform on a shelf with books of larger size.

stipple engraving: a combination of *etching* and *engraving*, qq.v. The outline of a design is made with a needle on a grained plate which is then etched and dried. A graver is next used to make small dots which give effects of light and shade as in pencil shading. This form of engraving was made popular in the 18th century by *Bartolozzi*, q.v., who came from Venice to London in 1764 when he worked for *John*

Boydell, q.v. It had, however, been used earlier by W. W. Ryland (1732–83) the royal engraver.

stitching: a term implying that the thread or wire passes through the whole contents of a book in one hit. If the book is in gathered sections the stitching will pass from side to side near the back (the book cannot thus be opened flat). If all sections are inserted (see *insert* (1)) the stitching is done through the back fold. Cf. *sewing*, which implies the individual sewing of each section to its neighbours.

In 1975 PIRA introduced a method of *adhesive stitch binding* as an alternative to thread sewing. It is based on stitching wire coated with a heat-activated plastic. The stitching head is fitted to the folding machine.   (With LK)

stock: 1. the printing trade term for paper.

2. the wet pulp of mixed ingredients before it enters the Fourdrinier to be formed into paper. Also known as *stuff*.

stockholding book wholesaler: a wholesaler having bulk stocks of titles from several publishers' list for sale to retail booktrade outlets.

Stockholm Protocol, 1967: a draft resulting from a conference in Stockholm held to revise the *Berne Convention*, q.v. Taking the *Model Copyright Law*, q.v., as their basis delegates considered demands from developing countries, and India in particular, for the unrestricted right to reprint copyright works if needed for educational purposes. It remains ineffective and has been overtaken by the *Paris Texts, 1971*, q.v. See also *International Copyright Information Centre*.

stock sizes: sizes of paper at the papermaker's. Sheets may or may not have been guillotine-trimmed and will normally require further trimming by the printer to final dimensions. See also *paper sizes*.

stone: 1. the stone or marble slab (later an iron plate) held in the *coffin*, q.v., of a hand-press. The forme of type rested on it during impression.

2. the heavy iron-topped bench (formerly a stone slab) on which the stone-hand imposes pages of type in a chase and locks them up to make a *forme*, q.v. The forme is also placed on the stone for correcting after proofing. See also *imposition*.

3. the slab of Bavarian limestone used, prior to the introduction of metal plates, as the image carrier for printing by *lithography*, q.v. See M. Twyman, 'Lithographic stone and the printing trade in the 19th century', *Jnl Printing Historical Society*, 8 1972.

stone engraving: engraving on lithographic stone; a hand process now little used except for script and line drawings in which sharpness and precision of line are more important than artistic expression, e.g. for maps.

Printing from a stone engraving can only be done in a hand-press, and editions are normally small. It is usual to transfer the image on the stone to a plate for printing.   (GU)

stone grinding: a lithographic stone must be treated to make its surface receptive to an image; the surface must be clean and flat. Grinding machines are used to grain the surface with fine sand and water by means of revolving flat plates; or hand grinding may be done by laying a second stone on the first, or by using a *levigator*, q.v.   (GU)

stone-hand: the printing craftsman who imposes type in a chase.

stone printing: 1. Chinese stone printing. About AD 175 Ts'ai Yung suggested that the six holy books of Confucius should be engraved on stone slabs to preserve them for posterity. According to tradition the earliest stone printing was done from these slabs. Since the 9th century this idea was adapted for printing pictures. A thin sheet of tough paper was laid on the engraved stone, thoroughly soaked, and pressed into the engraving with a brush or felt and hammer so that it covered the stone like a skin. Indian ink was spread over the paper, care being taken that it did not penetrate into the depressions. When the paper dried it was prised off the stone to reveal a light script or image on a dark ground.

2. Printing from stone on which an image had been made with thick ink was the original form of lithographic printing. Stone printing is still in occasional use, but the term lithography is extended to include printing from grained zinc, aluminium or plastic plates. See *lithography, Senefelder*.

Stone, Reynolds, b. 1909: a British master letterer and wood engraver internationally known for his distinctive renderings of the roman and italic alphabets. Precise cutting, graceful swashes and harmonious arrangement mark his work.

On joining Cambridge University Press in 1930 as an apprentice he learned typography and punchcutting (his Minerva roman and italic face was issued by Linotype in 1955 and is shown in Appendix A). But it was a brief working visit to *Eric Gill*, q.v., at Pigotts which determined his career as a wood engraver. In 1934 he commenced designing the title-pages, bookplates, devices and labels which subsequently won him public recognition (his awards include CBE, ARA and RDI). His vignettes and illustrations have appeared *inter alia* in books published by Cambridge University Press, Faber, The Limited Editions Club and Nonesuch Press. A conspectus of his work was published by John Murray in 1977 as 'Reynolds Stone engravings, with an introduction by the artist and an appreciation by Kenneth Clark'.

Dedication panel for the first edition of this Glossary, engraved by Reynolds Stone

Stonyhurst Gospel: a version of the Gospel of St John written in Northumbria in an uncial script. It is not decorated. The ninety surviving leaves, in a binding which is thought by some to be 7th-century work, are preserved in Stonyhurst College, Lancashire.

stop-cylinder press: a cylinder machine in which the paper-carrying cylinder stops after completing one revolution (in some older models one-half or one-third of a revolution), and is stationary during the return of the bed bearing the forme. During this pause fresh paper is fed. The cylinder is driven by gear racks on the bed which mesh with corresponding gears on the cylinder during printing. When the bed passes the cylinder, the outermost tooth of the gear rim loses contact with the gear rails of the bed and the rotary movement of the cylinder is intercepted by the pawl clutch which, with the cylinder brake, stops it. The pawl clutch also re-starts the cylinder when the bed is at its extreme end.

König & Bauer press, late 19th century

König's first cylinder machine (1812) was a stop-cylinder machine and the main principles of his model have survived to the present day. (See illustration.)

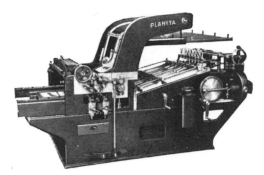

Stop-cylinder press

Modern stop-cylinder machines are arranged for pile delivery with space for a delivery table which can be lowered automatically as the pile increases. The best known English model is the *Wharfedale machine,* q.v. (GU)

stopping out: covering with varnish such parts of an etching plate as are not to be further etched by acid during its repeated dipping in the acid bath. Cf. *staging out.*

Stowe MSS: a valuable collection of nearly 1,000 volumes of historical papers, works on heraldry, genealogy, topography, Anglo-Saxon charters, King Alfred's Psalter, etc. The majority were assembled in the late 18th century by the palaeographer and antiquary Thomas Astle (1735–1803), Keeper of the Records in the Tower. In accordance with his will the collection was offered for £500 to George Grenville, first Marquis of Buckingham, of Stowe House. The collection was there enlarged by the acquisition of the Essex Papers and the Irish MSS of C. O'Connor.

In 1849 the Stowe MSS were sold to the Earl of Ashburnham. After his death they were bought by the Government for £50,000; the important Irish works went to the Royal Academy in Dublin, the remainder to the British Museum.

Stower, Caleb, d. 1816: a London printer who wrote several books on his craft. One was on proof correcting, but most important was his 'Printers' grammar', 1787, (2nd ed. 1808).

straight-grain morocco: goatskin which is moistened and then worked over with a ridged board to make the grain run in parallel straight lines. Roger Payne may have originated the style about 1766. In France, where it was known as *English morocco,* it had a great vogue between 1800 and 1840. Usual shades were green or red, though after 1810 or thereabouts dark blue and black were used. It is still made, but the skin is not always goat. Also known as *boarded leather*. See also *graining boards*.

straight matter: a normal piece of typesetting which does not contain display or tabular matter.

Straube, Kaspar: an itinerant Bavarian printer credited with being the first printer in Poland where he issued a Calendar for 1474 and an edition of Turrecremata 'Explanatio in Psalterium', *c.* 1475. Straube is not named, the edition bearing the place-name 'Cracis impressa'.

Strawberry Hill Press: the press established by Horace Walpole at his villa near Twickenham, London. It was also known as 'Officina Arbuteana'. He employed William Robinson and Thomas Kirgate to print for him a succession of books, pamphlets and broadsides. Caslon types were used. An important collection of Walpoliana is that assembled by Wilmarth Lewis for his 'Museum Arbuteanum' at Farmington, Conn., U.S.A. See A. T. Hazen, 'A bibliography of the Strawberry Hill Press', Yale U.P.: O.U.P., 1942.

strawboards: cheap boards made from unbleached straw or, in inferior grades, from re-pulped waste paper. They are used for book covers, but not by hand-binders who prefer *millboards*, q.v.

streamer: an item of publishers' publicity material supplied to booksellers chiefly for use in counter and window displays. It is usually a strip of paper (e.g. 300mm × 120mm) designed by striking wording to draw attention to a display of books over which or in front of which it is positioned. Cf. *crowner*.

stream feeder: see *feeder*.

strike: a piece of polished copper into which a steel punch, bearing an engraved character, has been struck by the punchcutter. After the laborious process of *justification*, q.v., the strike is known as a *matrix*, and from it type is cast.

Sets of unjustified strikes were sold to printers who attended the fairs at Frankfurt. In this way a fount of type from one set of punches could be dispersed to printers in several countries. An alternative name is *drive*. See also *stake*.

strike-on composition: a name for typewriter-style composition using such machines as the IBM Composer which has 'golf ball' heads.

strike through: a fault caused when the oily medium

in printing ink soaks into and through the paper, making it translucent. Cf. *show through*.

striking: a term used in calligraphy for the elaborate freehand flourishes swiftly made with the hand raised off the paper and without a guiding underdrawing. This dexterous form of embellishment was perfected in 1605 by *Jan van den Velde*, q.v. It is also known as *by command of hand*.

striking off: 1. the making by hand of stereo matrices.

2. making a proof from set up type before it is put on the press. A sheet of damp paper is positioned over the inked forme and beaten with a hard brush. The result is known as a *strike off*.

stripping: the removal of a negative from its original wet plate for mounting on a larger glass sheet. This is done in the *iodized collodion process*, q.v., when combining line and half-tone work, or doing fine line work.

stroke in: the action of hand-feeding a sheet of paper into a flatbed machine. This is done by the layer-on.

Stromeir, Ulman, d. 1407: a merchant and member of the Nuremberg senate who, about 1389, set up the first known papermill in Germany. He employed Italians from Lombardy, all being sworn to secrecy. About 1394 he leased the mill to Jorg Tyrmann. No paper was made there after 1463.

strongfold papers: coated papers with a strong base stock, e.g. kraft or manilla. The coating does not crack when the paper is folded or scored.

stub: 1. the first column of matter set in tabular form.

2. the narrow margin remaining in a book when a cancel has been removed and on to which a corrected leaf is fixed.

stuff: the wet pulp of mixed ingredients which is ready to be flowed on to the wire of the Fourdrinier. Also known as *slurry* or *stock*. See also *half-stuff*.

stuffer: a printed leaflet advertising one or more forthcoming books which is inserted at random by booksellers in whatever book they are selling to a customer, either over the counter or by post. Publishers enclose stuffers when sending statements of account to take up the weight allowance for minimum postage.

style of the house: the customary style of spelling (see *English spelling by printers*), punctuation, spacing, etc., used in a printing house. Compositors will follow in-house rules and style when setting type unless contrary instructions have been specified by the publisher. Cf. *follow copy*.

stylus: or *stilus*, the earliest writing implement, being a broad-headed stick of bone, metal, reed or wood. It came into use about *c.* 3500 BC in Mesopotamia where the sharp edge of a stylus was used to impress crude pictographic writing on clay tablets. It continued in use in the Near East and in ancient western Asia until about the 6th century BC. It was then replaced by the brush, pen and quill as the material for writing upon changed from clay to papyrus, parchment and paper; it was this change which made possible the writing of curved strokes for alphabets.

sub-heads: headings for the divisions of a chapter: size of type, position in relation to the text and leading are factors to be considered when setting them. See also *cross-heads, cut-in heads, margins, side-heads, shoulder-heads*.

subject books: a term used in the London book trade during the 1890s for books 'subject' to the usual discount of 15 to 25% which booksellers might allow a customer as distinct from 'net' books on which no discount was to be given.

subject series: a number of books, often written by different authors, which are uniform in format, scope and method. They are usually published under the name of a general editor.

subscribing a book: the showing by a publisher's representative of new books to booksellers and wholesalers prior to publication. See also *advance copies, subscription terms*.

subscription terms: terms up to 35% discount offered on general books by a publisher to booksellers on orders placed for a title prior to first publication. This is to allow for the extra risk they take in stocking copies of a work before its sales possibilities have been tested. See also *terms* (1).

subscription works: books which, because there may be doubts about sales potential, are only published when a sufficient number of subscribers or guarantors has been found in advance. In England the idea took hold in the 17th century, examples being 'Guide into tongues', privately printed for its compiler John Minsheu in 1617, and a polyglot Bible in six folio volumes printed by Thomas Roycroft, 1653–7, for Brian Walton, Bishop of Chester. See also *Chapter books, conger, privately printed, privately published, serial, subscription terms, vanity publishing*.

subsidiaries: parts of a book excluding the preliminaries and text, i.e. appendix, notes (if collected at the end), glossary, bibliography, index, plates and maps (if collected at the end), the publisher's advertisements, etc. Also known as *back matter, end-matter,* or *postlims*.

subsidiary rights: rights in copyright material other than the *volume rights*, q.v., which are the primary subject of the original agreement between copyright holder and publisher. Such rights may be handled by the publisher on behalf of the copyright owner, or by the copyright owner or his agents. Subsidiary rights include serialization in a newspaper or magazine, TV and film, re-issue in paperback form, lengthy quotation in an anthology, and so on. Formerly known as *outside rights*. See also *permissions copy*.

substance: see *paper substance*.

substrate: a supporting base. The word gained currency in printing trade literature in the 1970s, being used, *inter alia*, for uncoated paper stock prior to coating; thin steel plates which are given a copper and then chromium deposit for use in lithography; the cellulose acetate base on which emulsions are deposited in photographic film-making; and any surface on which inked type or an inked plate leave an image, either by direct contact or indirectly by the offset principle.

subtitle: wording, which is often explanatory, following the title on the title-page. It is usually set in a smaller type. The title-page of this Glossary provides an example.

suite: a series, as for example, of illustrations for a book.

sulphate pulp: a variety of *chemical wood pulp*, q.v., for which the digesting agent consists principally of caustic soda and sodium sulphide or certain other sulphur compounds. Paper made with it is strong, and is often used unbleached, but it can be bleached to a very white colour.

sulphite pulp: pulp used in making paper in which chipped wood is boiled with bisulphite of lime to separate the fibres. Such pulps are clean and bleach easily. A form of the process was devised in 1866 by two Americans, the brothers B. C. and R. Tilghmann. Commercial development by a Swede, C. D. Ekman, followed in 1872: he came to England and in 1886 established the Northfleet Paper & Pulp Co. in Kent.

summa: a collection of theological treatises.

sun and satellite format: see *drum cylinder press*.

sunken cords: cords or leather thongs laid in grooves sawn across the assembled sections of a book. Two grooves were usual. After sewing and lacing to the boards the spine of the book was flat.

This practice began in England in the late 16th century, fell into disuse for a time, but has continued since the late 18th century for hand-bound books.

The cords now used are thinner than those for raised cord sewing, but still thinner, and thereby weaker, cords were used for the method popular in the mid-19th century described under *sunken flexible*.

Also known as *recessed cords*. See also *flexible sewing*, *raised bands*, *thongs*.

sunken flexible: a manner of sewing the sections of a book in which grooves are sawn in them as far as the innermost fold. The thin cords which lie in these grooves are then completely encircled with the sewing thread, not crossed. The result is a *saw back* or *sawn-in back*.

sunk joints: see *french joints*.

super: the American term for *mull*, q.v.

super-calender: a calender which is separate from the papermaking machine. It consists of a stack of from five to sixteen rolls. These may be of cast iron or of heated burnished iron and compressed paper (or cotton) rolls arranged alternately, with two paper rolls together in the middle. Only one roll is power-driven, friction driving the others. Paper is passed through under pressure to be given a highly glazed finish. See also *bowls*, *calender*, *crown* (2), *finish*.

super-calendered paper: paper which has been given an extra smooth finish in a *super-calender*, q.v.

superior figures: small figures or letters printed above a word, e.g. to draw the reader's attention to a foot-note. They are cast above the mean line and often on the same body as the type with which they appear. See also *inferior figures*, *reference marks*.

supplement: matter forming part of a work already published and either printed immediately following the text pages of a new edition or issued with its own title-page and covers. See also *addendum*.

supralibros: a mark of ownership stamped, usually in gold, on the front or rear cover of a book. Heraldic designs typify most, but portraits were not unknown, particularly in 16th century Germany. Also known as *super ex-libris*.

surface papers: see *coated papers*.

surface sizing: the papermaking process of applying

size after the sheet or web has been formed (in which state it is called *waterleaf*). This can be done in a vertical or horizontal *size press* linked with the drying section of a *Fourdrinier*, q.v. Both sides of the paper are treated, size being forced in by rolls. Factors affecting the absorption of size in the press include degree of beating, prior engine sizing, paper surface, porosity, moisture control and temperature of the size solution.

Certain kinds of starch-latex coating can also be applied on the size press.

Prior to the introduction of the size press waterleaf was *tub-sized*, q.v., in a separate unit and this is still done for some high quality or hand-made papers. Nowadays tub-sizing baths can be linked to the last drying cylinder of the Fourdrinier, followed by hot-air drying and reeling units. See also *animal-sized*, *size* (2), *soft-sized*.

Sutherland bindings: the name given to a group of bindings made for the Duchess of Sutherland by G. T. Bagguley of Newcastle-under-Lyme who in 1896 patented his method of tooling in colour. After blinding-in the design, usually on vellum doublures, resin was brushed in the impression, colours were sprinkled on and tooled. Highlight dots and small circles in gold completed the effect. Typical designs which Léon V. Solon made for these books had all-over patterns of flowers and leaves.

s.v.: an abbreviation for the Latin *sub verbo* which means 'under the word' and can be used when referring a reader to an article in an encyclopaedia or other alphabetically arranged work instead of giving the volume or page number.

Swan, Sir Joseph Wilson, 1828–1914: an English physicist (originally a chemist in Newcastle) who as early as 1860 invented a carbon filament lamp. He improved electric accumulators and photographic dry plates and worked out several galvanic methods. In 1862 he patented an improved carbon print process and is regarded as the inventor of carbon tissue. Swan founded the Autotype Co., London, for the manufacture of carbon tissue. In 1879 he patented a double-line screen for half-tone work.

See also *photogravure*.   (GU)

The Swan Press: a small press which was developed, about 1921, by Sidney Matthewman as a branch of his father's jobbing printing establishment in Leeds. Although the press mostly issued pamphlet editions of verse by local writers, works by Laurence Binyon, Arthur Symons, and Swinburne were also published. Activity ceased about 1931.

swash letters: ornamental italic capitals with decora-

466

tive tails and flourishes, e.g. some letters of the Caslon Old Face italic and similar founts.

swelled rules: ornamental rules for the division of matter on the title-page and elsewhere. Their use in England and America developed in the 18th century,

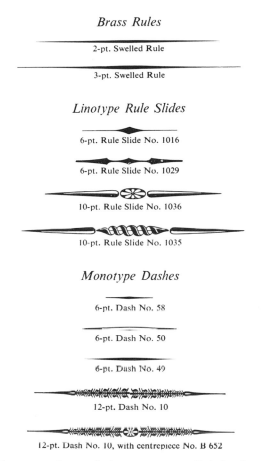

Brass Rules

2-pt. Swelled Rule

3-pt. Swelled Rule

Linotype Rule Slides

6-pt. Rule Slide No. 1016

6-pt. Rule Slide No. 1029

10-pt. Rule Slide No. 1036

10-pt. Rule Slide No. 1035

Monotype Dashes

6-pt. Dash No. 58

6-pt. Dash No. 50

6-pt. Dash No. 49

12-pt. Dash No. 10

12-pt. Dash No. 10, with centrepiece No. B 652

when proprietary designs were supplied by brass-founders. Modern examples are shown. Also known as *French dashes*.

Sweynheym, Conrad, fl.1465–73: a printer of Mainz who, with his colleague from the same place *Arnold Pannartz*, introduced into Italy the craft of printing. Their first press was established in 1465 at the Benedictine house Santa Scolastica, Subiaco, about thirty miles from Rome. It was here they issued the first book printed in Italy to bear a date: this was 'De divinis institutionibus' of Lactantius in which they made the first successful use of greek type, to which accents were added by hand. (It was preceded by an undated Cicero's 'De oratore', and a Donatus of which no copy survives.) They also printed here St Augustine's 'De civitate Dei'. For their Subiaco

books they used a calligraphic roman type showing the influence of humanistic script: it was a forerunner of the purer roman letter of Venice. A modern derivation of it by Emery Walker and Sydney Cockerell was made for the *Ashendene Press*, q.v.

In 1467 they moved to Rome where they established a press in the Palazzo Massimi, and in this busy year they issued Torquemada's 'Meditationes' illustrated with German woodcuts. In 1469 they printed the first edition of Apuleius, works by Caesar, Cicero and Virgil. The type they used in Rome was nearer in style to the roman of Venice than the Subiaco fount. In 1471 they issued the first printed Bible in Italian.

Most of the twenty-nine works they issued were in editions of 275 copies, but even so their business was commercially unsuccessful and they complained that their house was full of unsold books. In 1473 Sweynheym withdrew from the partnership and worked for a short time as an engraver. Pannartz printed alone until 1476.

Swiney Prize: since 1849, a prize of £100 cash, and a silver cup of the same value, awarded quinquennially for a published essay on jurisprudence. The Royal Society of Arts administers a sum of money left for this purpose by George Swiney (*c.* 1786–1844).

Symmen, Henric, van: a supplier of matrices and types who about 1488 was in the employ of *Gerard Leeu*, q.v., at Antwerp. It was after a quarrel arising when Henric wished to set up his own business that he killed Leeu in 1493.

Black letter types believed to be his were in use by the printers Jan van Breda and Matthias van der Goes. By 1500 nine printers in the Low Countries were using them and others used them there until the 1580s. John Day had a fount of his black letter. Between 1496 and 1511 Henric published about fifteen works, probably sometimes as specimens of his type.

Some scholars hold that Henric van Symmen, Henric de Lettersnijder and Henric Pieterszoon were different names used by one man.

Sympson, Benjamin, fl.1597: a Londoner, and the first independent letter-founder in England of whom records exist (viz. his bond in 1597 to the Stationers' Company). In general, English printers used letters cast in their printing shops, and the Star Chamber Decree of 1637 only allowed four independent Founders of Letters to practise their trade. In France, typefounding had been legally recognized as a separate trade in 1539.

synaxary: a collection of lives of the saints. Such works were first compiled in Constantinople in the 10th century and led to an increase in the portrayal of saints in the margins of psalters and in the inclusion of incidents from their lives in menologia.

Syndics: the governors of the Cambridge University Press, being a syndicate of senior members appointed by the Senate for a period of years to approve, on behalf of the University, every manuscript accepted for publication. Governors to the Press were first appointed in 1698, the first syndicate in 1737. See also *Cambridge University Press, Curatores Praeli Typographici.*

synopsis: a concise version of any piece of writing in which only the essential matter of the original is retained.

synthetic hot melts: see *back lining, hot-melt adhesives.*

system diagram: in technical-book illustration, a diagram showing the relative positions of the units which comprise a machine or installation.

Syst-o-colour: a system of four-colour ink standardization originated in Holland by Paul Schuitema and announced in 1965.

T

table book: 1. an obsolete term for a note-book. (Mentioned in Pepys's Diary, 10 May 1667.)

2. an elaborately decorated edition of a book, often covered in silk or velvet, for drawing-room display. Popular in the 19th century. See also *coffee-table book*.

table press: a small platen printing press which could be placed on a table. Although formerly not uncommon, these machines are now limited to small jobs.

table talk: see *ana*.

tabular work: matter set in columns, either with or without rules. The first column, which is called the *stub*, gives guiding information such as, for example, the vertical list of inter-terminal stations in a railway timetable. Each adjacent column is topped by a heading which identifies the data set below. In narrow columns head wording may be set vertically. Matter set in the columns under the row of heads is known as the *body* of the table. Tabular matter not set within ruled columns, e.g. a genealogical table, may call for a combination of hand and machine setting or even for artist's work.

tack: the stickiness of printing ink. If an ink has insufficient tack it will not print sharply. One which is too tacky may tend to pluck the paper surface and not remain smoothly upon it.

Low tack inks permit the use of lower quality paper for running at higher press speeds without picking problems.

tack marks: small dots incorporated in imposing schemes for sheets printed *work and turn*, q.v. One dot is used for the first side printed and two dots for the second side printed. Tack marks are also used to indicate the printer's *side lay*, in which case the dot is placed on the edge of the paper and bleeds off. (LK)

TAGA (Technical Association of Graphic Arts): an American association for the printing and allied trades. The annual report is in technical and scientific terms, but is an important guide to new technical ideas in the U.S.A.

Tagliente, Giovantonio, fl.1491–1531: an Italian writing master who in 1492 was appointed instructor to the Doge's chancery in Venice. He remained there for thirty-two years, training other scribes. His manual 'Lo presente libro insegna . . .', Venice, 1524, included plates engraved by Eustachio Celebrino to illustrate various alphabets including Arabic and Hebrew. Some of the pages were set in italic type cut to imitate script. Centuries later his work influenced *Alfred Fairbank*, q.v., for example in the 'Woodside' writing cards he issued in 1932. See also *Arrighi*.

tail: 1. the *margin*, q.v., at the foot of the page.
2. the bottom edge of a book.
3. the curved terminal stroke of such letters as Q, R, K.

tailband: the correct name for a *headband*, q.v., when this is affixed also to the foot of a book, although in modern usage 'headbands' includes both head and foot. There are also publishers who use the word *bottomband*.

tail cap: the nipped-over fold of leather at the foot of the spine where it forms a protecting cover for the tailband.

tail-end hook: see *back-edge curl*.

taille-douce: the French term for a *copperplate engraving*.

tail-piece: a decorative device printed in the blank space which follows a chapter. Designs may be specially drawn or built up from flowers. Cf. *head-piece*. The French term is *cul de lampe*.

take: the amount of copy taken by a compositor to set up in type at one time. Cf. *token*.

take down: to prepare a book for re-binding. This includes removing the cover, boards, and end-papers, all sewing threads and lining, cleaning, bleaching paper, and repairing any damage. When the book is reduced to its original separate sections it is said to be *pulled* or *taken down*.

take-over: the acquisition of exclusive rights in a book by one publishing house after it has first been published by another.

taking out turns: inserting correct types where the twin black foot-marks on a galley proof indicate that a *turned sort*, q.v., has been used.

Talbot, William Henry Fox, 1800–77: a British scientist and the inventor of several important photographic and reproduction methods. In 1839 he published his invention of a negative-positive process. In 1841 he patented a process he named *calotype* in which a negative was produced on iodized silver paper developed with gallic acid. Printing was done on silver chloride paper. Talbot used calotype for illustrating several books, e.g. 'The pencil of nature', 1844. The pictures, which he advertized as 'Talbotypes', tended to fade.

In 1852 Talbot discovered the sensitivity to light of a compound of dichromate and gelatine which gave rise to several reproduction methods. He also worked on photogravure or heliogravure and introduced etching with ferric chloride. He was one of the pioneers of the screen distribution of half-tones, and in 1852 patented a muslin screen and suggested dusting glass with fine powder as a form of grained screen. See H. J. P. Arnold, 'William Henry Fox Talbot: pioneer of photography and man of science', Hutchinson, 1977.

See also *chromate process*. (With GU)

tall copy: a book having larger head and foot margins than other copies from the same printing. Cf. *narrow copy*.

Talmud: the oldest extant code of post-biblical Jewish civil and traditional law. It is in two parts: the *Mishnah*, a codification of unwritten laws compiled and probably set down in the early 3rd century, and the *Gemara*, a compilation of commentaries and interpretations by sages and teachers. The word Talmud originally referred only to the Gemara of which there are two versions: the *Jerusalem Talmud*, written in Western Aramaic prior to 408 in which each section of the Gemara is preceded by the Mishnah text, and the *Babylonian Talmud* (Talmud Babli), written in Eastern Aramaic, on which work ended about 500. It is the latter, a very much larger work, which is strictly the Talmud. See also *Bomberg, Hebrew printing prior to 1600*.

tanned leather: animal skin which has been turned into leather by steeping it in an infusion of oak bark, which stains it dark brown, or of sumach. Goat skins so treated were used for book covers from Coptic times (7th-11th century). In England tanned goat and deer skins are found on books surviving from the 8th century onwards, most notably on the stamped Romanesque bindings of the 12th century (at which time more general use was made of *tawed leather*) and from 1450 onwards. Sumach and chrome have largely replaced oak bark for tanning skins. Vegetable tanned skins deteriorate in a polluted atmosphere. Cf. *tawing*.

tapes: strips of a closely woven cotton material, about ½in. wide, on to which the sections of a book may be sewn. Two are usual, but there may be as many as five. The use of tapes has diminished in publishers' binding.

Tate, John, d. 1507: a mercer of London who about 1484 established at or near Hertford the first paper-mill in England. His watermark was a star within two concentric circles. The paper was remarkably fine and was used c. 1494 by Wynkyn de Worde for printing Bartholomaeus' 'De proprietatibus rerum' (STC 1536) and Voragine's 'Legenda aurea', 1498, (STC 24876). There is no evidence of the mill after 1498.

Tauchnitz, Christian Bernhard, 1816–95: the founder in 1837 of a Leipzig printing and publishing firm famous for its cheap reprints in English of English books. The series 'Collection of British authors' began in 1841 with Bulwer's 'Pelham'.

After negotiations in London during 1843 Tauchnitz made agreements with authors and publishers for the sole rights to print their works in Germany. He agreed not to sell his editions in England or the Colonies. Dickens, Ainsworth, Disraeli and Thackeray were among those with whom he had agreements.

His project prospered, and the paperbacked Tauchnitz editions, selling for about 1/6d, were known throughout Europe and ultimately included nearly 4,000 volumes. The business was continued by his son *Karl Bernhard* (1841–1921), being finally destroyed by bombing in 1943. See also *Albatross Library*.

Tavernier, Ameet, c. 1522–70: punchcutter, founder and printer of Ghent and Antwerp where he was a contemporary of Plantin who used some of his types. In 1563 Tavernier printed a curious commonplace book by Lowys Porquin, part of which continued to be reprinted as a school textbook until the 18th century. The first edition was printed in Tavernier's version of *civilité* type, q.v.

tawing: the treatment of animal skins with salts of iron or chromium and alum; the skins are rendered white and supple. For bookbinding purposes alum tawed skins have greater resistance to atmospheric deterioration than tanned skins and they were often used for the covers and thongs of 12th century books.

The natural white finish was sometimes stained with red dye obtained from the kermes insect. In England it was used for binding from c. 1150 to 1450 and in Germany for panel-stamped bindings in the 16th century.

Tawed leather is also known as *Hungarian leather.* Cf. *tanned leather.*

Taylor, Samuel, fl.1765–81: a bookbinder and stationer of Berwick-upon-Tweed who about 1764 emigrated to America. He set up premises in Philadelphia. The only remarkable feature of his binding work was his use of large elegantly engraved labels to identify it.

Tchemerzine, Avenir, 1877–1963: a Russian colonel who left Russia during the 1917 Revolution and settled in Paris. There he compiled several studies on French printing. Notable were his 'Bibliographie d'éditions originales ou rares d'auteurs français des XVe, XVIe, XVIIe et XVIIIe siècles, contenant 6,000 fac-similés de titres et de gravures', 10 vols, 1927–33, (amended reprint, Paris, 1977), and 'Répertoire de livres à figures rares et précieux édités en France au XVIIe siècle' (in the Versailles Library), 1933. Incomplete when he died were a bibliography of science and one of medicine.

technical book illustration: see *artwork, bleach-out, block diagram, cake diagram, component-location diagram, cut-away, figure* (1), *glyph, ideogram, inset, isotype, linear flow diagram, model, pictogram, schematic, system diagram, tabular work, theoretical circuit diagram, thrown clear, thrown out.*

Techniplate: the trade name for a bonded copper-plastic printing plate introduced in the early 1960s. Such plates are used by process engraving firms to make wraparound plates for sheet-fed rotary presses. They can be proofed flat.

t.e.g.: see *top edge gilt.*

teleordering system: an automated book-ordering system. The first of several was the micro-processor controlled Libri Tele Ordering System (*Litos*), developed in the early 1970s for the German wholesaler Lingenbrink (*Libri*) of Frankfurt by Lager-Organisations-System. Litos is based on telephone links between word processing terminals held by booksellers and by Libri. Libri assigns the book identifying numbers used for ordering and supplies subscribers with a catalogue listing them. By early 1978 Libri was linked on either a trial or regular basis with Litos terminals in Austria, France, Japan and Luxembourg.

In America the R. R. Bowker Company of New York announced in 1977 that their alphanumeric *Computerized Acquisition System* was being investigated by the trade. It offered a book-ordering service for librarians and book dealers, based on Bowker's computer-held book files. Ordering could be by ISBNs or by author and title.

Between 1976 and 1978 the British booktrade considered the feasibility of teleordering schemes (see *The Bookseller*, 1976–8, Nos 3667, 3725, 3752, 3754–6, 3760–1). An integral component of whichever scheme would be adopted would be BBIP as a master data base. A *Litos* terminal, linked with Libri, was installed in a London bookshop (Dillons) in early 1978 as part of the IBIS field trials.

teletypesetting: a semi-automatic system of typesetting by remote control. It combines a QWERTY keyboard, named 'multiface perforator', with the teleprinter principle, and an operating unit which is used on Intertype and Linotype casters fitted with adaptor keyboards. The Teletypesetter was invented in America by Walter Morey in the early 1930s.

As copy is tapped off on the perforator keyboard a strip of tough paper about 22cm wide is punched with perforations based on a six-unit code. As tapping proceeds a pointer shows on a scale the cumulative width of characters in a line. When the line is complete the operator strikes 'return' and 'elevate' keys before proceeding with the next line.

Finished tape can be fed into a mechanical operating unit attached to the line caster: this automatically operates the keyboard and sends away the line of matrices for slug casting. Alternatively, the tape can be used for transmitting electrical impulses, by radio or wire, to a receiver or re-perforator which will convert them into a duplicate of the original tape. For the simultaneous production of newspapers or periodicals such transmissions can be sent to several offices over a wide area.

There is also a page printer machine, with or without a keyboard, which transmits and receives copy typed in upper and lower case. This enables a proof to be read and a correction tape made before casting begins.

The advantages of the TTS in bookwork include increased composing machine output, a saving in proofing costs, and the elimination of standing type or plate storage charges. See also *computer-assisted typesetting.*

Temple Sheen Press: a hand-press founded by Arthur K. Sabin at East Sheen, London, in 1911, but moved to Bethnal Green, London, in 1922. Editions were very small, sometimes for private circulation only, but produced with careful craftsmanship. See also *Samurai Press.*

Tenison Psalter: see *Psalter of Alphonso.*

471

tensile strength: in testing paper for strength, the weight necessary to apply to a given strip of paper to break it. (ML)

Term catalogues: the 17th century catalogues of new books of which the pioneer was 'Mercurius Librarius', issued at the end of Michaelmas Term 1668 in London by John Starkey and Robert Clavell. As their name implies, Term catalogues were issued four times a year (Hilary, Easter, Trinity and Michaelmas). See also *Arber*.

terms: 1. for the terms offered by publishers to book-sellers see *half see safe, journey terms, on sale or return, partial remainders, remainders, return on full credit, returns, see safe, subscription terms, trade terms.*
2. for general terms and conditions of supply, discounts, etc., see *courtesy terms, Library Licence, Net Book Agreement, net net, non-net books, Quantity Book-Buying Scheme, subject books.*

ternion: a gathering of three sheets, folded once, in which form some manuscripts and early printed books were assembled. See also *quaternion*.

tetraevangelium: a book containing the four Gospels, written in Greek.

tetralogy: a group of four related dramatic works, in particular three Greek tragedies and a satiric comedy.

text: 1. the main body of a book, excluding the pre-liminaries and subsidiaries. See also *display*.
2. paper which is generally suitable for the main body of a book.

textbook: a book prescribed for study. The organizers of an exhibition held in 1960 at the National Book League, London, defined a textbook as one intended to be used by a number of pupils receiving instruction at the same time, and dealing with any recognized subject of instruction at any level from the infant school to GCE 'O' level, and up to any form of tertiary level teaching, or their equivalents in other countries. See also *ad usum Delphini, in usum scholarum, paper-books, Primer, School edition.*

text editing system: see *video display unit*.

text hand: the medieval script of northern Europe which, as fully developed by the end of the 12th century, continued in use until the Renaissance for books. It was a compressed angular script, written with a broad-nibbed pen, with thick vertical strokes and hair-line linking strokes instead of curves. Also known as *gothic*. Cf. *Court hand*.

472

textile bindings: bindings with covers of fabric. There were in Europe two distinct periods and styles. From the 12th–15th century the wealthy laity, particularly in France, found an elegant alternative to the crudity of thick calf in covers made of silk brocade and velvet with silver or gold clasps. They were not durable and few survive. The second period was during the 16th and 17th centuries when *embroidered bindings*, q.v., were made.
The following extract from a binder's bill of about 1610 gives an idea of the cost:
'Item for binding 31 (books) in velvet edged with gold lace and lined with tafity silk stringes £20 : 13 : 4d.'

text illustrations: illustrations printed within pages of text as distinct from separately printed plates or insets. Also known as *cuts* or *figures*.

text letter: see *black letter* or *gothic*.

text string: a group of words, particularly those on the screen of a CRT proof-reading and correcting terminal where characters are displayed in type-written line format as text is read in from coded paper tape.

textualis: see *textus*.

Textur: the German name for *lettre de forme*, q.v.

textus: a formal gothic script used in the 12th and 13th centuries for liturgical books. The two main forms were *textus prescissus* and *textus quadratus*.
The first was a somewhat compressed letter with an emphasis on strong vertical strokes, the broad pen used to make them being held straight. 'Prescissus' means 'cut off' and refers to the abrupt termination on the base line of the upright strokes of most letters except descenders, i.e. the foot stroke or dot usual in most Gothic letters was absent.
The second form of textus was even more formal and mechanical in effect. Most of the usually rounded letters, e.g. e, p, o, etc., were made without curves, and instead of terminating with a curve or serif ended with a diamond-shaped dot. It was this script which became the basis of 15th century black-letter types.

textus receptus: or *received text*, the version of an author's text which, in the absence of conclusive proof, is agreed by scholars to be more likely than other extant versions to represent his intentions.
Particularly in the days when texts were circulated in manuscript form, often without a date or indica-tion of who penned the words, variant readings could result from careless copying and even deliberate changes by unknown scribes.
Similar difficulties in establishing just what an

author intended or wrote may occur when considering books printed without benefit of his proof reading or in the absence of a holograph text. Shakespeare's plays are a notable example of such difficulty. See also *collating machine*.

theoretical circuit diagram: in technical-book illustration, a diagram of electrical components with symbols and connecting lines to indicate the sequence of operations in a circuit. It is not representational.

thermoplastic binder: a machine for use in *adhesive binding*, q.v.

thermoplastic plates: printing plates made from any plastic which becomes soft in heating and sets again when cooled, in contrast to thermosetting material which is relatively soft when received but becomes hard when heated and remains hard whether hot or cold. It is usual to make moulds from type or blocks using thermosetting material, e.g. bakelite, and from these moulds to make thermoplastic plates. See also *plastic plates*.

thesaurus: literally, a treasury or storehouse of knowledge. The term is now particularly associated with Peter Mark Roget's 'Thesaurus of English words and phrases . . .', which Longman and partners first published in 1852. The first twenty-five editions were revised by the author. Other editions by his descendants followed until 1950 when Longmans bought the copyright.

The first American 'Thesaurus', edited by Barnas Sears, was issued in Boston in 1854. In 1886 Crowell & Co. published their first American edition based on that of J. L. Roget. In 1911 they issued Sylvester Mawson's completely Americanized edition, the basis of subsequent versions.

For an account of the several thesauri now available in the English-speaking world see D. L. Emblem, 'Peter Mark Roget, the word and the man', Longman, 1971.

Theuerdank: a work which has been described as the greatest German book of the Renaissance, being a fictionalized epic of part of Emperor Maximilian I's life, prepared during twelve years by his secretary Marx Treitzsauerwein and Melchior Pfinzing of Nuremberg. It was the first, and only completed volume, of a series of three which was planned to record the events of Maximilian's reign.

The first edition, printed by Johann Schönsperger, was issued in 1517 for private distribution. An edition for general sale appeared in 1519. The work was remarkable for its suite of fine woodcuts, mostly by Leonard Beck (77), Hans Schäufelein (20), and Hans Burgkmair (13), and cut by Jost de Negker. The special type used, based on a gothic script used in the Imperial chancery, was in its later form known as *Fraktur*, q.v.

An excellent folio facsimile edition was published by Müller & Schindler of Stuttgart in 1968.

thickening: the spread of printing ink from the image areas of a lithographic plate.

thickness copy: a publisher's dummy of a book made up of the actual number of pages it will require and using the same paper. It is used, *inter alia*, for designing the jacket and planning lettering for the spine.

thirty-twomo: written 32mo. A book size resulting from (notionally) folding a sheet of paper with five right-angle folds, thus giving a page size of one thirty-second of the sheet. In practice it is seldom practicable to fold paper more than four times, thus a half sheet folded four times would normally be used. From Crown paper the resulting size would be $3\frac{3}{4}$in. × $2\frac{1}{2}$in., viz. Crown 32mo. Also called trigesimo-secundo. (LK)

Thomas, Isaiah, 1749–1831: a general printer and publisher of Worcester, Mass. It was here that he made America's first wove paper, using it for his edition of Charlotte Smith's 'Elegiac sonnets'. Earlier, in 1771, he printed and published the influential weekly *Massachusetts Spy*. He was then living in Boston, but in April 1775, just prior to the Revolutionary War, he moved to Worcester, developing his business there until at one time he had 1,200 employees. His attractive specimen book of 1785 showed mostly Caslon types.

In 1791 he issued a fine Folio Bible, America's first, and in 1810 he published in two volumes his 'History of printing in America' which he claimed was the first of its kind. He also founded the American Antiquarian Society. See C. K. Skipton, 'Isaiah Thomas, printer, patriot, philanthropist', New York, Leo Hart, 1948.

Thomason, George, c. 1601–66: a London bookseller who between 1640 and 1661 assembled a unique and important collection of pamphlets, newspapers and fugitive pieces dealing with daily events in those troubled years.

The Thomason Tracts, as the 22,000 or more pieces are known, were given to the British Museum by George III in 1762.

Thompson, Henry Yates, 1838–1928: an English bibliophile. In 1880 he acquired the *Pall Mall Gazette* from his father-in-law, George Smith. Thompson's main interests as a bibliophile were illuminated manuscripts and books printed on parchment. In 1897 he bought for £30,000 part of the Ashburnham collection, and in 1902 items from John Ruskin's library. At a series of auction sales (1919–21) he sold about a hundred works for £150,000.

thongs: strips of leather to which the sections of a book were sewn, after which the ends of the thongs were laced through holes in the boards and secured on the inner side with wooden pegs or wedges.

This method of securing the body of a book to its covers was used in England from about the 12th century. In the beginning the portion of the thong which lay over the back of the sections was split into two, the sewing thread passing round each in turn. The ends for lacing in the boards were not split. By the mid-16th century thongs used for smaller books were not so split, but the binding was not as strong. After the later 16th century cords gradually replaced thongs. See also *cords, raised bands.*

Thorne, Robert, fl.1794–1820: a London typefounder who was apprenticed to *Thomas Cottrell*, q.v., and whose foundry he acquired in 1794. He is remembered for his fat-face jobbing founts, the popularity of which he did much to further. His skill led the Imprimerie Nationale, Paris, to commission a fount of fat face from his foundry.

Thorne's Fann Street Foundry was subsequently bought by *William Thorowgood*, q.v.

Thorold, Sir John, 1734–1815: a book collector who began his library at Syston Park about 1785. His son of the same name (1773–1831) was a great collector of incunabula, having the Mainz Psalter, Gutenberg Bible, and many Aldines. Most of the latter were rebound in red morocco stamped with a dolphin and anchor by S. Ridge and Richard Storr of Grantham ('the worst provincial binders that England has ever known'. Ricci.)

Thorowgood, William, fl.1820–49: a London type-founder whose first connection with the craft was the purchase in 1820 of the Fann Street Foundry of *Robert Thorne*, q.v., yet within two years he was appointed Letter-Founder to George IV. In 1828 he acquired the foundry of Dr Edmund Fry, and with it an important collection of oriental and greek founts. About 1838 he took Robert Besley (1794–1876) into partnership. Thorowgood retired in 1849 and the firm operated as Robert Besley & Co. Besley's partner, Benjamin Fox, was in 1845 responsible for the heavy egyptian face known as *Clarendon*. In 1861 the firm was joined by the printer Charles Reed (1819–81).

On the death of Fox in 1877 the name was changed to Sir Charles Reed & Sons (one of whom was the type historian and writer Talbot Baines Reed). The firm was sold in 1905 to *Stephenson Blake & Co.*, q.v., of Sheffield.

Thouvenin, Joseph, 1790–1834: a famous Parisian

binder who had been a pupil of the younger *Bozérian,* q.v. Thouvenin was noted for his excellent forwarding as well as, in his later years, for the copies of styles originated by the Padeloups, the Deromes and Le Gascon which he made for his chief patron Nodier. He sought in these revivals to excel the originators. Cathedral bindings were also among those he made for English, Russian and French customers. See also *fanfare.*

thread: see *sewing thread.*

thread sealing: an East German mechanical binding innovation of the 1960s. It reduces the number of processes in case binding by inserting separate U-shaped staples of plastic thread which are adhesive sealed between the second and third stations of a Brehmer-Leipzig folder. Thread-sealed signatures are then gathered and have a gauze lining glued to the back folds. The sections, it will be appreciated, are not sewn to each other or through the gauze. Also known as *fold sealing.*

Three Candles Press: see *O Lochlainn, Colm.*

three-colour reproduction: almost all colour can be reproduced by the superimposing of three colours: yellow, blue green (cyan) and magenta (red). Such plates are obtained by photography through filters of the complementary colours, i.e. red for cyan, blue for yellow and green for magenta ('red'). The possibility of three-colour reproduction is dependent upon the nature of human colour vision. This provides a convenient and economical method for colour printing. The use of a fourth, black printer, is not a technical necessity but in practice makes it much easier to retain good quality. The eye is very sensitive to slight changes of hue such as may occur due to slight variations on one of three colours. The use of a black printing makes it easier to obtain neutral shadows and brightens the picture by making the dense shadows more intense.

It is still difficult to make a perfect black plate and perfect four-colour reproduction would make use of the following facts: a dull green in three colours would be obtained by use of nearly solid yellow and cyan printings with an appreciable magenta printing. The same result could be obtained by use of black instead of the magenta and slightly less yellow and blue. If this could be carried out easily, although four print-ings were used, in any one spot no more than three would be present and in the brightest places only two. Brown would consist of yellow and magenta with a little black and so on.

Not only is it theoretically possible to match any colour with three printings out of the four mentioned above, but unless the colour is an exceptionally bright one the hues of ink are not critical, although to match a particular colour the duller the three primary inks the less black will be required. Until recently it has in fact been the custom to use inks which depart some way from the theoretically desirable. The yellow, although not always the same, was not markedly wrong, but the magenta was often red and the cyan often redder and darker than theory would require. In fact, these colour errors were less serious than might be expected and only caused practical difficulty when bright greens or bright purples were required. As the techniques of colour reproduction still involved a large amount of retouching or fine etching according to the process used there were no added difficulties in obtaining good colour reproduction, except for the bright colours mentioned above. Few scenes in nature and few great paintings contain any of these very bright colours.

The reasons for using such inks were partly lack of good pigments, but probably mostly due to a failure to understand the theoretical requirement. The use of the words 'red' and 'blue' rather than 'magenta' and 'cyan' does emphasize the misunderstanding. It was common to vary the exact hue to suit the subjects. This did not matter when single subjects were printed, but caused serious difficulty when several subjects were printed together.

Today, when rapid scientific development is taking place in colour correction by masking or electronic methods, and when it is normal practice to print many subjects together, the use of standard colours is even more important than the use of theoretically correct colours. Colour letterpress and colour lithographic inks are both standardized in a number of countries including Britain and Germany. The use of the brighter and more correct inks makes much cleaner greens, purples and blues possible, but it also makes even inking more important for the printer, as slight variations in any one ink will cause greater variation in the resultant colour.

The eye, although very critical in its judgement of two objects side by side is in other respects very tolerant. It is well known that the eye adapts itself easily to different lighting systems, e.g. daylight or incandescent, but it is also true that two subjects printed together will require much more careful colour correction and printing than if seen separately, even if the nature of the subject is quite different. The fact that one has a greenish cast and the other a reddish cast may only be obvious when they are side by side. The measurement of colour by physical instruments is still not easily carried out with an accuracy which would satisfy an ordinary man with ordinary colour vision. The critic must realize that the scientific reproduction of colour has still some way to go before it can reproduce all colour accurately and his own judgement may in fact be at fault sometimes, owing to conditions in which he is viewing the reproduction. The use of black or white or coloured surrounds will each cause the picture to appear different.

Although to the layman colour accuracy may seem the most important factor, tone accuracy or good choice of tone separation is even more important. One reproduction may be correct in colour but seem dead when compared with another which is less accurate in colour. A typical example is the reproduction of an oil painting with dense glossy shadows.

Colours affect each other. A colour adjacent to white appears paler than one adjacent to black; red and green each appear much brighter than if side by side. These and other changes can be noticeable enough to cause the same colour to appear markedly different in hue and strength. See also *colour photography*, *colour systems*, *two-colour reproduction*. (HJJ)

three-decker novel: three octavo volumes which, in the early 19th century, became the standard form for publishing fiction. They usually had paper-covered boards and a paper label bearing the title and were not illustrated. In their heyday, 1850–70, format was better, with cloth boards and gold lettering. Circulating libraries were big purchasers ensuring publishers a guaranteed minimum sale. However, production declined in the nineties when the demand for cheap reprints by a public unable to afford either a library subscription or the high cost of a three-decker forced publishers to issue cheap editions. See also *fiction series*, *yellow backs*.

Three Mountains Press: an avant-garde private press established in Paris by the American journalist-publisher William Bird in 1922. After learning to print he bought a Mathieu press and some Caslon type. He engaged Ezra Pound as editor. The two were later joined by Robert McAlmon and Ford Madox Ford who edited the *Transatlantic Review*. Contributors to it included Pound, Gertrude Stein and Ernest Hemingway. Bird sold the press in 1928.

3M Scotchprint: the trade name of a plastic film coated on one side to make it ink receptive. It is translucent and dimensionally stable and used for reproduction pulls of letterpress material (type, half-tones, stereos and electros) for conversion to litho plates. Any good short letterpress black ink is suitable for the pull which, after drying, is placed print-side down on a sheet of litho film and exposed in a contact printing frame. The resulting positive is processed on a litho plate by usual methods.

three-quarter binding: a binding style with the spine and a generous portion of the sides covered in leather or cloth, the rest of the sides being in another coloured cloth or paper.

thrown clear: a map, plan, or illustration printed with

475

a blank page-width guard and folded into the book. The whole of the opened map can thus be thrown clear of the page area for easy reference while the relevant text is being read. Cf. *thrown out*.

thrown out: an illustration printed on paper wider than the pages of the book to which it belongs. The extension beyond page width is folded in. This is the printer's method of accommodating an illustration too wide for the normal page, and thus differs in function from an illustration which is *thrown clear*, q.v. Also known as a *fold-out*.

thumb index: an alphabetical or subject guide to an index or other work of reference, its purpose being to facilitate consultation. It is cut into the fore-edge of a book and is seen as a series of steps or small printed tickets which are positioned and attached by hand.

Thurneysser, Leonhard, 1530–96: an alchemist, author, and sometime printer (of no great merit) who was born in Basle where he first worked as a goldsmith. In 1574 he set up a press and foundry in Berlin, developing his business until at one time he had 200 employees. Orientalia were his speciality and some of his exotic founts were shown in his 'Magna alchymia' 1583. His printing press was taken over by his chief compositor Michael Hentzke, and in 1584 he left for Florence to work as an alchemist.

ticket: a small paper label bearing the printed or engraved name of a bookbinder. They are usually found at the head or foot of the front or rear pastedown. This means of signing a binding occurs in English and French work of the early 18th century, and is still practised. Booksellers also use similar tickets.

Tickhill Psalter: an English Psalter of the early 14th century written, according to an inscription in it (but not universally accepted as genuine), by John Tickyll, Prior of Worksop, Notts. It is thought more probable that he merely applied and burnished the gold. It was skilfully illuminated by others. Features of the illustrations are scrolls which form the basis of nearly every page; the scenes depicted are based on the Old Testament. The figures are characterized by a certain simplicity, and drawings from nature of flowers also appear. The work is now in the New York Public Library.

tied letters: see *ligature*.

Tieffenbach, E. W.: see *Officina Serpentis*.

Tiemann, Walter, 1876–1951: a German book illustrator and typographer. From 1920–45 he directed

the Staatliche Akademie für graphische Künste, Leipzig. Tiemann illustrated books for the *Insel-Verlag*, and designed at least sixteen type-faces for *Klingspor*, qq.v. He was associated with Carl Ernst Poeschel in founding the *Janus-Presse*, q.v.

(With GU)

ties: 1. tapes fixed to the front edges of a book cover to facilitate handling and to secure a volume of unbound plates. Their use is common with vellum bindings which tend to warp. A form of leather strap was used for this purpose by Coptic binders in 9th century Egypt, and plaited thongs were so used in England from the 12th century. See also *clasps*.

2. terminations to lines tooled on each side of raised bands on the spine of a book which are continued on to the upper and lower covers as an ornamental feature.

tight back: a book cover which is glued to the body of the book at the back, a style used for flexibly sewn and library bindings. No supporting hollow is formed

Tight back

when the book is opened. A weakness is that the spinal lettering tends to crack with use and the style is rarely used today. Cf. *hollow back*. See also *sawn-in back*.

Timperley, Charles, 1794–*c*. 1873: a London printer remembered for two books on his craft, 'Printers' manual', 1838, and 'Dictionary of printers and printing', 1839.

tint blocks: blocks for printing flat background colours; they may be engraved in various patterns or stipples to give an illusion of colour, depth, or tone. See also *mechanical tints*.

tinted lithographs: monochrome lithographic prints enriched by being given a second printing from a stone bearing semi-transparent ink in shades of straw or beige. This was done to soften the sharp contrast of black ink and white paper. Senefelder may have invented the tinted lithograph, though the idea of tinting prints in a buff tone to soften them had been used by William Gilpin for his aquatints of the 1770s.

The popularity in England of tinted lithographs was probably influenced by the publication in Munich, from 1817, of reproductions of paintings in the King of Bavaria's collections at Munich and Schleissheim, printed by J. Strixner and F. Piloty. For some of these two tint-stones were used, and for some, part of the tint was removed to enhance the highlights. Ackermann's first tinted lithograph was issued in London in 1817, but the artist-publisher *Hullmandel*, q.v., was the principal worker in this medium. After 1820, when the introduction of india paper (which had a natural buff tint) made the use of a tinting stone less necessary, the popularity of the process waned until the mid-1830s when a collection of James Harding's drawings led a revival with better techniques. These included the addition of three or four tones to the black working as seen in David Robert's 'The Holy Land', 1842–9. Cf. *lithotint*.

tip: a thin flat brush consisting of a few camel or squirrel hairs fixed between two pieces of card. It is used for taking up gold leaf and laying it on a surface to be gilded.

Tipografia Camerale: from 1549 the earliest privileged printing office for the Vatican. Soon after printing began in Rome the Popes commissioned work from several craftsmen, but from 1515 Antonio Blado held an exclusive privilege and in 1549 was given the title 'Tipografo Camerale'. Blado, who printed the suppressed 'Index expurgatorius' in 1557 and the approved edition in 1559, was succeeded by his heirs who held the privilege until 1593.

In 1610 the Tipografia Camerale and the Typographia Apostolica Vaticana were combined as the *Stamperia Vaticana*, q.v. See also *Congregatio de Propaganda Fide*.

Tipografia del Popolo Romano: the special press set up in Rome in 1560 at the instigation of Pius IV. It was to work under direct Papal control, and particularly to print the decrees and other papers issued by the Council of Trent. Paulus Manutius was invited from Venice to direct it which he did from 1561 to 1570. The first imprint used was 'in aedibus Popolo Romano'. The press ceased to function shortly after 1570.

Tipografia Poliglotta Vaticana: see *Stamperia Vaticana*.

Tipografia Vaticana: see *Typographia Apostolica Vaticana*.

tipped in: said of separately printed illustrations or maps which are trimmed to the page size of the book, the inner margins being pasted into the text before gathering. An illustration so affixed is also known as a *paste in*.

tipping machine: a bookbinding machine for the gluing of end-papers or single plates on to folded sheets. There are several models. Usually the folded section and end-paper or plate are fed in separately from left to right, edged with paste along the back edge, and pressed together. (GU)

Tipping machine

Tiptoft, John, Earl of Worcester, *c.* 1427–70: a classical and humanist scholar and a wealthy bibliophile who was accused of having sacked the libraries of Italy in order to enrich England with beautiful books. He certainly bought books from Vespasiano da Bisticci in Florence, and commissioned the writing and embellishing of others in Padua. He bequeathed his books to the universities of Cambridge and Oxford where eleven of them have been identified.

Tiptoft was beheaded for treason. Of this Thomas Fuller wrote 'Then did the axe at one blow cut off more learning in England than was left in the heads of all surviving nobility.'

tissued plate: see *interleaved* (2).

titanium dioxide pigments: fine white fillers added to paper pulp to improve the opacity and brightness.

title-page: the page at the beginning of a book giving the title and sub-title, the author's name and his qualifications, the publisher's imprint, and sometimes a colophon and the date of publication. The back often states the edition or impression, printer's name, statement of copyright, and occasionally typographical information.

The development of the title-page was gradual and may be said to have begun with 'Bulla cruciatae contra turcos . . .' printed by Fust and Schöffer in 1463; this, however, was a *label title*, q.v. A further approach to the title-page proper was in the 'Kalendarius' of Johannes Müller, called Regiomontanus, issued in 1476 at Venice by Ratdolt and Maler; the introductory verse on the first page was surrounded by a graceful woodcut border of flower and leaf designs while the printers, place of printing and date were stated. The first book to include on its title-page

Dialogue de la bie et de
La Mort, Composé en Toscan par
Maistre Innocent Ringhiere
Gentilhomme Boulongnois.

Nouvellement traduit en Francoys par Jehan
Lonntan Recteur de Chastillon & Gembes.

A Lyon,
De L'Imprimerie de Robert Granjon.
Mil. D.c. L.vij.

Robert Granjon 1557

D. JUNII

JUVENALIS

ET

AULI

PERSII FLACCI

SATYRAE.

BIRMINGHAMIAE:
Typis JOHANNIS BASKERVILLE.
M DCC LXI.

1761

THE

HOLY BIBLE

Containing the Old and New
Testaments : Translated out
of the Original Tongues and
with the former Translations
diligently compared and revised by His Majesty's special
Command

Appointed to be read in Churches

OXFORD
Printed at the University Press
1935

Bruce Rogers

JUDY EGERTON

GEORGE STUBBS

anatomist and animal painter

1976   THE TATE GALLERY 1976

the information now customary (see above) was printed by Wolfgang Stöckel of Leipzig in 1500.

The first English book with a title-page was Canutus's 'A passing gode lityll boke . . . agenst the pestilence', printed by W. de Machlinia, *c.* 1490.

The possibilities of the title-page for decorative display were realized quite early in the 16th century. Not a few 16th-century title-pages had as the basic element of their design the Roman columned portico, the lettering being printed between the pillars. This was common to books printed in all European countries where printing was then practised, and may be thought to signify that by reading the succeeding pages one entered the classical world (it will be remembered that most books of the period were classics or written in Latin). An important subsidiary decorative feature was the medallion, based on Roman coins. Early Spanish title-pages in particular are typified by large heraldic emblems.

The colophon, which from ancient Egyptian times had supplied the author's name and title, gradually fell into disuse. See also *incipit, initia, label title.*

title-page border: a pattern built up from type ornaments set round the matter on the title-page.

title signature: a signature mark is not printed on the first sheet of a book, this being termed the *title sheet,* thus the term *signature A (or 1)* is not used. The second sheet, however, is printed with the mark *B (or 2),* thereby indicating that there is a section to precede it.
(LK)

titling alphabet: a fount of capital letters cast without shoulders so that the strokes of the character extend to the limits of the body, there being no beard. This is done to balance the space between lines. Ranging numerals and punctuation marks are included, but not lower-case letters.

titulus: introductory words traditionally written in capital letters at the head of chapters in manuscript books. They often filled several lines. When marking up a blank page space was reserved for the titulus to be added after the text had been written. For an important manuscript the titulus was written in gold ink by a chrysographer, otherwise in red or blue ink by a rubrisher. A large initial capital was added last. See also *incipit.*

token: a printer's unit of work done, being the number of impressions made per hour by two pressmen working a hand-press. Prior to the 19th century this was the basis of calculating their wages. The token was notionally 250 unbacked sheets. Achieving this rate depended on the nature of copy, the size of type used, the size of sheet, ink stiffness, the quality desired and so on. Difficult copy was charged more. The term passed out of use with the advent of the powered printing machine.

An early reference to the speed of working a press occurs in the colophon of Abraham Conat's edition of 'Arba'a turim', Mantua, 6 June 1476, where it is stated that the book was printed at the rate of 250 perfected sheets a day. See also *take.*

Tom-Gallon Trust: an award made in alternate years by the Trust administrators, the Society of Authors, being about £100 a year for two years paid to a novelist of modest means.

tonal colour: the effect of lightness or heaviness on a printed page. Among factors affecting this are the type face used, e.g. Caslon and Perpetua have light faces, Bodoni and Plantin dark; the use of leads, which increase lightness; paper surface, e.g. an antique paper will make the type appear darker, and the intensity of the ink used. See also *full colour.*

toned paper: printing paper of a light buff or cream colour.

tone engraving: see *wood engraving.*

Tonson, Jacob, fl. 1678–1736: an eminent Restoration publisher and bookseller who issued works by Congreve, Dryden, Milton and Pope. In 1709 he published Rowe's edition of Shakespeare in six octavo volumes, illustrated with forty-five engravings. This was the first small format Shakespeare, the first to be illustrated, and remained the standard edition for many years.

Tonson did much to systematize publisher-author relations and to develop the public's reading habits and taste. He was secretary of the blue-blood Kit Cat Club, and in 1712 became co-publisher of the famous political journal *The Spectator.*

About 1720 he retired and was succeeded by his nephew *Jacob II.* When the latter died in 1736 his son *Jacob III,* co-publisher of Johnson's Shakespeare, continued the business until his death in 1767. It then ceased. See H. M. Geduld, 'Prince of publishers: a study of the work and career of Jacob Tonson', Indiana U.P., 1969, and K. Lynch, 'Jacob Tonson, Kit-Cat publisher', Knoxville, Tenn., 1971.

tooling: the impressing by hand of lettering and decoration on book covers. The work is done by the *finisher* who uses heated brass letters, dies, pallets and roll tools. Cloth bindings are given little decoration, often only the author's name and title, lettered on the spine.

Blind tooling is done with heated tools but no gold or foil; for *gold tooling,* q.v., gold in leaf or spool form is used. The use of a press and large dies is known as *blocking.*

The finisher at work
The book is held in a clamp while decoration on the spine is impressed with a heated iron

The main stages of tooling are: (a) *preparing*, which includes marking with a bone folder the position of the chief lines, *blinding in*, the object being to enable the priming to be done at the precise place for the decoration, washing over with very thin paste and water to fill the pores before *priming* with glair, and rubbing over with vaseline; (b) *laying-on*, which means applying the leaf so that there is an unbroken layer of gold over the whole surface to be decorated; (c) *pressing the gold* with heated tools (which should just cease to hiss before use), whereupon the albumen in the glair coagulates and fixes the gold to the leather; (d) *cleaning and polishing*, the surplus gold being wiped off with a rubber from which it is later recovered, any vaseline is wiped off with petrol and cottonwool, and the finished decoration is cleaned, polished and pressed between polished nickel plates. See also *skewings*.

(With GU)

top edge gilt: a book having only the top edge gilded, the fore and foot edges being left plain.
Abbreviated *t.e.g.*

The finisher's hand tools
Top, book clamp, two irons, three rolls, four pallets and a laying-on wheel. Below, three small dies and a lettering pallet

topical headline: a running head printed at the top of a page. It may be the chapter title or briefly descriptive of a page subject.

Topié, Michel, fl.1488–1502: of Pyrmont; a printer who worked in Lyons with *Jacques Heremberck*, q.v., from 1488 until 1492. In 1495 he worked with *Johann Neumeister*, q.v., to whose business he succeeded in 1498. Together they printed a fine Uzès Missal in 1495 with interesting pictorial woodcut initials.

tops and tails: an expression used in some printing offices for preliminary and subsidiary matter.

Toribio-Medina, José, 1852–1931: a Chilean scholar and bibliographer whose 'La imprenta en Mexico: 1539–1821', 8 vols, Santiago, 1907–12 and other writings are the foundation of Hispano-American bibliography. In 1926 he gave his collection of 40,000 books to the National Library of Chile. His 77 volume 'Bibliotheca Hispano-Americana, 1493–1810', published between 1898 and 1907, was reprinted in 1967.

Torresano, Andrea, 1451–1528: a printer of Venice who in 1481 bought the punches, matrices and types of Jenson on the latter's death. In 1499 his daughter married Aldus Manutius and subsequently a business association was established. Books bore the imprint 'In aedibus Aldi et Andreae Asolani Soceri'. The Torresano family continued to manage the press after the death of Aldus, a five-volume edition of Galen's works, 1525, being their most important production. See D. Bernoni, 'Dei Torresani, Blado, e Ragazzoni . . .', Milan, 1890, repr. 1968.

Tory, Geofroy, *c.* 1480–1533: of Bourges, a bookseller, engraver and royal printer. Before opening his shop in Paris, *c.* 1522, he ·edited Latin texts for Parisian printers. His studies in Italy inspired his designs for the roman alphabet, and also for the simple and clear woodcut border decorations characteristic of his title-pages. His printing from his own press may date from 1529 when his 'Champ fleury' appeared. This work of interest to all letter designers is available in an English translation by George B. Ives, N.Y., Grolier Club, 1927, repr. Dover Publications, 1967. See also *entrelac initials, pot cassé.*

total publication: a feature of modern publishing whereby a publisher will issue an author's work in hard-cover form and also, but not necessarily at the same time, as a mass-market paperback under the publisher's own and separate paperback imprint. An example is Collins of Glasgow who own the Fontana paperback imprint. This is the publisher's alternative to leasing paperback rights to an independent publisher for a royalty of which as much as 50% to 60% is given to the author.

The term does not apply to simultaneous first publication under one imprint in hard-cover and softback form, or to publication subsequent to first issue of a 'quality' paperback edition with text and illustrations unchanged from the hard-cover edition.

Tottel, Richard, fl.1553–93: a London printer and an original member of the Stationers' Company in which he held office.

He had a patent for all common law books, but is remembered now for his literary publications. Notable were More's 'Dialogue of comfort', 1553; Lydgate's 'Fall of princes', 1554; and Grimald's translation of Cicero's 'De officiis', 1556. In June he brought out his famous 'Miscellany' of 271 poems: included were the poems of Sir Thomas Wyatt and Henry Howard, Earl of Surrey – the only form in which their verse survived for posterity. Wyatt developed the Elizabethan sonnet, and Surrey was the first to use blank verse. The Miscellany, entitled 'Songes and sonettes, written by the ryght honorable Lorde Henry Haward late Earle of Surrey, and other' was a significant book in our literature. The first edition survives in a single copy, now in the Bodleian Library. It was issued with additions and deletions in the same year. A Scolar Press facsimile of the first edition was issued in 1970.

Totum: a complete Roman Breviary.

Tour, Henri du: see *Keere, Hendrik van den.*

Tournes, Jean, de, 1504–64: an important scholar-printer of Lyons whose printing and publishing business survived in the family until 1780 (after 1585 in Geneva). De Tournes was trained by Sébastien Gryphius before setting up his own press in 1540. His books were carefully printed, being noted both for their scholarship and elegance, and in the last decade of his life he was probably the leading French printer. Books issuing from his press were remarkable for the beauty of the title-pages, the suites of floriated and historiated initials, the delicate woodcut borders and headpieces of arabesque fleurons, later to be cast as types by Robert Granjon. Much of his illustrative material was the work of *Bernard Salomon*, q.v.

De Tournes' major works were editions of Petrarch, 1545; Dante, 1552; Froissart, 1559–60; and Claude Paradin's 'Les Alliances généalogiques des rois de France', 1561, with its exceptionally imaginative *mise en page*. His son of the same name succeeded him and effected the move to Geneva. See A. Cartier, 'Bibliographie des éditions des de Tournes', 2 vols, Paris, 1937–8.

toy books: the generic name given by American and English publishers during the 19th century to small illustrated books for young children. The first toy books usually had eight leaves of hand-coloured pictures with minimal text and were issued in series to encourage collecting. Alphabets and simply told fairy tales were popular themes. As early as 1830 when Mahlor Day of New York advertized twenty-nine of his children's titles as 'six-cent toys' he already had 150 on his list. The lively coloured pictures and simple text of most later toy books were anticipated by Heinrich Hoffmann's 'Lustige Geschichten und drolliger Bilder', Frankfurt am Main, *c.* 1844. The chromolitho illustrations were by Hoffmann. With the third edition the title was changed to 'Strewwelpeter' and is so known the world over. An edition in English was printed in Leipzig in 1848.

The first toy books printed in colour in America were manufactured by John and Edmund McLoughlin of New York who began a flourishing trade in them in the mid-1850s.

The earliest toy book publisher of note in England was the firm of Frederick Warne and his one-time partner George Routledge. Warne's popular 'Aunt Louisa' series was mostly printed by J. M. Kronheim. The artist Walter Crane had his own series of 'Crane's Toy Books' of which the first, 'Railroad alphabet', 1865, was followed by nearly fifty others before 1886. His publisher was Routledge who began his 'sixpenny series' in 1866. In that year he issued 'Sing a song of sixpence' for which Crane designed cover, title-page, illustrations and text. The main printer for Routledge was Edward Evans who from 1877 commissioned Randolph Caldecott (first book 'John Gilpin', 1878) and Kate Greenaway (first book 'Under the window', 1878). Both worked for him for several years and enjoyed considerable fame and success.

Toy books were usually issued singly in paper covers, at first printed black on drab paper but later lithographed in colour on yellow paper. Collections of them were bound up for the Christmas trade with cover styles ranging from glazed printed boards to heavily stamped and gilded cloth inlaid with coloured pictures.

There were also *rag books* of untearable cloth. The cloth was printed on one side only and the page edges were crimped at head and foot, bolts uncut. These began about 1855 and at first had hand-coloured pictures. They continue to be made.

Another variation, known as *pop-up books* or *stand-up books*, had panoramas or stage settings in which several layers of thick paper were automatically raised when the book was opened to give an effect of perspective to the cut-out characters of the story.

Flicker books were popular in Britain in the 1930s. They were of small size and contained cartoon stories in which a sequence of figures drawn against a static background appeared to be animated as the pages were quickly flipped over from cover to cover.

The spirit of the Victorian toy book, if not the name, was revived when James Clegg (1905–76) began his by now world famous 'Ladybird' series of brightly coloured small books for young children. From 1940 they were published by his employers Wills & Hepworth Ltd of Loughborough. In 1961 Clegg acquired the company and expanded the business until its take-over in 1971 by the Pearson Longman Group. Books were all of one size, a single printed sheet folded into one section, and were remarkably cheap. The series of some 400 titles in print offers entertainment and instruction to young children in many countries who collect and cherish them as well-loved toys. By the mid-70s annual sales were twenty-five million. See also *Newbery*.

Toy, Robert, fl.1540–56: a London printer. From his premises in St Paul's churchyard he issued several theological works, Matthew's folio Bible, 1551, and a reprint of Thynne's Chaucer in 1555. He was a member and benefactor of the Stationers' Company.

His son *Humphrey* (*c*. 1540–77) succeeded to the business and was an occasional official of the Company. He issued works in Welsh, and also William Salusbury's 'A playne and a familiar introduction, teachyng how to pronounce Welshe', printed for him by H. Denham in 1567 (STC 21615).

tract: 1. a book or pamphlet devoted to one subject, usually of a religious or political nature. Also known as a *tractate*.

2. a pamphlet made from a single sheet.

Tracy, Walter: a newspaper type face designer, printing consultant and RDI, who began his career in 1930 as an apprentice compositor, studying at London's Central School of Arts and Crafts prior to working at the Baynard Press from 1935 to 1947.

In 1947 he joined the Linotype company for whom he planned the house magazine *Linotype Matrix* and subsequently designed several newspaper text faces, notably Jubilee, 1954 (named for the firm's fiftieth anniversary and first used by the *Glasgow Herald*); Adsans, 1958, a $4\frac{3}{4}$-point type used for advertisements, as was his wide-face Maximus, 1967. His Linotype Modern, 1969, was chosen by the *Daily Telegraph* as a substitute for Jubilee in which the paper had been printed since 1962. Linotype Modern, which was inspired by the Didot modern of 1784, has since been renamed Telegraph Modern.

In 1971 *The Times* announced that his Times-Europa (of which there was a trial showing at IPEX 1971) would replace the famous Morison Times Roman of 1929. The reason given for the change was that the 8-point size, used for most newspapers, with its small x-height, fine serifs and high ascenders, imposed limitations on ease of reading incompatible with the faster printing with newly formulated inks on thinner paper which were in use by the end of the 1960s. Tracy gave Europa characters strengthened serifs, a larger x-height, increased width and a better proportion between upper and lower case letters. The first issue of *The Times* set in the new type was dated 9 October 1972. See A. Hutt, 'Walter Tracy, type designer', *Penrose Annual*, 1973.

trade binding: 1. the plain calf or sheep bindings in which books were sold in England from the 15th–18th century: they only rarely had spinal lettering. As an alternative, and until the 19th century, the purchaser usually bought a book unbound or enclosed in wrappers for later binding to his order. See also *in boards*.

2. another name for publisher's binding.

Trade books: see *Chapter books*.

trade books: an imprecise term generally taken to include adult fiction and nonfiction, paperbacks and children's books. It does not include educational textbooks, scientific, medical and technical books.

trade catalogues: lists of books, systematically arranged by author or subject, and issued by publishers for the use of booksellers, or by booksellers for making their stocks known to the public. Georg Willer, an Augsburg bookseller, issued the first-known catalogue of this kind; this was a subject list of 256 titles, dated 1564. Catalogues were also issued at the great German book trade fairs of Leipzig (the first was by Henning Gross, 1595) and Frankfurt (1564): the fairs are still held.

In England, Andrew Maunsell (*d*. 1596), a bookseller of St Paul's, was the first publisher of an important alphabetical trade list of books. His earliest was a list of religious works; his second, medical and scientific. See also *Term catalogues*.

trade edition: copies of a standard work which are regularly printed and supplied to booksellers at wholesale rates.

trade sales: auction sales of publishers' remainders at which only booksellers were invited to bid. The practice of disposing in this way of surplus stocks may have begun in late 17th-century Britain. After 1820 such sales also took place in Philadelphia and Boston, U.S.A. The practice of holding large-scale auctions for the trade appears to have ceased about 1870.

A special type of sale to booksellers was apparently originated in London in the mid-18th century by Andrew Millar and his successor in business Thomas Cadell as a means of disposing of surplus stock. Millar invited a number of leading booksellers to dinner at a tavern. After the meal lists of books were circulated to the guests who were then invited to bid for them. The first recorded sale was in 1753, and they were usually held in November. As much as £19,000 was reached at one dinner. John Murray, one of several publishers who held similar sales in the 19th century, realised £15,000 for his publications in March 1836. They continued until later in the century. See also *remainders*.

trade terms: publishers' discount scales and payment dates allowed to booksellers.

trade typesetter: a business house which maintains an extensive mechanical typesetting plant manned by skilled compositors, and a wide range of type faces including many for foreign languages, as well as the special sorts required for mathematical and technical setting. Small printing firms send special jobs to a trade typesetter and then machine the result. Minor correcting can be done by the customer, extensive alterations can be returned for a re-set. The cost per thousand ens varies according to the type face specified, its size and availability.

trailing-blade coater: an off-machine paper-coating device, commercially introduced by the Rice Barton Corporation of America, which uses a thin flexible blade, trailing in the direction of web travel, to scrape off surplus coating. It is suitable for high-speed mass production, working best with light weight clay-casein-latex coatings, though medium or heavy coatings can also be applied.

The base paper can be pre-coated on the Fourdrinier to give a good foundation for the final coating. Speeds of up to 2,000 feet per minute are possible. High-velocity air drying hardens the surface before the paper is fed into the supercalender. See also *Champion coater*, *coater*.

Trajanus-Presse: the private press of the Frankfurt typefounding firm D. Stempel A.G. It was established by Gotthard de Beauclair in 1951 for the production of newsletters, type specimens, etc., in addition to occasional books printed on paper specially made by the Hahnemühle and hand bound by Willy Pingel. Beauclair designed the early books, but after 1960 when his duties as managing director of the *Insel-Verlag*, q.v., left insufficient time, Wolfgang Tiessen assisted.

The excellence and high standard of these books has led to their collection by typophiles and others. A feature of many has been the use of wood engravings by young illustrators. A notable edition of 'Die Frösche' by Aristophanes, issued in 1962, included engravings by *Imre Reiner*, q.v.

tranchefile: extra wires parallel to the chains at each end of the papermaking mould, and spaced a short distance from them. They leave an impression in the paper about half-way between the outer chain lines and the edges of the sheet. These are particularly noticeable in certain French papers.

transfer: a surfaced paper bearing a thickly inked image taken from an impression on a non-lithographic surface for transferring to a lithographic plate or stone. Lithographic transfers can be made from engraved plates, music on pewter plates, letterpress (including half-tone blocks) and drawings made with lithographic crayons or ink on transfer papers or on hard-sized papers. A transfer made from an existing lithographic forme is properly termed a *retransfer*, q.v.

(GU)

transfer lettering: dry-ink images of letters, numerals, rules and so on which are carried on the underside oe semi-transparent sheets. Pressure applied above the letter required will cause it to adhere to a surfacf below. An example is *Letraset*.

A wide range of proprietary makes and type faces is available. Such sheets are invaluable in the publisher's production department for art work and for adding display lettering to jackets instead of setting up type. Also known as *rub-off lettering*.

transfer paper: the paper on which an inked impression is brought to a lithographic surface where it then becomes the printing forme. It is usually a fairly thin, semi-gummed paper bearing a surface coating of substances soluble in water: there are many varieties.

(GU)

transfer press: a lithographic hand-press in which pressure is exerted by means of a scraper, i.e. a narrow disc standing on edge, usually of hard wood covered with leather. The scraper is placed against the plate or sheet of cardboard which covers the transfer paper resting on the flat forme; the bed is then rolled forward under the scraper. Hand or motor power may be used. Presses of larger size, intended for transferring on to large machine plates, sometimes have a steel roller instead of a scraper.   (GU)

transitional: a name sometimes given to the type-face designed by *John Baskerville*, q.v., and its derivatives. While retaining the bracketed serifs of old face it suggests in its precision the engraved quality of modern-face types.

transliterate: to render the letters or characters of one alphabet by those of another so as to represent the same sounds.

transparent bindings: books covered with vellum which has been treated with pearl ash to make it transparent. This process was patented by *Edwards of Halifax*, q.v., in 1785.

transpose: the instruction written in the margin of proofs as *trs.* to indicate that the order of lines, words or letters must be changed.

trapping: a printing fault formerly known as *crystallization*, q.v.

Trattner, Johann Thomas, 1717–98: a Viennese printer, publisher and typefounder. He published several books on the history of printing. Of the extensive range of type ornaments he cut his celebrated 'angel' is shown under *flowers*, q.v. See also his 'Abdruck von . . . Röslein und Zierrathen', Vienna, 1760, repr. 1927.

Trautz, Georges, 1808–79: born at Pforzheim in Germany. Between 1822 and 1825 he learned binding in Heidelberg, and worked in other German towns including Munich and Stuttgart before coming to Paris in 1830. He worked as a gilder with Kleinhans and Debès until 1833 when he entered the employ of *Bauzonnet*, q.v., becoming his partner by 1840, and continuing alone after 1851.

He avoided the current fashion for straight-grained morocco and the coarser decorative features of the mass binding trade, turning instead to the sound forwarding of Boyet, the richness of the Èves, and the elegance of the Padeloups for his inspiration. Although Trautz did not invent styles his personal interpretations of those by the great master binders were freed by their brilliance from the taint of plagiarism.

The firm's bindings made between 1840 and 1851

were signed Bauzonnet-Trautz: after 1851 they were signed Trautz-Bauzonnet.

For nearly forty years Trautz was the most fashionable binder of Europe. His dazzling creations, sumptuous and costly, were commissioned by none but the wealthiest book-collectors of Europe and America. They were imitated and counterfeited both during and after his lifetime; nor was he without detractors, and it was said 'Avec lui, le livre fut ferme au toucher, lourd à peser, dur à ouvrir . . . et délicieusement ovoïde'.

In 1869 he was awarded the cross of the Légion d'honneur, the first binder to be so recognised, and he died at the height of his fame.

traveller's samples: formerly certain signatures of a book, case-bound and jacketed, for submission to prospective buyers. Proofs and jackets now serve the purpose. Cf. *blad*.

travelling tympan: see *shifting tympan*.

tree-marbled calf: calf book covers decorated with a pattern resembling a tree and its branches. With the book clamped in an inclined position water is flowed down the leather to a central point at the bottom of each board. When the area which is to form the trunk and branches is thoroughly wet copperas and salts of tartar are spinkled on it in turn. These act chemically to form a permanent dark stain on the leather. The spine is not treated. After drying, the boards are filled in, pressed and highly polished. Chemical action may continue for years leading to disintegration of the covers.

The style is found in England from about 1775, and its introduction has been attributed to *Johann Baumgarten*, q.v. It was in occasional use until the mid-20th century. See also *Etruscan bindings*, *marbled calf*, *mottled calf*.

Trevecca Press: a printing press established about 1770 at Trevecca, near Talgarth in Wales, as part of the Methodist revival there. The press appears to have been erected at the instigation of Howell Harris who led the Methodist community. The name of the first printer is unknown, but Thomas Roberts, his apprentice, was printer until *c*. 1796. 'E. Roberts & Co.' and 'Hughes & Co.' were subsequent imprints until 1805 when the press was moved to Talgarth, remaining in operation until at least 1829.

Many of the hundred or so works issued between 1770 and 1805 were Welsh hymn-books, religious propaganda, and elegies (marwnadau). Small pica and long primer were the two sizes of type used and there was a case of ornaments for borders, initials and tailpieces.

A collection of Trevecca Press publications is in Cardiff Public Library.

Treveris, Peter, fl.1522–32: a printer of Southwark, London. He is remembered for several small grammatical tracts; an edition of Robert Whittinton's 'Syntaxis', 1522; a 'Grete herball', 1526 (STC 13176); and John de Trevisa's translation into English of Higden's 'Polychronicon', 1527.

Tridentine Index: an alternative name for the *Index librorum prohibitorum*, q.v.

trigesimo-secundo: see *thirty-twomo*.

Trilith N: the trade name of a British pre-sensitized multi-metal negative printing plate. The plate of steel, copper and chrome is factory coated with a negative-working light-sensitive resin. It is claimed that these plates will give consistent quality of colour during long runs on web-offset machines.

trimmed edges: properly, said of a book having a cut top edge, and with only the larger projecting leaves of the tail and fore-edge trimmed down; they are thus left with a rough appearance. Cf. *cut edges*.

trimmed flush: see *cut flush*.

trimmers: various tools for planing and cutting used when casting types, stereos, or making blocks, etc., to ensure that adjacent surfaces will all be at right-angles and fit flush. Also known as *dressers*. See also *edge trimmer* (1).   (GU)

trimming: the bookbinding process of shearing away about ⅛in. from each edge of a sewn book: the folds are thereby removed. Cf. *cutting*. See also *edge trimmer* (2), *guillotine*.

trindle: an iron fork. Two are used by a forwarder when cutting the fore-edge of a book. They are inserted between the spine and the boards which are folded back.

triple lining: a method of *lining up*, q.v., used for better-quality cased books. The work is done mechanically in seven stages. Briefly, these are the first coating of the back with glue; application of a strip of mull, inset slightly from the top and bottom edges of the back; second gluing; application of a broad strip of three-taped mull which has a carry-over on either side of the back for securing to the case; third gluing; positioning and securing of a crepe manila lining, with head- and tailbands if required; and rubbing down with pneumatic rollers.

Troper: a book containing the musical interpolations or tropes. Tropes were the words or verses of embellishment to the text of a Mass, and they were discontinued when the Roman Missal was revised under Pius V (1566–72).

Trovillion Press: a private press established in 1908 at Herrin, Illinois, by Hal Trovillion, newspaper editor and proprietor. Some years later his wife partnered him. When the press closed in the early 1960s they had issued more than fifty books, some by British authors, including reprints of 16th and 17th century herbals. Copies may be seen in the British Library. See H. Schauinger, 'A bibliography of Trovillion private press', Herrin, 1943.

ts.: *typescript*, q.v.

TS: the abbreviation for *tub-sized*, q.v.

Tschichold, Jan, 1902–74: one of Europe's leading calligraphers and typographers. He studied for three years at the Leipzig Akademie für graphische Künste und Buchgewerbe, returning there to teach calligraphy after a period in Dresden. At the same time (1921) he worked as a graphic artist under the guidance of Walter Tiemann at the Insel-Verlag. From 1927–33 he lectured on typography in Munich and then settled in Basle as a refugee immigrant, working as a book designer and consultant.

In 1935 he came to England as a consultant to Lund Humphries designing, *inter alia*, the 1938 *Penrose Annual*. After war years in Basle he returned to London in 1947 as adviser to Penguin Books Ltd., being 'put in charge of Penguin production, and many printers will remember what a stimulating, painful and almost alarming impact he had on composing rooms up and down the country. No detail of production was overlooked . . . meticulous and immensely detailed layouts were followed by revises without number . . .' ('Penguins progress, 1935–1960').

In his 'Die neue Typographie', 1928, which was a fundamental statement of book design emphasising above all the importance of attention to details, he advocated asymmetrical typography and the use of sanserif type for text setting, but this idea was never widely accepted and he later abandoned it. His several books on lettering, type and book design have been highly regarded in Europe and also America where he was awarded the American Institute of Graphic Arts gold medal in 1954. Britain appointed him an honorary RDI in 1965, and in the same year he received the Gutenberg Prize from his native Leipzig.

Early types designed by him included Transito, 1931, cut as a display fount for Typefoundry Amsterdam, and Saskia, 1931, for Schelter and Giesecke. In 1960 he began designing the multi-purpose type Sabon for joint manufacture by the German house of Linotype, Britain's Monotype and Stempel A.G. of Frankfurt. It is named after *Jacques Sabon*, q.v., its inspiration being a roman of Garamont and an italic of Granjon which had both appeared on the 1592 specimen sheet of the Egenolff-Berner foundry. It was probably the first face to be specially designed for photosetters, casting machines and foundry type. First use of Sabon was by Gotthard de Beauclair at his Trajanus-Presse in 1966. See R. McLean, 'Jan Tschichold: typographer', Lund Humphries, 1975.

tub-sized: hand-made sheets of waterleaf which have been dipped into a tub of animal glue, gelatine or a prepared starch (or a combination of these). Sheets are dried on ropes of cow-hair or hessian (once known as *trebles*). They are then glazed. When tub-sizing machine-made papers the roll coming from the Four-drinier is unwound and fed into a tub of size from which it emerges to be rolled, dried and calendered. Tub-sized paper is strong and has a high resistance to moisture. Abbreviated as *TS*. Cf. *animal-sized, engine sized*. See also *surface sizing*.

tumbler scheme: the method of perfecting sheets printed from a forme imposed in the oblong or land-scape manner. To obtain correct page sequence the sheet must be turned, or tumbled, in its short direction. See also *work and tumble*.

tummy band: a detachable strip of paper folded round a book and intended by its bright colour and arresting lettering to attract purchasers' attention at points of sale. Books which have been filmed are often so treated.

tung: a wood oil used as an alternative to linseed oil in printing ink.

Türkenkalender, 1454: a minor work attributed to the press of Gutenberg, known from the unique copy in Munich (missing since 1945). It begins 'Eyn manung der cristenheit widder die durken . . .' and under each month gives a call in verse for various people to fight the Turks. The text ends with the words 'Eyn gut selig nuwe Jar', the first New Year's greeting to be printed. The calendar was for 1455.

The type used was an early version of the 42-line Bible fount, and is found in the Donatus grammar and other small pieces ascribed to Gutenberg as well as in the 36-line Bible. The Kalender is held to be the first example of printing in German.

Turkey leather: also known simply as *turkey*; the name given to leather prepared from goatskins first imported from Turkey to Venice in the early 16th century and used for bookbinding. The skins were prepared with oil before the hair was removed, and further treatment included staining them in a distinctive shade of red before tanning with sumach. For nearly two centuries most goatskins used for fine

486

Türkenkalender, 1454 (Reduced)

binding in Europe came from Turkey (in a range of colours), but long after their import diminished the names *Turkey morocco* and *Levant morocco* were given to goatskins finished with a fine hard grain or a bold cross grain wherever produced. See also *morocco*.

Turkish manuscript painting: the majority of Turkish manuscripts which survive in European collections are not illustrated even though, in the case of the Koran, they may be illuminated. In Istanbul during the 15th century (i.e. the post-Byzantine era) calligraphers were numerous and honoured: painters were not.

The finest Turkish work was done in the 16th and early 17th centuries after the conquest of the Persians by Sultan Selim I in 1514 led to an influx of Persian craftsmen, including scribes and painters, into Istanbul. Although much of its inspiration derived from Persia Turkish manuscript painting was less concerned with the depiction of romantic scenes. Panoramas of battles against the infidels were tolerated as were those which realistically chronicled local events and festivals. The colouring was very vivid, had little of the delicate brushwork of Persian art, and often had disproportionately large human figures. Architectural detail was important. Not until the 18th century was there any marked Western influence. See also *Islamic illumination*.

Turkish printing: see *Ibrahim Müteferrika*.

turned chain lines: anomalously positioned chain lines in paper, e.g. horizontally in a folio section, which occur when sheets have been made two at a time in a divided mould. They also occur if a sheet double the size required for a printing job has been cut in half beforehand. Both practices are particular to the late 17th and 18th centuries.

turned sort: a type character used feet uppermost instead of one not to hand or not known when type is being composed, e.g. a page number in a footnote which cannot be identified until the whole text of a book has been set. See also *taking out turns*.

turning-in corners: in hand binding, the stage when thinly pared leather is pasted and stretched over the corners of the upper and lower boards where neatly mitred joints are made.

turnsole: the plant *heliotropium* from which was derived the purple dye used in classical and medieval times to stain the background of vellum leaves prior to writing on it with gold or silver ink. It was usually reserved for Gospels and Psalters intended for ceremonial purposes.

It was once thought that purple dye came only from the *murex* shellfish, but chemical analysis in the present century has shown that both were used. See F. Flieder, 'La Conservation des documents graphiques: recherches expérimentales', Paris, 1969.

turtles: an American term for the segmented chases used in the *type revolving machine*, q.v.

tusche: a greasy ink suitable for working on lithographic stones or plates.

twelvemo: written 12mo. The book size resulting from folding a sheet into twelve leaves (twenty-four pages) by means of right-angle folds. To define fully the size, the size of the paper must also be stated, e.g. Royal 12mo. Also called *duodecimo*. (LK)

twenty-fourmo: written 24mo. The book size resulting from folding a sheet into twenty-four leaves (forty-eight pages) by means of right-angle folds. To define fully the size, the size of the paper must also be stated, e.g. Royal 24mo. Also called *vigesimo-quarto*. (LK)

twin-wire binder: a machine which secures a number of single leaves plus a front and back cover by means of a comb of coiled wire or plastic-coated loops. Resulting books can be opened flat and the large number of twin-wire loops per inch gives a secure and neat finish. Semi-automatic and fully automatic models were announced in 1973, the latter with electronic sensing and synchronising equipment to control automatic feeding, wire-cutting and removal at speeds up to 3,600 per hour. See also *spirex binding*.

twin-wire paper: paper made on a Fourdrinier with twin 'wet ends' so that by bringing the two wet webs together, wire side innermost, a single sheet is formed with two top or felt sides. Such paper is eminently suitable for offset printing. Also known as *duplex paper*.

two-colour press: a machine printing two colours at one time. Most offset printing today is carried out on two-colour machines as the construction of a rotary two-colour machine is a straightforward engineering proposition, although the actual cylinder arrangements vary considerably in different makes. See also *Huber colour press*.

two-colour reproduction: this can often resemble full three-colour printing. The colours used are generally green or blue, and orange. The economy of using only two colours is obvious, but subjects must be chosen carefully, as results can sometimes be crude.

two-line letters: capital letters having a body depth extending over two lines of the type with which they are used, e.g. as an initial capital for the first word of a chapter.

two-line long primer: see *paragon*.

two-revolution press: a flat-bed cylinder machine in which the cylinder which carries the paper makes two revolutions for each impression. Printing is done during the first revolution, the bed with the forme returning during the second (the cylinder being kept raised), also during this second revolution the sheet is delivered. The cylinder revolves at a constant speed on early models, however, on later models of both two-revolution and single-revolution machines this principle was abandoned, the aim being to allow longer time for the actual printing while quickening the return of the bed, in some cases with a varying cylinder speed in consequence.

Early two-revolution presses were constructed by König in 1814 and David Napier in 1828. As the cylinder makes two revolutions between each impression the feeding can be done from one side of it and delivery from the other; it was some time, however, before machines were built with the advantage of front delivery, and on the first models delivery was arranged approximately as in the old stop-cylinder machines. Flyer-stick (rack) delivery by which the sheet is turned so that the printed side is underneath can be arranged; or, by using tapes delivery is done with the printed side uppermost which is preferable since the quality of the impression can be watched. The sheet is allowed to drop freely on the table at the

487

speed given by the tape transporter. The delivery constructed by Babcock is in general use, with tapes running over a pair of rollers. The tape carrier conveys the sheet forward over the delivery table and as the carrier moves away the tapes unroll so that the sheet lays itself on the table or on the pile which is lowered automatically. (See *printing press*.)

The inking system in a two-revolution machine is a pyramid of rollers, a duct, and a slab. The forme is taken in on the bed under the feeding table. The cylinder is usually set in motion by a gear driven directly from the main axle, while the carriage with the bed is driven by a double shuttle action, i.e. a toothed wheel revolving at a constant speed operates alternately an upper and lower gear track on the under-side of the bed. The moving bed is slowed, stopped and reversed by a crank drive; this arrangement was conceived by *Robert Miehle, 1883–88*, and he is regarded as the real originator of the modern two-revolution press. Air-buffers are often fitted to assist braking.

The cylinder is equipped with grippers and stretching devices for securing the packing. In order to maintain a high speed, two-revolution machines are equipped with swinging lays which grip the sheet lying on the feeding table and give it a speed which coincides with the speed of the cylinder grippers when it is gripped. At the moment of printing the periphery speed of the cylinder must be the same as that of the bed.

To ensure precise correspondence in the mutual position of cylinder and forme, which is critical in colour printing, the cylinder has register fingers and the bed an adjustable rack; these come into operation immediately before impression. (GU)

two-set: the setting of two jobs in one forme. One impression gives two signatures, subsequently separated.

two-sheets on: a method of hand-sewing a book made up of thin sections. Two are treated as a unit, and one length of thread attaches them to the tapes or cords. This avoids bulk at the back but the book is not so strong as when sewn normally. The work is best done in a sewing press.

two-up: the processing of two books as a single unit from the forme through all binding stages until they are separated by the trimmer. Used for the mass-production of paperbacks.

tying up: securing type after making it up into pages by tying each page with page-cord. This remains in position until the page is surrounded with furniture in the chase. See also *Quick-S*.

tympan and packing: 1. on a *hand-press* the tympan is the frame covered with a sheet of parchment on which a leaf of paper to be printed is positioned and held by the *frisket* during impression.

2. In letterpress printing on a *platen press* tympan is the name given to the packing on the platen which is fitted with a tight base-sheet, some filler sheets of MF paper, some card and a top cover sheet. Collectively they form the *dressing*, the purpose of which is to provide support for the paper to be printed. After a trial impression any make-ready needed is inserted under the top sheet, one or more filler sheets being removed to maintain the overall precise thickness needed for effective impression.

3. For the impression cylinder of a *cylinder machine* there is a *bottom*, or permanent, packing usually consisting of several oiled manila sheets, one of glazed linen and an upper sheet of damped manila (known as a *draw sheet*) which is drawn tightly over the whole by the first draw-bar. The bottom packing remains in position during repeated use and may not require renewal more than twice a year.

The *top*, or temporary, packing can be hard or soft according to the nature of the job in hand, the paper to be used, the length of the run, etc. In many cases it comprises up to twelve sheets of printing paper with a draw sheet held fast at the rear edge of the second draw-bar. All sheets are pasted or drawn tight to the gripper edge, while only the upper draw sheet is secured at the rear edge by a draw-bar or by pasting. In the top packing the number of sheets is reduced as patching is added during *make-ready*, q.v., since the total thickness must remain constant to ensure correct impression. The hardness of the packing may be varied. A harder packing gives a sharper and cleaner impression but requires more careful make-ready. The elasticity of the packing is of importance for improving printing quality.

4. The packing in a *rotary machine* is similar but simpler as the need for accurate thickness is less than with a cylinder press. See also *frisket*, *pre-press work*.

Tyndale, William, *c.* 1494–1536: the translator of the first New Testament to be printed in the English language (see *Bible printing in England*). He was strangled and burnt as a heretic at the town of Vilvorde near Brussels.

Typary machine: a machine devised in the 1920s as an alternative to setting up type in metal. As copy was tapped off inked characters were impressed on paper for reproduction by the *Typon process*, q.v. In its experimental stages several books were produced by it.

type: a rectangular metal casting, taken from a matrix, and having on one end of it the reversed image in relief of any one of the characters used in letterpress printing. Known to compositors as a *stamp*.

Parts of type

a *height to paper* h *line to back*
b *body, shank or stem* i *face*
c *front* j *bevel or neck*
d *feet* k *serif*
e *groove* l *shoulder*
f *nicks* j+1 *beard*
g *counter*

type and typefounding terminology: see *agate, antiqua, arabic type, ascenders, astronomical symbols, back-slanted type, baked, bastard, bastarda, belly, Bengali printing and typography, bevel, black letter, blooming letters, body-em, body type, botanical symbols, bourgeois, breaking-off boy, brevier, brilliant, capitals, caps and smalls, card fount, casting, chancery, cicero, civilité, clarendon, clumps, cock-up initial, cold type, composition fount, condensed face, contra italic, crabs, cup, cursive, cyrillic, depth of strike, descenders, devanagari, Didot point, digit, display type, Domesday characters, double character, dressers, drive, drop initial, egyptian, em, emerald, English, engraved face, en quad, ethiopic type, exotic types, expanded type, factotum, family, fat-face type, feet, fere-humanistica, fitting, flowers, foot, former, founder's type, fount, fount scheme, Fraktur, french nick, full on the body, fusible, gem, gothic, great primer, grecs du roi, greek type, groove, grotesque, hair-spaces, hand-matrix, hand-set, hanging figures, heavy type, Hebrew printing, height to paper, hot type, humanistic scripts, inferior figures, inline letters, inverted commas, Irish type and printing, italic, kerned letters, lapidary, laying the fount, leads, legibility, letra de Tortis, lettera Venetae, letters – forms and styles, lettre bâtarde, lettre de forme, lettre de somme, ligature, light face, logography, lombard, long-bodied type, long descenders, long s, lower case, majuscule, matrix, mean line, Mediaan, medical and pharmaceutical symbols, medium* (4), *meteorological symbols, millimétrique, minion, minuscule, missal caps, modern face, monogram, mould, movable type, neck, nonpareil, Old English, old face, old style, open letters, outline letters, paragon, parts of type, pearl, peculiars, peg, pica, point, primes, printer's ornaments, publicity faces, punch, punchcutter, punchcutting machine, punctuation marks, quadrata, quads,* *quotation marks, ranging figures, reference marks, reversed lettering, romain du roi, roman, ronde, Röslein, rotunda, ruby, rule, runners, sand letters, sanserif, Schwabacher, script, secretary, series, set, shaded letters, shoulder, slab serifs, small capitals, small pica, smoke, sorts, spaces, special sorts, split fractions, stake, stamp, strike, superior figures, swash letters, titling alphabet, transitional, trimmers, two-line letters, type family, type height, type metal, type ornaments, type sizes, typographer, typography, upper case letters, venetian types, weight, white letter, woodletter type.*

typecasting: the casting by a typefounder of type for hand composition. This was probably the essential contribution of Gutenberg to printing. His first mould

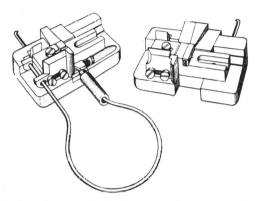

Hand-casting mould. Left, rear; right, front. In the middle of the latter is the cast type H *with its jet*

for casting type may have been primitive, but since the 16th century designs have changed little in principle up to the present day (though mechanical casters have made them obsolete). The mould as used in the 18th and 19th centuries was made up of two halves, each consisting of a bottom piece with a sliding core fixed on top, a sidepiece and other details, all made of brass or iron (see diagram). When the mould is assembled the surfaces of the bottom pieces and cores, turned inwards and smoothly ground, form the space in which the type is cast. Its body dimension is determined by the thickness of the core, and its width by the distance between the two cores. The casting space is closed at one end by the *matrix*, tightly held in the mould by adjustable sidepieces, so that the image of the character in the matrix is in the centre of the width of the type. In the second place adjustment is made by means of the movable back gauge against which one end of the matrix rests. The back gauge and its regulating screw are on that half of the mould which supports the *spring*, a steel wire of horseshoe shape for holding the matrix to the mould. On the bottom piece of either half of the mould, on the side opposite the matrix, pieces of metal are fitted

489

so shaped that they form a funnel-like opening (or jet) through which the metal is poured. They slide, so that the width of the casting hole can be varied according to the size of type. By placing partitions between them and the bottom piece the height of the type can be altered. To enable the founder to handle the halves of the mould at high temperatures they are encased in wooden covers. On either half of the lining is a pointed steel hook, a means of removing the cast type from the mould.

Matrices consist of metal plates, about 40mm. long and 9mm. thick, with a smoothly ground surface into which the image of the character is struck with a steel punch. A *counter-punch* bearing the inner enclosed portions of a letter is first made. This is cut by hand with the inner shape of a letter, e.g. the bowl of an o, q, p, etc., or the space between the strokes of an n, m, h, etc., and then hardened. After punching with a counter-punch on the end of a steel shank the inside contour of a letter, the outside is filed and cut away, and the steel tempered.

Both halves of the mould are put together and the matrix placed between the sidepieces where it is held firmly by means of the spring. The founder holds the mould in one hand and lifts the type metal in a casting ladle from a pot with the other, and applies it to the mouth of the mould. By giving the mould a jerk at the moment of casting the metal penetrates all parts of it. Enough metal is poured in to fill the opening, and a *jet* or *tang* is formed. When the mould is opened, the solidified type is released. The exact adjustment of mould and matrix must be checked by trial castings.

By tradition, letters 'm' and 'o' were cast first as a standard for adjusting the engraving on the type. A good founder could make about 5,000 units a day.

In finishing the cast type the jet is first broken off, after which the body sides are ground by hand. The types are arranged in a wooden composing stick, face downwards, for the *dresser* to plane off the jet-break

Steel die
(*punch*)

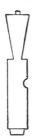

Type, as cast. The upper portion, known as 'jet' or 'tang', is broken off, leaving the body with a nick in the side, and the face at the bottom

at the foot of the types and ensure they are of standard type height. The channel on the side of the type, which serves as a *nick* in typesetting, can also be made here if not already done when casting. After any necessary planing of the type shoulders, the sides are scraped in a scraping stick.

The metal used for typecasting seems from the time of Gutenberg to have been an alloy of lead and tin. In the 16th century bismuth was added as a hardening ingredient and was later replaced by antimony. (See *type metal*.)

In the 15th century printers cast their own type, and handwriting was the model they sought to imitate in print. But casting and typesetting methods necessitated a certain system in shaping typographical material, and there could be little question of uniformity when every printer considered it an advantage to have type differing from that of other printers, if only to reduce the risk of theft and plagiarism: thus it was that heights varied. By degrees, however, typefoundries were established which had no direct connection with the printing trade. The first independent foundry in Germany was founded in 1571 at Frankfurt by *Jacques Sabon*, and in France by *Guillaume Le Bé* (died 1599), qq.v., whose foundry passed to the Fournier family in the 18th century. Later it became more and more usual for printers to buy their type from special typefoundries, and the demand thus grew both for a uniform scale of sizes and a productive capacity which could not be satisfied by hand-casting tools. In 1819 Henri Didot of Paris invented a casting tool in which, by using a matrix bar and a trough mould, several units of type could be cast simultaneously at the rate of from 300 to 400 a minute.

An early mechanical typecaster was invented by *William Church*, q.v. See also *logography*, *punch*.

In 1830 G. W. Bower and H. A. Bacon of Sheffield invented a pumping device for the metal-pot, so that the metal could be forced into the mould under pressure.

About 1838 David Bruce of New York and the Dane Laurids Brandt invented a hand-casting machine which, after a single adjustment, required only a few simple manipulations for casting a large number of types in rapid succession. A model was probably used in the Edinburgh foundry of James Marr & Co. The finishing of type was still carried out in the old way until 1859 when John Robert Johnson and John Staines Atkinson constructed the first machine for dressing types after casting: this was improved in 1862. In 1881 an improved casting machine was built for the Bauersche Giesserei by John Mair Hepburn, but it was not until 1883 that the first complete casting machine appeared which delivered entirely finished type which required no further work at all. It was built by Foucher frères, who exhibited a double casting machine of still greater capacity in Paris in 1894. In many private foundries type is cast for use in

Monotype casting machines; the output is from 6,000 to 10,000 units an hour according to size.

As already mentioned, matrices were formerly produced by striking with a steel punch engraved by hand. The material generally consisted of copper, but also of lead, especially for larger sizes. After the introduction of electrotyping with a galvanic battery in 1838 this method was employed, about 1845, for making matrices from cast type. Both electrotype and nickeltype were used. Nowadays the original type for this purpose is made by engraving in a boring machine. Original matrices are also engraved directly in a similar machine. A punchcutting machine was invented in 1885 by *Linn Boyd Benton* in Milwaukee, q.v. In principle it consists of a vertical pantograph with a revolving cutting tool at the upper end, and a pilot pin (the follower) which is guided around the outline of an enlarged metal pattern at the lower end.

When a new script has been designed the type-face is cut or engraved in one standard size (see *fusible*). After samples of type have been cast, and the stencils finally established for this size of type, they cannot immediately be used for other sizes. Diminution and enlargement of the image may affect the balance and proportions of the character. Only three or four sizes of matrices are therefore engraved from one set of stencils, while for others new designs and new stencils must be made. (GU)

typecasting machine: originally, a machine for the mechanical casting of single type units which were then set up in a stick by hand. *Typesetting machines*, q.v., were also invented which did not cast the type they set.

Such modern machines as the *Intertype, Linotype, Monotype*, and also the *teletypesetting* process, qq.v., both set and cast.

type classification: see *Vox classification*.

type composing: see *hand composition*.

type-composing machine: see *typesetting machine*.

type face: see *face*.

type face copyright: an international agreement for the protection for up to twenty-five years of original type faces, signed by ten countries at the Vienna Congress on Industrial Property, 1973.

Protection covers the unauthorized reproduction and sale of type designs, whether identical or slightly modified, intended to provide means for composing texts by graphic methods irrespective of the technical process or material used. Britain, France and Germany were early signatories. See 'The Vienna Agreement for the protection of type faces and their international deposit and protocol during the term of protection, Vienna, 1973', HMSO, 1974. See also *Association Typographique Internationale*.

type family: characters of one basic design which are available in upper and lower case roman, with companion italic, bold, semi-bold, small capitals, titling. An example is Univers. See also *fount*.

Typefoundry Amsterdam: established in 1851 by N. Tetterode, and later one of the world's biggest type manufacturers. Proprietary types known in Britain include De Roos roman, Egmont, Libra and Rondo. Additionally the firm has the Dutch agency for an extensive range of printing presses and equipment.

In Holland the firm is known as *Lettergieterij en Machinehandel v/h N. Tetterode-Nederland N.V.*

type height: 1. the height of a type from the feet on which it rests to the printing surface, i.e. 0·918in. (23·317mm).

2. the height to which a printing plate is mounted on a wooden block for use in letterpress work, i.e. 0·918in. (23·317mm).

type holder: see *pallet*.

type matter: see *matter*.

type metal: an alloy of varying composition, used for typographic material. The basic metal is lead with different admixtures of tin and antimony, as well as such other metals as copper at times. Metal alloys were already in use for this purpose in the 15th century.

Lead by itself is too soft and too difficult to melt to be of use. By the addition of antimony it becomes harder, and by that of tin more easily melted, although both these substances affect the end product. The two essential qualities of type metal are that it must be fluid at temperatures which will not burn the matrix, and it must expand slightly at the moment of solidification so as to give a sharp impression of the mould.

Relatively large additions of antimony are often made to founders' type, and copper is also added to increase the hardness. Such type contains up to 24% antimony, up to 12% tin, 1% copper, and 63% lead. *Stereotype metal*, q.v., has normally between 5% tin with 14% antimony or 7% tin with 18% antimony. For rotary stereotype up to 12% tin is used, but antimony should not exceed 15%.

Stephenson Blake & Co. Ltd of Sheffield use 26% antimony, 25% tin, 1% copper and 48% lead for their type alloy. For Monotype casting machines proportions are from 6 to 10% tin, and 15 to 19% antimony, the balance of lead. A low tin content can be used for spacing, while the antimony content is kept high to maintain resistance to wear and tear

(3 % tin with 18 % antimony is usual). See also *zinc type*.

type ornaments: see *brace ends, bracket, brass rule, cock, corners, dash, entrelac initials, flowers, head-piece, hooks, Oxford corners, parentheses, swelled rules, tail-piece, title-page border.*

type parts: see *parts of type.*

type revolving machine: a sheet-fed letterpress machine in which columns of type held in narrow segmented chases were secured across a large drum (*c.* 180cm diameter). The machine was designed for newspaper printing and represented a stage between the flat-bed and the rotary.

In England Augustus Applegath had his first machine operating by 1848: in America an independently conceived machine built by *Robert Hoe* began printing in 1847. See also *turtles.*

typescript: an author's original typed manuscript, or a professionally typed copy of it which he or his publisher may commission. Abbreviated as *ts.*

typesetting machine: a machine for the selection, assembling and spacing of typefounders' letterpress printing types, these being arranged and stored in channels instead of cases. About 200 experimental models of such machines were patented between 1820 and 1883, mostly in America. The basic idea was a keyboard connected with the storage channels in such a way that by each stroke of a key a single type was ejected and carried to an assembly point where the types were lined up. In most of the machines type was assembled in an endless row which an operator made up and justified into lines of the required measure. A third worker was often needed to replenish the type channels. As the compositor needed two assistants such typesetting by machinery was hardly more economical than setting by hand. See also *Church.*

Distributing machines were also constructed, notable being that of the Dane Christian Sörensen, *c.* 1850, who gave the various types special nicks by which they slid automatically down channels with corresponding mouths on the outside of a revolving cylinder; his machine was shown in the Great Exhibition of 1851. It was not until the 1880s that inventors solved the problem of justification: the Americans James W. Paige and Alexander Dow were among others to succeed, and, with a simpler system, Paul Cox. The latter used quad material of corrugated lead which, at the stroke of a key for each inter-word space, was cut off from a long rolled strip of lead. The line was set rather wider than required and then compressed to the measure.

The most successful typesetting machine was the Simplex or Unitype which required only one operator. It was constructed by Joseph Thorne who built a prototype in 1880 which included several earlier ideas, especially those of Sörensen. After various improvements and alterations the Thorne machine was given the name Simplex, and large numbers were sold about the year 1900. In 1898 it was combined with an improved spacing system by Cox and appeared under the name of Unitype, 1903. The Simplex machine consisted of two vertical cylinders placed above one another; vertical channels were let into their surfaces, and the shape of the channel mouths leading to the lower cylinder corresponded to special nicks on the back of the type, thus each type could only enter its correct channel. The matter to be distributed was placed in the channels of the upper cylinder, so that the type lay horizontally. During typesetting the upper cylinder revolved step by step, causing the channels on the upper and lower cylinders to meet in turn, so that the type was made to drop in this way into its proper channel from which it was released for subsequent setting by depressing a key. 10,000 types could be set in an hour.   (GU)

See also *typecasting machine, Wicks.*

type sizes: from the early years of printing until the late 19th century various names were used to describe type sizes and faces. It is thought that their association with a particular class of work determined the choice.

Names formerly used in English foundries are listed here with their approximate equivalents in *point*, q.v.:

Canon, Four-line Pica	48
Two-line Double Pica	44
Two-line Great Primer	36
Two-line English	28
Two-line Pica	24
Double Pica	22
Paragon	20
Great Primer	18
Two-line Brevier (Columbian in U.S.A.)	16
English	14
Pica	12
Small Pica	11
Long Primer	10
Bourgeois	9
Brevier	8
Minion	7
Emerald	$6\frac{1}{2}$
Nonpareil	6
Ruby (Agate in U.S.A.)	$5\frac{1}{2}$
Pearl	5
Diamond	$4\frac{1}{2}$
Gem	4
Brilliant, Half-minion	$3\frac{1}{2}$
Minikin, Semi-nonpareil	3

type-specimen book: see *specimen sheet.*

typewriter composing machine: a machine which produces a simulation of letterpress on material suitable for photographic reproduction and subsequent printing. In addition to ordinary typewriters a number of special machines have been made such as the *IBM 72 Composer* and the *Justowriter*, qq.v. They are used in the business world for in-house printing on small litho presses. Not only is copy cheaper to produce than when sent out for conventional type-setting, but its preparation is quicker and there is greater security for confidential matter.

typographer: a person qualified by his knowledge of letter designing, punchcutting, typefounding and printing processes, as well as by a flair for design, to plan a proposed printing work in a manner suited to the subject and purpose of it as well as to the materials and processes to be used.

The definition of John Moxon in 1683 is not without point today: ' . . . one who by his own judgement, from solid reasoning within himself, can either perform, or direct others to perform from the beginning to the end, all the handy-works and physical operations relating to typographic.' See also *copy fitting*.

Typographia Apostolica Vaticana: the printing press established by Sixtus V in 1587 in the apostolic palace next to the Vatican Library. The Venetian master printer Domenico Basa assisted by Aldus Manutius II (grandson of Aldus I) were engaged to print texts chosen by popes. The press owned a foundry, notable for the oriental and other types cut for it by Robert Granjon.

In 1610 it ceased to operate independently and was merged with the *Tipografia Camerale*, q.v., to form the *Stamperia Vaticana*. In 1825 the T. A. V. was re-established by Leo XII and in 1868 a portion of it was taken into the Vatican for use by the Council and named *Tipografia Vaticana*.

Typographia Linguarum Externarum: see *Stamperia Orientale Medicea*.

Typographia Medicea: another name for the *Stamperia Orientale Medicea*, q.v.

Typographica: an authoritive conspectus of modern typographic and graphic arts in Europe, edited by Herbert Spencer, RDI, with articles by authors from many countries. It was printed and published by Lund Humphries of Bradford and first appeared in 1949, continuing in two series, each of sixteen issues, until 1967 when publication ceased.

The Typographical Association: the trade union of the provincial letterpress printing industry in Britain, established in 1849. There had been other unions of printers in the early 19th century, notably the Northern Typographical Union (est. 1830), the Scottish Typographical Association (est. 1836), the Irish Typographical Union (est. 1836), and the London Union of Compositors (est. 1834), re-formed as London Society of Compositors in 1848.

The common aims of these unions had been to regulate the number of hours worked and wages paid; to limit the number of apprentices so that they were not used as a source of cheap labour; to lay down a policy with regard to the various new mechanical printing presses and composing machines which were being developed; to give financial help during strikes; to discourage 'unfair' printing offices which paid less than the established ('stab') rates and employed non-union journeymen; and to help unemployed printers who tramped the country seeking work (this assistance was known as 'tramp relief' and was a sum of money varying from 9d. to 5/-). See A. E. Musson, 'The Typographical Association: origins and history up to 1949', O.U.P., 1954.

The activities of the T.A. are now encompassed by the National Graphical Association.

typography: 1. the craft of printing; embracing composition, imposition and presswork.
2. the skilled planning of printed matter, including choice of paper, type face and size, and layout of the printed and blank areas to make a balanced and attractive whole. See also *copy fitting*, *margins*.

typometer: a gauge for measuring the body and thickness of type in comparison with a standard.

Typon process: properly, the name of a series of processes, variable according to the user's needs, for making flexible negatives or positives on paper or film. Out of print books can be photographed page by page for making up into litho plates.

Film negatives can be made by photographing in a camera, or by contact exposure in a printing frame in which the page to be reproduced is pressed into contact with the sensitized side of a sheet of reflex paper. Subsequent stages result in a negative with sharp clear lettering on a black ground. The process was originated by the Baltisch Papier-Industrie AG.

Typophiles of New York: a group of enthusiastic printers, designers, typographers and others who 'practice or appreciate the graphic arts'. Their activities were for many years guided by Paul A. Bennett (1897–1966). Since 1940 the group has issued a series of 'Chap Books', many containing original texts by such authorities as Bradley, Goudy, Hofer, Krimpen, and Ruzicka. The St Bride Printing Library in London has a complete set.

u

u.c.: the abbreviation for *upper case*, q.v.

Uffenbach, Zacharias Conrad von, 1683–1734: a German bibliophile whose private library in Frankfurt of 12,000 volumes and 30,000 autograph letters was available to scholars. His interesting account of the tour of libraries he made in 1709/10, published posthumously as 'Merkwürd. Reisen durch Niedersachsen, Holland, und Engelland', Ulm, 1753/4, has many references to the poor calibre of English academic libraries. See also *Bodley, calf, Sheldonian Theatre*.

ultrasonic binding: a binding process without the use of adhesives devised by the Leipzig Institute of Printing Machinery. Briefly, cut sheets are put under pressure tension in a clamp and then given a vibratory motion by a rotating disc. This results in a bonding together of the fibres at the point of pressure.

By 1965 experiments were being made to bind books on this principle.

ultrasonic cleaning of type: a method of cleaning dried ink from letterpress printing type and plates which obviates the damage done by normal methods of brushing and lye washing. The equipment consists essentially of a generator which produces an ultrasonic signal, transducers which convert the electrical signal into mechanical vibrations, and a stainless steel tank (of varying size) to contain the agitated solvent. The generator operates in the frequency range from 36 to 40 kilocycles per second, giving a succession of up to 40,000 pressure waves every second.

Briefly, it works as follows. Electrical signals from the generator cause the transducer to expand and contract at the frequency of the current supplied to it. If put in a tank of liquid, the constant expansion and contraction in the transducer will cause rapid pressure changes in the surrounding fluid. The result is the rapid generation and collapse of millions of tiny vapour bubbles. Bubbles tend to form round any nearby solid surface (this is known as cavitation), thus when a printing plate is immersed in the tank the bubbles will penetrate the smallest type or the finest line blocks where their agitation will dislodge caked dirt and dried ink. Warm solvent is more

494

efficient than cold, and solvents containing creosol, e.g. Magnasol, give best results. Type or plates are finally removed from the tank and rinsed in warm tap water. See also *chamber lye, washing up*.

Ulverstonian press: a printing press designed by Stephen Soulsby about 1850. It was made for him by Dawson and Payne of Otley, better known for their *Wharfedale machine*, q.v.

umbilicus: the stick about which a manuscript roll was wound. See also *volumen*.

unauthorized edition: an edition printed without the consent of the owner of the copyright.

uncials: a term of disputed origin for the majuscule form of writing used for the earliest extant Biblical codices, e.g. the 4th century *Codex Sinaiticus*, q.v. The script is also known as *Biblical uncial* although it was used for non-Christian works two centuries previously. After the 6th century uncial as a book hand was superseded by *half uncial*, q.v.

Distinctive features of uncial are rounded forms of a, d, e, m and u, also the minuscule forms of h, l and q. See E. A. Lowe, 'English uncial', O.U.P., 1960.

uncut: a book is said to be uncut if the edges of the paper have not been cut with the plough or guillotine. Cf. *unopened*. See also *witness* (2).

underbanding: the affixing of *false bands*, q.v.

undercut: the distance between the surface of a printing cylinder and the height of the bearers. This factor is important when setting the printing overpressure between the plate and blanket cylinders on an offset press (0.003in.). Gauges and a micrometer are used to check and set cylinders during makeready.

undercutting: the faulty etching of a block by which the metal carrying the lines or dots of the image is pitted from the side. This gives the block poor strength in printing, and makes it difficult or impossible to take from it matrices for stereotypes or electrotypes.

(GU)

underlaying: the placing of a sheet or sheets of paper or thin card under the forme and under the mounts of blocks to bring them to the required level for printing evenly. See also *make-ready.*

Uneoprint: the registered name of the utility printing process devised by Unwin Brothers Ltd. Briefly, copy is typed on an IBM Executive electric typewriter the keyboards of which can be supplemented by attachments carrying additional characters. The resulting matter is then photoreduced from its initial 12-point to the size required, transferred on to a presensitised aluminium plate and printed offset.

Text is not normally justified but this can be done by photographing each line with a different horizontal reduction.

Uneoprint is particularly suitable for complex technical composition, for lists and tables, and for informational and reference works where letterpress is too slow or costly yet office copying would be inadequate or impractical. See also *Cartoprint.*

Unger, Johann Friedrich, 1753–1804: a Berlin printer, woodcutter and typefounder who was much interested in type design. The light Fraktur which bears his name was perfected in 1794 (for a specimen see *letters–forms and styles*). He was the sole German agent for Didot's modern face roman. In 1800 he was appointed professor of woodcutting at the Berlin Academy.

ungrained plates: zinc plates for use in lithographic printing which, while not quite smooth, are considerably less rough than normal plates surfaced in a graining machine.

Ungrained deep-etch zinc plates are designed to increase the range of darker tones in a reproduction and to improve the overall merging of tones (this is particularly important for the successful rendering of half-tone dots).

It is the graining on normal lithographic plates which holds the water in the non-image areas and the ink for printing; if the graining is largely to be dispensed with the condition of water/grease repellency must be achieved by other means. One of these is to treat the image areas of the deep-etch plate with a non-blinding lacquer to increase their ink-receptivity, thus making greater the contrast with the non-image area which is densensitized with cellulose gum.

A second method is to use pre-sensitized plates in which chemically treated aluminium foil is applied as a base and water-absorbent area, with a diazo-type coating as the image area. A third method is to use bi-metallic plates with copper as the ink-receptive image area, and aluminium, chromium or stainless steel for the non-image area. If such a plate is immersed in a bath of phosphoric acid (20%) the above properties will result. Such plates are costly, but suitable for long runs.

Ungrained plates require more care on the press in such matters as roller adjustment, pressure and ink consistency (it should be stiff). Smooth or coated stock are recommended as being the most suitable.

Unicorn Press: a private press founded in 1895 by Ernest Oldmeadow (1867–1949) and the Rev. Joseph Dawson of London. The output was only small, and the press closed in 1905. Unicorn Press was strictly a publishing imprint and commercial firms did the printing.

In addition to some limited editions and general books, including a series 'Artist's Library' edited by Laurence Binyon, the press published a journal of the arts *The Dome,* 1897–1900, to which such writers and musicians as Binyon, Delius, Elgar, Laurence Housman, Arthur Symons and Yeats contributed. *The Dome* owed much to the inspiration of Alice Meynell at whose house Oldmeadow and most of his contributors met.

uniform edition: a set or series of books all composed, bound and jacketed in the same style.

Uniprint: an alternative to copper photogravure. In the 1950s a means was found of replacing the costly copper cylinder by one of vulcanized rubber about which a photographic colloidal matrix bearing the image is wrapped. The image is transferred by heat. Being cheaper it can be used for shorter runs than are usual for copper photogravure.

unit perfecting press: see *blanket-to-blanket press.*

unit principle: an arrangement used for colour printing in which each of from two to four offset printing units has its own inking system, plate cylinder, blanket cylinder and impression cylinder. In sheet-fed work a large transfer cylinder, equipped with grippers and positioned between each pair of units, effects passage of the paper from one impression cylinder to the next. A different method of sheet transfer is by chain mechanism in which one set of grippers holds the sheet from feed to delivery.

The unit principle can also be used for *blanket-to-blanket* machine installations, q.v.

Universal Copyright Convention, 1952: a convention on copyright organized by UNESCO at which thirty-six countries agreed with its conclusions. Britain ratified it in 1957 and by 1973 (in which year the U.S.S.R. joined) there were some sixty-five member countries.

The most important article is perhaps No. II which provides that published works of nationals of any contracting State, and works published in that State, shall enjoy in each other contracting State the same protection that other State accords to its nationals first published in its own territory.

In effect this means that members give protection for not less than twenty-five years from first publication, with exclusive rights of translation for seven years from the same date. The UCC was revised in 1971 (see *Paris Texts, 1971*).

The main difference between the UCC and the *Berne Convention*, q.v., is that copyright in Europe is attendant on first publication. In Pan-American countries formal registration of copyright was required. See also *All rights reserved, Copyright Act, copyright notice*.

University Mailing Service: see *International Book Information Service*.

unjustified setting: see *ragged right*.

unopened: a book sold with the bolts uncut, to be hand-slit by the purchaser with a paper-knife. It is then said to be opened. Cf. *uncut*.

unsewn binding: see *adhesive binding*.

untouched: said of incunabula which have not been rubricated or illuminated.

untouched edges: a bookbinding term for edges which are neither trimmed nor cut. The leaves have to be opened with a paper-knife by the purchaser. Synonymous with *unopened*. Cf. *uncut*.   (LK)

Updike, Daniel Berkeley, 1860–1941: an eminent American printer and type historian whose 'Printing types: their history, forms and use', 1922, is still a standard textbook though in need of revision and updating. It was reprinted in 1962.

From 1880–93 he worked for the Boston publishers Houghton, Mifflin & Co., the last two years being spent at their Riverside Press, Cambridge, Mass. In 1893 he set up the *Merrymount Press* 'to make work better for its purpose than was commonly thought worthwhile'. His associate John Bianchi was taken into partnership in 1915. Among the special types used were the Merrymount, designed by *Bertram G. Goodhue*, q.v., about 1895; the Mountjoye, 1903, from John Bell's transitional fount of 1788; and the Montallegro, designed by Herbert P. Horne and cut by *E. P. Prince*, q.v., in 1904.

The press was in no sense private, but achieved a reputation for the extraordinary care taken over details; it was said that every sheet printed was examined by one of the two partners before being delivered to the customer. In 1949 the press closed. See D. B. Updike, 'Notes on the Merrymount Press and its work', reprinted with bibliographies of the Press, 1893–1933, by J. P. Smith, and 1934–49, by D. B. Bianchi, 1975.

upper case: the part of the compositor's type case in which capital letters, reference marks and accents are kept. Cf. *lower case*.

upper case letters: capital letters or *majuscules*. Abbreviated as *u.c.*

upper end boy: the boy who assists the coucher (in a hand-made paper works) when the vat is on a very long sort. The boy helps to put the long felt on the *post*, q.v., and lightly squeezes down the mould as it is being couched. The upper end of the mould is that farthest from the coucher.

Utrecht Psalter: a manuscript of the Gallican version of the Psalms, written and illustrated at the Abbaye de Hautvillers near Rheims about 830. It is now in Utrecht University Library but at some time in the 9th or 10th century was brought to Canterbury where a copy was made about 1000 (now in the British Library). A second copy survives as the *Eadwine Psalter*, q.v., while a third, made in the early 13th century, is now in Paris.

The Rheims version was illustrated by brown ink drawings of figures set among landscape backgrounds. But while the original was the inspiration for the copies neither the economy of its style nor the liveliness and charming delicacy of its depictions survived transmission. In the BL copy, while the iconography was unchanged the figures were somewhat distorted and landscapes were ornamental rather than naturalistic. Greater emphasis on decorative pattern is a feature of the Eadwine version, and in the BN copy the pictures were painted in the heavier colours traditional in Gothic art. The copies were coloured: the original was not. See E. T. De Wald, 'The illustrations of the Utrecht Psalter', Princeton U.P., 1933.

Utterson, E. V.: see *Beldornie Press*.

V

vacuum frame: a copying frame used in process engraving for *printing down*, q.v. It may be vertical or horizontal and consists of a rubber-covered flat base. On this is laid a sensitized metal plate with the negative to be copied on top. Next comes a glass plate. The air between the rubber and glass is withdrawn by a pump, causing a vacuum in which the metal and negative are pressed together. Several plates of varying thickness and their accompanying negatives can be put in the frame at one time. Exposure is by arc, mercury vapour or pulsed xenon light.
See also *photolithographic plate*.   (With GU)

Valdarfer, Christopher, fl.1470–88: of Ratisbon. He was the third printer at Venice where his first book was Cicero's 'De oratore', 1470, followed by Aesop's 'Fabulae', 1470/1 and other translations into Latin of Greek classics. He used a rounded roman type with a distinctive 'h'. From 1474 to 1488 he worked in Milan (with a working visit to Basle in 1479) mostly printing Latin classics.

Val de Lagat: a French village, famous for its paper-mill, operating now as it did when built in the 13th century.   (ML)

Vale Press: a press founded in London in 1896 by *Charles Ricketts*, q.v., and Charles Haslewood Shannon (1863–1937) with the object of producing fine editions of the English classics. They had from 1889 collaborated to produce *The Dial*, a journal. Ricketts supervised the printing by Ballantyne & Hanson of the books he designed; special types used were the Vale, King's and Avon. Ricketts also embellished and illustrated many of the books with wood engravings which he drew and cut.
'The early poems of John Milton', 1896, was the first book to be printed in their special type, but 'Daphnis and Chloë', 1893 was the first book to bear the Vale imprint. The press closed in 1903 by which time eighty-five volumes had been published.

Vallet, Jacques, c. 1612–72: a typefounder born in Geneva who worked in Amsterdam and London (where he may have died). In 1670 Dr Fell's agent Thomas Marshall bought matrices of French design from the Van Dijck foundry. Two years later he acquired roman, italic, musical notation and flowers from Vallet as an alternative to further purchases of the costlier Van Dijck types.

Valleyre, Gabriel: see *stereotype*.

Van den Keere, Hendrik: see *Keere, Hendrik van den*.

Van de Velde, Henry: see *Velde, Henry van de*.

Van Dijck, Christoffel: see *Dijck, Christoffel van*.

Van Gelder paper: a fine quality all-rag paper manufactured since 1870 by the Dutch firm Koninklijke Papierfabrieken Van Gelder Zonen, established in 1784. It was and is widely used in Europe for de luxe editions, especially in France where it is known as *papier de Hollande*.

vanity publisher: a publishing concern whose main business is the issuing of books entirely paid for by their authors. Such firms flourish particularly in America, catering for thousands of unsuccessful writers unwilling to accept the implications of a stream of rejection slips from regular publishers, for the wealthy who consider they have a message for the world, for aspiring poets and so on.
That the author's return may cover no more than the cost of printing a single page is no discouragement, and one of such firms issues 400 or so books a year. Bookshops and reviewers tend to avoid vanity books, arguing that if a book had any worth it would have been published by a regular firm. Very often, too, an author will be invited to buy unsold stock to clear the publisher's warehouse, thus paying for his work twice.
Vanity publishing in England is not so extensive, being mostly limited to poetry. Also known as *subsidy publishing*.

Van Krimpen, Jan: see *Krimpen, Jan van*.

vantage: a blank page on a sheet.

variant: 1. in MSS, a difference in the text of a handwritten manuscript and copies made from it. Such variants resulted from careless copying. See also *hic nullus est defectus*.

2. in books, a textual variation noticed in two copies of the same impression of a work. This is the result of correcting a minor mistake noticed during printing; only the later sheets bear the corrections, the earlier ones being issued without alteration. The variant can also be caused accidentally. Cf. *state* (1). See also *collating machine*.

3. see *binding variants*.

variorum edition: an issue of a work containing the notes or opinions of several editors or commentators.

varnish: a general description of liquid substances which dry as hard films, insoluble in water, when applied in thin layers to various surfaces. Of special importance in the graphic industries are varieties of thick, viscous linseed oil varnish which form the binding agents in inks for letterpress and lithographic printing; while for gravure and aniline printing there are varnishes made of resins contained in evaporating solvents.

varnishing: usually, the application of a single coat of oleoresinous varnish over printed matter, e.g. paperback covers. This is a cheap process and is done either on the press or on a separate machine. The coating enhances the surface and increases resistance to moisture, handling and abrasion.

The two main grades of varnish are *overprint* and *gloss*. The first, which is cheap, is a quick-drying varnish which gives a gloss to the printed areas and a tolerable appearance to the surrounding blanks. The second is made of better materials and gives an overall smooth film which is equally glossy over the printed and the unprinted areas.

There are several models of varnishing machine, some being equipped with infra-red dryers. A separate machine for glazing or heat calendering will give a mirror-like finish to the coated sheet. Special varnishes are needed for this; they are based on synthetic polymeric materials and I.C.I.'s latex BC1 is an example. The printed sheet, coated with latex, is glazed between heated polished platens. This process is known as *plate glaze varnishing*. See also *lamination, nitrocellulose lacquering*.

Vascosan, Michel de, fl.1530–77: of Amiens. A Parisian printer-publisher, son-in-law of *Badius*, q.v., and in 1561 the royal printer. He specialized in the printing of classics, especially Cicero and Plutarch, 1541, for which he used an excellent type and small format. Notable was his Caesar of 1543.

In 1556 he printed an elegant edition of Oronce Finé's 'De rebus mathematicis' with beautiful initials and decorations designed by the author. For the most part Vascosan preferred simple typographic title-pages without ornament.

Vatican Virgil: one of the earliest illustrated codices, of which portions of Georgics and Aeneid survive on seventy-six vellum leaves. Six of the fifty miniatures fill a whole page: they were probably painted by two or more artists who used thick, deep and rich colours. There are interesting landscape and architectural details. From stylistic affinities with other works of art it has been assigned to the early 5th century. The text is in rustic capitals.

Since 1600 the work has been in the Vatican (Cod.Vat.Lat.3225). See also *Roman Virgil*.

vatman: the craftsman who dips the mould into a vat of pulp and skilfully shakes it into a sheet of paper.

vat paper: an alternative name for *hand-made paper*, q.v.

Vautroullier, Thomas, fl.1564–87: born at Troyes in France. A bookseller-printer who settled in London in 1562. In 1567 he briefly shared with Jean Desserans the London sales agency for Plantin press books. He was a skilled printer whose extensive output included, in addition to educational books, writings by Calvin, Luther, Cicero and, with the title 'Lives of the noble Grecians and Romanes', Sir Thomas North's translation of Amyot's rendering of Plutarch's 'Vitae illustrium virorum'. This handsome folio with medallion portraits of each life was issued in 1579.

Noteworthy also were two writing books he printed, Beauchesne's 'A booke containing divers sortes of hands', 1570, which was frequently reprinted, and in 1574 'A newe booke of copies . . .', of which the Lion and Art Press in London issued a facsimile edition in 1959. He is assumed to have published Francis Clement's 'Petie schole', 1576, which was the first writing manual entirely in English. In the earliest edition of which copies survive, that of 1587, it was claimed that it would teach a 'childe to read perfectly within one moneth'.

Vautroullier was licensed to employ in his London premises six French or Dutch assistants and one apprentice. In 1580 the Scottish General Assembly gave him a licence to sell books in Edinburgh where he set up a press in 1584. He returned to London in 1586.

After his death in 1587 his wife Jacqueline continued the business. It is possible that she was a qualified printer as in March 1588 the Stationers' Company forbade her to print. In that year three books were issued with the imprint 'By I. Vautrollier for R. Field'. This was the former apprentice *Richard Field*, q.v., whom she married later in 1588. Two of Vautroullier's four sons also worked in the book trade.

In the 16th century, when the spelling of names was not consistent, Vautroullier is also found as *Vautrollier* and *Vautrouillier*.

vehicle: the medium in which printing ink pigments are dispersed. Vegetable oils (chiefly linseed) are the most used, but soft synthetic resins, which allow more control in drying, may be chosen for quick-set inks to be printed on coated papers.

Velde, Henry van de, 1863–1957: a Belgian artist, designer and creator of the German *Jugendstil*. In 1895 he had a private press in Brussels on which he printed small editions of poetry, designing title-pages and abstract ornamentation in the style known in England as *art nouveau*. His typography showed the influence of William Morris and his bindings of Cobden-Sanderson. In the 1890s he made many designs for the Belgian craftsman-binder P. Claessens.

In 1898 he began an association with Harry Kessler, designing, *inter alia*, the layout and ornaments for the Cranach-Presse 'Also sprach Zarathustra', 1908. He also worked for Kippenberg's *Insel-Verlag*, q.v. See A. M. Hammacher, 'Die Welt Henry van de Velde', Köln, 1968.

Velde, Jan van den, 1568–1623: an important Dutch calligrapher whose 'Spieghel der Schrijfkonste' with copper engravings, Amsterdam, 1605, was the first of a magnificent series of similar works he prepared. He was the innovator and master of the script capital which began and ended in a whirl of freehand flourishes. This style was studied and adopted by calligraphers in France (by Louis Barbedor, c. 1589–1670), in England (notably by Edward Cocker, 1631–76, and John Seddon in the 1690s), in Italy (by Agostino Tensini in the 1680s), and in Germany from its inception to the present day. See also *striking*.

Veldener, Johann, fl.1472–83: of Würzburg, an itinerant typecutter, printer and publisher who may have worked with Ulrich Zel in Cologne before setting up the first press at Louvain in 1473. Although the printer has not been identified a work by de Gambilionibus dated 1475 has been ascribed to Veldener in Louvain. He issued Rolewinck's 'Fasciclus temporum' in the same year. This was the first printed book in the Netherlands to include illustrations.

About 1477 he moved to Utrecht where he issued a Dutch version of the Gospels and Epistles; a second edition, in Dutch, of Rolewinck, 1481, with additional cuts, and also in 1481 the 'Epistelen en Evangelien' with Biblical illustration and one of the famous 'Speculum' blocks (cut in two).

In 1483 he moved to Kuilenberg issuing in the same year a quarto edition in Dutch of the 'Speculum humanae salvationis'. For this he used all the woodcuts of the anonymous earlier folio editions, being obliged to cut the blocks to fit the smaller page. He added twelve new ones.

The close affinity between Veldener's first Louvain type and that used in the 'De proprietatibus rerum' by Bartholomaeus Anglicus, on which Wynkyn de Worde claimed Caxton worked at Cologne about 1472, has led to its attribution to Veldener and thus to his possible association with Caxton. Veldener may have supplied the coarse *lettre bâtarde* used by Caxton (his types Nos 1, 2, and 3), also types to the Fratres Vitae Communis in Brussels, to Machlinia in London, and to others.

vélin: the French term for wove paper.

vellum: the skin of the newly born calf, kid or lamb prepared for writing upon by stretching and polishing with alum. Calf-skin vellums were used by Irish scribes from the 7th to 9th century for MSS, and later elsewhere in Europe for small *Books of Hours*, q.v.

Modern vellum is usually unsplit calf and, when used for bindings, the hair follicles are visible on spine and cover. The boards of such books have a tendency to warp. See also *art vellum, Japanese vellum, parchment, ties.*

vellum binding trade: a former name for what is now known as *stationery binding*. At one time the sections of account books and ledgers were sewn on vellum tapes, and the back folds of the first and last sections were strengthened by having a strip of vellum pasted round the outsides. Linen webbing, which takes the glue better, is now substituted.

velvet bindings: bindings covered in velvet. In England they belong to the era 1500–1670, often being used for prayer books and, towards the end of the period, for *sombre bindings*, q.v. See also *embroidered bindings*.

Venetian bindings: bindings made in Venice at the end of the 15th century, showing the influence of the migrant oriental craftsmen who presumably made them. Goatskin or morocco-covered wood or cardboard were used, and some bindings were given double boards, front and back, so that a recessed panel could be cut for the main decoration.

Many books printed by Aldus about this time featured his leaf motif and small dolphins in blind and gold. More ambitious were the *Ducali bindings*, q.v.

venetian types: roman type cut in Venice in the late 15th century based on earlier Italian humanist hands. Bold serifs gave a balanced squareness to the capitals, lower-case letters had a wide set, and there was no italic. They were used by Jenson and da Spira. For a specimen see *letters – forms and styles*.

499

Vérard, Antoine, fl.1485–1512: an important figure in the Parisian booktrade whose scriptorium was extended to include printed book production. It is possible that Vérard did not operate presses but commissioned other printers. In 'Débuts de l'imprimerie en France', 1904, Christian writes of him as one who 'a passé longtemps pour être imprimeur, mais qui, en réalité, n'a été qu'un éditeur'.

The first printed work he issued, a translation by Laurent Premierfait of Boccaccio's 'Il Decamerone', was printed by Jean du Pré in 1485. Included among other well known printers who served him were Pierre Levet, Guy Marchant, and Jean Morand. In 1507 he was appointed bookseller to Louis XII. His French edition of the Epistles of St Paul, 1507–8, contains one of the earliest known privileges, granting him the sole right for three years to print, sell and distribute the work, with penalities for infringers.

Unlike his contemporaries who issued classical texts for scholars Vérard published extensively in French. He was noted for his printed *Books of Hours*, q.v., issuing some two hundred editions with special copies for royalty (*Heures royales*) pulled on vellum and illuminated. Fine woodcuts illustrated many of his books, and to him as much as any other publisher the early development of the illustrated book in France is due.

In the vellum presentation set of his three volume 'Les Grandes chroniques de France', 1493, the woodcut decorations of ordinary copies were replaced by nearly a thousand miniatures attributed to a disciple of the master François. The first volume had a traditional frontispiece scene of Vérard kneeling before the king to offer his book, a reminder that Vérard purveyed both written and printed works.

His son *Barthélemy*, who continued the business, was one of the first French printers whose work was influenced by the Italian Renaissance as in his 'Les Triumphes messire françoys petracque' (Petrarch), 1514, in which he combined his father's gothic type and some of his blocks with other cuts in the Italian style. See J. MacFarlane, 'Antoine Vérard', London, 1900.

verbatim et literatim: a Latin phrase meaning word for word, letter for letter; a literal translation.

Vereeniging ter bevordering van de belangen des Boekhandels: founded in 1815 as the Dutch booksellers and publishers association for the advancement of the interests of the book trade. Working in close cooperation with this association are the *Koninklijke Nederlandsche Uitgeversbond*, founded in 1880, and the *Nederlandse Boekverkopersbond*, founded in 1907, which are the separate organizations of publishers and booksellers respectively.

The association is largely concerned with trade organization and retail price maintenance and the establishment of professional standards. Only booksellers and publishers who have successfully completed a two-year diploma course are recognised by it.

The association also runs certain trade institutions, notably a trade clearing house, and a central stock house of over 40,000 titles (which combine to form the *Bestelhuis* or Orders Clearing House), and a library. It publishes the trade weekly 'Nieuwsblad voor de Boekhandel', the counterpart of Britain's *The Bookseller*.

vergé: the French term for laid paper.

vernis mou: an alternative name for *soft-ground etching*. See *etching*.

vernis sans odeur: a name descriptive of a group of lacquered bindings made in Paris. The Parisian binder associated with most of the twenty-one extant examples was Theodore Pierre Bertin, fl.1800–18, who had patented his process of making 'reliures vernisées' in the late 18th century.

Covers of calf were painted in a neo-classical style, gilded and lacquered. On the earliest specimens only the sides were varnished, the spine being of tooled leather with mosaic decoration; on most of the later examples the spines were decorated to match the sides and then varnished.

This method is also known as *vernis Martin*, supposedly after the Parisian Simon-Etienne Martin who developed a brilliant translucent lacquer which he patented in 1730. It was used for decorating furniture in the oriental manner, coach panels, boxes of all kinds, and on at least one known binding with gilt and coloured flowers under the lacquer of *c.* 1744.

For an illustrated note on these bindings see A. Ehrman, 'Les Reliures vernis sans odeur, autrement dit *vernis Martin*', *Book Collector*, Winter 1965.

Verovio, Simone: an Italian printer credited with being the first to have printed music from engraved copper plates. In 1586 he issued a collection of canzonette 'Diletto spirituale' from engraved plates attributed to Martin van Buyten.

versals: ornamental capital letters written marginally or partly in the text to mark the beginnings of paragraphs, verses or important passages in a manuscript. In early examples the ornamentation was simple, being mostly flourishes, dotted outlines or a contrasting colour. In the 15th century they became much more elaborate and developed into illuminated initials. Versals ranged over several lines of text but the top of the capital was approximately aligned with the minuscules of the word to which it belonged. See also *illumination*.

versificator regis: see *Poet Laureate*.

verso: 1. the reverse of a single unfolded printed sheet. See also *dorse, leaf* (3).

2. the left-hand page of an opening. Left-hand pages bear even numbers. Cf. *recto*.

vertical camera: a reproduction camera with a horizontal copy board and the camera permanently focussed for photographing through a prism. The lens is usually in a fixed position, and the copyboard and back of the camera (the position of the dark plate) are movable, their movements being correlated for automatic focussing. (GU)

vertical house: a publishing house with hard cover and paperback facilities.

vertical press: one with a vertical forme instead of a lateral one. See *platen press*.

vertical title labels: see *labels*.

Vicentino: see *Arrighi*.

Vidal, Pascual: see *Carsi y Vidal, Pascual*.

vide infra: the Latin for 'see below'. When this instruction to the reader is required in books in English 'see below' is preferable.

video display unit: or *VDU*, a correction and make-up device incorporating a keyboard and a cathode-ray tube on which lines of characters can be generated. One common use is for reading and correcting paper tape. Tape is fed into the unit and a group of characters representing the codes on the tape is displayed on a green phosphor screen. Characters can be added, deleted or moved by a cursor or light pen and the corrected version be punched out on fresh tape. As the tape is progressed the top of the lines scroll off the top of the screen and fresh lines scroll on to the bottom.

Such devices are also used on-line to a computer so that stored data can be called up for amendment, or fresh data be checked before entry. Also known as a *video display terminal* or a *visual display terminal* (somewhat anomalously since anything displayed must be visual). See also *word processing*.

vide supra: the Latin for 'see above'. The English form is preferable.

Vienna Dioscorides: a Greek herbal, being a parchment codex of 491 folios written in uncial script and illustrated with coloured drawings of plants, animals and birds. There are 392 whole-page pictures and 87 in the text. Most of the book is an alphabetically arranged sequence of drawings of plants with a description of each, and the text was largely the work of a Greek physician *Pedanios Dioscorides*, (fl. AD 54–68) who came from Anazarba in Cilicia (South Turkey), but writings by *Claudius Galen* and *Krateuas* are also included.

The scribe and artist(s) responsible for this great Byzantine manuscript are unknown, but it was completed before 513 since one of the drawings has a dedicatory inscription to Princess Anicia Juliana in gratitude for the building of a church at Honoratae, a suburb of Byzantium. Church historians say this was completed about 512–13, thus establishing the date of the codex with some certainty. The pictures of plants are mostly copied from 1st century BC originals.

The codex was rebound by Johannes Chortasmenos in 1406. It passed to the Turks after 1453, and Arabic and Turkish plant names were added in arabic script by unknown hands. In the 16th century Hebraic transcriptions were added, probably by Hamon, the Jewish doctor to Suleiman II. In 1569 the doctor's son sold the book for 100 gold ducats to Augerius Ghislain von Busbeck who brought it from Constantinople to Kaiser Maxmilian II in Vienna, where it may now be seen in the Österreichische Nationalbibliothek (Codex Vindobonensis, Med.gracc.1). In the late 1960s this great work was given new freshness by the skilful restoration of Professor Otto Wächter. A faithful facsimile was published in 1970 at Graz.

The first translation into Latin, by Petrus Paduanensis, was published at Colle in 1478, and Aldus Manutius issued the first printed Greek edition in 1499. Nearly eighty of the hundred or so editions issued between 1478 and 1800 were printed in the 17th century, in particular in the version entitled 'De materia medica' translated and edited by Pietro Mattioli (1500–77) of Siena. An interlinear English translation of the Aldine Greek was made by John Goodyer between 1652 and 1655. It was not published until 1934 when R. T. Gunther's edition with F. A. Boustead's black and white drawings of the Vienna codex was printed for him by O.U.P.

Vienna Genesis: the book of Genesis as depicted in a series of forty-eight pictures painted on twenty-four parchment leaves (there were originally about ninety-six) in the late 6th century, probably at Antioch (Antakya, South Turkey). The work of eight artists can be traced. The leaves are of a dark purple-brown, but the colours of the paintings are still remarkably fresh. The text is in silver uncials.

From notes on some of the leaves the work is known to have been in Italy during the Middle Ages; since 1664 it has been in the Imperial Library, Vienna (now Österreichische Nationalbibliothek).

For a contemporary work see also *Codex Rossanensis*. See E. Wellesz, 'The Vienna Genesis', Faber, 1960.

vigesimo-quarto: see *twenty-fourmo*.

vignette: 1. an illustration in which the edges of the picture shade off into the surrounding paper, there being no limiting border or frame. Title-pages and chapter heads of 18th and 19th-century books were often illustrated with engravings printed in this form. A modern vignetted illustration is shown under *half-tone*, q.v. See also *livres à vignettes*.

2. an initial capital letter decorated with vine-leaves and tendrils as painted in a handwritten book.

vignettes de fonte: small typographic ornaments used to decorate the head and foot of pages and elsewhere. Their use was begun by *Gabriel Giolito* in Venice, q.v., but it was Fournier le jeune who employed them most elegantly. See also *Fournier*.

Village Press: see *Goudy*.

Vinegar Bible: a soubriquet given to the edition of the Bible printed by John Basket in 1717 because of an error in the running title of Luke XX which reads: 'The parable of the vinegar' instead of 'The parable of the vineyard'. This edition has also been referred to as 'A basket-full of errors' as a pun on the printer-publisher's name.

Vine Press: an amateur private press established in 1956 by Peter Foster and John Peters at Hemingford, Hunts. Since their first book 'Vitis vera', printed in 1957, they have issued several small editions on hand-made paper, commissioning mechanical typesetting and a trade binder. The last book from their press was Evelyn Ansell's 'Twenty-five poems', 1963, which had wood engravings by Diana Bloomfield.

John Peters is also known for the Castellar titling fount he designed for the Monotype Corporation. It is shown in Appendix A.

Vinland Map: a vellum map of the world, probably drawn at or near Basle about 1440, which, 'if authentic and correctly dated, is evidence of the belief in mid-15th century Europe that *Vinlandia insula*, a large island situated a fair distance to the west of Greenland, was the Vinland stated in the sagas to have been discovered and temporarily settled by the Norseman Leif Eiriksson' in the early 11th century.

It is claimed in the monograph cited below that the map 'records in graphic form the only documented pre-Columbian discovery of America'. This provocative challenge to the primacy of Columbus was understandably dismissed in Madrid as a Viking myth, but it is conceivable that Columbus knew of the map and sought to investigate Eiriksson's voyage.

The manuscript text accompanying the map was written on paper which, after radioisotope exposure in the 1960s, was identified as having been made about 1460 in the Piedmontese town of Caselle, and in 1974 small particle chemical analysis of the ink on the map led experts to pronounce it a 20th century forgery. By whom remains unsolved. See R. S. Skelton and others, 'The Vinland map *and* The Tartar relation', Yale U.P., 1965.

vinnet: the name used in the 17th century for what was later known as a *vignette*, q.v.

vinyl binding materials: the generic term for book covering materials marketed under several proprietary names. They are (or should be) pliable, non-cracking, suitable for blocking and printing by letterpress or offset, as well as resistant to insects, damp and scuffing. See also *non-woven binding materials*.

viscosity: the resistance of a liquid to flow. The unit for measuring it is the *poise*, named after the Frenchman Jean Poiseulle who formulated it in 1842. The viscosity of letterpress printing is varied according to the machine on which it will be used, ranging from stiff inks (500 or more poises) for slow hand-fed machines to thin inks (6–12 poises) for high-speed rotaries. The SI unit for testing viscosity is the Newton second per metre squared: $1 \text{ Ns/m}^2 = 10$ poises.

visualizer: a name given in some publishers' production departments in the 1970s to their graphic designers of jackets, layouts, and so on, i.e. *visuals*.

viz.: an abbreviation for the Latin 'videlicet', i.e. namely.

Vizetelly, Henry, 1820–94: a London printer and engraver working from 1841–49 in partnership with his brother James, later alone. He was commissioned to produce illustrated books for several publishers, issued the first English edition of 'Uncle Tom's cabin' in 1853, and acted as Paris correspondent of the *Illustrated London News* (which he had helped to found in 1842).

Vizlant, Jakob, d. 1475: a German merchant who, with his brother Philip, may have financed the setting up of one of the early printing presses in Valencia. He employed John of Salzburg and Paul Hurus of Constance to operate it; this was in 1474. A year later the two printers set up the first press in Barcelona.

vocabulary: a systematically arranged list of words with explanations of their meaning. The term is mostly applied to lists in books for studying a contemporary language, and is less comprehensive than a *dictionary*, q.v. A vocabulary differs from a *glossary*, q.v., which explains the words of a particular subject or a classical language.

Vollard, Ambroise, 1869–1939: a Parisian art dealer and publisher of limited and de luxe editions of books in which the text was subordinate to the illustrations. His first publication was Paul Verlaine's 'Parallèlement', 1900, with lithographs by Pierre Bonnard. Chagall, Dufy, Picasso and Rouault were among others he commissioned, the last named illustrating Vollard's finest publication 'Cirque de l'étoile filante', 1938. See also *livres de peintres*. See U. E. Johnson, 'Ambroise Vollard éditeur: an appreciation and catalogue', N.Y., Wittenborn, 1944.

volume: a book distinguished from other books, or other parts of the same work, by having its own title-page and usually, though not necessarily by independent pagination. It is British Library practice to count such works as volumes whether or not they have separate covers.

volumen: a papyrus or vellum roll bearing columns of writing which, when not being read, was wound round an *umbilicus*, q.v. Each roll was identified by a ticket when closed.

The name 'volumen' is the Latin word for 'a thing rolled up', but in medieval times it was also applied to a book in codex form.

volume rights: the right to publish a work in any volume form. More particularly, it means that the rights granted include both cased and paperback publication.

volvelle: a composite woodcut diagram with movable parts. The parts are superimposed circles or segments of a circle, bearing printed information, and rotated from a central axis. The 16th century Italian Damianus Zenarius published works with woodcut volvelle diagrams which could be manipulated to show the positions of the sun, moon and planets.

Voskens, Bartholomeus, fl.1641–70: a typefounder of Rotterdam who with his brother *Reinhard* began work about 1641. He later moved to Hamburg, but by 1666 was established in Amsterdam. His son *Dirk*, who bought the Blaeu foundry, continued the business until about 1700 when it passed to his son *Bartholomeus II*. They had a considerable reputation and their types were used throughout Europe. Two of their English clients were John Fell (see *Fell types*) and *Thomas James*, q.v. In addition to the usual roman and gothic founts they sold a range of exotic types. See also *cyrillic*.

At the sale of the family business in 1780 Adam Mappa bought part of the equipment. In 1789 he took it to New York where it passed later to *Archibald Binny*, q.v., whose foundry in Philadelphia began in 1796.

Reinhard Voskens opened an independent foundry in Frankfurt which was sold to Johann Adolf Schmidt about 1670.

Vostre, Simon, fl.1486–1520: a Parisian publisher, remembered principally for his numerous editions of Books of Hours. About 1491 he seems to have begun a long association with *Philippe Pigouchet*, q.v. Many of the Horae which Vostre published had borders made up of several small blocks forming compartments. Towards the end of the 15th century Pigouchet used border blocks which included classical urns, acanthus leaves and other Renaissance motifs. Most of the Horae were 'ad usum Romanum', but Vostre also issued a Sarum Horae in 1498, and other local usages.

votive binding: a lavishly decorated binding, usually enclosing a copy of the Gospels, given to a church in return for prayers to be said for the giver's soul or that of a departed relative.

voucher body: a copy of a book which, because it includes material quoted with permission from a work issued by another publisher, is sent to the latter on publication day. This is done as evidence that the use made of such copyright material has been as agreed, and is comparable to the practice in periodicals publishing of sending an advertiser in a magazine a free (voucher) copy of the issue containing the advertisement he paid for.

In book publishing the term is often loosely and erroneously used in the trade for copies sent to editors for review, and for the six copies of his work given on publication to an author. Although supplied free they are not voucher copies. Also known as a *permissions copy*.

Vox classification: a scheme announced in 1954 by the French typographer and graphic artist Maximilien Vox whereby any type face could be classified according to its visual characteristics in one of ten categories to which he gave synthetic designations. As listed below the Vox names are shown with the group numbers given in 1962 when the Association Typographique Internationale (A Typ I) adopted the scheme.

Humane (A Typ I Group I) Revivals or derivatives of the roman letter of the late 15th century, known in England as 'venetians', and of the inscriptional capitals of classical Rome. E.g. Centaur, Cloister, Lutetia, Minerva.

Garalde (A Typ I Group II) Most old-face types. E.g. Bembo, Caslon, Garamond.

Réale (A Typ I Group III) Types known in English as transitionals and modern redrawings of old faces. E.g. Baskerville, Fournier, Perpetua, Times Roman.

Didone (A Typ I Group IV) Types known in English as modern face. E.g. Bodoni, Didot, Scotch Roman, Walbaum.

Mécane (A Typ I Group V) Antiques, clarendons, and egyptians having strokes of almost even thickness and slab serifs. E.g. Cairo, Egizio, Nero Tondo, Rockwell.

Linéale (A Typ I Group VI) Sanserif types of all kinds. E.g. Futura, Gill, Univers.

Incise (A Typ I Group VII) Types with a chiselled effect and a slight thickening of terminal strokes. E.g. Bold Latin Condensed, Thorne Shaded, Weiss Lapidar.

Scripte (A Typ I Group VIII) Calligraphic faces, either with joined letters as in most copperplate scripts, or with unjoined letters. E.g. Francesca, Trafton.

Manuaire (A Typ I Group IX) Types based on manuscript hands, and also formal unjoined pen or brush letters as distinct from scripts, E.g. Albertus, Klang, Othello.

Fracture (A Typ I Group X) All black letter types and their derivatives. E.g. Caxton, Fraktur, Old English Text. (Vox absorbed this group in his 'Manuaires': it has been separated as Group X by A Typ I.)

If a type does not fit clearly into one group a double name should be given, thus Ashley Script becomes Manuaire-Scripte. Several European founders use the classification in their catalogues, notable being Typefoundry Amsterdam.

Vox, Maximilien, 1894–1974: born Samuel Monod who, as M. Vox, began his long career as a journalist, graphic artist and typographer in 1913, followed from 1924 by work as a cover designer for the publisher Bernard Grasset. Vox was subsequently artistic adviser to Deberny et Peignot under whose auspices he produced the journal *Les Divertissements typographiques.* In 1945 he founded with Emmanuel Olive the journal *Caractère,* followed in 1950 by the sumptuous revue *Caractère Noël* which appeared annually until 1964.

His international reputation was consolidated with the founding in 1953 of the École de Lure, an international assembly of printers and graphic designers who met at a village in Haute Provence to discuss new printing techniques. A result of these proceedings was the *Vox classification* scheme for type described above.

Vulgate: the Latin version of the Bible as translated by St Jerome *c.* 380–405. Of surviving manuscript copies the *Codex Amiatinus,* q.v., is perhaps most important. Various recensions have been made for the Catholic Church, notable being the Toletus revision authorized by Clement VIII (1592–1605) which is still the approved text. See also *Bible printing in England, Gutenberg.*

W

wagoner: a nautical manual and atlas of charts for maritime use. The name may derive from 'Spiegel der Zeevaerdt', printed at Leyden by Plantin and published by the compiler, Lucas Jansz. Waghenaer, in 1584. Part one had twenty-three maritime charts and was the first printed illustrated manual of navigation. Part two, published in 1585, had a further twenty-two maps. An English translation by Anthony Ashley was published in London in 1588 with the title 'The mariners mirrour' (STC 11097).

The term wagoner or waggoner continued in use for similar publications throughout the 17th and 18th centuries. See also *Hondius, periplus, portolano, ruttier book, wind rose.*

Walbaum, Justus Erich, 1768–1837: the leading German typefounder of the early 19th century. He worked for a time as a plate engraver for the music publisher Johann Peter Spehr of Brunswick. In 1796 he successfully applied for the licence to establish a typefoundry at Goslar. This licence had been granted earlier in the same year to a printer, Gottlieb Kircher, who had renounced his claim without practising as founder. In 1803 Walbaum moved to Weimar where his business became famous. He sold it in 1836 to F. A. Brockhaus of Leipzig where his punches remained until 1918 when they were bought by the Berthold foundry of Berlin.

The modern face Monotype Walbaum, series 374, is based on Walbaum's Antiqua. It was begun in 1930. (See Appendix A.)

Waldegrave, Robert, c. 1554–1603: at one time a printer for the secret Marprelate Press which in the 1580s issued Puritan tracts (thereby necessitating its removal from place to place). In 1590 he was appointed King's Scottish Printer to James I, and for some years issued mostly theological works from his Edinburgh press. He may have returned to London when James ascended the English throne in 1603, publishing books there. The Edinburgh shop and privileges were acquired by Thomas Finlayson.

Waldow, Alexander: a printer of Leipzig who wrote several practical works on printing, published between 1864 and 1884. Most important was his 'Illustrierte Enzyklopaedie der Graphischen Künste', 1884, which at the time of its publication was judged to be the most comprehensive book of its kind to have appeared in any language.

Waldseemüller, Martin, c. 1470–1518: a German geographer who studied in Freiburg before settling at St Dié in Lorraine. In his book 'Introductio cosmographiae', printed by Gaultier Lud and associates, St Dié, 1507, Waldseemüller named the New World 'America' after Amerigo Vespucci, a Latin translation of whose 'Four voyages' describing the discovery of a new continent (actually South America) formed part of the 'Introductio'. This was the first use of the name which also appeared on the two maps to which the 'Introductio' was a commentary. One of these was an uncoloured map of the world in twelve elliptical segments, known as 'gores', designed to cover a sphere, and printed from a single wood block. Only two copies are known: one is in the University of Minnesota Library, the other was sold to Kraus of New York in 1960 for £12,500.

Waldseemüller later realised that the true discoverer of the New World was Columbus, so in his edition of Ptolemy's 'Cosmographia', published by Johannes Schott, Strasbourg, 1513, he substituted the name 'Prasilia sive Terra Papagalli', but the misnomer became the accepted name.

Waldvoghel, Procopius: a Prague goldsmith who at Avignon in France experimented with some form of 'artificial writing' about the years 1444–6. This was later than Gutenberg's invention of printing from movable type in 1436–9 but before the latter issued any work in the early 1450s. Waldvoghel is reported to have had equipment which included letters cut in copper, zinc, brass and iron as well as other instruments 'künstlich zu schreiben'. Nothing is known to survive from his endeavours, but legal documents exist which make it clear that he was experimenting. The two men Vitalis and Ferrose of Trier who paid to be associated with his project were sworn not to reveal what they had learned at Avignon.

Waldvoghel took over from the Jew David de Caderousse some hebrew letters cut in iron and the tools to make them. He also had to promise silence. While there have been conjectures that Waldvoghel either met Gutenberg or at least heard of his experiments the matter is likely to remain unsolved as there is no evidence that the former attempted to multiply copies of a text. See also *Brito*.

Walker, Sir Emery, 1851–1933: a London socialist, printer and photoengraver who was associated with the private press movement in England and Germany. In 1873 he joined Alfred Dawson's Typographic Etching Company, eventually becoming a recognised and widely consulted authority on printing processes with his own printing and photoengraving business. He lectured, and was concerned with the establishment of schools of printing in London. He advocated close-set type, now common practice, and sought to reform school handwriting.

Walker's friendship with William Morris began in 1884 when they were neighbours in Hammersmith. A lecture on letterpress printing which Walker gave to the Arts and Crafts Exhibition Society in 1888 was the touchstone which inspired Morris to set up his Kelmscott Press. Although not a partner in the enterprise Walker was closely associated as an adviser.

Later, as the partner of Cobden-Sanderson, Walker was responsible for the distinction of the Doves Press Bible, still considered a landmark in English printing. By his long friendship with the famous punchcutter E. P. Prince his influence pervaded the whole private press movement. Walker supplied Prince with working drawings and supervised the cutting of the Doves type, based on the Jenson original. He designed a venetian and accompanying italic for the Cranach-Presse edition of Virgil, and with Sir Sydney Cockerell prepared a version of the Subiaco roman for the Ashendene Press.

When in 1905 the German Insel-Verlag began the revival of good book production Walker designed the format for the series of reprints of national classics. He was also adviser to Count Harry Kessler of the Cranach-Presse.

One of the last books associated with him was Homer's 'Odyssey', translated by T. E. Lawrence, with typographical styling by Bruce Rogers who crossed the Atlantic specially to work with Walker. The book was issued in 1932.

Walker's knighthood in 1930 was for services to printing. Sir Sydney Cockerell, a friend and partner, wrote of him 'his influence, direct or indirect, can be discerned in nearly every well designed page of text that now appears, and to him, more than to any other man, this country's great improvement in book production is due'.

See C. Franklin 'Emery Walker: some light on his theories of printing . . .', C.U.P., (Privately printed), 1973. See also *Mall Press*.

wallet edged: said of a limp-bound book when the back cover is extended to enclose the fore-edge and fasten into a slot in the front cover.

Walpergen, Peter de, *c.* 1646–1703: a native of Frankfurt who in 1671 was engaged by the Dutch East India Company to work in Java as a typefounder and printer, but it was from Holland that he came in 1676 as typefounder to Oxford University. He made extra sorts for founts already there, while punches and matrices for his several founts of roman, italic, exotics and a graceful music type survive at the University Press. Some of his types are still cast and used.

For specimens see H. Hart, 'Notes on a century of typography at the University Press, Oxford, 1693–1794', 1900; reprinted with introduction and notes by Harry Carter, O.U.P., 1970.

Walter, John, 1738–1812: founder of the newspaper *Daily Universal Register* in 1785, the name being changed in 1788 to *The Times*. It was his son *John* (1776–1847) who established the fame of this paper. He sought to improve printing machinery and installed an early model of König's cylinder press. The founder's grandson, also *John*, was similarly interested in the development of printing machinery.

Walter press: an early rotary press for printing on rolls of paper. It was constructed at the instigation of J. Walter, the owner of *The Times*, by J. C. MacDonald and J. Calverley, 1866, and was later given a folding device. The reel of paper was moistened on both sides before printing, and the press could deliver 12,000 copies of the newspaper an hour. In the 1870s models were in use throughout Europe. See also *Applegath*.

(GU)

Walther, Henry, fl.1790–1840: a London bookbinder of considerable taste and skill. To generalize, he favoured the use of dark blue morocco with simple straight line tooling, and he also used a series of architectural tools. Other bindings attributed to him have an all-over pattern of crossed lines forming diamonds, i.e. *diced*.

Wanley, Humfrey, 1672–1726: Anglo-Saxonist, palaeographer and librarian who worked in the Bodleian from 1697–99. In 1705 he issued an important catalogue of Anglo-Saxon manuscripts, and it was about this time that he began to advise *Robert Harley*, q.v., on purchases for his collection. From 1708 he assumed the duties of full-time librarian to the Harleys, father and son.

From the diary which Wanley kept intermittently between 1715 and 1726 we get an interesting account of 18th century book collecting. Wanley supervised the binding, in calf for most of the manuscripts, but for the more important books in morocco specially obtained from Fez, via Gibraltar, whence came in 1720/1 two gross skins at £72. They were issued to the binders as required. It is recorded that when Chapman wished to buy these skins cheaply but to charge the usual binding rates he was told 'my Lord will not turn Leather-Seller; & therefore he must bring his proposals for Binding with my Lords Marocco-Skins; otherwise his Lordship will appoint some other Binder to do so'. There were also frequent complaints of badly done lettering.

Warde, Beatrice, 1900–69: a writer and lecturer on typography who in 1925 came to England from her native America where she had worked and learned in the library of the *American Type Founders Company*, q.v. She came into prominence when under the pen name Paul Beaujon she wrote for *The Fleuron* an article on the types of Garamont.

For many years she was publicity manager to the Monotype Corporation and edited the *Monotype Recorder*, making that publication of far more interest and importance to typographers than the usual house journal, while the superb broadsheet 'This is a printing office . . .' which she wrote and designed to display Eric Gill's Perpetua Titling series is known the world over. See "I am a communicator": a selection of writings and talks', *Monotype Recorder*, 44 1 1970; and 'The crystal goblet: an invitation to typography', 1947.

Warde, Frederic, 1894–1939: from 1921–4 printer to Princeton University Press, U.S.A., and known in Britain for the Arrighi italic he designed to accompany the Centaur roman of Bruce Rogers. This was cut for hand setting in Paris in 1925, the Monotype version appearing in 1929. He was the husband of *Beatrice Warde*, q.v.

warehouse copies: books damaged by careless handling in a publisher's or wholesale warehouse. They are sold cheaply through the trade as *partial remainders*, q.v.

warehouse work: the handling of paper in a printing establishment before and after it is machined, i.e. printed.

Pre-printing. The receipt, checking and storage in a printer's *white-paper warehouse* of his stock of paper. If prior cutting is needed it is done here. The head of the warehouse calculates and issues the quantity of paper for a job, calling for a knowledge of paper qualities, inks, and printing processes.

Post-printing. 1. The finishing processes which convert printed sheets into books, periodicals or other sectional matter. They include everything from jogging the sheets through to packing and despatch. See also *bookbinding methods and processes, print converters*.

2. The storing by a printer in his *printed-paper warehouse*, or by an edition binder, of unbound printed sheets. Binding up an edition may be spread over several years depending on the sales of a book, and the binder will charge the publisher for storage.

warping: the distortion of book covers after binding or casing so that they do not lie flat. Research has shown that this is due to the differing expansion and contraction of the various components of the cover, viz. cloth, boards, end-papers, and to a lesser extent the film of adhesive. On newly bound books these causes are at work due to the drying out of the adhesives, and later further stresses may occur due to climatic changes. Among practical means of minimizing warping are the use of well-matured boards, end-papers having the grain running from head to tail, the use of adhesives with a minimum water content, and adequate pressing of the books. (LK)

wash-drawing: a brush-drawing which contains grey tones in addition to blacks and whites.

washing up: 1. in binding, lightly sponging covers with glair to assist in the adherance of gold leaf. This is also done when blocking cased books. (LK)

2. in printing, the removal of ink from the forme, inking system, or offset rubber blanket. Normally petrol or benzol is used for washing up the forme, photogen for cleaning the inking system with or without subsequent washing with petrol, and petrol or special washing solutions containing sulphur for the offset rubber blanket.

Remains of ink are removed from a forme on completing printing by washing with lye. Steam is also used for removing grease and also baths of such detergent solutions as sodium sesquisilicate in water, heated by steam. After immersion in such a bath the forme is washed in clean water, dried and lightly oiled. The great disadvantage of the once popular caustic soda was its tendency to leave a film on the metal, quite apart from its offensive smell. (See also *chamber lye*.)

wash-out process: any process using photopolymer printing plates (e.g. Dycril, Nyloprint) from which the non-image areas are washed out after exposure. The need for routing out those areas is thus avoided.

waste paper conversion: the re-use of waste paper to make new paper or board. Every year British printing houses yield over 100,000 tons of printers' shavings and other waste paper which can be pulped and substituted for wood pulp in the manufacture of certain grades of paper and board.

A problem in the re-use of this waste for making better quality papers is the presence of pernicious contraries. These may include plastic coatings, hot-melt adhesives, or reinforcing fibres. If not discovered in time they can ruin a making of paper.

The British Waste Paper Utilisation Council has campaigned for the adoption by paper users of a system of marks to indicate whether or not a paper product is suitable for re-use. The Council introduced

507

its *Not Easily Pulpable* scheme (NEP) which uses labels, tags, or a printed symbol for tracing and identifying contrary papers through all stages of printing and conversion, and BS 3340 recommends a mark to be used for indicating freedom from contraries. Their widespread adoption could be an important factor in increasing the supply of usable waste paper. See also *recycled paper*.

water-colour inks: thin transparent inks, made without oil, which may be used when printing in colours from a rubber surface. As they remain soluble when printed their impression would be spoiled by accidental wetting as, for example, on a jacket.

watered silk: silk with a wavy or damask-like pattern: it is sometimes used for doublures.

water finish: heavily loaded paper which is given a high finish by alternately damping each side of the roll of paper with water and passing it through heated rolls. The process is used when making *imitation art paper*, q.v.

waterleaf: unsized paper which is semi-absorbent and requires sizing before use.

water lines: another name for the laid and chain lines of *laid paper*, q.v.

watermark: a distinguishing mark, lettering, or design made in paper during manufacture and visible when the sheet is held up to light. Watermarks were used in Italy during the 13th century, being made from wire twisted into simple geometric shapes. While originally used as trade-marks, in the course of time they developed into designations of size, hence *pott* had a jug as watermark, *foolscap* had a cap and bells, *post* had a post-horn, etc.

In hand-made paper the wire design is sewn or soldered to the mould on which the sheet is formed, causing the fibres to lie thinner where they touch it. Early watermarks were copied and many appear confusingly similar. In these instances the position of dots, occurring at each of the many places where a thread of wire was used to fasten the watermark to the mesh, will assist in identifying sheets made on one mould.

In machine-made papers the design is sewn to the dandy roll and impresses itself on the moist web by displacing fibres at a point in the machine where sufficient water has drained away for this displacement to set.

A function of modern watermarks is to give security against forgery (on stamps, cheques, banknotes, etc.). They are also of considerable help when tracing the date and place of a book, and reference should be made to Briquet's 'Les Filigranes' which reproduces 16,000 watermarks of the period 1282–1600. Should a mark be obscured by printing a radioactive sheet of plastic can be placed on the upper side of the leaf to be examined and a photographic film on the other. Carbon-14 embedded in the plastic emits electrons which pass through the thinner (watermark) areas of the paper and leave an impression on the film. No damage is done to the paper. See also *countermark*, *cut ahead*, *cut to register*, *impressed watermark*.

watermark reproduction: watermarks in paper have long been recognised as a possible means of dating an undated book and of locating the source of the paper used. For the collections of watermarks issued in book form (e.g. Briquet) tracing or photography have been the usual methods, the former being liable to inaccuracy, the latter being unsatisfactory because of the text printed over the mark.

In 1958 the Soviet Academy of Sciences in Leningrad published a report by D. P. Erastov on a new technique. Briefly, a radioactive calcium isotope preparation is put on a glass plate. The plate is positioned over the watermarked paper, and both are laid over a photographic film. After exposure for several hours the film shows clearly the places on the paper where the fibres lie thinner, i.e. the watermark. Printed or written matter is completely by-passed. Safety precautions are necessary in using isotopes.

A method of watermark copying by using secondary electrons emitted by the X-ray tube of a standard therapy plant is described in *Book Collector*, Summer 1965, 217.

water-reducible inks: letterpress inks developed by Coates Bros of Britain. They are quick-drying combinations of solvents and resins in a vehicle which, although stable on the machine, is made to set after impression by chemical reaction to the paper surface. The ink can be reduced with water and the press can be washed with water, yet the printed surface will not be affected by accidental wetting.

Watt, Robert, 1774–1819: a Glasgow physician remembered for his 'Bibliotheca Britannica', 2 vols, Edinburgh, 1824. This was a list of some 50,000 titles arranged by authors and subjects. Selected non-British works were included, as were articles on art and science from important periodicals.

Publication in parts began in the year Watts died and the work was seen through the press by his assistants. The venture was a financial failure, but the work doubtless inspired *W. T. Lowndes*, q.v. The 'Bibliotheca' was reprinted in New York in 1965.

Sir James Wattie Book of the Year Awards: since 1968, a series of cash awards founded and administered by private enterprise in New Zealand. Awards are made at the annual N.Z. Book Week.

Wauquelin, Jean, d. *c.* 1452: a professional translator and adaptor into prose of early verse tales who was employed by Philip the Good, Duke of Burgundy. Prior to the 15th century popular literature had been written in verse, but now prose became fashionable: it was also easier to read. Wealthy patrons, such as Philip, commissioned writers to adapt favourite 'chansons de geste' and the like.

Wauquelin's translation of Geoffrey of Monmouth's '*Brut*', q.v., and similar works still survive, but his prose owed too much to its originals to have either style or individuality. He was also, in a sense, a publisher, and employed copyists and illuminators in his Bruges atelier. A superb example of his work is the 'Chroniques de Hainaut', now in the Royal Library, Brussels, of which only the first of its three volumes was completed before Wauquelin died. See also *Weyden*.

waygoose: originally the name of the annual feast given by a master printer for his journeymen and apprentices. Writing in 1683 Moxon stated 'These Way-gooses are always kept about Bartholomew-tide. And till the Master-Printer have given this Way-goose, the Journey-men do not use to Work by Candle-Light.'

The term is still used to describe the annual outing or dinner held by or for the members of a printing works. The word, which is also spelled *Wayzgoose*, is of obscure origin, but if it is ever discovered that the many French printers who worked in England in the early 16th century still ate the traditionally French dish goose (Fr. *oie*) at their communal feasts, the source of this, as of so many printing trade terms may have been traced. Records show that in 16th century Antwerp the word *gansdach* (goose day) was used for a printers' feast.

Wayland, John, *c.* 1508–72: a printer and scrivener of London. He began printing about 1537, issuing Bishop John Hilsey's 'Primer' and four other devotional books before 1539 when he sold his stock to John Mayler. He worked as a bookseller and scrivener until 1553 when he resumed printing. He held a privilege for prayers and primers. Of importance was his reprint about 1555 of the Pynson edition of Lydgate's 'Falles of princes' (Boccaccio).

web breaks: the breaking of paper while printing. Breaks may be caused by calender cuts, damaged edges, or contraries, all of which start a tear. Low strength properties are often blamed for web breaks but as the stresses of calendering and reeling are greater than on the rotary press paper strength alone is not a factor.

web fed: any printing machine into which paper is fed from a reel. Cf. *sheet fed*.

web-fed flatbed machine: a flatbed web perfecting press which prints direct from flat formes. Paper is fed from a reel and after impression the web is automatically cut, folded, and delivered. It is used for newspaper printing. A pioneer model was the American *Duplex*, designed in 1889 by Paul Cox of Battle Creek, Mich. This (and its competitors) was frequently improved and was later made in Britain by the Vickers Group. Its British rival, the *Cossar*, was designed about 1900 by Thomas Cossar of Glasgow. This was also much improved and in its last form was made by *George Mann*, q.v. It had two stationary type beds (or decks) mounted one above the other, and two impression cylinders for each. When the Vickers Group absorbed both George Mann and Gordon & Gotch (makers of the Duplex) production of the Cossar ceased in 1968.

Webster, Noah: see *dictionary*.

Wechel, Christian, fl.1520–54: a Parisian printer-publisher, mostly of medical works and the classics. His son *Andreas* continued the business after 1554, moving to Frankfurt in 1572 where he worked until his death in 1581. Other members of the family were active as printers until 1629, also in Hanau and Basle.

Weiditz, Hans, fl.1518–36: or Johannes Guidictius, a talented German professional book illustrator who worked for publishers in Augsburg and Strasbourg. He is remembered for his naturalistic illustrations (made as water colours) for the popular 'Herbarum vivae eicones' of Otto Brunfels, Strasbourg, 1530–6, and his earlier contribution to the 'Theuerdank' of 1517. It is held that the Brunfels work began modern scientific botanical drawing (Blunt, 'The art of botanical illustration', Collins, 1950).

weight: 'the degree of blackness of a typeface' (BS 2961). Types in a *family*, q.v., may vary in weight, e.g. extra-light, light, semi-light, medium, semi-bold, bold, extra-bold, ultra-bold. Paper, ink and method of printing are factors to be considered when choosing a weight of type.

Weir, Richard: a London bookbinder who was associated for a time with *Roger Payne*, q.v. Between *c.* 1774–80 he was employed by Count MacCarthy-Reagh of Toulouse to bind books for the latter's library.

Weiss, Emil Rudolf, 1875–1943: a distinguished German painter, poet and type designer who worked for the Bauersche Giesserei and for Klingspor. For Bauer he designed several notable types, a Fraktur from 1911–14, a roman from 1924–31, a gothic in 1936 and a round gothic in 1937. He was also a book designer.

509

well closed: said of paper which when examined is found to have the stuff properly shaken into a sheet, with parallel, clump-free fibres.

Welsh printing and publishing: the pioneers of the Welsh press were Englishmen working in London. The first Welsh book, a collection of the Creed, Lord's prayer, and Commandants known by its incipit as 'Yny Lhyvyr hwnny' (in this book), was published by Edward Whitchurch in 1547 (STC 20310). William Salesbury published a Welsh-English dictionary in 1547 (STC 21616). He was granted a patent under which he issued the Epistles and Gospels in 1551 (STC 21617), the N.T. (STC 2960) and Book of Common Prayer (STC 16435), both printed in 1567 by Henry Denham for Robert Toy. They were all in Welsh and were financed by Thomas Myddelton.

The complete Bible in Welsh, in a translation supervised by William Morgan, was published in 1588 by the assigns of Christopher Barker (STC 2347). A revision of the Morgan Bible appeared in 1620: this had a wide acceptance and did much to preserve the pure Welsh.

During the 17th and 18th centuries printers at Oxford and Shrewsbury supplied the Welsh market. The first press in Wales of which we know was set up at Montgomery about 1648. It was one of the presses that followed the army, recording its doings in a broadsheet, usually called a 'Mercurie'.

Welsh books were occasionally printed on the Continent, as, for example, Griffith Roberts's 'Dosparth byrr ar . . . ramadeg cymraeg', Milan, 1567, and Rosier Smyth's translation of Petrus Canisius's 'Cathechisme', Paris, 1609.

It is believed that Isaac Carter set up the first press at which books were printed. This was in 1719 at Trefhedyn, and the first book was 'Eglurhad o Gatechism byrraf y Gymmanfa'. He later moved to Carmarthen which became the centre of the Welsh book trade.

Early Welsh printers were often Englishmen and of little skill; while due to the generally low level of education in Wales at that time there was little demand for their products, John Ross, fl.1743, of Carmarthen, was a London printer who took the trouble to learn Welsh. He described himself in his imprints as 'the only printer in these parts properly brought up to the trade'.

An early Welsh private press was that of Thomas Johnes, established on his estate at Hafod. (See *Hafod Press*.)

Printing and publishing were more vigorously practised in the 19th century, but regionalism and denominationalism still circumscribed the areas of sales. Dissenting author-ministers would often arrange lengthy preaching tours, selling copies of their works after speaking.

See J. I. Jones, 'A history of printing and printers in Wales to 1810, and of successive and related printers to 1923'. Cardiff, Lewis, 1925. See also *Denham*, *Gregynog Press*, *Toy*, *Trevecca Press*.

Wenssler, Michael, fl.1472–98: a printer of Basle and Lyons who was born in Strasbourg. During the 1470s, when his business in Basle was at its most active, he issued a series of law folios and a number of service books for various places including Cologne, Utrecht and Salisbury. About 1477 he worked in association with Richel and Ruppel, the large 'Super libros decretalium' of Panormitanus being their joint work.

In 1485 he issued the first complete edition of the 'Summa theologica' by Thomas Aquinas, the great medieval philosopher. In the later 1480s his business declined and he was sued for debt, finally selling his printing equipment to Jacob Steinacher for whom he printed until 1491. He then moved to Lyons, hiring printing materials from Matthias Huss. These he took to Cluny and Mâcon to print service books in each place. Back in Lyons he issued further legal works up to 1498.

Westminster Press: a printing press founded by Lord Archibald Douglas in 1878, and from 1899 managed by *Gerard Meynell*, q.v. In 1913 the press issued *The Imprint*, a journal on printing. About the same time poster printing was undertaken, in addition to the normal book production commissioned by various publishers.

Westphalia, Johannes de: see *De Westfalia, Johannes*.

wet end: the part of a Fourdrinier where the paper is formed, and extending to the first drying cylinder. Cf. *dry end*.

wet-on-wet printing: printing in two or more colours where the ink film of the first colour to be printed is still wet when the paper receives a second or subsequent impression. The consistency of the successive inks must be progressively less tacky.

wet pick: the picking or plucking of re-run coated stock on an offset press. The first run will have been pick free, but the stresses on the paper during impression and delivery may have so weakened the coating that picking occurs during subsequent runs.

wet plate: a photographic plate made by coating a piece of glass with collodion and sensitizing it by immersion in a solution of silver nitrate. Plates so made are always exposed wet, hence their name.

wet printing process inks: quick-drying inks for use in multi-colour printing. The ink of the last colour to be printed binds them all.

wet strength: a property of certain papers for which 5% or more of melamine or urea-formaldehyde has been added to the stuff in the beater. This gives increased strength for the moist conditions of lithographic printing, and such paper is used for map printing.

Weyden, Rogier van der, fl.1430–64: a painter of Tournai who about 1435 established his atelier at Brussels where it became one of the most famous of the time. From 1439 his principal patron was Philip, Duke of Burgundy. His best-known work (within the scope of this book) is to be seen in the copy of Wauquelin's translation of the 'Chronique du Hainaut' where a splendid presentation miniature shows Philip, surrounded by his knights of the Golden Fleece, receiving the work. The composition, portraiture and colouring skilfully combine to make this picture of knightly chivalry a document of historical importance. The work was completed in 1448 and is now in the Royal Library, Brussels.

It is probable that the drawings for the Brussels 'Biblia pauperum', 1465, and the 'Speculum' of 1466 were made in his atelier.

w.f.: an abbreviation for *wrong fount,* q.v.

Wharfedale machine: a stop-cylinder printing press (as distinct from a two-revolution cylinder which turns twice for each printing) devised about 1858 by *William Dawson,* q.v., of Otley in Wharfedale. The first model was built for a Glasgow printer. Type was carried on a travelling flat bed which passed under inkers to the paper-bearing cylinder. Much developed models are still in production. See also *Mann.*

Whatman, James, 1741–98: papermaker, of Turkey Mill, near Maidstone. His father, James Whatman I (1702–59), acquired the co-tenancy of Turkey Mill in 1740; a papermill since 1693. He developed the business until he was one of England's leading paper-makers. The first manufacture in Europe of *wove paper,* q.v., is attributed to him, and he may have invented the wove-wire mould about 1756.

James Whatman II continued his father's traditions. He made paper for such important customers as the Fourdriniers and Grosvenor Chater. To him was apprenticed William Balston in 1774. In 1794 Whatman retired and sold the mill to Thomas and Finch Hollingworth. Balston remained at the mill and became a partner. The business operated as Hollingworths & Balston. The partnership was dissolved in 1806, but the Hollingworths used the countermark 'J. Whatman, Turkey Mill' on their hand-made papers until 1859. See T. Balston, 'James Whatman, father and son', Methuen, 1957.

Whatman paper: a fine-quality English hand-made wove paper which was first made by James Whatman at Maidstone, *c.* 1770. It is used by artists as well as publishers of fine editions (it was used by *John Boydell,* q.v.).

In recent years much of the paper has been made on a mould machine by W. & R. Balston Ltd, the successors of Whatman's business.

Whethamstede, John, d. 1465: abbot of St Albans from 1420–40 and again from 1452–65. He was a notable ecclesiastical book collector and scholar. Subjects represented in his library were Latin classics, translations into Latin of Greek classics, and the writings of Italian humanists. He probably acquired many on visits to Italy. Whethamstede was a friend of Humphrey, Duke of Gloucester, to whom he gave several books.

He presented many of his books to St Albans and others to Gloucester College, Oxford.

whipstitching: a method of stitching books consisting of single leaves or plates. (See *overcasting.*)

whirler: an apparatus for spreading evenly a sensitized layer on to metal plates or lithographic stones used for printing in reproduction process work. The plate revolves horizontally about an axle. The preparation solution is distributed evenly over the surface by rotation. Heating devices are installed for drying the layer. In addition to horizontal whirlers there are vertical models in which the solution is applied with a spray.

Whitaker's Cumulative Book List: since 1924, quarterly and annual cumulations of the trade lists of British books which are published weekly in *The Bookseller.* There are also occasional larger volumes covering a number of years.

Whitbread Literary Awards: announced in 1971, being three annual awards of £1,500 each for a biography, novel, and volume of poetry written within the mainstream of English literary tradition by a British author or one domiciled in Britain for five years. The scheme is administered by the Booksellers Association. In subsequent years categories varied, thus in 1972 children's books replaced poetry.

Whitchurch, Edward, fl.1537–62: a London publisher-printer who, with Richard Grafton, sponsored the sale in England of the illustrated Matthew Bible, printed at Antwerp by Matthew Crom. The text was a combination of Tyndale and Coverdale's translations, with annotations by John Rogers, a theologian who used the pseudonymn Thomas Matthew, hence the name by which the edition is known. Whitchurch had supervised the printing of this as he was to do in Paris in 1538 when Francois Regnault printed the Great

Bible. In December of that year, when printing was proceeding, the Inquisitor-General of France stopped the work. Grafton and Whitchurch fled to London, leaving the sheets in possession of the Inquisitor who, says Foxe in his 'Acts and monuments', 'sold four great dry vats of them to a haberdasher to lap in caps, and these were bought again, but the rest were burned . . .' Grafton and Whitchurch returned to Paris and brought Regnault's presses, type and workmen to England where they finished the Bible in 1539. In London Whitchurch printed Cranmer's edition of this Bible in 1540, and there were five further printings within a year. Either Whitchurch or Grafton may have printed 'The workes of Geffray Chaucer', published by Wyllyam Bonham in 1542.

In January 1544 the partners held a patent for printing service books. In 1549 Whitchurch printed the first edition of the Book of Common Prayer of Edward VI which, in revised form, became second only to the Bible in popularity. See also *Welsh printing and publishing*.

white letter: the name given by early printers to roman type as distinct from *black letter* or gothic.

white line: a line filled with quads, blank slugs or leads. The space separating a page heading from the text below it is known as a *white line*, as also is the space below the text. Sometimes referred to as *blank line*.

white-lined black letter: see *inline letters*.

white out: to open out composed type with spacing or blanks to improve the appearance or fill an allotted area.

White Paper: an official British Government statement issued in a white paper cover.

white-paper forme: the *outer forme*, used for printing the first side of a sheet. The inner forme, used for backing up that sheet, is a *reiteration forme*. See also *sheet work*.

white vine: or *bianchi girari*, stems and leaves of the vine plant painted white on a coloured background. As a decorative motif in books the white vine, with its greater emphasis on the stalk than the leaves or fruit, traces its origins to St Gall illumination of the second half of the 9th century, usage subsequently spreading to Germany and Italy (home of the vine stem as a pre-Christian art motif). In the 14th century white vines were used to embellish capitals in manuscripts, especially in Italy, and in the 15th they were the main border decoration of Florentine manuscripts, particularly classical or humanistic texts, and were often inhabited by birds, animals or putti.

512

The woodcut capitals and borders used by some 16th century printers continued the tradition. See also *acanthus*.

white water: an alternative name for *backwater*, q.v.

whittawing: see *tawing*.

Whittingham, Charles, 1767–1840: born at Culledon in Warwickshire. In 1779 he was apprenticed to a Coventry printer and worked as a journeyman in Birmingham and London before opening his own business in Fetter Lane in 1789.

Whittingham was a close friend of William Caslon III from whom in the 1790s he bought large quantities of type, selling some to other printers, and for whom he printed the specimen books of 1795 and '96. He also printed the first book on what is now known as *india paper*, q.v., and was the first user of paper from his friend Fourdrinier's machine. From 1809 Whittingham supplied him with paper-stock from his works at Chiswick. In 1804 he bought one of the first Stanhope presses. He was clearly a man of enterprise.

A long association as one of Thomas Longman's printers began in 1797 with an edition of 'Pity's gift', an unremarkable work, but showing his first use of wood engravings, a later feature of his work. Whittingham paid great attention to the quality of his materials and to perfecting make-ready.

His first use of the imprint *Chiswick Press*, q.v., was in 1811, a year after setting up business there. The site was moved to College House, also in Chiswick, in 1818. In 1824 he trained and took into brief partnership his nephew Charles Whittingham II (1795–1876) who in 1828 set up his own business in Took's Court near Chancery Lane. Much of the fame of this new press stemmed from the nephew's close business association with *William Pickering*, q.v. To decorate his books, as distinct from illustrating them, the nephew had the borders of Tory, Holbein and Dürer copied or adapted by his daughters for the skilled engraving in wood of Mary Byfield.

On the death of his uncle the nephew managed both offices until 1852, then combining them at Took's Court. See also *McCreery*.

Whittinton, Robert: a Lichfield schoolmaster remembered for his Latin textbooks, widely used in grammar schools. His 'Syntaxis', printed by de Worde in 1517, showed the first greek (cut in wood) in an English printed book. A bound collection of his epigrams was the earliest English binding with gilt decoration. This was of brown calf with two panel stamps, one of St George and the dragon, the other of Tudor emblems. It was made about 1519 for Cardinal Wolsey (MS. Bodley 523).

Writing in *The Library*, 5th ser., vii 1952 121, H. M. Nixon suggests that heated panels were blocked without gold, glair was painted over the impressions, and gold leaf laid on before it dried. The cold block was lightly pressed again, causing the gold to adhere.

whole bound: see *full bound*.

wholesale bookseller: one whose main business is to supply retail booksellers.

Wickersham quoins: expanding steel quoins, adjusted with a key, which are inserted together with furniture at the side and foot of a chase.

Wicks, Frederick: of Glasgow, known for his invention in 1878 of a typecasting machine which was a considerable improvement on its predecessors of the 1850s. The large quantities of type produced by its battery of a hundred moulds made it particularly useful for newspaper work. When his rotary typecaster was introduced to the trade in 1881 fresh type was cast daily for *The Times* which used them between 1886 and 1908.

In his composing machine of 1880 Wicks devised a method of storing type in vertical channels, to be released by a keyboard operator. This inventive man included logotypes for common word endings and soft-metal spacing which on compression justified lines of type. See also *typecasting, typesetting machine*.

Widener, Henry Elkins: an American bibliophile who assembled an important collection devoted largely to Dickens, Stevenson and the Cruikshanks. After his death in the 'Titanic' his mother erected a library at Harvard in his memory and commissioned Rosenbach to prepare a catalogue of its contents.

widow line: a line of text set at the head of a page, e.g. the concluding words of a paragraph. Fewer than three lines in this position are considered bad setting. Cf. *club line*.

Wiebking, Robert, d. *c.* 1925: a German punchcutter and matrix maker who settled in Chicago in 1881. He engraved matrices for both *Goudy* and *Rogers*, qq.v., as well as designing types, e.g. the display face Artcraft. For a time he worked with the Barnhart Bros. & Spindler foundry, later with the Ludlow Typograph Company for whom he developed a matrix making machine.

Wiegand, Willi: see *Bremer Presse*.

Wiegendruck: the German term for *incunabulum*, q.v.

Wiemeler, Ignatz, 1895–1952: an important German craftsman-binder who was taught at the Landeskunstschule, Hamburg by Franz Weisse. Wiemeler subsequently taught bookbinding at graphic art schools in Offenbach (1921–25), Leipzig (1925–45), and Hamburg (1946–52) and his influence was considerable.

Of his three hundred or so known bindings the largest collection is in the Klingspor Museum at Offenbach.

Wiener Genesis: see *Vienna Genesis*.

Laura Ingalls Wilder Award: since 1954, a quinquennial award made to a writer or illustrator whose books, published in the United States, have made a significant contribution to literature for children. The award winner is chosen by the Children's Services Division of the American Library Association and commemorates the well-known writer of autobiographical stories for children.

Wilkins, Charles: see *arabic type, devanagari*.

Wilson, Alexander, 1714–86: a Scottish doctor, astronomer and typefounder who in partnership with John Baine established a foundry at St Andrews in 1742. Two years later they moved to Glasgow. In 1747 Baine opened a branch in Dublin and withdrew from the partnership in 1749.

Wilson and his descendants continued the business, subsequently known as the *Glasgow Letter-Foundry*. They supplied types to most Scottish and many Irish printers. Perhaps the most famous of Dr Wilson's types were the greek face used in the Foulis edition of Homer, 1756–8, and a double-pica roman first used in 1768 for Gray's poems.

After the death in 1830 of his son *Andrew* the business passed to his grandsons *Alexander* and *Patrick*. In 1834 they moved to London, trading as *Alex. Wilson & Sons*. Of considerable popularity in America were types known as Scotch face which they cut and cast to the order of Samuel Dickenson, a Boston typefounder-printer who completed the design in 1837.

By 1845 the surviving Wilsons were bankrupt and in 1850 they joined the Caslon foundry which had bought the business at auction.

Wilson, Halsey William, 1868–1954: born in Wilmington, Ver. His entry into the book trade began in 1889 when, with a partner, he opened a bookshop in Minnesota. In 1898 he began publication of the *Cumulative Book Index: a world list of books in the English Language* (quarterly with annual cumulations). In 1903 he incorporated the *H. W. Wilson Company*, moving to central New York in 1917 where it became one of the two leading bibliographical publishers in America. See also *Bowker, R. R.*

Wilson, John, 1802–68: a Glasgow printer who in 1823 moved to Belfast. His 'Treatise on English punctuation', 1826, was a guide for printers and had reached its twenty-third edition by 1871. It included rules for capitalization, abbreviations, etc.

In 1846 Wilson took his business to Boston, moving to Cambridge, Mass. in 1865. He and his son *John II* did much official work for Harvard as part of their general activity.

Winchester Bible: a fine example of English late Romanesque illumination, *c.* 1140–90 or later. The superb painted initials were done at different periods by various artists. Sumptuous colours, and the flowing draperies which divide the curving bodies of their wearers into ovals, typify the earlier work. The extensive use of purple, a diapered background to one of the pictures and simpler garments for the restrained figures which also show more character in their faces, are later, and some may be early 13th-century work: with gold backgrounds, they reveal the influence of Byzantium. See 'Artists of the Winchester Bible', by Walter Oakeshott, Faber, 1945.

Winchester School: a name given to the style of illumination characteristic of manuscripts originating in southern England during the era 950–1100.

In 954 Aethelwold founded a monastery at Abingdon where he gathered around him skilled monks whose influence on contemporary illumination resulted in the finest development of this art in Anglo-Saxon England. As Bishop of Winchester, 963–84, he continued his patronage.

Elaborate borders of acanthus leaves within two gold lines, brilliant initials filled with interlaced foliage and occasional animal heads, and figures with fluttering draperies are perhaps the main features of an art which sought to refine the barbaric traditions of Northumbria with the softer graces of classical painting, and make the page a splendid pattern of colour rather than merely a decoration. A Continental influence is suggested by the first use in England of Caroline minuscule, and features of Rheims and Metz work.

The Charter of the New Minster at Winchester, 966, is the earliest important work in the new style, while the *Benedictional of St Aethelwold*, q.v., is held to be the finest.

The special features of *Romanesque illumination*, q.v., characterized a second school of painting at Winchester, of which the finest survivals are the three-volume *Winchester Bible*, q.v., and a Psalter (B.L., *Nero*, C.iv). The latter, made for Henry of Blois (Bishop of Winchester, 1129–71), includes thirty-six whole-page scenes from the Old and New Testaments, a Jesse tree, and other scenes.

See F. Wormald, 'The Winchester Psalter', Miller & Medcalf, 1973. See also *Canterbury School*.

wind rose: or compass rose, the thirty-two pointed star which forms the centre of a compass dial or card.

The wind rose originated with the concept of eight symmetrical named winds featured in the Horologion (Tower of Winds) built at Athens by Andronicos of Cyrrhus in the 1st century B.C. The eight winds appeared as points, or rhumbs, in early portolani: of these the North was represented by a spearhead. By 1240 the wind rose compass was divided into thirty-two points. From the 16th to the 18th century the North was indicated on compass dials, tide tables, and maps by a fleur-de-lis (whence the custom among 16th century mariners of calling the wind rose a *flye*). The East was indicated by a cross or an ornamented scroll, though the use of the Cross was less common and was abandoned sooner. It was usual for the four cardinal points of the compass to be coloured blue and the half-cardinal points red: this standardization helped quick identification. See also *periplus, portolano*.

Wing, D.: see *Short-Title Catalogue*.

Wing, John, 1845–1917: an American publisher whose extensive collection of books on printing and its history is now in the Newberry Library, Chicago.

winter: the stout horizontal beam forming the principal support and strengthener of the *cheeks*, q.v., on a wooden printing press.

wipe: a printing fault seen as a blurred or even double image. The ink may be pushed across the forme instead of being deposited as a thin, even film, and thus leave thin ridges at the edge of type. In high-speed machine running it may be caused by a false movement between rollers and forme, and is also probable when printing on hard-surfaced paper from polyurethane rollers which have been carelessly set. As these rollers tend to heat up and expand during long runs it is necessary to re-set them every two or three hours.

Wipe may also occur if the forme rollers are set too low, and if the ink is too thin or too greasy.

wipe-on plates: lithographic plates of polished or very fine-grained aluminium, chemically treated, which prior to use are sponged over with a sensitizing mixture of a diazo powder in polyvinyl alcohol. After printing down a lacquer developer is applied which adheres to the image and removes unexposed coating.

Such plates are cheaper than factory *pre-sensitized plates*, q.v. They are suitable for short run work, and are available for negative or positive working.

wire: the continuous band of woven phosphor-bronze wire (or nylon) gauze which forms the *moulding unit* of a papermaking machine. The mesh is selected according to the type of paper to be made and varies from 12 to 40 wires per cm. The wire is supported at one end by the *breast roll* and at the other by the *couch roll*. The latter is powered and contains a suction box. A series of small rollers under the moving wire support it and maintain tension, and a number of suction boxes draw water through the wire.

The width of the paper being formed is known as the *deckle*, and on slow-moving machines rubber deckle straps may be fitted part way down the length of each side of the wire to prevent the pulp overflowing. Shortly before the web of paper reaches the couch roll it passes under the *dandy roll*, q.v. See also *Fourdrinier*, *twin-wire paper*, *wire-mark*.

wire-mark: the slight impression made by the wire gauze on the underside of paper as the sheet is formed on the Fourdrinier. The under, or *wire-side* of the paper has a lower surface strength and is less smooth than the upper or *felt side*, and may be thought to have a less satisfactory surface for printing upon. This difference between the two sides can be lessened if the web of paper is passed through a linked reversing press as soon as it leaves the wire. An alternative is to use *twin-wire paper*, q.v.

wire stabbing: a cheap process of mechanically side-stitching a book by forcing one or more wire staples through a number of leaves or sections, normally set about ⅛th in. in the back margin. This reduces the back margin, and stabbed books cannot be opened flat. Cf. *saddle-stitched*.

wire stitching: in a bindery, the mechanical insertion of wire staples through one or more folded sections to secure them. The process, commonly known as *wiring*, is much used for pamphlets and periodicals.

Depending on the substance of the paper an octavo pamphlet of 96 pages plus cover can satisfactorily be stitched by passing two staples through the opened back. For a work in several sections side *stabbing* is usual.

As sections to be stitched are fed to the machine tin-plated steel wire is passed automatically from spools to a row of stitching heads where it is cut, bent into staples and forced through the paper. The staples are closed by head-cups.

In 1877 August Brehmer brought from Philadelphia to London his patent machine which wire-stitched both pamphlets and books. The books were stapled to tapes across the backs, but as the wire tended to rust and disfigure the pages their use for books lapsed. See also *stitching*.

Wise, Thomas J., 1859–1937: a British bibliophile, bibliographer, biblioklept and literary forger. Concentrating on first editions of Romantic and Victorian verse and drama he assembled a major library which after his death was sold to the British Museum for £66,000. He named his collection the Ashley Library after the road in Crouch Hill, London where he once lived. Wise made a serious study of the writers he collected and published an important series of bibliographies as well as several catalogues of his own library. He was a President of the Bibliographical Society and a member of the Roxburghe Club.

For his forgeries he had the ingenious idea of printing in pamphlet form part of an already published edition and giving it an earlier date, thus creating first editions for profitable sale to trusting collectors and libraries. More than fifty examples were exposed as frauds by John Carter and Graham Pollard in 1934. Best known, and most lucrative, was an edition of Elizabeth Barrett Browning's 'Sonnets from the Portuguese' which he dated 'Reading, 1847', whereas records prove they were unknown to Robert Browning before 1849.

See W. Partington, 'Thomas J. Wise in the original cloth', Hale, 1946, and the eleven volume reprint of the Ashley Library catalogue issued in 1971.

witness: 1. bibliography. A term for the particular version of a manuscript or incunabulum which is accepted by scholars as authoritative.

2. printing and binding. Said of a book with fore-edges so slightly trimmed that some of these are still rough. Also known as *binding proof*. See also *uncut*.

Wolfe, John, fl.1579–1601: a London printer. He was apprenticed to John Day in 1562, then studied printing in Florence becoming an accomplished printer of Italian. He regularly sent books to the Frankfurt fair. By 1579 he was printing in London, frequently infringing other men's privileges. He owned five of the fifty-three presses then licensed in London. In 1587 he was appointed Beadle (or searcher) of the Stationers' Company. After 1593 he ceased printing and published books printed by others. His printing material was acquired by Adam Islip and John Windet.

Well-known books issued by Wolfe included Robert Greene's 'Quip for an upstart courtier', 1592; the first edition of John Stow's 'Survey of London', 1598; and John Hayward's 'Life and raigne of King Henrie IIII', 1599, for which author and printer were put in prison owing to certain passages which were held to be treasonable. He also published, after 1589, a series of news reports in pamphlet form, a forerunner of the later corantos.

Wolfe, Reginald (or **Reyner**), fl.1536–73: a native of Strasbourg who about 1536 settled in England and was several times Master of the Stationers' Company. He was King's Printer for Latin, Greek, and Hebrew to Edward VI.

Wolgemut, Michael, 1434–1519: a Nuremberg painter, famous for his designs for woodcuts. His finest achievement was a series of illustrations for 'Schatz-behalter der wahren Reichtümer des Heils und der ewigen Seligkeit', 1491 (Hain 14507), which had ninety-six full-page cuts and is considered outstanding for the period. Another great work was the equally famous 'Die Weltchronik' (Nuremberg Chronicle) of Hartmann Schedel and Georg Alt, printed by Anton Koberger (in Latin, 1493, and German, 1493, Hain 14508 and 14510). His stepson Wilhelm Pleydenwurff collaborated with Wolgemut on the 1,809 woodcuts for this last work. Albrecht Dürer was a pupil of Wolgemut (whose name is sometimes spelled *Wohlgemuth*. (With GU)

Wolpe, Berthold, 1905–   : an eminent engraver and type-designer, born in Germany where he studied with *Rudolph Koch*, q.v. In 1935 Wolpe came to England and has for many years been associated with Faber and Faber Ltd and the Lion and Unicorn Press of the Royal College of Art. He is known as the designer of the Albertus family of titling and display types, of which the earliest, Albertus Titling, was cut in 1935 and issued by Monotype in the following year. In 1960 Faber published 'Renaissance handwriting' in which Wolpe collaborated with Alfred Fairbank.

Wolpe was made a Royal Designer for Industry in 1959. See C. Mozley, 'Wolperiana . . .', Merrion P., 1960.

women in bookbinding: an early reference to a female binder is given in the account books of Jean II le Bon, king of France (1350–64) which record payments to Marguerite 'la relieresse'. In England evidence of women bindery owners is given in a record of 1685 when the Bishop of London ordered the seizure of 'counterfeit Primmrrs' from the premises of Mrs Harris, Binder. However, this is one of several instances where a widow continued her husband's business, binding being done by a foreman.

Extensive use of low-paid women was made in the 19th century binding trade in which they worked up to sixty hours a week as gatherers, folders, sewers and gilders, not always without male opposition.

For a further note on women in the bookbinding trade see *Aitken, Society of Women Employed in Bookbinding*. For artistic binders see *Katharine Adams, Guild of Women-Binders, S. T. Prideaux, Sybil Pye*.

women in papermaking: although women master papermakers seem to have been rare the account book of Sir James Foulis for 1705 records the receipt in 1704 of £85 from a Mrs Isabel Lithgow for the lease of the Upper Spylaw papermill at Colinton near Edinburgh, started in 1681 by James Lithgow (d. 1703). She also owed him three reams of paper for 1704 and four for earlier years. She continued the lease until about 1707, but it is possible that her nephew Robert Haliburton was the actual maker.

However, the paper trade in general has long made use of female labour as rag sorters and shredders, in the boiling room, the cutting room and the salle. So extensive was this practice in Victorian England that by 1844 out of 7,160 persons employed in papermills 2,028 were girls and women (Parliamentary Papers). They were wretchedly paid and their working day often continued from six in the morning until midnight.

women in printing: before the end of the 15th century women, often wives, might help as compositors and correctors. Many printers' widows married their husbands' foremen and took them into partnership. By trade custom the widow of a freeman of the Stationers' Company became a freewoman and took apprentices; thus in 1601 John Adams was bound for eight years to widow Alice Wolfe. In the 16th and 17th centuries several women are named in the Calendar of State Papers as printers or publishers. Some held patents, such as Hester Ogden for the printing of Dr Fulkes' translation of the New Testament, 1633.

Among Stationers' Register entries implying that women printed is this: 'It is agreed that Thomas Vautroullier his wife shall finish this present impression which she is in hand withall in her husband's absence, of Tullie's Epistles . . .'. In 1635 the Company forbade master printers to employ 'Girles' to remove printed sheets from the press. The earliest record of a girl being apprenticed concerns Joanna Nye, bound in 1666 to Thomas Minshall, engraver.

In 1695 Dinah Nuthead, widow of William Nuthead, re-opened her husband's press in Annapolis, Maryland, receiving a licence to print in 1696. Several women printers and publishers were active in Colonial America during the 18th century, the best known being *Mary Katharine Goddard*, q.v.

In London Miss Emily Faithfull's Victoria Press, founded in 1860, at first employed only women and girls, but after opposition from various quarters, they were withdrawn from actual printing but continued to feed paper into the presses and fold the printed sheets. In the present century certain British and American private presses have included women craftsmen.

See J. Bogardus, 'Some bibliographical notes about women in printing', New York, 1936. See also *Apud Sanctum Jacobum de Ripoli, layer-on, Stanbrook Abbey Press*.

Woodburytype: an obsolete photomechanical process in which a hardened gelatine relief image, taken from a photographic negative, was impressed into a lead plate by a hydraulic press. The plate was flooded with pigmented gelatine before being printed in a platen press. Paper was laid on top and the platen applied. When the gelatine set the paper was removed and dried. The process was invented in 1865 by W. B. Woodbury and had a limited use for book illustrations.

Detail of a wooden block of an ancient Chinese woodcut

woodcut: the earliest form of printed illustration in which an impression is taken from an inked forme cut in wood. Bold black lines or areas depict a design against a white background. The block for printing is made of soft, smooth-grained wood, usually type high, the design being drawn or transferred on to it for cutting with wood-carving tools along the plank grain; the non-image areas are cut away leaving the lines in relief.

The art is of ancient origin, in China at least before the birth of Christ. In Europe it was practised by monks in the late 14th century for depicting representations of saints, but the oldest dated sheet known is from 1418. The best known of early dated European woodcuts is the Buxheim 'Saint Christopher', 1423, which survives in a unique copy in the John Rylands Library, Manchester (though it has been argued that the style is that of work being done in the 1440s and merely depicts an event of 1423). One of the earliest books to be illustrated with woodcuts was Ulrich Boner's 'Fables' printed in 1461 by *Pfister* of Bamberg, q.v. At that time the text was printed first, and then the illustrations in spaces left for them; it was not for a few years that the idea of cutting the block to type height was conceived, permitting text and illustrations to be printed together.

Blocks of pear tree were used at first, cut along the length of the tree. The design was drawn or traced in reverse along the planed surface of the block, after which the white areas were cut away leaving the design in relief. The woodcutter used various knives and fine

Full-scale reproduction of a woodcut from the first printed book with illustrations 'Der Edelstein' (Fables) by Ulrich Boner, printed in 1461 by Albrecht Pfister of Bamberg. The original was hand-coloured, probably in the printer's shop

517

Detail of a woodcut in Dürer's Apocalypse series, 1498. In this full-scale reproduction the great advance which Dürer's art represented, both technically and artistically, is easily seen when compared with 'Der Edelstein'

chisels as tools, and worked towards his body. The block was inked by hand with a dabber, and then a damp sheet of paper was laid over it and pressed to the block with a leather ball stuffed with horsehair. The wooden block was later printed with type in a hand-press. Colouring was also done by hand until the beginning of the 16th century when separate blocks for the different colours were used.

The artist's work had to be adapted to the technique, and very often the cutting of the block was done by another person (Ger. Formschneider) whose task it was to cut the details of the drawing in wood with the greatest possible accuracy, line by line.

Artistic woodcutting may be said to have developed with Michael Wolgemut, Albrecht Dürer, and their successors in the 16th century. In the 17th century the only truly famous craftsman was Christoffel Jegher (1596-1652), a German-Dutchman, remembered for his woodcuts of Rubens's paintings, emblem books, initials and printers' devices. Owing to the increased popularity of *copper engraving*, q.v., woodcutting declined in the 18th century, to be revived, however, in the 19th under the influence of the Japanese woodcut. The Japanese worked mainly in many colours, preferably printed, so that the grain of the wood stood out. Colour was put on the block with a paint-brush which made toning possible. Water-colours with different vehicles were most used and printing was done in a simple hand-press. Japanese mulberry paper is highly absorbent and was used in both a damp and dry state. Modern European engravers, too, are fond of using Japan paper and Japanese water-colours for their original wood engravings, i.e., engravings drawn, cut and printed by the artist.

As wood blocks will only stand the printing of comparatively small editions, it is usual to make stereos or electros which are set up with type as ordinary blocks; in England the use of stereos for this purpose dates from the 1830s.   (With GU)

See A. M. Hind, 'An introduction to a history of woodcuts, with a detailed survey of work done in the 15th century', Constable, 1926, repr. N.Y., Dover, 1963; and P. Kristeller, 'Kupferstich und Holzschnitt in vier Jahrhunderten', Berlin, 1922. See also *block book, Colonna, Florentine woodcuts, Formschneider, wood engraving*.

woodcut bindings: early bindings of which the decorative feature was a woodcut. The woodcuts, one each for the upper and lower cover, were pasted to two or three thicknesses of paper to form a wrapper. The paper spine which was left blank was probably pasted to the back of the sewn sections. The title and date were printed in the centre panel formed by the surrounding woodcut border.

Few of these frail covers survive, but there is a copy of 'Das Buch der Lehrenrecht' printed in 1493 by Ratdolt of Augsburg now in the British Library: the wrapper is dated 1494.

Woodcut covers were also used in Ferrara and Venice early in the 16th century. They were either pasted on to books sewn on thongs which were laced into pasteboard instead of leather, or the cuts were pasted on thin board to form a case which was attached to the back by sewing through the spine. Unlike the Augsburg examples these woodcuts were used as a cheap means of decorating any suitable book: the former were printed for a specific title. See W. A. Jackson, 'Printed wrappers of the 15th to 18th centuries' (*sic*), *Harvard Library Bulletin*, 1952 313-21.

wood engraving: an impression from a block of wood on the surface on which the lines of a design, cut with a steel graver, are recessed below type height and so do not receive ink. Thus white outlines depict the image on a textured, toned, or black background. The development and subsequent popularity for book illustration of this process was due to *Thomas Bewick*, q.v., who found that sections of boxwood sawn across the grain gave a close-textured surface suitable for fine work.

Before use the block was coated with a solution of zinc white in gum arabic and then the artist drew his design. For tonal effects the relevant parts of the block were washed with ink of varying strength, after which it was left to the technical skill of the engraver (if not the artist) with his gouges, gravers and scaupers (worked away from the body) to reproduce the design in lines and dots.

Originally, inch thick slices of boxwood were sawn into small square or oblong blocks, thus for pictures

Bewick engraving. Original size.
From 'History of quadrupeds', 1790

with a larger dimension than about 20cm blocks were glued together, each carrying a portion of the whole design. Later, bolts were used to secure them. The whole block was then positioned with any accompanying text and locked up for printing. Composite blocks made possible the full-page illustrations which from 1842 featured in such popular periodicals as the *Illustrated London News*. Particularly sensational was Antoine Claudet's panoramic daguerreotype of London which the *Illustrated London News* published as an engraving on 7 January 1843. To make it nineteen engravers worked day and night in shifts for two months to cut the sixty pieces of boxwood on to which Claudet's daguerreotypes had been transferred. They were bolted together to make a composite block, and the resulting prints measured 127cm × 91cm.

If large, and urgently needed for a publishing deadline, the composite block was incised with main guiding cuts across the joints and then divided among several craftsmen. After reassembly the master engraver would work over the whole to harmonize the texture. Instances occurred where a block was separated even as drawing proceeded, so that the artist never saw the whole of his design until it was printed.

After 1860 photographs of artists' drawings were printed directly on to sensitized block surfaces for engraving. Probably the first commercially reproduced were in Winkworth's 'Lyra Germanica' printed by John Leighton in 1861.

By the end of the 19th century photo-mechanical processes had made hand crafted wood engraving uneconomic for general illustration work, but it continues today in private press productions and in fine bookwork where the unity of text and illustrations is particularly satisfying. Printing is now done from electros of original blocks, permitting bigger editions without loss of quality.

wood-free: paper made without mechanical wood pulp. *Chemical wood* paper, q.v., is wood free. Also known as *pure*.

woodletter type: poster size letters of hardwood. They are measured in lines of 12-point, thus 10-line equals 120-point. See also *sand letters*.

wood pulp: the principal ingredient of many kinds of paper. The two classes of wood pulp are *mechanical* or ground wood as used in newsprint, and *chemical* pulp produced by various processes including soda, sulphate and sulphite. The use of wood for paper dates from 1843 when it was patented in Germany by Friedrich Keller of Hainichen in Saxony although machinery for making it in commercial quantities was developed by Heinrich Völter.

word division: see *division of words*.

Worde, Wynkyn de, fl.1477–1530: a printer of Worth in Alsace who may have accompanied *Caxton*, q.v., when he came to London from Bruges in 1476. He became his chief assistant, continuing the Westminster business on Caxton's death in 1491. An edition of 'Liber festivalis' by Mirk, 1493, was one of his earliest

independent works. Between that date and 1500, when he moved to Fleet Street, Worde issued about 110 works, some known only by fragments. From Fleet Street he issued about 700 (including broadsheets and reprints). His finest publication is perhaps 'De proprietatibus rerum' by Bartholomaeus, *c.* 1495.

The black letter type he used influenced other printers of the day. He was the first London printer to use borders of type ornaments and to use italic type: this last was in Elyot's translation of Lucian's 'Complures dialogi', *c.* 1528. His illustrative material was less successful.

The Sarum Book of Hours, extant in only one copy, which he printed in red and black in 1510, included four pages written in gothic script, presumably written in his shop. In 1517, in another pioneer effort, he printed some Greek words from wooden blocks in Whittinton's 'De concinnitate grammatices', and in 1528 some arabic words, also from wood (see *arabic type*). He printed several of Whittinton's textbooks and also many school primers to meet the demand which marked the general spread of education. De Worde died in 1534. See H. R. Plomer, 'Wynkyn de Worde and his contemporaries from the death of Caxton to 1535', London, 1926. See also *Lucidarius*.

word processing: in the 1950s, when the term was adopted, the use of machines to make an error-free print-out of copy on paper, magnetic tape, discs or cassettes. Included were dictating machines, typewriters (manual, electric or automatic/memory), text editing terminals and composers.

The inputting of that copy to photosetters fitted with computer memories for text recall and keyed instructions, a development of the 1960s, was of interest to in-house printers but not, at that time to book printers. See also *ink-jet printing*.

work and back: see *sheet work*.

work and tumble: perfecting a sheet by feeding the opposite long edge to the grippers for the second impression from the same forme.

work and turn: a printing method suitable for long runs whereby the matter for both sides of a sheet is set in one forme. Paper double the size of the sheet required is first printed on one side and then turned over end for end and backed up from the same forme. Each printed sheet will then contain two perfected impressions of half its size, the halves being identical. The two halves are separated by slitting in the printing machine or in a guillotine.

Also known as *half-sheet imposition*.   (LK)

working: any forme on the press and being run off.

work in progress: work in hand at the printer's.

work off: to print a job.

work up: spacing material which has risen to type height in the forme causing a 'black' on the sheet.

World Intellectual Property Organization: since 1971 the name for the former Berne Copyright Bureau.

worm-eaten books: books damaged by the larvae of various beetles, especially *Anobium hirtum*. If books are tightly shelved and remain unused over a period of years worms may eat their way through an entire shelf of them. To fumigate worm-eaten books put a jar of paradichlorobenzine with the books in a tin. Seal it and leave for a week. Books infested with silver fish or mites require the same treatment. Lacquer paint containing Dieldrin or a similar substance should be used to paint the shelves: it will remain toxic for three years, even if scrubbed. Circulating air, dusting and use are the best preventives.

Wotton, Thomas, 1521–87: a patron of learning and a bibliophile. Many of the books bound for his library bore interlaced painted strapwork in the style of those bound for *Jean Grolier*, q.v., which, with his habit of having them lettered THOMAE WOTTONI ET AMICORUM stamped on the boards of some led to his being known as the 'English Grolier'. See G. Eland, 'Thomas Wotton's letter book, 1574–86', O.U.P., 1960.

wove paper: paper which when held up to light is seen to have an even or regular pattern of fine mesh but with none of the lines which distinguish *laid paper*, q.v. This is caused by the weave of the dandy roll. Variations in the quality of wove paper are due to the mesh; 60 to 65 strands per inch of screen for newsprint and 70 to 80 for other printing papers being usual.

James Whatman was probably the first manufacturer, if not the inventor, of wove paper. Its first-known use for bookwork was in 1757 when John Baskerville printed his Virgil upon it. See also *Isaiah Thomas*.

wraparound plates: 1. illustrations for a book, printed separately from the text, which during gathering are placed around the sections with which they are to be sewn. This is an alternative to placing them in the middle of the sections.

2. thin flexible shallow-relief plates of plastic or fine-gauge metal. They are used on a *wraparound press*, q.v. The thinner the plate the closer it will fit the cylinder. Thin plates can be etched flat: thicker ones are etched after curving in a bending machine. Thicknesses vary, but plates 0·032in. are common.

wraparound press: a sheet-fed rotary press developed in America in the 1950s for direct letterpress printing from shallow-relief plates. (See *wraparound plates*) Typical of such presses is the Harris Model 130 LE.

The elimination of make-ready and considerably increased running speeds are the main advantages, while for certain classes of work it is claimed that the clean impression of traditional letterpress can be achieved.

wrapped round: see *insert*.

wrapper: a paper cover attached to a book or pamphlet as an integral part of it. While often separately printed on heavier paper than that used for the work it completes and protects it can be of the same stock as the text sheets and be machined and folded with them, i.e. a *self-wrapper*. See also *wrappering*. Cf. *jacket*.

wrappered and overlapped: see *wrappering*.

wrappering: the process of gluing an unstiffened paper cover to the spine of a book. Alternative methods are to trim the wrappered book on three edges leaving it *cut flush*, to trim before covering so that the cover has narrow projecting edges, or to leave large flaps at the fore-edge which are then folded in over the first and last leaves to give extra strength without stiffening, (known as *wrappered and overlapped*). To hide the wire stitches of books which have them it is usual to crease the cover, forming side hinges which are glued and pressed.

The process is used for cheap and usually thin school books which are then said to be *wrappered* or to have *drawn-on covers*. Cf. *covering*.

writing manual: a book of instruction in handwriting containing reproductions printed from wooden blocks or engraved plates to show various styles of script, and with notes on ink preparation and how to cut and hold the quill or pen.

Writing manuals originated in Italy where the earliest known printed example was Fanti's 'Theoretica et practica', Venice, 1514. Among its predecessors was a work on letter design printed by Damianus Moyllis of Parma (fl.1477–83). His alphabet, printed on single sides of sheets which were then folded, was probably intended as a teaching manual. There was also the humanist Fra Luca da Pacioli (*c.* 1440–1509) who added his theory of the proportion and construction of letters to his 'De divina proportione', printed at Venice by Paganino de Paganini in 1509. It was illustrated with a woodcut alphabet. These were not strictly writing manuals.

The writing masters sought to standardize and extend the use of the elegant cursive scripts adopted for official purposes in the many chanceries, and although the spread of printing made unnecessary the labour of scribes to copy out texts for the book trade there remained, for a while, a moneyed society which still wished to have finely-written and illuminated manuscript books for the pleasure they gave.

Inevitably, an interest in Italian cursive writing and the means of acquiring skill in it spread to other countries, and writing manuals were made in England, France, Germany, Holland and Spain. In America the first writing manual to be printed was George Fisher's 'American instructor', Philadelphia, 1748, based on an English work. A second of note was Isaiah Thomas's 'The writing scholar's assistant', Worcester, 1785. The earliest wholly American copy book was probably that of John Jenkins, 'The art of writing', 3 parts, Boston, 1791–1817.

For notes on famous writing masters see under *Arrighi, Barbédor, Beauchesne, Bickham, Billingsley, Cocker, Cresci, Fanti, Hercolani, Mario, Mercator, Neudörffer, Palatino, Ruano, Sallando, Salutati, Taglienti, Velde, Yciar*. See Sir Ambrose Heal, 'The English writing-masters and their copy-books, 1570–1800', C.U.P., 1931; W. Doede, 'Bibliographie deutscher Schreibmeisterbücher, 1519–1800', Hamburg, Hauswedell, 1948; R. Nash, 'American writing masters and copy books', Boston, 1959; '2000 years of calligraphy', Baltimore, 1965; and A. S. Osley, 'Luminario . . . Italian writing-books of the 16th and 17th centuries', Holland, 1972. See also *calligraphy, cursive, humanistic scripts, letters – forms and styles*.

writings: paper sized to take writing ink and usually stocked in sizes known as *writing sizes* as distinct from *printings* which may not be suitable for writing upon and are stocked in an entirely different range of sizes.

wrong fount: a mistake in composition in which a letter of the wrong size or face is set. When proof correcting the letters 'w.f.' are written marginally to draw attention to such faults.

Wyer, Robert, fl.1529–56: an enterprising if undistinguished printer and bookseller living near Charing Cross, London, who developed a market for short cheap books on popular scientific subjects in additon to medical and religious works. These were mostly issued as roughly printed brochures illustrated with simple woodcuts, and he was essentially a printer for the general public. Notable works were a translation by Whitford of 'De Imitatione Christi', *c.* 1531, and William Marshall's 'Defence of peace', 1535.

Wynkyn de Worde Society: founded in London in 1957, being a social group instituted for the meeting at luncheon and other gatherings of persons associated with the creation and production of 'print', the promotion of mutual understanding, and the exchange and dissemination of information on printing and allied subjects. In 1960 the Society published James Moran's 'Wynkyn de Worde: father of Fleet Street'. See also *Worde*.

XYZ

xenon lamp: a quartz tube filled with low-pressure xenon and pulsed at a sufficiently high frequency to give the effect of continuous light (*c.* 30–35 lumens per watt), and having a spectral output close to sunlight. Xenon lamps are used in graphic technology as an alternative to carbon arc lamps.

xerography: literally 'dry writing', and the name given to the electrostatic process for reproducing or copying an original without the use of ink, pressure or rollers. It was patented by Chester F. Carlson (1906–68) of New York. In 1944 the Battelle Memorial Institute of Ohio began to develop the invention. The Haloid Company of Rochester N.Y. (later the Xerox Corporation) financed commercial development which was achieved by 1958. The British Rank-Xerox Company was formed in 1956.

Briefly, a selenium-coated surface is given a positive electrostatic charge and an image is then exposed to it through a camera. Where light is reflected the charge will be dissipated, leaving the positive charge in the image areas. When a negatively-charged black resinous powder is cascaded over the selenium it is attracted to the charged areas. If paper is now placed over the selenium and charged positively the powder image will be transferred to it, and the image can then be made permanent by heat and vapour fusing.

The process is of considerable importance, among other uses, for the reproduction of out-of-print books. Diagrams and line drawings reproduce well, but not half-tones.

x-height: the height of lower-case letters (excluding ascenders and descenders), i.e., the height of a lower-case x; a term used to describe the apparent size of a type. In a 12-point type this may vary from 0·056in to 0·080in. Walbaum, Perpetua and Centaur have small x-heights, Times and Plantin have large.

xylo-chirographic: an error, sometimes seen, for *chiroxylographic*, q.v.

xylograph: 1. a wood engraving.
2. a block book.

xylographic colour printing: see *chiaroscuro*.

Yapp: a style of limp-leather binding with overlapping flaps or edges on three sides. Named after William Yapp who between 1854 and 1875 had a Bible warehouse in London. He designed a limp binding suitable for Bibles to be carried in the pocket. This was made for him by Samuel Bagster, through whose catalogues the description and style 'Yapp binding' became known. However, bindings with tooled edges in this style were made in the mid-16th century. See also *circuit edges*.

Yciar, Juan de, fl.1548–55: born at Durango. The greatest Spanish writing master who lived at Saragossa where he worked as a teacher and writer of church service books.

His manual 'Orthographia pratica: Arte subtilissima, por la qual se ensña a escrevir perfectamente', Caracoga, 1548, made him known. This was improved in the second edition of 1550. The calligraphic specimens are seen against decorative backgrounds which were cut on blocks of hawthorn by Juan de Vingles, born in 1498, of the printing family of Lyons.

Notable too was Yciar's 'Libro de letras', 1555, in which he displayed several woodcut alphabets, each letter superimposed on a Biblical scene.

The Lion and Unicorn Press published a facsimile of the 1550 edition of 'Arte subtilissima' in 1958; O.U.P. edition, 1960.

yearbook: synonymous with *annuals* (1), q.v.

Year Books: collected reports of law cases, Term by Term, written in French, from the reign of Edward I onwards (1272–1307). They were circulated in manuscript versions until the 1480s when early printed reports were issued by *Machlinia* and *Pynson*, qq.v. Other printers of them were Rastell, Redman, Berthelet and Tottell. Various abridgements were issued. By 1560 some 260 volumes had been published, and they remain an important source of medieval common law.

yellow backs: books published in boards covered with glazed yellow paper and having a woodcut printed in three colours on the front. The style was originated by the London engraver and colour printer Edmund Evans in 1853 with an edition of Henry Mayhew's

'Letters left at the pastry-cooks'. Yellow backs were popular for cheap reprints until the turn of the century.

The Yellow Book: a quarterly magazine in book form published from 1894–7 by John Lane and Elkin Matthews. It epitomized in its writing and illustrations the aesthetic movement known as Art Nouveau. Aubrey Beardsley's brilliant if decadent pen and ink drawings added not a little to its short-lived fame.

Ye Sette of Odd Volumes: a London dining society founded in 1878 by Bernard Quaritch. The forty-two members met to dine and read papers on literary, artistic and scientific subjects. Some of their 'opuscula' have been printed, and R. Straus compiled 'An odd bibliography' listing those which appeared between 1878 and 1924.

Young-Delcambre: a composing machine made in Belgium in 1840. Assistance with technical details was given by Henry Bessemer, but the patent was taken out by James Hadden Young and Adrien Delcambre of Lille. The machine, known as the *Pianotype*, was keyboard operated, founder's type being released into converging channels where it was justified by hand. Maximum speed was 6,000 ens an hour. There was a good deal of opposition to the machine from London compositors and it never went into general manufacture and use.

Young Managing Printers: the name assumed in 1974 by the former *Young Master Printers*. The organization began in 1925 when a group of thirty-five master-printers' sons and young master printers met to discuss the structure of the industry, the role of employers' and workers' organizations in it, and the training of managers. This meeting was near Beaconsfield, Bucks.

Alliances of master printers elsewhere in Britain met similarly in the later 1920s. In 1931 the BFMP, now BPIF, approved the setting up of a standing YMP committee. Annual conferences and summer schools were held. By 1975 membership stood at 1,200 from 600 or so firms. The YMP remains an integral part of the Federation.

Young, Patrick, d. 1652: Royal Librarian to Charles I. He is remembered for his preparatory work on a complete facsimile edition of the *Codex Alexandrinus*, q.v., but did not live to complete it. The Codex had been brought from Constantinople to London in 1631 as a gift to King Charles.

He began the project with the publication in Greek and Latin of 'Ad Corinthios epistola prior', printed at the King's Printing House in 1633, and his notes as far as Numbers XIV were used by Bishop Walton for his Polyglot Bible of 1657.

Zaehnsdorf, Joseph, 1816–86: an Austro-Hungarian craftsman-binder (born in Budapest) who learned his craft in Stuttgart and Vienna. He came to London in 1837, working for Westley & Co. until 1842 when he founded the London firm of hand-binders long renowned for fine bindings. His forwarding and finishing were of the highest order, and a further speciality of the firm was the restoration of rare books.

Joseph William Zaehnsdorf (1853–1930), son of the founder, directed the firm for some time before his father's death and by the end of the 19th century was acknowledged to be the leading English binder. He was the author of 'The art of bookbinding', 1880. This was for long a standard textbook for apprentices. A reprint of the 1890 revised edition was published in 1968. In 1920 control of the business passed to the founder's grandson *Ernest* who directed it until 1945.

Zainer, Günther, fl.1468–78: of Reutlingen, who worked in Strasbourg, probably with Mentelin, before setting up in 1468 the first printing press at Augsburg. His first book was Bonaventura's 'Meditationes vitae Christi', 1468, followed a year later by the 'Catholicon' of Johannes Balbus. For some time he was not allowed by the local guild of woodcutters to illustrate his books with cuts; the licence he later obtained stipulated that guild members must be employed. However, after 1471 he issued a succession of illustrated books, many showing a fine balance between type and illustration. Notable was his Latin-German edition of the 'Speculum humanae salvationis', printed in 1473 on the press set up by Abbot Melchior von Stamheim at the monastery of SS Ulrich and Afra. The fifty-four cuts were hand-coloured. Zainer may have designed the attractive initials found in many of his books.

By 1472 he introduced one of the earliest roman founts to be cut in Germany, the first book in which it appeared being Isidore's encyclopaedic 'Etymologiae'. In 1475/6 he issued a folio German Bible with fine historiated initials at the commencement of each book. These were imitated a year later by Sensenschmidt and Frisner at Nuremberg. In 1475/6 Zainer also printed Steinhöwel's German translation of the 'Speculum humanae vitae' under the title 'Spiegel des menschlichen Lebens' illustrated with fifty-four woodcuts of country life.

In 1474 and 1476 he issued advertisements of his books, among the earliest known. On his death his former apprentice Anton Sorg acquired his equipment.

Zainer, Johann, fl.1472–93: of Reutlingen, and a kinsman of Günther, who after learning his craft in Strasbourg during the 1460s established the first printing press at Ulm in 1472. Zainer was one of the earliest among several publisher-printers who during the next fifty years were to seek the aid of scholars to edit or correct their productions, and in Dr Heinrich

Steinhöwel, medical officer and humanist, he found a learned collaborator. Thus his first book was Steinhöwel's 'Regimen wider die Pestilenz', 1473. Among other important books issued in the same year were Francesco Petrarca's 'Historia Griseldis' in Latin and German editions, a German edition of Boccaccio's 'Il Decamerone' and his 'De claris mulieribus'. The latter appeared in a Latin edition and in a German translation by Steinhöwel entitled 'Von etlichen frowen', both illustrated by some eighty excellent woodcuts deriving from French manuscript prototypes. These, and many other Zainer blocks, were widely copied throughout northern Europe.

Of greater artistic importance were the 193 cuts for Aesop's 'Vita et fabulae', issued in the original Latin and in Steinhöwel's German translation in 1476/7. The blocks were reprinted at Ausburg by his kinsman in 1477/8, by Anton Sorg in 1479, and in a derived form by Caxton in 1484. In general Zainer included attractive capitals and border decoration in most of his books. In 1493 his creditors forced him to flee Ulm, but either he or a relative of the same name may have returned to continue printing from 1496 to 1523.

Zapf, Hermann, 1918– : born in Nuremberg. In 1938 he worked in the studio of Paul Koch before becoming a free-lance calligrapher, book and type designer. His first type, a Fraktur, was shown in 1939. After 1945 he was retained by the Stempel foundry which had close ties with the German Linotype house, being art director between 1947 and 1957. This association extended the currency of the several roman faces he designed. Notable among Zapf's types are Palatino (1950), the titling face Sistina (1951), the newspaper type Mellor (1952), the text face Aldus (1954), and the important serifless roman Optima (cut 1955, shown 1958) originally a clear and graceful jobbing type but later reworked as a type for offset, letterpress and gravure. He has also designed faces for photosetting. In Britain Zapf's Melior, Optima and Sistina types are made under licence by the Monotype Corporation Ltd.

Recent designs include Scriptura (Hallmark) 1972, Orion (Linotype) 1974, Comenius S (Berthold) 1975, and Noris Script (Stempel) 1976.

Among his published writings are 'Pen and graver', 1952; 'Manuale typographicum', 1954, repr. 1970; 'About alphabets', 1960, new ed. 1970; and 'Typographic variations', 1964. All were issued in the United States where he teaches lettering, as well as in Germany. His wife Gudrun is also a type designer. See G. K. Schauer, 'Hermann Zapf, calligrapher and book designer', *Book Design and Production*', II 4 1959.

Zel, Ulrich, fl.1466–1507: a native of Hanau who may have learned printing with Schöffer at Mainz before setting himself up as the first printer of Cologne where his earliest signed and dated book, an edition of St Chrysostom's 'Liber primus super psalmum . . .', was issued in 1466. His large output of about 180 works included twenty-one editions of Johannes Gerson and such staple publications of the day as 'Gesta Romanorum', 'Legenda Aurea', Thomas à Kempis, and the writings of Johannes Nider.

Many of his books were undated, but even after printing for twenty years he was content to leave the addition of initial capitals, paragraph marks and so on to the hand of a rubricator. His printing, of which none was in the vernacular, was adequate but he was rarely inspired to ornament his pages with woodcuts or even to import fashionable Italian type.

Not a little of his present day notoriety comes from an account of the early history of printing which the anonymous compiler of the Cologne Chronicle, 1499, reported as being communicated to him by Master Ulric Zel of Hanau. It includes references to Strasbourg and to the Dutch Donatuses as harbingers of the discovery of printing about 1440 by 'Junker Johan Gudenburch van Mentz' whose work culminated years later in a Latin Bible. Both pro-Coster and pro-Gutenberg supporters claim this establishes priority of discovery for their man. See also *Caxton, Veldener.*

zig-zag guard: an alternative name for *continuous guard*, q.v.

Zilverdistel Press: the first modern Dutch private press, founded at The Hague, originally as an association of poets who commissioned Enschedé to print their works, but directed from 1910 by Jean François van Royen (1878–1942). His early books show the influence of the British private press movement. Special types designed for the press were the Zilver type of De Roos, 1915, and the Distel type of Lucien Pissarro, 1917, cut by E. P. Prince.

Van Royen's Albion press, other printing material and a collection of his books are preserved in the Meermanno-Westreenianum Museum, The Hague.

In 1923 the name was changed to *Kunera Press* (or *Pers*).

zinco: 1. an abbreviation for *zincograph*, q.v.

2. a cheap alternative to a *binder's brass*, q.v. It is less durable than brass and the impression made with it lacks sharpness.

zincograph: a zinc etching. See also *line block.*

zincography: an obsolete term for lithography, used regardless of the plate material.

zinc plates: photoengraving plates used for half-tone and line reproduction. They are an alternative to copper or magnesium alloy plates. Fine-grain micro-zinc plates are most used: they were patented by

W. H. Finkaldey in 1930. The older type of zinc plate is not suitable for fine-screen work. Cf. *copper plates*. See also *ungrained plates*.

zinc type: an alloy of 94% zinc, 4% aluminium and 2% magnesium introduced in the Soviet Union about 1950 for typecasting. Its melting point of between 340° and 365°C calls for modifications to casting machines. It is claimed to be cheap and durable.

Zip-a-tone: or *Zipatone*, a series of *mechanical tints*, q.v., printed on cellophane. They are used by artists and draughtsmen when preparing originals for reproduction. Tints are available in various textures and can be cut to any shape for stripping in with the artist's pen lines. This enables him to control the design to an extent not possible if tint laying is left to the process engraver. Zip-a-tone tints were patented in the U.S.A. in 1913 and are made in Britain under licence.

The American firm also makes *transfer lettering*, q.v.

zodiacal signs: see *astronomical symbols*.

SOME TYPE SPECIMENS

A Selection by Ronald Eames

See also the entry on *Letter forms*

GOTHIC FACES (BLACK LETTER)

Caxton Black

An imitation of the original Caxton face. V. J. Figgins 1904. 10 pt

ABCDEFGHIJKLMNOPQR
STUVWXYZ abcdefghijklmnopqrst
uvwxyz 1234567890

Fraktur

Monotype 1904. 12 pt

ABCDEFGHIJKLMNOPQRSTUVW
XYZÄÖÜ& 1234567890
abcdefghijklmnopqrstuvwxyzäöüchck
fififlllsfffßtß

Old English Text No. 2

Monotype 1934. 12 pt

ABCDEFGHIJKLMNOPQRST
UVWXYZ& abcdefghijklmnopqrst
uvwxyzæœ fiflffffifflffchckllsfistflßß
1234567890

Schwabacher

Monotype 1910. 12 pt

ABCDEFGHIJKLMNOPQRSTUVWXYZ
ÄÖÜ&
abcdefghijklmnopqrstuvwxyzäöü chckfiffflllsi
sfistßß 1234567890

VENETIAN FACES

Centaur

Designed by Bruce Rogers, 1915. Based on Jenson's original of 1470. Shown with Warde's italic. Monotype 1929. 12 pt

ABCDEFGHIJKLMNOPQRSTUVWXYZ

abcdefghijklmnopqrstuvwxyzæœ 1234567890

ABCDEFGHIJKLMNOPQRSTUVWXYZ

abcdefghijklmnopqrstuvwxyzæœ 1234567890

ABCDEFGHIJKLMNOPQRSTUVWXYZÆŒ

Cloister Old Style

Designed by Morris Benton after Jenson's roman. Monotype 1914. 12 pt

ABCDEFGHIJKLMNOPQRSTUVWXYZ

& abcdefghijklmnopqrstuvwxyz 1234567890

ABCDEFGHIJKLMNOPQRSTUVWXYZ 1234567890

ABCDEFGHIJKLMNOPQRSTUVWXYZ

abcdefghijklmnopqrstuvwxyzæœ 1234567890
1234567890

Goudy Old Style

Designed by F. W. Goudy. American Type Founders 1915–16; Monotype. 14 pt

ABCDEFGHIJKLMNOPQ
RSTUVWXYZ abcdefghijkl
mnopqrstuvwxyz 1234567890
ABCDEFGHIJKLMNOPQ
RSTUVWXYZ abcdefghijklm
nopqrstuvwxyz 1234567890

OLD FACES

Bembo

Griffo's roman originally cut for Aldus Manutius and first used in Cardinal Bembo's *De Aetna*. Redesigned by Monotype, 1929. 12 pt

ABCDEFGHIJKLMNOPQRSTUV
WXYZ abcdefghijklmnopqrstuvwxyz
1234567890
ABCDEFGHIJKLMNOPQRSTU
VWXYZ abcdefghijklmnopqrstuvwxyz
1234567890
ABCDEFGHIJKLMNOPQRSTUVWXYZ
ABCDEFGHIJKLMNOPQRST
UVWXYZ abcdefghijklmnopqrs
tuvwxyz 1234567890

Caslon Old Face

Once the most popular English Old Face. Introduced by William Caslon in 1725. Caslon. 12 pt

ABCDEFGHIJKLMNOPQRS TUVWXYZ abcdefghijklmnopqr stuvwxyz 1234567890
ABCDEFGHIJKLMNOPQRST UVWXYZ abcdefghijklmnopqrstu vwxyz
ABCDEFGHIJKLMNOPQRSTUVWXYZ
ABCDEFGHIJKLMNOPQR STUVWXYZ abcdefghijklmn opqrstuvwxyz 1234567890

Ehrhardt

A regularized version of a type by Nicholas Kis, 1672. Monotype 1938. 12 pt

ABCDEFGHIJKLMNOPQRSTUV WXYZ&
ABCDEFGHIJKLMNOPQRSTUVWXYZ abcdefghijklmnopqrstuvwxyz
1234567890   1234567890
ABCDEFGHIJKLMNOPQRSTUVWX YZ&ÆŒabcdefghijklmnopqrstuvwxyzæœ 1234567890
ABCDEFGHIJKLMNOPQRSTUV WXYZ&ÆŒ abcdefghijklmnopqrst uvwxyz 1234567890

Garamond

Based on types of the Imprimerie Nationale, not in fact cut by Garamont but by Jean Jannon (Mrs. B. Warde *Fleuron* No. 5) Monotype 1922. 12 pt

ABCDEFGHIJKLMNOPQRST UVWXYZ abcdefghijklmnopqrs tuvwxyz 1234567890
ABCDEFGHIJKLMNOPQRS TUVWXYZ abcdefghijklmnopqrst uvwxyz 1234567890
ABCDEFGHIJKLMNOPQRSTUVWXYZ
ABCDEFGHIJKLMNOPQRSTU VWXYZ&ÆŒ abcdefghijklmnopq rstuvwxyzæœfiflffifflff 1234567890

Janson

Originally cut by Nicholas Kis, *c.* 1690, and re-cut by C. H. Griffiths for Linotype, 1937. 12 pt

ABCDEFGHIJKLMNOPQRST VWXYZ abcdefghijklmnopqrstu vwxyz 1234567890

528

ABCDEFGHIJKLMNOPQRSTU VWXYZ abcdefghijklmnopqrstu vwxyz 1234567890
ABCDEFGHIJKLMNOPQRSTUVWXYZ

Plantin

Based by F. H. Pierpont on a Granjon face used in the 16th century by Plantin's contemporaries but not by him. 12 pt

ABCDEFGHIJKLMNOPQRS TUVWXYZ abcdefghijklmnopqr stuvwxyz 1234567890
ABCDEFGHIJKLMNOPQRS TUVWXYZ abcdefghijklmnopqrs tuvwxyz 1234567890
ABCDEFGHIJKLMNOPQRSTUVWXYZ
ABCDEFGHIJKLMNOPQRSTU VWXYZ& abcdefghijklmnopqrstuvwxyz 1234567890 1234567890

Van Dijck

Based, under the guidance of J. van Krimpen, on type used for a Dutch edition of Ovid, 1671, but not cut by Van Dijck. Caslon used a Van Dijck model for his Old Face. Monotype 1935. 12 pt

ABCDEFGHIJKLMNOPQRSTUVWX YZ&
abcdefghijklmnopqrstuvwxyzæœ 1234567890
ABCDEFGHIJKLMNOPQRSTUVW XYZ& abcdefghijklmnopqrstuvwxyzæœ 1234567890
ABCDEFGHIJKLMNOPQRSTUVWXYZ

TRANSITIONAL FACES

Baskerville

The English 18th-century face cut by John Baskerville. The original punches are now in the possession of Cambridge University Press. Monotype 1923. 12 pt

ABCDEFGHIJKLMNOPQRS TUVWXYZ abcdefghijklmnopq rstuvwxyz 1234567890

*ABCDEFGHIJKLMNOPQRST
UVWXYZ abcdefghijklmnopqrstuv
wxyz 1234567890*
ABCDEFGHIJKLMNOPQRSTUVWXYZ
**ABCDEFGHIJKLMNOPQRST
UVWXYZ
abcdefghijklmnopqrstuvwxyz**

Bell

Cut by Richard Austin in 1788. Monotype 1931. 12 pt
ABCDEFGHIJKLMNOPQRST
UVWXYZ abcdefghijklmnopqrst
uvwxyz 1234567890
*ABCDEFGHIJKLMNOPQRS
TUVWXYZ abcdefghijklmnopqrst
uvwxyz 1234567890*
ABCDEFGHIJKLMNOPQRSTUVWXYZ

Fournier

Based on the new roman designed by Pierre-Simon
Fournier in the 1740's, under the influence of the 'romains
du roi'. Monotype 1925. 12 pt

ABCDEFGHIJKLMNOPQRSTU
VWXYZ abcdefghijklmnopqrstuvwx
yz 1234567890
*ABCDEFGHIJKLMNOPQRST
UVWXYZ abcdefghijklmnopqrstuvw
xyz 1234567890*
ABCDEFGHIJKLMNOPQRSTUVWXYZ

MODERN FACES

Bodoni

The Modern of Giambattista Bodoni. Now offered by
most founders in many weights for book and display
purposes. Monotype, 1921. 12 pt
ABCDEFGHIJKLMNOPQRST
UVWXYZ abcdefghijklmnopqrs
tuvwxyz 1234567890
*ABCDEFGHIJKLMNOPQRS
TUVWXYZ abcdefghijklmnopqr
stuvwxyz 1234567890*

ABCDEFGHIJKLMNOPQRSTUVWXYZ
**ABCDEFGHIJKLMNOPQRSTU
VWXYZ abcdefghijklmnopqrstuv
wxyz 1234567890**

De Vinne

First cut in 1894 by G. Schroeder for what became the
American Type Founders Company. Intertype 1914.
12 pt
ABCDEFGHIJKLMNOPQR
STUVWXYZ abcdefghijklm
nopqrstuvwxyz 1234567890
*ABCDEFGHIJKLMNOPQR
STUVWXYZ abcdefghijklm
nopqrstuvwxyz 1234567890*
ABCDEFGHIJKLMNOPQRSTUVWXYZ

Walbaum

A German type inspired by Walbaum's Antiqua, intro-
duced into England by the Curwen Press in 1925. Mono-
type 1930. 11 pt (Didot)
ABCDEFGHIJKLMNOPQRSTU
VWXYZ abcdefghijklmnopqrstuv
wxyz 1234567890
*ABCDEFGHIJKLMNOPQRST
UVWXYZ abcdefghijklmnopqrstu
vwxyz*
ABCDEFGHIJKLMNOPQRSTUVWXYZ
**ABCDEFGHIJKLMNOPQRSTUVWX
YZ
abcdefghijklmnopqrstuvwxyzæœ
1234567890**

CONTEMPORARY FACES

Caledonia

Designed by W. A. Dwiggins. Inspired by Scotch Roman
and also types made by William Martin about 1790.
Linotype 1949. 12 pt
ABCDEFGHIJKLMNOPQRSTU
VWXYZ abcdefghijklmnopqrstu
vwxyz 1234567890

ABCDEFGHIJKLMNOPQRSTU VWXYZ abcdefghijklmnopqrstu vwxyz 1234567890

ABCDEFGHIJKLMNOPQRSTUVWXYZ

ABCDEFGHIJKLMNOPQRSTU VWXYZ abcdefghijklmnopqrstu vwxyz 1234567890

Cornell

Designed by George F. Trenholm. Intertype 1935. 12 pt

ABCDEFGHIJKLMNOPQRSTU VWXYZ abcdefghijklmnopqrst uvwxyz 1234567890

ABCDEFGHIJKLMNOPQRSTU VWXYZ abcdefghijklmnopqrst uvwxyz 1234567890

ABCDEFGHIJKLMNOPQRSTUVWXYZ

Dante

Designed by Giovanni Mardersteig and cut by Charles Malin for use at the Officina Bodoni in 1954. Now generally available. Monotype 1958. 12 pt

ABCDEFGHIJKLMNOPQRSTUVW XYZ&

abcdefghijklmnopqrstuvwxyzæœ 1234567890

ABCDEFGHIJKLMNOPQRSTUVWXYZ& abcdefghijklmnopqrstuvwxyzæœ 1234567890

ABCDEFGHIJKLMNOPQRSTUVWXYZ

Egmont

Designed by S. H. De Roos in 1933. Intertype 1937. 10 pt

ABCDEFGHIJKLMNOPQRSTUV WXYZ abcdefghijklmnopqrstuvwxyz 1234567890 1234567890

ABCDEFGHIJKLMNOPQRSTUV WXYZ abcdefghijklmnopqrstuvwxyz 1234567890 1234567890

ABCDEFGHIJKLMNOPQRSTUVWXYZ

ABCDEFGHIJKLMNOPQRSTUV WXYZ abcdefghijklmnopqrstuvwxyz 1234567890

ABCDEFGHIJKLMNOPQRSTUVWXYZ

ABCDEFGHIJKLMNOPQRSTUV WXYZ abcdefghijklmnopqrstuvwxyz 1234567890

ABCDEFGHIJKLMNOPQRSTUVWXYZ

Imprint

Modelled on an 18th-century Old Face to the instructions of J. H. Mason and Gerard Meynell specifically for *The Imprint* but now in general use. Monotype 1913. 12 pt

ABCDEFGHIJKLMNOPQRS TUVWXYZ abcdefghijklmnopqr stuvwxyz 1234567890

ABCDEFGHIJKLMNOPQRS TUVWXYZ abcdefghijklmnopqr stuvwxyz

ABCDEFGHIJKLMNOPQRSTUVWXYZ

ABCDEFGHIJKLMNOPQRSTUV WXYZ abcdefghijklmnopqrstuvwxyz 1234567890

Juliana

A narrow face designed by S. L. Hartz. Linotype 1958. 12 pt

ABCDEFGHIJKLMNOPQRSTU VWXYZ abcdefghijklmnopqrstu vwxyz 1234567890

ABCDEFGHIJKLMNOPQRSTU VWXYZ abcdefghijklmnopqrstu vwxyz 1234567890

ABCDEFGHIJKLMNOPQRSTUVWXYZ

Perpetua

Most popular of Eric Gill's Roman faces. Monotype 1929–30. 12 pt

ABCDEFGHIJKLMNOPQRSTUV WXYZ abcdefghijklmnopqrstuvwxyz 1234567890

ABCDEFGHIJKLMNOPQRSTUVW XYZ abcdefghijklmnopqrstuvwxyz 1234567890

ABCDEFGHIJKLMNOPQRSTUVWXYZ

ABCDEFGHIJKLMNOPQRSTUV WXYZ abcdefghijklmnopqrstuv wxyz 1234567890

Pilgrim

Designed by Eric Gill for a book published by The Limited Editions Club, New York. It was then called Bunyan. Now in general use. Linotype 1953. 12 pt

ABCDEFGHIJKLMNOPQRSTUVW
XYZ abcdefghijklmnopqrstuvwx
yz 1234567890
ABCDEFGHIJKLMNOPQRSTUVW
XYZ abcdefghijklmnopqrstuvwx
yz 1234567890
ABCDEFGHIJKLMNOPQRSTUVWXYZ
ABCDEFGHIJKLMNOPQRSTUVWXYZ

Spectrum

Designed by Jan van Krimpen. Enschedé 1952; Monotype 1956. 12 pt

ABCDEFGHIJKLMNOPQRSTUV
WXYZ abcdefghijklmnopqrstuvw
xyz 1234567890
ABCDEFGHIJKLMNOPQRSTUV
WXYZ abcdefghijklmnopqrstuvwxyz
1234567890
ABCDEFGHIJKLMNOPQRSTUVWXYZ

Times New Roman

Designed under the direction of Stanley Morison for the restyling of *The Times* newspaper, but universally adopted for book use. Monotype, Linotype 1932. 12 pt

ABCDEFGHIJKLMNOPQRS
TUVWXYZ abcdefghijklmnopq
rstuvwxyz 1234567890
ABCDEFGHIJKLMNOPQRST
UVWXYZ abcdefghijklmnopqrst
uvwxyz 1234567890
ABCDEFGHIJKLMNOPQRSTUVWXYZ
ABCDEFGHIJKLMNOPQRS
TUVWXYZ abcdefghijklmnopqr
stuvwxyz 1234567890

SANS SERIF

Gill Sans

Designed by Eric Gill. Available in many variations and four different weights. Monotype 1928–30. 12 pt

ABCDEFGHIJKLMNOPQRSTUVW
XYZ abcdefghijklmnopqrstuvwxyz
1234567890

ABCDEFGHIJKLMNOPQRSTUVWXYZ
abcdefghijklmnopqrstuvwxyz
1234567890

Univers

Designed by Adrian Frutiger. Monotype 1961-63. 12 pt

ABCDEFGHIJKLMNOPQRSTUV
WXYZ abcdefghijklmnopqrstuvw
xyz 1234567890

**ABCDEFGHIJKLMNOPQRSTU
VWXYZ abcdefghijklmnopqr
stuvwxyz 1234567890**

**ABCDEFGHIJKLMNOPQRSTUVWXYZ
abcdefghijklmnopqrstuvwxyz 123456
7890**

Vogue

Designed originally for *Vogue* magazine. Intertype 1932. 12 pt

ABCDEFGHIJKLMNOPQRSTUV
WXYZ abcdefghijklmnopqrstuv
wxyz 1234567890

ABCDEFGHIJKLMNOPQRSTUV
WXYZ abcdefghijklmnopqrstuv
wxyz 1234567890

EGYPTIAN

Cairo

Intertype 1933. 12 pt

ABCDEFGHIJKLMNOPQRSTU
VWXYZ abcdefghijklmnopqr
stuvwxyz 1234567890

**ABCDEFGHIJKLMNOPQRSTU
VWXYZ abcdefghijklmnopqr
stuvwxyz 1234567890**

Rockwell

In four weights with condensed and shadow versions. Monotype 1934. 12 pt

ABCDEFGHIJKLMNOPQRSTUV
WXYZ
abcdefghijklmnopqrstuvwxyz
1234567890

*ABCDEFGHIJKLMNOPQRSTUVWX
YZ abcdefghijklmnopqrstuvwxyz
1234567890*

FAT FACE

Ultra Bodoni
American Type Founders 1928, Monotype 1936. 14 pt

**ABCDEFGHIJKLMNOP
QRSTUVWXYZ
abcdefghijklmnopqrstuvw
xyz
1234567890**
*ABCDEFGHIJKLMNOP
QRSTUVWXYZ
abcdefghijklmnopqrstuv
wxyz*

EXOTIC

Amharic (Ethiopic)
Monotype 1966. 14 pt (Didot)

የሚከተለው ፡ አጭር ፡ ታሪክ ፡
ሞኖታይፕ ፡ የተባለው ፡ የፊደል ፡
መልቀሚያ ፡ መኪና ፡ መጀመሪያ ፡
ከወጣበት ፡ ከ፲፰፻፺፯ ፡ ዓ ፡ ም ፡ እንደ ፡
አውሮፓ ፡ አቆጣጠር ፡ ወዲህ

Arabic Naskh Accented
Monotype 1956. 24 pt (Didot)

فِى عَامِ ١٨٩٧ وَصَلَ إِلَى إِنْجِلْتِرَا
أُنْمُوذَجٌ مُسْتَحْدَثٌ لِآلَةٍ جَدِيدَةٍ كَانَ
الْمُخْتَرِعُ الْأَمْرِيكِيُّ تَلْبِرْتْ لَانْسْتُنْ
قَدِ ابْتَكَرَهَا مِنْ قَبْلُ. وَهِىَ آلَةٌ تَقْطَعُ
مِنْ سَبَائِكِ الرَّصَاصِ الْبَارِدِ أَنْوَاعاً

Bengali Bold
Monotype 1967. 14 pt

১৮৯৭ খ্রীস্টাব্দে আধুনিক মডেলের একটি
নূতন ও উন্নত ধরনের যন্ত্র আগাম নমুনা
হিসাবে ইংলণ্ডে আনা হয় । ছিদ্রিত কাগজের
রিবনের সাহায্যে ঠাণ্ডা সীসার পাত হইতে
বিভিন্ন অক্ষর (টাইপ) প্রস্তুত করার জন্য এই

Devanagari Bold
Monotype 1965. 14 pt

सन् १८९७ में इंगलैंड में एक नयी मशीन का अधिक
सफल माडेल आया । इसमें अभी और उन्नति
होनी थी । सब से पहिले अमेरिका के अनुसंधानक
टालबर्ट लैन्स्टन को इसके बारे में सूझी । उन्होंने
इसे छिद्रयुक्त रिबन के कागज में गुंथी एक ठंढी

Hebrew: Peninim
Monotype 1963. 14 pt

ויענו אנשי המצבה את
יונתן ואת נשא כליו ויאמרו
עלו אלינו ונודיעה אתכם
דבר ויאתר יונמן אל נשא
כליו עלה אחרי כי

Old Bulgarian
Monotype. 12 pt

АБВГДЄЖSЗZИИКЛМНОПРСТѸФ
ХѾѠЩЧШЪЫЬѢЮꙖꙘꙐѦѪꙖꙖꙞꙌ
ѰОⴸ абвгдєнюжsзꙁⰋꙇⰺⰠклмнопрстѸфх
хѿѡщчшъꙑꙑꙑꙑꙑꙑꙑꙑꙑꙑꙞꙞꙞꙌѰοⴸꙟ

Times Cyrillic
Monotype 1956. 12 pt

АБВГДЕЖЗИКЛМНОПРСТУФ
ХЦЧШЩЪЫЬЭЮЯЂЖЋЈЉЊЋ
Џ абвгдежзиклмнопрстуфхцчшщ
ъыьэюяѕђђјљњћџ

Times Upright Greek
Monotype 1956. 12 pt
ΑΒΓΔΕΖΗΘΙΚΛΜΝΞΟΠΡΣΤΥΦΧ
ΨΩς αβγδεζηθικλμνξοπρστυφχψως

DISPLAY FACES

ALBERTUS Albertus
TITLING

Berthold Wolpe. Monotype 1932–40

Ashley Script

Ashley Havinden. Monotype 1955

CASTELLAR

Designed by John Peters. Monotype 1957

Chisel

Robert Harling. Stephenson Blake 1939–56

Colonna

Monotype 1927

COLUMNA

Bauersche Giesserei 1955

CONSORT

After the Fann Street Foundry's extended Clarendon
of 1845. Stephenson Blake 1956

CORVINUS SKYLINE

Imre Reiner. Bauersche Giesserei 1929–34

EGMONT
INLINE

De Roos. Typefoundry Amsterdam 1934

Egyptian
Condensed
Expanded

Monotype (expanded Miller & Richard, *c.* 1850,
Stephenson Blake, *c.* 1950)

ERBAR Light

Jakob Erbar. Ludwig and Mayer 1922–30

FESTIVAL

Phillip Boydell. Monotype 1951

Francesca Ronde

Stephenson Blake 1948

Fry's BASKERVILLE

Stephenson Blake originally cut by Isaac Moore
1768

GILL TITLING
Bold Condensed
Extra bold, Line
SHADOW TITLING

Eric Gill. Monotype 1928–30

GRAVURE OPEN

Typefoundry Amsterdam

Grotesque (No. 9)

Stephenson Blake, 1909

Imprint Shadow

Monotype, 1926

Klang

Will Carter. Monotype 1955

LIBRA

De Roos. Typefoundry Amsterdam 1938

Marina

Stephenson Blake 1936

MINERVA *Italic* **Bold**

Reynolds Stone. Linotype 1955

MOLÉ FOLIATE

Stephenson Blake. Originally cut in 1819 in Paris

OLD FACE OPEN

Stephenson Blake. Originally cut in the 1790s

ONYX

Gerry Powell. American Type Founders 1937

OTHELLO

Monotype

PERPETUA TITLING

Eric Gill. Monotype 1928

PROFIL

Eugen Lenz. Haas'sche Schriftgiesserei 1943

Rockwell
Bold
Italic
Bold Condensed

Lanston Monotype 1934

ROMULUS OPEN

Jan van Krimpen. Enschedé 1956

ROSART

Enschedé 1759

**SANS SERIF
SHADED**

William Thorowgood, 1839. Re-cast by Stephenson Blake 1938. Issued 1948

SELECT

Albert Augspurg. Typefoundry Amsterdam 1936

Society Script

Stephenson Blake

Swing Bold

Monotype, 1955

Temple Script
Monotype 1937

THORNE SHADED

Robert Thorne, *c.* 1810. Re-issued Stephenson Blake 1936

Thorowgood *Thorowgood*

Thorowgood, after Thorne, 1836. Stephenson Blake, 1953

TIMES HEAVY TITLING

Monotype

Trafton Script

Howard Trafton. Bauersche 1933

Ultra Bodoni *Italic*

Monotype

Union Pearl

Oldest English decorated type. James Grover, *c.* 1690. Re-cast for 'The Fleuron', 1928. Available from Stephenson Blake since 1950

VENDÔME Bold

François Ganeau. Olive 1950

TRANSFER LETTERING

PIONEER

Letraset 1970

Dynamo

After the type designed by K. Sommer for Ludwig & Mayer, 1930. Letraset 1968

PHOTO LETTERING

Perpetua Bold Shadow

Photoset

Appendix B

LATIN PLACE NAMES AS USED IN THE IMPRINTS OF EARLY PRINTED BOOKS

Both the Latin and English forms of a place name are used as entry words in the single alphabetical sequence which follows, the former being printed in capitals. Where, however, this would result in the two entries for a place being adjacent, only the Latin into English is given. While Latin names usually occurred in the locative case, adjectival or possessive forms are not uncommon.

Aachen	AQUISGRANUM
ABBATISVILLA	Abbeville
ABBENDONIA	Abingdon
ABREDONIA	Aberdeen
ALBANI VILLA	St Albans
ALBIBURGI	Wittenberg
Alcalà de Henares	COMPLUTUM
AMSTELODAMUM	Amsterdam
ANDREAPOLIS	St Andrews
ANEDA	Edinburgh
ANTUERPIA	Antwerp
AQUISGRANUM	Aachen
ARGENTINA	Strasbourg
ARGENTORATUM	Strasbourg
ASCULUM PICENUM	Ascoli Piceno
ASTURICA	Astorga (Spain)
ATHENAE RAURACAE	Basle
Augsburg	AUGUSTA VINDELICORUM
AUGUSTA PERUSIA	Perugia
AUGUSTA TIBERII	Regensburg
AUGUSTA TRINOBANTIUM	London
AUGUSTA VINDELICORUM	Augsburg
AURELIA ALLOBROGUM	Geneva
AURELIACUM	Orleans
AVENIO	Avignon
BABENBERGA	Bamberg
Bamberg	GRAVIONATIUM
BARCHINO	Barcelona
BASILEA	Basle
Basle	ATHENAE RAURACAE
Basle	BASILEA
Basle	COLONIA MUNATIANA
BEROLINUM	Berlin
Besançon	VESUNTIO
BISUNTIA	Besançon
BITTURIS	Bourges
Bologna	FELSINA
BONONIA	Bologna
BORBETOMAGUS	Worms
Bourges	BITTURIS

Breslau	VRATISLAVIA
BRIXIA	Brescia
BRUXELLEN	Brussels
CADOMUM	Caen
CANTABRIGIA	Cambridge
Canterbury	DUROVERNUM
Chester	DEVA
Chichester	REGUM
Cologne	UBII
COLONIA AGRIPPINA	Cologne
COLONIA ALLOBROGUM	Geneva
COLONIA CLAUDIA	Cologne
COLONIA MUNATIANA	Basle
COLONIA UBIORUM	Cologne
COMPLUTUM	Alcalà de Henares
Copenhagen	HAFNIA
Copenhagen	HAVNIA
COSMOPOLIS	a fictitious imprint
DANTISCUM	Danzig
DEVA	Chester
DIVIO	Dijon
DORDRACUM	Dordrecht
DUACUM	Douai
Dublin	EBLANA
DUNELMIA	Durham
DUROBRIVAE	Rochester
DUROCORTORUM	Rheims
DUROVERNUM	Canterbury
EBLANA	Dublin
EBORACUM	York
Edinburgh	ANEDA
EDINBURGUM	Edinburgh
ELEUTHEROPOLIS	a 'free city', usually an illegal book
ELVETIORUM ARGENTINA	Strasbourg
ERFORDIA	Erfurt
ERIDANIUM	Milan
Exeter	ISCA
EXONIA	Exeter
FELSINA	Bologna

536

Foligno	FULGENTIUM	Mainz	MOGUNTIA
FRANCOFURTUM AD MOENUM	Frankfurt am Main	MANTUA CARPETANORUM	Madrid
		MEDIOLANUM	Milan
Frankfurt am Main	HELENOPOLIS	Milan	ERIDANIUM
Frankfurt an der Oder	TRAJECTUM AD VIADRUM	Milan	MEDIOLANUM
FULGENTIUM	Foligno	Modena	MUTINA
GANDAVUM	Ghent	MOGUNTIA	Mainz
GEBENNA	Geneva	MONACHIUM	Munich
GENABUM	Orleans	Munich	MONACHIUM
Geneva	AURELIA ALLOBROGUM	MUTINA	Modena
Geneva	COLONIA ALLOBROGUM	NANNETES	Nantes
Geneva	GEBENNA	Naples	PARTHENOPE
Genoa	IANUA	NEAPOLIS	Naples
Ghent	GANDAVUM	NICAEA	Nice
GIPPESWICUM	Ipswich	NORDOVICUM	Norwich
GLASCUA	Glasgow	NORICA	Nuremberg
GOTORUM	Lund	NORIMBERGA	Nuremberg
GRAVIONATIUM	Bamberg	Norwich	NORDOVICUM
HAFNIA	Copenhagen	OLYSSIPO	Lisbon
HAGA COMITUM	The Hague	Orleans	AURELIACUM
HAMMONA	Hamburg	Orleans	GENABUM
HAVNIA	Copenhagen	OXONIA	Oxford
HELENOPOLIS	Frankfurt am Main	Padua	PATAVIUM
HERBIPOLIS	Würzburg	PANORMUM	Palermo
HISPALIS	Seville	PAPIA	Pavia
IANUA	Genoa	Paris	LUTETIA
INSULIS	Lille	PARISIIS	Paris
Ipswich	GIPPESWICUM	PARISIUS	Paris
ISCA	Exeter	PARTHENOPE	Naples
Langres	LINGONENSIS, CIVITAS	PATAVIA	Passau
Leghorn	LIBURNUM	PATAVIUM	Padua
LEIDA	Leiden	Pavia	PAPIA
Leiden	LUGDUNUM BATAVORUM	Pavia	TICINI
Leipzig	LIPSIA	Perugia	AUGUSTA PERUSIA
LEMOVICENSE CASTRUM	Limoges	PETRIBURGUM	Peterborough
LEODIUM	Liège	PISAE	Pisa
LIBURNUM	Leghorn	RATISBONA	Regensburg
Liège	LEODIUM	Regensburg	AUGUSTA TIBERII
Lille	INSULLIS	Regensburg	RATISBONA
Limoges	LEMOVICENSE CASTRUM	REGUM	Chichester
LINGONENSIS, CIVITAS	Langres	Rheims	DUROCORTORUM
LIPSIA	Leipzig	Rochester	DUROBRIVAE
Lisbon	OLYSSIPO	ROTOMAGUS	Rouen
Lisbon	ULYSSIPO	SAENA	Siena
LONDINIUM	London	St Albans	ALBANI VILLA
LONDINIUM SCANORUM	Lund	St Albans	VILLA SANCTA ALBANI
London	AUGUSTA TRINOBANTUM	St Andrews	ANDREAPOLIS
London	LONDINIUM	CALIDONIA	Salzburg
LOVANIUM	Louvain	SARUM	Salisbury
LUBICENSIS	Lübeck	SENAE	Siena
LUGDUNUM	Lyons	Seville	HISPALIS
LUGDUNUM BATAVORUM	Leiden	Siena	SAENA
Lund	GOTORUM	Siena	SENAE
Lund	LONDINIUM SCANORUM	Strasbourg	ARGENTINA
LUTETIA	Paris	Strasbourg	ARGENTORATUM
Lyons	LUGDUNUM	Strasbourg	ELVETIORUM ARGENTINA
Madrid	MANTUA CARPETANORUM	SUBLACENSE MONASTERIUM	Subiaco
MAGUNTIA	Mainz		

537

TAURINUM	Turin	VESUNTIO	Besançon
THOLOSA	Toulouse	VICENTIA	Vicenza
TICINI	Pavia	Vienna	VINDOBONA
TIGURUM	Zürich	VILLA SANCTA ALBANI	St Albans
Tours	TURONIS	VINDOBONA	Vienna
TRAJECTUM AD RHENUM	Utrecht	VIRCEBURGUM	Würzburg
TRAJECTUM AD VIADRUM	Frankfurt am Oder	VORMATIA	Worms
TRAJECTUM INFERIUS	Utrecht	VRATISLAVIA	Breslau
TREVIRI	Trier	Warsaw	VARSAVIA
TURIGUM	Zürich	WESTMONASTERIUM	Westminster
Turin	TAURINUM	WIGORNUM	Worcester
TURONIS	Tours	Winchester	VENTA BELGARUM
UBII	Cologne	Wittenberg	ALBIBURGI
ULTRAJECTUM	Utrecht	Worcester	WIGORNUM
ULYSSIPO	Lisbon	Worms	BORBETOMAGUS
Utrecht	TRAJECTUM AD RHENUM	Worms	VORMATIA
Utrecht	TRAJECTUM INFERIUS	Würzburg	HERBIPOLIS
Utrecht	ULTRAJECTUM	Würzburg	VIRCEBURGUM
VARSAVIA	Warsaw	York	EBORACUM
VENETIAE	Venice	Zürich	TIGURUM
VENTA BELGARUM	Winchester	Zürich	TURIGUM

Appendix C

PROOF CORRECTION SYMBOLS

The British Standards Institution has very kindly authorised the reprinting here of an extract from BS 5261: Part 2: 1976. Complete copies can be obtained from the Institution, 2 Park Street, London W1A 2BS.

Notes on the use of the marks

1. For each marking-up or proof correction instruction a distinct mark is to be made:

    (a) in the text: to indicate the exact place to which the instruction refers;

    (b) in the margin: to signify or amplify the meaning of the instruction.

It should be noted that some instructions have a combined textual and marginal mark.

2. Where a number of instructions occur in one line, the marginal marks are to be divided between the left and right margins where possible, the order being from left to right in both margins.

3. Specification details, comments and instructions may be written on the copy or proof to complement the textual and marginal marks. Such written matter is to be clearly distinguishable from the copy and from any corrections made to the proof. Normally this is done by encircling the matter and/or by the appropriate use of colour (see below).

4. Proof corrections shall be made in coloured ink thus:

    (a) printer's literal errors marked by the printer for correction: green;

    (b) printer's literal errors marked by the customer and his agents for correction: red;

    (c) alterations and instructions made by the customer and his agents: black or dark blue.

Classified list of marks (Table 1 from BS 5261 : Part 2)

NOTE: The letters M and P in the notes column indicate marks for marking-up copy and for correcting proofs respectively.

Group A   General

Number	Instruction	Textual mark	Marginal mark	Notes
A1	Correction is concluded	None	/	P Make after each correction
A2	Leave unchanged	– – – – – – under characters to remain	(✓)	M P
A3	Remove extraneous marks	Encircle marks to be removed	✕	P e.g. film or paper edges visible between lines on bromide or diazo proofs
A3.1	Push down risen spacing material	Encircle blemish	⊥	P
A4	Refer to appropriate authority anything of doubtful accuracy	Encircle word(s) affected	(?)	P

Group B   Deletion, insertion and substitution

Number	Instruction	Textual mark	Marginal mark	Notes
B1	Insert in text the matter indicated in the margin	⅄	New matter followed by ⅄	M P Identical to B2
B2	Insert additional matter identified by a letter in a diamond	⅄	⅄ Followed by for example ◇A	M P The relevant section of the copy should be supplied with the corresponding letter marked on it in a diamond e.g. ◇A
B3	Delete	/ through character(s) or ⊢——⊣ through words to be deleted	ð	M P
B4	Delete and close up	⌒/⌄ through character or ⊢——⊣ through character e.g. chara̷cter charaᴃᴃcter	ð̑	M P

Number	Instruction	Textual mark	Marginal mark	Notes
B5	Substitute character or substitute part of one or more word(s)	/ through character or ⊢———⊣ through word(s)	New character or new word(s)	M P
B6	Wrong fount. Replace by character(s) of correct fount	Encircle character(s) to be changed	⊗	P
B6.1	Change damaged character(s)	Encircle character(s) to be changed	✕	P This mark is identical to A3
B7	Set in or change to italic	———— under character(s) to be set or changed	⊔⊔	M P Where space does not permit textual marks encircle the affected area instead
B8	Set in or change to capital letters	≡≡≡ under character(s) to be set or changed	≡	
B9	Set in or change to small capital letters	══ under character(s) to be set or changed	══	
B9.1	Set in or change to capital letters for initial letters and small capital letters for the rest of the words	≡≡ under initial letters and ══ under rest of word(s)	≡══	
B10	Set in or change to bold type	∿∿∿∿ under character(s) to be set or changed	∿	
B11	Set in or change to bold italic type	∿∿∿∿ under character(s) to be set or changed	⊔⊔ ∿	
B12	Change capital letters to lower case letters	Encircle character(s) to be changed	≠	P For use when B5 is inappropriate
B12.1	Change small capital letters to lower case letters	Encircle character(s) to be changed	≠	P For use when B5 is inappropriate

Number	Instruction	Textual mark	Marginal mark	Notes
B13	Change italic to upright type	Encircle character(s) to be changed	山	P
B14	Invert type	Encircle character to be inverted	↻	P
B15	Substitute or insert character in 'superior' position	/ through character or ∧ where required	⌐ under character e.g. ²⌐	P
B16	Substitute or insert character in 'inferior' position	/ through character or ∧ where required	∟ over character e.g. ∟₂	P
B17	Substitute ligature e.g. ffi for separate letters	⊢———⊣ through characters affected	⌣ e.g. ⌢ffi	P
B17.1	Substitute separate letters for ligature	⊢———⊣	Write out separate letters	P
B18	Substitute or insert full stop or decimal point	/ through character or ∧ where required	(·)	M P
B18.1	Substitute or insert colon	/ through character or ∧ where required	(⋮)	M P
B18.2	Substitute or insert semi-colon	/ through character or ∧ where required	;	M P
B18.3	Substitute or insert comma	/ through character or ∧ where required	'	M P

Number	Instruction	Textual mark	Marginal mark	Notes
B18.4	Substitute or insert apostrophe	/ through character or Λ where required	＇	M P
B18.5	Substitute or insert single quotation marks	/ through character or Λ where required	＇ and/or ＇	M P
B18.6	Substitute or insert double quotation marks	/ through character or Λ where required	＇＇ and/or ＇＇	M P
B19	Substitute or insert ellipsis	/ through character or Λ where required	. . .	M P
B20	Substitute or insert leader dots	/ through character or Λ where required	(. . .)	M P Give the measure of the leader when necessary
B21	Substitute or insert hyphen	/ through character or Λ where required	⊢—⊣	M P
B22	Substitute or insert rule	/ through character or Λ where required	⊢—⊣	M P Give the size of the rule in the marginal mark e.g. ⊢1 em⊣ ⊢4 mm⊣
B23	Substitute or insert oblique	/ through character or Λ where required	(/)	M P

Group C   Positioning and spacing

Number	Instruction	Textual mark	Marginal mark	Notes
C1	Start new paragraph			M P
C2	Run on (no new paragraph)			M P
C3	Transpose characters or words	between characters or words, numbered when necessary		M P
C4	Transpose a number of characters or words	3 2 1	1 2 3	M P To be used when the sequence cannot be clearly indicated by the use of C3. The vertical strokes are made through the characters or words to be transposed and numbered in the correct sequence
C5	Transpose lines			M P
C6	Transpose a number of lines	——— 3 ——— 2 ——— 1		P To be used when the sequence cannot be clearly indicated by C5. Rules extend from the margin into the text with each line to be transplanted numbered in the correct sequence
C7	Centre	enclosing matter to be centred		M P
C8	Indent			P Give the amount of the indent in the marginal mark
C9	Cancel indent			P
C10	Set line justified to specified measure	and/or		P Give the exact dimensions when necessary

Number	Instruction	Textual mark	Marginal mark	Notes
C11	Set column justified to specified measure	←——→	←→	M P Give the exact dimensions when necessary
C12	Move matter specified distance to the right	enclosing matter to be moved to the right →		P Give the exact dimensions when necessary
C13	Move matter specified distance to the left	← enclosing matter to be moved to the left		P Give the exact dimensions when necessary
C14	Take over character(s), word(s) or line to next line, column or page			P The textual mark surrounds the matter to be taken over and extends into the margin
C15	Take back character(s), word(s), or line to previous line, column or page			P The textual mark surrounds the matter to be taken back and extends into the margin
C16	Raise matter	↑ over matter to be raised under matter to be raised		P Give the exact dimensions when necessary. (Use C28 for insertion of space between lines or paragraph in text)
C17	Lower matter	over matter to be lowered ↓ under matter to be lowered		P Give the exact dimensions when necessary. (Use C29 for reduction of space between lines or paragraphs in text)
C18	Move matter to position indicated	Enclose matter to be moved and indicate new position		P Give the exact dimensions when necessary
C19	Correct vertical alignment	‖ ‖	‖ ‖	P
C20	Correct horizontal alignment	Single line above and below misaligned matter e.g. mi_saligned	═══	P The marginal mark is placed level with the head and foot of the relevant line

Number	Instruction	Textual mark	Marginal mark	Notes
C21	Close up. Delete space between characters or words	linking ⌒⌣ characters	⌒⌣	M P
C22	Insert space between characters	| between characters affected	Y	M P Give the size of the space to be inserted when necessary
C23	Insert space between words	Y between words affected	Y	M P Give the size of the space to be inserted when necessary
C24	Reduce space between characters	| between characters affected	⋀	MP Give the amount by which the space is to be reduced when necessary
C25	Reduce space between words	⋀ between words affected	⋀	M P Give amount by which the space is to be reduced when necessary
C26	Make space appear equal between characters or words	| between characters or words affected	⅄	M P
C27	Close up to normal interline spacing	(each side of column linking lines)		MP The textual marks extend into the margin
C28	Insert space between lines or paragraphs	—⊂ or ⊃—		M P The marginal mark extends between the lines of text. Give the size of the space to be inserted when necessary
C29	Reduce space between lines or paragraphs	—⊃ or ⊂—		M P The marginal mark extends between the lines of text. Give the amount by which the space is to be reduced when necessary

Appendix D

A SHORT READING LIST

Books referred to in Glossary entries are excluded

ARRANGEMENT OF THE SECTIONS

The Manuscript Book: Calligraphy: Illumination
The Book Trade: Publishing: Bookselling: Reading
Printing History
Printing Technology and Management
Book Design: Typography: Illustration: Private Presses
Bookbinding
Paper Technology

The Manuscript Book: Calligraphy: Illumination

ANDERSON, D. M. *The art of written forms: the theory and practice of calligraphy.* N.Y., Holt Rinehart, 1969.

CHILD, H. *Calligraphy today.* 2nd ed. Studio Vista, 1976.

DAWSON, G. E., AND KENNEDY-SKIPTON, L. *Elizabethan handwriting, 1500–1650.* N.Y., Norton, 1966.

DELAISSE, G. F. *A century (1400–1500) of Dutch manuscript illumination.* C.U.P., 1968.

DIRINGER, D. *The illuminated book: its history and production.* 2nd ed. Faber, 1967.

DRIVER, G. R. *Semitic writing from pictograph to alphabet.* 3rd ed. O.U.P., 1976.

FAIRBANK, A. *The story of handwriting: origins and development.* Faber, 1970.

HECTOR, L. C. *The handwriting of English documents.* 2nd ed. Arnold, 1966.

JENSEN, H. *Sign, symbol and script.* George Allen & Unwin, 1970.

LAMB, C. M. *The calligrapher's handbook.* 2nd ed. Faber, 1969.

LINGS, M. *The Quranic art of calligraphy and illumination.* World of Islam Festival Trust, 1977.

LOWE, E. A. *Codices Latinae antiquiores.* 11 vols, O.U.P., 1934–66.

MAHLER, J. G. *Oriental miniatures: Persian, Indian, Turkish.* Wellcome, 1965.

MITCHELL, C. A. *Documents and their scientific examination.* Griffin, 1935.

NASH, R. *American writing masters and copybooks.* Boston, 1959.

NESBITT, A. *The history and technique of lettering.* N.Y., Dover, 1957.

OAKESHOTT, W. *The sequence of English medieval art.* Faber, 1950.

ROBB, D. M. *The art of the illuminated manuscript.* New Jersey, 1974.

ROTHE, E. *Medieval book illumination in Europe: 400–1600.* Thames & Hudson, 1968.

SAUNDERS, O. E. *English illumination.* 2 vols, Florence, 1928.

THOMSON, S. H. *Latin bookhands in the later Middle Ages.* 1970.

TSCHICHOLD, J. *An illustrated history of writing and lettering.* Zwemmer, 1946.

VALENTINE, L. N. *Ornament in medieval manuscripts: a glossary.* Faber, 1965.

WARDROP, J. *The script of humanism: some aspects of humanist script, 1460–1560.* O.U.P., 1963.

WHALLEY, J. *English handwriting, 1540–1853.* H.M.S.O., 1969.

WRIGHT, C. E. *English vernacular hands from the 12th to the 15th centuries.* O.U.P., 1960.

The Book Trade, Publishing, Bookselling, Reading

ADBURGHAM, A. *Women in print.* George Allen & Unwin, 1972.

ALTICK, R. D. *The English common reader.* U. of Chicago P., 1957.

BAILEY, H. S. *The art and science of book publishing.* N.Y., Harper, 1971.

BARNES, J. J. *Free trade in books: a study of the London book trade since 1800.* O.U.P., 1964.

BARTLETT, G. *Better bookselling . . . a series of nine pamphlets.* Hutchinson, 1965–8.

BENNETT, H. S. *English books and readers, 1475–1640.* 3 vols, C.U.P., 1965–70.

BINGLEY, C. *Book publishing practice.* Lockwood, 1966.

BRIGGS, A. ed. *Essays in the history of publishing, in celebration of the 250th anniversary of the House of Longman, 1724–1974.* Longman, 1974.

CARTER, J. *ABC for book collectors.* 5th ed. Hart-Davis, 1972.

CARTER, J. *Taste and technique in book collecting.* 3rd ed. Private Libraries Association, 1970.

CARTER, J., AND MUIR, P. H. *Printing and the mind of man: a descriptive catalogue illustrating the impact of print on the evolution of Western civilization during five centuries.* Cassell, 1967.

CASSELL'S *directory of publishing.* 8th ed. 1976–7.

FAXON, F. W. *Literary annuals and gift books: a bibliography, 1823–1903.* Boston, 1912, repr. Private Libraries Association, 1974.

FEBVRE, L., AND MARTIN, H-J. *L'Apparition du livre.* Paris, 1958.

GRANNIS, C. B. *What happens in book publishing.* 2nd ed. N.Y., Columbia U.P., 1967.

HATTERY, L. H., AND BUSH, G. P. *Automation and electronics in publishing.* Macmillan, 1965.

HEYS, H. *The preparation and production of technical handbooks.* Pitman, 1965.

JOY, T. *The bookselling business.* Pitman, 1974.

KUJOTH, J. S. ed. *Book publishing: inside views.* N.Y., Bailey, 1971.

LITERARY *and library prizes.* 9th ed. N.Y., Bowker, 1976.

MADISON, C. *Book publishing in America.* N.Y., McGraw, 1966.

MUMBY, F. A., AND NORRIE, I. *Book publishing, 1870–1970.* 5th ed. Cape, 1974.

MYERS, R. *The British book trade.* Deutsch, 1973.

PLANT, M. *The English book trade: an economic history of the making and sale of books.* 2nd ed. George Allen & Unwin, 1965.

POWELL, C. *A passion for books.* Constable, 1958.

ROSCOE, S. *John Newbery and his successors, 1740–1814.* Five Owls P., 1974.

SMITH, D. C. *A guide to book publishing.* N.Y., Bowker, 1966.

SMITH, F. S. *Bibliography in the bookshop.* Deutsch, 1964.

TEBBEL, J. *History of book publishing in the United States.* 4 Vols. N.Y., Bowker, 1972– (in progress).

TANSELLE, G. T. *Guide to the study of U.S. imprints.* 2 vols. Cambridge, Mass., 1971.

THOMAS, D. *A long time burning: the history of literary censorship in England.* Routledge, 1969.

UNWIN, SIR STANLEY. *The truth about a publisher.* George Allen & Unwin, 1960.

UNWIN, SIR STANLEY. *The truth about publishing.* 8th ed. George Allen & Unwin, 1976.

UNWIN, P. *The publishing Unwins.* Heinemann, 1972.

WELCH, d'A. *Bibliography of American children's books printed prior to 1821.* Worcester, Mass., American Antiquarian Society, 1972.

WIDMAN, H. *Der deutsche Buchhandel in Urkunden und Quellen.* Hamburg, 1965.

WILLIAMS, H. *Book clubs and printing societies of Great Britain and Ireland.* 1929, repr. Detroit, 1971.

WINTERICH, J. T., AND RANDALL, D. *A primer of book collecting.* 3rd ed. George Allen & Unwin, 1966.

Printing History

ARS TYPOGRAPHIA LIBRARY. Edited by J. Moran. London, in progress.

BERRY, W. T., AND POOLE, H. *Annals of printing: a chronological encyclopaedia from the earliest times to 1960.* Blandford, 1966.

BIBLIOTHÈQUE NATIONALE. *L'Art du livre à l'Imprimerie nationale.* Paris, 1974.

BIGMORE, E. C., AND WYMAN, C. *A bibliography of printing.* Quaritch, 1884–6, repr. Duschnes, 1945.

BLUMENTHAL, J. *The art of the printed book, 1455–1955.* Bodley Head, 1974.

BLUMENTHAL, J. *The printed book in America.* Scolar P., 1978.

BOHATTA, H. *Bibliographie der Breviere, 1501–1850.* Stuttgart, 1937, repr. 1963.

BRUN, R. *Le Livre français.* Paris, 1969.

BUHLER, C. F. *The fifteenth-century book: the scribes, the printers, the decorators.* Penn., Philadelphia U.P., 1960.

CHAUVET, P. *Les Ouvriers du livre en France des origines à la revolution de 1789.* Paris, Presses Universitaires, 1959.

CHRISTIAN, A. *Débuts de l'imprimerie en France.* Paris, Imprimerie Nationale, 1904.

CLAIR, C. *A chronology of printing.* Cassell, 1969.

CLAIR, C. *History of printing in Britain.* Cassell, 1965.

CLAIR, C. *History of European printing.* Academic P., 1976.

GASKELL, P. *A new introduction to bibliography.* O.U.P., 1972.

GERNLAITIS, L. *Printing and publishing in 15th century Venice.* Mansell, 1976.

HAEBLER, K. *The study of incunabula.* N.Y., 1933, repr. 1967.

HANDOVER, P. *Printing in London from 1476 to modern times.* George Allen & Unwin, 1960.

HOWE, E. *The London compositor: documents relating to wages, working conditions and customs of the London printing trade, 1785–1900.* Bibliographical Society, 1947.

HUSS, R. E. *Development of printers' mechanical typesetting methods, 1822–1925.* U.P. of Virginia, 1973.

KIRCHNER, J. *Lexicon des Buchwesens.* 2nd ed. 4 vols. Stuttgart Hiersemann, 1952–56.

MCMURTRIE, D. *The book: the story of printing and bookmaking.* 3rd ed. O.U.P., 1943.

MORAN, J. *The composition of reading matter: a history from case to computer.* Wace, 1965.

MORAN, J. *Printing presses: history and development from the fifteenth century to modern times.* Faber, 1973.

MOREAU, B. *Inventaire chronologique des éditions parisiennes XVI siècle. I. 1505–1510.* Paris, Imprimerie municipale, 1972.

MORTIMER, R. *Catalogue of books and manuscripts. Pt I. French 16th century books. Pt II. Italian 16th century books.* Cambridge, Mass., Harvard U.P., 1964 & 1974.

NORTON, F. J. *Descriptive catalogue of printing in Spain and Portugal, 1501–1520.* C.U.P., 1978.

NORTON, F. J. *Printing in Spain, 1501–1520.* C.U.P., 1966.

PATENT OFFICE. *Printing patents: abridgements of patent specifications relating to printing, 1617–1857.* 1858, repr. P.H.S., 1969.

PLOMER, H. R. *A dictionary of the booksellers and printers who were at work in England, Scotland and Ireland from 1641–1775.* 3 vols, Bibliographical Society, repr. 1968.

RENOUARD, P. *Répertoire des imprimeurs parisiens.* 2nd ed. Paris, Minard, 1965.

RICHAUDEAU, F., AND DREYFUS, J., ed. *La Chose imprimée,* Paris, Editions Retz, 1977.

SADLEIR, M. ed. *Bibliographia: a series of studies in book history and book construction, 1750–1900.* Constable, 1930.

SAUGRAIN, C. *Code de la librairie et imprimerie de Paris . . .* Paris, 1744, repr. Gregg, 1971.

SILVER, R. G. *The American printer, 1785–1825.* U.P. of Virginia, 1967.

STEINBERG, S. H. *Five hundred years of printing.* 3rd ed. Faber, 1974.

THOMAS, A. G. *Great books and book collectors.* Weidenfeld, 1975.

TWYMAN, M. *Printing, 1770–1970.* Eyre & Spottiswoode, 1970.

TWYMAN, W. B. *Lithography, 1800–1850: the techniques of drawing on stone in England and France and their application in works of topography.* O.U.P., 1970.

UNWIN, P. *The printing Unwins: a short history . . . 1826–1976.* George Allen & Unwin, 1976.

UNWIN, P. *The Stationers' Company, 1918–1977.* Benn, 1978.

WEBER, W. *A history of lithography.* Thames & Hudson, 1966.

Printing Technology and Management

ADAMS, J. M. *Optical measurements in the printing industry.* Pergamon, 1965.

AVIS, F. C. *Printing machine and paper problems.* 2nd ed. Avis, 1967.

AVIS, F. C. *Printers' arithmetic.* 2nd ed. Avis, 1971.

BANKS, W. H. *Problems in high speed printing.* Pergamon, 1962.

BARNETT, M. P. *Computer typesetting: experiments and prospects.* Cambridge, Mass., M.I.T., 1965.

BREWER, R. *Approach to print: a basic guide to the printing processes.* Blandford, 1971.

BRITISH PRINTER. *Specification manual of printing machinery and equipment.* Annually.

BPIF. *Customs of the trade for the manufacture of books.* Regularly.

BPIF. *Estimating for printers.* Regularly revised.

BPIF. *Tables and data for printers and binders.* Regularly revised.

BURDEN, J. *Graphic reproduction photography.* Focal P., 1973.

CARR, F. *Guide to screen process printing.* Vista, 1961.

CARTWRIGHT, H. *Ilford graphic arts manual. I. Photoengraving.* Ilford, 1962.

CHAMBERS, H. *The management of small-offset print departments: a guide to setting up and running internal and trade offset printing.* Business Books, 1969.

CLOWES, W. *Guide to printing: an introduction for print buyers.* Heinemann, 1964.

CUMMING, R., AND KILLICK, W. *Single colour lithographic machine operating.* Pergamon, 1969.

CURWEN, H. *Processes of graphic reproduction in printing.* 4th ed. Faber, 1967.

DELAFONS, A. *Structure of the printing industry.* Macdonald, 1965.

DELLER, J. *Printers' rollers: their manufacture, use and care.* Skilton, 1960.

DURRANT, W. R. *Machine printing.* Focal P., 1973.

HURST, C., AND LAWRENCE, F. *Letterpress composition and machine work.* Benn, 1963.

MARTIN, A. G. *Finishing processes in printing.* Focal P., 1972.

MIDDLETON, H. K. *Silk screen process production.* 5th ed. Blandford, 1967.

MORTON, A. *Mechanical composition.* Pergamon, 1969.

O'CONNOR, J. *Introducing relief printing.* Batsford, 1973.

PATEMAN, F., AND YOUNG, L. *Printing science.* 2nd ed. Pitman, 1969.

PRACTICAL *printing and binding.* Odhams, 1972.

SIMON, H. *Introduction to printing: the craft of letterpress.* Faber, 1968.

SPECTOR, C. *Management in the printing industry.* Longman, 1967.

STRAUSS, V. *The printing industry.* N.Y., Bowker, 1967.

VICARY, R. *Manual of lithography.* Thames & Hudson, 1976.

VICARY, R. *Manual of advanced lithography.* Thames & Hudson, 1977.

WALLIS, F., AND CANNON, R. *Letterpress platemaking.* Pergamon, 1969.

WOOLDRIDGE, D. *Letter assembly in printing.* Focal P., 1972.

YOUNG, L. C. *Materials in printing processes.* Focal P., 1973.

YULE, J. *Principles of colour reproduction applied to photomechanical reproduction.* N.Y., Wiley, 1967.

Book Design: Typography: Illustration: Private Presses

ANNENBERG, M. *Type foundries in America and their catalogs.* Baltimore, 1975.

AUDIN, M. *Les Livrets typographiques des fonderies françaises.* Paris, 1934, repr. with supplement by E. Howe, Amsterdam, 1964.

AVIS, F. C. *Type face terminology.* Avis, 1965.

BAIN, E. *Display typography.* Focal P., 1972.

BANISTER, M. *Lithographic prints from stone and plate.* Ward Lock, 1973.

BENNETT, P. *Books and printing: a treasury for typophiles.* Rev. ed. Forum, 1963.

BERRY, W. T., AND JOHNSON, A. F. eds. *Catalogue of specimens of printing types by English and Scottish printers and founders, 1665–1830.* O.U.P., 1935.

BIGGS, J. R. *Basic typography.* Faber, 1968.

BIGGS, J. R. *Letter-forms and lettering.* Blandford, 1976.

BLAND, D. *A history of book illustration: the illuminated manuscript and the printed book.* 2nd ed. Faber, 1969.

BROOK, S. *A bibliography of the Gehenna Press, 1942–1975.* Northampton, Mass, 1977.

CANNON, R., AND WALLIS, F. *Graphic reproduction: copy preparation and processes.* Vista, 1963.

CARTER, H. *A view of early typography up to about 1600.* O.U.P., 1969.

CRAIG, J. *Production for the graphic designer.* Pitman, 1975.

DAVIS, A. *Graphics: design into production.* Faber, 1973.

DAY, K., ed. *Book typography, 1815–1965, in Europe and the United States of America.* Benn, 1966.

DOWDING, G. *An introduction to the history of printing types.* Wace, 1962.

DOWDING, G. *Finer points in the spacing and arrangement of type.* 3rd ed. Wace, 1966.

DREYFUS, J. *Type specimen facsimiles.* Bowes, 1963.

FEAVER, W. *When we were young: two centuries of children's book illustration.* Thames & Hudson, 1976.

FLOYD, O. ed. *Artwork and colour reproduction.* Planned Action, 1972.

FRANKLIN, C. *The private press.* Studio, 1969.

FYFFE, C. *Basic copy fitting.* Studio, 1969.

GRAY, N. *XIXth century ornamental types and title pages.* 2nd ed. with a chapter on ornamented types in America by Ray Nash, Faber, 1976.

GROSS, A. *Etching, engraving and intaglio printing.* 2nd ed. O.U.P., 1973.

HAMILTON, E. *Graphic design for the computer age.* N.Y., Van Nostrand, 1970.

HAMMELMANN, H., AND BOASE, T. *Book illustrators in eighteenth-century England.* Yale U.P., 1975.

HEWITT, R. A. *Style for print and proof correcting.* Blandford, 1958.

HODNETT, E. *Francis Barlow: first master of English book illustration.* Scolar P., 1978.

HOLLOWAY, O. *French rococo book illustration.* Tiranti, 1969.

HUTCHINGS, E. A. *Designer's handbook of printing techniques.* Studio Vista, 1969.

HUTCHINGS, R. *The western heritage of type design.* Cory, 1963.

HUTCHINS, M. *Typographics: a designer's handbook.* Studio, 1969.

JARRETT, J. *Printing style.* George Allen & Unwin, 1960.

JASPERT, W., AND BERRY, W. T. *Encyclopaedia of type faces.* 4th ed. Blandford, 1971.

JENNETT, S. *The making of books.* 5th ed. Faber, 1974.

JOHNSON, A. F. *Type designs: their history and development.* 3rd ed. Deutsch, 1967.

KELLY, R. R. *American wood type, 1828–1900.* N.Y. Van Nostrand, 1969.

KINDERSLEY, D. *Optical letterspacing.* Lund Humphries, 1976.

LEHNER, E. *Alphabets and ornaments.* N.V., Dover, 1968.

LEWIS, J. *The graphic reproduction and photography of works of art.* Faber, 1969.

LEWIS, J. *The twentieth century book: its illustration and design.* Studio, 1967.

LEWIS, J. *Typography: basic principles, influence and trends since the 19th century.* Studio, 1964.

MORISON, S. *First principles of typography.* 2nd ed. C.U.P., 1967.

MORISON, S. *Politics and script.* O.U.P., 1972.

MORISON, S. *A tally of types.* 2nd ed. C.U.P., 1973.

MORISON, S., AND DAY, K. *The typographic book, 1450–1935.* Benn, 1964.

MUIR, P. *Victorian illustrated books.* Batsford, 1971.

NESBITT, A. *200 decorative title-pages.* N.Y., Dover, 1964.

PHOTO-LETTERING INC. *Alphabet thesaurus.* N.Y., Reinhold, 1960.

PRIVATE PRESS BOOKS. Private Libraries Association. Annually since 1959.

RAY, G. N. *The illustrator and the book in England from 1790 to 1914.* N.Y., Pierpont Morgan Library, 1976.

RICHAUDEAU, F. *La Lettre et l'esprit: vers une typographie logique.* Paris, Planète, 1965.

RODENBERG, J. *Deutsche Pressen: eine Bibliographie.* Vienna, Amalthea V., 1925.

SCHAUER, G. *Deutsche Buchkunst, 1890 bis 1960.* 2 vols. Hamburg, Maximilien, 1964.

SILVER, R. G. *Typefounding in America, 1787–1825.* U. of Virginia Press, 1965.

SIMON, O., AND RODENBERG, J. *Printing today: an illustrated survey of post-war typography in Europe and the United States.* Davies, 1928.

SPENCER, H. *Pioneers of modern typography.* Lund Humphries, 1968.

SPENCER, H. *The visible word.* Lund Humphries, 1969.

SUTTON, J., AND BARTRAM, A. *An atlas of type forms.* Lund Humphries, 1968. (A really splendid compilation.)

TAYLOR, J. *The Art Nouveau book in Britain.* Methuen, 1966.

THOMPSON, S. O. *William Morris and American book design.* Bowker, 1977.

TOMKINSON, G. S. *Select bibliography of the principal modern presses, public and private, in Great Britain and Ireland,* 1928, repr. San Francisco, Alan Wofsy Fine Arts, 1975.

TURNBULL, A. *The graphics of communication: typography, layout, design.* 2nd ed. N.Y., Rinehart, 1968.

UNIVERSITY OF CHICAGO PRESS. *A manual of style for authors, editors and copywriters.* 12th ed. Chicago, 1969.

WAKEMAN, G. *Victorian book illustration: the technical revolution.* David & Charles, 1973.

WARDE, F. *Printers' ornaments applied to the composition of decorative borders, panels and patterns.* Monotype Corporation, 1928.

WILLIAMSON, H. *Methods of book design: the practice of an industrial craft.* 2nd ed. O.U.P., 1966.

WILSON, A. *The design of books.* N.Y., Reinhold, 1967.

Bookbinding

BODLEIAN LIBRARY. *Fine bindings 1500–1700 from Oxford libraries.* Oxford, B.L., 1968.

BURDETT, E. *The craft of bookbinding: a practical handbook.* David & Charles, 1975.

CARTER, J. *Publisher's cloth: an outline history of publisher's binding in England, 1820–1900.* Constable, 1935.

DARLEY, L. S. *Introduction to book-binding.* Faber, 1965.

EARLY *American bookbindings from the collection of Michael Papantonio.* N.Y., Pierpont Morgan Library, 1972.

ESMERIAN, R. *Reliures de quelques ateliers du XVIIe et XVIIIe siècles.* (Sale catalogue in 3 parts), Paris, Blaizot, 1972.

GELDNER, F. *Buchelnbände aus elf Jahrhunderten.* Munich, Bruckmann, 1958.

HARTHAN, J. P. *Bookbindings (in the V. & A. Museum).* 2nd ed. H.M.S.O., 1961.

HOWE, E. *List of London bookbinders, 1648–1815.* Bibliographical Society, 1950.

JOHNSON, A. W. *Bookbinding.* Thames & Hudson, 1976.

LEHMANN-HAUPT, H. *Bookbinding in America: three essays.* Rev. ed. N.Y., Bowker, 1967.

MCLEAN, R. *Victorian publishers bookbindings.* Fraser, 1974.

MARINIS, T. DE. *La Legatura artistica in Italia nei secoli XV e XVI.* 3 vols. Florence, 1960.

MITCHELL, W. S. *A history of Scottish bookbinding, 1432–1650.* Aberdeen U.P., 1955.

NIXON, H. M. *Broxbourne Library: style and designs of bookbindings from the 12th to the 20th century.* Maggs, 1950.

NIXON, H. M. *Sixteenth century gold-tooled bookbindings in the Pierpont Morgan Library.* N.Y., 1971.

NIXON, H. M. *Five centuries of English bookbinding.* Scolar P., 1978.

SARRE, F. *Islamic bookbindings.* Kegan Paul, n.d. (c. 1923).

SMITH, C. P. *New directions in bookbinding.* Studio Vista, 1975.

THE STUDIO. *Modern book-bindings and their designers.* The Studio, Winter number, 1899–1900.

TOWN, L. *Bookbinding by hand.* 2nd ed. Faber, 1963.

VAUGHAN, A. *Modern bookbinding: a treatise covering both letterpress and stationery branches of the trade.* 4th ed. Skilton, 1960.

VEZIN, J. *La Technique de la reliure médiévale.* Paris, B.N., 1973.

WALTERS ART GALLERY. *History of bookbinding, 525–1950 A.D., an exhibition catalogue.* Baltimore, 1958.

Paper Technology

BATTISTA, O. *Synthetic fibres in papermaking.* N.Y., Interscience, 1964.

BROWN, T. *Introducing paper: a guide for the newcomer to the paper trade.* 5th ed. Whitaker, 1966.

GRANT, J. *Laboratory handbook of pulp and paper manufacture.* 2nd ed. Arnold, 1961.

HIGHAM, R. R. *A handbook of papermaking: the technology of pulp, paper and board manufacture.* 2nd ed. Business Books, 1968.

HUNTER, D. *Paper-making: the history and technique of an ancient craft.* 2nd ed. Cresset, 1957.

JOINT TEXTBOOK COMMITTEE OF THE PAPER INDUSTRY. *Pulp and paper manufacture.* 2nd ed. 2 vols, N.Y., McGraw, 1969.

LABARRE, E. J. *Dictionary of paper and paper-making terms.* 2nd ed. O.U.P., 1952.

NATIONAL ASSOCIATION OF PAPER MERCHANTS. *Paper: its making, merchanting and usage.* 2nd ed. N.A.P.M., 1965.

NUTTALL, G. H. *Theory and operation of the Fourdrinier paper machine.* Phillips, 1967.

SHORTER, A. H. *Papermaking in the British Isles.* David & Charles, 1971.